On Race

ON RACE

34 Conversations in a Time of Crisis

George Yancy

OXFORD
UNIVERSITY PRESS

Oxford University Press is a department of the University of Oxford. It furthers
the University's objective of excellence in research, scholarship, and education
by publishing worldwide. Oxford is a registered trade mark of Oxford University
Press in the UK and certain other countries.

Published in the United States of America by Oxford University Press
198 Madison Avenue, New York, NY 10016, United States of America.

Library of Congress Cataloging-in-Publication Data
Names: Yancy, George, interviewer.
Title: On race : 34 conversations in a time of crisis / George Yancy.
Description: New York : Oxford University Press, 2017. |
Includes bibliographical references and index.
Identifiers: LCCN 2017002553 (print) | LCCN 2017033270 (ebook) |
ISBN 9780190498566 (updf) | ISBN 9780190498573 (ebook) |
ISBN 9780190498559 (hbk. : alk. paper)
Subjects: LCSH: Race—Philosophy. | Race awareness.
Classification: LCC HT1521 (ebook) | LCC HT1521 .Y363 2017 (print) | DDC 305.8—dc23
LC record available at https://lccn.loc.gov/2017002553

9 8 7 6 5 4 3 2 1

Printed by Sheridan Books, Inc., United States of America

In loving memory of Manomano M. M. Mukungurutse

My dear friend, a remarkable human being, a brilliant philosopher

TABLE OF CONTENTS

ACKNOWLEDGMENTS

I thank Lucy Randall, editor at Oxford University Press, for taking such a keen interest in this project. Your enthusiasm for this text, its deep relevance and importance, made the process of bringing it to fruition all the more exciting. Hannah Doyle, editorial assistant at OUP, thanks for your wonderful logistical help. Emma Clements, project manager, and her team are to be thanked for their expertise and enthusiasm. A special thanks to Asha Fradkin for her keen eyes. Thanks to the anonymous readers/reviewers for their deep excitement for this project. I'm appreciative.

Thanks to philosopher Simon Critchley and editor Peter Catapano at the *New York Times*, cofounders of *The Stone*, who have provided an indispensable, historical, philosophical, and metaphilosophical space for engaging philosophy outside the confines of the academy. My work with the two of you has been a real honor. Simon, thanks for your philosophical acuity and adventurous ideas. Peter, thanks for your deep editorial insight, knowing where to cut and where to emphasize. Personally, I would also like to thank Peter for being such an incredible human being and for reminding me of just how vital it is for me to, at important times, remain silent, stay calm, and appreciate complex processes that happen beyond my ego.

To all 34 contributors, thanks for your time, your energy, and your commitment. These conversations are gifts for which I am very thankful. I have learned much and have modified my thinking accordingly. Your courage is appreciated during this time of crisis. I am deeply honored for the opportunity to share this space of dialogue. Given your busy schedules and other commitments, sharing your time with me was generous and much appreciated. And thanks in advance to all of the readers who will join this specific conversation by engaging this text, engaging the questions raised, and the ideas advanced. You, too, are part of this conversation. We all are.

I send special thanks and appreciation to philosopher Kelsey Ward who, under serious time constraints, came through for me and this project. She read through the entire manuscript within a very short period of time, developed conceptually rich discussion questions for all eight sections of the book, and did so with deep insight, creativity, and philosophical nuance. As Cicero would say, "A Friend is, as it were, a second self." Thanks for being a friend, and thanks for being a philosopher and colleague.

I would also like to thank Susan and the Yancy boys for your love. For Susan, I appreciate all your help with the technical aspects of this project and many others. For my boys, know that I'm proud of what you are becoming. Know that you must fight injustice where you see it, and know that there are forms of injustice that you don't see, and may not want to see. But it exists and it may need you to speak its name. Do so with as much brilliance, passion, and anger (if need be) as you can muster.

Mano, this book is dedicated to you. Man, you know that we talked of this moment. We spoke of life and we spoke of death. In fact, we spoke of so many things between the two. You are greatly missed. You didn't share much of what I call my hopeful theism. But that's fine. I hope to see you again, anyway. So, there you have it. As you often said to me—"Love Yah!"

CONTRIBUTOR BIOGRAPHIES

Linda Martín Alcoff is professor of philosophy at Hunter College and the CUNY Graduate Center. She was the president of the American Philosophical Association, Eastern Division, in 2012–2013. Her recent books include *Visible Identities: Race, Gender, and the Self* and *The Future of Whiteness*. Her website is www.alcoff.com.

Kwame Anthony Appiah was born in London and raised in Kumasi, Ghana. He studied philosophy at Cambridge University and is professor of philosophy and law at NYU. He has been the president of the American Philosophical Association, Eastern Division, and of the PEN American Center. He is the author of numerous books, including, most recently, *Lines of Descent: W. E. B. Du Bois and the Emergence of Identity*.

Molefi Kete Asante is professor and chair of African-American studies at Temple University and is known for his pioneering work in the area of Afrocentricity. He is the author of more than seventy books, including *As I Run Toward Africa: A Memoir*; *The Afrocentric Idea*; *The History of Africa*; and *African Pyramids of Knowledge*. Asante received his PhD from the University of California, Los Angeles, created the first doctoral program in African-American Studies, initiated the Afrocentric school of thought, and founded the Molefi Kete Asante Institute for Afrocentric Studies, and was the founding editor of the *Journal of Black Studies*. Asante holds distinguished professorships at the University of South Africa and the Zhejiang University in Hangzhou, China. He is completing a book on *Revolutionary Pedagogy*.

Alison Bailey is professor of philosophy at Illinois State University, where she also directs the Women's and Gender Studies Program. Her scholarship engages broadly with questions in feminist ethics and epistemologies, with a focus on applied issues related to social privilege, intersectionality, reproductive justice, and ignorance. She coedited *The Feminist Philosophy Reader* with Chris J. Cuomo. Her scholarship appears in *Hypatia: A Journal of Feminist Philosophy*; *The Journal of Social Philosophy*; *Social Epistemology Review and*

Reply Collective; The Journal of Peace and Justice Studies; South African Journal of Philosophy; and in collections such as *Race and Epistemologies of Ignorance; The Center Must Not Hold: White Women Philosophers on the Whiteness of Philosophy*; and *White Self-Criticality beyond Anti-Racism: How Does It Feel to Be a White Problem?* Her current research is on anger and epistemic injustice.

Seyla Benhabib, born in Istanbul, Turkey, has been the Eugene Meyer Professor of Political Science and Philosophy at Yale University since 2001 and has been a lecturer in the Yale Law School for six terms. She is the chair of the Scientific Committee of Reset-Dialogues on Civilizations and a member of the Executive Committee of Istanbul Seminars. Her work has been translated into thirteen languages. Her most recent books include *The Reluctant Modernism of Hannah Arendt; The Claims of Culture: Equality and Diversity in the Global Era; The Rights of Others: Aliens, Citizens and Residents*, winner of the Ralph Bunche award of the American Political Science Association and the North American Society for Social Philosophy award; *Another Cosmopolitanism: Hospitality, Sovereignty and Democratic Iterations*, with responses by Jeremy Waldron, Bonnie Honig, and Will Kymlicka; *Dignity in Adversity: Human Rights in Troubled Times; Gleichheit und Differenz: Die Würde des Menschen und die Souveränitätsansprüche der Völker* (bilingual edition in English and German); *Kosmopolitismus ohne Ilusionen: Menschenrechte in turbulenten Zeiten*; and *Exile, Statelessness, Migration: Jewish Themes in Political Thought* (forthcoming). She holds honorary degrees from the Universities of Utrecht (2004), Valencia (2010), Bogazici University in Istanbul (2012), and Georgetown University (2014).

Lawrence Blum is Emeritus Professor of Philosophy and Distinguished Professor of Liberal Arts and Education at the University of Massachusetts, Boston. His scholarly interests are in race theory, moral philosophy, moral psychology, moral education, multiculturalism, social and political philosophy, philosophy of education, the philosophy of Simone Weil, and, more recently, philosophy and the Holocaust, and ethics and race in film. He is the author of five books, including *Friendship, Altruism, and Morality; "I'm Not a Racist, But . . .": The Moral Quandary of Race* (winner of the Social Philosophy Book of the Year from the North American Society of Social Philosophy); and *High Schools, Race, and America's Future: What Students Can Teach Us about Morality, Diversity, and Community*. He also teaches professional development courses for elementary- and secondary-school teachers and has consulted with groups doing antiracist work with K–12 teachers.

Judith Butler is Maxine Elliot Professor in the Department of Comparative Literature and the Program in Critical Theory at the University of California, Berkeley. She received her PhD in philosophy from Yale University in 1984. She is the author of numerous influential books, including *Gender Trouble: Feminism and the Subversion of Identity; Bodies that Matter: On the*

Discursive Limits of "Sex"; The Psychic Life of Power: Theories of Subjection; Excitable Speech; Antigone's Claim: Kinship Between Life and Death; Precarious Life: Powers of Violence and Mourning; Frames of War: When Is Life Grievable?; Parting Ways: Jewishness and the Critique of Zionism; Dispossession: The Performative in the Political, coauthored with Athena Athanasiou; *Notes toward a Performative Theory of Assembly*; and *Vulnerability in Resistance*. Her books have been translated into more than twenty languages. She presently has a Mellon Foundation Grant to establish an International Consortium of Critical Theory Programs. She has served on the Executive Council of the Modern Languages Association and chaired its committee on Academic Freedom. Butler is active in several human rights organizations, serving on the board of the Center for Constitutional Rights in New York and the advisory board of Jewish Voice for Peace. She was the recipient of the Andrew Mellon Award for Distinguished Academic Achievement in the Humanities (2009–2013).

John D. Caputo, the Thomas J. Watson Professor of Religion Emeritus at Syracuse University and David R. Cook Professor of Philosophy Emeritus at Villanova University, writes and lectures in the area of postmodern theory and theology for both academic and general audiences. His latest books are *Hoping against Hope: Confessions of a Postmodern Pilgrim; The Folly of God: A Theology of the Unconditional; The Insistence of God: A Theology of Perhaps*; and *Truth: Philosophy in Transit*. His next book, *Interpretation from the Margins: The Pelican Guide to Postmodern Hermeneutics*, is scheduled to appear in 2017.

Noam Chomsky was born in Philadelphia, Pennsylvania, on December 7, 1928. He studied linguistics, mathematics, and philosophy at the University of Pennsylvania. In 1955, he received his PhD from the University of Pennsylvania. Chomsky has taught at Massachusetts Institute of Technology, where he is Institute Professor (Emeritus) in the Department of Linguistics and Philosophy, for the past fifty years. His work is widely credited with having revolutionized the field of modern linguistics. Chomsky is the author of numerous best-selling political works, which have been translated into scores of languages worldwide. Among his most recent books are *Hegemony or Survival; Failed States; Hopes and Prospects; Masters of Mankind*; and *Who Rules the World?*

Patricia Hill Collins is Distinguished University Professor of Sociology at the University of Maryland, College Park and Charles Phelps Taft Emeritus Professor of Sociology within the Department of African-American Studies at the University of Cincinnati. Her award-winning books include *Black Feminist Thought: Knowledge, Consciousness, and the Politics of Empowerment*, which received both the Jessie Bernard Award of the American Sociological Association (ASA) and the C. Wright Mills Award of the Society for the Study of Social Problems; and *Black Sexual Politics: African-Americans, Gender, and the New Racism*, which received ASA's 2007 Distinguished Publication Award. She is also author of *Fighting Words: Black Women and the Search for Justice; From Black Power to Hip Hop: Racism, Nationalism, and Feminism; Another Kind of Public Education: Race, Schools, the Media, and Democratic Possibilities; The Handbook of Race and Ethnic Studies*, edited with John Solomos; and *On Intellectual Activism*. Her anthology *Race, Class, and Gender: An Anthology, 9th edition*, edited with Margaret Andersen, is widely used in undergraduate classrooms in over two hundred colleges and universities. Professor Collins has taught at several institutions, held editorial positions with professional journals, lectured widely in the United States and internationally, served in many capacities in professional organizations, most recently as a judge for the 2015 National Book Award, and has acted as consultant for a number of community organizations. In 2008, she became the hundredth president of the American Sociological Association, the first African-American woman elected to this position in the organization's 104-year history. *Intersectionality*, her most recent book coauthored with Sirma Bilge, was published in 2016 as part of Polity Press's Key Concepts series.

Joe Feagin has been a sociologist and a leading researcher of racism in the United States for more than forty-five years. He is Distinguished University Professor and Ella C. McFadden Professor in sociology at Texas A&M University, and has done much internationally recognized research on US racism, sexism, and urban issues for fifty years now. He has written sixty-nine scholarly books and two-hundred-plus scholarly articles and reports in his social science areas. His single-authored and coauthored books include *Systemic Racism; Liberation Sociology; White Party, White Government; The White Racial Frame; Latinos Facing Racism; Racist America*; and *Elite White Men Ruling*. He is the recipient of a 2012 Soka Gakkai International-USA Social Justice Award, the 2013 American Association for Affirmative Action's Arthur Fletcher Lifetime Achievement Award, and the American Sociological Association's 2013 W. E. B. Du Bois Career of Distinguished Scholarship Award. He was the 1999–2000 president of the American Sociological Association.

Dan Flory is professor of philosophy at Montana State University, Bozeman and author of *Philosophy, Black Film, Film Noir*. He is also coeditor (with Mary K. Bloodsworth-Lugo) of *Race, Philosophy, and Film*. He has written more than twenty essays on philosophy, critical race theory, and film, which have appeared in numerous scholarly works such as the *Journal of Aesthetics and Art Criticism; Projections: The Journal for Movies and Mind; Film and Philosophy; American Quarterly; The Blackwell Companion to Film Noir; The Philosophy of Spike Lee*; and *The Routledge Companion to Philosophy and Film*. In 2007–2008, he was visiting associate professor of philosophy at the American University in Cairo, Egypt. He is working on a new book about the philosophy of the emotions, race, and film.

Nancy Fraser is Henry A. and Louise Loeb Professor of Political and Social Science and professor of philosophy at the New School for Social Research in New York City, president-elect of the American Philosophical Association, Eastern Division, and holder of an international research chair at the Collège d'études mondiales, Paris. Her most recent book is *Fortunes of Feminism: From State-Managed Capitalism to Neoliberal Crisis*. Her new book, *Capitalism: A Critical Theory*, coauthored with Rahel Jaeggi, will be published by Polity Press in autumn 2017. Fraser's work has been translated into more than twenty languages and was cited twice by the Brazilian Supreme Court (in decisions upholding marriage equality and affirmative action).

Paul Gilroy is professor of American and English literature at King's College London in the UK. He has previously taught at the London School of Economics, Yale, and Goldsmiths College. He is the author of numerous books, including *The Black Atlantic: Modernity and Double Consciousness*.

David Theo Goldberg is the director of the system-wide University of California Humanities Research Institute and professor of comparative literature, anthropology, and criminology, law and society at the University of California, Irvine. Formerly director and professor of the School of Justice Studies, a law and social science program at Arizona State University, he is the author of *Racist Culture: Philosophy and the Politics of Meaning; Racial Subjects: Writing on Race in America; Ethical Theory and Social Issues; The Racial State; The Threat of Race*; and *Are We All Postracial Yet?*; and coauthor of *The Future of Thinking*. He edited *Anatomy of Racism; Multiculturalism: A Critical Reader*; and coedited *Between Humanities and the Digital; Race Critical Theories; Rethinking Postcolonialism; Companion on Gender Studies*; and *Companion on Race and Ethnic Studies*. He was the founding coeditor of *Social Identities: Journal for the Study of Race, Nation and Culture*. He has written, among other things, extensively on race and racism in a global context and on critical and race theory, on the contemporary university, on the impacts of the digital especially on the future of learning, and on the place of the humanities in the academy.

Clevis Headley is associate professor of philosophy at Florida Atlantic University. He has served in various positions during his tenure at Florida Atlantic University: chair of the Department of Philosophy, director of the Ethnic Studies Certificate Program, director of the Master's in Liberal Studies, and special assistant to the dean for diversity. Professionally, he was a founding member and served as the first vice president and treasurer of the Caribbean Philosophical Association. Professor Headley has published widely in the areas of critical philosophy of race, Africana/Afro-Caribbean philosophy, and analytic philosophy.

bell hooks is an acclaimed intellectual, feminist theorist, cultural critic, artist, and writer. hooks has authored over three dozen books and has published works that span several genres, including cultural criticism, personal memoirs, poetry collections, and children's books. Her writings cover topics of gender, race, class, spirituality, teaching, and the significance of media in contemporary culture. Born Gloria Jean Watkins in Hopkinsville, Kentucky, bell hooks adopted the pen name of her maternal great-grandmother, a woman known for speaking her mind. hooks received her BA from Stanford University, her MA from the University of Wisconsin, and her PhD from the University of California, Santa Cruz. She is currently the Distinguished Professor in Residence in Appalachian Studies at Berea College. Her books include *Ain't I a Woman: Black Women and Feminism; Rock My Soul: Black People and Self-Esteem; Teaching to Transgress: Education as the Practice of Freedom; Feminism Is for Everybody: Passionate Politics; Teaching Community: A Pedagogy of Hope; Where We Stand: Class Matters*; and *We Real Cool: Black Men and Masculinity*. The bell hooks Institute was founded in 2014. http://www.bellhooksinstitute.com/#/about/.

Craig Irvine is a founder and academic director of the Program in Narrative Medicine and program director of the Master's Program in Narrative Medicine at Columbia University. He holds his PhD in philosophy from the Pennsylvania State University. For almost twenty years, he has been designing and teaching cultural competency, ethics, narrative medicine, and humanities and medicine curricula for residents, medical students, physicians, nurses, social workers, chaplains, dentists, and other health professionals. He has thirty years of experience teaching philosophy, ethics, humanities, and narrative medicine. He is co-author of *The Principles and Practice of Narrative Medicine* and has published articles in the areas of ethics, residency education, and narrative medicine, and has presented at numerous national and international conferences on these and other topics.

Joy James is Francis Christopher Oakley Third Century Professor of Humanities and professor in political science at Williams College. She is the author of *Resisting State Violence; Transcending the Talented Tenth; Shadowboxing: Representations of Black Feminist Politics*; and *Seeking the Beloved Community: A Feminist Race Reader*. James has edited volumes on politics and incarceration, including *Imprisoned Intellectuals* and *The New Abolitionists*.

Charles Johnson is University of Washington (Seattle) professor emeritus and the author of twenty-two books, a novelist, philosopher, essayist, literary scholar, short-story writer, cartoonist and illustrator, an author of children's literature, and a screen-and-teleplay writer. A MacArthur fellow, Johnson has received a 2002 American Academy of Arts and Letters Award for Literature, a 1990 National Book Award for his novel *Middle Passage*, a 1985 Writers Guild award for his PBS teleplay *Booker*, the 2016 W. E. B. Du Bois Award at the National Black Writers Conference, and many other awards. The Charles

Johnson Society at the American Literature Association was founded in 2003. In November, 2016, Pegasus Theater in Chicago debuted its play adaptation of *Middle Passage*, entitled *Rutherford's Travels*. Dr. Johnson recently published *Taming the Ox: Buddhist Stories and Reflections on Politics, Race, Culture, and Spiritual Practice*. His most recent book is *The Way of the Writer: Reflections on the Art and Craft of Storytelling*.

David Haekwon Kim is associate professor of philosophy and the director of the Global Humanities program at the University of San Francisco. He has published widely in the area of philosophy of race, especially on issues concerning Asian American experience. His research interests also include philosophy of emotion, postcolonialism, and comparative philosophy.

Bill E. Lawson is Emeritus Distinguished Professor of Philosophy at the University of Memphis and 2011–2012 Fulbright-Liverpool University Scholar. He received his PhD in philosophy from the University of North Carolina at Chapel Hill. His area of specialization is African-American philosophy and social and political philosophy. His published works include *Between Slavery and Freedom*, coauthored with Howard McGary; *Pragmatism and the Problem of Race*, edited with Donald Koch; *Faces of Environmental Racism*, edited with Laura Westra; *Frederick Douglass: A Critical Reader*, edited with Frank Kirkland; and numerous scholarly articles. He served in the US Army in Viet Nam between 1968 and 1969. He has testified before a United States Congressional Subcommittee on the issue of welfare reform.

Emily S. Lee is associate professor of philosophy at the California State University, Fullerton. Her research interests include feminist philosophy, philosophy of race, and phenomenology, especially the works of Maurice Merleau-Ponty. She is the editor of *Living Alterities: Phenomenology, Embodiment, and Race*. She has published articles on phenomenology and epistemology in regards to the embodiment and subjectivity of women of color in journals, including *Hypatia: A Journal of Feminist Philosophy*; *The Southern Journal of Philosophy*; and *Philosophy Today*.

Eduardo Mendieta is professor of philosophy, associate director of the Rock Ethics Institute, and affiliate professor in the School of International Affairs at Penn State University. He is the author of *The Adventures of Transcendental Philosophy*; *Global Fragments: Globalizations, Latinamericanisms, and Critical Theory*; and *The Philosophical Animal: On Zoopoetics and Interspecies Cosmopolitanism*. He is also coeditor of *The Power of Religion in the Public Sphere* with Jonathan VanAntwerpen; *Habermas and Religion* with Craig Calhoun and Jonathan VanAntwerpen; and *Reading Kant's Geography* with Stuart Elden. He recently finished a book entitled *The Philosophical Animal*, which will be published by SUNY Press in 2017, and he is presently at work on another book entitled *Philosophy's War: Logos, Polemos, Topos*.

Charles Mills is Distinguished Professor of Philosophy at the CUNY Graduate Center. He works in the general area of oppositional political theory, with a special focus on race. He is the author of numerous journal articles and book chapters, and six books, including *The Racial Contract*. His most recent book is *Black Rights/White Wrongs: The Critique of Racial Liberalism*.

Fiona Nicoll is associate professor and research chair in Gambling Policy with the Alberta Gambling Research Institute and the Department of Political Science at the University of Alberta. She is one of the founding members of and former vice president of the Australian Critical Race and Whiteness Studies Association (ACRAWSA). She was also the inaugural editor of the *ACRAWSA Journal*. She is coeditor of *Transnational Whiteness Matters* and *Courting Blackness: Recalibrating Knowledge in the Sandstone University*, and has published numerous chapters and articles on reconciliation, Indigenous sovereignty activism, and whiteness in the Australian context. Her areas of research also include cultural studies, critical race and whiteness studies, queer theory, Indigenous sovereignty theory, gambling studies, cultural economy, and twentieth-century Australian nationalism. She has worked with contemporary Indigenous artists and community leaders on public education and art projects. These include *Aunty Nance*, a social history exhibition on the life of a survivor of the stolen generations of Aboriginal and Torres Strait Islander people who gave a speech to the New South Wales parliament on the occasion of its formal apology (2001–2002) and an installation of art by Karla Dickens, Archie Moore, Christian Thompson, Michael Cook, Ryan Presley, r e a, Megan Cope, and Natalie Harkin in the Great Court of the University of Queensland, which was curated by Fiona Foley (2015).

Lucius T. Outlaw Jr. is professor of philosophy, African-American and diaspora studies, and of human and organizational development (Peabody College) at Vanderbilt University, having joined the faculty in July of 2000. (He was formerly the T. Wistar Brown Professor of Philosophy at Haverford College Haverford, Pennsylvania.). He teaches, researches, and writes about race and ethnicity, American philosophy, Africana philosophy, critical social theory, social and political philosophy, and the history of philosophy in the "West." Born in Starkville, Mississippi, he is a graduate of Fisk University (BA, 1967) and of the Graduate School of Arts and Sciences of Boston College (PhD, philosophy, 1972). He is the author of *On Race and Philosophy* and *Critical Social Theory in the Interest of Black Folks* and other writings.

Falguni A. Sheth is associate professor of Women's, Gender, and Sexuality Studies at Emory University. Her research is in the areas of continental and political philosophy, legal and critical race theory, and philosophy of race, postcolonial theory, and subaltern and gender studies. Her books are *Race, Liberalism, and Economics*, coedited with David Colander and Robert E. Prasch, and *Toward a Political Philosophy of Race*. Sheth is an organizer of the California Roundtable on Philosophy and Race. She is currently writing a book on race, technologies of violence, and political vulnerability.

Peter Singer is Ira W. DeCamp Professor of Bioethics in the University Center for Human Values at Princeton University, a position that he now combines with the position of Laureate Professor at the University of Melbourne. His books include *Animal Liberation; Practical Ethics; The Life You Can Save; The Point of View of the Universe*; and *The Most Good You Can Do*. In 2014, the Gottlieb Duttweiler Institute ranked him third on its list of Global Thought Leaders, and *Time* has included him among the world's one hundred most influential people. An Australian, in 2012 he was made a Companion to the Order of Australia, his country's highest civilian honor.

Hortense Spillers is the Gertrude Conaway Vanderbilt Professor at Vanderbilt University. She is a prominent Black feminist scholar, literary critic, and cognoscente of the African diaspora. She is the author of *Black, White, and in Color: Essays on American Literature and Culture*.

Shannon Sullivan is professor and chairperson in the Department of Philosophy at the University of North Carolina, Charlotte. She specializes in feminist philosophy, critical philosophy of race, American philosophy, and continental philosophy. She is the author of four books, most recently *Good White People: The Problem with Middle-Class White Anti-Racism* and *The Physiology of Sexist and Racist Oppression*. She also is coeditor of four books, including *Race and Epistemologies of Ignorance* and *Feminist Interpretations of William James*.

Cornel West is currently Professor of the Practice of Public Philosophy at Harvard University. He is a prominent and provocative democratic intellectual. He has taught at Yale, Harvard, the University of Paris, Princeton, and, most recently, Union Theological Seminary. He graduated Magna Cum Laude from Harvard in three years and obtained his MA and PhD in philosophy at Princeton. He has written twenty books and has edited thirteen. He is best known for his classics, *Race Matters* and *Democracy Matters*, and his memoir, *Brother West: Living and Loving Out Loud*. He appears frequently on the *Bill Maher Show*, CNN, C-Span, and on Tavis Smiley's PBS TV Show. Cornel West has a passion to communicate to a vast variety of publics in order to keep alive the legacy of Martin Luther King Jr.—a legacy of telling the truth and bearing witness to love and justice.

Traci C. West is the James W. Pearsall Professor of Christian Ethics and African-American Studies at Drew University Theological School. She is the author of *Disruptive Christian Ethics: When Racism and Women's Lives Matter; Wounds of the Spirit: Black Women, Violence, and Resistance Ethics*; editor of *Our*

Family Values: Same-Sex Marriage and Religion; many essays on gender-based violence, white supremacy, sexuality, and religion, as well as the coeditor of the *Journal of Feminist Studies in Religion*. She is a scholar-activist whose work includes teaching in New Jersey state prisons and a current research focus on transnational Africana gender violence resistance.

George Yancy is professor of philosophy at Emory University. He received his PhD (with distinction) in philosophy from Duquesne University where he was the first McAnulty Fellow. He received his first MA in philosophy from Yale University and his second MA in Africana Studies from NYU, where he received the prestigious McCracken Fellowship. He received his BA (cum laude) in philosophy from the University of Pittsburgh. He works primarily in the areas of critical philosophy of race, critical whiteness studies, and philosophy of the Black experience. He has authored many academic articles and book chapters. He has authored, edited, or coedited over nineteen books, which include *Exploring Race in Predominantly White Classrooms: Scholars of Color Reflect; Pursuing Trayvon Martin: Historical Contexts and Contemporary Manifestations of Racial Dynamics; Look, A White! Philosophical Essays on Whiteness*; and *Critical Perspectives on bell hooks*. The first edition of *Black Bodies, White Gazes* received an honorable mention from the Gustavus Myers Center for the Study of Bigotry and Human Rights, and three of his edited books have received *CHOICE* outstanding academic book awards. Yancy's work has been cited nationally and internationally in places like Turkey, South Africa, Sweden, and Australia. He is editor of the Philosophy of Race Book Series at Lexington Books, and is known for his influential interviews and controversial articles on the subject of race at *The Stone, New York Times*. He has twice won the American Philosophical Association Committee on Public Philosophy's Op-Ed Contest. His recent publications include the second edition of *Black Bodies, White Gazes*, and a new coedited book entitled *Our Black Sons Matter*. He is working on a book entitled *Dear White America*.

Naomi Zack received her PhD in philosophy from Columbia University and has been professor of philosophy at the University of Oregon since 2001. Zack's newest book is *The Theory of Applicative Justice: An Empirical Pragmatic Approach to Correcting Racial Injustice*. Related recent books are *White Privilege and Black Rights: The Injustice of US Police Racial Profiling and Homicide* and *The Ethics and Mores of Race: Equality after the History of Philosophy*. Additional monographs include *Ethics for Disaster; Inclusive Feminism: A Third Wave Theory of Women's Commonality*; the short textbook, *Thinking About Race; Bachelors of Science: 17th Century Identity Then and Now; Philosophy of Science and Race*; and *Race and Mixed Race*. Most recent is a fifty-one-contributor *Oxford Handbook of Philosophy and Race*.

On Race

Introduction

Dangerous Conversations

GEORGE YANCY

We are confronted with the fierce urgency of now.
    —Dr. Martin Luther King, Jr., *"Beyond Vietnam: A Time to Break Silence"*

What we face is a human emergency.
    —Abraham Joshua Heschel, *"Religion and Race"*

To act is to be committed, and to be committed is to be in danger.
    —James Baldwin, *The Fire Next Time*

Initially, I had the straightforward plan to open this introduction to *On Race: 34 Conversations in a Time of Crisis* with an explanation of the book's genesis, its scope, and some of its aims. However, a few days before I began to write, I was, to use Dr. Martin Luther King's phrase, "confronted with the fierce urgency of now" after receiving a message that was in response to the publication of "Dear White America."[1] The message was sent to my university email address. As I read the message aloud for the first time during an important special postelection discussion sponsored by the Program in Global and Postcolonial Studies here at Emory University, one that was designed to discuss and share ways in which faculty and students can engage in critical political work beyond the ballot, I experienced a disturbing affective intensity that shook my body. After I read it, the small group of faculty and students gathered were silent; the room was filled with the heavy air of disbelief. Disbelief, even though just days before America was inundated with news reports of swastikas being spray-painted on buildings and vehicles, Muslims being referred to as "vile" and "filthy," calls to make America white again, and claims that Black lives *don't* matter. In fact, according to the Southern Poverty Law Center, there were 867 cases that were counted "of hateful harassment or intimidation in the United States in the 10 days after the November 8 election."[2]

Within that room, there was a shared trepidation of what was to come when we finally move beyond 2016. The silence was in contrast to the applause received from those gathered after the first two presenters had delivered their short talks. As I read aloud the message sent to me, I could feel my voice tremble.

The subject heading on the email message read, "FUCK OFF BOY." I guess that I could have deleted the message before opening it, but I didn't. This jolting, antiquated usage of "BOY" recalled a bygone white supremacist "past" in which Black men were denied the respect due to other adult men and reduced to caricatures—rendered childlike vis-à-vis the quintessential white *man*, the white paternal figure, an exaggerated white male masculinity that needed to prove itself "superior" by beating, castrating, and lynching Black bodies. It was in the early 1920s, almost one hundred years ago, that philosopher Alain Locke, when referring to the withering away of white racist depictions of Black people, wrote that "the popular melodrama has about played itself out, and it is time to scrap the fictions, garret the bogeys and settle down to a realistic facing of the facts."[3] The optimism Locke expressed is evident in the phrase, "*has about* played itself out" (emphasis mine). Yet, "FUCK OFF BOY" pointed to a form of relentless white racist hatred, and proved it was hardly in our past. It was traveling through time, from the author of this hateful email to me, right here in 2016.

I felt like a prisoner of a merciless temporality—one in which this word and all that it carried had never faded into the past. There was no feeling of progressive linearity concerning race matters, but a form of vicious return, a cyclical cruelty. Already decades after Locke had expressed his optimism, in 1963, fifty-four years ago, Dr. King noted some of the cruelties as to why Black people couldn't wait for justice any longer. In addition to noting that one's wife and mother would never be given the respect of being called "Mrs.," he also noted "when your first name becomes 'nigger' and your middle name becomes 'boy' (however old you are),"[4] you can't wait. I opened the message and it read,

> I read your rant regarding white people, and I'm proud to inform you that I will never feel any guilt or shame for being white or who I am. FUCK YOU, you race baiting piece of shit! You're just another nigger with a chip on his shoulder that's looking for excuses to justify his hatred, and guess what asshole NOBODY WHITE GIVES A FUCK WHAT YOU THINK. My only regret is that I didn't hear your bullshit in person so that I could call you a FUCKING NIGGER to your face you worthless bitch, and then kick your black ass until you were half dead. FUCK OFF BOY.[5]

I wanted those gathered to share the weight that I felt; I wanted them to be confronted with the fierce urgency of now. For me, there was both a feeling of fear, because I'm afraid of racial fanaticism, and anger, because anger grounds me; it keeps me focused. Counterintuitively, anger can provide clarity, especially within a context where my Blackness is taken as sufficient evidence that I am guilty of something, that I am disposable.

To feel the sense of fierce urgency, some readers might want to tarry longer with the words of the message, with the intent of the message, to reflect on the perverse pleasure that the writer may have obtained when the message was composed. This time, however, try reading it aloud, reading it slowly, allowing the magnitude of the violence expressed in the words to touch your conscience or sense of moral outrage.

As Black, I am apparently excrement, waste, refuse. That is an attack on my humanity. My writings on the subjects of race and white privilege are allegedly designed to induce white people to feel bad about themselves. Rather than being genuinely concerned with interrogating whiteness as a site of privilege, power, and social injustice, as a way of attempting to improve forms of human relationality, my aim is to "bait" white people, to lure them. That is an attack on my scholarship and its complexity. The writer also says "NOBODY WHITE" cares what I think. Well, that is a lot of white people. So, the writer speaks for *all* white people. That is an insult to white people. The content of what I write is referred to as 'bullshit,' which implies a form of exaggerated nonsense. That is an attack on the philosophical integrity of what I write. 'Nigger' is a grotesque term that reminds me of Black bodies swinging from the end of a rope; the word is traumatic and assaultive in its impact. Yet, I'm also a "fucking nigger," which adds intensification to the word 'nigger.' And note that the writer desires to say this to my face. This would be, I imagine, for greater confrontational effect. By 'fucking nigger,' I assume that the writer means that I'm *really* or *very much so* a "nigger." Then again, perhaps the writer meant that I'm a "worthless nigger." If so, then by white racist logic, that is simply a tautology. And then by calling me a 'worthless bitch,' the message is aimed at my sense of masculinity. I get it. In many testosterone-driven male spaces, 'bitch' signifies that I'm weak, afraid, a wuss. The writer, though, attempts to degrade me and by extension also degrades women. The modifier 'worthless' engenders the question: what is a "worthwhile bitch"? So, while I understand the hypermasculine lingua franca, I just don't have anything to prove. That one just washes off. In addition to all of these insults, however, the writer desires to kick my black ass until I'm half dead. That is an attack on my life! The existential stakes are now higher. That is an attack on all Black life! That is beyond the pale of discursive insult, but not beyond the facts of American history and not beyond the pale of the white imaginary to enact forms of grave physical violence: maim, brutalize, and murder Black bodies.

There is a part of me that would like to relegate this kind of discursive violence to media trolls who have nothing better to do with their time. I've seen this behavior many times already. After all, after the publication of "Dear White America" for the *Times*, I received hundreds of messages that were filled with white racist vitriol. But when bullying and caustic insults communicated through social media are erratically and incessantly engaged in by President Donald Trump, giving legitimacy to deploy the medium as a site for harassing others, the neofascist and existential stakes are raised. As Henry A. Giroux writes, "Trump has done more than bring a vicious online harassment culture into the mainstream, he has also legitimated the worst dimensions of politics and brought out of the shadows white nationalists, racist militia types, social media trolls, overt misogynists and a variety of reactionaries who have turned their hate-filled discourse into a weaponized element of political culture."[6]

Unlike any other presidential election in recent history, what we have witnessed is Faustian in nature—millions of predominantly white people were willing and prepared to sell their souls to a white man who had already confirmed their loyalty, saying he could shoot somebody and wouldn't lose any voters. That is the signature of a narcissist, one who is reckless, who can do no wrong in his eyes or in the eyes of others. That kind of self-obsession places ethics and democracy in abeyance; it is the stuff of totalitarianism and genocide. Perhaps many of us would rather be in a state of what Jean-Paul Sartre called "bad faith," which is our attempt to lie to ourselves about an unpleasant reality. In this case, though, it is more than an unpleasant reality. It is the stuff of Orwellian nightmares, the reality of unadulterated political madness and *shameless* white nativism. What we are witnessing in America is the birth of a monstrous presidential figure, one who has promised to make America "great again" and bring "law and order." These are tropes that signify, for some of us, a time in American history of de jure racism. There was a time when Germany needed to be made "great again," subjected to "law and order," made "racially pure" vis-à-vis the "chaos" of difference. Being made "great again," "racially pure," and subjected to "law and order" bespeaks the horrors of apotheosis and mass murder. And many were, sadly, in the case of Germany, convinced by the messenger. This is why, inter alia, we are confronted with the fierce urgency of now.

White people who voted for Trump, in my view, demonstrated a willingness to subordinate their freedom to a political idol regardless of his actions. Political idolatry bespeaks fanaticism and neofascism. Our current political situation might be said to be a species of D. W. Griffith's *The Birth of a Nation* (1915), which is a film about the rise and valorization of the Ku Klux Klan, and the problematic demonization of the Black male as a "sexual predator." Keep in mind that white male Dylann Roof, who on June 17, 2015, viciously murdered nine Black people holding a prayer meeting at the historic Emmanuel Methodist Episcopal Church in Charleston, South Carolina, is reported to have said, "I have to do it. You rape our [white] women and you're taking over our [white] country. And you have to go."[7] Both 'our women' and 'our country' are hallmarks of the white racist imaginary. It was also through the logics of the white racist imaginary that Trump, in 1989, purchased several ads in New York newspapers calling for the return of the death penalty and an increase in police presence after four Black males and one Latino were wrongly convicted in the Central Park Five case. Even now, after all five have been found innocent of any wrongdoing, Trump refuses to believe that they are innocent despite the evidence. Then again, some of us, in Trump's eyes, are *"the Blacks."*[8] We are always already stereotypically known. As Patricia J. Williams writes, "Culturally, blackness signifies the realm of the always known, as well as the not worth knowing. A space of the entirely judged. This prejudice is a practice of the nonreligious; it is profane, the ultimate profanity of presuming to know it all."[9] As the entirely judged, Trump "knew" about Black people's so-called monolithic economic plight and social pathology. This is partly why he said that we had nothing to lose by voting for him. Without any sophisticated analysis of Black social mobility or how structural racism adversely impacts Black life, Trump said, "You live in your poverty, your schools are no good. You have no jobs. What the hell do you have to lose?"[10] That was an insult to Black America, just as Trump's five-year-long birtherism lie was an insult to our first African-America President and by extension Black people. If the stakes were not so high, I might, as Frantz Fanon said, "laugh myself to tears."[11] But, as with Fanon, "that laughter [has] become impossible."[12]

It is certainly not a laughing matter when David Duke, once the Grand Wizard of the KKK, tweets, "Our people played a huge role in electing Trump!" It is the "our" that is so frightening. To my knowledge, Trump has not unequivocally called Duke out as a *racist*. It is Trump's reticence and perhaps unwillingness to name racism, sexism, and xenophobia that helps to form the mortar that will now scaffold the birth of this "new nation." It is Stephen K. Bannon, now Trump's chief strategist and senior counselor, who said that *Breitbart News* is "the platform for the alt-right,"[13] otherwise known as white nationalism/white nativism. It is Michael Flynn, who accepted Trump's offer of national security advisor, who said that "Fear of Muslims is rational."[14] And it is Jeff Sessions, whom Trump has selected as Attorney General, who is the same Sessions who denounced the 1965 Voting Rights Act, and who had branded the American Civil Liberties Union and the NAACP as "un-American." He also said that such organizations "forced civil rights down the throats of people."[15] And along with the racism, sexism, xenophobia, and ableism, Trump represents an existential threat because of his denial of climate change.[16] Furthermore, if we love our children and our planet, remember that Trump, when it comes to the use of nuclear weapons, does not want to take the cards off the table.[17] In a nuclear exchange, there will be no cards and no table. To play that hand places us squarely within the space of the profane, the unholy. Given what we have witnessed in his unpredictability, perhaps that is partly what constitutes the crime. Hence, the trauma that so many of us felt after the election of Trump is not some temporary uneasiness induced by a "peaceful" transfer of power. It is a form of mourning that cuts to the bone.

It should be noted that when Donald Trump became president-elect, America *didn't* suddenly become a nation predicated upon white supremacy. For those of us who have endured the hatred, the noblesse oblige of "good, God-fearing" white people, we didn't unexpectedly enter into a new and unforeseen nightmare. We didn't have the privilege to live in a twilight zone, a world of fantasy where things are unreal, where we get to wallow in what Richard Wright calls a form of white mania for mere trinkets. Wright says that the words of the souls of white people are "the syllables of popular songs,"[18] superficial distractions that speak to *nonracialized* suffering and mourning. To be fair, though, I have tried to empathize with the pain of working-class white America, those within what we all now know as the Rust Belt. I have tried to understand their feelings of exclusion and being treated as the "rural other" and as the "noncollege educated." And I have tried to understand their specific economic anxieties and how they perceive the failure of "the establishment" to address their interests. And even as I am concerned about their economic plight, and how they have experienced alienation, as we all should be, my sense is that their vote for Trump has created a set of conditions that will further mark differently vulnerable bodies in ways that will expose us to deeper forms of social pain and suffering, ostracization, and expulsion. Part of the problem is that their class suffering was not an isolated metric used in their decision to vote for Trump. I realize that race can't explain everything, but, on my view, even as they suffered, they always knew that they were *not* Black and thereby assumed that they were *entitled* to reap the benefits of white America. Part of their frustration (for them) is that they *are white* and that they continue to be treated like "niggers." That is their shame. Their suffering was never just economic; it was and is linked to a white vanguard mentality that has not materialized for them. So, even as they struggle economically, they voraciously feed on Trump's racist and xenophobic discourse.

As a Black person, I know that white America has always been a nightmare, a country filled with white terror, white brutality, white nativism, white hubris, white paranoia, and white privilege and power. So, for me, and for most Black people and people of color, the existential malaise that a "Trump victory" has produced is not new. Gifted with second-sight, as W. E. B. Du Bois would say,[19] we have always seen how whiteness operates within this country. So, for those white people who are disgusted and unhinged by Trump's election, just know that Black people and people of color have been living in the pre-Trump belly of the beast called white America for years. And for those of us who continue to believe that President Obama should have been far more vocal and interventionist (and should have transformed policy) when it came to racism in America, and especially anti-Black racism, remember that there were times when Obama demonstrated incredible moments of critique of our polity when he seemed to argue, for example, that white racism is systemic. In a revealing and candid interview for the podcast "WTF with Marc Maron," Obama said, "Racism, we are not cured of it. And it's not just a matter of it not being polite to say nigger in public."[20] He went on to say, "That's not the measure of whether racism still exists or not. It's not just a matter of overt discrimination. Societies don't, overnight, completely erase everything that happened 200 to 300 years prior."[21] My sense is that even Obama didn't see Trump coming; he didn't see the full extent of the whitelash.[22] And it is that whitelash, the likes of which we have yet to see fully, that drives home the fierce urgency of now. The "browning" of America will soon become "the [site of the] great unwashed"[23] vis-à-vis Trump's personal, egomaniacal white "exceptionalism." Joel Olson writes, "White tyranny does not contradict the democratic will but is an expression of it."[24]

Socrates caught hell for practicing philosophy in public spaces, for daring to speak to Athenians who would prefer to sleep. As a gadfly that stings, he refused to let them remain unconscious of their narrowness of vision and preoccupation with distractions from living a virtuous and just life. He became a victim of those who preferred to remain in Plato's cave, those who were prisoners of that cave and saw only shadows that they took to be real. The more that I talk with many white people about the reality of race in America, the more that I realize that they have been seduced by the shadows of a "postracial" American cave, as it were. They have failed to see the reality of how race operates in insidious ways and how they are complicit with it. They reside in a cave filled with shadows that placate their white identities as free of racism. We must continue to find the appropriate discourse and metaphors to communicate to our good liberal white friends that race continues to touch every aspect of their lives despite the fact that they didn't, even for moral, antiracist reasons, vote for Trump. Now with the alt-right in the White House, it will be perhaps even easier for many goodwill whites[25] to obfuscate the ways in which their own whiteness continues to perpetuate racial injustice. But it is often dangerous to call into question the ways in which shadows substitute for reality, the ways in which white people have created larger institutional structures that "validate" those shadows. To be committed to fighting against racial injustice is to be in danger. At the same time, though, how can I be true to the process of loving wisdom if I only address my fellow academics? At a time of crisis such as this, how can I avoid the importance of the value of philosophy to public discourse? How can I not wrestle with those social and existential matters that we would rather pretend are not real or are said by my fellow philosophers to be outside of philosophy? It is courageous speech, the fight against racial injustices, the belief that philosophy has a public role to play in critically engaging ideas, and the demand for clarity regarding race, that are some of the elements that drive this book. And while all of the interviews were conducted prior to Trump becoming president-elect, each interview is shaped by a shared ethos—the realization that we are living (and have lived) in a time of crisis when it comes to race. It was this sense of crisis that led to my sense of urgency to interview prominent philosophers and public intellectuals on the theme of race. As it turns out, the crises that took place as I continued these interviews would later only seem like the beginning.

In 2014, I began reading interviews of scholars, conducted by philosopher Gary Gutting, on the subject of religion. I was intrigued by the engaged level of conversation and the conceptual accessibility that took place at the *New York Times'* philosophy column, *The Stone*. I felt this would be an important venue for engaging in conversations about race. Since 2012, I had been carrying around the weight of the tragic killing of the unarmed seventeen-year-old Black male, Trayvon Martin. I wept upon hearing about his death. At that time, I had no idea that this was just the beginning of what felt like the systematic disposability of Black bodies, a cyclical nightmare. While this is not a new phenomenon, the widespread attention brought to these killings through the exposure on social media is new. There was the killing of the unarmed seventeen-year-old Black male Jordan Davis also in 2012 by a white man. There was the killing of the unarmed twenty-four-year-old Jonathan Ferrell and the killing of the unarmed nineteen-year-old Black female Renisha McBride, each in 2013 and both by white men, Ferrell being killed by a police officer. There was also the emergence of the Black Lives Matter movement in 2013 after the acquittal of George Zimmerman in the killing of Trayvon Martin. Continuing in 2014, there were the white police killings of the unarmed forty-three-year-old Eric Garner, the twenty-three-year-old John Crawford (who held a 22BB gun in a Walmart store), the unarmed eighteen-year-old Michael Brown (along with the resultant Ferguson protests), and the seventeen-year-old Laquan McDonald (who we later discovered was shot sixteen times as he held a three-inch blade and was walking away from police officers). There didn't seem to be any end in sight.[26] I needed to critically discuss race through a medium that drew broad attention to the existential malaise and racial violence that was occurring.[27] There was that fierce urgency of now.

So, I decided to contact the cofounders of *The Stone*, philosopher Simon Critchley and Peter Catapano, the award-winning opinion editor at the *New York Times*. I asked if they would be interested in me interviewing philosophers on race for their column. Both were enthusiastic about the idea, but none of us realized just how powerful the impact of the interviews would be. After a few interviews appeared, it was clear, from the positive responses that I began to receive, that the impact was major. To my knowledge, this was the first time that race had been discussed at a prominent site like the *New York Times* through an actual series of critical interviews with philosophers and public intellectuals on race. It was important for me to engage philosophers on the theme of race, as I believe that they have a moral responsibility, as framed through a Socratic lens, to use their critical capacities and critical tools to clarify the messiness of concepts, especially the concept of race. Engaging the views of philosophers on race was also important to me, as this engagement demonstrated just how socially and politically relevant philosophy can and ought to be, and how philosophy is a practice that all of us, as human beings, engage in. So, with Peter's enthusiasm, I conducted and we ran a total of nineteen interviews. The response was phenomenal, not just nationally, but internationally. I received email messages from many readers who had read interviews and had come to anticipate the interviews that would come out next. And the comment section of *The Stone* demonstrated not just how important and publicly enriching the interviews were, but also how race is such an emotionally and politically charged subject with great philosophical complexity. My aim was to do what *The Stone* does so well. It was to demonstrate the social relevance of philosophy, but to do so regarding an issue that may, to our national regret, cause "the fire next time."

On Race: 34 Conversations in a Time of Crisis is an expanded version of the series that began at *The Stone*. Picking up where the original nineteen interviews left off, the text is shaped by important assumptions regarding the social relevance of philosophy, that is, its need to tarry within the space of the everyday problems of human existence. In fact, philosophy as ideal theory, especially when this is taken to be its sole end or what is most exciting about it, fails us and trivializes our quotidian experiences. Philosophy as ideal theory fails to speak to the actual, often deeply tragic, experiences that we endure. As Adrienne Rich writes, "Theory can be a dew that rises from the earth and collects in the rain cloud and returns to earth over and over. But if it doesn't smell of the earth, it isn't good for the earth."[28] Philosophy must, if it is to be more than conceptual self-stimulation, smell of the earth, get dirty. Otherwise, it becomes a form of academic monasticism that remains trapped in its own hermetic silence. As Paulo Freire reminds us, "Human beings are not built in silence, but in word, in work, in action-reflection."[29] This, by the way, is not an a priori account of philosophy and its aims, but a self-conscious historical positioning of my understanding of philosophy as that which ought to change the world, to help to rid the world of oppression and hatred. For me, philosophy is a site of suffering. I suffer when I attempt to dwell within the emotional space of human pain and agony. The weight of the mystery of human existence, and the weight of the pain we impose upon each other, is, for me, about pathos. This means, of course, that philosophy must involve deeply uncomfortable, and many times dangerous conversations, and that is what you hold in your hands. *On Race: 34 Conversations in a Time of Crisis* consists of dangerous conversations; dangerous because they not only relentlessly mark the *tragic realities* of how race has operated and continues to operate in our world, in our lives, but they challenge the ways in which so many of us are complicit with such tragic realities and how many of us would rather remain oblivious to the realities of race. This book asks that you join in this conversation, especially in this time of crisis. It is an invitation, an entreaty to join in this dangerous conversation as we experience, globally, the fierce urgency of now.

NOTES

1. George Yancy, "Dear White America," *New York Times*, December 24, 2015, https://opinionator.blogs.nytimes.com/2015/12/24/dear-white-america/?_r=1.
2. Holly Yan, Kristina Sgueglia, and Kylie Walker, "'Make America White Again': Hate Speech and Crimes Post-Election," *CNN*, December 22, 2016, http://www.cnn.com/2016/11/10/us/post-election-hate-crimes-and-fears-trnd/.
3. Alain Locke, with an introduction by Arnold Rampersad, *The New Negro: Voices of the Harlem Renaissance* (New York: Simon & Schuster, 1992), 5.
4. James M. Washington, ed., *A Testament of Hope: The Essential Writings and Speeches of Martin Luther King, Jr.* (New York: Harper San Francisco, 1986), 293.
5. Email message to author, sent November 22, 2016.
6. Henry A. Giroux, "The Authoritarian Politics of Resentment in Trump's America," *Truthout*, November 13, 2016, http://www.truth-out.org/opinion/item/38351-the-authoritarian-politics-of-resentment-in-trump-s-america.
7. Lisa Wade, "How 'Benevolent Sexism' Drove Dylann Roof's Racist Massacre," *Washington Post*, June 21, 2015, https://www.washingtonpost.com/posteverything/wp/2015/06/21/how-benevolent-sexism-drove-dylann-roofs-racist-massacre/?utm_term=.3b20b02dc414.
8. Kathleen Parker, "Donald Trump and 'the Blacks,'" *Chicago Tribune*, August 31, 2016, http://www.chicagotribune.com/suburbs/daily-southtown/opinion/ct-sta-parker-trump-st-0901-20160831-story.html.
9. Patricia J. Williams, *Seeing a Color-Blind Future: The Paradox of Race* (New York: Farrar, Straus and Giroux, 1997), 74.
10. Michael Gerson, "Trump's Bad 'Law and Order' Rerun," *Washington Post*, August 29, 2016, https://www.washingtonpost.com/opinions/trumps-bad-law-and-order-rerun/2016/08/29/672fa4e2-6e18-11e6-9705-23e51a2f424d_story.html?utm_term=.fcae257e0db9.
11. Frantz Fanon, *Black Skin, White Masks*, trans. Charles Lam Markmann (New York: Grove Press, 1967), 112.
12. Fanon, *Black Skin, White Masks*, 112.
13. Sarah Posner, "How Donald Trump's New Campaign Chief Created an Online Haven for White Nationalists," *Mother Jones*, August 22, 2016, http://www.motherjones.com/politics/2016/08/stephen-bannon-donald-trump-alt-right-breitbart-news.
14. Thomas Gibbons-Neff, "'Fear of Muslims is Rational': What Trump's New National Security Adviser Has Said Online," *Washington Post*, November 18, 2016, https://www.washingtonpost.com/news/checkpoint/wp/2016/11/18/trumps-new-national-security-adviser-has-said-some-incendiary-things-on-the-internet/?utm_term=.66faa2c67351.
15. Phil Mattingly, Eric Bradner, "Trump Picks Sessions for Attorney General," *CNN*, November 18, 2016, http://www.cnn.com/2016/11/17/politics/jeff-sessions-attorney-general-donald-trump-consideration/index.html.

16. Jeremy Schulman, "Every Insane Thing Donald Trump Has Said about Global Warming," *Mother Jones*, December 5, 2016, http://www.motherjones.com/environment/2016/11/trump-climate-timeline.

17. "Trump on Using Nukes: 'Don't Want to Take Everything Off the Table,'" *Newsmax*, March 30, 2016, http://www.newsmax.com/Politics/trump-nuclear-dont-take-off-table-hesitant/2016/03/30/id/721571/.

18. Richard Wright, "The Man Who Went to Chicago," in *Eight Men,* introduction by Paul Gilroy (New York: Harper Perennial, 1996), 214.

19. W. E. B. Du Bois, *The Souls of Black Folk* (New York: New American Library, [1903] 1982), 45.

20. Deena Zaru, "Obama Uses N-Word, Says We Are 'Not Cured' of Racism," *CNN*, June 22, 2015, http://www.cnn.com/2015/06/22/politics/barack-obama-n-word-race-relations-marc-maron-interview/index.html.

21. Zaru, "Obama Uses N-Word."

22. Josiah Ryan, "'This Was a Whitelash': Van Jones' Take on the Election Results," *CNN*, November 9, 2016, http://www.cnn.com/2016/11/09/politics/van-jones-results-disappointment-cnntv/index.html.

23. Paulo Friere, *Pedagogy of the Oppressed* (New York: The Continuum Publishing Company, [1970] 2000), 90.

24. Joel Olson, *The Abolition of White Democracy* (Minneapolis: University of Minnesota Press, 2004), 51.

25. 'Goodwill whites' is a term used by philosopher Janine Jones in "The Impairment of Empathy of Goodwill Whites for African Americans," in *What White Looks Like: African American Philosophers on the Whiteness Question*, ed. G. Yancy (New York: Routledge, 2004), 65–86.

26. For an important collection of powerful voices of mothers of Black sons, mothers who refuse to accept the disposability of their Black sons by the state and its proxies, see *Our Black Sons Matter: Mothers Talk About Fears, Sorrows, and Hopes,* eds., George Yancy, Maria del Guadalupe, and Susan Hadley (Lanham, MD: Rowman & Littlefield, 2016).

27. In the second and expanded edition of my book, *Black Bodies, White Gazes: The Continuing Significance of Race in America* (Lanham, MD: Rowman & Littlefield, 2016), I examine a number of these tragic deaths through the theorization of the white gaze. See especially chapters 1 and 8.

28. Adrienne Rich, "Notes toward a Politics of Location" (1984), in *Blood, Bread, and Poetry: Selected Prose, 1979–1985* (New York: Norton, 1986), 211–31, quote from 218–19.

29. Paulo Friere, *Pedagogy of the Oppressed* (New York: The Continuum Publishing Company, [1970] 2000), 88.

PART I

Race and the Critical Space of Black Women's Voices

bell hooks

George Yancy: Over the years, you have used the expression 'imperialist white supremacist capitalist patriarchy' to describe the power structure underlying the social order. Why tie those terms together as opposed to stressing any one of them in isolation?

bell hooks: We can't begin to understand the nature of domination if we don't understand how these systems connect with one another. Significantly, this phrase has always moved me because it doesn't value one system over another. For so many years in the feminist movement, women were saying that gender is the only aspect of identity that really matters, that domination only came into the world because of rape. Then we had so many race-oriented folks who were saying, "Race is the most important thing. We don't even need to be talking about class or gender." So for me, that phrase always reminds me of a global context, of the context of class, of empire, of capitalism, of racism, and of patriarchy. Those things are all linked—an interlocking system.

G. Y.: I've heard you speak many times and I noticed that you do so with a very keen sense of humor. What is the role of humor in your work?

b. h.: We cannot have a meaningful revolution without humor. Every time we see the left or any group trying to move forward politically in a radical way, when they're humorless, they fail. Humor is essential to the integrative balance that we need to deal with diversity and difference and the building of community. For example, I love to be in conversation with Cornel West. We always go high and we go low, and we always bring the joyful humor in. The last talk he and I gave together, many people were upset because we were silly together. But I consider it a high holy calling that we can be humorous together. How many times do we see an African-American man and an African-American woman talking together, critiquing one another, and yet having delicious, humorous delight? It's a miracle.

G. Y.: What is your view of the feminist movement today, and how has your relationship to it changed over time?

b. h.: My militant commitment to feminism remains strong, and the main reason is that feminism has been the contemporary social movement that has most embraced self-interrogation. When we, women of color, began to tell white women that females were not a homogenous group, that we had to face the reality of racial difference, many white women stepped up to the plate. I'm a feminist in solidarity with white women today for that reason, because I saw these women grow in their willingness to open their minds and change the whole direction of feminist thought, writing, and action. This continues to be one of the most remarkable, awesome aspects of the contemporary feminist movement. The left has not done this, radical Black men have not done this, where someone comes in and says, "Look, what you're pushing, the ideology, is all messed up. You've got to shift your perspective." Feminism made that paradigm shift, though not without hostility, not without some women feeling we were forcing race on them. This change still amazes me.

G. Y.: What should we do in our daily lives to combat, in that phrase of yours, the power and influence of imperialist white supremacist capitalist patriarchy? What can be done on the proverbial ground?

b. h.: I live in a small, predominantly white town in the Bible Belt. Rather than saying, "What would Jesus do?," I always think, "What does Martin Luther King want me to do today?" Then I decide what Martin Luther King wants me to do today is to go out into the world and in every way that I can, small and large, build a beloved community. As a Buddhist Christian, I also think of Buddhist monk Thich Nhat Hanh who talks about throwing a pebble into the water, and while it may not go far in the beginning, it will ripple out. So, every day, I'm challenging myself. "What are you doing, bell, for the creation of the beloved community?" Because that's the underground, local insistence that I be a fundamental part of the world that I'm in. I've been to the Farmer's Market, I've been to the church bazaar this morning. I really push myself to relate to people, that is, people that I might not feel as comfortable relating to. There are many Kentucky hillbilly white persons who look at me with contempt. They cannot turn me around. I am doing the same thing as those civil rights activists, those Black folk and those white folk who sat in at those diners and who marched.

It's about humanization. And I can't think of another way to imagine how we're going to get out of the crisis of racial hatred if it's not through the will to humanize. Personally, I draw incredible strength from the images of Black people and white people in social movements. I personally did not think *Selma* was a great film, but the strength that I gained from the film was thinking about all of those people, those white folks who see *Selma* and say, "My God, this is unjust! Let's go do our part." And it's awesome when we're called. There are many times in this life of mine when I ask myself, "What are you willing to give your life for, bell? When are you willing to get out in the streets knowing that you're risking your health?" And if those older Black women who were there in Selma, Alabama, can do this stuff, it just reminds you how incredibly vital this history of struggle has been toward allowing you and me to be in the state of privilege that we live within today.

G. Y.: That point hits home, especially as I think about my own intellectual identity and yet often fail to think about the privilege that comes with it.

b. h.: I am a total intellectual. I tell people that intellectual work is the laboratory that I go into every day. Without all of those people engaged in civil rights struggles, I would not be here in this laboratory. I mean, how many Black women have had the good fortune to write more than thirty books? When I wake up at four or five in the morning, I do my prayers and meditations, and then I have what I call my "study hours." I try to read a book a day, a nonfiction book, and then I get to read total trash for the rest of the day. That's luxury, that's privilege of a high order—the privilege to think critically, and then the privilege to be able to act on what you know.

G. Y.: Absolutely. You've talked about how theory can function as a place of healing. Can you say more about that?

b. h.: I always start with children. Most children are amazing critical thinkers before we silence them. I think that theory is essentially a way to make sense of the world. As a gifted child growing up in a dysfunctional family, where giftedness was not appreciated, what held me above water was the idea of thinking through, "Why are Mom and Dad the way they are?" And those are questions that are at the heart of critical thinking. And that's why I think critical thinking and theory can be such a source of healing. It moves us forward. And, of course, I don't know about other thinkers and writers, but I have the good fortune every day of my life to have somebody contacting me, either on the streets or by mail, telling me about how my work has changed their life, how it has enabled them to go forward. And what greater gift to be had as a thinker-theorist, than that?

G. Y.: How do you prevent yourself from being seduced by that? I think that there is that temptation by intellectuals/scholars, who are well known, to be seduced into a state of narcissism. How do you resist that?

b. h.: First of all, I live in a city of twelve thousand people where most of them don't have a clue about who bell hooks is for the most part, or where someone asks, "Is bell hooks a person?" There is humility in the life that I lead, because one thing about having my given name, Gloria Jean, which is such a great Appalachian hillbilly name, is that I'm not walking around in my daily life usually as bell hooks. I'm walking around in the dailiness of my life as just the ordinary Gloria Jean. That's changing a bit in the little town that I live in because more of me as a thinker, writer, and artist is coming out into the world of the town that I live in.

I think that I've been coming out more and more in the fact that the work that I'm writing is about spirituality, because one of the central aspects that has kept me grounded in my life has been spirituality. Growing up, when my mom used to tell me, "You're really smart, but you're not better than anyone else," I used to think, "Why does she go on about that?" And, of course, now I see why. It was to keep me grounded and to keep me respecting the different ways of knowing and the knowledges of other people, and not thinking "Oh, I am *so* smart," which I think can happen to many well-known intellectuals.

I always kind of chuckle at people labeling me a public intellectual. I chuckle because people used to say, "How have you written so much?" and I'd say, "By not having a life." There is nothing public about the energy, the discipline, and solitude it takes to produce so much writing. I think of public intellectuals as very different, because I think that they're airing their work for that public engagement. Really, in all the years of my writing, that was not my intention. It was to produce theory that people could use. I have this phrase that I use, 'working with the work.' So if somebody comes up to me, and they have one of those bell hooks books that's abused and battered, and every page is underlined, I know they've been working with the work. And that's where it is for me.

G. Y.: Is there a connection between teaching as a space of healing and your understanding of love?

b. h.: Well, I believe whole-heartedly that the only way out of domination is love, and the only way into really being able to connect with others, and to know how to be, is to be participating in every aspect of your life as a sacrament of love, and that includes teaching. I don't do a lot of teaching these days. I am semiretired. Because, like any act of love, it takes a lot of your energy.

I was just talking with a neighbor about what it feels like to be working at a need-based college like Berea, where none of our students pay tuition, and many of them come from the hills of Appalachia. We often get discouraged any time we feel that our college isn't living up to its history of integration and of racial inclusion. But then we'd see we have students who are doing such amazing things, from the hills of Virginia, or Tennessee. You just know, I am right where I am meant to be, doing what I should be doing, and giving and receiving the love that comes anytime we do that work well.

G. Y.: You've conceptualized love as the opposite of estrangement. Can you say something about that?

b. h.: When we engage love as action, you can't act without connecting. I often think of that phrase, *only connect*. In terms of white supremacy right now, for instance, the police stopped me a few weeks ago here in Berea, because I was doing something wrong. I initially felt fear, and I was thinking about the fact that in all of my sixty-some years of my life in this country, I have never felt afraid of policemen before, but I feel afraid now. He was just total sweetness. And yet I thought, what a horrible change in our society that that level of estrangement has taken place that was not there before.

I know that the essential experience of Black men and women has always been different, but from the time I was a girl to now, I never thought the police were my enemy. Yet, what Black woman witnessing the incredible abuse of Sandra Bland can't shake in her boots if she's being stopped by the police? When I was watching that video, I was amazed the police didn't shoot her on the spot! White supremacist white people are crazy.

I used to talk about patriarchy as a mental illness of disordered desire, but white supremacy is equally a serious and profound mental illness, and it leads people to do completely and utterly insane things. I think one of the things that is going on in our society is the normalization of mental illness, and the normalization of white supremacy, and the evocation and the spreading of this is part of that mental illness. So remember that we are a culture in crisis. Our crisis is as much a spiritual crisis as it is a political crisis, and that's why Martin Luther King Jr. was so profoundly prescient in describing how the work of love would be necessary to have a transformative impact.

G. Y.: And of course, that doesn't mean that you don't find an important place in your work for rage, as in your book *Killing Rage*?

b. h.: Oh, absolutely. The first time that I got to be with Thich Nhat Hanh, I had just been longing to meet him. I was like, I'm going to meet this incredibly holy man. On the day that I was going to him, every step of the way I felt that I was encountering some kind of racism or sexism. When I got to him, the first thing out of my mouth was "I am *so angry!*" And he, of course, Mr. Calm himself, Mr. Peace, said, "Well, you know, hold on to your anger, and use it as compost for your garden." And I thought, "Yes, yes, I can do that!" I tell that story to people all the time. I was telling him about the struggles I was having with my male partner at the time and he said, "It is OK to say I want to kill you, but then you need to step back from that, and remember what brought you to this person in the first place." And I think that if we think of anger as compost, we think of it as energy that can be recycled in the direction of our good. It is an empowering force. If we don't think about it that way, it becomes a debilitating and destructive force.

G. Y.: Since you mentioned Sandra Bland, and there are so many other cases that we can mention, how can we use the trauma that Black people are experiencing, or reconfigure that trauma into compost? How can Black people do that? What does that look like therapeutically or collectively?

b. h.: We have to be willing to be truthful. And to be truthful, we have to say, the problem that Black people face, the trauma of white supremacy in our lives, is not limited to police brutality. That's just one aspect. I often say that the issue for young Black males is the street. If you only have the streets, you encounter violence on all sides: Black on Black violence, the violence of addiction, and the violence of police brutality. So the question is why at this stage of our history, with so many wealthy Black people, and so many gifted Black people, is it that we don't provide a place other than the streets for Black males? And it is so gendered, because the street, in an imperialist white supremacist capitalist patriarchy, is male, especially when it is dark. There is so much feeling of being lost that it is beyond the trauma of racism. It is the trauma of imperialist white supremacist capitalist patriarchy, because poverty has become infinitely more violent than it ever was when I was a girl. You lived next door to very poor Black people, but they had very joyful lives. That's not the poverty of today.

G. Y.: How is the poverty of today different?

b. h.: Let's face it, one of the things white people gave us when they gave us integration was full access to the tormenting reality of desire, and the expectation of constant consumption. So part of the difference of poverty today is this sort of world of fantasy—fantasizing that you'll win the lottery, fantasizing that money will come. I always cling to Lorraine Hansberry's Mama saying in *A Raisin in the Sun*, "Since when did money become life?" I think that with the poverty of my growing up that I lived with and among, we were always made to feel like money is not what life is all about. That's the total difference for everyone living right now, because most people in our culture believe money is everything. That is the big tie, the connecting tie to Black, white, Hispanic, native people, Asian people—the greed and the materialism that we all invest in and share.

G. Y.: When you make that claim, I can see some readers saying that bell is pathologizing Black spaces.

b. h.: As I said, we have normalized mental illness in this society. So it's not the pathologizing of Black spaces; it's saying that the majority of cultural spaces in our society are infused with pathology. That's why it's so hard to get out of it, because it has become the culture that is being fed to us every day. None of us can escape it unless we do so by conscious living and conscious loving, and that's become harder for everybody. I don't have a problem stating the fact that trauma creates wounds, and most of our wounds are not healed as African-Americans. We're not really different in that way from all the others who are wounded. Let's face it—wounded white people frequently can cover up their wounds, because they have greater access to material power.

I find it fascinating that every day you go to the supermarket, and you look at the people, and you look at us, and you look at all of this media that is parading the sorrows and the mental illnesses of the white rich in our society. And it's like everybody just skips over that. Nobody would raise the question, "Why don't we pathologize the rich?" We actually believe that they suffer from mental illness, and that they deserve healing. The issue for us as Black people is that very few people feel that we deserve healing. Which is why we have very few systems that promote healing in our lives. The primary system that ever promoted healing in Black people is the church, and we see what is going on in most churches today. They've become an extension of that material greed.

One of the reasons for why so many Black rebel antiracist movements failed is because they didn't take care of the home as a site of resistance.

G. Y.: As you shared being stopped by police, I thought of your book *Black Looks: Race and Representation*, where you describe whiteness as a site of terror. Has that changed for you?

b. h.: I don't think that has changed for most Black people. That particular essay, "Representations of Whiteness in the Black Imagination," talks about whiteness, the Black imagination, and how many of us live in fear of whiteness. And I emphasize the story about the policeman because, for many of us, that fear of whiteness has intensified. I think that white people, for the most part, never think about Black people wanting to be in Black-only spaces, because we do not feel safe.

In my last book, *Writing Beyond Race: Living Theory and Practice*, I really wanted to raise and problematize the question: Where do we feel safe as Black people? I definitely return to the home as a place of spiritual possibility, home as a holy place.

I bought my current house from a conservative white male capitalist who lives across the street from me, and I'm so happy in my little home. I tell people, when I open the doors of my house, it's like these arms come out, and they're just embracing me. I think that is part of our radical resistance to the culture of domination. I know that I'm not who he imagined in this little house. He imagined a nice white family with two kids, and I think on some level it was very hard for him to sell his house to a radical Black woman, a radical Black feminist woman. I think all of us, in terms of houses, have our idea, when we love our home, of who we want to be in it. But I think Black folks in general across class have to restore that sense of resistance in the home.

When we look at the history of antiracist rebels among Black people, so much organizing happened in people's homes. I always think about Mary McLeod Bethune : "Let's just start the college in your living room." Self-determination really does begin at home. We're finding out that one of the reasons for why so many Black rebel antiracist movements failed is because they didn't take care of the home as a site of resistance. So, you have very wounded people trying to lead movements in a world beyond the home, but they were simply not psychologically fit to lead.

G. Y.: That's an important segue to the question about your concept of "soul healing" with respect to Black men. What does soul healing among Black men look like? And what role do you think Black women play in helping to nurture that soul healing?

b. h.: Every now and then, George, I write a book that hardly anyone pays any attention to. One such book in my life is my book on Black masculinity, *We Real Cool: Black Men and Masculinity*. An aspect of that book that I found deeply moving is when I use the metaphor of Isis and Osiris. Osiris is attacked, and his body parts are spread all over. Isis, the stern mother, sister, and lover, goes and fetches those parts and puts him back together again. That sort of metaphor of harmony and friction that can be soul-healing for Black people is so real to me. Often I feel sad, because I think we are in a culture that keeps Black men and women further apart from one another, rather than meeting us in that place of shared history, shared story.

I am so grateful for the Black male friends in my life. Like so many professional Black women, I don't have a partner. I would like to have one, but I've been grateful for having conscious, caring, Black male comrades and friends, who keep me from any kind of integration of Black masculinity, who just keep me in this space of loving Blackness.

To have that kind of bonding is precious. These are the constructive moments of our time, and they're not televised. When Malcolm X said we have to see each other with new eyes, I think that's where self-determination begins and how we are with one another. Let's face it, so many Black males and females have suffered mental abandonment, and more than police brutality, that's the core for many of us of our trauma. Betrayal is always about abandonment. And many of us have been emotionally abandoned. These are the wounds we have yet to correctly attend to so both Black children and biracial children can have the opportunity to truly care for themselves in a way that's optimal for all.

G. Y.: How are your Buddhist practices and your feminist practices mutually reinforcing?

b. h.: Well, I would have to say my Buddhist Christian practice challenges me, as does feminism. Buddhism continues to inspire me because there is such an emphasis on practice. What are you doing? Right livelihood, right action. We are back to that self-interrogation that is so crucial. It's funny that you would link Buddhism and feminism, because I think one of the things that I'm grappling with at this stage of my life is how much of the core grounding in ethical-spiritual values has been the solid ground on which I stood. That ground is from both Buddhism and Christianity, and then feminism that helped me as a young woman to find and appreciate that ground. The spirituality piece came up for me in my love of Beat poetry. I came to Buddhism through the Beats, through Gary Snyder and Jack Kerouac—they all sort of gave me this other space of groundedness.

I talk about spirituality more now than ever before, because I see my students suffering more than ever before, especially women students who feel like so much is expected of them. They've got to be the equals of men, but then they've got to be submissive if they are heteronormative; they have to find a partner. It's just so much demand that has led them to depression, to addiction, or suicide. And it's amazing how spirituality grounds them.

Feminism does not ground me. It is the discipline that comes from spiritual practice that is the foundation of my life. If we talk about what a disciplined writer I have been and hope to continue to be, that discipline starts with a spiritual practice. It's just every day, every day, every day.

Patricia Hill Collins

George Yancy: Speak to the contemporary importance of Black feminist thought and its relevance to making our society aware of the *intersectional* dimensions of Black women's oppression.

Patricia Hill Collins: Black feminist thought centers on a few simple ideas. At its essence, Black feminist thought examines how Black women's ideas, experiences and actions reflect their social location within racism, sexism, class exploitation and similar intersecting systems of oppression. These intersecting oppressions structure social inequalities, which in turn result in specific social issues such as wage inequality, stereotypical and demeaning media images, limited educational opportunities, and differential access to health services. Because individuals, as well as the social groups to which they belong, are differentially positioned within power relations, their analyses of, experiences with and actions in response to social inequalities vary greatly. Drawing from the distinctive social location of African-American women at the intersection of racism, class exploitation, sexism, and heterosexism as systems of power, Black feminism argues that trying to address the social problems that Black women encounter through mono-categorical lenses is inadequate.

In the United States, Black feminism has highlighted the particular intersections of race, class, nation, gender, and sexuality. Yet within this broader intersectional framework, race and racism constitute foundational systems that, by law or by custom, have regulated everything from where African-American women could live, the schools they attend, the opportunities they encounter, to whether they could keep their children. Black feminist thought thus brings a more complex view of racism to the forefront of analysis, as well as how a more complex understanding of racism might shape social problems and solutions to them. Yet the core ideas of Black feminist thought concerning intersecting power relations, complex forms of social inequality and the particularities of social problems can be and have been broadly applied. Specifically, the saliency of particular intersecting power relations reflects particular histories. Across diverse social contexts, varying combinations of ethnicity, religion, age, and nationality are all possible.

Many people think that Black feminist thought is primarily for and about African-American women. Black women are at the center of Black feminism, yet the ideas of Black feminist thought have travelled far beyond the forms they've taken within the US context. The term *intersectionality* has been closely associated with US Black feminism, in part because African-American women have consistently advanced this interpretive framework as a way of thinking more expansively about inequality. Yet intersectionality is applicable beyond the experiences of African-American women. The tools of intersectional analysis, with its emphasis on intersecting systems of power as foundational to social justice, appear within such contexts as diverse as global Human Rights initiatives, within social media, across academic fields, as well as within policy venues.

Rather than seeing Black women primarily as victims of oppression, a broader intersectional lens also examines Black women's actions as political actors in resisting multiple oppressions. Black feminism exists not simply to document oppression, but also to do something about it. Rather than being a victim-claiming discourse that teaches Black women how oppressed they really are, Black feminism aims to empower Black women by showing all the ways that Black women have resisted oppression.

Black women's resistance to intersecting oppressions can take multiple forms. It can be something as simple as my mother's insistence that I needed to go to school every day. She convinced me that reading was fundamental and that, although she didn't say it, words could serve as powerful weapons against racism and sexism. Through their activities as mothers, artists, grandmothers, teachers, community other-mothers, intellectuals, and leaders, numerous Black women have taken on the task of nurturing children of African descent and carrying the weight for assaults on Black populations. For example, African-American women who show a powerful commitment to their families in the face of policies of the mass incarceration of their sons, brothers, and grandsons exemplify this resistance. Most understand on some level how power relations of race, class, gender, and sexuality coalesce in shaping not only their own experiences as African-American women but also those around them.

G. Y.: In your book, *Black Feminist Thought*, you write, "One key feature about the treatment of Black women in the nineteenth century was how their bodies were objects of display. In the antebellum American South white men did not have to look at pornographic pictures of women because they could become voyeurs of Black women on the auction block." In the various ways in which Tennis player Serena Williams, for example, has been the object of racist and sexist caricature, one might argue that she has been returned to a symbolic "auction block" despite her success and athletic genius. In what ways do you think Black women, in the twenty-first century, continue to be objects of sexual oppression?

P. H. C.: Because I don't routinely separate out racial oppression and sexual oppression, it's hard to parse out the specific effects of sexism. I'll begin to answer this question by examining how the body politics that construct ideas about Black femininity and Black masculinity are central to intersecting systems of oppressions of race, class, gender, and sexuality. Privileged, straight white men encounter a distinctive form of body politics that ironically disembodies them by attributing characteristics such as intelligence and leadership ability to those inhabiting these idealized white, straight male bodies. People of color and women encounter a different body politics, one that attributes characteristics such as lack of intelligence, hypersexuality, and a lack of leadership ability to those who are ostensibly ruled by their female and/or colored bodies. An intersectional framework provides a more finely-tuned analysis of how diverse social locations contribute to the different body politics.

For example, young African-American men and women living in poor or working-class urban neighborhoods encounter an historically specific form of body politics that reflects their placement within intersecting oppressions— how police, teachers, social workers, and judges perceive the bodies of young Black people contributes to the gender-specific treatment they receive. The easiest way to see the workings of body politics is to consider changing places with someone who inhabits a different body. How many white men would consider changing places with Black women, or Black straight men with Black lesbians? Would they recognize themselves as the person they understand themselves to be if their lived experiences occurred a different body?

Like most African-American women, for reasons of survival, Serena Williams has developed her own interpretations of the body politics that permeate racism, sexism, heterosexism and class exploitation. In this context, the issue of representations of Serena Williams is more complex than her being watched on an auction block by consumers who fetishize her body as a pornographic object. Certainly some viewers will do this, but contemporary mass media has facilitated new understandings of auction blocks and viewers who enjoy them as entertainment. In *Black Feminist Thought*, I wrote about the power of controlling images that aim to influence how we think about each other's and our own bodies. Controlling images are most effective when they create pornographic representations of African-Americans that in turn dehumanize Black people. Yet African-American women who are armed with an analysis of how controlling images work in shaping our daily experiences often bring different analyses to the same set of images and, via these oppositional interpretations, undercut the power of controlling images.

The case of actual Black people who were displayed on auction blocks during slavery and of representations of Black people within contemporary mass
media spectacles of sports in particular resemble one another, yet they are not
the same. First, Serena Williams and her sister, Venus Williams retain their
agency in how they take the stage. Over the course of their careers, they have
consistently worked to strip the tennis court of its power to function as a
"symbolic auction block." Venus and Serena Williams reject the uniformity of
tennis whites, choosing instead bright colors, unusual outfits, and ostensibly black hairstyles such as African-influenced beads and colorful weaves. The
Williams sisters have rejected the social scripts of how women tennis players
should look and perform. Neither Venus nor Serena can hide the fact that
they are Black women, nor do they try. They are strong and athletic. And they
win. There's visible agency in all of their choices. This was not the case for
enslaved African women. The important idea here is that ideas and images do
not "make" anyone do anything. Society may provide social scripts and derog-
atory interpretations of how Black women are supposed to look and act if they
want to be successful. Yet it's up to Black women whether we choose to believe
and act on them.

Second, by claiming control over her own image while on the court, Serena
Williams demonstrates her resistance to longstanding body politics in wom-
en's tennis. We will never know with certainty how the women on the actual
auction block felt about their nakedness and treatment and what strategies
they deployed to protect their dignity. Yet, because the awareness of always
being under surveillance has long been a core theme within Black feminist
thought, we do know much about how contemporary African-American
women use the inordinate attention given to their bodies in public space.
The Williams sisters have broken new ground in women's tennis, but they are
not alone. Popular culture icons such as Nicki Minaj, Viola Davis, Beyoncé
Knowles, and Janelle Monae all claim their representations in public space
and use that space differently. Behind the scenes, the cultural production
of African-American women artists and filmmakers such as Shonda Rhimes
turn traditional scripts concerning Black womanhood on their heads. Serena
Williams is but one figure in this universe of African-American women who
lay claim to representational space.

Third, Serena did not prevail in women's tennis as a solitary individual.
Venus and Serena Williams both competed and won. Neither could be discredited as the exceptional individual—here were *two* exceptional individuals.
I suspect that because they had each other, the Williams sisters were better
able to ward off the crippling effects of hypersurveillance and the negative
treatment both encountered during their long and stellar careers. Serena's
success is her own, but she did not do it alone. Moreover, Serena and Venus
Williams may be sisters, but they are also quite different from one another. As
individuals, they each unsettle notions of the exceptional Black woman who

must hew to one set of standards for acceptance. Each sister is the exception to the rule that the other seemingly invokes.

The case of the Williams sisters suggests that Black women's resistance to oppression generally, and the hypersurveillance of mass media venues, can occur in public areas with longstanding rules of body politics. There is something empowering about knowing the history of one's group, because it helps make sense of the present. For example, Venus and Serena Williams play championship tennis in part because they are talented, work hard, and show a passion for their sport, and in part because they are mentally equipped to reject the "symbolic auction block." But as young Black women, they knew that they would be judged by a different set of standards. They seemingly learned not to take the racism and sexism that they experienced personally because the differential treatment they received had little to do with them as individuals. In this context, their brilliance within women's tennis by challenging the body politics of championship tennis has also redefined representations of excellence.

G. Y.: Define how you understand an Afrocentric feminist perspective and how it functions as a critical framework for resisting and fighting against such oppressive assumptions about Black women.

P. H. C.: I don't use the term 'Afrocentric feminist perspective' any more, in part, because the term 'Afrocentric' became redefined and subsequently devalued in the 1990s in ways that didn't resemble my understanding of the concept. My original use referred to cultural continuities that were taken up differently by people of African descent in a diasporic context in response to heterogeneous experiences with colonialism, slavery, and imperialism. This usage positions African-American women's experiences in relationship to those of Black women in the Caribbean, Latin America, especially Brazil, continental Africa, and Black diasporic populations in Europe. It focuses on how culture can empower and draws upon the work of complex approaches to culture of Frantz Fanon and similar anticolonial theorists. In the face of structural oppressions, culture can become a weapon, but it can also become a confining straightjacket if understood as a static bundle of performed traditions. Unfortunately some strands of Afrocentric thinking in the US embraced static notions of black authenticity that manufactured ideas about a glorious African past that was more imagined than real. Unfortunately, these strands also incorporated patriarchal and heterosexist ideas that I categorically reject.

I also have moved away from the phrase because my own thinking has evolved, in part because Black feminists in the late twentieth century were successful in carving out a space for Black feminist thought; and in part because poststructuralist social theory offered a set of conceptual tools for examining constructed social realities generally, and the meaning of Blackness. In my earlier work, I was concerned with the political difficulties of carving out a clear space for African-American women to do intellectual work. Racism operated by categorizing Black women as inferior and then dismissing our ideas and experiences. We had to create the conditions that made our own intellectual production possible. I wrote the first edition of *Black Feminist Thought* in that narrow context. In contrast, the current expansive space enjoyed by contemporary Black women to critically engage a host of issues speaks to the success of earlier struggles for voice.

One no longer has to refute claims that anything associated with Blackness is worthless. Now there is space to analyze varying understandings of Blackness, including Afrocentric approaches. I now see Blackness as a political category, one that carries cultural meaning but that cannot be reduced to culture itself. The idea of Blackness is clearly tied to racism—there were no populations of actual Black people before slavery, colonialism and imperialism. The varying ethnicities of African descent carried distinctive names and cultures. Blackness emerges in the context of white supremacy, yet has never been a mere reaction to racism. Instead, Blackness has carried, since its inception, inherently political meanings. By queering categories of power, poststructuralism provides a vocabulary for examining hegemonic understandings of Blackness and how Black people shape interpretions of Blackness from one context to the next. Given the scope of lived experience with white supremacy and the depth of intellectual tools that are now available, performing some version of an authentic Afrocentric identity grounded in a cultural African identity seems ill equipped to handle contemporary social problems.

Cultural continuities, an idea that is central to Afrocentric analysis, are important. Yet when it comes to understanding Blackness as a political entity, continuities of Black social movements and of Black activism may be even more significant. A new generation of Black women has made real strides in applying Black feminism to contemporary social, economic and political challenges. The field of Black women's studies has progressed to the point where a new generation of young Black women embrace heterogeneous understandings of Blackness, including Afrocentrism, and use the tools of Black feminism to shape their contemporary political activism. Many of these women have moved beyond misguided views that view feminism as the property of white women or Afrocentrism as the litmus test for authentic Black womanhood. The idea of women's empowerment expressed within transnational feminism is rapidly putting the white/Black version of feminism honed within a US- or European-based race-relations framework to rest. In its place, a Black feminism that embraces a critical intersectional framework has the potential to offer much in challenging not only African-American women's oppression but also global injustices. Political resistance to social injustice as understood through intersectional frameworks is emerging as one important dimension of a Black diasporic feminism that is actively engaged in decolonizing thought and practice.

In the US, the emergence of visible political activism by young African-American women and their allies caught many by surprise. The tremendous growth of grassroots organizations for social justice such as the Black Youth Project 100 in Chicago or the Black Lives Matter Movement speaks to the aspirations of a new generation of Black people for equity and equality. Yet media coverage of this activism routinely depicts African-American women as the penultimate victims of police brutality, poor schooling, and limited job opportunities and looks to men as leaders of social movement organizations. In this context, intersectionality serves as a corrective to either/or thinking that reduces complex ideas to a matter of simple choice of race over gender or vice versa. Stated differently, elevating Black men above Black women, or straight Black people above LGBTQ people is unlikely to bring social justice to anyone.

Today, the Black Lives Matter movement is still in its infancy. Yet its four-year emergence in 2012 from a hashtag responding to the death of Trayvon Martin to its organizational reponses to urban unrest in Ferguson, Missouri (2014) and Baltimore, Maryland (2015), shows its commitment to resisting and fighting public policies and representations that derogate Black people. Moreover, since African-American women constitute a substantial part of this movement, both as participants in local struggles and as leaders of grassroots initiatives and the national organization, the Black Lives Matter movement exemplifies the ways in which intersectionality contributes to contemporary Black feminist projects.

G. Y.: Speaking of the Black Lives Matter movement, what do we say to mothers of Black sons who constantly fear the possibility that their sons could be another Trayvon Martin or Tamir Rice? It seems to be that mothers of Black sons are experiencing forms of trauma that will need to be addressed.

P. H. C.: I think the issue is less what the assumed "we" of academics, policy makers, community leaders, or political pundits say *to* Black women, women of color, mothers of Black children, poor people, and similarly located groups who care about Black youth, than what this group can say to the seeming experts about the routinized violence that targets Black youth. The experts on any given topic, in this case, the challenges that face the mothers of Black sons, or daughters for that matter, need not be the army of academics who have claimed expertise about race, gender, family, trauma, and a host of topics. The cottage industry of pundits on talk radio and television are not much help either. My sense of the Black Lives Matter movement, for all its heterogeneity and growing pains, is that everyday people who embrace the projects that are the bedrock of the Black Lives Matter movement recognize that they are the "experts" on their own lives. They exemplify identity politics, the idea of critically analyzing and speaking from the specifics of one's social location, that constitutes one fundamental tenet of Black feminism itself.

The Black Lives Matter movement challenges the social hierarchies that produce experts and victims in order to build new intellectual and political communities. Black feminist thought and intersectionality thus directly influence the Black Lives Matter movement. An intersectional framework is rarely decontextualized—one need be neither a mother nor African-American to be concerned about the precarious status of Black boys and youth in the United States. Mothers of Black boys are front-line actors and, as such, have a distinctive standpoint on the challenges that face their sons. The question is more one of who has their backs, not whose latest book on their lives reaches the *New York Times* best-seller list.

The vast majority of Black boys are raised by their Black mothers, but not all Black youth live in African American families. Many Black youth are raised by their grandparents, their fathers, other relatives, the state or are in foster care. Still other Black youth live in multiracial, multiethnic families. Despite this variability, Black mothers not only carry a disproportionate responsibility for protecting their children from racial oppression, they see how racial oppression affects their sons and daughters differently. Charged with helping their children live to adulthood, Black mothers confront the vulnerabilities that their LGBTQ children face. Some Black mothers living in poverty have gone under, whereas others have found a way to "make a way out of no way." African-American mothers of Black children can draw on prior generations' experiences with navigating the challenges of white supremacy—Black mothers have always had to fear for our children.

Black children and youth in the US, especially those who are poor and working class and who live in urban areas, experience overt or subtle forms of macro- or microaggressions that limit their opportunities. Regardless of social class, Black youth are pressured to go to their assigned places. Adolescent boys and young men on the street encounter a heightened and often tragic version of these general social relations. Specifically, differential policing contributes to their being far more likely to have criminal records than other groups, and to be injured or killed by police. Adolescent girls and young women are differently vulnerable; they encounter gender-specific yet equally harmful mechanisms of enforcement. Sexual assault of young Black girls in private spaces of families, churches, and communities, often by the very people who should be protecting them, can leave wounds that are just as damaging as the bruises on young Black men who have been victimized by the police. Many African-American mothers sense these dangers that lie ahead for their children.

Albeit a much smaller group, White mothers of Black and/or biracial children encounter a different set of issues, especially those who are middle class. White, middle-class mothers are more likely to have resources that provide important forms of protection for their children, yet neither white parents nor money provide the full level of protection of having white skin. Many white mothers are surprised by the differential albeit often more subtle treatment their Black and/or biracial children receive, even in the best of neighbor-hoods and schools. The same gender-specific processes affect their children, not because people actively discriminate against them. Rather, the seemingly hardwired residue of racism makes their children vulnerable as well. The fact of Blackness in the US means that if you are obviously identifiable as Black, Latino, and/or Muslim, if you are young, and male, and are in the wrong place at the wrong time, you are at risk.

When will American adults begin to see that the current treatment of children constitutes a failure of the democratic possibilities of the American Dream? Placing Black children in the precarious position of fearing for their lives from one generation to the next impoverishes us all. No child should live in fear and poverty; the fact that children do so in a global context, espe-cially children of color, is more than a trauma for those who love them—it is a tragedy.

G. Y.: You've discussed the importance of love in reference to the work of June Jordon, Katie G. Cannon, and Toni Morrison. What does political work look like when it is fueled by love?

P. H. C.: My comments about the kinds of advocacy we must do on behalf of Black children and youth, children and youth of color, and children living in poverty stems from this kind of deep love. The notion of privatized love, of seeing one's own child as one's own private property to do with whatever one wishes, contributes to a host of social problems.

I aim to draw upon traditions among African-American women of caring for the community's children, a commitment to youth and the next gener-ation that is fueled by a form of love. I remain awed by what Black women have and can do on behalf of children. This is a politics that stems not solely from the intellect, but from the heart. It can be a focused, razor-sharp analysis where a Black mother confronts an uninformed and unsympathetic teacher because her child's future is at stake; or acts of organized political activism, as is the case in the work of Ella Baker, Septima Clark, and other important yet-lesser-known figures of the Civil Rights Movement. Neither romantic nor sentimental, this kind of love is fueled by a passion for social justice.

The problem is that far too few of us go above and beyond what is expected. This kind of love can easily slide into exploitation, one where everyone expects African-American women to take care of others before they care for them-selves, with little reciprocity in mind. I am heartened to hear the leaders of the Black Lives Matter movement raise issues of self-care. They realize that they cannot continue their political work that is grounded in this kind of love with-out the support of allies, friends, colleagues, and communities; they cannot sustain political work that is not fueled by love.

G. Y.: You've also talked about the importance of spirituality. In *Fighting Words: Black Women & the Search for Justice*, you write, "Spirituality broadly defined continues to move countless African-American women like Sojourner Truth to struggle in everyday life."[1] In what way does spirituality play a role within your scholarship, your life?

P. H. C.: There are many forms of spirituality, some religiously inspired, others less so. The term 'spirituality' is not one that I apply to my everyday life or to my scholarship. I have a deep respect for people who manage to claim forms of spirituality that work for them, yet when it comes to my work, I aim to retain space that can accommodate womanist theologians, Muslim clerics, Christian evangelicals and atheists. Any system of ideas that so powerfully draws people into political engagement cannot be uncritically censured and condemned or, alternately, uncritically followed as truth.

I do think that living by ethical principles is important and that this notion of ethics differs from general understandings of spirituality. Stated differently, I see a third space between the secularism of the the academy and the religiosity of oppressed peoples who often call upon a Supreme Being to get through times of trouble. In my own work, I rely on a short list of ethical principles to shape my everyday decision-making. Social justice is one of them. I'm especially drawn to Ida B. Wells-Barnett, Pauli Murray, and similar Black women intellectual-activists who have expressed a passion for justice. The idea of justice was not a philosophical construct, but was something that permeated their everyday lives. They breathed life into the idea of social justice by the actions they took in their everyday lives. This perspective draws upon experience as the crucible for testing beliefs. I see ethical work as neither a dogma of applying a theology or ideology to society and following the rules, nor as a way of working that is untethered from ethical considerations.

G. Y.: What are some conceptual gaps and problems vis-à-vis the sociological imagination that you would like to see critically engaged when it comes to the issue of race in America. Of course, I'm thinking of race through an intersectional lens.

P. H. C.: Quite frankly, the US has a wonderful vision of what society should be. Equity and opportunity—it's that simple for me and, most likely, for many new immigrant populations who strive to come to America despite significant personal or financial cost. People want to live in a society with opportunities, and they want those opportunities to be fairly distributed. Yet because the denial of both opportunity and equity in the US fosters intergenerational social inequalities, participatory democracy in the US is potentially unstable and most likely unsustainable. Despite the specific topics we study, the broader issue of social justice should inform our sociological imaginations. No one has all the answers because no one can see the myriad configurations of the social problems that accompany social injustice.

No one wins within a society characterized by bitter partisan politics that pits one political party against the other; or who engages in endless arguments to rank *either* racism *or* sexism *or* class exploitation as a more fundamental oppression; or the frontier mentality in some urban neighborhoods that pressures twelve-year-olds of color to choose their gang colors for safe passage to a failing public school. Holding fast to a worldview of winners and losers makes losers of us all.

The way forward regarding racism in America lies, in part, in critically analyzing our most cherished assumptions about what we think we know to be true. For many people living in the US, our media experiences are far more desegregated than anything we experience in everyday life. Intersectionality can help with this. No one wants to be wrong, but sometimes we are. We'll never know how wrong or right our ideas actually are until we listen to alternative perspectives. Remaining within insulated social groups with threadbare explanations that doing so protects our children, or that we just want to be with our kind of people ring hollow. Refusing to settle for the status quo and imagining something different, or at least believing in the possibility of such, begins with individual commitment to critical thinking.

The way forward regarding racism in America lies in choosing to commit to building something new. We have to commit to something bigger than ourselves. People of color have a long history of being on the front lines of antiracist projects, primarily because our safety and futures depend on it. African-Americans who want to see our children and grandchildren not only survive but also thrive know we cannot do it alone. Like the Black mothers discussed earlier, we do this work without expectation of praise or acknowledgement. I would like to see an army of quiet, committed, everyday activists, who get up every day and try to do the right thing, especially when no one is looking.

NOTE

1. Patricia Hill Collins, *Fighting Words: Black Women & the Search for Justice* (Minneapolis: University of Minnesota Press, 1998), 247.

Hortense Spillers

George Yancy: In perhaps your most frequently cited essay, "Mama's Baby, Papa's Maybe: An American Grammar Book," you discuss how, as a marked woman, you are nominated as "Peaches," "Brown Sugar," "Sapphire," "Earth Mother," "Aunty," a "Miss Ebony First," and so on. Within this context, you show, quite powerfully, that Black women have been stereotyped through a certain racist and masculinist discourse or grammar. Since the publication of that essay in 1987, in what ways has that grammar book expanded? In what ways are Black women or women of color still overdetermined by what you call "nominative properties"?

Hortense Spillers: My genuine surprise is that the picture whose outlines were rather starkly clear to me in 1987 has not been radically displaced or replaced by a different synthesis of discursive elements. Even though the public image horde of faces has been multiplied across the color line—in the movies, on television, and in other symptoms of media presence, i.e., cyberspace—the fundamental "grammars" of interracial relations and exchange still mandate "Blackness" as social deficit. We know this primarily by way of the acute outbreak of racist pathology that has shadowed and accompanied the presidency of Barack Obama; that it is still possible to draw him in malicious effigy and to mock the features of the First Lady as an exercise in denegation; that police brutality not only persists, but appears to have increased to the point of deliberate systematicity and provocation. All of this suggests, to my mind, that the mechanisms of public relations and belonging that situate individuals in the general economy of citizenship have not been sufficiently altered or even challenged. It is simply not enough that Black names and faces have been "added" to the national imaginary so much so that they are now no longer "alien" to the dream life of the nation, but whether or not such appearances have reconfigured the scale of value—in other words, the count or account in *quantity* must be subtended by a respect of persons that would disallow the everyday re-embrace of toxic misnaming. The fraternity jingle concocted by the frat boys at the University of Oklahoma recently lends a case in point—one can say such things just as a matter of course!

G. Y.: The point that you raise about First Lady Michelle Obama is an important one. She has also been caricatured as a male. I'm also reminded of what Shamil Tarpischev, Russian president of the Tennis Federation, said regarding the Williams sisters. He referred to them as "the Williams brothers" and said that it is "frightening" to play against them. Here we've got the masculinization of Black women's bodies in the twenty-first century, which perpetuates forms of toxic misnaming. Is this way of denigrating Black women's bodies still implicated in the nineteenth-century assumptions of the Cult of True Womanhood, especially with respect to the denial of any measure of "femininity" to Black women?

H. S.: Something quite peculiar has taken place: the "Cult of True Womanhood" no longer fits the ambitions of any American demographic, I would say, but its values have been absorbed into the national imaginary in such a way that the old "cult" has generated powerful surrogates that perform overtime. Today's "powerful" female, or "power" woman, is all the more fetching and seductive because she is presented *contrastively* to the outgoing "feminine mystique." As far as I can tell, African-American women, as a national demographic, do not participate in this mythos, or myth-making, except as a glaring absence. When one speaks of, or thinks of, women "overcoming," they usually do not mean Black women at all. It just occurred to me again that the major beneficiaries of the Civil Rights era, or we could say, the major "subjects" or "symptoms" of the Civil Rights era, which I'd say runs from 1948 (and Truman's Executive Order that mandated the desegregation of the armed forces of the United States), through the *Brown v. Board* Supreme Court case in 1954, to the presidential election of Ronald Reagan in 1980, were Black men and white women. Relatedly, the measure of the nation's success as an open and assimilative engine is determined by these subjects' access to the public sphere. Supposedly, one relinquishes "femininity" in achieving public standing, but it seems to me that it is precisely the *denial* of the feminine that rethreads it because one can now appreciate the "new" woman only insofar as she repeats the "old" one, *by contrast, by contradiction.* There seems to me an element of deep erotic (and male?) pleasure attached to this reel of a "wonder woman" with beautiful tits, or a queen in armor, wielding it over the guys in her band as a "femme fatal." It only appears to be female empowerment, while in truth it is a delicious disguise that fools no one, although we pretend to be deceived. And that's part of the fun, of the joke, that a critically emancipatory scheme has sadly become.

G. Y.: As you put it, this toxic misnaming is also evident in the racist chant that was captured on video of members of the University of Oklahoma's Sigma Alpha Epsilon chapter where "nigger" is used and where there is reference to lynching Black people. Say more about how you see anti-Black racism as not merely an aberration, but as something far more pervasive and systemic.

H. S.: Since Trayvon Martin's murder by a citizen-vigilante, the incidence of Black men shot down by police force seems to have soared. If you ask me, we are in the midst of a veritable pandemic of such killings. Need we be reminded that this pandemic is taking place, despite the fact that there is now a considerable number of Black law enforcement officers across the country and up and down it, that the Department of Justice is currently headed by a Black person, and if Attorney Loretta Lynch is ever confirmed, will continue to be? What does this mean? It is nearly unbearable that perhaps it doesn't mean very much in terms of actual power. We can certainly not say with unalterable conviction that it doesn't mean zip because a Black attorney general does hold tremendous *symbolic* power. But such power has not yet wielded sufficient *real* power enough to stare down anti-Black racism. I cannot get over those US senators and their letter to the Iranian government, for example, or the congressional approval that lent a stage to a foreign prime minister in defiance of the President of the United States. This stuff goes deep, and I cannot for a moment imagine it happening to a Bill Clinton or a Bush, the elder or the younger; the racial antipathy in these cases goes well beyond party and strikes at the very heart of the republic and its constitutional order. The President of the United States takes an oath of office to defend the country against *all enemies, foreign and domestic*. But are we keeping quiet because we're looking an enemy in the face, and it is us? We're quiet because it's true and to do something about it would move our heaven and our earth. That's how deep anti-Black racism is: we can't even talk about it, but only nibble around the edges.

G. Y.: I recall US Representative Joe Wilson, though I understand that he apologized, saying to President Obama in 2009 during his health care speech, "You lie!" Is it possible to disconnect this sort of outburst from the exercise of white male power? What does this sort of disrespect say about mere *symbolic* power?

H. S.: Actual power strikes fear while symbolic power does not necessarily do so. As I understand it, symbolic power is akin to something nice. One can take it or leave it, while what I am calling actual power or material power has genuine consequences. As far as I remember, nothing about the life of Representative Wilson changed as a result of his outburst. He was neither booted out of office or prosecuted for anything, nor lost life, limb, or income. I'm not necessarily saying that any of that would have been a desirable result in this case, but I am saying that *consequences* matter, and everybody understands that they do, and especially a congressman!

G. Y.: If it is true that we are keeping quiet because the enemy is us, what should we be saying? What is it that we should be admitting to ourselves, especially when it comes to the issue of race?

H. S.: It's hard to say all at once what we should be saying because there would be too much to try to sum up here. In thinking about an answer to this question, it occurred to me that the crisis of race, as old and time-honored as it is, cannot be "answered" all the time at the place of race, if that makes sense. In other words, certain race matters might be cleared up if we were more conscious about our own lives—what goes into our minds and bodies; James Baldwin says everywhere in his work, especially "Notes of a Native Son,"[1] that white America has a problem with Blackness because it evades and avoids dealing with its own denial of death, its own inability to face its vulnerabilities, its humanness. The determination to confront one's own demons is what I mean by greater consciousness. Racism seems to come out of a profound self-ignorance that expresses itself variously, e.g., a congressman yelling out in public space, the arrogance of power, etc. It also occurs to me that racism is one kind of problem, but actually, there is another and related one that I would call a form of "tribalism," which disorder appears to affect and infect metropolitan police departments in particular. This is an infantile view of the world, really, that demands, indeed *expects*, to find little replicas of itself repeated all over the place. For the "tribalist," the world is no bigger than his den and everybody in it looks like his mama and daddy and sisters and brothers, or ought to, and when they don't, he is disturbed! This family model of gaining access to the world through the assumptions and lenses of one's own family meets neither the requirements of modern living, nor the strenuous cordiality, let's call it, of fellow citizenship; in the latter case, the citizenry does not always, does not most of the time, repeat me, or give me back a friendly or exact image of myself, and coexistence is the game of learning to live with that. We call it "difference," and I suppose that's what it is, but to say difference is to speak about having to accept the dire fact that the world is big, and everybody in it does not know me. But some theorists suggest that learning to live with such ideas is what it means to live in a nation-state, which is not based on ethnicity and race, but rather the *political* idea. For example, American citizenship is not based on race or blood, at least not in its *theory* about itself. In other words, we are *constitutionally* defined, which has nothing to do with the way we look, the color of our skin, what God we serve, etc. The "tribalist" didn't get the memo, however!

G. Y.: I think that what Baldwin says is profound and important. So, how do we get white people to love themselves?

H. S.: George, if I knew the answer to that one, I'd patent it and retire a rich woman! I really don't know the answer to that question at all. But my guess is that it has something to do with parenting and working at eliminating all the funky little tyrannies and cruelties that begin, ironically enough, with family at the parental knee! But that's the chicken and the egg debate, isn't it? Better education? Greater self-esteem? I think I can catch hold of this question only *after* the tide comes in: my observation is that predominantly white organizations or units, for example—many of them academic—tolerate a lot of abuse, a great deal of *psychological* violence, carried out by immature actors, or people we'd call "a-holes," really; what we've isolated as "domestic" and "spousal" abuse, mostly directed at women and children, seems to identify a much broader pattern of dominance and timidity and willful surrender that expresses itself as the unhealthy status quo of many of our institutions. Probably wider spread than we realize, the kind of violence I am talking about often finds displacement in debates about the worth and significance of intellectual work, and because our highest value is critical intelligence and the production of knowledge, we often overlook conduct, which we read as "personal" or noninstitutional. The only conduct that we outright invigilate in our precincts is known as "sexual harassment," but it is clearer and clearer to me that there are whole provinces of the ethical that go untended in, for example, administrators' relations to faculty and staff, and in the latter's relations with each other. When this stuff crosses racial lines, you will discover, if you look closely enough, that the racial angle is often only the most visible and dramatic layer of an underlying fault line of fear and malice that racism allows to be staged. I'm certainly not saying that academic institutional racism is not real, but rather that it scratches the surface sometime of a more encompassing dis-ease. If academic white people, as a portion of a much larger human sample, cannot practice charity and intelligence in mutual human contact, then we really shouldn't be all that surprised that greater numbers do not either, those who supposedly don't know any better. I am suggesting that Baldwin was right to maintain that some of the racist cure would have to be sought elsewhere, in combatting the failures of self-love and regard. In racism, one finds distraction from the one subject that he utterly refuses to confront precisely because it is so repulsive to him! Baldwin, however, was no less vigilant and articulate about the spiritual health of Black folk in part because that of white folk was so poor.

G. Y.: Given what you've said about Black men and white women, perhaps when it comes to Black women, we need to ask a more specifically intersectional question: Do the lives of Black women, especially *poor Black women*, matter in America?

H. S.: The truth is that—and this is my strengthening impression—no one matters in America anymore! That's a far-out statement, but when you think about what's happening to our bought-off, bought-out political class, what I am suggesting gains some force. If you need two billion dollars nowadays to run for presidential office, that means that the office is out of the people's hands and into the hands of those who can afford to play the game. That is a transformation in American political life that we'd better pay careful attention to. What kind of system is it where those who rule are those who can pay? This has a name, and it is too fearful to repeat. Under such conditions, it might not be ridiculous to say that the posture of poor Black women is representative for any number of others.

G. Y.: And, yet, despite the claim that "no one matters in America anymore," which I think is indicative of moral decay, Black men continue to go missing. As one recent article has shown, "For every 100 Black women not in jail, there are only 83 Black men. The remaining men—1.5 million of them—are, in a sense, missing."[2] The concept of missing suggests the sense of having been abducted, or missing in action, or having been stolen.

H. S.: Yes, you've hit on a key narrative of Black presence in the West and the demographic and other complexities that such presence has assumed over the centuries. But it's interesting to me that what "begins" in abduction, if we think of the slave trade as a sustained story of theft and alienation, continues on this side of Middle Passage; I have often wondered what geographers might tell us if they could guess what the percentages of African losses have been since the fifteenth century when the transatlantic trade opens by way of Lisbon. If I'm not mistaken, this marks a pre-Columbian conjuncture that gathers speed and momentum as time passes, and the African Continent never recovers. I'd be curious to know how this massive human gap might be explained, compared to rates of growth in other parts of the world. I guess I'm asking a kind of counter-intuitive question that defies words, but it goes something like this: all things being equal and correcting for natural and man-made disasters, what would be the number of African peoples on planet Earth today if the transatlantic trade had not happened, or had been definitively interrupted sooner than the early nineteenth century? Closer to home, we wonder what the implications of that missing million and half men might be today—for sure, a lot of people don't get born, but even more importantly, those who do are not always properly nurtured and cared for. In the final analysis, that, to my mind, is the real import of "Black Lives Matter": in other words, Black life is not spawned or self-generating like amoeba (this seems to have been the idea of slavery), but must actually come into *birth*, and that is a supremely social idea. We can have children, can have generations, but what *happens* to them?

NOTES

1. James Baldwin, *Notes of a Native Son* (New York: Beacon Press, 1965).
2. Dartagnan, "The Unspoken American Experience: 1,500,000 Missing Black Men," *Daily Kos*, April 21, 2015, http://www.dailykos.com/story/2015/4/21/1379162/ -The-Unspoken-American-Experience-1-500-000-Missing-Black-Men.

Joy James

George Yancy: There are times when I've asked myself if philosophy can console in times of pain and suffering. Among my friends and colleagues of all races, the killings of Michael Brown, Akai Gurley, Tamir Rice, and Eric Garner and so many others like them have caused emotional pain—feelings of being sick and hurt, feelings of depression, angst, hopelessness. It's crazy.

Joy James: That's grief. And yes, it is crazy. Welcome to Black life under white supremacy.

Grief as a painful historical trajectory is one thing; to grieve intensely in the misery of the present moment is another. Ferguson, Staten Island, Brooklyn, and Cleveland (we can add Detroit for seven-year-old Aiyana Stanley-Jones, and Bastrop, Texas for Yvette Smith)—these dispersed sites have forced diverse people around the country and internationally to huddle closer together as we scrutinize laws and policies that reward police violence with immunity.

Being denigrated and victimized by your designated protectors is shocking to the core, because their job is to protect and serve. We're stunned because our trust in law is violated; police departments tolerate hyperaggressive officers by underreporting and underdisciplining them. These officers are not "going rogue" in wealthy, white communities because those communities have the economic and political resources to discipline them.

Police are our employees whom we have to obey ostensibly for our own safety and that of the general good; but also because they will hurt us, often with impunity, if we don't and sometimes even when we do obey.

Of course, police crime and the duplicity of law are not new to America. During the convict prison lease system and Jim Crow, a Black person could easily be arrested for not stepping off the sidewalk to let a white person pass. In Ferguson, it appears that not stepping on the sidewalk to let a white person pass—one whose salary was paid in part by Blacks—sparked the encounter that ended Michael Brown's life.

Nonetheless, despite how disturbing these structural and episodic assaults are, they also work as catalysts for substantive change. Police incompetence, malfeasance, and murder inspire outrage.

G. Y.: What are your thoughts on the killings of officers Wenjian Liu and Raphael Ramos? Does it complicate these issues?

J. J.: The murders of these New York City police officers highlight the dangers that both police and public face. When Ismaaiyl Brinsley first shot his former female partner in a domestic violence dispute in Baltimore then traveled to Brooklyn to randomly kill police officers, he invoked the killings of Michael Brown and Eric Garner as motivation. This invocation has been denounced by the Brown and Garner families, civil rights activists, the president and attorney general, and city leaders. What any mentally ill or criminal person does is not representative of a movement for human rights.

G. Y.: What are the implications of the suffering amid police violence?

J. J.: In a democracy, the implications for an ill-informed citizenry are grim. The recent tragedies remind us that this violence is sadly familiar to those who have a complex memory. We've grappled with racial animus and hatred from overseers, Klansmen and women, police, segregationists, integrationists, and various sectors of society from academia to athletics.

The implications of public servants and deputized vigilantes violating Black life with impunity are profound, especially for young Black people. If police are sending some message indicating that, despite having a Black president and attorney general, in regards to anti-Black violence, the police have immunity and a renewable license to overcriminalize, overprosecute, traumatize, and kill, then their position has been noted in social media throughout the globe.

We need to publicly debate whether it is just, moral, and appropriate, or even safe and sane, to believe in modern policing given the fallibility, corruption, and danger present in the institution. Police agencies have a history of racial bias and violence that has been investigated and condemned by governments as well as civil and human rights organizations. Citizens are supposed to flee or fight criminals, not the police. But reality teaches you that in Black life you need to be ever vigilant for both.

We have diverse strategies. Some offer extensive documentation on how the legal system adversely and disproportionately affects Black life due to gender and racial-economic bias. Some debate those who deny crises structured through state-sanctioned violence. Others expand the civil rights struggle into international human rights, using petitions to the UN and testimony before the UN Committee Against Torture (CAT).

Many instruct their children about the meanings of teenagers and children dying violently at the hands of those seemingly "above the law": the

Michael Browns, Tamir Rices, Renisha McBrides, Aiyana Stanley-Joneses, Trayvon Martins. A few have the ironic pleasure of false hope fading into realism when they see that their children can instruct them; for example, the Deacons for Defense Robert Williams audio-documentary they are listening to is not a courageous NPR special report sensitively attuning its listeners to the historic place and need for Black self-defense from racist violence, but a CD offering slipped into the player by an inquisitive six-year-old, a random act of grace.

G. Y.: What do we do with despair at the moment regarding these killings? What do we do to avoid feelings of implosion?

J. J.: We mix sorrow with something else. We've historically done that as a people. Ida B. Wells as an antilynching activist, who was eventually marginalized by more integrated and institutionally powerful Blacks, always said she would sell her life "dearly" to a lyncher. She didn't have to (apparently she died from exhaustion and lack of support for her radical opposition to racism). Ida B. Wells loved, deeply and immensely; traumatized and transformed by the Memphis lynching of Thomas Moss, the father of her goddaughter, she became an activist. Targeted for economic competition with whites, Moss was lynched in 1892 with other Black men following the exchange of gunfire with white, unidentified policemen who approached the Black grocer's store at night, through a dark alley, with their guns drawn. Realizing the injured men were police, Moss and his associates went to the police to explain the mistake. Their murders at the hands of mob and police sparked an antilynching movement.

Decades later, just before Rosa Parks refused to give up her seat because, she stated, she thought of Emmett Till, Mamie Till defied the law and held an open casket for her mutilated fourteen-year-old son, Emmett, who broke "law" and custom by allegedly whistling at a white woman. He had a lisp; and later, in 2017, the press reported that the woman felt "tender sorrow" for lying in court that the teen had accosted her. Emmett was subsequently tortured and murdered; his white killers acquitted, later confessed to the crime for a $3000 payment in a LIFE interview. Women activists such as Till and Parks loved life, family, and community and inspired the courageous reinvention of America through social and political movements.

People sometimes miss that outrage and resistance are guided by love and the desire to bring honor to life brutally taken. We continue to remember atrocities through demonstrations and protests in sports, although traumatized by social and domestic violence and struggling with depression or lack of resources, Black communities still organize forums against gun violence, unequal educational resources, drug addictions, gentrification, employment and housing discrimination.

G. Y.: Why has racism persisted so long within the North American context?

J. J.: Because it is desirable and profitable. As the late great civil rights leader and historian Vincent Harding noted, this crisis is structural and endemic. But it is not evenly felt and for some it is enjoyable. Anti-Black prejudicial bias exists not only in policing but also in education, employment, health, and housing. "The law" has been an impediment to Black lives mattering since the "three-fifths clause" to the US Constitution legalized bodily theft to build a democracy favoring white property holders placing presidential power disproportionately into the hands of southern slave owners who benefited from the electoral college counting of nonvoting enslaved. The Thirteenth Amendment, known as the emancipation amendment, legalized slavery for those duly convicted of crimes, establishing the foundation for the convict prison lease system where Blacks died faster in freedom than they had on plantations as they were worked to death to benefit northern capital, emergent southern state economies, and an expansion of the white middle class through the trade of Black bodies via policing, courts, agricultural and infrastructure development. Jim Crow, foster care disproportionality, racially fashioned policing and incarceration and—as Marvin Gaye notes in "Inner City Blues (Make Me Wanna Holler)"—"trigger-happy policing" are all part of the fabric of American life that has a historical relation to Black lives based on consumption.

North American (Canadian, US, Mexican) racisms have violent directives tied to genocidal wars of annihilation and capture of Native and African Americans. In the ambitions of assimilation, one of the fastest ways to become "American" is to become "white." So, various ethnic groups position themselves along the continuum in which Blacks and Blackness are the antithesis of white as civic virtue and economic wealth. Racism is also economically and existentially profitable. Proximity to "whiteness" helps, as studies have shown, in obtaining jobs, housing, promotions; just as gender and sexism lead to differential pay for women, race and racism create differentials in the acquisition of resources.

Racism is sexualized, embedded with racial–sexual slander, and micro- and macroaggressions against Blacks (males and females, trans and gender fluid people). Normative as entertainment, fungible and edible, we are key to the American "libidinal" economy. For some, Black suffering is enjoyable as spectacle; and so for Black people in public or private life, there is in first and all encounters no suffering or confusion that is sacred or worth protection.

G. Y.: How does your understanding of that persistence relate to the current situation?

J. J.: Now, as historically, there is inadequate public thought and language about institutional, interpersonal, and internalized violence consuming Black people and society in general.

2014 is our 1892 (the year whose atrocities sparked Ida B. Wells's anti-lynching crusades). In 2014, we saw more clearly the "crazy" of our social order and how important and necessary international interventions are, such as CAT (which ruled that the US needed to de-militarize its police; address torture of minorities in police custody and diminish rape in prison). In October 2014, former Chicago police commissioner Jon Burge was released from prison, after running a torture ring that imprisoned over one hundred Black men. For over twenty years, Burge, who is white, led an anti-Black torture ring to obtain false confessions. Torture included cattle prods to their genitals, and near suffocation through plastic bags over their heads (some of the tactics evoke the report on the CIA's interrogation techniques). Due to the statute of limitations, Burge was convicted of perjury in 2010 and sentenced to four and a half years in prison. The officer-torturers now reportedly collect millions in pensions; and Chicago has settled more in compensation to their victims. Where the nation compensates racial and sexual predators by keeping them on the taxpayers' rolls, restorative justice remains elusive and structural accountability is rarely possible. Talking about the tragic murder rate in Chicago of mostly Black males is empty talk if it is severed from predatory policing, exploitative governance, the scarcity of decent jobs, housing, food, and schooling.

Restorative justice is complex. It is also unnecessarily complicated by police structures that claim omnipotence in the face of Black lives. In the absence of a clear line between criminal and police behavior, fear is the enforcer. Ironically, Black Americans are regularly taxed to pay salaries, pensions, and benefits to police forces that disproportionately target Black life through penalties and fines, brutality, and disrespect. We are also, like other Americans, taxed to pay for military interventions waged for geopolitical dominance rather than the expansion of human rights. In 2014 as our 1892, the Senate Intelligence Committee's report on CIA interrogation reported that the CIA lied to the public and government about its use of torture, and that its human rights violations rendered the United States not safer but more barbaric. Why would state and local police expect a different outcome if they treat Black communities as "enemies" and against whom excessive force can be legitimately deployed?

G. Y.: So, where do we go from here?

J. J.: When Congressman John Lewis, a former SNCC (Student Nonviolent Coordinating Committee) activist, stated at the beginning of the rebellion that Ferguson may have sparked another Civil Rights Movement, he was initially met with skepticims from the president through media to the local preacher. One constant is that older generations, and nonactivists, tend to underestimate the power of outraged, young Black people who demand justice. During the twentieth-century Civil Rights Movement, Ella Baker emphasized that the movement was about "more than a hamburger," that is, its goals aspired to more than access to consumer society at the highest levels. Historical leadership of Ella Baker, Fannie Lou Hamer, Rosa Parks, Audre Lorde prepared us for the present moment.

We've witnessed, feared and contested police violence for centuries. Resistance is resilient until it is broken; then for a time, it becomes dormant, but it always reappears. Today more attention is paid to sexual and physical assaults against Black women and girls, and structural, social, and interpersonal violence against transwomen, girls, women, boys and men, by state and society. The demands for institutional and communal goals of "zero death" and "zero trauma" increase as we better understand our real vulnerabilities and our desires to transcend them.

Black lives matter as a coda is both an assertion and a desire. The women who crossed gender divisions to follow in and bend traditions of political leadership to make this a shared language maintain that Black lives matter because we make them matter. Yet, all Black lives do not equally matter even to us. Propertied and impoverished Blacks are exhausted by legal and policing apparatuses that have historically preyed upon Black life. Transgressions into Black lives cut across class lines, but disproportionately the poor and working class are the most vulnerable to violence.

If we as ideologically diverse Black people have a no-divorce clause with US democracy, the site of our battery, then where do we go from here? The divide between de jure and de facto justice concerning Blacks in the Americas is a chasm. Our struggles are opportunities to bridge or jump; either way we are engaged in movement for security, justice, and a greater democracy.

PART I DISCUSSION QUESTIONS

1. Hortense Spillers and Patricia Hill Collins discuss the divisive tendency of some forms of love and love's privatization. Love of this sort appears to bring about and perpetuate racial hate. The inclusive, public, and expansive kind of love that bell hooks discusses is likely crucial in overcoming racial hate, but it also requires vulnerability. George Yancy asks Hortense Spillers how we can get white people to love themselves; but how do we even secure the condition for the possibility of love, namely that white people become vulnerable with respect to race?
2. How can we incorporate self-criticality among white people that encourages self-awareness without fueling counterproductive self-hatred?
3. Joy James points out that civil and human rights movements are about more than acquisition through consumerism, or, in reference to Ella Baker's assertion: "the movement was about 'more than a hamburger.'" How might we redirect consumer society's (surplus) consumption and excess toward a public ethics focused on universal access to healthcare, economic decency and employment, and the right to life and security from violence and neglect?

4. One of the strengths of Black Feminist thought is its intersectional capabilities and the ability to appreciate and account for the multiplicity of suffering beneath layers of oppression. How can one avoid falling into relativism when including many intersections of oppression and injustice in a single person's experience? Does ideology play a role in our analysis of intersectionality?

Race and the Naming of Whiteness

Judith Butler

George Yancy: In your 2004 book, *Precarious Life: The Powers of Mourning and Violence*, you wrote, "The question that preoccupies me in the light of recent global violence is, Who counts as human? Whose lives count as lives?"[1] You wrote that about the post-9/11 world, but it appears to also apply to the racial situation here in the United States. In the wake of the recent killings of unarmed Black men and women by police, and the failure to prosecute the killers, the message being sent to Black communities is that they don't matter, that they are "disposable." Posters reading "Black Lives Matter," "Hands Up. Don't Shoot," "I Can't Breathe," communicate the reality of a specific kind of racial vulnerability that Black people experience on a daily basis. How does all this communicate to Black people that their lives don't matter?

Judith Butler: Perhaps we can think about the phrase, "Black lives matter." What is implied by this statement, a statement that should be obviously true, but apparently is not? If Black lives do not matter, then they are not really regarded as lives, since a life is supposed to matter. So what we see is that some lives matter more than others, that some lives matter so much that they need to be protected at all costs, and that other lives matter less, or not at all. And when that becomes the situation, then the lives that do not matter so much, or do not matter at all, can be killed or lost, can be exposed to conditions of destitution, and there is no concern, or even worse, that is regarded as the way it is supposed to be. The callous killing of Tamir Rice and the abandonment of his body on the street is an astonishing example of the police murdering someone considered disposable and fundamentally ungrievable.

When we are taking about racism, and anti-Black racism in the United States, we have to remember that under slavery Black lives were considered only a fraction of a human life, so the prevailing way of valuing lives assumed that some lives mattered more, were more human, more worthy, more deserving of life and freedom, where freedom meant minimally the freedom to move and thrive without being subjected to coercive force. But when and where did Black lives ever really get free of coercive force? One reason the chant "Black Lives Matter" is so important is that it states the obvious but the obvious has not yet been historically realized. So it is a statement of outrage and a demand for equality, for the right to live free of constraint, but also a chant that links the history of slavery, of debt peonage, of segregation, and of a prison system geared toward the containment, neutralization, and degradation of Black lives, to a police system that more and more easily and often can take away a Black life in a flash all because some officer perceives a threat.

So let us think about what this is: the perception of a threat. One man is leaving a store unarmed, but he is perceived as a threat. Another man is in a chokehold and states that he cannot breathe, and the chokehold is not relaxed, and the man dies because he is perceived as a threat. Mike Brown and Eric Garner. We can name them, but in the space of this interview, we cannot name all the Black men and women whose lives are snuffed out all because a police officer perceives a threat, sees the threat in the person, sees the person as pure threat. Perceived as a threat even when unarmed or completely physically subdued, or lying in the ground, as Rodney King clearly was, or coming back home from a party on the train and having the audacity to say to a policeman that he was not doing anything wrong and should not be detained: Oscar Grant. We can see the videos and know what is obviously true, but it is also obviously true that police and the juries that support them obviously do not see what is obvious, or do not wish to see.

So the police see a threat when there is no gun to see, or someone is subdued and crying out for his life, when they are moving away or cannot move. These figures are perceived as threats even when they do not threaten, when they have no weapon, and the video footage that shows precisely this is taken to be a ratification of the police's perception. The perception is then ratified as a public perception, at which point we not only must insist on the dignity of Black lives, but name the racism that has become ratified as public perception.

In fact, the point is not just that Black lives can be disposed of so easily: they are targeted and hunted by a police force that is becoming increasingly emboldened to wage its race war by every grand jury decision that ratifies the point of view of state violence. Justifying lethal violence in the name of self-defense is reserved for those who have a publicly recognized self to defend. But those whose lives are not considered to matter, whose lives are perceived as a threat to the life that embodies white privilege, can be destroyed in the name of that life. That can only happen when a recurrent and institutionalized form of racism has become a way of seeing, entering into the presentation of visual evidence to justify hateful and unjustified and heart-breaking murder.

So it is not just that Black lives matter, though that must be said again and again. It is also that stand-your-ground and racist killings are becoming increasingly normalized, which is why intelligent forms of collective outrage have become obligatory.

G. Y.: The chant "Black Lives Matter" is also a form of what you would call "a mode of address." You discuss questions of address in your essay, "Violence, Nonviolence: Sartre on Fanon,"[2] where Fanon, for example, raises significant questions about sociality in talking about his freedom in relationship to a "you." "Black Lives Matter" says something like, "*You*—white police officers—recognize my/our humanity!" But what if the "you," in this case, fails to be moved, refuses to be touched by that embodied chant? And given that "racism has become a way of seeing," is it not necessary that we—as you say in your essay "Endangered/Endangering: Schematic Racism and White Paranoia"—install "an antiracist hegemony over the visual field"?[3]

J. B.: Sometimes a mode of address is quite simply a way of speaking to or about someone. But a mode of address may also describe a general way of approaching another such that one presumes who the other is, even the meaning and value of their existence. We address each other with gesture, signs, and movement, but also through media and technology. We make such assumptions all the time about who that other is when we hail someone on the street (or we do not hail them). That is someone I greet; the other is someone I avoid. That other may well be someone whose very existence makes me cross to the other side of the road.

Indeed, in the case of schematic racism, anti-Black racism figures Black people through a certain lens and filter, one that can quite easily construe a Black person, or another racial minority, who is walking toward us as someone who is potentially, or actually, threatening, or is considered, in his or very being, a threat. In fact, as we can doubtless see from the videos that have swept across the global media, it may be that even when a Black man is moving away from the police, that man is still considered to be a threat or worth killing, as if that person were actually moving toward the police brandishing a weapon. Or it could be that a Black man or woman is reaching for his or her identification papers to show to the police, and the police see in that gesture of compliance—hand moving toward pocket—a reach for a gun. Is that because, in the perception of the police, to be Black is already to be reaching for a gun? Or a Black person is sleeping on the couch, standing, walking, or even running, clearly brandishing no gun, and there turns out to be evidence that there is no gun, but still that life is snuffed out—why? Is the gun imagined into the scene, or retrospectively attributed to the standing or fleeing figure (and the grand jury nods, saying "this is plausible")? And why when that person is down, already on the ground, and seeks to lift himself, or seated against a subway grate, and seeks to speak on his own behalf, or is utterly subdued and imperiled by a chokehold, does he never stop looming as a threat to security, prompting a policeman to beat him or gun him down?

It may be important to see the twisted vision and the inverted assumptions that are made in the course of building a "case" that the police acted in self-defense or were sufficiently provoked to use lethal force. The fleeing figure is coming this way; the nearly strangled person is about to unleash force; the man on the ground will suddenly spring to life and threaten the life of the one who therefore takes his life.

These are war zones of the mind that play out on the street. At least in these cases that have galvanized the nation and the world in protest, we all see the twisted logic that results in the exoneration of the police who take away the lives of unarmed Black men and women. And why is that the case? It is not because what the police and their lawyers present as their thinking in the midst of the situation is very reasonable. No, it is because that form of thinking is *becoming more "reasonable" all the time*. In other words, every time a grand jury or a police review board accepts this form of reasoning, they ratify the idea that Blacks are a population against which society must be defended, and that the police defend themselves and (white) society, when they preemptively shoot unarmed Black men in public space. At stake is a way that Black people are figured as a threat even when they are simply living their lives, walking the street, leaving the convenience store, riding the subway, because in those instances this is only a threatening life, or a threat to the only kind of life, white life, that is recognized.

G. Y.: What has led us to this place?

J. B.: Racism has complex origins, and it is important that we learn the history of racism to know what has led us to this terrible place. But racism is also reproduced in the present, in the prison system, new forms of population control, increasing economic inequality that affects people of color disproportionately. These forms of institutionalized destitution and inequality are reproduced through daily encounters—the disproportionate numbers of minorities stopped and detained by the police, and the rising number of those who fall victim to police violence. The figure of the Black person as threat, as criminal, as someone who is, no matter where he is going, already-on-the-way-to-prison, conditions these preemptive strikes, attributing lethal aggression to the very figure who suffers it most. The lives taken in this way are not lives worth grieving; they belong to the increasing number of those who are understood as ungrievable, whose lives are thought not to be worth preserving.

But, of course, what we are also seeing in the recent and continuing assemblies, rallies, and vigils is an open mourning for those whose lives were cut short and, without cause, brutally extinguished. The practices of public mourning and political demonstration converge: when lives are considered ungrievable, to grieve them openly is to protest. So when people assemble in the street, arrive at rallies or vigils, demonstrate with the aim of opposing this form of racist violence, they are "speaking back" to this mode of address, insisting on what should be obvious but is not, namely, that these lost lives are unacceptable losses.

On the one hand, there is a message, "Black Lives Matter," which always risks being misheard ("What? Only *Black* lives matter?") or not heard at all ("these are just people who will protest anything"). On the other hand, the assembly, even without words, enacts the message in its own way. For it is often in public spaces where such violence takes place, so reclaiming public space to oppose both racism and violence is an act that reverberates throughout the public sphere through various media.

G. Y.: I've heard that some white people have held signs that read, "All Lives Matter."

J. B.: When some people rejoin with "All Lives Matter," they misunderstand the problem, but not because their message is untrue. It is true that all lives matter, but it is equally true that not all lives are understood to matter, which is precisely why it is most important to name the lives that have not mattered, and are struggling to matter in the way they deserve.

Claiming that "all lives matter" does not immediately mark or enable Black lives only because they have not been fully recognized as having lives that matter. I do not mean this as an obscure riddle. I mean only to say that we cannot have a race-blind approach to the questions: which lives matter? Or, which lives are worth valuing? If we jump too quickly to the universal formulation "all lives matter," then we miss the fact that Black people have not yet been included in the idea of "all lives." That said, it is true that all lives matter (we can then debate about when life begins or ends). But to make that universal formulation concrete, to make that into a living formulation, one that truly extends to all people, we have to foreground those lives that are not mattering now, to mark that exclusion, and militate against it. Achieving that universal, "all lives matter," is a struggle, and that is part of what we are seeing on the streets. For on the streets we see a complex set of solidarities across color lines that seek to show what a concrete and living sense of bodies that matter can be.

G. Y: When you talk about lives that matter, are you talking about how whiteness and white bodies are valorized? In *Gender Trouble: Feminism and the Subversion of Identity*, you discuss gender as "a stylized repetition of acts."[4] Do you also see whiteness as "a stylized repetition of acts" that solidifies and privileges white bodies, or even leads to naïve, "postracial" universal formulations like "all lives matter"?

J. B.: Yes, we can certainly talk about "doing whiteness" as a way of putting racial categories into action, since whiteness is part of what we call "race," and is often implicitly or explicitly part of a race project that seeks to achieve and maintain dominance for white people. One way this happens is by establishing whiteness as the norm for the human, and Blackness as a deviation from the human or even as a threat to the human, or as something not quite human. Under such perceptual conditions built up through the history of racism, it becomes increasingly easy for white people to accept the destruction of Black lives as the status quo, since those lives do not fit the norm of "human life" they defend. It is true that Frantz Fanon sometimes understood whiteness in gendered terms: a Black man is not a man, according to the white norms that define manhood, and yet other times the Black man is figured as the threat of rape, hypermasculinized, threatening the "virgin sanctity" of whiteness.

In that last formulation, whiteness is figured as a young virgin whose future husband is white; this characterization ratifies the sentiments that oppose miscegenation and defend norms or racial purity. But whose sexuality is imperiled in this scene? After all, Black women and girls were the ones who were raped, humiliated, and disposed of under conditions of slavery, and it was Black families who were forcibly destroyed: Black kinship was not recognized as kinship that matters. Women of color, and Black feminists in particular, have struggled for years against being the sexual property of either white male power or Black masculinity, against poverty, and against the prison industry, so there are many reasons why it is necessary to define racism in ways that acknowledge the specific forms it takes against men, women, and transgendered people of color.

Let us remember, of course, that many Black women's lives are taken by police and by prisons. We can name a few: Yvette Smith, forty-eight, in Texas, unarmed, and killed by police; or Aiyana Stanley-Jones, age seven, killed while sleeping on her father's couch in Detroit. After all, all of those are remembered by the people on the street, outraged and demonstrating, opposing a lethal power that is becoming more and more normalized and, to that degree, more and more outrageous.

Whiteness is less a property of the skin than a social power reproducing its dominance in both explicit and implicit ways. When whiteness is a practice of superiority over minorities, it monopolizes the power of destroying or demeaning bodies of color. The legal system is engaged in reproducing whiteness when it decides that the Black person can and will be punished more severely than the white person who commits the same infraction, or when that same differential is at work in the question, Who can and will be detained? And who can and will be sent to prison with a life sentence or the death penalty? Angela Davis has shown the disproportionate number of Americans of color (Black and Latino) who are detained, imprisoned, and on death row. This has become a "norm" that effectively says, "Black lives do not matter," one that is built up over time, through daily practices, modes of address, through the organization of schools, work, prison, law, and media. Those are all ways that the conceit of white superiority is constructed.

G. Y.: Yes. Whiteness, as a set of historical practices, extends beyond the skin. And yet, when a person with white skin walks into a store, it is assumed that she is not a threat. So, there is an entire visual technology that is complicit here, where the skin itself, as it were, is the marker of innocence. It is a visual technology that reinforces not only her sense of innocence, but that organizes the ways in which she gets to walk through space without being profiled or stopped. Hence, she contributes to the perpetuation of racial injustice even if she is unaware of doing so.

J. B.: Well, of course, class is also there as a marker of how anyone is perceived entering the door to the public building, the office, the post office, the convenience story. Class is in play when white people fail to look "monied" or are considered as working class, poor, or homeless, so we have to be clear that the "white" person we may be talking about can be struggling with inequality of another kind: whiteness has its own internal hierarchies, to be sure. Of course there are white people who may be very convinced that they are not racist, but that does not necessarily mean that they have examined, or worked though, how whiteness organizes their lives, values, the institutions they support, how they are implicated in ways of talking, seeing, and doing that constantly and tacitly discriminate. Undoing whiteness has to be difficult work, but it starts, I think, with humility, with learning history, with white people learning how the history of racism persists in the everyday vicissitudes of the present, even as some of us may think we are "beyond" such a history, or even convinced that we have magically become "postracial." It is difficult and ongoing work, calling on an ethical disposition and political solidarity that risks error in the practice of solidarity.

Whiteness is not an abstraction; its claim to dominance is fortified through daily acts that may not seem racist at all precisely because they are considered "normal." But just as certain kinds of violence and inequality get established as "normal" through the proceedings that exonerate police of the lethal use of force against unarmed Black people, so whiteness, or rather its claim to privilege, can be disestablished over time. This is why there must be a collective reflection on, and opposition to, the way whiteness takes hold of our ideas about whose lives matter. The norm of whiteness that supports both violence and inequality insinuates itself into the normal and the obvious. Understood as the sometimes tacit and sometimes explicit power to define the boundaries of kinship, community, and nation, whiteness inflects all those frameworks within which certain lives are made to matter less than others.

It is always possible to do whiteness otherwise, to engage in a sustained and collective practice to question how racial differentiation enters into our daily evaluations of which lives deserve to be supported, to flourish, and which do not. But it is probably an error, in my view, for white people to become paralyzed with guilt and self-scrutiny. The point is rather to consider those ways of valuing and devaluing life that govern our own thinking and acting, understanding the social and historical reach of those ways of valuing. It is probably important, and satisfying as well, to let one's whiteness recede by joining in acts of solidarity with all those who oppose racism. There are ways of fading out whiteness, withdrawing from its implicit and explicit claims to racial privilege. Demonstrations have the potential to embody forms of equality that we want to see realized in the world more broadly. Working against those practices and institutions that refuse to recognize and mark the powers of state racism in particular, assemblies gather to mourn and resist the deadly consequences of such powers. When people engage in concerted actions across racial lines to build communities based on equality, they defend the rights of those who are disproportionately imperiled to have a chance to live without the fear of dying suddenly at the hands of the police. There are many ways to do this, in the street, the office, the home, and in the media. Only through such an ever-growing cross-racial struggle against racism can we begin to achieve a sense of all the lives that really do matter.

NOTES

1. Judith Butler, *Precarious Life: The Powers of Mourning and Violence* (New York: Verso, 2006), 20.
2. Judith Butler, "Violence, Nonviolence: Sartre on Fanon," in *Senses of the Subject* (New York: Fordham University Press, 2015), 171–98.
3. Judith Butler, "Endangered/Endangering: Schematic Racism and White Paranoia," in *Reading Rodney King/Reading Urban Uprising*, ed. Robert Gooding-Williams (New York: Routledge, 1993), 15–22; 17.
4. Judith Butler, *Gender Trouble: Feminism and the Subversion of Identity* (New York: Routledge, [1990] 1999), 179.

Alison Bailey

George Yancy: I came across an important endnote in your chapter entitled "Strategic Ignorance." You wrote, "Whites may be privilege-cognizant but metaphysically comfortable."[1] What exactly do you mean by 'metaphysically comfortable'?

Alison Bailey: That's an important endnote and one that requires some unpacking, so please bear with me! In the early days of critical whiteness studies, Ruth Frankenberg made a useful distinction between the privilege-*cognizant* and privilege-*evasive* responses that white women gave to a series of questions about how whiteness was lived, discussed, and experienced. She was one of the first scholars who prompted me to notice how much we can learn about white ways of knowing and being, by listening to how white people talk about race. Privilege-cognizant responses acknowledge and engage white privilege (e.g., "I understand how my whiteness is an asset for any move I want to make in life"). These responses are epistemically opening; they offer us an epistemic traction that moves conversations forward. Privilege-evasive responses are defensive, epistemically closing moves that maintain white ignorance. What Alice Macintyre calls "white talk" (e.g., "I'm not racist, most of my friends are Latinx," or "I get stopped by the police too!") are examples of this. These engagements offer no epistemic traction in social justice discussions. The endnote that caught your attention asks readers to look deeply at the common metaphysical foundation that underwrites *both* sets of responses.

Robin DiAngelo's account of "white fragility" has advanced my understanding of the deep and abiding hold metaphysical comfort has on white folks' sense of ourselves as so-called white people. White people live in a social environment that insulates us from race-based anxiety and stress. This protective environment fosters expectations of racial comfort. We feel entitled to be racially at ease most of the time, and indeed most of us have the freedom to structure our daily lives and movements to ensure that we are. In general, white fragility triggers a constellation of behaviors that work to steer us back to places where we feel whole, comfortable, innocent, and good. These expectations of racial comfort mean that, with few exceptions, white folks have a low tolerance for racial stress. This deep urge to remain metaphysically comfortable drives *both* privilege-evasiveness and privilege-cognizance. Also, privilege-evasive responses are privilege preserving: they maintain white comfort through denial and defensiveness. Consider the anger-laced claims such as "I am the *least* racist person you've ever met." These responses are a form of worldview protection—they work to resist new information that deeply unsettles white folks' sense of entitlement to comfort and how we understand our place in the social order. When a particular core belief—say about the United States being a meritocracy—is challenged, we become deeply agitated, unsettled, and defensive. We attempt to bolster our metaphysical wholeness with stories about our merit-based accomplishments, family immigration history, or the long hours we've worked. These narratives are one way that we keep ourselves intact.

The urge for metaphysical comfort also drives privilege-cognizant white responses, but this point seems counterintuitive, so it's easy to miss. Most white people resist doing deep critical antiracist work. We have a tendency, as Sara Ahmed puts it, to "flee the unfinished history"[2] of racism. Highlighting white goodness and innocence masks our fragility; it allows us to embrace whiteness in ways that don't threaten our metaphysical comfort. We engage racial injustice movements *in safe ways* by steering conversations back to our good deeds, quoting people of color, taking minimal emotional risks, whitewashing our family histories, and following *#BlackLivesMatter* on Twitter, but not in our community. The energy we put into assuring others that we are good-hearted and loyal allies is another means of holding white selves together. These moves are, in a subtle way, also privilege preserving: they bolster our metaphysical invulnerability by insulating us from race-based anxiety.

I am continually astounded by the persistence and depth of these yearnings in my own conversations with folks of color, and how often, despite my efforts to be mindful of the twin lures of defensiveness and goodness, I've caught myself steering a particular conversation back to a more comfortable place. White folks' efforts to work toward privilege-cognizance in ways that preserve metaphysical comfort worry me. I think that for white people to do deep, meaningful, antiracist work, that we need to not be afraid to fall apart.

G. Y.: I see. But these moves illustrate how white people keep it together. What would it really look like for white people to "fall apart"? I like your use of this metaphor because it implies a form of crisis.

A. B.: Yes, I think crisis is an accurate description here. Crises throw us into spaces where the center doesn't hold. These spaces produce anxiety, fear, panic, and foment an urgency to repair the situation by restoring the world to *exactly* the way it was before the crisis. The image that comes to mind for me is the town that gets hit by a tornado and decides to rebuild their community using the original city plan, hiring the same architects, keeping the old street names, building the same houses in the same places, and painting them the same colors. White defensiveness and retreats to goodness are responses to crisis in this sense of the word. The responses aim at restoring the comfort of the old order, and that's not what I'm after here.

Your own use of 'crisis' is closer to its Greek origins in 'decision.' Decisions are represented geographically as crossroads or turning points. I have mixed feelings about these metaphors. On the one hand, I like the way that they direct our attention away from panicked attempts at restorative repair and toward places of openness and possibility. On the other hand, I worry that they narrowly characterize decision making as a strictly cognitive process directed at choosing among structured pre-existing roads. For white selves to fall apart, we need to go "off road," so to speak. We need to make a concerted effort to leave the locations, texts, values, aesthetics, metaphysics, and epistemologies where we are at ease. We need to work with an understanding of crisis/repair that is transformative rather than merely restorative.

I'm attracted to borderland theory in general, and to the work of Gloria Anzaldúa and María Lugones in particular, because these scholars/activists offer a conceptual vocabulary that foregrounds the transformative sense of repair. In her later work, Anzaldúa uses the Náhuatl word 'nepantla' to describe an *unstructured* liminal space that facilitates transformation. It is a psychic, spiritual, epistemic, and sometimes geographic space characterized by intense confusion, anxiety, and loss of control. It describes a moment or span of time when our beliefs, worldviews, and self-identities crumble. *Nepantla* is messy, confusing, painful, and chaotic; it signals unexpected, uncontrollable shifts, transitions, and changes. This is something you feel with your heart and body. It's a precognitive response to the fear of losing your ontological bearings that slowly works its way up into your head. Eventually you surrender. The old worldviews, beliefs, perspectives, and ontologies that once grounded you are but memories, and you find yourself working on a new epistemic home terrain.

In *nepantla*, we shift and a resistant self emerges; that is, a self that now can "see through" the old social order and resists reconstruction along the old lines of that order. Consider the shift that happens for most LGBTQ people during the coming-out process, or during religious conversions, or when someone comes to have a class consciousness or feminist consciousness. You can't go back because you've seen through the fictions of heteronormativity, a godless life, white supremacy, capitalism, or patriarchy.

G. Y.: Yes, you and I agree here about crisis. I mean not only the sense of losing one's footing, of *losing one's way*, or a process of disorientation, but also the etymological sense of the word crisis (from Greek *krisis*, that is, decision). Crisis, as I am using the term, is a species of *metanoia*, a kind of perceptual breakdown. It isn't about an immediate repair, but involves tarrying within that space of breakdown. It is within that space that there is a powerful sense of loss; in fact, there is a process of *kenosis* or emptying, even if the empting can't be complete and so must be repeated. So, the idea that I have of crisis is not about recovery vis-à-vis the familiar, but something radically new. Crisis is a site of dispossession. So, the concept of *deciding* denotes a life of commitment to "undo," to "trouble," over and over again, the complex psychic and socio-ontological ways in which one is embedded in whiteness. The decision is one that is made over and over again perhaps even for the rest of one's life. And, yes, crisis, this process of *metanoia* and *kenosis*, is perplexing, painful, and chaotic. It must be, because it involves facing an unfamiliar psychic terrain. You know, though, my fear here is that some well-meaning whites might believe that they can *willfully* "fall apart" and that this involves some *voluntary act* when in fact whiteness involves such a deep resistant historical embeddedness.

A. B.: Exactly. Your account of crisis resonates deeply with most of the elements present in *nepantla*—the disorientation, the perceptual breakdown, and the pain. I very much like your image of losing one's footing; borderlands are indeed rough terrain.

I also share your concern about white folks' desire to force a crisis through voluntary acts. Our desire to be good drives this, but it ends up looking like ontological white flight—I picture well-meaning white selves actively driving around in search of a new neighborhood in which to reconstruct ourselves more favorably. We can't think our way out of whiteness. White fragility and the desire for metaphysical comfort, however, mean that we are constantly drawn to spaces where our identities are secure. So, resistance requires a good amount of volition on our part. For white folks to shift, we need to leave those spaces, philosophies, texts, geographies, politics, aesthetics, and worlds that keep us whole.

So, in both *nepantla* and your definition of crisis, the shift in self comes from choosing to remain in uncomfortable places. Buddhists, such as Pema Chödrön, describe this as walking into "the places that scare you."[3] You describe this as "tarrying," a kind of lingering with the truth about white selves, white supremacy, and the how these constructions are part and parcel of the colonial structures that continue to oppress people of color. And María Lugones advocates for the practice of leaving "worlds" (e.g., social spaces where you are at ease because you are fluent in the culture, history, and social practices), and hanging out in "worlds" where you are rendered strange. This travel between and among "worlds" must be animated by loving perception and playfulness of spirit.

The practice of "playful, loving 'world' travel" has political, ontological, and epistemic goals. Politically, women of color (and white women) travel to one another's worlds as a way to learn to love one another and to form friendships and alliances. Ontologically, travel from one world to another is a shift in self, something very similar to a Du Boisian double-consciousness. The aim of this practice is to reduce arrogant perception and to allow what she thinks of as a "plural self" to emerge. In "travel" you have a double-image of yourself because you have a memory of yourself having an attribute in one world and not having that attribute in another world. For example, in 'worlds' where I'm at ease I'm seen as an easygoing vibrant person with a great sense of humor, but when I spend time in hostile worlds where I'm not at ease, I'm read as reserved, arrogant, quiet, or humble. Playful, loving, 'world' travel makes this plurality visible. I am a humorous-arrogant-humble-easygoing self. Epistemically, this practice teaches us to see ourselves as others see us. At one point, Lugones implores white women to acknowledge that women of color are "faithful mirrors" that show white women as no other mirror can show us.[4] It's not that they reflect back to us who we really are. They show us some of the many selves that we are. They reflect back our plurality, which she says is something that may in itself be frightening to us. Walking into these fearful reflections brings on crisis.

I think "'world' travel" can help facilitate *nepantla* moments. My first glimpse of the plurality of whiteness surfaced when I read John Langston Gwaltney's *Drylongso: A Self-Portrait of Black America* and read descriptions of white folks as greedy, hateful, arrogant, cheap, lying, immodest, empty people who should be regarded with suspicion. These words threw me. In your words, they caused me to lose my footing. The tension between the narratives in this collection and the narrative of white goodness that I was raised to believe taught me the importance of understanding white identity as plural. White folks are good-hearted-greedy-well-meaning-ignorant-lying-empty . . . .etc. beings.

Now, I want to tie this plurality to your point about historical embeddedness. It's so important to keep the deep recalcitrant historical embeddedness of whiteness in mind when reflecting on these *nepantla* moments. Let me offer an example that I hope doesn't sound too forced. In the spring of 1992 I was finishing my graduate degree in Cincinnati and taking a Black feminist thought seminar. The four LA police officers who brutally beat Rodney King had just been acquitted and the LA uprising/riots had just begun. I remember Professor Hill Collins asking the white students in the seminar to make a practice of sitting next to Black and Brown people in public places and to focus on what came up for us. I was surprised by the depth of discomfort and fear that surfaced in me during this assignment. I wondered about the origins of my fear and how it came to inhabit my body so deeply. It was an abiding fear that was awakened in the aftermath of the violence done to King. I came to understand this fearful presence neither as a character flaw nor lack of vigilance on my part, but as a recalcitrant colonial artifact. My fear had an affective ancestry that was part and parcel of racial formation projects that traded, and continue to trade, on the fear of Black, Brown, and Native bodies. It was embedded deeply in my whiteness.

Making this connection threw me off center. It forced me to address the white fear that was in my body that had escaped my notice. A fear that people of color certainly notice in me, a fear that, if I had to guess, was deeply tied to folks of colors' fear of white bodies. I became hyperaware of how I saw myself and how I imagined some folks of color saw me when I took my seat on the bus: I was at once fearful and feared. I worked to unpack the relationship between these fears with friends of color in the peace movement and in our seminar discussions. As we named these intertwined fears, I came to realize that our fears had very different textures. Nonetheless the fear of white terror and my own fear of Black bodies had deeply common historical roots.

G. Y.: You link the fear that people of color noticed in you to a fear that is deeply tied to folks of colors' fear of white bodies. Say more about this. Are you conflating the fears here?

A. B.: I don't mean to conflate the fears that were circulating on the bus that afternoon. I have no way of experiencing what it must have felt like to ride the bus as a Black woman or man on that day, but the heaviness of the violence done to King felt very present to me in that space. Emotions are never pure. They are complex and come in clusters. I imagine, but cannot be certain, that the fear that Black Cincinnatians felt after King's arrest and during the trial must have felt complex, perhaps a deeply mournful, grief-laden fear mixed with a righteous anger not just over police violence, but the knowledge that white fear visible in white bodies is the greatest killer of Black bodies. I think the fear I felt that day was a fear of confrontation, revenge, a fear of violence against my own person. I felt white fragility, but I did *not* feel the terror of whiteness. An old colonial script was at play in that space. One that continues to be animated over and over again. So, I want to point out the deep historical relations between these fears without collapsing them.

G. Y.: How might we facilitate *nepantla* moments when white police officers approach Black people? And here I'm thinking about Tamir Rice and Sandra Bland. Those police officers in each case didn't risk the importance of "'world' travel." My guess is that there was no trepidation of losing their ontological bearings.

A. B.: You can't. Lugones's conceptual framework cannot be stretched to cover these cases. Her account of "playful, loving, 'world' travel" is offered as a correction to arrogant perception and a means of building alliances across differences for those who are willing to do this work. The travel must be animated by loving perception and playfulness. These conditions don't hold during the policing of Black, Brown, or Native bodies. Lugones recognizes that most US women of color practice world travelling as a matter of necessity and that much of it is done unwillingly to hostile worlds. The officers who pulled over Sandra Bland and who shot Tamir Rice perceived them with arrogant eyes. The survival of people of color requires learning to navigate hostile worlds safely, skillfully, and creatively. You can't be playful with conquerors when you stumble into and move through their worlds. You have to navigate these worlds with care and an intense amount of awareness.

In fact, your question has me thinking about how impossibly complex it is to navigate hostile worlds. All the creative strategies that you think would work regularly fail. The case of Charles Kinsey, a Black therapist who was shot in the leg by a North Miami police officer while trying to calm an autistic patient is a case in point. He was lying down with his hands up; what more could he have done to communicate that he was unarmed and not a threat?

G. Y.: Of course the idea of 'world' travel has to be respectful. So, how do white people even begin to engage Black spaces and people of color spaces without the latter feeling imposed upon?

A. B.: This is a very important point. 'World' travel is not a form of tourism. It's also not about making people into spectacles for your education, entertainment, and consumption. It's a loving way of being and living. The question of how white people should engage spaces of color is a challenging one, because it depends upon whether we are talking about neighborhoods, the Howard university campus, the women of color caucus at a conference, or an event at a local mosque. Public spaces are the most challenging because white folks often treat so-called ethnic neighborhoods as cultural playgrounds. Of course white folks should be respectful when walking through so-called non-white spaces, but in my experience most of us are not. 'World' travel, however, is not just about going into those spaces to look around. It requires that we interact and hang out with folks in those spaces. So, it's easier for me to think about your question in terms of community efforts to facilitate world travel as a means of inoculating the larger community against violence. I'm thinking about what happened in my own community in response to the June 12, 2016 mass shooting of LGBTQ people at the Pulse Nightclub in Orlando, Florida. Communities of faith, queer organizations, and our local Not in Our Town chapter coordinated a series of open houses at local churches, mosques, and synagogues, so that all members of the community could come hang out and get to know members of the Muslim, Jewish, Queer Unitarian, and other Christian communities. It was an invitation to 'world' travel and to interact with members of the community that was respectful.

G. Y.: White resistance to 'world' traveling is linked to maintaining the fiction of white "wholeness." There is a kind of ontology of self-sufficiency and even purity. For those of us who teach courses where white students think of themselves as atomic, neoliberal subjects, how might we get them to see that they are far more relational and, as you might say, multiple?

A. B.: I've not had much immediate success with this. Getting white students to make sense of white identity relationally takes a long time; semesters are short, and the privilege-evasiveness among most of the white students on our campus is fiercely stubborn. So, I start with their resistance for a few reasons. First, I think you get further working with privilege-evasiveness than you do trying to push back against it. I've made it my short-term goal to get white students to become mindful of the discursive, embodied, and affective habits they deploy to maintain the fiction of whiteness. I want white students to learn to notice how much energy they are putting into holding whiteness together, and to think about what would happen if they took risks and just walked into places that scare them. Next, I think that permitting white students' resistance to circulate as if it were a legitimate form of critical engagement with questions and race is incredibly stressful for students of color in the class.

I also make space for students of colors' resistance (e.g., silence, deciding to be absent, declaring that they don't have the energy for the conversation that day) and we talk about the different textures of their resistance.

Like you, I believe that classrooms are not safe spaces. They are places where ignorance and knowledge circulate with equal vigor. I've recently started to think about what it would look like for philosophers to work with a pedagogy of discomfort; so much of our teaching is geared toward the comforts of rules and certainty. Yet if metaphysical comfort continues to shape how white students engage questions of racial justice, then we need a pedagogy of discomfort. I work to make emotions and somatic expressions of these feelings visible during our discussions. I also work with students to identify what I call "shadow texts" as a way of engaging the privilege-evasive moves we discussed earlier in the interview. Let me give a quick example and then briefly introduce the concept and pedagogy.

Our class is discussing the Black Lives Matter movement in the wake of the Laquan McDonald shooting by Chicago police. I begin, "What does it mean to say that *Black* Lives Matter?" Eventually a white student predictably adds her opinion that "all lives matter" to the discussion. I don't want to shame her by pointing out that she had not answered my question. This is not the discomfort I'm after here. I don't want to silence her resistance/ignorance. I want to make the logic of white discomfort visible by naming and engaging it. I want the class to understand how these discursive detours and distractions signal epistemic closure; that is, they tell listeners, "I'm not going there. My white comfort zone demands that we neutralize race in this discussion of police violence."

So, I treat "all lives matter" as a shadow text. "Shadow texts" direct our attention to the ways epistemic resistance circulates during classroom discussions. The word 'shadow' is intended to call to mind the image of something walking closely alongside another thing without engaging it, which is what these responses do. They stalk the question in an attempt to reframe it along more comfortable lines. Shadows are regions of epistemic opacity. They function as obstacles that block access to pursuing further certain questions, problems, and curiosities that threaten dominant worldviews. They offer no epistemic friction. Shadow texts are certainly *reactions* to course content, but I prefer to think of them as *being called up by* the deeply affective-cognitive responses to the material. So, I get white students to think about the tension between my original question and the shadow text. Where does the reply "No! All lives matter" take us? Why do white students feel more comfortable talking about "all lives" than we do about "Black lives"? What's going on in their bodies when we focus on "Black lives"? How do members of the class feel when race is drained from the conversation?

White students must come to recognize the whitely habits of repair in themselves and to understand how these habits of invulnerability block vulnerability. I introduce Erinn Gilson's notion of vuln*erability* as potential, and we talk about the ways in which risk taking moves conversations forward. It's only at this point that I ask them to get out of their comfort zones by spending time in so-called "nonwhite" spaces and texts. Sometimes I coordinate a short 'world' travel exercise on campus, where students attend open meetings of identity-based student organizations.

G. Y.: As we engage in this conversation, I recognize that you are a privilege-cognizant white person. I also realize that you should not be (and that you don't want to be) praised by Black people or people of color for your cognizance. In contrast, how do we engage racist white people like the Klan who don't give a damn about striving to be privilege-cognizant? After the publication of my article "Dear White America" in the column *The Stone*, in the *New York Times* (2015), I received on my university answering machine, and noticed on some white supremacist websites, some really sick racist responses. I can't fathom how we might facilitate *nepantla* moments or what I'm calling *metanoia* and *kenosis* with those whites who show little or no desire to transform. Such radical moments wouldn't even get off the proverbial ground. So, what is to be done with the Klan or even Klan-like whites who may not be card-carrying members of the Klan and yet who hate Black people and people of color?

A. B.: I first want to express my compassion for your continued suffering around the "Dear White America" article. It's very difficult and dangerous to engage these hate groups. It's also impossible to ignore them. You and I can't control another person's criminal behavior. There may be ways in the social world to change or limit the effects of this hatred, but this is a complex empirical question, and I don't know how to really answer it, so I'll offer an anecdotal response, because I remain forever hopeful that people can change.

The work we do takes a great deal of time and emotional energy. We need to be smart about where we focus our attention and how long we sustain it. We also need to be sensible about our expectations. Outside the classroom I practice a form of triage: privilege-cognizant whites are on board, so I organize with them. Privilege-evasive white folks can be brought around. It takes time and patience, but I think that it is time well invested. Think about Lee Mun Wah's film *The Color of Fear*. It took six men of color an entire week to finally get David, the well-meaning but clueless straight white man, to understand that the America he lived in was not the same as the America that people of color lived in. When he accepted this, he shifted.

But, what about the hard-core haters that belong to white identity groups? The logic of triage requires that we ignore these groups, but this creates a dilemma at least for me as a white woman. In the past I've engaged their actions and not their persons. When a Peoria white supremacist group leafleted our neighborhood, we took down the flyers and met with the mayor, but this does not foment change of character.

Some white supremacists have experienced *metanoia* on their own, so the question is, How did that happen? I'm thinking about Arno Michealis, who grew up in an alcoholic household where emotional violence was the norm. He became involved in the white power movement when he was seventeen, founded the largest racist skinhead organization in the world, and became the lead singer in a race-metal band. He eventually left the movement and now runs two antiracist/antihatred projects and works with young people. At some point he started to shift. It happened in moments. The Black woman at McDonalds who saw his swastika tattoo smiled and said, "You're better than that. I know that's not who you are." He began noticing how, time after time, he was "graced with great kindness and forgiveness"[5] by groups of people that he had been openly hostile toward. He now felt shame about harming people who had done nothing to him. He experienced the weight of hate and how it exhausted him. He became a single father. He watched friends die and go to prison. Fissures continued to appear in his world until his skinhead-self crumbled.

Now, I know it will be of little comfort to you as someone who continues to experience backlash from your *New York Times* piece. Michealis's story offers us one instance of what *metanoia* looks like from the perspective of a hard-core hater who somehow transformed himself into a peacemaker.

I don't think there is much we can do to facilitate this, but I do hang on to the hope that hundreds of small interventions can foment long-term change. In the past I've always thought, "What do you say to someone like that? Where do you begin?" I think of the power behind the remark "You're better than that. I know that's not who you are." I think about the questions I would have asked the young white man working on my roof a few summers back, who, to my surprise, took off his shirt on a hot July morning to reveal a palimpsest of white supremacist tattoos. What if, instead of saying, "I need you to put your shirt back on . . . NOW!" I'd said, "Tell me about your ink? Whose words are on your skin? Do you find that the hate in those words is too heavy to carry at times? I know that's not who you are." I wonder if that conversation would have given him some pause. I don't know. I just don't know.

NOTES

1. Alison Bailey, "Strategic Ignorance," in *Race and Epistemologies of Ignorance*, eds. Nancy Tuana and Shannon Sullivan (Albany, NY: SUNY Press, 2007), 77–94.
2. Sara Ahmed, "The Phenomenology of Whiteness," *Feminist Theory* 8, no. 2 (2007): 149–68; 165.
3. Pema Chödrön, *The Places that Scare You: A Guide to Fearlessness in Difficult Times* (Boston: Shambala Publications, 2005).
4. María Lugones, *Pilgrimages/Peregrinajes: Theorizing Coalition against Multiple Oppressions* (Lanham, MD: Rowman and Littlefield, 2003), 67.
5. "Arno Michaelis," *The Forgiveness Project*, November 7, 2011, http://theforgivenessproject.com/stories/arno-michaels-usa/.

John D. Caputo

George Yancy: I'd like to begin with an observation—maybe an obvious one—that the task of engaging race or whiteness in philosophy has been taken up almost exclusively by nonwhite philosophers. My sense is that this is partly because whiteness is a site of privilege that makes it invisible to many white philosophers. I also think that some white philosophers would rather avoid thinking about how their own whiteness raises deeper philosophical questions about identity, power, and hegemony, as this raises the question of personal responsibility. I have found that it is often very difficult to convince white philosophers that they should also take up this project in their work—they tend to avoid it, or don't consider it philosophically relevant. Do you agree?

John D. Caputo: 'White' is of the utmost relevance to philosophy, and postmodern theory helps us to see why. I was once criticized for using the expression 'true north.' It reflected my Nordo-centrism, my critic said, and my insensitivity to people who live in the Southern Hemisphere. Of course, no such thing had ever crossed my mind, but that points to the problem. We tend to say "we" and to assume who "we" are, which once simply meant "we white male Euro-Christians."

Postmodern theory tries to interrupt that expression at every stop, to put every word in scare quotes, to put our own presuppositions into question, to make us worry about the murderousness of "we," and so to get in the habit of asking, "we, who?" I think that what modern philosophers call "pure" reason—the Cartesian ego cogito and Kant's transcendental consciousness—is a white male Euro-Christian construction.

White is not "neutral." "Pure" reason is lily white, as if white is not a color or is closest to the purity of the sun, and everything else is "colored." Purification is a name for terror and deportation, and "white" is a thick, dense, potent cultural signifier that is closely linked to rationalism and colonialism. What is not white is not rational. So white is philosophically relevant and needs to be philosophically critiqued—it affects what we mean by "reason"—and "we" white philosophers cannot ignore it.

G. Y.: Do you think that this avoidance of race among white philosophers is rooted in fear?

J. D. C.: I think that racism arises from a profound fear of the other, and fear is not far from hatred. But my experience is that most philosophers, most academics, are quite progressive in their thinking about race and sexuality and politics generally, and they are often active in progressive causes. My guess is that if they don't write professionally about racism—I suspect it is often part of their teaching—it is in part because of a certain thoughtlessness, like my "Nordo-centrism." I am not afraid of the Southern Hemisphere; it just didn't hit me that this expression assumes "we" all live in the Northern one!

But I also think we have to take account of the professionalization and corporatization of the university, where our livelihood depends upon becoming furiously specialized technicians who publish in very narrow areas. Racism—like sexism, homophobia, xenophobia, religious discrimination, mistreatment of animals, environmental destruction, economic inequality—is a complex problem. All these problems demand to be addressed responsibly, and that requires expertise, a command of the literature, a knowledge of history, and so forth. No one can do all that, especially people trying to find jobs and later on get tenure and promotion, unless it intersects with their specialty in some pertinent way.

It is usually the damage done by religious dogmatism that occupies my attention. So I am at least as guilty as other white philosophers. My own work has always involved theorizing the "other," the claim made upon us by those who are excluded by the prevailing system, so I am always on the verge of mentioning race and even have race and other powers of exclusion in mind.

My shortcoming is that I lack the expertise to get down in the dirt with most of these problems; the advantage is that my work has a suggestiveness to a lot of people on the front lines in different life situations, who grasp its application and tell me it helps them with their work.

G. Y.: Given that you claim above that white philosophers cannot responsibly ignore the subject of race, what do you think must be done to get them—and the ways they understand philosophy—to change?

J. D. C.: More often than not I do not analyze race explicitly unless I am asked to; it's only then I find there are new things for me to say. I guess that means that one solution is to do what you're doing now—ask us! Interrupt us. Stop us and ask, "To what extent is everything you just said a function of being white?" There's a fair chance we never asked ourselves that question. And get the courses that do raise this question into the curriculum.

G. Y.: You mentioned that most philosophers and most academics are quite progressive, but often slip into a kind of unintentional thoughtlessness. Still, the recipients of such thoughtlessness can suffer deeply. And even "progressives" can continue to perpetuate deep systemic forms of discrimination in problematic ways. Do you think that thoughtlessness can function as an "excuse" for not engaging more rigorously in combating various structures of systemic power?

J. D. C.: No doubt. We all learned from Hannah Arendt a long time ago about the long arm of thoughtlessness, which she ventured to say reaches as far as the death camps. Every time I am asked to say something about race—or the environment or sexism or these other issues we've mentioned—I feel like Augustine in the *Confessions* praying and weeping over his sins. In these matters I follow Levinas.[1] When he analyzes ethics as an asymmetric relationship to the other—that means the other overtakes us, lays claim to us with or without our consent—he says a good conscience is fraudulent. This means our responsibility never ends and we can never say it has been discharged. It is when we think that things are fine that we are not thinking. It's just when we say "peace, peace" that the lack of peace descends on us. We coast on the status quo and we need the unrelenting provocation of responsible intellectuals, artists, journalists, and the media to remind us of our complacency about the suffering that is all around us.

G. Y.: You've argued that true religion or prophetic religion engages the real, involves a process of risk, especially as it demands, as you've said, serving those who have been oppressed, marginalized, orphaned. Etymologically, religion comes from *religare*, which means to "bind fast." I wonder if that process of binding fast is with those who are the strangers, the orphans, the unarmed Black men recently killed by police, women who are sexually objectified, the poor, and others.

J. D. C.: Yes, it is, of course. In the Gospels, Luke has Jesus announce his ministry by saying he has come to proclaim good news to the poor and imprisoned and the year of the Jubilee (Luke 4:18), which meant massive economic redistribution every fiftieth year! Can you imagine the Christian Right voting for that? The great scandal of the United States is that it has produced an anti-Gospel, the extremes of appalling wealth and poverty. But instead of playing the prophetic role of Amos denouncing the American Jeroboam, instead of working to close that gap, the policies of the right wing are exacerbating it.

That has been felt in a particularly cruel way among Black men and women and children, where poverty is the most entrenched and life is the most desperate. The popularity of such cruel ideas, their success in the ballot box, is terrifying to me. The trigger-happy practices of the police, not all police, but too many police, on the streets of Black America should alert everyone to how profoundly adrift American democracy has become—attacking the poor as freeloaders and criminals, a distorted and grotesque ideological exaggeration of freedom over equality. The scandal is that the Christian Right has too often been complicit with a politics of greed and hatred of the other.

To be sure, younger evangelicals are becoming critical of their elders on this point, and I am trying to reach them in my own work, and there are also many examples of prophetic religion, like the Catholic parish in a North Philadelphia ghetto that I wrote about in "What Would Jesus Deconstruct?" The secular Left, on the other hand, won't touch religion with a stick and abandons the ground of religion to the Right. So both the Left and the Right have a hand around the throat of prophetic religion.

G. Y.: You raise a few important issues here. I wonder what it would look like for a white police officer to see an unarmed Black man/boy through the eyes of prophetic religion. On an international stage, I imagine that both Palestinians and Jews would begin to see each other differently, where each would feel the deep ethical weight of the other.

J. D. C.: Prophetic does not mean the ability to foretell the future. It means the call for justice for "the widow, the orphan, and the stranger" (Deut. 10:18), the affirmation that the mark of God is on the face of everyone who is down and out, and a prophetic sensibility requires walking a mile in the shoes of the other.

I remember years ago, the president of a local college (in the Quaker tradition) took a year's leave of absence to work as a trash collector. I think you are hitting on an irreducible element in the phenomenology of "alterity," the very nub of it: were I there, there would be "here." That is a simple thought whose depth we never plumb. In my own work I cite it frequently to criticize the idea of "the one true religion." We have seven grandchildren, and when the last one was born I remember thinking that a little Black child was also being born that day, as dear and innocent as our granddaughter, who was going home to a desperate situation where the odds will be stacked against her. We begin with an originary natal equality and then we crush it. "Switched at birth" stories, like Mark Twain's *The Tragedy of Pudd'nhead Wilson*, have a deep ethical and political import. Were I there, there would be here. That should transform everything.

G. Y.: On June 17, 2015, a white male shot and killed nine people in the historic African-American Emanuel AME Baptist Church in Charleston, South Carolina. There was no apparent capacity on the part of this white male to walk in the shoes of the other, to envision Black life as anything other than disposable.

J. D. C.: Exactly. This was a white man declaring these lives not merely worthless but, still worse, a threat to the "natural order"—what form of oppression does not hide behind the "natural order?"—of the supremacy of the so-called white race. There is a qualitative difference here. This was not the result of a split-second miscalculation or a misunderstanding by a policeman in a tense situation. This was a ruthless execution. Here the other does not overtake me but lies beneath me, contemptible and abject. This is pure hatred of the other.

G. Y.: Staying on the theme of walking in the shoes of the other, can you speak to the recent revelation regarding Rachel Dolezal passing as Black? Do you see this as a genuine dwelling with the other or as a form of appropriation?

J. D. C.: I can only assume her intentions were good, but I think she was misguided. You can't be an "intentional" victim, adopt it freely, because that means you are always free to walk away from it if the going gets rough, take a few weeks off for a holiday, or just change your mind. So it ends up making a mockery of the oppressed—the biting edge of oppression is that is not of your own choosing! People who try to walk a mile in the shoes of the other, to live among and dedicate their lives to working with the oppressed, are also sensitive to the fact of their own privilege. They know they can never truly identify with them. They understand this paradox, but it doesn't paralyze them. This problem also comes up in Christian theology—God intentionally assumed our mortal condition, but it wasn't an inescapable plight visited upon the divine being without its consent.

G. Y.: Is there a version of philosophy that "binds us" philosophers to the real, one that requires risking our necks for the least of these?

J. D. C.: That is the attraction of postmodern philosophy to me, which is a philosophy of radical pluralism. It theorizes alterity, calls for unrelenting sensitivity to difference, and teaches us about the danger of our own power, our freedom, our "we." I think that philosophy is not only a work of the mind but also of the heart, and it deals with ultimate matters about which we cannot be disinterested observers. So at a certain point in my career I decided to let my heart have a word, to write in a more heartfelt way, which of course is to push against the protocols of the academy. That is why I advised my graduate students, only half in jest, that it would be too risky for them to write like that, and safer to wait until they were tenured full professors!

Furthermore, we do not merely write; we teach. Teaching means interacting in a fully embodied and engaged way with young people at a very precious moment in their life—when they are most ready to hear something different. Here philosophy professors brush up against what I consider the religious and prophetic quality of their work, even if they resist those words. Our work is a vocation before it is a form of employment.

Of course, this is possible in any philosophical style or tradition, but this is the special attraction of "continental" philosophy for me. This style of thinking irrupted in the nineteenth century with Kierkegaard and Nietzsche, who wrote with their blood, as we say, and the young Marx, and stretched from phenomenology to poststructuralism in the twentieth century, and came to a head under the name of postmodernism, the affirmation of difference and plurality in a dizzying digitalized world. This tradition speaks from the heart, speaks to the heart.

I came to philosophy through religion and theology, and as a result philosophy has always had a salvific and prophetic quality for me. It has always been a way to save myself, even as in antiquity philosophy did not mean an academic specialty but a way of living wisely. This is all threatened today by the professionalization of the university, of our teaching and our writing.

G. Y.: The twentieth-century French philosopher Jean-Francois Lyotard claimed that postmodernism involved a resistance toward and critical questioning of metanarratives—"big stories" like the Enlightenment, the march of scientific progress, or the supremacy of the West, that legitimate nations or cultures. I think postmodernism has tremendous value in terms of critically engaging racism. Yet, metanarratives are also powerful, and resistant to being undone. Besides encouraging white people to become more thoughtful, how do we do the deeper ethical work of *dwelling near* each other, recognizing our shared humanity?

J. D. C.: "Emancipation" is a prophetic call that never stops calling. If we take it as a metanarrative, then we run the danger of being lulled into a myth of progress, and we have seen how successful the Right has been in reversing progress in civil rights and fair elections. But if I am dubious about metanarratives, I am not dubious about prophetic action, which lies in singular sustained acts of resistance.

I have several times used the example of Rosa Parks. She did not one day, out of the blue, refuse to give up her seat and move to the back of the bus, nor was she even the first one to do that. What she did that day was another in a long line of acts of resistance, but this one worked. This one "linked," as Lyotard would put it.[2] It set off a city-wide bus boycott in Montgomery, Alabama, which was led by a young pastor no one ever heard of who ran a local church, a fellow named Martin Luther King Jr. The rest is history—a history the Right would like to undo. So Rosa Parks did the right thing at the right time in the right place. She set off the "perfect storm"—for racists!

I have a hope against hope not in metanarratives but in singular actions like that. Singular, but consistent and resolute.

G. Y.: Lastly, do you think that we need more prophetic voices in the world? What sort of *Bildung* or educational cultivation might help to generate more prophetic voices as opposed to those voices that appear to be seduced by power and narrow thinking?

J. D. C.: The prophetic voices are often the voices of obscure people who have no idea they're prophets, who produce changes they never dreamed possible. So massive changes, structural changes, tend to be a function of mini-changes, singular deeds of singular people. We require a massive change in a culture of greed and selfishness, where the concept of the "common good" is moribund, never even mentioned.

One place this change should be focused is the children, investing in the schools, lifting up a generation of desperately disadvantaged children in the ghettos, which I think is the best shot we have to break the cycle of poverty. There is no better place to experience the prophetic call of the other than in the face of a child in need, no better way to "dwell near" the other, as you put it.

Right now, with electoral districts gerrymandered against the poor, and with the unchecked flow of right-wing wealth into political campaigns, the electoral process that is supposed to address these problems has been profoundly distorted and corrupted. Right now, I fear it will take a generation to correct that. But the whole idea of prophetic action is that it is precisely when we are sure that things can never be changed that a woman refuses to sit in the back of the bus and the whole world changes. I also have hope in contemporary systems of communication. If we can keep them open, otherwise invisible individual acts of resistance—and oppression—become visible. That will keep the future open. That is our hope against hope.

NOTES

1. Hannah Arendt, *Eichmann in Jersusalem* (New York: Viking Books, 1963); Emmanuel Levinas, *Totality and Infinity*, trans. Alphonso Lingis (Pittsburgh: Duquesne University Press, 1969).
2. Jean-François Lyotard, *Just Gaming*, trans. Vlad Gozich (Minneapolis: University of Minnesota Press, 1985).

Shannon Sullivan

George Yancy: What motivated you to engage "whiteness" in your work as a philosopher?

Shannon Sullivan: It was teaching feminist philosophy for the first time or two and trying to figure out how to reach the handful of men in the class—white men, now that I think of it. They tended to be skeptical at best and openly hostile at worst to the feminist ideas we were discussing. They felt attacked and put up a lot of defenses. I was trying to see things from their perspective, not to endorse it (it was often quite sexist!), but to be more effective as a teacher. And so I thought about my whiteness and how I might feel and respond in a class that critically addressed race in ways that implicated me personally. Not that race and gender are the same or can be captured through analogies, but it was a first step toward grappling with my whiteness and trying to use it.

What really strikes me now, as I think about your question, is how old I was—around thirty—before I ever engaged whiteness philosophically, or personally, for that matter. Three decades where that question never came up, and yet the unjust advantages whiteness generally provides white people fully shaped my life, including my philosophical training and work.

G. Y.: How did whiteness shape your philosophical training? When I speak to my white graduate philosophy students about this, they have no sense that they are being shaped by the "whiteness" of philosophy. They are under the impression that they are doing philosophy, pure and simple, which is probably a function of the power of whiteness.

S. S.: I think I'm only just discovering this and probably am only aware of the tip of the iceberg. Here is some of what I've learned, thanks to the work of Charles Mills, Linda Martín Alcoff, Kathryn Gines, Tommy Curry, and many other philosophers of color: It's not just that in grad school I didn't read many philosophers outside a white, Eurocentric canon (or maybe *any*—wow, I'm thinking hard here, but the answer might be zero). It's also that as a result of that training, my philosophical habits of thinking, of where to go in the literature and the history of philosophy for help ruminating on a philosophical topic—even that of race—predisposed me toward white philosophers. Rebuilding different philosophical habits can be done, but it's a slow and frustrating process. It would have been better to develop different philosophical habits from the get-go.

My professional identity and whether I count as a full person in the discipline is bound up with my middle-class whiteness, even as my being a woman jeopardizes that identity somewhat. Whiteness has colonized "doing philosophy, pure and simple," which has a significant bearing on what it means to be a "real" philosopher. Graduate students tend to be deeply anxious about whether they are or will eventually count as real philosophers, and whiteness functions through that anxiety even as that anxiety can seem to be totally unrelated to race (to white people anyway—I'm not sure it seems that unrelated to graduate students of color).

G. Y.: For many whites, the question of their whiteness never comes up or only comes up when they are much older, as it did in your case. And yet, as you say, there is the accrual of unjust white advantages. What are some reasons that white people fail to come to terms with the fact that they benefit from whiteness?

S. S.: That's a tough one, and there probably are lots of reasons, including beliefs in boot-strap individualism, meritocracy, and the like. Another answer, I think, has to do with class differences among white people. A lot of poor white people haven't benefitted as much from whiteness as middle- and upper-class white people have. Poor white people's "failure" to come to terms with the benefits of their whiteness isn't as obvious, I guess I'd say. I'm not talking about a kind of utilitarian calculus where we can add up and compare quantities of white advantage, but there are differences.

I'm thinking here of an article I just read in the *Charlotte Observer* that my new home state of North Carolina is the first one to financially compensate victims of an aggressive program of forced sterilization, one that ran from the Great Depression all the way through the Nixon presidency. (A headline on an editorial in the *Observer* called the state's payouts "eugenics checks.") The so-called feeble-minded who were targeted included poor and other vulnerable people of all races, even as sterilization rates apparently increased in areas of North Carolina as those areas' Black populations increased. My point is that eugenics programs in the United States often patrolled the borders of proper whiteness by regulating the bodies and lives of the white "failures" who were allegedly too poor, stupid, and uneducated to do whiteness right.

Even though psychological wages of whiteness do exist for poor white people, those wages pay pennies on the dollar compared to those for financially comfortable white people. So coming to terms with whiteness's benefits can mean really different things, as can failing to do so. I think focusing the target on middle-class white people's failure is important. Which might just bring me right back to your question!

G. Y.: And yet for so many poor people of color there is not only the fact that the wages pay less than pennies, as it were, but that Black life continues to be valued as less. Is there a history of that racial differential wage between poor whites and poor Blacks or people of color?

S. S.: Yes, definitely. Class and poverty are real factors here, but they don't erase the effects of race and racism, at least not in the United States and not in a lot of other countries with histories (and presents) of white domination. The challenge philosophically and personally is to keep all the relevant factors in play in thinking about these issues. In that complex tangle, you hit the nail on the head when you said that Black life continues to be valued as less. Poor white people's lives aren't valued for much either, but at least in their case it seems that something went wrong, that there was something of potential value that was lost.

Let's put it even more bluntly: America is fundamentally shaped by white domination, and as such it does not care about the lives of Black people, period. It never has, it doesn't now, and it makes me wonder about whether it ever will.

Here is an important question: What would it mean to face up to the fact that the United States doesn't really care much about Black people? I think a lot about Derrick Bell's racial realism nowadays, especially after reading some recent empirical work about the detrimental effects of hope in the lives of Black men—hope, that is, that progress against racial discrimination and injustice is being made. How would strategies for fighting white domination and ensuring the flourishing of people of color change if Black people gave up that hope? If strategies for living and thriving were pegged to the hard truth that white-saturated societies don't and might not ever value Black lives? Except perhaps as instruments for white people's financial, psychological, and other advantages—we have a long history of that, of course.

G. Y.: We're all aware of the recent nonindictments of the Ferguson police officer Darren Wilson, who killed Michael Brown, and the New York City police officer Daniel Pantaleo, who killed Eric Garner in Staten Island. How do we critically engage people who see this as another blow to Black humanity, another blow to hope?

S. S.: It *is* another blow to Black humanity. I don't see any way around that. And also another blow to hope. But that doesn't mean that despair is the only alternative. I admit it's hard to see beyond that dichotomy—hope or despair—and I struggle to see beyond it. But maybe it's a false dichotomy, pegged to hopes that the legal system, including civil rights struggles, can get us out of this mess. What if we operated instead from the hypothesis that the legal system cannot do this, at least not at this moment in history? One thing that both Ferguson and the failure to indict in the Eric Garner case tell us is that "we" must come up with other alternatives or else "we" (I have to underscore the question of who the "we" is here) risk driving people to violence. Even when "they" don't necessarily wish to resort to violence, I think that also is important to underscore. I don't think that anyone particularly wants violence in its own right, but what happens when there aren't other options to ensure that Black people are considered full persons?

G. Y.: The critique of hope, as you suggest above, appears to be based on the assumption that the system of white supremacy and the devaluation of Black life will not fundamentally change. In this case, Black hope is just spinning its wheels. And yet, President Obama speaks of the audacity of hope. In what way do you square his hope with the pervasive feeling of a lack of hope among Black people when it comes to the end of racial injustice?

S. S.: When you talk of Black hope as spinning its wheels, I can't help but think of South Africa, which has just celebrated the twentieth anniversary of the end of apartheid and mourned the death of its first postapartheid president, Nelson Mandela. Its government is predominantly Black, including its current president, Jacob Zuma. It's a remarkable transformation, one that seems to provide the world with hope. But living conditions for most Black South Africans have not changed, and brutal patterns of racial segregation are still firmly in place. In fact, Black poverty and racial inequalities in income have actually increased since the end of legal segregation.

The answer of course is *not* to return to apartheid. I feel like I have to say that, especially as a white person skeptical of Black hope for equality! But liberal hope in racial progress isn't going to cut it. Again, there have to be other options, and then the question becomes whether violent revolution is the only other option.

The potential for racial conflagration is very real, I think, even beyond what we recently have seen in Ferguson. Would it be effective in changing the institutional, national, global, and personal habits that need to be changed to take down white supremacy? I worry that violence is a shortcut that doesn't help remake habits, racial or otherwise, and so it won't solve the long-term problem. At the same time, you and I should be suspicious of that worry. It's very convenient, isn't it, for a white person to have philosophical reservations about the effectiveness of violent Black resistance? I am not endorsing violence. What I'd like to do instead is shift the subject; I think that the issue of violence is something of a red herring. The urgent question in the United

States is not whether violence in response to Ferguson or elsewhere is justi-fied. That question distracts us from the more important issue of how to make sure that Black men aren't perceived as inherently criminal.

As for the audacity of hope promoted by Obama, I worry that in the end it has backfired. I too felt the buoyancy of hope in 2008. But electing the first Black president did not shift the scales of racial justice in the United States very much, if at all. This is not an argument against Obama's election, but one that many of us were naïve in thinking that Black exceptionalism wouldn't rear its ugly head if the "exception" in question was the president himself.

G. Y.: If it is true that we live in a white-saturated society, how do you con-ceptualize your role, especially as a white person who grapples with whiteness philosophically and existentially?

S. S.: I think that white people have a small but important role to play in combating white domination. Small, because the idea isn't that white people are going to lead that work; they need to be following the work and leadership of people of color. But important because, given de facto racial segregation, there still are many pockets of whiteness—in neighborhoods, businesses, classrooms, philosophy departments—where you need white people who are going to challenge racism when it pops up. Which it often does.

But I think I have to add that this role is absurd. I mean absurd in the tech-nical existentialist sense that, for example, Kierkegaard and Camus gave it. I don't have a lot of hope that our white-saturated society is ever going to change, and at the same time it is crucial that one struggles for that change. Those two things don't rationally fit together, I realize. It's absurd to struggle for something that you don't think can happen, and yet we (people of all races) should.

It's like Camus's main character in *The Plague*, the doctor who realizes that the plague will never completely go away. It—death, the atrocities of Nazi Germany—always wins in the end, even if one achieves some minor victories against it. We could add white supremacy to Camus's list. It's crucial to fight it even if total victory is impossible, to care for those who suffer because of it. And we all suffer because of it. The plague spares no one even as it hits differ-ent groups and individuals in different ways.

G. Y.: You know, many white readers will respond to this interview and argue that you desire white people to feel guilt or shame. I would argue that this is *not* your aim at all. Yet, is it an easy tactic for denying the legitimacy of what you've argued?

S. S.: You're right that I'm not trying to cultivate white guilt or shame. This will get me in hot water, but I don't think those are emotions that will help white people effectively struggle for racial justice in the long haul. I'm not saying that white people should never feel guilty or ashamed because of their race, and I don't think that not feeling guilty or ashamed is a way to let white people off the hook. But guilt and shame are toxic just as hatred and greed are, and we sure don't need to increase the toxicity of white people. James Baldwin said it best when he argued that white people will have to learn how to love themselves and each other before they can let go of their need for Black inferiority.

Craig Irvine

George Yancy: How did you become interested in narrative medicine?

Craig Irvine: I moved to New York in 1995, a year after completing my doctorate. I loved the city and had long dreamed of living there. Since I didn't yet have a job, it was a good time to make the move. For the first couple of years, I worked as an adjunct at several colleges, while working also as an office temp. Then in 1998 a friend who worked at the Center for Family Medicine at Columbia University told me about an opening for an administrative position. My friend knew that the family physician who was hiring, Vincent Silenzio, was interested in philosophy and thought we might make a good match. The job involved managing accounts, schedules, spreadsheets—the usual sort of thing—but Vince also wanted someone who could teach and write. Shortly after I was hired, Vince and I set to work writing grants to buy me out of my administrative work. One of the first was a Residency Training in Primary Care grant through the Health Resources and Services Administration (HRSA). HRSA was requesting proposals to support ethics training for residents; we proposed developing a narrative ethics curriculum in Columbia's family medicine residency program. That seemed somewhat risky at the time, as narrative ethics would have been relatively unknown in the medical academy. In writing the grant, we worked closely with Rita Charon, an internist with a PhD in literature who had been working in the field broadly designated "humanities and medicine" at Columbia since 1983. The grant received an excellent score from HRSA, and we initiated the curriculum in 2000. That same year, Dr. Charon coined the term 'narrative medicine' as a way to distinguish the work being done at Columbia from humanities training at other medical academies, and in 2003 the National Endowment for the Humanities awarded her a grant to support the further development of this work. By then, I'd been teaching philosophy courses for Dr. Charon's Program in Narrative Medicine (every medical student is required to take one six-week-long narrative medicine "selective") for several years. She funded a portion of my salary with the NEH grant, which established an intensive collaborative learning seminar at Columbia. The core seminar group included scholars from diverse disciplines, including psychoanalysis, pediatrics, literary and film studies, internal medicine, fiction writing, and philosophy. For over two years, our group met twice monthly to investigate the fundamental role of storytelling in clinical practice across all healthcare professions. Each of the seminar participants proposed contributions that her or his discipline might make to the theoretical foundations for the application of narrative to healthcare practices. Together we explored the relationality inherent in the close reading of literature, the power of creative writing to grant access to feelings and reframe experience, the ethics of giving and receiving accounts of self, and the relevance of all of these topics to health, illness, and disability. The core NEH seminar group also developed narrative medicine pedagogy, with a view toward enhancing the narrative skills fundamental to effective clinical practice. In 2006 we began offering narrative medicine workshops for nurses, physicians, social workers, psychologists, chaplains, and other clinicians, as well as academics, writers, artists, and others interested in the intersection of narrative and medicine. In 2009, we developed the Master's Program in Narrative Medicine, of which I have been the Director since 2010.

G. Y.: How would you specifically define narrative medicine and some of its philosophical assumptions?

C. I.: Put simply, narrative medicine is medicine practiced with narrative competence, or the skills of recognizing, absorbing, interpreting, and being moved to action by stories of illness.

A fundamental philosophical assumption of this field is that stories are the primordial means through which we experience and convey the meaning of our lives. We share Paul Ricoeur's conviction that our lives are always already "entangled" in stories, challenging the notion that life happens first and stories come after.[1] For Ricoeur, experience is not some sort of bare biological phenomenon onto which stories are grafted from the outside, after the fact, as a retrospective representation. Rather, from the beginning we experience life *in* stories—stories told by our families, nations, cultures, literatures, religions, and more. Their narration drives our constantly evolving process of identity formation. Indeed, Ricoeur contends that life is the process of constructing a narrative identity. Gadamer's notion of the "fusion of horizons" is helpful here.[2] Visiting your grandparents during a break from college, you ask them to tell you again about the itinerants who came to their door during the Depression, seeking work or just a meal and a place to rest. Your grandparents were Dustbowl farmers, barely scraping by, but they had more than the folks on the road, and they always shared what they could. You hear this story *inside* another story: the parable of the Samaritan, which you first heard on a Sunday morning before your earliest memory. In high school you read *The Grapes of Wrath*, and this story now nests inside your grandparent's story nested inside the Good Samaritan's. Each of these stories is a world opening before you a horizon of possible experience. Leaving your grandparent's house, you live inside all of these worlds, following paths extending to the edge of their fused horizons. You are the living embodiment of national, cultural, familial, religious, literary narratives, their forms the very shape of your identity.

Taking up this notion of narrative identity, we challenge the hegemony of a reductionist medicine for which alleviating suffering seems to require silencing the voices of those who suffer. I am particularly inspired by Emmanuel Levinas, who brings attention to the responsibility to answer the call of the suffering Other. Medical science developed as a response to this call. Descartes writes in his *Discourse on Method* that the entire focus of his work—the principal goal for developing a unified science—is to acquire knowledge of nature that would allow for the development of more reliable rules for medicine.[3] Mission accomplished! Medicine has certainly done more than any other human endeavor to address human suffering. Yet medical science, like all forms of conceptualization, naturally tends toward closure: it is allergic to alterity, hostile to whatever falls outside its totalizing gaze. For Cartesian medical science, the body is a complicated machine, an "extended thing" fundamentally separate from the self, which is an essentially *thinking* substance. Medicine therefore abstracts its treatment of the body, or of the fractured systems and organs of the body, from the *selfhood* of the person who is suffering. The patient is not a unique person, but an instance of a generic dysfunction: "the diabetic in Room 237." Who among us has not experienced the effects of this objectification, this alienation from our own bodies, under the clinical gaze?

Narrative medicine draws on the work of Merleau-Ponty to help medicine rethink the Cartesian separation of self from body. For Merleau-Ponty, consciousness is essentially embodied. I do not experience my body as an object alongside other objects in objective space, like a rock, a chair, or even a very complicated machine. My body is my very consciousness, my self. Merleau-Ponty makes the abstractions of science secondary to the primary, prereflective, prescientific, embodied experience of consciousness. He encourages us to *describe* rather than to *explain* this experience. Inspired by Merleau-Ponty's work, contemporary phenomenologists like Havi Carel, Richard Zaner, and S. Kay Toombs help us to recognize that, for the sufferer, illness and disability are not experienced as a disruption of an objective body separate from the self, but as a disruption of the *lived body* that threatens my very identity. If the heart of who I am lives in stories—Ricoeur's narrative identity—then one cannot hope to respond to the lifeworld-altering aspects of illness without close attention not only to the "objective" conclusions of the differential diagnosis but to the singular, specific stories of each patient.

G. Y.: Talk about some of the factors (social, personal) that shaped your consciousness about race.

C. I.: I grew up in southern Minnesota, on a small family farm five miles from a town of six hundred souls peacefully slumbering in what Ta-Nehisi Coates calls "the Dream."[4] In other words, I had no consciousness of race whatsoever throughout my childhood. I knew no people of color, and no one I knew, knew any people of color. I watched a lot of TV without even the vaguest consciousness that the world flickering there in black and white was in truth entirely white. I moved through a world of whiteness, blissfully taking for granted that this was simply the world as such, the "universal" world, the world open and available to one and all.

At the time, southern Minnesota was quite liberal. My father and mother and all their friends were diehard members of the DFL (Democratic-Farmer-Labor Party). My siblings and I and all our friends shared our parents' sympathies. Our hero was Hubert Humphrey, the man responsible for adding the first proposal to end racial segregation to the national platform of the Democratic party (in 1948, ten years before I was born) and lead author of the Civil Rights Act of 1964. Everyone in our rural, white bubble would have assured you we were not racist. We believed all humans were created equal, that everyone had the right to life, liberty, and the pursuit of happiness. We loved Sidney Poitier! (We fully supported his right to marry that nice, rich, liberal white girl who invited him to dinner.) We deplored the rhetoric of George Wallace, were outraged by the reports of lynchings, wept over the images of church bombings. Racism was an evil that flourished far from the enlightened North, perpetrated by backward Southerners—cowards who raped and brutalized and murdered under cover of sheets or mobs or Jim Crow laws. We believed we were on the side of the angels.

We weren't racist, but it never occurred to us to imagine that all of those angels hovering around a white Jesus enthroned beside His white Father were anything but white. On the authority of our *Children's Illustrated Bible*, from which mom read to us every night, Black angels were devils.

We weren't racist, but *Gone with the Wind* was our family's favorite movie. Our parents first took us when I was nine years old. It was 1967, and it was still the most popular movie in history, white people lining up around the block to see it. The theater was packed, so we had to split up: I was the youngest, so my next-oldest sister and I sat on either side of my mother in the front row. The movie was deeply imprinted on my psyche; I still recall the title card that scrolls down the screen at the opening: "There was a land of Cavaliers and Cotton Fields called the Old South. Here on this pretty world Gallantry took its last bow. Here was the last ever to be seen of Knights and their Ladies Fair, of Master and of Slave. Look for it in books, for it is no more than a dream remembered. A civilization gone with the wind." It only gets worse from there, but hearing the film's grand opening strains still brings me to tears.

We weren't racist, but whenever we had to choose someone to be "it" in tag, we'd chant,

Eeeny, meeny, miny, moe,
Catch a nigger by the toe,
If he hollers, let him go,
Eeny, meeny, miny, moe.

I was so unconscious about the racist meaning of that chant that I was well into my twenties before the shock of realizing what we'd been chanting finally registered.

All in the Family debuted in 1971. Like most of America, we congratulated ourselves for feeling superior to Archie, while experiencing a frisson of titillation at his overt racism. (We cheered when Sammy Davis Jr. kissed him.) While the show certainly broke ground, and all due respect to Norman Lear, we, and much of liberal white America, ignorant of our own racism, laughed at the ignorance of an obviously racist character, thus reinforcing the dominant narrative of liberal white progress that only further fortified our own ignorance. When the Jeffersons moved to the East Side, we didn't wake from our dream—we just spun them into our story and continued to sleep like babies.

I went to an overwhelmingly white college, and after I graduated in 1980 I spent four years in an overwhelmingly white monastery. When I came out of the closet as a gay man and left the monastic community, I moved to a predominantly white neighborhood in Minneapolis and worked at an all-white group home (staff and residents) for developmentally disabled adults. A couple years later I went to graduate school at Penn State; there were no students of color matriculating in the gradute philosophy program at the time, and the faculty was entirely white. During all of this time, I had no Black friends. And yet I carried with me, through all of these experiences, the conviction that I was not racist.

The only significant experience around race I can recall during all of those years occurred in 1981, when I was still in the monastery. I traveled to New York (monks are allowed to take vacations) to visit my friend Michael. Michael had a Black friend, Sherman, who lived in a brownstone in Crown Heights. On a particularly hot August day, Sherman took us on a driving tour of Brooklyn; while we were cruising through Bedford-Stuyvesant, he asked me if I'd like to get a soda. I was thirsty, so he pulled over and pointed to a bodega on the other side of the street. I panicked. This was a "bad" neighborhood: I hadn't seen a white person in block after block. I started to tell Sherman that I'd changed my mind, that I wasn't thirsty after all, but then

I felt foolish and weak, so I opened the door and stepped out of the car. I can still vividly recall the flush of fear, my heart hammering, palms wet. I felt as if eyes were following me from every direction. Danger on all sides. I passed a group of men hanging outside the bodega; I kept my eyes forward, feeling dizzy, trying not to stumble. I grabbed the first soda I saw, even though the can had one of those big bulges on the bottom that made it tilt sidewise in the cooler, paid without looking up, and walked back to the car as quickly as I could, forcing myself not to break into a run. For years afterward, when I told this story, I would always add that what I'd experienced that day "must be what Black people feel like most of the time."

I know now that this is not the case. Thanks to your work, George, and that of other whiteness theorists, which I began reading just a few short years ago, I know that I carried my whiteness into Bed-Stuy. I know that I continued to move through a white world, even in a space predominantly occupied by Black bodies. I know that I could not then and cannot now step over to the "other side," because my whiteness is transcendental—the norm that defines itself in dialectical *opposition* to the "other side" (good angels are not-Black; the ones who choose are not-Black; safe neighborhoods are not-Black). And I know that knowing this is not enough to free me from the whiteness of my being-in-the-world, or what you've aptly called "whitely-being-in-the-world." Knowing this does not mean that I cease to live and perpetuate the privileges of whiteness. Knowing this does not mean that my whiteness no longer perpetuates violence against Black lives. Knowing this does not mean that I am free from ignorance, that I no longer live in a dream. What would it mean to wake? As a white man, I am a phantom being living in a phantom world. This isn't the Matrix—there is no "real world" to wake into when someone pulls the plug. To face this means, as you have stressed, to live without hope.

G. Y.: That's powerful, Craig. So, how does race, especially the subject of whiteness, relate to narrative medicine?

C. I.: The United States healthcare system is broken. Even that isn't strong enough, because "broken" implies that it was once whole. It is undeniable that those who suffer most from the inequities, abuses, and dehumanization of our profit-driven healthcare system are people of color. Tuskegee was not an aberration. Studies consistently show deep health disparities based on race, despite decades of efforts to address them. African-Americans suffer the lowest life expectancy, highest infant mortality, highest rates of disability and preventable diseases, and highest rates of death from cancer, heart disease, asthma complications, and diabetes among all groups. These disparities exist even when such factors as age, severity of conditions, insurance status, and income are comparable. There is no question that bias, stereotyping, and prejudice contribute greatly to racial and ethnic disparities in healthcare. When polled, however, the overwhelming majority of physicians (75 percent of whom are white, non-Hispanic, and only 5 percent Black) report that they are not biased and that they treat all their patients the same, regardless of race. How can bias be so pervasive yet remain almost completely unacknowledged by its perpetrators despite decades of efforts to introduce "cultural competency" training into health professions curricula? And if it lives in all these good, liberal doctors, how might racism live in me, in the life I live, in all of my relationships, in the work to which I've dedicated myself professionally? It was facing these questions that moved me to begin to study race and whiteness theory.

That's how I discovered your work, George. I had been teaching Merleau-Ponty and other phenomenologists in a course called Bodies, Illness, and Care for several years. This seemed the ideal context to begin exploring how racism thrives as an embodied phenomenon despite or perhaps even because of the liberal ideology of those who perpetuate it. I asked a philosopher friend if she might recommend something, and she pointed me to *Black Bodies, White Gazes*. I found there much more than I'd bargained for. Your work asked me to recognize my *own* whiteness as the normative, relationally lived phenomenon that sustains all racist practices, including those perpetuated by the healthcare system narrative medicine seeks to reform. As a philosopher, I am quite comfortable living in my head, even when teaching phenomenology. Your work brought me into my body in an entirely new way. To challenge racism and the role whiteness plays in perpetuating racist practices requires more, as you stress, than a cognitive shift. It requires work on the somatic level. It doesn't matter how many lectures are delivered or articles published by well-meaning healthcare reformers about the evils of racial disparities; until white researchers, clinicians, and the reformers themselves begin to engage in a continuous effort to perform our bodies' racialized interactions with the world differently, meaningful healthcare reform will never take place.

In your work, you explicitly address the role white racist narrative plays in sustaining whitely-being-in-the world. This is, of course, of particular importance to narrative medicine. In *Black Bodies, White Gazes*, you write about narrative's power to communicate the lived and imaginative dimensions of experience, beyond abstract reflection. This is a central conviction of our work in narrative medicine. You teach us how to apply this conviction to the interrogation of the racist distal narratives—familial, national, religious, literary, and more—that shape the meaning of the Black body under healthcare's white gaze, perpetuating its racist practices. You guide us in reading literature—like Toni Morrison's *The Bluest Eye*—that imaginatively communicates the lived experience of the dehumanizing, brutalizing power of the white gaze. Your work is required reading in our core masters curriculum, and your Narrative Medicine Grand Rounds lecture at Columbia last year (2015) is a seminal event in the evolution of our program.

G. Y.: By integrating critical analyses of whiteness into the work that you do, have you found that white students are receptive or defensive or perhaps a bit of both? Speak to this.

C. I.: More than a bit of both, I'd say. Whether working with undergraduates, masters students, medical students, residents, or experienced clinicians, I experience a broad range of responses from white students, from assertions that they "don't see race, everyone is equal, racism would disappear if we just stopped talking about it" to honest, critical analyses of the ways their everyday interactions in and with the world constitute and perpetuate the normative hegemony of whiteness. Not surprisingly, I've found that the most effective means of moving white students out of the former position—to encourage them to begin to see the unseen—is to talk about my own experience, elaborating on what I've discussed above, regarding the formation of my identity as a white. Even then, of course, I don't bring everyone along. There are white students who are anxious to distance themselves from me, insisting that their own backgrounds are very different from mine: "I grew up in New York City"; "My brother was adopted from Ethiopia"; "My parents would never have let us use 'that word.'" Other white students seek to undermine the interpretations of critical race theory by offering "opposing" interpretations: "I cross a dark street because the person approaching me is a man, not because he is Black," or "My Black friend doesn't agree with Yancy." I certainly understand these attempts to evade, to cling to faith in one's enlightenment, to maintain one's exceptionality. I understand, because I struggle daily—hourly—to peel the scales from my own eyes. At least once every day I feel a satisfying rush of angry indignation as I excoriate Trump's supporters. Blaming the "bad whites," as you write, is an effective strategy for refusing to recognize my own center of power. There will be no end to my struggle to see, and thus to find ways to teach, the unseen contingency of my whiteness when every moment of every waking hour my ignorance is so richly rewarded.

G. Y.: So, how would you speak to a latent skepticism from students of color that a white male is able to speak in honest and transgressive ways to white power?

C. I.: I would never challenge the skepticism from students of color that a white male is able to speak in honest and transgressive ways to white power. Any judgments they might make regarding my honesty or dishonesty, my collusion or transgression, are based on a lived experience of racism—including acute observations of the performance of whiteness—to which I only have access by listening to the stories that inform their judgments. I still struggle to find effective ways to facilitate the telling of these stories, whether in the auditorium, the clinic, the classroom, or the hospital. It is my race and gender that have placed me in the position of facilitator. If I'm being honest, then I have to admit that the scope and acuity of my honesty and the range and effectiveness of my transgression are limited by the all-embracing, structural operations of whiteness from which I continue to benefit, whether visible to me or not. Students of color understand this; to pretend otherwise only further compromises trust.

G. Y.: If you were able to speak to white America and the narratives that so many of them live by, what would you say?

C. I.: Most of the narratives we live by as white Americans support the normativity of whiteness. This normativity brutalizes, marginalizes, impoverishes, rapes, subjugates, imprisons, and traumatizes people of color. As antiracist theorist Tim Wise has argued, it is also bad for the majority of whites, because it supports structures of power that enrich those at the top while feeding those on the bottom a myth of superiority that suppresses their sense of injustice. This myth is narrated in the histories of our families, in the primers that teach us to read, in the sagas of our country's founding, and the lyrics of our popular songs. It is narrated in the great majority of television shows and movies, fictional and documentary. It is narrated in morning and evening news reports—in the coverage of politics, disasters, celebrity gossip, and sports. Some of the media may be new, but the narratives themselves are very old. We've been telling them for centuries—monstrous children, infantilized by our own fairy tales, oblivious to the suffering we cause. So much suffering for so long. This isn't inevitable. It does not have to continue. It is time to practice what my colleague Sayantani DasGupta has termed "narrative humility."[5] Time to open ourselves to the stories of those we continue to hurt, while engaging in the difficult work of narrative self-evaluation, self-critique. If we are to stop hurting others, we must be completely unmade. It is time to be split wide open—time for a narrative identity crisis.

NOTES

1. Paul Ricoeur, "Life in Quest of Narrative," in *On Paul Ricoeur: Narrative and Interpretation*, ed. David Wood (London: Routledge, 1991), 20–33.
2. Hans-Georg Gadamer, *Truth and Method*, trans. Joel Weinsheimer and Donald G. Marshall (New York: Continuum International, 2004).
3. René Descartes, *Discourse on Method and Meditations on First Philosoph*, trans. Donald A. Cress (Indianapolis: Hacke, 1998), 44.
4. Ta-Nehisi Coates, *Between the World and Me* (New York: Random House, 2015).
5. Sayantani DasGupta, "Narrative Humility," *Lancet* 371, no. 9617 (2008): 980–81.

Joe Feagin

George Yancy: To what extent does your work as a sociologist overlap or pertain to what we might concern ourselves with as philosophers?

Joe Feagin: I have been deeply concerned with issues of social and moral philosophy since college. I majored in philosophy as an undergraduate and then went to Harvard Divinity School, where I worked with philosopher-theologians in social ethics, European theology, and comparative religions. I studied with James Luther Adams, Paul Tillich, Richard R. Niebuhr, Arthur Darby Nock, and others. When I switched to doctoral work in sociology at Harvard, I studied with the theoreticians Talcott Parsons, George Homans, Robert Bellah, Charles Tilly, and Gordon Allport. Allport and his young colleague Tom Pettigrew got me seriously interested in studying racial-ethnic theory in social science as well as the empirical reality of racism in the United States. During this decade (the 1960s) I was also greatly influenced by major African American social analysts of racism, like W. E. B. Du Bois, Stokely Carmichael, and Charles Hamilton. More recently, my work has been used by philosophers of race, including Lewis Gordon, Charles Mills, Linda Alcoff, Tommy Curry—and yourself.

G. Y.: In your book *The White Racial Frame*, you argue for a new paradigm that will help to explain the nature of racism. What is that new paradigm, and what does it reveal about race in America?

J. F.: To understand well the realities of North American racism, one must adopt an analytical perspective focused on the what, why, and who of the systemic white racism that is central and foundational to this society. Most mainstream social scientists dealing with racism issues have relied heavily on inadequate analytical concepts like prejudice, bias, animus, stereotyping, and intolerance. Such concepts are often useful, but were long ago crafted by white social scientists focusing on individual racial and ethnic issues, not on society's systemic racism. To fully understand (white) racism in the United States, one has to go to the centuries-old counter-system tradition of African American analysts and other analysts of color who have done the most sustained and penetrating analyses of institutional and systemic racism.

G. Y.: So, are you suggesting that racial prejudices are only half the story? Does the question of the systemic nature of racism make white people complicit regardless of racial prejudices?

J. F.: Prejudice is much less than half the story. Because prejudice is only one part of the larger white racial frame that is central to rationalizing and maintaining systemic racism, one can be less racially prejudiced and still operate out of many other aspects of that dominant frame. That white racial frame includes not only racist prejudices and stereotypes of conventional analyses, but also racist ideologies, narratives, images, and emotions, as well as individual and small-group inclinations to discriminate shaped by the other features. Additionally, all whites, no matter what their racial prejudices and other racial framings entail, benefit from many racial privileges routinely granted by this country's major institutions to whites.

G. Y.: The NAACP called the murder of nine African Americans in the historic Emanuel AME Baptist Church in Charleston, South Carolina, an "act of racial terrorism"? Do you think that definition is correct?

J. F.: According to media reports, the convicted murderer Dylann Roof has aggressively expressed numerous ideas, narratives, symbols, and emotions from an openly white supremacist version of that old white racial frame. The NAACP terminology is justified, given that the oldest terrorist group still active on the planet is the white supremacist Ku Klux Klan. We must also emphasize the larger societal context of recurring white supremacist actions, which implicates white Americans more generally. Mainstream media commentators and politicians have mostly missed the critical point that much of the serious anti-Black and prowhite framing proclaimed by supremacist groups is still shared, publicly or privately, by many other whites. The latter include many whites horrified at what these white terrorist groups have recently done.

G. Y.: I realize that this question would take more space than we have here, but what specific insights about race can you share after five decades of research?

J. F.: Let me mention just two. First, I have learned much about how this country's racial oppression became well-institutionalized and thoroughly systemic over many generations, including how it has been rationalized and maintained for centuries by the broad white racist framing just mentioned. Another key insight is about how long this country's timeline of racial oppression, and resistance to that oppression by Americans of color, actually is. Most whites, and many others, do not understand that about 80 percent of this country's four centuries have involved extreme racialized slavery and extreme Jim Crow legal segregation.

As a result, major racial inequalities have been deeply institutionalized over about twenty generations. One key feature of systemic racism is how it has been socially reproduced by individuals, groups, and institutions for many generations. Most whites think racial inequalities reflect differences they see as real—superior work ethic, greater intelligence, or other meritorious abilities of whites. Social science research is clear that white-Black inequalities today are substantially the result of a majority of whites socially inheriting unjust enrichments (money, land, home equities, social capital, etc.) from numerous previous white generations—the majority of whom benefited from the racialized slavery system and/or the de jure (Jim Crow) and de facto overt racial oppression that followed slavery for nearly a century, indeed until the late 1960s.

G. Y.: What then are we to make of the concept of American meritocracy and the Horatio Alger narrative—the rags-to-riches narrative?

J. F.: These are often just convenient social fictions, not societal realities. For centuries they have been circulated to justify why whites as a group have superior socioeconomic and power positions in American society. In the white frame's pro-white subframe, whites are said to be the hardest working and most meritorious group. Yet the sociologist Nancy DiTomaso has found in many interviews with whites that a substantial majority have used networks of white acquaintances, friends, and family to find most jobs over their lifetimes. They have mostly avoided real market competition and secured good jobs using racially segregated networks, not just on their "merit." Not one interviewee openly saw anything wrong with their use of this widespread system of white favoritism, which involves "social capital" passed along numerous white generations.

G. Y.: Can we talk about race in America without inevitably talking about racism?

J. F.: No, we cannot. In its modern racialized sense, the term 'race' was created by white American and European analysts in the seventeenth and eighteenth centuries in order to explain how they, as "good Christians," could so extensively and brutally oppress, initially, indigenous and African Americans. There was no well-developed American hierarchy of "races," a key feature of systemic racism, before white Europeans and white Americans made that the societal reality in the Americas by means of the Atlantic slave trade and the genocidal theft of indigenous peoples' lands. Whites were soon framed as the virtuous and "superior race," while those oppressed were dehumanized as the "inferior races."

G. Y.: There are some who argue that slavery existed in Africa before the arrival of Europeans. Assuming that this is true, was it different or similar to forms of slavery in the Americas?

J. F.: Many white analysts, and some analysts of color operating out of the white frame, like to immediately bring up this subject of slavery somewhere else when US slavery should be at issue. In such cases, it is usually an argument designed to avoid dealing forthrightly with the subject of this country's economic and political foundation on one of the worst types of slavery systems ever created in any society.

My answer is this: Let us first fully confront and understand the horrific reality of two-plus centuries of our extreme enslavement system, its great immorality, and its many horrific legacies persisting through the Jim Crow era and still operative in the present day, and then we can deal with the issue of comparative slavery systems. By no means have we as scholars and citizens accomplished this first and far more important task. Indeed, relatively few whites today know or care about the terrible legacies of our slavery and Jim Crow systems, including the fact that we still live under an undemocratic constitution undemocratically made, and early implemented, by leading white slaveholders.

G. Y.: What implications does the white racial frame have for Blacks, Asians, Latinos, and those from the Middle East, in our contemporary moment?

J. F.: There are many implications. Consider that the white frame is made up of two key types of subframes: The most noted and most researched are those negatively targeting people of color. In addition, the most central subframe, often the hardest to "see," especially by whites, is that reinforcing the idea of white virtuousness in a myriad ways, including superior white values and institutions, the white work ethic, and white intelligence. This white-virtue framing is so strong that it affects the thinking not only of whites, but also of many people of color here and overseas. Good examples are the dominant American culture's standard of "female beauty," and the attempts of many people of color to look, speak, or act as "white" as they can so as to do better in our white-dominated institutions.

G. Y.: In your book *The First R: How Children Learn Race and Racism* (coauthored with Debra Van Ausdale), there is a section on children and how they learn about race and racism, and examples of children exhibiting explicitly racist behavior at very young ages. What did you learn about how young children learn ways of racial framing?

J. F.: One major discovery from nearly a year of field observations that Debra did in that multiracial daycare center was that white children learn major elements of the dominant white racial frame at an earlier age than many previous and influential researchers had recognized. This is now backed up by much other social science research. We know that many white children as young as two to four years old have already learned and used key features of the white racist frame. Our research shows that these children have learned not only elements of the antiothers subframes, but also the strong white-virtue subframe.

One example of this latter subframe involved a white child confronting an Asian child who was starting to pull a school wagon. She put her hands on her hips and arrogantly made the assertion that "only white Americans can pull this wagon." In these field observations, we also found that young children of all backgrounds gain knowledge of racial framing from peers in classrooms and play settings, not just from relatives in home settings. Moreover, in everyday interactions they frequently did much more than imitate what they had heard or seen from others. They regularly acted on their racist framing in their own creative ways.

G. Y.: You've mentioned images and emotions and how they are linked to the racial frame. There have been studies that demonstrate a strong relationship between ape images of Black people that are emotion laden for those who project such images. Say a bit about these findings.

J. F.: That commonplace ape framing involves vicious stereotyping, narratives, and emotion-laden imagery. That complexity is why we need a broader white racial frame concept. Only a little research and theorizing have been done on the emotions of that white frame, but in my research they clearly include at least white anger, hostility, disgust, fear, envy, and greed. There is research linking ape imagery to white reactions to Black faces and white attributions of Black criminality. For more than two centuries that Blacks-as-apes imagery has been part of the dehumanizing process enabling whites, who see themselves as "good people," to engage in extensive racial oppression. Our most famous white "founder," Thomas Jefferson, in his major book, *Notes on the State of Virginia*, even suggested that Africans had sex with apes.

G. Y.: Has there been similar research that shows racist images that are emotion laden when it comes to images of Asian Americans, Latinos, and others?

J. F.: Much research on Asian Americans, Latinos, and other groups shows there are numerous racist images of these groups as well, although the white racist emotions that are unmistakably attached to them have again been little studied. One good example of this emotionally laden framing that has some research is the extraordinarily racist sexualization that white men often direct at Asian women, Asian American women, and US and other Latinas, such as on the internet websites exoticizing these women for white male sexual and related purposes.

G. Y.: Has research revealed that Black people also have such racist images and value-laden frames when it comes to their perception of white people?

J. F.: The research explicitly on such Black framing of whites is less extensive, but the substantial research interviewing of Black Americans that my colleagues and I have done over recent decades strongly suggests that Black framing of whites is usually different and generally more direct-experience-related. There are very few generic jokes stereotyping whites in our hundreds of interviews with Blacks, and what pained joking there is, is mostly about the actual discrimination that the Black interviewees have experienced from whites.

Analyzing white and Black college student diaries about racial events in everyday life, my talented colleague Leslie Houts Picca and I found that the white students mostly described racist conversations and other racist actions of white acquaintances, friends, and relatives that targeted people of color, such as whites telling N-word jokes or racially taunting Black people in public settings. In significant contrast, most Black and other student-of-color diaries from students at these same colleges recorded white racist actions targeting the diarists themselves or acquaintances and relatives. Black understandings of whites are typically based on much negative and discriminatory experience with whites. The reverse rarely seems to be the case in our extensive field interviewing.

G. Y.: Briefly distinguish between what you call backstage racism and frontstage racism. What does backstage racism tell us about the insidious nature of racism?

J. F.: The in-depth data my colleagues and I have collected over the last few decades strongly indicate that the anti-Black and prowhite framing of most whites has changed much less than is often asserted, including by researchers depending on brief attitudinal measures and opinion polls. The appearance of major change in white racist framing is created by the fact that many whites have learned to suppress a frontstage expression of some or much of their overtly racist framing—such as in public settings where there are people present who are unknown to them. However, data such as that noted previously for white college students reveal that a great many whites still assert and perform a blatantly racist framing of people of color in backstage settings—that is, where only whites such as friends and relatives are present.

G. Y.: Given your emphasis upon racial frames, in what ways can people begin to undo those racial frames?

J. F.: That is the difficult question for the social health and democratic future of this country. We have a modest research literature dealing with successful deframing and reframing of people's racist views, one much smaller than that measuring racial stereotyping and prejudice. One reason is that we have been handicapped by the narrow and individualistic concepts of stereotyping and prejudice, and few researchers have adopted a perspective problematizing a broader and dominant white racial framing. Getting rid of a few racial stereotypes is hard enough, and there has been some success at that, but when they are connected to hundreds of other "bits" of racist stereotyping, ideology, imagery, emotions, and narratives of that white racial frame, it is even harder to begin a successful process of substantial deframing and reframing toward an authentic liberty-and-justice framing. Such reframing takes great effort and a long period of time in my experience. Nonetheless, some social science research is encouraging in regard to changing at least limited aspects of that dominant white frame.

G. Y.: Lastly, what does social science have to teach philosophers when it comes to thinking about the reality of race and racism?

J. F.: We all have a lot to learn from the best social science dealing empirically and theoretically with the centuries-old reality of this country's white racism, especially that revealing well its systemic and foundational character and how it has been routinely reproduced over twenty generations. Also, in my view, the best philosophers on such white racism matters, among them you and my talented young colleague Tommy Curry, are ahead of most social scientists on such critical societal issues. So, social scientists, indeed all of us, have much to learn from the best philosophical analysts as well!

PART II DISCUSSION QUESTIONS

1. Joe Feagin draws on the concept of white racist framing in his work. What is entailed in the "white racial frame" that *all* white people seem to share, and how might it inform the mode of address that *all* white people take up? How might the frame of the white supremacist differ from the well-meaning and privilege-cognizant white person, and how would the two translate into different modes of address, if any?

2. There appear to be two theaters for research concerning race. One is the intimate, personal space of phenomenological work and narrative. Historical and statistical records of racist acts or structures and their effects characterize the other. Both seem necessary, so how can the two best be reconciled to provide a discursive space for lived experience without sacrificing the need for more broad, impersonal, structural analysis?

3. Anti-Black racism, Craig Irvine claims, "thrives . . . despite or perhaps because of the liberal ideology of those who perpetrate it." Whiteness is often characterized by self-ignorance. This ignorance and its privilege-evasive responses, including white fragility, shadow texts, and the unwillingness and/or inability to experience *nepantla* or "world" travel, resemble one of the oldest images in Western philosophy: Plato's cave. Discuss the ways in which white privilege keeps its possessors in a cave of ignorance, the difficulties of ascending out of ignorance, and also the difficulties of returning to the cave, this time as one who has, as Alison Bailey puts it, "seen through the fictions of heteronormativity, a godless life, white supremacy, capitalism, or patriarchy." How can white people best prepare to make this journey?

4. The elusive "perception of a threat" that Judith Butler discusses in her interview is a tool that white people use to justify violence done to Black bodies in "self-defense," real or perceived. It poses a special challenge insofar as it is *"becoming more 'reasonable' all the time,"* gaining momentum with every acquittal that legitimates the "perception of a threat." Can an education in whiteness rely on reason, if whiteness possesses an exceptional ability to use reason to cover its own tracks?

Race, Pedagogy, and the Domain of the Cultural

Lawrence Blum

George Yancy: Larry, explain how you became interested in issues regarding race and philosophy. What were some of the specific influences?

Lawrence Blum: I got into race relatively late, I am not proud to admit. I was one of those philosophers who didn't quite get how race could be dealt with within philosophy, though I had always been somewhat interested in race as a social issue, and I participated in a small way in the Civil Rights Movement. For a time I definitely had that "it's not philosophy" attitude. When Howard McGary, Laurence Thomas, Anita Allen, Leonard Harris, Bernard Boxill, Bill Lawson, Lucius Outlaw, Adrian Piper, and other African-American philosophers started writing in the 1980s I started to see, albeit still too slowly, how race could be a philosophical topic. In the late '80s I was talking with my African-American departmental colleague, the Hobbes scholar Tommy Lott, and he asked me if I had heard of Olaudah Equiano. I had never heard of him. Tommy told me who he was, and for some reason that was an "Aha" moment for me. I realized that there was something wrong with my education and outlook for not knowing about this important slave narrative and that I should and wanted to engage professionally with work on race and philosophy. That was a turning point.

G. Y.: What were some of the explicit and implicit assumptions about your understanding of philosophy such that you were one of those philosophers who didn't quite get how race could be dealt with within philosophy?

L. B.: It's hard to reconstruct that, George. It probably had to do with the alleged universality and timelessness of philosophical concerns, and perhaps connected with something about philosophical "methodology" as that was understood (and maybe still is by some people).

I do want to add that I see "philosophical race studies" as deeply informed by other disciplines. I don't think a "pure philosophy" approach can take us very far in the race area. Philosophers of race need to know something about history, sociology, political science. Certainly "applied ethics" recognizes the need to have substantial knowledge of nonphilosophy domains. But as Charles Mills has emphasized, race work is not just "applied philosophy." It involves shifting the way we think about the big picture of society and the world. In recent years many philosophers have seen value in psychology, social psychology, and cognitive science. Race work requires engagement with an even broader range of social sciences.

G. Y.: That's an excellent point, Larry. This is why I really admire and respect the work of sociologist Joe Feagin. He is a sociologist who does theory and empirical research on race. He engages that broader range of social sciences. Back to questions of identity, though, you came to the question of the philosophical significance of race late. Did you also come late to the question of how identity, more generally, impacts our philosophical intuitions and focus? For example, did your Jewish identity impact how you thought about philosophy and its aims? Of course, this question, generally speaking, is consistent with the assumptions behind standpoint epistemology.

L. B.: I came even later to issues about identity, and even then I was more interested in the social and political issues dealt with in multicultural theory than the epistemic ones in standpoint theory. I don't think my identity as Jewish really had any explicit influence or interest to me within philosophy, especially at that time. Now I am much more interested in all these issues.

G. Y.: In our contemporary moment, there has only been a modicum of growth in the professional field of philosophy regarding the philosophical significance of race. When you began to think about and write about race philosophically, did you ever encounter resistance from the profession?

L. B.: Not really, and I'm sure there is an element of white privilege in that. I was already an established moral philosopher. Maybe some people thought I was deserting "philosophy" in moving into the race area but I never really suffered for it. I think I benefited from teaching at a nonelite institution without a graduate program, in a very pluralistic department where a lot of people worked, and still work, in nonstandard areas and where we were encouraged to "follow our muse" and not to worry about where our department stands in the rankings.

G. Y.: Say more about how you understand the element of white privilege within that context.

L. B.: I was thinking that being white probably protected my professional standing from being diminished by working in what were then very marginal areas (of race).

G. Y.: Who were some of your philosophical allies at that time?

L. B.: By the early '90s I had gotten to know Anthony Appiah and was in a discussion group with him. I attended the tiny number of APA sessions on race in that period and started to get to know some of the African-American philosophers I mentioned earlier. And in 1993–1994 Jorge Garcia and I were fellows together in a professional ethics program, and our many wonderful conversations about philosophical racial issues really helped me get more deeply into the field.

G. Y.: In what ways do you see the profession of philosophy changing in its openness to questions of race?

L. B.: Well, we've made a bit of progress in the past twenty years or so. There are certainly more sessions on race at our professional organizations. The California Roundtable on Philosophy and Race meets every year and has nurtured and supported younger scholars of color and work on race. The journal *Critical Philosophy of Race* is an important new presence. Graduate students have been organizing Minorities and Philosophy (MAP) groups. The recent APA leadership has included some important race scholars, and the APA is taking serious and focused steps to diversify the profession. More departments are looking to offer courses in race and philosophy. Often they are more interested in enrollments than in acknowledging race studies as an important philosophical field; but it still helps move us forward.

Still, there is very little work on race in the very top journals—*Philosophy and Public Affairs, Ethics*—and the field still seems pretty marginalized. The number of people whose primary scholarly specialty is race seems pretty small. We've got a long way to go.

G. Y.: Despite this relative progress, I think that you are correct. We still have long way to go. What do you see as necessary for making the concept of race more philosophically relevant?

L. B.: Well, one thing is bringing people into philosophy who find these racial issues interesting and intellectually exciting. And another is challenging the "color-blind" way some gatekeepers still think about philosophy. I think the relatively recent PIKSI ("Philosophy in an Inclusive Key Summer Institute") programs (and Howard McGary's longer-standing Rutgers summer program) are tremendously valuable in that regard. (My university is very involved in the new Boston-area PIKSI.) These programs nurture, encourage, and mentor undergraduates of color to envision going on in philosophy. Although by no means do all of them want to do work on race, many do, and a larger number recognize racial issues as important. Hopefully bringing more students of all racial groups who are interested in race into the profession will help spread the word, as well as challenging the profession to see the intellectual necessity of dealing with race.

A related point is that more philosophers are able to see their specific subdisciplines as entrées to work on race. Initially almost all race philosophy was done by social and political philosophers (as I am), but now you find philosophers of biology, and of science more generally, and philosophers of language and even metaphysicians weighing in. This is a positive development in getting more people to see race as an intellectually engaging and significant subject.

G. Y.: Since the publication of your important book, *"I'm Not a Racist, But . . .,"* have you come to rethink your understanding of the meaning of racism?

L. B.: I am much less involved in the issue of the meaning of the term "racism" than I was in that book. I do still agree with the more general point I tried to make in that discussion—that the overuse of the single term 'racism' inhibits our ability to clarify the manifold types of wrong involved in race-related systems, practices, actions, statements, and thoughts. We need a richer and more varied moral vocabulary to do that work.

G. Y.: I see. I also think that there is a way in which 'racism' can be deployed to denude the term of its vitriol. Yet, isn't it also important that we don't define how those who are the recipients of white prejudice, especially Black people, understand racism, given their multiple experiences of pain and suffering? There are some who would argue that to do otherwise would be to define their reality.

L. B.: That's a really important point, and I don't think I can do it justice in the context of this interview. I certainly think white people working in the race area need to be aware of how Black people are experiencing racial prejudice and injustice, and how they talk about that experience. I don't think my analysis of racism takes anything away from the pain and suffering Black people experience from racial mistreatment by whites or other non-Blacks. But the issue of how people conceptualize their own experience, and where they are getting the concepts they use for doing so, is very complicated. Experience is never "pure" and unconceptualized. Philosophers try to explore, clarify, and systematize concepts that may then inform how people think about, and even experience, their experiences. This is the spirit of what I was trying to do in my book on "racism."

G. Y.: I've integrated work on whiteness and pedagogy in my scholarship that has proven important to scholars in the area of critical pedagogy. With the publication of your book *High Schools, Race, and America's Future*, you've managed to provide a template, as it were, for those of us who desire to engage race critically and engagingly with our students. Talk about what motivated this important book and your desire to teach a classroom course entitled Race and Racism.

L. B.: The book is based on a high-school course that I taught at my local high school, which is also the school my three children attended. I had been working in the area of education a bit at my university and was teaching one course in which my students were mostly in-service and preservice teachers. I was feeling a bit fraudulent because I had never spent any time teaching in a precollege classroom. I wasn't sure what to do about that, but one day I was talking to the social studies coordinator at the high school and asked her if I could run an after-school discussion group on race with a racially and ethnically mixed group of students. She proposed instead that I teach a whole course on Race and Racism. After the first offering of that course, I was invited back to teach it three more times. (I give my university credit for seeing that teaching a high-school course was worthy of support and one course release.) It was a really astonishing experience. I learned a tremendous amount from my students.

I was able to arrange with the high school for the racial demographics of my class to roughly mirror the school's—at that time about 40 percent Black, 33 percent white, 15 percent Latino, 8 percent Asian, and various others (including racially mixed students). Each time I was assisted by a UMass undergraduate or graduate student of color interested in going into teaching. The course was an advanced-level course but did not have the "official status" of an Advanced Placement course, known for being helpful for admission to selective colleges. I tried to get the guidance counselors to send me students who were "reaching for college" but were not necessarily from families where it would be totally taken for granted that they would go to college. Since the counselors had only partial influence in who actually signed up for the course, I always ended up with a class whose aspirations, previous attainments, and educational backgrounds were all over the map. There were always a few students who did not end up going to college after graduation, and a few who went to quite selective colleges, even though I did not seek out the latter type of student.

I built the course around very intellectually challenging material. A main text was Audrey Smedley's *Race in North America*, but I also used Ira Berlin's history of slavery, *Many Thousands Gone*. (Smedley is a Black woman, who writes in an academic voice not revealing of her racial identity, and this became a focus of attention and surprise in the class.) We explored the history of slavery both in itself and in connection with the developing idea of race over the course of several centuries. We read the slave narrative, *The History of Mary Prince, a West Indian Slave*, one of the first female slave narratives, and one (unlike Frederick Douglass's) I could assume the students would not have encountered. We read portions of David Walker's *Appeal*, a searing critique of slavery, and an influential, partly philosophical, and altogether fascinating Abolitionist tract from 1829. We also looked at the scientific critique of race—very difficult material. (The book provides the whole syllabus.)

I wanted to give a course that could introduce largely Black and Latino students to college-level work; Black and Latino students are not provided with anything like the same opportunities for intellectual challenge in secondary school as are whites and Asians. Like many schools with mixed populations, the classes designated as advanced were dominated by white (mostly) and

Asian students. I wanted the Black and Latino students to have an experience of an advanced class in which they were the majority. But I also wanted the full racial mix of the school inside my class, because I wanted to work on their communicating with each other about racial issues across that racial divide.

The school had other courses on racial topics—African-American history, African-American literature, Caribbean literature, and I'm sure others, occasionally taught by white faculty but usually not. But none of the students in my classes had taken a whole course on race as a subject of academic inquiry. I wanted them to see the topic of race as intellectually engaging, exciting, and challenging, and also as a pathway to help them understand their own experiences and the society they lived in.

The conversations in class did not always stay "on topic" and sometimes drifted onto more current racial experiences and issues, which were also the subject of some contemporary readings. But I also kept the intellectual focus of the course front and center. I reproduce some of the fascinating conversations among the students, both about the specific course material and the other topics, in the book.

G. Y.: One student, Antonine, says to you, "I thought that you'd be a Black guy, Professor." You know, I get something similar. Because I teach undergraduate and graduate courses on race, there is an assumption that I *must* be Black. So, there is a kind of stereotyping operating here. How were you able to work through this? That is, what are some of interpersonal issues at stake here? Because as you put it, there is that question of "credibility" as a white person teaching students of color about race.

L. B.: I think the identity connection is more important to high-school than college students. The high school did not have enough teachers of color when I was teaching there, but the few who were there played very important mentoring and role-modeling functions for the students of their specific racial group. I could not duplicate that. But at the same time the students did not think that only people of color could teach about race. Perhaps especially because the course was historical, and had science in it, they more readily accepted me as a legitimate "expert." I'm sure it also helped that I was a college professor. But I also worked very hard to establish individual relations with each student (the class was capped at around twenty). Remember that high-school courses have more than twice as many contact hours per week as college courses. I worked especially hard to show that I believed the students of color when they spoke in class, outside of class, or in their journals about racial mistreatment. High-school students also care more about their relationship with their teachers than college students do; and research shows that Black students are more concerned about that than are whites. While race never stopped affecting my relationships with the class and with particular students, I think they basically accepted my authority in the class and with respect to the material, and knew that I cared about them and their learning. Having said that, I can think of a few students, all Black and female, of the eighty or so students I taught over the four years, with whom I was never able to establish a real connection.

G. Y.: One question that I'm often asked is how to get students to actually talk about such a sensitive and potentially explosive topic as race, especially within the context of a diverse classroom, which is what you faced. Any advice?

L. B.: In one respect this is more of an issue in high school than college because the students are less mature. But they are also less inhibited and are sometimes more able to roll with expressed insensitivity on the part of their classmates. But I want to make three points here. First, the emphasis on academic study, with the implication (that I made explicit) that they all had something important to learn and that they were not likely to know it beforehand, helped with the dynamic. It would have been different if we were doing material that drew first and foremost on their current racialized experiences. Second, we had some discussions about "rules of engagement," recognizing that the material is very charged and trying to come up with rules or guidelines to keep things constructive. Students suggested things like "Don't say anything that may hurt someone's feelings" or "Don't say anything racist." Others replied that you don't always know beforehand what will hurt someone's feelings or is racist, and that is one of the things we were learning about in the class. So some said we couldn't put any constraints on what people said. Although we couldn't come up with any definite rules, having the conversation was very helpful in raising everyone's consciousness about how what they say might be heard or experienced by others. I also had a periodic "open journal" assignment where they could write about anything at all, that related in some way to the course. This allowed them to express irritation, anger, or outrage at something one of their classmates said.

A third general guideline or goal I aimed for was a balance between having everyone feel that we were a learning community where all had to be able to speak and be treated with respect by others, and that whites especially (but really everyone) had areas of ignorance and misunderstanding that they could help to correct through the learning and discussions in the class.

G. Y.: I'm often accused of being stuck in the Black/white binary. While I can defend my position, I do think that it is important to raise the issue of how the dynamics of race transcends that binary. How did you manage to transcend that binary in the classroom?

L. B.: I was concerned about this issue because I had students from all groups, not only whites and Blacks. However, I wanted them to recognize that the course was not an "equal time for every group" course, in a multicultural mode. If you are dealing with race historically, especially with a primary focus on the US, there is no way to avoid the fact that slavery and the expulsion and genocide of indigenous peoples on the part of whites form the foundation for that history. It isn't really intellectually responsible to deny that framework. I insisted that the students needed to understand US history and that all were in the same boat about that.

At the same time, I did a unit comparing the slave systems of the US and of Latin America (including the Spanish, though also Anglophone, Caribbean); and we looked at the different notions of race that emerged from the different settlement patterns and forms of slavery. And I did a unit on the Supreme Court cases Ian Haney-Lopez discusses in his book *White by Law*, in the 1910–1920 period, in which Japanese and Indian immigrants tried to naturalize as "white" as their only option (besides being Black) for gaining citizenship under the 1790 Naturalization Act. In those ways I tried to bring historical Asian and Latino experience into the course. Also, many of the "spillover" conversations raised issues outside of the Black/white binary. In addition, we discussed ethnic and national origin differences within the US Black population, which was reflected in the class composition also, which contained a significant number of Haitian Americans and a very small number of Africans, in addition to African-Americans.

G. Y.: In the book you make it clear that after reading the book, you hope that other teachers, including college professors, will desire to teach such a course. As a Black philosopher who teaches such courses, there is an added weight, especially when teaching within predominantly white academic institutions as I do. There is the weight of so much denial by white students that racism is real. There is also the pressure of being the only Black body in that white space talking to white students about their race privileges, which they also deny. So, while I agree with you that there needs to be more of us teachers engaging race within the classroom, I think that it is important to mark the difference encountered by Black teachers and teachers of color when they teach such courses. Any thoughts on this?

L. B.: The demographics of the classes really make a lot of difference. And so does the race of the instructor. What you say is entirely right about that. When I have talked about teaching this course to different audiences, especially those working in K–12 settings, I acknowledge that it is completely different for a white teacher to teach classes with a minority of white students than ones with, say, 90 percent white students. As you say, a Black teacher with the latter demographic, or even worse, with 100 percent white students, would face a very different situation. My focus is on encouraging white teachers to teach about race, to help develop the racial literacy all high-school graduates need to face the society they live in. My own (nonelite) university is quite diverse, though not of course as much as the high school. My classes on race seldom have fewer than 40 percent students of color, and I realize this is a much more favorable teaching environment.

I want to clarify that what I encouraged in the book was not so much professors teaching courses on race at their colleges but specifically at the high-school level. (As you note, I also aimed this message to high-school teachers.) I don't think it would ever occur to most college instructors to even consider doing that. In general, high schools are more racially diverse, and in particular less white, than are US colleges. I hope the book conveys how rewarding, challenging, and exciting it is to teach about race and racism to high-school students.

G. Y.: Given the dynamic nature of these conversations, I thought it necessary to ask one additional question, especially with respect to your pedagogy regarding race. As you know, two Black men were recently killed, one in Baton Rouge and another in St. Paul. There were also five police officers killed in Dallas. Of course, this has again energized the Black Lives Matter Movement. I have had Black students in the past say to me, "Racism will never end in the US. So, why are we discussing it?" Pedagogically, how might you negotiate such a question, in such a way that you honor those real feelings of hopelessness and yet encourage a sense of hope?

L. B.: Certainly the killings of Sperling and Castile, on top of the police killings of the past few years, can lead anyone including our students to think, "Not again! This is never going to end." But as their teachers, we can inject a historical and social-movement perspective that puts current horrors in a larger context. The system of legally mandated Segregation seemed impregnable through much of its history. There was certainly as much or more reason to feel hopeless about that as there is now about police violence. But courageous Black people in various eras fought against it, struggled and sacrificed, and finally brought it down. Black Lives Matter is an extremely hopeful movement for our times. In shining a light on Black lives lost as a result of police violence, it has very much helped to raise the consciousness of white Americans about police mistreatment of Blacks, and of racial justice more generally. I read that according to a late 2015 Pew survey, white Americans who agreed with the statement "Our country needs to continue making changes to give blacks equal rights with whites"[1] went from 39 percent to 53 percent in one year. And in fact more than a few police departments have put various programs and policies in place that are intended to reduce disparities in treatment of Blacks and whites.

There is always a "half full/half empty" dimension here, and we need to help our students do justice to both perspectives. It is disheartening that only 53 percent of whites signed on to that statement; but it is still a tremendous improvement. Another example: the Black high-school graduation rate in 2013 was 71 percent, up four points from two years before, and the highest it has ever been, and increasing at a higher rate than the white graduation rate; but the gap between white and Black is still large—15 percent. Half full, half empty. Measured by an "end of racism" standard, yes, we will never make that standard, any more than we will make an "end of terrorism," or "end of evil" standard. But would students think we shouldn't discuss terrorism or evil?

Of course, hopelessness cannot be assessed according to a strictly rational criterion, and I agree that we have to listen to our students' feelings of hopelessness and take them seriously. But I also hope we can help students recognize the sources and signs of change, historically and in the present.

NOTE

1. "Across Racial Lines, More Say Nation Needs to Make Changes to Achieve Racial Equality," *PewResearchCenter*, April 5, 2015, http://www.people-press.org/2015/08/05/across-racial-lines-more-say-nation-needs-to-make-changes-to-achieve-racial-equality/.

Dan Flory

George Yancy: At what point in your philosophical growth did you become interested in philosophy of film?

Dan Flory: It was a drawn-out process rather than any sort of discreet moment. During the 1980s I avidly read film theory and criticism with a combination of attraction and ambivalence. I was a graduate student at the time and had had a long-standing interest in movies that I wanted to develop philosophically but couldn't figure out how to do it in a way that I liked. I appreciated the way that what was then contemporary film theory could derive fascinating results that I often agreed with politically. But I was dubious of its reliance on Lacan and psychoanalysis, which I felt were based in antiquated, nineteenth-century theories of mind. I also read Stanley Cavell's *The World Viewed* (1979), George Wilson's *Narration in Light* (1986), and Gilles Deleuze's *Cinema I and II* (1986, 1989). But I couldn't envision then how I might continue on in terms of philosophy of film from what these thinkers had written. Cavell's book is a wonderful philosophical memoir about going to the movies that was a difficult act to follow in terms of how one might theorize about film, and that I didn't fully understand until years after I first read it. Deleuze basically reimagines how to theorize about film to the point when he was writing, partly as a result of thoughts and experiences similar to Cavell's, but I didn't fully grasp what he was doing until years later, either. Wilson's book is an engaging series of film interpretations that never quite develops a full-blown film theory (which he did later in *Seeing Fictions in Film* [2012]), so I was unsure at the time how I might build on the foundation he offered as well. In addition, philosophy of film was then predominantly looked at as not quite "real" or reputable philosophy, so I wasn't exactly encouraged to pursue it. No one taught or even talked about philosophy of film at the University of Minnesota in those days, where I was doing my graduate work.

When Noël Carroll published *The Philosophy of Horror* in 1990, however, what it did for me was offer a philosophical film theory to which I could envision myself contributing. His later work, as well as that of others, continued to elaborate this framework in a way I could embrace. By the early 1990s I also discovered the Society for the Philosophic Study of the Contemporary Visual Arts, which had been founded by philosophers who wanted to write about film but were frustrated by the lack of outlets in the discipline. I began presenting papers at their group sessions during APA meetings and publishing in their journal, *Film and Philosophy*. By the late 1990s I realized that I had developed a specialty in the philosophy of film, but getting to that point took nearly two decades of gradual development that was entirely on the side from what I had been taking courses in and writing about as a graduate student, as well as what I had been encouraged to do as a newly minted professional philosopher.

G. Y.: At what point did you begin to think critically about philosophy of film vis-à-vis race?

D. F.: After I turned in my dissertation in November 1995 (I took a long time to finish), I felt an overwhelming desire to write an essay about a series of African-American films that had stunned me over the previous few years. Movies like *Deep Cover* (1992), *One False Move* (1992), *Devil in a Blue Dress* (1995), and *Clockers* (1995) fascinated me by the way they used film noir tropes and techniques to articulate problems of race, and I wanted to analyze philosophically how they had done it. At the time I thought it would require no more than a standard-length article, but deciding to write that essay turned out to be pivotal for me professionally. Very few people were analyzing race in the philosophy of film at the time, and even then mostly in asides or passing references. In a way, I just kept researching because the way race could be articulated through film noir interested me. Another reason I kept researching race in film is that I had also been exploring the role of race in philosophy. A fellow graduate student, Jim Glassman, told me in the early 1980s about Richard Popkin's and Harry Bracken's articles from a few years earlier concerning Hume's and Locke's racism, which I tracked down and read.[1] I was, of course, shocked and appalled that I'd never been told or given opportunities to discuss these aspects of their work before. Weren't we in graduate school to study and analyze these sorts of problems? Over the years I dug more and more deeply on my own into the ways in which race had deformed and distorted the Western philosophical canon. For the most part, I had to explore this topic from outside philosophy itself because so few people in the field were exploring it, and even those explorations were hard to get (this was years before the Internet). I read Edward Said's *Orientalism* (1978), Martin Bernal's *Black Athena I and II* (1987, 1991), and other materials, and thought about the ways in which what was argued in these works applied to philosophy. Eventually I found that my interest in critical race theory dovetailed with my interest in philosophy of film to form what I've mainly been interested in and researched since.

Almost none of this, of course, was encouraged by the vast majority of my peers. Most of them felt that it was deeply inappropriate to explore these parts of philosophy, and publishing on race was like airing the discipline's dirty laundry in public. But with the encouragement of a few scholars doing critical race theory, like Charles Mills and Leonard Harris, and Tom Wartenberg in philosophy of film, I kept at it because it seemed worthwhile to do, even if it was marginalized from the mainstream of philosophy.

G. Y.: What are some of the complications in using the critical lens of philosophy to examine film when Western philosophy is itself so racially saturated?

D. F.: One complication is the circumstance I just mentioned: marginalization. With regard to race, that marginalization is typically cashed out by being shunned by one's peers. As some recent studies have underscored, professional philosophers remain deeply reluctant to explore the implications of race for philosophy itself, opting instead for what they see as the "high road" of ignoring remarks by figures like Hume, Kant, or Hegel about race and idealizing those thinkers' theories in ways that make the ideas seem as if they applied universally, rather than exclusively to white men—something these philosophers themselves were quite explicit about. It's the same "dirty laundry" problem that I encountered while in graduate school. Partly this reluctance is a result of the fact that even in 2016 more than 85 percent of the American Philosophical Association is white, so philosophers in the US generally feel that any critique of the whiteness of philosophy is also a critique of them (and they are not completely wrong to feel that way!). But that means when as a scholar you present about race in philosophy, you are often met with silence, avoidance, or sullen hostility. No one tells you to your face anymore that they wish you weren't doing this, but a lot of them make you feel that way. They avoid your talks, change the subject when race comes up, ask *sotto voce* whether it's really appropriate to be doing what you're doing, argue that they are exceptions to everything you've just said, or snub you after they hear racial criticisms that sting their sense of having a white self.

I've always been sort of an outsider, so I think it took me longer than perhaps it should have to grasp what was happening. But eventually I realized that the way a lot of people resisted, skipped over, or avoided the role of race in philosophy was the result of the depth of their discomfort with the topic. It's been an uphill battle over the last thirty years to get other philosophers to pay attention to the problem and really listen, but it finally seems that the realization is dawning on a significant number of members in the discipline that race is a topic they can no longer duck. I'm hopeful that that means a lot more progress can be made regarding race in philosophy than has been typical previously.

G. Y.: In your introduction to *Race, Philosophy, and Film*, you write about imagining how Christopher Nolan's *Batman* trilogy (2005–2012) would not have been the same had a Black or African-American actor played the role of Batman. How do you think a mainstream audience would respond?

D. F.: Well, I think immediately there would be questions in viewers' minds about where Bruce Wayne got his wealth and why he was acting as a vigilante. Mainstream audiences have no problem imagining that a white man—especially someone who can be perceived as a WASP such as actors Christian Bale or Michael Keaton—might be filthy rich and had inherited his wealth from his family. Northern European whites still most paradigmatically represent the universal human in cinema in terms of physiognomy, so WASPish-appearing actors remain much more able to represent a wide variety of human traits, such as being incredibly rich and seeking justice through vigilantism. But the normalcy of those presumptions is much harder for mainstream audiences to accept when it comes to Blacks and African-Americans. Typically, I think, there would be questions or suspicions on the part of many audience members that perhaps Bruce Wayne's money had been obtained illicitly if Batman were Black. Mainstream audiences are used to thinking of African-Americans as stereotypically poor or disadvantaged, so how a Black man could be so rich that he could become a playboy would have to be addressed in some way in order to allay those suspicions. (Was he or his father a drug dealer who cashed out? Is he an ex-rapper whose shady past contributed to his success? How can he live so large?) Either that or Bruce Wayne couldn't be rich. His origins story would have to be different; for example, that he arose from a neighborhood of grinding poverty and gained his loathing for crime from something other than seeing his rich parents gunned down by a thug might strike mainstream audiences as plausible. (This, by the way, is how Marvel comics introduces the new Black teenage girl who takes over the Iron Man character.) Perhaps as well—although it might remain a stretch for a lot of white viewers—he could be depicted as having arisen from a solidly middle-class family that had somehow been laid low by a thief who couldn't be prosecuted. But making such a backstory plausible to viewers who initially did not share that presumption as a likely possibility for Blacks would take a lot of exposition that might well not make the final cut of a film, given how blockbuster series like *Batman* have to immediately grab and hold your interest. In a way, it's a narrative shortcut to simply make the Black superhero an African prince like Black Panther in the most recent *Captain America* movie, or rely on other stereotypical scenarios instead of building a narrative character bit by bit from the ground up.

A different set of presumptions arises when thinking about a Black man being a vigilante for justice. Because of widespread presumptions that associate Black men with criminality, the use of violence by a Black Avenger would perhaps not be a stretch for mainstream audiences, but using it for the general public good probably would require additional narrative exposition. Blacks can readily be seen, I think, as plausibly using violence for personal or race-based ends, but it would be much harder to induce viewers to presume and accept that a Black man was using the appropriate amount of violence at the right time, at the right place, and regarding the right people to fight corruption and achieve universal, impartial justice. Again, to make Batman a Black vigilante superhero, its plausibility would have to be addressed and elaborated in the narrative (as it was in *Hancock* [2008] by making him an Ancient lesser god—and even then Hancock started out as a Black stereotype!), or Batman would have to be more of a criminal—more thuggish and prone to excess—to make him fit with mainstream racial sensibilities.

These problems of mainstream audience response have to do with what are now being explored as implicit racial biases. American culture, as you yourself have documented, is saturated with presumptions about what Black men are like: propensities to criminality, the myth of the Black rapist, and so on. However, these presumptions aren't explicit and haven't been for a long time. Instead, they've become submerged into behaviors that most of us are trained to follow from before the time we can talk, and they result in embodied predispositions like you've written about as the "elevator effect," where whites tense up and clutch their purses or briefcases when they find themselves in confined spaces with Black men, even when those Black men are immaculately dressed in three-piece suits and carry briefcases themselves!

Those sorts of embodied predispositions arise in most mainstream movie viewers as well. If Batman were Black, those presumptions would have to be addressed in order to make the story plausible for mainstream audience members, and even then many of them would probably resist or reject imagining anything that conflicted with their embodied presumptions. In order to make any divergences narratively plausible, those presumptions would have to be carefully addressed in the story, more for some than for others, so it would be a difficult balancing act trying to come up with the right amount of narrative exposition in order to overcome the imaginative resistance that most mainstream audience members have regarding Black men as potentially having the sorts of positive moral traits that Batman had in the Christopher Nolan trilogy.

G. Y.: Within the context of my previous question, I think about how, in the entire *James Bond* series, 007 is played by a white British male. My students have said to me that they would think that Black actor Idris Elba might change all of this. I'm skeptical. After all, imagine a Black male (on the big screen) seducing white women, and blending into the British Secret Service. As white, Bond can fit into any situation. As Black, he would already appear conspicuous.

Also, in a believable scenario where Bond is Black, his enemies would have to call him a "nigger." All of a sudden, Bond would be marked racially. Any thoughts?

D. F.: I think that I'm somewhere between you and your students regarding such a casting choice. I think it is possible to work out how James Bond might be played by a Black actor, but it would be difficult to do so successfully and, for the present, very unlikely. Like your students, I was intrigued last summer (2015) when those internet rumors made the rounds suggesting that Elba would be a great James Bond. Personally I loved the idea because I thought it would completely upend nearly all the presumptions we had about Bond as a character and the way the Bond series has maintained a subtly racist Cold War ideology since it began in the early 1960s, even if filmmakers have had to update or disguise that ideology over the years. Nearly everything would have to be reconfigured in the standard Bond narrative to accommodate a Black Bond, and I liked the prospect of those changes. It would be aesthetically, cinematically, and politically refreshing if it could be done in the right way, and the proposed casting of Elba, with his past roles as Stringer Bell in *The Wire* (2002–2008) and John Luther in the BBC series (2010–2015), as well as his gravitas and acting range, made a certain sort of sense to me, especially in the wake of Daniel Craig's casting as a rougher, more working-class Bond.

But portraying Bond as Black could also easily have the implications that you note. Seducing white women would look very different to mainstream viewers if Bond were Black and no other narrative changes were made, as would his relationships with other members of the British Secret Service like M or Q. Inevitably, I think it would be an almost irresistible temptation on the part of the screenwriters to have his enemies use the n-word to refer to him, if for no better reason than to see them as utterly evil so that Bond could beat them up, vanquish, and/or kill them without the audience feeling guilty about cheering Bond on while he pulverizes them.

But again, if the filmmakers were willing to build a sufficiently elaborate backstory that spelled out why a Black Bond made sense (something that I think unlikely at this time and for the immediate future), they might be able to assuage the default presumptions that most mainstream audience members have about Black men. His seduction of white women would have to be grounded and played out very differently from the way Bond typically seduces women, or he'd look like Max Julien in *The Mack* (1973). Similarly, his working relationships with MI6 members would need to be depicted in ways that either dealt with potential racial tensions, stereotypical presumptions of Black incompetence (except, perhaps, with respect to violence), questions of loyalty to the British Crown, or instilled a sense of workplace equality, none of which is so imperative to deal with when Bond is played by a white British male, who can be presumed, as you say, to "fit in" with his white British Secret

Intelligence Service peers, even if there may be a few minor bumps along the way, as were depicted when Daniel Craig took over the Bond role.

Moreover, the backstory would have to work against implicit racial biases that exist not only in the US and Great Britain, but also the world, because Hollywood, its standard narrational strategies, and the presumptions that go with them have worked their way into the perceiving habits of viewers across the globe, inclining people to see at least partly according to the "white gaze," as Fanon called it, even when it is not in their best interests. Presumptions about Blacks such as we typically have in the US may vary in strength, and they may be far stronger and more prevalent in America and Europe than elsewhere, but they are not absent because viewers across the globe have learned to see Hollywood-style movies at least to some extent from a white point of view. Some viewers may resist or reject this viewing stance (bell hooks and Tommy Lott have described this sort of phenomenon), but others have taken it on and do not even realize that they are perceiving from the perspective of the white gaze. You can see this in, for example, the "Darkie" toothpaste that was sold for decades in China and other parts of Asia. This toothpaste has more recently undergone a minor name change to "Darlie" or "Black person" toothpaste, but still uses a vaguely minstrel logo to advertise its product. Moreover, at the time that the name was changed, commercials and advertisements assured Asian consumers that it remained the same toothpaste, allegedly providing the same white teeth that blackface minstrelsy stereotypically represents. We've globally exported our implicit racial biases along with our entertainments, and a Black Bond would have to confront that fact as well—which makes it all the more unlikely, for the time being, that the producers who own the rights to the *James Bond* series would choose to fill that role with anyone but a white British male actor. It wouldn't be in their economic interests because it would not guarantee the prospect of huge profits in the way that casting a white British male actor currently does. For now, a white female Bond would seem more a possibility than a Black male Bond because there would be fewer implicit biases to overcome. But even that would be an uphill battle to depict without raising hackles on many mainstream viewers around the world.

But let me also note that embodied presumptions regarding race seem to be eroding. Generationally, our students represent a cohort that is much more at ease with people of different races interacting and mixing, so there may come a point in the future when a Black Bond makes sense to them in terms of their default presumptions about race and character in movies. If and when their implicit racial biases reach a point where they are sufficiently eroded, then a Black James Bond would make sense as a possibility because the target audience—which is, after all, young people who happily go out and buy tickets in movie theaters, not aging, stay-at-home baby boomers like you and me—would be ready to accept it. The James Bond series could even be at the forefront of effecting such a change if its producers wanted it to be. For example, I think of Gulliermo del Toro's *Pacific Rim* (2013) and the recent Broadway hit *Hamilton* (2015) as representing small steps in that direction because they treat race in ways that encourage us (albeit in modest ways) to think about and overcome our current implicit biases. But taking a similar step in the Bond series would represent a major change in direction that for the present seems pretty unlikely.

G. Y.: A Black female Bond might be beyond the pale of our default presumptions. In personal conversations with the literary figure and philosopher Charles Johnson, we talked about how Black people have a kind of double narrative intelligence. We are not only invited to imagine the fictional worlds of whites, but of Blacks as well. Yet, white folk are not necessarily challenged at this level of critically engaging these multiple ways of seeing. I'm very skeptical about the eradication of the white gaze. How can film be used as a venue through which to, as you've written, *de*-activate various behavioral dispositions and affective white propensities?

D. F.: I agree with you and Charles Johnson that Black people typically have a double narrative intelligence and that white people generally don't. Black people are not only invited, but in many ways compelled, to imagine the many worlds of whites, both fictional and real, if for no better reason than to have improved opportunities for survival and flourishing. Being able to imagine white social worlds helps Blacks to get by better in white-dominated societies because they often have no choice but to negotiate situations filled or controlled by whites. Moreover, that double narrative intelligence can be applied to mass art like movies. So we see Black directors, for example, doing creditable jobs portraying fictional worlds dominated by whites, such as Carl Franklin with *One True Thing* (1998) or F. Gary Gray with *The Italian Job* (2003). By contrast, whites in the US and most of Europe are rarely required to step out of their comfort zones and negotiate nonwhite worlds, or even imagine what it might be like to exist as a nonwhite human being. Often, on the rare occasions that they do, they can't manage it in a full-bodied way because their imaginative skills regarding race are so poorly developed. They can't envision how the world might work differently outside the white bubble that is their primary locus of experience. That's one of the perks of white privilege, as Peggy McIntosh pointed out decades ago.

But the very fact that Black people can develop a double narrative intelligence and frequently do with tremendous richness means that it is a *human* capacity, so whites are capable of doing it, too. But the fact of the matter is that, if whites live in a white-dominated society like the US or Europe, they get very few opportunities to practice the sorts of skills that would enable them to actualize that capacity with respect to race—and often have at their disposal powerful ways to distort or interfere with developing it. If you are a white viewer watching a film about nonwhites, I think it's often very tempting to interpret it though the usual white racial lens, rather than make any effort to see it in a new way, even when the film encourages it. Instead, one indulges in a form of cognitive laziness that arguably has its roots in evolutionary theory: we generally don't develop alternative interpretive frameworks unless we are forced to by a realization that the old ones aren't working.

Yet this possibility is where I see film as offering a venue for deactivating white behavioral tendencies and affective propensities and generating new ones. Movies are by no means a panacea, but allowing one to imaginatively enter into a world different from one's own and see the people in it in a different way is one of the possibilities that movies can take up best. We get to enter into fictional worlds we've never experienced before and find out something of what the characters in them and their social relations are like through vivid cinematic portrayals. And it's much like Aristotle said with regard to Greek tragedy: the portrayal of that world does not have to be literal history, but it has to depict circumstances that are possible according to our standards of probability and necessity, depicting events that we understand *could* occur, so the filmmakers can't lose us in the differences and contrasts they depict, but must offer cognitive links and connections so that we can find our way around and build bridges in order to understand how that world is different.

However, the existence of this possibility doesn't mean that it will be done well or that viewers will take it up. They as well as filmmakers themselves can easily slip into cognitive laziness and simply perceive or depict these fictional worlds through the white gaze. In addition, some movies that challenge the viewer's ability to complacently see through the white gaze, such as *Do the Right Thing* (1989), end up just pissing a lot of white people off because of the frustrations they experience at trying to see it through a white lens. At the same time, one of the reasons that I think some other whites have seen that movie as transformative for them regarding race is that it deftly resists interpretations that cast it according to the white gaze and encourages us to figure out how to see it in a new, more coherent way. That may frustrate or anger some people who don't want to make the effort, but for others it provides opportunities for reflecting on the white gaze itself and constructing ways to overcome it. One of the reasons I wanted to write about the African-American films noirs that I mentioned earlier is that I thought they were similar to *Do the Right Thing* in the sense that they resisted efforts to be interpreted according to the same old white gaze I had been using to watch movies and encouraged me, but also viewers in general, to contemplate some of the racial ways through which we saw movies and build new cognitive frameworks in order to make sense of the stories that these Black noirs told. There's an invitation extended by many Black noirs to enter into a world of being African-American about which most whites know little or nothing and learn how it is different. And that sort of invitation has modestly expanded to international films, like

City of God (2002) and *Children of Men* (2006), as I've argued elsewhere. Films like these can help white viewers to discover that nonwhites are just like them but suffer egregious forms of racial injustice, sometimes on an everyday basis. That's a good thing, I think, because it begins to encourage whites to question their default presumptions regarding how they see movies, including their affective propensities and behavioral dispositions regarding people of color, and find new ways to see. And those propensities and dispositions are ones they typically use in the real world as well, so their coming to question them in their experience of movies and construct new ways of seeing will typically spill over into their day-to-day lives as well.

Will such imaginative opportunities eradicate the white gaze? Well, the white gaze is pretty powerfully entrenched, so I'm not going to predict its imminent demise. But I am modestly hopeful, if for no better reason than that it's less powerful now than it was fifty, eighty, or one hundred years ago. For example, mainstream audiences see *The Birth of a Nation* (1915) very differently from the way they did when it was first released and they cheered the Klan's victory at the end. Similarly, the old Johnny Weismuller *Tarzan* movies can be pretty hard to watch these days for most whites, and these modest changes in perception make me modestly hopeful that the white gaze will continue to weaken. At the very least, these historical changes show that, logically speaking, the dominant white gaze *can* change for the better. Still, continuing that trend will never be a walk in the park: it's always going to be contested because it's so firmly entrenched, and the possibility that it could get worse is ever present as well, because sometimes in the past the white gaze has gotten worse, as in the later nineteenth and early twentieth centuries when portrayals of the Black characters in *Uncle Tom's Cabin* stage performances got worse and worse and white mainstream audiences ate it up.

But I will say that I think that cinematic opportunites for whites to enter into nonwhite worlds and begin to develop the skills required to have a double narrative intelligence—something I see as a dimension of what Linda Martín Alcoff calls developing a white double consciousness—can help to make the white gaze a lot less pernicious, so movies have a role in deactivating implicit racial biases and reducing the power of the white gaze. But getting white audiences to see those sorts of movies willingly, rather than watch them as some sort of medicine they have to take because they are sick in their racialized thinking (which they are, but most don't know it), is a difficult trick. There's a tendency to not want to do all the work required to construct an alternative affective and cognitive framework regarding race. Some (me, I suppose) do it willingly, but others flat-out refuse, and others still avoid it as too much effort and will do so only when they feel compelled to do so; and still another category of whites won't even realize they need to make the effort. These other categories are the more difficult cases that need to be addressed artistically in ways that get viewers to think about how they see in racially white ways and need to construct new ways of seeing the world as ones that include nonwhites as full partners rather than as subordinates, without these viewers realizing that they are being induced to do so. And movies can help do that, especially when artists accept that challenge, as many nonwhite artists working in film have done.

G. Y.: When I think about the deaths of unarmed Black men by the state, and the ways in which those Black bodies are perceived as "bestial," "criminal," sites of "disgust," it is hard for me to imagine how the medium of film might militate against such perceptions, and how the Black body can be treated as having full humanity. After all, we're talking about centuries of white perceptual practices. You've also noted how Fox News journalist Megyn Kelly proclaimed Santa Claus "just is white" and so was Jesus.[2] There is something deeply insidious going on here. So, how is it that you are optimistic about the possibilities of film to disrupt white perceptual practices?

D. F.: I'm cautiously optimistic because even though I agree that there's something deeply insidious about the centuries-long, entrenched white habits of perceiving Black people, there are still movies like *Fruitvale Station* (2013), *Selma* (2014), *Dear White People* (2014), and even *Straight Outta Compton* (2015) that manage to get made, even as they aim specifically at disrupting white perceptual practices. In addition, these films have broken into public consciousness in terms of their popularity and generated discussion of the critical racial points that they raise. In particular, a significant number of white people end up talking about them, even if it's to dismiss them with excuses that many I think are also beginning to sense are wearing thin. Plus, the "Oscars So White" and the "Black Lives Matter" movements have created amazing and immediate pushback on social media against business-as-usual white ignorance in ways that couldn't have happened a few years ago, and the former movement seems to have recently yielded some modest successes. Even Megyn Kelly took a lot of heat for her ridiculous Santa Claus comment, which not so long ago would have gone unremarked except in outraged op-ed pieces in Black or left-wing newspapers. Now it's all over the Internet almost instantly and gets picked up as a problematic claim in Twitter feeds and news analyses. (Why does Santa Claus have to be white anyway? He's based on a fourth-century Christian saint who lived in present-day Turkey and would probably at best now be considered merely "borderline" white. And why are his helpers in Belgium and the Netherlands *"Zwarte Pieten"* [Black Peters], who are decked out like blackface minstrels?) It doesn't take much digging to realize that "Santa Claus" is a social construction; and the same is true of the standard Western iconography of a white Jesus.

There's also been some noticeable influence on movies by critical race theory and Black studies courses: students who took those classes are now beginning to be green-lighted to make movies and TV shows, and in the process are showing what they have learned through the narratives they create. The injustice of racial profiling has even made its way into Disney animation: *Zootopia* (2016) metaphorically takes up police stereotypes about criminals by critically viewing the "normalized" assumptions against predators in its fictional world and showing how they distort perceptions of lion, fox, and weasel characters in the story. It strikes me as a major step forward once prejudices about bestiality, crime, and race make their way into movies aimed at children. As always, there's tons more to do, but milestones like these shouldn't go unremarked.

Here I think it's important to note as well that movies are only part of the overall picture, but that talking about them can give us insight into other powerful media. Television, for example, has moved much faster than movies in looking more critically at race, probably because production costs are lower and TV shows can aim at smaller target audiences and still be economically viable. Now we have programs like *Black-ish, Underground, How to Get Away With Murder*, and *Fresh Off the Boat* that deal directly with confronting and disrupting white perceptual practices and encouraging viewers to construct alternatives to seeing nonwhites in the usual way. Moreover, a number of these series have sufficient quality that they have become hard to ignore, especially for white viewers. Critics praise these shows in ways that make them difficult to avoid, and one of the things they confront white viewers with is thinking about how they are different from the standard fare of moving images that unexceptionally presume a white gaze.

In general, I think that surrounding ourselves with better images will be crucial to disrupting standard white perceptual practices and encouraging viewers to construct new ones, so not only film but also television, advertising, video games, and other moving image media need to disrupt white perceptual practices as well. And those media have gotten modestly better in the past few decades. Of course, none of these advances mean we are home free, because there is constant pushback against them, from the many clever strategies for upholding the white gaze to our tendency to not want to put in the effort to change our ways of thinking and perceiving, but we should at least recognize the modest positive advances that have been made because they mean we've gotten somewhere.

G. Y.: How do we nurture a robust form of imagination that might counter what you've called forms of "racialized imaginative resistance"?

D. F.: I feel that I can only speak for the part of the "we" who are white because that's what I've thought about the most. In general, whites should begin by cultivating a willingness to learn new things about race, a sense of openness to self-criticsm, and a moral humility when it comes to race. A lot of whites resist the possibility that nonwhites might be able to tell them something about race that differs from what they already know. This amounts to a kind of racial arrogance, which is a hangover from explicit white supremacy but continues on in present-day white privilege. So opening one's self to the possibility that one could be wrong about one's understanding of race, and that nonwhites could tell you something useful about it, requires these three initial steps. Then, whites would have to seek out things that challenged their white senses of self, in order to see whether that sense stood up to the challenge and subsequent scrutiny. Here, certain movies, TV shows, and other moving-image media would fit in as "test cases" for where one's white sense of self stood.

For those who are nonwhite, it's a different story, and one that I only partly understand. I defer to others to best describe how nonwhites might best cultivate robust forms of imagination in terms of race.

G. Y.: For those philosophers who engage race critically, especially whiteness, provide the titles of a select few films that you think help to explicate the complexities of whiteness and briefly explain why.

D. F.: As someone who knows best American popular movies, as opposed to art film or European cinema, I can only give recommendations that cover a limited part of the field. But that said, I'd recommend the best of Spike Lee's oeuvre. As the late Roger Ebert pointed out decades ago, Lee has tremendous empathy for all his characters, but it's especially important to remember that he has it for his white characters, whose shortcomings, excuses, and ignorance he presents with a gimlet eye even as he treats them compassionately. I've already mentioned some of the reasons to watch *Do the Right Thing*, but I'll also note how *Summer of Sam* (1999) analyses xenophobia and how it can be generated in whites, including how it overlaps with race. In addition, *Bamboozled* (2000) forcefully depicts the power of blackface minstrelsy and how it has permeated American entertainment. I'd also recommend some of the Black noirs that I've mentioned above. *One False Move* perceptively explores good-old-boy Southern whiteness in haunting, complicated ways, and the other Black noirs mentioned challenge the white gaze regarding racial profiling, the color line, and differences between white and Black perceptions of white dominance. Steve McQueen's European art film set in antebellum America, *12 Years a Slave* (2013), is worth watching because of its focus on how Blacks were forced to live under different oppressive regimes of whiteness. For those whose tastes run more to comedy, I've had luck showing Chris Rock's documentary *Good Hair* (2009) to my students as a critique of white standards of beauty, and *Dear White People* openly appeals to millennials by updating many of the insights earlier African-American films explored. I'll also add that 2016 was a banner year for documentaries about race—*O.J.: Made in America, 13th, I Am Not Your Negro*—as well as offering us some good to amazing fiction films about race, such as *Moonlight, Hidden Figures, Fences, Queen of Katwe, Free State of Jones, Loving*, and *Embrace of the Serpent*.

Again, key to viewing these films is seeing how they not only challenge old white ways of seeing, but also provide clues to constructing a new perception of race. However, these films don't do all the work for us. It's still up to us to rebuild our own affective and cognitive frameworks in ways that are more equitable and less interlaced with our implicit racial biases. These films provide us with opportunities to think, reflect, and untangle the intricate ways we continue to see the world through a racial lens—one that is as much a racial construction as Megyn Kelly's ideas regarding Santa Claus or Jesus.

NOTES

1. Richard Popkin, "Hume's Racism," *The Philosophical Forum* 9, no. 2–3 (1977–1978): 211–26; Richard Popkin, "The Philosophical Bases of Modern Racism" (1974), reprinted in *The High Road to Pyrrhonism*, ed. Richard A. Watson and James E. Force (San Diego: Austin Hill Press, 1980), 79–102; Harry M. Bracken, "Essence, Accident, and Race," *Hermathena* 116 (1973): 81–96; and Harry M. Bracken, "Philosophy and Racism," *Philosophia* 8 (1978): 241–60.
2. Dan Flory, "Imaginative Resistance, Racialized Disgust, and African-American Cinema," paper presented at the American Philosophical Association-Central Division Conference, Chicago, IL, February 27, 2014. (The reference is to a December 12, 2013 discussion on the Fox News program *The Kelly File* regarding Santa's race, during which Megyn Kelly flatly asserted the racial whiteness of both Santa Claus and Jesus.)

David Theo Goldberg

George Yancy: I only recently learned that you began your own music-video production company. Did this interest in music-video production precede your important work on race?

David Theo Goldberg: Actually it was a small film production and distribution company, Metafilms. When I arrived in New York in 1978 to do a PhD in Philosophy, my oldest friend from childhood in Cape Town, Michael Oblowitz, was already at film school in the city. We started making independent films together, including an internationally award-winning film on Robben Island as a metaphor for South Africa under apartheid. We were basically on the ground floor when music videos began airing on television. Michael Jackson threatened to withhold the video of "Thriller" from MTV in 1983 unless they played more videos by Black artists. MTV was receiving heat also from the likes of David Bowie, to his credit too. We happened to have just completed the music video for Polygram of Kurtis Blow's "Basketball," his paean to the greats of the game. Our assistant cameraman's mother was the lover of J. J. Jackson, the only African-American among the original MTV VJs. They needed material badly, the song was relatively innocuous by the standards of the day, with a cameo appearance by The Fat Boys, no less. The first rap video to air on MTV. The marriage of networking and luck, how the industry still functions.

The film and video production emerged more or less coterminously with my earliest work on race. I was writing my dissertation on "the philosophical foundations of racism." Gerry Cohen, the analytic Marxist philosopher, asked me in the early 1980s if racism had any. I guess analytic Marxism suffered the same veil of ignorance as classic liberalism at the time. While I had been thinking about race and racism for a good while already—any modestly thinking person growing up in South Africa could hardly avoid it—outlining a theory began around the time the music-video production work took off.

Just prior to this, I met Howard McGary and Bill Lawson, young faculty members at Rutgers and Delaware respectively then, at a regional philosophy conference in New Jersey, it must have been February 1982. Instead of attending the next boring session, we sat for three hours in Bill's little car in the pouring rain discussing race and racism in the context of moral and political theory, engine running to keep us from freezing. The contrast with Gerry Cohen couldn't be more palpable. They generously introduced me to the New York Society for the Study of Black Philosophy, run by Al Prettyman out of his apartment on Broadway on the Upper West Side. It was there I would meet Cornel West, Lucius Outlaw, Tommy Lee Lott, Leonard Harris, among others. We read and discussed each other's work, and it was from and through them I would learn enormously in ways unavailable from my PhD program faculty. The Society folk were incredibly welcoming but also uncompromisingly committed to the critical discussion of the ideas and conditions central to Black Philosophy and thought more generally. I was moved as a consequence—even forced, just to keep up!—to read the invisible canon living in the shadows of the conventional philosophical one. It would open me to ways of thinking, to a critical understanding of race, its structures and experiences, that has profoundly underpinned and shaped my subsequent work. And this was occurring precisely as rap was taking hold in the city, in the air, and as a subject of philosophical reflection. A double shaping, interwoven with each other, to be sure.

G. Y.: Did you have an interest in rap music and hip-hop culture in light of working with Kurtis Blow?

D. T. G.: We were already listening to the music, on the airwaves, in the Mudd Club, but in a sense rap was "invading" Manhattan from the outer boroughs ("Freaks come out at night"!). The independent film scene was deeply embedded with the Soho art scene, both residentially and recreationally. We were listening to the likes of Grandmaster Flash, Run-DMC, The Fat Boys, Chuck D and Public Enemy, Ice T. It was a big deal when Flavor Flav showed up at the Gaghosian Art Gallery in Soho for an opening, in something like 1981. Avant-garde and politically insurgent art forms were playing off each other. Something dynamic was at play, where the likes of Julian Schnabel's expressionism and the political and commercial critique of Barbara Kruger were beginning to dance with the radical critique from rap. William Burroughs was in conversation with The Last Poets, Kathy Acker and Jean-Marie Basquiat were emerging from intersecting cauldrons, the play of high theory with underground culture represented at the time in the pages of Sylvere Lotringer's *Semiotexte*. Heady times.

Our work with Kurtis Blow emerged out of rather than led to this engagement. We were two young white guys from South Africa hustling academically, intellectually, culturally, cinematically in the big bad world of downtown

Manhattan. The presence of Black folk in the Soho cultural scene, both in terms of artistic and cinematic production at the time, was minimal. The hip musical developments, as always, were being forged by Black artists. Cinema generally and independent filmmaking in particular was overwhelmingly white, the Hudlin's notwithstanding. Spike Lee burst onto the scene with his first feature in the mid-1980s. (I actually curated a film exhibition as part of an art show on race at Hunter College Art Gallery put together with Maurice Berger and Johnetta Cole around this time, and included *The Answer*, his compelling student remake of *The Birth of a Nation*.) We just happened to be at the intersection of these creative trends in 1983, having already made our film about the politics of South Africa. It was cut to the beat of driving South African jazz as its musical soundtrack. We perhaps fit the Polygram image of a cheap but creative date for Kurtis Blow, a bit less weighed down as we all were by American racial history.

G. Y.: In what ways do you understand the relationship between race and music videos, their production, their content, marketing, and so on?

D. T. G.: There are some obvious lines of racial demarcation. Music-video production was seen by the recording industry at the outset of the 1980s as a medium mainly to promote contemporary rock music. There's a longer history of filmic representation of musical expression, dating to the 1920s. And in the 1960s and 1970s, experimentation with image accompaniment to music increased. D. A. Pennebaker and Godard were working with the likes of Bob Dylan and the Rolling Stones. Music animation also took off: recall The Beatles' *Yellow Submarine*.

This is a shorthand way of saying that the recording, advertising, and film industries have long been controlled by white men (think *Mad Men*). And we know the long history of the music industry's exploitation of great Black artists across all genres of popular and experimental musics. Many a charge of theft has been expressed and more often than not borne out. A former graduate student of mine, Dimitri Bogazianos, who himself had had some limited success as a rap recording artist, writes of the fight to control artistic production and profitability between "the suites" and "the streets." One could extend the analysis to music-video production. MTV initially favored the music of white youth, rock, as the standard bearer for music videos, a fact they then used to rationalize why there were almost no initial videos of Black musical talent aired before Michael Jackson threatened to strike. So built into the very formation of the existing industries and their interplay is the structure of racial arrangement and exclusion already fashioning the output.

This structure is further cemented by the fact that musics are racially marketed, the videos reproducing and reinforcing racial expectation and by extension racial response. Music videos have tended to reflect this rather crass understanding both of the musics and their marketability, reinforcing

them. This is in part a product of the parochialism of the industry functionaries and in part an instrumentalizing calculation to maximize profitability.
Black, white, Latino, or for that matter Jewish musics, however, are hardly
untouched by the environments out of which they emerge, in which they
flourish. Musical tastes are not necessarily bounded by racial identification.
Tastes travel, reflecting much more complicated histories of formation: think
of the blues, jazz, rap, but also rock, opera, classical music. But think too of
that whitest of genres, country music, in the counterform of Dom Flemons
and the Carolina Chocolate Drops. Far from sacred, the boundaries of race are
there to be profanely transgressed!

Just as rock before it, rap has expressed in evolving fashion the sensibilities of a time, of our youth culture over the past three-plus decades now.
Implicit in much of the best of political rap, and the slam-poetry movement
to which hip-hop culture gave rise, is a racial critique. They fashion a political
commentary, an extended rejection of the forces of racially structured capital and the violence of its norm-enforcement that undercuts the all-too-easy
dismissal by conventional forces that youth today are apolitical. Take just one
small example: Too Short is an artist better known for his cruder lyrics about
sex and women. Nevertheless, "The Ghetto" (1990) offers a searing reading
over a Gil Scott-Heron chorus line of ghettoization and its modes of destructive containment that capitalism reproduces. The longer version includes lines
from The Last Poets' "Die Nigga." Race, music-making, video production, and
expressive culture come together in the form of critique and not just capital
reproduction.

G. Y.: What are some of the influences, both academic and nonacademic, that
shaped your critical engagement with race theory?

D. T. G.: I grew up in Cape Town, South Africa, from the early 1950s and
the formative years of formal apartheid through the youth-led uprisings in
Soweto and other cities in 1976, before leaving in late 1977. So my experiences from childhood "innocence" through teenage and student political consciousness were forged really by discovering the racial order of the city and
society, coming into critical self-consciousness, as Hegel might say, as I came
of age. In trying to make sense of the relation between antiapartheid and anticolonial struggles, we were already reading Fanon's *Wretched of the Earth* as
undergraduates, *A Dying Colonialism*, and *Towards an African Revolution*, and
only secondarily *Black Skin, White Masks*. We were also engaged with formative anticolonial intellectuals like Ngugi wa Thiongo. In the early 1970s, there
was a raging race-class debate for understanding the dynamics of apartheid.
White Marxists who prevailed in the social sciences and humanities argued for
the epiphenomenality of race. We were reading Sartre, especially *Anti-Semite
and Jew* and *Critique of Dialectical Reason*, Memmi, and Arendt as counters
to the reductionism. Jeremy Cronin, who after 1994 would become Secretary

General of the South African Communist Party, returned in the mid-1970s from studying with Althusser to teach us before being arrested. He had written a really interesting Althusserian analysis of "Afrikaner Nationalist ideology" as structuring the "ideological state apparatuses" in the country and offered a more sophisticated understanding of both race and class.[1] Black consciousness and Biko's work especially provided important critical comprehension regarding race around the time he was killed in 1977. When I arrived in New York in late 1978, both *Black Skin, White Masks* and Althusser were just starting to circulate seriously. Said's *Orientalism* appeared around that time, offering a very different way of approaching the conceptual complications concerning race.

There was still pitifully little on race and racism from analytic philosophers. Kantians like Kurt Baier and Rawlsians still viewed race as a morally irrelevant category. Chomsky and Bracken misleadingly dismissed empiricism and by implication utilitarianism as more conducive to racism than rationalism. The folks around the New York Society were far more important to my development. It was through them I started reading seriously the likes of Du Bois, Alain Locke, writers from Langston Hughes and Zora Neale Hurston to Richard Wright and Baldwin. Later I would have long discussions with Laurence Thomas on slavery and the Holocaust, and Tommy Lott on race and relatedly on jazz, which have stuck with me since. Angela Davis's *Women, Race and Class*, appearing in 1981 too, insisted on reading race, gender, and class together. Over the following decades, Angela would become a very dear friend who has continued to push my thinking throughout.

I discovered Stuart Hall just as I started formulating my dissertation at the beginning of the 1980s, first the work on the state and articulation (his own break with reductionist Marxism) and then fairly quickly his theorizing of Thatcherism and neoliberalism as well as the earlier work on policing. In the second half of the 1980s, the frame widened further. I was in conversation with Anthony Appiah and Skip Gates, not least regarding the cultural articulations of the racial. I started corresponding with Balibar on race and nation. All along I was reading Foucault closely, a generative influence, and in conversation with Ann Stoler. I've been characterized as a racial Foucauldian, though this is much too reductive, needing to reduce thinkers to a prevailing or singular influence. Obviously, that's just not me.

On a trip to London, in 1988, I met Paul Gilroy, who had just published *There Ain't No Black in the Union Jack*. We have remained in conversation since. In the US, critical race theory emerged in the late 1980s. Kim Crenshaw exemplified what it takes to analyze intersectionally; Patricia Williams and Mari Matsuda enabled creative thinking about racial formations at the complex intersections of law with the sociological and political. A little later, Cheryl Harris offered the hugely insightful analysis of whiteness as property as a more complicated critical account than emergent whiteness studies at the time. There have obviously been many more recent interlocutors, but in the past decade and a half, two have had ongoing generative impact on my thinking about race and much else: Achille Mbembe, my dear friend, and my extraordinary partner, Philomena Essed.

So, never narrowly philosophical, my thinking about the racial was quite complexly formed, always at the interfaces of political economy, law, philosophy, political theory, sociology, anthropology, and culture. I am perhaps a "macrohumanist," to coin a phrase prompted by economics and sociology.

G. Y.: That is a very impactful intellectual trajectory. What critical tools do you think are needed for understanding the recent killings of so many unarmed Black men, even boys, in the US, by the state or proxies of the state?

D. T. G.: This may come as a surprise, not least for humanists. First, the necessity of critically reading data. It is especially imperative given the proliferation of data sources floating around the web, some obviously far less reliable than others. There's a real necessity to recognize the reliability of the source, the assumptions on which the data were collected, how the data were compiled and composed, what implications are being drawn.

The latter suggests the associated need to develop the capacity to recognize arguments and the assorted fallacies so often embedded or resorted to. There's a critical urgency to discern the often unarticulated and untested assumptions—the presumptions—on which arguments are based, from which they jump off. For example, counterclaims have begun to proliferate that there is no evidence of police discriminating against Blacks in America. But the only reason there is no such evidence is that there is a complete paucity of data in this regard, and any argument suggesting no police racial discrimination is built on quicksand.

So there is a need also to recognize relationalities. Not just comparisons but the critical revealing of connections without which trajectories and trends go undetected. This includes being able to discern the connections between the contemporary and historical, to identify the "remainders of race," as Ash Amin characterizes it.[2] And so to understand the legacy, the ongoing impact, that these "remains" have on people's lives, we need to understand how such persistent inheritance positions people as more vulnerable to social forces, including policing, in ways that, as Ruthie Gilmore puts it in defining racism, foreshortens Black life.[3]

Third, the Internet has proliferated visual resources, in many ways privileging them over the written and textual. This entails the necessity to be schooled in reading—in critically comprehending—what is being conveyed in seemingly competing recordings of a deadly event like a police shooting. There is the first-order need to read from the sequence of two-dimensional representations of moving events what in fact has transpired in their three-dimensional actualization. So camera angles, representational details and their significance, and voiced exchanges become imperative in the reading of the moving image.

Consider Eyal Weizman's compelling methodology of critical forensics—he calls it "forensic architecture"[4]—that involves how to read the causal conditions of deadly events in and from the materialities in which they are embedded. This includes the contextual landscape or seascape, the built infrastructure, historical and contemporary, as it impacts people's bodies, racially defined. Critical forensics concerns reading the conditions against the grain of authoritative representations. To understand how many seconds have elapsed between being stopped by a police officer and the culpability involved in the fatal shots going off. Who was where and what actions were transpiring, what was said or not, where the person was shot and from what angle, where the bullet(s) pierced and exited and became embedded, the lapse between being shot and treated, shot and handcuffed, shooting and calling in to report. A critical forensics is a "weapon of the weak" (this from James Scott) made powerful.

All this, in short, can be summarized under the rubric of *how*, not what, to think today conceptually, analytically, visually, interpretatively, indeed critically. Not least in a more and more complicated ecology of thinking itself.

G. Y.: Part of the problem of course is due to the lack of trust between white police officers and Black communities and communities of color. Yet, this "mutual" lack of trust, it seems to me, flattens out the ways in which Black people justifiably experience a lack of trust because of the systemic nature of white supremacy. So, how do we engage in a conversation that helps to create some level of mutual trust while making it clear that white supremacy is the problem, not Black people in their "moral failure" to trust?

D. T. G.: As you suggest, George, this erosion of trust is not just dispositional or attitudinal. The trust deficit is linked to underlying socio-material conditions of experience. The cliché, "just the facts, please," is implicated in the flattening. First, it overridingly individualizes the facts to the conditions of the particular case being adjudicated. "Black man, stopped by the police, reaches for his pocket where there is a bulge looking like a gun. Fearing for his safety, officer shot suspect four times." Or "police failed to buckle arrestee into back of police car because fearing for their safety from gathering mob." So there's a ready script, designed to establish bureaucratic inculpability. No need to alter the script when it works every time! When civil suits brought by the families of the deceased invariably get settled in the favor of the police, it exacerbates the mistrust. It reduces responsibility to the bureaucracy—usually the city council in question—letting the individual police completely off the hook. So police officers face almost no consequences likely to alter conduct.

The first thing to establish for police and publics is the deep constitutive relation between being Black and brown in America, the disposability to official and public suspiciousness historically sedimented, the increased like-lihood of being apprehended for no or little good reason, the implication of police training, sentiment, and practice in the (re)production of this disposa-bility and its actualization in events.

The evident need for a shift in policing practices requires addressing what and who policing is for. Communally anchored and engaged policing would structure training very differently while also involving rigorous investigations of wrongdoing and agency oversight. The less adversarial this relationship, the more mutually engaged and transformative, the more driven by the impera-tives of communal dignity, the more likely it will enable the building—one can't even call it "re-building"—of trust. It would help to give this an appeal-ing moniker, to contrast it with "law and order" policing. "Community polic-ing" is the usual characterization, but this still suggests police work is to keep the community in line. Perhaps "safe policing" captures the doubling of the reach: a policing structured to ensure safety of all, and a policing that in its actualization and effects is safe for all, police included.

The police force is, among many things, a bureaucracy. Bureaucracies organ-izationally tend to act for the purposes of self-protection, self-perpetuation, and self-reproduction. More money, more "cops," better equipment, more protective gear, body-cams. This, of course, becomes especially poignant for a profession literally risking life and limb round the clock. It behooves us all to have the police feel and be safer. And it behooves the police to ensure the public—those they serve—to be and feel more at ease both in their daily lives and interacting with their local police.

A key implication here, both as instrumentalization and evidence of change, would be to reduce the radically disproportionate stops by police of Black people. Black folk are stopped far more readily than whites. If police stopped whites at the rate of Blacks, white incidence of crime would be sig-nificantly higher too. Tim Rice, the only Black Republican US Senator, said he has been stopped seven times this past year by police, including in the halls of Congress. I haven't been stopped seven times in the nearly forty years I have lived in America. I am not saying I should be stopped at the rate Rice has been; he should be stopped, for cause, no more than me.

Police are sometimes, but far from always, understandably impatient. A police stop is fraught, for the apprehended and for the apprehending police. Both parties grow taut, the apprehended sometimes to the point of freezing up, police occasionally to the point of acting violently. Police are characteristi-cally suspicious, the more so of Black people because both of the misdirected (not to mention racist) media rhetoric about Black criminality and supposed disposition to violence, and relatedly the long history of surveillance and sus-picion to which Black people have been subjected. Consider, here, Simone Brown's compelling book on the subject, *Dark Matters*. Hence the imperative of a call for patience, and against unnecessary use of force.

Police have a special responsibility to defuse the build-up of tension. In a routine stop like a traffic violation, things start off calmly enough. But the accusatory tone and the suspicion that immediately accompanies having to show identification heightens nervousness. Police need to be trained and practiced in maintaining an even keel, talking people down from their nervousness, not to take nervousness necessarily as a sign of wrongdoing. When the Black therapist of an autistic patient was shot in the leg, without provocation, by a policeman in the street in North Miami, he asked the policeman why he had shot. The response: "I don't know." Really?

Philando Castille, a dreadlocked Black man, was with his girlfriend and her four-year-old daughter, both also African-American, when he was stopped for an apparently broken taillight in suburban Minneapolis. It was, staggeringly, his fifty-second traffic stop in recent years. When the policeman asked for his identification, Castille quietly mentioned he was licensed to carry a gun, which was in his pocket, and politely asked if he could reach into his back pocket to get his wallet. Tension rose, the officer pulled out his gun, barking orders to see Castille's identification. Castille reached back to oblige, and the officer immediately shot him in the arm four times, leaving him in the wake to bleed to death as his girlfriend and her daughter distressingly looked on. No racial provocation? The shooting officer, himself Latino, is reported to have stopped Castille not for a broken taillight but because a robbery suspect in the area had "a broad nose" and Castille was the first person he came across who might fit the all-too-generically-coded description for a Black man.

What might have been done differently? For one, not being stopped at all for the crime of having a generic nose. But, once stopped, there was a second officer. The first could easily have said, "Look, with a gun things are more tense. So, sir, keep your hands on the wheel where I can see them. My partner will come around the other side and have the young lady and child exit the car. I'm sure all will be fine, but let's all be careful. My partner will then reach into your pocket to get the gun just so we can defuse the tension. If all is above board, we will return the gun to you in due course. Okay?" The outcome would have been vastly different than a decent young man losing his life completely unnecessarily before the desperate eyes of his girlfriend and her daughter, unable to do anything.

A few days after this I was stopped by a young Latino policeman near my home in university housing in California. I had not fully stopped at a stop sign. The exchange was very courteous, even friendly. It helped that he, a university police officer, recognized my name (not sure that's necessarily a good thing). After showing my ID and papers, we had a brief exchange about vacation time (it was summer, I was returning from an early morning surf, board in car), and he left me, reasonably, with a warning. But would it have been different had I been a younger, dreadlocked, Black faculty person, or an undocumented Latino doing home renovation in the area?

So the need is to redirect training and generalize a sense of civility and reasonable response to all. Far less impatience for protestors, even those of policing excesses. A no-tolerance policy for any police person who engages, publicly or privately, in racist expression, on the job or on social media, whether generally intended or directed at a fellow policeman or private citizen. Racist expression or behavior should suffice to cost perpetrators their jobs.

We cannot expect police to fix their own practices. It requires recognition also by lawmakers and courts that negligent, reckless, and discriminatory policing violence requires being addressed, individually and institutionally. "Fear for one's life" loses its credibility if trumping all reasonable counterconsideration, every time.

G. Y.: Are there similarities between antiapartheid and anticolonial struggles and the sort of protests that we've been witnessing, especially in terms of the Black Lives Matter Movement? Speak to this.

D. T. G.: #BLM represents the leading edge of the third historical antiracist movement in the country. The first, abolition through Reconstruction, straddled much of the nineteenth century. The pushback from the standing forces of racist power was segregation, ordering American life from the 1880s into the 1950s. The Civil Rights Movement both resisted this renewed extension of racism and crafted a vision and a politics at once nonracial and antiracist. Like the anticolonial and antiapartheid struggles, it was Black-led yet significantly cross-racially coalitional. All three of these overlapping movements had important international support and impact. They all premised their respective struggles on the insistence on equality and the dignity of all, notably on racial grounds. They each linked socioeconomic, political, and cultural considerations with legal transformation. And they saw the reinforcing impacts for their respective struggles from both the challenges and successes of the other two.

#BLM is no different on each of these indices, indeed, building on the legacies and lessons of these historical antecedents. It exactly seeks to complete the institutionalization of the reach for racial equality and dignity on which the historical antiracist movements were predicated. And it has linked these local struggles to codirectional commitments wherever they are occurring, from Brazil to South Africa, Europe to Palestine.

There is one significant distinction represented by #BLM that speaks to our contemporary moment. Each of the historical movements were led by groups of notable, recognizable figures, strong personalities and visionary leaders (though invariably men). They were also often deeply interactive with each other. #BLM's disavowal of leading personalities, even if there is some deference to the founding trio of three young women, is democratically principled and a major challenge to consistent application of principles, movement growth, and sustainability. This organizational diffusion and radical decentralization nevertheless challenge the movement's sustaining an uncompromising commitment to its core principles and their modes of activation.

G. Y.: I continue to be hit with the rhetoric that we are a color-blind US, and that racism, if it exists at all, is a mere aberration. I get this mainly from white students (occasionally, from students of color). How might you respond to this way of thinking that we have achieved a color-blind society?

D. T. G.: The core data regarding every index of social well-being and life condition evidence that, structurally, the US is far from a color-blind society, conventionally understood: income and wealth inequality, housing and mortgage access, cost of car loans, schooling quality, discriminatory employment, reliable health care, police stops, incarceration rates, life span all bear this out. And the rhetoric of major politicians as well as the proliferation of racist nastiness on the web are broad indications of the wide distribution of racist venom circulating. Google "Obama, racism, images" to get a quick sense of how explicit racist ugliness continues to proliferate.

The history of the term "color-blind" is at best mixed. It first appears in the late nineteenth century as both an aspiration to social justice and a rationalization of the racial status quo. Justice Harlan captures something of the latter in his famous dissent to the constitutional affirmation of "separate but equal" in *Plessy v. Ferguson* (1896) that legally underpinned segregation for the next half century. Harlan writes (I paraphrase) that in so far as whites are and will always remain so far advanced over Black folk in intelligence and skill, they have nothing competitively to fear from the imperative to advance color-blindness. Racism remains embedded historically within the formulation of the concept. Insisting aspirationally on institutionalizing color-blindness oblivious nevertheless to the society's racially founded and inscribed inequality serves only to cement racial inequity and iniquity more deeply in place. And it simultaneously makes the identification of those enduring inequalities, as Charles Tilly once put it, increasingly obscure by erasing the critical terms by which to identify those inequities.

This, as I have elaborated extensively elsewhere, is exactly how the logics of "postraciality" operate today: The complete erasure of the terms for identifying racial inequity and perniciousness; the dehistoricization of racially inscribed events thus radically individuating them, rendering them mere social anomalies; state protection (in the name of free speech) of all private racist expression; the denial of any racist intentionality and the denial of that denial when confronted about it; racial reversibilities in the sense that prejudice against whites is now being pushed as racism's most egregious expression; and the blaming of the victims of racism for bringing it on themselves. We are indeed all postracial already not in any affirming aspirational sense but because this mode of postraciality has become the driving logic and expression of raciality for our time. Postraciality is the defining modality of contemporary racism.

G. Y.: Do you see an important role that universities/colleges, especially philosophy departments, might play in effectively getting white students to understand the importance of how race and racism function in their lives? From my own experience, especially as I teach at predominantly white institutions, white students are ill-equipped to engage critically questions about white privilege, complicity, institutional racism, and so on.

D. T. G.: We have come to think of the university as somehow separate, even protected from society, the "real world," when in fact it is both very much reflective of and impacted by the social in which it is embedded. Universities have a mixed record on diversity, and philosophy programs often fare even worse. Those colleges that have done reasonably well on diversifying the student body nevertheless suffer the funnel effect through faculty ranks and upper administrative personnel. So the driving need is to ensure a welcoming environment for more faculty who can speak to the impacts and workings of racism in nontrivial ways. That faculty will very likely end up being more heterogeneous. There are examples of programs and institutions having a much more effective diversifying strategy without a formal "affirmative action program" in place precisely by opening up the admissions process from a narrow focus on grades, testing scores, and racially networked references to a broader array of qualifying considerations like work and life experience, capacity to contribute to the student body and university experience, and likelihood of making compelling social contributions.

I am not a fan of mandated courses on such subject matter. For one, the mandating can cause resentment; and the success of such a course, as with courses generally, will depend on who is teaching them and how they are taught. The point would be to have terrifically appealing critical courses on racial matters students will want to take.

That said, there are two related contributions philosophy might make to embedding critical address of race and racism within and across curricula components. First, as indicated earlier, philosophy has a special role in training students how to think critically. It would help to reinvent the model popular in the 1970s and 1980s requiring every undergraduate to take a course in critical thinking or practical reasoning. Today, this would involve ensuring a significant course focus on racism, gender discrimination, and so on. But to think more creatively about the content of such courses by including interesting cultural contributions from a diverse array of literary and visual culture to music and politics.

Second, there is a great tradition of philosophers speaking compellingly to driving social issues, not least race and racism, from Du Bois, Alain Locke, Fanon, Arendt, and Sartre to Angela Davis, Anthony Appiah, Judith Butler, Cornel West, and Achille Mbembe, among others. The range and depth of this legacy offer a rich archive on which to draw, one with the potential to fascinate a broad range of students. Giving an account of the extraordinary history of Pan-African congresses across the first half of the twentieth century will prove of interest not just to African and African-American students but equally to students of Asian- and Latin-American backgrounds when it is revealed to them that anticolonial leaders from those backgrounds attended the Congresses and engaged in common struggles at home. Nor would students of European background feel left out when understanding why those meetings were taking place in Manchester, Brussels, Paris, and the like.

This is quite different from the more scholastic focus on whether race is "biologically real" or a "social construction" that dominated professional philosophical debates on race from the later 1980s until recently. So there is a responsibility as much for us as for students to rise to the challenge in crafting learning programs and environments that are diversely attractive while drawing also on the multimedia resources and capacities our students today find compelling.

NOTES

1. This article was written in the mid-1970s. The piece was never actually published—it circulated underground in South Africa at the time and was banned, especially after Cronin himself was imprisoned.
2. Ash Amin, "The Remainders of Race," *Theory, Culture and Society* 27, no. 1 (2010): 1–23.
3. Ruth Wilson Gilmore, *Golden Gulag: Prisons, Surplus, Crisis and Opposition in Globalizing California* (Berkeley: University of California Press, 2007), 28.
4. Eyal Weizman, *Forensic Architecture, Notes from Fields and Forums: 100 Notes, 100 Thoughts: Documenta Series 062* (Berlin: Hatje Cantz, 2012).

PART III DISCUSSION QUESTIONS

1. David Theo Goldberg points out that music production is in many ways determined by what are considered likely consumer trends by those who already control the industry. In film, Dan Flory explains that products that can be marketed and consumed with great profit are prioritized over other, more challenging ones. To what extent is the production of cultural media a self-regulating hegemonic machine that perpetuates whiteness in the domain of music and film, particularly given that the influence of Hollywood-style movies has effectively deployed the white gaze to operate across the globe? How concerned should we be that such modes of cultural expression are necessarily a part of education from a young age, and that they seem inescapable?

2. One of the difficult and problematic features of whiteness is its capacity to preserve itself through self-regulating hegemonic mechanisms. Discuss the extent to which these mechanisms are present in our cultural surroundings with respect to Goldberg's discussion of music production, Flory's discussion of film, and institutions of education and policing in Blum's discussion.
3. Lawrence Blum engages his students in a discussion of possible "rules of engagement" to enhance "everyone's consciousness about how what they say might be heard or experienced by others" in his courses about race. The awareness of how one is perceived by others is also present in Charles Johnson's concept of "double narrative intelligence," as is made clear in Dan Flory's interview, in which Black people already (must) navigate a world dominated by the white gaze. How might the "rules" by which we are most aware of ourselves operating in the world make it possible or perhaps make it easier to develop multiple narratives?

Race, History, Capitalism, Ethics, and Neoliberalism

Noam Chomsky

George Yancy: When I think about the title of your book *On Western Terrorism*, I'm reminded of the fact that many Black people in the United States have had a long history of being terrorized by white racism, from random beatings to the lynching of more than three thousand Black people (including women) between 1882 and 1968. This is why in 2003, when I read about the dehumanizing acts committed at Abu Ghraib prison, I wasn't surprised. I recall that after the photos appeared, President George W. Bush said "This is not the America I know." But isn't this the America Black people have always known?

Noam Chomsky: The America that "Black people have always known" is not an attractive one. The first Black slaves were brought to the colonies four hundred years ago. We cannot allow ourselves to forget that during this long period there have been only a few decades when African-Americans, apart from a few, had some limited possibilities for entering the mainstream of American society.

We also cannot allow ourselves to forget that the hideous slave labor camps of the new "empire of liberty" were a primary source for the wealth and privilege of American society, as well as England and the continent. The industrial revolution was based on cotton, produced primarily in the slave labor camps of the United States.

As is now known, they were highly efficient. Productivity increased even faster than in industry, thanks to the technology of the bullwhip and pistol, and the efficient practice of brutal torture, as Edward Baptist demonstrates in his recent study, *The Half Has Never Been Told*.[1] The achievement includes not only the great wealth of the planter aristocracy but also American and British manufacturing, commerce and the financial institutions of modern state capitalism.

It is, or should be, well known that the United States developed by flatly rejecting the principles of "sound economics" preached to it by the leading economists of the day, and familiar in today's sober instructions to latecomers in development. Instead, the newly liberated colonies followed the model of England with radical state intervention in the economy, including high tariffs to protect infant industry, first textiles, later steel and others.

There was also another "virtual tariff." In 1807, President Jefferson signed a bill banning the importation of slaves from abroad. His state of Virginia was the richest and most powerful of the states, and had exhausted its need for slaves. Rather, it was beginning to produce this valuable commodity for the expanding slave territories of the South. Banning import of these cotton-picking machines was thus a considerable boost to the Virginia economy. That was understood. Speaking for the slave importers, Charles Pinckney charged that "Virginia will gain by stopping the importations. Her slaves will rise in value, and she has more than she wants." And Virginia indeed became a major exporter of slaves to the expanding slave society.

Some of the slave-owners, like Jefferson, appreciated the moral turpitude on which the economy relied. But he feared the liberation of slaves, who have "ten thousand recollections"[2] of the crimes to which they were subjected. Fears that the victims might rise up and take revenge are deeply rooted in American culture, with reverberations to the present.

The Thirteenth Amendment formally ended slavery, but a decade later "slavery by another name," the title of an important study by Douglas A. Blackmon, was introduced. Black life was criminalized by overly harsh Black codes that targeted Black people. Soon an even more valuable form of slavery was available for agribusiness, mining, steel—more valuable because the state, not the capitalist, was responsible for sustaining the enslaved labor force, meaning that Blacks were arrested without real cause and prisoners were put to work for these business interests. The system provided a major contribution to the rapid industrial development from the late nineteenth century.

That system remained pretty much in place until World War II led to a need for free labor for the war industry. Then followed a few decades of rapid and relatively egalitarian growth, with the state playing an even more critical role in economic development than before. A Black man might get a decent job in a unionized factory, buy a house, send his children to college, along with other opportunities. The Civil Rights Movement opened other doors, though in limited ways. One illustration was the fate of Martin Luther King's efforts to confront Northern racism and develop a movement of the poor, which was effectively blocked.

The neoliberal reaction that set in from the late '70s, escalating under Reagan and his successors, hit the poorest and most oppressed sectors of the society even more than the large majority, who have suffered relative stagnation or decline while wealth accumulates in very few hands. Reagan's drug war, deeply racist in conception and execution, initiated a new Jim Crow, Michelle Alexander's apt term for the revived criminalization of Black life, evident in the shocking incarceration rates and the devastating impact on Black society.

Reality is of course more complex than any simple recapitulation, but this is, unfortunately, a reasonably accurate first approximation to one of the two founding crimes of American society, alongside of the expulsion or extermination of the indigenous nations and destruction of their complex and rich civilizations.

G. Y.: While Jefferson may have understood the moral turpitude upon which slavery was based, in his *Notes on the State of Virginia*, he says that Black people are dull in imagination, inferior in reasoning to whites, and that the male orangutans even prefer Black women over their own. These myths, along with the Black codes following the Civil War, functioned to continue to oppress and police Black people. What would you say are the contemporary myths and codes that are enacted to continue to oppress and police Black people today?

N. C.: Unfortunately, Jefferson was far from alone. No need to review the shocking racism in otherwise enlightened circles until all too recently. On "contemporary myths and codes," I would rather defer to the many eloquent voices of those who observe and often experience these bitter residues of a disgraceful past.

Perhaps the most appalling contemporary myth is that none of this happened. The title of Baptist's book is all too apt, and the aftermath is much too little known and understood.

There is also a common variant of what has sometimes been called "intentional ignorance" of what it is inconvenient to know: "Yes, bad things happened in the past, but let us put all of that behind us and march on to a glorious future, all sharing equally in the rights and opportunities of citizenry." The appalling statistics of today's circumstances of African-American life can be confronted by other bitter residues of a shameful past, laments about Black cultural inferiority, or worse, forgetting how our wealth and privilege was created in no small part by the centuries of torture and degradation of which we are the beneficiaries and they remain the victims. As for the very partial and hopelessly inadequate compensation that decency would require—that lies somewhere between the memory hole and anathema.

Jefferson, to his credit, at least recognized that the slavery in which he participated was "the most unremitting despotism on the one part, and degrading submissions on the other."[3] And the Jefferson Memorial in Washington displays his words that "indeed I tremble for my country when I reflect that God is just: that his justice cannot sleep forever."[4] Words that should stand in our consciousness alongside of John Quincy Adams's reflections on the parallel founding crime over centuries, the fate of "that hapless race of native Americans, which we are exterminating with such merciless and perfidious cruelty . . . among the heinous sins of this nation, for which I believe God will one day bring [it] to judgment."[5]

What matters is our judgment, too long and too deeply suppressed, and the just reaction to it that is as yet barely contemplated.

G. Y.: This "intentional ignorance" regarding inconvenient truths about the suffering of African-Americans can also be used to frame the genocide of Native Americans. It was eighteenth-century Swedish taxonomist Carolus Linnaeus who argued that Native Americans were governed by traits such as being "prone to anger," a convenient myth for justifying the need for Native Americans to be "civilized" by whites. So, there are myths here as well. How does North America's "amnesia" contribute to forms of racism directed uniquely toward Native Americans in our present moment and to their continual genocide?

N. C.: The useful myths began early on, and continue to the present. One of the first myths was formally established right after the King of England granted a Charter to the Massachusetts Bay Colony in 1629, declaring that conversion of the Indians to Christianity is "the principle end of this plantation." The colonists at once created the Great Seal of the Colony, which depicts an Indian holding a spear pointing downward in a sign of peace, with a scroll coming from his mouth pleading with the colonists to "Come over and help us." This may have been the first case of "humanitarian intervention"—and, curiously, it turned out like so many others.

Years later, Supreme Court Justice Joseph Story mused about "the wisdom of Providence" that caused the natives to disappear like "the withered leaves of autumn" even though the colonists had "constantly respected" them.[6] Needless to say, the colonists who did not choose "intentional ignorance" knew much better, and the most knowledgeable described "the utter extirpation of all the Indians in most populous parts of the Union [by means] more destructive to the Indian natives than the conduct of the conquerors of Mexico and Peru."[7]

Knox went on to warn that "a future historian may mark the causes of this destruction of the human race in sable colors."[8] There were a few—very few—who did so, like the heroic Helen Jackson, who in 1880 provided a detailed account of that "sad revelation of broken faith, of violated treaties, and of inhuman acts of violence [that] will bring a flush of shame to the cheeks of those who love their country."[9] Jackson's important book barely sold. She was neglected and dismissed in favor of the version presented by Theodore Roosevelt, who explained that "The expansion of the peoples of white, or European, blood during the past four centuries . . . has been fraught with lasting benefit to most of the peoples already dwelling in the lands over which the expansion took place," notably those who had been "extirpated" or expelled to destitution and misery.[10]

The national poet Walt Whitman captured the general understanding when he wrote that "the nigger, like the Injun, will be eliminated; it is the law of the races, history. . . . A superior grade of rats come and then all the minor rats are cleared out."[11] It wasn't until the 1960s that the scale of the atrocities and their character began to enter even scholarship, and to some extent popular consciousness, though there is a long way to go.

That's only a bare beginning of the shocking record of the Anglosphere and its settler-colonial version of imperialism, a form of imperialism that leads quite naturally to the "utter extirpation" of the indigenous population—and to "intentional ignorance" on the part of beneficiaries of the crimes.

G. Y.: Your response raises the issue of colonization as a form of occupation. James Baldwin, in his 1966 essay, "A Report from Occupied Territory," wrote, "Harlem is policed like occupied territory."[12] This quote made me think of Ferguson, Missouri. Some of the protesters in Ferguson even compared what they were seeing to the Gaza Strip. Can you speak to this comparative discourse of occupation?

N. C.: All kinds of comparisons are possible. When I went to the Gaza Strip a few years ago, what came to mind very quickly was the experience of being in jail (for civil disobedience, many times): the feeling, very strange to people who have had privileged lives, that you are totally under the control of some external authority, arbitrary and if it so chooses, cruel. But the differences between the two cases are, of course, vast.

More generally, I'm somewhat skeptical about the value of comparisons of the kind mentioned. There will of course be features common to the many diverse kinds of illegitimate authority, repression, and violence. Sometimes they can be illuminating; for example, Michelle Alexander's analogy of a new Jim Crow, mentioned earlier. Often they may efface crucial distinctions. I don't frankly see anything general to say of much value. Each comparison has to be evaluated on its own.

G. Y.: These differences are vast, and I certainly don't want to conflate them. Post-9/11 seems to have ushered in an important space for making some comparisons. Some seem to think that Muslims of Arab descent have replaced African Americans as the pariah in the United States. What are your views on this?

N. C.: Anti-Arab/Muslim racism has a long history, and there's been a fair amount of literature about it. Jack Shaheen's studies of stereotyping in visual media, for example. And there's no doubt that it's increased in recent years. To give just one vivid current example, audiences are now flocking in record-breaking numbers to a film, described in *The New York Times* Arts section as "a patriotic, pro-family picture," about a sniper who claims to hold the championship in killing Iraqis during the United States invasion, and proudly describes his targets as "savage, despicable, evil, . . . really no other way to describe what we encountered there." This was referring specifically to his first kill, a woman holding a grenade when under attack by United States forces.

What's important is not just the mentality of the sniper, but the reaction to such exploits at home when we invade and destroy a foreign country, hardly distinguishing one "raghead" from another. These attitudes go back to the "merciless Indian savages" of the Declaration of Independence and the savagery and fiendishness of others who have been in the way ever since, particularly when some "racial" element can be invoked—as when Lyndon Johnson lamented that if we let down our guard, we'll be at the mercy of "every yellow dwarf with a pocket knife."[13] But within the United States, though there have been deplorable incidents, anti-Arab/Muslim racism among the public has been fairly restrained, I think.

G. Y.: Lastly, the reality of racism (whether it's anti-Black, anti-Arab, anti-Jewish, etc.) is toxic. While there is no single solution to racism, especially in terms of its various manifestations, what do you see as some of the necessary requirements for ending racist hatred?

N. C.: It's easy to rattle off the usual answers: education, exploring and addressing the sources of the malady, joining together in common enterprises—labor struggles have been an important case—and so on. The answers are right, and have achieved a lot. Racism is far from eradicated, but it is not what it was not very long ago, thanks to such efforts. It's a long hard road. No magic wand, as far as I know.

NOTES

1. Edward Baptist, *The Half Has Never Been Told: Slavery and the Making of American Capitalism* (New York: Basic Books, 2014).
2. Thomas Jefferson, *Notes on the State of Virginia* (New York: Penguin Classics, 1998), 145.
3. Jefferson, *Notes on the State of Virginia*, Query XIII, Manners, 168.
4. Jefferson, *Notes on the State of Virginia*, Query XIII, Manners, 169.
5. Cited in William Earl Weeks, *John Quincy Adams and American Global Empire* (Lexington: Kentucky, 1992), 193.
6. Cited in Nicholas Guyatt, *Providence and the Invention of the United States, 1607–1876* (New York: Cambridge University Press, 2007).
7. General Henry Knox, first US Secretary of War, cited in Reginald Horsman, *Expansion and American Indian Policy* (Lansing, MI: Michigan State University Press, 1967).
8. Knox, cited in Horsman, *Expansion and American Indian Policy*.
9. Bishop H. B. Whipple, introduction to Helen Jackson, *A Century of Dishonor* (Echo Library, [1881] 2016).
10. Theodore Roosevelt, Address at the celebration of the African Diamond Jubilee of the Methodist Episcopal Church, Washington, DC, January 18 , 1909.

11. Commentary: Disciples, *The Walt Whitman Archive*, 283, http://whitmanarchive. org/criticism/disciples/traubel/WWWiC/2/med.00002.56.html.
12. James Baldwin, "A Report from Occupied Territory." *Nation* 203, no. 2 (1966): 39–43.
13. Lyndon B. Johnson, speeches on November 1 and 2, 1966. Public Papers of the Presidents of the United States, 1966, Book II (Washington, DC, 1967), 563, 568.

Nancy Fraser

George Yancy: In what way have discussions of race shaped your thinking over the years?

Nancy Fraser: Race has shaped my thinking profoundly, and from a fairly young age. As a teenager, I was shaken out of my comfortable and rather boring life in a white middle-class suburb of Baltimore by the eruption of the Civil Rights Movement. Drawn quickly into the struggle for desegregation, I experienced a major existential reorientation. Suddenly, my family's move from the city to the suburbs appeared in a new light, as did my relation to our live-in Black maid, who had to wait in the car while we ate in restaurants on vacation road trips. The encounter changed me forever. The Civil Rights Movement provided my first political engagement, my first taste of solidarity in a community of struggle, and my first experience of the power of critique to dissolve blinders. And it informed the whole of my subsequent development, including my gravitation to the radical, anti-imperialist, and antiracist wing of the anti-Vietnam War movement, to a Marxian strand of Students for a Democratic Society, to socialist and antiracist currents of feminism, and eventually to Critical Theory as a genre of intellectual work aimed at disclosing the systemic bases of oppression and the prospects for overcoming it through social struggle.

G. Y.: In what ways have you come to specifically rethink the fact that you had a live-in Black maid? I ask this because there are ways in which when we acquire a critical consciousness things take on a different meaning, especially the past.

N. F.: Yes, that is exactly what I wanted to suggest. I was caught up in a nexus of racial oppression literally from birth, long before I could name it and subject it to critical assessment. That we were "white" and in a position to be *served* by a Black woman was simply the way things were. That she lived most of the week with us, in close proximity and engaged with the most intimate aspects of our daily lives (preparing our food, cleaning our dirt), and yet was not a member of our family and did not eat with us—indeed, was someone we held at a *distance*—all that too belonged to the taken-for-granted reality of my childhood. As I grew up, I absorbed but did not grasp the meaning of these everyday experiences: that she was pretty much the only person I knew who rode the public bus, that everyone I saw waiting to be picked up at the bus stop was Black, that she came to our house on a long bus ride from another part of the city, where she had a home and a family, a whole other life, about which I knew next to nothing. I did, as a young child, question certain things—above all, that she couldn't eat with us in restaurants on road trips; and I stored away for future use my parents' reply that this was the law but it was wrong. In retrospect I can see that I was storing up a lot of information until the time arrived when I could decode it. And as I said before, that time began with the Civil Rights Movement. I now believe that my whole upbringing primed me to jump into the struggle. On the one hand, I was living up close and personal with institutionalized racism. But on the other hand, I was hearing from my parents—solid FDR liberals, who nevertheless went along with the Jim Crow system—that it was wrong. My early antiracist activism was informed not only by a passion for justice, but also by adolescent rage at my parents' hypocrisy, their willingness to tolerate social arrangements they disapproved.

So yes, you are right, there is (if we are lucky!) an understanding that arrives late, like Hegel's Owl of Minerva, to provide a retroactive rereading of what we have lived. I think it is largely a process of self-decentering, of stepping back from lived experience and trying to grasp one's reality from the outside, by locating oneself in a social system, a system, if truth be told, of domination. When that happens, one's whole sense of who one is gets radically altered.

The most powerful account I know of this is Christa Wolf's "fictional autobiography," *Patterns of Childhood*.[1] In this extraordinary book, the adult narrator struggles to reconstruct what it was like to be a young German girl growing up in a "normal Nazi family," and eventually to own that experience, to integrate her childhood and adult selves, which at first are split off from one another, marked in the text by two different pronouns, "I" and "she." Another book that deals brilliantly with related issues is Marlene Van Niekerk's novel *Agaat*, which reads the whole forty-plus-year history of South African apartheid through the intimate and almost unbearably painful relation between Milla, an Afrikaner farmwife, and Agaat, her Black housekeeper. Milla brought Agaat to her farmstead and treated her as a substitute for the child she couldn't have, only to convert her into a servant a few years later when Milla became pregnant. In the novel's present, the Afrikaner woman lies dying from ALS. Unable to speak and immersed in her memories, she has no choice but to listen as Agaat reads aloud from her (Milla's) youthful diaries. Hearing her own words, pregnant with evasion and loss, Milla is hit by the full force of what she has done, of her love for Agaat, and of the way this most enduring and important relation of her life has been irredeemably twisted.[2] These are two of the deepest books I've ever read. In both cases, the authors are grappling with their own implication in brutal oppression as members of the perpetrator groups. Both of them explore the dynamics of retroactive self-understanding and responsibility. And both enact that decentering of subjectivity that is, in my view, the necessary starting point for critique.

G. Y.: How has race specifically shaped your philosophical work?

N. F.: I am widely viewed as a feminist and critical theorist—and rightly so. Nevertheless, my philosophical work has often attended to racism in one way or another. As I reflect on that now, it occurs to me that I have dealt with issues of race in four different ways. I have treated race, first, as a pervasive dimension of capitalist society, which informs every aspect of it and must be reckoned with in every social inquiry. When writing in this mode, I have sought to reveal the footprint of racialization in matters that could, at first glance, seem far removed from it. Thus, one aim of my early work on the welfare state was to disclose the racial subtext of social programs, along with the gender subtext. An example is my 1994 essay, coauthored with Linda Gordon, on then-fashionable criticisms of "welfare dependency." In that essay, Gordon and I exhumed racialized strands of dependency discourse, examined their imbrication with class-oriented and gendered strands, and situated them in terms of two major historical shifts—first, from preindustrial society to industrial capitalism, and then to postindustrial (or neoliberal) capitalism.[3]

But I have also approached race in a second, almost opposite, way—namely, as a feature of "common sense" that can suck up all the oxygen and occlude other forms of domination. In work of this sort, I have analyzed the use of racializing discourse to screen out gender and class, an approach that is especially revelatory with respect to class, which is so often occulted and disavowed in US politics. An example is my 1992 essay on the Clarence Thomas-Anita Hill confrontation, which drew on Habermas's theory of the public sphere to clarify the power dynamics behind Thomas's notorious claim that he was the victim of a "high-tech lynching."[4]

Then too, I have approached race in a third way, as a "case" that can disclose general features of social oppression. In writings of this type, I have examined racial injustice in order to illuminate injustice more broadly and to concretize my analysis of it. An example is my work on recognition and redistribution, which parsed race as a "two-dimensional" power asymmetry, forged from both culture and political economy, and combining features of both status and class. My aim there was twofold: to understand race for its own sake and to bring home the general point that struggles for recognition are not by themselves sufficient to overcome structural injustice.[5]

Finally, I have approached race in a head-on way, as a primary focus of investigation. In work of this type, I have lifted racial dynamics out from their larger social matrix and moved them to center stage. An example is my 1998 essay on Alain Locke's early effort to develop a critical race theory *avant la lettre*. There I sought to excavate Locke's largely forgotten but still unsurpassed insights, especially his brilliant disaggregation of the concept of "race" into three subconcepts: biological, political, and social.[6] Also in this category is a recent (2016) paper in which I try to explain why capitalist society has always been entangled with racial oppression. Proposing a systemic explanation, I argue that capitalism's official, foreground dynamic of exploitation depends on an equally central but disavowed background process of "expropriation," and that the distinction between those two "exes" corresponds to the color line.[7] In these cases, I have sought to contribute directly to critical race theory—generally by replacing conventional identitarian framings with a focus on historicized capitalism.

G. Y.: There is the argument that class trumps race. Some who have argued this position assume some variation of Marxism. Yet, racism involves more than exploitation, yes? Please elaborate on how you understand the difference between the terms "exploitation" and "expropriation" and how the latter term outstrips an analysis of oppression based upon class alone.

N. F.: Racism definitely involves more than exploitation. It is no mere "secondary contradiction" of capitalism and cannot be reduced to class oppression. But to reject those vulgar, orthodox views is not necessarily to abandon Marxism. To the contrary, I have proposed an account of racial oppression that belongs to the Marxist tradition, or perhaps I should say, to its "Black Marxist" current, which includes such towering thinkers as C. L. R. James, W. E. B. Du Bois, Eric Williams, Oliver Cromwell Cox, Stuart Hall, Walter Rodney, Angela Davis, Manning Marable, Barbara Fields, Cedric Robinson, David Roediger, Adolph Reed, and Cornel West.[8] This strand of Marxism takes us far beyond conventional economistic, class-essentialist, and color-blind orthodoxy, but without throwing out the baby with the bathwater.

My contribution turns on the distinction between capitalism's foreground economy and the latter's background conditions of possibility. According to the official Marxian view, capital is accumulated via the exploitation of "workers": free but propertyless "producers" contract to exchange their "labor power" for wages, while the "surplus value" their labor produces accrues to the capitalist. This view accurately depicts a central process of capitalism. But it gives us only the system's "front-story" while leaving unexamined its equally fundamental "back-story." If, as I said, the front-story is about exploitation, then the back-story concerns *expropriation*; and the distinction between those two "exes" is vital for understanding racial oppression. Whereas exploitation transfers value to capital under the guise of a free contractual exchange, expropriation dispenses with all such niceties in favor of brute confiscation—of labor, to be sure, but also of land, animals, tools, mineral and energy deposits, and even of human beings, their sexual and reproductive capacities, their children and bodily organs. Moreover, whereas exploited workers are accorded the status of rights-bearing individuals and citizens who enjoy state protection and can freely dispose of their own labor power, those subject to expropriation are constituted as unfree, dependent beings who are stripped of political protection and rendered defenseless—as, for example, in the cases of chattel slaves, colonized subjects, "natives," debt peons, "illegals," and convicted felons. Thus, the distinction between the two "exes" is at once "economic" and "political." It has to do not only with two different *mechanisms of accumulation* but also with two different *modes of subjectivation,* which fabricate two distinct categories of persons, one suitable for "mere" exploitation, the other destined for brute expropriation.

So I am claiming that expropriation is a built-in feature of capitalism, as constitutive of it as exploitation—and that it correlates strongly with racial oppression. The link is clear in practices widely associated with capitalism's early history but still ongoing, such as territorial conquest, land annexation, enslavement, coerced labor, child labor, child abduction, and rape. But expropriation also assumes more "modern" forms—such as prison labor, transnational sex trafficking, corporate land grabs, and foreclosures on predatory debt, which are also linked with racial oppression. Finally, expropriation plays a role in the construction of distinctive, explicitly racialized forms of exploitation—as, for example, when a prior history of enslavement casts its shadow on the wage contract, segmenting labor markets and levying a confiscatory premium on exploited proletarians who carry the mark of "race" long after their "emancipation."

Here, then, is my argument in a nutshell: capitalism harbors a deep structural distinction, at once economic and political, between exploitation and expropriation, a distinction that coincides with "the color line." I can also state the point in a different way: the racializing dynamics of capitalist society are crystalized in the "mark" that distinguishes *free subjects of exploitation* from *dependent subjects of expropriation.*

G. Y.: How do you see the relationship between capitalism and racism? Is racism a byproduct of capitalism or is it something far more integral to the expansionist structure inherent in capitalist circuits of desire?

N. F.: I see the connection as integral. The first clue is that racial oppression has always been part and parcel of capitalist society—just as expropriation has always accompanied exploitation in capitalism's history. We are not talking only about the period of racial slavery and modern colonialism. On the contrary, the relation between the two "exes" persisted throughout the era of Jim Crow and decolonization, when value was confiscated from racialized populations through sharecropping and debt peonage, through the "super-exploitation" of Black workers in dual labor markets, and through neoimperial "unequal exchange." And racialized expropriation continues today, despite the appearance of equal citizenship and despite lip service to equal rights. In the Global South it assumes the guise of corporate land grabs and dispossession by debt, while in the Global North it operates through for-profit prisons and prison services and through predatory subprime and payday loans. This ongoing history belies the orthodox interpretation of "primitive accumulation," which limits expropriation to the initial stockpiling of capital at the system's beginnings.[9]

But my claim is not simply that racialized expropriation persists throughout capitalism's history. As I see it, the history reflects a deeper, more structural connection. The link is in part "economic." A system devoted to the limitless expansion and private appropriation of surplus value gives the owners of capital a deep-seated interest in confiscating labor and means of production from subject populations. Expropriation raises their profits by lowering costs of production, including the wage bill—and it does so in at least two ways: on the one hand, by supplying cheap inputs, such as energy and raw materials; on the other, by providing low-cost means of subsistence, such as food and textiles, which permit them to pay lower wages. Thus, by confiscating resources and capacities from unfree or dependent subjects, capitalists can more profitably exploit "free workers." And so the two "exes" are deeply intertwined. In the memorable phrase of Jason Moore, "behind Manchester stands Mississippi."[10]

But not everything can be reduced to economics. Political dynamics play an indispensable role in entrenching racial oppression in capitalist society. Capitalism's economy has always depended on public, political powers to secure the conditions for accumulation. No one doubts that such powers supply the legal frameworks that guarantee property rights, enforce contracts, and adjudicate disputes, as well as the repressive forces that can be called on to suppress rebellions, maintain order, and manage dissent. But that is not all. Public powers also engage in political subjectivation: they codify the status hierarchies that distinguish citizens from subjects, nationals from aliens, freemen from slaves, "Europeans" from "natives," "whites" from "Blacks," entitled workers from dependent scroungers. Forged politically, such status hierarchies are essential for accumulation, as they mark off groups subject to brute expropriation from those destined for "mere" exploitation. And so that distinction is as much "political" as it is "economic."

What all of this entails, finally, is that expropriation and exploitation are not simply separate, parallel processes. Rather, the two "exes" are systemically imbricated—they are deeply intertwined and mutually calibrated engines of a single capitalist world system. The conclusion I draw is that the *racialized subjection* of those whom capital *expropriates* is a hidden condition of possibility for the *freedom* of those whom it *exploits*. And that tells us that racial oppression stands in a systemic, nonaccidental relation to capitalist society, that the connection between them is inherent.

G. Y.: In *Black Skin, White Masks*, Frantz Fanon argues that "Jean-Paul Sartre forgets that the black man suffers in his body quite differently from the white man."[11] For you, how does the Black body suffer in ways that the wage-earning white proletariat doesn't?

N. F.: Well, I would start by unpacking the phrase "to suffer in one's body." One obvious meaning is to be subject to physical violence, and there is no question that that condition afflicts people of color (both women and men!) disproportionately. Members of racialized groups are far more likely than "whites" to be murdered, assaulted, harassed, and raped; and the violence they suffer is far more likely to go unpunished. Worse still, those who are supposed to prevent and punish violence are, in the case of Black Americans, too often the perpetrators of it. And that fact compounds the violence. It sends the message that Black lives *don't* matter, that they can be maimed and extinguished with impunity, that there is no protection and no recourse, that attempts at self-defense will be branded as criminal and crushed by still more violence. All of this has recently erupted into full view in the United States; and the Black Lives Matter movement deserves enormous credit for insisting that we face it squarely, without averting our gaze. But none of it is new. The vulnerability of racialized people to *socially tolerated* violence is at least as old as this country. Everyone knows that it was an enduring feature of slavery and that it persisted (for example, in the form of lynching) long after abolition. But we should not forget that it has also been a constant for native peoples and for "illegals" and immigrants of color, as well as for LGBT people. Nor should we forget that susceptibility to socially tolerated violence is gendered—a fact that Fanon appreciated in the case of Black men, but obfuscated in the case of Black women.[12] To correct his blind spot, we need only mention the systematic rape of enslaved women, including the instrumentalization of their childbearing capacity for breeding, and the targeting of women of color for forced sterilization, transnational sex trafficking, sexual harassment, and sexual assault (both domestic and otherwise). No less than that directed against racialized men, this violence too has been socially tolerated in the United States—indeed throughout the capitalist world system.

We hear far too much of the word 'terrorism' today, but I can't resist using it here. To be susceptible to socially tolerated violence is precisely to be terrorized, to be constantly bracing oneself in expectation of a blow, without knowing when or whence it will come. This internal tension borne of anticipated violence is itself a form of "suffering in one's body," even apart from, or in the absence of, any blow. Simultaneously psychical and physical, it is a suffering that explodes the mind-body distinction. But the same is true of other historic forms of institutionalized racism: disfranchisement, segregation, exclusion, rejection, coerced labor—these also wound body and soul in ways that testify to their ultimate unity. Thus, we should take an expansive view of Fanon's phrase. What is sometimes called symbolic or cultural violence is not without its effects on racialized bodies. This was Fanon's great insight: that racialization imprisons people of color in their bodies; "race" itself is a form of bodily harm and bodily suffering.

But that is not all. People of color also disproportionately suffer in their bodies from what Rob Nixon has called "slow violence."[13] That phrase is meant to signal the long-term effects of the ordinary, everyday living conditions of impoverished racialized people: mal- or poor nutrition, lack of or poor health care, unsanitary water, unsafe housing or homelessness, exposure to pollution and other environmental hazards, dangerous and toxic work. The effects of these conditions unfold very slowly in many cases, but they are nevertheless lethal. So this is "slow violence," akin to "environmental racism." And it is also a form of suffering in one's body. Working gradually and imperceptibly, it stunts the growth, impairs the health, and shortens the lives of people of color across the globe.

When I try to put all of this together, I can't help but return to the idea of expropriation. Part of what I mean by that term, in contradistinction from exploitation, is exposure, the inability to set limits to what others can do to you, the incapacity to draw boundaries and invoke protections. The condition of *expropriability*, of being defenseless and subject to violation, seems to me to lie at the core of racialization and racial oppression. And that is why I said earlier that "race" is the mark that distinguishes free subjects of exploitation from dependent subjects of expropriation in capitalist society.

G. Y.: You argued earlier that capitalist society has always been entangled with racial oppression. Attacking racist ideological assumptions, while necessary, will not be sufficient to effectively eliminate racism, assuming that it will ever be eliminated. To engage in something far more radical, in what specific ways must capitalism, because it is always already linked to racism, be restructured? If racism must go, then what does this means for capitalism?

N. F.: Well, that's just about the hardest question you could possibly ask me! And I can't provide a fully satisfying answer. But let me suggest a way of thinking about it that draws on the conception of capitalism I've been sketching here. Assuming this conception, which encompasses expropriation as well as exploitation, politics as well as economics, I would like to address your question in its most classical and pointed form: is it possible to abolish racial oppression without abolishing capitalism? The short answer is: in theory, yes; in practice, given capitalism's history, almost certainly no. Let me explain.

A major consideration has to do with the ontology of "race." Like many critical race theorists, I hold that "race" does not exist apart from racialization, which is to say, apart from the political mechanisms of subjectivation that sort populations into different categories, suited to different functional roles and social locations. If that is right, then "race" just *is* that differential marking of capitalism's subjects, in the one case for exploitation, in the other for expropriation. Absent that political marking, it wouldn't exist. By the same token, however, "race" *must* exist in one form or another wherever social arrangements constitute expropriation and exploitation as distinct and separate processes assigned to distinct and separate populations. In those situations, *whoever* is constituted as expropriable will be racialized, constructed as dependent and inherently violable, deprived of rights and protections, and on that basis oppressed—even if the people in question are not disproportionately of African descent. If "race" is understood in this pragmatic, de-substantialized way, and if capitalism requires both expropriation and exploitation, as well as their mutual separation, then it cannot be detached from racial oppression.

But before we embrace that conclusion, we should consider another possibility: that while capitalism *does* require both expropriation and exploitation, it does *not* require that they be clearly separated from one another. Suppose, accordingly, that a new form of capitalism emerges, one that does *not* assign the two exes to distinct populations. Such a regime would conscript nearly all adults into wage labor, but pay the overwhelming majority less than the socially necessary costs of their reproduction. Reducing the "social wage" by dismantling public provision, it would entangle the bulk of the population in massive debt, empowering creditors to evict them from their homes and their land, to garnish their wages and seize their assets, including their personal capacities and bodily liberty. Universalizing precarity, the new regime would compel most households to rely on multiple earners working long hours at multiple jobs and thus to sacrifice health, family life, education, sleep, nutrition, leisure, and retirement in order to service their loans and meet their most pressing needs as best they can. In this new form of capitalism, the line between exploitation and expropriation would blur. Virtually everyone would be subjected to both those processes of value extraction, which would no longer be clearly separated from one another. Neither subjects of expropriation nor subjects of exploitation would exist as such. Those "pure" positions would be replaced by a new, nearly universal hybrid status: the exploitable-and-expropriable citizen-worker, formally free, but deeply vulnerable and highly dependent. Certainly, this type of capitalism would be no picnic. But in overcoming the dichotomous separation of the two exes, it would have transcended the historic basis of racial oppression in capitalist society.

The regime I've just imagined is logically possible, to be sure, which is why I said at the outset that a nonracial capitalism is possible in theory. For all practical purposes, however, we can rule it out. The reason has to do with path dependency, the constraints of history on real possibility, and with the dynamics of transition, the process of getting from here to there. Given the accumulated weight of racialization in capitalism's history and barring some unimaginable cataclysm, I can discern no practicable path to a regime of accumulation in which the burdens of expropriation are equitably shared across the color line.

To see why, we need only compare my hypothetical scenario to the really existing capitalism of the present era, with which it has clear similarities. Today's financialized capitalism is indeed a regime of universalized expropriation: of government "austerity," falling real wages, ballooning consumer debt, precarious employment, and increased hours of waged work per household. And the situation of "white" citizen-workers, previously protected from such expropriation, has badly deteriorated. Structurally, their circumstances now encompass both of the "exes," just like their counterparts of color, many of whom joined the ranks of exploited wage labor long ago, but without fully escaping expropriation. Today, accordingly, the relation between the two exes has changed. What once was a stark dichotomy, separating two distinct classes of subjects, now resembles a continuum. The hybrid status of the (disempowered, precarious) exploitable-and-expropriable citizen-worker, previously restricted to people of color, has now been generalized to virtually the entire non-property-owning population. In these respects, present-day financialized capitalism resembles the hypothetical postracial scenario I sketched above.

And yet: present-day capitalism is anything but postracial. The burdens of expropriation still fall disproportionately on people of color, who remain racialized and far more likely than others to be unemployed, homeless, poor, and sick; to be victimized by crime and predatory loans; to be incarcerated and sentenced to death, harassed and murdered by police; to be used as cannon fodder in endless wars. Racial oppression persists despite the advent of a new, less dichotomous configuration of the two exes. And that configuration may even aggravate racial animosity. When centuries of stigma and violation meet finance capital's voracious need for subjects to expropriate, the result is intense insecurity and paranoia—hence, a desperate scramble for safety—and exacerbated racialization. Certainly, "whites" are less than eager to share the burden of violation—and not simply because they are racists, although some of them are. It is also that they, too, have legitimate grievances, which come out in one way or another—as well they should. In the absence of a cross-racial movement to abolish a system that requires expropriation as well as exploitation, their grievances find expression in the growing ranks of right-wing authoritarian populism. Those movements, which flourish in virtually every country of capitalism's historic core, represent the entirely predictable response to the hegemonic "progressive neoliberalism" of the present era. The latter cynically deploys appeals to "fairness" as a cover for extending and exacerbating expropriation. In effect, it asks those who were once protected from it by their standing as "whites" and "Europeans" to give up that favored status, embrace their growing precarity, and surrender to violation, all while funneling their assets to private investors and offering them nothing in return beyond moral approval. In the dog-eat-dog world of financialized capitalism, marked both by the historical weight of centuries of racialization and by intensified expropriation-cum-exploitation, it is practically impossible to envision a "democratic" path to nonracial capitalism.

Nor, of course, is it easy to envision a path to a nonracial *post*capitalist society. But the kernel of the project is clear. Contra traditional understandings of socialism, an exclusive focus on exploitation cannot emancipate working people of any color; it is necessary also to target expropriation, to which exploitation is in any case tied. By the same token, contra liberal and "progressive" antiracists, an exclusive focus on discrimination, ideology, and law is not the royal road to overcoming racial oppression; it is also necessary to challenge capitalism's stubborn nexus of expropriation and exploitation. Both projects require a deeper radicalism—one aimed at structural transformation of the overall social matrix, at overcoming both of capitalism's exes by abolishing the system that generates their symbiosis.

Perhaps we can find some grounds for hope in the current situation. Today, when the exploited are also the expropriated and vice-versa, it might be possible, finally, to envision an alliance of populations that were too easily pitted against one another in earlier eras, when the two exes were more clearly separated. Perhaps in blurring the line between them, financialized capitalism is creating the conditions for their joint abolition.

NOTES

1. Christa Wolf, *Patterns of Childhood*, trans. Ursule Molinaro and Hedwig Rappolt (New York: Farrar, Straus and Giroux, 1984; originally published as *Kindheitsmuster* [Berlin: Aufbau-Verlag, 1976]).
2. Marlene Van Niekerk, *Agaat*, trans. Michiel Heyns (Portland and New York: Tin House Books, 2010; originally published in Afrikaans [Cape Town: Tafelberg Publishers, 2004]).
3. Nancy Fraser and Linda Gordon, "A Genealogy of 'Dependency': Tracing a Keyword of the US Welfare State," *Signs: Journal of Women in Culture and Society* 19, no. 2 (Winter 1994): 309–36; reprinted in Nancy Fraser, *Fortunes of Feminism: From State-Managed Capitalism to Neoliberal Crisis* (London and New York: Verso Books, 2013), 83–110.
4. Nancy Fraser, "Sex, Lies, and the Public Sphere: Some Reflections on the Confirmation of Clarence Thomas," *Critical Inquiry* 18 (Spring 1992): 595–612.
5. Nancy Fraser, "From Redistribution to Recognition? Dilemmas of Justice in a 'Postsocialist' Age," *New Left Review* 212 (July/August 1995): 68–93; reprinted in Nancy Fraser, *Justice Interruptus: Critical Reflections on the "Postsocialist" Condition* (New York and London: Routledge, 1997), 11–40. For a more extended discussion, see also my chapter 1 of Nancy Fraser and Axel Honneth, *Redistribution or Recognition? A Political-Philosophical Exchange*, trans. Joel Golb, James Ingram, and Christiane Wilke (London: Verso, 2003), 7–109.

6. Nancy Fraser, "Another Pragmatism: Alain Locke, Critical 'Race' Theory, and the Politics of Culture," in *The Revival of Pragmatism: New Essays on Social Thought, Law, and Culture*, ed. Morris Dickstein (Durham, NC: Duke University Press, 1998), 157–75.

7. Nancy Fraser, "Expropriation and Exploitation in Racialized Capitalism: A Reply to Michael Dawson," *Critical Historical Studies* 3, no.1 (Spring 2016): 163–78.

8. C. L. R. James, *The Black Jacobins* (London: Penguin Books, 1938); W. E. B. Du Bois, *Black Reconstruction in America, 1860–1880* (New York: Harcourt, Brace and Co., 1935); Eric Williams, *Capitalism and Slavery* (Chapel Hill: University of North Carolina Press, 1944); Oliver Cromwell Cox, *Caste, Class and Race: A Study of Social Dynamics* (New York: Monthly Review Press, 1948); Stuart Hall, "Race, Articulation and Societies Structured in Dominance," in *Sociological Theories: Race and Colonialism*, ed. UNESCO (Paris: UNESCO, 1980), 305–45; Walter Rodney, *How Europe Underdeveloped Africa* (Washington, DC: Howard University Press, 1981); Angela Davis, *Women, Race, and Class* (London: The Women's Press, 1982); Manning Marable, *How Capitalism Underdeveloped Black America* (Brooklyn: South End Press, 1983); Barbara Fields, "Slavery, Race and Ideology in the United States of America," *New Left Review* I/181 (May–June 1990): 95–118; Cedric Robinson, *Black Marxism* (Chapel Hill: University of North Carolina Press, 1999); David Roediger, *The Wages of Whiteness* (London: Verso, 1999); Cornel West, "The Indispensability yet Insufficiency of Marxist Theory," and "Race and Social Theory," both in *The Cornel West Reader* (New York: Basic Civitas Books, 1999), 213–30, and 251–67; and Adolph Reed Jr., "Unraveling the Relation of Race and Class in American Politics," *Political Power and Social Theory* 15 (2002): 265–74. I should explain that I understand Black Marxism as a political-theoretical perspective, not an identity category—which is why I include Roediger in this list and why I myself can hope to contribute to it.

9. Karl Marx, *Capital Volume I*, trans. Ben Fowkes (London: Penguin Books, 1976), 873ff.

10. Jason W. Moore, *Capitalism in the Web of Life* (London and New York: Verso, 2015).

11. Frantz Fanon, *Black Skin, White Masks* (New York: Grove Press, 2008; originally published as Peau Noire [Paris: Éditions du Seuil]), 117.

12. Gwen Bergner, "Who is that Masked Woman? Or, the Role of Gender in Fanon's *Black Skin, White Masks*," *PMLA* 110, no. 1 (1995): 75–88; Diana Fuss, "Interior Colonies: Frantz Fanon and the Politics of Identification," *Diacritics* 24, nos. 2/3 (1994): 19–42; T. Denean Sharpley-Whiting, *Frantz Fanon: Conflicts and Feminisms* (Lanham, MD: Rowman & Littlefield, 1998).

13. Rob Nixon, *Slow Violence and the Environmentalism of the Poor* (Cambridge, MA: Harvard University Press, 2013).

Peter Singer

George Yancy: You have popularized the concept of speciesism, which, I believe, was first used by animal activist Richard Ryder. Briefly, define that term and how do you see it as similar or different from racism?

Peter Singer: Speciesism is an attitude of bias against a being because of the species to which it belongs. Typically, humans show speciesism when they give less weight to the interests of nonhuman animals than they give to the similar interests of human beings. Note the requirement that the interests in question be "similar." It's not speciesism to say that normal humans have an interest in continuing to live that is different from the interests that nonhuman animals have. One might, for instance, argue that a being with the ability to think of itself as existing over time, and therefore to plan its life, and to work for future achievements, has a greater interest in continuing to live than a being who lacks such capacities.

On that basis, one might argue that to kill a normal human being who wants to go on living is more seriously wrong than killing a nonhuman animal. Whether this claim is or is not sound, it is not speciesist. But given that some human beings—most obviously, those with profound intellectual impairment—lack this capacity, or have it to a lower degree than some nonhuman animals, it would be speciesist to claim that it is *always* more seriously wrong to kill a member of the species *Homo sapiens* than it is to kill a nonhuman animal.

G. Y.: While I think that it is ethically important to discuss the issue of failing to extend to other (nonhuman) animals the principle of equality, we continue to fail miserably in the ways in which we extend that principle to Black people, the disabled, women, and others, here in the United States and around the world. What is it that motivates the failure or the refusal to extend this principle to other human beings in ethically robust ways? I'm especially thinking here in terms of the reality of racism.

P. S.: Although it is true, of course, that we have not overcome racism, sexism, or discrimination against people with disabilities, there is at least widespread acceptance that such discrimination is wrong, and there are laws that seek to prevent it. With speciesism, we are very far from reaching that point. If we were to compare attitudes about speciesism today with past racist attitudes, we would have to say that we are back in the days in which the slave trade was still legal, although under challenge by some enlightened voices.

Why do racism, sexism, and discrimination against people with disabilities still exist, despite the widespread acceptance that they are wrong? There are several reasons, but surely one is that many people act unthinkingly on the basis of their emotional impulses, without reflecting on the ethics of what they are doing. That, of course, invites us to discuss why some people have these negative emotional impulses toward people of other races, and that in turn leads to the old debate whether such prejudices are innate or are learned from one's culture and environment. There is evidence that even babies are attracted to faces that look more like those of the people they see around them all the time, so there could be an evolved innate element, but culture certainly plays a very significant role.

G. Y.: I think that it is important to keep in mind that American slavery was partly constituted by a white racist ideology that held that Africans were subpersons. There was also the European notion that nonwhites were incapable of planning their own lives and had to be paternalistically ruled over. So, in many ways, for Black people, the distinction between the human and the subhuman (even nonhuman) didn't hold in the face of white racist mythos. As a white Australian, do you think that there are parallels in terms of how the indigenous people of Australia have been treated, especially in terms of subpersonhood, and paternalism?

P. S.: Yes, unfortunately there are parallels. The early European settlers regarded the indigenous people as an inferior race, living a miserable existence. Because the indigenous people were nomadic, they were regarded as having no ownership of their land, which in British colonial law therefore belonged to nobody—the legal term was *terra nullius*—and so, very conveniently, could be occupied by Europeans. In some cases, when indigenous people killed cattle that were grazing on their traditional lands, Europeans went out in "shooting parties," killing them indiscriminately, as they would animals. Some of the Europeans justified this on the grounds that the indigenous people, like animals, had no souls. Although such killings were never permitted in law, enforcement was another matter.

When the Commonwealth of Australia was formed from the separate colonies in 1901, indigenous people were not able to vote, nor were they included in the census. Voting rights were achieved in stages over the next sixty years. The *terra nullius* doctrine was only overturned by the High Court of Australia in 1992, and indigenous communities then became able to claim rights over traditional land still in the possession of the government.

Australian government policy toward indigenous people became more benevolent, but it remained paternalistic until well into the twentieth century, and some argue, to the present day. Restrictions on the sale of alcohol in Australia's Northern Territory, where many indigenous people live, can be seen as evidence that paternalism still prevails, even though the restrictions do not, on their face, take into account the race of the person purchasing alcohol. Against that, it has to be said, many self-governing indigenous communities, acutely aware of the devastation that alcohol has caused to their people, restrict its use in the areas under their control. Indeed, some indigenous leaders have themselves promoted a swing back to more paternalistic policies.

G. Y.: Yet, it seems to me that the issue of alcohol abuse would perhaps be moot had indigenous people in Australia not been subjected to forms of oppression and marginalization in the first place. This is not to deny choice, but to acknowledge that structural forms of oppression, poverty, and marginalization should be taken into account when discussing alcoholism within the context of the lives of indigenous people in Australia. It's also important to note that Native Americans and First Nations people in Alaska also have huge problems with alcoholism. Some indigenous people in Australia are even sniffing petrol, which has it own specific devastating consequences. In what ways do you think that the alcoholism and the substance abuse described above are linked to these larger structural issues that disproportionately impact indigenous people?

P. S.: You are correct that the situation of Australia's indigenous people is in some respects similar to that of Native Americans and First Nations in Alaska, or for that matter in Canada too. The destruction of indigenous culture, and of the way of life that for thousands of years gave meaning and a social structure to the lives of indigenous people, obviously plays a role in leading some of them to drink or try to get high on petrol fumes. Indigenous Australians receive housing, health care, and sufficient income to meet their needs, but what has been taken away can never be restored. The problem goes so deep— and is now often compounded, as we have been saying, with alcohol and petrol abuse, which in turn lead to domestic violence and serious health damage— that it is hard to know how the situation can be turned around.

G. Y.: Above, you mentioned "emotional impulses," but don't you think that white racism is also based upon institutional structures, and not just people acting on the basis of their emotional impulses? In fact, there need not be any immediately identifiable emotional impulses; the institutional system, which includes inertial racist practices that are expressed systemically through banks, education, the prison industrial complex, health care, and so on, just needs to keep functioning, privileging and empowering some (white people) and oppressing and degrading others (Black people). Historically, the concept of institutional racism was systematically deployed during the Black Power Movement in the 1960s and was popularized by Stokely Carmichael (later known as Kwame Toure) and Charles V. Hamilton.

P. S.: What you are here referring to as "the institutional system" includes distinct sectors of society, and each of these sectors has its own divisions and subdivisions. The extent to which they are racist will vary, and it would take detailed evidence and analysis to demonstrate that each of these sectors, and each of its divisions and subdivisions, involves or expresses racist practices. So all I can say, without getting into all the detailed evidence that would be needed to consider each sector and then build back to an overall picture, is that where there is institutional racism, it can take the place of racist emotional impulses. Often, however, there will be racist emotional attitudes as well, and they will then support the institutional structures, making them more difficult to change.

G. Y.: And, in turn, can we say that institutional structures can instill and support certain racist emotional impulses?

P. S.: Yes. Where racist institutional structures continue to exist, they will provide a specific channel for racist feelings and attitudes, and in some situations, will serve to legitimate and reinforce them. But we cannot say how important this is without first determining which institutional structures are still racist, and to what extent and in what ways they are racist.

G. Y.: There is, however, data that shows that Black people suffer disproportionately with respect to bank lending practices, quality of education, quality of health care, arrest rates for nonviolent drug offenses, and so on. However, returning to what you said earlier, do you think that racism is innate or cultural? Even if there appears to be a proclivity toward a kind of xenophobic tribalism expressed within the human species, racism seems to be of a different order, yes?

P. S.: Racism is certainly different from xenophobia, or tribalism. Racism develops its own ideology and, as you pointed out, institutional structures. But if by 'a different order' you mean that racism and xenophobic tribalism have distinct origins, I am not sure about that. It's possible that xenophobia is the underlying impulse that, in different cultures, expresses itself in varying forms, and racism is one of those forms.

G. Y.: Yes. I think that racism may very well have its roots in a kind of xenophobic tribalism, but white racism expresses itself in all sorts of perverse ways and is perhaps motivated from psychic needs/places that transcend xenophobic tribalism.

P. S.: Maybe. We have strong hierarchical tendencies. We like to think that there is always someone below us, and for many people, having power over others seems, regrettably, to reaffirm their sense of self-importance and thus to make them feel good. That may be a psychic need that finds an outlet in racism. For some people, it also finds an outlet in the abuse of animals. In particular, jobs in in factory farms and poultry processing plants are poorly paid, high pressure, and low status. That may be why, year after year, undercover investigators in factory farms and slaughterhouses continue to find evidence of the most atrocious abuse, like workers bashing pigs with steel pipes, or using live chickens as footballs.[1]

G. Y.: To what extent do you think that biases against nonhuman animals are grounded within a certain unethical stewardship toward nature itself? Do you think that this is a specifically Western approach to nature where nature is conceived as an "object" over which we ought to have absolute control? Certainly, Francis Bacon seems to have had this idea. Of course, then there was René Descartes, who argued that nonhuman animals are mere machines.

P. S.: It is true that Western thinking emphasizes the gulf between humans and nature, and also between humans and animals, to a far greater extent than Eastern thinking, or the thinking that is characteristic of indigenous peoples. Yet it is also true that the treatment of both animals and nature is, today, generally worse in the East than in the West. Every visitor to Beijing has breathed in evidence of what China has allowed its industries to do to the air. Laws protecting the welfare of animals in Europe are far in advance of those in Eastern countries, including those with strong Buddhist traditions like Japan and Thailand. China still doesn't even have a national animal welfare law. So if the domination of nature and of animals was originally a Western idea, the sad fact is that it is being taken up avidly in the East, precisely at the time when it is being vigorously challenged in the West.

G. Y.: Black people in the US have been compared to subhuman animals. Even, on various occasions, President Obama has been depicted as a monkey. These charges are meant to degrade. And this attempt to degrade must be understood against the backdrop of Black people in the US fighting against precisely what we see a reduction of our humanity. In 2015, Black people are still fighting to be recognized as fully human, and that our lives matter. How can Black people, on the one hand, reject the reduction of, say, Obama to a monkey, and yet be against speciesism?

P. S.: I don't see any problem in opposing both racism and speciesism. Indeed, to me the greater intellectual difficulty lies in trying to reject one form of prejudice and oppression while accepting and even practicing the other. And here we should again mention another of these deeply rooted, widespread forms of prejudice and oppression, sexism. If we think that simply being a member of the species *Homo sapiens* justifies us in giving more weight to the interests of members of our own species than we give to members of other species, what are we to say to the racists or sexists who make the same claim on behalf of their race or sex?

The more perceptive social critics recognize that these are all aspects of the same phenomenon. The African American comedian Dick Gregory, who worked with Martin Luther King as a civil rights activist, has written that when he looks at circus animals, he thinks of slavery: "Animals in circuses represent the domination and oppression we have fought against for so long. They wear the same chains and shackles."[2] Alice Walker, the African-American author of *The Color Purple,* also has a memorable quote: "The animals of the world exist for their own reasons. They were not made for humans any more than black people were made for white, or women were created for men."[3]

G. Y.: Given that we have not even figured out how to treat those of our own species with dignity and respect, as someone who continues to fight against speciesism, do you have thoughts on how we might effectively dismantle racism?

P. S.: With all of these "isms"—racism, sexism, and speciesism—I'm an optimist about making progress, but a pessimist about achieving complete success any time soon. I'm encouraged by the facts compiled by Steven Pinker in *The Better Angels of Our Nature.* Pinker draws on and completes the argument of my own work, *The Expanding Circle.* I do believe that we are slowly expanding the circle of our moral concern. Pinker provides evidence for the claim that, notwithstanding the media headlines, we are living in less violent and more enlightened times than any previous century. This will surely help marginalized, disempowered, and oppressed groups. We can hope to isolate and reduce the impact of racism and sexism, but eliminating them altogether is going to be a long struggle. With speciesism, unfortunately, we still have much further to go, because it remains the mainstream view.

NOTES

1. See Mercy for Animals, https://www.mercyforanimals.org/investigations.aspx; and Donald G. McNeil, Jr., "KFC Supplier Accused of Animal Cruelty," *New York Times,* July 20, 2004, http://www.nytimes.com/2004/07/20/business/kfc-supplier-accused-of-animal-cruelty.html.
2. Dick Gregory, "The Circus: It's Modern Slavery," *Marin Independent Journal,* April 28, 1998, http://www.peta.org/living/entertainment/dick-gregory-circuses/.
3. Foreword to Marjorie Spiegel, *The Dreaded Comparison: Animal Slavery and Human Slavery* (New York: Mirror Books, 1996), 14.

Seyla Benhabib

George Yancy: How do you see the importance of the public sphere as a site for critically discussing issues regarding the persistence and reality of race in America?

Seyla Benhabib: We are conducting this conversation in the aftermath of the church shootings in South Carolina, the moving and inspiring memorial services to the victims, and the removal of the Confederate flag from the grounds of the South Carolina state capitol. These are events that have raised some of the most significant debates about racial symbolism in the North American public sphere. We have all been reminded of the presence of the past, and to paraphrase William Faulkner, "The past is never dead. It is not even past."[1]

I did not know, for example, that the Confederate flag was revived in Southern states during and after the Civil Rights Movement in clear defiance of racial equality and integration. This was not just a flag that Confederate soldiers fought and died under. It became, as some South Carolinian representatives told us, a symbol of defiance and hatred, and a reminder that the Civil War may have been won but that the battle for overcoming racial prejudice has not ended.

G. Y.: Yes. Within our world, though not restricted to signs and symbols of hatred, we are bombarded by racist signs and symbols.

S. B.: We live in televisual societies that are drowning in messages, images, and symbols that circulate at the click of a mouse. The Internet creates iconic images immediately, and these can have a galvanizing force—for good and for bad. Think of the image of Neda, the young Iranian girl shot in 2009 during antiregime demonstrations in Teheran, or Mohamed Bouazizi, the Tunisian vegetable vendor who in 2011 set himself on fire and whose death prompted the so-called Arab Spring. Images such as these indicate the power of electronic and televisual communication in public culture at large.

These new technologies of the public sphere also challenge democratic societies in that the speed of the circulation of images often overwhelms the communicative and deliberative processes that need to take place among all those affected to unpack and understand what is being implied by these images; whether they mean the same to all involved; and if not, how or why not? In societies that are still strongly divided—even if not legally and constitutionally—along racial and ethnic lines, this public conversation becomes all the more significant for learning to live together. As we saw in the case of the South Carolina massacre, sometimes sorrow and grief, which tear apart the fabric of everydayness, are powerful teachers. They can bring forth unexpected empathy and solidarity.

G. Y.: We far too often fail to understand each other across racial divides. A "postracial" discourse might even occlude the effort to do so. How do we create spaces for understanding the conditions of others, especially within the context of racial boundaries that divide us?

S. B.: Let me begin with a personal memory: I first came to this country from Istanbul, Turkey, as a foreign scholarship student in 1970 to Brandeis University. The program that sponsored me, the Larry Wien International Program, had great outreach success in African countries, and there were many African Wien students like myself. Yet, when we sat in the student cafeteria, the African students would sit in the company of African-American students, and effectively we self-segregated in one of the most progressive institutions of its time in the country.

G. Y.: What was your response to this?

S. B.: I was almost offended by this. I came from a country that was divided along all sorts of ethnic and religious lines, but not the color line. Having been active in the Student Movement of '68 and beyond, to me it was incomprehensible that at least those of us who shared similar political views could not be friends and colleagues. Brandeis, like much of North America at the time, was in the grips of Black separatisms. Angela Davis had been a student of Herbert Marcuse at Brandeis, and I had come to study with Marcuse, not realizing that he had already left for University of California at San Diego! It was not until I attended Yale Graduate School and formed friendships with Lorenzo Simpson and Robert Gooding-Williams that I began to fathom something about depth and hurt of the color line in this country.

I share this anecdote with you because, as the late Iris Marion Young reminded us, to understand one another across racial and many other divides we have to begin by "greeting" and "story-telling." One of the worst offenses of racism is that it blinds us to who the individual person is—the color of your skin becomes the mask that I see and, often, behind which I do not want to see the real person. And as Du Bois, a student of Hegel, reminds us, the one who is in the dominated position is aware of the perspective of the master: she is conscious of herself as being seen by the other, while her perspective is often irrelevant for the master. It is this double-consciousness that we must learn to understand. We must learn to see each other—to use terms that I introduced in *Situating the Self* both as "the generalized" and "the concrete other."[2]

As humans, we are like one another, equally entitled to respect and dignity; but we are also different from one another because of our concrete psychological histories, abilities, racial and gender characteristics, and so forth. Ethics and politics are about negotiating this identity-in-difference across all divides. We live in a "postracial" society only in the sense that we are all generalized others in the eyes of the law; but not in the eyes of those who administer the law—as we learn painfully. Think also of the bank clerk who denies a mortgage loan or even, to use Cornel West's famous example, the New York taxi driver who refuses to pick up the Black man on the curb and drives by! The history of discrimination, domination, and power struggles among the concrete others trumps the standpoint of the generalized other.

G. Y.: In *Feminist Contentions: A Philosophical Exchange*, you observe, "But in its deepest categories Western philosophy obliterates differences of gender as these shape and structure the experiences and subjectivity of the self."[3] Is it also true that Western philosophy obliterates differences of race and how this social category shapes the experiences of nonwhites?

S. B.: Western philosophy, as distinguished from myth, literature, drama, and many other forms of human expression, speaks in the name of the universal. Philosophy emerges when Socrates and Plato show how we have to free ourselves from the "idols of the city," and when the pre-Socratics ask what constitutes matter and the universe, and reject the answers provided by the Greek polytheistic myths. There is something subversive in this philosophical impulse, and even when Plato reinscribes differences of natural talent and ability into the order of the city, he does so by subverting the established order of the Greek polis, in which only the free male heads of households, who were also slave-owners, were free citizens. According to *The Republic*, differences in the city will not be based on social and economic status but on talents and capabilities shown by children differentially at birth: some are bronze, some are silver, and only the very few are gold!

G. Y.: Yes, this is Plato's Noble Lie.

S. B.: Yes. It is important to hold on to these moments in the birth of our discipline because rather than denouncing the Western philosophical tradition as the canon produced by "dead, white men," we need to remember that moment of opening and closure, subversion and restoration, freedom and domination that are present in these texts that we love: from *The Republic* to Hegel's *Philosophy of Right*. From Aristotle's *Politics* to Locke's *Second Treatise of Civil Government* and Rousseau's *Social Contract* and *Emile*, this dynamic of opening and closure holds. And it is in the context of this dynamic of freedom for some and domination for others that we need to understand both gender and racialized difference.

G. Y.: Perhaps we can think here of Hegel's claim that Black people have no *Geist*, and Locke's investment in the slave trade.

S. B.: John Locke was also Tutor and Secretary to the Earl of Shaftesbury, and he wrote the Constitution of the Carolinas for him. Locke is a colonizer, who believes that the white man's labor in appropriating and working the land will create a condition that will be beneficial to all. But who exactly is working the land? Not the master but the servant, and we know historically that there not only were indentured white servants during Locke's time in the British colonies, but also enslaved Black people. In view of the presence of these "others," who haunt the text, what do we make of Locke's theory of consent, equality, and rationality? How many of these ideals are "polluted" by the presence of the many whose equal rationality is never presumed? This is the kind of question that the critical investigation of race in these texts leads us to ask.

Unlike Locke, who is a natural rights theorist, Hegel has a deep sense of history and is a great social realist. I never know quite what to make of the *Lectures on the Philosophy of History*, where he discusses Africa and claims that Black people have no *Geist*. Clearly, he was ignorant. These were popular and popularizing lectures, simplistic in the extreme. Unlike Locke, who was familiar with the realities of colonialism and the slave trade, Hegel does discuss "Lordship and Bondage" in a most sublimated and abstract way in *The Phenomenology of Spirit* without much reference to the colonization of the New World. Yet, he has a great deal to say about the fact that persons cannot be property and that slavery is against human freedom and reason in *The Philosophy of Right*.

All this complicates the question of how to read Hegel, and even more importantly, how to appropriate him for critical philosophy and race theory. Obviously, Du Bois did so brilliantly by separating the power of Hegelian categories from Hegel's own limited historical knowledge and personal prejudice. Du Bois, in *The Souls of Black Folk*, even deployed the concept of *Volksgeist* for Black people, to investigate their own achievements and collective spirit.

G. Y.: I think that it is important to mention that within the Western philosophical tradition, the mind, coded as white and male, is privileged over the body, coded as female or a signification of Blackness, creating a false, disembodied practice.

S. B.: Of course, I agree with you. The master also shows "mastery" over his own feelings and emotions, where domination over the other means domination over the otherness within. As Adorno and Horkheimer argued brilliantly in the *Dialectic of Enlightenment*, in Western philosophy reason is understood as "*ratio*," as instrumental reason, which in Descartes's famous words intends to render us "masters and possessors of Nature."[4] Such *ratio* is an instrument for the social domination of others. And the slave, whether Black or not, is always represented as part of the order of nature that needs to be mastered and subjugated. Such an understanding of rationality brings with it the dualism of mind/body.

Yet we also have to remember that there is a different view of the relation of reason to the emotions, and of body to soul which is more one of education and formation and shaping—not domination. I would argue that from Aristotle to Hume to Smith and even the early Hegel, we find another model of rationality as "embodied intelligence," as the shaping of emotion by reason rather than its domination. John Dewey is the most articulate philosopher of this alternative understanding of rationality.

G. Y.: As a political theorist, do you think democracy is really able to deliver equality to Black people, to fully translate universalistic human rights into real change for them, especially as they have, for hundreds of years, been deemed subpersons?

S. B.: I don't think that it is democracy that is failing Black people in the United States, but the assault on democracy itself through the forces of a global corporate capitalism run amok and the rise of a vindictive and racist conservative movement that is unraveling the civic compact. Democracy is impossible without some form of socioeconomic equality among citizens. Instead, in the United States in the last two decades, the gap between the top 1 percent and the rest has increased; voting rights and union rights have been embattled. There is rampant criminal neglect of public goods such as highways, railroads, and bridges—not to mention the brazen onslaught of big money to buy off elections since the Supreme Court's *Citizens United* decision. We have become a mass democracy that is producing gridlock in representative institutions precisely because it is in the interest of global corporate capitalism to render representative institutions ineffective.

I fear for the future of democracy in the United States, and am grateful that, unlike in other countries, we have a military that believes in democracy and is not inclined to carry out a coup. But there are other forces that are undermining democratic institutions. Democracy can only survive as social democracy, and that is what we are lacking in the United States. Under conditions of growing inequality and plutocratic attacks on democracy, it is the most vulnerable populations such as urban or rural Black communities that are most affected.

NOTES

1. William Faulkner, *Requiem for a Nun* (New York: Vintage, [1950] 2011).
2. Seyla Benhabib, "The Generalized and the Concrete Other: The Kohlberg-Gilligan Controversy and Moral Theory," in *Situating the Self: Gender,*

Community and Postmodernism in Contemporary Ethics (New York: Routledge, 1992), 148–178.

3. Seyla Benhabib, Judith Butler, Drucilla Cornell, and Nancy Fraser, *Feminist Contentions: A Philosophical Exchange* (New York: Routledge, 2013), 19.

4. René Descartes, *Discourse on Method and Meditations on First Philosophy*, trans. Donald A Cress (Indianapolis: Hackett, 1998), 54.

Naomi Zack

George Yancy: What motivates you to work as a philosopher in the area of race?

Naomi Zack: I am mainly motivated by a great need to work and not to be bored, and I have a critical bent. I think there is a lot of work to be done concerning race in the United States and a lot of ignorance and unfairness that still needs to be uncovered and corrected. I received my doctorate in philosophy from Columbia University in 1970 and then became absent from academia until 1990. When I returned it had become possible to write about real issues and apply analytic skills to social ills and other practical forms of injustice. My first book, *Race and Mixed Race* (1991), was an analysis of the incoherence of US Black/white racial categories in their failure to allow for mixed race. In *Philosophy of Science and Race*, I examined the lack of a scientific foundation for biological notions of human races, and in *The Ethics and Mores of Race*, I turned to the absence of ideas of universal human equality in the Western philosophical tradition.

I'm also interested in the role of the university in homelessness and have begun to organize an ongoing project for the University of Oregon's Community Philosophy Institute, with a unique website.

G. Y.: How can critical philosophy of race shed unique light on what has happening, and is still happening in Ferguson, Missouri?

N. Z.: Critical philosophy of race, like critical race theory in legal studies, seeks to understand the disadvantages of nonwhite racial groups in society (Blacks especially) by understanding social customs, laws, and legal practices. What's happening in Ferguson is the result of several recent historical factors and deeply entrenched racial attitudes, as well as a breakdown in participatory democracy.

G. Y.: Would you put this in more concrete terms?

N. Z.: Let's work backward on this. Middle-class and poor Blacks in the United States do less well than whites with the same income on many measures of human well-being: educational attainment, family wealth, employment, health, longevity, and infant mortality. You would think that in a democracy, people in such circumstances would vote for political representatives on all levels of government who would be their advocates. But the United States, along with other rich Western consumer societies, has lost its active electorate (for a number of reasons that I won't go into here). So when something goes wrong, when a blatant race-related injustice occurs, people get involved in whatever political action is accessible to them. They take to the streets, and if they do that persistently and in large enough numbers, first the talking heads and then the big media start to pay attention. And that gets the attention of politicians who want to stay in office.

It's too soon to tell, but "Hands Up, Don't Shoot" could become a real political movement—or it could peter out as the morally outraged self-expression of the moment, like "Occupy Wall Street."

But the value of money pales in contrast to the tragedy this country is now forced to deal with. A tragedy is the result of a mistake, of an error in judgment that is based on habit and character, which brings ruin. In recent years, it seems as though more unarmed young Black men are shot by local police who believe they are doing their duty and whose actions are for the most part within established law.

In Ferguson, the American public has awakened to images of local police, fully decked out in surplus military gear from our recent wars in Iraq and Afghanistan, who are deploying all that in accordance with a now widespread "broken windows" policy, which was established on the hypothesis that if small crimes and misdemeanors are checked in certain neighborhoods, more serious crimes will be deterred. But this policy quickly intersected with police racial profiling already in existence to result in what has recently become evident as a propensity to shoot first. All of that surplus military gear now stands behind such actions, and should offend all members of the civilian public.

G. Y.: How does this "broken windows" policy relate to the tragic deaths of young Black men/boys?

N. Z.: People are now stopped by the police for suspicion of misdemeanor offenses, and those encounters quickly escalate. The death of Michael Brown, like the death of Trayvon Martin before him and the death of Oscar Grant before him, may be but the tip of an iceberg. Young Black men are the convenient target of choice in the tragic intersection of the broken windows policy, the domestic effects of the war on terror, and police racial profiling.

G. Y.: Why do you think that young Black men are disproportionately targeted?

N. Z.: Exactly why unarmed young Black men are the target of choice, as opposed to unarmed young white women, or unarmed old Black women, or even unarmed middle-aged college professors, is an expression of a long American tradition of suspicion and terrorization of members of those groups who have the lowest status in our society and have suffered the most extreme forms of oppression, for centuries. What's happening now in Ferguson is the crystallization of our grief.

We also need to understand the basic motives of whole human beings, especially those with power. The local police have a lot of power—they are "the law" for all practical purposes.

Police in the United States are mostly white and mostly male. Some confuse their work roles with their own characters. As young males, they naturally pick out other young male opponents. They have to win, because they are the law, and they have the moral charge of protecting. So young Black males, who have less status than they do, and are already more likely to be imprisoned than young white males, are natural suspects.

G. Y.: But aren't young Black males also stereotyped according to white racist assumptions?

N. Z.: Yes. Besides the police, a large segment of the white American public believes they are in danger from Blacks, especially young Black men, who they think want to rape young white women. This is an old piece of American mythology that has been invoked to justify crimes against Black men, going back to lynching. The perceived danger of Blacks becomes very intense when Blacks are harmed. And so today, whenever an unarmed Black man is shot by a police officer and the Black community protests, whites in the area buy more guns.

This whole scenario is insane. The recent unarmed young Black male victims of police and auxiliary police shootings have not been criminals. Their initial reactions to being confronted by police are surprise and outrage, because they cannot believe they are suspects or that merely looking Black makes them suspicious. Maybe their grandfathers told them terrible stories, but after the Civil Rights Movements and advancement for middle-class Blacks, we are supposed to be beyond legally sanctioned racial persecution. Their parents may not have taught them the protocol for surviving police intervention. And right now the airwaves and Internet are buzzing with the anxiety of parents of young Black men. They now have to caution their sons: "Yes, I know you don't get into trouble, and I know you are going to college, but you have to listen to me about what to do and what not to do if you are ever stopped by the police. Your life depends on it. . . . Don't roll your eyes at me, have you heard what happened to Trayvon Martin and Michael Brown?"

G. Y.: We can safely assume white parents don't need to have this talk with their children. Do you think white privilege is at work in this context?

N. Z.: The term 'white privilege' is misleading. A privilege is special treatment that goes beyond a right. It's not so much that being white confers privilege but that not being white means being without rights in many cases. Not fearing that the police will kill your child for no reason isn't a privilege. It's a right. But I think that is what 'white privilege' is meant to convey, that whites don't have many of the worries nonwhites, especially Blacks, do. I was talking to a white friend of mine earlier today. He has always lived in the New York City area. He couldn't see how the Michael Brown case had anything to do with him. I guess that would be an example of white privilege. Other examples of white privilege include all of the ways that whites are unlikely to end up in prison for some of the same things Blacks do, not having to worry about skin-color bias, not having to worry about being pulled over by the police while driving or stopped and frisked while walking in predominantly white neighborhoods, having more family wealth because your parents and other forebears were not subject to Jim Crow and slavery. Probably all of the ways in which whites are better off than Blacks in our society are forms of white privilege. In the normal course of events, in the fullness of time, these differences will even out. But the sudden killings of innocent, unarmed youth bring it all to a head.

G. Y.: The fear of Black bodies—the racist mythopoetic constructions of Black bodies—has been perpetuated throughout the history of America. The myth of the Black male rapist, for example, in *Birth of a Nation*. But even after the Civil Rights Movements and other instances of raised awareness and progress, Black bodies continue to be considered "phobogenic objects," as Frantz Fanon would say.

N. Z.: Fanon, in his *Black Skin, White Masks*, first published in France in 1952, quoted the reaction of a white child to him: "Look, a Negro! . . . Mama, see the Negro! I'm frightened!" Over half a century later, it hasn't changed much in the United States. Black people are still imagined to have a hyperphysicality in sports, entertainment, crime, sex, politics, and on the street. Black people are not seen as people with hearts and minds and hopes and skills but as cyphers that can stand in for anything whites themselves don't want to be or think they can't be. And so, from a Black perspective, the Black self that whites serve up to them is not who they are as human beings. This exaggeration of Black physicality is dehumanizing.

G. Y.: Given this, why have so many adopted the idea that we live in a postracial moment in America?

N. Z.: I don't know where the idea of "postracial" America came from. It may have begun when minorities were encouraged to buy homes they could not afford so that bankers could bet against their ability to make their mortgage payments, before the real estate crash of 2007–2008. It sounds like media hype to make Black people feel more secure so that they will be more predictable consumers—if they can forget about the fact Blacks are about four times as likely as whites to be in the criminal justice system. If America is going to become postracial, it will be important to get the police on board with that. But it's not that difficult to do. A number of minority communities have peaceful and respectful relations with their local police. Usually it requires negotiation, bargaining, dialogue—all of which can be set up at very little cost. In addition, police departments could use intelligent camera-equipped robots or drones to question suspects before human police officers approach them. It's the human contact that is deadly here, because it lacks humanity. Indeed, the whole American system of race has always lacked humanity because it's based on fantastic biological speculations that scientists have now discarded, for all empirical purposes.

G. Y.: So is it your position that race is a social construct? If so, why don't we just abandon the concept?

N. Z.: Yes, race is through and through a social construct, previously constructed by science, now by society, including its most extreme victims. But, WE CANNOT ABANDON RACE, because people would still discriminate and there would be no nonwhite identities from which to resist. Also, many people just don't want to abandon race, and they have a fundamental right to their beliefs. So race remains with us as something that needs to be put right.

Charles Mills

George Yancy: You are a philosopher who thinks very deeply about issues of race. Can you provide a sense of your work?

Charles Mills: I think a simple way to sum it up would be as the transition from white Marxism to (what I have recently started calling) Black radical liberalism.

G. Y.: So, how does "white" modify Marxism? And what is it about the modification that helps to account for the transition to what you're now calling Black radical liberalism?

C. M.: Mainstream Marxism has (with a few honorable exceptions) been "white" in the sense that it has not historically realized or acknowledged the extent to which European expansionism in the modern period (late fifteenth century onward) creates a racialized world, so that class categories have to share theoretical space with categories of personhood and subpersonhood. Modernity is supposed to usher in the epoch of individualism. The Marxist critique is then that the elimination of feudal estates still leaves intact material/economic differences (capitalist and worker) between nominally classless and normatively equal individuals. But the racial critique points out that people of color don't even attain *normative* equality.

In the new language of the time of "men" or "persons" (displacing citizens and slaves, lords and serfs), they are not even full persons. So a theorization of the implications of a globally racially partitioned personhood becomes crucial, and liberalism—once informed by and revised in the light of the Black experience—can be very valuable in working this out. In my recent (2017) essay collection for Oxford University Press, *Black Rights/White Wrongs: The Critique of Racial Liberalism*, I try to make a case for this retrieval—the deracialization of a liberalism historically racialized.

G. Y.: So what then is left of the value of Marxism? And does your point mean that there is, historically, a fundamental relationship (perhaps tension) between the political ideals of modernity, the phenomenon of white supremacy, and the subhuman racialization of Black people?

C. M.: Marxism is still of value in various ways: its mapping of the revolutionary transformative effects of capitalism on the modern world; its diagnosis of trends of concentration of wealth and poverty in capitalist societies (Thomas Piketty's 2014 bestseller, *Capital in the Twenty-First Century*, pays tribute to Marx's insights, while distancing itself from some of his conclusions); its warning of the influence of the material economic sphere on the legal, cultural, political, and ideational realms.

It also has various weaknesses, the recounting of which would be too long to get into here. Yes, I would claim that the tension between recognizing (some) people as "individuals" in modernity while subordinating others through expropriation, chattel slavery, and colonialism requires a dichotomization in the ranks of the human. So we get what I termed above a "racial" liberalism, that extends personhood on a racially restricted basis. White supremacy can then be seen as a system of domination that, by the start of the twentieth century, becomes global and which is predicated on the denial of equal normative status to people of color. As members of what was originally seen as a "slave race" (the grandchildren of Ham), Blacks have generally been at the bottom of these hierarchies. But the exclusions were broader, even if other nonwhite races were positioned higher on the normative ladder. At the 1919 post-World War I Versailles Conference, for example, the Japanese delegation's proposal to incorporate a racial equality clause in the League of Nations' Covenant was vetoed by the six "Anglo-Saxon" nations (Britain, the United States, Canada, South Africa, Australia, and New Zealand).[1] So this event brings out in a wonderfully clear-cut way the reality of a global polity normatively divided between racial equals and racial unequals.

G. Y.: How do you understand the meaning of white supremacy? And why is it that the reality of white supremacy has escaped traditional and perhaps contemporary political philosophers and philosophy? I wonder if there isn't a subtle, as you say, "dichotomization in the ranks of the human" operating even here.[2]

C. M.: By 'white supremacy' I mean a system of sociopolitical domination, whether formal (de jure) or informal (de facto), that is characterized by racial exploitation and the denial of equal opportunities to nonwhites, thereby privileging whites both nationally and globally. Historically, I would say that it *was* recognized by traditional (modern) political philosophy, but it was generally taken for granted and positively valorized. After World War II and decolonization, of course, the public expression of such views becomes impolitic. So you then have a retroactive sanitization of the racist past and the role of the leading Western political philosophers and ethicists in justifying Western domination.

In the fields of political theory and international relations, there's now a growing body of revisionist work documenting this history, for example Jennifer Pitts's *A Turn to Empire: The Rise of Imperial Liberalism in Britain and France* (2005), John M. Hobson's *The Eurocentric Conception of World Politics: Western International Theory, 1760–2010* (2012), and Alexander Anievas, Nivi Manchanda, and Robbie Shilliam's coedited *Race and Racism in International Relations: Confronting the Global Colour Line* (2014). Unfortunately, mainstream political philosophy is lagging behind the times in its refusal to admit the significance of this colonial and imperial past, the way it has shaped the modern world, and its implications for conceptualizing justice, both nationally and globally. Here in the United States, for example, we have the absurd situation of a huge philosophical literature on social justice in which racial injustice—the most salient of American injustices—is barely mentioned.

G. Y.: In your 1997 book *The Racial Contract*, you discuss the concept of an "epistemology of ignorance," a term which I believe you actually coined.[3] What is meant by that term? And how do you account for the complete thematic marginalization of racial justice? Does an epistemology of ignorance help to explain it?

C. M.: Yes, I believe it does help to explain it, but first let me say something about the term. The phrasing ('epistemology of ignorance') was calculatedly designed by me to be attention-getting through appearing to be oxymoronic. I was trying to capture the idea of norms of cognition that so function as to work *against* successful cognition. Systems of domination affect us not merely in terms of material advantage and disadvantage, but also in terms of likelihoods of getting things right or wrong, since unfair social privilege reproduces itself in part through people learning to see and feel about the world in ways that accommodate to injustice. "Ignorance" is actively reproduced and is resistant to elimination. This is, of course, an old insight of the left tradition with respect to class. I was just translating it into a different vocabulary and applying it to race. So one can see the idea (and my later work on "white ignorance") as my attempt to contribute to the new "social epistemology" that breaks with traditional Cartesian epistemological individualism, but in my opinion needs to focus more on social oppression than it currently does.

Ignorance as a subject worthy of investigation in its own right has, by the way, become so academically important that in 2015 Routledge published a big reference volume on the topic, the *Routledge International Handbook of Ignorance Studies*, edited by Matthias Gross and Linsey McGoey. The book covers numerous varieties of ignorance over a wide range of different areas and divergent etiologies, but my own invited contribution ("Global White

Ignorance") appears in the section on ignorance and social oppression. In this chapter, I argue that modernity is cognitively marked by a broad pattern in which whites generally endorse racist views (one type of ignorance) in the period of formal global white domination, and then (roughly from the post-World War II, decolonial period onward) shift to the endorsement of views that nominally decry racism, but downplay the impact of the racist past on the present configuration of wealth and opportunities (another type of ignorance). So remedial measures of racial justice are not necessary, and white privilege from illicit structural advantage, historic and ongoing, can remain intact and unthreatened. Insofar as mainstream "white" American political philosophy ignores these realities (and there are, of course, praiseworthy exceptions, like Elizabeth Anderson's 2010 *The Imperative of Integration*), it can be judged, in my opinion, to be maintaining this tradition.

G. Y.: So, would it be fair to say that contemporary political philosophy, as engaged by many white philosophers, is a species of white racism?

C. M.: That would be too strong, though I certainly wouldn't want to discount the ongoing influence of personal racism (now more likely to be culturalist than biological—that's another aspect of the postwar shift), especially given the alarming recent findings of cognitive psychology about the pervasiveness of implicit bias. But racialized causality can work more indirectly and structurally. You have a historically white discipline—in the United States, about 97 percent white demographically (and it's worse in Europe), with no or hardly any people of color to raise awkward questions; you have a disciplinary bent toward abstraction, which in conjunction with the unrepresentative demographic base facilitates *idealizing* abstractions that abstract away from racial and other subordinations (this is Onora O'Neill's insight from many years ago); you have a Western social justice tradition which for more than 90 percent of its history has excluded the majority of the population from equal consideration (see my former colleague Samuel Fleischacker's 2004 *A Short History of Distributive Justice*, that demonstrates how recent the concept actually is); and of course you have norms of professional socialization which school the aspirant philosopher in what is supposed to be the appropriate way of approaching political philosophy, which over the past forty years has been overwhelmingly shaped by Rawlsian "ideal theory," the theory of a perfectly just society.

Rawls himself said in the opening pages of *A Theory of Justice* that we had to start with ideal theory because it was necessary for properly doing the really important thing: nonideal theory, including the "pressing and urgent matter" of remedying injustice.[4] But what was originally supposed to have been merely a tool has become an end in itself; the presumed antechamber to the real hall of debate is now its main site. Effectively, then, within the geography of the normative, ideal theory functions as a form of white flight. You don't want to deal with the problems of race and the legacy of white supremacy, so, meta-phorically, within the discourse of justice, you retreat from any spaces worry-ingly close to the inner cities and move instead to the safe and comfortable white spaces, the gated moral communities, of the segregated suburbs, from which they become normatively invisible.

G. Y.: So, part of what I hear you saying is the need to make important metaphilosophical shifts regarding the whiteness of political philosophy, in particular, and the whiteness of the profession of philosophy, more generally. What are a few of these shifts?

C. M.: Yes, by its very nature, political philosophy is going to have a metadi-mension, in that the drawing of the boundaries of the political is itself often a political act. The best-known example in recent decades of such a challenge is feminist political theory, which classically argued that the conventional liberal division between the public and the private spheres needed to be rethought, since as it stood, gender injustice was obfuscated by the relegation of the family to the "apolitical" realm of the domestic. More recently, we've seen the challenges of postcolonial theory and queer theory, though they have-n't had much of an impact in philosophy circles, and certainly not in analytic political philosophy circles. In the case of race, we need to do various things, like exposing the racism of most of the important liberal theorists (such as Kant), asking what the actual color-coded (rather than sanitized for later pub-lic consumption) versions of their theories are saying (are Blacks full persons for Kant, for example?),[5] and how these racially partitioned norms justified a white-dominant colonial world. As I said above, we need to recognize and investigate the workings of racial liberalism/imperial liberalism, since this is the actual version of liberalism that has made the modern world, and that, more subtly today, is continuing to help maintain its topography of illicit racialized privilege and disadvantage. In the title of one of my (unpublished) papers, we need to be "Liberalizing Illiberal Liberalism," a metareconstruction of liberal theory. Likewise, we need to ask how it came about, and has come to seem normal, that "social justice" as a philosophical concept has become so detached from the concerns of actual social justice movements. Certainly it's not the case that if people in the civil rights community were planning a conference on racial justice next month that they would be heatedly debating which philosophers to invite! Rather, mainstream political philosophy is seen as irrelevant to such forums because of the bizarre way it has developed since Rawls (a bizarreness not recognized as such by its practitioners because of the aforementioned norms of disciplinary socialization). Social justice theory should be reconnected with its real-world roots, the correction of injustices, which means that rectificatory justice in nonideal societies should be the the-oretical priority, not distributive justice in ideal societies. Political philosophy needs to exit Rawlsland—a fantasy world in the same extraterrestrial league as Wonderland, Oz, and Middle-Earth (if not as much fun)—and return to Planet Earth.

G. Y.: Earlier, you mentioned Black radical liberalism. I'm assuming that this position critiques Rawls's ideal theory. If this is so, how does this position engage nonideal theory via-à-vis the historical legacy of white supremacy and its impact on contemporary nonwhite persons? Indeed, what sort of *normative theory* comes out of Black radical liberalism in terms of speaking to solutions to contemporary forms of anti-Black racism?

C. M.: It's a normative theory that, as you correctly say, is centrally located in the realm of nonideal theory, and as such makes rectificatory justice its priority. As a Black radical *liberalism*, it is committed to *moral* individualism (the individual as the locus of value), but this does not require, I would claim, any corresponding commitment to *descriptive* individualism (the individual as an atomic asocial entity). Rather, it recognizes—as a *Black radical* liberalism— that the social ontology of a racialized world is different from the social ontology of an ideal world, so that races are social existents (social constructs) that need to be incorporated into the liberal apparatus. (For ideal-theory liberalism, races don't even exist, since the processes of discrimination that would construct them are absent. This metaphysical divergence is part of the reason why Rawlsian ideal theory is so unhelpful in dealing with these matters.) Likewise, instead of a Rawlsian ideal-theory framing of society as "a cooperative venture for mutual advantage," it begins from the nonideal reality of societies as systems of group domination, with the focus here on racial domination (though of course in intersectional relationships with other kinds of domination). The principles of justice we are then seeking are the principles of nonideal normative theory that would correct for this legacy of domination, as manifest, for example, in second-class citizenship, racial exploitation, and social disrespect. So, as emphasized, they are principles of corrective justice, rather than Rawlsian principles of ideal distributive justice. How does one arrive at them? In other work, for example my 2007 book *Contract and Domination*, coauthored with Carole Pateman (though with separately authored chapters, given our disagreements), I have argued that we can modify Rawls's apparatus so as to use veiled prudential choice as he does, but in the different context of correcting for injustice. So our starting point is not the "original position," but the "later position" of a white-dominant sociopolitical order.

G. Y.: In terms of correcting for racial injustice, does the possibility of reparations fit within your framework, or does this belie any possibility of veiling, as it were?

C. M.: Yes, in the same book with Carole Pateman, *Contract and Domination*, I argue that behind the veil, worried that when it lifts we might turn out to be Black (or some other subordinated racial group), we would endorse principles of corrective justice that would include reparations. We would be mindful—in a way that the orthodox Rawlsian version of the thought-experiment is not (being a "device of representation" for *ideal* theory)—of the risks of ending up as a Black or Latina person in the ghettoes of Chicago, or a Native American on the reservation. So the thought-experiment is modified in such a way as to make the correction of racial injustice central and imperative, rather than being deferred (as it is in the Rawls literature) to a tomorrow that never comes.

G. Y.: How has "standard" (white) political philosophy responded to *The Racial Contract*?

C. M.: In twenty years there has been no response that I'm aware of. The panel discussions that did take place were organized by Black philosophers, or radical white philosophers, or political scientists. Three discussion forums were later published from these panels, one in 1998 in the postcolonial theory journal *Small Axe*, one in a 2003 conference volume on race, and a retrospective forum in 2015 in the new APSA journal *Politics, Groups, and Identities* in which the contributors are all political theorists, and as indicated the journal is a political theory journal. The book has achieved widespread course adoption and corresponding sales in courses in many disciplines across the US, including philosophy. But in certain respects I think it's more recognized outside of philosophy than within it.

G. Y.: How does your work speak to the situation going on in Ferguson, Missouri, and in other places in the United States where racial injustice and conflict is flaring?

C. M.: I would say that unfortunately it brings home the extent to which— in the second decade of the twenty-first century, 150 years after the end of the Civil War and even with a Black president in office—Black citizens are still differentially vulnerable to police violence, thereby illustrating their (our) second-class citizenship. The "racial contract" as a theory of the actual nonideal workings of society and the polity is obviously going to be a far more illuminating framework for understanding and redressing these problems than an idealized social contract which takes socially recognized moral equality and corresponding equitable treatment, independent of race, to be the norm.

G. Y.: Finally, you mentioned the alarming information coming out of cognitive psychology regarding implicit bias. I recall reading recently an article that suggested some Black Americans think that the Secret Service's failure to protect President Obama is due to the fact that he is Black. Why do you think that these perceptions continue to exist? Are they reasonable? I ask this especially because your epistemology of ignorance position does suggest that Black people will have a different epistemic perspective on reality—right?

C. M.: The radically divergent perspectives on reality of Blacks and whites are a straightforward reflection of the radically different realities in which they live. Segregation has deep cognitive consequences as well as the more familiar consequences for one's chances at a good education, home ownership in good neighborhoods, being able to escape gang violence, and so on. That doesn't mean that Black majority opinion is always going to be right, of course. But you would expect that those more subject to the inequities of the system will in general be the ones more likely to have a realistic perspective on it. Whites have not merely an unrepresentative group experience, but a vested group interest in self-deception. Sociologists have documented the remarkable extent to which large numbers of white Americans get the most basic things wrong about their society once race is involved. (See, for some hilarious examples, Eduardo Bonilla-Silva's *Racism without Racists*, now [2017] in its fifth edition.) My favorite example, from a poll a few years ago, is that a majority of white Americans now believe that *whites* are the race most likely to be the victims of racial discrimination! If that's not an epistemology of ignorance at work, I don't know what would be.

NOTES

1. For a detailed account, see chapter 12 of Marilyn Lake and Henry Reynolds, *Drawing the Global Colour Line: White Men's Countries and the International Challenge of Racial Equality* (New York: Cambridge University Press, 2008).
2. Charles W. Mills, *The Racial Contract* (Ithaca, NY: Cornell University Press, 1997), 23.
3. Mills, *Racial Contract*, 18–19.
4. John Rawls, *A Theory of Justice*, rev. ed. (Cambridge, MA: Harvard University Press, 1999), 8.
5. See Charles W. Mills, "Kant and Race, *Redux*," *Graduate Faculty Philosophy Journal* 35 (special issue on race and philosophy), nos. 1–2 (2014): 125–57.

Falguni A. Sheth

George Yancy: Can you discuss your own view of your "racial" identity and how that identity is linked to your critical explorations into the philosophical and political significance of race?

Falguni A. Sheth: Until 2001, I thought of my identity in terms of ethnicity rather than race. I was an immigrant, and in the American imaginary, immigrants were rarely discussed in terms of race. After September 11, 2001, I tried to reconcile what I saw as the profound racist treatment of people (often Arab, Middle Eastern and South Asian migrants) who were perceived as Muslim, with a politically neutral understanding of "racial identity," but it didn't work. That's when I began to explore race as a critical category of political philosophy, and as a product of political institutions. The biggest surprise was my coming to understand that "liberalism" and systematic racism were not antithetical, but inherently compatible, and that systemic racism was even necessary to liberalism. Soon after, I read Charles Mills's *The Racial Contract*, which supported that view.

G. Y.: In what ways do you see liberalism and systemic racism as complementary?

F. A. S.: There isn't a simple link. I am seen as a brown woman, but also as racially ambiguous, which has its own set of problems, as Linda Martín Alcoff discusses.[1] Gender is a key component of racial identity. I suppose that if I were less racially ambiguous, I might have been affected by the Asian "model minority" myth, which identifies Asian women as "good" or "docile," or "smart." But to both whites and nonwhites (including South Asians), my visible, physical self doesn't easily lend itself to that stereotype.

Racial identity is also complicated by class: I went to a public high school in a mostly Irish- and Polish-American working-class town with a large emerging population of brown and Black kids: Puerto Ricans, migrant kids of Mexican,

Colombian, Salvadoran, Nicaraguan, Brazilian, and Portuguese descent. I felt more comfortable there with the brown kids than I did in my middle-class grammar school composed almost entirely of white kids, many of whom, as I realized only as an adult, were racial bullies. To this day, I exhibit personality traits that are stereotypically "Jersey working class," which make it rather awkward to fit into the "genteel academic" circles in which I often find myself these days.

Aside from the cultural hostilities that are foisted upon brown people, my nonambiguous brownness sensitizes me to the vulnerabilities—the lack of rights, security, safety, legal protection—of being nonwhite in a polity that understands "good" and "deserving" members as being white and upper- or at least middle-class men and women. I remember my mother being treated roughly by police when she was in a traffic accident and, again, their indifference when she was targeted by the "Dotbusters," a self-appointed gang of racial nationalists that was assaulting Asian Indians in northern New Jersey in the late 1980s.

When I was finally granted an interview for US citizenship in December 2000, I asked a relative to accompany me in the event that there was trouble. The interview was demanded by the government during the American Philosophical Association meetings in December 2000 (it was virtually impossible to renegotiate the appointment without a long, punishing delay). Despite a heavy snowfall, we arrived an hour early. The INS interviewer was over an hour late in opening up the office, and cheerfully told me that I was lucky he had decided to show up. Conversationally and with a broad smile, he told me a series of stories about the various applicants he had had deported, even if they—like myself—had been in the United States since they were toddlers or infants, even if they knew no one from their countries of birth, and even if they stood to be in danger there. He emphasized how few protections immigrants had, and his message was this: The United States will deport without a second thought, and hey, it's the immigrant's problem, not theirs.

Through such experiences, I have come to understand identity not as racial, but racialized, through populations' relations, and vulnerability, to the state, which also is the basis of my book. The political framework of liberalism, which promises equality and universal protection for "all," depends on people to *believe* those promises, so that racial discrimination, brutality, violence, and dehumanization can be written off as accidental, incidental, a problem with the application of liberal theory rather than part of the deep structure of liberalism.

My book attempts to show that racism, racial exclusion, and racial violence are part and parcel of liberalism. For example, we see the exclusions in early liberal writings: In John Locke's *Second Treatise of Civil Government*, he discusses the social contract and the equal opportunity to "earn" property for everyone, except the "lunatics and idiots," women, and "madmen," or those incapable of reason, and therefore of creating property.[2] The treatise also offers a "just war" theory of slavery.[3] Locke helped write the "Fundamental Constitutions of Carolina," which afforded slave owners complete control over their slaves, alongside representative government. These key ideas are both, "compatibly," in that document.[4]

G. Y.: When you mention vulnerability to the state, I'm reminded of the American eugenics movement in the early twentieth century. Is there a connection here? I'm also reminded of Michel Foucault's concept of bio-power and its relevance within the American eugenics context. How does your work speak to this sort of policing of certain bodies?

F. A. S.: Certainly, that's one example. Political vulnerability is intrinsic to any society, but the rhetoric of universal and equal protection conceals the systematic impulse to exclude certain populations at any given time. The groups who are vulnerable are subject to change, depending upon how threatening they are, and/or how useful it would be to those in power to discard them. In the 1990s, the legal scholar Dorothy Roberts drew attention to how the bodies of American Black women were policed.[5] For example, if they were using drugs while pregnant, they were subject to being charged with crimes and thrown in prison.[6] Vulnerability goes beyond bio-power.

Other examples include the internment of Americans, Peruvians, and other Latin Americans of Japanese origin during the Second World War, or the deportation of Chinese migrants from the United States in the 1880s, and the disfranchisement of Asians from their United States-purchased land in the early 1900s. And needless to say, the wide-scale disfranchising of Muslims in the post-9/11 United States is but another recent example. In each of these cases, they are deprived of protections because they are perceived as threats in some way, and so they become—explicitly or not so explicitly—subject to laws intended to constrain, dehumanize, and criminalize them. It is a gradual process, but they are increasingly vilified, demonized, and dehumanized, which then rationalizes the move to strip them of protections under the mantle of "legality." That is what my work explores.

G. Y.: Given the continuing racial tensions across the nation, how do you see these events as deep problems endemic to liberalism? Or, are such events just a "misapplication" of liberal theory?

F. A. S.: The charge of "misapplication" of liberal theory is, I think, a desire to see selectively—to see only the best possible articulation of liberalism. But liberal frameworks are fundamentally predicated on violence or on rationalizing its effects, such as the conquest of *terra nullius*, of justifying enslavement, or the privation of rights to "idiots," "madmen," and "women." And it's not just Locke's theory that is a problem. Rousseau's very beautiful *Social Contract* must be read alongside his novel, *Émile*, in which Sophie is raised to support Émile's political existence as a true citizen. It is a remarkably sexist, if not misogynistic, understanding of women. But even more to the point, for Rousseau, these are not contradictory; they are rather compatible ideas.

While we can make corrections to "ideal" liberal theory, these corrections are at base additive. They don't fundamentally restructure the foundation of liberal society—namely the promise of universal and equal protections alongside a systematic impulse to violence in the name of "civilizing" the heathens, or for the purposes of maintaining "law and order." At base, this is what the killing of Michael Brown, and the ensuing encounters between the police and protesters in Ferguson, Missouri, have exposed: peace, safety, recognition of one's humanity, law, order, rights will be doled out—or withheld—only in terms that allow those in authority, those with wealth, to remain comfortable. Consider the recent Supreme Court decision to allow restrictive voter ID requirements in Texas—which hurts the poorest citizens. But—and here's the kicker—until we confront the repeated incidents of dehumanization as systematic, and not just a proliferation of accidental violations of humanity, we won't be able to address or challenge the fundamental flaw of liberalism: the "compatibility" between the promise of universal protections for some groups, and violence for others.

G. Y.: The discourse of a "postracial" and a "colorblind" America has been invoked since the election of President Obama. How do you see white power and white privilege as continuing to operate as sites of white sovereign authority?

F. A. S.: The idea of a "postracial" United States is quite bizarre, but it seems to reflect a narrative of distraction: Electing one, two, or even fifty politicians or hiring multiple bureaucrats of color doesn't end systemic racial inequality or discrimination, although it does provide a convenient (if superficial) defense against charges of racism. It also assumes that those politicians or functionaries are actively interested and focused—let alone "authorized" or empowered—to change racially problematic policies. In itself, that is a problematic assumption to make, since racism is systemic and deeply embedded in cultural outlooks, laws, ways of life, and traditions.

The political philosopher Charles Mills's understanding of white supremacy is useful here. Mills uses the term to note that the social contract is predicated on a racial hierarchy where whites are at the top, and Blacks and nonwhites below. I want to clarify that, in terms of political institutions, "whiteness" is a category of power based on a general, but not universal, correlation between those in power and general racial identity. In my work, "whiteness" is not about any individual specifically but about groups in power, and it is negotiated and contoured by factors of gender, class, ethnic identity, and institutional and historical factors—such as how certain groups are understood at various moments.

In "postracial" America, white supremacy continues by ensuring that those in bureaucratic, lawmaking, executive, policy-making functions continue to do what those in the top 5 percent—and others who benefit from white supremacy—need to remain on top: ensure that bankers are not punished; pretend that minorities weren't duped into taking on subprime loans or balloon-payment mortgages; justify rampant invasive surveillance and war-mongering in the name of national security; and arrest and detain immigrants—not just adults, but children! Laws and policies that support these events enable at least two things: the siphoning of money away from poorer, darker, vulnerable, vilified populations who have been subject to racism, violence, and police brutality, and a distraction from the real, everyday problems that affect those populations.

Even in "postracial" America, the US government has continued to wage war on Muslims and Arab populations: detainees still remain in Guantánamo Bay without charges. Some of them are still being force-fed, but the United States military deliberately no longer offers updates on their status; the current administration has created the "disposition matrix," and expanded the drone program, which has killed hundreds, if not thousands, of Yemeni, Somali, and Pakistani civilians. And there is a noticeable absence of a reprimand for the most recent Israeli attacks on Gaza. There is vocal, visible support for these policies, not through invocations of racism but through appeals to national security or "helping bring democracy" to "backward" regions, through justifications about saving "women and children" or innocent "civilians." The institutional effect is that Muslims and Arabs and South Asians are still systematically suffering at a greatly disproportionate rate to any possible "transgressions." It seems that "postracial" America continues to racialize and dehumanize.

G. Y.: How does an epistemology of ignorance work within this context—in, for instance, the comparison between the experience of Black Americans and Asian-Americans?

F. A. S.: As Mills has argued (and as many feminist philosophers and philosophers of race argue), pervasive racial inequality—understood within the frames of legal, social, and political systems—persists because "whites themselves are unable to understand the world that they themselves have made." Here's what that looks like: "Slavery's over. Why are we still discussing it? What does this have to do with poverty? After all, look at all those Asian immigrants: They're not asking for handouts. They're doing very well for themselves."

But such a comparison ignores history and context: Asians who migrated post-1965 to 1985 were a different class of migrants. They were migrating as professionals, or for graduate study, and did not have a history of slavery in the United States, nor a vivid history of racism (ironically, because they were almost entirely prevented from migrating to the United States for forty years, and therefore were largely invisible). They were not migrating on H1B-visas, as many South Asians do today (which restrict access to the full complement of economic and legal protections that permanent residents are eligible to receive). Such a comparison also doesn't acknowledge that white wealth was built not only on the backs of Black slaves, but on the backs of their "free" and mightily persecuted descendants, nor that whites as a group benefit from *not* being recipients of racist treatment. And of course, it neglects the very pointed goal of redlining, which was to block the entry of Blacks into white neighborhoods, and thereby access to better schools for their children, among other benefits. It neglects the specific history of targeted harassment toward Blacks, whether in the South, or after they migrated North, as Ta-Nehisi Coates details in his excellent article in *The Atlantic*, "The Case for Reparations."[7]

And perhaps most importantly, such a comparison falsely focuses on poverty and wealth as a consequence of individual character, rather than as the result of policies that benefit those who already have, while hurting those who have little. This is why I think discussing racism as a "matter of the heart," or individual cultural attitudes is useful but limiting. It inhibits us from considering systemic analyses, and thereby systemic solutions to systemic problems.

G. Y.: There are some theorists who continue to want to reduce race to class. My sense is that W. E. B. Du Bois was correct regarding his claim that even poor whites possess whiteness. Do you think that such a distinction has any relevance in our contemporary moment in American history?

F. A. S.: In *Black Reconstruction in America: 1860–1880*, Du Bois discussed the wages of whiteness paid to white workers by the Southern white bourgeoisie— through the vehicle of racial apartheid—in order to divide and conquer the working class, and get white and Black workers to hate and fear each other, despite, as he says, "their practically identical interests."[8] There is certainly truth in the claim for today, but it also depends on context, geography, historical moment, and situation—and the racial perspectives of those in power.

Poor whites won't be racially profiled by white police, or store clerks, or white or nonwhite landlords to the same degree as darker men across economic classes will be. Yet, thinking institutionally, because economic policies adversely impact those who are already disadvantaged, poor Blacks and poor whites will both suffer that impact. However, those in power and positions of authority will most often blame working-class and poor Blacks for various moral character flaws. We have seen it countless times: from Daniel Moynihan's infamous 1965 report that traces poverty to character flaws of African-Americans to Ronald Reagan's vilification of poor Black women who then came to be referred to as "welfare queens," to President Obama's multiple admonitions to Black men to be more responsible fathers. This is despite the fact that we have ample evidence illustrating that Black men are incarcerated six times as often as white men, and that they suffer from racial profiling and discrimination and unfair laws like "stop and frisk," which collectively inhibit them from finding employment, housing, or economic success.

Presumably, if poor Blacks suffer from "character flaws," then so do poor whites and other populations of color, but we rarely hear the same moral admonitions directed toward them.

G. Y.: Lastly, from what you've argued, engaging in a critical overthrow of white supremacy as a system will certainly involve a *systemic* approach. Yet, people of color must deal with virulent manifestations of white racism on an everyday basis, even enacted by "well-intentioned" whites.

F. A. S.: Certainly. Those, it seems to me, are but symptoms of institutional aggressions, manifestations of virulent racism that are expressed through the larger structures of our society. How can those aggressions disappear without the simultaneous coextensive reform of our larger juridical, legal institutions, and federal laws and policies that, at some level, endorse and approve those microaggressions? While it is important to note those microaggressions, I think, reform and redress have to occur at the macrolevel, with policies that address socioeconomic, and political change. Many people take their cues from the laws under which they live; if the laws reflect respect and dignity, then . . .

NOTES

1. Linda Martín Alcoff, *Visible Identities: Race, Gender and the Self* (New York: Oxford University Press, 2006).
2. John Locke, *Two Treatises of Government* (New York: Hafner Press, 1947), par. 60; 61.
3. Locke, *Two Treatises*, chapter 3.
4. The Fundamental Constitutions of Carolina: March 1, 1669, http://avalon.law. yale.edu/17th_century/nc05.asp. Regarding slave ownership, see clauses 107 and 110.
5. Dorothy E. Roberts, *Killing the Black Body: Race, Reproduction, and the Meaning of Liberty*, 1st ed. (New York: Vintage, 1997).
6. Roberts, *Killing the Black Body*, ch 4.
7. Ta-Nehisi Coates, "The Case for Reparations," *The Atlantic*, June 2014, https:// www.theatlantic.com/magazine/archive/2014/06/the-case-for-reparations/ 361631/.
8. W. E. B. Du Bois, *Black Reconstruction in America 1860–1880* (New York: Free Press, 1998), 700–1.

PART IV DISCUSSION QUESTIONS

1. Noam Chomsky suggests that "intentional ignorance" is characterized by the desire and efforts to whitewash the past to erode uncomfortable or inconvenient truths. Thomas Jefferson and John Quincy Adams are

symbols of this tendency insofar as they know first-hand the atrocities in which they are participants and in fact recognize the moral repugnancy of slavery and genocide even as they engage in them. In our time, "intentional ignorance" has flourished in multiple and complex forms. Charles Mills identifies his concept of "epistemology of ignorance" in the global trend to adhere first to racist views and then to "shift to the endorsement of views that nominally decry racism, but downplay the impact of the racist past on the present configuration of wealth and opportunities." Another manifestation of this ignorance is evident in Falguni A. Sheth's discussion of the "narrative of distraction." In what ways are claims about a "postracial" America, expressed in "colorblindness" at the level of the individual, distractions from the racial injustices that currently exist and have existed in the past?

2. Charles Mills explains that Rawls employs ideal theory for the sake of developing nonideal theory, but that the latter's ideal theory has mistakenly become an end in itself. Radical Black liberalism dwells in the nonideal reality in which race necessarily impacts social ontology. Radical Black liberalism seeks "principles of justice . . . [that] are the principles of nonideal normative theory that would correct for this legacy of domination, as manifest, for example, in second-class citizenship, racial exploitation, and social disrespect." The emphasis, Mills explains, is on corrective rather that distributive justice, and would include reparations, for example. Develop an account for what a "nonideal normative theory" is, and determine what might constitute the principles of such a theory.

3. Nancy Fraser addresses the question, "Is it possible to abolish racial oppression without abolishing capitalism?" She argues that it is theoretically possible, but nearly impossible in practice. The difficulty is rooted in part in capitalism's exceptional ability to nourish subjectivation through both exploitation and expropriation. Fraser explains that "in the absence of a cross-racial movement to abolish a system that requires expropriation as well as exploitation, their grievances find expression in the growing ranks of rightwing authoritarian populism." Naomi Zack suggests that loss of agency fuels fear and its attended hatred for the other. She notes as one example that when young Black men are shot by police officers and there is popular protest in response, neighboring whites buy more firearms. Falguni A. Sheth's personal experience following the terror attacks on September 11, 2001 and the widespread disfranchising of Muslim Americans further supports Zack's suggestion. Selya Benhabib expresses concern over the future of democracy that is being damaged by global capitalist structures "run amok" and the corresponding "rise of a vindictive and racist conservative movement." In this complex framework, the ebb and flow dynamic of progress and pushback, loss of agency and vicious retaliation cannot be ignored. Thus it seems necessary to address loss of agency and its toxic

effects if we want to dismantle racial oppression without abolishing capitalism. How do we get started with this work, and what might we use to replace the oppressive support system on which that capitalism currently depends?

4. Peter Singer discusses the role of emotional impulse in perpetuating racism, despite the widespread rational acceptance that racism is wrong. On the one hand, unthinking emotional reactions without ethical reflection make education, progress, and tolerance impossible. On the other hand, emotion's counterpoint cannot be "pure" reason. Mastery of emotion and reason itself are used to render the other docile. Seyla Benhabib discusses this destructive and subjugating role of reason in the history of philosophy in Descartes's desire to make us "masters and possessors of Nature" and Hegel's master-slave dialectic. Reason is, she writes, "an instrument for the social domination of others." Since emotion and reason can both be used to fight against or galvanize a white racist framework, how can we best direct them against that framework? The relationship between emotion and reason is further complicated concerning race with respect to terror. To be terrorized is fundamentally "to be susceptible to socially tolerated violence . . . to be constantly bracing oneself in expectation of a blow, without knowing when or whence it will come," in Nancy Fraser's words. Can we effectively diffuse the toxic effects of the vicious emotional outbursts that Singer discusses when terror characterizes the mode of living for an individual in a terrorizing environment? Can we effectively diffuse those effects when terror becomes an abstract entity that characterizes a country's domestic and international policy and infiltrates its social structures?

5. Discuss the central concept of dehumanization that discussions of race, history, capitalism, ethics, and neoliberalism have in common. What tools might the different disciplines provide to address the problem of dehumanization and restore humanity to those living within a matrix of both oppressive ideologies and structures as well as human ethical and epistemological failures?

Race Beyond the Black/White Binary

Linda Martín Alcoff

George Yancy: What is the relationship between your identity as a Latina philosopher and the philosophical interrogation of race in your work?

Linda Martín Alcoff: Every single person has a racial identity, at least in Western societies, and so one might imagine that the topic of race is of universal interest. Yet while whites can sometimes avoid the topic, for those of us who are not white—or less fully white, shall I say—the reality of race is shoved in our faces in particularly unsettling ways, often from an early age. This can spark reflection as well as nascent social critique.

The relationship between my identity and my philosophical interest in race is simply a continuation through the tools of philosophy of the pursuit that I began as a kid, growing up in Florida in the 1960s, watching the Civil Rights Movement as it was portrayed in the media and perceived by the various parts of my family, white and nonwhite. I experienced school desegregation, the end of Jim Crow, and the war in Indochina, a war that also made apparent the racial categories used to differentiate peoples, at enormous cost. It was clear to me from a young age that it was too often the case that white North Americans were the ones with no value for life, at least the life of those who were not white.

My sister and I came to the southern United States from Panama as young children and had to negotiate our complex identities (mixed-race Latina and white) within a social world where racial borders were being challenged and renegotiated and, as a result, ceaselessly patrolled and violently defended.

G. Y.: So, given these early experiences, were you drawn to philosophical questions of racial identity?

L. M. A.: In philosophy I was drawn to topics of knowledge (epistemology) and metaphysics, never ethics, which may seem odd given this background. But the issue of metaphysics raised questions about how we name what is, and the issue of epistemology raised questions about how we know what we think we know. Hence, these subfields opened the way for me to consider the contestations over reality as well as over authority. Of course, the received canon in philosophy was both useful and infuriatingly silent on the topics I was most interested in: bodies showed up little, and difference was routinely set aside, and yet the debates over mereological essentialism and other concepts illustrated the possibility of multiple right answers and of a social and practical context silently guiding the debate. Quine was in vogue and his ideas about contingent rather than necessary ways to name what is was a short step from the political analysis of dominant ways of naming that I was interested in.

For many years, my personal and my philosophical life were lived as parallel tracks with little overt interaction. I went to demonstrations and then came home to finish my Heidegger homework. I glanced across the fence now and then, but did not attempt serious philosophical engagement with race until I had published enough that had nothing to do with race or gender or Latin American philosophy to establish a foothold in the profession. Tenure set me free, and I immediately began a project on the metaphysics of mixed-race identities.

G. Y.: You mentioned how questions of embodiment were not treated in any substantive way in your early philosophical training. Why is it that the profession of philosophy, generally speaking, is still resistant to questions of embodiment and by extension questions of race?

L. M. A.: In my view this is primarily a methodological problem. Philosophers of nearly all persuasions—analytic, continental, pragmatist—aim for general and generalizable theories that can explain human experience of all sorts. And the ultimate aim, of course, is not description but prescription: how can we come to understand ourselves better, to know better, to understand our world better, and to treat each other better? Worthy goals, but they are usually pursued with a decontextualized approach, as if the best answers would work for everyone. To get at that metalevel of generality, some aspects of one's context need to be set aside, lopped off, cut out of the picture, and this has traditionally meant the concrete materiality of human existence as we actually experience it in embodied human form.

This is just a way of saying that the body *had* to be ignored except in so far as we could imagine our bodies to be essentially the same. And to achieve that trick of imagination—to imagine all of our wild diversity in embodiment to be irrelevant—required a bad faith that can be seen throughout the canon: racist asides and ridiculous theories about women alongside generic pronouncements about justice and beauty and the route to truth.

I call it bad faith because, on the one hand, nearly all the great philosophers divided human beings into moral and intellectual hierarchies even while, on the other hand, they presumed, from their consciously particularist space, to speak for all. Hence, methodologically, the problem for philosophy is how to speak *for* all when one does not, in fact, speak *to* all. And the solution is to enact a doublespeak in which one justifies not speaking to the mass of humanity at the same time that one imagines oneself to be speaking for the human core that exists in all of us. The body, and difference, is simultaneously acknowledged and disavowed.

This is why philosophers such as Bartolome de Las Casas in the sixteenth century and W. E. B. Du Bois from even his early writings in the nineteenth century are such powerful figures: they each explore their own specificity and its impact on how they view the world and others, even to how they formulate moral questions. They model a discourse that can become part of a general dialogue in which others can have a voice as well.

G. Y.: Yes. I understand your point about methodology and bad faith. Speak to how this presumption to speak for others, to place under erasure our diversity of embodiment, is something that is linked specifically to whiteness, especially within the context of our field that continues to be dominated by white males.

L. M. A.: Entitlement is a core feature of white subjectivity, as numerous works by sociologists such as Joel Feagin document. There is a sense of entitlement to rights and resources, comfort and attention, access to space and to deference, or being granted presumptive credibility until proven otherwise. Entitlement is always complicated and modified by class, gender, religion, and sexuality; poor whites, for example, learn early on to defer to others. But white people as a whole, or as an imagined grouping, are the presumed paradigms of rights-bearing American citizens. And this seeps into one's consciousness.

It is inevitable that these social realities will find some manifestation in white-majority (or even exclusively white) philosophy classrooms. This is especially so given the fact that philosophy curricular requirements almost never include course topics that might enhance students' knowledge or capacity to reflect about these realities. So it should be no surprise that the work (teaching and scholarship) produced by a white-majority philosophy profession manifests, in general, an assumed entitlement to rights and resources, comfort and attention, access to space, and deference. They assume the ability to access all knowledge, and resent (and resist) theories that might restrict that access, on the grounds, for example, that one's identity and experience play a formative role in what one can understand on some matters. They assume the right to dominate the space—literal and figurative—of philosophical thought and discussion. They assume the right to have attention, and they assume this is nonreciprocal: others should be reading their work even while they neglect to read the work of nonwhites. I am speaking in gross generalities that will be unfair to numerous individuals, but the patterns I am describing are, I suggest, familiar to marginalized philosophers.

G. Y.: In what way has Latin American philosophy challenged such bad faith and the proclivity to be so methodologically narrow?

L. M. A.: The philosophies developed in the colonized world during the emergence of European modernity have not had the luxury of such universalist pretensions or obliviousness. Philosophy in Latin America is very diverse, but one can discern a running thread of decolonial self-consciousness and aspiration. Thinkers from Europe and the United States persist even today in dismissing Latin American philosophy, and as a result, Latin American philosophers have had to justify their prerogative, and their ability, to contribute to normative debates over the good, the right, and the true. But this has had the beneficial result of making visible the context in which philosophy occurs, and of disabling the usual pretensions of making transcendent abstractions removed from all concrete realities.

All of the great thinkers, from Simon Bolivar to José Martí, José Carlos Mariátegui, José Vasconcelos, Leopoldo Zea, Che Guevara, and Enrique Dussel, have had to develop philosophical arguments within a contextual consciousness ever mindful of colonialism's effects in the realm of thought. Since the social identities—racial and ethnic—of their contexts were made grounds for dismissing claims to self-determination or original thought, each of these thinkers engaged with the question of Latin American cultural, racial, and ethnic identities and histories. It's a rich tradition. Knowledge requires self-knowledge. Philosophy's lack of diversity in North America has compromised its capacities for both self-knowledge and knowledge.

G. Y.: Your very last point raises issues of standpoint epistemology, the idea that one's social identity is sometimes relevant to what one notices and how one makes judgments. I'm thinking here in terms of Supreme Court Justice Sonia Sotomayor's comment that her experience being a wise Latina woman would help her to reach better legal conclusions than a white male. My sense is that there still exists within America the assumption (inside and outside the academy) that Latino/a voices and Black voices are biased/inferior voices. Yet, both within and outside of the academy, it seems that there is a positive relationship between "racialized" identities and the production of knowledge. I think that this question also speaks to the "reality" of race as lived. What is your view on this?

L. M. A.: One can make an analogy between how Latin American thinkers have had to theoretically reflect about the intellectual and political effects of their geographical location and ethno-racial identities, and the way everyone who is not white in North America has had to engage similar questions just as a necessity of survival in a white supremacist society. So as a result, outside of white dominant spaces, the set of debates and discussions about such topics is much richer, older, and more developed, especially in the African-American philosophical tradition, than anywhere else. Knowledge is not an automatic product of the experiences engendered by different identities, I would suggest. But there is more motivation to pursue certain kinds of knowledge, and one often has willing and able interlocutors in one's immediate home and community environments who are comfortable with such topics and have reflected on and debated them. And it is also true that simply the experience of being nonwhite provides a kind of raw data for analysis.

Sotomayor received so much vitriol for her claims about the link between identity and judgment that she was forced to renege on them in order to be appointed to the Supreme Court. But the view she expressed is quite a common-sense view most everyone actually accepts. Of course it is the case that our differences of background and experience can affect what we are likely to know already without having to do a Google search, and these differences also influence what we may be motivated to find out. There is a wealth of empirical work on jury selection that bears this out, and the congressmen and lawyers grilling Sotomayor knew this literature. But there is a taboo on speaking about the epistemic salience of identity in our public domains of discourse, although it is a taboo that primarily plays out only for nonwhites, women, and other groups generally considered lower on our unspoken epistemic hierarchies.

During the Sotomayor kerfuffle, Jon Stewart helpfully played back clips of all the Congressmen who played up their veteran status in their political campaigns, and even Supreme Court nominees who talked about their own modest class backgrounds as relevant to their appointment to the Court. It is only accepted for whites, and white men in particular, to use their particularity to augment their epistemic authority in this way, to generate a heightened trust in their judgment, and almost never for others to do the same.

This is itself an interesting issue to explore. Why can the mainstream media acknowledge the positive epistemic contributions of white particularities but no others? I believe the answer is that it would simply be too dangerous to the social status quo. Admitting the relevance of diversity to knowledge would require too much social change at every level and in nearly every social institution.

Some believe that capitalism will solve this problem with its natural tendency to maximize profit over all other considerations, such that if racism and sexism thwart product development, capital will promote inclusion. I am skeptical of this. For one thing, capitalism profits too much from racism and sexism to let go. And secondly, the need of corporations to diversify their management pool has more to do with the need to manage effectively a diversity of low-paid workers than anything else. And if racism and sexism helps maintain the disempowered and underpaid conditions of those workers, capitalism wins both ways.

If we were to acknowledge the relevance of identity to knowledge, the solution would not be simplistic diversity quotas, but a real engagement with the question of how our unspoken epistemic hierarchies have distorted our educational institutions, research projects, academic and scientific fields of inquiry, and general public discourse across all of our diverse forms of media. And then we could pursue a thorough attempt at solutions. Philosophers working in many domains—concerning epistemology, the social ontology of identity, moral psychology, the philosophy of science, and others—could contribute to these efforts, but philosophy must first direct such efforts internally.

G. Y.: Lastly, what do you say to those philosophers of color who might feel the pain of rejection, especially because, for them, their racialized identities are so important to their philosophical practice/projects? And, more generally, what advice do you have for our profession in terms of challenging those "unspoken epistemic hierarchies"?

L. M. A.: Our profession continues to be an inhospitable climate for philosophers of color working on race, so the first thing to do is to acknowledge this. Some significant progress has been made, it is true, and there are a few high-profile individuals, but one can no more imagine that these individual successes show that the climate is now open and fair than we can imagine that Oprah's and Beyoncé's successes prove that all is fine for Black working women. Too many philosophers still operate with depoliticized notions of "real" philosophy and consider both feminist and critical race work suspect because they are politically motivated rather than concerned only with truth. The result is a lot of microaggressions, as well as general neglect of the emerging scholarship.

I am not optimistic about convincing the mainstream. I don't believe that if we just do serious and good philosophical work that its merit will shine through. To believe that one would have to believe that philosophy is a true intellectual meritocracy, that philosophers are immune from racism and sexism and implicit bias, and that long-standing framing assumptions about the depolitical nature of philosophy will not skew judgment.

A better solution lies in working multiple strategies: (1) carving out, and regularly nurturing, those spaces—journals, professional societies, conferences—in which all who are interested in the subfield of critical race philosophy can develop our work within a constructively critical community; (2) developing our understanding of the sociology of the profession, in other words, the extent, causes, and effects of its demographic challenges and hostile climate. We need to develop this understanding in a philosophical way, which might include, for example, new and more realistic norms of epistemic justification and argumentation that can provide some redress for our nonideal context of work; (3) doing as much as we can to widen and strengthen the stream of young people of color who make a choice, an informed choice, hopefully, to try their hand at philosophy. The burden is on the marginalized and our allies to do this work. What else is new?

But what I would also say to young philosophers is that this is actually a great time to join the discipline. We have the beginnings of a critical mass, a beachhead, with multiple conferences now each year, several organizations such as the Society for the Study of Africana Philosophy, the Caribbean Philosophical Association, and the California Roundtable on Race. There is a new journal, *Critical Philosophy of Race*, as well as some receptivity in existing journals. And there is a growing community of frankly rather brilliant people busily working to advance our collective understanding of race, racism, and colonialism. Also, there are many students in undergraduate classrooms receptive to these questions. The margins are flourishing and growing. In this sense, it is a positive moment.

Eduardo Mendieta

George Yancy: How do you understand the logic of a postrace discourse in our contemporary moment?

Eduardo Mendieta: Let me begin by saying that we are no more "postrace" because of Obama's presidency than we would be "postgender" if Hillary Clinton is elected to the White House.

I do agree that shortly after Obama's election there was a triumphalist rhetoric that reveled in the idea that "we" had left behind the shame of racism, that somehow Obama's election had redeemed the nation and elevated us beyond the still-too-evident indications that we had not. I am not sure that discourse is convincing, although it still has slivers of America in its grip. Nonetheless, I think ideologies are not only epistemic veils; they are also diagnostic. They point to certain tendencies in our society.

G. Y.: In the case of "postracialism," provide a few examples.

E. M.: I would single out four factors. First, I think "postrace" is symptomatic of the hegemony of the gospel of "neoliberalism" that has spelled the dismantling of the social welfare state—that is, the retrenchment and elimination of social programs aimed at remedying and alleviating social inequities through the intervention of programs underwritten by Federal and State governments. Postliberalism is an economic dogma that says that the best economy is the least steered or balanced by government intervention. It is also a political ideology that says that the best politics is the least politics, or rather that the best politics is when we leave politics alone. Neoliberalism means the uncoupling of economics from politics. In this sense, neoliberalism is an antipolitical politics. Neoliberalism is an ideology, and as such it is also prescriptive; it is a prescription that says that we need to think of social agents as financial assets, as economic units, as, let us say, "hedge funds." This is what has been called the "entrepreneurial self." I think these dimensions of "neoliberalism" were captured aptly by the '80s and '90s discourse of the "contract with America." Evidently, this language dissimulates the ways contracts are always between "solvent" and "credible" creditors that could be signatories to an "exchange" that allegedly would be symmetrically beneficial. Mesmerized by this ideology, we are unable to comprehend the persistence of race. We are lulled into thinking that racialized subjects remain in their positions of disadvantage and marginalization not because of institutional and societal constraints, and deliberate discrimination, but due to individual failures. Neoliberalism says that if one is disadvantaged, marginalized, deprived, poor, victimized, and so on, it is because the individual is culpable, completely responsible for their situation; he or she has failed to properly take care of themselves, has failed to properly make of themselves their own asset; which continues the big lie: that the system as such is designed to enable everyone to be their own entrepeneurs. Neoliberalism, as a form of economic reductionism, atomizes race into an individual choice, while depoliticizing the causes of racist institutions. Neoliberalism reduces race to this: If you invoke race, it is because you want to come up with an alibi for your failure.

Second, I think "postrace" expresses a malaise or confusion that has arisen from the dramatic demographic changes of the US population over the last three to four decades. In many states, mostly on both coasts of the country, and the so-called Sun Belt, whites have become minorities and minorities have become majorities. This is what has been called, invidiously, the "Browning of America." Latino/as are now the largest minority, and are projected to become a quarter of the US population by 2050. This demographic transformation would seem to indicate that the racial matrix of "Black/white" has been displaced, or at least called into question, from the center of the imaginary of the US. This is what "postracialists" seem to think, namely, that we are "postrace" because now "Blacks" and "whites" are minorities within minorities. But these demographic shifts have neither displaced nor abolished the "white/ Black" racial matrix; instead they have shifted the racial boundary to one side or another of the "color line," and they have mutated it into new modalities of racializing discourses, and above all practices and technologies. Let us take the "Latino/a" or "Hispanic" label, which operates both as an ethnic and as a racial label, which is played against the "Black" label. Latino/as are neither "Black" nor "white," but they are treated as though they were "Black." We have the birth of a third race, an ethnorace.

There is, then, a third factor that dictates the "logic"—as you call it—of "postracialism," and this has to do with the mythologizations, or mirages, of our hypermediatized culture. Here I would appeal to Patricia Williams's important insights into what she calls the "dynamics of display" that bounces Blacks between "hypervisibility and oblivion."[1] We see "Blacks" everywhere on the Media, as actors, as athletes, as secretaries of defense, as Supreme Court justices, as the face of American popular culture, as the therapists and cultural arbiters of US culture, as the poets and Nobel Prize writers who are our ambassadors to the world of letters, while we don't see all the faces "at the bottom of the well," the faces and bodies exiled to the carceral archipelagos of the prison industrial complex, to use Angela Davis's language, the families of generations consigned to the "Gray Wastes"—the assemblage of institutions that link poor ghettos, unemployment lines, detention centers, prisons, and of course, the postprison branding institutions—as Ta-Nehesi Coates refers to them.[2] As you point out in your own work, "Blacks" are seen and not seen. It is as though Blacks were afflicted by an epidermal malady: they are a reflecting surface that reflects back only what the white eye wants to see, not what it must see or could see." So, "postrace" names this double malady: we see only what we want to see and not what we must and can see.

The fourth factor has to do with something that was diagnosed, at least for me, by Cornel West in his pioneering book *The American Evasion of Philosophy: A Genealogy of Pragmatism* (1989), namely the ideology of "Adamic Innocence" that undergirds the deeply ingrained myth about the newness and innocence of this country. I think the relative youth of our country has licensed the myth that, in contrast to Europe, and the Motherland in general, we are not weighted by the sins of feudalism, colonialism, totalitarianism, genocides, and the slave trade. I think this theologically sanctioned "Adamic Innocence" has resulted in what I would call "Promethean Amnesia." We are the country of the short history, and thus, of the collective imaginary that dispenses with the weight of its own history. "Promethean Amnesia," furthermore, is potentiated by the demographic shifts that, like waves of the sea, continue to wash away innocently and without remorse the sins of our past. We, and I count myself among them, the new generation of assimilated immigrants and children of immigrants, take up the mantle of "American," step up on the pedestal of a protean America, but without assuming its history. We are not the latecomers, but the newcomers who renew the nation's mythological innocence. But, of course, history is not simply a narrative that we weave to make sense of our collective self; it is also the very material house that slavery, Jim Crow, the Ghetto, the Japanese internment camps, the Chinese Exclusion Act, the Prison Industrial complex, and the Gray Wastes, the many Proposition 187s, the many Immigration Acts of Congress that criminalize immigrants from certain specific parts of the world, all of which continue to reproduce race in the US.

I think these four factors are what nourish the fiction that we are "postracial." But, at the same time, I think these factors have proven to be poor nutrients, as they are all unsustainable and indefensible. Let me say one last thing about why I am deeply skeptical of "post" discourses in general. They all operate on a certain way of thinking about history specifically, and temporality in general. The "post" discourses assume that history is homogeneous, synchronous, directional, and teleological. That at its core, history is driven by a developmentalist logic, each stage building on the prior while superseding it. History is the great ladder of ever-advancing and progressing humanity; at each moment, we can throw away that ladder and be content to have climbed to the heights we have allegedly ascended. But, in fact, we can no more say that we are "post" racial than we can say that race in the US has remained unchanged since the postbellum "Reconstruction" and the de-constitutionalization of "Jim Crow." History is not a ladder. It is certainly not a theodicy, that is, the belief that any modicum of progress is built on the suffering of the many and the most destitute—in fact, neoliberalism is the latest version of Christian theodicy. It is more like a haunted plantation, a crumbling ghetto, Alcatraz, La Frontera, the roads built by leased prison labor, in which the past is barely past, and in which the future is mortgaged to the dream of the "Dreamers," the dream of those who refuse to carry the weight of our history.

G. Y.: You know, on this point about the "Browning of America," one might think that this is an inherent threat to white power, privilege, and hegemony. It seems to me that this is a non sequitur. I think that "post-Apartheid" South Africa is a counter to such an assumption. Whites there continue to have most of the real power. Whites in the US can continue to flourish existentially, politically, and economically despite the "Browning" process.

E. M.: Yes, yes, I agree, especially if we think of South Africa, and I would say Brazil as well, as counterexamples. Notwithstanding what I generally take to be a salutary effect of Latino/as on the whole racial discourse in the US, there are ways in which Latino/as contribute to the entrenchment of white power and privilege. Some of "my" people totally buy the "Dreamers" dream. Like the Irish, Italians, and to a certain extent the Jews, some Latino/as would like to become white. But, then, too many of us are really Black folk, mixed like a creole dish, or a Sancocho—poor people stew. *Mestizaje* is the crucible that made us, already before Colon left Europe to "discover" the new world. But that is another story.

G. Y.: Returning to President Obama's tenure for the last eight years, do you think that his longevity has helped to underwrite such a "postrace" discourse?

E. M.: Let me begin by noting, or confessing, that I was one of the many Americans who volunteered to canvass for Obama back in the summer of 2008 when he was first running for office. At the time, I lived on Long Island, certainly not a bastion of liberalism, much less of pro-Black political sentiment. Still, I remember that after I volunteered I was sent to canvass in the north districts of Philadelphia, in mostly white but also some racially mixed neighborhoods. It was a beautiful and powerful experience. My then wife and I had voted for Nader in the 2000 election that gave us Bush, and we felt guilty and partly responsible for the debacle that befell us. So, this time around I felt that I had to do something. I had to put shoulder to the boulder, or shut up.

In any event, it was a great civic education for me. Many people welcomed me into their houses, and we talked politics, about the candidates, and about Obama. I remember that many were skeptical, but not for "racist" reasons; others were truly energized by Obama's very presence as a candidate. Now, mind you, I was sent to canvass in middle-class areas, in areas of Pennsylvania that are liberal and perhaps even Democratic strongholds, though I did come across some Republicans. I also remember very distinctly arriving in California for a conference as the election was taking place. I had been traveling on a red eye, and was getting bits and pieces of the news about the ballot results. But, when I took BART to San Francisco, there was a sense of collective joy. I saw people smiling, some were even tearing up—I myself teared up in joy and a bit of self-congratulation, as Obama was declared President-Elect. I felt part of a great moment in our history. I had done my bit in shifting "Our America" in what seemed like a better direction. I think many felt that way. Again, San Francisco is probably not a good place to get the pulse of the nation, but at least there we all seemed to exude an aroma of accomplishment, and our faces smiled with hope.

But almost immediately, Obama became entangled with the bailout of the banks and the scandals in the banking industry, the protracted pull out of Iraq, the contraction of troops in Afghanistan, the blocked attempt to close Guantánamo, and of course, the drone policy. But I am sanguine enough to recognize that Obama stepped into a situation with tremendous institutional constraints. As much as Obama wanted to thwart the discourse of neoliberalism, he had to cavil to its institutional forces and constraints. He could not talk about poor, working-class America. He had to talk about the middle class. Why? Because poor America is Black and Brown America. The middle class is a code word for white America. He was trapped in that discursive logic of our public language.

Now, let me recall that whenever Obama did attempt to talk about "race" in America, he was immediately chided, censored, and attacked. The vitriol that was spewed because of his "relationship" to Jeremiah Wright is just emblematic of how Obama was boxed into a certain way of viewing Blacks in the US. I also distinctly remember the pre- and postelection discourse about Obama not being an American citizen, and the invocations and incitements to violence. To his credit, his opponent, Senator McCain, criticized such discourses and worked hard to stop it. Many of us feared that some white supremacist would kill Obama. In general, I think very few presidents have had to face the kind of racially motivated, ad hominen attacks that Obama has had to deal with—the catalogue of the defamations, offensive caricatures of both him and Michelle Obama, is unmatched, I bet you, by the caricatures of any other president in our history. Even so-called respectable politicians used racial innuendos that left as little to the imagination as a *Hustler* spread leaves to the pornographic mind, as when Newt Gingrich called Obama a "food stamp" president (!). I remember very indelibly when Obama had to intervene on behalf of preeminent scholar and Harvard professor Henry Louis Gates Jr., and he got in trouble with the police and many, many white Americans. I remember his statement shortly after the shooting of Trayvon Martin by a Latino vigilante, and he got flack, major backlash because of his authentic expression of condolences and deeply felt shame and sorrow for the killing of a young Black American. I remember very clearly the hot waters he got into because of his nomination and defense of now Justice Sonia Sotomayor.

Obama has tried, like no president, to get us to have a "civil," honest, intro-spective, and healing public discussion about race; but, in my assessment, "America" has not let him. In order to attempt to jumpstart this discussion, Obama had to take distance from many constituencies in the racially progres-sive Black and white movements of the US. He had to distance himself from the Black Church, from Black intellectuals like West, or even Gates, notwith-standing his initial solidarity with them. In the process, he has had to isolate himself. I can't imagine how "alone" Obama must feel. He has had to retreat into the "Washington Machine," and there his moral soul has gotten lost in the labyrinths of the Pentagon. Still, I don't want to get carried away with that metaphor. Even in the midst of the fog of war, a war that he inherited, and the wars he refused to fight, one can still glimmer a fundamentally moral pres-ident. Recently I have been reading Scott Shane's *Objective Troy: A Terrorist, A President, and the Rise of the Drone* (2015), because I have been trying to philosophize about what the "drone" means as both a military weapon and a political device. In this carefully researched, investigative journalism, we discovered an incredibly engaged and scrupulous Obama presidency. This book led me to reread Obama's speech before the 2013 graduating class at the National Defense University. I have never read anything like this by an American president in my lifetime—a time that included Nixon, Ford, Carter, Clinton and Bush. There are many important and historic speeches by Obama, but this one is particularly important. Here a president avows his responsi-bility for authorizing and commanding the killing of an American citizen, while also assuming responsibility for the "collateral damage" of the killing of two innocent bystanders. Now, let me be clear, I am not sanctioning Obama's actions. I am trying to foreground the issue that Obama is here pulling us into the space of giving moral reasons. This speech is not moralizing, but rather both an exemplar of how politics is and must be underwritten by moral rea-sons, and how we must either agree or disagree with these moral reasons. Of course, I disagree with the moral reasons given by Obama; but that Obama invites us as citizens to be part of this moral reasoning is breathtaking. I have no doubts that all the "drone attacks" Obama authorized weigh heavily on his soul, in ways that evidently all the killings of "shock and awe," and the torture and assassinations signed by Bush, Cheney, and Rumsfeld don't register on their moral radars.

But I really have not answered your question. I wanted to qualify why perhaps I have a very biased disposition. Still, let me attempt to answer it by saying that unwittingly Obama partly has contributed to the "postrace" discourse. Or, rather, he has been unwillingly dragged into the witness stand of this ideological trial. Returning to what Williams calls the "dynamic of display,"[3] Obama is evidently hypervisible, but yet we refuse to see him as a "Black" president. He is caught in the great machinations of the neoliberal machine that runs Washington from Wall Street, offshore bank accounts, and multinationals with headquarters in London, Frankfurt, and Geneva. As a mixed-race American, he is also part of what I called before the demographic transformation of the US. Here, however, I would have to interject a qualification. Obama may be suspect as a "Black" president, but First Lady Obama certainly is not suspect. I wish we could talk about Michelle Obama, but that is another long story. Let me just say quickly that her presence in the White House has the character of a tectonic shift, namely, slow, but profound. I think that as a high-power lawyer, an accomplished professional, along with her beauty, elegance, poise, intelligence, and commitments, Michelle Obama is a formidable role model, an unsurpassed historical figure. And all of this has not been properly acknowledged. But her distinct qualities certainly shed a unique halo on the President. If he is our "Black President," it is in large part due to Michelle Obama. Here is a hypothetical question: would he have been electable had he been married to a white Woman?

Finally, to his credit, I think that Obama has refused to invoke the grammar of the "Adamic Innocence" rhetoric that underwrites so much of our public religion and theodicy. I think that his speech on the occasion of the Wright controversy is testimony to this refusal. I am referring to his speech, "A More Perfect Union," from March of 2008.

G. Y.: In answer to your question, I would say, "Hell, no!" Given this country's white violent history against sexually intimate (real and imagined) and conjugal relations between Black men and white women, Obama would not have been elected, and had he been he may have even been killed. I mean, think about the young Emmett Till. You know, it is my sense that there is something always already racialized about the office of the presidency in the US. In other words, the highest office in the world is already in some sense normatively white. If this is true, then a robust discussion of race by the president is ipso facto precluded. If I'm right here, how much could we have expected of Obama? The proverbial deck is already stacked against him.

E. M.: I totally agree that the "proverbial deck is already stacked against him." I think that Obama has had a mighty fight with that stacked deck, and he still has managed to do some impressive things. But I am not sure I agree with the diagnosis that the office of the presidency in the US is "normatively white." If it were, Obama would never have been elected. OK, there are many Americans who do not accept Obama as our legitimate president, notwithstanding his election to two terms in the White House. In fact, there are many who do not think of him as a US citizen, and thus suspect his citizenship. But those who believe this are not operating within mainstream American political culture. I agree that the office of the president is "overdetermined," that is, that it is the site for the negotiation of a lot of "racial" fantasies, as well as masculinity, and religious, and purity, and all kinds of imperial and Manifest Destiny fantasies. But does that mean that the body of the president is "normatively male," and "normatively protestant"? Evidently, for a long time Americans could not countenance to elect a Catholic president, but we did. Evidently, for a long time many Americans thought that women were to be consigned to the private realm, and could only be in the White House as wives, servants, and mistresses, but we are about to elect a woman to the highest office in the United States.

Here I would want to appeal to your own work, as well as that of the rich, majestic, encyclopedic, uniquely American, African-American, Black, Negro, call it what you will, philosophical, historical, theological, feminist traditions that have taught us to see through the historicity of race, through its constructedness, its archeology, its contingency, but also its endurance, its renewal, its vitality, its viscosity, its capillarity. I don't know, when we dive into the deep waters of Douglas, Du Bois, Wells, Hurston, hooks, Davis, West, Williams, Yancy, Gooding-Williams, we come out not as Kantian/Rawlsian subjects, baptized into "Promethean Amnesia," but as good political genealogists and phenomenologists, who know that we do need norms to discern between what is allowed and disallowed, but who also know that those norms are products of struggles, of transformations of our imaginaries, of the expansion of our moral horizons. Normativity is not a standpoint, but a horizon, one that is expanded or contracted by our acts of imagination. It just occurred to me that perhaps that is what you mean by "normative whiteness"—namely, let us assume that in fact the office of the presidency were "normatively White," what would that mean? Something like an Einsteinian "thought experiment." But, perhaps you should just correct me or let me know what you mean by 'normatively White.'

G. Y.: By 'normatively white,' I don't mean that the most powerful office in the world is fixed; as you imply, there is too much of the historically informed in my work. Take the space in my home office where I study. It has become dialectically expressive of my presence, my movements. I have left a trace; it speaks of my being, my unconscious and conscious motility, my moods, how I arrange objects, and why. Indeed, my study is the kind of space such that were you or someone else to enter that space, you might find it alienating or even resistant to your way of inhabiting space. So, I think of the presidency in this way. It is a site, a space, configured by whiteness. Just as my room is structured by my being there. That Obama actually became president doesn't deny the reality that the presidency is normatively white no more than that my being hired at Emory (or you at Penn State) makes those institutions less normatively white. They can accommodate us, just as the presidency has accommodated Obama. And it is this white sedimentation of configured space, with its normative assumptions, ways of being, that I see as always already operating against Obama. Perhaps this is linked to my next question. Do you think that racism has abated or increased since we've had an African-American president?

E. M.: I have to split my answer. On the one hand, I think that straight-out racism has become intolerable, or at least unacceptable, as part of the civil and public language of our society. I think that the blunt and explicit racism that we saw and heard not so long ago has acquired a rancid, unpalatable, uncouth taste and smell. Look, I was also shocked by all the images of Black bodies being submitted to obscene violence, enacted by the police. Yet, we don't have lynchings, those public rituals of blood and racial punishment that should certainly make us ponder whether we have come a long way after all. When white supremacists hang nooses from trees in college campuses, there are immediate responses condemning such acts. On the other hand, given what I read about how the African-American community, as a whole, is treated, and how Latino/as are treated, I would have to say that racism remains vibrant and that its effects have grown more intense. I read some years ago that African-Americans, collectively, are worse off than they were before the sixties. I can believe this. Given the ways that two generations of African-Americans have been caught in the crushing wheels of the Prison Industrial Complex, I can only assume that racism has increased, but as an institutional, material, economic, political, and social phenomenon. I think that US neoliberalism has contributed to the exacerbation of racism, while also throwing a fog of obfuscation in front of its nefarious and long-lasting effects. Michelle Alexander is right to talk about the *New Jim Crow*, that is, new regimes of exclusion, expropriation, and marginalization that build on past such regimes.[4]

G. Y.: There is a way in which Obama's election was symbolically important, a feel-good moment in North American history. Yet, his presidency seemed to unleash all sorts of racist hatred and racist myth-making. How do you explain this apparent paradox?

E. M.: Yes, Obama's election was profoundly symbolic, and it was certainly a feel-good moment for many Americans. But for the very reason that he is representative of certain forces, tendencies, and ideals of progressive American society, he has also become the object on which forces of anti-Black racism have performed a cathexis, a transfer and fixation, of their resentment, their virulent and visceral rejection of what he stands for. At the same time, Obama stands as a reminder of how much has been accomplished symbolically, if not materially and institutionally, against racism, and thus he has become an alibi for unleashing all kinds of violence, both macro and micro, against Blacks and Latino/as. I think you are right to refer to these dual responses to Obama as an "apparent" paradox. I think Obama means many things, many opposite things to many different Americans, but I am not sure all of these different and opposing meanings are held together for the same reasons by the same persons. I think how you see Obama, and how you talk about his presidency, is a kind of litmus test about your stand on race and your views about what America means. I do agree that Obama's Blackness has invited some shameful behavior not only against him, but also other Black Americans. But this violence comes from those sectors that questioned his citizenship, his religious loyalty to America's public religion, his competency, his impartiality, his commitment to defend the heartland, his fealty to American empire, and there I only see apple pie, resilient, rejuvenated American racism.

G. Y.: Finally, neoliberalism has deep ties not only to a certain ways of thinking about markets and responsibility, but it seems to offer us a deeply problematic and morally corrosive philosophical anthropology. While I know that it is difficult to be brief given the gravitas of this question, what is needed as an alternative?

E. M.: First, we need to revitalize the agency of citizens. Citizens must take back control of their government, but not through populism, which appeals to the worst aspects of identities, resentments, and fears, as we are witnessing in this 2016 election. Second, we have to recover the language and spirit of the Civil Rights Movement with its commitment to nonviolence, and to legal and political transformation that appealed to the best of the political morality of our country. In fact, I think that the Civil Rights Movement is one of the most important political, social, cultural, and moral movements we have had in this nation, along with the abolition, women's suffrage, and the anti-nukes movements. The Civil Rights Movement remains an open agenda. Third, we have to initiate and sustain a Black and Latino/a coalition and dialogue about how to take up the civil rights agenda again. Fourth, we have to reject, philosophically, politically, and morally, the reduction of the political and moral to the economic. It is important to note that economics was always part of moral philosophy or applied philosophy. Today, we seem to subordinate everything to the chaos of the economic. And finally, we have to continue to reject the illusion that race is a thing of the past, and face up to the fact that we have become the nation we are because of race, as that which has subordinated many, and as that which has been relentlessly resisted, giving birth to new vocabularies of emancipation and political agency.

NOTES

1. Patricia J. Williams, *Seeing a Color-Blind Future: The Paradox of Race* (New York: The Noonday Press, 1997), 17.
2. Ta-Nehesi Coates, "The Black Family in the Age of Mass Incarceration," in *The Atlantic*, 316, no. 3 (October 2015): 60–84; 64.
3. Williams, *Seeing a Color-Blind Future*, 17.
4. Michelle Alexander, *The New Jim Crow: Mass Incarceration in the Age of Colorblindness* (New York: The New Press, 2012).

David Haekwon Kim

George Yancy: A great deal of philosophical work on race begins with the white/Black binary. In what ways does race mediate or impact your philosophical identity as a Korean American?

David Haekwon Kim: In doing philosophy, I often approach normative issues with concerns about lived experience, cultural difference, political subordination, and social movements changing conditions of agency. I think these sensibilities are due in large part to my experience of growing up bicultural, raced, and gendered in the US, a country that has never really faced up to its exclusionary and often violent anti-Asian practices. In fact, I am sometimes amazed that I have left so many tense racialized encounters with both my life and all my teeth. In other contexts, life and limb were not at issue, but I did not emerge with my self-respect intact.

These sensibilities have also been formed by learning a history of Asian Americans that is more complex than the conventional watered-down immigrant narrative. This more discerning, haunting, and occasionally beautiful history includes reference to institutional anti-Asian racism, a cultural legacy of sexualized racism, a colonial US presence in East Asia and the Pacific Islands, and some truly inspiring social struggles by Asians, Asian-Americans, and other communities of color.

It's a challenge to convey this sort of lived experience, and this too has shaped my philosophical identity. So little has been said in philosophy and public life about the situation of Asian Americans that we don't have much in the way of common understandings that are accurate and illuminating. Making matters worse is that the void is filled by many misleading notions about race in general, which includes such notions like our country being beyond race, that critiquing white privilege is hating whites, that any race talk is racist, and so on.

There is also problematic discourse about Asian Americans in particular, like the Model Minority myth. This popular notion posits Asian Americans as being successful along many indices of assimilation and socioeconomic well-being and thus a model for other nonwhites. Its veracity aside, its actual political function is to excuse anti-Black and anti-Latino racism and prevent interracial solidarity. In any case, I believe the invisibility of Asian Americans in our culture has been so deep and enduring that Asian Americans themselves are often ambivalent about how they would like to see themselves portrayed and perhaps even uncomfortable about being portrayed at all. It will be interesting to see how the new sitcom, *Fresh Off the Boat*, which features the assimilation woes of a Taiwanese-American family, develops over the coming months. Will it repeat conventional narratives, only in a funnier way? Or will humor and a richer truth unite?

G. Y.: In what ways has Asian American philosophy had to legitimate itself within or even against a philosophical myopia that focuses on Western traditions?

D. H. K.: As I see it, the undoing of this hegemony requires at least two sorts of diversification, and ultimately these efforts have to be integrated. One has to do with race, gender, sexuality, class, disability, and other identities related to subordination and social justice. The other concerns the study of non-Western conceptual traditions, like those found in Buddhist, Confucian, Vedic, Ubuntu, Nahuatl, and Islamicate perspectives, as well as modern hybrid traditions of the non-Western world. If we look at philosophy journals and requirements for the philosophy major and for graduate school in philosophy, it's hard to deny that white, Euro-American male perspectives and Euro-American traditions form the center of the profession both historically and presently, and descriptively and normatively. It's just silly to deny this.

Given this context, I think Asian American philosophy as philosophy of Asian American experiences or conditions faces a steep uphill struggle. Insofar as Asian American philosophy seeks to draw from indigenous Asian traditions, and I think it should, it faces Eurocentrism and the traditions diversification problem I mentioned. Furthermore, if Asian American philosophy tries to expand the justice dialogue and the traditions dialogue simultaneously, it may take on a damaging burden. Just think of what a dissertation or tenure committee would say to a philosopher putting forward, say, a Confucian theory of racial shame or a Buddhist critique of the exoticization of Asian women. Such a philosopher has committed professional harakiri.

G. Y.: And yet, by remaining so philosophically insular, I wonder if Anglo-American and European philosophy will, perhaps, die by its own hand in light of the "browning" or even "yellowing" of America.

D. H. K.: As the US becomes a majority nonwhite nation, a transition from insularity to obsolescence is a vital concern for the profession. We are already seeing setbacks to philosophy departments in the wider tide against the humanities. So if philosophy wants to avoid the diminishing trajectory of classics departments, then among other things, it must fully commit to social justice diversification. It should have done so yesterday!

However, I think it is also quite possible that insularity and hegemony unite and create a professional membership consisting largely of dark bodies and Westernized minds. The idea that philosophy simply is Western philosophy, be it analytic or continental, is such a deep structure of the profession. In fact, I don't think it's such a strange future in which we have a statistical majority of Blacks, Latinos, Asians, Native Americans, and Middle Easterners in the American Philosophical Association, nearly all members of which work primarily in the Western canon. Even philosophy addressing race, gender, and class inequality can rely solely on Rawls or Foucault, or on analytic moral psychology or Heideggerian phenomenology, out of more ideological than pragmatic reasons. Such a future would mean a terrible loss of opportunity. Ending formal Western imperialism was difficult; ending Eurocentrism may prove to be still more challenging. So, as I see it, there may yet be a sense in which Anglo- and Euro-American philosophy persists as the center, even in a profession filled with a darker professoriate.

And transformative efforts face a complex legacy of insularity. For example, currently, there is an increasing presence of "East-West" comparative philosophy in the profession. Unfortunately, the wider picture, one including a "North-South" axis, reveals that non-Asian non-Western philosophies, like those found under the headings of Africana philosophy, Native American philosophy, and Latin American philosophy, do not even make it onto the map in the Western profession of philosophy. I think it's no coincidence that these exclusions are of philosophies of colonized peoples. And it should be pointed out that Asian peoples and philosophies too have been enmeshed in colonial conditions. A sign of significant progress would be the robust development of what we might call "East-South" philosophy. In fact, I propose that we operationalize this idea and build it into the infrastructure of the American Philosophical Association. This would not only indicate the admission of "South" philosophy into the profession, but also "South" philosophy's engagement with "East" philosophy would imply a strong decentering of Western philosophy. Perhaps all this is to say that I long for the day when we let the world teach us about the world.

G. Y.: A Chinese student of mine said to me recently that she was told by a white male to go back to her own country. The fear of the "Yellow-Peril" is well known. What are some of the ways in which you see this playing itself out in our contemporary moment?

D. H. K.: I think Yellow Perilism, or anti-Asianism more generally, persists. This is especially clear if we look beyond large coastal cities, like San Francisco, or contexts like the academy. There is a whole lot of America between the urban dots in which Asian Americans are beginning to appear more familiar, and there are many realms of life outside of the university, a place where Asian Americans are regarded as a model minority. In many of these other locations and contexts, Asian Americans are often not welcome. And in these places as well as the ones where they are more familiar, they are often welcomed in a conditional fashion: they have to be "good" Asians, politically compliant and sometimes even white-identified.

Sometimes the exclusion is crass or violent with classic racist elements. Historically, this is often linked to the state of our foreign policy. So if we continue to see a large influx of Asian immigrants and tensions with China and North Korea persist or worsen, then predictably we'll see a spike in Yellow Perilism. We have already seen a terrible rise in hate crimes and arguably state crimes against many members of Muslim, Middle Eastern, and South Asian peoples since 9/11.

G. Y.: I recall that once at a conference you mentioned being called "Ching Chong." How did you resist this sort of racist vitriol and slur? And what sort of psychic scars does this sort of thing leave?

D. H. K.: To your first question, honestly, the answer is: poorly! I sometimes hear Asian Americans and other people of color insisting on matching the vitriol in kind. I have often resisted in this way simply because I couldn't control my outrage or contempt.

However, I would not insist upon this sort of resistance. It can quickly escalate the nastiness of the situation, and one may end up beaten, humiliated, even killed. And whatever else may be true, we do not need more people of color degraded or killed by racism. Also, at the end of the day, we need to have community, in some wide sense of the word, with racists. I don't know if I'm saying something controversial here or simply identifying part of the agony of race in this country. But, as W. E. B. Du Bois mournfully noted, as infuriated as we may get by violent or structural racism, we must be reminded by the end of the day that racists are human, even all too human.

Having said all this, I do think that a decently effective response to racist vitriol is needed because a lack of resistance can deepen the stereotype of Asian passivity, which can encourage more such racism elsewhere. Also, not resisting can have corrosive effects in which one begins to internalize the image of oneself conveyed by the racist, which gets at your point about scarring. There is something about constantly returning to the site of degradation in one's memory and imagination that has really baleful effects on one's sense of self. Perhaps we can get help by thinking about all this in terms of practices with aims. I think typically the aim of the antagonism is to goad the victim into anger, fear, or agitation, the expressions of which incite pleasure and more such ridicule, intimidation, or violence. So I think in many such cases an alternative to countervitriol is performing a kind of imperturbability with a calm indignation or even a kind of composed hostility.

I have sometimes folded my arms in front of my chest and calmly glared at antagonistic racists, trying to convey with my face and comportment two things: you don't unsettle me, and you're pathetic. Sometimes, I even smile a little and say in my own mind, "Uh uh, no, you're an idiot." The problem with this strategy is that sometimes I cannot end the performance, and afterward I continue to feel animosity and contempt. There are clearly other, and no doubt better, strategies that can be used. Importantly, given the support offered by the wider context of racial and gender hierarchy, it may actually be impossible to win this battle of wills.

Perhaps the hardest part of all this is contending with a distinctive kind of vulnerability, one that can also cause scarring. Following a Fanonian line of thought, one that resonates with some Confucian themes of the ritualization of the social self, I am thinking of a very basic kind of sociopolitical affiliation or identification process, a subject-forming sense of attunement to and belongingness within a community, which subsequently conditions, often invisibly, one's social encounters in everyday life.

This process often unfolds as naturally and unconsciously as breathing air, but it forms one of the many fundamental bases of the self. In broad outline, this is not so different from how philosophers talk about how basic kinds of background, embodiment, or know-how are more fundamental than, and condition more consciously, explicit propositional knowledge or know-that. The problem, then, is when this subject-forming sociopolitical affiliation is directed toward the very community in which racists are important members. One of the very bases of the social self makes the subject deeply vulnerable to racist vitriol and to the more pervasive context of racist exclusion.

To appreciate this point, it can be useful to contrast two Asian Americans, one who has mostly grown up in the United States and one who recently immigrated here. Both can be angry at racist insults, fearful of racist assaults, and can worry over racist exclusions. Thus, they are both vulnerable to racism. But insofar as the "American" in "Asian American" plays a significant role in the former's subject-forming sense of sociality, whereas it is, say, China, Korea, or Vietnam that plays a parallel role in the latter's sense of self, then the former can be more deeply, we might say existentially, unsettled by racism than the former. This, I believe, is one of the points of contention between immigrant parents and their children who are raised here. The parents puzzle over how much their children are impacted by racism and sometimes even flee from any cultural affiliation with their homeland. The deep unsettling effects of racism can be relatively easily described, but are very difficult to appreciate with a kind of lived understanding. And here, I'm afraid only structural changes to society can significantly remove the vulnerability I've just described.

G. Y.: What has to change in America, more generally, for you, as an Asian American, to feel affirmed? And what, specifically, in the professional field of philosophy?

D. H. K.: I think the sort of affirmation that's salient here isn't a sense of feel-good multiculturalism but an ethical affirmation that concerns social transformation and political accountability. In regards to the profession of philosophy, I would go back to the two processes of diversification noted earlier. I am certain that less than 1 percent of philosophy departments across North America have students pursuing majors or minors, to say nothing about graduate students, required to take courses that could be considered part of either justice or traditions diversification, like feminism and Buddhism, respectively. But if even 10 percent did, I would have an energized sense of hope.

In regards to national changes, and to limit myself, two things come to mind. First, I think we need to align the implicit sense of history in our civic affairs with the best history produced by our Asian Americanist scholars and others doing the work of justice diversification. Stories of anti-Asian institutional racism, American imperialism, and Asian American democratic struggles must be a part of the basic infrastructure of our historic self-understanding in our K–12 education and our civic narratives, rather than being relegated to an elective history seminar in college.

Second, Asian Americans have to see themselves as part of a larger community of color. We are often hoodwinked into believing the model minority story and that we should be grateful for our successes. Note that such gratitude, apparently compulsory, frames our interests or affiliations in an unethically narrow fashion and invites a kind of political affiliation with whiteness. But the America of Blacks, Latinos, Native Americans, Middle Easterners, and so on is also a part of our America. The killings of Trayvon Martin and Michael Brown are but the tip of the iceberg of anti-Black racism; Latinos are hunted by ICE (Immigration and Enforcement Customs), and the tragedy of border crossing is a human rights issue for which subsequent generations will judge us; Asians have arrived on an already occupied land, one filled by peoples for whom virtually every treaty was violated. And with the same logic as the Japanese Internment, so many Middle Easterners, Arabs, and Muslims are being held without trial, and more generally they are profoundly ostracized in our "War on Terror." Thus, with a wider sense of ethical community, I'll have to reserve my gratitude for the day when a deeper democracy is achieved.

Emily S. Lee

George Yancy: You work at the intersection of race and phenomenology. What got you interested in this area?

Emily S. Lee: Well, I've always been interested in how people can live in close proximity, share experiences, even within a family, and yet draw very different conclusions from the experience. So when I began reading French philosopher M. Merleau-Ponty's *Phenomenology of Perception*, I really appreciated his care and attention to how this phenomenon can occur. Because an experience is not directly drawn from the empirical circumstances, it is also structured by the accumulated history and aspirations of each of the subjects undergoing the experience. Merleau-Ponty's work helps to systematically understand how one can share an experience, and yet still take away different conclusions.

It was with luck that while I was reading Merleau-Ponty's book, I was also reading the critical race theorist Patricia Williams's book, *The Alchemy of Race and Rights*. I found some of her descriptions and analysis demonstrating the chasms of understanding among different "races" incredibly enlightening. I thought an explanation for many of the racial phenomena that Williams described in terms of the inexplicable dearth of understanding among various racialized subjects could be facilitated with the phenomenological framework.

G. Y.: I think that what you suggest above really opens up an important way of accounting for differential understandings of race and racism in the United States. Many white people fail to grasp what it means for people of color who experience living in this country very differently—whether it be people of color undergoing experiences of racist microaggression or overt racist physical violence. Is there a way to make sense of this through a phenomenological lens?

E. S. L.: I think that the question and the problem is determining—that is, having people agree—that something constitutes racism and what constitutes a microaggression or a macroaggression, although I do hope that the latter is clearer by now. I like the phenomenological framework because it highlights the entire lens, orientation, or framework through which to recognize something as racist. Keep in mind that expressions of racism have not been static, and hence they creatively change.

Perhaps the following example might help—and it goes beyond the black/white binary. As Korean American, I came to the provinces of the US, specifically Guam, when I was five or six. I came to the mainland of the US, specifically New York City, at the age of ten. So, as someone who is Korean American, I still cringe when told that I "speak good English," and I must point out that blacks as well as whites have said this to me. Half the time, I want to correct their grammar, to let them know that they should say that I "speak English *well*." But so far, I've refrained from this. The person speaking to me usually thinks they are giving me a compliment. But I recognize this statement as their inability or unwillingness to understand that Asian Americans have been living in the United States and have been citizens for well over one hundred years. This unwillingness or inability to recognize Asian Americans as Americans has the result of insistently casting Asian Americans as foreigners or people who do not belong here.

I recognize this "compliment" as *macroaggressive*, not microaggressive, setting the stage to treat Asian Americans as not quite deserving of the same rights as Americans, because Asian Americans are, after all, only "immigrants." Considering the controversy even over the Dream Act, immigrants can clearly be maltreated. But of course I also recognize that this "compliment" can only be the result of a specific socially constructed understanding of the history of the United States, so I do attempt to be more understanding of it. Nevertheless, such a "compliment" is problematic.

People may not accept the above scenario as a macroaggression, but rather that perhaps I'm being too sensitive, that I'm making a mountain out of a molehill and that the above scenario only constitutes at most a microaggression. I am absolutely sure that there are even Asian Americans who would insist I am being much too sensitive. I think that stereotypes and jokes about stereotypes function much in the same way. They may be about small characteristics, but they are part of a bigger framework. It is in this sense that I think the problem is in determining what constitutes a racist act and what constitutes a microaggression or macroaggression.

After all, to cast something as a microaggression is to suggest somehow that these aggressions are not too damaging, that they are not that important, and, hence, "understandable." And it is here, where people occupy a crossroad, where people may simply disagree and not see eye to eye, that phenomenology can be helpful. Because of the priority of phenomenology's framework of describing the world, not simply the material conditions of the world, but also the subject's very ambiguous, contextual, situated conditions of being-in-the-world, phenomenology can be helpful in describing why or how people can so completely diverge in understanding an event as racist, or aggressive, in a micro or macro sense.

G. Y.: Your point about speaking "good English" reminded me of the "I, too, am Harvard" Photo Campaign, where students of color at Harvard were tired of the institutional and microaggressive racism that they experienced on a daily basis. As a philosophical approach, how might phenomenology help them to make sense of their situation? I'm reminded of Frantz Fanon's *Black Skin, White Masks*, where he describes the *lived experience* of black bodies.

E. S. L.: I am reminded that Fanon recognized that alienation for the black male professional is different from the alienation of the black male worker. In other words, I appreciate Fanon's attention to the different forms of alienation because of class. I guess I especially like this because as much as I sympathize with the students at Harvard and their sense of alienation, their alienation is distinctly different from the alienation of the working class. I read Fanon as utilizing and critiquing both dialectical and phenomenological frameworks. And as you hint at here, yes, his work (as well as your work) deploys a necessary phenomenological approach to describe the lived experience of the black man and woman, though when it comes to women, his work is not without controversy. But I also appreciate phenomenology not only in terms of its descriptive capabilities—in describing the functioning of perception, embodiment, and experience—but hopefully in its normative possibilities. In other words, I appreciate phenomenology in making explicit the functioning of these three lens through which we engage the world. With this accomplishment or some advancement in this area, we can move toward making ethical and political decisions with lasting changes.

G. Y.: Speaking of lived experience, I have shared with my white philosophy graduate students how alienating it can be within a profession like philosophy that is predominantly white. What is this alienation like for you as an Asian American woman philosopher?

E. S. L.: I guess that I'm still not quite sure how to describe this experience of being an Asian American woman philosopher. Working on the American Philosophical Association Committee on Asian and Asian American philosophy and philosophers, I am very much aware of how few of us there are in the discipline. I'm still left wondering if some of my experiences are from being a woman, especially as philosophy really is still a good ol' boys' network. Or, I wonder if some of my experiences occur from being Asian American, in the ways people stereotypically assume that I must specialize in certain areas of philosophy or behave in specific ways, such as being quiet and subdued. At times, it appears if I speak at all, people immediately assume I'm aggressive.

I know these expectations about behavior make a significant difference because, in academia especially, a clear boundary between work colleagues and friends does not exist. I think sometimes at conferences, people just don't know what to make of me, though at times people seem to react with genuine effort to be inclusive. But I guess to the extent that there is discrimination, I feel it most in two ways.

First, I feel it in the sense of not being regarded as a philosopher, or as a good philosopher, and as someone who just accidentally or barely made it into the discipline. I am always left questioning my intelligence and my ability to think as well as the others who look like they are members of the discipline. The questioning by others in the discipline of whether I belong becomes internalized, making me question myself and second-guess myself about whether I can do this.

Second, I work on feminist and race philosophy. People both within and outside the discipline do not regard these areas as "true" philosophy because they presume to guard the boundaries of what constitutes and does not constitute real philosophy. These presumptions challenge my understanding of philosophy and my legitimacy as a philosopher.

G. Y.: Why are there so few Asian American professional philosophers in the United States?

E. S. L.: The philosopher David H. Kim has written on this.[1] Kim speculates that part of the reason may be because Asian Americans are primed by their parents to enter more lucrative positions such as law or medicine, or more secure positions like engineering or computer science. He also acknowledges that stereotypes about what talents Asian Americans possess, that is, the sciences and math-related fields, may prime some Asian Americans themselves not to enter the humanities. However, the burgeoning field of American Studies, and the specialization of Asian American studies, seems to suggest that it isn't that Asian Americans are averse to studying and working in the humanities. I believe that Kim suggested that the field of philosophy itself, in terms of the professors encouraging or discouraging Asian American youth from furthering their studies in philosophy, or other sorts of subtle signals, is discouraging more Asian Americans from entering philosophy.

Recently, Carole Lee has empirically traced the numbers and attempts to provide an answer as to why there are so few Asian American professional philosophers. So I think the conclusion is that influences within the discipline of philosophy as well as broader social forces provide an explanation for the paucity of Asian American philosophers.

G. Y.: In *Black Skin, White Masks*, Fanon describes what it was like for him, while in France riding on a train, to experience his body as a problem when a little white child, in its mother's arms, exclaims, "Look, a Negro!" When you think about the profession's policing of the boundaries of what philosophy "really" looks like, do you ever feel as if the profession communicates to you, "Look, an Asian!"? Of course, what comes with this is that sense of being reduced to one's body.

E. S. L.: It's interesting, because since moving to Southern California, I do not feel the sense of being noticed for being Asian as much as I did while living in New York City and in the northern parts of New York State. There I definitely felt the sense that my Asian features defined me and spoke for me. Even I would note if I saw an Asian person on the street. Here in Southern California the population is so diverse that I don't feel the sense of overdetermination of my body all the time. But more specifically within the discipline of philosophy, at conferences, I think at this point in my career, I've found enough circles of collegial philosophers—admittedly mostly philosophers of color—among whom I do not feel reduced to my body. So, whether I am reduced to the racial features of my body depends on the context. I am glad to say that I've participated in niche conferences such as at the Society for Women in Philosophy meetings, at the Future Directions in Feminist Phenomenology, or at the Korean Modernities/Colonialities Workshop where I thoroughly enjoyed myself while engaging in thought-provoking conversations and learning a great deal.

But at some of the larger mainstream conferences, yes, I definitely feel self-conscious both as an Asian and as a woman. I think to some extent I am aware of being a woman more than being Asian. I say this because the Asian racialized identity works in ways I cannot quite pinpoint yet. I am aware that there are claims out there that Asians are becoming "white." I do not want to fall into this scenario. I think the racialization of Asian Americans is distinctly different from whiteness, but not so different from whiteness as blackness is—perhaps different but not different enough? The identity functions between denigration and exoticism. Perhaps this difference functions ambiguously enough that I still do not fully understand it.

If anything, I want the difference to be acknowledged, I do not want the sense that my identity does not matter. I do not want acceptance on the condition of reducing my differences away.

G. Y.: There are experiences that African American, Afro-Caribbean, Latin American, Native American, and Asian American philosophers share as minority philosophers (or even graduate students) in a profession that is still predominantly white and male. What are some shared philosophical themes or topics that you think would be relevant for these minority groups to critically engage as a collective, a collective that would be mutually empowering? And what positive impact do you think that such a collective would have on our profession's understanding of itself?

E. S. L.: This is a hard question. I want to begin by noting that I know that we have shared experiences; I know this because one of the first books that woke me up to the question of race and deeply rang true for me was Richard Wright's *Black Boy* and Audrey Lorde's *Zami*. I don't know what is the shared experience, in that I think it is not just feelings of alienation or marginalization.

I hope it is more a sense of knowing there is more than the prevailing structures of existence and knowledge.

But in terms of philosophical themes that it would be relevant to critically engage—I'm going to answer by describing my experiences, and hopefully it will speak to this concern. I guess I am a phenomenologist: I want to leave open the question of which topics and themes to engage, because I do not want to presume to be able to speak for others. I feel like the experience of participating in academia as a philosopher has been similar to teaching a class on philosophy of race. Because in my institution the class is a general education requirement, I get quite a few students who are resistant to the material and as a result attack my pedagogy and my abilities to teach. I have read enough material indicating that this experience is quite common among professors who teach material on race. At one point, it was so difficult that I considered not teaching the class. But then I recalled the students, not many, but a significant number, who personally expressed how important the class was to them. If I did not teach the class, these students might be left in a vacuum. I decided I want to continue teaching this class to meet these students. Now, the class is a pleasure to teach.

I think in the same sense, it's been a difficult journey getting here, and it continues to be challenging, but I must say that the few philosophers of color (and white philosophers who are more "enlightened," let's say, or who at least try) with whom I now engage philosophically and socially, really make the journey worthwhile. In a deep sense, I know I made the right decision becoming a philosopher.

NOTE

1. David Haekwon Kim, "Asian American Philosophers: Absence, Politics, and Identity," *American Philosophical Association Newsletter* 1, no. 2 (Spring 2002): 25–28.

PART V DISCUSSION QUESTIONS

1. Eduardo Mendieta explains that "normativity is not a standpoint, but a horizon, one that is expanded or contracted by our acts of imagination." The word 'horizon' is often used to represent opportunity or possibility, and sometimes carries with it the implication of a destination. Discuss the notion of horizon as it applies to racialization, one's identity as "Black," "white," and so on.
2. Out of its own struggle for philosophical legitimacy, philosophy in Latin America has made "visible the context in which philosophy occurs,"

according to Linda Martín Alcoff. She suggests that throughout the diverse range of Latin American philosophy "one can discern a running thread of decolonial self-consciousness and aspiration." The works of the great Latin American thinkers that Alcoff identifies all seem to share an origin and discursive center in self-knowledge. To what extent does the role of the United States as a colonizing, imperial power make its own philosophers reluctant to know themselves?

3. In many cases, it seems like the discussion of race cannot get off of the ground because we lack the prerequisite education. In some cases, as for example the anti-Asian policy and practices in the United States noted by David Haekwon Kim, shameful aspects of American history are rarely addressed in standard curricula. In the same way, we fail to understand the full picture of race and culture in the present. The "insularity and hegemony" of disciplines like philosophy continue to exclude non-Western, nonwhite, nonmale modes of philosophy, as attested to by Kim and Alcoff, Mendieta, and Emily Lee. Thus, in addition to the failure to understand what Lee discusses as macro- and microaggressions when they occur, we also deny them access in discourse. To what extent can we account for Western myopia in terms of the failure of the education system in the United States, intentional ignorance on the part of the white racist structures and the people who live among them, and the "Promethean Amnesia" that Mendieta describes? Is this enduring failure to understand or even acknowledge racism, to the point of excluding pluralistic philosophy, a form of micro- or macroaggression?

Race and Africana Social and Political Frames

Molefi Kete Asante

George Yancy: From an Afrocentric perspective, how do you define race in America?

Molefi Kete Asante: Race in America is a psychological, physical, and social location for determining the conditions of one's current and future life. This is because America's benefits and privileges have been structured around race and its markers for difference. Those markers, largely physical, identify some people as being privileged and others as being victims. As a central concept in America's history, race has always been an arena for selecting who will eat and who will not eat or for determining the quality and condition of a group's possibilities.

G. Y.: Given the recent killings of unarmed Black people by white police officers, does Afrocentricity provide a prescription of any sort for eliminating racism?

M. K. A.: Afrocentricity as an intellectual idea takes no authority to prescribe anything; it is neither a religion nor a belief system. It is a paradigm that suggests all discourse about African people should be grounded in the centrality of Africans in their own narratives. However, the warrant "given the recent killings of unarmed Black people by white police officers" is part of a continuing drama in America; its contemporary emergence is simply a recent exposure through popular media.

When one asks about the elimination of racism, then the concentration cannot be on African people but on the perpetrators of racism. Who acculturates racists? What does a white child learn about privilege? How can we dismantle the apparatus that supports white *exceptionalism* in a multicultural society? It will take really bold and courageous action to bring about several key components of a national will to overcome racism. It must mean an acceptance of the fact that racism is a principal fact of American life.

It also necessitates an embrace of all national cultures in the country in a defiant act of seeking to contest ignorance in all arenas. This is what the brilliant people of Starbucks attempted to do recently by having their baristas engage customers in conversations about race—to the utter disgust of the racist class. Thus, in the end, to eliminate racism will also require a rewriting of our understanding of the United States of America from the perspective of the oppressed, the violated, and the marginalized. The Native Americans must be folded into the discussion of racism because they lost an entire continent based on racism as a location of what their future conditions should be.

Of course, you cannot do any of this if you seek to whitewash the facts of American history. Institutions should and could support the least powerful and thereby redress a thousand wrongs. I would like to see politicians open the discussion on reparations for 246 years of enslavement.

The question of the killing of Black men by police is not a recent one; it is more in view now because of the new social media. I am afraid that the country has not overcome the pockets of racist fearmongers who are happy to kill African-Americans in the tradition of the old KKK. I personally believe that some KKK-style racists have found homes inside police forces and are now called "systematic failures." Removing racists, these "systematic failures," from police departments is rightly the work of criminal justice scholars, some of whom spend too much time seeking to criminalize Black people. Consequently, statements about mechanized forces, better training, mistaken shootings by reserve deputy police, and aggravated behavior miss the point of dealing with rogue police officers who get an "adrenalin charge" by subduing Black males with deadly force.

G. Y.: On your view, who is it that, as you point out, acculturates racists, and what does a white child learn about privilege?

M. K. A.: Let me remind you of a recent event. A white policeman in New Richmond, Ohio refused to shoot a white man begging to be shot. The policeman, Jesse Kidder, is praised for demonstrating restraint in refusing to shoot the man, Michael Wilcox, who had been accused of killing his fiancée. Pundits and commentators announced gleefully that Kidder's action was exceptional and certainly an example of good police behavior. Few would dispute the fact that the police used restraint, but the lesson to the white child and to the Black child, I should add, is that police can show restraint when the suspect is white, even if he is suspected of murder.

The point that I am making is that almost everyday, perhaps hundreds of times per day, white children learn how special they are in the society and how unspecial Blacks are to whites who control the society. Racism begins to assert itself quite early, and children learn at an early age, perhaps as early as three to four years of age, that people are different and they are treated differently. If you are a white child, it is extremely obvious that you have privileges that a Black child does not have because you are surrounded by privilege, opportunities, and power buttons that are often denied to African-descended children. Thus the white child finds three aspects of privilege immediately in a racist society. They are secure in their physical and psychological situations; they are protected in their living spaces; and they have the freedom to explore every conceivable adventure without fear or trepidation. On top of this, they are granted audacity that is condemned in Black children. Furthermore, white people have the privilege of being blinded to their privilege by the protocols of the society. It is like the white view of the police as good guys and the general Black view of suspicion of the police. The blindness comes because the police in a racist society make racial judgments and decisions. They decide to stop and arrest Blacks at a rate greater than that of whites. They decide to harass young Black males and to send young white males home to their parents. This blindness to racism is an inherent part of the meanness of the system of privilege. Alas, Black children are rarely protected and are not secure in their spaces.

G. Y.: I have heard from both white and Black pundits that Black people ought to spend the same level of energy protesting "Black-on-Black" crime. Other scholars with whom I've spoken see this move as a way of avoiding a critical discussion of the fact that some white police officers, who have sworn to protect citizens across race, actually see Black lives as disposable. What are your thoughts?

M. K. A.: "Black-on-Black" crime is not an anomaly; most crimes are committed in the communities where victims are found, and since most Blacks live among other Blacks, the criminals and the victims will tend to be Black. But this is only part of the issue; it is a small part of the bigger problem that is the cause of violence in the African-American community. There is a morbid philosophy of demise operating in a systemic way to destroy the elements that maintain Black communities.

Here is what I mean. Unemployment, racial profiling, housing discrimination, educational shabbiness, exploitation of the poor, and the rampant physical abuse by the authorities create a cauldron of frustration and fear. The brew is violent and its manifestation engulfs those who enter the madness of this arena of violence. It cannot be justified, but it must be understood for us to continue to find a solution.

G. Y.: You stated above that Afrocentricity "is a paradigm that suggests all discourse about African people should be grounded in the centrality of Africans in their own narratives." Given this time of grief, suffering, and sadness that so many African-Americans are feeling as we continue to hear about (and in some cases actually see) one killing after another of unarmed Black people by white police officers, what are some of our "own narratives" that might be drawn upon to bring about a sense of empowerment during these times?

M. K. A.: In the worst of times there are always victories, even if they are small ones. So when we are whipped, broken in culture and spirit, effectively destroyed physically, we can still manage to sing, to laugh, to rebel, and to join revolution; this is the victory of those whose lives are wounded by brutality. You remember the Middle Passage crossing? When our ancestors sat on those ships they were not all dejected; some were defiant, others nodded in solidarity to their daughters or sons and gave them signs of victory. Those who leaped over board and drowned themselves were also gaining victories over the criminal kidnappers. The key to centering is situational; that is, one must claim space or take space, intellectually or physically, in any situation, however difficult and dire it may be seen.

What are we to do if we are in bad situations where our freedoms are stolen? We are to resist and the best way to resist is to claim our space, even if it is in short bursts of time to assert ourselves and consequently to become the subjects of our own narratives.

G. Y.: Speak to how you do or do not see the protests taking place, as of this interview, in Baltimore, as an example of Black people claiming space.

M. K. A.: In my book *The Afrocentric Idea*, I suggested that the objective of the oppressed, the victimized, and the exploited is always to "seize" the accoutrements of power in order to correct the imbalance when the mastering force least expects assaults on the ramparts of villainy that seek to marginalize them. The youth of Baltimore seized the space and the time when they went to the streets and posed the threat of violence; it is always the threat of violence, not violence itself, that unnerves the system because of the uncertainty that comes when a people hold in their hands the potential of competing for power. Thus, the claiming of space adjusts the narrative of confrontation so that you no longer have a hierarchical symbolism but a more balanced position, even if only temporarily, that allows the oppressed to establish itself as a contestant for attention and power.

This is what the demonstrative protests brought into play in Baltimore, because the people took to the streets and seized the space, the time, the limelight of the media, and the assertive rhetoric of action that demanded change in the system. Those few who burned down buildings and destroyed cars *were not* demonstrating; they were much too literal to pose a threat. In effect, they took advantage of the seizure of space and corrupted it to an obvious provocation that could and did draw down the awesome power of the state. Without military capacity, protesters are in no position to survive a literal confrontation; this is why the threat of violence with its potentiality is a more effective strategy for gaining change.

G. Y.: If you were speaking to young Black boys and Black men about the recent killings of unarmed boys and men who look like them, what would you say?

M. K. A.: There would be two points I would make to them, the same two points I made to my own son, some years ago. The first is "The United States has always been a dangerous nation for African boys and men." The second is that "you must always be on the side of fighting for transformation in the society." Actually the intent of the enslavement was to kill us, to work us to death, to dispense with us in one way or the other, or to conspire against our success, or to hang us from a tree because of the inherent threat that the Black male body posed for the society. Young Black boys must know their power and learn to respect it, to be amused by the fear that they cause in those who reflect on the violence they have measured against us. Young Black boys bring a sense of unease to many whites who expect them to do something, to say something; it is the same unease that rides on the shoulders of the police who have been trained in a culture that disrespects Black people.

And yet I would say to them that they must resist narcissism because journalists and social media love to fetishize them. Once you are fetishized, you are ready to be destroyed, overturned, subverted, interrogated, and incarcerated. The Baltimore mother who reacted emotionally to save her son from arrest by beating him away from the protests appeared to do something wholly parental because she was saying that she was not going to lose her son. However, the media saw the beating of the Black male body, not the mother's love, as the main story. I would also insist that young Black boys and men undestand that we must be on the side of justice, progress, and transformation. What is correct for us is correct for others, and we must fight all forms of human oppression; this is truly the legacy of African ancestors in the Americas whose destinies have always been tied up with those of the abused, harmed, hurt, and brutalized. In the end, they should know that they should be careful, but have no fear; be confident but not arrogant, and let no one separate them from goodness, character, and justice.

G. Y.: Returning to your point about space, there is also canonical or curricular space. As a professional philosopher, I was primarily taught European and Anglo-American philosophy. In what ways does Afrocentricity seek to rethink the canon of Western intellectual and philosophical space?

M. K. A.: Yes, George, you are right about Afrocentricity rethinking the canon. There is nothing really wrong about the European canon; it is what it is, the European canon. I think that often African and to a lesser degree Asian scholars are asking Europeans to do what others have not done. We privilege Europe and European people as the ones who should set the canon, but just allow us inside with one or two books of our own. Afrocentricity understands that the European project is not something that we should change; we could, for example, suggest items for the canon, but in the end its purpose is to canonize European thought and thinkers.

Yet in a diverse society like ours we must have space for all people who share this land with us. This requires knowledge and generosity. Thales must be paired with Imhotep, and the pyramids must be seen as the monumental icons of the ancient world long before the creation of the *Iliad* and the *Odyssey*. You cannot have a canon, however, in the United States that avoids the profound works of David Walker, Marcus Garvey, W. E. B. Du Bois, James Baldwin, James Weldon Johnson, Toni Morrison, Zora Neale Hurston, Langston Hughes, and E. Franklin Frazier, for example.

I think it is important to say that Afrocentricity is in opposition to the imposition of particularisms as if they are universal. There has to be cultural and intellectual opportunity in the curriculum for cultures and people other than European. Who created the calendar that we use today? Who established the foundations of geometry? If we do not know the answers to these questions, it is because what has been imposed as if it were universal may be only those items and achievements that are European-derived.

Intellectual space must be shared because all humans have contributed to human civilization. The ancient African philosophers such as Amenhotep, the son of Hapu, Imhotep, Ptahhotep, Amenemhat, Merikare, and Akhenaten lived hundreds, even thousands of years before Socrates, Plato, and Aristotle. Why is it that children do not learn that the African Imhotep built the first pyramid? Our children do not know that Hypatia, Plotinus, and St. Augustine were born in Africa.

Bill E. Lawson

George Yancy: Why do race and racism continue to be a problem in the US? Also, talk about why critical discussions of race and racism are still relatively marginal points of philosophical discussion within the context of professional philosophy.

Bill E. Lawson: These questions seem to have a lasting hold on people in the United States. My basic answer is that the reasons are complex. Nonetheless, I think that there is a certain aspect of American culture and history that maintains racism as a problem. But first, we must understand what is the problem regarding race and racism in the United States. Straightforwardly, the problem is at least two-fold, the failure of national, state and local governments to ensure that the rights of Blacks, as full members of the state, were respected, and the failure of the state to ensure that employment and educational opportunities were afforded to Blacks collectively. I contend that these problems are interrelated. There is a general lack of regard for the opinions and rights of those people who are descendants of American chattel slavery. The history of the United States is replete with examples of this lack of regard for the rights of Black people. This lack of respect was in play before there was a United States. As early as 1669, The Fundamental Constitutions of the Carolinas gave the slaveholder absolute and complete power over their African slaves. After the founding of the country, the legal sanctions and public policies regarding the social inclusion of Blacks have always had a bias toward keeping Blacks in their place, that is, no Negro could be better situated than a white person. The central problem of the United States regarding Black people after the Civil War was and still is, What to do with the Negro? The Negro Problem remains.

Let me be clear here: none of this means that there have not been whites who sought or seek to respect Blacks as fellow humans and citizens, but only to note that there has been a consistent and prevailing anti-Black bias in the treatment of Blacks as both humans and citizens in the United States. This anti-Black bias has given rise to negative views of Blacks as persons and citizens. This anti-Black bias permeates every aspect of life in the United States. It has been particularly embedded in the educational and academic life of the country. I would hate to guess how many trees have been sacrificed to record the manner in which Black people do not measure up to white standards. All of the academic disciplines have taken their turn explaining why Blacks and Black culture are of no value and that Blacks cannot be scholars of note. For an interesting discussion on this point, read John Hope Franklin's "The Dilemma of the American Negro Scholar."[1] In this regard, philosophy is no different. The Black experience has not been seen as a source of philosophical exploration or enlightenment. Since philosophers are supposed to be part of the intellectual elite and their intellectual investigations are the height of intellectual acumen, only the best of humankind can be philosophers, and this means that people from marginalized groups with marginalized histories bring nothing to the academic table. Thus, there is no reason to respect these people or their experiences as having philosophical importance. The problem of race and racism continues because of a racist social climate that influences all aspects of social life in the United States, and academic philosophy is no exception.

G. Y.: In fact, one might argue that philosophy is one of the "whitest" of the professions in the humanities. Why is this? And can it be inferred that Black humanity is in some sense least respected in philosophy, especially historically?

B. E. L.: George, that is an interesting way to put the question. Why not ask, Would you argue that philosophy is one of the "whitest" of the disciplines and professions in the humanities? My answer would be yes, it is. It is the whitest in regards to the relative number of philosophers who are white, and it is the whitest in terms of the persons and areas of interest researched. Unlike the other disciplines in the humanities, there could be no call for a philosopher to teach the writings of W. E. B. Du Bois, Richard Wright, or Ida B. Wells. These scholars were not considered philosophers and thus had nothing to say about the real-world problems of philosophy. Plus, they were not white. People often teach what they were taught. Most of our professors in graduate school knew little and cared less about the people and concerns we brought to graduate school. (Alain Locke was never presented as a philosopher to study.) One should not be surprised. Philosophy as a discipline is situated in the racist history of this country. Why would white philosophers be concerned with the writings of people deemed intellectually and morally inferior? Does this mean that all white philosophers avoided issues of race and racism in the profession? No! While there have been mainstream white philosophers who took issues of race and racism seriously as subjects of study, for the most part, Black people and the Black experience have been avoided. Would I infer that this reflects how philosophers fail to respect the humanity of Blacks? Yes. It seems as if it was thought that there was nothing in the experience of this group of humans that warranted philosophical exploration, or could bring philosophical insight. This does not mean that the Black experience should permeate every area of philosophy. There are questions of social and political philosophy and ethics that could use the insights gained from the Black experience to make moral and political theories more attuned to the social reality of many people, not just Black people. But because the prevailing way of thinking discounts the Black experience, we lose these insights. It has been mainly through the work of the African-American philosophers who came into the profession beginning about forty years ago that we see at least some acknowledgement of the Black experience as philosophically relevant. This is not to discount the handful of academically trained Black philosophers who were in the profession before the mid-1960s, but only to note that between the early 1970s and the late 1980s there were at least two handfuls of Black philosophers. Departments that had progressive white colleagues were often at the forefront of the recruitment of Blacks into the profession as colleagues and graduate students. The numbers of Black philosophers was still low. The paucity of Blacks in the profession meant that more often than not the Black philosopher was the only person of color in their department. White philosophers did not see this as strange because they had tried to get the best Black in their department, and, of course, you only need one Black to show that your department was not racist and socially concerned. These were hard times. As bad as it was for Black men, it was hell for many Black women, both as professors and graduate students. This is a story that also must be told. Fortunately, there are younger white philosophers who are trying to make the future of philosophy more inclusive on all fronts than was its history. Still, *one* might argue that historically philosophy, as an academic discipline and profession, has *worked* to maintain its "whiteness."

G. Y.: Frederick Douglass endured the absurdity and dehumanization of American slavery. Given your work on Douglass, in what way does he offer a set of experiences and conceptual frames of reference that can inform philosophy?

B. E. L.: I think that Frederick Douglass's life experiences do have something to tell us about the profession and the doing of philosophy. Douglass is interesting, as is anyone who lived so long and wrote so much. From his life as a slave to elder statesman, Douglass experienced the best and worst of United States history from before the Civil War to the late 1890s. Douglass's life gives us reason to reflect on both the practice of philosophy and the profession of philosophy. First, Frederick Douglass is not often thought of as a philosopher. He is considered an abolitionist, civil rights advocate, women's rights supporter, and humanitarian. Yet a careful reading of Douglass's work shows that he exhibits all of the academic attributes of a trained philosopher. This was one of the reasons I, along with Frank Kirkland, chose to do an anthology of articles by philosophers looking at the writings of Douglass as a philosopher *by philosophers*.[2] In part it was Douglass's commitment to arguments that were sustained and substantive that made this project possible.

Douglass in his speeches and writings reflected on the social and political status of Blacks in the United States, the meaning of racial difference, the meaning of democracy, what it means to be human, and the role of art in the push for social and racial progress. In fact, in his speech "Pictures and Progress," he notes that he is doing philosophy of art. I am in the process of working through Douglass's theory of art. I see a line of reasoning about the role of art that runs from Douglass through the works of Booker T. Washington to the aesthetic writings of Alain Locke. So not only was Douglass a philosopher, but his writings influenced later generations of Black scholars. Frederick Douglass was both an activist and a scholar.

I would contend that those in the philosophy profession did not examine his writings because it would be assumed that his writings were not philosophical. Of course, no one would take the time to read his work because it was about race, and until recently there *had not been* a sustained treatment of issues regarding race in the profession of philosophy. Issues regarding race were not the subject matter of philosophy. Rather, other areas of the humanities and the social sciences were the arenas for research on race. Douglass's work and life raise questions about who can do philosophy and what should be counted as philosophy. Those concerns still haunt Blacks in the philosophy profession today. I would suggest reading Kristie Dotson's "How Is This Paper Philosophy?"[3] and my paper "Philosophical Playa Hatin': Race, Respect, and the Philosophy Game,"[4] as examples of these concerns.

G. Y.: We generally ask what Martin Luther King Jr. would think about race relations in America if he were still alive. But what would Douglass think, especially within a context in which Black people continue to feel existential pain and suffering on so many indices (employment, poverty, healthcare, police profiling, etc.)?

B. E. L.: If Douglass were still alive, he would be 196 years old. He would have lived through the *Plessy* decision, the lynching of Black soldiers returning from WWI and WWII, the massive racial segregating of America, the *Brown* decision, *Brown II*, the Civil Rights Movement, the killing of Martin Luther King Jr., the rise of someone like Oprah, the election of President Obama, the increasing wealth disparity between Blacks and whites over the past 25 years, and the shooting of Michael Brown. What would Douglass think about the state of race relations in the United States today? Douglass was born into slavery and lived to see that horrible institution dismantled. He was, I think, at the end of his life, disappointed in the way race relations in the United States were going. In 1871, he realized that without some form of affirmative action, qualified Blacks would not get employment; in 1888, he questioned the value of the Emancipation Proclamation; in 1890, he addressed the race problem and noted that it was not Blacks who were the problem but white attitudes toward the rights of Blacks. In 1895, a year before his death, he again addresses the problem of Blacks being upright citizens when national, state, and local governments do nothing to protect their rights. You can read his reflections in the speech "The Lessons of the Hour." In this speech, Douglass notes that the Supreme Court has surrendered. State sovereignty has been restored, and the Republican party has become the party of money and things rather that a party of morals and justice. He concludes with the question, What next? We know what came next. The nation became more racially segregated, Jim Crow Laws, governmental sanction segregation, sundown towns and neighborhoods, lack of political protection for Black citizens, and, of course, racial violence against Blacks in the form of lynching. It may be argued that these are not the times we live in now. Douglass, I contend, understood the manner in which laws and social practices impact on the attitudes of people. Three hundred years of anti-Black thought cannot be eradicated in fifty years. Even if people want to claim that Douglass would be hopeful, it must be remembered that he would also have thought that the country could have treated Black people differently than it did. It could have treated Blacks like the full citizens they were and protected their rights and opportunities. Douglass died in 1895, and in 1896 we had the *Plessy* decision. Given this history, he might be disheartened at the current state of race relations.

G. Y.: Yes, but what would we make of Douglass's hope in light of the recent killings of not only Michael Brown, but Eric Garner, Tamir Rice, and now Walter Scott and Eric Harris? There is a pervasive feeling of panic and angst (across race) at this time.

B. E. L.: Some people look at the social and political status of Black people now and marvel as to how far the country has come in regards to race relations. I do not think that most people either know or understand the depth of anti-Black thinking in this country. Events of late have caused many Blacks and whites to re-evaluate the meaning of racial progress. Some whites feel that given all the country has done for Blacks, many Blacks seem strangely ungrateful. "Hell," they say, "we let them into our neighborhoods, our schools, our jobs; we even let them marry our daughters. What more do they want?" On the other hand, the current level of anti-Black thought shocks many Blacks and whites. "How can these overtly racist actions be happing in 2014–2015? My God! We have a Black President of the United States!" Both of these views ignored the deeply racist history of this country and how difficult it is to overcome the impact of that history. Remember that it was only seventy years ago that *An American Dilemma: The Negro Problem and Modern Democracy* was published.[5] By the time of its publication, Douglass had been dead for fifty years. Douglass's hope has to be seen in light of his having been born into slavery. He saw the social and political attitudes turn from supporting slavery to being anti-Black. Yet, he remained hopeful. Douglass understood that resolution of the race problem required the full political and moral weight of the United States government.

I think that you are correct that there is panic and angst across and on both sides of the racial divide. What does hope mean in these times? It depends on what you hope for and how you access the possibility of the situation hoped for to materialize. Hopes can be weak or strong. I have examined the position of Martin Luther King Jr. and Derrick Bell on hope in "The Aporia of Hope: King and Bell on the Ending of Racism,"[6] and would contend that King's hope, like Douglass's,was based on a belief in faith, reason, and the adhering to liberal principles of respect for the individual, along with hard social and political work would bring about the beloved community. Bell, on the other hand, had little hope that the beloved community will be established in the United States. Thus, Bell has a permanence of racism thesis. The killings of Michael Brown, Eric Garner, Tamir Rice, and others push many people to Bell's position. Whether you agree with King or Bell, one's understanding of United States history is important. In sum, the current panic and angst is rooted in the racist history of this country that has never been addressed because of a tradition of being ahistorical when it comes to issues of race and racism.

G. Y.: When confronted by the "slave breaker" Covey in 1833, Douglass physically resists him. Yet, when the white abolitionist John Brown calls upon Douglass to join him in a war against white slave-holders, Douglass backs down. What has Douglass to teach us about tactics when it comes to resisting racial injustice in our contemporary moment?

B. E. L.: Frederick Douglass teaches us that given the history of racism in this country, people concerned with racial justice have to know when to act and when not to act. In other words, don't be stupid!

NOTES

1. John Hope Franklin, "The Dilemma of the American Negro Scholar," in *Soon One Morning*, ed. Herbert Hill (New York: Knopf, 1963).
2. Bill E. Lawson and Frank M. Kirkland, *Frederick Douglass: A Critical Reader* (Malden, MA: Blackwell, 1999).
3. Kristie Dotson, "How Is This Paper Philosophy?" *Comparative Philosophy* 3, no. 1 (2012): 3–29.
4. Bill E. Lawson, "Philosophical Playa Hatin' Race, Respect and the Philosophy Game," in *Reframing the Practice of Philosophy: Bodies of Color, Bodies of Knowledge* (Albany: State University of New York Press, 2012), 181–202.

5. Gunnar Myrdal, Richard Sterner, Arnold Marshall Rose, and Robert L. Harris, *An American Dilemma: The Negro Problem and Modern Democracy* (Norwalk: Easton Press, 1993).
6. Bill E. Lawson, "The Aporia of Hope: King and Bell on the Ending of Racism," in *The Liberatory Thought of Martin Luther King Jr.: Critical Essays on the Philosopher King* (Lanham, MD: Lexington Books, 2012), 321–40.

Lucius T. Outlaw Jr.

George Yancy: Your work has played a major role in introducing the critical examination of race within the professional field of philosophy. Briefly, what sort of resistance did you encounter early on in terms of introducing the philosophical significance of race, and would you say there are still forms of resistance in the profession that deem philosophical treatments of race unimportant or nonphilosophical?

Lucius T. Outlaw, Jr.: If I interpret your question correctly, George, as asking me to comment on what resistance I encountered to my endeavoring to focus thematic philosophical efforts of analysis and critique on conceptualizations and praxes involving raciality, then I must say that your question doesn't seem to call attention to efforts on my part, efforts joined and led by more than a few others, to call attention to various ways in which investments in raciality were distorting the discipline and profession of philosophy, efforts that preceded the emergence of "philosophy of race." In my judgment, struggles against *racism* (and other impediments) in the profession of philosophy were a precursor to, and prepared the way for, the forging of discursive contexts through which a more structured and persistent subfield, "philosophy of race," has been developed. "Philosophy of race" grew, to some extent, out of efforts to forge what has become the now-multidimensional subfield of Africana philosophy. In other ways, "philosophy of race" has been part of a larger insurgent intellectual venture—antiracist "critical race theory/studies"—advanced by critical thinkers in several other disciplines (law, literary studies, political theory/philosophy, sociology, Liberation Theology, etc.). In short, it is crucial to have an understanding of the extent to which there had to be successes in antiracist struggles to win and secure the presence and legitimacy in disciplines and professions in addition to philosophy of *persons* of particular racialities (and other important identifying characteristics), persons for whom those identities were significant for/in critical philosophizing, as the social basis for engaging in and legitimating discursive foci as disciplinary fields or subfields.

There was strong resistance to those early efforts to secure places in the profession (through appointments, reappointments, tenure, and promotions) of those waging efforts to forge and legitimate discursive contexts for Black/African-American/African/Caribbean/Africana philosophy. Of particular significance were the many years when virtually all publishers of works of philosophy that would have booths at divisional meetings of the American Philosophical Association and were approached with inquiries or formal proposals for projects that were the focus of the insurgent discourses refused, some repeatedly, to publish offered works. So, too, editors of many journals.

But, there has been substantial success, so much so that, several decades ago, the American Philosophical Association added "Africana philosophy" to its list of recognized subfields and added "Philosophy and the Black Experience" to its roster of newsletters. And today there are more works of Africana philosophy, broadly conceived, being published that I can keep up with. No small matters, these. Still, not all departments of philosophy, those with graduate programs especially, honor the recognition or publications in their curricula, hiring of new faculty, regard for publications, and so forth. Moreover, I suspect that a substantial number of professional philosophers, distinguishable to some extent by their areas of specialty and the years of their training in philosophy, continue to nurture the idea, the aspirational ideal, that philosophizing at its best is not influenced by the philosopher's investments in raciality, a matter that is "morally irrelevant" and without "scientific" (empirical) grounding. For more than a few of these, as for many other thoughtful persons, to best be done with racism we should be done with any and all investments in raciality. Persons so persuaded continue to be resistant.

G. Y.: So, what would be a productive way to address those who would conflate investments in raciality with the continuation of racism?

L. T. O. Jr.: Well, I wouldn't consider the situation as involving persons "conflating investments in raciality with the continuation of racism." Rather, I think that there are particular (by no means all) investments in raciality, too often unacknowledged and/or denied, that contribute to the continuation of instances and institutionalizations of racism (i.e., invidious racial judgments and valorizations manifested in behaviors and practices), sometimes inadvertently, sometimes willfully.

Addressing such instances would require deliberately structured occasions of discussion (structured by shared commitments to regulating practices by shared principles of disciplined respect, openness, courage, and cooperation guided by the ideal of a shared mission) devoted to working together to identify, explore critically, propose renovations of, and implement and continuously evaluate the consequences of implementations of revisions to, or eliminations of, the instances of shared life conditioned by investments in raciality that are invidious or produce invidious consequences. As well, such critical interventions would be especially productive if efforts were also devoted to identifying and fortifying all instances of shared life that currently (or during previous times and conditions) nurture and enhance shared life in positive ways for all concerned, for those, especially, who suffered from invidious investments. Of course, such explorations would also benefit from considerations of instances of shared life in other contexts (departments, programs, disciplines, institutions, organizations; in different life-worlds and cultural traditions, etc.) that critical examinations persuade those involved that there are lessons from which to learn, examples to be followed, with appropriate modifications for the situations under review.

In short: addressing such instances motivated by the shared desire—and the shared commitment—to change things for the better requires a shared commitment to shared learning, growth, and adaptive reorganization of (particular aspects of) shared life, a shared commitment, that is, to work together to foster directed personal and social coevolution.

G. Y.: So, for you, what are some of the "invidious racial judgments and valorizations manifested in behaviors and practices" that continue to sustain (whether deliberately or not) racism as manifested, for example, in the field of philosophy here in the US?

L. T. O. Jr.: An appropriate response requires knowledge growing out of empirical data regarding behaviors and practices, accumulated and analyzed systematically, drawn, at least, from a credible representative sample of persons, institutionalizations, and organizations of academic and professional philosophy, in the USA, for example. I have neither such data nor such an analysis. Nor, to my knowledge, has any organization of professional academic philosophers—the American Philosophical Association, the Society for Phenomenological and Existential Philosophy, for example—undertaken the tasks of gathering and analyzing such data in order to contribute to the development of a synthetic and diachronic empirically informed understanding of behaviors and practices, the conceptions and valorizations that give rise to and sustain (and are sustained by) behaviors and practices, constitutive of academic and professional philosophy and philosophizing. I am left, then, to take on the risks of offering considerations drawn from my limited experiences of more than four decades of engagements in academic and professional philosophy and philosophizing in the contexts of departments in colleges and universities (in four as a full-time member, in four others as a visitor); organizations (the APA and SPEP, among others: several of the organizations' committees; being a participant and member of the audience in many, many of the organizations' sponsored and hosted sessions); local, national, and international conferences sponsored and hosted by various departments, institutions, and organizations.

So, then, let's begin with historical and genealogical accounts of the emergence of "philosophy" that tend to be put forward in texts and recapitulated in introductory courses in the discipline: "Philosophy began in Greece . . . subsequently spread to Europe . . . then to . . . " Such accounts tend to be more than historical when serving to valorize certain peoples/civilizations as having given unique "gifts" to the world never before produced by any other peoples/civilizations. And to the extent that "philosophy" becomes identified with the exercising of reasoning capabilities to such accomplishment as to be the realization of "Reason," then those canonized as exemplars of such reasoning serve as paradigmatic representatives of the peoples/civilizations producing the unique "gifts." The histories of such peoples/civilizations, then, of the practices of reasoning and the products thereof, have been valorized and canonized as achievements that distinguish the producers (and their practices, institutions, cultures, nations, nation-states, continental regions, peoples, races) from, and as better achievers, than all other peoples/civilizations (and their practices, institutions, cultures, nations, nation-states, continental regions, peoples, races). Such, I hazard to believe, constitutes much of the disciplinary self-understanding and professional identity-formation that are cultivated in the education/socialization organized and mediated in a great many of the departments of philosophy in our country.

To the extent that this is the case, there continue to be valorized and valorizing cultivation and mediation of invidious considerations of both favored and disfavored peoples/civilizations, the favorings and disfavorings often, I suspect, being highly correlated with invidious racial identifications and characterizations of peoples/civilizations. What tend to be regarded as basic notions of "what it is to be human" are made problematic by limited and/ or distorted comparative considerations of projects of reasoning by peoples/ civilizations excluded from study. Likewise for conceptions of the agendas of reasoning in the diversity of circumstances in which, across the history of the evolution of our species, humans, across successive generations, have survived and adapted. It is across the whole of the species, then, to which our careful studies of adaptive reasoning should be oriented in order to learn about learning while refining our capabilities for critical comparisons leading to fallible judgments that are to be continuously subjected to review as we make history. Such an orientation would require very substantial renovations of much of our curricula, of much of our research practice, of much of our pedagogy, of much of our guiding agendas for philosophizing. One of the most substantial efforts to wrestle with these matters has been taken on by Elizabeth Kamarck Minnich, insights from which she shares in her *Transforming Knowledge*. Very highly recommended.

G. Y.: Yes. I think that Minnich's view not only questions and critiques epistemic sites that are exclusionary of other legitimate sites of knowledge production, but her view (as well as what you've argued above) raises deep philosophical anthropological issues. I recall reading recently where North Korea's state media referred to President Obama as a "wicked black monkey." And we have footage of a white police officer in Ferguson, Missouri saying to a group of Black protesters, "Bring it, all you fucking animals! Bring it!" How can Black people even begin to be seen as producers of knowledge and civilization, when there is this relatively fixed image of Black people as subhuman persons?

L. T. O. Jr.: The economist Paul Samuelson has been credited with the insight that theory advances funeral by funeral. Similarly, a fuller appreciation of contributions by persons of African descent, to knowledge production as well, will come with the succession of older generations by newer ones comprised of persons many of whom will have been educated, formally and informally, across the full range of contexts of education, by teachers and mentors who themselves have acquired knowledge that has facilitated their cultivation of appreciations for peoples African and African-descended and their many contributions.

We are farther along in this development than in previous decades and centuries, but have a ways to go still. The electoral successes yesterday of Republicans are in important ways indicative, I believe. Republican strategists and operatives guided Republican candidates in waging successful campaigns to persuade willing voters that President Obama is a "failed leader" who has accomplished nothing worthwhile and is "bad for the country." And this after Republicans waged a successful campaign of obstruction in the US House and Senate to deny the President any significant legislative successes, a campaign that was launched over dinner in a local Washington, DC establishment while the just-inaugurated President and his wife were making the rounds attending celebratory balls.

This strategy has a long and inglorious history, and was diagnosed insightfully by Swedish social scientist Gunnar Myrdal, who was recruited to lead the massive study of "the Negro problem" during the 1940s, the results of which were published under his editorial guidance as *An American Dilemma: The Negro Problem and Modern Democracy*. Foundational to "the Negro problem," Myrdal concluded, was white racial prejudice, the manifestations of which he understood as "dynamic causation" formally identified as a "principle of cumulation" or "vicious circle": "White prejudice and discrimination keep the Negro low in standards of living, health, education, manners and morals. This, in turn, gives support to white prejudice. White prejudice and Negro standards thus mutually 'cause' each other."[1]

Myrdal's conclusion, after the education he gained through the studies he directed, led him to propose the need for a "virtuous circle" as a corrective for the "vicious circle." He was convinced, however, that because the "dynamic causation" had many factors, no attempted corrective would be effective if directed at one factor alone, or if directed at what was thought to be the primary determining factor (economic conditions, for example). All factors had to be addressed, in a coordinated fashion, within and among all the contexts of life and social interactions: work, play, worship, entertainment, education, "manners and morals,"[2] and so forth. Virtually all modes of knowledge-production can be resources on which to draw, philosophy included, though there are no privileged resources in the latter to guide and structure the long, slow, renovative and replacement work. For the discipline of philosophy has had to be subjected to renovation. Here, too, the work is not finished. And it will not be finished even after the funerals that will memorialize the lives ended of my generation and those but slightly ahead of us.

G. Y.: But don't you think that there is something far more racist and vicious at play here? It seems to me that the discourse of "failed leader" and "bad for the country" can function as tropes for anti-Black racism where the real charge is that it is because Obama is Black that he is really, quite frankly, "incompetent."

L. T. O. Jr.: Well, George, drawing on personal and shared histories of experiences of folks African and African-descended, I have a heightened suspicion—a working hypothesis—that, indeed, for many white folks, even for many folks of color, judgments and expectations regarding particular competencies are racially construed. So it is after nearly four centuries of social constructions of realities[3] grounded on and shaped by ideologies of White Racial Supremacy and negro/black racial inferiority. And while important changes have produced liberating reductions and transformations in the forms and forces of such ideologies, there are continuing modalities of changed ideologies such that, perhaps, voting for Barack Obama as a presidential candidate involved, I suspect, exaggerated assessments of him and heightened expectations for his performance: he was, for many, an *exceptional* Black man, *unusually* well qualified (in part, for some folks, *because* his mother was white). When, then, his performance in any arena is judged by some as less than extraordinary, there is a quick and all-too-easy regression by some of those judging to the not-yet-eradicated presumption of racial inferiority—or, less perniciously, to a presumption of racially induced subpar competencies brought to light by subpar performance, accomplishments otherwise notwithstanding.

Such are my suspicions, my hypotheses. I need the assistance of social scientists accomplished at empirical research, social psychologists especially skilled at researching opinions and sentiments not often made explicit or even acknowledged by those harboring them, in order to determine whether my suspicions/hypotheses are cogent, or not, and for whom they are true, more or less, if at all.

G. Y.: Lastly, what role do you see for white philosophers (within the more immediate context of our profession) in generating forms of knowledge production toward the end of creating a less hostile space for philosophers of color? Of course, this question bleeds over into the whole of American race relations and the responsibility that white people have to engage in antiracist practices.

L. T. O. Jr.: All folks "white" have not, do not, take up "being white" in the same ways. Even at the heights of white racist dominance in the United States of America, there were white folks who became willful, courageous traitors to projects of impositions, institutionalizations, and perpetuations of White Racial Supremacy.

There are persons in the profession of academic philosophy who have continued these legacies of courage. The development of "Africana Philosophy" has benefitted substantially from the support of numerous white philosophers, scholar-practitioners in other disciplines, administrators in institutions of higher education, and officials in foundations and federal agencies. Already, then, the emergence of new modes of knowledge-production less constrained and less distorted by white racism is under way; so, too, the lifting up of philosophically significant articulations of insights and wisdom by Black folks heretofore unheralded in our profession. The publication of this and other interviews you have conducted with the likes of me for publication via *The Stone* is yet another milestone of these historic developments.

Meanwhile, slowly but significantly, more undergraduate and graduate students are partaking of these developments in regular and special courses; through attendance at and participation in lectures, conferences, symposia; through engagements with texts and other media; through direct encounters and engagements with white teachers who lead them into discoveries of learnings through engagements with productions of articulations and creative expressions by persons African or of African descent. Of particular significance, through several signal anthology projects, you have forged provocative queries in response to which white philosophers have drawn on their courage as well as their philosophical competencies to explore racist whiteness as contributions to disclosures that, when taken up critically, warrant revisions of attitudes, beliefs, passions, habits, and behavior such that white racism can be reduced and more respect for nonwhite peoples and persons, their life-worlds, can be forged and lived.

The very hard work of creating less hostile spaces for philosophers of color is thus well underway. I suspect—I hypothesize—that, gradually, as older generations are replaced by younger generations, funeral by funeral, more and more white philosophers will share in this challenging work.

NOTES

1. Gunnar Myrdal, *An American Dilemma: The Negro Problem and Modern Democracy* (New Brunswick, New Jersey: Transaction Publishers, [1944] 1996), 75.
2. Myrdal, *An American Dilemma*, 75.
3. Peter Berger and Thomas Luckmann, *The Social Construction of Reality: A Treatise in the Sociology of Knowledge* (New York: Doubleday, 1957).

Cornel West

George Yancy: One of your newest books is entitled *Black Prophetic Fire*, which has a conversational structure. Define what you mean by 'Black prophetic fire.'

Cornel West: Black prophetic fire is the hypersensitivity to the suffering of others that generates a righteous indignation that results in the willingness to live and die for freedom.

G. Y.: When I think of black prophetic fire, I think of David Walker, Frederick Douglass, Sojourner Truth, Audre Lorde, Malcolm X, Medgar Evers, Martin L. King Jr, James Baldwin, and so many others. In recent weeks, some have favorably compared the writer Ta-Nehisi Coates to Baldwin. I know that you publicly criticized this comparison. What was the nature of your critique?

C. W.: In a phone conversation I had with Brother Coates not long ago, I told him that the Black prophetic tradition is the collective fightback of sustained compassion in the face of sustained catastrophe. It has the highest standards of excellence, and we all fall short. So a passionate defense of Baldwin—or John Coltrane or Toni Morrison—is crucial in this age of Ferguson.

G. Y.: In what ways do you think the concept of Black prophetic fire speaks to—or ought to speak to—events like the tragic murder of nine people at the Emanuel African Methodist Episcopal Church in Charleston, South Carolina?

C. W.: I think in many ways we have to begin with the younger generation, the generation of Ferguson, Baltimore, Staten Island, and Oakland. There is not just a rekindling, but a reinvigoration taking place among the younger generation that enacts and enables prophetic fire. We've been in an ice age. If you go from the 1960s and 1970s—that's my generation. But there was also an ice age called the neoliberal epoch, an ice age where it was no longer a beautiful thing to be on fire. It was a beautiful thing to have money. It was a beautiful thing to have status. It was a beautiful thing to have public reputation without a whole lot of commitment to social justice, whereas the younger generation is now catching the fire of the generation of the 1960s and 1970s.

Charleston is part and parcel of the ugly manifestation of the vicious legacy of white supremacy, and the younger generation—who have been wrestling with arbitrary police power, arbitrary corporate power, gentrification, the land-grabbing, the power-grabbing in and of the black community, and arbitrary cultural power in terms of white supremacist stereotypes promoted on television, radio, and so forth—has become what I call the "marvelous new militancy," and they embody this prophetic fire. The beautiful thing is that this "marvelous new militancy" is true for vanilla brothers and sisters; it's true for all colors in the younger generation, though it is disproportionately Black, disproportionately women, and, significantly, disproportionately Black, queer women.

G. Y.: Why the metaphor of 'fire'?

C. W.: That's just my tradition, brother. Fire really means a certain kind of burning in the soul that one can no longer tolerate when one is pushed against a wall. So, you straighten your back up, you take your stand, you speak your truth, you bear your witness and, most important, you are willing to live and die. Fire is very much about fruits as opposed to foliage. The ice age was all about foliage: "Look at me, look at me." It was the peacock syndrome. Fire is about fruits, which is Biblical, but also Marxist. It's about praxis and what kind of life you live, what kind of costs you're willing to bear, what kind of price you're willing to pay, what kind of death you're willing to embrace.

That was a great insight that Marcus Garvey had. Remember, Garvey often began his rallies with a Black man or woman carrying a sign that read, *"The Negro is not afraid."* Once you break the back of fear, you're on fire. You need that fire. Even if that Negro carrying that sign is still shaking, the way that the lyrical genius Kanye West was shaking when he talked about George W. Bush not caring about Black people, you're still trying to overcome that fear, work through that fear.

The problem is that during the neoliberal epoch and during the ice age you've got the process of "niggerization," which is designed to keep Black people afraid. Keep them scared. Keep them intimidated. Keep them bowing and scraping. And Malcolm X understood this better than anybody, other than Ida B. Wells—they represented two of the highest moments of Black prophetic fire in the twentieth century. Ida, with a bounty on her head, was still full of fire. And Malcolm, we don't even have a language for his fire.

G. Y.: Does this process of "niggerization" in American culture partly involve white supremacist myths being internalized by Black people?

C. W.: Yes. When you teach Black people they are less beautiful, less moral, less intelligent, and as a result you defer to the white supremacist status quo, you rationalize your accommodation to the status quo, you lose your fire, you become much more tied to producing foliage, what *appears* to be the case. And, of course, in late capitalist culture, the culture of superficial spectacle, driven by capital, driven by money, driven by the market, it's all about image and interest, anyway. In other words, principle drops out. Any conception of being a person of integrity is laughed at because what is central is image, what is central is interest. And, of course, interest is tied to money, and image is tied to the peacock projection, of what you appear to be.

G. Y.: Can we assume then that you would emphasize a form of education that would critique a certain kind of hyperrealism that is obsessed with images and nonmarket values.

C. W.: That's right; absolutely. It's the kind of thing that my dear brother Henry Giroux talks about with such insight. He's written many books providing such a powerful critique of neoliberal market models of education. Stanley Aronowitz, of course, goes right along with Giroux's critique in that regard. The notion has to do precisely with that critical consciousness that the great Paulo Freire talks about, or the great Myles Horton talked about, or the great bell hooks talks about in her works. How do you generate that kind of courageous critical consciousness that cuts against the grain and that discloses the operations of market interests and images, capitalist forms of wealth inequality, massive surveillance, imperial policies, drones dropping bombs on innocent people, ecological catastrophe, and escalating nuclear catastrophe?

All of these various issues are very much tied into a kind of market model of education that reinforces the capitalist civilization, one that is more and more obsessed with just interest and image.

G. Y.: What do you see as the foremost challenge in creating a common cause between the past generation and the current generation now "catching fire," as you put it?

C. W.: For me, it is the dialectical interplay between the old school and prophetic thought and action. I'm an old Coltrane disciple just like I'm a Christian. You can be full of fire, but that fire has to be lit by a deep love of the people. And if that love is not in it, then the fire actually becomes just a sounding brass and tinkling cymbal that doesn't get at the real moral substance and spiritual content that keeps anybody going, but especially people who have been hated for so long and in so many ways, as Black people have.

For me, the love ethic is at the very center of it. It can be the love ethic of James Baldwin, Audre Lorde, Toni Morrison, Marvin Gaye, John Coltrane, or Curtis Mayfield, but it has to have that central focus on loving the people. And when you love people, you hate the fact that they're being treated unfairly. You tell the truth. You sacrifice your popularity for integrity. There is a willingness to give your life back to the people given that, in the end, they basically gave it to you, because we are who we are because somebody loved us anyway.

G. Y.: This question relates to the collection of Dr. King's writings you edited, called *The Radical King*. Why did you undertake the job of curating and editing the book?

C. W.: Because Martin had been so sanitized and sterilized. He has been so Santa Claus-ified, turned into an old man with a smile, toys in his bag to give out, and leaving everybody feeling so good. It was like we were living in Disneyland rather than in the nightmare that the present-day America is for so many poor working people, especially poor Black working people. So, we needed a kind of crystallization.

But there has been a variety of different voices talking about the radical King. You know my closest friend in the world, James Melvin Washington, was the only person that the King family allowed to bring the collection of sermons and writings together. Clayborne Carson was another scholar who early on published King's sermons, speeches, and writings. It's one of the greatest honors for me to be one of the few that the King family allowed to bring those kinds of writings together across the board, laying out a framework. You've got James Melvin Washington's *A Testament of Hope*. You've got other wonderful scholars like James Cone, Lewis Baldwin, and others who have done magnificent work in their own way. But, you know, as I pass off the stage of space and time, I want to be able to leave these love letters to the younger generation. I want to tell them that they're part of a great tradition, a grand tradition of struggle, critical, intellectual struggle, of moral and political struggle, and a spiritual struggle in music and the arts, and so on.

Contrary to when people talk about King every January, there is in *The Radical King* in fact a particular understanding of this moral titan, spiritual giant, and great crusader for justice. So you get a sense of who he *really* was beyond all of the sanitizing and sterilizing that are trotted out every year in celebration of him.

G. Y.: How does *The Radical King* compare with other books that you've written or produced?

C. W.: That, for me, is the most important book I've ever done. That's why I dedicated it to my blood brother who is the closest person to me in the world. He is the most Coltrane-like, Christ-like, and the most Curtis Mayfield-like person I've ever met in my life. He just happened to be the person I grew up with and slept in the same bedroom with and talked to every day. That's grace right there, brother. It's a gift. I'm not responsible for that. I just showed up.

G. Y.: King is well known for quoting the American reformer and abolitionist Theodore Parker's words, "the arc of the moral universe is long, but it bends toward justice." What's your assessment of King's claim now, in 2015, particularly in the light of the kind of existential plight and angst that Black people and poor people are experiencing? Is there an arc of the moral universe?

C. W.: I think King had a very thick metaphysics when it came to history being the canvas upon which God was in full control. As you know, I don't have such a thick metaphysics. I am closer to Anton Chekhov, Samuel Beckett, and a bluesman. I think that King at the end of his life became more of a bluesman. He began to think, "Lord, have mercy. That arc might be bending, but it sure is bending the wrong way." After all, he's dealing with white supremacist backlash, patriarchal backlash, and capitalist backlash against working people and the possibility of ecological catastrophe. He was already wrestling with the possible nonexistence of life on the earth in terms of the nuclear catastrophe that we were on the brink of. So, he made a leap of faith grounded in a certain conception of history that was heading toward justice. I don't accept that. I just do it because it's right. I do it because integrity, honesty, and decency are in and of themselves enough reward that I'd rather go under, trying to do what's right, even if it has no chance at all. Or, if it has the chance of a snowball in hell, I'll do it anyway. I'm not a consequentialist in that sense, either theologically or politically or anything else. So, my view is much, much darker than brother Martin's view. It's just that he and I made the same leap, where the leap has to do with telling the truth, bearing witness, and dealing with whatever scars and bruises that go along with it. It's a process of trying to listen to critics, but also, keeping track of the "sell-out" folk who demonize you. I go right back at them and pull the cover from over their own hypocrisy, mendacity, and their willingness to defer to the powers that be.

G. Y.: I was thinking about your existentialist sensibilities that would in fact be critical of the claim that the universe is moral at all. Yet, both you and King share a blues sensibility that places emphasis on touching the pain and yet transcending the pain, and also the importance of the Christian good news.

C. W.: Oh, absolutely, we are both very similar in terms of never allowing hatred to have the last word, not allowing despair to have the last word, telling the truth about structures of domination of various sorts, keeping track of the variety of forms of oppression so we don't become ghettoized and tied to just one single issue. Yet, at the same time, we're trying to sustain hope by being a hope. Hope is not simply something that you have; hope is something that you are. So, when Curtis Mayfield says, "Keep on pushing," that's not an abstract conception about optimism in the world. That is an imperative to be a hope for others in the way Christians in the past used *to be* a blessing—not the idea of praying for a blessings, but *being* a blessing.

John Coltrane says *be* a force for good. Don't just talk about forces for good; be a force. So it's an ontological state. So, in the end, all we have is who we are. If you end up being cowardly, then you end up losing the best of your world, or your society, or your community, or yourself. If you're courageous, you protect, try, and preserve the best of it. Now, you might preserve the best, and still not be good enough to triumph over evil. Hey, that's the way it is. You did the best you could do. T. S. Eliot says, "For us, there is only the trying. The rest is not our business."

G. Y.: Indeed. When it comes to race in America in 2015, what is to be done?

C. W.: Well, the first thing, of course, is you've got to shatter denial, avoidance, and evasion. That's part of my criticism of the president. For seven years, he just hasn't or refused to hit it head-on. It looks like he's now beginning to find his voice. But in finding his voice, it's either too late or he's lost his moral authority. He can't drop drones on hundreds of innocent children and then talk about how upset he is when innocent people are killed. You can't reshape the world in the image of corporate interest and image with Trans-Pacific Partnership and then say that you're in deep solidarity with working people and poor people. You can't engage in massive surveillance, keeping track of phone calls across the board, targeting Edward Snowden and Chelsea Manning and others, and then turn right back around and say you're against secrecy, you're against clandestine policy.

So that, unfortunately, if he had come right in and asserted his moral authority over against Fox News, over against right-wing, conservative folk who were coming at him—even if he lost—he would have let the world know what his deep moral convictions are. But he came in as a Machiavellian. He came in with political calculation. That's why he brought in Machiavellians like Rahm Emanuel and Larry Summers, and others. So, it was clear it was going to be political calculation, not moral conviction.

How can anyone take your word seriously after seven years about how we need to put a spotlight on racism when, for seven years, you've been engaged in political calculation about racism? But then you send out your lieutenants. You send out all your Obama cheerleaders and bootlickers and they say to his critics that he is president of all of America, not black America. And we say white supremacy is a matter of truth. Are you interested in truth? It's a matter of justice. Are you interested in justice? It's a matter of national security. Are you interested in national security? Well, we talk about Black America. We're not talking about some ghettoized group that's just an interest group that you have to engage in political calculation about. When you talk about Black people, you're talking about wrestling with lies and injustice coming at them and their quest for truth and justice. If you're not interested in truth and justice, no politician ought to be in office, and not just the president. And that's true in our classrooms, as you know. Should we study Black history, or brown history, indigenous people? Are you interested in truth and knowledge and justice? Then you're going to have to come to terms with them. You're not doing us a favor. You're talking about your commitment to truth. Well, the same is true for the President. So, we've actually had a major setback in seven years; a lost opportunity.

One of the grandest public intellectuals, brother David Bromwich, said it so well in "What Went Wrong," which is published in *Harper's Magazine*.[1] What a lost opportunity we've had for progressives and for people concerned with poor people and working people. Look at the Israeli-Palestinian situation. Five hundred babies killed in fifty days and the President can't say a mumbling word? And not a politician can say a mumbling word? What kind of moral authority can anybody have, if you can't say a word? "Well, that's the way American politics is." No, no, no, we know we've got Jewish brothers and sisters willing to engage in critique of vicious Israeli occupation and bomb-dropping on innocent people. They're human beings, too. And if they are not willing to come to terms with it, let them engage in an argument, but you have to make the effort. That's part of my being so upset about brother Martin being in the Oval Office. You can't have Martin staring at you every day and you're losing moral authority in regard to drones, Wall Street, massive surveillance. Being re-elected and talking about race after seven years. I would say that even when it comes to our precious gay brothers and lesbian sisters and bisexuals and trans-folk. It was just three years ago that both Hillary Clinton and Obama were defending the Marriage Act. And then finally, when they were pushed because Joe Biden made his move. No, no, take a moral stand! Is it right or is it wrong? How are the states going to deal with it if in fact you're taking a moral stand and you know they have a right to equality, and you know they have a right to have their dignity affirmed, then the federal government ought to come in. "No, it's a matter of the polls." We're back to Machiavellian calculation again. And, you know, the gay brothers and lesbian sisters know this. You either take a stand or you don't. You can't just ride the wave at the end when the movement is successful. That's just wrong. And for me, that's what prophetic fire is all about. And then people say, "Well, that sounds self-righteous. You do understand how American politics functions. You have to grow up to come to terms with the limits of any historical situation." I say, BS. If that were the case we'd still be enslaved, women would still be dealing with patriarchal households, and workers would still be unorganized. We can go right down the row in terms of the various struggles for freedom around the world. Colonized people would still be dealing with empires on their backs. You've got to be willing to try to tell the truth, engaging in witness bearing, organizing, and then, in the end, pass it on to the next generation. The greatest example, of course, is W. E. B. Du Bois. The greatest, the best, is Du Bois, and where did Du Bois end up? 31 Grace Court, Brooklyn Heights. One major visitor, a giant named Paul Robeson, was under house arrest in Philadelphia. Both of them, pariahs; viewed as people who lost their minds because they wanted to tell the truth. The world is still trying to catch up with Du Bois and Robeson, even as I speak, in terms of their critique of capitalist civilization, their critique of how deep white supremacy cuts. And they were concerned about the Dalit people in India, working people and poor people in Tel Aviv as well as the plight of Palestinians. They had a universal and humanistic orientation, but it led them to cut so radically against the grain that we're still trying to catch up. See, that's my tradition right there. And Du Bois was wrong about the Soviet Union, no doubt about that. But I'm talking about their critique of capitalism which we're still coming to terms with, even today.

G. Y.: But is it really possible to speak courageous speech while acting as the most powerful country in the world? Of course, we also have to admit the history of racism preceded Obama's tenure and will exceed it. My point is that there is a deep tension that exists for someone who desires to embody prophetic fire and yet be in charge of an empire.

C. W.: I think that's true for most politicians, actually. Now when it comes to the intellectuals who rationalize their deference to the politician, so they want to pose as prophetic even though they are very much deferential to the powers that be, they need to be criticized in a very intense way. That's why I'm very hard on the Obama cheerleaders, you see, but when it comes to the politicians themselves, *it is* very difficult to be a prophetic politician the way in which Harold Washington was or the way Paul Wellstone was or the way Shirley Chisolm was, or the way my dear brother Bernie Sanders actually is. He is a prophetic politician. He speaks the truth about wealth and equality. He speaks the truth about Wall Street. He speaks the truth about working and poor people being afterthoughts in terms of the kind of calculations of the oligarchs of our day. He shows that it's possible to be a politician who speaks the truth.

Once you occupy the White House, you are head of the empire. Then you have a choice. We've had two grand candidates in the history of the United States. We've had Abraham Lincoln and we've had Franklin D. Roosevelt. Both of them are full of flaws, full of faults, full of many, many blind spots. But they pushed the American experiment in a progressive way, even given their faults. And that's what we thought Obama was going to do. We were looking for Lincoln, and we got another Clinton, and that is in no way satisfying.

That's what I mean by, we were looking for a Coltrane and we ended up getting a Kenny G. You can't help but be profoundly disappointed. But also ready for more fightback in post-Obama America!

NOTE

1. David Bromwich, "What Went Wrong? Assessing Obama's Legacy," *Harper's Magazine*, June 2015, http://harpers.org/archive/2015/06/what-went-wrong/.

Kwame Anthony Appiah

George Yancy: How did you become interested, philosophically, in the question of race? Did it grow out of something like a conceptual problem of reference, or did it come more out of lived experience? Or, perhaps this disjunction is a false start?

Kwame Anthony Appiah: I'm always skeptical when intellectuals give accounts of how they came about their interests! So you should take what I have to say as a set of hypotheses about my own past, not as the results of introspection, which yields nothing about this.

When I first started teaching in the United States in 1981, I had a joint appointment at Yale, in African and African-American studies, on the one hand, and philosophy, on the other, and I was casting about for things to do on the African and African-American side of my work, both as a teacher and as a scholar. I had been an undergraduate student at Cambridge in medical sciences for one year, and philosophy for two, and I was puzzled, as a newcomer to the United States, by the fact that many people appeared to think "race" was a biological concept, whereas I had been taught in my brief career in the life sciences to think it was not.

So I looked to see what there was of a philosophical sort to teach on this topic and discovered not very much. And since "race" was a rather central concept in the field of African-American Studies, it seemed to me that thinking a bit about it was a contribution that someone with my training could make.

Since my dissertation had been in the philosophy of mind and language, issues about reference seemed like one thing to take up, but I began mostly with explorations that were less technical, just trying to get across why it was that the life sciences had given up on race and what the best conceptual and empirical evidence suggested about whether they were right. Eventually I got to see that the concept had a life in many fields—or rather that many concepts travel under the flag of the word "race." So I've written about it as a topic in literary studies as well as in biology, the social sciences and metaphysics.

G. Y.: In your new book, *Lines of Descent*, you write that W. E. B. Du Bois saw himself as an American and a Negro (as opposed to an African-American). You state correctly how being an "American" and being a "Negro" did not fit well for him. I'm reminded of Du Bois's encounter in *The Souls of Black Folk* with the tall (white) newcomer and how she refused to exchange visiting cards with him and how this signified early on in his life a deep tension in his sense of "racial" identity.[1] Do you think contemporary African-Americans also find themselves possessed by, as Du Bois describes it, "two warring ideals in one dark body, whose dogged strength alone keeps them from being torn asunder"?[2]

K. A. A.: I think that Du Bois's way of thinking about this, which was informed by nineteenth-century German social philosophy, can be put like this: each people, each *Volk*, has a soul, a *Geist*, that is the bearer of a folk culture and of what he called spiritual "strivings." American Negroes were possessed of the soul of America and the soul of the Negro. Since America's folk culture was racist, they were possessed by a spirit that was, in some respects, hostile to them. The Negro soul gave them the resources for a positive sense of self, which helped to resist this, but it also gave them various other gifts.

I don't believe in the *Volksgeist* myself. (Big surprise.) So I would translate all this into perhaps less exciting terms. But to begin with I'd have to challenge one of the tendencies of this German Romantic line of thought—which is to think that there's a kind of wholeness and homogeneity to the collective soul. Because it seems to me that Black identity in America brings with it a whole host of contradictory forces, which are not easily parsed either as American or as Black. And how they play out for you depends on other things about who you are—a woman, a skilled laborer, a philosopher, a bisexual, a Catholic, and so on.

But there are surely many contemporary Black Americans who are taken up in an American concern for individuality but frustrated by the undeniable obstacles to success for Black people in a way that most Americans can't be. (Though Hispanics, I think, increasingly are as well.) And similarly, many Black Americans draw on Black traditions of community, based in churches and mosques, that are thicker than much white religiosity. So, though I don't think it's the case that you can parse African-American life as *one* tension between the two sides of the hyphen, I do think that there clearly are characteristic sources of racial storm and stress, but that class and gender and other factors mean that it's a different story for different subgroups.

G. Y.: Even if one agrees, as I do, that there is not really anything like a "collective Negro soul"—and especially not in the metaphysical sense—isn't there a way we can still hold on to something like "Black identity"? In other words, aren't there ways in which to be Black in America is based upon shared traditions of resistance, shared pain and angst, shared assumptions about things like the racial policing of our bodies or white supremacy, and so on?

K. A. A.: One reason I'm a nominalist about identities is that you can say that there's a shared label, then say that what it does, both in the mind of the bearer and in her treatment by others, has elements that are shared and elements that are distinct. So what makes the identity *one* identity is its label, I think, more than what is done with them.

Similar complexities surround the idea of a Black culture. Black Americans can certainly draw on cultures transmitted within communities of Black people, and those cultural traditions may have elements shared across the board. Black adults, for example, tend to teach Black children ways to handle American racism. The Black label explains part of why they do this: bearing the label brings with it the risk of racist responses. So we could then say that teaching kids to deal with racism is part of Black culture.

Then there's the equally vexed issue of shared experiences. The sense in which a Black American in New York now shares the pain of the lynch victim in Georgia one hundred years ago is importantly figurative rather than literal. And it is a difficult question how much Booker T. Washington shares the traditions of resistance of Frederick Douglass. An idea, a practice, a response can be marked as Black in various ways, without its being shared among Black people. The advantage of abandoning the *Volksgeist* is that we can ask what is and isn't actually shared.

G. Y.: I'm also thinking about Du Bois's essay "The Souls of White Folk," where he says he is "singularly clairvoyant" when it comes to understanding white people.[3] "White folk" isn't just a nominal concept here; it has political, psychological, and existential content. His claim about knowing the ways of white folk is an epistemic claim that is grounded upon his own identity as an oppressed Black person who is part of a suffering group, one who rides the Jim Crow car, but who in his clairvoyance also sees what I don't think we want to deny—that is, a collective white supremacist *identity*. What do you think?

K. A. A.: One thing that I think is absolutely true in Du Bois's remark is the recognition that the oppressed often have a deeper understanding of the lives of oppressors than vice versa, because they have to make sense of the powerful to survive. (If you want to know how the marriage of a person with servants is going, don't ask their friends; ask the servants.) But again, I'd be a nominalist about white identity. And I'd agree that the role of whiteness in white supremacy is part of the story. But John Brown, like many other white abolitionists, wasn't participating in the supremacist narrative; he was trying to undo it. So while white people share an identity, it isn't going to follow that they share an agenda, or beliefs or values in virtue of that fact.

G. Y.: You also wrote in *Lines of Descent* that Du Bois would say that the race concept should be retained, or that a Black identity should be preserved, until justice and freedom reigns on earth.[4] Yet, this seems to confine Black identity to a kind of master-slave relationship; once the white master disappears, there will be no need for a Black identity. Do you think there are legitimate ways in which Black people can hold on to their "racial identities" after, let's say, the collapse of white supremacy? Isn't Black identity certainly more than being forced to ride the Jim Crow car or being disproportionately profiled by white police officers?

K. A. A.: I think it would take an imagination more powerful than mine to know what would be possible once white supremacy came to an end everywhere. Identities shift their meanings all the time, and a Black identity in a world without white supremacist institutions or practices would undoubtedly mean something different. What would happen to the way the identity relates to transnational forms—Pan-Africanism, Black churches—and how it would change within our country would be worked out by real people in real time. So while racism gives Black and white identities a central role in their particular current inflections, who knows what they would mean in a future without racism?

And even in the present, as you say, the meaning of the Black label for particular people and communities has to do with a great deal more than the experience of racial insult and injustice. We have vibrant Black cultures in music, film, literature, sport, dance, the visual arts, and one's relation to these forms is psychologically and sociologically mediated by a Black identity. You can think of these things as "ours" through the Black label, the Black identity. And there's no obvious reason why any of this would stop just because we got, say, institutionalized racism under control.

G. Y.: There are not enough John Browns fighting against white supremacy (even if one disagrees with his method) and all the subtle ways in which it has continued to exist. To invoke Du Bois again, how have you experienced what he says is an unasked question—How does it feel to be a problem? And in what ways do you personally negotiate that question and what it implies?

K. A. A.: Well, I should begin by saying that I think that a background of class privilege on both sides of my family has protected both my sisters and me from some of the worst challenges of living in a racist world. (They have also had the advantage of living much of their lives in various parts of Africa!) I was born in London but moved with my family to Ghana when I was one. My sisters were all born there. When I was an undergraduate at college in England, Skip Gates and I and a Nigerian philosophy student we knew were the only Black people in our college. But I had white upper-middle-class high-school friends and upper-middle-class English cousins around, so I guess I didn't feel that there was any question as to my right to be there, and I don't think anyone else thought so either. (And I wouldn't have cared if they did!)

As a young person in Ghana, many people I met in my daily life in my home-town knew my family, and knew why I was brown and not Black. They knew my mother was an Englishwoman (and white) and my father was Ashanti (and Black). And throughout my childhood in Ghana, the Asantehene, the king of Ashanti, whose capital was my hometown, was my great-uncle by marriage. (To those who didn't know me, though, I was a "*broni kokoo*," a "red [skinned] foreigner"; "*broni*" is often mistranslated these days as "white person.") So, in a way, the most interesting "problem" for me, having been in America and then an American citizen for much of my adult life (since 1997), has been how to figure out a Black identity having come from two places where my color had a very different significance.

One of the things that I have always been most grateful to this country for is the sense of welcome I have often felt from African-Americans as a person of African descent. There's no necessity about this: my ancestors—and not so many generations back—were in the business of capturing and selling other Black people into the Atlantic slave trade (and some of my mother's kinfolk back then were no doubt in the business of buying and shipping them). So one thing that race does in the world is bring Black people together in spite of these divided histories. But I suppose that the main effect of my being Black has been to draw me to Black subject matter, Black issues, and to give me an interest—in both senses of the term, an intellectual engagement and a stake—in pursuing them. Without this connection to the world of Africa and her diaspora I would just be someone else.

G. Y.: One central premise or conviction of cosmopolitanism, which you wrote about in your book *Cosmopolitanism: Ethics in a World of Strangers*, is that all human lives matter. Yet in 2015 we continue to witness the need to declare "Black Lives Matter." Has America failed to embrace this conviction when it comes to Black people and other "strangers"?

K. A. A.: No society has yet lived up to the principle that everybody matters. Our American failures have indeed been around race and gender and religion and sexual orientation and disability, but we mostly move in the right direc-tion over the long haul, though too slowly for anyone who cares about this principle. It ought, by the way, to worry morally serious conservatives that conservatism has been on the wrong side of so many of the struggles around these issues, even when they have eventually come round. Our defections are particularly scandalous, I think, because we *began* with the proposition that we're all created equal.

It is just preposterous that in 2015 we have to be in the business of insist-ing that Black Lives Matter. It ought not to be necessary to say that the rela-tive invisibility of Black suffering and the racially oppressive character of our institutions, especially as they face the Black poor, is a huge problem. But it is necessary, alas. And surely one of the greatest scandals in the world today is the fact that the "home of the free" has more people incarcerated per capita than any other nation—OK, except the Seychelles islands—and while less than half of our prisoners are (non-Hispanic) Blacks, you've got to believe that the general indifference to this vast prison population has something to do with its racial composition. What kind of person would want to live in a society where half the male population has been arrested at least once by the time they're in their mid-twenties, which is the situation for African America? (Actually, what kind of country has arrested more than a third of its male population of any race by that age?) I think the general tolerance for the level of poverty in this very rich country is probably connected with the association of poverty with Black people as well. So, as Du Bois pointed out a long time ago, among the victims of American racism are many of the white poor. My blood pressure literally rises in indignation whenever I think about the depraved indifference of too many of our politicians and too much of our media to these problems. I've argued (in *The Honor Code*) that patriotism is above all about having a stake in the honor of your country. So let me put it this way: on these questions, we Americans should be ashamed of ourselves.

G. Y.: I'm sure you are aware that the South Carolina police officer Michael Slager has been charged with the murder of Walter Scott, a Black male, after a video of Slater shooting Scott in the back as he fled surfaced on the Internet. Some see this as a kind of turning point in the situation between white police officers and Black people in the United States. Do you?

K. A. A.: We'll see. Certainly, the response of the authorities in the town has so far been exemplary. But this was a very extreme case. An independent witness filmed the whole thing. The murder involved shooting a man in the back, a man who posed no threat because he was clearly running away. Officer Slager seems to have lied about what happened, and appears, in the video, to have planted evidence. So, of course, it's a good thing that he will be charged and tried—and, of course, his trial, just to be clear, should start with the presumption of innocence—but I don't know that the evidence will be so overwhelming the next time something like this happens. Without that iPhone video, it might just have been another case where the cop claimed self-defense. So who knows if a prosecutor or a grand jury would have believed him.

Of course, we'll never know for sure what would have happened. Maybe the bullets in the back fired from a distance would have worried the coroner, but there have been more than two hundred shootings of suspects, both Black and white, by police in South Carolina in the last five years; only a few have been investigated, and there has not been one conviction of an officer. Still, one story often helps people to understand what a whole lot of argument doesn't. So, let's hope that this story helps people understand why too many Black people are right not to trust too many police officers. Then, perhaps, we can develop the political will to do something about it.

NOTES

1. W. E. B. Du Bois, *The Souls of Black Folks*, with introductions by Nathan Hare and Alvin F. Poussaint (New York and Scarborough, Ontario: New American Library, [1903] 1982).
2. Du Bois, *The Souls of Black Folks*.
3. W. E. B. Du Bois, William Edward Burghardt, and David Levering Lewis, *W. E. B. Du Bois: A Reader* (New York: Macmillan, 1995).
4. Kwame Anthony Appiah, *Lines of Descent: W. E. B. Du Bois and the Emergence of Identity* (Cambridge, MA: Harvard University Press, 2014).

Clevis Headley

George Yancy: At what point in your philosophical training did you realize that race was an important philosophical concept that needed to be clarified?

Clevis Headley: I first came to the realization that race was an important philosophical concept in need of clarification after I became disillusioned by the complacent declarations by philosophers and other intellectuals that the concept of race is both semantically and ontologically illegitimate. Among other things, I came to realize that these thinkers were uncritically invoking various problematic assumptions about meaning and reference. Indeed, while employing naïve realist convictions about the relation between language and the world, those in the grips of this uncritical realism glibly denounce the concept of race, arguing that the term 'race' fails to designate an independent entity in the world. Accordingly, they argue that, since the concept of race is ontologically vacuous, it is also semantically empty. It was this kind of uncritical philosophizing about race that led me to the realization that it is important to develop an approach to concept formation and use that is favorable to socio-historical/cultural concepts such a race. Put differently, formal, abstract analyses of the concept of race distort and render invisible the historical, existential, and experiential features of the concept of race. Any philosophical analysis or approach to race that is blind to its historical, existential, and experiential realities is philosophically derelict.

It should be noted that there are some courageous philosophers who actively pursue other approaches to race. These philosophers, convinced about the philosophical relevance of race, provide stimulating and insightful examples of concrete and existential phenomenological studies of race and racism. Two of these outstanding philosophers are you and Lewis Gordon.

G. Y.: Do you think that professional philosophy is still resistant to treating race and racism as legitimate philosophical concerns? If so, why? I recall that as an undergraduate at the University of Pittsburgh, there was no philosophical treatment of race. So, perhaps there is something specific about the philosophical legitimation practices in analytic philosophy that avoids race.

C. H.: Yes, I do believe that professional philosophy is still resistant to treating race and racism as legitimate philosophical concerns. There are a number of reasons for this resistance. First, within professional analytic philosophy, there exists the ideological contention that "real philosophy" deals only with perennial philosophical problems. Since the concept of race is not a perennial philosophical problem, analytic philosophers do not consider it to be a legitimate philosophical concern. In other words, to the extent that race is, among other things, a historical and cultural problem, those analytical philosophers who are philosophical purists do not involve themselves with race. Second, analytic philosophers have not promoted a "race industry" in philosophy because of the long-held conviction that the concept of race is a vague concept and one that is so obviously flawed that there is nothing of philosophical significance to be gained from philosophical studies of race. Third, analytic philosophers are also inclined to resist treating race and racism as legitimate philosophical concerns because of their uncritical loyalty to liberalism. An unthinking allegiance to the liberal mantra that society is an aggregate of autonomous, atomistic, rational, and free individuals has led many philosophers to conclude that, since individuals are socially and ontologically primary, all that is necessary is to extend to all individuals the same sets of rights. This conviction has led to a full embrace of color blindness as a norm. In turn, the norm of color blindness has enabled philosophers to argue that race or racial determinations are philosophically irrelevant, in so far as they do not capture the true essence of individuals, namely rationality and autonomy. Again, both race and racism are considered analytically and theoretically exhausted as determined by the liberal paradigm. Thus, race and racism do not qualify for any special philosophical attention, since liberalism has already supplied the vocabulary and conceptual framework for dealing with race and racism. Any philosophical interest in race and racism is thus not considered to be bona fide or pure philosophy but mere applied philosophy, at best.

G. Y.: What must be done at the level of rethinking the Western philosophical canon in order to trouble the philosophical biases against race as a philosophically rich phenomenon?

C. H.: In order to trouble the philosophical biases against race as a philosophically rich phenomenon, a number of strategies must be pursued: (1) We need to radically rethink traditional notions about ontology. Instead of grounding our ontology upon notions of permanence, sameness, identity, and so forth, we need to embrace ontological assumptions that are historically informed, that are sensitive to time, process, development, and change. (2) Rather than embrace the traditional conviction that our ontology must be consistent with classical Aristotelian logic, we need to investigate the philosophical merit of the Hegelian notion that logic and ontology are complementary. (3) We need to rethink traditional assumptions about the meaningfulness of concepts. Thus, on the traditional view, a concept is legitimate if its application does not violate the law of the excluded middle or the law of bivalence. (4) Rather than denouncing concepts whose application violates these laws as being vague, we need to better understand the ways in which vagueness is not a defect of socio-historical/cultural concepts. (5) We also need to cultivate a greater appreciation for the pragmatic, contingent, and historical character of concept formation and use. In other words, instead of viewing concepts as naming transcendent essences or as being legitimate when they satisfy the norms of scientific usage, we need to focus more on the complex practices of concept construction and application, from the perspective of actual human existence. To this end, our analysis of concepts should develop either a philosophical morphology or, from a different perspective, a chemistry of concept formation, and (6) the sort of philosophical naturalism championed by John Dewey would create an atmosphere in which philosophers could pursue the sorts of interdisciplinary activities that would enable philosophers to escape the obsession with a priori methods so often incapable of capturing the dynamic reality of race.

G. Y.: Given that the professional field of philosophy continues to be largely white and male, do you see a connection between this demographic, on the one hand, and the resistance to or silence regarding race as philosophically relevant, on the other?

C. H.: If one subscribes to the view that racial, gender, class, and other so-called contingent factors are irrelevant both to being a person and to the discipline of philosophy, then one would have to deny the existence of any connection between the predominance of white males in philosophy and the resistance to race as philosophically relevant. I hold the view that individuals are neither disembodied beings, totally removed from culture, nor totally determined by cultural, racial, or historical factors. Rather, individuals must critically negotiate with a socio-historical/cultural world. They must critically interact with the socio-historical/cultural world, in which they find themselves, and this world in turn influences individuals. This kind of inescapable dialectical exchange entails that the biographies of individuals are not existentially irrelevant. Indeed, the existential structure of their biography influences their philosophical interests. Again, because of the complex narrative histories that shape and facilitate individuals' efforts to make sense of their existence, this kind of narrative intelligibility cannot be mechanically erased when one becomes a philosopher.

It seems then that philosophy is the kind of discipline that should embrace and aggressively promote epistemological pluralism. If, as Wilfrid Sellars maintains, "the aim of philosophy, abstractly formulated, is to understand how things in the broadest possible sense of the term hang together in the broadest possible sense of the term,"[1] then it follows that philosophy would be better served by the kind of demographic diversity that could guarantee the posing of new and different questions, as well as the creation of novel research agendas by persons from different narrative traditions. Hence, epistemological pluralism is not a call for philosophical fragmentation or for the end of philosophy; rather, it is a call for the flourishing of plural epistemological paradigms. Demographic pluralism should encourage the kind of epistemological pluralism in which philosophers could creatively and imaginatively interact by seeking cross-fertilization of philosophical practice, questioning, and investigation. Epistemological monism encourages philosophical illiteracy regarding race and racism. A literate pluralism, on the other hand, would create conditions for the cultivation of meaningful knowledge about race and racism and, in the words of Lewis Gordon, would put an end to the current "disciplinary decadence"[2] that encourages lost knowledge concerning race and racism.

G. Y.: I agree with your critique of society as *not* being an aggregate of autonomous, atomistic, rational, and free individuals. I tend to stress the heteronomous, the socially embedded nature of who we are. As someone who teaches courses on race, how do you engage students, especially white students, who tend to have already been seduced by the Horatio Alger narrative, to rethink their identities in ways that trouble a neoliberal, atomic understanding of the white self?

C. H.: First of all, since people find it difficult to discuss race, I always attempt to put my students at ease. Indeed, the effort to unsettle the notion of being a self-sustaining individual entails debunking aspects of a social mythology concerning, among other things, the ways in which one fulfills one's ambitions. The challenge to invite students to rethink their identities in ways that trouble a neoliberal, atomic understanding of the white self requires that one turn to history. I explain to students that although they did not participate in the original decision to use race as a category of exclusion and inclusion, and as a basis for political, social, and economic participation, they, nevertheless, were born into a world structured on the basis of race. The fact that they played no role in the original creation of what Charles Mills calls the racial contract does not mean that they can arbitrarily opt out of the racial contract. One can easily nullify the terms of a legal contract if one has good reasons to believe that it is not in his/her interest to uphold the terms of the contract. However, an individual cannot simply opt out of the racial contract simply by declaring that he/she does not believe in race and does not want to be considered as being white. Objectivities, such as racial identities, do not easily lend themselves to isolated individual protestation and elimination. As I referenced above, I emphasize the importance of critical negotiation in terms of how one must deal with realities not of our own choosing.

Hence, the turn to history is necessary in order to enable white students to understand that although white individuals are represented as race-less, whiteness is an identity, that is, a historically constructed identity. To be more specific, I utilize history to establish that the significance of whiteness is not exclusively biological or for that matter metaphysical, but ontological in the manifold sense of whiteness as property, a very suggestive metaphor pioneered by Cheryl Harris. Here Harris emphasizes, among other things, the historical fact that the possibility of accumulating property required that one first be recognized as white. This phenomenon was made possible by constitutional fiat, not by biology, by nature, or even by God. Again, the retreat to history is to make clear to students that dominant narratives about self-made individuals are decontextualized constructions that distort the historical background of how and why certain groups enjoyed abundant success and why other groups are confined to situations of subordination.

G. Y.: How do you respond to white students who argue that they didn't own slaves and therefore can't be responsible for perpetuating racial injustice? I imagine that the atomic conception of the self is also operating within such contexts.

C. H.: It is indeed true that the atomic conception of the self is immediately invoked by some whites in protestations against any possible charges of responsibility for racial injustice. As a matter of fact, even the very notion of responsibility is contaminated with the ontological pretensions of atomistic individualism. The argument goes: if it is true that individuals are responsible only for their actions, then only the concept of individual responsibility makes sense. Consequently, if an individual did not directly participate in slavery, he or she has no responsibility for the historical consequences of slavery. Only perpetrators of harm are responsible for compensating the victims of the harm. Since current whites did not own slaves, they are not responsible for the racial injustices of slavery.

Alternatively, while adamantly invoking individual responsibility, students often express their support for the idea that it is impossible for there to be any coherent notion of collective, generational, or historical responsibility. Since the notion of collective, generational, or historical responsibility is incoherent, the only viable sense of responsibility is individual responsibility. Accordingly, one can hide behind the notion of individual responsibility to nullify individual responsibility for the actions of the distant past even if one lives in a society that functions in a way that accords one benefits resulting from historical injustice.

From another perspective, denying any responsibility for perpetuating racial injustice is possible if one actively embraces the phenomenon of blindness to history. Blindness to history not only explains why individual whites view themselves as not culpable for perpetuating racial injustice but also the fact that they are the beneficiaries of past racial injustice. Hence, I attempt to enable students to acknowledge and to appreciate the extent to which history is real and how it effects the present and shapes the future. Of course, my attempt to reach students, as you know and already appreciate, is not a matter of promoting absurd views. Rather, the goal is to get them to critically confront the past or use the past to illuminate the present. The challenge then is to help white students to become ethically aware such that they can think critically about how they can transform the world for the better. Here taking responsibility for the past is a matter of seeking to obtain a greater understanding of how the past inserts itself into the present. It is also a matter of appreciating that a failure to understand the persistence of history is not a sign of liberation and autonomy but, rather, of rendering oneself a prisoner of the past, even becoming vulnerable to the possibility of suffering blindness to history as a terminal existential condition.

G. Y.: I've also heard from white Americans who say, "Look, I have no power. I'm poor." How do we address such claims while also trying to make the case for white privilege?

C. H.: While clearly understanding that there are differences of class between Blacks, as well as differences of class among whites, the simple response to claims of common victimhood or parity of suffering is to point out the complexities of unjustifiable differences in treatment between Blacks and whites as they respectively interact with and negotiate the dominant institutions of society. For example, we know that because of the phenomenon of implicit bias, a white single mother is more likely to be viewed as deserving of assistance than a Black single mother.

A second response is to utilize the notion of "false equivalence" to explain the mistaken attempt to locate all individuals on the same social and political plane, all in the name of formal equality. There exists abundant empirical evidence indicating that persistent differences separate a Black society from a white society. Here I am thinking about Andrew Hacker's *Two Nations: Black and White, Separate, Hostile, Unequal.* Hacker points out that being white is a major privilege in American society and that despite how degraded the life of a white individual, that white individual would not seriously consider voluntarily becoming a black individual.[3] Hacker intimates that most whites attribute great value to their whiteness and would not easily surrender their whiteness. Michelle Alexander's *The New Jim Crow: Mass Incarceration in the Age of Colorblindness* chronicles the severe racial inequalities perpetrated by the criminal justice system. And, finally, we learn from *Chain Reaction: The Impact of Race, Rights, and Taxes on American Politics*, by Byrne Edsall and Mary D. Edsall, the extent to which race plays a vital role in shaping the views of white Americans on outstanding political matters. Again, it is necessary to keep in mind that blind faith in or uncritical allegiance to individualism prevents people from understanding the extent to which the complexities of the political, economic, and social world cannot be semantically reduced to mere individual initiative. We know that the neighborhood that you are born into determines the quality of one's early education, and we know that one's early education will determine one's success in college and ultimately one's professional success. However, since whites and Blacks live in segregated communities and since white communities have greater access to more resources than do Black communities, individual initiative is not potent enough to consistently overcome these structural barriers. Some scholars have used the term 'hoarding' to explain why whites tend to have greater access to resources and opportunities than Blacks. In other words, our residential patterns facilitate the ability of whites to hoard opportunities and resources, hence exposing the idea of there being total racial equality.

I want to end my response to this question by introducing the notion of an epistemology of ignorance that some philosophers have used to explain why whites would see themselves as not having power and as being just as poor as Blacks. Many thinkers have interpreted the notion of an epistemology of ignorance as an attempt by whites to claim not to know what they should know or deliberately refusing to unlearn certain things in order to maintain power. In other words, a white individual can believe that racial discrimination does not exist and that whites and Blacks are treated equally in society. However, when confronted with evidence concerning the great disparities in wealth, education, income, and so on, between Blacks and whites, the white individual can declare ignorance of these facts or even refuse to be epistemologically impacted by them. Although the notion of an epistemology of ignorance can explain certain trivial aspects of the daily lives of both Blacks and whites, it remains to be seen if the appeal to this notion is sufficiently adequate to coherently explain the persistence of Black racial subordination and the survival of white privilege. Among other things, a certain question emerges: what does it mean for whites to either not know or feign ignorance of the daily racial realities of American society when it is analytically assumed that their very identities are shaped by these realities?

G. Y.: Why would white folk even want to admit to their racial privilege, to challenge it? To do so seems counter to their own interests. So, how does one make the case that it is in their "best" interest to dismantle their white privilege?

C. H.: It is probably the case that there are whites who have a genuine desire to dismantle white privilege. The problem, however, is that the basic theoretical assumptions, ontological presuppositions, and analytical devices of the law, political theory, economic theory, social philosophy, and so on, are all grounded on the primacy of individualism. Consequently, even if certain whites desire to dismantle white privilege, they lack the vocabulary and theoretical tools that would allow them to gain a fair hearing in society. Indeed, we all use the common vocabulary of liberalism to discuss matters of race. The problem is that this vocabulary works by translating historical and group-related issues into issues of abstract individualism. As a matter of fact, notions such as group rights or collective responsibility, when viewed from the perspective of dominant narratives, are unintelligible. The general point is as follows: that those whites who view themselves as mere individuals and as race-less, and who are opposed to notions of group rights or collective responsibility, will argue that they are entitled to what they have because they have earned it. For example, the courts will judge in favor of white individuals who challenge efforts to extend opportunities to Blacks precisely because, again, the law recognizes individual rights not group rights. So, although there is much evidence to substantiate the idea of white privilege, any discursive practice grounded in individualism will be unable to dismantle white privilege. Finally, even if we were to focus on creating the appropriate vocabulary, it might not be possible to rationally convince many whites to surrender or dismantle their white privilege. We tend to invest a great deal of value in rational argumentation while denigrating the role of imagination, emotions, and affectivity in politics. However, as James Baldwin has intimated, perhaps we need to think more in terms of love and not the exhausted abstractions that offer us "false clarity" and invite us to erase the complexity and messiness of the actual world in which we exist.

G. Y.: I want to return to your point about epistemology of ignorance. I appreciate your point. Of course, it could be that whites are also persistently blinded to (or epistemically failing to see) their own relative successes vis-à-vis Blacks and people of color. Yet, I want to say, surely, they see this! You raise an important point here. For example, I'm thinking of the recent tragic killings in St. Paul and Baton Rouge. There seems to be something else going on other than an epistemology of white ignorance. What else is going on?

C. H.: It is extremely difficult to analytically discuss the institution of the police in American society, especially with regard to the relation between the police and race. Nevertheless, I will approach this issue from a philosophical perspective and not from the perspective of an activist or a social movement. Most people prematurely denounced the Black Lives Matter Movement because they uncritically interpreted this movement as a particularism that is opposed to the universalist view that all lives matter. The problem is that most people fail to realize that, although the slogan "Black Lives Matter" is a particularlist statement, it is in fact an unabashed endorsement of the universal recognition that all lives do indeed matter. We live in a society that gives lip service to this universalist recognition but behaves as though Black lives are irrelevant and are, therefore, excluded from the universalist position. Thus, the only way to include Black lives into the universalist position is to explicitly assert that Black lives matter. So, instead of being a negation of the universal recognition of the value of all lives, the slogan 'Black Lives Matter' is undeniably consistent with the universality of all lives as having value and as mattering. Accordingly, it expresses this recognition by calling attention to the fact that the universal declaration of the value of all lives is atrociously empty if the lives of Black people are not equally valued. If society remains largely apathetic to the killing of innocent Black men and women by law-enforcement officers, then the universal declaration that "All Lives Matter" is hollow. Hence, to correctly understand the ethical thrust of the statement 'Black Lives Matter,' at least as I understand it, does not and should be interpreted as condoning the denigration of the value of the lives of non-Blacks or police officers.

The difficulty of talking about the relation between the police and the Black community is made greater by the tendency of the media to sensationalize this particular issue. There is also the risk of being accused of encouraging violence against police officers. And then there is the unquestioned assumption that Black people cannot dispassionately discuss this issue without becoming excessively emotional. Of course, even the institutionalized discursive practices that go by the name of 'criminal justice' are burdened by a theoretical concoction of descriptive generalizations that masquerade as solid science.

So, back to your question: What else is going on other than the epistemology of ignorance? The discussion concerning the police and the Black community is almost always severely decontextualized, continuously removed from the history of the society. We can solve this problem by contextualizing this discussion. That is, by carefully situating it within the multiple layers of history that are relevant to this issue. In other words, any discussion concerning the relation between the Black community and the police should be contextualized relative to the history of slavery, reconstruction, Jim Crow, the "law and order" debate of the 1960s, the phenomenal escalation of the prison industrial complex, and the war on drugs of the 1980s and 1990s. The common thread variously connecting these historical events is the use of state power to monitor and discipline Black bodies. You have brilliantly discussed this issue in your book *Black Bodies, White Gazes*.

So, instead of reducing tragic incidents of unarmed Black people being shot by the police or dying under suspicious conditions while in police custody to isolated cases of individual culpability, we need to do a better job of understanding that individual police officers do not function in a historical void. Rather, they are operating within an institution of policing that is tainted by the historical and structural denigration of the lives of Black people. Even white police officers who are not compromised by implicit racial bias and who hold no racist animus toward Blacks may, nevertheless, become complicit in supporting policies and engaging in practices that have horrendous racist impact. It is not then simply a matter of better training police officers or improving race relations, even if these initiatives are helpful; we need to critically evaluate and modify the persistent structures that support and sustain the institution of policing in American society. This approach should not be interpreted as being against the institution of policing but, rather, should be seen as a manifestation of our active support of democracy, as well as a realistic embrace of the institution of the police.

Finally, another reason why there is so much confusion and misinformation concerning the relation between the institution of policing and the Black community is a failure to properly contextualize the political status of the police in modern democratic societies. The mainstream debate regarding the police and the Black community is often translated into a certain philosophical vocabulary. Most people feel confident in what they construe as the neutral and patriotic support of the police because they assume that the police are ontologically prior to the citizenry. Put differently, they seem to assume that the institution of the police is a transcendental condition of the possibility of civil society. It seems to me that this ontological ordering is misleading. Consistent with social contract theory, the citizenry is ontologically prior and the institution of the police is ontologically secondary, meaning the possibility of the police is secondary to the prior agreement among free individuals to enter a social contract to establish society. Hence, the institution of the police is not the ontological equal of the citizenry but must answer to the citizenry; the police is a creation of free citizens. It is not the case that the people are dependent upon the police in order to recognize themselves as having rights. Clearly, then, it is not whether one supports the police, for there is no sense to be made of not supporting the institution of the police in a modern, democratic society. Rather, we need to do a better job of making sure that those hired by citizens to enforce the laws created by the representatives of the people understand that citizens always have a metalevel function to perform in holding agents of the state accountable. The use of force is not a unilateral matter outside the scope of critical scrutiny by the citizenry. And citizens must shoulder and recognize their responsibility for assuming the burden of sustaining civil society. This point is a corrective to the commonly held view that the police constitute a thin blue line separating civil society from the state of nature. Hence, triumphalist calls for law and order, when Black citizens lose their lives in unfortunate circumstances involving law-enforcement officers, is an unethical repudiation of our collective responsibility as citizens to subject the use of force by agents of the State to the strictest scrutiny possible.

G. Y.: What is it like for you (here I'm thinking about how Fanon engages the *lived* experience of Black people) to understand that your life within a white supremacist society *doesn't* matter relative to white lives?

C. H.: This is a very important question, the kind of question that any think-ing Black person should take the time to critically work through, while avoid-ing the extremes of denial or acting out. I have two quick responses to this intriguing question—a question that infused and inspired so much of Fanon's writings: First, I am reminded of Hannah Arendt's idea of one being viewed as an "objective enemy" of the dominant society.[4] I think that this notion correctly connotes the sense of certain individuals simply by virtue of their birth being classified as guilty; in other words, their sin is having been born. Hence, the relative value of the life of a Black person in comparison to the life of a white person is an indication of this phenomenon of one's existence as a crime, an existential mishap. Under these circumstances, that mutated existence, that life (Black life) that is considered a deviation from the norm is not valued as being of equal value as the life (white life), which is a repre-sentation of the norm. Consequently, in a white supremacist society, Black lives are less valuable than white lives. Second, I am reminded of a phrase that Marina Banchetti, my wife, shared with me: "Daseining while Black." I inter-pret this phrase as the existential equivalent of the common phrase, "driving while Black." So, the idea of "Daseining while Black" essentially connotes the dangers one confronts as a person "existing while Black." The question pres-ents itself in the form: what does it mean to exist while Black? What does it mean to be in-the-world while Black, especially when the world is skeptical of your existence?

I deal with the realization that my life within a white supremacist society *doesn't* matter relative to white lives by adopting a radical existential attitude. By this I mean that I affirm the absurdity, contingency, and unpredictability of life. This approach is not a retreat into nihilism. Rather, it is matter of under-standing that objectively speaking, the world has no absolute, objective mean-ing or purpose. Hence, to consider white lives as more valuable than Black lives in a white supremacist society is a matter of a choice, something decided by human beings. And although this choice is a reality, it does not follow that I am necessarily obligated to embrace or affirm this choice. I do not have to become complicit in the choice; I do not have to engage in the bad faith of assuming that Black life and existence are less valuable than the lives of oth-ers simply because these others believe that they are totally complete, or that they possess an exclusive rational faculty.

As a Black person I tend to focus on validating and affirming my exist-ence by utilizing the amazing resources of the Black existential tradition, the resources found in the tradition of jazz, gospel, the blues, and reggae. For me it is not so much an issue of being obsessed with how I am perceived but, rather, with making sure that I put into practice the Black existential imperative of improvising, the importance of enduring suffering but not being crushed by the unfortunate events of life. As you know, that great novelist and existential philosopher Ralph Ellison dealt brilliantly with the issue of the value of Black lives in a white supremacist society. Ellison, among other things, warned about the dangers of Blacks embracing the pathologies of existence that the dominant society always imposed upon Blacks. Baldwin also validated his existence by maintaining a vigil against the denigration of Black existence, the tendency of describing Black existence through the medium of statistics, graphs, and numbers. This kind of existential erasure through quantification is one way in which the devaluation of Black life takes place.

But even as Blacks must contend with their situation, they should realize that there is a flip side to this issue. To be more specific, there is an ethical challenge that they must pose to the white other. Just as Blacks must confront the devaluation of their lives in a white supremacist society, white individuals also must contend with the ethical implications of having to treat others as less than oneself. Put differently, what harm or damage is done to the white self when whites assume that their lives are, objectively speaking, more valuable than the lives of others? It seems to me that philosophers and other intellectuals must focus more attention on the existential damage of the assumption of the absolute value of the rightness of whiteness. We need to investigate the implications of what Du Bois called "the psychological wages of whiteness."[5] Why would a group of people tolerate the indignities of economic injustice only to feel a sense of superiority because they are not Black but are white?

I want to conclude by suggesting that unlike those thinkers who have called for an elimination of white identity and Black identity in order to resolve the issue of white supremacy, I do not think that this idea is in any way an indication of deep, effective thinking. We should accept that white lives are considered as being more valuable than Black lives. Similarly, Blacks should not surrender the existential faith that is so deeply rooted in the Black existential tradition, nor allow themselves to become mesmerized by the illusion of absolute whiteness. What seems to me to be a more realistic attitude is to accept the persistence of whiteness. However, the challenge is to invite whites to critically work thorough their whiteness. For those whites who approach whiteness as metaphysical or transcendental, they most likely will view white lives as being more valuable than Black lives. However, those whites who understand whiteness as a choice, as a construction, as a historical project, will realize that whiteness can be critically worked through and that being white need not entail that one must automatically assume the "rightness" of whiteness. Rather, these whites can come to view whiteness as just another fragile identity among other identities, identities constructed by vulnerable human beings as they struggle in the dark to make sense of their existence.

G. Y.: Lastly, I want to return to your reference to love. As you know, Baldwin doesn't mean anything like superficial Hollywood romance. What does love look like to you when operating politically?

C. H.: You are correct: Baldwin did not reduce love to romantic lust. He also refused to construe love in politics as an exercise in the pathology of the dialectics of recognition. Hence, Baldwin did not believe that Blacks were in need of paternalistic love from whites. Indeed, his reverence for love partly explains his condemnation of the cheap sentimentalism of *Uncle Tom's Cabin*.

Baldwin infused his conception of love with strong and abiding existential insights. Love, as he understood it, was not the superficial, good-feeling nonsense advertisers exploit to promote and encourage greater conspicuous consumption. Baldwin explained love in dynamic terms; consequently he framed it in terms of the realities of growth, courage, forgiveness, risk-taking, decentering selfishness, centering the other, and the importance of greeting others as a singular *Thou* and not an abstract *It*. Since I think that Baldwin has a very suggestive notion of love, I will use his position to describe what love looks like when it operates politically.

An essential element of Baldwin's existential conception of love pertains to the transformative power of love, specifically the ability of love to alter the state of one's existence. I interpret Baldwin as intimating the following: the individual who has the courage to truly love another person, the individual who earnestly dedicates his/her life to love, will be ontologically transformed into being a more ethically aware and authentic human being. This point relates to the redemptive affectivity of love. Love, Baldwin declares, actively contributes to growth, flourishing, and maturity.[6] Hence, the individual who is incapable of loving is existentially impaired. Baldwin explains that he used the word 'love' "not merely in the personal sense but as a state of being, or a state of grace—not in the infantile . . . sense of being made happy but in the tough and universal sense of quest and daring and growth."[7] He also adds in "In Search of a Majority," in *Nobody Knows My Name*, "Love does not begin and end the way we seem to think it does. Love is a battle, love is a war; love is growing up."[8] In another context, in David Leeming's *James Baldwin: A Biography*, Baldwin declared that "love . . . means *responsibility to each other* [my italics]."[9] Baldwin also thought that love should be more prominent in our social and political thinking. He despised the tendency of social scientists to hide behind categories and abstractions, while ignoring flesh-and-blood human beings. Baldwin does not offer an alternative theory of social pathology; nor does he introduce a new method to facilitate the substitution of one individual for another, which would entail, again, not being required to confront concrete individuals. The answer, as far as Baldwin is concerned, is love. David Leeming sums up Baldwin's position as follows: "Without . . . love people are unable to learn to see real human beings behind the categories, labels, and prejudices created by the loveless and the horrible results of such blindness are evident in . . . history."[10]

Clearly, then, a politics of love, would be a call to surrender the comfort of hiding behind the mazes of pathologies, stereotypes, and monstrous assumptions that enable the dominant society to promote as natural and normal what can best be described as a "friendly" and voluntary style of apartheid as an experiment in democratic living.

NOTES

1. Wilfrid Sellers, *Empiricism and the Philosophy of Mind* (London: Routledge & Kegan Paul Ltd, 1963), 1.
2. Lewis Gordon, *Disciplinary Decadence: Living Thought in Trying Times* (New York: Routledge, 2007).
3. See Andrew Hacker, *Two Nations: Black and White, Separate, Hostile, Unequal* (New York: Scribner's, 1992), chapter 3.
4. Hannah Arendt, *The Origins of Totalitarianism* (New York: Harcourt, Brace and Co., 1951), 426–427.
5. W. E. B. Du Bois, *Black Reconstruction in America, 1860–1880* (New York: Harcourt, Brace and Co., 1935).
6. James Baldwin, "Down at the Cross: Letter From a Region in my Mind," in *The Fire Next Time* (New York: Vintage, 1993), 95.
7. Baldwin, "Down at the Cross," 95.
8. James Baldwin, "In Search of a Majority," in *Nobody Knows My Name* (New York: Vintage, 1993), 136.
9. David Leeming, *James Baldwin: A Biography* (New York: Arcade Publishing, 2015), 322.
10. Leeming, *James Baldwin*, 200.

PART VI DISCUSSION QUESTIONS

1. When Molefi Kete Asante discusses protests against police violence and the recent police shooting deaths of young Black men, he suggests that the most effective mode of demonstration is one that bears "the threat of violence, not violence itself." Demonstrating that one has "the potential of competing for power" is the best way, he explains, to shake the foundations of current power structures and demand changes in the system as it exists. A demonstration that implies an actual threat of violence, though dangerous for people of color, seems to be one manifestation of "the collective fightback of sustained compassion in the face of sustained catastrophe," that is, Cornel West's notion of "Black prophetic fire." Those who cause violence and destroy property are not demonstrators at all, explains Asante, but in fact they undermine demonstration because they require the state to intervene by force. Such behaviors might also be prohibited when one is filled with "Black prophetic fire" because that "fire has to be lit by a deep love of the people." Yet we cannot ignore that it is the (alleged) *perceived* threat of violence that results in innumerable killings of people of color, especially

young Black men. Bill E. Lawson underscores this point when he cautions, "People concerned with racial justice have to know when to act and when not to act. In other words, don't be stupid!" Is it currently possible to support the threat of violence, driven by West's "Black prophetic fire," without taking unnecessary risks, or risks that are too likely to harm demonstrators? In what ways is the "threat of violence, not violence itself" compatible with Cornel West's notion of "Black prophetic fire" as manifested in the philosophies and actions of Martin Luther King Jr., Malcolm X, Marcus Garvey, and Ida B. Wells, among others?

2. One of the difficulties in taking seriously the reality of racism and the importance of racial discourse in the United States is the problem of responsibility. Clevis Headley explains that many people appeal to individual responsibility to account for their innocence. Whites born in the twentieth century did not hold slaves. Because they did not themselves directly buy, sell, or forcibly breed Black bodies for profit, they think they have "no responsibility for the historical consequences of slavery." Simultaneously, Headley points out, they deny the possibility of collective responsibility, effectively eliminating all related concepts other than atomistic individualism. This naturally contributes to the continuation of an epistemology of ignorance on the part of whites and the limitation of discourse of race to the vocabulary of liberalism that in turn supports blind faith in individualism that allows white people to avoid "the complexities of the political, economic, and social world" that are necessary in discussing race. At the other end of the spectrum, Kwame Anthony Appiah discusses the meaning of *Volkgeist* in Du Bois's work. Appiah offers a modification of Du Bois's notion of a "collective soul" that is whole and homogenous across a people, but that can take different directions depending on the forces at work for each individual person. Lucius T. Outlaw Jr.'s claim that "all folks 'white' have not, do not, take up 'being white' in the same ways" seems consistent with this view. Could some notion of a "collective soul" that allows for some individual difference or other shared identity overcome the strong inclinations toward atomistic individualism in the United States? To what extent might this be a way to improve racial discourse or possibly improve a discussion vis-à-vis some notion of shared responsibility?

PART VII

Race Beyond the United States

Fiona Nicoll

George Yancy: Provide a sense of the origin of your interest in critical race and whiteness studies, especially given your identity as a white woman.

Fiona Nicoll: There are three formative moments in this origin story. The first was a deep sense of rupture from everyday whiteness at the age of thirteen when my parents—practicing Christians—decided to take a year away from Australia "in mission," as teachers at a Protestant denomination senior school in a remote part of Papua New Guinea. The year was 1980. This was five years after the nation had gained independence from Australia, but where I was located there seemed to be a significant continuation of colonial relations. As white people, we were spatially and culturally separated from the Indigenous people. They were called "nationals," while we were called "expatriates" or "expats" for short. As white children, my sister and I studied via correspondence, while "nationals" lived and studied in the school. I completed my correspondence subjects within the first six months; after this my mental health began to suffer because I was socially isolated with nothing much to do. I asked my parents, who subsequently asked the white principal, if I could study with the nationals for the second part of the year. My request was granted, and I had the unusual experience of being the only white student in a school of around three hundred students.

G. Y.: What was the impact of that experience?

F. N.: This revived my interest in life generally, and I became aware of a whole other world to which I had only partial access as a white child. I also became cognizant of race as a mode of colonial power; it was the white expats in the remote island who occupied most of the positions of control at the school, and it was the Chinese traders who owned most of the stores on the small island. I actually found it quite traumatic when I returned to Australia because being white had ceased to feel "natural" in the same way as it had been prior to my leaving. I simultaneously experienced a welcome opening to a wider world of human experience and a lack of confidence in the unexamined white race privilege conferred on me through birth as a white Australian citizen. It's hard to describe this experience except to say that I was no longer able to *believe* in whiteness in the way that I had prior to leaving the country; I also became aware of the way that most of my peers, friends, and teachers accepted whiteness as a fundamental trait connected with *being Australian*.

The second origin story explaining my interest begins eight years later in 1988 when I took a year out from my university studies and travelled around Australia. This was the bicentenary of Australia's origins in a British penal settlement in 1788, and there was considerable Indigenous activism from all over the continent, converging in large protests in Sydney. Somehow I got hold of a paperback book entitled *We Call for a Treaty*. Written by a group of prominent non-Indigenous Australian public servants, academics, and writers, this book explained the precarious standing of my nation within international law both during the time of British declaration of sovereignty and through to the late twentieth century. It was only many years later that I realized this book was, in part, a response to the successful human rights advocacy of Indigenous people from the nineteenth century onward. And, most specifically, it was a response to the Aboriginal men and women who established an Aboriginal Tent Embassy on the lawns of the national parliament house in Canberra in 1972. A highlight of my career a few years ago was being invited to contribute to an edited book that included writings and archival material from activists of that era. It was a privilege to interview Michael Anderson, one of the original group of men who established the Tent Embassy who has dedicated a lifetime as a lawyer and grassroots community organizer to agitating for the recognition of Indigenous sovereignty both in Australia and in international forums.

The third story relating specifically to the creation of a critical race and whiteness studies association in Australia was my meeting with Aileen Moreton-Robinson. A lifetime activist, brilliant academic, and superior strategist, Aileen brought critical race studies to Australia in the late 1990s with her sociological work on how the subject position of 'middle-class white woman' was formative of antiracist discourses limited by unrecognized white race privilege. After reading her early work, I was able to understand why, in spite of the very best intentions, white supporters of Indigenous rights struggles rarely achieved the changes we purported to seek in our national political life. I began to suspect that our good intentions were part of the problem. We became close colleagues when we formed, together with a small group of other people writing on whiteness and race, the Australian Critical Race and Whiteness Studies Association (ACRAWSA). Aileen was the founding president, and I was the founding vice president and editor of the inaugural Association journal. Through conferences, a website, and an academic journal, we aimed to generate new conversations about race in Australia, from the starting point that "whiteness" was a problem that needed to be known, owned, and worked through by scholars from all disciplines.

Other formative thinkers for me at this time were Sara Ahmed, Ghassan Hage, and Cheryl Harris. Sara demonstrated the centrality of whiteness to the way that embodied others appeared as "strangers" in postcolonial encounters, while Ghassan highlighted the racial work of the liberal value of "tolerance" in debates about migration in a multicultural Australia. Through Cheryl Harris's pioneering work on whiteness as a form of personal property protected in law, I began to understand embodied intersections between state and subject formation in settler-colonial contexts.

G. Y.: What were some of the philosophical and personal challenges that you faced as you began to pursue such issues?

F. N.: One philosophical challenge is the simultaneous necessity and impossibility of this work for me as a middle-class, white Australian woman. The epistemological challenge is to engage with Indigenous Australia both materially and ontologically while attending to the difficulties of this project. For example, 'Indigenous' and 'Aboriginal' are terms that *unname* human ways of knowing and connecting to the life of this continent over tens of thousands of years. But at the same time, they are terms to which histories of struggle, of loss, of pride, of creativity have been attached by individuals since the British took possession. A potent expression of this is the Aboriginal flag designed by Harold Thomas in 1971. As a non-Indigenous Australian, I cannot appropriate this Indigenous history as my own national story; but I must equally articulate an ethical and authentic relationship to it. Otherwise whiteness will remain at the ontological and epistemological heart of what Australia means and of what it means to be Australian. The most important philosophical contribution to working through these quandaries is the book *Indigenous Sovereignty and the Being of the Occupier: Manifesto for a White Australian Philosophy of Origins* by Toula Nicolacopoulos and George Vassilacopoulos. The authors demonstrate how the construction of Australia as a container for particular kinds of immigrant subjects has historically precluded negotiation of Indigenous sovereignty, and they argue persuasively that this is required for the nation to become itself.

G. Y.: And what of the more personal challenges?

F. N.: There have been many personal challenges in this work. The academic environment into which critical race and whiteness studies entered was heavily infused by poststructuralism and postcolonial theoretical frameworks, which tended to be critical of approaches where identity was interrogated rather than problematized as such. As an aspiring queer theorist, I was at once embedded in this environment and attuned to its limitations for scholars positioned outside the scope of normative white assumptions about knowledge formation and dissemination. As an early-career academic working in Australian universities, I would be continually struck by other white academics' indifference toward or dismissal of the subtle work of theorists of whiteness like Moreton-Robinson, Ahmed, and Hage. Their work was dismissed as "essentialist" or as driven by "political" rather than "intellectual" agendas. It wasn't until I read Cheryl Harris's penetrating study "Whiteness as Property" that I began to see how the discontent of white academics with critical race and whiteness studies was structured by a possessive relationship to knowledge. Indigenous and nonwhite scholars were welcomed into the academic community with the proviso that their views should be "tolerable" rather than unsettling to business as usual. Racial ways of seeing, doing, and being in the academy became increasingly evident as part of my everyday working life through my active involvement in different projects connected to critical race and whiteness studies. After being explicitly and implicitly warned off from deepening my involvement in this area, there were two paths available to me. I could accept that my privileged position as white required me to perform a kind of "professional" distancing from knowledge and knowers seen as marked by their racial difference and/or "political" agendas. Or I could get in deeper. At the risk of appearing (and being disciplined) as excessively willful, I chose the latter.

After I completed my PhD, my first academic job was to deliver an academic course on contemporary Indigenous art. This began my experience of working together with Indigenous people to produce new knowledge for *all* university students and researchers rather than delivering knowledge about *them* for and by people like *me*. In concrete terms, this involves resistance to two kinds of more or less explicit demands that hold whiteness in place institutionally. I refuse to speak *for or on behalf of* Indigenous people and positions even when it would be professionally rewarding for me to do so. I refuse to *contain the scope* of Indigenous projects on which I collaborate as a non-Indigenous researcher, curator, or project manager. While diligent in fulfilling all that is required from funding bodies and auspicing institutions, I am not prepared to contain *perceived* risks of Indigenous proximity to students, staff, and other stakeholders. I strongly believe that unless white Australians are prepared and allowed to experience some discomfort or disorientation as we connect with Indigenous Australians, the best-intentioned projects will fail to achieve transformation within established fields of social power.

Life is too short for projects that are merely decorative or documentary; I hope to see meaningful treaties negotiated between Indigenous nations and the communities where they are located in my lifetime. Two related dangers that haunt the kind of work I do are failure and overcommitment. Failure comes from getting involved in projects that I am ill equipped to contribute to or from weakness within networks of participants, while overcommitment comes from a belief that I am uniquely qualified and committed to follow through every aspect of a project. Having pulled off some significant collaborative projects including two major exhibitions in my career, I feel the need to invest more in cultivating distributed leadership among white people and in developing digital communication infrastructure to facilitate ongoing outcomes of collaboration.

My sense is that for changes to hold on the ground of racially structured power relationships, collaborative processes are more important than individually determined and owned outcomes. Of course this can pose personal challenges to the degree that academic institutions only count individual inputs and outputs. I have been part of universities where one or two senior leaders have found ways to count collaborative work as well as universities where this work is seen as extraneous—and potentially hostile—to their business model. Another challenge I've experienced is the way that individuals within white institutions can be rewarded for playing one Indigenous individual or group against another to achieve their own objectives. This strategy is as old as colonization itself and requires careful ethical negotiation by anyone who considers themselves a "white ally." This ethical negotiation should not be confused with or performed with reference to values of "objectivity." It can involve a *refusal* to masquerade as neutral or uninvested in outcomes of conflict staged between Indigenous people. And it demands transparency about who you are standing with and why in any given conflict. Unless we "go there," as white Australians, significant social transformation of the colonial relationships will be forever deferred. In my research and pedagogy, I always try to remember that we cannot stand aside or beyond the issues that afflict Indigenous people; we are a constitutive element part of these issues, whether we acknowledge it or not.

G. Y.: What does Indigenous sovereignty theory look like within the context of Australia?

F. N.: In Australia, Indigenous sovereignty theory is significantly structured in response to a legacy of dispossession that was retrospectively justified by colonial administrators through a legal doctrine of *terra nullius*: the racial proposition that the people living on the continent at the time the British declared sovereignty were not—in a meaningful sense—owners of their countries. Part of the task of Indigenous sovereignty theory is to demonstrate that *terra nullius* is not just a failure of cross-cultural understanding with devastating and continuing impacts on Indigenous people, but is symptomatic of *racial* ways of seeing, thinking, and acting through which white Australia produces Aboriginality as a subhuman condition. The Crown is a key concept for Indigenous sovereignty theory in Australia because it is the site from which authority flows both historically and symbolically. For example, colonial practices included the designation of particular Indigenous individuals as "queens" and "kings" through the use of brass breastplates. Colonists would deal with these individuals in the process of land acquisition and settlement. Another component of British sovereign power was the spectacular public punishment of warriors who organized armed resistance to invasion. I would also include more recent dimensions such as delegations of Indigenous leaders to meet Queen Elizabeth II, to discuss various matters including ongoing sovereignty claims and requests for the return of human remains held in British institutions. I am curious about whether the recent decision of a not-so-United Kingdom to leave the EU will alter the agenda for these ongoing discussions. Another significant aspect of Indigenous sovereignty theory is the reclamation by Indigenous people of their countries, their languages, and naming rights as lawful and regenerative practices in everyday life. Indigenous sovereignty is not only about a process of grieving for the many lives taken and destroyed over nearly 250 years of colonial occupation; it is equally about knowledge passed along through generations and the capacity of subsequent generations to value and transform this knowledge so it remains relevant and imbued with political agency.

Another important focus of Indigenous sovereignty theory in Australia is identity. My understanding of Indigenous identity is that *connection* lies at its heart. This identity is not "prehistorical" or narrowly "cultural," but rather it is embodied, familial, and takes the elements, plants, and animal life as aspects of what it means to be human rather than being opposed to it as "nature" available for expropriation. So an important political struggle is to ensure that Indigenous knowledge (of plant properties for example) is not simply approached as a resource for transnational knowledge corporations (including universities) to "rediscover" and package for sale as commercial Intellectual Property.

G. Y.: How do you understand the concept of Indigeneity in the twenty-first century? I'm thinking here in terms of its epistemological and empowering implications for Indigenous people in Australia.

F. N.: Very broadly. I think that the concept of Indigeneity as a site of political struggle concerns the right to name and resist the containment of being on the part of those people around the world who encountered European imperial expansion from the seventeenth century. However, there seems to be a difference between nations where Indigenous people signed onto treaties with colonial powers and those, including Australia, where this is yet to occur. In New Zealand, for example, Indigenous sovereignty theory and practice is linked to the politics of the Waitangi Treaty as a foundational national document. The problems that Maori people face there seem linked to debates over the terms of the Treaty and to continuing social disadvantage and marginalization. The fragile legal situation for Aboriginal and Torres Strait Islanders in Australia seems to allow their citizenship rights to be more easily overlooked. In 2007, for example, remote Indigenous communities in the Northern Territory were targeted for a Federal government "Intervention". This included global bans on alcohol and pornography and compulsory sexual health checks for all children. And in 2015 the Western Australian government threatened Indigenous people living in basic conditions on their remote countries with closure of basic services including electricity and water. Whereas in Australia the struggle to claim Indigenous identity as both valuable and rights bearing remains a site of activism, the struggle in nations with treaties seems more focused on what this identity means today and on aligning rights with social justice principles rather than settling for the bare minimum of resources that white settler states are prepared to grant to their "domestic nations."

A common thread in the literature on Indigeneity is the insistence that Indigenous people should not be approached as containers of a feared or fetishized cultural "difference" but, rather, respected as embodying a living and evolving presence that is more or less reckoned with by various nation states. This has important implications for epistemology insofar as Indigenous people have been historically defined as objects of Western knowledge systems that, in turn, stake powerful claims for universality. Indigenous academics from different nations around the world have mounted powerful challenges to such claims. One way they have done this is to demonstrate how local Indigenous terms and ideas can generate new understandings of an array of global problems, from poverty and illness to global warming and housing. In Australia, the concept of Indigeneity is used through practices of education, language revival, arts, and political activism to produce a visible and legible social presence with which Australian governments may ultimately form treaties. One way that this concept is countered by white Australians possessively invested in ownership of the nation is by assuming the right to define who is or is not "authentically" Indigenous. Considerable cultural work is expended in policing the boundaries of acceptable Aboriginality—on the one hand—and suspect or "inauthentic" Aboriginality—on the other. For example, several years ago an Australian commentator attacked the legitimacy of awards granted to several high-achieving Indigenous people. He argued that, since they could plausibly "pass" as white, their recognition came at the expense of their darker-skinned counterparts. Indigenous opportunity was presented as a zero-sum game in which only the suitably embodied should be eligible to participate.

G. Y.: There are specific ways in which whiteness in the US gets expressed through unarmed Black bodies being killed by mostly white police. In fact, in the US, we are currently mourning the deaths of the killing of two Black men, Philando Castile in St. Paul, Minnesota and Alton Sterling, in Baton Rouge, Louisiana. There are also the five officers in Dallas who were sadly killed. Talk about the ways in which Black bodies in Australia are treated by law enforcement.

F. N.: As with the current situation in the US, violence against Black bodies by law enforcement is a significant problem. Rather than incidents involving shootings, the main problem in Australia is discriminatory policing and Aboriginal deaths in police custody. Having lived for a short time in New Orleans in my twenties, I'm aware of the ways that race in the US is powerfully registered through the spatial demarcation of cities. Together with the criminalization of petty offences, in particular those involving drugs or vehicle registration and maintenance, hostilities between law enforcement and specific Black communities seem to be reproduced and exacerbated in more overt ways than in the Australian context, where Indigenous people are a more or less visible minority. Racial violence in Australia often has a more secretive character, and this is linked, in my view, to the ongoing force of *terra nullius,* whereby ways of seeing and acting toward Indigenous people in particular render them sub- or not-quite human. There has been organized protest about police violence and deaths in custody for over three decades. Government responses include a Royal Commission in 1990 and a decade-long process of "reconciliation" from 1991–2001. Yet Indigenous people continue to be brutalized and to die in police custody at horrendously high rates. If police shootings in the US could be described as racial crimes of commission, Aboriginal deaths in custody are often crimes of omission. Examples that come to mind in recent years include an elderly man dying while being transported hundreds of kilometres in temperatures of close to 50°C (122°F) in an airless van without air conditioning; a young woman, ignored after complaining of feeling ill and asking for hospital treatment, and dying a few days later; a man arrested for being drunk who passed away in a holding cell because officers forgot to make regular checks on his welfare.

In addition to physical harms inflicted by law enforcement, there are many examples of psychological and cultural violence against Indigenous people while in custody. My partner, Sandi Peel, an Indigenous woman from South Australia, wrote a song entitled "Living Hell" based on the experience of one of her neighbors. This young woman, a member of the 'stolen generations', was taken into custody and before being locked in a cell she was stripped of all her clothes. When she asked the custodial officers why she had been stripped, they claimed it was a protective measure to prevent suicide. The chorus of Sandi's song is powerful:

> Lying, naked in a cell.
> The hurt, the pain, the shame, this is a living hell.
> Stripped of her clothes, her culture and her dignity.[1]

G. Y.: That's powerful. You know, many in the US have no sense that indigenous Black bodies in Australia are also marked, oppressed, and brutalized. Talk about some of the *specific* similarities and differences between white Australian racism and white US racism.

F. N.: I've discussed the similarities above to some extent, but two areas where I see specific difference can fall under the headings of "guns" and "euphemisms." Guns make a difference because of their power to anchor crime and law enforcement in threats and acts of lethal violence. They also significantly increase the risk of innocent victims being killed by misattributed identity or in crossfire. There is a deep cultural attachment to guns in the US and this makes it very difficult to remove them from equations about racial violence. In Australia, while lethal force is to some extent an issue because firearms are legal for police and there have been police shootings, other kinds of injuries and inexplicable 'suicides' of Indigenous people in custody are more common. Images of juvenile offenders, many of them on remand, being brutalized and restrained in the Northern Territory, were revealed in an investigative media report in late July of 2016. Several young men were tear-gassed inside the detention center building while others were strapped to chairs for hours with their heads covered with hoods, allegedly to prevent them from spitting at guards. While the Prime Minister rightly expressed his outrage about these images and called immediately for a Royal Commission to ascertain types and levels of the abuse of young Indigenous people in detention, events that followed this call demonstrate the power of whiteness to reproduce *terra nullius* in everyday life. The man appointed to lead the Royal Commissioner was a former Chief Justice of the Territory (where the abuses had occurred), and no Indigenous leaders were consulted about the terms of reference or invited to serve as co-Commissioners. This demonstrates a disturbing failure to acknowledge how existing institutions contribute to the brutalization of Indigenous people and to imagine that Indigenous people might have a fundamental role in making these institutions more humane. In this context I have argued elsewhere that Carl von Clauswitz's famous formulation about war being the continuation of "policy by other means"[2] needs to be inverted to account for race and sovereignty issues in Australia. When it comes to Indigenous Australia, policy and its institutions of enforcement have long been charged with the prosecution of an undeclared war.

I think this is partly because the Australian Constitution still enables separate laws to be passed that specifically target them. And this means that racial values are hardwired into the nation-state in ways that profoundly shape experiences of everyday life. For example, I have heard direct reports from tourists of local white people discouraging them from giving money to Indigenous people in Alice Springs "because they're like pigeons. If you give them some, they'll come back with all their relations and ask you for more." I've also heard white people in remote areas refer to Indigenous people as a separate "species" who are uniquely unable to tolerate alcohol. This dehumanizing terminology has disturbing origins in early processes of colonial settlement on the East Coast of Australia; armed parties of white men, often relying on the navigational skills of Aboriginal "trackers" or "native police," would go on expeditions and kill entire clans in reprisal for attacks against settlers or their property. The purpose of these trips was sometimes euphemistically referred to in local newspapers as "dispersing" a group of Blacks.

A common thread linking historical racism against Indigenous bodies to current manifestations in law enforcement is the myth that Indigenous people represent a "prehistoric" or "uncivilized" state of existence and that the only way to stop the violence is for them to accept assimilation into the wider Australian society. Certain white politicians and public intellectuals, together with a small handful of Indigenous spokespeople, have promoted the view that Indigenous rights activism is somehow linked to poor outcomes across social indicators such as unemployment, incarceration, and poor health. Implicit in their arguments is the notion that letting go of the struggle for Indigenous sovereignty will lead to more social acceptance and greater prosperity for individuals and their families. There is a disturbingly performative element of this kind of talk; those Indigenous people who refuse to accept the prescribed quiescence are often treated as "trouble-makers" and their views are disregarded. To conservative Australian politicians and media commentators, Indigenous sovereignty claims appear (and are represented) as a travesty of the "civilized" political system held in place by *terra nullius* and racial conceptions of "British" values. This can create problems for Indigenous public intellectuals, as supporting treaty and sovereignty claims is quickly framed as being nationally "divisive." Stan Grant is one prominent public intellectual, an internationally successful Indigenous journalist swayed by the coverage of the custodial treatment of young Indigenous people that I related above to call for a Truth and Reconciliation Commission and lend his support to a Treaty rather than settling for the constitutional "recognition" of Indigenous people.

Relating his response to the filmed scenes, he said,

> This week I have struggled to contain a pulsating rage. . . . I have moved from boiling anger to simmering resentment; but the feeling has not passed, nor have I wanted it to. . . . What offences we've seen this past week.
>
> How can I stand here and speak to the idea of our place in an indissoluble Commonwealth, when this week my people have been reminded yet again that our place is so often behind this nation's bars? This week, my people know what Australia looks like. This week, Australia is a boy in a hood in a cell.
>
> Treaty, even unattainable, sings to the heart of Indigenous people here in a way that recognition cannot. We need to infuse it with the urgency of now. It needs to speak to substance, not symbolism.
>
> It needs to speak with hope to the hooded, beaten boys in dark prison cells.[3]

One of the most frustrating aspects of the work we do in ACRAWSA is the slow pace of social and political transformation. Because we engage with controversial issues discussed above but also others such as the incarceration of asylum seekers offshore and legal and social practices that target Muslim communities, our critique targets powerful and sometimes litigious individuals and institutions. In the academy, it sometimes feels as though we are repeating ourselves in the face of those who would love to see us "move on"; as Sara Ahmed observes, racism and sexism are sites of pressure in academic debates which often approach them as "overed."[4] Having noted this, genuine rewards come through the satisfaction of creating and fostering innovative work and discussions and when our students "get it" and become energized by a passionate determination not to reproduce the prevailing racial order. I accept that the way they "get it" will be unique to the racialized context of their everyday lives. My own experience of white embodiment in the "postcolonial" context of Papua New Guinea where I was neither normal nor invisible, together with my reading of a book calling for a treaty with Indigenous Australians, altered the course of my life. So I must trust that students' encounters with the creative and research projects I've delivered with Indigenous Australians will alter the course of their lives in ways that are impossible to predict.

NOTES

1. Sandi Peel, "Living Hell," 1998. Reproduced with permission by Sandi Peel.
2. Carl von Clausewitz, *On War*, trans. J. J. Graham (London: Penguin, 1982), 402.
3. Grant, cited in Christine Kearney, "Four Corners: Stan Grant Speaks of 'Boiling Anger,' 'Simmering Resentment' over Detention Abuse Videos," *ABC News*, July 30, 2016, http://www.abc.net.au/news/2016-07-30/stan-grant-speaks-of-'boiling-anger'-over-detention-footage/7674778.
4. Sara Ahmed, *On Being Included: Racism and Diversity in Institutional Life* (Durham, NC and London: Duke University Press, 2012), 179–80.

Paul Gilroy

George Yancy: In a review of the 2013 movie *12 Years a Slave*, you critiqued neoliberalism as that which "decrees that racism no longer presents a significant obstacle either to individual success or to collective self-realisation. . . . Racism is presented as anachronistic—nothing more than a flimsy impediment to the machinery of colourless, managerial meritocracy."[1] I certainly agree with your critique of neoliberalism, especially as neoliberalism interprets racism as anomalous, something that stems from a few "bad apples" as opposed to the reality that racism is systemic and constitutes the very fabric of our polity, where racism is business as usual. Events like the killing in April, 2015, of Walter Scott, a Black man who was shot in the back eight times by a white police officer in Charleston, South Carolina, and so many other incidents like this one, show us that there is nothing anachronistic about American racism. It is alive and well. From your perspective in Britain, how do you understand events like the Scott killing within the context of American race relations?

Paul Gilroy: I don't come to the United States very often, but I happened to be visiting when Walter Scott was shot by another trigger-happy police officer. I was angry and upset. I hope I don't need to emphasize that I am a firm supporter of the movement that has arisen in response to this sequence of killings exposed by the ubiquity of the cameraphone and the communicative resources of social media. Britain isn't a gun-loving or toting nation. Racism in our country doesn't operate on the same scale as the racial organization of law and sovereign power in the United States, but our recent history also includes a long list of Black people who've lost their lives following contact with the forces of law and order. Similarly, our police and their various private proxies have never been held to account for those deaths, so this is very familiar ground. Police in many polities can kill with impunity, and racial hierarchy augments their essentially permissive relationship with the law. The officer in this case was charged with murder. We will have to see whether he is found guilty. That would be a very rare outcome indeed.

Of course, to say that neoliberalism presents racism as anachronistic was not to say that racism *is* anachronistic. Confronting racism is a timely, urgent matter. The casual killing of Black people appears to be a pursuit that originated in an earlier phase of American history. In his epochal analysis of historical and cultural process, the prolific Welsh novelist and academic Raymond Williams drew an important distinction in the way that social and cultural formations develop. Drawing upon him, we can say that we live with neoliberalism but it might not yet be fully dominant. There is certainly worse to come. Neoliberalism could still be emergent, while what appears to be the casual habit of murdering people who come into contact with the police might belong to its prehistory and could be considered either dominant or residual depending on your point of view.

What was especially interesting to me when I was here in April was how the video of Walter Scott's death was being replayed continuously on television (and certainly shared innumerable times on the Internet) as if, by sheer repetition, it would disclose a hidden or secret detail that might make it somehow legitimate. Perhaps the iteration was a means to deaden spectators and drain the spectacle of its full horror? Perhaps there are obscure pleasures in those patterns of identification, for both Black and white viewers of this racial pornography. The replays were often accompanied by neurotic speculation as to what the killer's courtroom defense might be. I'm almost as concerned by the constant, compulsive replaying of the event as I am by the event itself. There is a complicity in that gesture that is also part of the way that racism becomes culture.

G. Y.: You've written about the Middle Passage, about that tragic transportation of African bodies across the Atlantic. Violent disciplining of the Black body, rendering it docile, was one mechanism at work during that passage. What ways to do you think contemporary Black people in the United States or in Britain continue to undergo forms of violent discipline?

P. G.: There are many connections between the ways that we inhabit and reproduce the contemporary racial order and the period of slavery. However, we are not slaves. It's important not to let slavery slip into being a metaphor and blur the difference between our condition and the predicament of the slaves. The racial *nomos* has changed since the eighteenth century. How racial hierarchy and the exploitation it sanctions and the terror it requires link the past to the present needs to be understood very carefully. I know I am stepping away from the political liturgy or code used in American discussions of race and politics, but I don't care for Manichean styles of thought. Abstract and reified magnitudes like "whiteness" aren't, in my view, very helpful in interpreting what is now going on around us. Racial categories have to be de-natured. We have to see, for example, how that whiteness is assembled and brought to actual and virtual life. What are its historical, economic and social conditions of existence? How does it become articulated to juridical, scientific, medical, aesthetic, military, and technological forms of expertise? These are concrete problems that open whiteness up to multilayered struggle.

G. Y.: I certainly understand your point. Yet Black people in America understand that, in so many instances, they are being shot and killed by white police officers who are sworn to protect them. They understand how white life matters differently. And even if that life is poor, it is still white. And they understand the reality of white privilege. Isn't there a way in which this is a real phenomenon to be reckoned with? Black people, it seems to me, are not responsible for creating a racial Manichean reality of "us" (Blacks) versus "them" (whites).

P. G.: In *Wretched of the Earth*, Frantz Fanon speaks powerfully about the need and the difficulty of getting beyond this Manichean perspective. He describes how the Manicheism of the colonizer creates the Manicheism of the colonized. That reaction cannot be avoided, but it is also a bad place to get stuck. You speak of privilege here. I know this is now the language many people use to talk about racial hierarchy, but I'm not comfortable with that as a shorthand term for capturing the complex machinery of inequality. It makes power simply a possession rather than a relationship.

G. Y.: It's my understanding that there are also fewer than one hundred Black professors in Britain. Of course, there is also the problem of not having a department of Black British Studies comparable to Black Studies or Africana Studies here in the United States. Within the context of the manifold problems in higher education, how does racism play a role in sustaining such realities there?

P. G.: Britain's educational system is failing at every level. Its betrayal of Black people is part of a much more comprehensive betrayal. It is being regimented, privatized, and cut so that it operates as a mechanism for deepening inequality and reducing opportunity across the board. Drafting in more Black professors is not going to fix it! Of course we need more Black professors, but we must be fiercely realistic about what we can expect that to achieve. These days, neoliberalism loves diversity. Corporate multiculturalism speaks to the needs of globalized capital hungry for new markets and investors. The decorative presence of Black professors, like that of Black cops, guarantees nothing at the level of institutional outcomes.

I have dreamed for years of building an institutional home for something like a multidisciplinary Black studies initiative in Europe, a place for archiving our histories, for indulging our curiosity, and honing our critique that could combine academic research with public advocacy. There seems not to be an opening for that sort of development at the moment. Our universities are beleaguered public bodies, not privately endowed operations. They estimate—and they might even be right—that there is no money to be made from anti-racist commitments. What is more, the younger Black people who do make it into the world of higher education mostly want to get their MBAs and start making money like everybody else. I recall during my years in the United States that there was a whole lot of culture/identity talk on our campus, but when it came to actual enrollments in African-American studies the numbers were disappointing. Perhaps the recent campaigning around these killings has changed that.

I wrote a lot about the cultural forms of British racism—how they connected with nationalism and the exclusionary impulses that resulted. It's only very recently that our political landscape has changed to the extent that Blacks are not expected to "go back home" whenever the problems we represent were identified. Nominally we were citizens, but we had to fight long and hard to be recognized as belonging to our country. That's quite different from the American situation where you've had to fight to make your citizenship meaningful but there are whole swathes of the country where African-Americans are the majority population. I've been to Alabama.

The wars of recent years have made Muslim into a racial category. That too has altered the kind of racism we have. It's often oriented by our burgeoning securitocracy. At the same time, the Black population of Caribbean heritage is declining. It is being replaced by a variety of different African peoples divided by language, faith, and nationality, and what counts as Blackness is clearly in transition.

Talking about the Middle Passage or the history of struggles against slavery cannot mean the same to people who have migrated or fled from Somalia, Nigeria, or Ghana. They have their own distinctive history and relationship to the political order of the British Empire that has brought them here. There are large numbers of Francophone Africans in London busy escaping from the problems they face in France. One result of all these developments is that there is a much greater reliance upon what I call *generic* racial identity. It's often created from the fantasy version of African-American culture that's been exported to the rest of the world. That blackness derives in large measure from the dreamworlds of global consumer capitalism. It is heavily mediated by the Internet and social media, and its dismal effects are compounded by the general crisis of political imagination.

G. Y.: In what ways do you see Black people in the United Kingdom and Black people in the United States as struggling with the same racial and racist issues? And how might they create new forms of solidarity and collective activism that confront anti-Black racism?

P. G.: Some of the issues are similar; some are different. We all have to face the problems of structural and institutional racism: the fact that our lives are valued differently, that we are vulnerable as a result of being consigned on racial grounds to infrahumanity. Solidarity is an altogether trickier thing. It has to be made rather than assumed on racial grounds. The effects of racism are insufficient to maintain solidarity. I'm glad that people can act in concert across national boundaries, but the routine effects of the online network are often mistaken for the stirrings of an actual movement. The movement from virtual to actual solidarity isn't automatic or even easy.

Let me raise a couple of difficult examples to illustrate the organizational and conceptual problems that we face in antiracist organizing. A couple of years ago, after the killing of Trayvon Martin, his mother came to Britain for a heavily publicized meeting with Baroness Lawrence, the mother of Stephen Lawrence. Her son was murdered by racists in a horrible, tragic case that has dominated the field of our racial politics for many years. The grieving mother whose loss has been compounded by the failure of the criminal justice system to bring redress is a very potent symbol. But when Anuj Bidve's parents came to Britain from India after his murder by racists in Manchester, I don't recall them meeting with anybody except the police and the mainstream politicians who were hungry for a photo op. The crisis of political imagination has real, disabling consequences.

Last autumn, many activists were so busy protesting against a white South African artist's exhibit at London's Barbican Center that the police shooting of forty-year-old Dean Joseph in Islington, a mile or two away, passed them by entirely. I don't know all the details of that case, but it was telling that it could be so comprehensively overlooked while there was so much antiracist energy crackling in the air.

What should and could be solidarity can lapse into a kind of mimicry. Circulated through the ether by phenomena like #Blacktwitter, American racial codes, rhetoric, and interpretations can begin, wrongly, to trump locally based analysis and priorities.

NOTE

1. Paul Gilroy, "12 Years a Slave: In Our 'Post-racial' Age the Legacy of Slavery Lives On, *Guardian*, November 10, 2013, https://www.theguardian.com/commentisfree/2013/nov/10/12-years-a-slave-mcqueen-film-legacy-slavery.

PART VII DISCUSSION QUESTIONS

1. Police violence directed against Black bodies recently has become a highly visible phenomenon in the United States. The use of social media to broadcast and replay footage of the violent police encounters both raises

awareness in making the events visible, but may also serve to "deaden spectators and drain the spectacle of its full horror," as Paul Gilroy suggests. In the UK, he explains that social media appears to have contributed to the uneven if not misguided attention paid ad hoc to racist acts. Though people have access to information about racial violence, some incidents are completely missed. This problem is frightening when considered alongside the fact that, Gilroy explains, "police in many polities can kill with impunity" and they have "never been held to account" for the police killings of non-white persons. Fiona Nicoll suggests that racial violence against Indigenous people in Australia is more secretive than racial violence against nonwhites in the United States, specifically in the abuse and death rates of Indigenous people in police custody. At the same time, she explains that the violence appears to be "hardwired" into Australian policy, law, and culture, which are highly public and visible. Discuss the dual-capacity of visibility both to aid in the process of identifying and eliminating racial violence, but also to undermine those processes. What alternative or additional measures should be taken to help make progress with respect to racial violence in places like Australia?

PART VIII

Race and Religion

At the Intersections

Charles Johnson

George Yancy: Talk about some of the creative ways in which your identity as a literary figure and as a philosopher intersect.

Charles Johnson: Both philosophy and literature offer interpretations of our experience delivered through language and a reasoning process specific to each discipline. I attempt to explain the reasoning process in both disciplines in my book, *The Way of the Writer: Reflections on the Art and Craft of Storytelling*. Moreover, philosophers are not just thinkers; they are also writers. And our finest storytellers, the ones who transform and deepen our understanding of the world, are not just writers; they are also engaged in the adventure of ideas, to borrow a phrase from Alfred North Whitehead.[1] As a philosopher, as a writer of stories, and as a visual artist, I find that these activities are concerned with two things—the process of discovery and problem-solving. Both philosophy and literature begin with wonder, in an interrogative mode. As you can probably tell, my Western philosophical orientation is phenomenology even as my spiritual practice is Buddhist and also informed by other Eastern philosophies.

G. Y.: Link your literary and philosophical identity with your being a Buddhist. By the way, I don't assume that any of these identities are separate for you.

C. J.: No, none of them are separate. They are streams that flow from the same source—the lifelong love of goodness, truth, and beauty. Buddhism is many things: a philosophy, a 2,600-year-old religion, a spiritual practice. As a way of life, it is nonmaterialistic, nonviolent, and nondualistic. It is "radical" in the sense of that word meaning a going to the root of things. As Paul Tillich once observed, it is one of the world's most competitive of religions precisely because it is noncompetitive. Buddhism is concerned, first and foremost (like phenomenology), with understanding consciousness and the operations of the mind. For many artists, the Buddhadharama has offered a liberation from our calcified ways of seeing, from our social and intellectual conditioning, and with what we call Beginner's Mind. It provides a fresh encounter with phenomena, a liberation of perception. That, of course, is what every artist strives for.

G. Y.: In what ways have literature, philosophy, and Buddhism helped you to elucidate the complex subject of race or racism?

C. J.: When creating philosophical works such as "A Phenomenology of the Black Body" (1975) or *Being and Race: Black Writing Since 1970* (1988), a philosophical slave narrative like *Oxherding Tale* (1982), or short fiction such as "The Weave" (2014), my concern is always with discovering the freshest profile (meaning) I can for the subject I'm investigating. In our conscious experience, when one profile or appearance (of an object or subject) is called forth, the others recede from view. Thus to reveal (a meaning) is also to conceal (other meanings). To describe an object (to *say*) is also to *show*. But that saying or showing renders other things unseen or "invisible." What that means in terms of my body of work is that I've attempted to show as many profiles (meanings) as possible, always after setting aside my presuppositions, assumptions, prejudices, and judgments about a subject. The first step, as a Buddhist and phenomenologist, is always to get "me" out of the way. We know, of course, that the field in which meanings unfold has an ever-receding horizon. In other words, we shall, as historically situated beings, never be able to describe all possible profiles or meanings for anything.

That is the approach that gave birth to my 1980 article in *Obsidian*, "Philosophy and Black Fiction," where I stated that:

> Our experience as black men and women completely outstrips our perception— black life, like all life, is ambiguous (it means *too* much) and a kaleidoscope of meanings rich, multisided, and what the authentic black writers does is despoil meaning to pin down the freshest interpretation given to him or her. This creates fiction of the highest order. And it is also hermeneutic philosophy in the sense the writer is an archeologist probing the Real for veiled sense.[2]

As a Buddhist and philosopher looking at racism, I described what I think are some of the invariant characteristics of racism in an interview conducted by poet E. Ethelbert Miller that appeared in the twenty-fifth anniversary edition of *Tricycle: The Buddhist Review*. Here is that description:

> Because most people live in Samsara, or the realm of ignorance and delusion, they will experience the world in terms of their fragile ego. Now, the ego wants to maintain its existence. It identifies with the physical body, with its sense of race and gender, and with its endless desires. Furthermore, the ego is always measuring itself against others because such measuring is how it survives and

avoids what it perceives to be dangerous or a threat to its continuation. It is for-ever wondering if it is inferior, equal, or superior to others. Always wondering, "Is mine bigger than yours?" Obviously, it prefers to feel bigger, superior to, and better than others—smarter, more beautiful, wealthier, more gifted, moral, etc. Something the ego especially dislikes is feeling itself to be in an inferior or sub-ordinate position to (and here I'll use a troublesome black phrase we hear too often these days) "someone who doesn't look like you."[3]

Such an ego—or monkey mind—is the root and fruit of racism. It is enor-mously difficult for most people to overcome, regardless of whether they are white or Black, Hutu or Tutsi, Muslim or Christian, male or female because the ego and its errors reside right at the center of the *I* and what we call per-sonal identity or the self, which for a Buddhist (and David Hume) is an empir-ically unverifiable social construct. What saves me from despair about this very human situation? It is simply the fact that while I am not *blind* to damage caused by the lived illusion of race, neither am I *bound* by it. And I know others need not be bound by it, too.

G. Y.: To entertain the loss of the "I" can be so fearful. Yet, I imagine that part of that fear grows precisely out of the structure of the "I." White supremacy is certainly predicated upon a "mine is bigger than yours" ideology. How do we get whites who are invested in white privilege and superiority not to fear loss of that fictive supremacist "I"? And while not a Buddhist, it seems to me that Martin Luther King Jr. was all too aware of how the white supremacist "I" can be morally destructive.

C. J.: King was acutely aware of the ego's role in racist thought. Nowhere does he express this more eloquently than in his powerful sermon, "The Drum Major Instinct." Most people live in fear of losing their "self," the ego or the *I*, because that means living without a safety net; it means a freedom (and uncertainty) most people are afraid to face. We know, obviously, that there are no safety nets. Buddhists understand this. In Sanskrit, the word 'Nirvana' is composed of *nir* ("out") and *vāna* ("blow"). It literally means to extinguish self-will, ego, and selfish desire. I often think of Nirvana in terms of a visual image—someone blowing out a burning candle and experiencing awakening and liberation. And the most complete state of freedom that any individual can imagine. A freedom even from Buddhism after one reaches a certain stage of development. This is captured in the old Buddhist trope of how we use a boat to cross the sea (of suffering). But once we reach land, we don't carry that boat (rules, precepts, concepts, intellectual tools, etc.) around on our backs, because it has served its purpose and is no longer needed. More than anything else, Shakyamuni Buddha wanted us all to be *truly* free. And let me dare to ask: Isn't freedom what we, as Black Americans, say we want?

Based on what I've just explained above, I will say that I believe the culmination of the three-hundred-year-old Black liberation struggle will be found in what Buddhists call the Three Jewels or Three Refuges: the Buddha, the Dharma, and the Sangha.

G. Y.: So, as one of the two best-known Black male Buddhists in the US (Lama Choyin Rangdrol being the other), say more about how these Three Jewels are linked to Black struggle.

C. J.: You use the phrase 'Black struggle' without defining it or giving examples, assuming I know what it means. I hate to make assumptions for, as the old saying goes, if I assume I know how you are using these terms or what they mean, I make an ASS out of U and ME. As a philosopher, you know we have to define our terms in order to have a dialogue that has substance and is meaningful.

G. Y.: I agree. Voltaire says, "If you wish to converse with me, define your terms." So, by 'Black struggle,' let's limit the question to two social phenomena. How might the Three Jewels have importance in terms of addressing shootings of unarmed young Black men by police and their proxies? And how might the Three Jewels be of importance to the Black Lives Matter Movement in terms of its specific attempt to bring attention to those killings?

C. J.: I think the answer to your question is contained within the "Fourteen Precepts of Engaged Buddhism," as expressed by Thich Nhat Hahn in his book *Interbeing*. Five of these, which are particularly relevant, I've provided below beginning with number 9.[4]

9. Do not say untruthful things for the sake of personal interest or to impress people. Do not utter words that cause division and hatred. Do not spread news that you do not know to be certain. Do not criticize or condemn things of which you are not sure. Always speak truthfully and constructively. Have the courage to speak out about situations of injustice, even when doing so may threaten your own safety.

10. Do not use the Buddhist community for personal gain or profit, or transform your community into a political party. A religious community, however, should take a clear stand against oppression and injustice and should strive to change the situation without engaging in partisan conflicts.

11. Do not live with a vocation that is harmful to humans and nature. Do not invest in companies that deprive others of their chance to live. Select a vocation that helps realize your ideal of compassion.

12. Do not kill. Do not let others kill. Find whatever means possible to protect life and prevent war.

13. Possess nothing that should belong to others. Respect the property of others, but prevent others from profiting from human suffering or the suffering of other species on Earth.

G. Y.: Black bodies are feared in virtue of being Black. They are profiled in truncating ways. You powerfully demonstrate this in your essay, "A Phenomenology of the Black Body." How do we re-educate police officers, for example, to engage in a kind of *epoché* or bracketing so that the rich and fluid meanings of Black bodies can become the foreground of perception? And might not the phenomenological *epoché* have deep ethical implications?

C. J.: Yes, Husserl, the father of phenomenology, well understood that the *epoché* was a radical first move in any investigation of phenomena, a move that clearly had ethical implications. The real question, it seems to me, is how do we get everyone—not just police officers—to approach others with a sense of what I call epistemological humility and egoless listening?

G. Y.: Say more about how you understand both epistemological humility and egoless listening.

C. J.: It's simple—it's all about getting yourself, your ego, out of the way. One way to think about this is to see that whatever it is you are dealing with, it is *you*. I'll say more about this in a moment.

G. Y.: What do you say to those who might argue that Buddhism is too passive, that it involves a kind of apolitical navel-gazing?

C. J.: I would say those people don't understand a damned thing about Buddhism. They do not understand—and probably never heard of—the Bodhissatva vow of Mahayana Buddhism, which is devoted to working toward the happiness and liberation from suffering of all sentient beings (and not just humans). They have probably never heard of the "engaged Buddhism" advocated by Thich Nhat Hahn and others in the world-wide sangha. Or the Edicts of King Ashoka. Or Nagarjuna's advice to King Udayi Shatavahana.[5] As a lay Buddhist, an *upasaka*, my entire day is devoted to living at the white-hot center of Samsara and helping as many others as I can and in every possible way. As Buddhists, we give and ask for nothing in return. I am not an especially political person because politics as we practice it is drenched in dualism, in a Them vs. Us partitioning of the world and our experience, and often the intention of "our" side is winning at any cost, even if that means behavior that is unethical or immoral. In my novel *Dreamer*, I reminded readers that Henry Adams called politics "the systematic organization of hatreds." In *Middle Passage*, Capt. Ebenezer Falcon sums up the consequences of dualism this way: "Mind was made for murder." I was raised as a cradle Christian, and a saying I've never forgotten from my childhood is this: "What shall it profit a man, if he shall gain the whole world, and lose his own soul?" Just look at the people, Republican and Democrat, running in 2016 to be president of the United States. Look at their speech—the lies, falsehoods, inflammatory rhetoric, their lust for power over others, their insults, their reliance on logical fallacies, and playing fast and loose with facts. This is Wrong Speech (the opposite of Right Speech in the Eightfold Path). No, anyone who tries to make a lame accusation that Buddhists are not involved every day in trying to make the world a better place is a brainless fool.

G. Y.: Given what you've insightfully delineated above, the uprooting of the ways in which politicians border on losing their souls as they gain the world would require an entire reconceptualization of politics, yes? What would that look like? I imagine that a Buddhist-inspired Donald Trump (or Hillary Clinton) would entail forms of "political" relationality that we have not seen before.

C. J.: Actually, it is something we have seen before. In various publications, I have described Martin Luther King's idea of "the beloved community" as a "sangha by another name." Taking that a step further, in my novel *Dreamer*, I isolated King's vision in terms of three ideas important to his fourteen-year public ministry: The values he asked us to live by place an emphasis on (1) nonviolence as a way of life; (2) integration as the life's blood of being; and (3) agape.

Putting aside the first two ideas for a moment, let's look more closely at agape, which traditionally is understood to be the unconditional love that God has for human beings. King put this into practice in much the same way that Gandhi did with his implementation of *satyagraha* ("soul force"). He knew the British had to leave India. But he understood that they must leave as a friend, not an enemy. His goal was to win over the hearts and minds of his opponents. See, this is the kind of love that a mother or father has for their children. There may be days, especially when a young person is going through growth at puberty, when the child is willful, defiant, and confused, when a parent loves that child but can't say he or she *likes* them on a particular day. But agape is, as I see it, a teleological love. It loves the potential in what we know that child can become—an enlightened, compassionate being. For example, George Wallace in the 1960s was not an especially loveable person. But by the 1970s he changed. Agape acknowledges that we and others are not nouns but verbs; not products but processes. So in what we as Black people are fond of calling "the struggle," we do not alienate others or attempt to defeat or humiliate or destroy them. Rather, and as we do with our children, we abandon the Us vs. Them mentality, deal with them always with respect, and provide the space for them to grow beyond their moment of confusion and one day enter into the beloved community.

I believe it's important to understand that politics is merely the skin of our social lives. It operates, conceptually, on a high level of abstraction and reification, one several stages removed from the immediacy of our daily, lived experience. That is where we really live on the ground of daily practice. I was a Marxist (in my early twenties), one you probably would not have liked because I was so argumentative and dogmatic. (My master's thesis was on the influence of Marx and Freud on Wilhelm Reich, and as a philosophy TA in the doctoral program at Stony Brook University, I taught a course entitled Radical Thought, which covered Marxist thought from the *1844 Manuscripts* through Chairman Mao.) But Marxism is an ideology, as Marx himself understood—and political, economic, gender, and race ideologies find it difficult to change based on new evidence or counterexamples; indeed they cannot do this by examining their presuppositions and fundamental premises. So I'm saying all that to say this: If we judge someone to be a racist, a homophobe, a sexist, a bourgeois, a proletarian, we have allowed codified language to present a single profile of them; we have employed language and concepts to essentialize their being, to do violence to their multifaceted and prismatic being. As a Buddhist, I am very suspicious of the narratives or stories we tell ourselves about ourselves and others. Ironically, as a writer, I am even suspicious of words, their power to distort our experiences. I don't trust them, and therefore I can't—and won't—base my actions on reified language. One might, for example, describe my wife as a Christian. (Or me as a Buddhist.) But what has that word given us? I've known my wife for forty-eight years, forty-six of those years as husband and wife. I have seen her change over almost half a century. I know her as a friend, mother, confidante, spiritual seeker, former teacher, and social worker. I know her medical history and results of her DNA testing. I know her birth in Buddhist terms to be a blessing unknown to either gods or hungry ghosts. But I can never know all her thoughts, feelings, and experiences even after a lifetime spent together. Do we ever truly "know" another well enough to define or judge them when each of us is, ontologically, a ceaseless play of patterns—physically, emotionally, perceptually, and in respect to consciousness? I think not. This is what I mean by epistemological humility. To some degree, the Other remains a wonderful mystery—even George Wallace or Donald Trump—that ever outstrips our concepts, feelings, and perceptions of him or her. My wife is, therefore, always new and surprising to me. We can say the same about ourselves. And in the face of such a mystery, as we contemplate ourselves and others, the Buddhist approach is to do so with egoless listening to how the Other presents herself, phenomenologically, to us moment by moment. (Her meaning is like the horizon, something we shall never arrive at.) We listen without attachment or desire or self-righteousness. Another name for such selfless listening is love.

Something I've never forgotten, that has stuck with me for decades, is a story I read once about a Westerner who described the horrors Hitler had created to a group of Buddhist nuns, who lived in a remote place and knew nothing about him. The Westerner expected them to say they hated a man whose actions were so monstrous. Instead, they quietly listened to the description of Hitler, and said they pitied him for his ignorance and delusion and the great harm he had caused. Hate, in their practice, was not an emotion they cultivated.

G. Y.: Are there specific challenges when it comes to be being a Black male Buddhist in the twenty-first century?

C. J.: The challenges are simply human ones—the challenge of being compassionate toward all sentient beings. The challenge of being humble enough to understand that our knowledge is limited and always provisional. Physicists tell us that 27 percent of this 13.8 billion-year-old universe consists of dark matter, and 68 percent is dark energy. That means the cosmos that we can measure and observe—what we can experience—is only 5 percent of what is out there. The challenge of loving truth strongly enough that we do not accept prefabricated thinking, ideology, intellectual kitsch, or uncritically take the judgments and interpretations of authorities but rather work—each of us as individuals—to confirm what is and is not true in the depths of our own experience. The challenge of knowing that, in the practice called *vipassana*, thoughts and feelings pass through our consciousness, but we are not those thoughts and feelings, just as we are not our bodies. The challenge of knowing how to observe and examine our thoughts and feelings dispassionately, letting go of those that are wrong or harmful, and returning to those that potentially will bring happiness and freedom from suffering (the two things that all human beings want) to others and ourselves.

G. Y.: You mention that you are suspicious of words. As a writer, how do you negotiate this, that is, how do you communicate with words about which you are suspicious, and, yet, for which I imagine you have a "love." One remarkable piece of advice that you give potential writers is to read the dictionary.

C. J.: As I say in the new book, *The Way of the Writer*, in the chapter entitled "Words," I see words as being the flesh of thought. Furthermore, words are the crystallization in language of thousands of years of experience across numerous cultures and civilizations, each word being the almost tangible skin in which thought is the tabernacle. Phenomenologically, the word *is* the Other. Language is a record of human experience. There is literally a word for every object, material or immaterial, every relation, and every process that human beings have experienced. As writers, words are our most basic tool. So, yes, I am a lover of language and read dictionaries—English and Sanskrit—for both personal pleasure and professional reasons.

But at the end of the day, and especially when I practice meditation, I accept the fact that words are only tools. In a classic Buddhist formulation, they can be "a finger pointing at the moon," but they are not—and cannot be—the experience of the moon itself. They cannot be a substitute for that. Ultimate truth (*paramārtha-satya* in Buddhism) is a nonconceptual and nondiscursive insight into ourselves and the world. Nirvana means letting go of all notions, and concepts to experience phenomenon with freshness.

I'm really delighted that you asked me a question about words, i.e., language, a question that directly relates to literary art, to storytelling and aesthetics, because that has been my primary field of study and focus for the last forty or fifty years, and the basis for my formal education as a philosopher and literary artist. I'm not a politician, a race writer, or even a political writer—just a storyteller, visual artist, and philosopher.

G. Y.: Most certainly. And you tell stories in ways that are philosophically rich and that engage phenomenology, Buddhism, and other powerful lenses. How do you characterize "a race writer" and why don't you consider yourself to be one?

C. J.: I've written about "race" for decades—since the late '60s, and usually because editors ask me to. They figure a Black writer or artist has an understanding of the subject that whites do not have. And they're right. As Black artists and philosophers, we can clarify race questions better than whites based on personal experience and study. And as one of my agents said to me, "Race sells." But there is a trap in this that every serious Black creator and thinker should think about avoiding, one I discussed at length in "The Role of the Black Intellectual in the 21st Century," which is in my book *Turning the Wheel: Essays on Buddhism and Writing*. I consider "race" to be a phenomenologically *lived* illusion (like the belief in an enduring self) that has caused immeasurable human suffering. Predictably, even progressive whites grant to Black intellectuals authority over this single territory—race—while they reserve for themselves the rest of the universe of subjects to explore and examine (including their own take on race). The result is that Black thinkers and artists become ghettoized, pigeonholed as one-trick ponies and never asked their understanding of, say, science or nonracial subjects. This has always felt to me to be like keeping Black artists and intellectuals "in their place," *i.e.*, only talking about themselves. Of course, since the 1970s whites will applaud a Black artist/thinker who so limits himself or herself, pay them handsomely, and offer them endowed chairs in the Academy. I've known many Black thinkers and artists who found this lure of self-limitation—and its social and professional rewards—to be an offer and opportunity they could not refuse, but I'll mention no names. I think, sadly, that this stunts their growth intellectually, artistically, and spiritually. Personally, I'm simply unable to limit my intellect, curiosity, and my talents in this or any other way.

G. Y.: Indeed! Returning to King, we should keep in mind that even as he put into effect the power of "soul force," he was murdered. For example, it's hard to tell people who are being slaughtered by their oppressors that a teleological love will eventuate in some sort of transformation of their oppressor. What are your thoughts on this?

C. J.: My thought is that while both King and Gandhi were murdered, the belief in "soul force" was what motivated them their entire lives. But we should not forget that both King and Gandhi were both profoundly religious men. They were men of unshakeable faith. They did not despair. When imprisoned by the

British, Gandhi had his followers read to him the *Bhagavad Gita* (a book I love), and King, as we know, was a Baptist minister who saw God as a power higher than the unjust laws of men. It might be interesting if we "flip" this question and ask if an atheist or someone with no spiritual practice would have this kind of faith in human beings, and in social and racial progress. Indeed, we might well ask if someone with no spiritual practice will be effective in "the struggle." Any kind of struggle, personal or political.

G. Y.: That is a powerful flip to consider. While I'm a hopeful theist, my guess is that an atheist can be sustained by faith in human beings and their potential to become fundamentally changed. I wonder if any of us is completely without some level of spiritual practice, broadly construed. Speaking of our potential to change for the better, do you think that America, given its history of classism, racism, sexism, and militarism, will ever achieve a beloved community?

C. J.: I don't have a crystal ball so I can't see into the future. But there are beloved communities that exist, here and there, in America today—the sangha is one example, and I consider myself blessed to belong, as an *upasaka* (or lay Buddhist) to the ever-evolving, multiracial sangha in this country. Will all three hundred million Americans ever constitute such a community? That may be asking for too much, based on what we know about human beings, the ego, and the monkey mind. As a wise abbot I interviewed in Thailand in 1997 said to me, some people will understand the Dharma after just seven days. Some will understand after seven months. Some after seven years. And others will still be struggling to understand this wisdom after seventy years.

NOTES

1. Alfred North Whitehead, *Adventures of Ideas* (New York: Simon and Schuster, 1967).
2. Charles Johnson, "Philosophy and Black Fiction," *Obsidian: Black Literature in Review* 6, no. 1–2 (1980): 55–61.
3. E. Ethelbert Miller, "Black Coffee Buddhism," *Tricycle: The Buddhist Review*, Fall 2016, https://tricycle.org/magazine/black-coffee-buddhism/.
4. Thich Nhat Hahn, *Interbeing* (Berkeley, CA: Parallax Press, 1987).
5. See Charles Johnson, "The Dharma of Social Transformation," in *Taming the Ox: Buddhist Stories, and Reflections on Politics, Race, Culture, and Spiritual Practice* (Boulder, CO: Shambhala Publications, 2014), 23, for more on this.

Traci C. West

George Yancy: What were some of the motivating factors that shaped your deep interests in theology and ethics?

Traci C. West: I cannot imagine answering this question about motivating factors without pointing to the person who had the earliest and therefore most formative impact on my understanding of Christianity and its engagement of the world: my mother. My mother had a dynamic personality, highly articulate style of speaking, and rigid understanding of strict parental control of her children. The air that I breathed every day in my family life was comprised of her unique amalgam of evangelical faith and justice-oriented racial politics.

I was thoroughly socialized by her spiritual and intellectual leadership. It combined public and private habits. She exhibited a vigilant antiracist engagement of the world in her routine interactions with whites, Latinos, and Blacks as a teacher's aide in public schools. This was combined with contemplative prayer and Bible study at dawn each day. I relished this time without my siblings that I was able to spend alone with her. Also in my household, daily family viewing of network television evening news was mandatory. I have vivid memories that deeply influenced my later vocational interests of watching embattled civil rights leaders on the nightly news, particularly Martin Luther King Jr. My view of these events was fed by my mother's emotional articulation of admiration and respect for what she understood as the civil rights leaders' divinely guided mission. She also organized a Sunday afternoon family and friends book reading group of Black power texts in which we (the children) were required to participate. This emphasis on reading Black power texts occurred simultaneously with active weekly involvement in our predominantly white local church that she chose for our family. Some of my most enduring questions and interests in theology and ethics were spawned by her complex example. Throughout my childhood I learned about the power of articulate, bold, Christian-faith-informed expressions of racial justice in public life by a poor, Black single mom.

G. Y.: Your mother had a powerful and beautiful impact on your life. How might she be said to have embodied a Black womanist or Black feminist ethics?

T. C. W.: I am intrigued by this question. But my response may seem somewhat surprising. I do not think that my mother embodied Black womanist or Black feminist ethics. I do not want to place the label of womanist or Black feminist on her ethics, nor on my description of her impact on my interests in theology and ethics. I find it specious to impose a political identity on historical figures when they did not claim this identity for themselves. Indeed there are contemporary Black women intellectuals who have significantly contributed to the birthing of my Black feminist commitments in religious scholarship and activism. They include leaders outside of the academic study of religion such as Audre Lorde, Michelle Wallace, Angela Davis, and bell hooks.

But the audacious Christian ethics that my mother embodied seems somehow devalued or shrunken if its worth can only be recognized by its embeddedness in Black feminism or womanism. I have inadequately described her influence if I have portrayed her as mainly having inspired an interest in making the primacy of Black women's subjectivity an essential aspect of my theology and ethics. Of course, my motivation for and the stamina of my Black feminist scholarly research and writing cannot be separated from her formative, disciplining social and Christian values. But how do I convey a broader understanding of her influence that makes it clear that her particular example of Christian faith and antiracism did not merely nurture interests that mirrored her particularity? I want to avoid a common form of white supremacist entrapment wherein the invoking of Black identity narrows rather than expands what one imagines it is possible to learn from Black women's subjectivity. But it may not be possible to do so.

G. Y.: Talk about some of the influences on your theology while a student at Union Theological Seminary. I ask this in light of the sociopolitical consciousness of so many of its scholar/teachers—Reinhold Niebuhr, Dietrich Bonhoeffer, Delores Williams, James Cone, Cornel West, and many others.

T. C. W.: One of the biggest influences was of course my academic adviser, Beverly Wildung Harrison, a white lesbian feminist pioneer of feminist Christian social ethics. I was inspired by the boldness of her vision in her Marxist-influenced social theory and iconoclastic critique of patriarchy in Christian thought and history, as well as her complex Christian theological conceptualization of abortion rights. Okay, you might wonder why I find the intellectual boldness of Harrison and other thought-leaders I met at Union to be so deeply inspiring. Note that I am not pointing to a self-aggrandizing boldness intended merely to shock or create a buzz in the media. Instead I am referring to a kind of boldness that courageously steps into those cultural spaces of fearmongering political and religious manipulation and then persistently, creatively refuses to acquiesce. We know all too well that fear is very effective in silencing dissent from our tolerance for violence against and suppression of poor people's rights, bodily freedoms, and dignity in public life, especially socioeconomically poor Brown and Black women. But fearfulness can hold great sway in academic discourse as well. Too often, a stifling fear reigns even among liberal or progressive academics, that is, a fear of having a voice that sounds too passionate or has too much of an association with messy realities and choices of women's everyday lives rather than well-worn traditional paths of so-called neutral categories of inquiry.

I also had the privilege of being a student in one of the first womanist theology courses ever offered in a seminary in the United States. The pioneering womanist theologian appointed to the Union Theological Seminary faculty, Delores Williams, was the professor. She also served on my dissertation committee. One of the many things I learned from Delores Williams was the importance of cultural critique as a core aspect of theological work. I recall one course with her where she assigned conservative cultural critiques that included ideas about race with which I vehemently disagreed. She consistently required her students to develop political theology and ethics with nuance and breadth attached to our political assertions. We had to account for cultural narratives that preserved white supremacist epistemologies and assumptions in public policy in our theological claims, but only after we had studied those who concertedly authored them.

I learned liberationist methods from these and other faculty mentors as well as an assertive community of Black women student peer activist-intellectuals. A few of those student peers constructed some of the earliest Black queer scholarly interventions in longstanding expressions of black Christianity. Because of the encouragement of certain faculty and student radical Christian innovators, I had the opportunity to experiment with crafting theological language and moral claims that took seriously women's bodies, histories, voices, and choices.

G. Y.: How do we change the violent forms of academic discourse that overlook or, indeed, deny, the importance of Black women's bodies and their concerns?

T. C. W.: That's a challenging question because of its scope and complexity related to the varied disciplinary and ideological traditions that would need to be carefully incorporated into an adequate response. A couple of ideas come to mind, but I readily admit that they are merely starting points for a much more in-depth conversation that is needed.

In any reflection upon "violent forms of academic discourse", I make the preliminary assumption of a degree of blurriness in the lines conventionally drawn between academic discourse and public discourse. I think that the questions academics choose to investigate and human conditions they deem worthy of study are deeply informed by dominant narratives of our broader sociopolitical ethos. Too often denial of the significance of how certain distorted characterizations of Black women's bodies and personhood are reflected in our sociopolitical practices can be cyclically reiterated in academic classrooms and texts.

To uproot violent victimization supported by language, symbolic metaphors, and conceptualizations, we must recognize the political relationship between particular and universal moral claims about human worth and dignity. That is, we must recognize how the particular and universal are indelibly imbricated in, for example, the manner in which broadly framed religious practices and moral values can nurture tolerance of violence against US-American Black lesbians and transgender women. An understanding of the particular experiences of stigma and dehumanization that incubate a disregard for their safety and freedoms facilitate and expand our understanding of universal moral life and truths about US society. Other starting points I would suggest for dismantling "violent forms of academic discourse" would include a commitment to exploring questions of empathy and protest. What kind of academic discourse engenders the possibility of empathy and solidarity? Antiracist critiques of the sexist and heteropatriarchal influences of Christianity could be a means of inciting empathy that counters and unseats tolerance of the violence. What are the imaginative or narrative rhetorics and dialogical, transdisciplinary, or memory-work methods that might enable it? In addition, academic habits that nurture a tolerance for violence reside in seemingly benign and even well-meaning scholarly studies and theoretical analyses. We must consciously develop academic discourse that insistently protests simplistic monolithic narratives about Black women's subjectivities as well as theological and ideological shibboleths superficially asserting common interests and shared power, glossing over the violence nurtured by inequalities.

G. Y.: At what point did you come to realize that race plays such a significant role in theology and that it raises all sorts of important ethical questions?

T. C. W.: In my work in religion, particularly on Christian faith and theology and violence against women, I became increasingly frustrated. Too often the racial dynamics that contributed to the perpetuation of intimate violence and its consequences were assumed to be negligible. Instead of attention to issues of race, I found that certain supposedly universal truths about the experience were asserted. Or in analyses of intimate violence that did incorporate some consideration of issues of race, I became frustrated with a frequent, generalized, almost rote, rejoinder expressing some version of "and for Black women this is worse." For a victim-survivor who is coping with the crisis of abuse or assault, her experience of racial identity and racism cannot be isolated from her experience of spiritual anguish, faith community support or lack of it (if she has such a community), or sexist interpretations of Christian biblical teachings that routinely seep into popular views of women and girls in our Christianity-dominated US American culture. The emphasis on God's expectation of self-sacrifice so centrally taught in Christian theology represents one example of many I could cite. It is preached and taught as standard criteria demonstrating authentic faith in Jesus Christ. For a Christian Black woman victim-survivor, this theology can conjointly reinforce justifications that may be articulated by her abuser, indicating that she has a "racial-loyalty-obligation" to endure his violence that results from the racism he encounters in the world as well as Black communal expectations that she should self-sacrificially refuse to report her Black male abusive partner to police and potentially subject him to racist policing tactics.

In short, I could find few theological resources that took seriously the role of race and racism in the experience, consequences, and prevention of intimate violence. Without an appreciation for the intricate manner in which issues of race and racism can infuse every element of the crisis of the varied forms of gender-based violence, we will have a greatly diminished ability to recognize how those issues exacerbate the harm to those victimized as well as to our broader, collective moral life.

G. Y: Why is the question of race so important theologically? There are some who might argue that theology concerns itself with deep metaphysical and divine issues and thereby is free of something as mundane as race.

T. C. W.: Well, who conceptualizes the theological claims about metaphysics and divinity? All such theological ideas are produced within some identifiable cultural context. It is precisely because theology attempts to offer the most expansive representations of divine, creaturely, and natural existence possible for our human imaginations that we must understand how particular cultural conditions such as race and racism discipline those attempts. To ignore the cultural locatedness of all theological endeavors undermines the seriousness of the theological project's quest to be truthful. All such theological ideas are produced by human bodies, birthed by a woman, physically abled in certain ways, sexually desiring in certain ways, emotionally in need of relational connection in certain ways, and so forth. Racial politics calibrates the worth and dignity of such embodiedness. Attending to embodiedness emboldens theological vision and narratives that can challenge dehumanizing calibrations.

G. Y.: At the moment, our country is experiencing a deep sense of mourning, anger, and violence over the killings in Baton Rouge, St. Paul, and Dallas. Much of this is deeply racially motivated. How might theology, one deeply informed by context and history, speak to this crisis?

T. C. W.: You have named the heart of crisis that so many Black and Brown people are experiencing. Their mourning, anger, and frustration are directly related to the acontextual and ahistorical understanding of the racism that prevails in the United States. The multiple forms of public erasure of historical patterns of white dominance and institutionally reinforced assumptions of white superiority form the context for incendiary dynamics we are witnessing in both the tragedies that make the headlines and those that do not. Liberationist Christian theological voices are uniquely equipped to speak to those in Christian faith communities and beyond who are directly impacted by this crisis of violence because we are so thoroughly invested in a tradition centered on God's intervention in history through the Jesus movement in the first century, on the side of those the state executed and violently repressed. For liberationist Christian theologians and ethicists, we are enabled in speaking to the dynamics of this crisis by our identification with a gospel tradition where the Roman state tortured and executed Jesus, a Palestinian Jew, to send a message to rebellious Jews. And a divinely empowered movement of Gentiles and Jews flourished in defiance of such forms of state terror and humiliation aimed at reinforcing social hierarchies.

G. Y.: So much attention is focused on unarmed Black males who were killed and continue to be by the police and their proxies. Yet, it is Black mothers who we see weeping in the media. I often think of Mamie Till-Mobley and her pain and courage after her son Emmett Till was brutally murdered in 1955. What message do you have for Black mothers who suffer the loss of their sons through state violence?

T. C. W.: Before I attempt to formulate any kind of message to the mothers, I want to mention a few preliminary thoughts that your question provokes.

You rightly point out that so much attention has been focused on "unarmed Black males who were killed and continue to be by the police and their proxies." Unarmed Black and Brown women and girls have also been targeted in killings and assaults by police and citizens acting as their proxies. These incidents include victims such as Miriam Carey, Mya Hall, Alexia Christian, Meagan Hockaday, Renisha McBride, and others. Why has there been less attention and public outrage about these assaults? I commend the work of the African-American Policy Forum based at Columbia University Law School for their ongoing refusal to allow these crimes against women to be ignored.

As I struggle with the idea of crafting an appropriate message to the mothers, a barrage of related historical dynamics come to mind. When you mentioned these Black mothers and their pain and courage glimpsed in the media, I am reminded of cultural and academic debates on the moral significance of Black motherhood that date back to the nineteenth century. W. E. B. Du Bois's notion of "the mother idea" portrayed Black mothers as Christian martyrs and a symbol of survival, dignity, and strength that represents the entire race of Black peoples. This idea was a defense of Black motherhood in the face of common assaults in American literature and discourse characterizing them as insatiably sexually promiscuous, broodmarish breeders of Black laborers,

asexual Mammies for white children, or some other dehumanized caricature. Moreover, Black single motherhood has been excoriated as a sign of
pathology in Black communities by influential scholars such as Black sociologist E. Franklin Frazier and white sociologist Daniel Patrick Moynihan,
as well as nationally elected political leaders who were architects of late
twentieth-century welfare-reform policies. But I do not want to respond to the
Black mothers who have suffered the loss of their sons or daughters through
state violence as symbolic representations of Black peoples who need to be
defended or disciplined.

When you mention that the mothers have been seen weeping in the media,
I can barely contain my anger about how little attention is paid by the media
to the content of their advocacy that accompanies those tears. Their public
witness also summons our recollection of the historical legacy of Black wom-
en's antiviolence activism, such as the leadership of media journalist and public intellectual Ida B. Wells that was centered on protesting brutal, widespread
lynchings of Black men by white men. But I feel like it would be an extremely
unfair burden to craft a message that praises these contemporary mothers in
any way that expects them to offer the kind of self-sacrificial extraordinary
leadership Ida B. Wells offered to our nation.

So I think that if I were to offer a message directed to the mothers of men and
women who have been killed and assaulted by state violence in the US, I am not
certain exactly how, but I would want to avoid trivializing clichés and patron-
izing advice-giving about what they must do for themselves or in behalf of the
memory of their sons and daughters or for the sake of the moral health of US
society imperiled by its white racism and violence. Instead, I would offer my support and care for them as they struggle with their grief in all the forms it takes.
I would want to linger in the space and time of lament crucial for acknowledging
the specificity of each mother's loss and mourning process. I would also want to
address the racialized pressure some may experience to exemplify some version
of the strong Black mother. I would seek words or actions that attempt to convey my belief that the fullness of their subjectivity and dignity must be honored
in a manner that recognizes their entitlement to feel weak, lost, angry, bitter, to
weep, to depend on others to hold them up, to be strong, bold, assertive, to offer
persevering leadership or whatever response they choose and need in the wake
of these devastating murders and societal betrayals.

PART VIII DISCUSSION QUESTIONS

1. Traci C. West says that she was inspired by the boldness of Beverly Wildung
   Harrison's ability to develop complex, rich theological frames of reference
   to ground her cultural critique and defense of various rights. She demonstrates West's concept of "a kind of boldness that courageously steps into

those cultural spaces of fearmongering political and religious manipulation and persistently, creatively refuses to acquiesce." Though some may think that Buddhism is too passive to be useful in confronting racism, Charles Johnson suggests that the ego is "the root and fruit of racism." Underlying racism and its violence is the fear most people share of losing the "self," or the "ego." The kind of freedom pursued in Buddhism is one that "literally means to extinguish self-will, ego, and selfish desire." As such, Buddhist ethics requires that the individual always interrupt injustice without self-concern. To what extent does Johnson's "epistemological humility and egoless listening" contribute to the self-surrendering embedded within Buddhist ethics? How does this kind of self-surrender compare to the kind of boldness that West discusses?

2. West points out that "unarmed Black and brown women and girls have also been targeted in killings and assaults by police and citizens acting as their proxies," but they receive significantly less media attention than victims who are Black and brown men and boys. Women of color are more readily included in the media as the grieving mothers of these men and boys, but even then their presence and their very identity is distorted. They are presented as having only deep hurt grounding their words, such that the "content of their advocacy that accompanies their tears" is ignored. How might the central ideas of Buddhism and West's account of Christian theological ethics restore the experience of Black and brown women from what West calls "multiple forms of public erasure"? The rift between what is experienced in this case and what is reported might be accounted for in the lack of what Johnson calls "teleological love," in which one's love for another is directed at the potential within every human being to become "an enlightened, compassionate human being." Can teleological love help to narrow the schism between the experience and perspective of women of color and their portrayal in the media? If so, how can we cultivate teleological love to redress this massive failure to appreciate the ongoing struggle and endlessly undervalued subjectivity of women of color?

SUPPLEMENTAL QUESTIONS

1. Lawrence Blum establishes "rules for engagement" before discussing race in his classes, and has noted the success in this practice for making people aware of the impact their words have on those around them, particularly in emotionally charged discourse. Rules in this context are an effective way to get students speaking productively on a difficult subject. They are also effective in creating space for rational argumentative progress in logic, and meaningful and playful interaction in games. Can the use of "rules" help

bring together the element of playfulness discussed in bell hooks with the engagement of difficult and emotionally volatile subjects?

2. The treatment of enslaved Black people and indigenous peoples in the early history of the United States is indisputably morally reprehensible. Yet there persists intentional ignorance and denial such that, in the words of Peter Singer, "Perhaps the most appalling contemporary myth is that none of this happened." The problem of dehumanization discussed in Part IV is reflected by the inability or unwillingness of whites individually and the United States government in general to recognize that atrocities that have been sanctioned and carried out by the United States government against indigenous peoples and other nonwhite peoples, and how the effects of those policies have benefited and continue to benefit white people. To what extent might the problems of continuing racism, sexism, and other dehumanizing practices be attributed to this lack of recognition? As such, is a memorial for the dehumanized and atonement on the part of the United States government a necessary first step before lasting progress can occur?

3. Linda Martín Alcoff explains that philosophy has a methodological flaw insofar as it aims for the most general, universal theories that account for human experience. To attain generalizability, philosophers sacrifice the context in which human experiences occur, especially experiences relating to embodiment, including gender and race. Clevis Headley returns to this idea throughout his interview insofar as discourse on race continues to fail because it is almost always engaged in without regard for historical context. Decontextualized, ahistoric perspectives on race necessarily involve abstraction that distorts and "[renders] invisible the historical, existential, and experiential features of the concept of race." How can we develop the tools to keep history and context present in conversations about race, and what might those tools look like? And what are the implications for Western philosophy's tendency toward abstraction and ideal theory?

4. Molefi Kete Asante emphasizes that victories can be claimed even in the worst moments. "The key," he explains, "[is that] one must claim space or take space, intellectually or physically, in any situation however difficult or dire it may be seen." Individuals need this space to "become subjects of [their] own narratives." The creation and maintenance of space is also important for Linda Martín Alcoff. She explains that "carving out, and regularly nurturing, those spaces—journals, professional societies, conferences—in which all who are interested in the subfield of critical race philosophy can develop our work within a constructively critical community" is likely a good strategy in substantially and meaningfully diversifying philosophy. Is there currently adequate space in daily American life to sustain a more robust discourse on race and substantial improvement for the lives of the excluded and oppressed? How might we make more space,

especially a space that has not been compromised by various forms of hegemony?

5. The interviews with Lucius T. Outlaw Jr., Bill E. Lawson, and Clevis Headley all suggest that philosophy should be deeply informed by other disciplines to make headway on the problem of race both as a subject of philosophical inquiry and as an inequity needing redress in the discipline itself. Is Western philosophy's inability to see its own flaws a self-evident refutation of, as a paradigmatic example, Kant's *Critique of Pure Reason* or the more general reputation of Western philosophy to see the "big picture"? Why is Western philosophy so resistant to self-knowledge and the project of determining it oversights?

6. What is the relationship between narrative as a process of identity development and as a process of self-obfuscation?

7. Is it possible to focus on narrative to access the injustices done to groups of people without abandoning all hope for some notion of "truth" that stands apart from narrative?

8. Can love of truth be liberated from the white supremacist drive for absolute, transcendent, objective truth?

9. What is the difference between narrative, myth-making, and intentional ignorance?

INDEX

anger
  convenient myths on, 150
  expression of, 113
  goading victims into, 228
  Grant on, 306
  hooks on, 19
  Nhat Hanh on, 19
  over media advocacy, 333
  over racially motivated killings, 331
  in privilege-evasive responses, 62
  of white people, 66, 101, 125
  Yancy on, 3
Anievas, Alexander, 187
anti-Arab/Muslim racism, 151–52
anti-Black racism
  collective activism and, 312
  community of color and, 230
  discussion questions on, 103
  normative theory and, 190
  Obama and, 7, 221, 260
  schematic racism and, 55
  Spillers on, 39
  in the United States, 53
antilynching activism/movement,
    45, 46
Anti-Semite and Jew (Sartre), 134
Anzaldúa, Gloria, 63
APA (American Philosophical
    Association), 109, 118, 119, 194,
    227, 233, 256, 257
apartheid, 84, 131, 134, 156, 198,
    216, 292
ape framing, of Black people, 101
"The Aporia of Hope: King and Bell
    on the Ending of Racism"
    (Lawson), 252
Appeal (Walker), 111
Appiah, Kwame Anthony
  background of, 274–75
  on Black identity, 272–74
  on Black Lives Matter
    movement, 275–76
  Blum and, 109
  contributor biography, xi
  *Cosmopolitanism: Ethics in a World of
    Strangers*, 275
  Goldberg and, 135
  on interest in philosophy of
    race, 271–72
  Lines of Descent, 272, 273

  on police killings of unarmed Black
    men, 276–77
  on social issues, 142
  on *Volksgeist*, 272, 293
  on white supremacist identity, 273
Arab Spring, 173
Arendt, Hannah, 75, 134, 142, 289
Aristotle, 246
Aronowitz, Stanley, 265
Asante, Molefi Kete
  on acculturation of racists, 242–43
  The Afrocentric Idea, 244
  on Afrocentricity, 241–42, 245–46
  on "Black-on-Black" crime, 243
  on claiming space/power, 244, 335
  contributor biography, xi
  on empowerment in times of
    grief, 243–44
  on killing of unarmed Black men,
    242, 244–45
  on protests against police
    violence, 292
  on race in America, 241
Augustine, 75
Australia. *See* Aboriginal people/
    Aboriginality; Indigenous people/
    communities
Australian Critical Race and Whiteness
    Studies Association (ACRAWSA),
    298, 306

Bacon, Francis, 171
Baier, Kurt, 135
Bailey, Alison
  on Black Lives Matter
    movement, 68–69
  on borderland theory, 63, 64
  contributor biography, xi–xii
  on crisis, 63–64
  on hate group engagement, 69–70
  on metaphysical comfort,
    61–62, 64, 68
  on "shadow texts," 68, 69
  on teaching white students, 68
  on travel between worlds, 64–67
  on white discomfort, 68
  on white fear, 65–66
  on white people "falling apart," 62–63
  on white privilege, 103
Baker, Ella, 33, 47

Baldwin, James, 1, 40, 41, 86, 135, 151, 246, 263, 265, 286, 290–91
Baldwin, Lewis, 266
Balibar, Étienne, 135
Baltimore, Maryland, 31
Bamboozled (film), 129
Banchetti, Marina, 289
Bannon, Stephen K., 5
Baptist, Edward, 147, 149
"Basketball" (music video), 131
Batman trilogy, 120
Being and Race: Black Writing Since 1970 (Johnson), 318
Bell, Derrick, 83, 252
Bellah, Robert, 97
beloved community/communities, 16, 252, 321, 322, 326
Benhabib, Seyla
 contributor biography, xii
 on democracy, 177, 200
 Feminist Contentions: A Philosophical Exchange, 175
 on racial divides/boundaries, 174
 on racial symbolism in public sphere, 173–74
 on role of reason, 201
 Situating the Self, 175
 on Western philosophical tradition, 175–77
Berea College, 18
Berlin, Ira, 111
Bernal, Martin, 118
Bethune, Mary McLeod, 21
The Better Angels of our Nature (Pinker), 172
Beyoncé (Knowles), 28, 210
"Beyond Vietnam: A Time to Break Silence" (King), 1
Biden, Joe, 269
Bidve, Anuj, 313
Biko, Steve, 135
birtherism, 5
The Birth of a Nation (film), 4, 126, 182
'bitch,' term usage, 3
Black Athena I and *II* (Bernal), 118
Black Bodies, White Gazes (Yancy), 93, 287
Black Boy (Wright), 235
Black feminist thought
 discussion questions on, 49
 intersectional dimensions of, 25–30

Black Feminist Thought: Knowledge, Consciousness, and the Politics of Empowerment (Hill Collins), 26, 27, 30
Black Lives Matter movement
 Bailey on, 68–69
 Blum on, 115
 emergence of, 8
 Flory on, 127
 Goldberg on, 140–41
 Headley on, 286–87
 Hill Collins on, 31–33
 James on, 48
 Spillers on, 42
"Black Lives Matter" phrase, 53–55, 57
Black Looks: Race and Representation (hooks), 21
Black men/masculinity. *See also* unarmed Black people, killing of
 body politics and, 27–29
 as film vigilantes for justice, 120–21
 hooks on, 22
 as "missing," 42
 targeting of, 180–81
Blackmon, Douglas A., 148
Blackness
 meaning/idea of, 29–30, 33
 as social deficit, 37
Black prophetic fire, 263–64, 292–93
Black Prophetic Fire (West), 263
Black Reconstruction in America: 1860-1880 (Du Bois), 198
Black Rights/ White Wrongs: The Critique of Racial Liberalism (Mills), 185
Black Skin, White Masks (Fanon), 134, 135, 161, 182, 233, 234
Black/white binary, 113–14
Black women/Black women's bodies
 in academic discourse, 329–330
 body politics and, 27–29
 intersectional dimensions of oppression, 25–27
 killing of, 334
 masculinization of, 38
 mothers/motherhood, 31–32, 332–33
 nominative properties and, 37
 as sexual property, 58
 socially tolerated violence against, 161
 Spillers on, 41–42

Humphrey, Hubert, 90
Hurston, Zora Neale, 135, 246
Husserl, Edmund, 321

ideal/non-ideal theory, 9, 188, 190–91, 200, 335
ignorance, epistemology of, 187, 191–92, 200, 285–86, 293
image, control of, 27–29
"I'm Not a Racist, But . . . ," (Blum), 110
'imperialist white supremacist capitalist patriarchy,' 15, 16, 20
Indigenous people/communities, 99, 114, 149, 151, 168–69, 171, 268, 297–300, 304–7, 314, 335
Indigenous Sovereignty and the Being of the Occupier: Manifesto for a White Australian Philosophy of Origins (Nicolacopoulos and Vassilacopoulos), 299
Indigenous sovereignty theory, 301–3
"Inner City Blues (Make Me Wanna Holler)" (Gaye), 46
institutional racism, 41, 142, 170, 230
intentional ignorance, 149–151, 199–200
Interbeing (Nhat Hahn), 320
intersectionality, 25–27, 30–32, 34–35, 41, 49, 135
Irvine, Craig
    on anti-Black racism, 103
    consciousness about race, 90–92
    contributor biography, xvi
    on narrative medicine, 87–89, 92–93
    on normativity of whiteness, 95
    on skepticism from students of color, 94–95
    on teaching white students, 94
The Italian Job (film), 124

Jackson, Helen, 150
Jackson, J. J., 131
Jackson, Michael, 131, 133
James, Joy
    on activism, 45
    on civil rights movements, 47
    contributor biography, xvi
    on grief, 43
    on persistence of racism, 45–46
    on police violence, 43, 48

on resistance, 48
on restorative justice, 47
James Baldwin: A Biography (Lemming), 291
James Bond series, 121–23
Jefferson, Thomas, 101, 148, 149, 199–200
Jesus, social construction of, 127, 130
Jim Crow, 43, 46, 98, 100, 149, 151, 156, 159, 182, 205, 215–16, 251, 273–74, 287
Johnson, Charles
    on *agape*, 322
    on beloved communities, 326
    on "Black struggle," 320
    Buddhist identity of, 317–19
    on challenges for Black male Buddhists, 324
    characterization of "a race writer," 325
    contributor biography, xvi–xvii
    "double narrative intelligence" concept, 124, 144
    on epistemological humility/egoless listening, 321, 334
    on Marxism, 322–23
    philosophical writings of, 318
    on philosophy/literature intersection, 317
    on "soul force," 325–26
    suspicion of words, 324–25
    on teleological love, 334
    Turning the Wheel: Essays on Buddhism and Writing, 325
    The Way of the Writer: Reflections on the Art and Craft of Storytelling, 317, 324
    on white supremacist "I," 319
Johnson, James Weldon, 246
Jordon, June, 33
Joseph, Dean, 313

Kant, Immanuel, 119, 336
Kelly, Megyn, 127, 130
Kierkegaard, Søren, 77, 85
killing, of unarmed Black people, 8, 53–54, 56, 58–59, 67, 75–76, 127, 136, 180–82, 241, 243–44, 287, 303, 320, 332, 334
Killing Rage (hooks), 19
Kim, David Haekwon

white supremacists/supremacy. *See also*
    'imperialist white supremacist
    capitalist patriarchy'
    engagement with, 69–71
    as mental illness, 19
    Mills on, 186, 189–190
    Trump's election and, 6
    usage of term "boy," 2
    value of Black lives under, 288–89
"white talk," 61
Whitman, Walt, 150
Williams, Delores, 328
Williams, Patricia J., 5, 135, 214,
    219, 231
Williams, Raymond, 310
Williams, Robert, 45
Williams, Serena, 26, 27, 28–29, 38
Williams, Venus, 28–29, 38
Wilson, Darren, 83
Wilson, George, 117
Wilson, Joe, 39
Wise, Tim, 95
Wolf, Christa, 156
women. *See* Black women/Black
    women's bodies
Women, Race and Class (Davis), 135
'world' travel, 64–65, 66–67
The World Viewed (Cavell), 117
Wretched of the Earth (Fanon), 134, 311
Wright, Jeremiah, 217, 219
Wright, Richard, 6, 135, 235, 248
*Writing Beyond Race: Living Theory and
    Practice* (hooks), 21

"WTF with Marc Maron" (podcast), 7

xenophobia/zenophobic tribalism, 5, 6,
    74, 129, 170

Yancy, George
    Black Bodies, White Gazes, 93, 287
    contributor biography, xx
Young, Iris Marion, 174
youth. *See* Black youth

Zack, Naomi
    on "broken windows" policy, 180
    contributor biography, xx
    The Ethics and Mores of Race, 179
    on Ferguson, Missouri, 179
    on loss of agency, 200
    motivation of, 179
    on participatory democracy,
    179–190
    Philosophy of Science and Race, 179
    on "postracial" idea, 182–83
    Race and Mixed Race, 179
    on race as social construct, 183
    on targeting of Black men,
    180–81
    on white privilege, 182
Zami (Lorde), 235
Zaner, Richard, 89
Zea, Leopoldo, 208
Zimmerman, George, 8
Zootopia (film), 128
Zuma, Jacob, 84

THE DOCTOR IN HISTORY

CHAPTER I

An Unknown Hero of Medicine

DISEASE is older than man.

There were no men in the Age of Reptiles, in those days before the surface of the land was for the last time covered with a blanket of ice. But there were diseases.

The story of disease is written in records of rock and soil. We find in the fossil remains of gigantic dinosaurs the signs of injuries. There are broken bones, the only record of some mighty struggle to the death enacted perhaps a hundred million years ago. There are traces to show that broken bones had healed in some great beast that once limped across a world man never saw.

Such injuries were to be expected; what is more important is that there are signs of infection. Dinosaurs, cave bears, and saber-toothed tigers had toothache; their fossil teeth show cavities and decay. In prehistoric bones there are roughened spongy places, traces left by a sort of rheumatism of the joints. In one skeleton of a horned dinosaur that has been uncovered there are marks of an abscess of the leg that once held nearly half a gallon of pus.

We know today that all infections are caused by living parasites that grow upon the flesh, parasites such as bacteria.

There were disease bacteria before there were men.

Many hundreds of centuries ago the forces were being marshaled, the scene set, for the great struggle which was in time to confront the human race—disease against man and man against disease.

Then like a curtain separating the acts in a play, the glacial period descended upon the Continent of Europe. For centuries the ice lay upon lands barren of life. Gradually it

began to melt. A new scene opened, another era began, and a new actor appeared upon the stage—man.

Thirty or forty thousand years ago the glacier was slowly moving back toward the mountains. Streams from the melting ice were cutting wide valleys in the land. The level of the ocean was rising, but still it had not yet covered the strip of land that connected England with the continent. There was no English Channel. The Baltic Sea was a great freshwater lake. The weather was still cold, but the air was becoming drier, and dust storms swept across the land. Along the seacoast forests were springing up; inland there were wind-swept prairies sparsely grown with grass, widening each year as the ice receded.

A bison painted on the wall of a cave by a prehistoric artist.

It was the grass, always the grass, that drew the animals to the new-found prairies. Slowly, over centuries, they came, first the warm fur animals; then, as the climate changed, the thin-coated grazing animals.

Their story, like that of the great reptiles before them, is

written in records of rock and soil. From fossil bones we can identify the woolly rhinoceros, the mammoth with enormous tusks, the musk-ox, the bison, the reindeer, and the wild horse. The horses came in droves, queer little ponies with tufted beards like goats.

In the wake of the grass-eaters followed the animals of prey; the bear, the fox, the cave hyena—and man. He came across North Africa, following the slow migration into the new lands of a changing world. These men who followed the reindeer and horses into France were not the first to live there. But they were the first men of whom we have record who looked like modern men. The earlier inhabitants were not handsome by our standards nor were they, we should judge, intelligent. They were short and stocky, with bowed legs, overhanging brows, receding chins. They were probably more savage, more primitive and beastlike than any people living today, even in the most remote jungle.

Our story concerns the reindeer men and they, at least in appearance, do not suffer by comparison with modern men, for they were giant fellows, well over six feet tall, straight bodied, strong limbed, large headed. We call them Cro-Magnon men because it was in the Cro-Magnon caves at Dordogne, France, that the remains they left were first discovered.

The reason why these people have an especial interest for our story is that among them we find the first record of a doctor.

Twenty thousand years ago the struggle between man and disease was already under way. A leader had been chosen to direct the forces that men employed to fight for health and life.

We have no records to tell us what sort of a struggle the earliest men, those bowlegged squat fellows of fifty thousand years ago, made against disease. But we can guess and guess closely. Certainly they had no doctors. Probably they had no tribes or tribal organization, but lived in scattered

families made up of a leader followed by a few women with their babies. Their life was hard and cruel and short. Men, women, and children suffered from accidents and diseases. But they knew, we are sure, little more about how to cure or prevent disease or treat the injuries from accidents than do brute beasts.

An animal struggles alone against disease or injury; none of its kind helps it. The crippled beast hides from others, lest it be torn to pieces; it licks its sores in solitude; sick, it crawls into a dark corner to die unattended. No doubt the earliest men behaved in the same way when confronted with accident and disease. The hale man killed the injured man and took for himself his skins and weapons; the sick savage died neglected, shunned by his companions. Such primitive men did not even bury their dead.

Sympathy, the willingness to aid the injured and the ill, to enlist in their defense against disease, was the first forward step in man's struggle against disease. No man can fight sickness alone, and least of all the man to whom disease has come.

This sympathy in some measure at least had developed among the Cro-Magnon people twenty thousand years and more ago, for, as we have said, their tribes had leaders in the struggle against disease—medicine men. We must not think of these primitive doctors as being like modern doctors. Their medical practice was as primitive as were their weapons and their homes. But they deserve a place in our story because as far as we know they were the first among men to join together in the struggle against disease. They gave us the first principle of medicine, a very important one: that there shall be men whose duty it is to devote themselves to the care of the sick and injured, to use their efforts to save their companions from disease. These primitive tribesmen originated the doctor.

Hundreds of centuries before the Christian Era, the Cro-Magnon people vanished; they either died off entirely or

were absorbed into other tribes of men that came later. The climate of the lands where they lived changed, forests grew up, the animals they had hunted disappeared. Forest tribesmen far more civilized than they came into their lands. In

The Cro-Magnon medicine man dressed in his ceremonial costume.

time from the East there arrived men in steel helmets—the Romans—advancing civilization, driving back the barbarians. Then in turn the barbarians drove back the Roman legions, but civilization lingered. Castles arose and feudal lords reigned, then kings. Wars were fought over the lands

where the Cro-Magnon men once chased wild horses. Cities grew, fields and orchards spread across the land. Factories were built, railroads spanned the countryside, automobiles sped over paved roads, perhaps carrying the modern doctor to his patient, and steamboats churned their way through rivers where the Cro-Magnon man had once speared fish. The panorama of recorded history unfolded over the land where he had lived and where he had enlisted in man's first organized struggle against disease.

For two hundred centuries the records of the Cro-Magnon people and their medicine men lay buried undisturbed in caves in the hills.

These people did not, like the savages before them, desert their dead; they buried them with ornaments and weapons. From the skeletons we know their stature and build. From the remains they left in the caves which were their homes— stone tools and weapons, carved bones and perforated skulls —we can tell something of how they lived. We can tell even more: how they looked and what they saw, for they have left amazing paintings on the smooth stone walls of deep caverns.

It was only in our time that men began to explore these caves, deserted for thousands of years. The entrances are often merely narrow clefts at the base of a hill, perhaps partially submerged in streams and now nearly sealed with stalactites formed by centuries of dripping water. From them the way leads into upper galleries, long, high-walled caves where there are hollowed rocks into which grease was once poured to form crude lamps. There are pictures on the walls of these chambers—bison in red and black, half-finished sketches of reindeer, and drawings of wild horses.

The paintings are mostly of animals—flat-looking one-sided pictures, lacking the foreshortening that gives perspective and a sense of depth. They are, in fact, much like the paintings made by the early American Indians.

You would hardly believe that these paintings could have

survived for twenty thousand years, but they have, and for a peculiar reason. The Cro-Magnon artists used grease paint, and the grease has preserved the colors against moist air and trickling water. The grease was the fat from some animal, tallow mixed with colored dirt and pushed inside a piece of broken bone—not a bad sort of paint tube for a primitive artist.

There is one cave in particular at Ariège, France, that holds our attention. It was discovered by the three sons of Count Begouën and is called in their honor *Trois Frères*—the three brothers. It contains one of the few prehistoric pictures of a man—a Cro-Magnon medicine man. This is the first known representation of a doctor.

He is shown dressed fantastically in the skin of an animal. On his head he wears the antlers of a reindeer; his ears look like those of a bear; on his hands are mittens with claws; a long flowing beard and the tail of a horse complete his costume.

He is half crouching as if in the step of a ceremonial dance, and he presides over the painted animals as he did in life, when through his magic he brought game to the hunters of his tribe and kept his people free from disease. He is the Cro-Magnon sorcerer—and doctor.

The Cro-Magnon people had no written or picture language. Such things came much later. We do not know, and never shall, the name of this primitive doctor. We shall never know what feats of magic he performed, what wonderful cures he effected. But we do know that his companions turned to him for aid in illness. He was the early leader in man's struggle against disease.

To him and his kind we today owe the principle of medicine: that there shall be doctors to lead men in a united warfare against disease.

CHAPTER II

Spirits, Demons, Ghosts, and Witches

WE owe to primitive man the origin of the doctor and the beginning of medicine. But such a queer creature is man that, having pointed the direction and taken the first steps toward the control of disease, he lost his way and wandered into a maze of bypaths that led him not to science but to magic and mystery and superstition. In consequence for hundreds of centuries he fought a sham battle with disease in a region where disease does not exist.

The thing that led him astray was a belief, a false belief which held back the progress of medicine for thousands of years. Until it was discarded, all the meager advances resulted from accident and chance.

Primitive man believed that disease came not from natural causes but from supernatural ones; that it arose from the action of unfriendly spirits, ghosts, and demons, or from witchcraft. It was accordingly to be prevented and treated by magic directed against supernatural forces.

The greatest single advance ever made in controlling disease was not the acquiring of something new but the giving up of something that was old—the discarding of a false belief. The great difference between the futile efforts of the Cro-Magnon medicine man and the success of the modern doctor in treating and preventing disease is not so much in their relative skills as in their opposing beliefs. The Cro-Magnon medicine man, because of his beliefs, attempted to treat disease by dealing with spirits and ghosts; the modern doctor attempts to deal with the facts of nature. The one fought a sham battle; the other meets the enemy in reality.

We have spoken here as if we knew what the beliefs of the Cro-Magnon medicine man were. The only record we have

of him is his picture. But in spite of that we do know what he believed about disease as well as if we had lived with him and spoken his language. His costume gives us the clue to his beliefs. It was the ceremonial dress he wore to frighten away the evil spirits that tormented his tribesmen with disease. We know his beliefs because of another reason—a curious one: All the medicine men of all primitive peoples in all times of which we have any record have held, and still hold the same beliefs about disease, and used the same measures to contend against it.

You could go as an explorer to some little-known tropical island where there are primitive people and learn the beliefs of the medicine man. You would find that he thought that disease was caused by spirits and demons and ghosts, and that his tribesmen believed that illness could be cured only by magic and witchcraft. Or you could land thousands of miles away in Africa and trek far into the interior to a people who had never heard of the Islanders, who spoke a different language, were a different race, and you would find that they too believed that disease was caused by spirits and demons and ghosts. Explore wherever you wish, among primitive peoples, and you will always discover beliefs similar to those held by the Cro-Magnon medicine man.

Turn to the records of our Indians. They once thought that spirits were the cause of disease. On page 12 is a picture of a medicine man of the Blackfoot tribe, dressed in his professional costume. He wears the hide of the uncommon yellow bear; strung to it are skins of snakes, frogs, and mice, the feathers of birds, and the hoofs of the deer and goat. In one hand he holds a decorated wand and in the other a rattle. When called to treat a sick man, he brandished the wand and shook the rattle, hopped and jumped about his patient, gave wild Indian yells, growled like a bear, and ordered the demon of disease to depart.

We find these same beliefs among the Druids of ancient Britain, among the barbarians who once roamed the forests

of Germany, and in the ancient records of Egypt, Babylon, Greece, and Rome. As we go on with our story we shall dis-

Medicine man of the Blackfoot Indians dressed
in his professional costume.

cover that the idea of the supernatural origin of disease has persisted in civilization and exists in our own time.

You perhaps may wonder—great scientists certainly have —how it happened that all primitive peoples, although they lived widely separated, shared this common belief concerning disease. Some scientists think that the idea was carried from a common center during ancient migrations of people or was spread by travel in days when there was more land above the water than there is now and tribes were not cut off and isolated. The Cro-Magnon men when they came out of North Africa brought their beliefs with them, as did the Lake Dwellers who migrated into Europe after them. The American Indians, the Eskimos, the Islanders, the Africans migrated centuries ago to the lands where they are now. We do not know where they came from. Did the basic idea concerning disease spring from one common meeting place and so spread everywhere? It is possible. Also it is true that once primitive peoples adopt a belief they do not readily change it, but keep it unaltered for centuries; they are the victims of tradition even more than are civilized men.

The theory of migration does not, however, explain at all where or why belief in spirits as a cause of disease arose, but merely tells how it may have spread.

Other scientists do not consider migration necessary to account for this uniform belief. They think that there may have been no common source, but that the idea arose many times quite independently and would occur naturally among any untutored men living the life of savages.

Men are very much alike everywhere. They differ, of course, in strength and size and color and certainly in intelligence, but always their natural tendency is to reason about the dangers of life in a certain way. This peculiarly human way of reasoning accounts for the ideas that made spirits the cause of disease.

By extensive education the natural faults of reasoning can be corrected. Native people were, of course, educated,

but not to this extent. They were trained in the folkways of their people and in tribal tradition. Beyond these things their education did not go. The child educated in civilized surroundings is, for the first ten or twelve years of his schooling, trained in precisely the same things—the folkways and traditions of his people. During the centuries of civilization many facts have been accumulated; folkways and traditions have changed. The school child of today has knowledge of many things unknown to the savages and, if he continues with his education, he may go beyond the stage of the mere acquiring of knowledge; he may learn to correct his faults of reasoning and to think independently. That is an ideal of education held only by civilized peoples.

Unfortunately, education is not hereditary; we are born ignorant and untrained. If a child of civilized and educated parents were placed among savages and raised by them, he would grow up to think and believe as they do. This has happened, and the child—unlike the heroes of some jungle tales—did not become superior in education to the natives, or teach himself to read and write, or learn to think logically. He remained an ignorant savage with the savage's beliefs and fears.

Primitive man is like a child not yet educated to think independently, but a child without parents to protect him. In spite of his ignorance he must take all responsibilities himself. He is a man; and he is confronted by the most serious things that can occur to men—disease, injury, and death. From these things he wants to escape, to protect himself. But his thoughts on the problems of health and disease, life and death, are guided only by the peculiar and natural qualities that are always in the human mind, that we are born with.

Curiosity is one of these qualities; no education is required for its attainment. Conceit or egotism is another. Egotism makes us believe that what we accomplish successfully is due to our own fine qualities, and that what we do poorly is

owing to no fault of our own but to some outside influence. Like the savage, we all wish to take credit for our success and to blame our failures on someone else.

Native peoples confronted by disease blamed their misfortunes on something other than their own ignorance, on something outside themselves. Because they were curious they sought the influences that brought their misfortunes. They found them in spirits.

Men from the very beginning have seen their companions killed or injured by falling trees, gored or trampled by animals, knocked down or murdered by other men. In each case there was a cause for the misfortune. The tree that fell, the animal that turned, the man that struck, were the visible agents of misfortune. But men also saw their companions fall ill, suffer, and die when nothing visible had injured them. Since, so reasoned the savage, the effects were there— the pain and death—there must be an agent. It was invisible but still it must exist—a malicious, vindictive "something."

Invisible forces then could bring misfortune. But where were they? What were they?

Dreams and motion supplied the material for the solution of the problem. In his dreams primitive man saw men he knew were far away or dead. He saw animals that threatened him. He awoke in fear, but the bodies of the men or animals were no longer there.

Men and animals, so reasoned the savage, have then something—let us call it a spirit—which can separate from them and travel long distances, which persists even after death.

He reasoned further: Men and animals have spirits; men and animals are alive; things that are alive move; movement means life. The water in the rivers moves, the clouds in the skies move, the branches of the trees move, the sun and moon and stars seem to move; the wind moves. These things must be alive; being alive they must have spirits.

Like a small child, the savage made no clear distinction

between living and nonliving things. When he stepped on a bent stick and the end flew up and struck him, he turned and kicked the stick to get even with it. When he slipped and fell in a mud puddle, he might throw a rock into the water for vengeance, because it had been unkind to him.

Primitive men think of everything about them as having the qualities of men. The trees can talk, the thunder is the voice of a great spirit, the sun eats up the moon each day, the rocks that men stumble over have deliberately crawled into the path. Such things sound much like fairy tales. And so they are. When the small child of today reads and prattles of whispering brooks and animals that talk, of good fairies and roaring giants, he is living over in play the things that were serious to savage men.

It was not in play that primitive man peopled the world with spirits. Spirits were the invisible agents of misfortune. A spirit could attack a man, hurt him, kill him.

Sometimes a man's own spirit left him for a time. Then the man fell down as if dead, but when his spirit returned, he came to life again. We should say he had fainted or was unconscious.

Occasionally a wandering spirit found its way into a man's body, crawled into it, and overcame the man's true spirit. Such a man might speak with a queer voice and behave in most peculiar ways. His body was possessed by a strange spirit, said the savage; we should say that he was insane.

Again a man thus possessed might throw himself on the ground and writhe and squirm and beat his arms and legs against the earth. Surely, reasoned the savage, no spirit would so abuse the body to which it rightfully belonged. Here, said he, is proof that an alien spirit has entered the body; we should say the man had a fit.

The belief in spirits offered an explanation for every misfortune that could happen to men. And what is more, it satisfied curiosity as to the cause of misfortune and it

pleased conceit. Misfortunes could be blamed on the spirits. It was a very satisfying belief indeed.

You would call these beliefs of the savage superstitions. And so they are if people hold them today. Among primitive peoples they were not superstitions. A superstition is a belief derived logically, but from ideas that are not consistent with generally prevailing knowledge. When a savage, seeing his image in a mirror, believed that it was his spirit looking at him, he was following the ideas thought to be true by all of his people. If he broke a mirror, he believed that bad luck would come to him, for he had injured his spirit. His reasoning was logical. He was not truly superstitious; he was ignorant. When, on the other hand, men learned the principles of optics and knew the image to be merely a reflection of light, then the belief that it was a spirit became a false idea, one no longer consistent with generally prevailing knowledge. To believe that a broken mirror brought bad luck thus became merely a superstition.

Nearly every superstition that exists today is a survival of the beliefs that primitive men developed to account for their misfortunes. You have seen superstitious people do something, such as tapping wood, to prevent the bad luck they expect. This is to drive away the evil spirits and the ghosts and demons that may be lingering about. A childish idea, of course, but a serious matter to ignorant peoples. Ideas like this guided primitive man in his struggle against disease.

For him there were literally thousands of things that he must or must not do to keep away the spirits that brought illness. Of course the details of these acts varied among different tribes, but they existed everywhere. Food must be eaten in a certain way, caves or tents entered in a special manner, spears stacked in a peculiar position, charms carried as lucky pieces, like a rabbit's foot, or like a horse-chestnut to prevent rheumatism, and so on through the range of every conceivable act. Today we sometimes think we are tram-

meled and cramped by the conventions of social etiquette, but we are free compared with primitive man who imposed upon himself prohibitions for every act of life.

When, in spite of constant "wood tapping and salt throwing," so to speak, bad luck came to the savage, as it often did, it was the business of the medicine man to set matters right. He was the one who was nearest to the spirits, who knew where they lived and how to frighten or bribe them away. He had developed many methods of controlling them. Some spirits disliked noises, others feared water, some dashed away when smoke was about, and many disappeared into thin air when certain magic words were spoken.

The medicine man built his treatment into a ceremony. He came to the patient and "made medicine." His efforts were always intended to remove the evil spirits that he imagined caused the illness. He dressed to impress the spirits and carried charms to make them obey him; he danced, he shouted, he shook his rattle, and made a frightful din about the sick man to frighten the demons away. Sometimes he threw water over the invalid or even dipped him in a stream. He filled the tent with smoke. He gave the man vile tasting medicines to make his body unpleasant for the spirits. And finally he mumbled curious words that no one except the medicine man and the spirit could understand, and produced weird and rare things to convince the spirits of his powers— a deformed frog, a snake with legs, or, in modern times, as a result of contact with civilized people, a broken dollar watch, or a collar button.

The antics of the medicine man had no influence upon the nonexistent spirits, but they did make a deep impression on those who watched him. The medicine man did everything possible to increase the awe in which he was held. He lived apart from other men, he behaved differently, he dressed differently. He never missed an opportunity to impress upon people that he was different from other men; he

controlled the spirits. It was this belief held by his companions.that gave him his main influence upon disease.

A medicine man of an African tribe driving away evil spirits.

He did have some effect on the illness of those he treated. In disease there is always an element that is purely mental; often it is the most unpleasant part of illness. The fears and discouragements of the sick man make his sufferings more severe. The medicine man encouraged him, comforted him, removed his fears; he took over responsibility for the disease and so relieved the patient's mind of responsibility. In consequence the sick man might feel better, and suffer less, become more confident of recovery because he believed in the medicine man. But the treatment affected the disease itself very little.

Almost everyone has played "medicine man." You have seen a small child fall down and bump his head. What did you do? First you picked up the child and looked to see how severely he was hurt. Then when you found his injury was slight, did you not use the medicine of the savage—make faces, try to stand on your head perhaps, shout to drown out his wails, and swing your watch in front of him to catch his attention, and make him "forget the pain"? After the tears stopped, perhaps you gave him a piece of candy to keep him from thinking of the hurt. The candy was like the savage's amulet, a charm to keep away disease. This kind of treatment for the child—or for the savage—while it may stop pain and fear and anxiety, does not heal a wound or cure an infection, nor does it prevent disease.

It seems never to have occurred to primitive peoples that wounds might heal of themselves and that a man might recover from disease without any treatment. Many people today do not realize the enormous recuperative ability of the human body. There are many diseases the modern doctor cannot cure, but he does help the sick man recover by aiding in every way the healing powers of the body.

Primitive peoples, however, as they always attributed the cause of disease to some outside force also attributed recovery to it. The medicine man controlled the healing agency.

He received full credit for curing every man who lived through an illness.

Some of his patients died, but such failures were quickly forgotten; only successes were remembered and talked about. People were pitifully eager to believe in the powers of the medicine man. Doubt and uncertainty are unpleasant. Confidence brings hope and peace of mind even when it is misplaced confidence.

Then, too, the medicine man always had ready an explanation for his failures. The most effective one was that some enemy of the sick man, in his tribe or perhaps in another tribe far away, had put a curse upon him, sent a spirit to torment him. The spirit of course could not be driven away until the enemy was found. Often the patient died before the search was finished.

This explanation for his failures brings up an unpleasant side of the medicine man, one on which we have not touched —that of black magic. When the medicine man tried to heal the sick by driving away evil spirits, he was practicing what is called white magic. But he was expected to aid his tribe not only by preventing their misfortunes but also by bringing misfortunes on their enemies. He then called on the spirits to cause disease. Such a practice is black magic.

It is doubtful whether the medicine man's efforts at black magic influenced the members of a tribe at a distance, but they did affect the people about him. They were in constant fear of offending him and so bringing down upon themselves his black magic. So strong was this belief that when the medicine man worked his magic on a member of his own tribe, the man might actually become ill and even die from fear.

In terror of this black magic or witchcraft, primitive peoples often carefully buried the parings of their finger nails, bits of loose hair, a tooth, or anything that had been a part of their bodies; they thought that if a sorcerer found

such things he could use them to work a magic spell and so send an evil spirit to torment them. Some peoples even believed that their names were as much a part of them as their eyes, or teeth, or arms. Consequently they were very cautious about telling their true names, often giving fictitious ones to strangers.

Such beliefs did not stop with primitive or barbarian peoples. They were carried on far into civilization. We shall meet black magic again under the names of sorcery and witchcraft. We shall find men making little wax images of their enemies, sticking pins in them, and melting them in order to cause disease. We shall find judges in courts of law in civilized countries, only a century or two ago, maintaining that men who were mentally ill were possessed by demons. We shall find epidemics of disease attributed to the wrath of the gods; men hanged in the belief that they have caused death by black magic; and poor, harmless old women burned as witches.

And yet amid the welter of false beliefs of early man there were hidden great principles of medicine, the very foundations of modern medicine. We saw in the first chapter how the tribesmen gave us the principle of the doctor— a man who devoted himself to the care of the sick and to the prevention of disease. In the next chapter we shall find that, in spite of their false beliefs, these same tribesmen laid the crude foundations of hygiene, the use of medicaments, of surgery, and even of medical education.

Theories and Facts

CENTURIES before the rise of civilization, primitive peoples developed what may be called a theory of disease. A theory affords an explanation for known facts. The theory concerning spirits served to explain every fact that primitive people knew about disease.

Theories, when correct, are very useful indeed, for they serve as guides in the search for new facts. But when incorrect, they obscure the truth.

In the early nineteenth century, as we shall see, most physicians held the theory that infectious diseases resulted from evil smells and peculiar conditions of the air. Their theory was wrong, and when they attempted to prevent disease by following it, they failed. Later in the century scientists advanced the theory that infection was caused by bacteria. They found that by preventing the spread of bacteria they could prevent the spread of disease, and so the theory was proved to be a fact. But without the theory the fact perhaps would not have been discovered.

Occasionally, even in following out a false theory, important facts may be stumbled upon by accident. Some primitive peoples believed that the sun was born each morning and was eaten up each night at dusk; the ancient Greeks believed that the sun was a glowing chariot driven across the sky by Apollo. Both theories were wrong; but that did not prevent men from discovering that they could tell the passage of time from the position of the sun. False theories do not alter facts.

Likewise even though primitive people followed an incorrect theory of the cause of illness, they nevertheless occasionally stumbled upon important facts about disease. The knowledge that we have gained since their time shows that

the explanation they gave for the facts was wrong, but the facts themselves remain unaltered.

Early man had stomach aches, just as we do, from eating indigestible things such as unripe fruit, but he had no one to tell him that indigestible material irritates and inflames

Humans changed to beasts by black magic.

the interior of the stomach and so causes pain. He did not even know he had a stomach. All that he was aware of was the pain. He explained it by saying that a spirit tormented him. That was his theory.

However, after many stomach aches from eating unripe fruit, the idea gradually dawned upon him that there was some connection between the fruit and the pain. The fruit, so he reasoned, following his theory, was the abode of an evil spirit. Evil spirits were to be shunned, and so he avoided the fruit.

Gradually in the same way he learned many facts concerning what we should call hygiene. He found that certain berries had in them spirits that killed men. He discovered that fish which had rotted in the sun acquired a particularly violent spirit that brought great pain to men: fish were to be eaten fresh and thrown away when stale. He found that when the leaves of certain trees, such as the swamp oak, or of certain vines, such as poison ivy, touched him, a spirit crept under his skin and made it raw and sore. Such plants were to be let alone.

He discovered that there were whole tracts of land, the home of buzzing flies which rose from the bushes to bite men and animals; in such places lived spirits that gave men a sleeping illness. There were marshes where spirits dwelt that caused men to shake in chills and burn with fever. These places were to be avoided.

Step by step from sad experience man gained practical knowledge of hygiene. This knowledge he handed on to his children.

In matters of hygiene, early man was not always either a careful or a critical observer. His fears and his false theories made him too ready to believe that harm lay where there was none. He often made mistakes in picking out the places. where evil spirits were to be found, and so prohibitions grew up about many things and many acts which were not harmful. His life was burdened with the host of things that he must or must not do to prevent misfortune.

Just as efforts to avoid evil spirits led to the first attempts at hygiene, so attempts to drive away the spirits after disease had occurred led to the first use of medicaments. Primi-

tive man in thinking of the spirits always imagined that their likes and dislikes were much the same as his own. He reasoned that bitter herbs, vile tasting messes, since they were unpleasant to man, should make his body unpleasant for the spirits and thus hasten their departure. Following this theory, he concocted medicaments from berries, barks, roots, dirt, the flesh of animals, anything in fact that seemed likely to rout the spirits. The vast majority of these concoctions had no real effect upon disease, but some made the sick man vomit, some were physics, and a very few were real remedies against disease or its symptoms.

Hemp and mistletoe and the juice of the poppy drove away the evil spirits of pain. The bark of the willow and the black birch relieved the aches of rheumatism. The fresh buds of hemlock cured the scurvy. A toad boiled in water, made into a mess like the witch's caldron of Macbeth and given to a man swollen with dropsy, seemed to benefit him. Pure fancy? That is what scientists thought until a few years ago when they discovered that the toad has in its skin a drug called bufonin that may actually be helpful in treating dropsy.

From ancient China came the belief that eating bits of dragons' bones drove away the evil spirit that caused babies to have fits. Foolish as this sounds, dragons' bones were really those of dinosaurs buried in the sands of the Gobi Desert. Today for a certain kind of convulsion that babies may have the doctor prescribes calcium, and the dinosaur bones, like all others, contain calcium!

Would you believe that the ashes from a burnt sponge could help relieve a swelling in the neck? Ashes were used, and they drove away the spirit that caused the swelling— according to the ancient theory. Modern science has shown that a swelling of the neck called a goiter may occur when there is too little iodine in the food and drinking water, as is the case in some parts of our country. Small amounts of

that everyone would do well to remember and apply as a test to his way of thinking.

Through this type of reasoning the medicine man of primitive peoples received credit for curing everyone who got well under his treatment. And because of it many worthless substances were used as medicaments long after belief in spirits as a cause of illness was given up.

When a man became sick, he was given medicine or treated in some way. If he recovered from his illness, it was, so it is always natural to believe, the medicine or the treatment which cured him. It is only in modern times that science has raised the questions: "Might not the man have recovered from his illness if he had taken no medicine, or some other medicine, or used some other treatment? Did the treatment cure him, or did he get well in spite of it?" Questions of this kind led to studies by "statistics" and control experiments. We shall have much more to say of these things when we have gone further in our story and reached the time when the useless medicaments of the savage were finally discarded. The remedies used by the modern physician have been proved to be beneficial by scientific tests. Science with means of experimental proof came late in civilization; it has altered many of our ways of thinking but it has not altered the fact that it was the savage who gave us the great principle of using medicines. Nor was this the only form of treatment we owe to him.

It was he who originated what is called physical treatment, or physiotherapy. Physiotherapy makes use of exercises, massage, baths, the application of heat and cold. It seems a far cry from belief in spirits as the cause of disease to using massage. But the savage originated massage when he tried to pound the spirits out of the flesh. He sometimes placed his patient on the ground and prodded and poked and pounded him in a manner that would make the massage of an athletic trainer seem gentle stroking. Often under this

treatment the evil spirits in stiff joints and sore muscles seemed actually put to flight. The joints became more limber and the soreness left the muscles.

Physical therapy is a useful form of treatment as applied by the modern doctor, but it was harmful as well as useful in the hands of the medicine man. Very definite harm may come from following the wrong theory in treating disease. The savage might use massage for any kind of illness, because he believed that all disease was due to a common cause. Today we know that rough massage may be harmful in certain diseases, especially infections, just as the wrong medicine may be harmful. The modern doctor must choose his treatment carefully to suit the disease.

Physiotherapy and medicaments by no means exhausted the list of treatments that the savage used and that we have adopted. As we have already said, he used suggestion. His magic and ceremony, his beating on the tom-tom and shouting did not impress the spirits, but they did impress the sick man and make him believe that he was getting well and that his pain was disappearing. Suggestion, the influence of the mind on the body, may be beneficial, or useless, or harmful. Primitive man made no distinctions, nor, as we shall see, did the healing priests of early civilization. The modern doctor has adopted the principle of suggestion which the savage originated, but again he must decide carefully when to apply this treatment.

Physiotherapy, medicaments, and psychotherapy (the medical term for mental treatment) were originated in crude form by native peoples, and so also was surgery.

Today surgery is looked upon as a method of repairing injured parts of the body, removing diseased flesh, and correcting abnormalities. The savage no doubt tried some of these things in a rough sort of way when he straightened out broken legs, but his interest even in surgery centered about the spirits. He mutilated the body rather than repaired it. Thus he might cut off the tip of a finger to pro-

vide a means of exit for a troublesome spirit, or bore a hole through the skull so that the spirit which caused headaches might escape. Explorers find in the ancient burial places skulls upon which this operation has been performed not only once but many times.

Present-day surgery is always associated in our minds with antiseptics, substances to destroy bacteria and hence to prevent infection. But antiseptics as we know them did not come into use until late in the nineteenth century. Nevertheless primitive man did have an antiseptic of a kind. It was fire. Fire was itself a spirit, one that could be used to frighten away other spirits. Burning embers or a red-hot stone held for a moment in a wound drove off evil spirits of disease, so the savage thought; and incidentally they did kill the bacteria of infection, of which he knew nothing.

A traveler to Russia some forty years ago relates how he saw fire thus applied by a native boy of the Yakuts. The boy had an infected finger. He and his friends had come to the conclusion that a spirit had established itself in the finger. To drive the spirit out, the boy took a burning coal and began to touch it to the place, while blowing upon it. When the burned flesh blistered and finally burst with a little crackle, the curious group which had crowded around to watch him jumped back with cries of terror, and the wounded boy with a smile of satisfaction said: "You saw how he jumped out."

Among civilized people fire continued in use as an antiseptic until the sixteenth century, not always because of belief in spirits, but because it was thought that some wounds were poisoned, and that fire destroyed the poison. We shall tell later how the great French war surgeon of the sixteenth century, Ambroise Paré, was the first to discourage the torture of wounded men with fire and boiling oil. But fire is used occasionally even today when nothing else is available and an especially strong antiseptic action is needed, as in the case of bites from mad dogs; now we call its use cauterizing.

Still another practice of primitive peoples which, like the use of fire, was carried over into civilization and then largely discarded, was bleeding. If you have read of Dr. Sangrado in the story of *Gil Blas* you know what is meant by that— the actual opening of a vein and letting out blood, with the idea that health is thus improved and disease prevented or cured. The method is now rarely resorted to, but even in the eighteenth century it was one of the commonest practices in medicine. It has been said that George Washington was bled to death by his physician, Dr. Craik, who treated him in his last illness; he was certainly bled, but since he had a severe throat infection, possibly diphtheria, the bleeding alone probably was not responsible for his death.

The practice of bleeding was originated by primitive peoples as a sort of peace offering to the ghosts and spirits. A man gave some of his blood to flatter them into favoring him. It was in miniature a duplication of the practice of human sacrifice to appease the gods, a practice that held so gruesome a place in the religions of savages and even, long ago, in those of civilized men.

Physicians in the time of Washington did not, of course, "bleed" for that reason; by that time the old belief had changed and been replaced by the theory that blood-letting removed impurities from the body—let out what some people still absurdly call "bad blood."

It is a long way from the hygiene, the medicines, the physiotherapy of primitive man to these same things in the hands of the modern doctor. The difference is as great as that between a rude straw hut and a skyscraper. Yet in that hut may be found all the principles of the skyscraper—the principle of the roof, the floor, the walls, the rooms, the windows, the doors, and even the stairs. We have simply elaborated, refined, extended the structure.

Today we have great medical schools where young men are trained to become physicians, and rigorous examinations given by the State before the doctor can treat the sick. Primi-

tive peoples, too, had these things in a crude form. We owe
them, then, still another principle.

In earliest times the medicine man was probably simply
the chosen leader, the strongest and the most intelligent man
of the tribe. Later, as tribal organization grew more complex
and there were both chiefs and medicine men, the choice was
sometimes made for other reasons. A man might be selected

A saint delivering a princess from a demon.

because of something in his appearance—physical disfigure-
ment by a birthmark perhaps, or crossed eyes, or even blindness. Even today some superstitious people talk of the "evil
eye" and fear one-eyed people, for as Dickens says, "Popular prejudice is in favor of two."

The way that one tribe of African natives chose a medicine man is related by an explorer: One of the natives
climbed a tree and chopped off the limb on which he was
seated. He fell to the ground, but although he fell a long

way, he landed on his feet unhurt. Obviously the spirits must have protected him and kept him from harm. He was therefore a friend of spirits and hence a medicine man.

Rarely, however, was the test so easy. These primitive physicians guarded their order jealously. They accumulated a great fund of beliefs and customs and methods which they handed on to young men, and sometimes young women as well, who studied with them as apprentices. And these pupils, before they were finally initiated into the order of medicine men, were forced to show before the assembled tribe the skill they had acquired in handling spirits.

To the accepted medicine man a life of ease and importance was assured. He did not labor in the fields; his food, his shelter were provided for him; he was respected, even venerated. The medicine man had leisure, and fortunately he sometimes used it profitably; he served as the artist and the historian of the tribe. These functions passed on to the priests of civilized people who, not so many centuries ago, were the only men in a whole kingdom able to read and write.

With the many advantages that went with the position of medicine man, one might think that any young man would choose to join such an order—but there was one drawback. The medicine man had to be successful. When disease or famine, flood or drought visited the tribe, he was responsible. Unless fortune favored him or he could explain away his failure, he might find himself in an uncomfortable position. Natives may be gullible, but they may also be violent. The medicine man who failed too often paid for his failures with his head.

What we have attempted in this chapter is to marshal many things both good and bad that find their places again and again in the story of medicine.

Long before the days of recorded history great principles of medicine were shaped by rude medicine men living in caves and jungles; but these men also originated false theo-

ries of disease. The modern doctor has accepted and used many of the beneficial principles, but discarded the false beliefs. These two, the savage medicine man and the modern doctor, lie at the extremes of a hundred, perhaps two hundred, centuries of medical progress. Our story covers the years between, and in these intervening years we shall recognize the old beliefs recurring in changing forms but, knowing their origin, we shall know their meaning.

We shall find belief in the supernatural origin of disease, in evil spirits, in demons, and in sorcery, magic, witchcraft, kept alive in civilization, in Egypt, Greece, Rome, and in Christian Europe.

The primitive medicine man with all his fears and his false reasoning stalks on for centuries in the midst of civilization. Finally the doctors outdistance him, acquiring fresh theories and knowledge, and using new and effective weapons in the age-long struggle of man against disease.

Part Two

IMHOTEP, THE GOD

ÆSCULAPIUS, THE MYTH

HIPPOCRATES, THE NAME

Imhotep, the God

THOUSANDS of years ago man first put his foot to the endless ladder of civilization and began his stumbling progress from the lowest savagery. We today still climb onward, rising from the steps reached by men before us. As we look down from our elevation far above the savage, far above the men of early civilization, we can see the steps they took. The savage climbed one rung when he first used fire, another when he chipped crude weapons and tools from stone. Then, each step a rung higher, the family group gave way to the tribe with a chief, animals were domesticated, crops were raised, rough dwellings built. Centuries went by while men worked out the barest rudiments of government and acquired the simplest elements of culture.

Civilization had its greatest growth when men built towns and cities. Wandering tribesmen had scant time to devote to art, or science; their ways of living remained crude and primitive as they are today among the Bedouins of the desert, or among the Eskimos. When men settled in cities, some of them had leisure to devote to what we call "culture," and in settled communities improvements could be made that were impossible among migrating tribes.

The settlements flourished best where the climate was warm and water abundant, and where there was natural protection against the men of the tribes that still wandered about. The valley watered by the river Nile, and protected by a desert on one side and by a sea on the other, afforded a place particularly suited to the growth of cities. Civilization flourished there at an early period.

In the more peaceful settled life of towns men progressed far beyond the culture of the wandering tribesmen and of

the cave dwellers before them. But this advance consisted less in finding new things than in improving and refining the old. The tribal chief became a king. The cave or rude hut became a house of stone or brick. The pictures daubed on the walls of caverns grew into writing.

Writing—the use of symbols to record the thoughts, the knowledge, and the deeds of men—marks perhaps the greatest of all steps in man's progress. It is the one thing beyond all others that marks him as civilized.

It is also the step that has given us history. History in contrast to legend has its beginning in written records. When knowledge was handed from generation to generation only by the spoken word, the stories told grew and changed in the telling, as happens today with gossip. But with the invention of writing the original facts could be found out as long as the writing was preserved.

In moist climates paper decays unless it is carefully preserved; inscriptions cut in stone or scratched on clay soon weather away. But in the dry climate of sandy Egypt, Assyria, and Babylon, buildings and writing too have been preserved through the centuries. We can decipher many of the inscriptions. We know from them what men of ancient Egypt did and thought and believed from actual records written by their hands.

Egypt is the burial ground of early civilization. Still hidden in the sands, or already uncovered by explorers, is the record of man's rise from the primitive state to one of high culture and art. There are the beginnings of masonry, and also, from much later periods, magnificently designed buildings, with water pipes and even sewers. There are rough attempts at carpentry and metal working buried almost side by side with exquisite furniture, tapestries, and wonderfully designed jewelry. Such seemingly modern devices as candles, razors, steam baths, manicure sets, and lip-sticks were known to ancient Egyptians.

The same dry climate and sandy soil that have preserved

the records of Egypt have also helped preserve some of the men themselves; men who lay buried for centuries with the things they wore and used when they were alive.

The art of preparing mummies grew out of the belief that after death the spirit of a man survived and would live on in another world. It would have need of a body and of food.

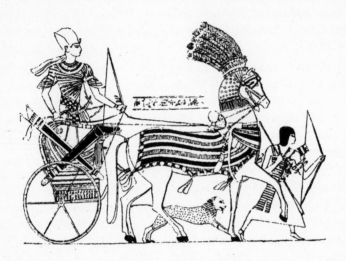

Rameses II and his chariot.

In preparing for the after-life the Egyptian learned by heart the *Book of the Dead*, a guide to the other world. And then at death his body was preserved, made into a mummy, and buried in a tomb with food and clothes and weapons. The earliest mummies were crudely prepared, but as time went on the art was perfected and became an elaborate ritual. First the brain was removed, the organs of the abdomen taken out, the space filled with spices, and the wound sewn up. Then the body was soaked for more than two months in a solution of salt or sodium bicarbonate. Next it was wrapped in bandages smeared with gum and resin and

placed in a coffin shaped to resemble a man. This coffin, together with four jars containing the organs removed from the abdomen, was then put carefully into the tomb.

From study of mummies we know something of the diseases from which the Egyptians suffered. There are signs of broken bones, infections, appendicitis, rheumatism, decayed teeth, and many other diseases that we have today.

One particular mummy holds additional interest for our story. It has not yet been found or identified, but we know that it lies buried in a tomb near Memphis. When it is discovered, we shall see the first physician of whom there is a written record—the physician Imhotep.

How different his story is from that of the Cro-Magnon medicine man whose picture is in the cave at Ariège in France! We know only how the medicine man appeared— nothing of what he actually did. Imhotep lived in the days of writing. We know from the records what he did and what he thought and how he treated his patients.

The records tell us that Imhotep, whose name means "he who comes in peace," lived about 5,000 years ago in the reign of King Zoser, a pharaoh of the Third Dynasty. His father was an architect. When Imhotep reached manhood, such were his abilities and learning that he became Grand Vizier to the Pharaoh. If you wonder what his duties were, these titles which he held may give the answer: "chief judge, overseer of the King's records, bearer of the royal seal, chief of all the works of the King, supervisor of that which Heaven brings, the Earth creates, and the Nile brings, and supervisor of everything in this entire land."

One might gather that, though the pharaoh held the higher position, the vizier did most of the work. Indeed, in the old kingdom of Egypt at least, the vizier seems to have been chosen because he was the wisest man in the land. And of all of the viziers Imhotep was the wisest.

It was probably he who designed the great Step Pyramid which still stands near Memphis, the earliest large stone

structure known to history. Imhotep also helped design the first temple of Edfu, one that preceded the temple standing there today.

It may have been in this ancient temple that Imhotep held

Facsimile of a portion of the Ebers papyrus

office as the high priest and magician, for Imhotep was a physician, and even in the civilization of Egypt, as among the Cro-Magnon people, the magician, the sorcerer, was the physician.

The physician was also the priest. It was his duty to deal

with the gods and spirits that caused disease, for the Egyptians, like primitive peoples, still believed disease to be of supernatural origin. But the spirit world of the Egyptians was more highly organized than that of the savage. Just as the society of men in becoming civilized had become more complex, so the spirit world had become more and more complicated.

The spirits were no longer crude creatures living in trees and rivers, in beasts and stones; they were denizens of another world, of various ranks, like soldiers in an army. And like soldiers, the spirits of lesser rank were led by powerful commanders, gods. Each village had its own patron god or goddess represented in the temple by an idol often wearing the head of some animal.

Just as soldiers change in rank, the gods of Egypt might gain or lose power. A local god might gain in reputation from the tales told by his priests and come to be feared or worshiped in other cities. So it happened in time that Ra, the Sun God, was worshiped throughout the whole of Egypt.

The enemy of Ra was Apop, the God of Darkness, who each morning fought with Ra to prevent the rising of the sun and was always defeated. These family squabbles among the gods were indirectly the cause of many misfortunes to man. The god Osiris quarreled with his brother Seth, the god of Upper Egypt, who in consequence of his defeat became a constant evildoer. He and his friends created evil and spread disease. Their tears, dropped upon the ground, made plants poisonous; and their sweat turned into scorpions and deadly snakes. At every chance these evil demons sought to inflict harm upon men, and could be kept away only by magic which brought protection from the gods friendly to man.

The gods of Egypt, like men, might suffer from disease. Ra occasionally had a disease of the eye, so that there was darkness for a time—an eclipse we should call it. He nearly died when stung in the heel by a scorpion. Horus, the son of

Isis, had headaches, and, like Ra, nearly lost his life from a scorpion's sting.

When a god was stricken with disease he turned for aid to his friends among the gods. That was precisely what men did. They turned to the gods. The sick went to the temples for aid.

The priests knew the mystery of the gods and the magic formulæ to drive away evil spirits. The priests of Egypt were medicine men. Their principles, for all their greater knowledge, were the same as those of the medicine man of primitive peoples. Only, the wild and grotesque behavior of the primitive medicine man had under the restraint of civilization given place to mystery and magic and charms.

The greatest of the priests of ancient Egypt, the man who best controlled the evil spirits of disease and brought the friendly gods to the aid of his fellow men, was Imhotep.

He not only treated the sick, but he wrote in proverbs the things he had learned of men and of life. So deeply were his countrymen impressed by his great learning that his words became a national tradition.

When he died, he was buried with the highest honors; and his reputation lived on. A man so kindly, so wise in life, so successful in healing, would surely continue to aid men in spirit from the other world. So people prayed to Imhotep. They called to him for help in illness. Statues of him were built, and these statues had healing powers. With each century after his death his reputation grew. Men placed him near the gods—he was a demigod. Finally 2500 years ago, when Egypt was conquered by the Persians under Cambyses, Imhotep had become a god—the Egyptian God of Healing and of Medicine. Temples were erected in his honor. These temples where he was worshiped were in a way hospitals; they were schools of medicine and of magic. The sick came to them, and the lame and the maimed, to pray to Imhotep, the beloved god. Upon these people the priests of Imhotep

worked their healing magic and prescribed such remedies as they knew.

The priests wrote on papyrus descriptions of the diseases they saw and the treatment they gave. One of these papyri, discovered by the archæologist Edwin Smith, is fifteen feet in length and describes forty-eight injuries, wounds, and broken bones, together with the treatment given and the magic formulæ used. These temple papyri were the first written records of medicine—the first medical books.

CHAPTER V

Æsculapius, the Myth

IN time civilizations grow old just as men do. As we
grow older our interest turns back to the past, to scenes
of earlier and more vigorous days. The old man talks of
his childhood; the old civilization adheres to its earlier customs and makes them into formal traditions. In each case
progress ceases.

Three thousand years ago the civilization of Egypt had
reached its peak and was declining, dying. Stiff with age,
its art, its architecture, its literature, had become formal,
unchanging. But this country of tombs and mummies became with the passage of centuries a vast storehouse of wisdom from which other and younger civilizations, more progressive, were to learn something of the mysteries of life
and death, of health and disease.

Such a civilization was rising to the north and west. There
a poet, a story-teller, blinded, so legend says, to keep him
from leaving the tribe he entertained, was singing of a new
civilization. Homer, as he was called, told tales of warlike,
sturdy barbarians, who in their wanderings had come upon
an ancient civilization on the shores of the Mediterranean
Sea and had conquered its cities. The barbarians had taken
over the civilization of their predecessors. They had settled
in towns. Homer's tale was only an incident in the age-long
conflict between the settler and the nomad.

New cities—Athens, Sparta, Thebes, and Corinth—grew
up where old ones had been. Although the people spoke a
common language, their cities were not united, but each was
ruled as a little state.

These men, the Hellenes, or as we should call them, the
Greeks, were a free and independent people who knew no
binding traditions. They were acquisitive, not only of lands

and riches, but of knowledge and beliefs as well. Their civilization was young.

They believed in gods and had gods of their own, but unlike the Egyptians they obeyed no rigid rule of the temple.

The Greeks were willing to respect the gods of all people, but they gave to no god a profound reverence. They were free-minded and open-minded. When at length their sailors and merchants came to Egypt, they saw in Imhotep not a rival deity but their own god under a different name. They called him Imuthes and linked his name with their own God of Healing, Æsculapius.

The Greeks, like their nomadic ancestors and like the Egyptians, believed in the supernatural origin of disease. They turned to their gods for aid in misfortune, for the cure and prevention of disease. Gods were supreme, powerful beings with enormous magic powers, but with all the bad habits and weaknesses of men. They could walk on earth, mingle with men, and enjoy men's pleasures. They were likable gods to whom one could speak as man to man.

In early times all the cities and villages had their own favorite gods and goddesses, but they respected each other's deities just as they did Imhotep. Gradually some of the gods grew in reputation and rose to supremacy. The legends that were built about them have come down to us—the legends of Zeus, and Apollo, and Artemis, and all the rest of the great galaxy that mirrored the adventurous and nature-loving spirit of the Greeks.

Apollo, the averter of ills, was chief god of healing. His arrows visited plagues and pestilence upon men, but he could, if he desired, recall them and free men from disease. He was physician, so Homer tells us, to the gods on Mount Olympus, and treated their wounds with the root of the peony. Some men believe that the name "Sons of Pæan," which is sometimes applied to physicians, comes from that story.

Apollo, so legend records, communicated all his knowl-

edge of healing to the son of Cronus, the centaur Chiron,
half horse, half man. Chiron, who was versed in history and
music as well as medicine, was intrusted with the education
of the heroes Jason, Hercules, Achilles, and, particularly,
Æsculapius, who was destined in time to become the great
healing god of Greece, greater even than Apollo.

Egyptian god modeling a man.

Everyone knows, of course, the legends of some of these
fabled heroes: Jason, who went in search of the Golden
Fleece; Hercules, the mighty son of Zeus, who accomplished
the twelve great tasks; and Achilles who could be wounded
only in the heel. But the story of Æsculapius is less well
known, and so here is one of the many versions of his life,
the myth found in the works of the Greek poet Hesiod, who
lived twenty-seven hundred years ago.

According to the story, Apollo was the father of Æsculapius; his mother was Coronis, a maiden from Thessaly.
Coronis was secretly married to the god, and being unable

to divulge the secret, was finally forced by her father into a wedding with her cousin Ischus.

Apollo heard of the marriage from his spy the raven. In anger the god first took vengeance upon the bearer of evil tidings. The raven, which had been white, he turned black, and ever since black has been the sign of mourning. Next he turned to the luckless but innocent husband, Ischus, and slew him with one of his far-reaching arrows. The unhappy Coronis was killed by Apollo's twin sister Artemis.

Then Apollo, his anger exhausted, was stricken with remorse and snatched his infant son from the funeral pyre of his mother and took him to Chiron, the centaur, on Mount Pelion.

From Chiron, the child Æsculapius learned the healing art. As he grew up, he did great deeds in medicine. But filled with pride—though some say for the love of gold—he ventured too far with his powers. From Athena he obtained the blood of the fabled Gorgon. He could do great magic with it, could cure all disease, even give life to the dead. It was this last, the raising of the dead, that brought him into trouble. Some legends say he accepted bribes, and others that Pluto, the God of the Underworld, complained to Zeus that Æsculapius by his magic threatened to depopulate Hades by bringing all its residents back to earth. Either in anger at his greed and as warning to all physicians to respect their art, or else to maintain the balance of population, Zeus punished Æsculapius. The poem says that great Zeus:

Was filled with wrath, and from Olympus top
With flaming thunderbolt cast down and slew
Latona's well-loved son—such was his ire.

Apollo, who, it would seem, had a very touchy temper, in grief for his son turned and slew those who had forged for Zeus the thunderbolt that had killed Æsculapius. And then he begged Zeus to place Æsculapius among the stars and so make him a god.

Æsculapius, while living on earth, legend says, was married and had a family. In most of the stories his wife was Epione, daughter of Merops, King of Cos. The best known of his children are two sons, Machaon and Podalirius, and two daughters, Hygieia and Panacea.

The names of the sons have not become a part of our lan-

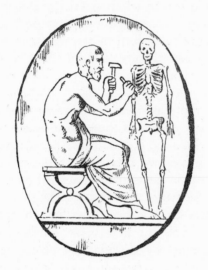

Prometheus carving out man's skeleton.

guage, but those of the daughters have. Hygieia was the Greek goddess of health, and from her name have come all words such as hygiene, hygienic, and hygienist. Panacea was the goddess of the healing powers found in herbs. Your dictionary will tell you that a panacea is a remedy that cures all diseases, a thing which your physician will tell you is quite as mythical as Panacea herself.

In the poems of Homer, Æsculapius is called a Thessalian prince; his sons Machaon and Podalirius are mentioned as commanders of sailing vessels and as good physicians practicing their art. In the fourth book of the Iliad, Machaon is

summoned to remove an arrow driven through the belt of the King of Sparta:

"When he perceived the wound, where the bitter shaft had fallen, having sucked out the blood, he skillfully sprinkled on it soothing remedies, which benevolent Chiron had formerly given his father."

As would be expected, wounds from weapons were of great interest to the warlike Greeks; the Iliad gives a detailed account of 147 such wounds. It does not speak well for the skill of the surgeons of those days that 114 of these wounds were fatal in spite of the sucking out of the blood and the application of soothing herbs recommended by the great Chiron. Indeed to us sucking a wound sounds like not only a rather unpleasant task but a most unsanitary form of treatment as well. Men of these times knew nothing of the cause of infection, and we shall find this practice of wound-sucking still in use two thousand years after the Iliad was written. It will be mentioned again in our story when we come to the adventures that Robert, the son of William the Conqueror, was supposed to have had at the Hospital at Salerno in the twelfth century after Christ.

The descendants of Æsculapius, or at least those who claimed such descent, controlled the healing art in Greece. Some of them, following the example of Machaon and Podalirius, devoted themselves mainly to surgery as private physicians; others became healing priests in the temples erected to the memory of their godlike ancestor.

Among the early Greeks, wounds were looked upon as being quite different from any other bodily ill. There was nothing mysterious about wounds, everyone could see the cause and effect, and there was no need to attribute them to gods and spirits, so they were treated in a practical if unsanitary manner. But all other illnesses were still held to be a matter of the malign influence of gods, and spirits and demons, and heroes. It was in the interests of the sick, rather than the injured, that the temples of Æsculapius were built.

These temples were sanatoria for the care of sick people. They were often beautiful stone buildings with shady colonnades and olive groves and great courtyards with fountains. The ruins of some of them exist today. The treatment given in them was in principle the same as that used in the Egyptian temple of Imhotep and in the caves of Cro-Magnon men. The priests of Æsculapius were "medicine men." They did not shout and dance like the savage, they did not use the weird magic of the Egyptians, but their results were obtained in the same way—by suggestion.

In each temple was a statue of Æsculapius holding in his hand a staff about which a snake was coiled—the staff and snake are still the emblem of the physician today. With the statue of the god there was often one of Hygieia.

From far and wide the sick came to the temple, but they must not be too ill, for it would be disrespectful to the god to die in his temple. Nor were they treated at once, but instead waited their turn for treatment, living in the meantime in inns outside the temple.

This delay, although they did not know it, was part of the treatment. While waiting, the sick man was made to observe certain rules for purifying himself before he saw the god. He must drink no wine, must rest and diet, and bathe in cold salt water. These practices often of themselves started an improvement in his health, although he probably did not notice it, for his attention was fixed upon something else, something that aroused his keenest interest and made him certain that he would recover.

Each day the waiting crowd assembled to see written on a tablet the list of the cures the god had performed that day. They read of men who had been lame or paralyzed for years and could now walk, of the blind who through the benevolence of the god could see; they heard of men whose pains and aches had left them at the touch of Æsculapius or even his dog.

What these poor people, eagerly anxious to believe, did

not know was that the men who walked and saw and whose pains were soothed were those who suffered from mental disturbances, diseases caused by what some people call "upset nerves" or hysteria. In addition to the fortunate few whose illnesses yielded to suggestion, there were other men and women and even children whose diseases were of the flesh; though they were made to feel better, encouraged, their diseases went on unarrested. But the crowd did not hear of such failures, did not want to know of them.

Perhaps unconsciously the priest of Æsculapius, like the medicine man of primitive peoples, was a good "showman." While people waited for treatment about the temple, he aroused in them the certain conviction that they would be cured. When at last they were led in groups into the sacred grounds each man felt himself nearly well. But the show went on. Led by a priest, the sick man was shown through the temple and told the stories of marvelous cures. The tablets and the mystic symbols that covered the walls were explained to him. An air of sanctity, of deep religious dignity, pervaded the whole temple. The patient was awed and he was certain, without a doubt, that he would recover from his sickness. Already his step felt lighter, his pains were soothed; and the mysterious events of the night to come would complete his cure.

At dusk the patient, dressed in white, lay down on a couch. Prayers were offered to the gods. The lamps were extinguished. Everyone was silent. Sleep came to the sick man as the priests had told him it would, and with sleep, just as they had promised, came dreams of Æsculapius and Hygieia, who stood before him, ministering to him. In the dim light of morning he awoke, and there beside his bed he saw a priest dressed in the costume of the god. With the priest were a snake and a dog. The snake crawled across the bed, the dog licked his hand, and the priest asked him questions about his illness, gave advice, prescribed medicaments, and

assured him that he would become well. The priest, the dog, the snake, passed to the next couch. A cure was completed.

Arising, with his pain gone, his lameness cured, the man rejoiced in the goodness of the god. He was convinced of his cure and in his enthusiasm he had the priests write his

Æsculapius.

story on the tablets while the eager crowd watched. He gave a testimonial. And often he also gave a votive offering to the temple—a little statue of metal or of clay showing where pain had been or in what part his body had been diseased. When he returned home he told his friends of the glory of Æsculapius. And they, too, in time of need, came to the temple.

The cult of Æsculapius spread in Greece. His temples throve. There were not enough descendants of Æsculapius to provide all the priests needed for the temple and all the physicians needed to treat the wounded in private practice. Young men were adopted into the families of the descendants and trained as healing priests and physicians. But the Æsculapian families were jealous of their reputation and fearful that someone thus adopted would bring discredit upon their good name as healers. There had been a warning, you remember—Zeus slew Æsculapius himself because he had become greedy and presumptuous.

When a young man was adopted and took up healing he had to swear to lead a life becoming to the family of Æsculapius. This oath in many different versions has come down through the centuries. In some medical schools of our country today the students on graduation take this same ancient oath. There could be none better for a young man who takes over the grave responsibilities that the practice of medicine brings, for this oath defines what are called "medical ethics." Ethics are concerned with moral duties or moral principles, and the ancient Greek medical oath, which is usually called the oath of Hippocrates, is the code of moral duties for the physician. It tells how he shall conduct his life and perform his duties so as to deserve the trust and confidence of all men and the respect of his fellow physicians.

A physician is trusted with the secrets of the people he treats, and these he must never tell. He is trusted with poisons, and these he must never use except to cure. Any beneficial treatment that he discovers he must make public for the aid of all sick people; he must not keep it secret in order to obtain money for it, like the inventor of a mechanical device who may patent his discovery and sell it. All these things and many more are dealt with in the code of medical ethics—established by the early Greek physicians and followed by the physicians of today. Here is a portion of the ancient oath, and you will see not only that it is a moral

code but also that the medical art in those days was a "family affair."

"I swear by Apollo the physician, and Æsculapius, Hygieia, and Panacea, and all the gods and goddesses that, according to my ability and judgment, I will keep this Oath and this stipulation—to reckon him who taught me this Art equally dear to me as my parents, to share my substance with him, and relieve his necessities if required; to look upon his offspring in the same footing as my own brothers, and to teach them this Art, if they shall wish to learn it, without fee or stipulation; and that by precept, lecture, and every other mode of instruction, I will impart a knowledge of the Art to my own sons . . . and to disciples bound by . . . oath according to the law of medicine, but to none others. I will follow that system of treatment which, according to my ability and judgment, I consider best for the benefit of my patients, and abstain from whatever is harmful and mischievous. I will give no deadly poisons to anyone if asked, nor suggest any such counsel. . . . With purity and with holiness I shall pass my life and practice my Art. . . . Whatever . . . I see or hear, in the life of men, which ought not to be spoken of abroad, I will not divulge, as reckoning that all such should be kept secret. While I continue to keep this Oath unviolated, may it be granted to me to enjoy life and the practice of the art, respected by all men, in all times! But should I trespass and violate this Oath, may the reverse be my lot!"

Since the days when the Greeks defined the conduct of the doctor, the ways of treating disease have changed; indeed, as we shall see in the next chapter, the whole principle of medicine was to change at the hands of the Greeks themselves—but the oath, the ethics, remain unaltered. It was the Greeks who gave the physician his most priceless possession: not worship, not veneration as the priest of a healing god; but honor. They saw the physician as an honorable man, as did also the ancient Hebrews. These words strongly

expressing the sentiment of the ancient oath were written in the Bible:

> *Honor the physician according to thy need of*
> *him with the honors due unto him . . .*

> *The skill of the physician shall lift up his head:*
> *And in the sight of great men he shall be admired.*

CHAPTER VI

Hippocrates, the Name

IN the fifth century before Christ, among the Greeks, there occurred the most important event in the history of medicine—perhaps in all history. It marked a change in the tide of battle against disease; from then on man, and not disease, was to be the victor.

This great discovery was not itself a cure or a means of preventing disease; it was merely a new way of studying disease. It was a belief, a philosophy. It told where the enemy was to be found and fought.

For a hundred centuries and more men had struggled against disease, but always with their attention fixed on spirits, ghosts, and demons; they had fought with shadows. Never once had they seen or touched the enemy in reality. In these years disease had flourished almost uncontrolled.

But now in the fifth century B.C. men at last turned from the supernatural in their search for the cause of disease, and sought it where it really is—in nature, in the workings of the body, in the earthly surroundings of man.

This turn in the battle against disease marks the beginning of modern medicine.

In the days when this great event occurred Athens was the supreme city of the Greek states; yet it was not there that the change had its beginning, but in Asia Minor, in the Greek colony called Ionia. And what a seemingly insignificant event it was! A man named Thales, who had been in Egypt studying with the priests, had returned to his home in the town of Miletus. The Athenians who gathered in crowds about the temple of Æsculapius would have laughed in derision if they had been told that Thales was shaping a force that was to destroy belief in the gods of healing and in the demons and spirits as causes of disease. And Thales

himself did not realize it. What he was doing was predicting that in the year 585 there would be a day of darkness, an eclipse.

Men were always foretelling things, predicting events by looking at the livers of slaughtered animals and by listening to the mysterious mutterings of oracles. But Thales said he could foresee a day of darkness by studying the position of the stars and sun and moon. There was no telling what sort of queer ideas might grow in the mind of a philosopher; such men were to be laughed at unless too many foolish fellows, deceived by words, began to believe their theories. It was time then to punish them for disrespect to the gods, who, as every reasonable man knew, were responsible for all the things that happened in the world and in the sky as well.

But the eclipse occurred. Surely some god must have whispered to Thales that the darkness was to come. Yet there he was, the foolish one, trying to tell men he had figured it out by himself.

Equally absurd was his idea that water was the primary element from which everything, even man, was derived. Surely the Ionians—so the good Athenians must have thought—were stupid to listen to such words. Everyone knew that Prometheus, the Titan, had created the first man out of clay, had breathed the spirit of life into him, and for his use had stolen fire from the heavens.

But other men in Ionia caught the fever of speculation; they were forming new philosophies of life in a most sacrilegious manner. They were beginning to doubt that the gods were responsible for what went on in the world; they were talking of things called nature and numbers. Empedocles of Akragas was saying that everything in the world was composed of four things: earth, air, fire, and water.

Pythagoras of Samos was trying to solve the riddle of life with mathematics. Ten was the perfect number; it included everything in the whole universe. Three and four

were also important numbers, especially four. There were four elements in the universe; earth, air, fire, and water. There were four conditions, or states, which all things might possess: heat, moisture, dryness, and coldness. There were four fluid substances in the body called humors: blood, phlegm, yellow bile, and black bile.

Here, most sacrilegious of all, the philosopher had pushed the gods and spirits and demons aside and said that disease was due to natural causes. When the four humors were in proper proportions, a man was healthy. But when the humors were out of balance, when there was too much or too little blood or bile, or phlegm, or when their condition was too wet, or cold, or dry, or hot, he was diseased. The way to treat disease was not to ask aid of the gods or to drive away the spirits, but to try to restore the humors to their proper balance.

Of course, you and I today, like most Athenians of the fifth century B.C., but for very different reasons, would say that such theories were silly. Yet these beliefs were destined to be the great guiding theories of medicine for centuries after the time of the Ionian philosophers. We shall meet the theory of humors and the theory of numbers again and again in our story. The important thing is not the theory but the fact that in the new ideas concerning disease the gods and spirits and demons were nowhere mentioned. Men for the first time in all the ages had stopped looking for the cause of disease in the air and the heavens and were searching for it in the flesh of man. They were hunting for a reasonable, a natural, explanation of disease. Their explanations, we know now, were wrong, but the direction in which they sought was the right one.

The new philosophies that were taking shape in Ionia, although perhaps men did not recognize the fact, were destined to place a great responsibility on human beings. When spirits and gods and demons were believed to be the cause of disease, man took no responsibility for his misfortunes.

He was merely the plaything of a host of creatures that might injure or help him. Disease was no fault of his, it was just bad luck.

But if what these philosophers were saying was true, then

Hippocrates as shown in the surgical works
of Ambroise Paré.

man was responsible for disease. If illness was caused by natural forces, then it was man's responsibility to discover these forces, learn the laws of nature, and find out how to control them.

As we have pointed out in Chapter II, where we talked

about egotism, most men are anxious to blame their misfortunes on something other than their own ignorance. That is, they are eager to avoid taking responsibility for their own faults. It was a hard road that the philosophers were pointing out for men to follow. It meant putting aside the childish, dreamlike myths like those of Apollo and his chariot, Æsculapius and his snake, Zeus and his thunderbolts, and all the host of gods and demons and spirits which had saved men from taking responsibility.

In the centuries that follow, as we shall see, men often strayed from this narrow road and shifted the responsibility back to the gods. But in the fifth century before Christ there were courageous men, keen and curious.

The new idea of a rational philosophy spread. It reached Athens at a fortunate time when the Greek cities were more closely united than they had ever been before. They had been driven by necessity to join forces against a common enemy, the Persians, who were led first by Darius and later by Xerxes. In the battle of Salamis in 480 and of Platæa and Mycale the following year, the Greeks had been victorious. Then followed a half century—very different from the past—in which the Greek cities were at peace among themselves.

In this period of prosperity Athens was governed by a wise statesman, Pericles. Men had leisure to think and study.

It was then that a philosopher named Anaxagoras came to Athens from Ionia. He attempted to explain to men the nature of eclipses, and of the rainbow, and of the stars and meteors. He told them that the earth was round. Quite naturally his teachings brought him into conflict with the religious beliefs of the Athenians. He could talk of any god he wished, believe in any one he cared to, but he must be respectful to all gods and not deny their deeds. He was arrested and tried. Pericles himself defended him. Anax-

agoras was forced to leave Athens, but his ideas remained behind.

In and about the city of Athens there soon formed the greatest group of thinkers that has ever existed. You know the names of some of them—Socrates, Plato, Aristotle. These men and many others sought behind the myths for truth.

Some of the philosophers were physicians, and they treated disease according to the explanations for its cause which they had developed from their speculations. They tried to correct the balance of the humors, or to work with numbers, or to apply the theory of heat and cold and wetness and dryness. They failed in their efforts. Their patients were not cured.

The philosophers could theorize about the movements of the planets, the origin of man, and the nature of matter, but their speculations, right or wrong, had no effect upon these things. The sun rose and set as regularly and shone as warmly, whether it was thought of as a chariot driven by Apollo or a burning mass around which the earth revolved. But disease was different. Merely to tell a man that he was ill because the humors were unbalanced, or that he had too much black bile, or that his blood was too warm, stopped no pain. Speculation alone cures no diseases. Men wanted their pains relieved, their children cured of illness.

Theories, as we have said before, are useful, indeed necessary, guides in finding or arranging facts, but the facts and not the theories are the important thing. When men only speculate, they often become so interested in their theories that they forget realities.

It is to the speculation of philosophers that we are indebted for the separation of disease from the supernatural, and medicine from religion. But after speculation had pointed the way to look for the cause of disease, it ceased to be useful. What was needed was fact. The facts of nature had to be found out and recorded. When, and only when,

the facts had been accumulated, could sound theories and explanations result.

It was a physician and philosopher named Hippocrates of Cos who rescued medicine from speculation and began the collection of facts about disease. Today we call him the father of medicine.

Hippocrates did what no physician had ever done before. He examined sick men carefully and recorded honestly the signs and symptoms of disease, without theorizing. He was not looking for spirits; he was not trying to show that the humors were out of balance; he was attempting to find out exactly how the sick man differed from the well man and how one sick man differed from another.

The chief importance of the work of Hippocrates lies in the fact that he observed and recorded the symptoms of disease. He began the accumulation of the facts concerning disease upon which the knowledge of modern medicine rests.

When the physician of today is called to visit a sick man, he follows the same general method that Hippocrates followed 2300 years ago. You have seen a doctor at the bedside of a patient—probably your own bedside. The first thing that he does is ask questions—how you feel, how old you are, what illnesses you have had before, what diseases you have been exposed to recently.

Next he examines you—looks in your throat, your eyes and ears, feels about your body for sore places, taps your chest, and listens to your heart.

The modern doctor is seeking, with the symptoms as clues, to find out from what disease the patient is suffering. He is making what is called a diagnosis. From his knowledge of the various diseases he is then able to prescribe the proper treatment.

Diagnosis is one of the important steps in dealing with disease, for without diagnosis there can be no sound basis for treatment. But diagnosis also depends on the knowledge that there are separate and distinct diseases which may affect

man. Physicians did not know this in the days of Hippocrates; it was not discovered until more than two thousand years after his time. But it was learned then by the method that Hippocrates originated—careful study of sick men, the recording of symptoms, and the accumulation of knowledge from actual observation.

Hippocrates believed, as indeed all men did until the seventeenth century A.D., that no matter what form the symptoms took, disease arose from some common disturbance in the body. Nevertheless he recognized that when a certain combination of symptoms appeared the illness seemed to follow one course and when another combination appeared it seemed to follow a different course. He wrote down the symptoms and the course of the illness in the cases he studied. Such records of how men appear and behave when affected by disease are called clinical histories. When he had collected many of these records, Hippocrates could draw general conclusions. He could say that when certain symptoms appeared the disease would follow a certain course.

He wrote down what he learned in the form of aphorisms or proverbs, such as these:

When sleep puts an end to delirium, it is a good sign.
Consumption comes on mostly from 18 to 35 years of age.
Apoplexy is commonest between the ages of 40 and 60.
Old persons bear fasting most easily, next adults, and young people yet less; least of all children, and of these least again those who are particularly lively.
Weariness without cause indicates disease.

Hippocrates was not able to make a diagnosis as the modern doctor would, but he was able to give a prognosis, a feature of medicine in which the Greeks were especially interested. Prognosis means a foretelling. It is the answer to the

questions that the sick man always asks: "What is going to happen to me? How long am I going to be in bed?"

And Hippocrates carried medicine beyond mere prognosis; he laid the basis for sound treatment. His clinical records showed him the benefit or lack of benefit derived from the various treatments given, and he was able to select from among them those treatments that were most beneficial.

But it is not because of the prognoses he made or the treatments he gave that we call Hippocrates the father of medicine. It is because of his method of studying disease, of describing and recording. He was the first to use the principle of science in medicine.

All the knowledge that physicians have gained of disease since the time of Hippocrates has been acquired by following the principle he laid down—careful observation. Hippocrates clearly expressed the difference between speculation and guesses on the one hand and on the other knowledge gained from observation of facts. He said: "To know is one thing; merely to believe one knows is another. To know is science, but merely to believe one knows is ignorance."

Now much has been said here of what Hippocrates did for medicine; more will be told as we go on with our story. But we have said nothing of Hippocrates himself. All that we actually know of him as a man can be told in a few short sentences. He was born on the island of Cos about 460 B.C. He was a member of the Guild of Æsculapidiæ, those men who claimed descent from Æsculapius or who were adopted into such families. He is said to have died about 360 B.C.

If so little is actually known of Hippocrates, how does it happen that we credit so much to him? The records of his own time make little mention of him: Plato and Aristotle name him merely as a prominent physician, no more. But in the centuries following his death Greek physicians, and later those of Rome, said he was the author of the writings in which appeared the principles we have discussed.

The manuscripts were written in his time and they were

written in the region where he lived and taught. But we have no way of knowing whether or not he was the sole author of them; certainly it would seem that he did not write all the books credited to him. And really it makes little difference.

Hippocrates exists as a name rather than as a man. Under that name we group all the great and now forgotten men of Greece who in the fifth century B.C. founded the scientific basis of medicine.

Hippocrates lived and died, but his name alone among perhaps many who lived and worked with him has come down through the years to symbolize the ideal physician. Each stage of medicine in each civilization has had its ideals and its god who personified these qualities. Imhotep with his magic expressed the ideal of Egyptian medicine; he became the god of healing. Æsculapius with his divine powers was the model for the healing priests of ancient Greece; he became the god of medicine. Hippocrates with his honesty, his insistence upon clear reasoning and upon observation of facts rather than speculation, expresses the ideal of our medicine; he is the demigod of modern medicine.

Part Three

THE PATH OF MEDICINE

THE BEARERS OF KNOWLEDGE

THE WAY DIVIDES—EAST AND WEST

The Path of Medicine

IN 430 B.C. an epidemic of some grave infectious disease broke out in Athens and lasted five years. Pericles, his power broken by political intrigue, saw first his sister and then his two sons contract the disease and die. Then in the year 429, he too fell victim to the epidemic.

In spite of changing local politics, in spite of epidemics, in spite of the loss of a powerful ruler, the medical advance started at Athens went on.

Ahead of the country itself lay tragedy. It was doomed to political extinction before a rising civilization to the west —Rome.

Except for chance, the example set in medicine by Hippocrates might have perished and all records of his work been lost in the ruins of war and conquest. No doubt many discoveries that would be of vast importance to us have been made in the past and have disappeared. But the principles laid down by Hippocrates were destined to be spread to the farthest corners of the ancient world and were finally to be carried in the stream of civilization down to our own time. They guide the medicine of today.

In the turmoil of changing politics, of war and conquest, through shifting scenes, we can trace the path that Greek medicine followed.

Almost in the year that Pericles died, two boys, who were called Plato and Xenophon, were born in Athens. Their destinies led them to widely different careers. Plato became a great philosopher and teacher in Athens. Xenophon as a young man joined with other Greeks in a war that Cyrus was waging against his brother, Artaxerxes II, ruler of Persia. The army of Cyrus was defeated in the year 401, and

the Greeks returned home under the command of Xenophon. He describes this expedition and the famous retreat of the "10,000" in his book, the *Anabasis*. Back in Greece the disbanded soldiers told their townsmen that Persia was a rich country for plunder and ill-prepared for war against a strong invading force.

Presently in the little country of Macedonia, north of Athens and beyond Thessaly where, according to legend, Æsculapius was born, two other young men embarked on careers as widely different as those of Plato and Xenophon. One was Philip, the son of the King of Macedonia; the other, Aristotle, the son of the king's physician. Aristotle went to Athens and there studied with Plato. Philip became King of Macedonia.

Each of these men made amazing progress in his chosen field. Philip spread the boundaries of his country wider and wider by conquest and finally united all the Greeks in a great war against Persia. Aristotle conceived the idea of studying nature in the way that Hippocrates studied disease —not by speculating about it, but by observing and describing it, and arranging his information in orderly fashion. He became the first natural historian. The tremendous task that he began of taking stock of the whole world goes on today; after all these years the study is still far from completed, although it has given us the vast fund of knowledge that we now have.

Philip was the greatest warrior of his day; Aristotle the greatest scientist. The careers of the two were united by a third young man, Philip's son Alexander. Philip asked Aristotle to return to Macedonia to tutor Alexander, and Aristotle taught his young pupil science and philosophy and developed in him a love of natural history. Philip proposed to the Athenians and the inhabitants of the other Greek towns that they join in a war against Persia. Some of the townsmen, remembering the stories told by the soldiers of Xenophon, were willing to go with him, but the Athenians

refused. Demosthenes, the orator, denounced Philip and his plans in his famous speeches, the Philippics. But the matter was not to be settled with words; the armies of the Macedonians and the Athenians met in battle, and Philip won. The conquest of Persia was to start under his leadership.

In the year 336 B.C., as the army of the united Greeks began its march, Philip was assassinated. Alexander, the pupil of Aristotle, became king, and the conquest went on under his command. Alexander did not forget the teachings of his famous schoolmaster. With the army went scientists to collect information from every country for Aristotle's great books of natural history.

Thirteen years later Alexander the Great had completed the conquest of Persia and the whole of the ancient world as far east as India. Then at the age of thirty-two he died of fever in the city of Babylon. After his death the empire he founded fell to pieces, but in each land he had left Greek rulers, Greek settlers, and Greek scholars.

Greek knowledge was thus scattered over the civilized world. But in one place particularly it took root and flourished. That was in Alexandria, in Egypt, near the delta of the Nile. Alexander had founded the city and left one of his companions, a man named Ptolemy, to govern it. The succeeding Ptolemies became the Greek rulers of Egypt; the famous Cleopatra, who was defeated by the Romans, was the last of them.

Under the guidance of the earlier Ptolemies a great museum and a library were erected at Alexandria, and a vast number of manuscripts of Greek scholars were collected. The museum was really the first university in the world. With its founding Athens ceased to be the center of learning. Students went instead to Alexandria. Euclid worked there upon his geometry; and it was there that Eratosthenes measured the size of the earth and came within a few hundred miles of being correct in his figures. It was at Alexan-

dria also that Archimedes studied his problems in engineering, and Heron built the first steam engine.

Not only literature, mathematics, and engineering flourished at Alexandria, but also medicine. In the third and second centuries before the Christian Era the leading doctors of all countries gathered there. They developed something new in medicine, and made the greatest advance since the days of Hippocrates—although it was to be forgotten. It was the study of human anatomy through dissection of the human body.

Such a thing would not seem unusual to us today, for we realize that a doctor cannot carry out his work unless he knows the structure of the body and all its organs. But in ancient times, and in fact until only about a century ago, there was intense opposition to dissection; one of the most lurid chapters in the history of medicine concerns, as we shall see, the "anatomy murderers," the anatomy riots, and grave robbers in the early years of the nineteenth century, before the present anatomy laws were passed.

In ancient times the Egyptians had held the body far too sacred, as you could guess from the care they took in embalming it, to allow dissection. The religious beliefs of the Greeks likewise forbade it. Hippocrates knew very little about the actual structure of the human body and though Aristotle, perhaps, knew more, he had never seen a human dissection. Both these men had studied only animals, and they drew their conclusions concerning human beings from what they found in animals.

But in Alexandria in the third and second centuries B.C., people from every part of the world met, beliefs were mingled, old religions were discarded, and new ones grew up. Traditions were changing, and for a short time dissections of the human body were performed without opposition.

One doctor at Alexandria, Herophilus, wrote a textbook of anatomy, telling what he found in the body and comparing human structures with those of animals. Although we

call it a book, it was really a hand-written manuscript, a roll of papyrus. There were, of course, in those days before printing, few copies of any work, because of the great labor involved in writing out each one by hand. The anatomy book of Herophilus was known to the men who lived in his time, but only fragments of it have come down to us.

It was Herophilus who discovered the nerves in the body; Aristotle had erroneously thought that nerves and tendons were the same, just as he had thought that arteries held air instead of blood. The word "artery" means a passage for air.

Knowledge of anatomy is the first step toward the discovery of the cause of disease. That step was made, but forgotten; and progress stopped for nearly 1800 years. Ancient medicine had reached its peak and was about to start on a period of decline.

The medicine of the Greeks, as we have seen, was spread widely by the conquests of Alexander. In the various countries changes were made in it. At Alexandria it was improved; in other cities queer local beliefs concerning the influence of stars, of colors, and of numbers on disease were added to it. Some of these notions were eventually to find their way into the medicine of Europe in astrology and other superstitions, but for a time our story does not concern them; rather we shall follow the stream of civilization that carried Greek medicine on to our time. And so for a moment we turn again from medicine to politics.

To the west of Greece lay a strip of land extending like a great boot out into the Mediterranean—the Italian peninsula. When Alexander was making his conquests, the foot of the peninsula and the island of Sicily next to the toe were inhabited by Greeks; their main cities were Tarentum and Syracuse. On the mainland of Africa, divided from Sicily by a narrow strip of water, was the city of Carthage, founded long before by the Phœnicians.

The greater part of Italy belonged to a people called the

Latins, or Romans, from their principal city, Rome. They were mainly farmers. For a long time they had struggled with a neighboring people, the Etruscans, and with the barbaric Gauls who lived in the north. In 290 B.C., thirty-three

Site of the Roman Temple of Æsculapius.

years after Alexander had completed his conquest, Rome became mistress of the whole central region of the peninsula.

The Romans at this time were far less civilized than their Greek neighbors; they were more like backwoodsmen. They worshiped gods that were almost the same, except in names, as those of the Greeks. Their medicine was still religious in character; indeed they had a god or goddess for nearly every symptom of disease. They had no physicians as did the Greeks.

In 293 B.C. a severe epidemic like the one that had occurred at Athens more than a century before, broke out in Rome. The Roman gods seemed powerless to control it, and

so a messenger was sent to the Greeks to borrow one of their gods for the occasion. A temple of Æsculapius was erected on an island in the river Tiber opposite the city of Rome. This temple is of importance in our story, for it was to become the first true hospital.

The Romans up to this time seem to have attracted little attention from their Greek neighbors. But during the next hundred years the farmers of Italy, successful in their battles against Carthage—the famous Punic wars—became a conquering people thirsty for land, for power, and for booty. Eventually they extended their conquests as far west as Britain and east over the countries that Alexander had ruled.

The Romans as conquerors were a far different people from the Greeks. They did not put men of science in the countries they defeated; indeed they had no scientists, for the Romans were "practical" people and regarded law and war and politics as the only honorable careers. Instead Greek physicians came to Rome, some as slaves and others as free men to make their fortunes there. It was after the fall of Corinth that Greek medicine finally reached Rome.

With the coming of Greek physicians, Greek medicine together with Greek customs and luxuries became popular at Rome. There were many of these physicians whose names have come down to us for the cures they wrought, the wealth they accumulated, and the public monuments they erected, but none, until the first and second centuries A.D., is important to our story. Let us see what the Romans themselves gave to medicine, for although they had no physicians of their own, they did contribute to the progress of medicine. Their contribution was in the field of what we should call public health, or sanitation.

The Greek cities were not equipped with sewers, nor did they always have good supplies of fresh water. For lack of sanitation they could not grow to any great size. The practical Romans, however, put in sewers and built aque-

ducts to bring fresh water to their city. When Rome was in her prime, nearly two hundred million gallons of fresh water flowed into the city each day. No modern city of equal size has a greater water supply than Rome had nearly 2000 years ago.

Sewers and water supply are not the only contributions to medicine made by the Romans—the greatest gift was the hospital. It was during the reign of the Emperor Claudius, from 41 to 54 A.D., that the first public hospital was founded.

When in an earlier chapter we told of the temples of Æsculapius, we did not call them hospitals. Sick people spent in them only a single night and that for religious reasons. The temples were not places where men, women, and children when seriously ill could be cared for over a long period of time. In Rome, before the days of the Emperors, there were no hospitals in the cities; some of the Greek physicians had offices where they performed operations, but the sick were cared for at home. If they had no relatives to look out for them, they received little or no attention. There were no nurses, in our sense of the word, who could be summoned into the home. And merely to give sick people clean, comfortable surroundings, to care for their wants, to provide them with proper food are some of the most important measures in treating disease.

The first institution of which we know that can be correctly called a hospital grew up on the island in the Tiber on which the Romans in 293 B.C. had erected the temple to Æsculapius.

In the intervening years it had been a cruel custom to put on this island slaves who were old or ill. The Roman author Suetonius says: "On this island of Æsculapius certain men exposed their ill and wornout slaves because of the trouble of treating them." The word "exposed" has, as he uses it, an unpleasant meaning. When a baby was deformed or simply not wanted in the home it was exposed on the steps of

some temple. "Exposed" meant that it was left until it had died of starvation.

Suetonius has more to say of this island and the practice of exposing sick slaves there: "The Emperor Claudius, however, decreed that such slaves were free, and, if they recovered, they should not return to the control of their masters."

In time the island became a place of refuge for all poor people who were ill. Care was given to them there. The old temple became a crude sort of hospital.

Soon other hospitals were built, and even free Roman citizens began to use them. The greatest development of the hospital, however, took place in the Roman army. Before the idea had originated, sick and wounded soldiers were sent home for treatment. But as the Roman Empire and the Roman army extended over wider territory, the journeys became too long, and so hospitals were erected at convenient places. The ruins of many of them still exist. They were planned and arranged in a manner far in advance of any subsequent hospitals until modern times.

These Roman hospitals were not charity hospitals. There are few indications indeed that the pagan Romans felt it their duty to provide medical care free of cost for poor people. But it was at Rome, after the rise of the Christian religion, that a lady named Fabiola founded the first charity hospital. We shall tell more of her later.

In this chapter we have followed the progress of medicine over a period of more than four hundred years. We have seen the origin of the study of natural history, the spread of Greek learning, the development of the school of Alexandria, the rise of the Roman Empire, and the founding of sanitation and the hospital. But we have said little of any medical heroes. So before we leave the Roman Empire to its gloomy fate at the hands of the barbarians, we shall turn in the next chapter to three men, two Greeks and a Roman—Dioscorides, Galen, and Pliny. There have been greater heroes of medicine than these three men, greater by

far, but their importance lies in the fact that they seemed to the people of the next ten centuries and more, the greatest. Each of these men wrote books on medical subjects. These books, rather than the original works of Hippocrates or Aristotle or Herophilus, became the guiding influence of medicine in the following centuries. Medicine was Greek medicine as interpreted by Pliny and Galen.

CHAPTER VIII

The Bearers of Knowledge, Dioscorides, Pliny, and Galen

IN the days when Alexander made his conquests, and even later when the Roman Empire rose, some men believed in science, but more believed in magic. Greek medicine and science, although they followed the army of Alexander and later came to Rome, did not rid people of superstition or of belief in spirits and demons and ghosts as a cause of disease. The medicine that we have described was practiced by only a few men. The great masses of people still clung to their age-old beliefs in healing gods and in the magic wrought by spells and charms.

In illness they did not turn to the Greek physicians, but to the remedies their forefathers had used, or else they went to the shops of the rhizotomists or "root cutters" for magic herbs. A "root cutter" was a man who gathered roots and herbs and sold them to people to use in treating disease. With the drugs he gave magic rituals to be carried out when the medicaments were taken. Likewise, when he gathered his herbs, he performed certain rites which were supposed to add to their healing powers.

The mandrake was a popular remedy with the rhizotomists. The plant had a root like a carrot, though it frequently was split into two parts so that by using one's imagination very vigorously it could be seen to resemble the body and legs of a man. This human shape was supposed to give it a special healing power, and according to the rhizotomists it was a dangerous plant to gather. When the mandrake was pulled from the ground, it gave a terrible shriek; anyone who heard the sound fell dead. Of course the question one asks is: How did anyone know this to be so, if everyone who

heard it died before he could tell anyone else? That we ask means simply that we are better educated and hence more critical than were the customers of the rhizotomists. They did not ask; they simply believed what they were told and marveled at the powers that such a wonderful drug must have over disease. The rhizotomists told people that the only way this root could be gathered was by tying one end of a string to the plant and the other to a dog. The owner of the dog tightly stopped his ears so that he might not hear the shriek of the mandrake and then called the dog. The dog pulled; the mandrake came from the ground and presumably shrieked, whereupon the dog died. No wonder such a drug brought a very high price.

In Shakespeare's *Romeo and Juliet*, in the fourth act, Juliet says, "And shrieks like mandrakes' torn out of the earth, that living mortals, hearing them, run mad." So we know that the legend of the mandrake was still current 1600 years and more after the time of the most famous of all the Greek rhizotomists, Crateuas.

Crateuas was private herb doctor to Mithridates VI, King of Pontus, in the last century before the Christian Era. He was famous, not for the medicines he prepared, but because, as far as we know, he was the first man to use drawings to illustrate descriptions of plants. His book, or rather the remnant of it that has survived, was filled with the usual magic spells that all rhizotomists used—but it differed in having pictures in it.

There had been men before Crateuas who had described plants, notably Theophrastus, a pupil of Aristotle, but none had used pictures to aid in recognizing them.

About a hundred years after the time of Crateuas, a surgeon in the army of the Emperor Nero named Dioscorides classified plants in a new way; he listed them under the diseases for which they were supposed to be beneficial and gave a short account of each plant, where it grew, what it looked like, and how it was to be used as a remedy.

We know little of the life of Dioscorides himself. Probably he was not an exceptional physician and certainly he would have been forgotten entirely if he had not hit upon this useful way of classifying medicinal plants. He founded what we call today *materia medica*, the materials of medicine, or the list of remedies to be used in treating disease.

A rhizotomist.

In his travels with the army, Dioscorides had the opportunity to study plants native to many countries, and his book contains descriptions of some six hundred plants and plant products. About one hundred and fifty of these were known to the Greek physicians in the time of Hippocrates; perhaps ninety of them are still used in medicine. It was not the plants he chose that made the work of Dioscorides important, but the manner in which he classified them.

His book, because of its practical nature, quickly became popular. Copies of it were prepared and illustrated as Crateuas' book had been.

The *materia medica* of Dioscorides came to be called an herbal, which means a book of botany. It was used by the physician, and also kept on the shelf in homes to be referred to in case of illness as a guide to the sort of remedy to be taken.

The pictures in some of the early copies of the book are really excellent works of art. But with each copying little errors crept in and tiny omissions were made, until finally after several centuries the pictures no longer had much resemblance to the plants they were supposed to represent.

Translated into nearly every language, the herbal continued in use for more than 1500 years. During all these centuries no one took the trouble to make the drawings fit the plants. This slavish copying of the old, regardless of error, is characteristic of the unprogressive state into which medicine passed during the years following the fall of the Roman Empire.

The herbal of Dioscorides and the *Natural History* of Pliny were the great sources of scientific information in the first 1400 years of the Christian Era.

Pliny was one of the few Romans who wrote on science. He was born at Como about 23 A.D. He was a learned man, and very well educated in the humanities and subjects considered essential in his time; that is, he had studied rhetoric and was familiar with the popular philosophy of his day, he was well versed in military and legal matters and had even studied botany in the gardens of Antonius Castor at Rome. But from our point of view Pliny was learned rather than well educated. He accepted without criticism everything that he heard or read, and wrote things down as facts without attempting to prove by trial or observation whether they were true or false. He had a great curiosity, and his curiosity took him into every field of knowledge. But somehow as we

read his writings the words of Hippocrates come to mind: "merely to think one knows is ignorance." Unfortunately the men who came after Pliny were as credulous and as uncritical as he was, and they too believed all that he had written.

If you wish to know how an energetic, studious Roman

The legend of the mandrake.

like Pliny spent his days, you can turn to the account which his nephew, Pliny the Younger, has left of his uncle's habits. He called upon the Emperor before daybreak (the Romans had no adequate artificial lighting and so, except in the case of a banquet or celebration, they went to bed early and rose before dawn). Pliny's call of ceremony over, he performed the necessary duties of the various government offices he held. These completed, he went home and had a

slave read to him or else take down in a kind of shorthand what he dictated. Next came luncheon, after which, unless official duties called him, he lay down and again listened while his slave read. Later in the afternoon he bathed, ate a light lunch, and took a nap. Then he often continued his studies until dinner time, which was just before dark. He rarely walked, so the nephew says, but was usually driven in a conveyance to save time. With his carriage went a secretary ready to take down his dictation.

Before we describe the book of natural history which he based on his reading of nearly two thousand different works by 146 Roman and 326 Greek authors, it is perhaps interesting to recount the story of his death. He died in a peculiar way, as a result of his curiosity, this time not to read but to see.

It happened in 79 A.D., when Pliny was fifty-six years old. At that time he was in command of the Roman fleet at Misenum and was on board a boat in the Bay of Naples. He saw the volcano Vesuvius begin to erupt, and wishing to get a closer view, he landed at Stabiæ with some friends. Though frightened, the party tried to hide their fears and dined cheerfully. In the middle of the night the house where they were staying was shaken by a great earthquake. Fearing that the building would collapse, they rushed outside; they were met by a shower of rocks and ashes. Hastily seizing cushions, they bound them over their heads and stumbled about in darkness lit now and again by flashes of flame from Vesuvius. They waited for morning, but no sunlight could penetrate the cloud of dust and smoke. With lighted torches they made their way to the shore. The sea was too rough to embark in small boats. Fumes of sulphur began to fill the air. Pliny, weak and choking, lay down and asked for water. Threatening flames shot through the pall of clouds. In fear the men roused Pliny; two slaves lifted him, but he collapsed. The slaves fled. The eruption grew more violent.

Molten lava flowed down the mountain sides and covered the famous city of Pompeii.

This great upheaval of nature which Pliny had seen with his own eyes he could never describe in his *Natural History*. When, two days later, his companions came back in search

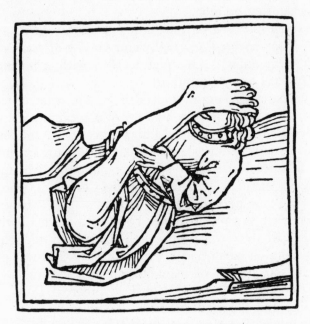

A man from the country of one-footed people.

of him, they found him in the very spot where the slaves had left him. There were no injuries on his body, but he was dead.

His great *Natural History* was copied and recopied and became the storehouse of knowledge for the men of fifty generations after his time.

The book, or rather books, for it is divided into thirty-seven parts, was intended as an encyclopedia of all physical knowledge. It contains much sound information, but min-

gled with fact is fancy and legend and what is for us superstition.

The book begins with a description of the universe. Pliny, like all learned men of his time, knew that the earth was round; but in spite of the general belief in his writings the men who came after him often doubted whether he was correct in that opinion.

Having disposed of the formation of the earth and the stars, Pliny covered geography and the rise of man; next he dealt with animals and plants, then with medicine, and finally with minerals and art.

The parts on botany and medicine are what concern us here. Pliny held the view that every plant had some special medicinal value if we could only discover it, and that for every disease there was a plant that would cure it. Indeed it was this peculiar sort of belief, or philosophy, of his that made his writings popular among the Christians, who in his day were gaining strength and who in a few centuries were to dominate Western Europe. The Christians held what we should call teleological beliefs. That is, they thought that everything on earth had a useful purpose and was created for the sole benefit of mankind, an idea that, as we shall see later, greatly influenced medical progress. Pliny wrote: "Nature and the earth fill us with admiration . . . as we contemplate that they are created for the wants or enjoyments of mankind." Pliny, although a pagan, seemed thus to hold Christian views and so his works were in great favor among the Christians.

The *Natural History* contains marvelous tales of men (living of course in a far distant country) whose feet turned the wrong way, of men who had no mouths but fed entirely on the fragrance of flowers, and of men whose feet were so large that they could hold them over their heads like parasols to shade themselves from the sun. Side by side with sound facts and science are stories of winged horses, unicorns, mermaids, and the almost human dolphins. Such fan-

ciful tales would be merely amusing if it were not for the fact that they were implicitly believed by later men. We find them scattered through the stories of the *Arabian Nights*, and in the folk tales of Europe and the beliefs of ignorant people of today, and we shall encounter them again

A man from the country of snake eaters.

and again in the medical beliefs of Europe as late as the sixteenth century. A famous king of France once paid an enormous sum of money for the horn of a unicorn to be used as a medicine. What the unscrupulous dealer sold him was probably the horn of a narwhal.

Pliny had a great influence on medicine after his time, though unfortunately he really knew little about the subject. He did not trust in theories; he was rather a "practical man," and believed in what he called "experience." But like so many "practical men" what he meant by experience

was what he had heard and what he himself believed. Untrained as he was in science, he often took for proofs of facts things that were neither proofs nor facts. He did not test his experience with experiments.

Here is one of his typical "proofs." "The herb dittany," he writes, "has the power to extract arrows. This was proved by stags who had been struck by these missiles which were loosened when they fed on this plant." If he had really desired proof, he could easily have tested his idea. With arrows he could have shot say a dozen stags but not fatally. To six of these he could then have fed dittany, but given none to the other six. If the arrows fell out of the flesh of those that ate dittany but did not fall out of the flesh of those that ate none, then he would have had a real proof of his statement.

It is unfair to Pliny, however, to criticize his failure to carry out experiments to prove theories. Few men before and equally few for centuries after his time, attempted any such thing. Today we look upon experiment as the natural way of finding out and demonstrating facts.

Of the three men whose work dominated the medicine of Europe for nearly 1500 years only one, Galen, attempted any experiments.

The story of Galen takes us first to the year 133 B.C., when there occurred one of the extraordinary events in history. In the rich Greek colony of Pergamum in Asia Minor the king, Attalus III, when he died, bequeathed his kingdom, for no known reason, to the Roman people. All its riches and its lands were to become the property of the citizens of Rome.

Imagine if you can the same thing being done today: the King of England, let us say, presenting Great Britain to the people of Italy! Of course today no king has such absolute power over his dominions as to be able to do anything like that. But Pergamum at the bequest of Attalus became Roman property.

In this Roman land of Pergamum a boy was born 264 years later who was destined to perhaps the greatest reputation that any physician, save Hippocrates, has ever achieved. His name was Galen, which means the calm, peaceful one. He was the son of Nicon, an engineer.

The boy Galen was carefully trained to be a philosopher. But when he was eighteen his father had a dream which led

A man from the country of headless people.

him to have his son study medicine. Dreams, as you know, were taken as omens in those days. Today telling the future from dreams is a practice limited to not very bright or well-instructed people, who read what are called "Dream Books," supposed to tell the significance of every sort of dream. Dreams may tell a great deal about the past and the dreamer's thoughts, but they tell nothing of the future. Yet in 149 A.D., when Galen was eighteen, even the most intelligent and educated men shaped their lives according to their dreams. Because of his father's dream, Galen turned from philosophy to medicine, and a great and influential physician was given to the world.

When Galen was twenty, his father died; but already the young man had acquired all the medical knowledge which his teachers were able to give him. There was nothing to keep him in Pergamum. And since it was the practice then for physicians who wished to gain wide experience to go from country to country studying with the leading doctors, Galen set out on his travels. For nearly ten years he wandered, staying here awhile and there awhile, but steadily nearing Alexandria, his goal.

Alexandria was no longer the great center of learning it had been nearly 500 years before when Herophilus and Archimedes and the other Greek scientists had worked there. But the skeletons used for dissections in the old days were still there, and from them a physician might learn the shape and arrangement of the human bones. This opportunity was lacking in the Greek and Roman cities; religious beliefs forbade such abuse of the body. Even at Alexandria Galen could not obtain a body to dissect, although he must have seen skeletons there and learned something of human structure. But he was forced to content himself with the dissection of hogs and apes to learn the form and arrangement of the internal organs. He assumed that man's organs were similar. This assumption, as we shall see later, had an unfortunate influence upon medicine for many centuries after Galen's time, for men believed that the human anatomy was like that of apes and hogs.

In 157 A.D. Galen returned to his native city of Pergamum, ready to start on his career as a physician. It was an amazing career, one that almost forces us to believe in luck.

Of course, many wise people tell us that there is no such thing as luck, that success and happiness in life come to those who work hard for them and seize their opportunities. It is certainly true that many people try to cover their own deficiencies and faults by calling them "bad luck." But that is not the sort of thing we mean. We mean that some men have the ability to seize fortunate opportunities. Galen was

a well-trained physician, he was highly intelligent, and he had, perhaps most important of all, a remarkable personality; people liked him and were impressed by him. He was very, very sure of himself—too sure, in fact. And he was willing to assume responsibilities. No doubt there were many other men of Greece and Rome as gifted as he. But fortune was with Galen.

When he returned to Pergamum, the summer gladiatorial shows were about to begin, but no one had been appointed to fill the important position of surgeon to the gladiators. Welcomed as the returning son of an honored man, Nicon, Galen was given this position. That was good fortune for a young man. Many gladiators were wounded, and wounded seriously, in the contests, but under Galen's care not one died. Galen was credited with their recovery. No doubt he was a good surgeon for his time, but often gladiators were so badly wounded that no medical care could save them. And for three years in succession Galen was appointed surgeon to the gladiators.

A man less ready to seize the opportunities of fortune might have stayed on in this important post, training, directing, treating the athletes and acquiring a great reputation in Pergamum. But Galen in the midst of his first success continued to study philosophy and medicine, trying to perfect himself; and he wrote, practicing the art of expressing himself in order that he might influence people.

In 161 A.D. he gave up his position in Pergamum and went to Rome, the great city which drew every ambitious man of the Empire. Rome for young Galen was a far different place from his home country, Pergamum. In Rome no one knew of him or of his father, Nicon. It must have seemed to him that there were countless physicians in the great city. Some were good, some bad, some modest and honest, some shrewd and self-exploiting, and every one of them fighting for his own success. Galen was an almost friendless country boy in a big city.

A lesser man than he might have failed and returned to Pergamum, but Galen watched for his chance. He called on fellow countrymen from Pergamum who had come to Rome and were established there. One of them, Eudemus by name, fell ill; he called in a famous physician to treat

Gladiators training.

him. But each day he grew worse, until at last his life was despaired of. Thinking he was soon to die, he sent for Galen. That young man with amazing courage disagreed with the great doctor who was in charge of the case. He said that the treatment was wrong, but that if Eudemus followed his advice, he would live. That was a grave responsibility to take, for if Eudemus died, Galen would be a ruined man.

It may have been Galen's skill, or his good fortune, or both—but at any rate the patient lived. And that Eudemus happened to be a prominent man at Rome, with many admirers, was certainly Galen's good fortune, for Eudemus told all his friends how the young doctor from Pergamum saved his life when the leading physician of Rome had given him up as hopeless.

Patients flocked to Galen. Jealous, the physicians of

Rome turned against him. He defended himself in speeches and with pamphlets. His patients believed in him and trusted him.

The wife of the Consul, Flavius Boethius, fell ill. Galen treated her, and she too recovered. Her husband became a firm friend and admirer of Galen. He set aside a room for the young physician where he might dissect animals and prepare a book on anatomy.

In four years the country boy who had come to Rome had reached the height of success in medicine. Only one step remained, and that was about to be taken. The Consul Boethius and another friend, Marcus Barbarus, son-in-law of the Emperor Marcus Aurelius, wished to have Galen appointed physician at court. Everything was in readiness for this last success when Galen did a peculiar thing. Probably no one will ever know why, but suddenly he left Rome, returned to Pergamum, and took up the practice of medicine there.

Many people have speculated as to why he left. Perhaps they wondered then, for a second curious thing occurred, and some men have said that his departure was closely connected with it. Within a few months a great epidemic of some infectious disease broke out in Rome, killing thousands of people. Did Galen leave to escape the approaching epidemic —did he run away? We can hardly blame him if he did, for his medicine, his skill could be of no avail against this great outbreak of disease which for sixteen years was to fill the streets of Rome with funerals and the homes with sorrow. But to run away is a thing that few physicians have ever done, as we shall see when we come to the story of the epidemics of the Black Death in Europe years later. Physicians stay and treat and comfort people even when they know they are giving their lives to their calling. It has been suggested that Galen went home to Pergamum because he felt that he would be needed there if the epidemic spread to that city.

He had been in Pergamum two years when a messenger from the Roman Emperor arrived there searching for him. Galen was ordered to join the army of the Emperor Marcus Aurelius and to become the court physician. He reached the army at Aquileia, then a large city situated near the upper end of the Adriatic Sea. The epidemic of disease, still spreading, swept down upon the Roman army. The Emperor Marcus Aurelius fled toward Rome, and with him went his adopted brother, the Emperor Verus. Marcus Aurelius reached Rome; Verus died on the way; Galen stayed at Aquileia.

Again Marcus Aurelius sent for Galen. He was to accompany the Emperor as his personal physician on a campaign against the barbarians to the north. But Galen convinced the Emperor that it would be better if he, the great physician, stayed in Rome to take care of the Emperor's son, Commodus.

Marcus Aurelius died some ten years later, still fighting the barbarians. Galen remained at Rome, writing, studying, and lecturing. Commodus came to the throne, and Galen was his court physician. Twelve years later Commodus was murdered, but Galen remained on at court, still working. Pertinax and Didius Julianus became emperors, and then Septimius Severus, and Galen continued as court physician —still writing, still studying. Finally in 200 A.D., in the reign of Septimius Severus, he died.

The volumes he wrote have lived as have the writings of few other physicians. As we read on in our story we shall find the name of Galen occurring again and again. It will be Galen this, and Galen that, and Galen said, and Galen can't be wrong.

Even in the sixteenth century when the Belgian, Vesalius, wrote the first true anatomy of the human body, men said he was wrong because Galen had not found things in the body as he found them. In the seventeenth century when William Harvey, physician to King Charles II of England,

discovered how blood circulated in the body, men said that he was wrong because Galen had found it otherwise.

Why were Galen's writings so popular? What was it

*Galen as shown in the surgical works
of Ambroise Paré.*

about them that made men believe in them? Certainly there had been greater physicians than he; Hippocrates was far greater.

There were two reasons. The first was his positiveness, and the second his love for systematizing everything. Galen

was very sure of himself, very certain that he was always right. There was never any doubt in his writings. He had an explanation for everything that might occur, and he was clever enough to make his explanations plausible. People, unless they are trained in science, often have a great liking for plausible explanations. They prevent doubt and so save thinking. Hippocrates, you will remember, was never really certain of anything except actual facts which he could observe. He knew that human reasoning was often faulty. One of his sayings on this very point has come down through the ages in nearly every language. Perhaps you are familiar with the first half of it: "Life is short and art is long." It goes on: "Experience is fallacious and judgment difficult." Hippocrates avoided explanations. He said in effect, "Observe and find out for yourself, and prove it so by many observations." Galen seemed to say, "I'll explain it for you."

Now it happened that after the time of Galen, science did not flourish again for many centuries; men turned passionately to religion, which taught faith, belief in the written word, belief in authority. And Galen was accepted as the supreme authority in medicine. His very positiveness made him so. He said he was right—and men believed him. Here are his actual words: "Never as yet have I gone astray, whether in treatment or in prognosis, as have so many other physicians of great reputation. If anyone wishes to gain fame . . . all that he needs is to accept what I have been able to establish."

Galen's purpose in writing was to bring system into all medical knowledge and to prove that everything was created for a useful purpose for man. He started with the works of Hippocrates, which he admired greatly, but which he felt were badly out of date. He intended to add to them all the knowledge gained in the six hundred years since Hippocrates' time. Then he would bind the whole together into a system, a theory, an explanation of everything that might happen to a man.

Not only did he bring together all the medical knowledge he knew of, but he included all the theories and speculations that had been evolved. To sound facts and observations he added the number lore of the Pythagoreans which we spoke of in the chapter on Hippocrates, the theory of the four humors, and the theory of the qualities. You will remember that the body of every man was supposed to have four qualities, heat and cold and wetness and dryness, and that it was believed that in health these qualities were balanced in the body. In disease they were unbalanced. If a man had fever, one need only say he had too much heat and not enough coldness—that was what ailed him. Everything in the world had one or more of these same qualities. Thus some vegetables were hot, some cold, some wet, and some dry. Cucumber seeds were cooling to the fourth degree—"cool as a cucumber"—and so Galen might give a man with fever cucumber seeds to balance with their coolness the excess of heat which made him sick. It was a simple system—and, as we see it, a foolish one.

We could perhaps laugh at it, if it were not for the sad fact that for fourteen or fifteen centuries after Galen's time sick men and women and children were dosed with the useless "herbs" that Galen had recommended. They were the sort of medicaments that old women in the country sometimes use even now for home remedies—horehound water and onion syrup, sassafras tea and tansy stew. Many of the prescriptions that the followers of Galen used contained hundreds of different herbs. They were what the modern physician calls "shotgun prescriptions"—many drugs shot at the disease in the hope that one of them may hit it. Even now herb drugs—and some few of them are of course very valuable in medicine—are called Galenicals.

If ever any man committed what Hippocrates called the sin of ignorance—"to know is science; merely to believe one knows is ignorance"—it was Galen. And great harm resulted from his "ignorance" spoken with the voice of au-

thority! He said that pus, matter that forms in infected sores, is a necessary part of the healing of wounds. Of course he knew nothing of bacteria or of infection—no one did in those days—but he made a positive statement. There were physicians, nine centuries and again thirteen centuries after his time who said that wounds should be treated so that pus did not form. But men paid no attention to them, for the great Galen had said otherwise. It was only late in the nineteenth century, almost in our time, that a great physician, Lister, showed that Galen was entirely wrong and that antiseptics could be used to prevent infection and the formation of pus.

When one thinks of all the thousands upon thousands of men and women and children who have suffered and perhaps died needlessly of infection because the great Galen had said that pus was necessary to healing, it is difficult to be sympathetic toward his work. But there was one side of it that deserves not only our sympathy but also our admiration.

Galen was the first experimenter in medicine. Men before him had observed facts, but Galen went further; he demonstrated facts. Thus men had observed that injury to the back sometimes led to paralysis of the legs. Galen by cutting the spinal cord showed that this paralysis was due to the injury of the nerves that went to the legs. By experiment he showed that the heart pumps blood and that the lungs draw in air when we breathe. These were great and important discoveries, and he used a great and important method for making discoveries—experiment.

The sad fact is that the men who came after him forgot his experiments, ignored the very thing that would have unlocked for them the secrets of nature, and remembered instead his useless theories and his foolish systems. Whom shall we blame? Galen held out the shiny dross of speculation and the dull gold of true science; men chose the dross.

CHAPTER IX

The Way Divides—East and West

THERE were evil portents in the city of Rome.
When Galen in his old age laid down his pen,
he had written *finis* to a chapter in medical progress. Men were no longer concerned with the search for facts,
or with science—even the kind of science that Pliny had
followed. It was not the diseases of men, but the diseases of
society that held their attention. An empire was dying.

The greatest physicians of the ancient world had once
come to Rome. But now there were few left in the city
whose names are worth recording.

On the streets where Galen had walked proudly there
were peddlers of drugs, magicians who pretended to cure
disease with charms, fortune tellers, stargazers—fakers all.
There are always men willing to profit from the ignorance
and the necessities of the most pitiful of all people, the sick
and the infirm. When civilization declines, when poverty
reigns, when life seems darkest and hardest, people turn
more and more to the false prophets of medicine who promise most and do least. And so it was in Rome. The peddlers,
magicians, and astrologers were practicing the kind of medicine that savage people had used. Civilization was moving
backwards.

We could turn from these scenes of a declining civilization and close the book upon Roman medicine if it were not
for one fact. The roots of our own civilization are buried in
Roman soil.

The events of those closing years of the Empire left their
impression on medicine for centuries to come. The kind of
lives people in Europe were to lead, the diseases they were
to have, the beliefs they were to hold, and the doctors they

were to employ were influenced by things that were occurring in the days when Rome was going to her ruin.

In Galen's time the Roman Empire had expanded to the greatest size it was ever to attain. The Roman eagle held sway over all the lands that touched on the Mediterranean Sea. On the map you will see a ring with Rome at its center, a ring made up of North Africa, Egypt, Palestine, Greece, Italy, France, and Spain. To the north and west the legions had pushed into the British Isles, and there the Romans had erected a wall to hold back the barbarians. Ruins of this farthest outpost of the ancient Empire still stand today in England.

From the conquered lands tribute poured into Rome— taxes and levies, slaves and plunder.

Outside the land held by the Roman Empire, in the great expanse to the north, were the tribesmen of the forests and plains whom the Greeks and Romans called barbarians— the Goths, the Vandals, the Angles, and the Saxons, and to the east the Huns. Although primitive in their way of living as compared to the luxurious Roman nobles, the barbarians loved liberty and freedom and admired strength and courage. The Romans had defeated some of these tribesmen, as Cæsar tells us in his story of the conquest of Gaul, and had made soldiers of them. In the Roman army the barbarians learned Roman ways of fighting. And now like a circle of hungry dogs eying another dog with a juicy bone, they eyed Rome. It was the age-old situation—the city dweller growing fat and soft, the virile nomad watching for a chance to seize and plunder.

But Rome was not only fat and soft; Rome was diseased, sick with the worst of social disorders, injustice and oppression.

The Roman Empire contained perhaps as many inhabitants as does our country today—a hundred million and more. The vast majority of these people were neither free nor independent; they were completely subject to Roman

rule; they worked and slaved and paid so that a comparatively few men, Roman citizens, might live in luxury. Wealthy Romans often bought their way into high office; they controlled the Empire; with part of the money they collected they built great stone roads extending from county to county; they erected magnificent public buildings; they

An illustration from one of the translations of Dioscorides.

hired an army to hold back the barbarians; they gave elaborate gladiatorial shows and circuses for the people; to the multitude of restless adventurers and ne'er-do-wells who migrated to Rome they handed out doles of oil and grain.

None of these things brought contentment or prosperity to the people of the conquered lands, who were little better than slaves. The poor and oppressed far outnumbered the Roman citizens. If they had risen under some great popular leader, they might have overthrown the government in a civil war. Such things have happened often in history. But He who had risen to unite the common people in a single cause was not a warrior counseling bloodshed. His message

was, "Love your enemies." His fame grew widely in the centuries after he had been condemned to death by the Roman judge of Palestine, Pontius Pilate. The words he had spoken to his disciples in the brief years when he walked the dusty roads of the Holy Land became full of meaning for the oppressed. He had said that all men were brothers; the Roman patrician and the slave were equal before God. He had preached peace and submission, with promise of reward in a future life.

The Christian religion was a solace to the oppressed. It offered hope to the downtrodden; it made a man of the slave. It grew and spread. Every effort of the emperors to stamp out the growing menace to Roman rule brought converts to the Christian fold. Men by thousands and millions were turning from the Empire of Rome to the Empire of God.

Among a people whose minds were fixed upon heaven, who looked for miracles and the help of God, there was no place for science or for medicine of the kind that Hippocrates or even Galen had known. Faith and hope and prayers were taking the place of science.

Among such a people, united in their misery by religion, there could be no patriotic fervor for the Empire of Rome. When the barbarians turned upon the legions, defeated them, and advanced on Rome, the common man did not rise to defend the state. To him the barbarians were merely other masters; none could be worse than the Romans. What did it matter to him if the rich were plundered, the pagan temples burned, and the gladiatorial amphitheaters ruined?

The capture of Rome by the Visigoths in 410 and its destruction by the Vandals in 455 were not events of enormous importance; they were merely announcements that the Empire in the west, long ill, was at last dead. Already the Vandals had settled in Spain, the Angles and Saxons had moved into Britain, the Huns from the east had migrated into France.

A century before the fall of Rome, the capital of the Roman Empire was transferred from Rome to a city to the east called Byzantium.

It was not the approach of the barbarians that drove the emperors to Byzantium, but the unsuitable position of Rome. The Romans were not seafaring people; they traveled by land and not by water. Italy projects far out from the mainland and a journey half the length of the peninsula was necessary when troops or messengers or the emperor himself wished to go from Rome to other provinces. Because of this fact the emperors in time of war had often set up temporary headquarters at some place more conveniently located. Constantine the Great, who ruled from 306 to 337, finally transferred the imperial power permanently to Byzantium, and the name of the city was changed to Constantinople.

Constantine was the first emperor to be baptized a Christian. In three centuries Christianity had spread from the hovels of slaves to the imperial court.

With the removal of the capital, the Empire split in two great divisions: a Greek-speaking eastern half and a Latin-speaking western half. The Western Empire fell to the barbarians, and that portion included southwestern Europe.

Our story of medicine divides now and runs for many centuries in two channels—one to the West, one to the East. In the East it will be the record of medicine in the Byzantine Empire and among the Arabs, who are soon to come in a conquering horde. In the West it will be the record of medicine in a barbaric civilization, but a civilization from which our own has sprung. Far along in our story the medicine of the East and of the West will finally meet and go on together.

First let us see what the conditions were in the Western Empire. The barbarians had entered the Roman towns; the tribesmen and the men who had lived under Roman rule occupied the same lands. There was a great mixing of the

population; barbarians and highly civilized men intermingled. The tribesmen from different regions spoke different languages, which gradually blended with the Latin of the Roman inhabitants. New languages were evolved, modifications of Latin which we now call French, Italian, Spanish, and Portuguese. And when Europe was in the making there was little communication and little travel between the small settlements of people, and so many different variations of the languages—dialects—grew up.

With the fall of the Roman Empire, Europe was left with no general controlling power. The scattered tribes of barbarians had for a time been united under leaders in their conquests, but as they settled they again broke into small groups, each one independent of the others. It was in effect a condition which still persists in some uncivilized countries, such as parts of Africa, where each town is the home of a tribe and each tribe is an independent unit. Conditions in Europe were in many ways similar to those in our own country during the gold rush of 1849, when rough and lawless men as well as worthy citizens migrated to the West and set up new towns. Because of the lack of a governing power, the strong preyed on the weak, and brigands made the lands between the towns unsafe for travelers. You will remember how in our own newly settled West, under the influence of the men who saw the need of law and order, vigilance committees were organized to stop crime, and officers were elected, laws drawn up, and order finally established.

Similarly in Europe in the early days there were, mingling with the barbarian invaders, men who had been under Roman rule and had ideas of civilization. Under their influence a form of government grew up that came to be known as the feudal system. Someone, because of his strength or cunning, became the feudal lord. The people on the neighboring farmlands swore allegiance to him; he became ruler, protector, and military leader. As a result of the growth of this system, Europe became a network of feudal

domains. Each had its lord with his castle and men at arms; in the surrounding lands over an area large or small, depending on the strength of the lord, the lesser people acknowledged his rule. In theory the feudal lord was the owner of all the land under his domain.

In time another ruling power appeared—the king, who, so it came to be believed, held all the land by divine right. The kings at first were usually feudal lords who had become powerful and expanded their domains by conquering other feudal lords and forcing them to acknowledge their overlordship.

The matters we discuss here may seem to be far more political than medical, but we cannot follow the course of medicine in the early days in Europe unless we know the conditions under which people lived.

The part that Christianity played in medicine was important, too, and to study it we must return for a moment to Rome in the closing years of the Empire. Christianity, as we have said, had spread among the people and even reached the palace when in the fourth century after Christ the Emperor Constantine was baptized. Now there was one feature of Christianity that linked it to medicine. Christ had taught self-sacrifice. Some of his followers interpreted this as mortification of the flesh. That is, they tried in every way to abolish all their earthly desires by tortures which they imposed upon themselves. Many of them left their families and their friends and went into desert regions to live alone in caves. They rarely ate, they whipped and tortured themselves, and they prayed long hours at a time. They thought that this mortification of the flesh, this suppression of all earthly pleasure, would make them pleasing in the sight of God and so assure them a place in heaven.

Men and women who gave a broader interpretation to the meaning of self-sacrifice, instead of becoming hermits, devoted their lives to caring for the poor, and the ill. The Roman Empire at this time needed such men and women

badly; century after century great epidemics of disease had
been spreading among the inhabitants. In the next chapter,
we shall describe one such epidemic, but here we are concerned only with the way the Christians behaved in the
presence of disease. The pagan Romans, when epidemics
broke out, had often fled in fear and left the sick to die

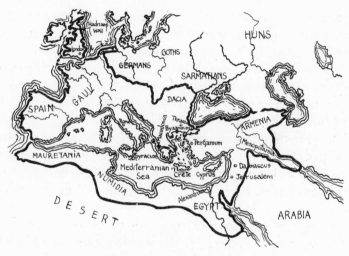

Map of the Roman Empire.

without care. Many of the Christians felt it a religious duty
to stay and nurse the sick, to sacrifice their own lives if
necessary in the service of the helpless.

Fabiola, whose conception of self-sacrifice inspired the
founding of the first charity hospital at Rome was a Christian.

In another chapter we told how the Romans founded the
first public hospital, built on the island where sick slaves
were left to die. But so far as we know, food and shelter and
medical care were not given there free of cost. Only those
who could afford to pay were welcomed. Fabiola created a

hospital where free care was given out of charity, as a Christian duty.

About a century after she had founded her hospital, when the feudal system was in its infancy, a young man whom we know as St. Benedict decided to become a Christian hermit. He went to a place fifty miles from Rome where Nero had once had a summer home, crawled into a cave, and scourged his flesh with whip and hair shirt. For three years he lived there; and during this time his reputation as a holy man spread over the countryside. People flocked to see him. Finally he emerged from the cave, gave up his self-torture and established monasteries in which young men were educated to be priests of the Christian religion. The monks in these monasteries extended charity and help to the poor and needy, and cared for the sick. The monasteries grew in number and spread throughout Europe. They were the sole centers in which education was kept alive; they served as hospitals; the monks, who were the only educated men—indeed the only men who could read and write—acted as physicians.

The Western Empire—Europe—as we leave it now to turn to the eastern channel of our story, was a country of feudal rule and monastic medicine. Its civilization was primitive, and so was its medicine. There were no medical schools, and no trained physicians. The well-meaning priests did what they could to help ailing people, but too often all they could do was pray and comfort.

In contrast to the primitive conditions in the West, the luxury of Roman life continued in the East. The emperors in their palace at Constantinople carried on the customs of Roman rule. But these people of the East were different from the Latins of Rome.

The traditions of the Eastern, or Byzantine Empire, were older than the Roman. They came from Egypt and Syria and Greece.

In the Eastern Empire there was a mingling of Greek

culture, Roman law, Christian religion, and Egyptian and Syrian magic.

In one respect, and it is a very important one for medicine, this Greek civilization differed from that of the time of Alexander. The Greek love for learning lasted, but the spirit of the search for truth was lost. The learned men of the Eastern Empire were mere copyists—repeating what other physicians had said, especially Galen and Dioscorides and Pliny. And into their writings crept beliefs that were held by the Christians of those days, belief in miracles and the effectiveness of prayer in curing disease, and belief in magic. This influence you can see in the writings of the doctors of the times. Aetius, physician to the Emperor Justinian I, prescribed as the best method for removing a bone from the throat saying in a loud voice to the bone, "As Jesus Christ drew Lazarus from the grave, and Jonah out of the whale, thus Blasius, the martyr and servant of God, commands, 'Bone come up or bone go down.'" The author of these foolish words occupied the same position in the Roman court of the East that Galen had held four hundred years before in Imperial Rome.

Beyond the description of the symptoms of a few diseases, there was no advance made in medicine in the Eastern Empire, no lives of medical heroes to record. But the scholars of Byzantium performed one service to medicine. In the palaces and in the monasteries the men who admired Greek learning but could not use it collected and copied the ancient medical books. The books were preserved—a store of knowledge which would be available when men knew how to use it.

Medicine, as we leave it here at the close of the sixth century, had declined far below the level to which Hippocrates raised it. It survived, but feebly, in the monasteries of the West; it was preserved in the documents in the libraries of the Eastern Empire, in the works of Galen, of Pliny, of Dioscorides, and in a few scattered manuscripts of Hippoc-

rates and Aristotle. Before medicine could progress again, it had to regain the ground it had lost. A thousand years and more had elapsed since the days of Aristotle and Hippocrates; a thousand more must pass before medicine would revive fully. And it is to the first of the quickening influences in this revival that we now turn. Our story leads us next to a people who have not yet crossed our pages—the Arabs. But before the Arabs descend to ravage the cities of the East there is another event to record—a tragic event—a great outbreak of a deadly disease.

Part Four

DISEASE AND CONQUEST

SCIENCE UNDER THE CALIPHS

MEDICINE FOLLOWS THE CRUSADES

CHAPTER X

Disease and Conquest

PLAGUE and pestilence dealing death in the home and in the street, or a barbaric enemy killing on the battlefield and plundering in the town—which is the more terrible? Both were to fall upon the Eastern Roman Empire.

The pestilence came first—a product of trade and commerce.

When people live in small communities isolated one from another, there can be little diffusion of acute infectious diseases. By an acute infection is meant one in which the illness develops quickly and is severe; it lasts a few days or weeks and then the man affected is either dead or on his way toward recovery. In either case he can no longer spread the disease. You are familiar with the milder forms of acute infectious diseases—tonsilitis, the head cold, measles, and chicken pox, and perhaps scarlet fever. There are others which are serious and deadly: smallpox, bubonic plague, and typhus fever.

There are also infectious diseases that are not acute, but that are called chronic. They may persist for years, during all of which time the sick man may spread the disease. Leprosy and tuberculosis are diseases of this kind. They can be spread even by slow commerce, but the acute infections cannot.

In a sparsely settled district where weeks or even months of travel lie between the towns, epidemics of acute infections rarely occur, for they are spread only by the contact of the sick man with the well. If, then, travelers with smallpox, let us say, started out for a distant city, they would be ill on the way. Some might die, but those who finally reached

their destination would have recovered so completely that
they would no longer spread the infection.

When large groups of people hold active commerce with

The planets that caused the plague.

each other, when cities are close together and means of
transportation rapid, then acute infectious diseases travel
along the same routes that men travel.

The Romans built paved roads throughout the Empire.

Their trade extended even to China, where Roman gold changed hands for silk. Trade and travel grew up before medicine had developed the means for controlling the more serious epidemics of disease. In the Empire extending along the shores of the Mediterranean, plague and typhus rode in the caravan of the traveler and in the ranks of the legions. Reaching the cities, disease would advance like a great conflagration, sweeping everyone before it. The population would flee in panic, leaving the sick to die unattended. Finally, when, like a fire that had burned out, the disease died down, the refugees would return. Many of their friends would be gone; some would have survived, crippled and broken in health. Again travel and commerce would begin and flourish. Then after a pause, perhaps a decade, perhaps a century or more, the plague and pestilence would again ride in the caravan of the traveler and in the ranks of legions and would wreak their frightful mortality upon the cities.

We have mentioned some of these epidemics of disease in earlier chapters. Pericles and his sons died in a pestilence that occurred at Athens. The Romans before their conquest of Greece suffered from epidemics; it was then, you will remember, that they erected on the island in the Tiber the temple to Æsculapius that was to become the first hospital. Again at Rome when Marcus Aurelius was Emperor there was another outbreak, the one that men said frightened Galen away and that killed the Emperor Verus. There were other epidemics in the closing years of the Western Empire, and unquestionably they contributed to the decline and eventual fall of the Empire. But when the barbarians conquered the Western Empire, trade and travel everywhere except in Italy itself slowed and stopped. The epidemics ceased.

In the Eastern Empire, commerce, war, and travel went on uninterrupted. The epidemics continued.

In the year 542, travelers coming to Constantinople, where the Emperor Justinian reigned, brought word that an

epidemic was raging in lower Egypt. Slowly the disease spread, following the coast line where traffic was most active. In 543 it reached Constantinople. There at its height it killed ten thousand of the inhabitants in a single day.

Justinian was at war with the barbarians who had migrated into Italy. He expelled the barbarians and in doing that he spread the plague. For fifteen years it tarried in the border regions of the Eastern Empire and then it moved slowly back toward Egypt. Again on its return it struck at Constantinople. This time the havoc was even greater than during the first outbreak. There were so many dead that the bodies could not be buried. Finally the roofs were taken off the towers of the walls that surrounded the city; into the space below were crammed thousands upon thousands of bodies. Then the roofs were replaced and sealed. Gibbon, who wrote *The History of the Decline and Fall of the Roman Empire*, says of this epidemic:

"No facts have been preserved to sustain an account, or even a conjecture, of the numbers that perished in this extraordinary mortality. I only find that, during three months, five and at length ten thousand persons died each day in Constantinople; that many cities in the East were left vacant, and that in several districts of Italy the harvest and the vintage withered on the ground."

For fifty-two years this outbreak of plague attacked the tortured people in recurring epidemics.

If the modern physician could control plague no better than the physician in Greek or Roman days, we too should suffer from the great epidemics. The diseases still exist, smoldering today in the Eastern lands from which they arose and spread in ancient times. Although we have commerce, active commerce, with those countries, the diseases do not reach us, for in the intervening centuries physicians have learned how to control them. But before that triumph was achieved, Europe only five, four, and three centuries ago was to suffer outbreaks of plague and pestilence greater even

than those which occurred at Constantinople in the years beginning with 543.

Now for a time we leave the Byzantine Empire, weakened by disease, and, following the retreating wave of the plague, we go eastward, although it is not disease or even medicine we are to consider, but politics again.

Our interest now is Arabia, a great tract of land lying between the Red Sea and the Persian Gulf and separated from the Mediterranean by Syria and the Holy Land. This country of Arabia is mostly rough pasture lands dotted here and there with fertile tracts; in the center is a great sandy desert. There are in the whole country only a few small walled towns, and of these only two are of any importance; one is Medina and the other Mecca. In the sixth century most of the inhabitants lived a nomadic life in tribes, knowing only the rule of their own chosen leader and worshiping among their gods an idol—a meteorite, built into a temple at Mecca.

In Mecca in the years when the great plague was still sweeping over the Eastern Empire, a man was born who was destined to unite the wandering tribes in a common cause. His name was Mohammed. His force for union was religion. He was the prophet of a living god, Allah.

Arabia was stirred by his words. Arguments were waged and battles fought over the gods of Mecca and the god of Mohammed. Slowly Mohammed's god won the allegiance of the people.

The outside world paid little attention to the turmoil in Arabia, a domestic row among flea-bitten riders of the desert. The rulers of the surrounding countries smiled when in 628 the envoys of Mohammed ordered them to surrender to his cause. But they did not smile when, less than ten years later, the forces of a united Arabia stormed their gates. The Arabian conquest was under way. Syria and the Holy Land fell before troops of horsemen shouting their war cry of "Allah, Allahuakbar."

The Persians under Rustam went down to defeat amid a stampede of their own trained war elephants. Egypt, Armenia, Turkestan, North Africa, and Spain were brought under Arabic rule.

Allah triumphed.

Constantinople survived the attack of the Arabs as it had survived the attacks of plague. But shorn of its great Empire by one and weakened by the other, it was dead so far as progress was concerned.

The great library at Alexandria was burned by the Arabs because the leader of the expedition said that there was no need of any books except the Koran, the bible of Arabia.

The glory of Athens had passed years before and little was left of the glory of Rome. But the stream of medical progress flowed on, no longer through Athens and Alexandria and Rome, but through Bagdad, Damascus, Cairo, and Cordova.

The center of progress and the center of medical advance in the eighth, ninth, tenth, and eleventh centuries lay among the Arabs.

CHAPTER XI

Science Under the Caliphs

THE story of Arabian conquest is again the story of the nomad and the settler. In the span of a single century the virile Arabs had engulfed the wide lands of an ancient civilization and had themselves been swallowed by that civilization.

They had come out of Arabia, a crude and ruthless people, simple and primitive in their ways of living, a people of tents and horses, subsisting on goat's milk, mare's milk, and dates.

Unlike the Romans they did not make slaves of the people they conquered. All that they demanded was acceptance of the words of Mohammed as written in the Koran. The men under their rule were of many nations and languages, but translation of the Koran was forbidden. The people must learn the Koran; hence they must learn Arabic, and so this language became the universal one of the lands ruled by the Arabs—the Moslem Empire.

Their conquests accomplished, the Arabs had time to take stock of the new and strange things they found about them. They were full of curiosity. They saw castles and bridges, aqueducts and engines of war; they tasted the sweets of a luxury unknown in their simple way of living; they found men of medicine whose potions stopped pain more surely than did the magic words of the wise men of the desert; they learned that the wisdom of great men was set down in books —but the writing was in a language unknown to them.

The Arab conquerors had gained great wealth from their plunders; wealth unlocked the secrets that had aroused their curiosity. Learned men—Jews, Persians, and Syrians— were offered gifts to translate into Arabic the books of the Greeks and Romans. Persians, Jews, Syrians, and even

Greek Christians, rather than the Arabs themselves, were the scientists of the Eastern Empire. It was indeed from the Christian followers of Nestorius, a priest of the Byzantine Empire, that the Arabs first obtained knowledge of Greek and Roman medicine. Nestorius had been a bishop in Constantinople, but he had been driven from that city with his followers because he differed with the accepted doctrines of the Eastern Church. He and his band finally found refuge in Persia. Strangers in a strange land, they turned to the care of the sick and so to the study of medicine—medicine of the kind that had survived in the Byzantine Empire. Under the patronage of the Arabs such men of science and medicine were not content to stop with the mere copying of the ancient books of the Greeks and Romans; they went further. Science flourished in Arabia as it had at Alexandria under Greek rule. The sciences of chemistry, geology, and algebra were founded. The numerals we use today in our arithmetic are the Arabic form. A great many herbs native to the Orient were put into medical use in addition to the remedies of Dioscorides. These substances were mainly spices, such as camphor, nutmeg, cloves, and musk; but at that time they were used to treat diseases, and so they have a place in our story.

Later, as we shall see, the medical knowledge of the Arabs passed into Europe. It was through the civilization of the Eastern Empire that the stream of knowledge flowed on to our own day and our own country. That is the reason why we have stopped here to talk of the Arabs and their medicine. We have said nothing of the medicine of China or of India, for it lay outside the channel in which ancient knowledge came on down through the centuries to us.

Because the medicine of Europe followed that of Arabia, the spices used as medicaments by the Arabic doctors were also used in Europe. Centuries later in our story we shall see King Charles II of England on his deathbed dosed with spices, with nutmeg, camphor, mace, and cloves.

A spice trade was established between the East and West, but it was really a drug trade. When Columbus tried to find a shorter route to India to obtain spices, and discovered America by a blunder, the spices he sought were not to be used by the cook but by doctors to treat sick people. It has often been said, but erroneously, that the spices of the East were used to preserve food in those days before ice boxes and the invention of canning. In reality they were too expensive to be used as preservatives; salt was cheaper and quite as effective.

Clear evidence of the fact that a great deal of our knowledge came from Arabia is seen in the words of our own language. Later in our story we shall find that men in Europe turned for information to the books written in Arabic—translations made from Greek and Syrian books by the learned men employed by the Arabic rulers. Because the Europeans could not read Arabic, they too employed translators to change the Arabic into Latin. But there were no Latin words for many of the things mentioned in the Arabic books and so the Arabic terms were kept. In our language the words alcohol, alfalfa, admiral, arsenal, azure, cipher, algebra, zero, zenith, syrup, julep, and many, many more are Arabic.

Nor are words the only things in everyday life we owe to the Arabs; like the Chinese they invented fireworks; they were the first to use windowpanes, to cultivate fruit, and to use street lights. As we have said, they were the founders of chemistry, and chemistry has since continued to be closely associated with medicine. The Arabian chemists discovered such important substances as alcohol, sulphuric and nitric acids, silver nitrate, and bichloride of mercury; but it was the philosophy behind their chemistry that influenced men of later times more than the chemicals they discovered.

Their chemistry was combined with astrology, and belief in the elixir of life which bestowed perpetual youth and cured all disease. According to their ideas, the seven heav-

enly bodies—the sun, moon, Mercury, Mars, Venus, Jupiter, and Saturn—corresponded to the seven days of the week and the seven metals that were known at that time: gold, silver, iron, mercury, tin, lead, and copper. All these metals were born in the earth from a common substance under the influence of the planets. The chemists, or rather alchemists, sought to find the secret of the birth of metals so that they could change lead and iron into gold. And further they sought to dissolve gold so that it could be eaten or drunk, for potable gold was an elixir of life.

Absurd as these ideas seem now, they nevertheless were considered serious matters up to a time within three centuries of our own. Men spent their lives and their fortunes trying to change lead into gold and to find the secret of perpetual youth. In their search and their experiments they discovered, by accident, many useful chemicals—but no one found the universal remedy or the secret of eternal life.

From Arabic chemistry grew in time some of the weirdest of all medical beliefs, particularly the idea that the seven planets ruled seven vital parts of the body. In antiquity, a planet was any heavenly body which appeared to move. Thus the sun was a planet; it ruled the heart, the moon the brain, Jupiter the liver, Saturn the spleen, Mercury the lungs, Mars the bile, and Venus the kidneys. The influence of the stars on diseases fills a great chapter in medical history and one that we shall deal with when we come to the beliefs current in Europe centuries later. Even today some almanacs, as you may have noticed, show pictures of the planets that rule the organs of the body; and some people still believe in astrology.

Early in this chapter we said that the Arabs came out of Arabia a rough and simple people, eager for knowledge. We have mentioned some of the things they learned and some of the things that were accomplished under their rule. The Arabs themselves were changing. Within a short time they had given up their desert ways. After a century they were

living in great cities, Cairo, Damascus, Bagdad, and Cordova in far-off Spain. The streets of these cities teemed with the traffic of caravans and were lined with the shops of merchants displaying beautifully woven cloth and rugs,

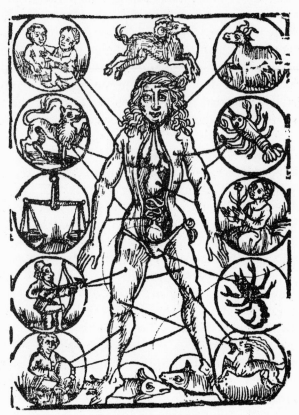

Astrological influence.

delicate metal work and jewelry, glassware, pottery, and sweetmeats. Under the shade of canopies the merchants and their friends sipped what was to become our lemonade and "soda water," for the Arabs were the first to use drinks flavored with essence of rose and lemon and spices. In the

shaded courtyards of private homes were wealth and luxury and comfort. There were beautiful public buildings, hospitals, schools, and colleges. These were the times told of in the *Arabian Nights*, the times of merchants, and princes, and emirs, and viziers, and caliphs, and wizards, and genii. This was the time of the great Caliph, Haroun Al-Raschid.

Turn to the pages of the *Arabian Nights* and you will find mention of the medical knowledge and science that we have been talking about. There is the tale of Abu Al-Husn and his slave girl Tawaddud. The young man, having lost his fortune, intended to sell her to the Caliph, who, to test her knowledge, asked her questions concerning religion, philosophy, astronomy, music, and medicine. The medicine that she glibly told of was the medicine of Galen.

Through Greece, Rome, Byzantium, Arabia and so into Europe wound the devious channel of the stream of medical knowledge. But there was one thing peculiar to Arabian medicine that distinguished it from all that had come before; it grew out of a characteristic of Eastern people. The Arab and the Persian loved to dispute, but they were not greatly concerned over the subject itself—merely the argument. Quibbling among them was a sort of game in which shrewdness and cleverness and subtlety were more admired than truth and solid fact. They split hairs, but often they made no real impression on the substance of the matter. Something of the Arabian love of argument as a substitute for the search for facts was, as we shall see, carried over into Europe with Arabian medicine.

Some of this showiness, this cleverness, this trickiness even, was admired in their doctors. And so we find that many Arabian physicians were tricksters who puffed up their own reputations by pretending to perform marvelous cures on men whom they hired to pose as patients. Sometimes a physician sent around confederates to find out what they could about sick people so that when he came, he would appear to have profound knowledge.

But along with the ostentatious Arabian physicians there were also many who were sober, earnest, sincere men. The names of two of them in particular have come down through the centuries. One was Rhazes and the other Avicenna.

Both these men were Persians and their real names were Abu Bekr Mohammed ibn Zakhariya Ar-Razi and Abu Ali al-Husain ibn Abdullah ibn Sina. But we shall continue to call them by Latin names—Rhazes from Ar-Razi, and Avicenna from ibn Sina.

Rhazes lived between the years 860 and 932. He devoted his youth to studying philosophy and music, and turned to medicine many years later. But his fame as a physician grew rapidly, and soon we find him called from his native city of Raj (the Razi of his name) to take charge of a new hospital that was to be built at Bagdad. His first task was to select the place where the hospital was to be erected. In making his choice, so the story goes, he hung up at many points about the city large pieces of meat and then watched them to see which would be the last to spoil. That place he chose for the site of the hospital, in the belief that the air there was better than at any of the other sites. Of course he knew nothing of bacteria or infection, but he must have realized that putrefaction and disease had something in common. The realization that this common element was bacteria came nearly a thousand years after the time of Rhazes, and with it came modern sanitation, the use of antiseptics, and all the sterile procedures that make modern surgery possible.

Rhazes is remembered only in legend for his association of disease and putrefaction; his contributions to medicine were his descriptions of the symptoms of disease. He was the first to thoroughly describe those of smallpox. He also wrote a book on the treatment of disease, following Galen's methods closely. It was in wide use in Europe as late as the seventeenth century.

Avicenna, called later "The Prince of Physicians," lived between the years 980 and 1037. He was, according to story,

one of those phenomenal young men whose brilliance seems almost superhuman. At ten he knew the Koran by heart; next he perfected himself in philosophy, law, and mathematics. At sixteen he turned to medicine; at eighteen he was famous as a physician. Thereafter his way led through the courts of the emirs; sometimes he had good fortune, sometimes bad; sometimes he was vizier and chief minister of state; sometimes he had to flee for his life in political turmoils.

Avicenna wrote extensively on medical matters. Galen was his authority, and like Galen he wished to make medicine into as sure and exact a system for treating disease as mathematics is for solving a problem in its field. His system had all the defects of Galen's and more besides, but since people like systems, even wrong ones, his writings were widely popular in Europe for centuries after his time. Indeed the medicine of Europe was to become very largely Galenic medicine interpreted by Avicenna.

None of the Arabian physicians dissected the body; their religious beliefs forbade this practice. Nor did they undertake surgery when they could avoid it. Indeed Avicenna taught that surgery was inferior to medical practice and was to be carried on by men of lower social rank.

This belief of his was also widely accepted in Europe years later, and so surgery was left to barbers, executioners, bathhouse keepers, and strolling fakers. The distinction between the superior physician and the inferior surgeon persisted until well into the seventeenth and eighteenth centuries.

Another thing that Avicenna taught and that was widely accepted was that the cautery—a red-hot iron—should be used in surgery instead of the knife. It seems a rather brutal thing to burn wounded and injured people, and that is exactly what a famous surgeon of the sixteenth century thought when he discarded the practice. We shall tell the story of this man, Ambroise Paré of France, and his adven-

tures in war in a later chapter. But perhaps Avicenna was right and Paré wrong. The fire hurt frightfully and made terrible wounds, but it also killed the bacteria that caused infection, in a time when no one knew of the use of antiseptics. It is probable that more men died of infection when cautery was given up in surgery than when it was in use.

It is curious that Rhazes should, without knowing the reason, connect putrefaction and disease, and that Avicenna, also without knowing the reason, should strongly advocate a kind of antiseptic against infection, heat. If only they or the men who followed soon after them could have seen deeper and recognized the truth that lay just behind these two things, medical progress might have been hastened by centuries.

But the men of Europe to whom we now turn saw only what was written in words—the words of Galen, Rhazes, and Avicenna.

CHAPTER XII

Medicine Follows the Crusades

WE have told how the followers of Mohammed, sword in hand, fought for the glory of Allah. They conquered an ancient civilization; they united it; they stimulated it to progress.

And now in the West much the same sort of change was taking place, but more slowly. Religion there also was turning to the sword to drive men into union.

The Christian religion in the days of the Western Roman Empire had taught submission—"Love thine enemies." But centuries had passed since then; in the intervening years the Cross had passed from the hands of the martyr to be borne as the banner of the warrior.

Let us trace briefly this changing attitude and see its consequences.

When Constantine moved the capital of the Roman Empire to Byzantium, the center of the Christian church remained behind at Rome. The Bishop of Rome was recognized as the head or patriarch of the Church, the Pope.

Although the Western Empire fell, the center of the Church still remained in Rome. Indeed the patriarch of the Church took over added powers and dignities as the representative of all the spiritual forces of Christendom. From the Pope in Rome emanated the influence which controlled the monks of the monasteries scattered over feudal Europe. Missionaries preached the Christian religion to the barbarians. Christianity spread, slowly, steadily. The barbarian rulers became converted to the faith; with them the Pope held overlordship as the leader of all Christians.

Thus Christianity gradually became the unifying force, the one thing in common, the controlling power over the scattered domains of Europe.

With religious unity there grew political unity. Kings were rising. The lands from Belgium to the Pyrenees were united in the Frankish kingdom, which was steadily becoming a Christian domain. But in one respect the Franks failed to develop the unity of the followers of Mohammed in the East. The universal language of the Mohammedans was Arabic; in the Frankish kingdom the people of the western half, present-day France, spoke dialects of Latin; those of the eastern half, now Germany, retained the language of the Germanic barbarians. Language was in time to be the insurmountable barrier to complete unity of the countries. But in those years from the fifth to the middle of the ninth century the different lands were held, though not very firmly, under the rule of the Frankish kings.

In the year 800 there came to the throne a man named Charles. On the day of his coronation he was crowned by the Christian church not as king but as emperor of the whole of Christendom. His only superior was the Pope. Charles the Great—or Charlemagne—was the warrior of the Church. His wars of conquest were wars for Christianity; with the sword he converted the barbarians. Christianity had become a warlike religion. What the followers of Mohammed had done in the East, the followers of Charlemagne were now doing in the West. The Arabs had said to the peoples of ancient civilizations, "Yield to Allah or die"; the Christians of the West were saying to the pagans of the Rhinelands, "Become Christians or die."

While Charlemagne conquered in the West, the Caliph Haroun Al-Raschid ruled in the East. These two, so stories tell us, were friendly; it is even said that Haroun Al-Raschid sent Charlemagne the keys to the Holy Sepulcher.

But friendship was not the force that was to bring the East and West together, to cut the channel for the westward flow of medical knowledge. It was to be war, and war in the cause of religion.

Haroun Al-Raschid allowed Christians, if they wished,

to visit the Holy Land, the early home of their religion. The stern rule of the followers of Mohammed had become relaxed; luxury, riches, political strife, had weakened a once rigorous, stern people. The Arabs had been nearly swal-

The medieval way of wrapping a baby.

lowed by the civilization they had seized. But off to the northeast, in Turkestan, Mohammedanism throve in the vigorous warlike form that Mohammed had preached. The Turks were far less civilized than their fellow Moslems of Syria, Palestine, Egypt, and Spain.

The closing centuries of the first thousand years after Christ were times of shifting populations and constant migration. So also were the opening years of the next millennium. In 1066 William led the Norman conquest of England; five years later the Turks descended upon Asia Minor and stormed the very gates of Constantinople.

The Holy Land was now in the hands of an intolerant

people, unfriendly to the Christians. No longer could Christian pilgrims visit Jerusalem; the Sepulcher was desecrated by the infidel. So the forces of militant Christianity turned for the first time to the East. A religious war was to be organized; all strife among Christians was to cease, and they were to unite under no political rule but under the banner of all Christendom to seize the Holy Sepulcher from the infidels.

Princes and knights were to put on their armor and followed by their men at arms go to war with the Moslems. Chivalry in its flower was to strike at the Saracens.

But that is not quite the way the matter turned out, for a peculiar character appeared among the people, preaching not a war but a true crusade. Into town after town of Germany and France there rode on a donkey a barefoot man clad in rough garments and bearing on his shoulder a huge cross. This was Peter the Hermit. He described the tortures of Christians who attempted to make pilgrimages to the Holy Land, and the profanation of holy ground.

During 1094 and 1095, the years that Peter the Hermit preached, there had been a famine and an outbreak of an infectious disease in Germany. People were excited; his words wrought them to a fever pitch. In great bands, without leaders, without food, without arms, with no plan except to reach the Holy Land, multitudes of people started eastward. The first two bands reached Hungary and were massacred there by the inhabitants. A third broke up in the same country. The fourth and fifth led by Peter reached Constantinople; they crossed the Bosporus and were slaughtered by the Turks in 1096.

The following year the first organized crusade moved in military fashion eastward and took Antioch after a long siege and then Jerusalem.

The Turks, aroused, fought to recapture the conquered lands; new crusades went forth. For two hundred years the

Knights of Christendom struggled back and forth across the Holy Land.

We need mention here only one crusade, and that formed no part of the channel through which the medical knowledge of the East came to the West. But it gives an idea of

Pope Urban preaching the Crusades.

the excitement of the times and the barbarity of the people. It was the Children's Crusade—a dreadful affair. A crowd of many thousands of boys from France and Germany left their homes to conquer the Turks and rescue the Holy Sepulcher. Those from France were lured on board ships by slave traders at Marseilles and sold in Egypt; some of those from Germany reached Italy, but most of them died on the way. It may have been from the story of the Children's Crusade

that there has come down to us the legend of the Pied Piper of Hamelin Town who, to the tune of his pipe, led the children away in a great crowd.

The Crusades were directly and indirectly responsible for the first feeble revival of medicine in the West. But not all the changes that resulted were favorable to medical progress, and we pause first to tell of two things growing out of them that retarded rather than advanced medicine.

You will remember that in the West after the fall of the Roman Empire medicine became monastic; that is, the monks acted as best they could as doctors, and the monasteries were often places of refuge for the sick. Among the barbarians of Germany healing was largely in the hands of the women of the tribes. In the towns of the Frankish kingdom there were strolling peddlers, mountebanks, who pretended to be surgeons and dentists; but there were really no good doctors, except occasional ones among the Jews who came as immigrants from Arabia. Unfortunately Christians were forbidden to employ Jewish doctors.

In the monasteries some of the monks studied medicine, but their only textbooks were the few manuscripts that had been preserved. Most of these they could not use, for without special schooling they were unable to understand the complicated works of Hippocrates and Galen.

In their stead the monks used merely books of recipes, herbals, and the simpler sort of medical books intended for home remedying, such as those of the rhizotomists.

As late as the tenth century there was no chance at all in the whole of Western Europe for a man to obtain an education in medicine except at a place in Italy called Salerno, of which we shall tell more shortly. Even if men outside the Church could have become trained doctors, they would have had difficulty in practicing. These were rough times and poor ones; the common people had little money with which to employ physicians; the knights, the feudal lords, and the members of royalty were uneducated and often intolerant

of failure. If a physician did not succeed in effecting a cure he often had to leave town quickly. Many a peddler who pretended to be a doctor lost his life, or, what was more common, had his eyes put out for rashly promising to cure some irritable nobleman, and failing.

In 580 Gutram, King of Burgundy, killed two surgeons because they could not save the life of the queen when she had plague; in 1337 John of Bohemia threw a surgeon into the river Oder because he failed to cure him of blindness.

The priests alone were free from risk in their charitable medical work, but in the year 1163 a law was passed by the Church which limited their efforts and, quite unintentionally, brought surgery into disrepute. The monks sometimes performed crude operations; there was, so the officials of the Church thought, a possibility that by accident a monk might, in his efforts at surgery, cause the death of some man —a very unpleasant responsibility for a Christian monk. Therefore, with the good intention of preventing such an occurrence, an edict was issued beginning with the words, *Ecclesia abhorret a sanguine*—the Church abhors the shedding of blood.

The edict went wide of its mark and was interpreted as meaning that surgery was not approved of, was not respectable—an idea, you will recall, that the Arabs also held.

In 1300 there was another edict, equally misread, that brought opposition to anatomical dissection. Pope Boniface VIII decreed that whoever dared to cut up a human body or boil it should fall under the ban of the Church. The ruling was intended to prohibit a practice which the crusaders occasionally used. When one of their number died in a far off country, his companions sometimes cut up his body and boiled it in order to obtain his bones, which could be easily carried back to friends at home for burial. The rule of the Church against this custom was understood to mean that there should be no dissection for medical study.

These two edicts, detrimental as they were, were more

than compensated for by benefits to medicine that arose from the Crusades. The greatest of these was the founding of many hospitals.

Men were wounded in the battles in the Holy Land; many more became ill during the journeys. You will remem-

A Hospitaler.

ber that Christians had peculiar ideas in regard to the sick and injured. In primitive times, in Greece and in Rome the diseased were looked upon with some contempt; they were disregarded, they were unlucky people, often outcasts. The strong and healthy man did not help the feeble and ill; it would have been a sign of weakness if he had. But the Christians believed that illness and pain brought man nearer to

God. The sufferer was a privileged person; he who helped him shared in his privilege and made himself more Christ-like. Christianity established the principle that to help the sick and needy is a sign of strength, not weakness.

To care for the men diseased and wounded during the Crusades, religious orders were founded, such as the Knights Hospitalers, and the Teutonic Knights. The men of these orders wore distinguishing costumes, and, like the Benedictines of recent times in the Alps, sometimes used dogs to help in their rescue of the wounded. They did valiant work in the Holy Land, and returning home, established hospitals on the lines of march and in the towns where they stopped.

We must not think of these places as being like modern hospitals—far from it. They were usually rough buildings with straw on the floor instead of beds. Food and shelter were given to the people who entered, but very little medical care. Patients with all sorts of illnesses or with none were mingled together, for in those days there was little knowledge of the way in which infectious diseases were spread. Eight diseases only were regarded as contagious: bubonic plague, tuberculosis, epilepsy (which is not contagious), the itch, erysipelas, the cattle disease—anthrax—the eye disease—trachoma—and leprosy.

Leprosy was connected with the Crusades. In speaking of the great epidemic of plague in the time of the Emperor Justinian of Constantinople, we said that a chronic disease such as leprosy could be spread even by slow travel. It can of course be spread still faster by rapid travel. Leprosy had come into Europe from the East at an early date, but now, with the passage of men back and forth from the Holy Land, it became widely prevalent. It spread just as it did among the Hawaiian Islanders after they began to trade with China.

Hospitals were erected by the monks to care for the lepers and to keep them from coming in contact with well people. These hospitals were called lazarettos, after Lazarus, the

leper of the Bible. How widely prevalent leprosy became you can judge from the fact that in France alone there were 2000 of these lazarettos and in England more than 200. The isolation of lepers which began 800 years ago eventually wiped out the disease in Europe, save for a few small centers of infection which still persist, mainly in the countries of Scandinavia.

Hospitals thus grew up as a result of the Crusades, and so did medical schools.

Earlier in this chapter we said that when the Crusades began there was only one place in all Europe where any medical education could be obtained and that was Salerno, a town near Naples.

Just how or why or when that tiny school was founded there no one knows. The only certain records we have of it are of a time when it came into prominence during the Crusades. It happened to be on the line of march to the Holy Land.

The School of Salerno was not part of a monastery; it was probably the first nonecclesiastical center of education in all Christian Europe. There in that little seashore town, known to the Romans as a health resort, a spark of Greek and Roman medicine had persisted in spite of the fall of the Western Empire. It was a feeble spark, but just at the time the Crusaders were marching it was fanned into a meager flame by a man named Constantine of Africa.

Constantine was born in Carthage about the year 1010. He traveled through Arabia and even India and learned the medicine of these lands. When he returned to Carthage, he was looked upon with suspicion because of his knowledge. He was thought to be a wizard, a doer of black magic, and was driven from the city. He fled to Salerno, disguised as a beggar. The King of Babylon, so the story says, passing through Salerno, recognized him and raised him from his lowly position. At any event Constantine finally found his way to the monastery of Monte Cassino and became a monk.

Since he knew both Latin and Arabic, he set himself to the task of translating the Arabic works of medicine into Latin.

Thus it was that some of the books of Galen and of Dioscorides made the short journey from Rome to Salerno by the roundabout way of Arabia. But in this journey the Greek and Roman writings had taken on the flavor of the East. The medicaments were spices; the methods of surgery, the knowledge of anatomy, were those which the Syrians and Persians of Arabia had used.

Under the influence of Constantine of Africa medicine began to flourish at Salerno. The doctors there wrote and rewrote the medical knowledge of the past and added to it some of the things they observed.

Even in the days of Constantine of Africa the bands of Crusaders began to pass through Salerno. The town's fame spread. Wounded knights and nobles came there for treatment. They carried away tales of the new medicine, and soon schools were started in other cities, recruiting their teachers from Salerno.

There are many legends, more indeed than facts, surrounding the history of the School of Salerno. One of these legends, although it is not at all true, is perhaps worth retelling, for it illustrates the kind of medicine that was practiced in Europe in the eleventh, twelfth, and thirteenth centuries and even later.

According to the story—and remember it is only a story—which we have copied from an old medical book: "Among the visitors of distinction who honored Salerno with their presence was Robert, Duke of Normandy [a son of William the Conqueror] who, having gone among the first Crusaders to Palestine and having been wounded there in the arm with an arrow, came to Salerno for medical advice in the year 1100 accompanied by his wife Sybillia, daughter of the Count of Conversana, a lady of distinguished beauty and accomplishments, for whose sake Robert had sacrificed his

chance of succeeding to the throne of England on the death of his brother, William Rufus, by wearing away his time with her in Italy when he should have been on his way to England."

After that long sentence let us say parenthetically that

Constantine of Africa.

there were no doctors or surgeons with the Crusaders. Robert was shot through the arm with an arrow and the wound became infected from lack of care. A little iodine put into the sore might have saved him a trip to Salerno, but iodine or any other antiseptic did not come into use until late in the nineteenth century.

To continue:

"Robert's wound had, from neglect, degenerated into a running sore. Upon a consultation among the medical men of Salerno, it was decided that the only means of extracting the poison which prevented the wound from healing was by sucking it out [wound sucking was sometimes a part of the surgeon's trade in those days!] could any person be found bold enough to undertake the office. The high-spirited and

Scene at the medical school of Salerno.

generous prince refused to listen to the proposal of a remedy which threatened the operator with danger; but the advice of the physicians coming to the ears of his wife whose affections were wedded with her hand to her husband, she resolved not to yield to him in generosity; and, taking advantage of an opportunity when his senses were locked in slumber, she extracted the poison from his wound with her own mouth, and thus rescued from the grave, at the price of her own existence, a husband without whom she felt the gift of life would have been valueless."

Very romantic! But even if Sybillia had carried out this unpleasant task, she would not have died in consequence; the old belief that infected wounds were poisoned has, of course, been given up. The point we want to make with this story is that this was what surgery was like in Europe 800 years ago.

The tale goes on to say that when Robert left Salerno, cured of course, the doctors wrote for him a medical book which he could give to any physician treating him in order that the doctor might have the last word in medicine of the year 1100.

The book actually exists, but it was not written for Robert; in fact it was probably written a century and a half after he died. It is called the *Regimen Sanitatis Salernitanum*, which translated very loosely means: A textbook of hygiene from Salerno.

It was probably the most popular medical book ever written. It was copied and recopied; and when printing came into use, it went into more than two hundred editions. It was still popular as a home health book in the time of Queen Elizabeth, and was in fact translated into English by her godson, Sir John Harington, and probably used in the education of the English royal children.

The book itself was written in Latin, as in the West, for reasons of which we shall speak in the next chapter, Latin was used by all doctors. It was composed in the form of short verses. In the days before printing, books were very scarce and very costly, and so the students were forced to memorize them. And verse is easier to learn by heart than prose.

Even today there are a few lines well worth remembering from this old book. One couplet goes thus:

> *Joy, temperance and repose,*
> *Slam the door on the doctor's nose.*

And another:

> *Use three doctors still, first Doctor* Quiet
> *Next Doctor* Merry-man, *and Doctor* Diet.

Here is a verse that reminds us of Galen and his herbs:

> *Six things, that here in order shall ensure,*
> *Against all poisons have a secret power,*
> *Pear, Garlick, Reddish-root, Nuts, Rape, and Rue,*
> *But Garlick chiefest; for they that it devour*
> *May drink, and care not who their drink do brew;*
> *May walk in airs infected every hour.*
> *Sith Garlick then hath power to save from death,*
> *Bear with it though it make unsavory breath;*
> *And scorn not Garlick, like to some that think*
> *It only makes men wink, and drink, and stink.*

And still another verse:

> *If in your teeth you hap to be tormented*
> *By means some little worms therein do breed:*
> *Which pain (if heed be taken) may be prevented,*
> *By keeping clean your teeth when as you feed,*
> *Burn Frankincense (a gum not evil scented)*
> *Put Henebane unto this, and onion seed,*
> *And in a Tunnel to the Tooth that's hollow,*
> *Convey the smoke thereof, and ease shall follow.*
> *By nuts, Oyles, Eels, and cold in head,*
> *By Apples and raw fruits is hoarseness bred.*

The belief that toothache and cavities are due to worms that eat away and rot the tooth just as worms do apples is a very ancient idea. It probably dates back to Egypt and Babylon; it appeared in the Roman medical books in the first century after Christ; and it was in the hygiene of Salerno a thousand years later. And here finally to complete its course is a line or two from an advertisement for a tooth

powder published in the year 1724 in a magazine called *The British Journal*.

"The Incomparable Powder for cleaning the teeth, which has given great satisfaction to most of the nobility and gentry for above these twenty years. Sold only at Mr. Palmer's Fan Shop in St. Michael's Church-Porch, Cornhill, Mr. Markham's Toy Shop, at the Seven Stars under St. Dunstan's Church in Fleet Street and nowhere else in England. It at one using makes the teeth as white as ivory, never black or yellow. It wonderfully cures the scurvey in the gums and kills worms at the root of the Teeth, and thereby hinders the toothache."

Medical knowledge and medical errors flowed through the same roundabout channels—primitive, Egyptian, Greek, Roman, Arabic, and finally European. And now in our story we are approaching the days when in Europe new knowledge is added to the old knowledge which has been regained. But before we leave the Middle Ages to come to the Revival of Learning, and the Renaissance, we must pause to describe life in the medieval cities and in the medieval universities and record another great epidemic of disease—perhaps the greatest—the Black Death and its fantastic companion, the Dancing Mania.

Part Five

TOWN AND GOWN

THE BLACK DEATH

THE MENTAL CONTAGIONS

CHAPTER XIII

Town and Gown

THE Revival of Learning and the Renaissance mark the beginning of a true scientific advance in the West. The Renaissance, which was at its height in the sixteenth century, did not spring up suddenly, fully under way. It grew slowly. There were important events in the twelfth and thirteenth centuries, the centuries of the Crusades, leading up to it. In these years the feudal system gave way to central rule, cities grew in size and number, and the great universities of Europe arose. Each of these events was a step toward the Renaissance from which our own progress has sprung; each had its influence directly or indirectly on medical matters.

You will remember that we mentioned the feudal system when we told of the fall of the Roman Empire. Feudalism arose then because there existed no central government strong enough to protect the common man, the small land owner, the farmer, the laborer, the merchant. Unable to defend himself against robbers, against invaders, against anyone in fact who wished to seize his lands, his goods, or even his family, he was forced to seek aid of some strong, rich neighbor, a great land owner, or a nobleman. In return for protection the feudal lord made lesser people his vassals, if they were gentry; his serfs, if they were laborers. The price of protection was paid by vassals in military service, by serfs in labor and shares of crops. Europe was dotted with these feudal domains, often hostile one to another. Under such conditions there could be little travel, little communication, little trade, and no general education at all.

In time, as we have said, kings gradually gained in power; they conquered the feudal lords, one by one over a period of

centuries, and made them their vassals. The kings became the supreme feudal lords.

Slowly central rule was again established; the nobles lost in power, but remained privileged characters of social importance. Their rights passed on from father to son in an hereditary nobility. Likewise the lot of the common man changed; if he had land, it became his own to be passed on to his sons. He ceased to be a serf and became a peasant or a merchant or a free craftsman. He still paid taxes to his lord, but now he paid in money, no longer in personal service. Money could be used to hire soldiers. In early feudal days when the lords went to war, each one, followed by his vassals, had formed a separate army unit. Under central rule the peasants stayed at home and worked their farms, and the fighting was done by professional soldiers.

With the breakdown of the feudal system and the rise of central authorities, trade and travel and communication increased. Cities grew in size and number. They could flourish only with the growth of a merchant class, the free farmer, and free craftsman.

When the Romans had inhabited Western Europe and fought there with the barbarians, they had built cities surrounded for protection by high stone walls. These walled cities and many new ones now became the market places to which the farmers of the outlying districts brought their produce for sale and where they bought in turn the merchandise of the traders and craftsmen. There were, of course, no factories in those days; each craftsman carried on his work in his own home. There were indeed few factories until late in the eighteenth century, when steam power came into use. But great churches were erected in the medieval towns, and the universities so important to our story of the progress of medicine grew up.

The conditions of life in the cities of the twelfth and thirteenth centuries were much the same in the fourteenth, fifteenth, and sixteenth. These conditions have significance

for our story of medicine and show us how disease goes with filth and vermin.

Cleanliness was not regarded highly in medieval Europe. The pagan Romans in the time of the Empire, at least those of the wealthy class, had been a cleanly people. Indeed they

A domestic scene in the Middle Ages—
removing head lice.

had made a luxury of bathing. Cleanliness, the care of the body, was to them a matter of comfort and pleasure. The early Christians in opposing the demoralizing luxuries of the pagans had also opposed the idea of cleanliness. Dirt and filth were to some of them indications that they ignored worldly matters and the flesh in order to develop the spirit. There were Christian saints who, to show their holiness, actually boasted that they had never bathed. And cleanliness in the Middle Ages was still looked upon as a sign of weakness and worldliness and luxury. It was not until the

modern discovery that bacteria are the cause of infection that there was any scientific reason given for cleanliness. In the last seventy-five years the civilized world has returned to the cleanliness and sanitation of the Romans, not only for the sake of comfort, but for the sake of health.

With our modern ideas of what a city should look like and smell like, the medieval cities—if we could see them now as they were five or six hundred years ago—would appall us. Those walled cities were unbelievably dirty. They were crowded. The streets were crooked and narrow; the second stories of the buildings projected over the sidewalks so far that the shop signs on opposite sides sometimes touched. The windows had no glass in them; some were merely barred, others were covered with oiled paper. There were no fly screens, and multitudes of flies crawled over the walls and ceilings, over the food on the table, and rose in a buzzing cloud when anyone walking on the rushes on the floor disturbed them in their feast of filth. There were no ice boxes in the kitchens, no running water piped to the houses, no bathrooms in the homes, and no sewers in the streets. The streets were the dumping grounds for all refuse. Each year, with the accumulation of filth, their level rose higher and higher. Hogs wandered about, rooting in the bubbling mire for refuse thrown from the shops and houses. Citizens often shared their homes with their horse or cow. In some places there were city herdsmen who each morning rounded up the squealing swine and drove them outside the walls of the town to feed on the pasture land. Pigs and pigpens were a normal part of the domestic scene of the city. The first regulation against allowing swine to wander on the streets was passed in 1281 in London; and the first to prohibit keeping swine in town was passed in 1481 in Frankfort on the Main. Leipzig followed in 1645. It is said that an occasional hog might be seen wandering on Broadway in New York City as late as the middle of the nineteenth century.

If you had gone into a prosperous home in a medieval walled town, you would have found the handsome, courteous, devout, but not well bathed, gentlemen and ladies living, and happily, in the midst of filth. You would have seen rushes strewn on the dining room floor, a few plates on the table. For the most part the food was served on slices of bread and eaten with the fingers and a knife—there were no forks. Refuse from the table was thrown on the floor to be eaten by the dog and cat or to rot among the rushes and draw swarms of flies from the stable. The smell of the open cesspool in the rear of the house would have spoiled your appetite, even if the sight of the dining room had not.

But manners have changed under the influence of modern medical discovery! Because of the danger of spreading disease, to spit on the sidewalk or in any public building is now against the law; spitting is, in consequence of changing custom, regarded as ill mannered. But it was not so in the days we are telling of here. There was no connection known then between the secretions of the body and the spread of disease. Saliva was thought to be a healing fluid. Pliny tells of its use in treating many diseases. And Christ, you will remember, used saliva mixed with dust to cure a man of blindness. In medieval times to spit anywhere and in any place was no more ill mannered than to cough or sneeze, and people then did not cover their mouths with their handkerchiefs when they coughed.

In fact handkerchiefs were not much in use. Neither for that matter were underwear and nightgowns and sheets. Men wore chiefly leather garments; women, dresses of heavy cloth. Only the wealthy had beds; ordinarily people slept on piles of straw. But there was one thing shared by all, rich and poor alike, and that was vermin. The houses and the inhabitants as well were overrun with fleas and lice. By our standards these medieval cities were horrible places in which to live. And the farmhouses of those days were no better.

It is little wonder that in such surroundings disease flour-

ished. In the thirteenth century the great epidemic of the
Black Death, which in one great wave was to wipe out
nearly half the population and leave the people broken and

A medieval professor of medicine.

demoralized, was slowly but relentlessly approaching the
walled cities. But before the epidemic came, the greatest
gift to us from medieval days had been made; the universities had been founded. Education had started to revive.

After the collapse of the Roman Empire, Western Europe
sank to the lowest point in the history of its intellectual life.

The period from the sixth to the ninth century has been called the Dark Ages. Europe during this time was isolated from the civilization of Byzantium and the East. Knowledge survived only in the monasteries, and even there education amounted to little more than literacy in most cases.

The monks of the monasteries of early medieval days could read and write. But few other men in Western Europe had mastered even the rudiments of an education. It was Latin that the monks used, for the services of the Church and the text of the Bible itself were in this language. The dialects of Latin and the Germanic tongues had not yet become written languages.

So rare was the ability to read and write in those days that a man with these simple accomplishments was given under the laws special privileges, called benefit of clergy. That is, he had the right to be tried before a Church court for any crime except treason. There were two kinds of courts of justice, one conducted by the Church and the other maintained by the town or state or nobleman. The Church, or ecclesiastical, court did not decree capital punishment, for the Church abhorred the shedding of blood. Except in case of heresy, for which men were burned, its penalties were usually very mild. The civil courts ordered the death penalty freely and for crimes that would seem to us rather minor offenses. As late as the eighteenth century, robbers, pickpockets, and counterfeiters when caught, were hanged; men of noble rank were spared this ignoble mode of death and beheaded instead, but usually only for political crimes.

Benefit of clergy was almost permission to commit murder with impunity. And this privilege, if you wish to call it such, was granted to men who could read and write. In those days the educated man was a cherished citizen.

It was the Emperor Charlemagne, he who united the countries of Europe in the eighth and ninth centuries, who first made an effort to extend education. He could probably read; it is doubtful that he ever learned to write. But he

decreed that there should be schools established in the monasteries of his realm. These monastic schools were the forerunners of the universities which sprang up in the twelfth and thirteenth centuries. Up to the time of Charlemagne it had been believed by Western Christians that much education was inconsistent with godliness. Charlemagne broke down this belief and made it possible for young men to study the seven liberal arts. The first three of these, the *trivium* as they were called, were grammar, rhetoric, and logic. Of these, logic was held in highest esteem. The remaining and less important four, the quadrivium, were arithmetic, music, geometry, and astronomy. The astronomy was really astrology; the arithmetic was very simple and elementary.

A teacher of any of these subjects might be called a *doctor scholasticus*, but usually the term doctor was reserved only for the men who taught logic. Finally, when the universities expanded, the degree of doctor was given to students who graduated in law and theology. But it was not until the fourteenth century that the term doctor came into use in medicine. In America as late as the eighteenth century physicians used only the title Mister.

The term university has likewise gone through changes in coming to its modern usage. The Latin word *universitas* was first applied to a corporation or guild of students. Sometimes the group moved from one place to another—and where the group was, there was the university. The actual site of the university, its buildings and its grounds, was called a *studium generale*, meaning a place where students came together from all directions.

As the country was opened up for travel, especially after the Crusades, the students came from many countries, often over long distances, to these medieval *studia*. They spoke different languages and dialects. Partly for that reason, but more because of the association of teaching with the Church, Latin was used as the common spoken and written language

in the universities. A boy wishing to enter a university first
went to a school of Latin; often his entrance examination to
the university consisted in presenting his case to the rector
in acceptable Latin and answering in the same language any
questions put to him. Once enrolled in the university, he
was usually required to speak only Latin, even when at play.
Often there were spies, called *lupi*, or wolves, whose duty
it was to detect for punishment those students who thought-
lessly spoke in their native tongue.

Students were not very different in behavior from those
of today, if one may judge from the regulations of the old
universities; there were solemn edicts against bringing bean
shooters into schoolrooms, pouring water on the heads of
people in the street below, whispering in class, and, as the
old rules say, against "heckling the public hangman in the
execution of his duty." But there was one thing that the
modern student would have missed sorely—and that was
games. They were considered irreligious; no student was
allowed to play ball, race, or even play chess. Exercises with
the sword, the bow and arrow, and the lance were the only
manly sports.

The buildings, too, would have given the modern student
much to think about—great bare stone halls, unheated,
lighted only with torches, and with no glass in the windows.
In the dormitories the students slept on straw piled on the
floor.

Then as now there were self-supporting students. They
earned their way by begging and they also stole. Begging
had been made respectable by sects of monks who supported
their monasteries in this manner; stealing came naturally to
the unruly youths. Anything along the road from university
to university that was not nailed down or tied down found
its way into the hands of needy students. Fortunately for
them they were protected by benefit of clergy.

As a result of the rise of universities, it became possible
for men to be trained in medicine. Soon then there were edu-

cated doctors, but they rarely practiced among the common people; they were in too great demand with the nobility and the officers of the Church.

As a rule these doctors did not perform surgical operations. Surgery was still of the crudest kind and performed

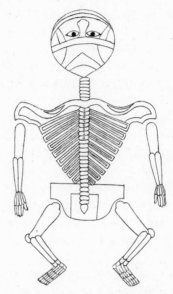

Medieval picture of the skeleton.

only in case of dire necessity. The surgeons used no anæsthetics and no antiseptics, and had little knowledge of the structure of the body, for human anatomy had not been studied since the days of Herophilus at Alexandria.

The physicians looked with contempt upon surgeons; few educated men cared to take up this branch of medical study. During four centuries, from 1100 to 1500, there were perhaps not more than a few dozen educated surgeons in the whole of Europe. These few in turn scorned the uneducated men—the barbers—who did most of the surgery.

The barber surgeons owed their origin indirectly to two

edicts of the Church. Most men of the day wore beards, but in 1092 the Church passed a ruling that monks and priests should be clean shaven. Consequently barbers were trained and kept at the monasteries to serve the clergy. Then in 1163 there came the famous edict forbidding churchmen to perform any surgical operations—*Ecclesia abhorret a sanguine*. So these tasks fell to barbers. They carried out the bleeding so much in use in treating disease, and performed any necessary surgical operations—lanced abscesses, reduced dislocations, splintered broken limbs, and amputated legs and arms. They were even the dentists, for they pulled teeth—there was no other dentistry.

The barber-surgeons, because they did not know Latin and had not studied at the universities, were called surgeons of the short robe to distinguish them from the educated surgeons of the long robe. In a later chapter we shall have much to say of the conflict that eventually occurred between the men of the long robe and the men of the short robe.

The important thing in medicine that resulted from the rise of universities was not the improvement in the practice of medicine, but the fact that medical education had been revived. That step was of itself a great advance over conditions that had existed earlier.

But there were peculiar limitations imposed upon medical study. Men could study Pliny and Dioscorides and Galen and Avicenna, but they were not allowed to question them. Everything in medicine had been settled by those authors; no new facts were to be sought, no new truths found. Under such conditions there could of course be no advance in medical science. And this stationary state of affairs in medicine was only one aspect of the whole approach to learning in the period.

In earlier chapters we have described how philosophy may act as a guiding influence and direct men toward or away from the path that leads to truth. The philosophy of primitive men led them to believe that disease was due to

spirits, to supernatural causes—false beliefs. The philosophy of Hippocrates and other great Greeks led to the belief that disease was due, not to supernatural, but to natural causes that could be found out by observation, reduced to almost mathematical rule, and so brought under control. This philosophy guides the beliefs of the doctor and the scientist of today.

The attitude of the Middle Ages, so far as medicine was concerned, lay almost midway between these two extremes. It was an attempt to combine the natural and the supernatural, to work out a system which would explain both. It was not science; it was speculation.

The supernatural was stressed in all medieval scholarship that had its origin in the monastic schools that Charlemagne had founded. The monks depended for knowledge almost wholly on the writings of the Christian saints whose works had become part of the New Testament. These men were concerned with spiritual matters, not with science or natural history. The monks followed them in believing that everything in the world was under the direct influence of divine control. Disease was due to the wrath of God and the sins of men. It was to be controlled by prayer and penance. In spite of the beautiful sincerity of these religious beliefs, the guiding medical philosophy was not at all different from that of primitive peoples. God, the saints, and their opposing force, the devil and his legions, had merely taken the place of the forces which brought good and ill fortune to the savage.

Knowledge of the natural world came almost entirely from fragments of the writings of the ancient Greeks and Romans. In medical matters, the words of Galen, of Pliny, of Avicenna and of Dioscorides became nearly as authoritative as the words of the Bible. It was sinful to doubt Galen even if his statements disagreed with common sense and common observation.

Aristotle had said quite mistakenly that women had fewer

teeth than men; in the Biblical story of creation, Adam lost
a rib and therefore men had one less than women. These
statements were accepted in spite of the fact that all one
had to do to disprove them was to look in the mouth and to
run a finger down the ribs. Men did not seek for truth even
in this simple way. They viewed the world not with their
own eyes but with the eyes of authority.

The task of the medieval scholar was not to add new
knowledge to what was given him by his authorities but to
codify and systematize their statements. With the help of
an elaborate training in logic, all sorts of tricks were devised
to make the authorities agree and to explain away their contradictions. Galen said one thing; Aristotle seemed to say
the opposite, while Pliny held a third view on the subject,
Avicenna perhaps a fourth, and the writings of a Christian
father presented a fifth. In reconciling the differences the
medieval logician started with a general proposition, let us
say: "Plague is an act of God." Then he collected the statements of the authorities on the subject. One had seen plague
follow earthquakes; another attributed it to air poisoned by
the fumes of volcanoes; a third considered it a Job-like penalty sent for the torment of mortal flesh; a fourth had seen
it spread from man to man in an army but spare the inhabitants of an island only a short distance away, and so on and
so on. Finally, after he had cited all the authorities the
scholar came to the most important part of his dissertation,
the argument. He carefully scrutinized and weighed each
word, each statement of the authorities. Where did it fit into
the scheme of the whole; what figurative interpretation
would it yield? In the end, by one way or another, each
authority was made to justify the general proposition.

Earthquakes and volcanoes were acts of God, and anything that resulted from an act of God was likewise an act
of God. In smiting the men of the army with plague, God,
in His infinite wisdom, had taken this means to direct political destiny into the beneficial channels which subsequent

events showed that it did take. And so on and on, until the conclusion finally emerged that, as shown by the authorities, the ways of God were manifold; His acts took diverse and infinite forms; the plague was an act of God.

The imperfect observations of ancient doctors had to be reconciled not only with each other but with the prevailing

Legal torture.

supernaturalism. Whether or not we now consider such a task worth doing, it was a tremendous undertaking, one which men found so fascinating that for centuries it entirely occupied their attention. They were too preoccupied with speculation of this sort—their system of scholasticism—to check the truth of ancient observations or to make new ones for themselves. Medical study in the Middle Ages was largely a matter of recapturing the knowledge of the past; only the spirit of observation which had made this knowledge possible was still lacking.

As time went on the medieval scholar obtained more manuscripts, more authorities, sometimes from an occasional

traveler and translator such as Constantine of Africa who went to Salerno. And on the Crusades, the men of the West met at first hand Eastern scholars versed in the science of the time. They marveled at the science of the Moslems. They obtained badly garbled translations of the *Natural History* of Aristotle; they secured more of the works of Galen and Pliny. But the writings of these men had passed through many hands before they reached the Christians; in the copying, recopying, and translating they had been altered and mixed up. To the West also came the medieval writings of Avicenna and with them his astrological beliefs. All these things had in turn to be worked over and made to harmonize with the general propositions.

The greatest mills were the universities. There the authoritative beliefs which were proper for Christians to hold were ground out by the clever argument and refined by the hair-splitting logic of medieval scholasticism.

To us, with our freedom of thought and our skepticism, such an attitude is almost incomprehensible. But remember that these men were not trained as we can be today; their beliefs were very different. All education from childhood onward, in the home, the school, and the Church, was dominated by the belief that life on earth was only a brief preparation for a future that might be vastly better or vastly worse. A heaven of infinite peace and security and a hell of everlasting torment were vividly real and ever-present in their minds. It did not follow that they were well behaved and free from vice—far from it. They were often turbulent, immoral, and cruel. But sins of the flesh could be forgiven if penance were done; such sins were mere individual weaknesses of frail mortals for whom God had compassion. Sins of thought were a different matter. To doubt, to disagree, was heresy. Heresy threatened the security of the Church, and undermined the very foundation of Christian faith. It must be met with the severest penalties. For heresy men

were excommunicated, even burned—and assured of hell everlasting.

Ignorant of methods of observing and recording facts such as Hippocrates used, men felt that magic and sorcery were the only ways of winning power over nature and securing knowledge of its secrets. But sorcery and magic were heresy, they were sinful.

The fact that medical matters, and indeed everything scientific, became involved in the theological beliefs of the times made medical progress impossible. When as late as the sixteenth century Andreas Vesalius, a Belgian of whom we shall have more to say later, showed the true anatomy of the human body, a great cry was raised against him for daring to disagree with Galen—the great "authority." When in the same century the astronomer Copernicus dared to say that the earth revolved about the sun, he was made to recant by Church dignitaries who knew from their authorities that the world was the center of the universe. When a whole century later William Harvey of England showed that the blood circulated through the arteries and veins, his work was denounced: Galen and Aristotle—the authorities—had said otherwise!

If progress in the science of medicine could not be made in the days when the minds of men were fixed exclusively on spiritual matters, it was equally impossible in those later years when they looked to the past and believed firmly in established authority.

From the fall of the Roman Empire until beyond the thirteenth century—nearly a thousand years—there is no advance in medical science to record in Western Europe. There were humanitarian advances like the hospital. There were scholastic advances like the university. But medical advance, no. It was a period in which the men of the West, with their eyes in turn on the heavens and on the past, sought to adjust themselves to the world they were living in. And now even the slow process of accumulating the knowl-

edge of the past was to be interrupted, for in the fourteenth century there reached the walled cities, the monasteries, and the universities that great sweeping wave of death—the bubonic plague.

CHAPTER XIV

The Black Death

ONE of the great marvels of the universe—so it seems to us—is that man appeared upon earth. It is an even greater marvel that he has managed to survive. Stronger, tougher animals than he have been exterminated in the hard struggle for existence, yet he has lived on and multiplied. He has survived not because of his physical strength but because of his superior intelligence.

The world that early men met, as we have said in an earlier chapter, was rough and terrifying. Life was severe, because man was ill suited physically to cope with its hardships. There were great beasts to prey upon him in his comparative defenselessness; there was uncertainty of food supply; there were diseases.

Man conquered the beasts; his physical strength was less, but his intelligence was greater than theirs. To defend himself he used what no other animal has ever used—weapons: the club, the knife, the spear, the bow and arrow, and, finally, the gun. And he was successful. His only unconquered "enemy" still existing is his fellow man, on whom he has so many times turned his weapons in the useless slaughter of war.

The same superior intelligence that prompted mankind to the invention of weapons led to the discovery of means for insuring his food supply. Man domesticated animals; raised crops, mastered the principles of husbandry.

Of the three great hazards to human existence only one then remained beyond control. That was disease. Man's intelligence failed to lead him to success against it as rapidly as against the other hazards. Disease was an invisible enemy, far harder to cope with than the great beasts that

roared in the forests. The spear and the club and the bow and arrow were of no avail against it. The only weapon with which it could be fought was knowledge, the knowledge of how disease is caused and how it can be controlled. It was far simpler to learn the ways of the land, the rudiments of agriculture, the planting of grain, the tilling of crops, than to learn the nature of the thing called disease.

The winning of that knowledge has been slow. What we have been telling and have yet to tell are the steps by which it has been acquired and is still being acquired. It is a story of false paths followed and of obstructions that man has put in the road to his own salvation. The philosophy of supernatural causes of disease was a false path; medieval scholasticism was an obstruction to progress. Fortunately for us, we live in a time when slowly gained, hard-earned knowledge is finally conquering disease. From our position today we can look back over the past and marvel that man has survived on earth. And we can look ahead to the future knowing that if he continues to seek and find knowledge he will win greater and greater victories over disease. His only weapon is knowledge.

As we tell of some of the diseases that afflicted men in the thirteenth and fourteenth centuries, let us at the same time look forward and see when the method of controlling them was discovered and precisely what it was. Often it was a simple thing, seemingly obvious now that we know it, and yet in its absence men suffered and died.

The diseases we shall speak of here are those that came in great terrifying epidemics—almost world-wide outbreaks—called pandemics. We are not yet ready to deal with the diseases that were always present, such as head colds, appendicitis, pneumonia, cancer, and the like. In medieval days there were epidemics of which most people nowadays have never even heard. One of them was called St. Anthony's fire. Sometimes this name was given to the disease erysipelas but more often to a cruel and crippling malady

that appeared oftenest among poor people. There would be a season when the rains were heavy and the summer damp and foggy. The harvest of grain, the rye from which the

St. Anthony and the victims of the "fire."

black bread was made, would be scanty and the seeds spotted with a mildew blight. Then late in the fall, perhaps at the gate of the town, some poor fellow would be found with his legs and arms black and shriveled, trying pitifully

to crawl to the monastery. People would run from him in terror; only the monks of St. Anthony would come to him and carry him to their monastery; they had devoted their lives to aiding such sufferers.

That day the town was quiet; men and women stayed indoors; no children played in the streets. In hushed voices they whispered that the fire of hell, St. Anthony's fire, moved through the land.

Soon in one house and then in another and another a child, a man, a woman would be stricken with the disease. Scarcely a home would escape.

The legs and the arms of the sufferers would grow cold and become frightfully painful. Then they would turn black. Some of the people would die; some would recover; but many of the latter would have lost an arm or a leg which had withered and dropped off. From a few the vicious disease would take both legs and arms, leaving nothing but the maimed trunk and head. It is small wonder that people feared the disease.

But what knowledge did they have with which to fight it? Some men believed that wet weather poisoned the air. The idea that disease was due to evil smells and bad air was very prevalent then; it was one that was to persist until well into the nineteenth century. The disease malaria, common then in Italy and spreading into Western Europe, got its name from the words meaning bad air, *mala aria*. Other men thought that epidemic disease was due to eclipses and falling stars and earthquakes. Some believed that it arose from the anger of God at the sins of men, and some were certain that the Jews had poisoned the wells. In the year 1161 the Jewish physicians in the town of Prague were accused of this crime and burned.

What did men do to control the disease? They prayed; they wore blessed charms; they took the medicines that Dioscorides had recommended in his herbal. But the disease swept on; it maimed and killed in spite of prayers and

charms and medicines. It would last for a year at a time; then the next fall with the new harvest it would cease, unless that year too had been wet and foggy.

We have said that St. Anthony's fire is held in check now by knowledge; it no longer occurs. The cause of it lay before the eyes of the people of those bygone days—lay in a fact already mentioned. It was not until 1597 that men guessed the cause, or until 1630 that they were sure of it. It took two more centuries for that knowledge to be put fully into effect. Then the disease ceased to occur entirely. And the knowledge was simply this: rye with mildew blight from the wet season is poisonous. The blight is a fungus growth of a kind called ergot. Ergot like some toadstools is a poison. Taken in large enough quantities it shrinks the blood vessels for a time until so little blood can flow to the arms and legs that they become starved and die. All men needed to know was: to avoid St. Anthony's fire do not eat blighted rye. Without that simple knowledge they prayed—and were crippled or died. With it today we face a world safe in a victory over one disease—and a rapacious one.

In the Middle Ages the epidemics of disease uncontrolled by knowledge made the average length of life far shorter than it is today. Some men, of course, escaped disease and lived as long as any people live today; but many more died young, while they were still babies or small children. The average length of life then was only about eight years; today it is nearly sixty. In the six hundred years that have passed since then, medical knowledge has added half a century to the average length of life.

In this connection one peculiar fact concerning human behavior has been true in all ages. When life is short and hard and uncertain, it seems to be valued least. In the last six hundred years, really in the last one hundred, men have grown far more humane than they were. We value life more highly today; we attempt more, far more, to prevent suffering, perhaps because we know now that it can be prevented.

In the days when St. Anthony's fire was common, many men and women lost legs and arms. There are old pictures and old wood carvings showing these crippled people. With the victims of the fire are those deformed by leprosy. But in

St. Roch treating plague sores.

that procession of the maimed were many who had been crippled deliberately at the will of men. Wars went on century after century. And those too were the days when the penalties of the law prescribed cutting off a hand or an arm for even slight crimes, and on mere suspicion of crime men were tortured with rack and boot. Next to disease, man has always had himself as his worst enemy.

St. Anthony's fire and leprosy were both great scourges of the Middle Ages, and there were others. What disease would you add to the list? The smallpox that killed its millions? That came later. Its great onslaught was after the fifteenth century; the knowledge for its control came in the eighteenth century. Perhaps you would name diphtheria, which once wrought such havoc throughout the world and killed Napoleon's wife Josephine, and perhaps George Washington. But that disease made its greatest ravages from the sixteenth to the twentieth century. The knowledge by which it is controlled came within the lifetime of the older of us living today. Again you might name tuberculosis, consumption, the disease once called the "captain of the men of death." Yes, it was present, always present, taking toll of the population year in and year out, but it never came in sweeping waves as did the "great mortalities."

Typhus fever was one of these pandemic diseases. The word typhus comes from the Greek and means smoke or a cloud, hence a dimness of consciousness, a stupor. Typhus fever was once confused with another disease—typhoid fever—which is quite different except that in it also there is fever with stupor. The word typhoid means "resembling typhus." But typhus is much more serious than typhoid. Typhus was a disease of war and famine, of prisons and jails and ships and of medieval cities. In war it killed more men than were ever killed with shot and sword. Its cause? People of the Middle Ages thought it an affliction from God; we know now that it is due to a germ carried from the sick man to the well man by body lice. The little typhus, typhoid, is spread by food or water contaminated with sewage. Medical science takes the glamor, the dignity away from the enemy disease and shows it in its crude reality. That bit of knowledge—that typhus is carried by the louse —was gained only in the twentieth century. It came barely in time to prevent the spread of the disease in the World War, the first great war in which typhus failed to take its

thousands and perhaps hundreds of thousands. In the East, in Serbia, there was typhus fever during the War. But the measures of medical science kept it from spreading in an epidemic to the men in the trenches on the Western front. And the means that medical science used was simply the establishing of delousing stations through which all travelers from the East to the West must pass and leave their lice behind. Disease often loses its terrifying aspects when medical knowledge points out its humble lurking places.

But there are still some infections which defy even modern knowledge. One of these came in repeated epidemics in the Middle Ages, and in all the centuries since the pandemics have continued, twenty or thirty years apart. It is a disease that we all know—influenza, the mildest of the great pandemics.

The term influenza is a clue to beliefs concerning its cause in bygone days: *influenza coelestia* was its full name, heavenly influence. Storms and earthquakes, shipwreck and war, comets and rains of blood were given as the causes of influenza. Those occasional rains of blood especially excited the imaginations of the people. They occurred in very rainy seasons; food and linen and even the walls of the houses were marked with tiny red spots like drops of blood. We today, less prone to look to the supernatural for the cause of everything unusual, should say that those drops of blood were a red moldy mildew—nothing more.

But this mildew, unlike that of St. Anthony's fire, had nothing to do with the disease. Influenza is caused by a germ passed from the sick to the well by coughing and sneezing. That we know, but we do not yet know how to prevent the spread of the germ. We still have epidemics of influenza.

It is the mildest of the great pandemics, but if you think of the last great epidemic, the one in 1918, you may be doubtful of its mildness. That year in the United States alone nearly forty million people had the disease; almost three hundred thousand died. Yet that was mild for a pan-

demic. Compare the figures with those that would have resulted if instead of influenza we had had an epidemic of the oriental bubonic plague like the one in the fourteenth century. Instead of three hundred thousand, fifty million people would have died. Every town, every city, every state would in the course of a few weeks have shrunk to half its popula-

The Black Death.

tion. Whole families would have been wiped out. We would not have been able to bury the dead. Bodies would have lain in the streets and in the fields and in the homes.

If such a pandemic should strike our country, our social and business life would be paralyzed. For want of men the factories and the railroads would stop; the fire companies could not respond to calls, fire would spread in the cities. Schools and stores would be closed, the streets deserted; the sick and dying would call for doctors. But half the doctors would be dead. It would take us a century, perhaps longer, to build our country up again after such an outbreak of disease.

This disease was the "great mortality" of the Middle

Ages. Uncontrolled by knowledge, it threatened to exterminate the human race.

We have told of the epidemic of bubonic plague that came to Constantinople in the year 543. But that epidemic did not spread far into Western Europe. At that time, soon after the fall of the Roman Empire, travel and commerce were almost at a standstill in the West. The disease was held in check by the isolation of the people. But by the fourteenth century travel and commerce were active. The countries were overrun with vagabonds; the students of the universities wandered from city to city; bands of soldiers moved across the countryside. It was a warlike century. Gunpowder was first used in battle in 1330; the Hundred Years' War began in 1336. Conditions were ideal for the spread of plague.

In the spring of 1347 the disease, coming out of Asia, reached Constantinople as had the epidemic of 543. By the autumn it had spread to Sicily, and by December to Naples, Genoa, and Marseilles. Early in 1348 it had extended over southern France, Italy and Spain. In June it reached Paris; in August, Britain and Ireland. It took the plague fifteen months to travel from Constantinople to London. But it did not stop there; it spread in all directions into the Netherlands, Germany, Scandinavia, and Russia.

Terror moved ahead of the ruthless march of the plague; its passage left the countries broken, demoralized, nearly depopulated. In the face of overwhelming calamity the customs that held men together grew lax; law and order almost disappeared; human nature followed its own dictates. Some men in panic fled from their families, gave their possessions to the Church, hid in the cathedrals, and prayed until the disease reached and killed them there. Others dashed to boats, sailed out to sea and died on shipboard, and the boats drifted derelict with crews of corpses. A heroic few gave their last days to comforting the sick and dying. Still others gave themselves up to revelry, drinking, feasting, and danc-

ing. Such was the behavior of the people of Jerusalem when threatened with an attack by Sennacherib and his army. It is described in the Bible. "The Lord God of Hosts called to weeping and to mourning and to baldness and to girding with sackcloth: and behold joy and gladness, slaying oxen, and killing sheep, eating flesh and drinking wine: let us eat and drink for tomorrow we shall die."

The Italian author Giovanni Boccaccio, who was one of the first men to write in Italian prose, was living in Florence at the time of the epidemic of the Black Death in 1348. He survived, and in one of his books, the *Decameron*, gives this description of the outbreak in Florence: "Such was the cruelty of Heaven and perhaps of Men [He believes, you see, in the divine origin of disease and yet his story is about a merry group of young people who hid in seclusion in the hope of escaping the disease. Ideas were mixed; God caused disease, but that the disease spread by infection seemed obvious.] that between March and July following it is supposed and made pretty certain that upwards of a hundred thousand souls perished in the city only, whereas before the calamity it was not supposed to contain so many inhabitants. What magnificent dwellings, what noble palaces were then depopulated to the last person, what families extinct, what rich and vast possessions left, and no known heir to inherit, what numbers of both sexes in the prime and vigor of youth —who in the morning Galen, Hippocrates, or Æsculapius himself would have declared in perfect health—after dining with their friends here have supped with their departed friends in the other world."

Disposal of the dead was one of the great problems for the survivors during outbreaks of the plague. At Avignon the Pope consecrated the river Rhône so that corpses could be sunk in it instead of being buried. In other cities they were thrown into the sea—often to be washed back on to the shores with the returning tide.

In these years, because of strife within the Church, the

Pope lived in the city of Avignon instead of Rome. This particular Pope, Clement VI, had in his service the most famous surgeon of the Middle Ages, Guy de Chauliac. At the outbreak of the plague Guy had the Pope lock himself

The Diseases and Casualties this Week.

Abortive	4	Imposthume	8
Aged	45	Infants	22
Breeding	1	Kingfevil	4
Broken legge	1	Lethargy	1
Broke her scull by a fall in the street at St. Mary Wool-church	1	Livergrown	1
		Meagcome	1
		Palfie	1
		Plague	4237
Childbed	38	Purples	2
Chrifomes	9	Quinfie	5
Confumption	126	Rickets	23
Convulfion	89	Rifing of the Lights	18
Cough	1	Rupture	1
Dropfie	53	Scurvy	3
Feaver	348	Shingles	1
Flox and Small-pox	18	Spotted Feaver	166
Flux	1	Stilborn	4
Frighted	2	Stone	2
Gowt	1	Stopping of the ftomach	17
Grief	3	Strangury	3
Griping in the Guts	79	Suddenly	2
Head-mould-fhot	1	Surfeit	74
Jaundies	7	Teeth	111
		Thrufh	6
		Tiffick	9
		Ulcer	1
		Vomiting	10
		Winde	4
		Wormes	20

Christned	Males — 90		Buried	Males — 2777	Plague — 4237
	Females — 81			Females — 2791	
	In all — 171			In all — 5568	

Increafed in the Burials this Week ———————— 249.

Parifhes clear of the Plague ——— 27 Parifhes Infected ——— 103

The Affize of Bread fet forth by Order of the Lord Mator and Court of Aldermen, A penny Wheaten Loaf to contain Nine Ounces and a half, and three half-penny White Loaves the like weight.

A bill of mortality during the epidemic of bubonic plague in England, 1665.

for the duration of the epidemic in a room in which there burned continuously an open fire to purify the air.

Here is Guy de Chauliac's description of the disease from which millions died. He says, "The great mortality appeared at Avignon, January, 1348, when I was in the service of Pope Clement VI. It was of two kinds. The first lasted two months, with continued fever and spitting of blood, and people died of it in three days. The second kind was all the rest of the time, also with continuous fever, and with swellings in the armpits and groin; and people died in five days. It was so contagious, especially that accompanied by spitting of blood, that not only by staying together, but even by looking at one another, people caught it, with the result that men died without attention and were buried without priests. The father did not visit his son, nor the son his father. Charity was dead and hope crushed.

"I call it great, because it covered the whole world, or lacked little of doing so. . . . And it was so great that it left scarcely a fourth part of the people. . . .

"Many were in doubt about the cause of this great mortality. In some places they thought that the Jews had poisoned the world: and so they killed them. In others, that it was the poor deformed people who were responsible: and they drove them out. In others that it was the nobles; and they feared to go abroad. Finally they reached the point where they kept guards in the cities and villages, permitting the entry of no one who was not well known. And if powders or salves were found on anyone, the owners, for fear that they were poisons, were forced to swallow them. . . ."

The swellings that Guy de Chauliac mentions as appearing in the armpits and groin were enlarged and infected lymph glands. A gland so infected is called a bubo—hence the term bubonic plague; plague itself means a blow. In many infections, often in mild ones, lymph glands became enlarged, as do those in the neck from sore throat. When a person had the bubonic plague the glands were not only

swollen, but if the patient lived long enough, they also became filled with pus, broke, and made running sores—plague sores.

The name Black Death was given to the plague because in its victims there appear little hemorrhages under the skin looking like tiny black and blue places—tokens of the plague, they were called.

Guy de Chauliac in his brief description makes one very important statement concerning control of the disease. Perhaps the line caught your attention—"Finally they reached the point where they kept guards in the cities and villages, permitting the entry of no one who was not well known." This was the first time that measures of the kind were put into effect—the first use of quarantine.

The idea of a quarantine which grew out of the epidemic persisted after the plague began to subside. Isolation was for various lengths of time; but beginning in 1383 travelers in ships suspected of infection were held for forty days in the harbor of Marseilles before they were allowed to land in that city. Quarantine means forty. We still use the measure and the name although the term has lost its original significance of forty days; the time of isolation now varies with the disease.

Bubonic plague still exists in the world today; thousands have died of it in this century in Asia. It has even reached our shores, and a few cases have occurred here. But the disease can be held in check, for we now know how it is caused and how it can be controlled. We have knowledge!

The tragic thing about the bit of knowledge that alone keeps us free from plague is that Avicenna, the great physician of Arabia in the tenth and eleventh centuries, came close to guessing it. He observed that before the plague spread, rats and mice came out of their burrows and staggered about as if drunk, and many died. Only late in the nineteenth century did the meaning of his observation become clear. The knowledge by which the bubonic plague can

be held in check is this: it is a disease of rats and mice and ground squirrels—of rodents. It is caused by a germ which rat fleas spread. The fleas bite the sick rat and acquire the germ. They leave the dying rat and with their bite infect other rats—or men.

The great difference between medieval times and our own is not so much in ways of living and acting as in ways of thinking and acquiring knowledge, the knowledge that makes us victorious over disease. We often pride ourselves on our material things: our great inventions, such as the radio and the aëroplane, our great cities with streets filled with automobiles, our great buildings lighted by electricity and heated with steam. But such things would be of no advantage if epidemics like the Black Death could sweep over us. The aëroplanes, the automobiles, the buildings, even the cities would be deserted in the face of the Black Death. We would behave just as did the people of the fourteenth century. Knowledge, medical knowledge, is man's most priceless possession; it is his greatest triumph in his struggle for existence, the struggle for safety, food, and health.

CHAPTER XV

The Mental Contagions

THE fourteenth century was the period of that great pestilence, the Black Death. The fifteenth century was the time of the Dancing Mania, the queerest emotional disorder that has ever affected large groups of human beings. It was a curious prelude to a period of contradiction. The century gave birth to Joan of Arc, and to her strange companion, the monstrous Gilles de Rais, to Leonardo da Vinci, the genius of art and science, and Christopher Columbus, the discoverer of America. The century opened with an epidemic of a horrible emotional disturbance; its close marks the beginning of modern times, for during that century printing was first used in Europe and the Revival of Learning and the Renaissance occurred.

We have said little in our story of how the diseases of individual men may affect the course of history. Everyone's behavior is influenced by physical infirmities and by mental peculiarities, and each of us recognizes that fact in his own actions. But we see it perhaps more clearly and certainly more critically in the actions of others. Usually the behavior of the individual affects only a small number of people, his family and those he meets in daily life. But some men are raised to positions of great influence as generals during a war or rulers or popular leaders, as was Peter the Hermit, who incited the people to the Crusades. Then their peculiarities may affect whole nations, even whole civilizations. The indigestion of a king may influence his policies more than the advice of his counselors; his toothache, occurring at a critical moment, may precipitate a civil war; his mental peculiarities may lead his country to ruin or triumph.

We could speculate on the infirmities of the great and wonder what the course of history would have been had

they been healthier—if Alexander the Great had not died when he was thirty-two; if William of Orange had not had tuberculosis; if Queen Anne's eyes had been stronger; if Louis XIII had not been feeble-minded; if Joan of Arc had

Gilles de Rais.

been a normal-minded peasant girl instead of one who had visions.

Joan of Arc, you remember, was finally burned as a witch, an act characteristic of the times. And Gilles de Rais? It sounds like an anti-climax, but if he had not had his mental peculiarities we, probably, should not have had the story of Bluebeard.

There have been monsters like the Baron of Rais before and since, but the reasons he gave for his actions are, like those for burning Joan, characteristic of the times. Gilles

wished, so he said, to replenish his fortune by magic; with the aid of the devil he sought to find gold.

As a young man he inherited wide lands in Brittany, which had once been a great feudal domain. His career started well; he joined the French king in the war against England. When Joan of Arc led the army to victory, he rode at her side and for his bravery was made a marshal of France. The war over, Gilles returned to Brittany and lived there in the most amazing splendor, lavishing his money on public feasts and entertainments for the people of the countryside. At last, when his fortune was nearly exhausted, he called to his aid the greatest alchemists and sorcerers of the day. Mysterious rites were performed in secret at his castle for the purpose of obtaining the philosophers' stone.

At the same time, in the country for miles around the castle, there occurred a series of mysterious disappearances. Small children, boys and girls of four and five and six and seven, left their homes to carry lunch to their fathers in the fields or to go on errands to neighboring farms and never returned. One such disappearance, even two or three, might have attracted no wide attention in a day when wolves and wild boars inhabited the thick forest; but when the number rose to dozens, scores, and even hundreds, sorrow gave way to excitement and horror. The country was bewitched. Children on the open road, in lane and lot, seemed to vanish into the air. One moment they were there; the next they were gone.

But one thing people noticed. Whenever a disappearance occurred, there had passed through the neighborhood at the time the mounted men of the Baron of Rais. Suspicion was aroused against the tall marshal with the blue-black beard. This was the fifteenth century; human lives were no longer sacrificed without protest at the mere word of a nobleman. The Baron was arrested. The bodies of some of the missing children, horribly mutilated, were discovered. Like savages, Gilles and his magicians had held blood orgies.

Gilles was tried before an ecclesiastical court for heresy and before a civil court for murder. He was found doubly guilty, excommunicated, and condemned to be hanged and burned. He did not fear death, but the penalty of excom-

The Dancing Mania.

munication which carried with it the certainty of eternal damnation in hell terrified him.

When we told of the methods of scholarship of the thirteenth century, we said that fear of excommunication kept men from daring to risk the heresy of free thought. Here in the fifteenth century this warrior, sorcerer, and murderer

broke down and begged in tears that he might die, but not
be excommunicated. His prayer was granted; his confession
was heard, and he was absolved of sin. He was simply
hanged and burned.

Led to the gibbet, he climbed on a high stool; a rope was
passed around his neck; the stool was pushed away. The
faggots about his feet were lighted. The flames mounted
over him and burned the rope. His body fell into the fire. At
this sight the sentiment of the people, even of those who had
lost their children, suddenly changed. A moment before they
had been eager for revenge; now they were softened. Women
from the crowd of spectators ran forward and rescued the
body. It was given Christian burial. On the spot where
Gilles died a shrine was erected. In time a legend grew about
it; it was said to possess miraculous powers. Women flocked
there to pray for abundance of milk that they might nurse
their babies well!

The story of Gilles lived on, but changed in the telling
and became confused with the tale of another monster of
Brittany who lived in the sixth century, Comorre the Cursed.
Gilles's blue-black beard stuck in men's memory. The garbled legend became the story of Bluebeard, written by the
Frenchman Charles Perrault, who also told the stories of
Cinderella and the Sleeping Beauty. What an ironical fate
for the strong and terrible Baron of Rais—that the spot of
his execution should become a magic shrine for mothers, and
the story of his life a nursery tale to amuse children!

The ways of human nature and human behavior and belief are at times seemingly inexplicable. And if in the case
of Gilles de Rais they seem strange, they were even stranger
in the case of the Dancing Mania of the same century.

Perhaps the Black Death may give a clue to the origin of
this strange phenomenon. The graves of the victims of that
mortality were covered, but the memory of the horror remained; it haunted the survivors. A sense of insecurity, of
panic, pervaded the people. The pent-up emotion broke out

first in the town of Aix-la-Chapelle. There, one morning, the inhabitants awoke to find their city invaded by a strange band of people who had come from Germany. Silently, intent only on their own purposes, they walked through the

Music for the tarantella.

streets until they came to an open square. Then, forming in a circle, they began to dance. But it was such a dance as no one in the city had ever seen. Slowly at first and then faster and faster the dancers contorted their bodies, until finally they were writhing and jumping in a frenzy, screaming, their eyes fixed, foam dripping from their mouths. One by

one they fell from exhaustion, but as they dropped their places were taken by the townspeople. The contagion of the Dancing Mania, a mental contagion, one of sympathy, of suggestion, was spread by the mere sight of the dancers.

Along country roads, from town to town, from city to city, went processions of the dancers. Shops were closed, farms neglected. Crowds followed in the wake of the dancers. Some were impelled by curiosity, but some were anxious parents seeking their children. And there were children crying pitifully as they crept among the hurrying feet of the spectators, seeking parents who had joined the dancers.

In 1418 the mental turmoil reached its climax in the city of Strasbourg. The priests of the church tried to comfort and soothe the victims of the mania. The sufferers took St. Vitus as their patron saint. They appealed to him to save them from their own wild outbreaks.

The Dancing Mania occurred five hundred years ago, but the term St. Vitus' dance still survives. It is applied now to a certain nervous disease called chorea in which there is twitching of the face and arms.

There is another word in the language that commemorates this wild outbreak that once spread over Europe. It is "tarantella," the name given to a lively form of Italian music which was originally played for those who were overcome by the Dancing Mania; music seemed to bring relief. Not knowing why they danced, people sought an explanation. They said that spiders bit them, tarantulas, and that the poison made them twist and squirm. The music of the tarantella healed them. This superstition lasted for three hundred years; to treat spider bites the village musicians were called to play on flute and oboe and Turkish drum the whirling music of the tarantella.

The strenuous exertion of the Dancing Mania was merely the physical expression of intense emotional excitement. Similar behavior has often been seen among people aroused

to great religious enthusiasm; the zealous have shaken and trembled and even fallen unconscious. Some religious sects have been named after the queer behavior which marked their earlier days—especially the Shakers, the Jumpers, the Rollers, the Quakers, and the *Convulsionnaires*, not to mention the whirling dervishes.

Most of the mental epidemics, and there have been many before and since the Dancing Mania, have taken some form other than mere purposeless muscular activity. The Crusades to the Holy Lands, especially those incited by Peter the Hermit, and certainly the Children's Crusade, were the outcome of mental epidemics. So, also, years later, was the Tulip Mania that centered in Holland during which, in a frenzy of speculation, ordinarily sensible men paid out their entire fortunes for a few tulip bulbs.

A far sadder epidemic than the latter was the persecution of witches which started in the fifteenth century and lasted well into the eighteenth. Thousands of harmless old women were burned to death or drowned in the belief that they were witches. America was far from escaping the craze. There were men who made a business of witch-hunting, and sought out suspected people, looking for small projections on their bodies called "witch spots." Mob excitement waxed high over witchcraft. In solemn courts of law robed judges listened seriously to fantastic tales worthy of savage and primitive people, and condemned harmless old ladies to death. Many of those were poor insane people who had the misfortune to live in a day when the humane care of the mentally ill had not yet begun.

People in all ages who have lived in tribes or cities or nations have felt the influence of mental contagion. No germ causes it; the mania is not a disease; it is simply one of the manifestations of strange human nature and human behavior transmitted by imitation.

Why is it that one idea or the example of one man may influence a whole group of people and incite them to some

peculiar course of action? Many years ago, in a nunnery in
Europe, one of the sisters began to mew like a cat; soon another and another joined her until all of the inmates were

Killing tarantulas with music.

mewing industriously. Threats of punishment failed to stop
them; they were whipped, but still they mewed on until the
petty mania wore itself out and ceased. In a thousand other
nunneries a sister might have mewed in vain—merely the
butt of ridicule.

Why did the mewing spread in this one nunnery? Conditions, you say, were ripe for it; the mental attitude receptive. Such words mean little. But manias, small and great, are very real. You have seen the milder ones—the sudden success of a fashion in clothing or in cosmetics or in slang expressions, or a wave of enthusiasm for some new popular song which is sung and sung and sung and then dropped and forgotten.

War, perhaps, is the greatest of all the epidemic manias. A wave of excited patriotism, a mental contagion, spreads through a country; men go out to maim and kill their fellow men whom they have never seen. Then the war subsides as the Dancing Mania did; men lose their hatred for their erstwhile enemies; the survivors return once more to peace and international commerce.

Not all mental contagions are bad or foolish; not all of them deserve the name "mania," which means unreasonable excitement. Some mental contagions which spread by example and imitation are good and beneficial. Although contagion always suggests disease, there is no phrase but mental contagion to explain how in a short time the opinion, the attitude, even the guiding belief, of a great body of people may be completely altered. By means of mental contagion Peter the Hermit aroused people to march on the First Crusade.

Great humanitarian reforms, such as the Red Cross agreement to care for the wounded in war time, humane care of the insane and of animals, have been effected by the contagion of an idea, which has spread until it has become accepted and established in ways of living. We shall tell of these advances in their place, and you will see then that although they are good and helpful, they too, like the useless and harmful manias, bear a relation to the mental contagions.

Our present attitude toward the world had its beginnings in a fashion that arose in Italy in the fifteenth century. Near

the end of the fourteenth century men for the first time discovered the beauty of the writings of classical antiquity. At first their attention was held by the Latin authors. But these authors themselves said so much about Greek literature that men were led to learn the language and discover the beauty of Homer, Plato, and the great Greek dramatists.

A wave of enthusiasm for the classics spread through Italy; classical literature and art became fashionable. To be a gentleman meant that a man was acquainted with scholarship and with the works of writers such as Plutarch, Isocrates, Virgil, Cicero, and Lucretius.

What is called a classical education had its beginnings then. In the colleges, the lecture rooms of the teachers of poetry and rhetoric were crowded. But the students did not attempt to follow deeply one single line of learning. Rather they learned a little of everything—a little medicine, a little philosophy, a little art—in order to develop the widest possible culture. They were not experts in anything.

In wealthy families, because of the new learning, tutors were employed to instruct boys in the works of poets and orators in order that they might quote them fluently in polished conversation and write prose and poetry in the ancient Latin style of Cicero.

With the discovery of the beauty of classical style came a wave of enthusiasm for the loveliness and grandeur of classical art and architecture. But men not only admired the technical beauty of style and the art of the ancients. They came for the first time to understand the Greek and Roman way of thinking about life. Greek influence was especially important. The Greeks had, as you recall, conceived life in the fullest sense of its possibilities and glories. Their art showed men and women ideally beautiful but still men and women. Their architecture was practical and direct; its beauty grew out of its very simplicity. The Greeks had looked at life face to face, and had tried to understand the real nature of man and the universe. The men of the Middle

Ages had shrouded all that was human with supernatural mystery; the Greeks had tried to make the supernatural less mysterious by making it more human.

The revival of ancient learning, carrying with it this point of view, opened the eyes of men to themselves and the world about them. Not only were the heavens good but so was the earth; man was good and nature was good; man was born

Illustration from a calendar printed in 1493.

with a right to use nature for his earthly benefit. These were ideas quite different from those held by medieval Christians.

From the intense emotional reaction of the Renaissance, there resulted in Italy some unpleasant social consequences. Men in a desire for earthly experience lost the restraint of piety which they had felt in the Middle Ages. The fear of excommunication which had frightened even the Baron of Rais no longer disturbed the Italian nobleman, who, yielding to the contagion of new ideals, yielded to the bad as well as the good. The somewhat refining experiences that we have gained since that time were lacking. There came a period when Italy was disgraced not only by political intrigue and dishonesty, but also by brutal assassinations and poisoning

at the hands of cultured gentlemen and gentlewomen. It was a period of extreme sophistication, when people had no guiding principles of decency as we know them. Cesare and Lucrezia Borgia and Lorenzo de' Medici made the pages of history bloody with their deeds. But in one thing they differed from the terrible Gilles de Rais of Brittany. He gave way to temptations; he sinned and knew it; he was afraid; he repented. The murderous Italians of the Renaissance flouted religion; they knew no sin; they feared no spiritual vengeance. Their basic ideal was not very different from that of today in some schools for small children; it was to give way to complete self-expression in order to develop all the natural qualities of the personality. Following it, some of the Italians behaved like vicious, spoiled children.

Fortunately these unpleasant by-products of the Renaissance were largely limited to Italy. But the contagion of the spirit of learning, of free thinking, spread through Europe. It was tremendously accelerated after the invention of printing with movable type. Manuscripts copied by hand were inaccurate and expensive; printed books were more accurate and far cheaper. Printing unquestionably was the most important of all agents in spreading the new doctrines of the Renaissance.

Printing began in Germany soon after 1440, and in 1462 the sack of the town of Mainz by Adolph of Nassau drove the German printers to take refuge in the cities of other countries of Europe. Books were being issued from many presses and some of the earliest to be printed were medical works. In 1457 a purgation calendar was printed which told when the stars were propitious for taking a physic. In 1462 a similar astrological work on blood-letting appeared. The writings of Avicenna were printed in 1479 and a year later the first of many editions of the Sanitary Regimen of Salerno.

These were old and well-known books that were merely distributed more widely by printing; soon an entirely dif-

ferent kind of medical work was to appear from the new printing presses. The wave of enthusiasm which led men to collect and translate the manuscripts of pagan poetry and oratory led them also to the classical medical writings. The works of Galen and Hippocrates were translated directly from the original Greek and printed. Men began to see how the words of the masters had been garbled in passing through many translations at the hands of Romans, Syrians, Persians, Arabs, and Hebrews.

The fifteenth century was for medicine a period of the revival of ancient learning. The new ideals of freedom of thought and criticism, which characterized the Renaissance, affected art and literature and politics and religion more quickly than medicine. The physicians of the fifteenth century were busy translating, comparing, learning, and had as yet no desire to work out scientific methods, make observations, and perform experiments.

But in the closing days of the fifteenth century, a single year after the discovery of America by Columbus, a man was born who was destined to awaken the scientific spirit among physicians and to spread the contagion of the Renaissance to the field of medicine. In the one thousand years that have passed since the fall of Rome he is the first European doctor we have mentioned. His name was Aureolus Theophrastus Bombastus von Hohenheim. In those days it was the practice of learned men to take a Latin name, and so he called himself Paracelsus after the Roman physician Celsus, and it is by this name that we shall speak of him.

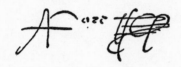

Part Six

PARACELSUS, THE CRITIC
VESALIUS, THE OBSERVER
PARÉ, THE EXPERIMENTER

CHAPTER XVI

Paracelsus, the Critic

EXPLORATION, trade, politics, war, religion, those ancient and dominating figures in the pageant of human history, stormed across the stage of the sixteenth century. And among their hulking shapes what a poor show the actors of medicine and science made; what a feeble voice they raised amid the din of loading ships, of rattling armor, of cries and shouts and exhortations! Medicine: one critic, one observer, and one experimenter. That strange character Paracelsus, moving across the stage with his crew of vagabond students; Vesalius, the courtier, glancing over his shoulder as he dissected in hiding a stolen body; and Paré, the barber, performing amazing feats of surgery on the battlefields of France.

And science? Gentle old Dr. Gilbert, who wrote his volume on that toy new to the West, the magnetic compass, and who was appointed physician to Queen Elizabeth, although he never treated her; she preferred the magic of the royal astronomer to the science of Gilbert. And Galileo, who climbed the leaning tower of Pisa to drop weights and so establish a law of physics and outrage the scholars of his day—for everyone knew that gentlemen settled matters of science by authority and argument, not by experiment.

Those whom we call heroes of medicine and science were humble men, pushed to one side, obscured in the onrush of exploration, trade, politics, war, religion. And why not? What indications were there then that these once lowly fellows of medicine and science would in time become leaders in the pageant of history?

Contrast them—one critic, one observer, one experimenter in medicine in a whole century—with the great men that history records for those years. There was Columbus, who

died in the early years of the century, died without knowing that he had discovered a new continent. After him there trooped to the lands that he had found a procession of swash-buckling Spanish adventurers who tramped over the country, exploring, betraying, killing for the sake of the stream of gold that they sent back to Spain. And Portuguese crews, rotten with scurvy, disembarked from their tiny ships on these new lands. Spain, so the Pope decreed, should rule all the lands of America west of the 50th parallel, and Portugal all the rest. A mighty event, this serving up of a continent as though it was a pie to be divided with one stroke of the knife. That alone dwarfed to insignificance a wandering doctor, a dissector, an army surgeon, a man who played with compasses, and one who dropped stones from a building badly out of plumb.

And trade? What a scramble there was for naval supremacy and sea trade! On the outcome hinged the destiny of nations. Sea power was the key to the greatness of England, and the rise of the British Empire. The only advantage that this commerce held for medicine, a scant one at best, was that the articles dealt in were chiefly drugs. Medicaments were the lightest, safest, most valuable cargo a ship could carry. Two ducats worth of cloves from the Moluccas brought eight hundred ducats in London. And there was cinnamon to be had from Ceylon; aloes and pepper from Cochin China; ginger and benzoin from Sumatra; nutmeg and mace from Banda; camphor, musk, and rhubarb from China. Spices we call them now, but they were medicines then; they were the native herbs of the East that Rhazes and Avicenna had added to the medicaments of Dioscorides. But with them were powdered "mummy," odd stone-like concretions from the intestines of goats, and the horns of narwhals, to be used in treating disease. This was the drug trade. In the ships of the explorers came coffee and tea and tobacco and potatoes. Coffee and tea were used to treat "acidity," tobacco was a medicament of which many a six-

teenth and seventeenth century physician wrote in highest praise; the potato sold for fabulous sums to cure disease and weakness. Gold and silver and drugs were the cargoes of that time—and human beings. The days of plantations were opening in the New World. The first African negroes were brought to the West Indies in 1502.

As for religion—this was the century in which Luther preached a Reformation, a century made bloody with religious strife. Men were exiled, tortured, slaughtered, not for the sake of Christianity, as they had been in Charlemagne's time, but for the sake of freedom of belief within the Christian religion.

In politics Machiavelian intrigue and war joined their bloody hands. Off to the East Suleiman the Magnificent ruled from Bagdad to Hungary. He besieged Vienna. But more important to the European kings and queens and princes and nobles than this outside enemy were their own intrigues. In England the much married Henry VIII held the throne, then the feeble and tuberculous Edward, next Bloody Mary, and finally Elizabeth. In France reigned Francis I, one of the few great kings ever captured and ransomed; next Henry II, who died in a tournament from a lance wound in his eye; then the feeble sons of the intriguing Florentine, Catherine de' Medici. In Spain and Germany there was that strange character whom no one understands very well, the Holy Roman Emperor Charles V, who ruled over nearly half of Europe and fought against the other half, whose troops sacked Rome to obtain their pay, and who as an old man finally turned over his kingdoms and his wars to his son Philip II in order that he might have leisure to eat like an epicure and worship like a monk. It was Philip's Armada that was sunk in the English channel.

Exploration, trade, politics, war, religion held the center of the stage. True there were in the background medical matters that now and again obtruded into the affairs of even kings and princes. There were four great pandemics of influ-

enza, one wide outbreak of the plague and a dozen or more minor ones. Typhus appeared in the camps of the armies and broke out in the law courts, where it spread from the prisoners to the judges and jury and spectators and killed without regard for rank and dignity. These terms of court were afterwards called the Black Assizes. Diphtheria spread through Spain and the Rhinelands. More and more each year smallpox was branding the people with its pitted marks. And although men did not recognize the fact, the pneumonia that we have today was then starting its great increase.

Where were the doctors to hold in check not only these terrifying diseases, but the other invisible enemies, the common diseases, the croups, the consumptions, and all the infections that crept unceasingly across the baby's crib, through the schoolroom, the home, the church, the ship at sea, the camp of war—and crept unhindered?

The physician of the sixteenth century, though trained in a university, knew no more what a disease really was than did the savage. Theories he learned in books; some helpful treatment, some valuable remedies, some beneficial surgery he found there, but mingled with them always the false theories of the past. These were his guides—the theories of the four humors, of the planets that controlled the functions of the body, of plethora that led to treatment by bleeding, the theory of colors, and the theory of numbers.

Dignified and scholarly physicians sat in consultation rooms strewn with strange relics which would have delighted a befeathered medicine man—stuffed alligators, narwhal horns, and bizarre animals from the New World. Through the heavy leather-bound spectacles of the day they peered at yellowed manuscripts and drew astrological charts, made their diagnoses and prescribed a medicine of a hundred ingredients without perhaps ever having seen their patient.

The educated surgeon, dressed in his long robe, disdained to touch the wounded man. With his cane he pointed to the place where the barber surgeon should cut.

Such doctors as these were not for the common people. For them there were quacks and tinkers, bathhouse keepers, strolling mountebanks, and old women. Failing these, there were the holy shrines where hope and prayer and faith brought ease of mind and suffering as they had in the temples of Æsculapius. But the shrines stopped no disease; dis-

Paracelsus.

ease was most rampant when faith in shrines and holy relics was the greatest.

Neither physician nor surgeon nor quack knew the human structure; few had seen inside the body; none had studied it. None knew the simplest facts of physiology— how the blood circulates, why man breathes. None had heard of bacteria.

The physician of the sixteenth century lacked knowledge. But his greatest fault was his failure to seek knowledge.

Instead he was content with his cherished authorities, those newly translated volumes of Galen, written thirteen hundred years before. He had to break with the past before he could turn to the future, before he could advance. And to shake him from his reverence of the antiquated a critic was needed who would sow the seeds of dissatisfaction.

The man destined to this rôle, the idol breaker, was Paracelsus.

He was born in the rough mountains of Switzerland, of a German father and a Swiss mother. The father was a physician, a lover of nature, a botanist. He named his boy Theophrastus after the first botanist, who had been a pupil of Aristotle. The revived learning of the ancients had spread from Italy across the Alps.

When the boy Theophrastus was ten years old, the family moved to the town of Villach in Austria. This was a mining region where there were iron smelters. Young Theophrastus watched the miners at their work and learned the principles of metallurgy and of chemistry, just as in his Swiss home he had learned the principles of botany.

And then about the time that the popular Prince Hal was mounting the throne of England as Henry VIII, Theophrastus went to college to become a scholar. He made the slow journey to Italy, where at Ferrara the teacher Leoniceno had recently translated from the Greek some of the writings of Hippocrates.

Theophrastus was educated after the manner of all medical students of those days. He did not, as the modern student does, spend long hours in the dissecting room, in the laboratory, and at bedsides in the hospital. Instead, he studied from books of the ancients, of Hippocrates and Galen and Avicenna, and spoke, read, and wrote Latin. He read the classical orators, poets, and grammarians; the geographers, historians, and philosophers. He had a classical education, tinctured, but only tinctured, with medicine. When he had completed his training, he was well equipped

to translate further works of the ancients and to dispute over their theories and their philosophies, but he was sadly equipped indeed to help his suffering fellow men as a physician or to contend hand to hand with the enemy disease.

However, in his short life Paracelsus was not destined to lead the sheltered and unreal existence of the scholar of medicine. Why was this so? We shall never know, but men have speculated as to the reason he became a critic; and it is a harmless speculation. Most investigators have concluded that his early training in Switzerland and his observations in the mines of Austria had made him too free and independent to be content with classrooms where there flitted only the ghosts of great men and of great observations. He wanted realities. These things are true no doubt, but there is more. The destinies of men are not shaped wholly by what men see and hear, but also by what is in them at birth.

Theophrastus was made of rebellious fiber. He was born to stand alone and lead, not follow. In war perhaps he would have been a doughty, impetuous, violent, and unruly hero. But he chose medicine. There was no battle to be waged there; all was submission to authority.

The schoolroom held him for a few years and then he was free. There was much to see in the world that the ancients had never dreamed of. He would see it. He threw away his scholarly costume and traveled far and wide as a simple wayfarer. Here then was a rarity, a trained scholar associating with common people, listening to them. Barber surgeons, bathhouse keepers, wise old women who treated the peasants, confided to him their funds of practical knowledge. These were things that the professors in the schoolrooms, getting their noses dusty in ancient tomes, had never heard. A mass of superstition, but mingled with it here and there sound knowledge made from observations by keen eyes unblinded by long reading of the old manuscripts.

Paracelsus had seen the miners break away the useless rocks from the rich ore. Like them he separated the useless

from the valuable. He listened, he observed, he thought; and there grew on him the conviction that there was much error and much nonsense in the theories of the ancients. Hippocrates alone had been a true observer. The others had made theories. The students in the classrooms were being crammed with traditions which, for all the polished language they were written in, were as false as the superstitions of the garrulous peasants.

As Paracelsus' ideas changed during his travels, so did his manners and his speech. He found the rough native tongue better suited to his palate than the Latin of his school days, and the vulgar company of the tavern more to his liking than that of gentlemen. He was coarsened, roughened. He no longer disputed; now he fought to prove to the dandified scholars that the traditions of their medicine were false. He wrote not in Latin but in German, so that all his country-men might learn what disease really was and how actual experience taught that it should be treated.

What he wrote seems to us now nearly as remote from the truth as were the theories of the ancients. Paracelsus for all his critical attitude was a product of the early sixteenth century. He believed in astrology and spirits (in fact he said he always carried one about in the hilt of his sword) and salamanders that walked through fire unscathed. He believed that nature had put on every plant the signature of the disease it would cure. He believed in weapon ointment, and here, perhaps, more clearly than anywhere else, we see his peculiar mixture of practical common sense, observation, and mystical nonsense. It was commonly believed that to cure a wound the healing ointment should be put not on the wound itself but on the blade of the weapon that caused the wound. The wound was left undisturbed or merely wrapped with linen. Paracelsus had observed that wounds actually healed better when treated this way—and he had observed correctly. But his ideas led him to find an explanation in a mysterious supernatural force which radiated from

the weapon to the wound. His theory was wrong; his observation right. The ointments intended for wounds were made up of filthy ingredients, often bits of decayed animals and even dung. A wound healed better when the ointment was applied anywhere else than upon the wound.

The experience that Paracelsus had had in the mines of Villach led him to use mineral substances for medicines. Revolting against the herbs that Galen had employed, he prescribed iron, sulphur, mercury, and mineral waters. It did not disturb him in the least that the ancients gave no authority for this kind of treatment. He believed in many things, but he did not believe in authority.

Out of his writings on the use of simple mineral remedies there grew in the next century a great conflict in medical practice—the conflict between the doctors who believed in Galenical herbs and those who followed the lead of Paracelsus. The herbs were largely useless; they were also harmless. The mineral substances were often beneficial; but they might also be poisons and grave harm might, and often did, follow their excessive use.

It is not, however, the fact that Paracelsus introduced new methods of medical treatment that makes him a hero of medicine. His greatest contribution lies in his criticism of authority, his breaking with the past. Even his new remedies helped do that.

In his wanderings he had seen much, thought much, written much. It was time now to get his books published. With written words for his cudgel, he would beat the authorities into submission; bully them out of existence—all except Hippocrates. Hippocrates was a man after his own heart. The slavish nincompoops (Paracelsus would have used some such word, probably a less polite one) of medicine, those scholarly doctors who believed that truth was to be found only in the traditional doctrines, should see how a man of brains, a man who trusted his own senses and his own reason went about settling the problems of medicine.

Getting books published was no easy matter. But Paracelsus was lucky in this respect—for a little while. You will
remember Galen's good fortune when he came to Rome and
was called to treat Eudemus. Paracelsus stopped his wander-

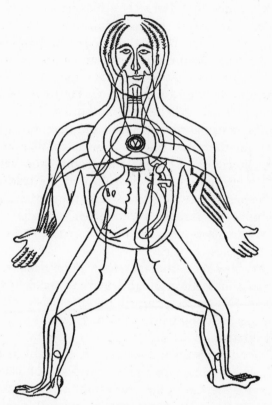

The nervous system as shown in a medieval manuscript.

ings and settled in Strasbourg, but his fame as a doctor who
succeeded where others failed reached to the town of Basel.
In Basel there was a wealthy printer by the name of Frobenius, who had for a long time suffered with a pain in his
foot. His physician recommended that his leg be cut off.

Operations in those days, of course, were done without anæsthetics, without antiseptics, and without adequate means for controlling the hemorrhage. Frobenius decided that before he submitted to the operation he would consult the doctor of Strasbourg who boasted so boldly of his successes.

Paracelsus went to Basel. He treated the leg; to the joy of Frobenius the pain went away. This fellow Paracelsus for all his rough exterior was no mere braggart.

With an influential patron now, Paracelsus could not only get his books published, but, as seemed fitting, for a man of his attainments, he could have the position of city physician and teach in the University as well.

Here at last was Paracelsus back in scholarship. Scholarship had not changed, but Paracelsus had. He would show these dry-as-dust delvers into books how medicine should be taught. He would tell them what he thought of them even before he started to teach. So he published a pamphlet not in scholarly Latin but in German, in order that all literate men might understand the great reform that he was going to bring about.

"Who is there who does not know," he wrote, "that doctors of today make frightful mistakes and greatly harm their patients? Who does not know that this is due to the fact that they cling firmly to the teachings of Galen, Avicenna, and such men?" I, Paracelsus, on the contrary "elucidate with industry and to the great advantage of all who will hear me, from books on the practice and the theory of medicine written by myself. I do not, like other medical authors, make these books up out of extracts from Hippocrates and Galen, but in never ending toil I create them anew upon the basis of experience, the supreme teacher of all things. If I want to prove anything, I do not try to do so by quoting authorities, but by observation and trial and reasoning. . . ."

This pamphlet was a bomb exploding in the scholarly precincts of the sedate University. There was no precedent

in the ancient authorities prescribing how to deal with such behavior, but for once the professors needed no authority. They would throw out this bullying quack. He could not stay at their University.

But Paracelsus did stay—for a time at least. And what is more—a then unheard-of thing—he gave his lectures not in Latin but in German, the native tongue, the vernacular, as would be done today.

It is said that to impress his students with his contempt for authority he publicly burned the books of Galen and Avicenna.

In his lectures he told the students the practical and useful observations he had made; but he told them also his vague and mystical theories of disease. And, becoming excited, he challenged the authorities of antiquity and bullied his students. He, Paracelsus, alone of all men, knew medicine and the way to truth in medicine. The truth was not to be found in the teachings of the learned doctors of the universities. "All the universities," he declared, "have less experience than my beard; the down on my neck is more learned than my auditors." And on another occasion, he said, "You must follow in my footsteps; I shall not go in yours. Not one of you [the professors] will find a corner so well hidden but that the dogs will come and lift their legs to defile you. I shall become monarch; mine will be the monarchy over which I shall rule to make you gird up your loins. . . . You will eat dirt."

Vulgar, crude, egotistical—but mingled with his raillery there was profound wisdom.

During his short stay in the University his students failed to appreciate the real meaning and significance of his words. They laughed at him, ridiculed him, and finally lampooned him in a scurrilous poem posted on the door of the lecture room.

Paracelsus, the exponent of freedom, amazing as it may seem, turned to the city council for protection against his

own students. But his bad manners counted against him. He treated the judges of the courts as contemptuously as he had the professors of the University. He was the great Paracelsus; they mere foolish, useless men of no consequence. He actually and sincerely believed this; it was his way of thinking.

In disgust at the treatment he received, Paracelsus left the University. If men would not listen to his words in lectures, they would read his words in books. He would write and demonstrate that the authorities themselves were men no greater than other men—certainly not as great as Paracelsus.

At the age of forty-eight he died. His enemies, and they were many, have said that he was killed in a drunken brawl, that he was deformed and physically abnormal; all that we really know is that he died, and we can be very sure that he died sadly misunderstood.

Who cared that in 1541 a vulgar man who boasted to his students and railed at his betters passed away? This was the century of great things—of exploration and trade, of kings, and princes, of wars and conquests; who cared that the first of the modern doctors died?—for Paracelsus was the first modern doctor. His ways were as different from those of the doctor of today as his times were from ours. But underneath his rough exterior he had the spirit of the modern doctor, the spirit of truth, progress, observation, independence, and self-reliance.

CHAPTER XVII

Vesalius, the Observer

IN 1514, when Paracelsus was twenty-one, a son was born to the Imperial Court apothecary of His Majesty the Emperor Charles V. The baby was christened Andreas. The father's family, though living now in Brussels, had come originally from Wesel and had taken as their name a Latinized form of this town—Vesalius. The boy, Andreas Vesalius, was destined to become the first critical observer in modern medicine, the father of anatomy.

How often the things we do in our youth affect our after life! Or is it that we do them because of something peculiar within ourselves, something in us that remains there all through our lives and shapes our actions in maturity as well as in youth? In the boy, can we see the man that is to come? I think so.

Young Vesalius, like most keen boys, had a hobby. It was a queer one, so it seemed in those days, but one that since then has fascinated many a budding young doctor. His hobby was dissection. Mice, and frogs, and even cats and dogs were his playthings; and he investigated them with that same irresistible desire to see what was inside that makes a modern boy take apart the mechanical toy and alarm clock. One can almost hear the voice of Andreas' nurse or tutor raised in protest—such nasty dirty things for a young gentleman to soil himself with—and always to be grubbing into the insides of rats and mice, and carrying them in his leather pouch!

Boys were not different then from now, nor were parents and nurses. And hobbies? Fortunately they existed then and still do—one of the most priceless things in any boy's life. Pity the poor mortal who has not some engrossing, soul-consuming interest!

Bloodthirsty, depraved, this hobby of dissection? Certainly not. What Vesalius saw in dissection was not blood and gore, but nature itself; his mind seethed with curiosity. The mangled rat, the half-skinned mouse to such a boy is a thing of beauty far beyond the flowers of the field. And it was in pursuit of his beloved study of anatomy that Vesalius went to Paris to the great school of medicine and to the greatest disappointment of his life.

In Paris in the year 1533 anatomy was taught, not by careful dissection, but instead as it had been in the Middle Ages by that old doctor of Bologna, Mondino de' Luzzi, who called himself Mundinus.

Before the opening of the Christian Era, the study of human anatomy died in Alexandria with Herophilus. Galen wrote a book of anatomy, an elaborate one, but he had not dissected the human body; there were religious reasons to prevent. Instead he used pigs and oxen and monkeys. But, being Galen and very sure that all God's creatures were created much alike, he did not admit that he had never dissected man himself. So when the Arabs translated his works, they stated positively that the things he described were all in man and had the shape and form he said they had. Galen described all the anatomy that any man need ever know—so thought the doctors of the past. But Mundinus held that a dissection, a demonstration now and then would make the facts stick better in the student's mind. And so early in the fourteenth century there began the first human dissections since Alexandrian days. The bodies used were those of condemned criminals, and at most only one or two were available to a medical school in a whole year.

The way in which the dissections were made was this: the professor of anatomy sat on a raised platform. Seated before him were the pupils. At his feet was the body and beside it a barber surgeon. The professor read aloud from Galen, and as he named a part of the body the barber surgeon pointed to it. In the days of Mundinus the affair—it would be ab-

surd to call it a dissection—took up only four class periods.
Today a medical student may spend on dissection four hours
a day for a whole school year.

Andreas Vesalius.

The way that Mundinus had taught anatomy, more than
a century before, was the way it was being taught when
Vesalius came to Paris. In his disappointment he called the
dissection he saw "an execrable rite." A careless barber sur-

geon mangled a body and an indifferent professor mumbled lines from Galen. It wasn't a dissection; it was a farce.

Vesalius was forced to study medicine as the other young men at the school did, but he wanted to study it differently. He wanted to do what no one in medicine had yet done. He wanted to specialize, give most of his time to one subject, anatomy, study it thoroughly, and become an expert. He made a vow that he would devote all his powers to the revival of anatomy and strive to reach a perfection of dissection, description, and understanding of the human body equal to that of the ancients.

From that very statement you see that Vesalius believed firmly that Galen's dissections and his descriptions were of human anatomy. This is a point to bear in mind, for his discovery later that Galen had not dissected human beings was the great turning point in his life.

As a young man in Paris Vesalius and a group of fellow students fired by his enthusiasm for anatomy searched through graveyards for bones—in those days coffins were of wood which rotted and the cemetery land was used century after century, so that sometimes a skull or a leg bone or an arm bone found its way to the surface; you will remember Hamlet and the skull over which he soliloquized. So thoroughly did Vesalius study the chance bones he found that he could identify each one by the mere sense of touch when he was blindfolded. But he had no such opportunity for studying the organs of the body or the muscles and nerves and blood vessels.

Twice he sat on the student benches and watched a barber surgeon hurriedly point to the main organs of the body while the professor recited snatches of Galen. On the third occasion—thanks to his zeal for anatomy—he was allowed to take the barber surgeon's place. But this was not dissection; this was merely a peep at those fascinating structures which he longed to study as he had studied the bones.

In 1536 war between France and Spain and Germany put

an end to Vesalius' schooling in Paris. His father, you will remember, was attached to the court of Emperor Charles V. Andreas went to Louvain to continue his studies. It was there that the most picturesque event of his life occurred.

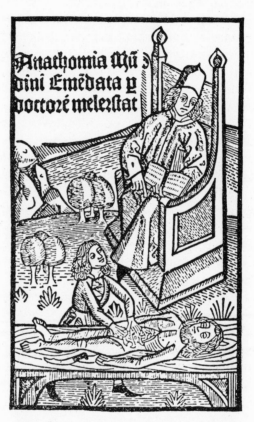

Title-page of the Anatomy *of Mundinus.*

In the dead of night he stole a skeleton from the gallows outside the city walls, the skeleton of a convict hanged in chains and left hanging, according to the custom, as a warning to all malefactors. If he had been caught in the act, he would no doubt have shared the same fate.

He spent a year in Louvain, and then went on to Venice. There he met a fellow countryman named Jan Calcar, a pupil of Titian, who could paint so adroitly that his work could hardly be told from that of his master. The two young men went on together to Padua. There at the University Vesalius completed his medical studies and received his doctor's degree. The day after he graduated he was made professor of surgery and anatomy. He was twenty-three years old.

In the following year, 1538, to aid his students, Vesalius published his first book of anatomy. It consisted of six large plates showing the skeleton, the blood vessels, and the organs of the body. His friend Calcar drew the pictures.

Now here is the peculiar thing about these pictures. The anatomy shown was exactly as Galen had described it. The breast bone of the skeleton had seven segments; the spleen was oblong in shape; the liver had five lobes. Vesalius had not seen the structures in this form in the human bodies he had examined, but who was he to compare his brief experience with the master, the great authority, Galen? Vesalius could be wrong—Galen never.

But as he conducted his dissections day after day in Padua, sometimes secretly on a body which he obtained we know not where, his wonder mounted, his perplexity grew. In all the bodies that he dissected the structures seemed the same, but they were not as Galen had described them.

And then one day in the year 1541 he found the answer to his dilemma. He was dissecting a monkey. On one of the vertebræ of its spine he noticed a small projection of the bone. That projection he had not been able to find in the vertebræ of human beings. Yet Galen had described it. Galen then had not dissected human beings, but only beasts. In all the centuries in between men had believed that it was human anatomy that Galen was describing. Instead of trusting their eyes they had been blinded by Galen's great authority.

It was preposterous! Here he had hoped to revive anatomy and make it as great as it was in Galen's day. And all the time he had known more anatomy, more human anatomy, than had Galen himself!

The enthusiasm that kept him at his work now had a new purpose. That purpose was to describe for the first time true human anatomy. His zeal redoubled. With Calcar at his side to draw and make the printing blocks of carved wood, he dissected, wrote, described. A year and a half of feverish activity and the great anatomy was ready for the press. Where should he publish it? Venice? No, at Basel, the very center of the printers' trade. Over the Alps went mules laden with the blocks for the pictures. Vesalius rode with them. He supervised each step of the printing. At last in June, 1543, there appeared complete the great book—*De Fabrica Humani Corporis*. It had 663 pages and more than 300 woodcuts.

Vesalius was twenty-eight years old. His work was done. In his twenty-one remaining years he did no more in anatomy. Henceforth there was to be no peace for him. He had dared to turn against the idol Galen. The scholarly physicians, the teachers of anatomy railed at him. If the anatomy of man was different from that described by Galen, then the anatomy of man had changed since Galen had described it! Strange, isn't it, how men will try to deny the facts? But that was not the worst. He was ostracized, his pupils left him, his fellows snubbed him, the authorities put difficulties in his way to embarrass him.

Vesalius in indignation burned his manuscripts. He left Padua, gave up anatomy, and became court physician to the Emperor Charles V. It would have been better had he borne the attacks against him and marked time until everything became quiet again. While Vesalius was buried at the court of Charles, men began timidly to look around to see if by chance he was right. They found that he was. Then forgetting Vesalius, so it seemed, they went on from where he had

stopped. Soon Vesalius was only a name. A court physician in retirement, he was dead to medicine.

Perhaps his unmerited oblivion rankled in his mind and

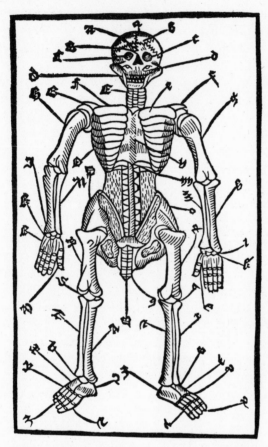

The skeleton according to Galen's description.

he longed to escape from the court, go back again and mingle with the men who were carrying on the work he loved. At any rate in 1563 he left the court and made his way to Venice. From this city twenty-six years before he had set

out with Calcar, carefree, happy, on his way to Padua and fame. This time, we do not know why, he took a ship to Palestine.

In 1564 he made the return journey, hastened, some say, because he had received an invitation to take over his post at Padua again. On the way he died.

CHAPTER XVIII

Paré, the Experimenter

IN 1559 King Henry II of the Valois family had been on the throne of France twelve years; he was just forty years old. An interruption had come in the wars with Spain and Germany; one of the many treaties of peace had been agreed upon. And now to seal the peace the King's daughter Elizabeth was to marry the King of Spain and his sister the Duke of Savoy. June of that year, 1559, was a month of festivals, of balls, hunts, and jousts at the court. The King, to show his good fellowship to his officers and his athletic prowess to the ladies of the gallery, entered the lists. He called upon Gabriel, Comte de Montgomery, Seigneur de Lorges, Lieutenant in the Scottish Guard, to break a lance with him. Reluctantly allowing his armor to be put on, Montgomery mounted his horse. There was little for him to gain; if he lost, he would be ridiculed; if he won—well, royal favor and royal prejudice were fickle things, and many a brave if indiscreet man had lost his hold at court by winning from the King. But fate had more in store here than reputation and favors; two lives were at stake.

The joust was run. Montgomery's lance struck the King's helmet and broke and splintered. A fragment passed through the vizor, penetrated the King's eye, and passed on into his brain. The King fell to the ground and was borne away unconscious to his bedroom. He died. Montgomery fled to escape the vengeance of the Queen, Catherine de' Medici. Some years later he was captured, tortured, and executed.

Alexander Dumas, author of *The Three Musketeers*, describes this incident in his romantic tales of France. And he tells of the medical treatment that the King received. Ambroise Paré, the royal surgeon was summoned. He examined the wound. He knew too little of the anatomy of the head

to dare attempt an operation in search of the splinter. So he sent for Andreas Vesalius. Loaned by the Spanish Court, the great anatomist rode night and day to reach Paris. After

Ambroise Paré.

greeting Paré, he examined the King, and then ordered the heads of two executed criminals brought to him at once. There in the sick room he and Paré carried out their dissections to obtain the precise knowledge of anatomy necessary

for the operation. But their efforts were in vain. The King died of an infection of the brain.

The tale of the meeting of Vesalius and Paré may be merely the invention of a romancer, but it has nevertheless a figurative significance. Paré's acquaintance with the anatomical knowledge of Vesalius resulted in a great advance in surgery. Paré applied to surgery the anatomy that Vesalius had described. He found surgery a degraded calling; he left it, if not a great profession, at least a dignified and competent branch of medicine. He was the first to start breaking down the attitude developed by the Arabs that the surgeon was a menial, far inferior to the physician.

Paré was quite a different kind of man from either of the other two medical heroes of the Renaissance with whom we have dealt. Paracelsus and Vesalius were well educated. The one had revolted against tradition and fought with all the violence of his personality against the theories of Galen; the other had painstakingly shown that Galen's facts were false. Ambroise Paré was not an educated man; he was a humble barber surgeon. The force that drove him on was not revolt, nor yet zeal for observation; it was love, the love arising from a deep compassion for those who suffer.

Paré was born about 1510. As a boy he was apprenticed to a barber. He was taught to clip hair and shave, and he learned the other duties of a barber of those days; to bleed, to pull teeth, to dress wounds. Surgery appealed to him, and so he went to Paris to work at the great hospital there, the Hôtel Dieu.

Being familiar with a modern hospital, you may have in mind an immaculately clean operating room, with tiled walls, an array of complicated, shiny instruments, and hallways where nurses move quickly and quietly in and out of rooms with neat white beds. But there were no such hospitals until late in the nineteenth century. The hospital that Paré went to, like all those of the time, was still a place of

refuge. It was a great stone building, badly lighted by narrow, dusty windows opening into long rooms with rows of canopied beds. Sometimes two or three or even four or five patients were put in a bed, with no regard to the diseases they might have. In the halls on piles of straw lay others— men, women, and children, too. And for nurses there were only the Sisters of Charity, untrained for such work, who

Scene in the Hôtel Dieu.

gave their services as a religious duty. The place was indescribably dirty; it was overrun with vermin; a vile smell of filth and disease and rotting flesh pervaded the building. The only operating room was a corner, a cubicle, or perhaps a dimly lighted vestibule.

In such a place Paré studied; there he learned to bandage wounds, put splints on broken limbs, and now and again to cut off a leg or an arm from some screaming fellow held down by strong men. Slim chance indeed did such patients have

for recovery. Infection usually killed them in spite of all his efforts.

In 1536 the war that drove Vesalius from Paris called Paré into the army. The forces of the French crossed the Alps and laid siege to Turin. Paré accompanied Marshal Montejan as regimental surgeon.

It was a new life for the young surgeon. He was, as he said, a greenhorn not yet hardened to the cruelties of war; this is the tale he tells of his first experience:

"We thronged at the city and passed over the dead bodies and some that were not yet dead, hearing them cry under the feet of our horses, which made a great pity in my heart, and truly I repented that I had gone forth from Paris to see so pitiful a spectacle. Being in the city, I entered a stable, thinking to lodge my horse, where I found four dead soldiers and two others who were not yet dead propped against the wall, their faces wholly disfigured, and they neither saw, nor heard, nor spoke, and their clothes yet flamed with the gunpowder which had burnt them. Beholding them with pity, there came an old soldier who asked me if there was any means of curing them. I told him no. At once he approached them and cut their throats gently and without anger. Seeing the great cruelty, I said to him that he was an evil man. He answered me that he prayed God that when he should be in such a case, he might find some one who would do the same for him, to the end that he might not languish miserably."

During this campaign Paré made the first of his great innovations in surgery; it concerned the treatment of gunshot wounds, which were a new feature of warfare. The muzzle-loading arquebus, shooting a ball as large as a walnut, inflicted horrible wounds. The sword, the lance, and the battle-ax made clean open wounds, usually only slightly infected. But the gunshot wound was deep and narrow, and bits of clothes and filth were carried into it. Such wounds became badly infected.

The leading scholarly writer on the surgery of the century was Giovanni di Vigo, who was physician to Pope Julius II. He had stated that gunshot wounds were poisoned with gunpowder. It was an ancient doctrine of Arabian surgery that "diseases not curable by iron were curable by fire." That is, if the surgeon could not give relief with his knife, he should use cautery. Since gunshot wounds, then, were thought to be poisoned burns (it was a century later that men discovered that bullets were not hot enough to burn the

Setting a broken leg on the battlefield.

flesh), they were to be treated at the first dressing by pouring into them oil boiling hot. Good logic, but from a false premise!

Here is Paré's first experience in treating wounds by the method then in vogue: "Now all the soldiers at the Chateau, seeing our men coming with great fury, did all they could to defend themselves and killed and wounded a great number of our soldiers with pikes, arquebuses, and stones, whereupon the surgeons had much work cut out for them. Now I was at that time an untried soldier; I had not yet seen wounds made by gunshot at the first dressing. It is true that I had read in Jean di Vigo that wounds made by firearms

were poisoned wounds, because of the powder, and for their cure he commands to cauterize them with oil of elder, scalding hot, in which should be mixed a little theriac; and in order not to err before using the oil, knowing that such a thing would bring great pain to the patient, I wished to know first, how the other surgeons did for the first dressing, which was to pour oil as hot as possible into the wounds, of whom I took courage to do as they did. At last my oil lacked and I was constrained to apply in its place a digestive made of the yolks of eggs, oil of roses, and turpentine. That night I could not sleep at my ease, fearing that by lack of cauterization I should find the wounded upon whom I had failed to put the oil dead or poisoned, which made me rise early to visit them, where beyond my hope I found those upon whom I had not put the oil feeling little pain, their wounds without inflammation or swelling, having rested fairly well throughout the night; the others, to whom I had applied the boiling oil, I found feverish, with great pain and swelling about their wounds. Then I resolved with myself never more to burn thus cruelly poor men wounded with gunshot."

Ambroise Paré was, you see, a rare surgeon for his day. He could do what so few men then could do; he could trust and follow his own intelligence and reasoning regardless of authority. He cared not what the noble Giovanni di Vigo, the Pope's physician, said. Paré saw with his own eyes—he never more would "burn thus cruelly poor men wounded with gunshot."

It was this same keenness and compassion that led Paré on to develop many other valuable methods for surgery. It was he who introduced, or rather reintroduced, for it had been used centuries before by the Romans, the ligature for stopping hemorrhage. In his day surgeons staunched the flow of blood with red-hot irons which seared the flesh and made a painful wound slow to heal. Paré used pieces of twine, ligatures, to tie shut the ends of the bleeding vessels. The surgeon of today uses the method he introduced.

A multitude of ingenious operations, artificial eyes, greatly improved artificial arms and legs, massage, and implanted teeth, are some of the things Paré gave to surgery. But the most important contribution he made was to anatomy. It

Making theriac.

was he who popularized for surgeons the anatomy that Vesalius had described.

It is unthinkable now for a surgeon to attempt an operation without knowing in exact detail the structure of the body. But in the days before Paré, the surgeon learned as craftsman a few simple operations; the trick of doing them was handed on from surgeon to surgeon by apprenticeship. The operations could not be varied to suit the needs of the patient; nor could new operations be developed. But with

knowledge of anatomy a whole new field was opened to the surgeon; his operations no longer needed to be merely the tricks of a trade; with a knowledge of what lay beneath his knife he could now plan operations intelligently and vary them to suit the occasion.

Paré, as we have said, made surgery a skilled craft. It remained as he left it for two hundred years, and we shall therefore have little to say of it until we come to the medical heroes of the eighteenth and nineteenth centuries—to the Scotchman, John Hunter, who made a science of surgery, and the Englishman, Joseph Lister, who introduced antiseptics to prevent infection, and the Americans, Long and Wells and Morton who gave us the blessing of anesthesia to abolish the pain of operation.

Before we tell more of Paré and his work, there are two terms that we have used that deserve explanation. One is theriac. You will remember that when Paré wrote of Di Vigo's treatment for gunshot wounds he said, "cauterize them with oil of elder, scalding hot, in which should be mixed a little theriac." This word theriac takes us back some sixteen centuries before the days of Paré. We mentioned Mithridates, King of Pontus, and his private herb doctor Crateuas. Mithridates was a dabbler in medicine; he wished to make himself immune to all poisons (a very useful state for a king of those days) by taking small but gradually increasing doses of the poisons. He was reputed to have discovered a universal antidote—a theriac. The theriac that Paré mentions was supposed to be made after the original formula; it contained vipers' flesh and some sixty-three other ingredients, none of which had any beneficial medicinal effect. Theriac was a most popular remedy until well into the eighteenth century.

The other term concerns an operation which we said Paré introduced: the implantation of teeth. The only dentists in Paré's time—if we exclude the bathhouse keepers, peddlers, and old women—were the barber surgeons. Dentistry at

their hands was merely the pulling of aching teeth. The extraction was performed with formidable instruments called pelicans and keys, which seized on the suffering tooth, and often one or two sound ones as well, as a pipe wrench seizes on a pipe. It was a brutal form of dentistry, but there was no other. In order to cover up the gap made by missirg teeth,

The legend of the bezoar stone.

artificial teeth carved from bone or ivory were sometimes wired in place. Paré's method of implantation was to pull the aching tooth and then insert into the wound in the jaw a sound tooth extracted from the mouth of some poor chap willing to sell a tooth. The tooth thus stuck in grew firmly to the bone and often lasted several years. Of course no one in those days dreamed of infection of the teeth or its consequences, nor were such things known until late in the nine-

teenth century. It was only then that modern dentistry began.

We have said that Paré raised surgery from a trade followed by menials to a skilled craft carried out by trained men. After his time instruction in surgery became more and more a part of medical education. The distinction between the surgeons of the long robe and those of the short robe was gradually broken down. Surgery became respectable.

It is hard to turn from Paré to the other medical heroes who await us in the centuries ahead. If you ever read the tales Paré wrote, you will know why. In reading them you see the man; you know and love him. To part with him is to leave a friend.

Paré was a man at home equally in the strife of the battlefield, the turmoil of the camp, and in the intrigue of a polished court. He lived beloved by the common soldiers, respected by kings. His unvarying purpose in life was the one that has moved all truly great doctors: the desire to help, to heal, to relieve the suffering of their fellow men. It was love—not maudlin sentiment, or the compassion of those who shrink from the sight of suffering—but the aggressive warfare of men who for love of their fellows devote their lives to the fight against the enemy disease.

Paré was a fighter of tough fiber, and yet he was not ashamed to show gentleness and humility. Nowhere is his gentle character more clearly seen than in the words with which he closed his descriptions of the cases he treated. They were: "I dressed his wounds; God healed him."

There remains yet one more thing to be said of Paré. He was one of the first men in modern medicine to perform experiments. Moreover, he used what is now called the method of the control experiment. Here is an instance.

In one of his army experiences he was called to treat a man who had been badly burned. He went to the supply tent to get a healing ointment but on the way he met an old woman among the camp followers of the army. She told

him that the best way to treat a burn (remember this is the sixteenth century and not today) was to put on the wound chopped-up onion. Paré never ignored suggestions. He tried the onion. The man's face healed well. The treatment seemed of benefit. A lesser man than Paré, one who did not possess that blessed thing called skepticism, would have

Animal portant le Bezoar

A bezoar stone and the animal from which it really came.

said, "the onion healed the burn." Because of that kind of uncritical reasoning, medicine since primitive times has been encumbered with its multitude of useless remedies and treatments. But Paré asked a question, the question that made him a scientist. It was: "Might not the burn have healed as quickly as it did even if the onion had not been put upon it? Did the onion help the healing or did the burn heal in spite of the onion?"

To answer that question he tried an experiment. Soon a

soldier came to him with his face burned on both sides. To one cheek Paré applied his chopped-up onion; but on the other he put nothing. The untreated cheek was his control, his standard of comparison. He found that the side treated with onion healed more quickly than the side untreated. Thus by sound experimental evidence he proved that the treatment was of benefit.

And here is another of Paré's experiments that gives an idea of the kind of remedies then in use. There were four medicaments in which the physicians of those times had great confidence. Theriac, of course, was one; then there were powdered "mummy" from Egypt to heal wounds, unicorns' horns to detect poison in wines, and bezoar stones as antidotes against poison. Paré wrote a scathing condemnation of "mummy"; as chief surgeon and counselor to the King he told His Majesty that the unicorn's horn which was dipped in the royal wine by the poison tester was useless; and he proved that the bezoar stone was not an antidote against poison. It is with the incident of the bezoar stone that we are concerned here. A bezoar was, so legend said, a crystallized tear from the eye of a deer bitten by a snake; it was in reality a concretion, a sort of gallstone, found in the stomachs and intestines of goats and similar animals. It had, of course, no medicinal value. But it was firmly believed that if one was poisoned, all he need do was swallow the stone and the poison would have no effect. A great many people who thought they were poisoned had swallowed stones and had recovered. But Paré raised the question: "Were they really poisoned, or did they merely think they were?"

King Charles IX, who, by the way, had been marked by smallpox so badly that his nose was split in two, possessed a valuable bezoar stone, one that he prized highly. Paré suggested an experiment that would prove or disprove its value as an antidote—try the stone on a condemned criminal given poison. The King sent for his provost and asked if

there was such a criminal in the prisons. He was told that there was a poor cook who had stolen two silver plates from his master and who in accord with the pitiless custom of the time was to be hanged and strangled. "The King," said Paré, "told the provost that he wished to experiment with a stone which they said was good against all poisons, and

A variety of unicorns.

that he should ask the cook if he would take a certain poison, and that they would at once give him an antidote; to which the cook very willingly agreed, saying that he liked much better to die of poison in the prison than to be strangled in view of the people." (Apparently the cook did not share the King's faith in the bezoar stone.)

The prisoner was given the poison and the bezoar. He died seven hours later. The stone was returned to the King. He is said to have thrown it in the fire.

'The method of the control experiment which Paré used is the one, although without the human subjects, by which

the medicaments and treatments used by modern physicians have been proved to be effective. Needless to say there are far fewer remedies in use today than there were in the sixteenth century or even the seventeenth and eighteenth.

It took many years for the experimental method to come into wide use in medicine. It would perhaps never have been used if such great doctors as Ambroise Paré and Paracelsus and Vesalius had not carried into medicine the spirit of independent observation, of criticism, and of progress which grew out of the Renaissance. But for the spirit and the practical results that have grown from it, you and I today would be dosed with horrid and useless concoctions, would read our fate in the stars, would scream in pain while we were mangled by the barber surgeons who knew no anatomy, have our teeth extracted by peddlers, and go to hospitals that were filthy and reeking with infection. But worst of all by far— we should be defenseless against disease, as defenseless as men were when the Black Death threatened to wipe out the human race.

Little more than three centuries lie ahead of us in our story, a mere moment in the vast expanse of time through which we have traced medicine. In these few years medicine and surgery and dentistry have grown from what they were in Paré's time to the highly developed sciences we know today.

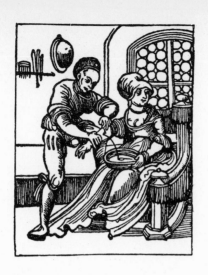

Part Seven

THE SCIENCE OF MEDICINE

THE SUPERSTITIONS OF MEDICINE

THE PRACTICE OF MEDICINE

CHAPTER XIX

The Science of Medicine

MANY, many years ago when men believed in the philosophers' stone that changed base metals into gold, there was a formula, said to be infallible, for obtaining the stone. Its sly author, though he lacked in science, was wise in understanding the contradictions of human ways. Go to a mountain top, said the directions, and mix together certain ingredients—their names are unimportant—and then sit for half an hour without once thinking of the word hippopotamus. That was the important thing, not to let that word hippopotamus slip into your mind; if it did, as it always did, the formula failed.

To Galileo the fateful and forbidden word was not hippopotamus but mathematics. You will remember Galileo, whom we have mentioned as dropping weights from the leaning tower to prove a law of physics. It was in 1581 that his father sent him as a boy of seventeen to the medical school of Pisa where he was to study to become a doctor.

The father, fearing that mathematics—then a most flourishing science—would catch and hold the boy's attention and take his interest from medicine, had kept him from studying the subject and warned him not to think of it when he went to college.

Galileo, dutiful and devout, sat one day in the cathedral of Pisa. He must not think of mathematics. But swinging enticingly before his eyes was a lamp hung on a chain from the ceiling. Back and forth like a pendulum it moved. One, two, three, four; its swing grew less; five, six, seven, eight; his finger strayed to the artery pulsing in his wrist; nine, ten, eleven, twelve; he could count the pulse and the pendulum together, so many swings, so many beats, so many swings, so many beats. The forbidden mathematics! But after all it

was important to know that there were always the same number of swings to the same number of beats, even though the distance of the swings grew less and less. No one had ever known before that the rate of the pendulum was largely independent of the range of its swing.

Galileo kept on with medicine; but again the forbidden mathematics intruded. He chanced to hear part of a lecture

Sanctorius.

on geometry. This was a fascinating subject; there were facts to be proved by mathematics, and things to be measured exactly. Compared to mathematics, medicine, the treating of disease, was a blundering, uncertain sort of business. Reluctantly the father yielded to the son's enthusiasm, and gave his permission; Galileo left medicine and took up instead the study of mathematics. And from this change science was to benefit. It owes to Galileo many principles of physics, the law of the swing of the pendulum, of falling bodies, of the movement of projectiles. It owes to him also great improvements in the telescope, and the invention of the microscope

and the thermometer. But most of all it owes to him a method of study. It is the method of making measurements to determine the facts of nature, of using mathematical proof to replace vague guesses and often wrong guesses.

It is indeed rare that we can count medicine as fortunate when a great man leaves its ranks; but that was true in Galileo's case. The physician of today, when he takes the temperature of his patient, counts his pulse and rate of breathing, determines the pressure of the blood in his arteries, weighs him, carries out any of the precise measurements that make modern medicine so vastly more exact than the medicine of the past, is following the method of Galileo. But what is more, the nature of the very bodily functions to which he applies his tests was found out in part at least by Galileo's method.

Medical science as we have traced it so far in our story has followed two methods only. Vesalius was using one when in his dissections he observed and described. Paré, when he experimented with remedies by trial and comparison, was using the second. And now in the seventeenth century there came into use a third, the method of Galileo, of measurement and mathematical proof.

The first man to apply the new method of science to the problems of medicine was a physician named Santorio Santorio; he is usually called by his Latinized name, Sanctorius. Graduated in 1582 from the famous School of Padua, he led a varied career; he was physician to the court of Poland, then a professor at Padua, and finally a private citizen of Venice, where he practiced medicine and carried on the scientific studies which so aroused his enthusiasm.

Men, for centuries before Sanctorius, had observed the fact that in illness there is fever, but no one had ever measured the rise in temperature nor was it certain that the body had a normally constant temperature. Sanctorius was the first physician to use a thermometer to measure body temperature. His thermometer was vastly different from the one

that the doctor of today draws from his pocket. It was a long twisted tube with a bulb nearly as large as an egg at the top; the open end at the bottom was placed in water. The patient held the bulb in his mouth; the air in it, becoming warmed, expanded and escaped through the water. When no more air leaked out, the bulb was taken from the mouth; on cooling, the air contracted and water rose in the tube. The height to which it rose was a measure of the air expelled and hence of the temperature that had been about the bulb—the patient's temperature.

For centuries, physicians had felt the pulse at the wrist; they had judged the nature of disease from the quality of the pulse, its firmness, its regularity. But no one had counted it to see how rapid it was. Galileo, some say, counted his pulse with the pendulum; but what he really did was to time a pendulum with his pulse. It was Sanctorius who counted the pulse. He did not use a watch, for a very good reason. Watches had been invented in 1510 but in the early years of the seventeenth century they had no second hand or even minute hand. Sanctorius used a pendulum and varied the length until the rate of the pendulum corresponded to that of the pulse. The rate of the pulse was recorded not in so many beats per minute, as we record it now, but as so many inches of pendulum length. I paused for a moment in writing these lines to measure my pulse: it beat twenty-six inches; my watch said seventy-two beats to the minute.

Sanctorius carried out many experiments in measurement. One of the most famous concerns the weight of the body. He had attached to the ceiling of his dining room a steel-yard to which his chair was hung. He weighed himself while he ate and recorded his loss of weight hour after hour from insensible perspiration.

The methods that Sanctorius used are by modern standards crude indeed, but the principle of these methods is the same as that used by the physicians of today in the most refined procedures of modern science, the principle of meas-

urement, of expressing facts in numbers—expressing them
objectively.

During the seventeenth century this method was used to
yield one of the greatest of all discoveries in medicine. It
was the discovery of the function of the heart. The English
physician William Harvey demonstrated that the heart

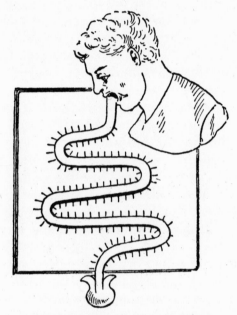

The thermometer of Sanctorius.

pumps blood and that the blood circulates in the blood vessels. He discovered these facts by observation, he demonstrated them experimentally, and he proved them mathematically—the three great methods of science.

We have said little so far concerning the function of any
organ of the body; but that does not mean that much had
not been said by the physicians and the philosophers in every
age. There was indeed a theory to explain every known

function of every known organ. But there was little fact in most of these theories. True, Galen had actually performed experiments to show the function of nerves and muscles. But he had performed none to show the function of the heart, and yet he gave an explanation of its action in an elaborate theory. It was the one held by every physician at the beginning of the seventeenth century.

The liver, so said Galen, was the center of the blood system. The food eaten was brought to the liver and changed in some mysterious way into an equally mysterious substance called "natural spirits." Blood containing the "natural spirits" flowed outward from the liver. But the word "flow" was not used in the sense in which we speak of the flow of blood; rather Galen meant a sort of tide that moved slowly out to every part of the body, distributing the "natural spirits." In the brain these spirits were changed to "animal spirits" and in that form passed out along the nerves, emptying from their tips back into the veins. The arteries throughout the body pulsated each time the heart beat. But in giving the beat that could be felt against the ribs on the left side, the heart was believed to expand just as did the arteries.

The heart itself was known to have two sets of chambers, one pair on the left side and the other on the right. To those on the right the veins holding bluish-black blood were connected and to those on the left the arteries holding bright vermilion blood. Between the two sides of the heart, so said Galen, there were minute pores through which the blue blood and the red blood mingled.

It had not occurred to Galen that the heart was a pump; instead, like Aristotle, he thought of it as a churn and a furnace. It heated the blood and stirred into it something called "vital spirits." The lungs were fans that cooled the blood.

Galen's theory gave support to the old idea that bleeding, the drawing off of blood, was beneficial in the treatment of

disease. That belief arose, as we have told, among primitive people; it was promoted by the false theories of ancient physicians; it was widely practiced by the physicians of the fifteenth, sixteenth, seventeenth and, sad to say, even of the eighteenth and early nineteenth centuries. Believing Galen's theory, men were unaware of the fact that there was only a small quantity of blood in the body, perhaps a gallon, rapidly circulated. They thought rather that it was continually formed and stagnated. To bleed relieved the body of "bad blood"; and new and good blood was made to take its place. Sometimes there was too much blood, so they thought, on one side of the body, and in order to establish a balance some was drawn off.

Bleeding at one time was the physician's chief method of treating disease. Read the story of *Gil Blas*, as we have suggested in an earlier chapter, and you will see to what excesses bleeding was carried by the famous character, Dr. Sangrado, "the tall, withered, wan executioner of the sisters three." The story is fiction, of course, but it is based on fact. In Paris in the seventeenth century a prominent physician named Guy Patin wrote that he bled himself seven times for a head cold, and his son twenty times in the course of a few days. His procedure was not exceptional.

The story of the discovery of the circulation of the blood takes us first to Padua—the Padua of Vesalius and of Sanctorius. The English boy, William Harvey, came there to study medicine after his graduation from Cambridge University. In 1602—the same year that Shakespeare's *Hamlet* was first played—Harvey received his doctor's degree from the University of Padua. But Padua gave him something in addition that no other school of that time could have given him, a love for anatomical observation. True to the memory of the great Vesalius, it was the leading school of anatomy.

While he was there Harvey may have read the famous lines that Vesalius wrote when he looked for the tiny pores

through which Galen had said the blue blood and the red blood were supposed to mingle—and did not find them: "We are driven to wonder at the handiwork of the Almighty, by means of which the blood sweats from the right into the

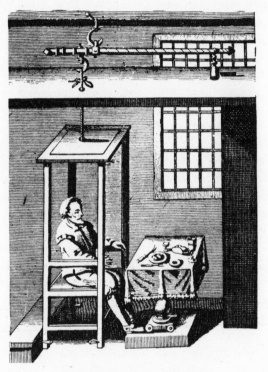

Sanctorius on the steelyard.

left ventricle through passages which escape human vision."

Perhaps Vesalius suspected even more than he implied. But his was a dangerous time in which to hint that ancient theories of how the organs of the body worked might be wrong. Such things were still closely linked to religious beliefs. Men could be burned for upsetting established views.

Another man, Miguel Serveto or Servetus, less prudent

than Vesalius, published his discovery that the blood passed from the right side to the left of the heart, not through the partition but through the lungs. And of all places he chose to print it in a book pointing out what he thought were errors in religion. Galen's mistake was one of the errors he enumerated. Servetus was burned to death in 1553.

Servetus' discovery did not by any means settle the problem of what the heart does. That was left for Harvey. This young man, newly made a doctor, was back in London practicing medicine.

The London of his day had a population of less than a quarter of a million. And it was a plague-ridden place; one outbreak after another tortured the people, until the greatest and last of all in 1665, a year before the fire that burned a large section of the city.

Between treating his patients, Harvey carried on the study of anatomy that he had begun at Padua. His interest centered on the heart. What was the meaning of its movement? He could see it move in fishes, in turtles, in frogs. And as he watched the living heart pulsate, he pondered. Here was something different from the descriptions of Galen and of Aristotle. Had they looked as carefully as he? They had said the heart expanded when they felt it beat against the ribs, when the pulse could be felt in the arteries. Instead he saw the heart contract. It was pushing out—squeezing out—the blood it held. The pulse in the artery was caused by the rhythmic onrush of the blood.

Then came a question. If the heart pushes out the blood, does the blood run back into the heart when it relaxes? An experiment was needed. He tied a cord about the forearm of a man. The cord pressed hard enough to shut off the flow of blood in the veins but not in the arteries. With each beat of the heart blood flowed into the arm; the veins of the hand were distended, the arm swollen. The veins above the band were collapsed. Clearly the experiment showed that the blood flowed from the heart through the arteries but did not

flow back through them when the heart relaxed. Instead it flowed from the arteries into the veins. This was science by the method of observation and experiment, but it alone did not supply the answers to the questions Harvey raised.

Where did the blood in the veins go? And, if the heart kept pumping blood where did the blood come from? Was it possible that it was the same blood being pumped round and round? Measurements, mathematics would supply the answers.

Harvey calculated that each time the heart squeezed down and emptied out its blood two ounces of blood went into the arteries. The heart of a man at rest beat some seventy-two times a minute. Seventy-two beats, 72 x 2 ounces, 144 ounces a minute; 540 pounds an hour; more than 16 tons in 24 hours! Absurd to think that the body produced that much blood. There could be only one answer; the blood circulated. It went from the left side of the heart into the arteries, from the arteries to the veins, from the veins to the right side of the heart and from the right side of the heart— as Servetus had shown—through the lungs and back to the starting point. The heart was a pump; the blood circulated.

In 1618 William Harvey had learned these facts. Ten years later, when he was certain beyond question of a doubt, he published them. His book, *Exercitatio anatomica de motu cordis et sanguinis in animalibus*, is one of the great landmarks of medicine.

We need hardly say that a storm of opposition met Harvey's statements. He had dared to doubt Galen. The repetition of that cry "You deny Galen?" may have become a bit tiresome even to the men of that time. Eighty-five years had passed since Vesalius had been driven from his post at Padua. Harvey lost some patients; he heard some uncomplimentary things about himself; but the storm soon passed. He stayed on in his post as royal physician to His Majesty King Charles I and lived to see his discoveries accepted.

And the man himself? Those who knew him said that he

was rather quick of temper when crossed in an argument, given to fingering the handle of the dagger he wore at his belt, and that "in person he was not tall but of the lowest stature; round-faced, olivaster complexion, little eyes, round, very black, full of spirit, his hair black as a raven,

William Harvey.

but quite white twenty years before he died." He died in 1657—four years too soon to know the answer to the question that must have puzzled him all his days. How did the blood flow from the arteries to the veins; how did it flow through the lungs?

It was the Italian physician Marcello Malpighi who solved the riddle. He used the method of observation but he

had at hand a new instrument—the microscope that Galileo had invented.

Under the lens of even the crude microscope of those days a whole new field of study was opened up by the physician. The tissues of the body had definite and important structures invisible to the unaided eye.

In the year 1661 Malpighi, then professor of anatomy at Bologna, reported that he had seen in the lungs and about the intestines of frogs, minute blood vessels, far too small to be visible to the naked eye, connecting the arteries and veins. In the flesh of a living animal he saw blood move through these capillary vessels, saw it flow from artery to vein.

Harvey, Servetus, and Malpighi supplied all the main facts concerning the circulation of the blood. Since their time only details have been added. But in spite of their knowledge, none of these men knew what functions the blood served in the body. The microscope showed it a clear, faintly yellow fluid in which were suspended many minute red disks; Malpighi had thought them drops of red fat. But what did the fluid do in the body; why was it circulated? Again theories. Since earliest times blood had been looked upon as a fluid denoting the very essence of life. It was the ingredient passed on in heredity to carry the family traits— witness, "blood relations." Men were distinguished temperamentally as "hot blooded" or "cold blooded." When in the seventeenth century the first crude transfusions of blood, the drawing of blood from the veins of one man and putting it into the veins of another, were performed, there was much speculation as to what would happen to the character of the recipient. Would a sheep bark when transfused with the blood of a dog; how would an English bishop behave if he were transfused with the blood of a Quaker?

Nowhere has modern science dealt more unkindly with old beliefs than with those concerning blood; to the modern physician blood is simply the least alive of all the tissues of

the body; it has nothing to do with temperament; notions that one hears even today of disease due to "bad blood" the physician knows are absurd. The one peculiarity of blood lies in the fact that it is a liquid and can escape when the body is wounded. The body needs its blood to carry oxygen

Title-page of De Motu Cordis.

and food and waste materials from one part of the system to another. Blood is merely a vehicle.

It was not until the nineteenth century that these facts were known fully, but in the seventeenth century the first step was taken toward finding them out. An Englishman from Cornwall, named John Mayow, showed that the bluish

blood found in veins turned red in passing through the lungs because it took something from the air. What that something was he did not know. He called it nitro-aërial— spirit of air; we call it oxygen, but oxygen had not been discovered in his day.

In reading here of Galileo, Sanctorius, Servetus, Harvey, Malpighi, and Mayow, you may have noticed a fact that in a way makes their work different from that of the medical heroes of the sixteenth century. Paracelsus, Vesalius, and Paré were reformers; they revolted against the medical beliefs of their time; they attempted to change the course of medicine; their achievements depended largely upon their peculiar personalities.

In the seventeenth century medical science was still in the hands of independent workers but there were the beginnings of close coöperation. Thus Harvey, following the anatomy of Vesalius and the method of Galileo, went on from where Servetus had left off and was able to demonstrate the circulation of blood; both Malpighi and Mayow followed with their contributions to this one problem. Individual contributions were becoming merely a part of a united whole that each year grew, and still grows, more nearly completed. From now on our story of medical science will deal less with the lives of men; their work, their contributions to the unfolding scheme of things, and not their personalities, become the dominating theme. Personality and chance shape the destiny of each great man; but the work that has come before likewise shapes his work. We are to find fewer reformers but many new contributors.

In recognition of this coöperation, this interdependence, the scientists of the seventeenth century were founding societies in which they might exchange ideas to their mutual benefit. Scientific journals were appearing; one of the greatest of them was the *Philosophical Transactions* of the Royal Society of London. The society itself was formed in 1645 and given a charter by Charles II in 1662; the *Transactions*

first appeared in 1664. In this journal a few years after its founding, a discovery was reported, the importance of which was not realized until almost two centuries had passed. A man named Leeuwenhoek of Delft had written a letter to the editor of the *Transactions*. He was not a physician but

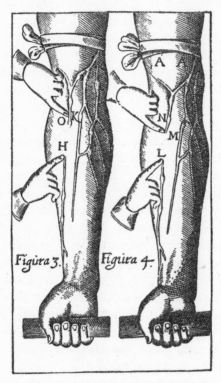

An illustration from De Motu Cordis.

the janitor of the city hall. He had, however, a profitable hobby, the microscope. He ground his own lenses, made his own microscopes, and turned them on everything he could find.

In 1683 he wrote that in scrapings from a tooth he had

seen what we call bacteria. He described them accurately. Bacteria were of no interest at all except as curiosities to physicians of those days. Leeuwenhoek's was an isolated fact of observation.

While Leeuwenhoek peered through his microscope, off in Italy another naturalist was studying flies, making his isolated contribution of a fact. Francesco Redi by experiment disproved a theory held strongly in his day—that maggots develop spontaneously in filth and rotting things. He placed some meat in jars; some of the jars he left open; others he covered with gauze. The meat decayed. Attracted by the smell, flies buzzed about the vessels. Soon there were maggots in the meat of the open jars; there were none in the meat of the jars covered with gauze. But on top of the gauze where eggs had been laid maggots appeared. Flies, not something in the rotten meat, were responsible for the maggots. Maggots were not generated spontaneously.

These observations of Leeuwenhoek and of Redi lay isolated for nearly two hundred years. Then in the nineteenth century the French chemist Pasteur built them into the scheme of science. He showed that bacteria, like maggots, did not arise spontaneously, but were produced by other bacteria; and he proved that bacteria were the cause of infectious disease. This was a revolutionary advance of medicine, but it had its beginnings in the work of scientists of the seventeenth century: Galileo who invented the microscope, Leeuwenhoek who described bacteria, and Redi who first disproved spontaneous generation.

This chapter which we have entitled "science" is really one act in the drama of medicine. The other two acts could be named, as we have named the next two chapters, "superstition" and "practice." The stage is set here for the seventeenth century; it could as well have been set for the eighteenth, nineteenth, or twentieth. We have chosen the seventeenth because then the contrasts between science, superstition, and practice were greatest.

The science of medicine is knowledge concerning the body in health and disease, knowledge proved by experiment and reduced to rules, precise, exact, unvarying.

The superstitions of medicine are the false beliefs concerning disease and its treatment that linger in the minds of many people.

Science and superstition are conflicting forces. One makes for progress; the other retards it.

The practice of medicine concerns all the ways in which the doctor deals not only with disease but also with the people who have disease. Behind him, supplying him with new facts, weapons with which to fight disease, is science. But science has not even yet told him all, far from it. The doctor must know not only science but men as well, with all their fears, their false beliefs, their superstitions.

A time may come perhaps, though not in your day or mine, when medicine will be a single thing—science. Superstitions will have died, and science will have reduced to rules not only the knowledge of how the body works and how disease can be prevented and cured but also how human beings behave.

In the seventeenth century little use was made in medical practice of the science that we have described in this chapter, vastly important though it was for later events.

CHAPTER XX

The Superstitions of Medicine

AN automobile mired in the unpaved streets of London in the seventeenth century; an aëroplane soaring over the modest homes of the Pilgrim fathers of New England, or those homes lighted with electricity—these things would be anachronisms.

But it is just as much an anachronism to bring forward in time something old and out of date as it is to move something back in time. A primitive medicine man in the surroundings of the Royal Court of England would be an anachronism. Standing there, his nakedness barely covered with bits of fur, he would be out of place among ladies dressed in the flowing gowns of the seventeenth century and gentlemen with tight satin breeches, velvet coats, and powdered wigs. In the decorous surroundings of civilization the medicine man shouting, gesticulating, carrying out his rites and incantations, would most certainly appear absurd. But suppose that we were to dress this medicine man in the costume of the times and change his rites and ceremonies, not in principle but only in form, so that they no longer seemed grotesque; then he would not appear as an absurdity but he still would be an anachronism. He would represent something old brought forward in time, misplaced.

With this idea in mind let us read from the diary of an English writer of the seventeenth century—John Evelyn, a cultured gentleman and friend of King Charles II. Here is what he said concerning an incident he witnessed on July 6, 1660:

"His Majesty began to touch for the Evil according to custom, thus: His Majesty sitting under his state in the banqueting house, the chirurgeons cause the sick to be brought, or led, up to the throne, where they kneel; the King

strokes their faces or cheeks with both hands at once, at which instance a chaplain in his formality says, 'He put his hands upon them, and he healed them.' . . . When they have been all touched, they come up again in the same order, and the other chaplain kneeling, and having angel gold strung on white ribbon on his arm, delivers them one by one to His Majesty, who puts them about the necks of the touched as they pass, while the chaplain repeats, 'That is the true light who come into the world.' Then follows an epistle with liturgy, prayers for the sick, lastly blessings; and then the Lord Chamberlain and the Comptroller of the Household bring a basin, ewer, and towel, for His Majesty to wash."

The same ceremony as described by Shakespeare in *Macbeth*, Act IV, Scene 3, reads:

> *—strangely-visited people,*
> *All swoln and ulcerous, pitiful to the eye;*
> *The mere despair of surgery, he cures;*
> *Hanging a golden stamp about their necks,*
> *Put on with holy prayers.*

These are faithful descriptions of the ceremony of the Royal Touch for the disease of the King's Evil. If it were carried out in some forest glade by a shouting, sweating savage, if the gold pieces were perforated shells on a grass string, the primitive nature of the ceremony would be apparent. In principle it was the same in the court of England in the days of the seventeenth century; for all its regal surroundings it was primitive, savage, superstitious medicine.

The King of England played the rôle of a primitive medicine man. He was only one in an unbroken succession that has carried the medical beliefs of the savage through all ages even to our day. In guise ever changed to suit the times but with principle unaltered, we shall meet these "primitive medicine men" again and again in the centuries that remain

before us in our story. They are the ignorant healers, the leaders of healing cults, the great quacks.

The Royal Touch for the King's Evil was merely one of many superstitions in the seventeenth century, but it was perhaps the most striking. The disease, the King's Evil, was scrofula; and scrofula, as we know now, is tuberculosis of the glands of the neck.

The belief in the power of the laying on of hands is an ancient one. The primitive medicine man stretched out his hand, touched the ailing place, and bade the tormenting spirit leave. In early civilization the priest was an emissary of the gods, sharing their healing powers; often he wrought cures by touch. Later when kings, so it was believed, ruled by divine right, they too had healing power. Why their virtues were limited to one disease, scrofula, we cannot say, but the fact remains that Edward the Confessor in England touched for this disease in the eleventh century.

From the time of Henry VII in 1465 to William of Orange in 1689 the Royal Touch was an accepted court ceremony. William, far from superstitious in this matter, touched only once and then greatly against his will. He laid his hands on the sick person and said, "May God give you better health; and more sense." In the eighteenth century, however, Queen Anne revived the practice. Dr. Johnson was one of the last persons she touched: it was done in his infancy; he retained his scrofula all his life.

The French kings from Clovis to Louis XVI also touched for the evil. In 1775 Louis XVI, the last king before the Revolution, touched 2400 sick persons on the day of his coronation. But men were becoming openly skeptical of the ancient practice. An investigation was made of the 2400 cases. In only five were there any signs whatever of improvement. In spite of skepticism the practice was revived in 1824 at the coronation of Charles X; he touched 121 sick people.

The Royal Touch has not been used now for more than a century, that is, not used by royalty; but the laying on of

hands is still performed as manipulation of the feet or spine by men who have a following for their primitive, superstitious medicine quite as great as was the king's in the past.

For a time in the seventeenth century there was no king on the English throne. The head of Charles I had fallen under the ax of the public executioner. Cromwell was in

KINGS-EVIL.

A broadside printed in 1697 showing King Charles touching for the evil.

power, but he refused to attempt the touch for the evil. And so the public turned to one of those odd characters who in every century, even the present, have carried on the healing of the primitive medicine man. It was Valentine Greatrakes, one of Cromwell's soldiers, who, so he said, was told in a dream that he possessed healing powers over the evil. He began to practice his art and was quite as successful as the kings had been. That is to say, he satisfied the people. By successive dreams it was revealed that his healing powers covered almost every disease. Thousands of people flocked

to him; he obligingly touched them; they were "cured."
Many prominent men, even Robert Boyle, the "father of
modern chemistry," spoke in praise of Greatrakes.

There in the countryside of England was an ignorant man
practicing in his quiet way the principle of healing that had
been used by the medicine men of primitive people, by the
magicians of Egypt, the priests of Æsculapius, and the sorcerers of Syria. The principle is the same regardless of the
way it is applied; the medicine man shouted and danced;
the magician drew his magic circles; the priest of Æsculapius commanded sleep and dreams; the kings of France and
England, and Greatrakes touched. After their times men
were to turn to still other means, to mesmerism, to electricity, to manipulation of joints, and even to healing philosophies. The principle remains unaltered; the primitive medicine man in ever-changing guise stalks down through the
centuries to become in a day of science an anachronism.

Whatever form the principle takes, the result is the same.
As we have said in earlier chapters, primitive medicine acts
largely through its effect upon the mind. If confidence is obtained and fear banished, the symptoms of disease may for a
time be relieved, but physical disease itself is not altered.
But the important thing here is the fact that the cure used
by the kings and Greatrakes and all of the superstitious
healers in all ages was applied to physical as well as mental
disturbances; no distinction was made. Only in the momentary wave of their enthusiasm did the physically ill feel
better and then, as their diseases progressed, they became
worse than they had been before they were treated.

Valentine Greatrakes for a few months was a tremendous
success; and then his prestige began to wane. The pains and
aches and infirmities which had yielded to confidence returned. His fame diminished; the crowds no longer sought
him.

Another of the medical superstitions of the seventeenth
century was the amazing powder of sympathy that was ex-

ploited by Sir Kenelm Digby. Digby was at various times a
student at Oxford, an English ambassador, a Commissioner
of the Navy, a follower of Cromwell, and a courtier of

The truly Learned and Hono.ble
S.r Kenelme Digby K.t Chancellor
to the Q: Mother
Aged 62.

Grose sculpsit

Sir Kenelm Digby who used the powder of sympathy.

James I, Charles I, and Charles II. Quite a checkered career.
He was energetic, he had wild schemes which he could present with amazing conviction. It is said that he hastened the
death of his sorely abused consumptive wife by trying out

on her a remedy made of vipers' flesh, intended to beautify her.

After he had traveled for some time on the continent he had returned to the court of King James with his amazing remedy, the powder of sympathy. It was a variant of the weapon ointment of which we have spoken in connection with Paracelsus. You will find mention of weapon ointment in Sir Walter Scott's "The Lay of the Last Minstrel," in the episode in which Lady Margaret finds William of Deloraine wounded:

> *She drew the splinter from the wound,*
> *And with a charm she stanched the blood.*
> *She bade the gash be cleansed and bound:*
> *No longer by his couch she stood;*
> *But she has ta'en the broken lance,*
> *And washed it from the clotted gore,*
> *And salved the splinter o'er and o'er.*

Now sometimes, as you may well imagine, it was difficult to obtain the weapon that caused the wound. The enemy might escape with his sword or dagger. It was in just such instances that the sympathetic powder of Sir Kenelm came in so helpfully. It was applied not to the weapon but to blood-stained clothing. Scraps of cloth were soaked in a solution of the powder; instantly pain stopped and the wound healed.

King James was particularly excited about the remedy and begged to be told its composition. Reluctantly Digby divulged it. This mysterious substance was iron sulphate, green vitriol.

Kings of those days had their personal medical superstitions. Henry VIII was interested especially in "cramp rings," rings to be worn to prevent stomach ache. But we can forgive him any superstitions he may have had in view of his one great gift to medicine. It was he who first decreed that births and deaths should be carefully recorded; later,

causes of death were added, and the way thus opened for medical statistics. Queen Elizabeth wore a magic locket about her neck that kept her free from infection; William of Orange used the dried ground-up eyes of crabs for a medicament (he had consumption); and Queen Anne's medical superstitions aside from the Royal Touch led to her making tailors and tinkers into eye specialists to treat her failing sight.

The most striking of Charles II's many connections with medical superstitions occurred while he was unconscious. We shall come to it soon when we talk of popular remedies; first, let us see some of the more common medical superstitions of the people at large. We could go on endlessly recounting local superstitions that prevailed in one region or another—a spider in a bag to cure fits; a horse chestnut carried in the pocket to prevent rheumatism; a cleft in a tree through which a child could be pushed to cure rickets; coral to drive off malarial fever and keep dogs from going mad; cobwebs to stop hemorrhage; a black snake put around the neck to cure goiter; the blood of a black hen killed in the dark of the moon to cure a variety of diseases; and so on and so on. There were literally thousands, yes, hundreds of thousands of these remarkable remedies. Many of them persist today.

There were, however, in the seventeenth century, three superstitions that were thoroughly believed in as influencing matters of health and disease. These were palmistry, astrology, and witchcraft.

Palmistry is one of the most ancient arts of divination. From the shape of the hands, from the swellings and depressions, and from the creases, the health of the individual, his character, and his future could be determined—so it had been believed from prehistoric times. The life line, the crease at the base of the thumb; the liver line across the wrist; and the heart line ending near the index finger were the most important in determining health, although perhaps

the heart line was studied more often in relation to the tender emotion supposed to be centered in this organ than in relation to diseases. Of course, the creases in the hands are simply places where the skin is firmly tied down to the

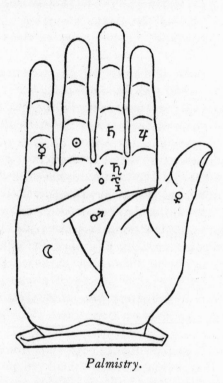

Palmistry.

underlying flesh; the lines are no more indicative of states of health than are finger prints.

In the seventeenth century astrology bulked large in medical superstitions. It was to hold its place until the eventful year 1758. Halley, the astronomer, calculated that the comet which now bears his name would appear in that year. It did. And men realized then that comets were not the gods' token of disease but instead were themselves under the rule of mathematics.

We mentioned astrology, the so-called science of the influence of the heavenly bodies on human life and health, when we talked about Arabian medicine. But astrology was older than the Arabian civilization; it probably arose among the Babylonians or Chaldeans. About the fourth century B.C. it spread to Greece and under Greek influence was woven into every phase of art and science and indeed every act of daily life. From Greece, astrology followed the stream of knowledge; it went into Egypt in a new form with the Ptolemies; it reached Rome shortly before the opening of the Christian Era; it spread to the Moslem Empire; it was carried into Western Europe and throve there from the thirteenth to the seventeenth centuries. Among ignorant people it still flourishes even in America of today. The almanacs of patent medicines still occasionally show the typical picture of a man surrounded by the constellations of the zodiac, from each of which a line extends to the organ that the particular constellation controls. Again in the columns of newspapers and magazines and over the radio, astrological advice is given concerning the indications of the stars for lucky days and ventures. Fortune tellers, in spite of laws prohibiting their practice, still for a fee draw horoscopes showing the fate of the individual as predicted from the position of the constellation at the moment of birth.

The absurdity of astrology is apparent to any moderately well educated and intelligent person of today; but three hundred years ago astrology was an accepted and serious part of medicine. The time for bleeding, the time for taking medicines, indeed, even the form of treatment used, as well as the kind of disease present, were often determined from the stars. The royal astrologer was a very important man at court.

In 1621 the scholar Robert Burton published an amazing book called the *Anatomy of Melancholy*. In it was his horoscope showing that his death would occur in 1640. He died on the twenty-fifth of January, 1640—some say at his own

hands so that his horoscope would come out correctly. Cromwell is said to have had his "lucky days," and the great astronomer Kepler occasionally drew horoscopes. But in the seventeenth century many people were becoming skeptical of astrology; astronomical discoveries were yielding a new conception of the stars and planets. It was just after the close of the seventeenth century that Jonathan Swift, the author of *Gulliver's Travels*, perpetrated a hoax on astrology that by ridicule hastened the discarding of the practice in England. Swift, as you know, wielded a satirical pen that could drive home his points by astute exaggeration. Thus in his paper *Modest Proposal for Preventing the Children of Poor People from being a Burden to their Parents or the Country*, he ridiculed the futile schemes of impractical writers on social problems. His suggestion was to fatten the children and eat them.

His astrological hoax was in the form of an announcement that on March 29, 1708, a certain Mr. Partridge would die. Instead of his own name on the announcement, Swift signed that of Isaac Bickerstaff. Mr. Partridge was a famous almanac maker and predictor of events. On March 30 Mr. Bickerstaff published a notice that his prediction was correct and that Partridge was dead. Partridge at once protested that he was alive; Bickerstaff denied it. The silliness of the controversy between the indignant Partridge and the sarcastic and insistent Bickerstaff amused the public. When a thing is ridiculed and parodied it is difficult ever again to view it seriously. Astrology declined rapidly.

But our language, which is in itself a record of the past, still keeps words derived from astrology. Lunatic is one of them—from luna, the moon that shone on men in their sleep and made them insane.

More pernicious by far than astrology was the superstitious belief, still existent in the seventeenth century, in witchcraft. By witchcraft, so it was thought, a spell could be cast upon some victim and disease and misfortune produced.

This, as you will recognize, was a belief that had persisted from the time of primitive people when the medicine man was supposed to be able to do black magic. There were many efforts made by men and women of the sixteenth and seventeenth centuries to dispose of their enemies or their rivals by using black magic. Sometimes little images were shaped in wax and needles stuck with proper ceremony in the part where the disease was to strike, or the image was melted to cause death. Needless to say no ill effects came from these

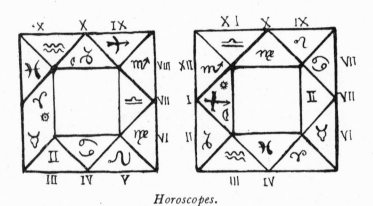

Horoscopes.

vindictive if harmless practices. But there was another aspect which was far from harmless. Sometimes when people had misfortunes or disease they believed them caused by black magic and accordingly sought to find the enemy who was attacking them. As like as not they hit on some poor wretch who was insane, who lived alone, was queer in her actions, and muttered meaningless words. She was accused of being a witch, and was drowned or burned.

Superstition in the seventeenth century still prevented men from realizing that the insane were really sick people. The savage superstition of possession by evil demons persisted in the midst of the elaborate civilizations of France, England, Germany, and Italy. Little kindness was shown to

the insane; they were often taken to be witches or else possessed. But some institutions had arisen for the care of the more violent and incurable cases. The most famous of all was the hospital of St. Mary's of Bethlehem in London. With the English genius for such things, the name was shortened to Bedlam; the word has come down to our time to signify a place of discord and turmoil—a lasting commentary on the conditions of this institution. It was super-

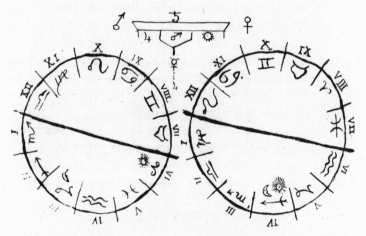

Horoscope in geometrical form.

stition, ancient savage beliefs, that prevented people from realizing that the insane man was a sick man, as deserving of care and sympathy as the man who was physically ill. Shakespeare had spoken of insanity as "a mind diseased," but three centuries were to pass—three centuries of stupid brutality—before this knowledge was to become widespread and the insane were to receive humane care. In the sixteenth century Bedlam, with its imprisoned, tortured inmates, was a sort of zoo where of a Sunday afternoon the curious could for a penny see the mad men. It was one of the sights of London.

When we spoke in passing of some of the minor personal superstitions of the kings and queens of the period—the cramp rings of Henry and the charmed locket of Elizabeth —we said that we would tell of the medical ritual in which Charles II was involved. It was a superstitious proceeding at the hands of his physician. Remember nearly a century had passed since the days when gentle old Ambroise Paré showed Charles IX how to test the bezoar stone by the method of control experiment. Here, on the other hand, are the remedies that the royal physicians applied to a dying king in the year 1685.

The records tell us that at eight o'clock on the morning of February second, King Charles fell unconscious while shaving in his bedroom. His physician, on being summoned, bled the King to the extent of a pint from his right arm. Next he drew eight ounces of blood from the left shoulder (Harvey had described the circulation of the blood fifty-seven years before), gave an emetic to make the King vomit, two physics and an enema containing antimony, rock salt, marsh-mallow leaves, violets, beet root, camomile flowers, fennel seed, linseed, cardamom seed, cinnamon, saffron, cochineal, and aloes. The King's head was then shaved and a blister raised on his scalp. A sneezing powder of hellebore root was given to purge his brain and a powder of cowslip administered to strengthen it, for it was the belief in those days that the nasal secretion came from the brain. The emetics were continued at frequent intervals and meanwhile a soothing drink given, composed of barley water, licorice, and sweet almonds, light wine, oil of wormwood, anise, thistle leaves, mint, rose, and angelica. A plaster of pitch and pigeon dung was put on the King's feet. Next there was more bleeding followed by the administration of melon seeds, manna, slippery elm, black cherry water, extract of lily of the valley, peony, lavender, pearls dissolved in vinegar, gentian root, nutmeg, and cloves. To this mixture were

added forty drops of the extract of human skull. Finally in desperation a bezoar stone was tried. The King died.

Hardly a single one of the medicines given the King had, as we know now, any effect upon the body whatever. The mixture of drugs sounds more like something prepared in a nightmare than in a drugstore.

We should call these remedies superstitious ones today; they were not then. A superstition, as we said many chapters earlier, is a belief inconsistent with generally prevailing knowledge. As we shall see in the next chapter the medicaments used on poor King Charles were unfortunately consistent with the knowledge of the time.

Few of the scientists of those days—such men as Harvey, Sanctorius, and Malpighi—had turned their attention to the treatment of disease. They were interested in finding out how the body worked rather than how to treat the sick man. The remedies of the seventeenth century, barring only a few, were nearly as unscientific as those that the savage used.

In 1618, the first *London Pharmacopœia* appeared. A pharmacopœia is a book listing the remedies used in treating disease and giving the recipes for their preparation. There were nearly two thousand remedies described in this book, the vast majority of which were herb medicaments. A few of the remedies were valuable beyond question and are in use today: there was quinine, the great medical discovery of the seventeenth century, and mercury salts, the potent mineral medicament that Paracelsus had advocated, and "steel" tonics for the treatment of anæmia. But with these few there were many showing only too clearly that five thousand years and more of civilization had not changed the beliefs of ignorant people. That the great inventions of movable type and ink and paper should be used to record such remedies was itself an anachronism. There were pills made of viper flesh, the dried lungs of foxes for shortness of breath, ground up jewels, oil squeezed from bricks, bear grease to grow hair, and snake oil to limber muscles, moss

scraped from the skull of a convict hanged in chains (a popular remedy), crabs' eyes, hoofs of animals, fly specks, the
dung of many different kinds of animals (crocodile dung
was especially beneficial), human sweat, saliva, spider's
webs, snake skins, lice, oil of puppies boiled with earth-
worms, and cat-fat ointment! The very witches' caldron was
brewed in the pharmacopœia of the seventeenth century.

CHAPTER XXI

The Practice of Medicine

IN the seventeenth century medicine as it was practiced was out of date. The satires of the great French dramatist Molière held the doctors up to ridicule before an amused public. It is said that Molière had a personal grievance against physicians; they were unable to cure him of the consumption from which he was dying; they had failed to save the life of his son, and of his dearest friend. Whatever his motive may have been, his keen satire dissected medical practice and laid bare its greatest fault. Medicine was out of date.

The doctors of the seventeenth century were trained as doctors had been trained in the Middle Ages. Disputation, hair-splitting argument over the authoritative statements of Galen and the Arabian physicians was still the essence of medical education. The great medical school of Paris allowed no student to read or discuss the works of Paracelsus. Medical practice was what it had been in the fourteenth, fifteenth, and sixteenth centuries. The doctors were educated, but they were not educated to treat diseases. They were the same scholarly and pompous gentlemen against whom a century before Paracelsus had directed his shafts.

In one scene of Molière's play, *L'Amour Médecin*, five physicians in their best professional manner bring all their powers of subtle disputation to bear upon the momentous subject of whether it fits their dignity better to ride to their patients on a horse or a mule. And that argument had truly as much importance as many upon which the doctors wasted their energies.

The last play written by Molière was *Le Malade Imaginaire;* it had to do with a man sick only in his imagination, a hypochondriac, who took all sorts of patent medicines and

consulted many doctors. The part that satirized medical practice dealt with the elaborate ceremony of graduation from a medical school, a form of ceremony that had sur-

Semeiotica Uranica :
OR, AN
ASTROLOGICAL JUDGEMENT
OF
DISEASES
From the Decumbiture of the sick
much Enlarged.

1. *From* Aven Ezra *by way of Introduction.*
2. *From* Noel Duret *by way of Direction.*

Wherein is laid down,
The way and manner of finding out the Cause, Change., and End of the disease. Also whether the sick be likely to live or die; and the time when Recovery or Death is to be expected.

With the Signs of Life or Death by the body of the Sick party, according to the judgment of *Hippocrates.*

Whereunto is added,

A Table of Logisticall Logarithmes, to find the exact time of the Crisis *HermesTrismegistus* upon the first Decumbiture of the sick: shewing the signs & conjectures of the disease, and of life and death, by the good or evil position of the Moon at the time of the Patients lying down, or demanding the question: Infallible signs to know of what complexion any person is whatsoever: With a compendious Treatise of Urine.

By NICHOLAS CULPEPER *Gent.*
Student in Physick and Astrologie.

Disce, sed ira cadat naso, rugosaque sanaa. Persius.

London, Printed for *Nath. Brookes* at the Golden Angel on *Cornhil*, neer the *Exchange*, 1658.

Diagnosis of disease from the stars.

vived from the Middle Ages. It actually took a week or more of banqueting, arguing, speech making, and parading before the student was pronounced a doctor. In Moliere's play the

graduation disputation is burlesqued by a ballet singing in a sort of "pig Latin." Latin was still the language of medicine, in spite of the efforts of Paracelsus to break down the tradition.

It was in the fourth performance of *Le Malade Imaginaire* that Molière, while playing his part, became weak and faint; he covered his hesitation with a forced laugh. After the play he was carried home; he died that night.

The seventeenth century was a period of scientific progress. There, for all to see, was an amazing contrast: on the one hand, science that flourished in the work of Vesalius, Sanctorius, Harvey, Malpighi; and, on the other, a practice of medicine that remained unchanged.

But the truth is, science did not help the doctor. It was of no assistance to him to learn that the blood circulated, for he did not know what function the blood served in the body; the knowledge of the circulation merely cast doubt on his cherished practice of bleeding. The measurements that Sanctorius had made did not help the doctor in the treatment of disease, for no one yet knew the significance of these measurements. The anatomy of Vesalius helped the surgeons, it is true, but not the physicians; there was as yet no connection between anatomy and disease except in the case of diseases curable with the knife.

The doctors were bewildered. The whole structure upon which they depended was being torn down about them. Galen was wrong; Arabian medicine was little better than superstition. The scientists told them that, but gave them nothing to replace the things they took away. Paracelsus said study Nature; the philosopher Descartes said the body was a machine to be studied as a machine; Van Helmont said it was a chemical reaction. The scientists could not even agree among themselves except in saying that Galen was wrong and the Arabs were wrong.

Science did no more for medicine than did the satire of

Molière. Both simply showed that medicine had not kept pace with the progress of the time. But the scientists themselves, when they practiced medicine, discarded their science and dealt with disease as Galen had directed. We have described the treatment given King Charles II; it was carried out in the same royal court in which half a century before Harvey himself had been physician.

This was the unfortunate situation when there entered upon the scene a man destined to start medical practice on the path of progress. What Hippocrates had done for the medicine of the fifth century B.C., Thomas Sydenham did for the medicine of the seventeenth century. He gave to medicine the form it holds today, he made it a discipline to which experimental science and mathematical science could make their contributions.

Sydenham was an English practitioner of medicine. He disclaimed the use of all science but nevertheless he was a scientist. He did not use the principle of experiment, he did not use mathematical proof, but he did observe and describe. He dealt with the practice of medicine in the same way that Vesalius had dealt with anatomy.

Sydenham was born in 1624, four years after the Pilgrims landed at Plymouth Rock. These were troublesome times for men of the Puritan faith; and Thomas had been brought up a Puritan. The year he entered Oxford University the Great Rebellion broke out. Leaving school he joined the forces against the king. Four years later the army disbanded, but Sydenham, then twenty-two, felt too old to start again in college. At a loss for a career, he decided to take up medicine. He entered the medical school of Oxford but he learned little there, for in the years that he had been campaigning he had forgotten his Latin. After two years of struggle with books and lectures, he was granted, largely through political influence, so it is said, the degree of bachelor of medicine. That was in the year 1648.

Almost at once war broke out again and Sydenham turned from medicine, with some relief we may suspect, to serve in the army, not as a surgeon, but as a captain of cavalry.

Events moved fast. In 1649 Charles I was beheaded; his son Charles II, then a refugee in Paris, took ship and landed first in Jersey and then in Scotland, where in 1651 he was crowned King of the Scots. The same year he was defeated by the army of Cromwell, and after many adventures he again escaped to France. In 1653 Oliver Cromwell became Lord Protector and Thomas Sydenham reluctantly settled down to practice medicine in Westminster. Politics still held his attention and he obtained an official position. But that was lost, and with it all hope of a political career, when in 1660 King Charles II was restored to the throne.

It looked very much as if Sydenham would have to practice medicine after all. He must have thought so himself, for he went for a year to the Medical School of Montpellier to make up some of the deficiencies of his education. Sydenham was thirty-nine when he passed his examination permitting him to practice medicine in London; he was fifty-two before he obtained his degree of doctor of medicine.

In his career with its many interruptions Sydenham had no opportunity to learn the science of the time, to study the anatomy of Vesalius, ponder over the discovery of Harvey, try the measurements of Sanctorius, or discuss the theories of Descartes. He was above all else a practical man, a soldier turned doctor. He approached the problem of medical practice with an open mind. The fact is that he had not had enough medical education to be spoiled by having drilled into him with all their weight the beliefs that the practitioners of medicine then held.

Education colors our views, determines the way we see and interpret the facts before us. If the views are false then we are actually blinded to realities; we cannot see them in their true importance and true relation. Instead, we see them

only through the tinted and distorting glasses which bad education has put before our eyes. Primitive man, trained to believe in spirits, interpreted every fact of nature as a manifestation of spirits; the doctors of the seventeenth century, trained in the beliefs of Galen and of the Arabian physicians, saw in sickness only what these men had pointed out.

Paracelsus, you will remember, with all the strength of his egotistical personality, revolted against this kind of education. He wanted to use his own eyes and to see clearly. He came near seeing what Sydenham saw, but he expressed himself in a fashion far too mystical for other physicians of his time to understand.

There was nothing mystical about Sydenham. It was his practical army training rather than his medical training that seemed to influence his views and determine the way he would attack the problem of disease.

From earliest times, men had looked upon disease as one common thing with many different manifestations in the body. What physicians, philosophers, scientists had sought for was the cause of disease; they wished to solve the problem of disease as a whole.

Sydenham saw the problem differently. He knew that a good general does not plan his attack against enemies as a whole, but against each enemy separately. In warfare the general finds out first all there is to be learned about the enemy he is facing. He must study his position, numbers, armament. Then only when he has obtained all necessary information about the particular enemy can he plan and execute a successful attack.

Sydenham recognized that the same principle applied to diseases. He said in effect: the human mind is far too limited in its ability and knowledge to settle the great problems of what disease is and why there should be disease. While we debate such questions there are sick men who need help and for whom we as physicians are "answerable to God." The

place to study disease is at the bedside of the sick man; by observation and experience we can learn the nature of diseases.

Hippocrates might have spoken these words. But there was one great difference between the method of Hippocrates

Sydenham.

and that of Sydenham. Hippocrates had studied the appearance and behavior of men who suffered from disease; he described how they looked and acted. From observation and experience he learned that when certain symptoms appeared the illness followed one course; with other symptoms it followed another course. He could thus judge, prognosticate, the probable outcome of the illness.

Sydenham on the contrary studied diseases. He believed that there was not one general illness with many different

forms but that there were many different diseases. Each one was as definite and separate as were the different species of plants and animals. By careful study the physician could recognize the particular disease that affected the man just as a biologist could recognize a plant or animal.

According to Sydenham the particular disease attacks the body; the body in turn resists the disease and tries to overcome it by its inherent healing powers. The symptoms of disease result from the struggle between the body and the disease. These symptoms—the pain, the fever, the weakness—are not the disease itself, they are merely signs of the struggle that is going on, they are part of the body's effort to overcome the disease. With each kind of disease the struggle made by the body is different; therefore the symptoms are different. By studying the course of the illness carefully from the appearance of the first symptoms to the disappearance of the last, it should be possible, so Sydenham thought, to write a description of the disease itself—to write, as it were, the natural history of each disease.

It was to this task that he set himself. In 1675 he gave the first full and accurate account of scarlet fever and measles. He described smallpox, malaria, and dysentery. His masterpiece, published in 1683, was a description of gout, a disease from which he himself suffered.

Sydenham based his treatment on the idea that the physician should attempt to assist the natural healing powers of the body, to help it overcome the particular disease that affected it, not merely to overcome the symptoms—the signs of the struggle. He had no use whatever for the vast array of herbs and vile concoctions with which the pharmacopœia of his day supplied the doctor. He used only the few remedies which observation and experience showed him to be definitely beneficial—iron for anæmia, quinine for malaria, and sedatives to give rest and sleep and so to restore strength. Instead of using many medicines, as was the common procedure in medical practice then—you will recall those used

on poor King Charles—he turned to other forms of treatment designed to build up the inherent self-healing powers of the body. He introduced such innovations as fresh air in the sick room, horseback riding for consumption, and cooling drinks for smallpox. Instead of attempting to adjust the disordered humors of the body or drive out disease with foul medicines, he tried to help the body heal itself.

The work of Sydenham brought system and order into medical practice to replace confusion. Since his time physicians have continued to describe diseases in the way that he did—separately.

If you look at an old textbook of medicine you will find it mainly a discussion of symptoms. One large section is devoted to fevers of all kinds, simple fevers, intermittent fevers, malignant fevers, fevers with eruptions, and so on. If then you turn to the pages of a modern text on the practice of medicine, you will find, thanks to Sydenham, not symptoms as the headings, but diseases, named, classified, and described so that they can be recognized.

Look under smallpox. You will find that smallpox is in brief an acute infection developing nine to fifteen days after exposure; that it begins with a chill, headache, pain in the back, and often vomiting followed by a rise in temperature and rapid pulse. Usually on the fourth day bright red spots appear, first on the face and arms and legs. The temperature falls. On the fifth or sixth day the red spots change to small blisters. About the eighth day pus appears in the blisters and the temperature again rises. In favorable cases the eruption subsides, the sores heal, often leaving scars, and normal health slowly returns. You will find much more detail, of course, for recognizing a disease even when it is fully described is sometimes difficult.

After reading a full description of smallpox and carefully examining many people with the disease, the physician has in mind a clear conception of the disease itself; he knows its natural history and its behavior and probable outcome. He

can differentiate and treat each disease separately and not waste his efforts trying to treat diseases in general. But to do so he must study each patient thoroughly.

This conception was new in medicine. Hippocrates had urged physicians to study the sick man; Paracelsus had told them to turn from books and theories to the study of the disease state. But it was Sydenham who told them what to look for, how to describe disease, how to classify it. Here then was something concrete and practical for the physician to deal with—the natural history of separate diseases.

Following the method of Sydenham, many physicians began to study their patients carefully, began the work of compiling the description of individual diseases.

In making the study every possible clue that would lead to a more thorough description of the disease was followed. It was here that the contributions of mathematical science had their place. In smallpox the pulse was rapid; there was fever. These were clues. The pulse must be counted, the temperature taken in all diseases and comparison made so that these clues could be used to help distinguish one disease from another. New methods of diagnosis made the separation of the diseases easier and more certain. In the centuries between the time of Sydenham and our own we shall see in our story the rise and development of means of diagnosis, the stethoscope, the art of percussion, the X-ray, the serum tests and all the array of precise methods at the command of the modern physician.

In the scheme of diseases that Sydenham presented there was another place for science; it was to determine what changes occurred in the organs and tissues of the body in the separate diseases. It was here that the anatomy of Vesalius and the microscope of Galileo were to play their parts. In the centuries ahead of us we shall see the rise of a new study in medicine called pathology, the study of the changes in the flesh caused by diseases, the changes from which the symptoms of disease arise. Into the same scheme fitted the

work of Harvey and all other scientists who were to study the functions of organs. How was the action of the heart affected by one disease or another; what was the significance of its altered action; what symptoms, what changes, what diseases even, arose from the disturbed function of the various organs? First the scientist must tell the physician what the organs did in the body, must describe their physiology.

And finally we shall come to still another study, of the cause of each separate disease, the thing which acts to produce the changes in the flesh and in the function. In that field, as we shall see, lies one of the greatest discoveries of modern science, the discovery of the bacterial cause of infectious diseases.

The great practical triumphs of modern medicine have been achieved in the years which lie between Sydenham's time and ours. For the majority of diseases there are precise descriptions, exact methods of diagnosis, an understanding of the changes within the body, and knowledge of means for prevention or treatment. It was Sydenham who pointed the way for the progress of medicine, who made it possible for medicine to keep up with science. Perhaps if Sydenham had not shown us how to attack the enemy disease, we today, in spite of science, might be as ignorant about diseases, as unhealthy, as short lived, as were the people of the seventeenth century.

Part Eight

EUROPEAN MEDICINE COMES TO AMERICA

A CENTURY IN AMERICA

DOCTORS IN LACES AND FRILLS

CHAPTER XXII

European Medicine Comes to America

IN early chapters we saw the stream of medical knowledge emerge from the spirit-infested swamp in which primitive man lived, and flow turbid, muddy with false beliefs, into the earliest civilizations. We followed it from Egypt to Greece where it was freshened and widened by new sources. From Greece we traced it westward with Alexander and still farther westward with the Roman conquests. And then with the fall of the Empire we saw it recede eastward, through Byzantium, Syria, and into the Arabian Empire. In the days of the Crusades we again followed it westward into Italy, Germany, France, and England, sluggish and slow, but gradually gaining impetus. Finally in the seventeenth century we saw it abruptly widen and quicken, still carrying some of the flotsam and jetsam of the past, some superstitions, but flowing broader and deeper and more swiftly than it ever had before.

In the seventeenth century it again turned westward. English settlers bore their medical knowledge to the eastern shores of the New World. And there on plain and in forest, wherever settler met Indian, a curious contrast could be found. Medical knowledge accumulated through five thousand years and more of progress was brought face to face with the source from which it sprang. The medicine of the Indian was the medicine of primitive peoples, unchanged in one hundred and fifty centuries. The medicine of the settlers was that of Europe in the seventeenth century.

In the opening years of the century both settler and Indian were confronted with conditions new to them. The Spanish explorers, earlier comers to the New World than the settlers of Virginia and Plymouth, had brought to the continent infectious diseases from which the Indians had

never before suffered. In great waves epidemics swept over the tribes, threatening to exterminate them.

What the disease or diseases were we do not know for sure; but it is certain that if the Indians had not been stricken they would have opposed more strongly than they did the landing of the colonists. Quite naturally, but rather uncharitably, the Pilgrims looked upon the affliction of the Indians as a special blessing sent by God to aid in the establishment upon these shores, as they said, of "a better stock."

The descriptions that eye-witnesses have left of the "prodigious pestilence" of the Indians are too meager and too biased to afford certain recognition. Some physicians of later date thought it smallpox, but that hardly seems likely, for the settlers were not affected at the time by the disease of the Indians, although in later years smallpox became a sore trial to them. Others have thought it bubonic plague, but certainly immigrants from plague-ridden London would have recognized that disease. And still others have believed it yellow fever, although it could not have been this disease, for yellow fever is carried only by a mosquito and the outbreaks occurred in the winter when there are no mosquitoes.

It seems very probable that the epidemic may have been measles. This is a disease that we consider one of the less important illnesses of childhood, but it can be very serious. There is a common belief among doctors that when a large part of the population of any country has suffered generation after generation from some disease, a partial resistance to it develops. The disease becomes as mild as measles is with us. But when this apparently mild disease is introduced to a people who have never had it, and hence are completely unresistant to it, it again becomes virulent and mortal.

In quite modern times an outbreak similar to that among the Indians occurred in the Fiji Islands. The King of Fiji, his family, and a number of his followers went aboard a British warship and were exposed to measles. The disease, which none of the natives had ever had, spread throughout

the Islands. Within a few months nearly a third of the population had died. But the question has been raised: did they die because this disease became for a time more deadly among them or from lack of care? In civilized surroundings measles attacks a majority of the population, but only a few are sick at any one time and these are mostly children cared for by parents who years before have had measles and become immune. There in the Fiji Islands, however, nearly all the natives fell sick at the same time. There was no one left to care for them. Many, too ill to provide for their own wants, actually died of starvation.

Whatever the pestilence of the American Indians may have been, it afflicted them severely; all writers of the times agree on that. Daniel Gookin in his account of the Indian tribes says of the outbreak among the Pawkunnawkutts: "This people were a potent nation in former times, and could raise . . . about three thousand men . . . a very great number of them were swept away by an epidemic and unwonted sickness, An. 1612 and 1613. [It was in reality 1616 and 1617.] Thereby divine providence made way for the quiet and peaceable settlement of the English in those nations."

Of the Pawtuckets he says: "They were also a considerable people heretofore, about three thousand men. . . . But they also were almost completely destroyed by the great sickness . . . ; so that at this day they are not above two hundred and fifty men, besides women and children."

Of the way in which the Indians treated infectious diseases we have a description in the writings of an English traveler, John Josselyn, who visited the early settlements. He writes: "Their physicians are the Powaws or Indian Priests who cure sometimes by charms or medicines, but in general infections they seldom come amongst them, therefore they use their own remedies, which is sweating, etc. Their manner is when they have the plague as smallpox amongst them to cover their Wigwams with Bark so close that no Air can enter in . . . and making a great fire till they

are in top sweat, and then run out in the Sea or River, and presently after they come into their Hutts again; they either recover or give up the Ghost."

John Lawson, who at the close of the century was surveyor-general of North Carolina, has left us an account of Indian surgery, although in this instance it is of a form hardly more beneficial than the common practice of scalping. He describes the way in which the Seneca Indians prevented prisoners from escaping:

"The Indian that put us in our path, had been a prisoner among the Sinnegars [Seneca Indians] but had outrun them, although they had cut his toes and half his feet away, which is a practice common amongst them. They first raise the skin, then cut away half the feet, and so wrap the skin over the stump and make a present cure of the wounds. This commonly disables them from making their escape, they being not so good travellers as before, and the impression of their half feet makes it easy to trace them."

Of the actual ministrations of the medicine man Lawson gives this account: "As soon as the doctor comes into the cabin, the sick person is set on a mat or skin stark naked, except some trifle. . . . In this manner the patient lies when the conjurer appears, and the King of that nation comes to attend him with a rattle made of a gourd with peas in it. This the King delivers into the doctor's hand whilst another brings a bowl of water and sets it down. Then the doctor begins and utters some few words very softly; afterwards he smells the patient's navel and belly; and sometimes scarifies him a little with a flint, or an instrument made of rattlesnake teeth for this purpose; then he sucks the patient and gets out a mouthful of blood and serum . . . which he spits in the bowl of water. Then he begins to mutter and talk apace, and at last to cut capers and clap his hands on his breech and sides, till he gets into a sweat, so that a stranger would think that he was running mad, now and then sucking the patient . . . still continuing his grimaces and antic

postures, which are not to be matched in Bedlam. At last
you will see the doctor all over of a dropping sweat, and
scarcely able to utter one word, having quite spent himself;
and then he will cease for awhile, and so begin again till he
comes in the same pitch of raving and seeming madness as

Matthew Hopkins, the famous "witch-finder."

before; all this time the sick body never so much as moves,
although doubtless the lancing and sucking must be a great
punishment to them. . . . At last the conjurer makes an
end, and tells the patient's friends whether the patient will
live or die; and then one that waits at this ceremony takes
the blood away . . . and buries it in the ground in a place
unknown to anyone but he that inters it."

Certainly the most famous example of the actual meeting

of primitive medicine and seventeenth-century medicine on
the shores of America was the treatment of the Indian chief
Massasoit. Word came to Plymouth that Massasoit, who
had befriended the colonists, was dying. Edward Winslow,
later Governor of the Plymouth Colony, and John Hamden
went to offer sympathy and help to the chief. Governor
Winslow in his *Good News from New England* tells of the
incident:

"When we came thither we found the house so full of
men as we could scarcely get in; though they used their best
diligence to make way for us. They were in the midst of
their charms for him making such a hellish noise, as to dis-
temper us that were well. . . . About him were six or eight
women, who chafed his arms, legs, and thighs, to keep heat
in him."

Winslow finally made his way through the milling Indians to the chief's side and offered help. Massasoit nodded
his consent. "And," says Winslow, "having a confection of
many comfortable conserves, etc.; on the point of my knife
I gave him some; which I could scarcely get through his
teeth. When it was dissolved in his mouth, he swallowed the
juice of it whereat those that were about him much rejoiced,
saying, he had not swallowed anything in two days before.
I then desired to see his mouth which was exceedingly
furred; and his tongue swelled in such a manner, as it was
not possible for him to eat such meat as they had, his
[throat] being stopped up. Then I washed his mouth and
scraped his tongue; and got abundance of corruption out of
the same. . . . Then he desired to drink; I dissolved some
of it [the confection] in water and gave him thereof. Within
half an hour, this wrought a great alteration in him, in the
eyes of all that beheld him." Next Winslow sent back to the
colony for a chicken for broth and "such physic as the Surgeon durst administer."

While waiting the return of the messenger, Massasoit
asked Winslow to go among the Indians, "requesting me to

wash their mouths also and give to each of them some of the same I gave him. . . . This pains I took with willingness; though it were much offensive to me, not being accustomed to such poisonous savours."

The cure of Massasoit, as you will remember, had a most fortunate outcome for the colonists. In gratitude the chief revealed to Winslow the details of a conspiracy among the Indians to murder the English.

Winslow was not a doctor, but in those early days every man in the colonies of necessity learned something of practical medicine, just as he learned carpentry, farming, fishing, and hunting.

In the early years of the century, while the Indians suffered from the epidemics, the settlers themselves were having a tragic time learning to live under the conditions which they found in America. The voyage across the sea was long and there was sickness on the boats, especially scurvy from the lack of fresh food. When Francis Blackwell sailed from Amsterdam in 1618, only 50 out of 180 of the crew and passengers reached Virginia. That was of course an exceptionally high mortality, but even after more fortunate passages the survivors were weak and ill-nourished—and, one cannot doubt, frightfully homesick. Nor did their troubles end with the voyage; far from it; privation and sickness were awaiting them.

The colonists who landed at Cape Henry, Virginia, on April 26, 1607, and settled at Jamestown, had made a voyage of some ninety-six days. They disembarked on a fair day when the land was fresh with the flowers and grass of spring. William Strachey, secretary and recorder of the colony, described the new country in glowing terms. It seems to have been a failing of the early colonists to write home to friends and relatives of the comforts and prosperity they were enjoying in America, when in reality they were suffering and dying. Perhaps they were whistling to keep up their flagging courage, for George Percy, brother of the Earl of

Northumberland and one of the first settlers in Jamestown, has left quite a different account of conditions in the colony. He wrote: "Our men are destroyed with cruel disease, as swellings, flixes, burning fevers, and by wars and some departed suddenly. But for the most part they died of mere famine. There were never Englishmen left in a foreign country in such misery as we were, in this newly discovered Virginia. We watched every three nights lying on the bare, cold ground, what weather soever came; working all the next day which brought our men to be most feeble wretches. Our food was but a small can of barley sod in water to five men a day; our drink cold water taken out of the river, which was at flood very salty, at a low tide full of slime and filth . . . our men night and day groaned in every corner of the fort most pitiful to hear. If there were any conscience in men it would make their hearts bleed to hear the pitiful murmurings and outcries of our sick men, without relief every night and day for the space of six weeks; some departed out of the world, many times three or four in a night, in the morning their bodies trailed out of their cabins like dogs to be buried."

It has been estimated that 4170 immigrants landed in Virginia between 1607 and 1621. In 1624 the actual population was 1800.

Out of the hundred Pilgrims who landed at Plymouth in December, 1620, only fifty were alive in March. The immigrants who settled at Charlestown, although they arrived in the summer, suffered nearly as badly. They became ill when they ate berries in the fields and forests; they became ill again when they tried to live on the salt meat they had brought with them. The country was far hotter than any climate they had experienced. Sickness spread through the camp.

The Plymouth colony, more fortunate in having a man who acted as physician, Samuel Fuller, loaned their medical man to the inhabitants of Charlestown. He was unable to

handle the situation there and wrote back, "Many are sick, and many are dead, the Lord in mercy look upon them." The immigrants, wholly ignorant of how a camp should be run, had allowed the grounds of their settlement to become filthy with decaying refuse. It was unfit for human habitation. The people deserted it and settled in what is now Boston.

Dr. Fuller of the Mayflower was not the first English physician to come to America; in fact he really held no medical degree. There is said to have been a doctor among the colonists of Jamestown. However he left soon and was replaced the following year by another who accompanied Captain John Smith on some of his voyages of exploration. After a few months his place was taken by still another doctor. None of these physicians appears to have remained long in the settlement. Perhaps they were merely recent medical graduates in search of experience. In those times it was common for such men to join a ship's company. In any event Captain Smith, when wounded in 1609 by an explosion of gunpowder, was forced to return to London for treatment, since at that date there were no physicians in the colony. Dr. John Pott was the first physician to live permanently in Virginia; he became governor in 1628.

With the growth of towns and harvesting of crops, the most trying days for the colonists were over. Immigrants came in ever increasing numbers and among them were a few trained physicians. Of these certainly the most famous was Dr. John Winthrop, Jr., first Governor of Connecticut and one of the early members of the Royal Society of England. Some of these early doctors were preachers as well; there was a strong tendency to combine the two callings. This situation may account at least in part for the fact that during epidemics of disease there were often proclaimed days for fasting and prayers of deliverance, to be followed by a feast of thanksgiving when the outbreak had passed. These spiritual appeals had something in common with

what we call public health. Today, however, with public health, we turn to quarantine, sewage disposal, and water purification instead of fast days.

The earliest of the fast days proclaimed against disease was July 3, 1644; the records do not state what the disease was, but merely that "there was much sickness in the land." In the course of an epidemic of "chin-cough"—whooping cough—in the Plymouth colony about the year 1649, a number of fast days were held.

One after another the more common infectious diseases found their way to America; some in the seventeenth century and some not until the eighteenth. Influenza was epidemic in 1647, and in the same year yellow fever appeared in Massachusetts; in the next century it was to decimate the inhabitants of Philadelphia. Yellow fever was then prevalent in the Barbados, and to prevent its further spread to the mainland the first quarantine regulation in America was put into effect. In 1665 this quarantine was extended to all boats coming from England, for that was the year of the last great epidemic of bubonic plague in London. Diphtheria first appeared in 1659, in Kingston, New Hampshire, so it is said, and spread from there through the colonies, causing a frightful mortality among children. Scarlet fever was first observed in 1783.

The most important date in the history of American epidemics is 1663. That year virulent smallpox appeared in the Dutch settlement of New Netherlands. Fast days were proclaimed in rapid succession as the disease spread from town to town. We shall follow the history of smallpox in America in the next chapter, for the most important developments connected with it occurred in the eighteenth century; it was then that inoculation was first used in America to control it, and then also that vaccination was discovered in England. Smallpox in the seventeenth century in the colonies is, however, connected with one event of at least historical importance. The wide interest in the disease occasioned by the

recurring epidemics led to the publication of the first medical book in America, the only one published here in the seventeenth century. It was written by a doctor-preacher of Boston named Thomas Thacher, and was called *Brief Rule to guide the Common People of New-England how to order themselves and theirs in the Small Pocks or Measels*. It consisted of a single page.

The first physicians who came to this country came before Sydenham's innovations had had any influence on medical education. They were trained in the theories of Galen; perhaps they knew something of the remedies of Paracelsus, and the anatomy of Vesalius, and the surgery of Paré. Oliver Wendell Holmes described a typical colonial physician:

"His pharmacopœia consisted mainly of simples, . . . St. John's wort and Clown's All-heal, with Spurge and Fennel, Saffron and Parsley, Elder and Snakeroot, with opium in some form, and roasted rhubarb and the Four Great Cold Seeds, and the two Resins . . . with the more familiar Scammony and Jalap and Black Hellebore. . . . He would order Iron now and then and possibly an occasional dose of Antimony. He would perhaps have had a rheumatic patient wrapped in the skin of a wolf or wild cat, and in case of a malignant fever with 'purples' . . . or of an obstinate king's evil he might have prescribed a certain black powder, which had been made by calcining toads in an earthen pot. . . . Sydenham had not yet cleansed the Pharmacopœia of its perilous stuff, but there is no doubt that the more sensible doctors of that day knew well enough that a good honest herb-tea which amused the patient and his nurse was all that was required to carry him through all common disorders."

Dr. Holmes used the words "sensible doctors," and certainly that applies to most of those who came to the colonies. Indeed there was about American medicine a practicality that distinguished it from European medicine, which in these years Molière was satirizing with his barbed pen. There was no appreciable audience for medical theorizers

in the colonies; life was very hard and very serious for people there. Doctors must help and struggle as everyone helped and struggled.

There were no medical schools in America until well into the eighteenth century; the immigrant doctors were far too few to care for the population. Some of the young men went back to England for medical training, but many more obtained it by apprenticeship. The boy who intended to devote his life to medicine became a doctor's assistant. He lived in the doctor's home; took care of the doctor's horse and carriage, and rolled pills and mixed powders. In his spare moments he read in the doctor's library and learned the theories of medicine. But his real training was gained when he accompanied the doctor on visits to his patients. There at the bedside the older man pointed out to him the symptoms of disease and the treatment. As they walked or rode on to the home of the next patient, they discussed the case. This was a far different kind of education from that which young men were receiving in Europe where they learned largely from books. The apprenticeship of colonial days was essentially the same as the training given in the hospitals of the modern medical school. It is what is known as clinical instruction, one of the greatest advances in medical education. In colonial days the young doctors learned their medicine in the great school of practical experience.

CHAPTER XXIII

A Century in America

COTTON MATHER, the Puritan preacher of Boston, and Benjamin Franklin, the printer, diplomat, and philosopher, both played prominent parts in the medicine of the colonies in the early eighteenth century. Neither of them was a doctor.

Cotton Mather was a son of the President of Harvard College, Increase Mather. He was hot-headed and energetic and although he was primarily concerned with religion, he turned his restless attention to every event of the day. He wrote on witchcraft, in which he believed firmly, and he was implicated in the Salem witchcraft trials of 1692; he dabbled in politics with no success, he wrote on religion, science, history, and he tried his hand at treating his parishioners' physical as well as spiritual ailments. It is said that his favorite remedy was "sow-bugs" drowned in wine, a remedy quite in line with many then in the pharmacopœia of London. His fame, not as a doctor, but as a scholar, became international, but in 1713 he was elected to the Royal Society of London.

That was the first of a train of events leading to the establishing of his medical importance. As a member of the Society he received copies of the *Transactions*. Some time in the spring of 1721 he read in that august journal two descriptions of how the people of Turkey "buy the smallpox." Now smallpox in those days both in America and Europe, had become a frightfully prevalent disease, a terrifying specter in every home where there were children. Few indeed escaped the infection; millions died—in Europe alone in the eighteenth century sixty million—and many millions more were left marked and deformed for life. According to the article in the *Transactions*, the people of Turkey avoided

the unpleasant consequences of the disease by a process called inoculation. Inoculation is not vaccination. The discovery of vaccination, the event with which we shall close the next chapter, came in 1798.

For an inoculation some of the pus was taken from the sores of a man actually sick with smallpox. A drop of this matter was then put in a scratch on the skin of a man who had not yet had smallpox. From this infection he soon developed the disease. But here is the important point: If he were to acquire smallpox by the usual means of infection, which seems to be connected with the salivary and nasal secretions, his illness would be severe indeed; of those who had smallpox, ten to seventy-five in every hundred died and those who survived were usually pockmarked. But when smallpox was given by inoculation the illness was mild; of those inoculated only one to three in every hundred died, and those who survived were not pockmarked. After smallpox by inoculation, as after smallpox by infection, there was immunity to the disease, that is, it was very rare for anyone to have a second attack. Inoculation was used by the people of Asia just as we now use vaccination—as a means of obtaining immunity to smallpox. There was, however, one great drawback to it. The people who "bought" the mild disease could spread the severe disease just as could those who acquired it by the usual mode of infection. Unless everyone were inoculated when very young, the practice tended to spread smallpox.

The description of inoculation that Cotton Mather read in the *Transactions* excited him immensely; here was a heaven-sent method for controlling a disease that at that moment was scourging the people of Boston. He would have them inoculated. But the procedure was beyond the medical skill of the enthusiastic Puritan—or perhaps for once in his life he did not want to take so great a responsibility. In any event he succeeded in obtaining the aid of a prominent Boston doctor, Zabdiel Boylston. Dr. Boylston, before he would

risk it on any of his patients, tried it first on his only son, a boy of thirteen, and two negro servants. That was on June 26, 1721. The young men inoculated suffered no ill effects nor did they take the smallpox when a few weeks later Dr. Boylston took them to the pesthouse and exposed them freely to the patients with the disease.

Quite unknown to the colonists, the same experiment had been tried in April of the same year in England. Lady Mary

INOCULATION.

THE subscriber respectfully informs the public that he has lately opened an Inoculation, at the pleasantly situated hospital in Glastenbury; Gentlemen and Ladies who wish to have the Small-Pox by this safe and easy method, may be boarded, and have faithful attendance paid them, by their obedient,

ASAPH COLEMAN.

March 23, 1797.

EIGHT months is allowed by the Court of Probate for the district of Hartford, for the creditors of the estate of Col Samuel Talcott, late of Hartford deceased;

An advertisement of an "inoculation farm."

Wortley Montagu, wife of the Ambassador to Turkey, had her son inoculated while the family was still in Turkey. Returning to England, she attempted to interest the doctors of London in the advantages of inoculation. She had little better success in her efforts than did Cotton Mather and Dr. Boylston in the colonies.

During the epidemic of 1721 and 1722, Dr. Boylston inoculated 247 people in Boston; 39 were inoculated by other physicians. Six died. During the same period, 5759 citizens (more than half the population of Boston) acquired the disease by infection. Of these, 844 died. Many of those who recovered were disfigured with scars and broken in health.

Scarcely had the epidemic subsided when a violent controversy arose over inoculation. The physicians themselves

turned against Dr. Boylston. The preachers from their pulpits and editors through their newspapers hurled invectives against inoculation. If a patient died, they said, the doctor who performed the inoculation should be hanged. Admittedly six patients had died. A bomb was thrown into Cotton Mather's home; Dr. Boylston was attacked on the streets; his house was set on fire, and a bomb was thrown into the parlor where his wife was sitting. The Massachusetts House of Representatives passed a bill to prohibit inoculation; but before it became a law, popular feeling had turned in favor of inoculation. Other epidemics of smallpox threatened.

Among the bitterest opponents of inoculation were the Franklin brothers, James and Benjamin, who in August of 1721 had established a paper called the *New England Courant*. The editorials in the journal were sensational for those days, and the denunciation of inoculation was particularly unsparing. Benjamin was then only sixteen years of age; as he grew older his views about inoculation changed. He had a son of his own who died of smallpox in 1736. In his famous *Autobiography* Franklin wrote: "A fine boy of four years old, by the smallpox, taken in the common way. I long regretted bitterly, and still regret I had not given it to him by inoculation. This I mention for the sake of parents who omit that operation, on the supposition that they should never forgive themselves, if a child died under it, my example showing that the regret may be the same either way, and therefore that the safer should be chosen."

Benjamin Franklin became one of the strongest supporters of inoculation; he urged the adoption of the practice in Philadelphia, where he set up his own printing press after leaving his brother James. The practice spread slowly, especially among those whom Franklin called "the common people of America." But opposition was not confined to them, for in 1747 Governor Clinton of New York issued a proclamation in which it was "strictly prohibited and for-

bidden all and every of the Doctors, Physicians, Surgeons and Practitioners of Physick . . . to inoculate for the small-pox any person or persons within the City and County of New York, on pain of being prosecuted to the utmost rigour of the law."

In equally stringent terms the practice is forbidden by law today, but for an entirely different reason. The modern laws were passed when at the close of the eighteenth century vaccination replaced inoculation. Smallpox cannot be spread by the person vaccinated, as it can by someone who has been inoculated.

In spite of Governor Clinton's proclamation the practice of inoculation grew, especially in Massachusetts, Connecticut, and Pennsylvania. In September, 1774, when the Continental Congress was in session, the physicians of Philadelphia agreed to inoculate no one during the time the visiting congressmen were there "as several of the Northern and Southern delegates are understood not to have had that disorder [smallpox]." It was feared that they might become infected from inoculated cases.

In Connecticut especially, judging from the advertisements in the papers, danger of infection was avoided by establishing "inoculation farms" out in the country, where "Ladies and Gentlemen who wish to have the smallpox by this safe and easy method may be boarded and have faithful attendance paid them."

George Washington was a strong advocate of inoculation and during the Revolutionary War ordered that all recruits to the Continental Army who had not already had smallpox should be inoculated. Martha Washington took the disease in this manner. In spite of the growing tolerance toward inoculation, it was by no means universally used; the epidemics of smallpox continued with frightful mortality among the uninoculated.

It was largely through the efforts of Benjamin Franklin that the first hospital was erected in the American colonies.

Franklin had come to Philadelphia in 1726 as an almost penniless young man. Twenty-five years later, wealthy and influential, he found time from his printing ventures to indulge in his many interests—politics, literature, philosophy,

To the Honorable

The CONGRESS of the United-States
of AMERICA,

And to every FRIEND and WELL-WISHER
To the Rights and Liberties of Mankind,

THE FOLLOWING

VINDICATION

OF HIS PUBLIC CHARACTER,

In the Station of DIRECTOR-GENERAL
Of the MILITARY HOSPITALS,

And PHYSICIAN in CHIEF
To the AMERICAN ARMY,

With all deference to Rank and Authority,
AND WITH ALL BECOMING FREEDOM,

CHEARFULLY SUBMITTED
BY

THEIR MOST RESPECTFUL
AND MOST OBEDIENT
HUMBLE SERVANT,

JOHN MORGAN

Title-page of Dr. Morgan's Vindication.

medicine, and science. He became known abroad for his demonstration that lightning was electricity and his invention of the lightning rod, and was recognized as America's leading citizen.

In 1751 the idea was suggested to him by a friend, Dr.

Thomas Bond, that Philadelphia, the metropolis of the colonies, needed a hospital. In Franklin's masterly hands the idea soon grew into a reality. The hospital was opened in 1752 in a rented building. A few years later it was moved to a building erected for the purpose which stands today and is called the Pennsylvania Hospital.

In this hospital—and this is strange for the eighteenth century—insane people were taken as patients. The antics of the insane seem to have attracted many idle people who gathered about the windows and teased the inmates. The board of managers had a fence built; but the crowd clamored outside for admission. A gate was put in the fence and a notice posted that "persons who came out of curiosity to visit the house should pay a sum of money, a Groat at least, for admission."

Although people ill with all sorts of disease were admitted to the hospital, it was the insane, caged in the cellar, who aroused the most interest. One incident connected with a patient named Polly shows the rather informal hospital care of the times and incidentally casts some light on the amusements of the residents of Philadelphia. The records kept by one of the managers are full of the exploits of Polly. Here is one anecdote:

". . . I was walking on the Commons and heard a great noise. Where it came from I could not tell, but list'ning Attentively, I discovered it was from the blue house, and directing my course there, I found it to be the shouting of a great number of people. They were assembled to a Bull baiting. . . . The Animal appeared to be in a great rage, tho' much exhausted by the Dogs, before I reached the Scene of Action. Soon after I got there, a Small Mastiff was sett on, which he threw about ten feet high, and fell to the ground with his upper Jaw broke and Every tooth Out.

"A short rest was now again given to the Bull, when a presumptious little Man, to shew what he could do, ran towards the Animal, but returned faster than he went, for

the creature took him under his breeches and tossed him about twelve feet from the end of the Rope.

"A new pack of dogs being procured to renew the fight, every Eye was turned to the Onset.

"At this moment Polly scaled the high fence, thro' the Crack of which she saw the battle and pitying the Bull, she pierced unseen thro' the Circle and ran up directly to the Ring; and without Shoes or Stockings; with her neck bare and her beautiful Ringlets wildly dangling over her Shoulders—her other Cloathing was her Shift only and a white petty coat; so that she appear'd more like a Ghost than a human Creature. When she reached the Bull (tho' almost before, he was in a Rage) she Accosted him—'Poor Bully! have they hurt you? they shall not hurt you any more,' and stroking his forehead and face she repeated 'they shall not, they shall not hurt thee.' This was indeed wonderful; but the Animal's behavior was not less so, for he no sooner saw her approach him, than he dropt his Head and became Mild and Gentle. As tho' he knew she was sent to deliver him.

"The whole Concourse of spectators saw it, and were Struck with Astonishment—not one of whom dared to enter into the Ring to save her; but stood trembling for Polly's life, afraid to stir a step and even to follow her on the Return, thro' the Midst of the dumb Struck Company, like an Arrow from the Bow Over the high fence again to the Hospital from which she eloped."

When this incident occurred, Philadelphia was the largest city in the colonies. Its population was about forty thousand; that of New York about thirty thousand; and that of the entire country less than four million.

It was in Philadelphia that the first medical school of the colonies was founded. Several of the more prominent physicians of Philadelphia had gone to Europe for their medical education, but many young men could not afford this expense. It was in their interest that Dr. John Morgan, on his return to Philadelphia from Europe, urged the founding of

a medical school. There was in the city the college that later
became the University of Pennsylvania; in 1765 in response
to Dr. Morgan's urging, it opened a department for instruction in medicine. In this first medical school the doctors who
were soon to become prominent in the Revolutionary War

EXTRACTS from LETTERS to the AUTHOR of the
METALLIC DISCOVERY,

PIERPONT EDWARDS, Efq. Diftrict Attorney
for the State of Connecticut.

DEAR SIR,   *New-Haven, October 7, 1796.*

I SHOULD have written you laft week, had I
then been able to afcertain certain facts, the rumor of
which I had heard. A Mrs. Beers, a near neighbor
to me, the wife of Eber Beers, and daughter of Capt.
Samuel Huggins, of this town, had been, for fourteen
weeks, exceedingly diftreffed with the Rheumatifm, to
fuch a degree that for the fourteen weeks, previous to
the 29th of laft month, fhe had not been able to walk
acrofs her room even with crutches, fave only once,
when fhe made out with the affiftance of crutches, to
hobble part of the way acrofs her room.—On the 29th
of September laft, fhe procured a fet of your Metallic
Subftances, and in lefs than an hour after fhe had begun to ufe them, in the manner directed by you, fhe
rofe from her chair, and walked about her houfe, and
on the next day fhe went abroad to her neighbors,
having thrown afide her crutches. I have this day

A testimonial for Perkins' tractors.

---

acted as teachers. They were Dr. Morgan, Dr. William
Shippen, Jr., and Dr. Benjamin Rush.

The beginning of the war, as you know, found the colonies in a state of unpreparedness. There was little military
organization, and there was no medical organization to care
for the sick and wounded, and no time to build hospitals or
to make surgical instruments. Each district sent out with its

fighting men such doctors as were available; some were good and some were useless; some had surgical and medical supplies and some had none.

The first step toward organizing a medical department of the Continental Army was made in July, 1775, when the Continental Congress passed a resolution creating such a department with a director-general and chief physician at its head. Dr. Benjamin Church of Boston was appointed to this office. In October of the same year he was tried for treason and found guilty. Probably the grounds for the accusation were not well founded, for those were chaotic times when a breath of suspicion was enough to damn a man as a Tory. Dr. Church was put in prison, but obtained permission to sail to the West Indies. His boat was wrecked and all aboard were drowned.

Dr. Morgan became the next director-general. He, too, was soon dismissed. His vigorous efforts to establish a really effective medical service aroused the animosity of many of the less efficient doctors. Through political intrigue they succeeded in having Congress deprive him of his post. Dr. William Shippen, Jr., was appointed to succeed him. Benjamin Rush served under Shippen as surgeon-general of the Middle Division.

In spite of the work of Morgan, Shippen, and Rush, medical care during the Revolution was pitifully inadequate. The hospitals improvised in public buildings and private houses were hotbeds of infectious disease. There was an almost complete lack of surgical instruments and all the men capable of making these were manufacturing guns. The sick and wounded suffered frightfully from lack of food and bedding and nursing.

There were heroic doctors in the Revolution, but they were hopelessly handicapped by the conditions under which they were forced to work. However, if patients profited little from the doctors, the doctors profited a good deal from the war. It was the first time that men trained in medicine

by apprenticeship in small towns were brought in contact with physicians educated in Europe. Ideas were exchanged, new interests aroused, and wider experience gained. American medicine grew up during the Revolution. In spirit at least the physicians were no longer colonial doctors of the backwoods; they were now doctors of a new country, the United States, and as such, they turned with a new vigor, a new feeling of union, to meet the scientific advances of the nineteenth century.

But before we come to that greatest of all centuries in medicine, there remains to be told the medical progress of Europe in the eighteenth century. We have dealt so far only with America. And there is also the story of America's first great contribution to medical quackery.

Science in America in the eighteenth century consisted of Benjamin Franklin's discoveries in electricity and some half dozen descriptions of diseases by American doctors after the manner of Sydenham. America aroused Europe's greatest interest with the amazing medical fad of Dr. Elisha Perkins. This was perhaps not extraordinary in view of the fact that medical superstition was more vigorous in Europe than in the colonies.

Elisha Perkins was graduated from Yale College late in the eighteenth century. He took up medicine, but in 1798 he developed a device that did away—so it seemed—with all further need for doctors. He invented the Perkins' tractor. The tractor consisted of a compass-like device of two rods, one sharp pointed and the other blunt. They were made of combinations of different kinds of metal, copper and zinc, gold and iron, or platinum and silver.

The tractor was stroked over the skin above the ailing place and the pain disappeared. The bimetallic rod suggested strongly a discovery that Luigi Galvani of Bologna had made in 1786; he observed that the legs of a dead frog twitched when brought in contact with two different metals. In 1792 the famous Alessandro Volta of Pavia, inventor of

the electric battery, had written on animal electricity; and in America Franklin had brought electricity out of the clouds. Electricity was the subject of much popular discussion and much speculation; there was as yet little knowledge about its properties. But people were willing to credit miracles to this mysterious thing; and they were willing to believe in Perkins' tractors.

Of course, after going this far in our story you know that almost any remedy or medical procedure that catches and holds interest will drive pain away and make many people think for a time that they are cured of disease. Perkins with his tractors was practicing the same kind of medicine that the medicine man of primitive people, and Valentine Greatrakes and all such healers had used. Dr. Perkins was entirely sincere in his belief in the benefit to be derived from the tractors, and so were many thousands of people who bought and used them and gave testimonials.

The fad spread to Europe. An Institute of Perkinism was erected in London. The Perkins' tractor was the sensation of the day.

But in Europe there had been a whole century of progress since the days of the Touch for the King's Evil. Some men were learning to be skeptical in matters of science and to test remedies.

A Dr. John Haygarth of England tested the tractors. He used a method that Ambroise Paré might have and that a modern doctor certainly would have used—the control experiment. He made a pair of tractors out of wood and painted them to resemble metal. When he applied these to ailing people, their pain disappeared and they recovered just as quickly as when the real bimetallic tractors were used. He, too, collected testimonials. And then he disclosed his deception. At once the enthusiasm for Perkins' tractors collapsed. People were willing to be impressed by something that suggested electricity, but they knew that a chip of wood scratched over the skin cured no disease.

CHAPTER XXIV

Doctors in Laces and Frills

IN the seventeenth century Molière ridiculed the doctors of Europe as pompous asses. But in that same century Harvey and Sydenham did their work. If Molière had lived and written in the eighteenth century, he certainly would have characterized the doctors as fashionable fops; and he would have found rich fields for his satire in the charlatans and their patent medicines, for this was the "golden age" of quacks. And yet this century gave us the great French scientist Lavoisier who supplied the answer to the question of why men breathe; Morgagni who showed the changes in the body due to diseases; and Jenner who provided the race with one of its great boons, vaccination against smallpox.

In manners and customs the eighteenth was a century of artificiality, of strong class distinction, of powdered wigs and lace ruffs, of elaborate etiquette and poverty and brutality. It was not with pen and ink that the revolt against the injustices of the times was written but with steel and blood—the pike and guillotine of the French Revolution, the sword and musket of the American Revolution.

The fashionable doctor of England dressed as became an aristocrat; he wore a red coat, satin breeches, silk stockings, buckled shoes, a powdered wig and a three-cornered hat; he carried a goldheaded cane and often a fur muff to protect the delicacy of his hands. Perhaps behind him as he walked, which he rarely did, there followed at a respectful distance a footman bearing his gloves and satchel. More often he rode in a fashionable carriage drawn by elegantly equipped horses. Many doctors, so it is said, made it part of their business to gallop about London for the admiration of the

people and to create the impression that they had very large practices.

Now when doctors pretended to the foppery of fashion it was easy for quacks to ape them, because what the public saw and admired in the doctor was not his skill in science but his polished behavior. All that the charlatan needed was an equal ostentation, an equal snobbery, an equal effrontery,

A mountebank dentist.

and he, as judged by the standards of the time, was likewise a great doctor. Many were the quacks who followed this device and made their fortunes.

The artist Hogarth in a satirical engraving has given us with others the likenesses of three of the greatest quacks of the century—"Spot" Ward, Chevalier Taylor, and Sally Mapp. The engraving is designed in heraldic fashion and is called the "Undertaker's Arms."

Joshua Ward, nicknamed "Spot" because of a birthmark on his face, took up medicine, but his preparation for it was

slight. He had failed first as a drysalter and then as politician. He invented a variety of medicaments which had great.
popularity. Among his "patients" were Lord Chesterfield,
Horace Walpole, and Edward Gibbon, the historian. He
had the very good luck to cure by a sudden pull a disloca-
tion of the thumb of King George II. After that his fortune
was made. He was given a room at Whitehall; he asked that
he might be buried in Westminster Abbey. His greatest
claim to lasting distinction is that the poet Pope, and the
lexicographer Johnson, deigned to notice him. Pope wrote
of him:

> *Of late, without the least pretence to skill,*
> *Ward's grown a famed physician by a pill.*

And Johnson said: "Taylor was the most ignorant man I
ever knew, but sprightly; Ward the dullest."

Taylor was the Chevalier Taylor of Hogarth's engraving.
He was an apothecary's assistant; but he set himself up as
an eye specialist. In this he did badly at first but he became
a success as a traveling mountebank, dressed in the height
of fashion, lecturing to the people from his carriage in inverted sentences to create, as he said, the impression that he
spoke like Cicero. Among his patients was Gibbon, who
seemed to have a failing for quacks, and Handel, the great
German composer. Taylor was appointed oculist to King
George II.

Taylor and Ward are shown in Hogarth's engraving
holding goldheaded canes; Mrs. Mapp is brandishing a
bone. Her claim to medical distinction lay in what is called
"bonesetting." Bonesetting in turn arose from the idea that
pain and illness result from bones slipping from their proper
places. The bonesetter manipulates the leg, or foot, or arm,
or spine, corrects the misplacement, and health is presumed
to follow. The whole procedure is a "laying on of hands"
but done with impressive force. Mrs. Mapp made a small

fortune out of such manipulation and rivaled the fashionable physician with the magnificence of her dress and carriage and footmen.

Probably the greatest medical absurdity of the eighteenth century was perpetrated by another English woman, Joanna Stevens. She had, so she claimed, a remedy that was a certain cure for stone in the bladder, a complaint common in those times. Being a public-spirited lady she consented to part with the secret for $25,000. The amazing thing is that the money was actually given to her in the interest of the public by Act of Parliament. When published in 1739 in the *London Gazette*, her "cure" turned out to be a mixture of eggshells, soap, snails, together with an assortment of weeds and herbs.

It was to the same public that hoped to benefit from her medicine that Perkins' tractors made so strong an appeal. But unfortunately for the American, he appeared late on the scene; by the end of the eighteenth century physicians at least were not quite as gullible as they were in the more fashionable days before the Revolution.

The medical troubles of the eighteenth century went deeper than the mere foibles of fashionable medical practice and quackery; they extended even into the theories of medicine. Some physicians, to the profit of medical progress, patiently followed the rigorous method that Sydenham had pointed out—studying disease at the bedside of the patient. But many more, carried away by the tendencies around them, turned to making systems and building up classifications of disease quite as artificial as the manners of the times.

The fashion for classification was set by a physician who is known best as a botanist, Carl von Linné or Linnæus. His interest in medicine was romantic rather than scientific. He fell in love with the daughter of a wealthy physician; and the father would only consent to her marrying a physician. Linnæus thereupon studied medicine, and then, duly wed, returned to botany and zoölogy. He gave us the best classi-

fication of plants and animals that had been made up to that time; one that though modified is still in use. It was he who

The "Undertaker's Arms."

classified man as an animal in the order of Primates and called him *Homo sapiens*—intelligent man.

Now man, for all of his intelligence, allows himself to be led easily from the arduous paths of search for facts. He

finds it simpler to pause and speculate, and systematize. The great usefulness of the system of classifications made by Linnæus served as an excuse for physicians to attempt similar classifications of diseases and their symptoms and indeed of all aspects of life itself. Medicine was advanced little by these attempts at systematizing on which men wasted their energies and over which they engaged in violent controversies.

Certainly the most silly and at the same time the most popular of all the systems was one devised by Dr. John Brown of England. It had a tremendous influence on medical thought. As late as 1802 the argument between the Brunonian and non-Brunonian medical students of the University of Göttingen became so violent that it broke into a riot which was quelled only by the militia. The Brunonian system had at least the advantage of simplicity. According to it the essential of life was excitability; in disease there was either too much or too little "excitement." The remedy was to reëstablish the proper degree of excitability. To do this Dr. Brown used mainly two medicaments, opium and alcohol. He died of an overdose of his favorite remedies.

In the seventeenth century the greatest advance made in physiology had been allied to mechanics—the discovery of the circulation of the blood by the physician Harvey. In the eighteenth century there was an equally important advance, but it came this time from the new and rapidly growing field of chemistry—the discovery of the significance of breathing.

The chemists of the eighteenth century were particularly interested in air. Here was a thing that had always been taken for granted, but only in its physical aspects—its movements. The winds drove the boats across the water and, blowing over the land, turned windmills. And it was known that man must have air to live; but the belief again concerned the physical properties: the lungs were bellows which moved the air, and the resulting breeze cooled the blood. It was in the seventeenth and especially the eighteenth cen-

turies that scientists began to realize that air had important chemical as well as physical properties. They were interested in the airlike substances to which the physician Van Helmont had given the name gases.

Robert Boyle, the English chemist, who took many but

Stephen Hales's windmill ventilator on Newgate Prison.

not all of the useless and unpleasant medicaments out of the pharmacopœia in the seventeenth century, performed an experiment to show that an animal could not live or a flame burn in a vacuum. It was more than a hundred and fifty years later that the French scientist Antoine Laurent Lavoisier showed that man and the flame needed air for the

same reason—because the process of living is one of combustion in which food is burned.

In the intervening years, clue after clue had been revealed to show the secret of breathing. Many of the more common gases had been discovered: those that we now call hydrogen, nitrogen, carbon dioxide and oxygen. It had been shown that an animal could be kept alive when air was blown through its lungs with a bellows, that the movement of the chest and lungs was not necessary to life. It had been shown also that the blood takes something from the air in passing through the lungs, and its color changes from purple to vermilion. Likewise men had learned that when a flame is burned in a closed vessel something is taken from the air so that what is left is no longer good for animals to breathe. In breathing, men and animals and fire not only took something from the air but they added something to it, something that made lime water turn white and turbid—the gas carbon dioxide.

Lavoisier took these separate observations and systematized them. He showed that nearly four-fifths of the volume of air is a gas, nitrogen, which will not support life; and one-fifth is a gas which he called oxygen, which is necessary to maintain life. It is the oxygen that combines with the blood in the lungs and changes its color. When a man breathes air into his lungs, part of the oxygen is taken up by his blood and in return another gas, carbon dioxide, is given off and breathed out. Lavosier showed that exactly this same exchange takes place when carbon such as charcoal is burned in air—oxygen from the air is used up and carbon dioxide formed.

Combustion, a burning of food, takes place then in the living body. The energy of the combustion appears as the heat that keeps the body warm, and as the work that the muscles perform. Air is necessary to life because oxygen is needed for the vital combustion. We breathe—not to cool the blood—but to obtain oxygen and to throw off carbon

dioxide. Although it is the mechanical part of breathing that is most apparent, it is the chemical part that is the essential.

Physicians had small part indeed in the great discovery of why men breathe. But they had at least a connection—an unfortunate one—with the discoverer. Lavoisier was condemned to death by one doctor and executed on a machine invented by another.

Lavoisier was wealthy, he was an aristocrat, he dabbled in politics, and he lived in France during the closing years of the eighteenth century. An unpleasant combination for those days when common men were revolting in violence against social injustices.

Jean Paul Marat, the firebrand of the French Revolution, was a physician, and it was he who brought against Lavoisier the charge that as farmer-general he had oppressed the people. Lavoisier was condemned to death. He died under the guillotine invented by Dr. Joseph Ignace Guillotin.

Physicians had not even this much connection with another discovery in physiology made in the eighteenth century. It is to an English preacher, Stephen Hales that medicine owes the first attempt to measure the pressure of blood in the arteries—the blood pressure. Hales diversified his religious duties with scientific investigation; he invented artificial ventilation. A law had been passed putting a tax on windows; and to avoid payment the windows of tenements and prisons, which were then operated as concessions by private individuals, were boarded up. An epidemic of typhus fever broke out. The typhus of course was attributed to "bad air" and unpleasant smells. Hales attempted to purify the air in Newgate Prison by erecting on its tower a large fan wheel driven by a windmill. In spite of the usefulness of the invention of artificial ventilation it failed its purpose in this case, for it did not affect the lice which, as we know now, were really responsible for the typhus.

Hales's measurement of the blood pressure was carried

out, not on a human being, but on his horse. He fastened a large glass tube directly to an artery. The blood rose in the tube to a height of six feet or more and pulsated with each beat of the heart. This was the first real advance in the

Edward Jenner.

physiology of the circulation of the blood since the days of Harvey, more than a century before. The physician of today finds in the measurement of the blood pressure one of his most useful methods of diagnosis, but needless to say he does not measure it on his patients as Hales did, but by a much simpler method, and a painless one. He finds out how tightly

the arm must be squeezed by a rubber cuff into which air is blown from a bulb, to shut off momentarily the flow of blood. The pressure needed is the same as the pressure of the blood in the arteries.

So far in our account of eighteenth-century medicine, we have not dealt kindly with the doctors of Europe; physiology we have seen in the hands of the chemists and of a preacher; the doctors were more interested in fashions and systems and theories than in discovering facts. These were defects of the period. But in any time strong and earnest men may overcome such handicaps. And there were strong men of medicine in the eighteenth century. Although they were not scientists in the sense that the chemist Lavoisier was, although they were not seeking the fundamental facts of physiology as he and Harvey did, they nevertheless made practical contributions of vast importance to the progress of medicine. Three such men were Giovanni Morgagni, John Hunter, and Edward Jenner.

Morgagni takes us again to the famous University of Padua where Vesalius had carried out his dissections, where Sanctorious had taught, and where Harvey had studied. Morgagni held the position of professor of anatomy, the same post that Vesalius had held two hundred years before. Vesalius had studied the normal structure of the body and from his work we gained the first true understanding of human anatomy. Morgagni's attention was held by the abnormal structures of the body, those that were caused by disease, and he gave us our first knowledge of what is called pathology.

Many physicians before Morgagni had noticed that changes in the normal structure had occurred in the bodies of men who had died from disease. They had seen strange growths; they had found stones in the gall bladder; they had seen lungs red and firm like the liver instead of soft and pink as is the normal lung. These for Morgagni were clues to his discoveries; and just as Lavoisier had disclosed the

secret of why men breathe, so Morgagni disclosed the reason why diseases give rise to symptoms.

Whenever he had the opportunity he dissected the bodies

AN

INQUIRY

INTO

THE CAUSES AND EFFECTS

OF

THE VARIOLÆ VACCINÆ,

A DISEASE

DISCOVERED IN SOME OF THE WESTERN COUNTIES OF ENGLAND,

PARTICULARLY

GLOUCESTERSHIRE,

AND KNOWN BY THE NAME OF

THE COW POX.

BY EDWARD JENNER, M.D. F.R.S. &c.

———— QUID NOBIS CERTIUS IPSIS
SENSIBUS ESSE POTEST, QUO VERA AC FALSA NOTEMUS.
LUCRETIUS.

London:

PRINTED, FOR THE AUTHOR.

BY SAMPSON LOW, N°. 7, BERWICK STREET, SOHO:

AND SOLD BY LAW, AVE-MARIA LANE; AND MURRAY AND HIGHLEY, FLEET STREET

1798.

Title-page of Jenner's announcement of vaccination.

of those who had died of disease. He found, as other men had, changes in the organs. But he went further; he studied these changes in relation to the disease from which the man had died and to the symptoms which his illness had shown.

As he gradually accumulated his observations concerning one disease after another, he wrote of them in letters to his numerous friends in medicine. They in turn studied and confirmed his findings. Finally, in 1761, when Morgagni was seventy-nine years old, he published his life's work in a book—the first book of pathology. Thus only one hundred and thirty-nine years before the beginning of the twentieth century, physicians for the first time learned something of the changes in the body caused by diseases and of the symptoms that arose from them. With the aid of this knowledge the physician, by merely studying the symptoms, could determine the changes in the body caused by the disease. In the progress of medicine Morgagni takes his place with the great leaders: Hippocrates described the symptoms of disease, Sydenham the nature of diseases, and Morgagni the changes caused by diseases.

Morgagni's work was only the beginning of the great study of pathology which year by year since his time has brought us nearer the answer to the problem of what disease is. He did not use a microscope in his study; his descriptions were only of the changes that appeared to the naked eye. It was past the middle of the nineteenth century that the great Prussian scientist, Rudolf Virchow, carried Morgagni's work forward another stride and showed the nature of the changes produced by disease in the cells that make up the tissues.

The first field of medicine to profit from the study of pathology was surgery. Surgery, as we know it now, aims to correct by operation disease states within the body. Without a knowledge of pathology, surgery is a mere skilled trade of amputating limbs, treating wounds, and correcting those disturbances that can be seen or felt from the surface. Surgery before the work of John Hunter was little more than that. In the opening years of the eighteenth century it was much as Ambroise Paré had left it in the sixteenth. The physician still looked upon the surgeon as a man of inferior rank. But that social barrier was being broken down. In America, by

force of necessity, the physician performed surgical operations. In France, in the early years of the eighteenth century,
the surgeons publicly revolted against the physicians, refusing to open the doors of their meeting room to the procession of doctors clad in full regalia with ermine-trimmed
robes. Left standing in the street in a snowstorm the ridiculous appearance of the doctors amused the spectators. The

*An anti-vaccination caricature published in 1800 intended to
discourage the use of vaccination.*

people sided with the surgeons and finally the fashionable
physicians admitted the surgeons to an equal standing with
them. In England a similar change was brought about in a
way vastly more important to the progress of surgery.

John Hunter based surgery upon pathology and physiology. At his hands it acquired the aims of modern surgery.
It was no longer sufficient for the surgeon to know merely
anatomy and the tricks of his trade. Instead he must study
physiology, pathology, diagnosis—in short, study all of
medicine—and learn the operations of surgery in addition.

Under the influence of John Hunter surgery became a profession.

But even with this change there was still a vast difference between surgery then and now. Two of the greatest discoveries were to come in the nineteenth century—the use of antiseptics to prevent infections, and of anæsthetics to abolish pain. Until the middle of the nineteenth century, people under operation bore their pain as best they could, and were held down in their struggles by powerful men. The almost universal infection that followed prevented surgeons from performing operations within the abdomen; infection there was more deadly in its effect than anywhere else in the body.

John Hunter, like Sydenham in the previous century, had only snatches of education. He refused flatly to learn Latin. As a young man failing to do well in various occupations, he was sent from his Scottish home to London to assist his brother William, a prominent surgeon and teacher. In the dissecting room John found his place. He worked indefatigably; he dissected not only men but every variety of animal he could find in order to compare the structures of their bodies. He collected an enormous museum of specimens which is preserved today in the Royal College of Surgeons. There you will find his two greatest curiosities: the skeleton of a Sicilian dwarf, a girl of ten who was only one foot, eight inches high, and the skeleton of the famous Irish giant who was seven feet, six and a half inches. And what a time he had getting that enormous skeleton of O'Brien! When the giant became ill, Hunter watched over him with such solicitude that the poor man suspected the surgeon's ulterior motives. He made his friends promise faithfully that when he died they would never lose sight of his body until they had sealed it in a lead casket and sunk it in the sea. Nevertheless the skeleton stands today in the Hunterian Collection.

John Hunter leads us directly to the last of our medical heroes of the eighteenth century—Edward Jenner. Jenner

was a pupil of Hunter, but, leaving him, he became a country practitioner in Gloucestershire. He was a man of pleasing appearance and kindly, gentle ways. He was also one of the greatest medical discoverers of all times. He gave us vaccination against smallpox.

A tradition among the dairy folks of the countryside led him to make his discovery. Now and again Jenner was called to inoculate against smallpox the members of some farmer's family. And often he could not succeed in giving the smallpox in this way to people who handled cows. "They've had the cowpox," said the farmers. That was the tradition. Those who had the disease called cowpox would never afterwards take the smallpox.

Cowpox appeared in the dairy cattle as small pus-filled sores on the skin. Men and girls handling the cattle sometimes acquired similar sores. Beyond the local effect which lasted only a short time, they were not ill. And yet tradition insisted that those who had had the cowpox never took the smallpox.

Here to Jenner was a thrilling possibility—something safe and simple to take the place of inoculation. But he had learned from John Hunter the principles of science. He could not jump at conclusions; he must obtain proof by experiment.

In 1796 cowpox broke out on a farm in Gloucestershire; a dairy maid named Sarah Nelmes contracted the disease. Jenner took from her sores a tiny drop of pus and put it in a scratch on the arm of an eight-year-old boy named James Phipps. Soon a small sore appeared on the boy's arm; he had the mark of cowpox only in that one place; it healed and left a tiny scar. Jenner waited. A month went by and then he again made a small scratch on the boy's arm; this time he rubbed over it the pus from the sores of a man with smallpox—he inoculated the boy. James did not become ill. Again a few months later Jenner inoculated him and still he did not take the smallpox. The tradition was true; cowpox

protected against smallpox. Jenner wrote an account of his experiment and sent it to the Royal Society for publication in the *Transactions*. His letter was returned unpublished. The observation, the members of the Society thought, was

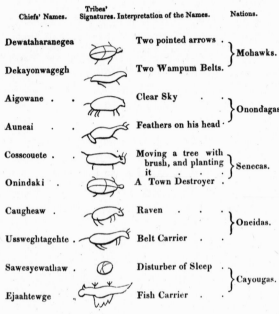

Chiefs' Names.	Tribes' Signatures.	Interpretation of the Names.	Nations.
Dewataharanegea		Two pointed arrows .	} Mohawks.
Dekayonwagegh		Two Wampum Belts.	
Aigowane . .		Clear Sky . .	} Onondagas.
Auneai . .		Feathers on his head .	
Cosscouete . .		Moving a tree with brush, and planting it . .	} Senecas.
Onindaki .		A Town Destroyer .	
Caugheaw .		Raven . .	} Oneidas.
Ussweghtagehte .		Belt Carrier . .	
Sawesyewathaw .		Disturber of Sleep .	} Cayougas.
Ejaahtewge		Fish Carrier . .	

Signatures of Indian chiefs on the tribute to Jenner.

too amazing to be true. It was a mere chance that James had not taken the smallpox.

Encouraged by John Hunter, Jenner repeated his experiment on other subjects. He got the same result: cowpox protected against smallpox.

The evidence was beyond question, and so in 1798 Jenner published a book called *An Inquiry into the Causes and Effects of the Variolæ Vaccinæ*. It is only seventy-five pages long, but it is one of the great masterpieces in medical literature. It is literally because of that book that you and I have

not had smallpox either from infection or by inoculation, which vaccination replaced.

Even Edward Jenner, in those closing years of the eighteenth century, could not in his writing wholly escape the affectation of his time. But fortunately he used most of it in the opening paragraphs of his book, which read:

"The deviation of Man from the state in which he was originally placed by Nature seems to have proved to him a prolific source of diseases. From the love of splendour, from indulgences of luxury, and from his fondness for amusement, he has familiarised himself with a great number of animals, which may not originally have been intended for his associates.

"The Wolf, disarmed of ferocity, is now pillowed in the lady's lap. The Cat, the little Tyger of our island, whose natural home is the forest, is equally domesticated and caressed. The Cow, the Hog, the Sheep, and the Horse, are all, for a variety of purposes, brought under his care and domination."

After this florid preamble leading up to cowpox, he discarded his fine style and reported as briefly and as clearly as would any scientist of today the experiments that demonstrated the validity of vaccination.

In the early days of the practice of vaccination, the procedure followed was in one respect vastly different from that of today. In Jenner's time no one knew anything about bacterial infection. The virus of the cowpox was taken from human subjects and passed from arm to arm. Infection sometimes followed, for bacteria were thus spread from one person to another. Today the virus is obtained only from calves kept in stables almost as clean as is the operating room of a hospital. The modern vaccine virus is a vastly purer product than the cleanest milk we drink.

In spite of crude methods, men of Jenner's time, faced constantly with the horrors of smallpox and the dangers of inoculation, could appreciate the blessing of vaccination.

From all over the world people paid tribute to Jenner. The American Indians sent a deputation to thank him personally and to bring him gifts. The Dowager Empress of Russia sent him a ring and gave the name Vaccinoff to the first child vaccinated in Russia. Napoleon ordered all the men of his great army vaccinated, just a little more than a quarter of a century after George Washington had ordered the men of the Continental Army inoculated.

The pathetic eagerness with which vaccination was welcomed by men who had seen their families ravaged with smallpox and the primitive way in which vaccination was given in the early years of the nineteenth century, led to one of the strangest of all voyages. In 1805, seven years after Jenner's announcement of his method for safely preventing smallpox, a ship set sail from Spain to the Spanish possessions in the New World. Its cargo was children. Each week two of the children were vaccinated from the sores on the arms of the two who had been vaccinated the week before. These children were the living bearers of vaccine virus to the lands where, nearly three hundred years before, the Spanish explorers had introduced the smallpox from Europe. Millions of people in the New World had died of the disease; millions of them are saved each year by the medical contribution of the eighteenth-century country doctor— Edward Jenner.

Florence Nightingale

Part Nine
MEDICINE AT THE BEDSIDE
IN THE OPERATING ROOM
IN BARRACKS AND PRISONS

CHAPTER XXV

Medicine at the Bedside

IN the year 1782 there was a vacancy in the staff of the
Necker Hospital in Paris. A young physician named
Jean Nicolas Corvisart presented himself before the
board of governors and applied for the post. His medical
qualifications were excellent, his recommendations the best.
But he was refused the position. He was rejected because he
wore no powdered wig!

But eighteenth-century emphasis on such matters was
near its end. The Reign of Terror began in 1793. Fashionable heads, stripped of their wigs, fell under the knife of
Dr. Guillotin's invention. These were days of chaos. All
corporations aided or controlled by the state were abolished.
There was no longer any regulation of medical practice;
anyone could call himself a doctor and treat the sick. There
was indeed no place where anyone could be trained in medicine; the medical schools were closed.

But doctors and especially surgeons were greatly needed.
France was at war with Austria; she was at war with herself.
The wounded must be cared for by trained men. New schools
must be established. The old ones had taught the traditions
of medicine from ancient texts long out of date. This was an
era of a new democracy and a new progress. Men with aris-
tocratic ways and old-fashioned ideas must yield to the new.

Medical education was a century—yes, three centuries—
behind the times. The learned doctors still quibbled over
the "authorities"; they ignored Paracelsus; they ignored
Sydenham and Harvey and Sanctorius and Morgagni. Men
were needed who would look not backward, but forward,
who would seize and use everything that the new sciences
offered for treating and preventing disease.

Medical education in the general form in which we know

it now grew out of the French Revolution. In the new schools of Paris there were laboratories for scientific study; students were taught at the bedside in the hospital, as Sydenham would have taught them. And it was Corvisart—he

A caricature of a superstition of the nineteenth century—phrenology.

who wore no wig—who did the teaching, for under the new *régime*, he had become the leading professor of medicine.

Observe—train the senses to perceive the symptoms of disease—that was his watchword. He collected accurate observations in order to learn the natural history of diseases. And when possible he followed the example of Morgagni and noted from dissection, from autopsy, the changes in the body that caused the symptoms of disease.

This was in spirit modern medical education, but in those opening years of the nineteenth century few of the modern aids of diagnosis were available to Corvisart. Like Hippocrates, like Sydenham, he used only his bare hands and his keen senses in studying disease. True, more fortunate than Sanctorius, he had a watch and could easily count the pulse. But he was eager for other methods to aid in the elusive study of diseases.

He discovered that in 1761—the same year that Morgagni's book appeared—a Viennese doctor named Leopold Auenbrugger had published a book on what is called percussion. It was a small book, only ninety-five pages. It had failed to impress physicians and had been nearly forgotten. But Corvisart saw in it the possibility of a greatly needed means of diagnosis. He translated the book and amplified it from his own observations until it grew to more than four hundred pages. Corvisart gave full credit for the discovery to Auenbrugger.

In the preface of his little book, *Inventum novum ex percussione thoracis humani*, Auenbrugger had written: "I here present the reader with a new sign which I have discovered for detecting diseases of the chest. This consists in the percussion of the human thorax, whereby according to the character of the particular sounds elicited, an opinion is formed of the internal state. . . . In making public my discoveries . . . I have not been unconscious of the dangers I must encounter, since it has always been the fate of those who have illustrated or improved the arts and sciences by their discoveries to be beset by envy, malice, hatred, destruction and calumny."

But Auenbrugger was wrong in his prediction. His discovery was first received with indifference and then actually revised with praise by Corvisart.

Percussion is today a commonplace of medicine, something with which everyone is familiar who has been examined by a doctor. The physician taps with his finger on the

chest and listens to detect the slight differences in the sounds as he percusses one place after another.

Over the lungs, since they are filled with air, the gentle tap on the chest elicits a reverberation like that of a muffled drum. Over the heart and liver the sound is dull. When there are diseased areas in the lungs they, too, may give out a dull note or one that sounds to the doctor's ear quite different from the reverberation of the normal chest. The percussion discovered by Auenbrugger and popularized by Corvisart, is one of the indispensable means of diagnosing disease in the lungs.

In 1807 Corvisart became the personal physician of Napoleon Bonaparte; he died in 1821. But the principles he taught were used by his pupils. And soon one of them discovered an instrument to aid in finding the symptoms of disease—the stethoscope—to be used in what is called auscultation, an art as indispensable to the modern physician as is that of percussion.

In auscultation the physician listens to the sounds that come from the lungs and from the heart. The gentle "swish" of air as it passes through the tiny bronchial tubes may be altered in disease, and harsh crackling or bubbling sounds appear; the regular "lub-dub" of the normal heart beat may be blurred with murmurs. These sounds allow the physician, with his trained ear, to "see" into the chest and find the seat of disease and learn its nature.

Long before the nineteenth-century physicians had occasionally practiced auscultation, but their observations had little meaning until the pathology of Morgagni showed the way of finding out the disease state from which the abnormal sounds arose. Even then, auscultation did not come into wide use; it was difficult indeed with the bare ear pressed to the chest to hear the faint sounds that denoted disease.

René Laënnec, physician-in-chief to the Necker Hospital —from which his teacher Corvisart had been turned away because he wore no wig—saw great possibilities in ausculta-

tion. He also found great difficulties in it. The patients in the hospital of those days, for all the seeming modernity of medicine, were often unwashed and infested with vermin.

René Laënnec.

Putting the ear to a dirty chest was far from pleasant for a fastidious physician such as Laënnec. And there were even greater difficulties. Some patients were so fat that the faint sounds from the chest were deadened and lost.

It was in fact this very difficulty that led Laënnec to the

invention of the stethoscope. He had as a patient a fat girl suffering from heart disease; not a sound could he get from her well-insulated chest. One day on his way to the hospital, Laënnec chanced to walk through the gardens of the Louvre. He paused to watch some children at play on a pile of lumber. One child put his ear to the end of a long beam; another went to the opposite end and tapped on the wood. The signal traveled through the beam. There Laënnec saw the answer to his problem. He walked quickly to the hospital and in the room of his fat patient he seized a paper-covered book, rolled it into a cylinder and to the amazement of the onlookers put one end of this crude instrument against the patient's chest and applied his ear to the other. To his joy he heard the heart sounds clearly and those of breathing louder than he had ever heard them before.

Soon Laënnec was making little wooden "trumpets" on a turning lathe. The stethoscope was well on its way toward its modern form—the one with which we are all familiar: a tiny funnel to be put against the chest, connected to the rubber tubes that go to the ears of the physician. And equally important, Laënnec each day found new uses for his invention.

It was invaluable in the diagnosis of the one disease in which he was especially interested—tuberculosis. Half the patients who came to the hospitals of those days had this disease, so the stethoscope disclosed. After more than a thousand autopsies, Laënnec knew nearly all that we know today of this disease, save one great fact—how it is caused. It was he, and a fellow-student Boyle, who showed that the disease could appear in any part of the body as small lumps which they called tubercles—hence tuberculosis. Nearly a half century was to pass before the German doctor, Robert Koch, showed that these lumps are caused by a certain kind of bacteria.

In 1819 Laënnec published his famous book, *Traité de l'auscultation médiate*. In 1826 he died of tuberculosis.

Percussion and auscultation, the physician's two great methods of examination, were first used in the opening years of the nineteenth century; a third—the most amazing of all methods—was discovered in the closing years of the same century: the X-ray. This time the discoverer was not a physician, but a physicist. In the intervening years the progress of medicine had become inseparably connected with the progress of physics and chemistry and, indeed, all branches of science. No sooner was a discovery made in science than the doctor seized upon it, searching to find in it some valuable use in the diagnosis, the treatment, or prevention of disease. Medicine had lost its old-fashioned ways, it had fallen into step with science. In the seventeenth century the thermometer and the pulse pendulum of Sanctorius lay neglected; in the closing years of the nineteenth century Wilhelm Konrad Roentgen's discovery of the X-ray was seized upon and used in medicine within a month after he had announced it.

Roentgen was a professor in the Department of Physics at the University of Würzburg in Germany. He experimented with electrical discharges from an induction coil through a bulb called a Crookes tube. When the electrical discharge was passed the bulb glowed with a yellowish, greenish light. If a piece of paper coated with certain metallic salts was held in the light the coating glowed with a curious phosphorescence.

On November 18, 1895, Roentgen, working in his darkened laboratory, chanced to cover the Crookes tube with black paper to exclude all light. Then, with the tube darkened, he turned on the electrical discharge. No visible light appeared, but the coated paper lying on the table suddenly glowed with a mysterious ghostly light. It shone as brightly as it had before he put the black paper over the tube. Roentgen picked up the paper and turned its coated surface away from the tube. It continued to glow. An invisible ray was shining through the paper. He held a piece of metal before

the paper; a shadow was cast; he held his hand before it and saw what no one had ever seen before—the shadow of the bones of his hand. The invisible ray that lighted up the paper passed through human flesh. And what is more, these same rays affected photographic film. It was possible to take

Laënnec using the stethoscope.

pictures of bone and structures beneath the surface of the skin.

Early in January, 1896, Professor Roentgen told a group of scientists at Würzburg of his discovery of what he called the X-ray. But even before that his secret had leaked out. Accounts appeared in the newspapers of all countries; but they were not accurate, and from them the reader got odd notions indeed of the new ray. It was believed that it could be used anywhere at any time. An English merchant promptly advertised X-ray proof clothes for modest ladies. A bill was introduced into the legislature of New Jersey prohibiting the use of X-rays in opera glasses at the theater and a professor in a New York university talked of using X-rays to penetrate the thick skulls of dull students and project knowledge directly into their brains. The doctors, however, were quick to sense the true possibilities of the X-ray.

In the four decades that have passed since Roentgen announced his discovery, the X-ray has become one of the most valuable methods of diagnosis—a method that allows the physician to actually see within the body and detect the changes which Morgagni first showed as foci of diseases.

By the time the X-ray had been discovered, medical education had been through nearly a century of progress since the days of Corvisart. Great schools had grown up throughout the world. Medical progress had become international. For a time, at the hands of some great teacher, one school or another grew supreme and became the Mecca for doctors —as England had been for the doctors of colonial America.

Following France, the schools of Vienna and Berlin led for a time in medical progress. In Berlin the pathology of Morgagni was carried a long step forward, as we have already said, by Dr. Rudolf Virchow. Virchow was born in 1821—the same year that Corvisart died; he graduated from medical school in 1843, and that year began his teaching as an assistant in the school in Berlin.

A great scientific discovery was in those years attracting the attention of physicians with its possibilities for a nearer approach to the nature of disease. Physicians recognized that organs, and even tissues of the body, might become disordered and appear abnormal; that the symptoms of disease might arise from these changes. But there was still the age-long question of what is disease? Why and how do the changes appear in the flesh? There was only a vague theory for answer. In these years so near our own, the theory of Hippocrates and Galen—of the disordered humors—was still advanced to explain the cause of disease.

In the seventeenth century when the microscope was a scientific novelty, men had seen that some plant substances seemed to be made up of tiny blocks or cells. Gradually, with the perfection of the microscope, details were seen in the structure of these units. And finally, in the nineteenth century, the microscope disclosed the fact that human flesh was likewise made up of cells. The cell was the smallest unit of living tissue. The tissues of the body were aggregations of cells; one tissue differed from another because of the differences in the cells of which they were constructed. When flesh grew, the increase in size was due to the multiplication of cells. When it was diseased—and this was Virchow's discovery—it was the cells that were changed and disordered. Their disorder in turn affected the appearance of the tissue to the naked eye—causing the changes which Morgagni had described.

With that knowledge, the microscope became another of the indispensable instruments for the study of disease. To-day the modern physician turns to his microscope to study the blood: to count the red cells, for if they are lacking anæmia exists; to count the white cells in order to judge from their number the possibility of a patient's having an infection; to examine tissues suspected of harboring that anarchy of cell growth that we call cancer. The microscope serves a thousand purposes in the study of disease.

Rudolf Virchow, who gave us the modern cellular theory of disease, lived until 1902.

Structure is only one aspect of tissues and organs; function is another. Physiology as well as pathology must make its contribution to medical progress. And one of the earliest

An early cartoon of Roentgen's discovery of the X-ray published in Life.

and most important of its advances takes us from the learned professors of the cities of Europe to a simple army surgeon in the backwoods of America. It was William Beaumont, stationed in the early years of the nineteenth century at the frontier post, Fort Mackinac, who gave us the first clear account of what happens in the stomach during the digestion of food.

There had been many theories to explain digestion. Some

men had thought that the food was ground up in the stomach; others that it "cooked" or simmered there; still others —and they had performed experiments on birds and dogs and even on themselves—were certain that the food underwent some sort of fermentation. But no one was certain. The stomach was looked upon as a mill, a fermenting vat, or a stewpan.

It was Beaumont who proved that digestion was a chemical process; his experiments were made possible by an accident.

Beaumont was born in 1785 at Lebanon, Connecticut. Leaving home in 1806 with all of his possessions—a horse and sled, a barrel of cider, and one hundred dollars—he set out to make his way alone in the world. For a time he taught school and then, becoming interested in medicine, he decided to be a doctor. He did not go to a medical school—American medical education was far behind that of Europe—but instead took an apprenticeship with a practicing physician. After two years of study, he enlisted in the army for the War of 1812 as an assistant surgeon.

After the war he was stationed at the trading post and fort on the island in the waters where Lake Michigan and Lake Huron unite. In the spring of the year, the traders and hunters and trappers of the surrounding woods came to Mackinac to sell their furs and replenish their stock of food. In the spring of 1822 a gun was discharged by accident into the midst of the crowd that filled the store. A French Canadian named Alexis St. Martin received the full charge in the abdomen. Surgeon Beaumont was called from the fort to treat him. It seemed impossible at first to save his life; a great gaping wound had been opened into his stomach. For three years Beaumont nursed him. Finally there came a day when Alexis, thin and pale, could walk about. But the wound had not healed completely, nor would it ever heal; a small flap of flesh covered an opening that led into the stomach; when the flap was pushed aside the interior of the

stomach could be seen. Beaumont realized the possibilities that existed for actually watching digestion and the movements of the stomach. He employed Alexis and day by day he carried on his investigations. He studied the rate at which various kinds of food were digested; he collected the secretion formed; he noted the effect of alcohol and of indigestible food. For two months the studies went on and then Alexis deserted Beaumont. He returned to Canada, married and had two children; there, after four years of search, Beaumont finally found him. Again the experiments were undertaken and carried on for two years. In 1833 Beaumont published his work: *Experiments and Observations on the Gastric Juice and the Physiology of Digestion*—the first medical contribution to experimental science to come from America and one that established the basis of our present knowledge of digestion in the stomach.

Beaumont died at the age of 68; his patient Alexis lived to be 83.

Chance alone gave Beaumont the opportunity to make his contribution to physiology. The study of that subject was carried on by the great French physiologist, Claude Bernard, who really founded what is called experimental medicine. But even his discoveries were often as much due to accident as was that of Beaumont. Thus it was by chance that he found that the liver stores, for future use, sugar brought to it from the digestion of food in the intestines. The studies that followed from that observation laid the groundwork for a great discovery of the twentieth century—a means for controlling the disease diabetes, in which the body fails to burn sugar. Discovery after discovery came from his investigations; knowledge of digestion in the intestines, the way the blood vessels are controlled in size, the first facts concerning what are called internal secretions (chemical substances that control the functions of the body), the action of certain poisons, and many, many more. But perhaps most important of all was the fact that it was he who made physi-

cians see for the first time that the organs of the body do not act independently but are linked together and work together and must be studied together. The liver, the heart, the lungs, were to be looked upon only in their relation to the man as a whole. This was a step that had a profound influence on the development of modern physiology.

In this chapter we have seen medical progress taking new

William Beaumont.

shape as the result of great discoveries and new conceptions and medical education well launched toward its modern form. The doctor of today was being shaped in the years that gave us Corvisart, Virchow, Beaumont, and Bernard. But medical education in the early part of the century was sometimes faced with a peculiar difficulty; it was one that led to a morbid chapter in medical history. There was intensive opposition to anatomical dissection and it was only

after the anatomy riots and the notorious murders of Burke and Hare, that the modern anatomy laws were passed. Under these laws the unclaimed bodies of paupers are turned over to medical schools for the dissection so essential to medical education.

In the eighteenth and early nineteenth centuries there were no laws of this kind in England or America. Bodies were sometimes obtained by robbing graves. And suspicion of grave robbery was often turned against those who taught anatomy. Dr. William Shippen, Jr., of Philadelphia, the surgeon-general in the American Revolution, was once shot at by a mob angered by rumors of grave robbery. In 1788 in New York City a mob stormed a hospital where dissections were performed and burned the anatomical collection. The doctors took refuge in jail and the militia was called out. Seven rioters were killed and several severely wounded. The following year the state legislature authorized the dissection of the bodies of men executed for burglary, arson, and murder.

In 1831 Massachusetts passed the first law in this country making available for dissection "deceased persons, required to be buried at publick expence." That law and those to come after it in most of the other states, were the aftermath of a great medical scandal that occurred in Edinburgh, Scotland, then a prominent center of anatomical instruction.

Men called "Resurrectionists" often supplied the schools by robbing graves. In 1827, William Hare and William Burke in partnership undertook a less laborious way of obtaining bodies—they used the simple expedient of murder. Sixteen bodies were obtained in this way and sold before they were detected. They were careful to attack only those whose disappearance would attract little attention. Suspicion was finally aroused when they murdered a good-natured but feeble-minded man, a character on the streets of Edinburgh, known as "Daft Jamie." They were arrested. Hare turned state's evidence; Burke was hanged in 1829 before

a gathering of thirty thousand people—among them it is said was Sir Walter Scott. This sensational and disreputable episode led to the passage of laws to provide for the dissection necessary in medical schools.

CHAPTER XXVI

In the Operating Room

THERE are men living today who were born before the time when means were found for relieving the pain of surgical operation. There are many people who can remember from their own experience when there was no way of preventing the infection that almost invariably followed any operation, or indeed, any wound. In those days, less than a lifetime removed from our own, surgical operation was the last resort of necessity, to be tried only when all other forms of treatment had failed.

Today most of us at some time in our lives are treated by surgery, but a vastly different surgery from what our grandfathers knew. We no longer need view an operation with horror, but rather with some calm and a genuine thankfulness that we live in a time when the discoveries of the nineteenth century have given us the oblivion of anæsthesia that does away with pain and the safety of antisepsis and asepsis that removes the danger of infection. These medical discoveries have kept from our lives many of the cruelest hardships our ancestors suffered.

From earliest time men had tried to overcome the pain of operation. Drugs and alcohol, numbing of flesh with cold or pressure, and hypnotism were all tried and none was successful. Pain was apparently inevitable, an ordeal not only for the patient, but for the surgeon. In compassion the surgeon attempted to shorten the agony by working with the greatest speed; and when an operation had to be completed in a few seconds, it could not be the careful and precise procedure that the best surgery requires.

It is strange how often discoveries lie already made before our eyes without our really seeing them. In 1800 the English chemist Sir Humphrey Davy recorded the fact that

inhalation of the gas nitrous oxide produced unconsciousness; he wrote: "It may probably be used with advantage in
surgical operations." But no one used it for nearly half a
century.

Surgical anæsthesia was an American discovery that was
discovered twice within a few years. The first physician to
use an anæsthetic for an operation was Crawford Long of
Georgia. He used ether. This substance had been known for
many years; some doctors even were aware of the fact that
if its vapors were inhaled, drunkenness and unconsciousness
might follow. Dr. Long was the first to put this chance observation to practical use.

In March, 1842, he removed a small tumor from the neck
of a patient; during the operation the man inhaled the
fumes of ether. He suffered no pain. Unfortunately, Dr.
Long did not publish a report of his success; indeed his discovery remained unknown until the effects of ether had been
rediscovered and anæsthesia had become an accepted part of
surgery.

Strange to say, before ether again came into use the anæsthetic effects of nitrous oxide were again discovered, and this
time by a dentist of Hartford, Connecticut, named Horace
Wells.

In the forties, lectures were a popular form of entertainment. And in 1844 a man named Colton gave a series of lectures in Hartford on the new discoveries of chemistry. He
demonstrated in his lectures the effects of nitrous oxide.
His advertisement in the newspapers announced that he
would allow members of the audience to inhale the gas
which would make them laugh and talk and sing. He promised to have twelve strong men in the front row to protect
the spectators against harm from the exuberant antics of
those who became drunk from the gas.

Horace Wells and a friend attended the lecture. The
friend volunteered as one of the subjects. Dazed from the
gas, he became pugnacious and, so the story says, jumped

from the stage to grapple with one of the "strong men" in the front row. The guardian of safety fled and after him went Wells's friend. To cut short the chase, he jumped over the back of a bench. He caught his leg and fell to the floor. Sobered by the blow he made his way shamefacedly back to his seat beside Wells. The lecture continued; and then suddenly the man with Wells noticed that his leg was bleeding.

A caricature of eighteenth-century surgery.

He pulled up his trousers to expose a ragged gash that he had received when he struck against the bench. He was surprised at the sight of the wound, for he had felt no pain. Wells questioned him closely; still he insisted that he had not felt the blow.

The next day Horace Wells prepared a bag of nitrous oxide; he had a tooth pulled as he inhaled the "laughing gas," and he felt nothing. Convinced that he had arrived at a long sought goal, he went to Boston to the Massachusetts General Hospital and offered to exhibit the properties of nitrous oxide. But there his efforts failed. Without special

apparatus nitrous oxide is difficult to administer; the patient whose tooth he extracted revived from the gas before the operation was over and screamed his pain. Wells went home discouraged.

But another dentist named William Morton, who knew Wells, continued where he left off. Morton was a student in the Harvard School of Medicine, as well as a dentist. One of his professors, a chemist named Jackson, suggested to him that he try ether instead of gas. Morton experimented on himself and on the family dog, and finally used ether with success as an anæsthetic for the extraction of teeth. He was ready then for his great venture, the use of ether for a major surgical operation. He asked Dr. Warren, chief surgeon of the Massachusetts General Hospital, for permission to make the test. The request was granted; the day was set for October 16. This was in 1846.

The story of that demonstration has become one of the classics of medicine. Rumor spread that some medical student had presumed to offer a method for abolishing the pain of operation. The gallery of the operating amphitheater was crowded with incredulous spectators. The patient was brought in. The surgeon waited, dressed in formal morning clothes—in those days surgeons did not wear white gowns, nor did they wash their hands before operating, but only afterward, for Lister had not yet shown that infection might come from dirty hands. At the appointed time the surgeon, the patient, the strong men to hold him down in his struggles, the spectators, were all ready, but Morton was not present. A quarter of an hour passed, and then Dr. Warren, taking his knife in hand, turned to the spectators and said, "As Dr. Morton has not arrived, I presume he is otherwise engaged." The audience smiled—they had been skeptical all along. Dr. Warren touched his knife to the skin of the shrinking patient. At that moment—so the story goes—the door opened and in came Morton. He had been delayed in completing an apparatus to administer the ether. Dr. War-

ren stepped back, pointed to the man strapped to the operating table, and said, "Well, sir, your patient is ready." Amid the silence of the spectators, surrounded by unsympathetic faces, Morton administered the ether. In a few minutes he looked up and said, "Dr. Warren, *your* patient is ready." The incredulous audience watched in silence as the operation was begun. The patient gave no sign of pain; he was obviously alive—everyone could see his breathing; he slept. With the completion of the operation, Dr. Warren turned to the spectators, and said, "Gentlemen, this is no humbug."

Anæsthesia for surgical operation was a demonstrated reality. But the men in that operating room did not call it anæsthesia; the phenomenon was new and there was no term in the language to describe it. Oliver Wendell Holmes later coined the words anæsthesia, anæsthetic, and anæsthetist.

The operating room at the Massachusetts General Hospital where the demonstration was made has stood unchanged ever since that day in 1846, a memorial to the first public demonstration of the blessing of anæsthesia. If by chance you visit it, you will realize that its very appearance also commemorates a second great discovery in surgery. It is an ordinary room of the period, with wooden floors, carpet strips and drab painted walls. It has no white tiles or shining metal, and none of the scrupulous cleanliness of the modern operating room. The story of the change with all that it embodies in freedom from infection takes us from America to Scotland.

In 1854 a young surgeon, an English Quaker named Joseph Lister, went to Edinburgh. Six years later he had risen to the position of professor of surgery in the University of Glasgow and embarked on the career that made him the greatest surgeon of all times. The problem that held his attention was infection in wounds. The formation of pus, the development of fever, were believed to be due to the state of the weather, and to evil smells in the air, or else were considered inevitable in all wounds resulting from vio-

lence and indeed, as we have seen, a regular part of healing. Infection, whatever its cause, made surgery a discouraging task. Lister operated skilfully and cared for his patients carefully; they did well for a day or two, and then the infection set in. Half or more died of what we should call blood poisoning. A surgical operation in Lister's hospital or in any other at the time was nearly as dangerous as bubonic plague. What made matters worse was that it seemed to make little difference whether the operation was grave or slight. In either case the infection came and the blood poisoning followed.

Lister, studying the problem, observed a curious fact which gave him the clue to his discovery. There were men in the wards with broken legs and broken arms. They were wounded, but the wound was under the skin. Such wounds did not become infected. The air did not reach them. Something from the air, reasoned Lister, poisoned the wound and caused infection.

The next clue came from the work of a French chemist, Louis Pasteur. He had been employed by the wine industry of France to study the diseases of wines. Wines sometimes became "sick," lost their pleasant odor and spoiled. Pasteur found that the sickness was due to the growth of bacteria that got into the wine from the air. To prevent the growth of these "germs," he had developed a process of treating the wine by heat. The process has ever since been known by his name, "Pasteurization."

Lister, reading of Pasteur's discovery, saw a similarity between the putrefaction of wine and the infection of wounds. The something from the air that caused the "putrefaction" in open wounds might well be bacteria. If that should prove true, then he had to prevent the bacteria from getting in the wound or, if that were impossible, kill them before they had multiplied and spread.

He decided to start his experiments with a wound that was already infected. But first he must find something with

A GRAND EXHIBITION of the effects produced by inhaling NITROUS OXIDE, EXHILARATING or LAUGHING GAS! will be given at UNION HALL, THIS (Tuesday) EVENING, Dec. 10th, 1844.

FORTY GALLONS OF GAS will be prepared and adminis-tered to all in the audience who desire to inhale it.

TWELVE YOUNG MEN have volunteered to inhale the Gas, to commence the entertainment.

EIGHT STRONG MEN are engaged to occupy the front seats, to protect those under the influence of the Gas from in-juring themselves or others. This course is adopted that no apprehension of danger may be entertained. Probably no one will attempt to fight.

THE EFFECT of the GAS is to make those who inhale it either Laugh, Sing, Dance, Speak or Fight, &c., &c., accord-ing to the leading trait of their character. They seem to re-tain consciousness enough to not say or do that which they would have occasion to regret.

N. B. The Gas will be administered only to gentlemen of the first respectability. The object is to make the enter-tainment in every respect a genteel affair.

MR. COLTON, who offers this entertainment, gave two of the same character last Spring, in the Broadway Taberna-cle, New York which were attended by over four thousand ladies and gentlemen, a full account of which may be found in the New Mirror of April 6th, by N P. Willis. Being on a visit to Hartford, he offers this entertainment at the earnest solicitation of friends. It is his wish and intention to *deserve* and receive the patronage of the first class. He believes he can make them laugh more than they have for six months previous. The entertainment is *scientific* to those who *make* it scientific.

Those who inhale the Gas once, are always anxious to in-hale it the second time. There is not an exception to this rule.

No language can describe the delightful sensation produc ed. Robert Southey, (poet) once said that "the atmosphere of the highest of all possible heavens must be composed of this Gas."

For a full account of the effect produced upon some of the most distinguished men of Europe, see Hooper's Medical Dictionary, under the head of Nitrogen.

MR. COLTON will be the first to inhale the Gas.

The History and properties of the Gas will be explained at the commencement of the entertainment.

The entertainment will close with a few of the most sur-prising CHEMICAL EXPERIMENTS.

MR. COLTON will give a private entertainment to those Ladies who desire to inhale the Gas, TUESDAY, between 12 and 1 o'clock, FREE. None but Ladies will be admit-ted. This is *intended* for those who desire to inhale the Gas although others will be admitted.

Entertainment to commence at 7 o'clock. Tickets 25 cents—for sale at the principal Bookstores and at the Door.

dec 10   1d

Colton's announcement in the Hartford Courant, *December 10, 1844.*

which to kill the bacteria; obviously he could not Pasteurize a man. He turned to chemical substances in the hope of finding one that would kill bacteria. Strangely enough, at this time his attention was called to the use of carbolic acid in treating sewage to prevent unpleasant odors. He decided to try it.

His preparations were now made, but he waited ten months for the arrival of a case in which he could feel justified in trying the experiment. Finally a man suffering from a compound fracture was brought to the hospital. A compound fracture is one in which the ends of the broken bone are forced through the flesh and skin, making an open wound. Simple fractures, those in which there is no opening to the air, healed in Lister's wards, as we have said, without infection. Compound fractures were always infected, and in Lister's time, for lack of a way to control the spread of infection, it was usually necessary to amputate the limb. Even then the result was often fatal.

Lister applied carbolic acid to the wound of the fracture and built a small tent over it to exclude the air. In spite of all these precautions, infection developed, blood poisoning followed, and the patient died. But Lister persisted. For later cases he washed his instruments in carbolic acid; he dipped his hands in the antiseptic, and sprayed a mist of it in the air about the room; he took every precaution to clean the wound and to keep bacteria from entering it. This time he succeeded; pus did not form or blood poisoning occur. The infection was controlled.

Soon he was using the spray of carbolic acid in the operating room and carrying out in all operations the procedure that had succeeded with the compound fracture. Infection and fever disappeared; the clean wounds healed quickly and safely. Vastly fewer deaths occurred.

In those early days Lister was convinced that the germs causing infection came from the air. In fact, so strongly did he insist upon the unpleasant spray of carbolic acid in the

air of the operating room that other surgeons thought he was trying to introduce a new medicine; their attention was distracted from the fundamental principle he was advocating —the principle of preventing the spread of infection by the use of antiseptics. Lister went his way calmly, indifferent to opposition, performing safely operations which other surgeons feared to do and saving the lives of the patients in his wards.

Reports of Lister's work spread to the continent and soon foreign surgeons came to visit him and learn his methods. The Franco-Prussian War broke out and antiseptics were used on the wounded with great success.

Gradually as experience grew, the belief that the germs of infection came from the air gave way to the knowledge that they came from filth ground into wounds, from the unclean hands and instruments of the surgeons, and from dirty bandages. So cleanliness—surgical cleanliness or asepsis— became the dominant idea of surgery. The modern operating room, the scrupulously clean hospital, the white-gowned surgeon, all are the result of Lister's discovery that infection in wounds is due to the presence of bacteria.

With the new safe surgery, freed from the fear of ever-present infection, surgeons for the first time could operate successfully on parts of the body where few had ever dared to operate—especially the abdomen and joints. Before Lister's time, men and women and children had appendicitis just as they do today. But the surgeon, even if he had fully understood the condition, could not have saved their lives by operation. The dangers of infection were far too great. A whole new field of surgery was opened up by Lister's discovery. And what is equally important, for the first time in all history, medicine had given a reason for cleanliness, in the home and office and factory as well as in the hospital and operating room. But cleanliness did not wholly replace the use of antiseptics even in the operating room. Instruments could be sterilized with heat, but not the surgeon's

hands or the patient's skin. For these antiseptics must be used. And besides, there were still wounds from accidents in which bacteria were present. Knowledge of the need of antiseptics spread, until now everyone knows of their necessity in the first aid treatment of even slight injuries. Fortunately we today have better and safer antiseptics than the carbolic acid that was first used.

Lister died in 1912—two years too soon to see the greatest vindication of his principles of antisepsis made in the World War, on the germ-ridden battlefields of France and Belgium. Thousands upon thousands of veterans who live today owe their lives to Lister, just as do hundreds of thousands of other men and women and children wounded in peacetime accidents or in operations.

CHAPTER XXVII

In Barracks and Prisons

AGAIN we return to the time of the French Revolution, to the events that gave Corvisart his opportunity for reorganizing medical education and that cost Lavoisier his head. Great national changes were underway: the States-General had assembled, the Bastille had been stormed, the Rights of Man proclaimed, the palace invaded, the king beheaded, and France was a republic. The Commune ruled. Out of fanaticism and patriotism and oratory, the members of that body shaped the policies of a nation and defined the Rights of Man. The extreme radicals were gaining power rapidly and the Reign of Terror was about to burst on France.

But an event perhaps more important to the future of the civilized world than those of politics and bloodshed was brought to pass amid the turmoil by a frail and timid doctor named Philippe Pinel. He had nerved himself to appear before the Commune and asked to be allowed to plead for the rights of his patients. He was repulsed. Again and again he came, and finally the burly Couthon, the firebrand of the Commune, condescended to listen to his plea.

Pinel told Couthon that if all men had equal rights then his poor insane patients in the prison of Bicêtre should share in them. They were chained in filthy dungeons; their fate was far more unjust than had been that of the common man at the hands of the aristocrat before the Revolution; they should be sheltered in kindness and given reasonable liberty.

Couthon, although he regarded Pinel as a wild visionary, was touched on a sensitive spot—his treasured reputation for equality. He consented to go with Pinel to the prison. Long used though he was to deal with the savage element of society, he flinched before the scene at the Bicêtre. In the

damp corridors of an underground prison he was greeted by
the shouts and execrations of three hundred lunatics, by the
creaking of chains, the pounding of manacles against iron
bars. Couthon exclaimed to Pinel, *"Ah, ça! citoyen, es-tu
fou toi-même de vouloir déchainer de pareils animaux?"*
(Citizen, are you crazy yourself to want to unchain such
beasts?). Pinel insisted. Retreating from the filthy cells,

Casting the demons into the swine.

Couthon said, "Do as you will; but your own life will be
sacrificed to this false mercy." Couthon left; Pinel began his
great experiment in the humane care of the mentally ill.

He commenced with an English captain who had been in
chains for forty years. The man had killed an attendant
with a blow from his manacles; the keepers approached him
cautiously watching his every move. But Pinel walked
ahead and entered his cell unattended. He talked to the man
quietly and offered him the freedom of the prison yard if he

would promise to behave "like a gentleman." The promise was given and the chains cut off. The poor man, for want of exercise, could not walk at first. Finally he managed to creep to the door. And he wept in ecstasy at the sight of the trees and sky.

Within a few days Pinel released from their chains more than fifty men who had been violently insane. The removal of restraint, the kindliness they received, wrought a change in them. They were still insane, still needed careful watching and help, but the violence of their mania, aggravated by chains and brutality, yielded to gentleness. They were no longer rebellious and disorderly.

Pinel's experiment, as we shall see, was destined to spread and grow into a great humanitarian movement which has completely altered not only the care of the insane, but also our attitude toward mental illness.

Pinel and Corvisart were the same age; they were friends, but two men could hardly have been more different in appearance and personality. Corvisart was stocky, round, vigorous, hail-fellow-well-met, and above all, practical. Pinel was slender, frail, retiring, meticulous in manner, visionary in his ideas. Corvisart set a useful, practical example in medical education and in diagnosis; Pinel originated a fundamental ethical change in civilization.

Pinel started his career as a student by entering a school of divinity, but he became interested in philosophy and then in natural history; it was only at the age of thirty that he finally decided that medicine should be his career. For a time he followed the fashions of the day and developed a classification of diseases. But again his interest shifted; one of his friends became insane and according to custom, was locked up and treated like a vicious animal. He escaped and hid in the woods; a few days later his skeleton was found; he had been devoured by wolves. The event made a horrible impression on Pinel; in the hope of benefiting men like his friend, he turned his medical interest to the study of insanity.

Under his influence the prison asylums of Paris, the Bicêtre and the Salpêtrière, became hospitals.

The brutality manifested toward the insane in the closing years of the eighteenth century was dictated by the belief that they were consciously unruly and destructive; that they

Driving out a demon.

were intentionally malicious. The insane were looked upon not at all as human beings; but literally as wild beasts to be brought to reason with chains and torture. There was no sympathy for them. The men of the early nineteenth century were compassionate to physical suffering and kind to animals; but they had not yet learned to sympathize with the mentally ill. There was no true understanding of the nature of mental disease.

In all ages the attitude toward the insane had been determined by the prevailing view concerning the cause of insanity. Among primitive peoples the insane were often held in high respect as being nearer to the spirits or gods than ordinary men. The insane man in his hallucinations heard voices—spirit voices—that no one else could hear; he talked to unseen creatures. He was superior to ordinary men. Even today in some Oriental countries the insane and feeble-minded are tolerated in kindness in the belief that their wits are already in Heaven.

But there was another belief regarding the insane which was to have unpleasant consequences. A spirit might enter a man's body and take possession of his faculties; he would then speak with the man's voice and hear with his ears. The man "possessed" could be brought back to normal only by driving out the spirit with medicine or magic ritual. The idea of possession dominated the attitude toward insanity for thousands of years.

The belief persisted after the appearance of the Christian religion, but views concerning spirits changed. Good spirits could no longer possess men, only evil ones, demons. The good spirits had taken the shape of angels, and although they could guide and advise men, they could not possess them.

Consequently, if the insane man's behavior took on a religious character, if he prayed and mortified the flesh, if he spoke with many holy words, he was not considered possessed; indeed he might be regarded as one deserving to be a saint. But if he were blasphemous, violent, or unruly, then indeed he was possessed of a demon. Exorcism with prayer and ritual was the treatment; if this failed, he might be beaten for his stubbornness in refusing to relinquish the demon.

At a still later date, another belief flourished that brought even less sympathy to the insane. It was the idea that witches made a voluntary bargain with the devil. As we

have said in earlier chapters, many of the witches burned were unfortunate insane people.

Gradually belief in "possession" and in witchcraft began

Exorcising an insane man.

to die out. But the lot of the insane was no better; indeed, if possible, it was worse. No longer were demons or the devil responsible for their victims; the victims themselves were to blame. They were like wild beasts: their irrational ways

were due to inherent maliciousness. And like beasts, they were to be brought under control by force.

Such was the state of affairs when Pinel asked permission from the French Commune to try the experiment of treating the insane as sick men.

His experiment, as we have seen, was a success. Under kindly care, violence and disorder diminished. It was still necessary to have institutions for the mentally ill, as it was to have hospitals for the physically ill. But these new institutions were to be truly hospitals for care and help, and not prisons.

Pinel's theory that insanity was a mental illness, deserving the same study and sympathy as physical sickness, spread slowly among physicians; here and there an institution was opened for the new treatment of the insane. But the idea did not reach the general population; their attitude remained unchanged; to them the insane were still not human beings.

It was in America that the great reform was extended to give the public the understanding that insanity was a form of sickness. At the beginning of the nineteenth century the United States had one asylum; it was located in Virginia; the hospital of Philadelphia had, as we have said, cells where the insane could be locked up. Forty years later there were eight institutions in America where the mentally ill could receive care, but few of them were hospitals supported by state funds. Most of the mentally ill, if violent, were still locked in barns and sheds, or jails, or county poor farms. If they were harmless, they were sometimes auctioned off to the bidder who would take the smallest sum for their care, or else turned loose on country roads to become tramps.

That was the situation when a seemingly insignificant event occurred, but one that was destined to spread the reform that Pinel had started throughout the world. On Sunday, March 28, 1841, a school teacher of Boston, Miss Dorothea Lynde Dix, was asked to give Sunday School instruction to the inmates of the East Cambridge House of Correc-

tion. Here for the first time she was brought in contact with the frightful conditions in the jails of that time. She found twenty women crowded together into one very dirty room. No provision was made for heat, for among them were several who were insane, and because of their violence, a stove was dangerous. Miss Dix was shocked. She decided to do what she could to remedy the condition.

In the forties of the last century aggressive women were

Burning a witch.

not looked upon with favor—a woman's place was in the home, not in public affairs. Accordingly Miss Dix asked a Dr. Howe of Boston to protest in his own name in the newspaper against the brutalities she had seen. His letter had no effect. Miss Dix set out quietly to visit every prison and poorhouse in the state of Massachusetts. It took her two years to do it. Then she wrote a memorial to the State Legislature. It began with these words: "About two years since . . . duty prompted me to visit the prisons and almshouses in the vicinity of this metropolis. . . . Every investigation

has given depth to the conviction that it is only by decided, prompt and vigorous legislation that the evils to which I refer, and which I shall proceed more fully to illustrate, can be remedied. I shall be obliged to speak with great plainness, and to reveal many things revolting to the taste, from which

Insane girl in prison.

my woman's nature shrinks with peculiar sensitiveness. But truth is the highest consideration. I shall tell what I have seen."

Her memorial goes on to describe specifically the revolting scenes in the jails and poor farms where the insane were chained in dungeons and often starved and frozen. It was a gruesome document, a veritable indictment of civilization. In response to it, action was prompt; the Massachusetts Legislature unanimously voted to appropriate funds to establish

state-supported hospitals and provide humane care for all the mentally ill of the state.

Miss Dix, however, realized that the abuses she had helped to correct in one state still existed in the others. Her work had barely begun. In the next forty years she visited every state in the Union, and England and Scotland as well. Her procedure was always the same—an investigation and a memorial. The response was always the same—the appropriation of funds and the erection of a hospital. In this country thirty-two new state institutions were started as a result of her work, and, what is equally important, under her disclosures the sentiment of the public changed. The people of this country—indeed of the whole civilized world—were made conscious of a grave abuse, and given a new ideal—sympathy for the mentally ill.

In spite of her great work, Dorothea Lynde Dix is little known today. The name of another medical humanitarian of the nineteenth century is much more familiar—a woman whom Longfellow has described in Santa Filomena:

> *On England's annals, through the long*
> *Hereafter of her speech and song,*
> *That light its rays shall cast*
> *From portals of the past.*
>
> *A Lady with a Lamp shall stand*
> *In the great history of the land,*
> *A noble type of good*
> *Heroic womanhood.*

The "Lady with the Lamp" was Florence Nightingale. In 1915, during the World War, a statuary group was unveiled in London in memory of an earlier conflict, the Crimean War. One of the figures in that group was Florence Nightingale. Except for members of royalty it was the first statue in honor of a woman to be erected in London.

During the Crimean War Florence Nightingale founded

modern trained nursing. She did not found nursing but she
made it a respected profession. Women in all centuries had
given their services to aid the sick and injured; but they
were rarely trained to this calling. The Sisters of Charity
of the Catholic Church had from early days devoted their
lives to nursing, but in the nineteenth century they were of

Hogarth's picture of Bedlam.

little practical use in the hospitals of England and America.
An absurd prudery had grown up. In consequence a series
of restrictions were imposed even upon the Sisters of Charity. They could watch the sick, maintain discipline in the
hospitals, but the actual care of the sick was carried out by
women who were too low in social caste or intelligence to
be ashamed of their degraded occupation of professional
nursing. These were the days before Lister's discovery; the
hospitals in the hands of slovenly drunken nurses were in-

describably filthy. No one went to a hospital when ill who could possibly avoid it; people stayed at home, even for surgical operations.

Florence Nightingale was a well-bred English girl of the nineteenth century, but she revolted against the idea that young women should live at home, without any means of earning their living, and wait to be married. One of her great interests in life was establishing the independence of women. To the utter outrage of her friends and family, her revolt took the form of a desire to nurse. To keep her from carrying out this notion, her mother took her on a trip to visit the fashionable summer resorts of the continent. But Florence ran away. She went to Kaiserswerth, a town near Düsseldorf, where a Lutheran pastor named Fliedner had started a school for discharged female prisoners whom he was attempting to train as nurses. Florence joined the group and there learned the first principles of nursing. Returning home, she became superintendent of a small hospital in London. But though she hoped for it, other women did not follow her example and show their independence by becoming nurses. She was simply regarded as "queer."

This same year, however, there started a series of events that was to change this view entirely. There was talk of war in the East—with Russia. The French and English fleets had steamed to a position at the mouth of the Dardanelles. A year later the western forces had joined with Turkey and the Crimean War began. Today we may turn to Tennyson's "Charge of the Light Brigade" for the story of the war; but in 1854, news of a far less romantic cast came to London from a newspaper correspondent named Russell. Before his reports were censored, he told some unpleasant facts about the conditions of the war hospitals. Among other things he said that there were no nurses whatever to take care of sick and wounded English soldiers.

The public was aroused. A call was issued for volunteers. Women responded; but none, save Florence Nightingale,

knew anything of organized nursing. Put in full charge of
the entire nursing service of the English Army she managed
to collect thirty-eight women, ten of whom were nuns, who
knew something of practical nursing. This little band was to
care for all the sick and wounded of the British Army.

On November 4, 1854, they landed at Scutari, a suburb
of Constantinople. The hospital there was a deserted bar-

Dorothea Lynde Dix.

racks intended to accommodate a thousand men. Four thousand sick and wounded soldiers were crowded into it. Four
miles of beds—and thirty-eight nurses! The beds were bare
boards on trestles; there was no other equipment in the hospital. Army regulations required each soldier to bring his
own clothing to the hospital; none was issued even to men
carried from the battlefield in rags. The windows of the
barracks were tightly closed. The floor was rotten and un-
swept. There was no laundry. The doors were shut at night

and opened only in the morning to pass out the dead. There was no one at all to care for the sick during the night.

Florence Nightingale undertook to remedy the situation. She was at once confronted by official red tape. The regulations must be obeyed. But Miss Nightingale, as we have implied, was a strong-minded lady. Her temper was as short as the colonel's; her sarcasm matched his. She took orders from no one; she gave them instead. Supplies were issued; the windows of the hospitals were opened; a laundry was built. To the army officer in command she must have seemed a raging demon, but to the wounded soldiers she was an angel of mercy. No sacrifice was too great in her work of "helping the patient to live." At night she walked through the long wards of the barracks, lamp in hand, ministering to the soldiers. The lamp became her emblem.

In 1856 the war ended. The troopers returned home. Thousands of men carried back the story of the "Lady with the Lamp" to whom they owed their lives. They were the advocates of trained nursing; before their appeal prudery crumbled. Soon funds were raised and schools opened where young women could be trained as nurses.

No practical advance ever made in medicine has brought greater comfort and greater help to the sick than the trained nursing founded by Florence Nightingale.

But her inspiration was destined to lead to an even greater humanitarian reform. In 1859, a Swiss named Henri Dunant stood on a hillside overlooking the battle of Magenta and Solferino. His mind, tortured by the scene before him, turned to Florence Nightingale's work of relief. Could it be extended to relieve the suffering on the battlefield? He conceived there the idea that grew to be the great humanitarian principle for which the Red Cross stands today.

On that June day, Dunant saw the allied armies of France and Italy under Napoleon III engaged in battle with the army of Austria. Forty thousand men were killed or wounded. There was no treaty to protect the doctors of the

armies; they, of necessity, followed the troops as the allies drove the Austrians from the field. The wounded lay unattended, deserted except by the people of the neighboring villages. The peasants came with carts; the wounded who had lain on the ground perhaps for days were loaded into them and carried over rough roads to the towns. There were no doctors or nurses to care for them; the women of the town ministered as best they could—but only to their own compatriots. From sheer neglect thousands of men died who could readily have been saved if provision had been made for their care.

Dunant went among the wounded, giving such help as he could. On the altar steps of a church he found an Austrian chasseur, horribly wounded, who had had nothing to eat for three days. He bathed his wounds and gave him bouillon to drink; the man lifted his benefactor's hand to his lips. Dunant, weeping, turned to the women of the town, and urged them to make no distinction in the care of the wounded, telling them that all wounded men were their brothers, no matter in what cause they had fought.

This was indeed a new ideal of humanity—a universal brotherhood with the ill and needy. In the past there had been a few attempts to put military hospitals under a flag of truce, but usually the wounded had been neglected or actually killed. The Knights Hospitalers of the Crusades and the Sisters of Charity had given their services without distinction to race or creed or nation. But Dunant was suggesting something greater—an international alliance which would raise the wounded above all ties of race or nation and make them brothers of every man. To that end he wanted not only the wounded, but the doctor, the nurse, and the hospital as well, to be fully protected by truce of war.

He wrote a book called *Un souvenir de Solferino;* in it he described the scenes he had witnessed, and set forth his ideas for an international alliance. He worked enthusiastically to bring the plan before the rulers of the European countries.

In 1863, four years after Solferino, his efforts were rewarded. A meeting was held at Geneva; fourteen countries were represented. Each agreed to follow Dunant's suggestion. These nations banded together in an international alliance to aid the wounded and to provide succor in time of disaster. They agreed that the injured man, the physician, and the nurse were thereafter to be considered neutrals, and the hospital a sanctuary.

An international army of a new kind—one that was dedicated to the interests of humanity—was founded. That army, too, was to have an emblem, a flag to rally under, a distinguishing mark that would be respected by all men in time of war and peace. In tribute to Dunant, the emblem chosen was the Swiss flag with colors reversed—the red cross on the white background.

H. Boerhaave

Part Ten

THE LABORATORY

THE FRONTIERS OF DISEASE

THE GOAL

CHAPTER XXVIII

The Laboratory

IN the nineteenth century a search that had been going on for more than one hundred and fifty centuries ended. The spirits which primitive man had thought responsible for pestilential disease were finally seen and identified as bacteria. When spread out on a thin slip of glass and viewed through a microscope, there was nothing supernatural about these creatures. Quite the contrary; they appeared harmless—merely tiny rods or minute spheres like infinitesimal berries, or slender filaments coiled into corkscrew forms.

Leeuwenhoek, in the seventeenth century, had seen these minute plants through his crude microscope. They were then merely scientific curiosities. Until late in the nineteenth century no one dreamed that they played a part in human affairs. It was the work of Pasteur, Lister, and Koch that brought bacteria into prominence and into disrepute. Since those days we have become painfully conscious of an invisible population of the world—a ruthless murderous population.

But this attitude is totally unfair to the great family of bacteria. By far the greater portion of them spend their humble lives toiling, as Pliny with his teleology would have said, in the interest of mankind. The fact is that without bacteria the human race could not exist. Nothing would decay; fallen plants, dead animals would not disintegrate into soil and so nourish other growths that nourish man. Most bacteria are the harmless benefactors of all visible living things. Most of them cannot thrive on living flesh; put into a wound they would die. It is the unfortunate ability of a few to grow on living human flesh that makes them disease bacteria. The insignificant presence of a few thou-

sand or even a million bacteria in the flesh, does not make them harmful; but rather their ability to grow there, to become billions and trillions until their overwhelming numbers force the body to recognize their presence. The body defends itself; the defence gives rise to the symptoms of disease.

The rogue bacteria, which through the centuries have learned to prey on human flesh, have each their special habits. Some are harmless except in open wounds; and there one kind may produce pus, another blood poisoning. Others cannot live in wounds, and find conditions suited to their growth only in the throat or perhaps the intestines. Different symptoms of disease result from these habits of growth of the various kinds of disease bacteria, giving rise to what are called specific infectious diseases. One kind and only one produces typhoid fever; a quite distinct variety gives rise to diphtheria; while still another produces scarlet fever.

It was Pasteur who taught us the life history of bacteria; Lister who found that they produced infection in wounds; and Koch who showed that they were the cause of the specific infectious diseases.

Louis Pasteur was not a physician; he was a chemist. Born at Dôle, France, in 1822, the son of a tanner, he went as a young man to Paris to the École Normale. There he showed such talent for science that he became an assistant to one of his teachers. Soon Pasteur made an important discovery: tartaric acid from wine existed in several forms; each was composed of exactly the same chemical elements in exactly the same amounts, but when a beam of light from a quartz prism was passed through the crystals of the acid, some turned the beam to the right, others to the left, and still others affected it not at all. This difference, as Pasteur was the first to demonstrate, was due to a difference in the arrangement of the elements that made up the acid.

Thus at the very beginning of his career, he founded a whole new branch of chemistry, one known as stereochemis-

try—based on the position of the atom in the molecule. His reputation was made, and he was offered teaching positions in other schools. For a time he taught at Dijon and then Strasbourg; but soon he was called to become dean of the

A caricature of Pasteur.

faculty of natural science at Lille. This city was the center for the manufacture of alcohol, and Pasteur turned his attention to the problem of fermentation.

It was known that sugar was converted into alcohol by the action of a microscopic plant called yeast. The living yeast used the sugar for food, and alcohol was formed as a

waste product. But there were other changes besides that of fermentation; wine soured, and so did milk; butter became rancid and meat putrefied. Were these alterations likewise due to living things?

Pasteur's microscope disclosed in all souring and spoiling food substances the presence of bacteria. But then came the question: were bacteria the cause of the change or the result; did they produce putrefaction or were they a product of it? Here again was the old problem of spontaneous generation of life. In the seventeenth century Redi had shown that maggots did not arise spontaneously in spoiled meat but came from the eggs of flies. In the nineteenth century Pasteur repeated the experiments using bacteria. Fluids such as wine or bouillon, that had been heated to kill any bacteria already present, did not sour or putrefy as long as air was excluded. But if air containing bacteria was allowed to come in contact with them, putrefaction began as soon as the bacteria multiplied in the fluid. Pasteur proved conclusively that bacteria come only from other bacteria.

The "sickness" of wine was caused by bacteria; it could be prevented by heating—"Pasteurization"—which killed the bacteria. That was a discovery of enormous value to the wine industry; it was the one, as we have seen, that guided Lister in his discovery of the cause of wound infection.

The bacterial population of the world, which up to this time had been ignored, now suddenly came into startling prominence. Did bacteria cause disease in men and animals? That was the question.

Pasteur first applied his discoveries not to human beings but to silk worms. Silk growing, like the manufacture of wines, was one of the great industries of France. A disease had broken out; the caterpillars were dying. Pasteur found out that certain bacteria were affecting the worms and showed the silk growers how to breed healthy stock.

Five years were taken up in the investigation that saved the silk industry of France and, even more important,

showed that bacteria could produce disease. By this time other men were becoming interested in bacteria, and particularly a German country physician named Robert Koch. He was twenty-one years younger than Pasteur and when Pasteur was showing that the disease of silk worms was caused by bacteria, he was just beginning his practice in the district of Wollstein. Koch had a hobby; he was a botanist of a kind, but the plants he studied were bacteria. His young wife had made him a present of a microscope; his office soon became a crude laboratory. Between calls on his patients he cultivated his collection of bacteria with all the enthusiasm that an amateur gardener spends on flowers or vegetables. Koch was learning the habits of bacteria, finding out how to raise them; he was establishing the principles of modern bacteriology.

In the countryside where Koch practiced there was prevalent a disease of sheep and cattle called splenic fever or anthrax. It sometimes spread as a fatal malady to the men who handled the animals or their hides. As early as 1849 a veterinary surgeon, examining animals which had died of anthrax had, through his microscope, seen in their blood large rod-shaped bacteria. In 1863 a physician had put some of the blood containing these bacteria into a sheep; the sheep developed anthrax and died. The experiment seemed to show conclusively that the disease was caused by the bacteria; it would have been proved except for one fact. The blood of the sick animals caused the disease even when no bacteria could be found in it. There again was the question that had confronted Pasteur—were the bacteria the cause or the result of the disease?

This problem Koch undertook to solve. In his laboratory he grew the bacteria from the blood of diseased animals; they appeared as long delicate threads in the nutrient fluids which he used for their cultivation. But if a drop of the fluid was put on a piece of glass and allowed to dry, a change took place in the filaments. Dot-like areas appeared on them.

The large bacteria shriveled and died but the minute dots persisted. When these were put in broth they grew like seeds and produced the large bacteria. These in turn multiplied so that from a few of the "spores," as the dots are called, a great number of bacteria could be produced.

Here then was a possible answer to the question why blood from sick animals that showed no bacteria could still produce disease. Only the minute spores were present. Experiments proved that. Anthrax was due to a specific bacterium, but one that had the peculiar property, shared by a few disease bacteria, of existing in two forms. The spores were far more resistant to drying, to heat, to antiseptics, than were the long rod-shaped forms that came with active growth. The spores clinging to the wool of sheep, or to the grass of pastures, could persist for many months. If they were eaten, or if they entered wounds, they developed into the tender rod-shaped form and multiplied. Anthrax resulted.

Koch made his discoveries known. He described the life history of the anthrax bacterium and proved it to be the cause of a specific infectious disease.

In time Koch became the director of the Institute for Infectious Diseases at Berlin, and it was there in 1882 that he made one of his greatest discoveries. He found the cause of tuberculosis. He showed that tuberculosis was not due, as men had supposed, to "bad" heredity or to weakened constitutions; it was caused by a bacterium, the tubercle bacillus. The swellings called tubercles that René Laënnec had found in the flesh of men sick with the disease were the result of the growth of these bacteria. Tuberculosis was an infection. Koch's discovery made possible for the first time the development of means to prevent consumption which until our time has killed more men than perhaps any other disease. Today it has lost its place as "captain of the men of Death"; each year it yields more and more to the efforts which point now to its eventual eradication—efforts to pre-

vent the spread of the bacteria which Koch discovered to be its cause.

After Koch had set the example the bacteria responsible for most of the infectious diseases were discovered in rapid succession—those of cholera, typhoid, bubonic plague, dysentery, and diphtheria, and many others.

At last a means of preventing infectious diseases—by controlling the spread of disease bacteria—had been found. Modern sanitation and modern public health grew out of the discoveries in bacteriology made late in the nineteenth century.

But the discoveries led into other channels as well—treatment and personal prevention. It was Pasteur who by chance observation discovered the possibilities of vaccines. He had isolated a bacterium that caused cholera in chickens and he was growing the organism in tubes of broth in his laboratory. Every few days he would take a drop from a tube and add it to fresh broth in another tube. Left too long, the bacteria by their prodigious multiplication would overcrowd the broth; they would apparently become weakened and, left long enough, would actually exterminate themselves.

A drop or two of the broth containing the actively growing bacteria, given to a chicken, caused it to sicken with cholera and die. But one day in his experiments Pasteur chanced to use an old culture, one in which the bacteria had lived for several weeks. This time the chickens, although they seemed sick for a day or two, did not die. Obviously the bacteria had been weakened by their own overcrowding and had lost their deadly properties. They could no longer multiply in the flesh of the chicken. That was a fact readily explained. But here was something else. Pasteur again gave these same chickens cholera germs, this time fresh and vigorous ones that killed quickly and certainly—but they did not kill these particular chickens. These chickens could not be given cholera; they could eat the bacteria with impunity. Why? The dose of weakened cholera germs had rendered

them immune to the disease. Their bodies had been able to cope with the weakened bacteria and had developed protection against a second attack. This was an immunity similar to that observed in nearly all infectious diseases: after we

Caricature of Dr. Koch "culturing" bacteria.

have once had a disease we are not likely to acquire it again. Weakened or even dead bacteria then might be used to produce immunity safely, produce it without the dangers of the disease itself.

Pasteur applied his discovery of what he called vaccines to the prevention of anthrax. He prepared a culture of the

anthrax bacilli and then made it harmless; that is, he killed the bacteria. His vaccine was a sort of soup of the vegetable called the anthrax bacillus. He injected some of the vaccine into half the cattle in a herd. After a few days he repeated the injection. And then into all the cattle he injected living and virulent anthrax bacteria. The untreated cattle sickened and died; those given the vaccine were not affected. The dead bacteria had rendered them immune.

Next came the question: what change did the vaccine produce in the body—what was the nature of immunity? That problem has not even now been answered fully, but in studying it, one of Koch's pupils, named Emil von Behring, made a great practical discovery. He found that some bacteria, as they grew on the flesh, formed poisons which were absorbed and carried into the blood, injuring the nerves or other delicate tissues of the body. In immunity there was something in the blood that neutralized this poison. It was an antidote or antitoxin. Thus blood of a man who had had diphtheria, because of the antitoxin it held, neutralized the poison given off by the diphtheria bacteria. This antitoxin could be produced in animals by injecting small and non-fatal amounts of the bacterial poison. The fluid of the blood, the serum, held the antitoxin. Here again was a new weapon in fighting disease. In diphtheria—then a prevalent and fatal disease— the child infected with the bacteria was making his own antitoxin, but often not as fast as the bacteria were producing the toxin. Help could be given by supplying antitoxin. Soon antitoxin was used by physicians in all civilized countries; the results were amazingly successful. Diphtheria ceased to be the dreaded disease it once was.

The principle applied to diphtheria yielded equally beneficent results with another and even more deadly disease —tetanus or lockjaw. Infection from this bacterium comes from filth and dirt ground into wounds or carried deep into the flesh in slender puncture wounds such as those made by nails or the prongs of rakes. The disease is so severe and can

so readily be prevented by antitoxin that this treatment is now a regular part of the medical care of accidental injuries.

One of the few diseases that rank with tetanus in its extremely deadly nature is hydrophobia, or rabies. And this disease, in time, was conquered by Pasteur.

In 1881 he reported to the French Academy of Science that the virus of rabies is found in the saliva of animals which have the disease. Year by year the progress of his work can be followed in the pages of the papers of the Academy. He told how he found the virus in nerves; how it traveled to the brain and there, acting on the nerve cells, caused madness.

It took weeks or months for the virus to travel from the bite to the brain. But Pasteur could produce rabies in animals quickly by putting the virus directly into the brain; or he could weaken the virus by passing it from one animal to another. And then by taking out and drying the nervous tissues that held it he made a vaccine. He injected dogs with the weakened virus. Then he put with them an equal number of dogs unprotected by vaccination, and turned a frantically mad dog loose among the group. All were bitten. The unprotected dogs developed rabies; those vaccinated did not. Here was a method that might eradicate rabies. Pasteur suggested that all the dogs in France be vaccinated. But there were obstacles; there were stray dogs that could not be captured and there were wolves that harbored rabies. It seemed that, after all, the treatment which offered so much hope might fail of practical use. Pasteur had not then thought of applying the vaccine to men already bitten.

It was the affair of a boy named Joseph Meister that gave Pasteur the idea of using the vaccine to stop the spread of the virus within the body. Joseph and his mother came from Alsace to Pasteur's laboratory. The nine-year-old boy had been bitten in fourteen places by a rabid dog. His death was almost certain. Pasteur was not a physician; he was a chemist. Doctors called in consultation recommended the experi-

ment of giving the vaccine, for the boy was doomed otherwise. On the evening of July 6, 1885, Pasteur made the first injection. He gave ten more. Joseph did not develop rabies.

Soon there was another patient, a shepherd boy named Jean Jupille who, seeing a mad dog throw itself upon a group of six young children, had taken his whip and rushed to their aid. The dog had seized his hand, but the boy threw the animal to the ground, forced open its mouth to release the mangled hand, and although bitten many times, held the dog until he could tie its mouth shut with the whip cord and beat it to death with his wooden shoe.

Jean was treated by Pasteur. He too survived. And today in the courtyard of the Pasteur Institute in Paris there is a statue showing this shepherd boy struggling with the mad dog. But the true memorials to Pasteur, Koch, and Von Behring are not in stone but in human beings who have been freed of suffering—who are alive even—because of their work.

CHAPTER XXIX

The Frontiers of Disease

THERE is a legend of a ghost ship called *The Flying Dutchman.* In southern waters on moonlight nights the sailors saw her, so they said, as, with sails filled, she glided by them without crew or helmsman. *The Flying Dutchman* was an evil omen; her legend was the sailors' picturesque way of expressing their dread of the "yellow jack"—that mysterious disease of the tropics. And there really were ships that became Flying Dutchmen of a kind. Yellow jack—the yellow fever—broke out on board; the crew perished to a man; the ship became a derelict carried before the winds, drifting with the currents.

Yellow fever, so it seemed, struck only at the white man. The negroes on the coast of Africa and in the West Indies never took the disease; only the sailors, soldiers, travelers, merchants who came to those places, died of it. When, just before the opening of the eighteenth century, the king's ship *Tiger* lay at the Barbados, her captain buried six hundred men in two years, although his full crew was only two hundred and twenty. He "pressed" sailors out of every merchant ship that came to the Islands to keep his own crew manned.

Yellow fever, carried in the merchant ships, reached the Atlantic coast of America in the eighteenth century; the inhabitants of Boston, New Haven, and Philadelphia more than once suffered from the disease. In the summer of 1793, nearly ten per cent of the population of Philadelphia died of the "American plague," as it was called. The city resembled London in the days of the bubonic plague. People fled, hoping to escape. New York and other cities posted armed guards to prevent the entrance of anyone from Philadelphia. Burial of the dead was carried out by negroes; they were

exempt from the disease; it was only the white man who suffered—or so it was believed.

In reality we know now that the exemption was not natural, but acquired. In the native home of the negroes, yellow fever was a nearly universal disease. Among children, as compared to adults, it was a mild malady. The native children all had it and obtained life-long immunity. But when the adult white man came to Africa, to the West Indies, or to parts of South America, or when the disease spread to northern cities and attacked adults, it assumed its severest form, and the mortality was high.

Yellow fever serves to illustrate what may be called a biological balance between bacteria and man; it also illustrates the penalties of disturbing the balances that nature imposes. What is true of yellow fever is true also of most of the infectious diseases.

Looked at in a wholly impersonal way, there is an element of fair play in the matter of infectious disease. Only a few such maladies are almost invariably fatal, like hydrophobia and tetanus; most are comparatively mild in children; and nearly all confer immunity with one attack.

These are the elements that enter into the natural biological balance that existed when disease was universally present and completely uncontrolled.

A baby at birth carries from its mother a temporary immunity against the diseases to which she is immune. That once meant all the common infectious diseases. For a few months the baby is protected against disease; then gradually the immunity diminishes. One after another in the past the disease bacteria gained a foothold, and specific infectious diseases appeared—measles, scarlet fever, smallpox, whooping cough, typhoid fever, typhus perhaps, cholera, and bubonic plague; and in the tropical regions, yellow fever, and, even in the temperate zone, malaria and nearly always tuberculosis. In all the diseases except malaria and tuberculosis, immunity resulted in those who did not die and even

for these two a tolerance of a sort developed. After the baptism of disease the child had little need of sanitation, little benefit from modern preventive medicine. He had paid his tribute to the bacterial world and thereafter he could live immune to it.

But there was one great drawback to satisfying this biological balance which gave safety to the adult. For all their comparative mildness in diseases of childhood, the bacteria often killed. Formerly more young people died than survived to obtain their immunities. Nature took heavy toll of life.

Modern prevention of infection began with the first sketchy attempts at quarantine; progressed with the efforts in the early nineteenth century to clean the towns and cover up the sewers; and bounded forward with tremendous impetus following the discoveries of Pasteur, Lister, and Koch. In consequence the lives of many boys and girls who in earlier generations would have died from infectious diseases were saved. During the nineteenth century the average length of life was doubled.

Save for vaccination against smallpox, the efforts of preventive medicine have been mainly to keep disease bacteria from reaching men and infecting them. In consequence there have grown up generations which, though they have escaped the penalties of disease and lived to adult years, have also lost the benefits—immunity to infection. Our ancestors, with their immunity to the diseases common in their time, were like the natives of the tropics in respect to yellow fever —we today are like the travelers, the sailors, the soldiers, and the merchants who went unprotected to the West Indies and to the coast of Africa.

In fact, this situation is exactly duplicated by the infections that we now call tropical diseases. There are in reality few diseases that are limited to any part of the world. Those that are, are mainly limited because they depend on some tropical insect for their transmission. The tsetse fly, which

causes the African sleeping sickness, is still peculiar to Africa, although its haunts have spread. Yellow fever appeared in Philadelphia but could not survive the winter there, for the mosquito that carried it died with the frost. The hookworm of the tropics and of our southern states, likewise is killed in the soil by freezing weather. But diseases that we now often consider wholly tropical—the malarias, the choleras, the plagues, the dysenteries—were all diseases that our ancestors knew well in their northern homes. They have been driven out of the temperate zone by an active civilization and intensive sanitation. But they have not been eliminated; they retreated to strongholds in less progressive regions—the tropics—and there in warmth and filth they flourish.

When the trader of the nineteenth or twentieth century went to tropical regions, he was moving backwards in sanitary history. There he met, not bizarre diseases, but those known to his own ancestors a hundred or two hundred years ago. He found the natives of the tropics living in the natural biological balance with disease, just as the inhabitants of Europe and of North America had lived—but the trader, reared in civilization, had sacrificed his immunity.

True he could shun the tropics and live only in those regions made safe for him by sanitation. But modern progress did not take that path.

Medicine, for its advance, had drawn on the natural sciences; it had developed preventive medicine. Engineering and invention, drawing on these same sources, had achieved the miracles of transportation and communication. The steamboat, the canal and the railroad, the telegraph and the cable, made the once enormous world grow smaller—not in miles but in hours. The journey from England to America changed from months to days; the once distant tropical wilderness moved closer to the northern regions. The frontiers of civilization expanded rapidly and extended beyond the shelter of medical protection. Planters and merchants and

travelers now went to regions once known only to explorers and soldiers. The white men met in the tropics the diseases of their own past. The conquest of the tropics meant a struggle, not against men, but against disease.

The tropical fevers bred in swamps were mostly malarias. And malaria was a disease known well to the ancient Romans, widely prevalent in France in the time of Louis XIV, and in England in the days of Charles II. It was the ague, the chills and fever, of the colonists of North America. The first step toward controlling it was taken in the tropics. About 1630 the Countess of Chinchon, visiting Lima where her husband was a viceroy of the Spanish possessions, sickened with malaria. In spite of all treatment she burned with the fever and shivered with chills of the disease. One day an Indian brought her the bark of a tree, the native remedy for the disease. There was a legend that years before a tribesman, nearly dead of fever, had fallen beside a pool of water in which lay a broken tree. Tortured with thirst, he dragged himself to the water and drank. The fluid was bitter with the taste of bark. But something in the bitter water drove away the fever; the man recovered. The bark of that kind of tree became the native remedy for fever. The countess took the bark, and her fever went away. Two years later the remedy was carried to Europe by the Jesuit priests; it was called Jesuit powder, or, in honor of the countess, chinchona bark. Its use was popularized in medical practice by Sydenham. We call its active element quinine.

For the milder forms of malarial fever quinine is a specific cure; it is also a preventive against the disease. Due to the use of quinine and the development of sanitation, the malaria of Europe and North America began to disappear; with the drug, the traveler, the missionary, and the soldier could go with far greater safety into the fever-infested regions of the tropics. But malaria in its severest form still existed there.

The knowledge that will lead to the eventual eradication

of the disease came in 1880. That year Alphonse Laveran, an army surgeon in Algeria, discovered in the blood of victims of malaria a microscopic animal parasite. It was not a bacterium but a single-celled form of animal life. In 1897 Ronald Ross of the Indian medical service discovered this same parasite in the stomach of Anopheles mosquitoes that had sucked the blood of men with malaria. The next year he showed that the parasites were in the saliva of the insect and were deposited in the blood of other men by the bite of the mosquito. Malaria did not spread from man to man by contact as did smallpox and diphtheria—an intermediary was required. This intermediary was that particular breed of mosquito called the Anopheles. The mosquito, considered formerly only a pest, now appeared in a new guise as the carrier of a deadly disease.

The attitude toward the louse and flea and even the common fly was to change just as the attitude toward the mosquito had. As carriers of disease these insects assumed a new importance in the scheme of life.

The discovery of the part that the mosquito played in infecting men with malaria made possible the control of the disease. Eradicate the mosquito; drain swamps; get rid of stagnant water or oil its surface so that mosquitoes could not breed in it—those were the essentials for controlling malaria.

Centuries ago the disease got its name, as we have said, from the Italian words meaning "bad air," for men had long known that the chills and fever came to those who lived near swamps and stagnant water. To avoid the mists and miasma, men had moved to healthier regions. In the closing years of the nineteenth century they learned to avoid the mosquito instead of the mist. The spade and the drainage ditch became the instruments of preventive medicine. The conquest of the tropics began. Typhoid and cholera also yielded before supplies of clean drinking water and the sewer.

There still remained the less widely spread but far more deadly yellow fever. Against it, quinine offered no relief. It remained a constant menace to the traveler in the West Indies and South America; and even in the early years of the twentieth century it reached our southern states in epidemics.

Expanding trade and commerce focused attention on a jungle region of South America. Speed could be gained, miles of journey saved, if a canal could be cut across the isthmus that tied the continents together. Late in the nineteenth century the great French engineer, De Lesseps, who had built the Suez Canal, undertook to separate the Americas. He failed. His engineering skill was adequate to the task, the means were available, but disease drove the workmen from the zone. Yellow fever made Panama "the white man's grave." The tropical jungle spread over the deserted machinery of the French; the railroad they had built rusted and crumbled away. It was said without exaggeration that under each crosstie lay the body of a workman, a sacrifice to the diseases which then had their stronghold in the tropics.

In 1904 the United States undertook to build the canal across the same region. It succeeded. Today the Panama Zone is one of the healthiest regions in the world. It is made healthy and kept healthy by the unremitting efforts of preventive medicine.

Most of the discoveries that have given us means for control of the diseases prevalent in the tropics have been made by physicians in the army medical service. It was an army commission headed by Major Walter Reed that in the year 1900 discovered how to control yellow fever.

The disease was present in Cuba during the Spanish-American War. Many soldiers lost their lives from it. At the close of the war a commission was appointed to investigate it and found that yellow fever was not caused by visible bacteria, or even a microscopic animal parasite. But there

was present in the blood of men who had been infected for twelve or fifteen days something that would produce the disease but that could not be seen even under the most powerful microscope and would pass through a filter of porcelain far too fine to allow the passage of the smallest known bacteria. The infectious substance was one called a virus—a filterable virus.

The most important question was: how was the virus transmitted? Dr. Carlos Finlay of Havana had suggested years before that mosquitoes might play a part. Walter Reed and his commission investigated the possibility. They experimented on men who volunteered to expose themselves to the bite of infected mosquitoes or to have the virus injected into their bodies. One member of the commission, Lezear, died of the fever contracted from an accidental mosquito bite in the yellow fever ward of the hospital.

The experiments proved conclusively that a certain species of mosquito, the *Aëdes ægypti*, was responsible for the spread of yellow fever. Its bite carried the virus from the sick to the well man.

This particular mosquito has habits different from the Anopheles that transmits malaria. *Aëdes ægypti* is far more domestic; it lives in water barrels about houses, in the water in discarded tin cans, in sagging drain pipes. It cannot survive the freezing weather of the north, and for that reason the outbreaks of yellow fever in the temperate zone had occurred only in the summer time. The yellow fever mosquito does not fly over long distances; those that had caused the northern outbreaks had been carried by ships from South America or the West Indies.

In 1901 Major William Gorgas put to use the knowledge supplied by Walter Reed and his commission to free Havana of yellow fever. He surrounded everyone who had the disease with screens to keep away mosquitoes, he drained the breeding places, cleaned up the city, screened water barrels, killed mosquitoes. Three months later, for the first time in

one hundred and fifty years there was not one case of yellow fever in Havana.

It was William Gorgas, now a general, who carried the same measures of sanitation to Panama and made "the white man's grave" a healthy place to live. But so long as infectious diseases still exist—and they do exist in the jungles on both sides of the zone of Panama—sanitation must continue unremittingly. If the medical measures that keep the Canal Zone healthy today were dropped, in a decade Panama would again be as fever ridden as it was at the opening of the twentieth century. We should not be able to use the Canal for fear of disease.

Today the visitors to Panama see in stone and steel and concrete a memorial to the engineering progress of the century. The medical triumph is not visible, or obvious. The greatest victories of medicine are negative—the absence of disease. Yet without these negative victories—so easily accepted and forgotten—the engineering miracle of steel and speed could not exist.

CHAPTER XXX

The Goal

IN the nineteenth century Darwin formulated the theory of evolution. Man, as well as everything else in the world, was changing, evolving. Human egotism and human hope interpreted change as progress. With scant evidence to support it, the belief was accepted and firmly held that the human race is moving generation by generation toward some desirable goal, improving its condition, growing better, and at the same time making the world a better place to live in.

Progress inevitably involves a goal toward which the progress is made. The mere fact, however, that there may be grave doubts concerning the goals we are seeking, strange to say, does not seem to affect belief in the inherent goodness of progress. Yet in matters pertaining to government, economics, and sociology there are today widely different views as to the desirable goal. It has even been questioned by some people whether invention with its multitude of amazing engineering achievements, pointed to and exclaimed over as the very acme of modern progress, has led us toward happier ways of living. And without a definite goal, progress is purposeless.

Medicine is in sharp contrast to these things. Its goal has never been uncertain. It is the control of disease, prevention of suffering and prolongation of life. That has been its aim since primitive man was first confronted with disease.

We have traced through our chapters the devious course that men have followed in striving for the goal of health. Today, more secure against disease than any previous generation of the race, we can look back in sympathy and pity to the centuries when men sought blindly for the goal that seems now almost within our grasp. Yet it is entirely pos-

sible that with the scientific revelations yet to come, future generations will in turn look back to our day with the same sympathy, the same pity.

But whatever happens, the opening of the twentieth century will continue to mark an epoch—the completion of a great cycle in the history of medicine. In these years in the midst of a rapid succession of discoveries, medicine suddenly went backwards. Instead of evolving a new form it assumed one long discarded—that in which the medicine of primitive people had appeared. Medicine, after the lapse of thousands of years, again took up its social leadership.

In the days before civilization medicine had been the pre-eminent social force. The medicine man led his tribe in its struggle against misfortune. He not only treated the individual patient in illness and injury, but in public ceremony he dispersed the spirits that threatened all his people with disease and pestilence.

Under the influence of civilization medicine shrank in importance. In earlier chapters we have traced the steps in the change. We have seen belief in spirits as the cause of disease discarded; we have seen religion separated from medicine. In that parting, religion assumed the social leadership; to medicine were left merely the maladies of the individual man. The priest in public ceremony guided the welfare of his people; he shaped their beliefs, their customs, their behavior. The physician on the contrary had nothing to offer to the general welfare. His place was in the seclusion of the sickroom. In times of pestilence men did not turn to the physician for protection; they turned in hope to the priest.

It was the great discoveries of the nineteenth century that brought the doctor from the bedside to take his place in social leadership. This time he was not to wage a futile war against the spirits, but armed with knowledge he was to fight successfully to preserve the health of nations—of all mankind.

In the few years of its new leadership medicine has profoundly altered the manners and customs of men, their beliefs, and their ideals.

We have seen the ethical concepts of civilization alter before the humanitarian innovations of Pinel and Dix and Nightingale and Dunant. But the greatest contribution of medicine to public welfare was intelligent cleanliness as a means of preventing the spread of infection. Modern sanitation had its origin in the discoveries of Pasteur, Lister, and Koch. Led by the physician, the civilized world began to clean up, and as it became cleaner the mortality from disease declined and the average length of life increased.

Sanitation extended into every phase of civilized life. The modern sewage system, the inspection of food, the pasteurization of milk, the purification of water, the disposal of refuse, the use of fly screens, refrigeration, the new doctrines of personal cleanliness, antiseptics to prevent wound infection, the individual drinking cup, and the individual towel—things commonplace to all of us—mark the influence of sanitation. Changing laws and changing customs indicate its progress; its successes are proved by the fact that the average length of life has tripled since the eighteenth century; they are felt in a sense of security against disease never before experienced by mankind.

There can be little question that the discovery of the bacterial causes of infection—made so near to our own day—ranks in importance with those fundamental discoveries made countless years ago that are the very basis of civilization—the use of fire, the principle of the wheel, the domestication of animals, the raising of crops, the invention of writing. Indeed, measured by its effects on the conditions of life, the bacterial cause of infection is the only discovery made during recorded history that takes its place among those fundamentals of civilization.

Sanitation has become a basic necessity of human existence. Today when disaster comes upon men, when lands are

desolated by fire, earthquake or volcano, the first call is for food; the second is for physicians to institute the measures which control the spread of pestilential disease.

The prevention of communicable disease by the sanitation arising from the discovery of the bacterial cause of infection has yielded such striking results that it has tended to obscure another and equally important social aspect of medicine—health promotion. Health is something more than the mere absence of disease. Health and vigor and growth to the utmost of the individual's capacity come only from satisfying the needs of the body. It has become the duty of the physician to define these requirements and to educate the public. This is his social obligation.

Modern knowledge of food values due to medical education has changed the dietary habits of civilized man. The result of one of these discoveries now greets nearly all babies soon after their arrival—the nursing bottle full of prepared milk. Only a little more than a hundred years ago bottle feeding was almost the equivalent of a death warrant. Even under the best conditions, sixty to seventy per cent of the babies deprived of mothers' milk died. Today, with the knowledge gained of diet, a baby suffers no serious handicap in being raised on a bottle and most of them are at least partially fed that way.

The modern knowledge of dietary requirements came from the same source as the discovery of the bacterial cause of infection—the application of the natural sciences to medical problems. Such terms as calories, proteins, carbohydrates, roughage, mineral needs, and vitamin requirements were only a few years ago the technical words of the research laboratory. Now they are household terms. The public has followed with eager interest the discovery of one vitamin after another; it has seen scurvy, the disease that killed the crews on the sailing vessels of the great explorers, yield to fruit juice—the same fruit juice that for the same reason a mother now feeds to her young baby. Disappearing rapidly,

too, is that disease in which the bones became deformed—rickets—for medicine has shown that this once mysterious disturbance yields to a vitamin. This vitamin is a peculiar one—the only one that can be formed in the human body; the ultra-violet light of sunshine produces it. Today the baby has his sun bath, or failing that, he drinks his sunshine from his bottle as vitamin D. Growth-promoting vitamin A has brought green vegetables and butter and milk to the table. And with these foods comes vitamin B, which prevents the disease beriberi and makes the muscle of the intestines more vigorous in its action.

Of the minerals the body needs, iron and calcium and iodine are the ones that medicine has shown to be most often lacking. In consequence, spinach, molasses, and milk have been given a new virtue in the home; and iodine has become a matter of legislation. In some sections of our country the tiny trace of iodine found in most drinking water is lacking; a swelling of the neck, a certain kind of goiter, may develop unless the deficiency is supplied. In consequence iodine is added to the table salt.

Almost as mysterious in action as the vitamins are those peculiar chemical substances described three quarters of a century ago by Claude Bernard—the internal secretions found in minute amounts within the body and poured into the blood to exert, as we know now, a profound influence on growth and health. Through lack of secretion from a gland of the neck, the thyroid, a child will fail to grow in stature and in mind, and will become a stunted imbecile. The dwarf and the giant of the side show suffer from a disturbance of a gland in the skull, the pituitary, the dwarf from too little secretion, the giant from too much. Medical discovery day by day is finding more of these secretions, isolating the chemical forces that control the human body. At least two secretions have already become valuable remedial substances. The child stunted by lack of secretion from the thyroid gland can be made to grow and become normal if

fed precisely the right amount of the thyroid gland of a sheep. But few of the internal secretions that have been discovered can be taken by mouth; they are destroyed by digestion. That is the case with the second of the commonly used secretions which is called for in the treatment of diabetes. In diabetes, the pancreas gland, which forms a digestive fluid for the intestines, is diseased. The digestive fluid is formed, but an internal secretion also made in the gland is lacking. The man so affected can digest sugar and starches but cannot use them in his body for fuel—and he sickens. In bygone days diabetes was often fatal. But now it need not be, for medical research has shown that this internal secretion of the pancreas can be used as a medicament and given with a hypodermic needle. It is called insulin.

The discoveries concerning the internal secretions have just begun—a whole unexplored field lies ahead.

In the enthusiasm for the social benefits of medical leadership, we have lost sight for a moment of the doctor at the bedside. Sanitation, public health, and public knowledge have not solved all the problems of disease, far from it. What we have witnessed in the three decades of the twentieth century is not so much elimination of diseases as a shift of diseases. As fast as one disease is conquered, another has risen to replace it. Inevitably this must be so. Every man must die; in the long run, there are always as many deaths as births. Few men if any die of "old age"; disease still claims them. But the diseases change. Only a few years ago tuberculosis was the leading cause of death; today it has fallen to fifth place. In its stead there are diseases of the heart and blood vessels and second to them a newcomer among the leaders of mortality—cancer.

There is an obvious reason for this change in the cause of death. The increase in cancer and disease of the heart and blood vessels is mainly a consequence of a longer average life, which is a result of greater freedom from infection. These diseases occur most often after middle life; infections

kill in early years. Boys and girls who fifty years ago would have died of diphtheria, typhoid, or tuberculosis now live long enough to develop cancer and disease of the heart and blood vessels.

The doctor of today, for all his successes in the field of social leadership, for all his conquests in the laboratory, still wrestles with diseases at the bedside of the individual patient just as did Hippocrates and Sydenham and all those generations of men who devoted their lives to ease the suffering of their fellow men. His problems still lie before him, complex and mysterious, some of them, as the problem of life itself, but the doctor confronts them today with an experience in art and science that has accumulated in the two hundred centuries our story has covered.

INDEX

DATE DUE

~~APR 4 '71~~			
~~Reserve~~ ~~ticket~~ ~~9/25/74~~			
~~reserve~~ ~~ticket~~ ~~10/5/77~~			
~~APR 2 5 1996~~			
~~NOV 2 4 2000~~			
DISCARDED			
GAYLORD			PRINTED IN U.S.A.

Part One

AN UNKNOWN HERO OF MEDICINE

SPIRITS, DEMONS, GHOSTS, AND WITCHES

THEORIES AND FACTS

Illustrations

Contents

low Paré through court intrigue and battle. I want them to recognize the primitive medicine man disguised as King of England, the mountebank of the street corner, and the quasi-scientist of today. I want them to witness the rise of mental contagions, and see civilizations crumble before disease and rise again with the aid of medical discovery. . . . I want them to follow the Doctor in History.

I wish to express here my thanks for the valuable suggestions and criticisms of my friends Professor Samuel Harvey and Professor Erwin Goodenough who read the manuscript in preparation. To Miss Ella Holliday of the Yale University Press I extend my gratitude for her tireless effort in checking dates and quotations.

HOWARD W. HAGGARD

New Haven, Conn.
  September 24, 1934

This educational aspect was once called hygiene—but hygiene of the kind we knew in school is a failure. I have taught for many years what is generally called hygiene and I have gained from the experience a thorough conviction of the inadequacy of the so-called rules of health. I should prefer my children to think logically and soundly on the social matters of medicine in these years of faddism, quackery, and commercially exploited "health appeal," than to be able to recite glibly the hygienic dicta of today, many of which will surely become the absurdities of tomorrow. On the other hand, the history of health is the clue to the logic of modern medicine; if people know the past they will be able to interpret the present.

That is what I had in mind when I wrote these pages. But having written them, I doubt my complete sincerity. I wonder, too, if Daudet and Chesterfield were wholly honest in their purpose. Was it entirely guidance they sought to give? Or were they led on by the hope, the parent's longing so often doomed to disappointment, that sons and daughters will feel a kindred enthusiasm for scenes and deeds that stirred the parent?

The scenes and deeds of medicine are not to be comprehended in the sentimental story of the "good fight" for the sake of humanity. They are part, rather, of the grim tale of man's ignorance and hope, his life and death. I want my children to see the reeking, sweating, savage medicine man struggling with the spirits of disease—the savage who gave us the principle of nearly everything we have in medicine today and much besides that we have tried to get rid of. I want them to join the temple throngs and pay their respects to Imhotep and Æsculapius; stand for a moment beside the philosophers who rescued medicine from religion and beside the physicians who rescued it from the philosophers. I want them to meet Galen, admire his intellect and condone his egotism. I want them to see the jigsaw puzzle of medieval scholasticism, hear the vulgar words of Paracelsus, and fol-

Preface

DAUDET, presumably with a view to their moral sophistication, wrote *Sapho* for his children to read when they were twenty-one. Chesterfield wrote his letters in the interest of his son's social elegance. I know nothing of the effect on Daudet's children; Chesterfield's son did not appear to benefit. Nevertheless, hopeful, as parents will be, I have followed the example and written this book for my children. Not, let me hasten to say, for their morals or their manners. Perhaps it is a reflection of changing times, or possibly merely of my own interests, that I am frankly concerned less with these matters than I am with some other aspects of their education and their health—especially their health.

What I have tried to write for them is a history of health.

I have little doubt that their generation will live to see this new kind of history come much to the front—the movement is rapid in that direction. History as the older of us knew it in school was almost wholly the story of man's struggle against man and against geographical barriers. We saw the pageant of human affairs through the eyes of the explorer, the warrior, the politician, the economist, the priest, even the refugee and the slave, but we did not see it with the doctor or the humanitarian. And that in spite of the fact that man's greatest and longest struggle has been to survive against disease.

Before us today an epoch in medicine is beginning. The physician is regaining a social leadership lost 2300 years ago when medicine was separated from religion. Medicine is rapidly ceasing to be a private matter of the bedchamber; it is becoming a guiding influence in everyday life. Now—and it will be even more obvious in the future—for the sake of health, medical matters must be known, must be interpreted correctly by the layman.

THIS BOOK

IS HOPEFULLY DEDICATED TO

HOWARD JR., WILLIAM II, AND MARJORIE MARIE

The
DOCTOR
in History

By

HOWARD W. HAGGARD

ASSOCIATE PROFESSOR OF APPLIED PHYSIOLOGY
IN YALE UNIVERSITY

New Haven
YALE UNIVERSITY PRESS
London, Humphrey Milford, Oxford University Press
1934

Preface to the Third Edition

WHEN THIS BOOK WAS FIRST CONCEIVED (MORE THAN 25 YEARS AGO) few mathematicians outside the Soviet Union recognized probability as a legitimate branch of mathematics. Applications were limited in scope, and the treatment of individual problems often led to incredible complications. Under these circumstances the book could not be written for an existing audience, or to satisfy conscious needs. The hope was rather to attract attention to little-known aspects of probability, to forge links between various parts, to develop unified methods, and to point to potential applications. Because of a growing interest in probability, the book found unexpectedly many users outside mathematical disciplines. Its widespread use was understandable as long as its point of view was new and its material was not otherwise available. But the popularity seems to persist even now, when the contents of most chapters are available in specialized works streamlined for particular needs. For this reason the character of the book remains unchanged in the new edition. I hope that it will continue to serve a variety of needs and, in particular, that it will continue to find readers who read it merely for enjoyment and enlightenment.

Throughout the years I was the grateful recipient of many communications from users, and these led to various improvements. Many sections were rewritten to facilitate study. Reading is also improved by a better typeface and the superior editing job by Mrs. H. McDougal: although a professional editor she has preserved a feeling for the requirements of readers and reason.

The greatest change is in chapter III. This chapter was introduced only in the second edition, which was in fact motivated principally by the unexpected discovery that its enticing material could be treated by elementary methods. But this treatment still depended on combinatorial artifices which have now been replaced by simpler and more natural probabilistic arguments. In essence this new chapter is new.

Most conspicuous among other additions are the new sections on branching processes, on Markov chains, and on the De Moivre-Laplace theorem. Chapter XIII has been rearranged, and throughout the book there appear minor changes as well as new examples and problems.

I regret the misleading nature of the author index, but I felt obliged to state explicitly whenever an idea or example could be traced to a particular source. Unfortunately this means that quotations usually refer to an incidental remark, and are rarely indicative of the nature of the paper quoted. Furthermore, many examples and problems were inspired by reading non-mathematical papers in which related situations are dealt with by different methods. (That newer texts now quote these non-mathematical papers as containing my examples shows how fast probability has developed, but also indicates the limited usefulness of quotations.) Lack of space as well as of competence precluded more adequate historical indications of how probability has changed from the semimysterious discussions of the 'twenties to its present flourishing state.

For a number of years I have been privileged to work with students and younger colleagues to whose help and inspiration I owe much. Much credit for this is due to the support by the U.S. Army Research Office for work in probability at Princeton University. My particular thanks are due to Jay Goldman for a thoughtful memorandum about his teaching experiences, and to Loren Pitt for devoted help with the proofs.

WILLIAM FELLER

July, 1967

Preface to the revised printing

IN CONTRAST TO THE FIRST EDITION, THE THIRD WAS MARRED BY A disturbing number of errata. In the present revised printing all discovered errata are corrected. Moreover, some formulations have been improved and hints to problems added where this could be done without resetting type. I am grateful to my publisher for permitting these costly changes which should make for much better readability.

Almost all changes were suggested either by Professor R. E. Machol and Dr. J. Croft working together in Chicago, Ill., or else by Lt. Col. Preben Kühl (now retired) of the Royal Danish Army. They have read the book with unusual care and understanding, and I have greatly profited by the ensuing enjoyable correspondence.

Princeton, N.J.
June, 1970

Preface to the First Edition

IT WAS THE AUTHOR'S ORIGINAL INTENTION TO WRITE A BOOK ON analytical methods in probability theory in which the latter was to be treated as a topic in pure mathematics. Such a treatment would have been more uniform and hence more satisfactory from an aesthetic point of view; it would also have been more appealing to pure mathematicians. However, the generous support by the Office of Naval Research of work in probability theory at Cornell University led the author to a more ambitious and less thankful undertaking of satisfying heterogeneous needs.

It is the purpose of this book to treat probability theory as a self-contained mathematical subject rigorously, avoiding non-mathematical concepts. At the same time, the book tries to describe the empirical background and to develop a feeling for the great variety of practical applications. This purpose is served by many special problems, numerical estimates, and examples which interrupt the main flow of the text. They are clearly set apart in print and are treated in a more picturesque language and with less formality. A number of special topics have been included in order to exhibit the power of general methods and to increase the usefulness of the book to specialists in various fields. To facilitate reading, detours from the main path are indicated by stars. The knowledge of starred sections is not assumed in the remainder.

A serious attempt has been made to unify methods. The specialist will find many simplifications of existing proofs and also new results. In particular, the theory of recurrent events has been developed for the purpose of this book. It leads to a new treatment of Markov chains which permits simplification even in the finite case.

The examples are accompanied by about 340 problems mostly with complete solutions. Some of them are simple exercises, but most of them serve as additional illustrative material to the text or contain various complements. One purpose of the examples and problems is to develop the reader's intuition and art of probabilistic formulation. Several previously treated examples show that apparently difficult problems may become almost trite once they are formulated in a natural way and put into the proper context.

There is a tendency in teaching to reduce probability problems to pure analysis as soon as possible and to forget the specific characteristics of probability theory itself. Such treatments are based on a poorly defined notion of random variables usually introduced at the outset. This book goes to the other extreme and dwells on the notion of sample space, without which random variables remain an artifice.

In order to present the true background unhampered by measurability questions and other purely analytic difficulties this volume is restricted to *discrete sample spaces*. This restriction is severe, but should be welcome to non-mathematical users. It permits the inclusion of special topics which are not easily accessible in the literature. At the same time, this arrangement makes it possible to begin in an elementary way and yet to include a fairly exhaustive treatment of such advanced topics as random walks and Markov chains. The general theory of random variables and their distributions, limit theorems, diffusion theory, etc., is deferred to a succeeding volume.

This book would not have been written without the support of the Office of Naval Research. One consequence of this support was a fairly regular personal contact with J. L. Doob, whose constant criticism and encouragement were invaluable. To him go my foremost thanks. The next thanks for help are due to John Riordan, who followed the manuscript through two versions. Numerous corrections and improvements were suggested by my wife who read both the manuscript and proof.

The author is also indebted to K. L. Chung, M. Donsker, and S. Goldberg, who read the manuscript and corrected various mistakes; the solutions to the majority of the problems were prepared by S. Goldberg. Finally, thanks are due to Kathryn Hollenbach for patient and expert typing help; to E. Elyash, W. Hoffman, and J. R. Kinney for help in proofreading.

WILLIAM FELLER

Cornell University
January 1950

Note on the Use of the Book

THE EXPOSITION CONTAINS MANY SIDE EXCURSIONS AND DOES NOT ALWAYS progress from the easy to the difficult; comparatively technical sections appear at the beginning and easy sections in chapters XV and XVII. Inexperienced readers should not attempt to follow many side lines, lest they lose sight of the forest for too many trees. Introductory remarks to the chapters and stars at the beginnings of sections should facilitate orientation and the choice of omissions. The unstarred sections form a self-contained whole in which the starred sections are not used.

A first introduction to the basic notions of probability is contained in chapters I, V, VI, IX; beginners should cover these with as few digressions as possible. Chapter II is designed to develop the student's technique and probabilistic intuition; some experience in its contents is desirable, but it is not necessary to cover the chapter systematically: it may prove more profitable to return to the elementary illustrations as occasion arises at later stages. For the purposes of a first introduction, the elementary theory of continuous distributions requires little supplementary explanation. (The elementary chapters of volume 2 now provide a suitable text.)

From chapter IX an introductory course may proceed directly to chapter XI, considering generating functions as an example of more general transforms. Chapter XI should be followed by some applications in chapters XIII (recurrent events) or XII (chain reactions, infinitely divisible distributions). Without generating functions it is possible to turn in one of the following directions: limit theorems and fluctuation theory (chapters VIII, X, III); stochastic processes (chapter XVII); random walks (chapter III and the main part of XIV). These chapters are almost independent of each other. The Markov chains of chapter XV depend conceptually on recurrent events, but they may be studied independently if the reader is willing to accept without proof the basic ergodic theorem.

Chapter III stands by itself. Its contents are appealing in their own right, but the chapter is also highly illustrative for new insights and new methods in probability theory. The results concerning fluctuations in coin tossing show that widely held beliefs about the law of large numbers are fallacious. They are so amazing and so at variance with common intuition that even sophisticated colleagues doubted that coins actually misbehave as theory predicts. The record of a simulated experiment is therefore included in section 6. The chapter treats only the simple coin-tossing game, but the results are representative of a fairly general situation.

The sign ▶ is used to indicate the end of a proof or of a collection of examples.

It is hoped that the extensive index will facilitate coordination between the several parts.

Contents

---

* Starred sections are not required for the understanding of the sequel and should be omitted at first reading.

INTRODUCTION

The Nature
of Probability Theory

1. THE BACKGROUND

Probability is a mathematical discipline with aims akin to those, for example, of geometry or analytical mechanics. In each field we must carefully distinguish three aspects of the theory: (*a*) the formal logical content, (*b*) the intuitive background, (*c*) the applications. The character, and the charm, of the whole structure cannot be appreciated without considering all three aspects in their proper relation.

(a) Formal Logical Content

Axiomatically, mathematics is concerned solely with relations among undefined things. This aspect is well illustrated by the game of chess. It is impossible to "define" chess otherwise than by stating a set of rules. The conventional shape of the pieces may be described to some extent, but it will not always be obvious which piece is intended for "king." The chessboard and the pieces are helpful, but they can be dispensed with. The essential thing is to know how the pieces move and act. It is meaningless to talk about the "definition" or the "true nature" of a pawn or a king. Similarly, geometry does not care what a point and a straight line "really are." They remain undefined notions, and the axioms of geometry specify the relations among them: two points determine a line, etc. These are the rules, and there is nothing sacred about them. Different forms of geometry are based on different sets of axioms, and the logical structure of non-Euclidean geometries is independent of their relation to reality. Physicists have studied the motion of bodies under laws of attraction different from Newton's, and such studies are meaningful even if Newton's law of attraction is accepted as true in nature.

(b) Intuitive Background

In contrast to chess, the axioms of geometry and of mechanics have an intuitive background. In fact, geometrical intuition is so strong that it is prone to run ahead of logical reasoning. The extent to which logic, intuition, and physical experience are interdependent is a problem into which we need not enter. It is certain that intuition can be trained and developed. The bewildered novice in chess moves cautiously, recalling individual rules, whereas the experienced player absorbs a complicated situation at a glance and is unable to account rationally for his intuition. In like manner mathematical intuition grows with experience, and it is possible to develop a natural feeling for concepts such as four-dimensional space.

Even the collective intuition of mankind appears to progress. Newton's notions of a field of force and of action at a distance and Maxwell's concept of electromagnetic waves were at first decried as "unthinkable" and "contrary to intuition." Modern technology and radio in the homes have popularized these notions to such an extent that they form part of the ordinary vocabulary. Similarly, the modern student has no appreciation of the modes of thinking, the prejudices, and other difficulties against which the theory of probability had to struggle when it was new. Nowadays newspapers report on samples of public opinion, and the magic of statistics embraces all phases of life to the extent that young girls watch the statistics of their chances to get married. Thus everyone has acquired a feeling for the meaning of statements such as "the chances are three in five." Vague as it is, this intuition serves as background and guide for the first step. It will be developed as the theory progresses and acquaintance is made with more sophisticated applications.

(c) Applications

The concepts of geometry and mechanics are in practice identified with certain physical objects, but the process is so flexible and variable that no general rules can be given. The notion of a rigid body is fundamental and useful, even though no physical object is rigid. Whether a given body can be treated as if it were rigid depends on the circumstances and the desired degree of approximation. Rubber is certainly not rigid, but in discussing the motion of automobiles on ice textbooks usually treat the rubber tires as rigid bodies. Depending on the purpose of the theory, we disregard the atomic structure of matter and treat the sun now as a ball of continuous matter, now as a single mass point.

In applications, the abstract mathematical models serve as tools, and different models can describe the same empirical situation. *The manner in which mathematical theories are applied does not depend on preconceived ideas; it is a purposeful technique depending on, and changing with, experience.* A philosophical analysis of such techniques is a legitimate study, but is is not within the realm of mathematics, physics, or statistics. The philosophy of the foundations of probability must be divorced from mathematics and statistics, exactly as the discussion of our intuitive space concept is now divorced from geometry.

2. PROCEDURE

The history of probability (and of mathematics in general) shows a stimulating interplay of theory and applications; theoretical progress opens new fields of applications, and in turn applications lead to new problems and fruitful research. The theory of probability is now applied in many diverse fields, and the flexibility of a general theory is required to provide appropriate tools for so great a variety of needs. We must therefore withstand the temptation (and the pressure) to build the theory, its terminology, and its arsenal too close to one particular sphere of interest. We wish instead to develop a mathematical theory in the way which has proved so successful in geometry and mechanics.

We shall start from the simplest experiences, such as tossing a coin or throwing dice, where all statements have an obvious intuitive meaning. This intuition will be translated into an abstract model to be generalized gradually and by degrees. Illustrative examples will be provided to explain the empirical background of the several models and to develop the reader's intuition, but the theory itself will be of a mathematical character. We shall no more attempt to explain the "true meaning" of probability than the modern physicist dwells on the "real meaning" of mass and energy or the geometer discusses the nature of a point. Instead, we shall prove theorems and show how they are applied.

Historically, the original purpose of the theory of probability was to describe the exceedingly narrow domain of experience connected with games of chance, and the main effort was directed to the calculation of certain probabilities. In the opening chapters we too shall calculate a few typical probabilities, but it should be borne in mind that numerical probabilities are not the principal object of the theory. Its aim is to discover general laws and to construct satisfactory theoretical models.

Probabilities play for us the same role as masses in mechanics. The motion of the planetary system can be discussed without knowledge of the individual masses and without contemplating methods for their actual measurements. Even models for non-existent planetary systems may be the object of a profitable and illuminating study. Similarly, practical and *useful probability models may refer to non-observable worlds.* For example, billions of dollars have been invested in automatic telephone exchanges. These are based on simple probability models in which various possible systems are compared. The theoretically best system is built and the others will never exist. In insurance, probability theory is used to calculate the probability of ruin; that is, the theory is used to avoid certain undesirable situations, and consequently it applies to situations that are not actually observed. Probability theory would be effective and useful even if not a single numerical value were accessible.

3. "STATISTICAL" PROBABILITY

The success of the modern mathematical theory of probability is bought at a price: the theory is limited to one particular aspect of "chance." The intuitive notion of probability is connected with inductive reasoning and with judgments such as "Paul is probably a happy man," "Probably this book will be a failure," "Fermat's conjecture is probably false." Judgments of this sort are of interest to the philosopher and the logician, and they are a legitimate object of a mathematical theory.[1] It must be understood, however, that we are concerned not with modes of inductive reasoning but with something that might be called physical or *statistical probability*. In a rough way we may characterize this concept by saying that our probabilities do not refer to judgments but to possible outcomes of a *conceptual experiment*. Before we speak of probabilities, we must agree on an idealized model of a particular conceptual experiment such as tossing a coin, sampling kangaroos on the moon, observing a particle under diffusion, counting the number of telephone calls. At the outset we must agree on the possible outcomes of this experiment (our *sample space*) and the probabilities associated with them. This is analogous to the procedure in mechanics where fictitious models involving two, three, or seventeen mass points are introduced, these points being devoid of individual properties. Similarly, in analyzing the coin tossing game we are not concerned with the accidental circumstances of an actual experiment: the object of our theory is sequences (or arrangements) of symbols such as "head, head, tail, head, ..." There is no place in our system for speculations concerning the probability that the sun will rise tomorrow. Before speaking of it we should have to agree on an (idealized) model which would presumably run along the lines "out of infinitely many worlds

---

[1] B. O. Koopman, *The axioms and algebra of intuitive probability*, Ann. of Math. (2), vol. 41 (1940), pp. 269–292, and *The bases of probability*, Bull. Amer. Math. Soc., vol. 46 (1940), pp. 763–774.

For a modern text based on subjective probabilities see L. J. Savage, *The foundations of statistics*, New York (John Wiley) 1954.

one is selected at random. . . ." Little imagination is required to construct such a model, but it appears both uninteresting and meaningless.

The astronomer speaks of measuring the temperature at the center of the sun or of travel to Sirius. These operations seem impossible, and yet it is not senseless to contemplate them. By the same token, we shall not worry whether or not our conceptual experiments can be performed; we shall analyze abstract models. In the back of our minds we keep an intuitive interpretation of probability which gains operational meaning in certain applications. We *imagine* the experiment performed a great many times. An event with probability 0.6 should be expected, in the long run, to occur sixty times out of a hundred. This description is deliberately vague but supplies a picturesque intuitive background sufficient for the more elementary applications. As the theory proceeds and grows more elaborate, the operational meaning and the intuitive picture will become more concrete.

4. SUMMARY

We shall be concerned with theoretical models in which probabilities enter as free parameters in much the same way as masses in mechanics. They are applied in many and variable ways. The technique of applications and the intuition develop with the theory.

This is the standard procedure accepted and fruitful in other mathematical disciplines. No alternative has been devised which could conceivably fill the manifold needs and requirements of *all* branches of the growing entity called probability theory and its applications.

We may fairly lament that intuitive probability is insufficient for scientific purposes, but it is a historical fact. In example I, (6.*b*), we shall discuss random distributions of particles in compartments. The appropriate, or "natural," probability distribution seemed perfectly clear to everyone and has been accepted without hesitation by physicists. It turned out, however, that physical particles are not trained in human common sense, and the "natural" (or Boltzmann) distribution has to be given up for the Einstein-Bose distribution in some cases, for the Fermi-Dirac distribution in others. No intuitive argument has been offered why photons should behave differently from protons and why they do not obey the "a priori" laws. *If* a justification could now be found, it would only show that intuition develops with theory. At any rate, even for applications freedom and flexibility are essential, and it would be pernicious to fetter the theory to fixed poles.

It has also been claimed that the modern theory of probability is too abstract and too general to be useful. This is the battle cry once raised by practical-minded people against Maxwell's field theory. The argument could be countered by pointing to the unexpected new applications opened by the abstract theory of stochastic processes, or to the new insights offered by the modern fluctuation theory which once more belies intuition and is leading to a revision of practical attitudes. However, the discussion is useless; it is too easy to condemn. Only yesterday the practical things of today were decried as impractical, and the theories which will be practical tomorrow will always be branded as valueless games by the practical men of today.

5. HISTORICAL NOTE

The statistical, or empirical, attitude toward probability has been developed mainly by R. A. Fisher and R. von Mises. The notion of sample space[2] comes from von Mises. This notion made it possible to build up a strictly mathematical theory of probability based on measure theory. Such an approach emerged gradually in the 'twenties under the influence of many authors. An axiomatic treatment representing the modern development was given by A. Kolmogorov.[3] We shall follow this line, but the term axiom appears too solemn inasmuch as the present volume deals only with the simple case of discrete probabilities.

---

[2] The German word is *Merkmalraum* (label space). von Mises' basic treatise *Wahrscheinlichkeitsrechnung* appeared in 1931. A modernized version (edited and complemented by Hilda Geiringer) appeared in 1964 under the title *Mathematical theory of probability and statistics*, New York (Academic Press). von Mises' philosophical ideas are best known from his earlier booklet of 1928, revised by H. Geiringer: *Probability, statistics and truth*, London (Macmillan), 1957.

[3] A. Kolmogoroff, *Grundbegriffe der Wahrscheinlichkeitsrechnung*, Berlin (Springer) 1933. An English translation (by N. Morrison) appeared in 1956: *Foundations of the theory of probability*, New York (Chelsea).

CHAPTER I

The Sample Space

1. THE EMPIRICAL BACKGROUND

The mathematical theory of probability gains practical value and an intuitive meaning in connection with real or conceptual experiments such as tossing a coin once, tossing a coin 100 times, throwing three dice, arranging a deck of cards, matching two decks of cards, playing roulette, observing the life span of a radioactive atom or a person, selecting a random sample of people and observing the number of left-handers in it, crossing two species of plants and observing the phenotypes of the offspring; or with phenomena such as the sex of a newborn baby, the number of busy trunklines in a telephone exchange, the number of calls on a telephone, random noise in an electrical communication system, routine quality control of a production process, frequency of accidents, the number of double stars in a region of the skies, the position of a particle under diffusion. All these descriptions are rather vague, and, in order to render the theory meaningful, we have to agree on what we mean by *possible results of the experiment or observation in question.*

When a coin is tossed, it does not necessarily fall heads or tails; it can roll away or stand on its edge. Nevertheless, we shall agree to regard "head" and "tail" as the only possible outcomes of the experiment. This convention simplifies the theory without affecting its applicability. Idealizations of this type are standard practice. It is impossible to measure the life span of an atom or a person without some error, but for theoretical purposes it is expedient to imagine that these quantities are exact numbers. The question then arises as to which numbers can actually represent the life span of a person. Is there a maximal age beyond which life is impossible, or is any age conceivable? We hesitate to admit that man can grow 1000 years old, and yet current actuarial practice admits no bounds to the possible duration of life. According to formulas on which modern mortality tables are based, the proportion of men surviving 1000 years is of the order of magnitude of one in $10^{10^{36}}$—a number with 10^{27} billions of zeros. This statement does not make sense from a biological or sociological point of view, but considered exclusively from a statistical standpoint it certainly does not contradict any experience. There are fewer than 10^{10} people born in a century. To test the contention statistically, more than $10^{10^{35}}$ centuries would be required, which is considerably more than $10^{10^{34}}$ lifetimes of the earth. Obviously, such extremely small probabilities are compatible with our notion of impossibility. Their use may appear utterly absurd, but it does no harm and is convenient in simplifying many formulas. Moreover, if we were seriously to discard the possibility of living 1000 years, we should have to accept the existence of maximum age, and the assumption that it should be possible to live x years and impossible to live x years and two seconds is as unappealing as the idea of unlimited life.

Any theory necessarily involves idealization, and our first idealization concerns the possible outcomes of an "experiment" or "observation." If we want to construct an abstract model, we must at the outset reach a decision about what consitutes a possible outcome of the (idealized) experiment.

For uniform terminology, the results of experiments or observations will be called *events*. Thus we shall speak of the event that of five coins tossed more than three fell heads. Similarly, the "experiment" of distributing the cards in bridge[1] may result in the "event" that North has two aces. The composition of a sample ("two left-handers in a sample of 85") and the result of a measurement ("temperature 120°," "seven trunklines busy") will each be called an event.

We shall distinguish between *compound* (or decomposable) and *simple* (or indecomposable) *events*. For example, saying that a throw with two dice resulted in "sum six" amounts to saying that it resulted in "(1, 5) or (2, 4) or (3, 3) or (4, 2) or (5, 1)," and this enumeration decomposes the event "sum six" into five simple events. Similarly, the event "two odd faces" admits of the decomposition "(1, 1) or (1, 3) or . . . or (5, 5)" into nine simple events. Note that if a throw results in (3, 3), then *the same throw* results also in the events "sum six" and "two odd faces"; these events are not mutually exclusive and hence may occur simultaneously.

---

[1] *Definition of bridge and poker.* A deck of bridge cards consists of 52 cards arranged in four suits of thirteen each. There are thirteen face values (2, 3, . . . , 10, jack, queen, king, ace) in each suit. The four suits are called spades, clubs, hearts, diamonds. The last two are red, the first two black. Cards of the same face value are called of the same kind. For our purposes, playing bridge means distributing the cards to four players, to be called North, South, East, and West (or N, S, E, W, for short) so that each receives thirteen cards. Playing poker, by definition, means selecting five cards out of the pack.

As a second example consider the age of a person. Every particular value x represents a *simple* event, whereas the statement that a person is in his fifties describes the compound event that x lies between 50 and 60. In this way every compound event can be decomposed into simple events, that is to say, a compound event is an *aggregate of certain simple events*.

If we want to speak about "experiments" or "observations" in a theoretical way and without ambiguity, we must first agree on the simple events representing the thinkable outcomes; *they define the idealized experiment.* In other words: The term simple (or indecomposable) event remains undefined in the same way as the terms point and line remain undefined in geometry. Following a general usage in mathematics *the simple events will be called sample points*, or *points* for short. By definition, *every indecomposable result of the (idealized) experiment is represented by one, and only one, sample point.* The aggregate of all sample points will be called the *sample space*. All events connected with a given (idealized) experiment can be described as aggregates of sample points.

Before formalizing these basic conventions, we proceed to discuss a few typical examples which will play a role further on.

2. EXAMPLES

(*a*) *Distribution of the three balls in three cells.* Table 1 describes all possible outcomes of the "experiment" of placing three balls into three cells.

Each of these arrangements represents a simple event, that is, a sample point. The event A "one cell is multiply occupied" is realized in the arrangements numbered 1–21, and we express this by saying that the event A is the aggregate of the sample points 1–21. Similarly, the event B "first cell is not empty" is the aggregate of the sample points 1, 4–15, 22–27.

TABLE 1

1. $\{abc \mid\ -\ \mid\ -\ \}$	10. $\{a \quad\mid\ bc \mid\ -\ \}$	19. $\{\ -\ \mid a \quad\mid\ bc\}$
2. $\{\ -\ \mid abc \mid\ -\ \}$	11. $\{\ b \mid a\ c \mid\ -\ \}$	20. $\{\ -\ \mid\ b \quad\mid a\ c\}$
3. $\{\ -\ \mid\ -\ \mid abc\}$	12. $\{\ c \mid ab \mid\ -\ \}$	21. $\{\ -\ \mid\quad c \mid ab\ \}$
4. $\{ab \mid\ c \mid\ -\ \}$	13. $\{a \quad\mid\ -\ \mid bc\}$	22. $\{a \quad\mid\ b \mid\ c\}$
5. $\{a\ c \mid\ b \mid\ -\ \}$	14. $\{\ b \mid\ -\ \mid a\ c\}$	23. $\{a \quad\mid\ c \mid\ b\}$
6. $\{\ bc \mid a \quad\mid\ -\ \}$	15. $\{\ c \mid\ -\ \mid ab\ \}$	24. $\{\ b \mid a \quad\mid\ c\}$
7. $\{ab \mid\ -\ \mid\ c\}$	16. $\{\ -\ \mid ab \mid\ c\}$	25. $\{\ b \mid\ c \mid a\ \}$
8. $\{a\ c \mid\ -\ \mid\ b\ \}$	17. $\{\ -\ \mid a\ c \mid\ b\ \}$	26. $\{\ c \mid a \quad\mid\ b\ \}$
9. $\{\ bc \mid\ -\ \mid a\ \}$	18. $\{\ -\ \mid\ bc \mid a\ \}$	27. $\{\ c \mid\ b \mid a\ \}.$

The event C defined by "both A and B occur" is the aggregate of the thirteen sample points 1, 4–15. In this particular example it so happens that each of the 27 points belongs to either A or B (or to both); therefore the event "either A or B or both occur" is the entire sample space and occurs with absolute certainty. The event D defined by "A does not occur" consists of the points 22–27 and can be described by the condition that no cell remains empty. The event "first cell empty and no cell multiply occupied" is impossible (does not occur) since no sample point satisfies these specifications.

(b) *Random placement of r balls in n cells.* The more general case of r balls in n cells can be studied in the same manner, except that the number of possible arrangements increases rapidly with r and n. For $r = 4$ balls in $n = 3$ cells, the sample space contains already 64 points, and for $r = n = 10$ there are 10^{10} sample points; a complete tabulation would require some hundred thousand big volumes.

We use this example to illustrate the important fact that the nature of the sample points is irrelevant for our theory. To us the sample space (together with the probability distribution defined in it) *defines* the idealized experiment. We use the picturesque language of balls and cells, but the same sample space admits of a great variety of different practical interpretations. To clarify this point, and also for further reference, *we list here a number of situations in which the intuitive background varies; all are, however, abstractly equivalent to the scheme of placing r balls into n cells, in the sense that the outcomes differ only in their verbal description.* The appropriate assignment of probabilities is not the same in all cases and will be discussed later on.

(b,1). *Birthdays.* The possible configurations of the birthdays of r people correspond to the different arrangements of r balls in $n = 365$ cells (assuming the year to have 365 days).

(b,2). *Accidents.* Classifying r accidents according to the weekdays when they occurred is equivalent to placing r balls into $n = 7$ cells.

(b,3). *In firing* at n targets, the hits correspond to balls, the targets to cells.

(b,4). *Sampling.* Let a group of r people be classified according to, say, age or profession. The classes play the role of our cells, the people that of balls.

(b,5). *Irradiation in biology.* When the cells in the retina of the eye are exposed to light, the light particles play the role of balls, and the actual cells are the "cells" of our model. Similarly, in the study of the genetic effect of irradiation, the chromosomes correspond to the cells of our model and α-particles to the balls.

(b,6). In *cosmic ray experiments* the particles reaching Geiger counters represent balls, and the counters function as cells.

(b,7). *An elevator* starts with r passengers and stops at n floors. The different arrangements of discharging the passengers are replicas of the different distributions of r balls in n cells.

(b,8). *Dice.* The possible outcomes of a throw with r dice correspond to placing r balls into $n = 6$ cells. When *tossing a coin* we are in effect dealing with only $n = 2$ cells.

(b,9). *Random digits.* The possible orderings of a sequence of r digits correspond to the distribution of r balls ($=$ places) into ten cells called 0, 1, ..., 9.

(b,10). The *sex distribution* of r persons. Here we have $n = 2$ cells and r balls.

(b,11). *Coupon collecting.* The different kinds of coupons represent the cells; the coupons collected represent the balls.

(b,12). *Aces in bridge.* The four players represent four cells, and we have $r = 4$ balls.

(b,13). *Gene distributions.* Each descendant of an individual (person, plant, or animal) inherits from the progenitor certain genes. If a particular gene can appear in n forms $A_1, ..., A_n$, then the descendants may be classified according to the type of the gene. The descendants correspond to the balls, the genotypes $A_1, ..., A_n$ to the cells.

(b,14). *Chemistry.* Suppose that a long-chain polymer reacts with oxygen. An individual chain may react with 0, 1, 2, ... oxygen molecules. Here the reacting oxygen molecules play the role of balls and the polymer chains the role of cells into which the balls are put.

(b,15). *Theory of photographic emulsions.* A photographic plate is covered with grains sensitive to light quanta: a grain reacts if it is hit by a certain number, r, of quanta. For the theory of black-white contrast we must know how many cells are likely to be hit by the r quanta. We have here an occupancy problem where the grains correspond to cells, and the light quanta to balls. (Actually the situation is more complicated since a plate usually contains grains of different sensitivity.)

(b,16). *Misprints.* The possible distributions of r misprints in the n pages of a book correspond to all the different distributions of r balls in n cells, provided r is smaller than the number of letters per page.

(c) *The case of indistinguishable balls.* Let us return to example (a) and suppose that the three balls are not distinguishable. This means that we no longer distinguish between three arrangements such as 4, 5, 6, and thus table 1 reduces to Table 2. The latter *defines* the sample space of the ideal experiment which we call "*placing three indistinguishable balls into three cells*," and a similar procedure applies to the case of r balls in n cells.

TABLE 2

1. $\{\ast\ast\ast \mid - \mid - \}$	6. $\{ \ast \mid \ast\ast \mid - \}$
2. $\{ - \mid \ast\ast\ast \mid - \}$	7. $\{ \ast \mid - \mid \ast\ast \}$
3. $\{ - \mid - \mid \ast\ast\ast\}$	8. $\{ - \mid \ast\ast \mid \ast \}$
4. $\{\ast\ast \mid \ast \mid - \}$	9. $\{ - \mid \ast \mid \ast\ast \}$
5. $\{\ast\ast \mid - \mid \ast \}$	10. $\{ \ast \mid \ast \mid \ast \}$.

Whether or not actual balls are in practice distinguishable is irrelevant for our theory. Even if they are, we may decide to treat them as indistinguishable. The aces in bridge [example $(b,12)$] or the people in an elevator [example $(b,7)$] certainly are distinguishable, and yet it is often preferable to treat them as indistinguishable. The dice of example $(b,8)$ may be colored to make them distinguishable, but whether in discussing a particular problem we use the model of distinguishable or indistinguishable balls is purely a matter of purpose and convenience. The nature of a concrete problem may dictate the choice, but under any circumstances our theory begins only after the appropriate model has been chosen, that is, after the sample space has been defined.

In the scheme above we have considered indistinguishable balls, but table 2 still refers to a first, second, third cell, and their order is essential. We can go a step further and assume that even the cells are indistinguishable (for example, the cell may be chosen at random without regard to its contents). With both balls and cells indistinguishable, only three different arrangements are possible, namely $\{\ast\ast\ast \mid - \mid - \}$, $\{\ast\ast \mid \ast \mid - \}$, $\{\ast \mid \ast \mid \ast \}$.

(*d*) *Sampling.* Suppose that a sample of 100 people is taken in order to estimate how many people smoke. The only property of the sample of interest in this connection is the number x of smokers; this may be an integer between 0 and 100. In this case we may agree that our sample space consists of the 101 "points" 0, 1, . . . , 100. Every particular sample or observation is completely described by stating the corresponding point x. An example of a compound event is the result that "the majority of the people sampled are smokers." This means that the experiment resulted in one of the fifty simple events 51, 52, . . . , 100, but it is not stated in which. Similarly, every property of the sample can be described in enumerating the corresponding cases or sample points. For uniform terminology we speak of events rather than properties of the sample. Mathematically, an event is simply the aggregate of the corresponding sample points.

(e) *Sampling* (*continued*). Suppose now that the 100 people in our sample are classified not only as smokers or non-smokers but also as males or females. The sample may now be characterized by a quadruple (M_s, F_s, M_n, F_n) of integers giving in order the number of male and female smokers, male and female non-smokers. For sample points we take the quadruples of integers lying between 0 and 100 and adding to 100. There are 176,851 such quadruples, and they constitute the sample space (cf. II, 5). The event "relatively more males than females smoke" means that in our sample the ratio M_s/M_n is greater than F_s/F_n. The point (73, 2, 8, 17) has this property, but (0, 1, 50, 49) has not. Our event can be described in principle by enumerating all quadruples with the desired property.

(f) *Coin tossing.*   For the experiment of tossing a coin three times, the sample space consists of eight points which may conveniently be represented by *HHH, HHT, HTH, THH, HTT, THT, TTH, TTT.* The event *A*, "two or more heads," is the aggregate of the first four points. The event *B*, "just one tail," means either *HHT*, or *HTH*, or *THH*; we say that *B* contains these three points.

(g) *Ages of a couple.*   An insurance company is interested in the age distribution of couples. Let x stand for the age of the husband, y for the age of the wife. Each observation results in a number-pair (x, y). For the sample space we take the first quadrant of the x,y-plane so that each point $x > 0, y > 0$ is a sample point. The event *A*, "husband is older than 40," is represented by all points to the right of the line $x = 40$; the event *B*, "husband is older than wife," is represented by the angular region between the x-axis and the bisector $y = x$, that is to say, by the aggregate of points with $x > y$; the event *C*, "wife is older than 40," is represented by the points above the line $y = 40$. A geometric representation of the joint age distributions of two couples requires a four-dimensional space.

(h) *Phase space.*   In statistical mechanics, each possible "state" of a system is called a "point in phase space." This is only a difference in terminology. The phase space is simply our sample space; its points are our sample points.

3. THE SAMPLE SPACE. EVENTS

It should be clear from the preceding that we shall never speak of probabilities except in relation to a given sample space (or, physically, in relation to a certain conceptual experiment). *We start with the notion of a sample space and its points; from now on they will be considered given. They are the primitive and undefined notions of the theory* precisely as the notions of "points" and "straight line" remain undefined in an axiomatic treatment of Euclidean geometry. The nature of the sample points does not enter our theory. The sample space provides a model of an ideal experiment in the sense that, by definition, *every thinkable outcome of the experiment is completely described by one, and only one, sample point.* It is meaningful to talk about an event *A* only when it is clear for *every* outcome of the experiment whether the event *A* has or has not occurred. The collection of all those sample points representing outcomes where *A* has occurred completely describes the event. Conversely, any given aggregate *A* containing one or more sample points can be called an event; this event does, or does not, occur according as the outcome of the experiment is, or is not, represented by a point of the aggregate *A*. We therefore define the word *event to mean the same as an aggregate of sample points.* We shall say that an *event A consists of (or contains) certain points,* namely those representing outcomes of the ideal experiment in which *A* occurs.

Example. In the sample space of example (2.*a*) consider the event *U* consisting of the points number 1, 7, 13. This is a formal and straightforward definition, but *U* can be described in many equivalent ways. For example, *U* may be defined as the event that the following three conditions are satisfied: (1) the second cell is empty, (2) the ball *a* is in the first cell, (3) the ball *b* does not appear after *c*. Each of these conditions itself describes an event. The event U_1 defined by the condition (1) alone consists of points 1, 3, 7–9, 13–15. The event U_2 defined by (2) consists of points 1, 4, 5, 7, 8, 10, 13, 22, 23; and the event U_3 defined by (3) contains the points 1–4, 6, 7, 9–11, 13, 14, 16, 18–20, 22, 24, 25. The event *U* can also be described as the *simultaneous realization* of all three events U_1, U_2, U_3.   ▶

The terms "sample point" and "event" have an intuitive appeal, but they refer to the notions of point and point set common to all parts of mathematics.

We have seen in the preceding example and in (2.*a*) that new events can be defined in terms of two or more given events. With these examples in mind we now proceed to introduce the notation of the formal *algebra of events* (that is, algebra of point sets).

4. RELATIONS AMONG EVENTS

We shall now suppose that an arbitrary, but fixed, sample space $\mathfrak{S}$ is given. We use capitals to denote *events*, that is, sets of sample points. The fact that a point *x* is contained in the event *A* is denoted by $x \in A$.

Thus $x \in \mathfrak{S}$ for every point x. We write $A = B$ only if the two events consist of exactly the same points.

In general, events will be defined by certain conditions on their points, and it is convenient to have a symbol to express the fact that no point satisfies a specified set of conditions. The next definition serves this purpose.

Definition 1. *We shall use the notation $A = 0$ to express that the event A contains no sample points (is impossible).* The zero must be interpreted in a symbolic sense and not as the numeral.

To every event A there corresponds another event defined by the condition "A does not occur." It contains all points not contained in A.

Definition 2. *The event consisting of all points not contained in the event A will be called the complementary event (or negation) of A and will be denoted by A'. In particular, $\mathfrak{S}' = 0$.*

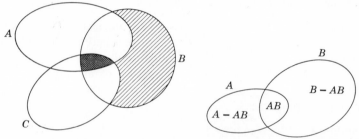

Figures 1 and 2. Illustrating relations among events. In Figure 1 the domain within heavy boundaries is the union $A \cup B \cup C$. The triangular (*heavily shaded*) domain is the intersection ABC. The moon-shaped (*lightly shaded*) domain is the intersection of B with the complement of $A \cup C$.

With any two events A and B we can associate two new events defined by the conditions "*both A and B occur*" and "*either A or B or both occur.*" These events will be denoted by AB and $A \cup B$, respectively. The event AB contains all sample points which are common to A and B. If A and B exclude each other, then there are no points common to A and B and the event AB is impossible; analytically, this situation is described by the equation

$$(4.1) \qquad\qquad AB = 0$$

which should be read "A and B are *mutually exclusive*." The event AB' means that both A and B' occur or, in other words, that A but not B occurs. Similarly, $A'B'$ means that neither A nor B occurs. The event $A \cup B$ means that at least one of the events A and B occurs;

it contains all sample points except those that belong neither to A nor to B.

In the theory of probability we can describe the event AB as the simultaneous occurrence of A and B. In standard mathematical terminology AB is called the (logical) intersection of A and B. Similarly, $A \cup B$ is the union of A and B. Our notion carries over to the case of events $A, B, C, D, \ldots$.

Definition 3. *To every collection $A, B, C, \ldots$ of events we define two new events as follows. The aggregate of the sample points which belong to all the given sets will be denoted by $ABC \ldots$ and called the intersection[2] (or simultaneous realization) of $A, B, C, \ldots$. The aggregate of sample points which belong to at least one of the given sets will be denoted by $A \cup B \cup C \ldots$ and called the union (or realization of at least one) of the given events. The events $A, B, C, \ldots$ are mutually exclusive if no two have a point in common, that is, if $AB = 0$, $AC = 0, \ldots$, $BC = 0, \ldots$.*

We still require a symbol to express the statement that A cannot occur without B occurring, that is, that the occurrence of A implies the occurrence of B. This means that every point of A is contained in B. Think of intuitive analogies like the aggregate of all mothers, which forms a part of the aggregate of all women: All mothers are women but not all women are mothers.

Definition 4. *The symbols $A \subset B$ and $B \supset A$ are equivalent and signify that every point of A is contained in B; they are read, respectively, "A implies B" and "B is implied by A". If this is the case, we shall also write $B - A$ instead of BA' to denote the event that B but not A occurs.*

The event $B - A$ contains all those points which are in B but not in A. With this notation we can write $A' = \mathfrak{S} - A$ and $A - A = 0$.

Examples. *(a)* If A and B are mutually exclusive, then the occurrence of A implies the non-occurrence of B and vice versa. Thus $AB = 0$ means the same as $A \subset B'$ and as $B \subset A'$.

(b) The event $A - AB$ means the occurrence of A but not of both A and B. Thus $A - AB = AB'$.

(c) In the example (2.g), the event AB means that the husband is older than 40 *and* older than his wife; AB' means that he is older than

---

[2] The standard mathematical notation for the intersection of two or more sets is $A \cap B$ or $A \cap B \cap C$, etc. This notation is more suitable for certain specific purposes (see IV, 1 of volume 2). At present we use the notation AB, ABC, etc., since it is less clumsy in print.

40 but *not* older than his wife. AB is represented by the infinite trapezoidal region between the x-axis and the lines $x = 40$ and $y = x$, and the event AB' is represented by the angular domain between the lines $x = 40$ and $y = x$, the latter boundary included. The event AC means that both husband and wife are older than 40. The event $A \cup C$ means that at least one of them is older than 40, and $A \cup B$ means that the husband is either older than 40 or, if not that, at least older than his wife (in official language, "husband's age exceeds 40 years or wife's age, whichever is smaller").

(*d*) In example (2.*a*) let E_i be the event that the cell number i is empty (here $i = 1, 2, 3$). Similarly, let S_i, D_i, T_i, respectively, denote the event that the cell number i is occupied simply, doubly, or triply. Then $E_1 E_2 = T_3$, and $S_1 S_2 \subset S_3$, and $D_1 D_2 = 0$. Note also that $T_1 \subset E_2$, etc. The event $D_1 \cup D_2 \cup D_3$ is defined by the condition that there exist at least one doubly occupied cell.

(*e*) *Bridge* (cf. footnote 1). Let A, B, C, D be the events, respectively, that North, South, East, West have at least one ace. It is clear that at least one player has an ace, so that one or more of the four events must occur. Hence $A \cup B \cup C \cup D = \mathfrak{S}$ is the whole sample space. The event $ABCD$ occurs if, and only if, each player has an ace. The event "West has all four aces" means that none of the three events A, B, C has occurred; this is the same as the simultaneous occurrence of A' and B' and C' or the event $A'B'C'$.

(*f*) In the example (2.*g*) we have $BC \subset A$: in words, "if husband is older than wife (B) and wife is older than 40 (C), then husband is older that 40 (A)." How can the event $A - BC$ be described in words? ▶

5. DISCRETE SAMPLE SPACES

The simplest sample spaces are those containing only a finite number, n, of points. If n is fairly small (as in the case of tossing a few coins), it is easy to visualize the space. The space of distributions of cards in bridge is more complicated, but we may imagine each sample point represented on a chip and may then consider the collection of these chips as representing the sample space. An event A (like "North has two aces") is represented by a certain set of chips, the complement A' by the remaining ones. It takes only one step from here to imagine a bowl with infinitely many chips or a sample space with an infinite sequence of points $E_1, E_2, E_3, \ldots$.

Examples. (*a*) Let us toss a coin as often as necessary to turn up one head. The points of the sample space are then $E_1 = H$, $E_2 = TH$, $E_3 = TTH$, $E_4 = TTTH$, etc. We may or may not consider as thinkable the possibility that H never appears. If we do, this possibility should be represented by a point E_0.

(*b*) Three players a, b, c take turns at a game, such as chess, according to the following rules. At the start a and b play while c is out. The loser is replaced by c and at the second trial the winner plays against c while the loser is out. The game continues in this way until a player wins twice in succession, thus becoming the winner of the game. For simplicity we disregard the possibility of ties at the individual trials. The possible outcomes of our game are then indicated by the following scheme:

(*)   *aa,   acc,   acbb,   acbaa,   acbacc,   acbacbb,   acbacbaa,* . . .

        bb,   bcc,   bcaa,   bcabb,   bcabcc,   bcabcaa,   bcabcabb, ...

In addition, it is thinkable that no player ever wins twice in succession, in which case the play continues indefinitely according to one of the patterns

(**)   *acbacbacbacb* . . . ,   *bcabcabcabca* . . . .

The sample space corresponding to our ideal "experiment" is defined by (*) and (**) and is infinite. It is clear that the sample points can be arranged in a simple sequence by taking first the two points (**) and continuing with the points of (*) in the order *aa, bb, acc, bcc,* . . . . [See problems 5–6, example V,(2.*a*), and problem 5 of XV,14.]   ▶

Definition. *A sample space is called discrete if it contains only finitely many points or infinitely many points which can be arranged into a simple sequence $E_1, E_2, \ldots .$*

Not every sample space is discrete. It is a known theorem (due to G. Cantor) that the sample space consisting of all positive numbers is not discrete. We are here confronted with a distinction familiar in mechanics. There it is usual first to consider discrete mass points with each individual point carrying a finite mass, and then to pass to the notion of a continuous mass distribution, where each individual point has zero mass. In the first case, the mass of a system is obtained simply by adding the masses of the individual points; in the second case, masses are computed by integration over mass densities. Quite similarly, the probabilities of events in discrete sample spaces are obtained by mere additions, whereas in other spaces integrations are necessary. Except for the technical tools required, there is no essential difference between the two cases. In order to present actual probability considerations unhampered by technical difficulties, we shall take up only discrete sample spaces. It will be seen that even this special case leads to many interesting and important results.

In this volume we shall consider only discrete sample spaces.

6. PROBABILITIES IN DISCRETE SAMPLE SPACES: PREPARATIONS

Probabilities are numbers of the same nature as distances in geometry or masses in mechanics. The theory assumes that they are given but need assume nothing about their actual numerical values or how they are measured in practice. Some of the most important applications are of a qualitative nature and independent of numerical values. In the relatively few instances where numerical values for probabilities are required, the procedures vary as widely as do the methods of determining distances. There is little in common in the practices of the carpenter, the practical surveyor, the pilot, and the astronomer when they measure distances. In our context, we may consider the diffusion constant, which is a notion of the theory of probability. To find its numerical value, physical considerations relating it to other theories are required; a direct measurement is impossible. By contrast, mortality tables are constructed from rather crude observations. In most actual applications the determination of probabilities, or the comparison of theory and observation, requires rather sophisticated statistical methods, which in turn are based on a refined probability theory. In other words, the intuitive meaning of probability is clear, but only as the theory proceeds shall we be able to see how it is applied. All possible "definitions" of probability fall far short of the actual practice.

When tossing a "good" coin we do not hesitate to associate probability $\frac{1}{2}$ with either head or tail. This amounts to saying that when a coin is tossed n times all 2^n possible results have the same probability. From a theoretical standpoint, this is a *convention*. Frequently, it has been contended that this convention is logically unavoidable and the only possible one. Yet there have been philosophers and statisticians defying the convention and starting from contradictory assumptions (uniformity or non-uniformity in nature). It has also been claimed that the probabilities $\frac{1}{2}$ are due to experience. As a matter of fact, whenever refined statistical methods have been used to check on actual coin tossing, the result has been invariably that head and tail are *not* equally likely. And yet we stick to our model of an "ideal" coin, even though no good coins exist. We preserve the model not merely for its logical simplicity, but essentially for its usefulness and applicability. In many applications it is sufficiently accurate to describe reality. More important is the empirical fact that departures from our scheme are always coupled with phenomena such as an eccentric position of the center of gravity. In this way our idealized model can be extremely useful even if it never applies exactly. For example, in modern statistical quality control based on Shewhart's methods, idealized probability models are used to discover "assignable causes" for flagrant departures from these models and thus to remove impending machine troubles and process irregularities at an early stage.

Similar remarks apply to other cases. The number of possible distributions of cards in bridge is almost 10^{30}. Usually we agree to consider them as equally probable. For a check of this convention more than 10^{30} experiments would be required—thousands of billions of years if every living person played one game every second, day and night. However, consequences of the assumption can be verified experimentally, for example, by observing the frequency of multiple aces in the hands at bridge. It turns out that for crude purposes the idealized model describes experience sufficiently well, provided the card shuffling is done better than is usual. It is more important that the idealized scheme, when it does not apply, permits the discovery of "assignable causes" for the discrepancies, for example, the reconstruction of the mode of shuffling. These are examples of limited importance, but they indicate the usefulness of assumed models. More interesting cases will appear only as the theory proceeds.

Examples. (*a*) *Distinguishable balls.* In example (2.*a*) it appears natural to assume that all sample points are *equally probable*, that is, that *each sample point has probability* $\frac{1}{27}$. We can start from this *definition* and investigate its consequences. Whether or not our model will come reasonably close to actual experience will depend on the type of phenomena to which it is applied. In some applications the assumption of equal probabilities is imposed by physical considerations; in others it is introduced to serve as the simplest model for a general orientation, even though it quite obviously represents only a crude first approximation [e.g., consider the examples (2.*b*,1), birthdays; (2.*b*,7), elevator problem; or (2.*b*,11) coupon collecting].

(*b*) *Indistinguishable balls: Bose-Einstein statistics.* We now turn to the example (2.*c*) of three indistinguishable balls in three cells. It is possible to argue that the actual physical experiment is unaffected by our failure to distinguish between the balls; physically there remain 27 different possibilities, even though only ten different forms are disinguishable. This consideration leads us to attribute the following probabilities to the ten points of table 2.

Point number:	1	2	3	4	5	6	7	8	9	10
Probability:	$\frac{1}{27}$	$\frac{1}{27}$	$\frac{1}{27}$	$\frac{1}{9}$	$\frac{1}{9}$	$\frac{1}{9}$	$\frac{1}{9}$	$\frac{1}{9}$	$\frac{1}{9}$	$\frac{2}{9}$.

It must be admitted that for most applications listed in example (2.*b*) this argument appears sound and the assignment of probabilities reasonable. Historically, our argument was accepted for a long time without question and served in statistical mechanics as the basis for the derivation of the *Maxwell-Boltzmann statistics* for the distribution of r balls in n cells. The greater was the surprise when Bose and Einstein showed that certain particles are subject to the *Bose-Einstein* statistics (for details see II,5). In our case with $r = n = 3$, this model attributes *probability* $\frac{1}{10}$ *to each of the ten sample points.*

This example shows that different assignments of probabilities are compatible with the same sample space and illustrates the intricate

TABLE 3

Trials number	Number of heads										Total
0– 1,000	54	46	53	55	46	54	41	48	51	53	501
– 2,000	48	46	40	53	49	49	48	54	53	45	485
– 3,000	43	52	58	51	51	50	52	50	53	49	509
– 4,000	58	60	54	55	50	48	47	57	52	55	536
– 5,000	48	51	51	49	44	52	50	46	53	41	485
– 6,000	49	50	45	52	52	48	47	47	47	51	488
– 7,000	45	47	41	51	49	59	50	55	53	50	500
– 8,000	53	52	46	52	44	51	48	51	46	54	497
– 9,000	45	47	46	52	47	48	59	57	45	48	494
–10,000	47	41	51	48	59	51	52	55	39	41	484

interrelation between theory and experience. In particular, it teaches us not to rely too much on a priori arguments and to be prepared to accept new and unforeseen schemes.

(c) *Coin tossing.* A frequency interpretation of the postulate of equal probabilities requires records of actual experiments. Now in reality every coin is biased, and it is possible to devise physical experiments which come much closer to the ideal model of coin tossing than real coins ever do. To give an idea of the fluctuations to be expected, we give the record of such a simulated experiment corresponding to 10,000 trials with a coin.[3] Table 3 contains the number of occurrences of "heads" in a series of 100 experiments each corresponding to a sequence of 100 trials with a coin. The grand total is 4979. Looking at these figures the reader is probably left with a vague feeling of: So what? The truth is that a more advanced

---

[3] The table actually records the frequency of even digits in a section of *A million random digits with 100,000 normal deviates*, by The RAND Corporation, Glencoe, Illinois (The Free Press), 1955.

theory is necessary to judge to what extent such empirical data agree with our abstract model. (Incidentally, we shall return to this material in III,6.) ▶

7. THE BASIC DEFINITIONS AND RULES

Fundamental Convention. *Given a discrete sample space $\mathfrak{S}$ with sample points $E_1, E_2, \ldots$, we shall assume that with each point E_j there is associated a number, called the probability of E_j and denoted by $\mathbf{P}\{E_j\}$. It is to be non-negative and such that*

$$(7.1) \qquad \mathbf{P}\{E_1\} + \mathbf{P}\{E_2\} + \cdots = 1.$$

Note that we do not exclude the possibility that a point has probability zero. This convention may appear artificial but is necessary to avoid complications. In discrete sample spaces probability zero is in practice interpreted as an impossibility, and any sample point known to have probability zero can, with impunity, be eliminated from the sample space. However, frequently the numerical values of the probabilities are not known in advance, and involved considerations are required to decide whether or not a certain sample point has positive probability.

Definition. *The probability $\mathbf{P}\{A\}$ of any event A is the sum of the probabilities of all sample points in it.*

By (7.1) the probability of the entire sample space $\mathfrak{S}$ is unity, or $\mathbf{P}\{\mathfrak{S}\} = 1$. It follows that for any event A

$$(7.2) \qquad 0 \leq \mathbf{P}\{A\} \leq 1.$$

Consider now two arbitrary events A_1 and A_2. To compute the probability $\mathbf{P}\{A_1 \cup A_2\}$ that either A_1 or A_2 or both occur, we have to add the probabilities of all sample points contained either in A_1 or in A_2, but each point is to be counted only once. We have, therefore,

$$(7.3) \qquad \mathbf{P}\{A_1 \cup A_2\} \leq \mathbf{P}\{A_1\} + \mathbf{P}\{A_2\}.$$

Now, if E is any point contained both in A_1 and in A_2, then $\mathbf{P}\{E\}$ occurs twice in the right-hand member but only once in the left-hand member. Therefore, the right side exceeds the left side by the amount $\mathbf{P}\{A_1 A_2\}$, and we have the simple but important

Theorem. *For any two events A_1 and A_2 the probability that either A_1 or A_2 or both occur is given by*

$$(7.4) \qquad \mathbf{P}\{A_1 \cup A_2\} = \mathbf{P}\{A_1\} + \mathbf{P}\{A_2\} - \mathbf{P}\{A_1 A_2\}.$$

$$P(A \cup B \cup C) = P(A) + P(B) + P(C) \\ - P(AB) - P(BC) - P(AC) \\ + P(ABC)$$

If $A_1A_2 = 0$, *that is, if* A_1 *and* A_2 *are mutually exclusive, then* (7.4) *reduces to*

$$(7.5) \qquad \mathbf{P}\{A_1 \cup A_2\} = \mathbf{P}\{A_1\} + \mathbf{P}\{A_2\}.$$

Example. A coin is tossed twice. For sample space we take the four points *HH, HT, TH, TT,* and associate with each probability $\frac{1}{4}$. Let A_1 and A_2 be, respectively, the events "head at first and second trial." Then A_1 consists of *HH* and *HT,* and A_2 of *TH* and *HH.* Furthermore $A = A_1 \cup A_2$ contains the three points *HH, HT,* and *TH,* whereas A_1A_2 consists of the single point *HH.* Thus

$$\mathbf{P}\{A_1 \cup A_2\} = \tfrac{1}{2} + \tfrac{1}{2} - \tfrac{1}{4} = \tfrac{3}{4}. \qquad \blacktriangleright$$

The probability $\mathbf{P}\{A_1 \cup A_2 \cup \cdots \cup A_n\}$ of the realization of at least one among n events can be computed by a formula analogous to (7.4), derived in IV,1. Here we note only that the argument leading to (7.3) applies to any number of terms. Thus *for arbitrary events* $A_1, A_2, \ldots$ *the inequality*

$$(7.6) \qquad \mathbf{P}\{A_1 \cup A_2 \cup \cdots\} \leq \mathbf{P}\{A_1\} + \mathbf{P}\{A_2\} + \cdots \quad \text{BOOLE's INEQUALITY}$$

holds. In the special case where the events $A_1, A_2, \ldots$ *are mutually exclusive, we have*

$$(7.7) \qquad \mathbf{P}\{A_1 \cup A_2 \cup \cdots\} = \mathbf{P}\{A_1\} + \mathbf{P}\{A_2\} + \cdots$$

Occasionally (7.6) is referred to as *Boole's inequality*.

We shall first investigate the simple special case where the sample space has a finite number, N, of points each having probability $1/N$. In this case, the probability of any event A equals the number of points in A divided by N. In the older literature, the points of the sample space were called "cases," and the points of A "favorable" cases (favorable for A). *If* all points have the same probability, then the probability of an event A is the ratio of the number of favorable cases to the total number of cases. Unfortunately, this statement has been much abused to provide a "definition" of probability. It is often contended that in *every* finite sample space probabilities of all points are equal. This is not so. For a single throw of an untrue coin, the sample space still contains only the two points, head and tail, but they may have arbitrary probabilities p and q, with $p + q = 1$. A newborn baby is a boy or girl, but in applications we have to admit that the two possibilities are not equally likely. A further counterexample is provided by (6.*b*). The usefulness of sample spaces in which all sample points have the same probability is restricted almost entirely to the study of games of chance and to combinatorial analysis.

8. PROBLEMS FOR SOLUTION

1. Among the digits 1, 2, 3, 4, 5 first one is chosen, and then a second selection is made among the remaining four digits. Assume that all twenty possible results have the same probability. Find the probability that an odd digit will be selected (a) the first time, (b) the second time, (c) both times.

2. In the sample space of example (2.a) attach equal probabilities to all 27 points. Using the notation of example (4.d), verify formula (7.4) for the two events $A_1 = S_1$ and $A_2 = S_2$. How many points does $S_1 S_2$ contain?

3. Consider the 24 possible arrangements (permutations) of the symbols 1234 and attach to each probability $\frac{1}{24}$. Let A_i be the event that the digit i appears at its natural place (where $i = 1, 2, 3, 4$). Verify formula (7.4).

4. A coin is tossed until for the first time the same result appears twice in succession. To every possible outcome requiring n tosses attribute probability $1/2^{n-1}$. Describe the sample space. Find the probability of the following events: (a) the experiment ends before the sixth toss, (b) an *even* number of tosses is required.

5. In the sample space of example (5.b) let us attribute to each point of (∗) containing exactly k letters probability $1/2^k$. (In other words, aa and bb carry probability $\frac{1}{4}$, acb has probability $\frac{1}{8}$, etc.) (a) Show that the probabilities of the points of (∗) add up to unity, whence the two points (∗∗) receive probability zero. (b) Show that the probability that a wins is $\frac{5}{14}$. The probability of b winning is the same, and c has probability $\frac{2}{7}$ of winning. (c) The probability that no decision is reached at or before the kth turn (game) is $1/2^{k-1}$.

6. Modify example (5.b) to take account of the possibility of ties at the individual games. Describe the appropriate sample space. How would you define probabilities?

7. In problem 3 show that $A_1 A_2 A_3 \subset A_4$ and $A_1 A_2 A_3' \subset A_4'$.

8. Using the notations of example (4.d) show that (a) $S_1 S_2 D_3 = 0$; (b) $S_1 D_2 \subset E_3$; (c) $E_3 - D_2 S_1 \supset S_2 D_1$.

9. Two dice are thrown. Let A be the event that the sum of the faces is odd, B the event of at least one ace. Describe the events AB, $A \cup B$, AB'. Find their probabilities assuming that all 36 sample points have equal probabilities.

10. In example (2.g), discuss the meaning of the following events:
(a) ABC,   (b) $A - AB$,   (c) $AB'C$.

11. In example (2.g), verify that $AC' \subset B$.

12. *Bridge* (cf. footnote 1). For $k = 1, 2, 3, 4$ let N_k be the event that North has at least k aces. Let S_k, E_k, W_k be the analogous events for South, East, West. Discuss the number x of aces in West's possession in the events
(a) W_1',   (b) $N_2 S_2$,   (c) $N_1' S_1' E_1'$,   (d) $W_2 - W_3$,
(e) $N_1 S_1 E_1 W_1$,   (f) $N_3 W_1$,   (g) $(N_2 \cup S_2) E_2$.

13. In the preceding problem verify that
(a) $S_3 \subset S_2$,   (b) $S_3 W_2 = 0$,   (c) $N_2 S_1 E_1 W_1 = 0$,
(d) $N_2 S_2 \subset W_1'$,   (e) $(N_2 \cup S_2) W_3 = 0$,   (f) $W_4 = N_1' S_1' E_1'$.

14. Verify the following relations.[4]

(a) $(A \cup B)' = A'B'$.

(b) $(A \cup B) - B = A - AB = AB'$.

(c) $AA = A \cup A = A$.

(d) $(A - AB) \cup B = A \cup B$.

(e) $(A \cup B) - AB = AB' \cup A'B$.

(f) $A' \cup B' = (AB)'$.

(g) $(A \cup B)C = AC \cup BC$.

15. Find simple expressions for

(a) $(A \cup B)(A \cup B')$, (b) $(A \cup B)(A' \cup B)(A \cup B')$, (c) $(A \cup B)(B \cup C)$.

16. State which of the following relations are correct and which incorrect:

(a) $(A \cup B) - C = A \cup (B - C)$.

(b) $ABC = AB(C \cup B)$.

(c) $A \cup B \cup C = A \cup (B - AB) \cup (C - AC)$.

(d) $A \cup B = (A - AB) \cup B$.

(e) $AB \cup BC \cup CA \supset ABC$.

(f) $(AB \cup BC \cup CA) \subset (A \cup B \cup C)$.

(g) $(A \cup B) - A = B$.

(h) $AB'C \subset A \cup B$.

(i) $(A \cup B \cup C)' = A'B'C'$.

(j) $(A \cup B)'C = A'C \cup B'C$.

(k) $(A \cup B)'C = A'B'C$.

(l) $(A \cup B)'C = C - C(A \cup B)$.

17. Let A, B, C be three arbitrary events. Find expressions for the events that of A, B, C:

(a) Only A occurs. $AB'C'$

(b) Both A and B, but not C, occur. ABC'

(c) All three events occur. ABC

(d) At least one occurs. $A \cup B \cup C$

(e) At least two occur. $(A \cup B)C'$

(f) One and no more occurs. $AB'C'$

(g) Two and no more occur.

(h) None occurs. $A'B'C'$

(i) Not more than two occur.

18. The union $A \cup B$ of two events can be expressed as the union of two mutually exclusive events, thus: $A \cup B = A \cup (B - AB)$. Express in a similar way the union of three events A, B, C.

19. Using the result of problem 18 prove that
$$P\{A \cup B \cup C\} =$$
$$= P\{A\} + P\{B\} + P\{C\} - P\{AB\} - P\{AC\} - P\{BC\} + P\{ABC\}$$
[This is a special case of IV, (1.5).]

---

[4] Notice that $(A \cup B)'$ denotes the complement of $A \cup B$, which is not the same as $A' \cup B'$. Similarly, $(AB)'$ is not the same as $A'B'$.

CHAPTER II

Elements
of Combinatorial Analysis

This chapter explains the basic notions of combinatorial analysis and develops the corresponding probabilistic background; the last part describes some simple analytic techniques. Not much combinatorial analysis is required for the further study of this book, and readers without special interest in it should pass as soon as possible to chapter V, where the main theoretical thread of chapter I is taken up again. It may be best to read the individual sections of the present chapter in conjunction with related topics in later chapters.

In the study of simple games of chance, sampling procedures, occupancy and order problems, etc., we are usually dealing with finite sample spaces in which the same probability is attributed to all points. To compute the probability of an event A we have then to divide the number of sample points in A ("favorable cases") by the total number of sample points ("possible cases"). This is facilitated by a systematic use of a few rules which we shall now proceed to review. Simplicity and economy of thought can be achieved by adhering to a few standard tools, and we shall follow this procedure instead of describing the shortest computational method in each special case.[1]

1. PRELIMINARIES

Pairs. *With m elements $a_1, \ldots, a_m$ and n elements $b_1, \ldots, b_n$, it is possible to form mn pairs (a_j, b_k) containing one element from each group.*

---

[1] The interested reader will find many topics of elementary combinatorial analysis treated in the classical textbook, *Choice and chance*, by W. A. Whitworth, fifth edition, London, 1901, reprinted by G. E. Stechert, New York, 1942. The companion volume by the same author, *DCC* exercises, reprinted New York, 1945, contains 700 problems with complete solutions.

Proof. Arrange the pairs in a rectangular array in the form of a multiplication table with m rows and n columns so that (a_j, b_k) stands at the intersection of the jth row and kth column. Then each pair appears once and only once, and the assertion becomes obvious.   ▶

Examples. (*a*) *Bridge cards* (cf. footnote 1 to chapter I). As sets of elements take the four suits and the thirteen face values, respectively. Each card is defined by its suit and its face value, and there exist $4 \cdot 13 = 52$ such combinations, or cards.

(*b*) "*Seven-way lamps.*" Some floor lamps so advertised contain 3 ordinary bulbs and also an indirect lighting fixture which can be operated on three levels but need not be used at all. Each of these four possibilities can be combined with 0, 1, 2, or 3 bulbs. Hence there are $4 \cdot 4 = 16$ possible combinations of which one, namely $(0, 0)$, means that no bulb is on. There remain fifteen (not seven) ways of operating the lamps.   ▶

Multiplets. *Given n_1 elements $a_1, \ldots, a_{n_1}$ and n_2 elements $b_1, \ldots, b_{n_2}$, etc., up to n_r elements $x_1, \ldots, x_{n_r}$; it is possible to form $n_1 \cdot n_2 \cdots n_r$ ordered r-tuplets $(a_{j_1}, b_{j_2} \ldots, x_{j_r})$ containing one element of each kind.*

Proof. If $r = 2$, the assertion reduces to the first rule. If $r = 3$, take the pair (a_i, b_j) as element of a new kind. There are $n_1 n_2$ such pairs and n_3 elements c_k. Each triple (a_i, b_j, c_k) is itself a pair consisting of (a_i, b_j) and an element c_k; the number of triplets is therefore $n_1 n_2 n_3$. Proceeding by induction, the assertion follows for every r.   ▶

Many applications are based on the following reformulation of the last theorem: *r successive selections (decisions) with exactly n_k choices possible at the kth step can produce a total of $n_1 \cdot n_2 \cdots n_r$ different results.*

Examples. (*c*) *Multiple classifications.* Suppose that people are classified according to sex, marital status, and profession. The various categories play the role of elements. If there are 17 professions, then we have $2 \cdot 2 \cdot 17 = 68$ classes in all.

(*d*) In an agricultural experiment three different treatments are to be tested (for example, the application of a fertilizer, a spray, and temperature). If these treatments can be applied on r_1, r_2, and r_3 levels or concentrations, respectively, then there exist a total of $r_1 r_2 r_3$ combinations, or ways of treatment.

(*e*) "*Placing balls into cells*" amounts to choosing one cell for each ball. With r balls we have r independent choices, and therefore *r balls can be placed into n cells in n^r different ways.* It will be recalled from example I,(2.*b*) that a great variety of conceptual experiments are abstractly equivalent to that of placing balls into cells. For example, considering the faces of a die as "cells," the last proposition implies that the experiment of throwing a die r times has 6^r possible outcomes, of which 5^r satisfy the condition that no ace turns up. Assuming that all outcomes are equally probable, the event "no ace in r throws" has therefore probability $(\frac{5}{6})^r$. We might expect naively that in six throws "an ace should turn up," but the probability of this event is only $1 - (\frac{5}{6})^6$ or less than $\frac{2}{3}$. [Cf. example (3.b).]

(f) *Display of flags.*[2] For a more sophisticated example suppose that r flags of different colors are to be displayed on n poles in a row. In how many ways can this be done? We disregard, of course, the absolute position of the flags on the poles and the practical limitations on the number of flags on a pole. We assume only that the flags on each pole are in a definite order from top to bottom.

The display can be planned by making r successive decisions for the individual flags. For the first flag we choose one among the n poles. This pole is thereby divided into two segments, and hence there are now $n + 1$ choices possible for the position of the second flag. In like manner it is seen that $n + 2$ choices are possible for the third flag, and so on. It follows that $n(n + 1)(n + 2) \cdots (n + r - 1)$ *different displays are possible.*

▶

2. ORDERED SAMPLES

Consider the set or "population" of n elements $a_1, a_2, \ldots, a_n$. Any ordered arrangement $a_{j_1}, a_{j_2}, \ldots, a_{j_r}$ of r symbols is called *an ordered sample of size r* drawn from our population. For an intuitive picture we can imagine that the elements are selected one by one. Two procedures are then possible. First, *sampling with replacement;* here each selection is made from the entire population, so that the same element can be drawn more than once. The samples are then arrangements in which repetitions are permitted. Second, *sampling without replacement;* here an element once chosen is removed from the population, so that the sample becomes an arrangement without repetitions. Obviously, in this case, the sample size r cannot exceed the population size n.

In sampling with replacement each of the r elements can be chosen in n ways: the number of possible samples is therefore n^r, as can be seen from the last theorem with $n_1 = n_2 = \cdots = n$. In sampling without replacement we have n possible choices for the first element, but only

---

[2] H. M. Finucan, *A teaching sequence for* ^nH_r, The Math. Gazette, vol. 48 (1964), pp. 440–441.

$n - 1$ for the second, $n - 2$ for the third, etc., and so there are $n(n-1) \cdots$ $(n-r+1)$ choices in all. Products of this type appear so often that it is convenient to introduce the notation[3]

$$(2.1) \qquad\qquad (n)_r = n(n-1) \cdots (n-r+1).$$

Clearly $(n)_r = 0$ for integers r, n such that $r > n$. We have thus:

Theorem. *For a population of n elements and a prescribed sample size r, there exist n^r different samples with replacement and $(n)_r$ samples without replacement.*

We note the special case where $r = n$. In sampling without replacement a sample of size n includes the whole population and represents a reordering (or *permutation*) of its elements. Accordingly, n elements $a_1, \ldots, a_n$ can be ordered in $(n)_n = n \cdot (n-1) \cdots 2 \cdot 1$ different ways. Instead of $(n)_n$ we write $n!$, which is the more usual notation. We see that our theorem has the following

Corollary. *The number of different orderings of n elements is*

$$(2.2) \qquad\qquad n! = n(n-1) \cdots 2 \cdot 1.$$

Examples. (*a*) Three persons A, B, and C form an ordered sample from the human population. Their birthdays are a sample from the population of calendar days; their ages are a sample of three numbers.

(*b*) If by "ten-letter word" is meant a (possibly meaningless) sequence of ten letters, then such a word represents a sample from the population of 26 letters. Since repetitions are permitted there are 26^{10} such words. On the other hand, in a printing press letters exist not only conceptually but also physically in the form of type. For simplicity let us assume that exactly 1,000 pieces of type are available for each letter. To set up a word in type the printer has to choose ten pieces of type, and here repetitions are excluded. A word can therefore be set up in $(26,000)_{10}$ different ways. This number is practically the same as $26,000^{10}$ and exceeds 10^{44}.

(*c*) Mr. and Mrs. Smith form a sample of size two drawn from the human population; at the same time, they form a sample of size one drawn from the population of all couples. The example shows that the sample size is defined only in relation to a given population. Tossing a coin r times is one way of obtaining a sample of size r drawn from the

---

[3] The notation $(n)_r$ is not standard but will be used consistently in this book *even when n is not an integer.*

population of the two letters H and T. The same arrangement of r letters H and T is a single sample point in the space corresponding to the experiment of tossing a coin r times.

(*d*) *Concerning ordering and sampling in practice.* When the smoking habits of a population are investigated by sampling one feels intuitively that the order within the sample should be irrelevant, and the beginner is therefore prone to think of samples as not being ordered. But conclusions from a sample are possible only on the basis of certain probabilistic assumptions, and for these it is necessary to have an appropriate model for the conceptual experiment of obtaining a sample. Now such an experiment obviously involves choices that can be distinguished from each other, meaning choices that are labeled in some way. For theoretical purposes it is simplest to use the integers as labels, and this amounts to ordering the sample. Other procedures may be preferable in practice, but even the reference to the "third guy interviewed by Jones on Tuesday" constitutes a labeling. In other words, even though the order within the samples may be ultimately disregarded, the conceptual experiment involves ordered samples, and we shall now see that this affects the appropriate assignment of probabilities.   ▶

Drawing in succession r elements from a population of size n is an experiment whose possible outcomes are samples of size r. Their number is n^r or $(n)_r$, depending on whether or not replacement is used. In either case, our conceptual experiment is described by a sample space in which each individual point represents a sample of size r.

So far we have not spoken of probabilities associated with our samples. Usually we shall assign equal probabilities to all of them and then speak of random samples. The word "random" is not well defined, but when applied to samples or selections it has a unqiue meaning. The term *random choice* is meant to imply that all outcomes are equally probable. Similarly, whenever we speak of *random samples of fixed size* r, *the adjective random is to imply that all possible samples have the same probability*, namely, n^{-r} in sampling with replacement and $1/(n)_r$ in sampling without replacement, n denoting the size of the population from which the sample is drawn. If n is large and r relatively small, the ratio $(n)_r/n^r$ is near unity. This leads us to expect that, for large populations and relatively small samples, the two ways of sampling are practically equivalent (cf. problems 11.1, 11.2, and problem 35 of VI, 10).

We have introduced a practical terminology but have made no statements about the applicability of our model of random sampling to reality. Tossing coins, throwing dice, and similar activities may be interpreted as experiments in practical random sampling with replacements, and our probabilities are numerically close to frequencies observed in long-run experiments, even though perfectly balanced coins or dice do not exist. Random sampling without replacement is typified by successive drawings of cards from a shuffled deck (provided shuffling is done much better than is usual). In sampling human populations the statistician encounters considerable and often unpredictable difficulties, and bitter experience has shown that it is difficult to obtain even a crude image of randomness.

Exercise. In sampling without replacement the probability for any fixed element of the population to be included in a random sample of size r is

$$1 - \frac{(n-1)_r}{(n)_r} = 1 - \frac{n-r}{n} = \frac{r}{n}.$$

In sampling with replacement the probability that an element be included at least once is $1 - (1 - 1/n)^r$.

3. EXAMPLES

The examples of this section represent special cases of the following problem. A random sample of size r with replacement is taken from a population of n elements. We seek the probability of the event that in the sample no element appears twice, that is, that our sample could have been obtained also by sampling without replacement. The last theorem shows that there exist n^r different samples in all, of which $(n)_r$ satisfy the stipulated condition. Assuming that all arrangements have equal probability, we conclude that *the probability of no repetition in our sample is*

(3.1) $$p = \frac{(n)_r}{n^r} = \frac{n(n-1) \cdots (n-r+1)}{n^r}.$$

The following concrete interpretations of this formula will reveal surprising features.

(a) *Random sampling numbers.* Let the population consist of the ten digits $0, 1, \ldots, 9$. Every succession of five digits represents a sample of size $r = 5$, and we assume that each such arrangement has probability 10^{-5}. By (3.1), *the probability that five consecutive random digits are all different is* $p = (10)_5 10^{-5} = 0.3024$.

We expect intuitively that in large mathematical tables having many decimal places the last five digits will have many properties of randomness. (In ordinary logarithmic and many other tables the tabular difference is nearly constant, and the last digit therefore varies regularly.) As an experiment, sixteen-place tables were selected and the entries were counted whose last five digits are all different. In the first twelve batches of a hundred entries each, the number of entries with five different digits varied as follows: 30, 27, 30, 34, 26, 32, 37, 36, 26, 31, 36, 32. Small-sample theory shows that the magnitude of the fluctuations is well within the expected limits. The average frequency is 0.3142, which is rather close to the theoretical probability, 0.3024 [cf. example VII, (4.g)].

Consider next the number $e = 2.71828\ldots$. The first 800 decimals[4] form 160 groups of five digits each, which we arrange in sixteen batches of ten each. In these sixteen batches the numbers of groups in which all five digits are different are as follows:

$$3, \quad 1, \quad 3, \quad 4, \quad 4, \quad 1, \quad 4, \quad 4, \quad 4, \quad 2, \quad 3, \quad 1, \quad 5, \quad 4, \quad 6, \quad 3.$$

The frequencies again oscillate around the value 0.3024, and small-sample theory confirms that the magnitude of the fluctuations is not larger than should be expected. The overall frequency of our event in the 160 groups is $\frac{52}{160} = 0.325$, which is reasonably close to $p = 0.3024$.

(b) *If n balls are randomly placed into n cells, the probability that each cell will be occupied equals $n!/n^n$.* It is surprisingly small: For $n = 7$ it is only $0.00612\ldots$. This means that *if in a city seven accidents occur each week, then* (assuming that all possible distributions are equally likely) *practically all weeks will contain days with two or more accidents, and on the average only one week out of 165 will show a uniform distribution of one accident per day.* This example reveals an unexpected characteristic of pure randomness. (All possible configurations of seven balls in seven cells are exhibited in table 1, section 5. The probability that two or more cells remain empty is about 0.87.) For $n = 6$ the probability $n!\, n^{-n}$ equals $0.01543\ldots$. This shows how extremely improbable it is that in six throws with a perfect die *all* faces turn up. [The probability that a particular face does not turn up is about $\frac{1}{3}$; cf. example (1.e).]

(c) *Elevator.* An elevator starts with $r = 7$ passengers and stops at $n = 10$ floors. What is the probability p that no two passengers leave at the same floor? To render the question precise, we assume that all arrangements of discharging the passengers have the same probability (which is a crude approximation). Then

$$p = 10^{-7}(10)_7 = (10\cdot9\cdot8\cdot7\cdot6\cdot5\cdot4)10^{-7} = 0.06048.$$

When the event was once observed, the occurrence was deemed remarkable

---

[4] For farther-going results obtained by modern computers see R. G. Stoneham, *A study of 60,000 digits of the transcendental e,* Amer. Math. Monthly, vol. 72 (1965), pp. 483–500 and R. K. Pathria, *A statistical study of the first 10,000 digits of π,* Mathematics of Computation, vol. 16 (1962), pp. 188–197.

and odds of 1000 to 1 were offered against a repetition. (Cf. the *answer* to problem 10.43.)

(*d*) *Birthdays.* The birthdays of r people form a sample of size r from the population of all days in the year. The years are not of equal length, and we know that the birth rates are not quite constant throughout the year. However, in a first approximation, we may take a random selection of people as equivalent to random selection of birthdays and consider the year as consisting of 365 days.

With these conventions we can interpret equation (3.1) to the effect *that the probability that all r birthdays are different equals*[5]

$$(3.2) \qquad p = \frac{(365)_r}{365^r} = \left(1 - \frac{1}{365}\right)\left(1 - \frac{2}{365}\right) \cdots \left(1 - \frac{r-1}{365}\right).$$

Again the numerical consequences are astounding. Thus for $r = 23$ people we have $p < \frac{1}{2}$, that is, *for 23 people the probability that at least two people have a common birthday exceeds* $\frac{1}{2}$.

Formula (3.2) looks forbidding, but it is easy to derive good numerical approximations to p. If r is small, we can neglect all cross products and have in first approximation[6]

$$(3.3) \qquad p \approx 1 - \frac{1 + 2 + \cdots + (r-1)}{365} = 1 - \frac{r(r-1)}{730}.$$

For $r = 10$ the correct value is $p = 0.883 \ldots$ whereas (3.3) gives the approximation 0.877.

For larger r we obtain a much better approximation by passing to logarithms. For small positive x we have $\log(1-x) \approx -x$, and thus from (3.2)

$$(3.4) \qquad \log p \approx -\frac{1 + 2 + \cdots + (r-1)}{365} = -\frac{r(r-1)}{730}.$$

For $r = 30$ this leads to the approximation 0.3037 whereas the correct value is $p = 0.294$. For $r \leq 40$ the error in (3.4) is less than 0.08. (For a continuation see section 7. See also answer to problem 10.44.)

---

[5] Cf. R. von Mises, *Ueber Aufteilungs- und Besetzungs-Wahrscheinlichkeiten*, Revue de la Faculté des Sciences de l'Université d'Istanbul, N. S. vol. 4 (1938–1939), pp. 145–163.

[6] The sign $\approx$ signifies that the equality is only approximate. Products of the form (3.2) occur frequently, and the described method of approximation is of wide use.

4. SUBPOPULATIONS AND PARTITIONS

As before, we use the term *population of size* n to denote an aggregate of n elements *without regard to their order.* Two populations are considered different only if one contains an element not contained in the other.

Consider a subpopulation of size r of a given population consisting of n elements. An arbitrary numbering of the elements of the subpopulation changes it into an ordered sample of size r and, conversely, every such sample can be obtained in this way. Since r elements can be numbered in $r!$ different ways, it follows that there are exactly $r!$ times as many samples as there are subpopulations of size r. The number of subpopulations of size r is therefore given by $(n)_r/r!$. Expressions of this kind are known as *binomial coefficients*, and the standard notation for them is

(4.1)
$$\binom{n}{r} = \frac{(n)_r}{r!} = \frac{n(n-1)\cdots(n-r+1)}{1\cdot 2\cdots(r-1)\cdot r}.$$

We have now proved

Theorem 1. *A population of n elements possesses $\binom{n}{r}$ different subpopulations of size $r \le n$.*

In other words, a subset of r elements can be chosen in $\binom{n}{r}$ different ways. Such a subset is uniquely determined by the $n - r$ elements *not* belonging to it, and these form a subpopulation of size $n - r$. It follows that there are exactly as many subpopulations of size r as there are subpopulations of size $n - r$, and hence for $1 \le r \le n$ we must have

(4.2)
$$\binom{n}{r} = \binom{n}{n-r}.$$

To prove equation (4.2) directly we observe that an alternative way of writing the binomial coefficient (4.1) is

(4.3)
$$\binom{n}{r} = \frac{n!}{r!\,(n-r)!}.$$

[This follows on multiplying numerator and denominator of (4.1) by $(n-r)!$.] Note that the left side in equation (4.2) is not defined for $r = 0$, but the right side is. In order to make equation (4.2) valid for all integers r such that $0 \le r \le n$, *we now define*

(4.4)
$$\binom{n}{0} = 1, \qquad 0! = 1,$$

and $(n)_0 = 1$.

Examples. (a) *Bridge and poker* (cf. footnote 1 of chapter I). The order of the cards in a hand is conventionally disregarded, and hence there exist $\binom{52}{13} = 635{,}013{,}559{,}600$ different hands at bridge, and $\binom{52}{5} = 2{,}598{,}960$ hands at poker. Let us calculate the probability, x, that a hand at poker contains five different face values. These face values can be chosen in $\binom{13}{5}$ ways, and corresponding to each card we are free to choose one of the four suits. It follows that $x = 4^5 \cdot \binom{13}{5} \big/ \binom{52}{5}$, which is approximately 0.5071. For bridge the probability of thirteen different face values is $4^{13} \big/ \binom{52}{13}$ or, approximately, 0.0001057.

(b) Each of the 50 states has two senators. We consider the events that in a committee of 50 senators chosen at random: (1) a given state is represented, (2) all states are represented.

In the first case it is better to calculate the probability q of the complementary event, namely, that the given state is *not* represented. There are 100 senators, and 98 not from the given state. Hence,

$$q = \binom{98}{50} \big/ \binom{100}{50} = \frac{50 \cdot 49}{100 \cdot 99} = 0.24747\ldots.$$

Next, the theorem of section 2 shows that a committee including one senator from each state can be chosen in 2^{50} different ways. The probability that *all* states are included in the committee is, therefore, $p = 2^{50} \big/ \binom{100}{50}$. Using Stirling's formula (cf. section 9), it can be shown that $p \approx \sqrt{2\pi} \cdot 5 \cdot 2^{-50} \approx 4.126 \cdot 10^{-14}$.

(c) *An occupancy problem.* Consider once more a random distribution of r balls in n cells (i.e., each of the n^r possible arrangements has probability n^{-r}). To find the *probability*, p_k, *that a specified cell contains exactly k balls* ($k = 0, 1, \ldots, r$) we note that the k balls can be chosen in $\binom{r}{k}$ ways, and the remaining $r - k$ balls can be placed into the remaining $n - 1$ cells in $(n-1)^{r-k}$ ways. It follows that

$$(4.5) \qquad p_k = \binom{r}{k} \cdot \frac{1}{n^r} \cdot (n-1)^{r-k} = \binom{r}{k} \cdot \frac{1}{n^k} \cdot \left(1 - \frac{1}{n}\right)^{r-k}.$$

This is a special case of the so-called *binomial distribution* which will be taken up in chapter VI. Numerical values will be found in table 3 of chapter IV.   ▶

The distinction between distinguishable and indistinguishable elements has similarities to the relationship between a subpopulation and the corresponding ordered samples. Deleting all subscripts in an arrangement (or grouping) of r elements $a_1, \ldots, a_r$ yields an arrangement of r indistinguishable letters. Conversely, an arbitrary numbering of the r letters in an arrangement of the latter kind produces an arrangement of the letters $a_1, \ldots, a_r$. This procedure yields $r!$ different arrangements provided, of course, that any interchange of a_i and a_k counts as rearrangement. The following examples show how this principle can be applied and extended to situations in which the elements a_k are only partially identified.

Examples. (*d*) *Flags of one or two colors.* In example (1.*f*) it was shown that r flags can be displayed on n poles in $N = n(n+1) \cdots (n+r-1)$ different ways. We now consider the same problem for flags of one color (considered indistinguishable). Numbering the flags of such a display yields exactly $r!$ displays of r distinguishable flags and *hence r flags of the same color can be displayed in $N/r!$ ways.*

Suppose next that p among the flags are red (and indistinguishable) and q are blue (where $p + q = r$). It is easily seen that every display of r numbered flags can be obtained by numbering the red flags from 1 to p and the blue flags from $p + 1$ to $p + q$. It follows that the number of different displays is now $N/(p! \, q!)$.

(*e*) *Orderings involving two kinds of elements.* Let us consider the number of sequences of length $p + q$ consisting of p alphas and q betas. Numbering the alphas from 1 to p and the betas from $p + 1$ to $p + q$ yields an ordered sequence of $p + q$ distinguishable elements. There are $(p+q)!$ such sequences, and exactly $p! \, q!$ among them correspond to the same ordering of alphas and betas. Accordingly, *p alphas and q betas can be arranged in exactly*

$$\frac{(p+q)!}{p! \, q!} = \binom{p+q}{p} = \binom{p+q}{q}$$

distinguishable ways.

The same result follows directly from theorem 1 and the fact that all orderings of p alphas and q betas can be obtained by choosing p among $p + q$ available places and assigning them to the alphas.

(*f*) The number of shortest polygonal paths (with horizontal and vertical segments) joining two diagonally opposite vertices of a chessboard equals $\binom{16}{8} = 12{,}870$.   ▶

Theorem 2. *Let* $r_1, \ldots, r_k$ *be integers such that*

$$(4.6) \qquad r_1 + r_2 + \cdots + r_k = n, \qquad\qquad r_i \geq 0.$$

The number of ways in which a population of n *elements can be divided into* k *ordered parts (partitioned into* k *subpopulations) of which the first contains* r_1 *elements, the second* r_2 *elements, etc., is*

$$(4.7) \qquad\qquad \frac{n!}{r_1!\, r_2! \cdots r_k!}.$$

[The numbers (4.7) are called *multinomial coefficients*.]

Note that the order of the subpopulations is essential in the sense that $(r_1 = 2, r_2 = 3)$ and $(r_1 = 3, r_2 = 2)$ represent different partitions; however, no attention is paid to the order within the groups. Note also that $0! = 1$ so that the vanishing r_i in no way affect formula (4.7). Since it is permitted that $r_i = 0$, the n elements are divided into k *or fewer* subpopulations. The case $r_i > 0$ of partitions into *exactly* k classes is treated in problem 11.7.

Proof. A repeated use of (4.3) will show that the number (4.7) may be rewritten in the form

$$(4.8) \qquad \binom{n}{r_1}\binom{n-r_1}{r_2}\binom{n-r_1-r_2}{r_3} \cdots \binom{n-r_1-\cdots-r_{k-2}}{r_{k-1}}$$

On the other hand, in order to effect the desired partition, we have first to select r_1 elements out of the given n; of the remaining $n - r_1$ elements we select a second group of size r_2, etc. After forming the $(k-1)$st group there remain $n - r_1 - r_2 - \cdots - r_{k-1} = r_k$ elements, and these form the last group. We conclude that (4.8) indeed represents the number of ways in which the operation can be performed. ▶

Examples. (*g*) *Bridge.* At a bridge table the 52 cards are partitioned into four equal groups and therefore the number of different situations is $52! \cdot (13!)^{-4} = (5.36\ldots) \cdot 10^{28}$. Let us now calculate the probability that each player has an ace. The four aces can be ordered in $4! = 24$ ways, and each order represents one possibility of giving one ace to each player. The remaining 48 cards can be distributed in $(48!)(12!)^{-4}$ ways. Hence the required probability is $24 \cdot 48! \cdot (13!)^4/52! = 0.105 \ldots$.

(*h*) *Dice.* A throw of twelve dice can result in 6^{12} different outcomes, to all of which we attribute equal probabilities. The event that each face appears twice can occur in as many ways as twelve dice can be arranged in six groups of two each. Hence the probability of the event is $12!/(2^6 \cdot 6^{12}) = 0.003438 \ldots$.

*5. APPLICATION TO OCCUPANCY PROBLEMS

The examples of chapter I, 2, indicate the wide applicability of the model of placing randomly r balls into n cells. In many situations it is necessary to treat the balls as *indistinguishable*. For example, in statistical studies of the distribution of accidents among weekdays, or of birthdays among calendar days, one is interested only in the number of occurrences, and not in the individuals involved. Again, throwing r dice is equivalent to a placement of r balls into $n = 6$ cells. Although it would be possible to keep track of the r individual results, one prefers usually to specify only the numbers of aces, twos, etc. In such situations we may still suppose the balls numbered, but we focus our attention on events that are independent of the numbering. Such an event is completely described by its *occupancy numbers* $r_1, r_2, \ldots, r_n$, where r_k stands for the number of balls in the kth cell. Every n-tuple of integers satisfying

$$(5.1) \qquad\qquad r_1 + r_2 + \cdots + r_n = r, \qquad\qquad r_k \geq 0$$

describes a possible configuration of occupancy numbers. *With indistinguishable balls two distributions are distinguishable only if the corresponding n-tuples $(r_1, \ldots, r_n)$ are not identical.* We now prove that:

(i) *The number of distinguishable distributions [i.e. the number of different solutions of equation (5.1)] is*[7]

$$(5.2) \qquad\qquad A_{r,n} = \binom{n+r-1}{r} = \binom{n+r-1}{n-1}.$$

(ii) *The number of distinguishable distributions in which no cell remains empty is* $\binom{r-1}{n-1}$.

Proof. We represent the balls by stars and indicate the n cells by the n spaces between $n + 1$ bars. Thus $| *** | * | | | | **** |$ is used as a symbol for a distribution of $r = 8$ balls in $n = 6$ cells with occupancy numbers 3, 1, 0, 0, 0, 4. Such a symbol necessarily starts and ends with a bar, but the remaining $n - 1$ bars and r stars can appear in an arbitrary order. In this way it becomes apparent that the number of distinguishable distributions equals the number of ways of selecting r places out of $n + r - 1$, namely $A_{r,n}$.

---

* The material of this section is useful and illuminating but will not be used explicitly in the sequel.

[7] The special case $r = 100$, $n = 4$ has been used in example I, (2.e).

The condition that no cell be empty imposes the restriction that no two bars be adjacent. The r stars leave $r - 1$ spaces of which $n - 1$ are to be occupied by bars: thus we have $\binom{r-1}{n-1}$ choices and the assertion is proved.   ▶

Examples. (a) There are $\binom{r+5}{5}$ distinguishable results of a throw with r indistinguishable dice.

(b) *Partial derivatives.* The partial derivatives of order r of an analytic function $f(x_1, \ldots, x_n)$ of n variables do not depend on the order of differentiation but only on the number of times that each variable appears. Thus each variable corresponds to a cell, and hence *there exist* $\binom{n+r-1}{r}$ *different partial derivatives of rth order.* A function of three variables has fifteen derivatives of fourth order and 21 derivatives of fifth order.   ▶

Consider now n fixed integers satisfying (5.1). The number of placements of r balls in n cells resulting in the occupancy numbers $r_1, \ldots, r_n$ is given by theorem 4.2. Assuming that all n^r possible placements are equally probable, *the probability to obtain the given occupancy numbers* $r_1, \ldots, r_n$ *equals*

$$(5.3) \qquad \frac{r!}{r_1! \, r_2! \cdots r_n!} \, n^{-r}.$$

This assignment of probabilities was used in all applications mentioned so far, and it used to be taken for granted that it is inherent to the intuitive notion of randomness. No alternative assignment has ever been suggested on probabilistic or intuitive grounds. It is therefore of considerable methodological interest that *experience* compelled physicists to replace the distribution (5.3) by others which originally came as a shock to intuition. This will be discussed in the next subsection. [In physics (5.3) is known as the *Maxwell-Boltzmann* distribution.]

In various connections it is necessary to go a step farther and to consider the cells themselves as indistinguishable; this amounts to disregarding the order among the occupancy numbers. The following example is intended to explain a routine method of solving problems arising in this way.

Example. (c) *Configurations of $r = 7$ balls in $n = 7$ cells.* (The cells may be interpreted as days of the week, the balls as calls, letters, accidents, etc.) For the sake of definiteness let us consider the distributions with occupancy numbers 2, 2, 1, 1, 1, 0, 0 *appearing in an arbitrary order.* These seven occupancy numbers induce a partition of the *seven cells* into three subpopulations (categories) consisting, respectively, of the two doubly occupied, the three singly occupied, and the two empty cells. Such a partition into three groups of size 2, 3, and 2 can be effected in $7! \div (2! \cdot 3! \cdot 2!)$

ways. To each particular assignment of our occupancy numbers to the seven cells there correspond $7! \div (2! \cdot 2! \cdot 1! \cdot 1! \cdot 1! \cdot 0! \cdot 0!) = 7! \div (2! \cdot 2!)$ different distributions of the $r = 7$ balls into the seven cells. Accordingly, *the total number of distributions such that the occupancy numbers coincide with* 2, 2, 1, 1, 1, 0, 0 *in some order is*

$$(5.4) \qquad \frac{7!}{2!\,3!\,2!} \times \frac{7!}{2!\,2!}.$$

It will be noticed that this result has been derived by a *double application of* (4.7), namely to balls and to cells. The same result can be derived and rewritten in many ways,

TABLE 1

RANDOM DISTRIBUTIONS OF 7 BALLS IN 7 CELLS

Occupancy numbers	Number of arrangements equals $7! \times 7!$ divided by	Probability (number of arrangements divided by 7^7)
1, 1, 1, 1, 1, 1, 1	$7! \times 1!$	0.006 120
2, 1, 1, 1, 1, 1, 0	$5! \times 2!$	0.128 518
2, 2, 1, 1, 1, 0, 0	$2!\,3!\,2! \times 2!\,2!$	0.321 295
2, 2, 2, 1, 0, 0, 0	$3!\,3! \times 2!\,2!\,2!$	0.107 098
3, 1, 1, 1, 1, 0, 0	$4!\,2! \times 3!$	0.107 098
3, 2, 1, 1, 0, 0, 0	$2!\,3! \times 3!\,2!$	0.214 197
3, 2, 2, 0, 0, 0, 0	$2!\,4! \times 3!\,2!\,2!$	0.026 775
3, 3, 1, 0, 0, 0, 0	$2!\,4! \times 3!\,3!$	0.017 850
4, 1, 1, 1, 0, 0, 0	$3!\,3! \times 4!$	0.035 699
4, 2, 1, 0, 0, 0, 0	$4! \times 4!\,2!$	0.026 775
4, 3, 0, 0, 0, 0, 0	$5! \times 4!\,3!$	0.001 785
5, 1, 1, 0, 0, 0, 0	$2!\,4! \times 5!$	0.005 355
5, 2, 0, 0, 0, 0, 0	$5! \times 5!\,2!$	0.001 071
6, 1, 0, 0, 0, 0, 0	$5! \times 6!$	0.000 357
7, 0, 0, 0, 0, 0, 0	$6! \times 7!$	0.000 008

but the present method provides the simplest routine technique for a great variety of problems. (Cf. problems 43–45 of section 10.) Table 1 contains the analogue to (5.4) and the probabilities for all possible configurations of occupancy numbers in the case $r = n = 7$.   ▶

(a) Bose-Einstein and Fermi-Dirac statistics

Consider a mechanical system of r indistinguishable particles. In statistical mechanics it is usual to subdivide the phase space into a large number, n, of small regions or cells so that each particle is assigned to one cell. In this way the state of the entire system is described in terms of a random distribution of the r particles in n cells. Offhand it would seem that (at least with an appropriate definition of the n cells) all n^r arrangements should have equal probabilities. If this is true, the physicist speaks of *Maxwell-Boltzmann statistics* (the term "statistics" is here used in a sense peculiar to physics). Numerous attempts have been made to prove that physical particles behave to accordance with Maxwell-Boltzmann statistics, but modern theory has shown beyond doubt that this statistics *does not apply to any known particles;* in no case are all n^r arrangements approximately equally probable. Two different probability models have been introduced, and each describes satisfactorily the behavior of one type of particle. The justification of either model depends on its success. Neither claims universality, and it is possible that some day a third model may be introduced for certain kinds of particles.

Remember that we are here concerned only with *indistinguishable* particles. We have r particles and n cells. *By Bose-Einstein statistics we mean that only distinguishable arrangements are considered and that each is assigned probability* $1/A_{r,n}$ with $A_{r,n}$ defined in (5.2). It is shown in statistical mechanics that this assumption holds true for photons, nuclei, and atoms containing an even number of elementary particles.[8] To describe other particles a third possible assignment of probabilities must be introduced. *Fermi-Dirac statistics* is based on these hypotheses: (1) *it is impossible for two or more particles to be in the same cell, and* (2) *all distinguishable arrangements satisfying the first condition have equal probabilities.* The first hypothesis requires that $r \leq n$. An arrangement is then completely described by stating which of the n cells contain a particle; and since there are r particles, the corresponding cells can be chosen in $\binom{n}{r}$ ways. Hence, with *Fermi-Dirac statistics there are in all* $\binom{n}{r}$ *possible arrangements, each having probability* $\binom{n}{r}^{-1}$. This model applies to electrons, neutrons, and protons. We have here an instructive example of the impossibility of selecting or justifying probability models by *a priori* arguments. In fact, no pure reasoning could tell that photons and protons would not obey the same probability laws. (Essential differences between Maxwell-Boltzmann and Bose-Einstein statistics are discussed in section 11, problems 14–19.)

To sum up: *the probability that cells number* $1, 2, \ldots, n$ *contain* $r_1, r_2, \ldots, r_n$ *balls, respectively (where* $r_1 + \cdots + r_n = r$) *is given by* (5.3) *under Maxwell-Boltzmann statistics; it is given by* $1/A_{r,n}$ *under Bose-Einstein statistics; and it equals* $\binom{n}{r}^{-1}$ *under Fermi-Dirac statistics provided each* r_j *equals 0 or 1.*

---

[8] Cf. H. Margenau and G. M. Murphy, *The mathematics of physics and chemistry*, New York (Van Nostrand), 1943, Chapter 12.

Examples. (a) Let $n = 5$, $r = 3$. The arrangement $(*\mid-\mid*\mid*\mid-)$ has probability $\frac{6}{125}$, $\frac{1}{35}$, or $\frac{1}{10}$, according to whether Maxwell-Boltzmann, Bose-Einstein, or Fermi-Dirac statistics is used. See also example I, (6.b).

(b) *Misprints.* A book contains n symbols (letters), of which r are misprinted. The distribution of misprints corresponds to a distribution of r balls in n cells with no cell containing more than one ball. It is therefore reasonable to suppose that, approximately, *the misprints obey the Fermi-Dirac statistics.* (Cf. problem 10.38.)   ▶

(b) Application to Runs

In any ordered sequence of elements of two kinds, each maximal subsequence of elements of like kind is called *a run.* For example, the sequence $\alpha\alpha\alpha\beta\alpha\alpha\beta\beta\beta\alpha$ opens with an alpha run of length 3; it is followed by runs of length 1, 2, 3, 1, respectively. The alpha and beta runs alternate so that the total number of runs is always one plus the number of conjunctions of *unlike neighbors* in the given sequence.

Examples of applications. The theory of runs is applied in statistics in many ways, but its principal uses are connected with tests of randomness or tests of homogeneity.

(a) In *testing randomness*, the problem is to decide whether a given observation is attributable to chance or whether a search for assignable causes is indicated. As a simple example suppose that an observation[9] yielded the following arrangement of empty and occupied seats along a lunch counter: *EOEEOEEEOEEEOEOE*. Note that no two occupied seats are adjacent. Can this be due to chance? With five occupied and eleven empty seats it is impossible to get more than eleven runs, and this number was actually observed. It will be shown later that if all arrangements were equally probable the probability of eleven runs would be 0.0578 . . . . This small probability to some extent confirms the hunch that the separations observed were intentional. This suspicion cannot be proved by statistical methods, but further evidence could be collected from continued observation. If the lunch counter were frequented by families, there would be a tendency for occupants to cluster together, and this would lead to relatively small numbers of runs. Similarly counting runs of boys and girls in a class-room might disclose the mixing to be better or worse than random. Improbable arrange-ments give clues to assignable causes; *an excess of runs points to intentional mixing, a paucity of runs to intentional clustering.* It is true that these conclusions are never foolproof, but efficient statistical techniques have been developed which in actual practice minimize the risk of incorrect conclusions.

The theory of runs is also useful in industrial quality control as introduced by Shewhart. As washers are produced, they will vary in thickness. Long runs of thick washers may suggest imperfections in the production process and lead to the removal of the causes; thus oncoming trouble may be forestalled and greater homogeneity of product achieved.

In biological field experiments successions of healthy and diseased plants are counted,

---

[9] F. S. Swed and C. Eisenhart, *Tables for testing randomness of grouping in a sequence of alternatives,* Ann. Math. Statist., vol. 14 (1943), pp. 66–87.

and long runs are suggestive of contagion. The meteorologist watches successions of dry and wet months[10] to discover clues to a tendency of the weather to persist.

(*b*) To understand a typical problem of *homogeneity*, suppose that two drugs have been applied to two sets of patients, or that we are interested in comparing the efficiency of two treatments (medical, agricultural, or industrial). In practice, we shall have two sets of observations, say, $\alpha_1, \alpha_2, \ldots, \alpha_a$ and $\beta_1, \beta_2, \ldots, \beta_b$ corresponding to the two treatments or representing a certain characteristic (such as weight) of the elements of two populations. The alphas and betas are *numbers* which we imagine ordered in increasing order of magnitude: $\alpha_1 \leq \alpha_2 \leq \cdots \leq \alpha_a$ and $\beta_1 \leq \beta_2 \leq \cdots \leq \beta_b$. We now pool the two sets into one sequence ordered according to magnitude. An extreme case is that all alphas precede all betas, and this may be taken as indicative of a significant difference between the two treatments or populations. On the other hand, if the two treatments are identical, the alphas and betas should appear more or less in random order. Wald and Wolfowitz[11] have shown that the theory of runs can be often advantageously applied to discover small systematic differences. (An illustrative example, but treated by a different method, will be found in III, 1.*b*.)   ▶

Many problems concerning runs can be solved in an exceedingly simple manner. Given *a* indistinguishable alphas and *b* indistinguishable betas, we know from example (4.*e*) that there are $\binom{a+b}{a}$ distinguishable orderings. If there are n_1 alpha runs, the number of beta runs is necessarily one of the numbers $n_1 \pm 1$ or n_1. Arranging the *a* alphas in n_1 runs is equivalent to arranging them into n_1 cells, none of which is empty. By the last lemma this can be done in $\binom{a-1}{n_1-1}$ distinguishable ways. It follows, for example, that there are $\binom{a-1}{n_1-1}\binom{b-1}{n_1}$ arrangements with n_1 alpha runs and n_1+1 beta runs (continued in problems 20–25 of section 11).

(*c*) In physics, the theory of runs is used in the study of cooperative phenomena. In Ising's theory of one-dimensional lattices the energy depends on the number of unlike neighbors, that is, the number of runs.   ▶

6. THE HYPERGEOMETRIC DISTRIBUTION

Many combinatorial problems can be reduced to the following form. In a population of n elements n_1 are red and $n_2 = n - n_1$ are black. A group of r elements is chosen at random. We seek the probability q_k that the group so chosen will contain exactly k red elements. Here k can be any integer between zero and n_1 or r, whichever is smaller.

To find q_k, we note that the chosen group contains k red and $r - k$

---

[10] W. G. Cochran, *An extension of Gold's method of examining the apparent persistence of one type of weather*, Quarterly Journal of the Royal Meteorological Society, vol. 64, No. 277 (1938), pp. 631–634.

[11] A. Wald and J. Wolfowitz, *On a test whether two samples are from the same population*, Ann. Math. Statist., vol. 2 (1940), pp. 147–162.

black elements. The red ones can be chosen in $\binom{n_1}{k}$ different ways and the black ones in $\binom{n-n_1}{r-k}$ ways. Since any choice of k red elements may be combined with any choice of black ones, we find

$$(6.1) \qquad q_k = \frac{\binom{n_1}{k}\binom{n-n_1}{r-k}}{\binom{n}{r}}.$$

The system of probabilities so defined is called the *hypergeometric distribution*.[12] Using (4.3), it is possible to rewrite (6.1) in the form

$$(6.2) \qquad q_k = \frac{\binom{r}{k}\binom{n-r}{n_1-k}}{\binom{n}{n_1}}.$$

Note. The probabilities q_k are defined only for k not exceeding r or n_1, but since $\binom{a}{b} = 0$ whenever $b > a$, formulas (6.1) and (6.2) give $q_k = 0$ if either $k > n_1$ or $k > r$. Accordingly, the definitions (6.1) and (6.2) may be used for all $k \geq 0$, provided the relation $q_k = 0$ is interpreted as impossibility.

Examples. (a) *Quality inspection.* In industrial quality control, lots of size n are subjected to sampling inspection. The defective items in the lot play the role of "red" elements. Their number n_1 is, of course, unknown. A sample of size r is taken, and the number k of defective items in it is determined. Formula (6.1) then permits us to draw inferences about the likely magnitude of n_1; this is a typical problem of statistical estimation, but is beyond the scope of the present book.

(b) In example (4.b), the population consists of $n = 100$ senators of whom $n_1 = 2$ represent the given state (are "red"). A group of $r = 50$ senators is chosen at random. It may include $k = 0, 1,$ or 2 senators from the given state. From (6.2) we find, remembering (4.4),

$$q_0 = q_2 = \frac{50 \cdot 49}{100 \cdot 99} = 0.24747 \ldots, \qquad q_1 = \frac{50}{99} = 0.50505 \ldots.$$

The value q_0 was obtained in a different way in example (4.b).

---

[12] The name is explained by the fact that the generating function (cf. chapter XI) of $\{q_k\}$ can be expressed in terms of hypergeometric functions.

(*c*) *Estimation of the size of an animal population from recapture data.*[13]
Suppose that 1000 fish caught in a lake are marked by red spots and
released. After a while a new catch of 1000 fish is made, and it is found
that 100 among them have red spots. What conclusions can be drawn
concerning the number of fish in the lake? This is a typical problem of
statistical estimation. It would lead us too far to describe the various
methods that a modern statistician might use, but we shall show how the
hypergeometric distribution gives us a clue to the solution of the problem.
We assume naturally that the two catches may be considered as random
samples from the population of all fish in the lake. (In practice this
assumption excludes situations where the two catches are made at one
locality and within a short time.) We also suppose that the number of fish
in the lake does not change between the two catches.

We generalize the problem by admitting arbitrary sample sizes. Let

n = the (unknown) number of fish in the lake.

n_1 = the number of fish in the first catch. They play the role of red balls.

r = the number of fish in the second catch.

k = the number of red fish in the second catch.

$q_k(n)$ = the probability that the second catch contains exactly k red fish.

In this formulation it is rather obvious that $q_k(n)$ is given by (6.1).
In practice n_1, r, and k can be observed, but n is unknown. Notice that
we consider n as an unknown fixed number which in no way depends on
chance. We know that $n_1 + r - k$ different fish were caught, and therefore
$n \geq n_1 + r - k$. This is all that can be said with certainty. In our
example we had $n_1 = r = 1000$ and $k = 100$; it is conceivable that the
lake contains only 1900 fish, but starting from this hypothesis, we are
led to the conclusion that an event of a fantastically small probability
has occurred. In fact, assuming that there are $n = 1900$ fish in all, the
probability that two samples of size 1000 each will between them exhaust
the entire population is by (6.1),

$$\binom{1000}{100}\binom{900}{900}\binom{1900}{1000}^{-1} = \frac{(1000!)^2}{100!\ 1900!}.$$

---

[13] This example was used in the first edition without knowledge that the method is
widely used in practice. Newer contributions to the literature include N. T. J. Bailey,
On estimating the size of mobile populations from recapture data, Biometrika, vol. 38
(1951), pp. 293–306, and D. G. Chapman, *Some properties of the hypergeometric
distribution with applications to zoological sample censuses*, University of California
Publications in Statistics, vol. 1 (1951), pp. 131–160.

Stirling's formula (cf. section 9) shows this probability to be of the order of magnitude 10^{-430}, and in this situation common sense bids us to reject our hypothesis as unreasonable. A similar reasoning would induce us to reject the hypothesis that n is very large, say, a million. This consideration leads us to seek the particular value of n for which $q_k(n)$ attains its largest value, since for that n our observation would have the greatest probability. For any particular set of observations n_1, r, k, the value of n for which $q_k(n)$ is largest is denoted by $\hat{n}$ and is called the *maximum likelihood estimate* of n. This notion was introduced by R. A. Fisher. To find $\hat{n}$ consider the ratio

$$(6.3) \qquad \frac{q_k(n)}{q_k(n-1)} = \frac{(n-n_1)(n-r)}{(n-n_1-r+k)n}.$$

A simple calculation shows that this ratio is greater than or smaller than unity, according as $nk < n_1r$ or $nk > n_1r$. This means that with increasing n the sequence $q_k(n)$ first increases and then decreases; it reaches its maximum when n is the largest integer short of n_1r/k, so that $\hat{n}$ equals about n_1r/k. In our particular example the maximum likelihood estimate of the number of fish is $\hat{n} = 10,000$.

The true number n may be larger or smaller, and we may ask for limits within which we may reasonably expect n to lie. For this purpose let us test the hypothesis that n is smaller than 8500. We substitute in (6.1) $n = 8500$, $n_1 = r = 1000$, and calculate the probability that the second sample contains 100 or fewer red fish. This probability is $x = q_0 + q_1 + \cdots + q_{100}$. A direct evaluation is cumbersome, but using the normal approximation of chapter VII, we find easily that $x = 0.04$. Similarly, if $n = 12,000$, the probability that the second sample contains 100 or more red fish is about 0.03. These figures would justify a bet that the true number n of fish lies somewhere between 8500 and 12,000. There exist other ways of formulating these conclusions and other methods of estimation, but we do not propose to discuss the details.   ▶

From the definition of the probabilities q_k it follows that

$$q_0 + q_1 + q_2 + \cdots = 1.$$

Formula (6.2) therefore implies that for any positive integers n, n_1, r

$$(6.4) \qquad \binom{r}{0}\binom{n-r}{n_1} + \binom{r}{1}\binom{n-r}{n_1-1} + \cdots + \binom{r}{n_1}\binom{n-r}{0} = \binom{n}{n_1}.$$

This identity is frequently useful. We have proved it only for positive integers n and r, but it holds true without this restriction for arbitrary positive or negative numbers n and r (it is meaningless if n_1 is not a positive integer). (An indication of two proofs is given in section 12, problems 8 and 9.)

The hypergeometric distribution can easily be generalized to the case where the original population of size n contains several classes of elements. For example, let the population contain three classes of sizes n_1, n_2, and $n - n_1 - n_2$, respectively. If a sample of size r is taken, the probability that it contains k_1 elements of the first, k_2 elements of the second, and $r - k_1 - k_2$ elements of the last class is, by analogy with (6.1),

$$(6.5) \qquad \binom{n_1}{k_1}\binom{n_2}{k_2}\binom{n-n_1-n_2}{r-k_1-k_2}\Big/\binom{n}{r}.$$

It is, of course, necessary that

$$k_1 \le n_1, \qquad k_2 \le n_2, \qquad r - k_1 - k_2 \le n - n_1 - n_2.$$

Example. (*d*) *Bridge.* The population of 52 cards consists of four classes, each of thirteen elements. The probability that a hand of thirteen cards consists of five spades, four hearts, three diamonds, and one club is

$$\binom{13}{5}\binom{13}{4}\binom{13}{3}\binom{13}{1}\Big/\binom{52}{13}. \qquad\blacktriangleright$$

7. EXAMPLES FOR WAITING TIMES

In this section we shall depart from the straight path of combinatorial analysis in order to consider some sample spaces of a novel type to which we are led by a simple variation of our occupancy problems. Consider once more the conceptual "experiment" of placing balls randomly into n cells. This time, however, we do not fix in advance the number r of balls but let the balls be placed one by one as long as necessary for a prescribed situation to arise. Two such possible situations will be discussed explicitly: (i) *The random placing of balls continues until for the first time a ball is placed into a cell already occupied.* The process terminates when the first duplication of this type occurs. (ii) *We fix a cell* (*say cell number* 1) *and continue the procedure of placing balls as long as this cell remains empty.* The process terminates when a ball is placed into the prescribed cell.

A few interpretations of this model will elucidate the problem.

Examples. (*a*) *Birthdays.* In the birthday example (3.*d*), the $n = 365$ days of the year correspond to cells, and people to balls. Our model (i) now amounts to this: If we select people at random one by one, how many people shall we have to sample in order to find a pair with a common birthday? Model (ii) corresponds to waiting for *my* birthday to turn up in the sample.

(*b*) *Key problem.* A man wants to open his door. He has n keys, of which only one fits the door. For reasons which can only be surmised, he tries the keys at random so that at each try each key has probability n^{-1} of being tried and all possible outcomes involving the same number of trials are equally likely. What is the probability that the man will succeed exactly at the rth trial? This is a special case of model (ii). It is interesting to compare this random search for the key with a more systematic approach (problem 11 of section 10; see also problem 5 in V, 8).

(*c*) In the preceding example we can replace the sampling of keys by a sampling from an arbitrary population, say by the *collecting of coupons*. Again we ask when the first duplication is to be expected and when a prescribed element will show up for the first time.

(*d*) *Coins and dice.* In example I, (5.*a*) a coin is tossed as often as necessary to turn up one head. This is a special case of model (ii) with $n = 2$. When a die is thrown until an ace turns up for the first time, the same question applies with $n = 6$. (Other waiting times are treated in problems 21, 22, and 36 of section 10, and 12 of section 11.)   ▶

We begin with the conceptually simpler model (i). It is convenient to use symbols of the form $(j_1, j_2, \ldots, j_r)$ to indicate that the first, second, ..., rth ball are placed in cells number $j_1, j_2, \ldots, j_r$ and that the process terminates at the rth step. This means that the j_i are integers between 1 and n; furthermore, $j_1, \ldots, j_{r-1}$ are all different, but j_r equals one among them. Every arrangement of this type represents a sample point. For r only the values $2, 3, \ldots, n + 1$ are possible, since a doubly occupied cell cannot appear before the second ball or after the $(n+1)$st ball is placed. The connection of our present problem with the old model of placing a fixed number of balls into the n cells leads us to attribute to each sample point $(j_1, \ldots, j_r)$ involving exactly r balls the probability n^{-r}. We proceed to show that this convention is permissible (i.e., that our probabilities add to unity) and that it leads to reasonable results.

For a fixed r the aggregate of all sample points $(j_1, \ldots, j_r)$ represents *the event that the process terminates at the rth step.* According to (2.1) the numbers $j_1, \ldots, j_{r-1}$ can be chosen in $(n)_{r-1}$ different ways; for j_r we have the choice of the $r - 1$ numbers $j_1, \ldots, j_{r-1}$. It follows that *the probability of the process terminating at the rth step is*

$$(7.1) \qquad q_r = \frac{(n)_{r-1} \cdot (r-1)}{n^r} = \left(1 - \frac{1}{n}\right) \cdots \left(1 - \frac{r-2}{n}\right) \cdot \frac{r-1}{n},$$

with $q_1 = 0$ and $q_2 = 1/n$. The probability that the process lasts for more *than r steps is* $p_r = 1 - (q_1 + q_2 + \cdots + q_r)$ *or* $p_1 = 1$ *and*

(7.2) $$p_r = \frac{(n)_r}{n^r} = \left(1 - \frac{1}{n}\right) \cdots \left(1 - \frac{r-1}{n}\right)$$

as can be seen by simple induction. In particular, $p_{n+1} = 0$ and $q_1 + \cdots + q_{n+1} = 1$, as is proper. Furthermore, when $n = 365$, formula (7.2) reduces to (3.2), and in general our new model leads to the same quantitative results as the previous model involving a fixed number of balls.

The model (ii) differs from (i) in that it depends on *an infinite sample space.* The sequences $(j_1, \ldots, j_r)$ are now subjected to the condition that the numbers $j_1, \ldots, j_{r-1}$ are different from a prescribed number $a \le n$, but $j_r = a$. Moreover, there is no a priori reason why the process should ever terminate. For a fixed r we attribute again to each sample point of the form $(j_1, \ldots, j_r)$ probability n^{-r}. For $j_1, \ldots, j_{r-1}$ we have $n - 1$ choices each, and for j_r no choice at all. For *the probability that the process terminates at the rth step* we get therefore

(7.3) $$q_r^* = \left(\frac{n-1}{n}\right)^{r-1} \cdot \frac{1}{n}, \qquad\qquad r = 1, 2, \ldots.$$

Summing this geometric series we find $q_1^* + q_2^* + \cdots = 1$. Thus the probabilities add to unity, and there is no necessity of introducing a sample point to represent the possibility that no ball will ever be placed into the prescribed cell number a. For *the probability*

$$p_r^* = 1 - (q_1^* + \cdots + q_r^*)$$

that the process lasts for more than r steps we get

(7.4) $$p_r^* = \left(1 - \frac{1}{n}\right)^r, \qquad\qquad r = 1, 2, \ldots$$

as was to be expected.

The median for the distribution $\{p_r\}$ *is that value of r for which* $p_1 + \ldots + p_{r-1} \le \frac{1}{2}$ *but* $p_1 + \ldots + p_r > \frac{1}{2}$; it is about as likely that the process continues beyond the median as that it stops before. [In the *birthday* example (3.d) the median is $r = 23$.] To calculate the median for $\{p_r\}$ we pass to logarithms as we did in (3.4). When r is small as compared to n, we see that $-\log p_r$ is close to $r^2/2n$. It follows that *the median to* $\{p_r\}$ *is close to* $\sqrt{n \cdot 2 \cdot \log 2}$ or approximately $\frac{6}{5}\sqrt{n}$. It is interesting that the median increases with the square root of the population size. By contrast, *the median for* $\{p_r^*\}$ *is close to* $n \cdot \log 2$ or $0.7n$ and increases linearly with n. The probability of the waiting time in model (ii) to exceed n is $(1 - n^{-1})^n$ or, approximately, $e^{-1} = 0.36788 \ldots$.

8. BINOMIAL COEFFICIENTS

We have used binomial coefficients $\binom{n}{r}$ only when n is a positive integer, but it is very convenient to extend their definition. The number $(x)_r$ introduced in equation (2.1), namely

$$(8.1) \qquad (x)_r = x(x-1) \cdots (x-r+1)$$

is well defined for all real x provided only that r is a positive integer. For $r = 0$ we put $(x)_0 = 1$. Then

$$(8.2) \qquad \binom{x}{r} = \frac{(x)_r}{r!} = \frac{x(x-1) \cdots (x-r+1)}{r!}$$

defines the binomial coefficients for all values of x and all positive integers r. For $r = 0$ we put, as in (4.4), $\binom{x}{0} = 1$ and $0! = 1$. For negative integers r we define

$$(8.3) \qquad \binom{x}{r} = 0, \qquad\qquad\qquad r < 0.$$

We shall never use the symbol $\binom{x}{r}$ if r is not an integer.

It is easily verified that with this definition we have, for example,

$$(8.4) \qquad \binom{-1}{r} = (-1)^r \qquad \binom{-2}{r} = (-1)^r (r+1).$$

Three important properties will be used in the sequel. First, for *any positive integer n*

$$(8.5) \qquad \binom{n}{r} = 0 \qquad \text{if either} \quad r > n \quad \text{or} \quad r < 0.$$

Second, *for any number x and any integer r*

$$(8.6) \qquad \binom{x}{r-1} + \binom{x}{r} = \binom{x+1}{r}.$$

These relations are easily verified from the definition. The proof of the next relation can be found in calculus textbooks: *for any number a and* *all values* $-1 < t < 1$, *we have Newton's binomial formula*

(8.7) $$(1+t)^a = 1 + \binom{a}{1}t + \binom{a}{2}t^2 + \binom{a}{3}t^3 + \cdots.$$

If a is a positive integer, all terms to the right containing powers higher than t^a vanish automatically and the formula is correct for all t. If a is not a positive integer, the right side represents an *infinite* series.

Using (8.4), we see that for $a = -1$ the expansion (8.7) reduces to the *geometric series*

(8.8) $$\frac{1}{1+t} = 1 - t + t^2 - t^3 + t^4 - + \cdots.$$

Integrating (8.8), we obtain another formula which will be useful in the sequel, namely, the *Taylor expansion of the natural logarithm*

(8.9) $$\log(1+t) = t - \tfrac{1}{2}t^2 + \tfrac{1}{3}t^3 - \tfrac{1}{4}t^4 + \cdots.$$

Two alternative forms for (8.9) are frequently used. Replacing t by $-t$ we get

(8.10) $$\log\frac{1}{1-t} = t + \tfrac{1}{2}t^2 + \tfrac{1}{3}t^3 + \tfrac{1}{4}t^4 + \cdots.$$

Adding the last two formulas we find

(8.11) $$\tfrac{1}{2}\log\frac{1+t}{1-t} = t + \tfrac{1}{3}t^3 + \tfrac{1}{5}t^5 + \cdots.$$

All these expansions are valid only for $-1 < t < 1$.

Section 12 contains many useful relations derived from (8.7). Here we mention only that when $a = n$ is an integer and $t = 1$, then (8.7) reduces to

(8.12) $$\binom{n}{0} + \binom{n}{1} + \binom{n}{2} + \cdots + \binom{n}{n} = 2^n.$$

This formula admits of a simple combinatorial interpretation: The left side represents the number of ways in which a population of n elements can be divided into two subpopulations if the size of the first group is permitted to be any number $k = 0, 1, \ldots, n$. On the other hand, such a division can be effected directly by deciding for each element whether it is to belong to the first or second group. [A similar argument shows that the multinomial coefficients (4.7) add to k^n.]

9. STIRLING'S FORMULA

An important tool of analytical probability theory is contained in a classical theorem[14] known as

Stirling's formula:

$$(9.1) \qquad n! \sim \sqrt{2\pi}\, n^{n+\frac{1}{2}} e^{-n}$$

where the sign $\sim$ is used to indicate that the ratio of the two sides tends to unity as $n \to \infty$.

This formula is invaluable for many theoretical purposes and can be used also to obtain excellent numerical approximations. It is true that the difference of the two sides in (9.1) increases over all bounds, but it is the percentage error which really matters. It decreases steadily, and Stirling's approximation is remarkably accurate even for small n. In fact, the right side of (9.1) approximates $1!$ by 0.9221 and $2!$ by 1.919 and $5! = 120$ by 118.019. The percentage errors are 8 and 4 and 2, respectively. For $10! = 3,628,800$ the approximation is 3,598,600 with an error of 0.8 per cent. For $100!$ the error is only 0.08 per cent.

Proof of Stirling's formula. Our first problem is to derive some sort of estimate for

$$(9.2) \qquad \log n! = \log 1 + \log 2 + \cdots + \log n.$$

Since $\log x$ is a monotone function of x we have

$$(9.3) \qquad \int_{k-1}^{k} \log x\, dx < \log k < \int_{k}^{k+1} \log x\, dx.$$

Summing over $k = 1, \ldots, n$ we get

$$(9.4) \qquad \int_{0}^{n} \log x\, dx < \log n! < \int_{1}^{n+1} \log x\, dx$$

or

$$(9.5) \qquad n \log n - n < \log n! < (n+1) \log (n+1) - n.$$

This double inequality suggests comparing $\log n!$ with some quantity close to the arithmetic mean of the extreme members. The simplest such

---

[14] James Stirling, *Methodus differentialis*, 1730.

quantity is $(n+\frac{1}{2})\log n - n$, and accordingly we proceed to estimate the difference[15]

(9.6) $$d_n = \log n! - (n+\tfrac{1}{2})\log n + n.$$

Note that

(9.7) $$d_n - d_{n+1} = (n+\tfrac{1}{2})\log\frac{n+1}{n} - 1.$$

But

(9.8) $$\frac{n+1}{n} = \frac{1 + \dfrac{1}{2n+1}}{1 - \dfrac{1}{2n+1}},$$

and using the expansion (8.11) we get

(9.9) $$d_n - d_{n+1} = \frac{1}{3(2n+1)^2} + \frac{1}{5(2n+1)^4} + \cdots.$$

By comparison of the right side with a geometric series with ratio $(2n+1)^{-2}$ one sees that

(9.10) $$0 < d_n - d_{n+1} < \frac{1}{3[(2n+1)^2 - 1]} = \frac{1}{12n} - \frac{1}{12(n+1)}.$$

From (9.9) we conclude that the sequence $\{d_n\}$ is decreasing, while (9.10) shows that the sequence $\{d_n - (12n)^{-1}\}$ is increasing. It follows that a finite limit

(9.11) $$C = \lim d_n$$

exists. But in view of (9.6) the relation $d_n \to C$ is equivalent to

(9.12) $$n! \sim e^C \cdot n^{n+\frac{1}{2}} e^{-n}.$$

This is Stirling's formula, except that the constant C is not yet specified. That $e^C = \sqrt{2\pi}$ will be proved in VII, 2. The proof is elementary and independent of the material in chapters IV–VI; it is postponed to chapter VII because it is naturally connected with the normal approximation theorem.[16]

---

[15] The following elegant argument and the inequality (9.14) are due to H. E. Robbins, Amer. Math. Monthly, vol. 62 (1955), pp. 26–29.

[16] The usual proof that $e^C = \sqrt{2\pi}$ relies on the formula of Wallis. For a simple direct proof see W. Feller, Amer. Math. Monthly (1967).

Refinements. The inequality (9.10) has a companion inequality in the reverse direction. Indeed, from (9.9) it is obvious that

$$(9.13) \qquad d_n - d_{n+1} > \frac{1}{3(2n+1)^2} > \frac{1}{12n+1} - \frac{1}{12(n+1)+1}.$$

It follows that the sequence $\{d_n - (12n+1)^{-1}\}$ decreases. Since $\{d_n - (12n)^{-1}\}$ increases this implies the double inequality

$$(9.14) \qquad C + \frac{1}{12n+1} < d_n < C + \frac{1}{12n}.$$

Substituting into (9.6), and anticipating that $e^C = \sqrt{2\pi}$, we get

$$(9.15) \qquad \sqrt{2\pi}\, n^{n+\frac{1}{2}} e^{-n} \cdot e^{(12n+1)^{-1}} < n! < \sqrt{2\pi}\, n^{n+\frac{1}{2}} e^{-n} \cdot e^{(12n)^{-1}}$$

This double inequality supplements Stirling's formula in a remarkable manner. The ratio of the extreme members is close to $1 - (12n^2)^{-1}$, and hence *the right-hand member in (9.15) overestimates* $n!$, *but with an error of less than* $9n^{-2}$ *per cent.* In reality the error is much smaller;[17] for $n = 2$ the right side in (9.15) yields 2.0007, for $n = 5$ we get 120.01.

PROBLEMS FOR SOLUTION

Note: Sections 11 and 12 contain problems of a different character and diverse complements to the text.

10. EXERCISES AND EXAMPLES

Note: *Assume in each case that all arrangements have the same probability.*

1. How many different sets of initials can be formed if every person has one surname and (*a*) exactly two given names, (*b*) at most two given names, (*c*) at most three given names?

2. Letters in the Morse code are formed by a succession of dashes and dots with repetitions permitted. How many letters is it possible to form with ten symbols or less?

3. Each domino piece is marked by two numbers. The pieces are symmetrical so that the number-pair is not ordered. How many different pieces can be made using the numbers $1, 2, \ldots, n$?

4. The numbers $1, 2, \ldots, n$ are arranged in random order. Find the probability that the digits (*a*) 1 and 2, (*b*) 1, 2, and 3, appear as neighbors in the order named.

---

[17] Starting from (9.9) it is possible to show that $d_n = C + (12n)^{-1} - (360n^3)^{-1} + \cdots$ where the dots indicate terms dominated by a multiple of n^{-4}.

5. *A* throws six dice and wins if he scores at least one ace. *B* throws twelve dice and wins if he scores at least two aces. Who has the greater probability to win?[18]

Hint: Calculate the probabilities to lose.

6. (*a*) Find the probability that among three random digits there appear exactly 1, 2, or 3 different ones. (*b*) Do the same for four random digits.

7. Find the probabilities p_r that in a sample of *r* random digits no two are equal. Estimate the numerical value of p_{10}, using Stirling's formula.

8. What is the probability that among *k* random digits (*a*) 0 does not appear; (*b*) 1 does not appear; (*c*) neither 0 nor 1 appears; (*d*) at least one of the two digits 0 and 1 does not appear? Let *A* and *B* represent the events in (*a*) and (*b*). Express the other events in terms of *A* and *B*.

9. If *n* balls are placed at random into *n* cells, find the probability that exactly one cell remains empty.

10. At a parking lot there are twelve places arranged in a row. A man observed that there were eight cars parked, and that the four empty places were adjacent to each other (formed *one* run). Given that there are four empty places, is this arrangement surprising (indicative of non-randomness)?

11. A man is given *n* keys of which only one fits his door. He tries them successively (sampling without replacement). This procedure may require 1, 2, . . . , *n* trials. Show that each of these *n* outcomes has probability n^{-1}.

12. Suppose that each of *n* sticks is broken into one long and one short part. The 2*n* parts are arranged into *n* pairs from which new sticks are formed. Find the probability (*a*) that the parts will be joined in the original order, (*b*) that all long parts are paired with short parts.[19]

13. *Testing a statistical hypothesis.* A Cornell professor got a ticket twelve times for illegal overnight parking. All twelve tickets were given either Tuesdays or Thursdays. Find the probability of this event. (Was his renting a garage only for Tuesdays and Thursdays justified?)

14. *Continuation.* Of twelve police tickets none was given on Sunday. Is this evidence that no tickets are given on Sundays?

15. A box contains ninety good and ten defective screws. If ten screws are used, what is the probability that none is defective?

16. From the population of five symbols *a, b, c, d, e,* a sample of size 25 is taken. Find the probability that the sample will contain five symbols of each

---

[18] This paraphrases a question addressed in 1693 to I. Newton by the famous Samuel Pepys. Newton answered that "an easy computation" shows *A* to be at an advantage. On prodding he later submitted the calculations, but he was unable to convince Pepys. For a short documented account see E. D. Schell, *Samuel Pepys, Isaac Newton, and probability*, The Amer. Statistician, vol. 14 (1960), pp. 27–30. There reference is made to *Private correspondence and miscellaneous papers of Samuel Pepys*, London (G. Bell and Sons), 1926.

[19] When cells are exposed to harmful radiation, some chromosomes break and play the role of our "sticks." The "long" side is the one containing the so-called centromere. If two "long" or two "short" parts unite, the cell dies. See D. G. Catcheside, *The effect of X-ray dosage upon the frequency of induced structural changes in the chromosomes of* Drosophila Melanogaster, Journal of Genetics, vol. 36 (1938), pp. 307–320.

kind. Check the result in tables of random numbers,[20] identifying the digits 0 and 1 with a, the digits 2 and 3 with b, etc.

17. If n men, among whom are A and B, stand in a row, what is the probability that there will be exactly r men between A and B? If they stand in a ring instead of in a row, show that the probability is independent of r and hence $1/(n-1)$. (In the circular arrangement consider only the arc leading from A to B in the positive direction.)

18. What is the probability that two throws with three dice each will show the same configuration if (a) the dice are distinguishable, (b) they are not?

19. Show that it is more probable to get at least one ace with four dice than at least one double ace in 24 throws of two dice. The answer is known as de Méré's paradox.[21]

20. From a population of n elements a sample of size r is taken. Find the probability that none of N prescribed elements will be included in the sample, assuming the sampling to be (a) without, (b) with replacement. Compare the numerical values for the two methods when (i) $n = 100$, $r = N = 3$, and (ii) $n = 100$, $r = N = 10$.

21. *Spread of rumors.* In a town of $n + 1$ inhabitants, a person tells a rumor to a second person, who in turn repeats it to a third person, etc. At each step the recipient of the rumor is chosen at random from the n people available. Find the probability that the rumor will be told r times without: (a) returning to the originator, (b) being repeated to any person. Do the same problem when at each step the rumor is told by one person to a gathering of N randomly chosen people. (The first question is the special case $N = 1$.)

22. *Chain letters.* In a population of $n + 1$ people a man, the "progenitor," sends out letters to two distinct persons, the "first generation." These repeat the performance and, generally, for each letter received the recipient sends out two letters to two persons chosen at random without regard to the past development. Find the probability that the generations number $1, 2, \ldots, r$ will not include the progenitor. Find the median of the distribution, supposing n to be large.

23. *A family problem.* In a certain family four girls take turns at washing dishes. Out of a total of four breakages, three were caused by the youngest girl, and she was thereafter called clumsy. Was she justified in attributing the frequency of her breakages to chance? Discuss the connection with random placements of balls.

24. What is the probability that (a) the birthdays of twelve people will fall in twelve different calendar months (assume equal probabilities for the twelve months), (b) the birthdays of six people will fall in exactly two calendar months?

---

[20] They are occasionally miraculously obliging: see J. A. Greenwood and E. E. Stuart, *Review of Dr. Feller's critique*, Journal for Parapsychology, vol. 4 (1940), pp. 298–319, in particular p. 306.

[21] An often repeated story asserts that the problem arose at the gambling table and that in 1654 de Méré proposed it to Pascal. This incident is supposed to have greatly stimulated the development of probability theory. The problem was in fact treated by Cardano (1501–1576). See O. Ore, *Pascal and the invention of probability theory*, Amer. Math. Monthly, vol. 67 (1960), pp. 409–419, and *Cardano, the gambling scholar*, Princeton (Princeton Univ. Press), 1953.

25. Given thirty people, find the probability that among the twelve months there are six containing two birthdays and six containing three.

26. A closet contains n pairs of shoes. If $2r$ shoes are chosen at random (with $2r < n$), what is the probability that there will be (a) no complete pair, (b) exactly one complete pair, (c) exactly two complete pairs among them?

27. A car is parked among N cars in a row, not at either end. On his return the owner finds that exactly r of the N places are still occupied. What is the probability that both neighboring places are empty?

28. A group of $2N$ boys and $2N$ girls is divided into two equal groups. Find the probability p that each group will be equally divided into boys and girls. Estimate p, using Stirling's formula.

29. In bridge, prove that the probability p of West's receiving exactly k aces is the same as the probability that an arbitrary hand of thirteen cards contains exactly k aces. (This is intuitively clear. Note, however, that the two probabilities refer to two different experiments, since in the second case thirteen cards are chosen at random and in the first case all 52 are distributed.)

30. The probability that in a bridge game East receives m and South n spades is the same as the probability that of two hands of thirteen cards each, drawn at random from a deck of bridge cards, the first contains m and the second n spades.

31. What is the probability that the bridge hands of North and South together contain exactly k aces, where $k = 0, 1, 2, 3, 4$?

32. Let a, b, c, d be four non-negative integers such that $a + b + c + d = 13$. Find the probability $p(a, b, c, d)$ that in a bridge game the players North, East, South, West have a, b, c, d spades, respectively. Formulate a scheme of placing red and black balls into cells that contains the problem as a special case.

33. Using the result of problem 32, find the probability that some player receives a, another b, a third c, and the last d spades if (a) $a = 5$, $b = 4$, $c = 3$, $d = 1$; (b) $a = b = c = 4$, $d = 1$; (c) $a = b = 4$, $c = 3$, $d = 2$. Note that the three cases are essentially different.

34. Let a, b, c, d be integers with $a + b + c + d = 13$. Find the probability $q(a, b, c, d)$ that a hand at bridge will consist of a spades, b hearts, c diamonds, and d clubs and show that the problem does *not* reduce to one of placing, at random, thirteen balls into four cells. Why?

35. *Distribution of aces among r bridge cards.* Calculate the probabilities $p_0(r), p_1(r), \ldots, p_4(r)$ that among r bridge cards drawn at random there are $0, 1, \ldots, 4$ aces, respectively. Verify that $p_0(r) = p_4(52 - r)$.

36. *Continuation: waiting times.* If the cards are drawn one by one, find the probabilities $f_1(r), \ldots, f_4(r)$ that the first, $\ldots$, fourth ace turns up at the rth trial. *Guess* at the *medians* of the waiting times for the first, $\ldots$, fourth ace and then calculate them.

37. Find the probability that each of two hands contains exactly k aces if the two hands are composed of r bridge cards each, and are drawn (a) from the same deck, (b) from two decks. Show that when $r = 13$ the probability in part (a) is the probability that two preassigned bridge players receive exactly k aces each.

38. *Misprints.* Each page of a book contains N symbols, possibly misprints. The book contains $n = 500$ pages and $r = 50$ misprints. Show that

(*a*) the probability that pages number 1, 2, ..., *n* contain, respectively, r_1, $r_2, \ldots, r_n$ misprints equals

$$\binom{N}{r_1}\binom{N}{r_2} \cdots \binom{N}{r_n} \bigg/ \binom{nN}{r} \; ;$$

(*b*) for large *N* this probability may be approximated by (5.3). Conclude that *the r misprints are distributed in the n pages approximately in accordance with a random distribution of r balls in n cells.* (*Note.* The distribution of the *r* misprints among the *N* available places follows the Fermi-Dirac statistics. Our assertion may be restated as a general limiting property of Fermi-Dirac statistics. Cf. section 5.*a*.)

Note: *The following problems refer to the material of section 5.*

39. If r_1 indistinguishable things of one kind and r_2 indistinguishable things of a second kind are placed into *n* cells, find the number of distinguishable arrangements.

40. If r_1 dice and r_2 coins are thrown, how many results can be distinguished?

41. In how many different distinguishable ways can r_1 white, r_2 black, and r_3 red balls be arranged?

42. Find the probability that in a random arrangement of 52 bridge cards no two aces are adjacent.

43. *Elevator.* In the example (3.*c*) the elevator starts with seven passengers and stops at ten floors. The various arrangements of discharge may be denoted by symbols like (3, 2, 2), to be interpreted as the event that three passengers leave together at a certain floor, two other passengers at another floor, and the last two at still another floor. Find the probabilities of the fifteen possible arrangements ranging from (7) to (1, 1, 1, 1, 1, 1, 1).

44. *Birthdays.* Find the probabilities for the various configurations of the birthdays of 22 people.

45. Find the probability for a *poker* hand to be a (*a*) royal flush (ten, jack, queen, king, ace in a single suit); (*b*) four of a kind (four cards of equal face values); (*c*) full house (one pair and one triple of cards with equal face values); (*d*) straight (five cards in sequence regardless of suit); (*e*) three of a kind (three equal face values plus two extra cards); (*f*) two pairs (two pairs of equal face values plus one other card); (*g*) one pair (one pair of equal face values plus three different cards).

11. PROBLEMS AND COMPLEMENTS OF A THEORETICAL CHARACTER

1. A population of *n* elements includes *np* red ones and *nq* black ones ($p + q = 1$). A random sample of size *r* is taken with replacement. Show that the probability of its including exactly *k* red elements is

(11.1) $$\binom{r}{k} p^k q^{r-k}.$$

2. *A limit theorem for the hypergeometric distribution.* If n is large and $n_1/n = p$, then the probability q_k given by (6.1) and (6.2) is close to (11.1). More precisely,

$$(11.2) \quad \binom{r}{k}\left(p - \frac{k}{n}\right)^k \left(q - \frac{r-k}{n}\right)^{r-k} < q_k < \binom{r}{k} p^k q^{r-k} \left(1 - \frac{r}{n}\right)^{-r}.$$

A comparison of this and the preceding problem shows: *For large populations there is practically no difference between sampling with and without replacement.*

3. A random sample of size r *without replacement* is taken from a population of n elements. The probability u_r that N given elements will all be included in the sample is

$$(11.3) \qquad u_r = \binom{n-N}{r-N} \Big/ \binom{n}{r}.$$

[The corresponding formula for sampling *with replacement* is given by (11.10) and cannot be derived by a direct argument. For an alternative form of (11.3) cf. problem 9 of IV, 6.]

4. *Limiting form.* If $n \to \infty$ and $r \to \infty$ so that $r/n \to p$, then $u_r \to p^N$ (cf. problem 13).

Note:[22] *Problems 5–13 refer to the classical occupancy problem (Boltzmann-Maxwell statistics): That is, r balls are distributed among n cells and each of the n^r possible distributions has probability n^{-r}.*

5. The probability p_k that a given cell contains exactly k balls is given by the binomial distribution (4.5). The most probable number is the integer v such that $(r-n+1)/n < v \leq (r+1)/n$. (In other words, it is asserted that $p_0 < p_1 < \cdots < p_{v-1} \leq p_v > p_{v+1} > \cdots > p_r$; cf. problem 15.)

6. *Limiting form.* If $n \to \infty$ and $r \to \infty$ so that the average number $\lambda = r/n$ of balls per cell remains constant, then

$$(11.4) \qquad p_k \to e^{-\lambda}\lambda^k/k!.$$

(This is the *Poisson distribution,* discussed in chapter VI; for the corresponding limit theorem for Bose-Einstein statistics see problem 16.)

7. Let $A(r, n)$ be the number of distributions leaving *none of the n cells empty.* Show by a combinatorial argument that

$$(11.5) \qquad A(r, n+1) = \sum_{k=1}^{r} \binom{r}{k} A(r-k, n).$$

---

[22] Problems 5–19 play a role in quantum statistics, the theory of photographic plates, G-M counters, etc. The formulas are therefore frequently discussed and discovered in the physical literature, usually without a realization of their classical and essentially elementary character. Probably all the problems occur (although in modified form) in the book by Whitworth quoted at the opening of this chapter.

Conclude that

(11.6) $$A(r, n) = \sum_{v=0}^{n} (-1)^v \binom{n}{v} (n-v)^r.$$

Hint: Use induction; assume (11.6) to hold and express $A(r-k, n)$ in (11.5) accordingly. Change the order of summation and use the binomial formula to express $A(r, n+1)$ as the difference of two simple sums. Replace in the second sum $v + 1$ by a new index of summation and use (8.6).

Note: *Formula (11.6) provides a theoretical solution to an old problem but obviously it would be a thankless task to use it for the calculation of the probability* x, *say, that in a village of* $r = 1900$ *people every day of the year is a birthday. In IV,2 we shall derive (11.6) by another method and shall obtain a simple approximation formula (showing, e.g., that* $x = 0.135$, *approximately).*

8. Show that *the number of distributions leaving exactly* m *cells empty is*

(11.7) $$E_m(r, n) = \binom{n}{m} A(r, n-m) = \binom{n}{m} \sum_{v=0}^{n-m} (-1)^v \binom{n-m}{v} (n-m-v)^r.$$

9. Show without using the preceding results that *the probability*

$$p_m(r, n) = n^{-r} E_m(r, n)$$

of finding exactly m *cells empty satisfies*

(11.8) $$p_m(r+1, n) = p_m(r, n) \frac{n-m}{n} + p_{m+1}(r, n) \frac{m+1}{n}.$$

10. Using the results of problems 7 and 8, show by direct calculation that (11.8) holds. Show that this method provides *a new derivation (by induction on* r) *of (11.6).*

11. From problem 8 conclude that *the probability* $x_m(r, n)$ *of finding* m *or more cells empty equals*

(11.9) $$\binom{n}{m} \sum_{v=0}^{n-m} (-1)^v \binom{n-m}{v} \left(1 - \frac{m+v}{n}\right)^r \frac{m}{m+v}.$$

(For $m \geq n$ this expression reduces to zero, as is proper.)

Hint: Show that $x_m(r, n) - p_m(r, n) = x_{m+1}(r, n).$

12. *The probability that each of* N *given cells is occupied is*

(11.10) $$u(r, n) = n^{-r} \sum_{k=0}^{r} \binom{r}{k} A(k, N)(n-N)^{r-k}$$

Conclude that

(11.11) $$u(r, n) = \sum_{v=0}^{N} (-1)^v \binom{N}{v} \left(1 - \frac{v}{n}\right)^r.$$

[Use the binomial theorem. For $N = n$ we have $u(r, n) = n^{-r}A(r, n)$. Note that (11.11) is the analogue of (11.3) for *sampling with replacement*.[23] For an alternative derivation see problem 8 of IV, 6.]

13. *Limiting form.* For the passage to the limit described in problem 4 one has $u(r, n) \to (1 - e^{-p})^N$.

Note: *In problems 14–19, r and n have the same meaning as above, but we assume that the balls are indistinguishable and that all distinguishable arrangements have equal probabilities (Bose-Einstein statistics).*

14. The probability that a given cell contains exactly k balls is

$$(11.12) \qquad q_k = \binom{n+r-k-2}{r-k} \bigg/ \binom{n+r-1}{r}.$$

15. Show that when $n > 2$ zero is the most probable number of balls in any specified cell, or more precisely, $q_0 > q_1 > \cdots$ (cf. problem 5).

16. *Limit theorem.* Let $n \to \infty$ and $r \to \infty$, so that the average number of particles per cell, r/n, tends to λ. Then

$$(11.13) \qquad q_k \to \frac{\lambda^k}{(1+\lambda)^{k+1}}.$$

(The right side is known as the *geometric distribution*.)

17. The probability that exactly m cells remain empty is

$$(11.14) \qquad p_m = \binom{n}{m}\binom{r-1}{n-m-1} \bigg/ \binom{n+r-1}{r}.$$

18. The probability that group of m prescribed cells contains a total of exactly j balls is

$$(11.15) \qquad q_j(m) = \binom{m+j-1}{m-1}\binom{n-m+r-j-1}{r-j} \bigg/ \binom{n+r-1}{r}.$$

---

[23] Note that $u(r, n)$ may be interpreted as the probability that the *waiting time* up to the moment when the Nth element joins the sample is less than r. The result may be applied to *random sampling digits:* here $u(r, 10) - u(r-1, 10)$ is the probability that a sequence of r elements must be observed to include the complete set of all ten digits. This can be used as a test of randomness. R. E. Greenwood [*Coupon collector's test for random digits*, Mathematical Tables and Other Aids to Computation, vol. 9 (1955), pp. 1–5] tabulated the distribution and compared it to actual counts for the corresponding waiting times for the first 2035 decimals of π and the first 2486 decimals of e. The median of the waiting time for a complete set of all ten digits is 27. The probability that this waiting time exceeds 50 is greater than 0.05, and the probability of the waiting time exceeding 75 is about 0.0037.

19. *Limiting form.* For the passage to the limit of problem 4 we have

$$(11.16) \qquad q_j(m) \rightarrow \binom{m+j-1}{m-1} \frac{p^j}{(1+p)^{m+j}}.$$

(The right side is a special case of the *negative binomial distribution* to be introduced in VI, 8.)

Theorems on Runs. *In problems 20–25 we consider arrangements of r_1 alphas and r_2 betas and assume that all arrangements are equally probable [see example (4.e)]. This group of problems refers to section 5b.*

20. The probability that the arrangement contains exactly k runs of either kind is

$$(11.17) \qquad P_{2\nu} = 2 \binom{r_1-1}{\nu-1}\binom{r_2-1}{\nu-1} \Big/ \binom{r_1+r_2}{r_1}$$

when $k = 2\nu$ is even, and

$$(11.18) \qquad P_{2\nu+1} = \left\{ \binom{r_1-1}{\nu}\binom{r_2-1}{\nu-1} + \binom{r_1-1}{\nu-1}\binom{r_2-1}{\nu} \right\} \Big/ \binom{r_1+r_2}{r_1}$$

when $k = 2\nu + 1$ is odd.

21. *Continuation.* Conclude that the most probable number of runs is an integer k such that $\dfrac{2r_1r_2}{r_1+r_2} < k < \dfrac{2r_1r_2}{r_1+r_2} + 3$. (*Hint:* Consider the ratios $P_{2\nu+2}/P_{2\nu}$ and $P_{2\nu+1}/P_{2\nu-1}$.)

22. The probability that the arrangement starts with an alpha run of length $\nu \geq 0$ is $(r_1)_\nu r_2/(r_1+r_2)_{\nu+1}$. (*Hint:* Choose the ν alphas and the beta which must follow it.) What does the theorem imply for $\nu = 0$?

23. The probability of having exactly k runs of alphas is

$$(11.19) \qquad \pi_k = \binom{r_1-1}{k-1}\binom{r_2+1}{k} \Big/ \binom{r_1+r_2}{r_1}.$$

Hint: This follows easily from the second part of the lemma of section 5. Alternatively (11.19) may be derived from (11.17) and (11.18), but this procedure is more laborious.

24. The probability that the nth alpha is preceded by exactly m betas is

$$(11.20) \qquad \binom{r_1+r_2-n-m}{r_2-m}\binom{m+n-1}{m} \Big/ \binom{r_1+r_2}{r_1}.$$

25. The probability for the alphas to be arranged in k runs of which k_1 are of length 1, k_2 of length 2, ..., k_ν of length ν (with $k_1 + \cdots + k_\nu = k$) is

$$(11.21) \qquad \frac{k!}{k_1!\,k_2!\cdots k_\nu!} \binom{r_2+1}{k} \Big/ \binom{r_1+r_2}{r_1}.$$

12. PROBLEMS AND IDENTITIES INVOLVING BINOMIAL COEFFICIENTS

1. For integral $n \geq 2$

$$1 - \binom{n}{1} + \binom{n}{2} - + \cdots = 0$$

$$\binom{n}{1} + 2\binom{n}{2} + 3\binom{n}{3} + \cdots = n2^{n-1}$$

(12.1)

$$\binom{n}{1} - 2\binom{n}{2} + 3\binom{n}{3} - + \cdots = 0,$$

$$2 \cdot 1 \binom{n}{2} + 3 \cdot 2 \binom{n}{3} + 4 \cdot 3 \binom{n}{4} + \cdots = n(n-1)2^{n-2}$$

Hint: Use the binomial formula.

2. Prove that for positive integers n, k

(12.2) $$\binom{n}{0}\binom{n}{k} - \binom{n}{1}\binom{n-1}{k-1} + \binom{n}{2}\binom{n-2}{k-2} \cdots \pm \binom{n}{k}\binom{n-k}{0} = 0.$$

More generally[24]

(12.3) $$\sum \binom{n}{\nu}\binom{n-\nu}{k-\nu} t^\nu = \binom{n}{k}(1+t)^k.$$

3. For any $a > 0$

(12.4) $$\binom{-a}{k} = (-1)^k \binom{a+k-1}{k}.$$

If a is an integer, this can be proved also by repeated differentiation of the geometric series $\sum x^k = (1-x)^{-1}$.

4. Prove that

(12.5) $$\binom{2n}{n} 2^{-2n} = (-1)^n \binom{-\frac{1}{2}}{n},$$

$$\frac{1}{n}\binom{2n-2}{n-1} 2^{-2n+1} = (-1)^{n-1}\binom{\frac{1}{2}}{n}.$$

5. For integral non-negative n and r and all real a

(12.6) $$\sum_{\nu=0}^{n} \binom{a-\nu}{r} = \binom{a+1}{r+1} - \binom{a-n}{r+1}.$$

Hint: Use (8.6). The special case $n = a$ is frequently used.

---

[24] The reader is reminded of the convention (8.5): *if ν runs through all integers,* only finitely many terms in the sum in (12.3) are different from zero.

6. For arbitrary a and integral $n \geq 0$

(12.7)
$$\sum_{v=0}^{n} (-1)^v \binom{a}{v} = (-1)^n \binom{a-1}{n}.$$

Hint: Use (8.6).

7. For positive integers r, k

(12.8)
$$\sum_{v=0}^{r} \binom{v+k-1}{k-1} = \binom{r+k}{k}.$$

(a) Prove this using (8.6). (b) Show that (12.8) is a special case of (12.7). (c) Show by an inductive argument that (12.8) leads to a new proof of the first part of the lemma of section 5. (d) Show that (12.8) is equivalent to

(12.8a)
$$\sum_{j=0}^{n} \binom{j}{m} = \binom{n+1}{m+1}.$$

8. In section 6 we remarked that the terms of the hypergeometric distribution should add to unity. This amounts to saying that for any positive integers a, b, n,

(12.9)
$$\binom{a}{0}\binom{b}{n} + \binom{a}{1}\binom{b}{n-1} + \cdots + \binom{a}{n}\binom{b}{0} = \binom{a+b}{n}.$$

Prove this by induction. *Hint:* Prove first that equation (12.9) holds for $a = 1$ and all b.

9. *Continuation.* By a comparison of the coefficients of t^n on both sides of

(12.10)
$$(1+t)^a(1+t)^b = (1+t)^{a+b}$$

prove more generally that (12.9) is true for arbitrary numbers a, b (and integral n).

10. Using (12.9), prove that

(12.11)
$$\binom{n}{0}^2 + \binom{n}{1}^2 + \binom{n}{2}^2 + \cdots + \binom{n}{n}^2 = \binom{2n}{n}.$$

11. Using (12.11), prove that

(12.12)
$$\sum_{v=0}^{n} \frac{(2n)!}{(v!)^2(n-v)!^2} = \binom{2n}{n}^2.$$

12. Prove that for integers $0 < a < b$

(12.13)
$$\sum_{k=1}^{a} (-1)^{a-k} \binom{a}{k}\binom{b+k}{b+1} = \binom{b}{a-1}.$$

Hint: Using (12.4) show that (12.11) is a special case of (12.9). Alternatively, compare the coefficients of t^{a-1} in $(1-t)^a(1-t)^{-b-2} = (1-t)^{a-b-2}$.

13. By specialization derive from (12.9) the identities

(12.14)
$$\binom{a}{k} - \binom{a}{k-1} + - \cdots \mp \binom{a}{1} \pm 1 = \binom{a-1}{k}$$

and

(12.15)
$$\sum_v (-1)^v \binom{a}{v}\binom{n-v}{r} = \binom{n-a}{n-r},$$

valid if k, n, and r are positive integers. *Hint:* Use (12.4).

14. Using (12.9), prove that[25] for arbitrary a, b and integral k

(12.16)
$$\sum_{j=0}^{k} \binom{a+k-j-1}{k-j}\binom{b+j-1}{j} = \binom{a+b+k-1}{k}.$$

Hint: Apply (12.4) back and forth. Alternatively, use (12.10) with changed signs of the exponents.

Note the important special cases $b = 1, 2$.

15. Referring to the problems of section 11, notice that (11.12), (11.14), (11.15), and (11.16) define probabilities. In each the quantities should therefore add to unity. Show that this is implied, respectively, by (12.8), (12.9), (12.16), and the binomial theorem.

16. From the definition of $A(r, n)$ in problem 7 of section 11 it follows that $A(r, n) = 0$ if $r < n$ and $A(n, n) = n!$. In other words

(12.17)
$$\sum_{k=0}^{n} (-1)^{n-k} \binom{n}{k} k^r = \begin{matrix} 0 & \text{if} \quad r < n \\ n! & \text{if} \quad r = n. \end{matrix}$$

(*a*) Prove (12.17) directly by reduction from n to $n - 1$. (*b*) Next prove (12.17) by considering the rth derivative of $(1-e^t)^n$ at $t = 0$. (*c*) Generalize (12.17) by starting from (11.11) instead of (11.6).

17. If $0 \le N \le n$ prove by induction that for each integer $r \ge 0$

(12.18)
$$\sum_{v=0}^{N} (-1)^v \binom{N}{v} (n-v)_r = \binom{n-N}{r-N} r!.$$

(Note that the right-hand member vanishes when $r < N$ and when $r > n$.) Verify (12.18) by considering the rth derivative of $t^{n-N}(t-1)^N$ at $t = 1$.

18. Prove by induction (using the binomial theorem)

(12.19)
$$\binom{n}{1}\frac{1}{1} - \binom{n}{2}\frac{1}{2} + \cdots + (-1)^{n-1} \binom{n}{n}\frac{1}{n} = 1 + \frac{1}{2} + \frac{1}{3} + \cdots + \frac{1}{n}.$$

Verify (12.19) by integrating the identity $\sum_{0}^{n-1} (1-t)^v = \{1 - (1-t)^n\}t^{-1}$.

---

[25] For a more elegant proof see problem 15 of IX, 9.

19. Show that for any positive integer m

(12.20) $$(x+y+z)^m = \sum \frac{m!}{a!\,b!\,c!}\,x^a y^b z^c$$

where the summation extends over all non-negative integers a, b, c, such that $a + b + c = m$.

20. Show that $\Gamma(a+1) = a\Gamma(a)$ for all $a > 0$, whence

(12.21) $$\binom{-a}{k} = (-1)^k \frac{\Gamma(a+k)}{k!\,\Gamma(a)}.$$

21. Prove that for any positive integers a and b

(12.22) $$\frac{(a+1)(a+2)\cdots(a+n)}{(b+1)(b+2)\cdots(b+n)} \sim \frac{b!}{a!}\,n^{a-b}.$$

22. The *gamma function* is defined by

(12.23) $$\Gamma(x) = \int_0^\infty t^{x-1} e^{-t}\, dt$$

where $x > 0$. Show that $\Gamma(x) \sim \sqrt{2\pi}\, e^{-x} x^{x-\frac{1}{2}}$. [Notice that if $x = n$ is an integer, $\Gamma(n) = (n-1)!$.]

23. Let a and r be arbitrary positive numbers and n a positive integer. Show that

(12.24) $$a(a+r)(a+2r)\cdots(a+nr) \sim Cr^{n+1} n^{n+\frac{1}{2}+a/r}.$$

$$\left[\text{The constant } C \text{ is equal to } \frac{\sqrt{2\pi}}{\Gamma(a/r)}.\right]$$

24. Using the results of the preceding problem, show that

(12.25) $$\frac{a(a+r)(a+2r)\cdots(a+nr)}{b(b+r)(b+2r)\cdots(b+nr)} \sim \frac{\Gamma(b/r)}{\Gamma(a/r)}\,n^{(a-b)/r}.$$

25. From (8.10) conclude

(12.26) $$e^{-t/(1-t)} < 1 - t = e^{-t}, \qquad\qquad 0 < t < 1.$$

CHAPTER III*

Fluctuations in Coin Tossing
and Random Walks

This chapter digresses from our main topic, which is taken up again only in chapter V. Its material has traditionally served as a first orientation and guide to more advanced theories. Simple methods will soon lead us to results of far-reaching theoretical and practical importance. We shall encounter theoretical conclusions which not only are unexpected but actually come as a shock to intuition and common sense. They will reveal that commonly accepted notions concerning chance fluctuations are without foundation and that the implications of the law of large numbers are widely misconstrued. For example, in various applications it is assumed that observations on an individual coin-tossing game during a long time interval will yield the same statistical characteristics as the observation of the results of a huge number of independent games at one given instant. This is not so. Indeed, using a currently popular jargon we reach the conclusion that in a population of normal coins the majority is necessarily maladjusted. [For empirical illustrations see section 6 and example (4.*b*).]

Until recently the material of this chapter used to be treated by analytic methods and, consequently, the results appeared rather deep. The elementary method[1] used in the sequel is therefore a good example of the newly discovered power of combinatorial methods. The results are fairly representative of a wider class of fluctuation phenomena[2] to be discussed

---

* This chapter may be omitted or read in conjunction with the following chapters. Reference to its contents will be made in chapters X (laws of large numbers), XI (first-passage times), XIII (recurrent events), and XIV (random walks), but the contents will not be used explicitly in the sequel.

[1] The discovery of the possibility of an elementary approach was the principal motivation for the second edition of this book (1957). The present version is new and greatly improved since it avoids various combinatorial tricks.

[2] See footnote 12.

in volume 2. All results will be derived anew, independently, by different methods. This chapter will therefore serve primarily readers who are not in a hurry to proceed with the systematic theory, or readers interested in the spirit of probability theory without wanting to specialize in it. For other readers a comparison of methods should prove instructive and interesting. Accordingly, *the present chapter should be read at the reader's discretion independently of, or parallel to, the remainder of the book.*

1. GENERAL ORIENTATION.
THE REFLECTION PRINCIPLE

From a formal point of view we shall be concerned with arrangements of finitely many plus ones and minus ones. Consider $n = p + q$ symbols $\epsilon_1, \ldots, \epsilon_n$, each standing either for $+1$ or for -1; suppose that there are p plus ones and q minus ones. The partial sum $s_k = \epsilon_1 + \cdots + \epsilon_k$ represents the difference between the number of pluses and minuses occurring at the first k places. Then

$$(1.1) \qquad s_k - s_{k-1} = \epsilon_k = \pm 1, \qquad s_0 = 0, \qquad s_n = p - q,$$

where $k = 1, 2, \ldots, n$.

We shall use a geometric terminology and refer to rectangular coordinates t, x; for definiteness we imagine the t-axis is horizontal, the x-axis vertical. The arrangement $(\epsilon_1, \ldots, \epsilon_n)$ will be represented by a polygonal line whose kth side has slope ϵ_k and whose kth vertex has ordinate s_k. Such lines will be called paths.

Definition. *Let $n > 0$ and x be integers. A path $(s_1, s_2, \ldots, s_n)$ from the origin to the point (n, x) is a polygonal line whose vertices have abscissas $0, 1, \ldots, n$ and ordinates $s_0, s_1, \ldots, s_n$ satisfying (1.1) with $s_n = x$.*

We shall refer to n as the *length* of the path. There are 2^n paths of length n. If p among the ϵ_k are positive and q are negative, then

$$(1.2) \qquad n = p + q, \qquad x = p - q.$$

A path from the origin to an arbitrary point (n, x) exists only if n and x are of the form (1.2). In this case the p places for the positive ϵ_k can be chosen from the $n = p + q$ available places in

$$(1.3) \qquad N_{n,x} = \binom{p+q}{p} = \binom{p+q}{q}$$

different ways. For convenience we *define $N_{n,x} = 0$ whenever n and x*

are not of the form (1.2). With this convention *there exist exactly* $N_{n,x}$ *different paths from the origin to an arbitrary point* (n, x).

Before turning to the principal topic of this chapter, namely the theory of random walks, we illustrate possible applications of our scheme.

Examples. (*a*) *The ballot theorem.* The following amusing proposition was proved in 1878 by W. A. Whitworth, and again in 1887 by J. Bertrand.

Suppose that, in a ballot, candidate P *scores* p *votes and candidate* Q *scores* q *votes, where* $p > q$. *The probability that throughout the counting there are always more votes for* P *than for* Q *equals* $(p-q)/(p+q)$.

Similar problems of arrangements have attracted the attention of students of combinatorial analysis under the name of ballot problems. The recent renaissance of combinatorial methods has increased their popularity, and it is now realized that a great many important problems may be reformulated as variants of some generalized ballot problem.[3]

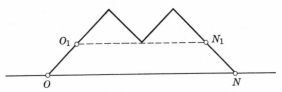

Figure 1. Illustrating positive paths. The figure shows also that there are exactly as many strictly positive paths from the origin to the point $(2n, 0)$ as there are nonnegative paths from the origin to $(2n-2, 0)$.

The whole voting record may be represented by a path of length $p + q$ in which $\epsilon_k = +1$ if the kth vote is for P; conversely, every path from the origin to the point $(p + q, p - q)$ can be interpreted as a record of a voting with the given totals p and q. Clearly s_k is the number of votes by which P leads, or trails, just after the kth vote is cast. The candidate P leads throughout the voting if, and only if, $s_1 > 0, \ldots, s_n > 0$, that is, if all vertices lie strictly above the t-axis. (The path from 0 to N_1 in figure 1 is of this type.) The ballot theorem assumes tacitly that all admissible paths are equally probable. The assertion then reduces to the theorem proved at the end of this section as an immediate consequence of the reflection lemma.

(*b*) *Galton's rank order test.*[4] Suppose that a quantity (such as the height

---

[3] A survey of the history and the literature may be found in *Some aspects of the random sequence*, by D. E. Barton and C. L. Mallows [Ann. Math. Statist., vol. 36 (1965), pp. 236–260]. These authors discuss also various applications. The most recent generalization with many applications in queuing theory is due to L. Takacs.

[4] J. L. Hodges, Biometrika, vol. 42 (1955), pp. 261–262.

of plants) is measured on each of r treated subjects, and also on each of r control subjects. Denote the measurements by $a_1, \ldots, a_r$ and $b_1, \ldots, b_r$, respectively. To fix ideas, suppose that each group is arranged in decreasing order: $a_1 > a_2 > \cdots$ and $b_1 > b_2 > \ldots$. (To avoid trivialities we assume that no two observations are equal.) Let us now combine the two sequences into one sequence of $n = 2r$ numbers arranged in decreasing order. For an extremely successful treatment all the a's should precede the b's, whereas a completely ineffectual treatment should result in a random placement of a's and b's. Thus the efficiency of the treatment can be judged by the number of different a's that precede the b of the same rank, that is, by the number of subscripts k for which $a_k > b_k$. This idea was first used in 1876 by F. Galton for data referred to him by Charles Darwin. In this case r equaled 15 and the a's were ahead 13 times. Without knowledge of the actual probabilities Galton concluded that the treatment *was* effective. But, assuming perfect randomness, the probability that the a's lead 13 times or more equals $\frac{3}{16}$. This means that in three out of sixteen cases a perfectly ineffectual treatment would appear as good or better than the treatment classified as effective by Galton. This shows that a quantitative analysis may be a valuable supplement to our rather shaky intuition.

For an interpretation in terms of paths write $\epsilon_k = +1$ or -1 according as the kth term of the combined sequence is an a or a b. The resulting path of length $2r$ joins the origin to the point $(2r, 0)$ of the t-axis. The event $a_k > b_k$ occurs if, and only if, s_{2k-1} contains at least k plus ones, that is, if $s_{2k-1} > 0$. This entails $s_{2k} \geq 0$, and so the $(2k-1)$st and the $2k$th sides are above the t-axis. It follows that the inequality $a_k > b_k$ holds ν times if, and only if, 2ν sides lie above the t-axis. In section 9 we shall prove the unexpected result that the probability for this is $1/(r+1)$, irrespective of ν. (For related tests based on the theory of runs see II, 5.*b*.)

(*c*) *Tests of the Kolmogorov-Smirnov type.* Suppose that we observe two populations of the same biological species (animals or plants) living at different places, or that we wish to compare the outputs of two similar machines. For definiteness let us consider just one measurable characteristic such as height, weight, or thickness, and suppose that for each of the two populations we are given a sample of r observations, say $a_1, \ldots, a_r$ and $b_1, \ldots, b_r$. The question is roughly whether these data are consistent with the hypothesis that the two populations are statistically identical. In this form the problem is vague, but for our purposes it is not necessary to discuss its more precise formulation in modern statistical theory. It suffices to say that the tests are based on a comparison of the two empirical distributions. For every t denote by $A(t)$ the fraction k/n of subscripts i for which $a_i \leq t$. The function so defined over the real axis is the *empirical distribution* of the *a*'s. The empirical distribution *B* is defined in like manner. A refined mathematical theory originated by N. V. Smirnov (1939) derives the probability distribution of the maximum of the discrepancies $|A(t) - B(t)|$ and of other quantities which can be used for testing the stated hypothesis. The theory is rather intricate, but was greatly simplified and made more intuitive by B. V. Gnedenko who had the lucky idea to connect it with the geometric theory of paths. As in the preceding example we associate with the two samples a path of length $2r$ leading from the origin to the point $(2r, 0)$. To say that the two populations are statistically indistinguishable amounts to saying that ideally the sampling experiment makes all possible paths equally probable. Now it is easily seen that $|A(t) - B(t)| > \xi$ for some t if, and only if, $|s_k| > \xi r$ for some k. The probability of this event is simply the probability that a path of length $2r$ leading from the origin to the point $(0, 2r)$ is not constrained to the interval between $\pm \xi r$. This probability has been known for a long time because it is connected with the ruin problem in random walks and with the physical problem of diffusion with absorbing barriers. (See problem 3.)

This example is beyond the scope of the present volume, but it illustrates how random walks can be applied to problems of an entirely different nature.

(*d*) *The ideal coin-tossing game and its relation to stochastic processes.* A path of length n can be interpreted as the record of an ideal experiment consisting of n successive tosses of a coin. If $+1$ stands for heads, then s_k equals the (positive or negative) excess of the accumulated number of heads over tails at the conclusion of the kth trial. The classical description introduces the fictitious gambler Peter who at each trial wins or loses a unit amount. The sequence $s_1, s_2, \ldots, s_n$ then represents Peter's successive cumulative gains. It will be seen presently that they are subject to chance fluctuations of a totally unexpected character.

The picturesque language of gambling should not detract from the general importance of the coin-tossing model. In fact, the model may serve as a first approximation to many more complicated chance-dependent processes in physics, economics, and learning theory. Quantities such as the energy of a physical particle, the wealth of an individual, or the accumulated learning of a rat are supposed to vary in consequence of successive collisions or random impulses of some sort. For purposes of a first orientation one assumes that the individual changes are of the same magnitude, and that their sign is regulated by a coin-tossing game. Refined models take into account that the changes and their probabilities vary from trial to trial, but even the simple coin-tossing model leads to surprising, indeed to shocking, results. They are of practical importance because they show that, contrary to generally accepted views, the laws governing a prolonged series of individual observations will show patterns and averages far removed from those derived for a whole population. In other words, currently popular psychological tests would lead one to say that in a population of "normal" coins most individual coins are "maladjusted."

It turns out that the chance fluctuations in coin tossing are typical for more general chance processes with cumulative effects. Anyhow, it stands to reason that if even the simple coin-tossing game leads to paradoxical results that contradict our intuition, the latter cannot serve as a reliable guide in more complicated situations. ◀

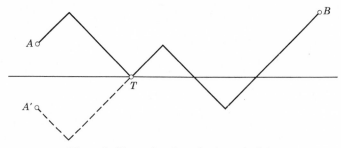

Figure 2. Illustrating the reflection principle.

It is as surprising as it is pleasing that most important conclusions can be drawn from the following simple lemma.

Let $A = (a, \alpha)$ and $B = (b, \beta)$ be integral points in the positive quadrant: $b > a \geq 0$, $\alpha > 0$, $\beta > 0$. By reflection of A on the t-axis is meant the point $A' = (a, -\alpha)$. (See figure 2.) A path from A to B is defined in the obvious manner.

Lemma.[5] (*Reflection principle.*) *The number of paths from A to B which touch or cross the x-axis equals the number of all paths from A' to B.*

Proof. Consider a path $(s_a = \alpha, s_{a+1}, \ldots, s_b = \beta)$ from A to B having one or more vertices on the t-axis. Let t be the abscissa of the first such vertex (see figure 2); that is, choose t so that $s_a > 0, \ldots, s_{t-1} > 0$, $s_t = 0$. Then $(-s_a, -s_{a+1}, \ldots, -s_{t-1}, s_t = 0, s_{t+1}, s_{t+2}, \ldots, s_b)$ is a

---

[5] The reflection principle is used frequently in various disguises, but without the geometrical interpretation it appears as an ingenious but incomprehensible trick. The probabilistic literature attributes it to D. André (1887). It appears in connection with the difference equations for random walks in XIV, 9. These are related to some partial differential equations where the reflection principle is a familiar tool called *method of images.* It is generally attributed to Maxwell and Lord Kelvin. For the use of repeated reflections see problems 2 and 3.

path leading from A' to B and having $T = (t, 0)$ as its first vertex on the t-axis. The sections AT and $A'T$ being reflections of each other, there exists a one-to-one correspondence between all paths from A' to B and such paths from A to B that have a vertex on the x-axis. This proves the lemma. ▶

As an immediate consequence we prove the result discussed in example (a). It will serve as starting point for the whole theory of this chapter.

The ballot theorem. *Let* n *and* x *be positive integers. There are exactly* $\dfrac{x}{n} N_{n,x}$ *paths* $(s_1, \ldots, s_n = x)$ *from the origin to the point* (n, x) *such that* $s_1 > 0, \ldots, s_n > 0$.

Proof. Clearly there exist exactly as many admissible paths as there are paths from the point $(1, 1)$ to (n, x) which neither touch or cross the t-axis. By the last lemma the number of such paths equals

$$N_{n-1,x-1} - N_{n-1,x+1} = \binom{p+q-1}{p-1} - \binom{p+q-1}{p}$$

with p and q defined in (1.2). A trite calculation shows that the right side equals $N_{n,x}(p-q)/(p+q)$, as asserted. ▶

2. RANDOM WALKS: BASIC NOTIONS AND NOTATIONS

The ideal coin-tossing game will now be described in the terminology of random walks which has greater intuitive appeal and is better suited for generalizations. As explained in the preceding example, when a path $(s_1, \ldots, s_\rho)$ is taken as record of ρ successive coin tossings the partial sums $s_1, \ldots, s_\rho$ represent the successive cumulative gains. For the geometric description it is convenient to pretend that the tossings are performed at a uniform rate so that the nth trial occurs at epoch[6] n. The successive partial sums $s_1, \ldots, s_n$ will be marked as points on the vertical x-axis; they will be called the positions of a "particle" performing a random walk. Note that the particle moves in unit steps, up or down, on a

---

[6] Following J. Riordan, the word *epoch* is used to denote *points* on the time axis because some contexts use the alternative terms (such as moment, time, point) in different meanings. Whenever used mathematically, the word time will refer to an interval or duration. A physical experiment may take some time, but our ideal trials are timeless and occur at epochs.

line. A path represents the record of such a movement. For example, the path from O to N in figure 1 stands for a random walk of six steps terminating by a return to the origin.

Each path of length ρ can be interpreted as the outcome of a random walk experiment; there are 2^ρ such paths, and we attribute probability $2^{-\rho}$ to each. (Different assignments will be introduced in chapter XIV. To distinguish it from others the present random walk is called *symmetric*.)

We have now completed the definition of the sample space and of the probabilities in it, but the dependence on the unspecified number ρ is disturbing. To see its role consider the event that the path passes through the point $(2, 2)$. The first two steps must be positive, and there are $2^{\rho-2}$ paths with this property. As could be expected, the probability of our event therefore equals $\frac{1}{4}$ regardless of the value of ρ. More generally, for any $k \leq \rho$ it is possible to prescribe arbitrarily the first k steps, and exactly $2^{\rho-k}$ paths will satisfy these k conditions. It follows that *an event determined by the first $k \leq \rho$ steps has a probability independent of ρ*. In practice, therefore, the number ρ plays no role provided it is sufficiently large. In other words, any path of length n can be taken as the initial section of a very long path, and there is no need to specify the latter length. Conceptually and formally it is most satisfactory to consider unending sequences of trials, but this would require the use of non-denumerable sample spaces. In the sequel it is therefore understood that the length ρ of the paths constituting the sample space is larger than the number of steps occurring in our formulas. Except for this we shall be permitted, and glad, to forget about ρ.

To conform with the notations to be used later on in the general theory we shall denote the individual steps generically by $\mathbf{X}_1, \mathbf{X}_2, \ldots$ and the positions of the particle by $\mathbf{S}_1, \mathbf{S}_2, \ldots$. Thus

$$(2.1) \qquad \mathbf{S}_n = \mathbf{X}_1 + \cdots + \mathbf{X}_n, \qquad \mathbf{S}_0 = 0.$$

From any particular path one can read off the corresponding values of $\mathbf{X}_1, \mathbf{X}_2, \ldots$; that is, the $\mathbf{X}_k$ are functions of the path.[7] For example, for the path of figure 1 clearly $\mathbf{X}_1 = \mathbf{X}_2 = \mathbf{X}_4 = 1$ and $\mathbf{X}_3 = \mathbf{X}_5 = \mathbf{X}_6 = -1$.

We shall generally describe all events by stating the appropriate conditions on the sums $\mathbf{S}_k$. Thus the event "at epoch n the particle is at the point r" will be denoted by $\{\mathbf{S}_n = r\}$. For its probability we write $p_{n,r}$. (For smoother language we shall describe this event as a "visit" to r at

---

[7] In the terminology to be introduced in chapter IX the $\mathbf{X}_k$ are random variables.

epoch n.) The number $N_{n,r}$ of paths from the origin to the point (n, r) is given by (1.3), and hence

$$(2.2) \qquad p_{n,r} = \mathbf{P}\{S_n = r\} = \binom{n}{\dfrac{n+r}{2}} 2^{-n},$$

where it is understood that the binomial coefficient is to be interpreted as zero unless $(n+r)/2$ is an integer between 0 and n, inclusive.

A *return to the origin* occurs at epoch k if $S_k = 0$. Here k is necessarily even, and for $k = 2\nu$ the probability of a return to the origin equals $p_{2\nu,0}$. Because of the frequent occurrence of this probability we denote it by $u_{2\nu}$. Thus

$$(2.3) \qquad u_{2\nu} = \binom{2\nu}{\nu} 2^{-2\nu}.$$

When the binomial coefficient is expressed in terms of factorials, Stirling's formula II, (9.1) shows directly that

$$(2.4) \qquad u_{2\nu} \sim \frac{1}{\sqrt{\pi\nu}}$$

where the sign $\sim$ indicates that the ratio of the two sides tends to 1 as $\nu \to \infty$; the right side serves as excellent approximation[8] to $u_{2\nu}$ even for moderate values of ν.

Among the returns to the origin the *first return* commands special attention. A first return occurs at epoch 2ν if

$$(2.5) \qquad S_1 \neq 0, \dots, S_{2\nu-1} \neq 0, \quad but \quad S_{2\nu} = 0.$$

The probability for this event will be denoted by $f_{2\nu}$. By definition $f_0 = 0$.

The probabilities f_{2n} and u_{2n} are related in a noteworthy manner. A visit to the origin at epoch $2n$ may be the first return, or else the first return occurs at an epoch $2k < 2n$ and is followed by a renewed return $2n - 2k$ time units later. The probability of the latter contingency is $f_{2k}u_{2n-2k}$ because there are $2^{2k}f_{2k}$ paths of length $2k$ ending with a first return, and $2^{2n-2k}u_{2n-2k}$ paths from the point $(2k, 0)$ to $(2n, 0)$. It follows that

$$(2.6) \qquad u_{2n} = f_2 u_{2n-2} + f_4 u_{2n-4} + \cdots + f_{2n}u_0, \qquad n \geq 1.$$

(See problem 5.)

---

[8] For the true value $u_{10} = 0.2461$ we get the approximation 0.2523; for $u_{20} = 0.1762$ the approximation is 0.1784. The per cent error decreases roughly in inverse proportion to ν.

The normal approximation. Formula (2.2) gives no direct clue as to the range within which $\mathbf{S}_n$ is likely to fall. An answer to this question is furnished by an approximation formula which represents a special case of the central limit theorem and will be proved[9] in VII, 2.

The probability that $a < \mathbf{S}_n < b$ is obtained by summing probabilities $p_{n,r}$ over all r between a and b. For the evaluation it suffices to know the probabilities for all inequalities of the form $\mathbf{S}_n > a$. Such probabilities can be estimated from the fact that for all x as $n \to \infty$

$$(2.7) \qquad \mathbf{P}\{\mathbf{S}_n > x\sqrt{n}\} \to 1 - \mathfrak{N}(x) = \frac{1}{\sqrt{2\pi}} \int_x^\infty e^{-\frac{1}{2}t^2}\, dt$$

where $\mathfrak{N}$ stands for the normal distribution function defined in VII, 1. Its nature is of no particular interest for our present purposes. The circumstance that the limit exists shows the important fact that for large n the ratios $\mathbf{S}_n/\sqrt{n}$ are governed approximately by the same probabilities and so the same approximation can be used for all large n.

The accompanying table gives a good idea of the probable range of $\mathbf{S}_n$. More and better values will be found in table 1 of chapter VII.

TABLE 1

x	0.5	1.0	1.5	2.0	2.5	3.0
$\mathbf{P}\{\mathbf{S}_n > x\sqrt{n}\}$	0.309	0.159	0.067	0.023	0.006	0.001

3. THE MAIN LEMMA

As we saw, the probability of a return to the origin at epoch 2ν equals the quantity $u_{2\nu}$ of (2.3). As the theory of fluctuations in random walks began to take shape it came as a surprise that almost all formulas involved this probability. One reason for this is furnished by the following simple lemma, which has a mild surprise value of its own and provides the key to the deeper theorems of the next section.

Lemma 1.[10] *The probability that no return to the origin occurs up to and including epoch $2n$ is the same as the probability that a return occurs at epoch $2n$. In symbols,*

$$(3.1) \qquad \mathbf{P}\{\mathbf{S}_1 \neq 0, \ldots, \mathbf{S}_{2n} \neq 0\} = \mathbf{P}\{\mathbf{S}_{2n} = 0\} = u_{2n}.$$

---

[9] The special case required in the sequel is treated *separately* in VII, 2 without reference to the general binomial distribution. The proof is simple and can be inserted at this place.

[10] This lemma is obvious from the form of the generating function $\Sigma f_{2k}s^{2k}$ [see XI, (3.6)] and has been noted for its curiosity value. The discovery of its significance is recent. For a geometric proof see problem 7.

Here, of course, $n > 0$. When the event on the left occurs either all the S_j are positive, or all are negative. The two contingencies being equally probable we can restate (3.1) in the form

(3.2) $$P\{S_1 > 0, \ldots, S_{2n} > 0\} = \tfrac{1}{2}u_{2n}.$$

Proof. Considering all the possible values of S_{2n} it is clear that

(3.3) $$P\{S_1 > 0, \ldots, S_{2n} > 0\} = \sum_{r=1}^{\infty} P\{S_1 > 0, \ldots, S_{2n-1} > 0, S_{2n} = 2r\}$$

(where all terms with $r > n$ vanish). By the ballot theorem the number of paths satisfying the condition indicated on the right side equals $N_{2n-1,2r-1} - N_{2n-1,2r+1}$, and so the rth term of the sum equals

$$\tfrac{1}{2}(p_{2n-1,2r-1} - p_{2n-1,2r+1}).$$

The negative part of the rth term cancels against the positive part of the $(r+1)$st term with the result that the sum in (3.3) reduces to $\tfrac{1}{2}p_{2n-1,1}$. It is easily verified that $p_{2n-1,1} = u_{2n}$ and this concludes the proof. ▶

The lemma can be restated in several ways; for example,

(3.4) $$P\{S_1 \geq 0, \ldots, S_{2n} \geq 0\} = u_{2n}.$$

Indeed, a path of length $2n$ with all vertices strictly above the x-axis passes through the point $(1, 1)$. Taking this point as new origin we obtain a path of length $2n - 1$ with all vertices above or on the new x-axis. It follows that

(3.5) $$P\{S_1 > 0, \ldots, S_{2n} > 0\} = \tfrac{1}{2}P\{S_1 \geq 0, \ldots, S_{2n-1} \geq 0\}.$$

But S_{2n-1} is an odd number, and hence $S_{2n-1} \geq 0$ implies that also $S_{2n} \geq 0$. The probability on the right in (3.5) is therefore the same as (3.4) and hence (3.4) is true. (See problem 8.)

Lemma 1 leads directly to an explicit expression for the probability distribution for the first return to the origin. Saying that a first return occurs at epoch $2n$ amounts to saying that the conditions

$$S_1 \neq 0, \ldots, S_{2k} \neq 0$$

are satisfied for $k = n - 1$, but not for $k = n$. In view of (3.1) this means that

(3.6) $$f_{2n} = u_{2n-2} - u_{2n}, \qquad\qquad n = 1, 2, \ldots.$$

A trite calculation reduces this expression to

$$(3.7) \qquad\qquad f_{2n} = \frac{1}{2n - 1} u_{2n}.$$

We have thus proved

Lemma 2. *The probability that the first return to the origin occurs at epoch 2n is given by* (3.6) *or* (3.7).

It follows from (3.6) that $f_2 + f_4 + \cdots = 1$. In the coin-tossing terminology this means that an ultimate equalization of the fortunes becomes practically certain if the game is prolonged sufficiently long. This was to be anticipated on intuitive grounds, except that the great number of trials necessary to achieve practical certainty comes as a surprise. For example, the probability that no equalization occurs in 100 tosses is about 0.08.

4. LAST VISIT AND LONG LEADS

We are now prepared for a closer analysis of the nature of chance fluctuations in random walks. The results are startling. According to widespread beliefs a so-called law of averages should ensure that in a long coin-tossing game each player will be on the winning side for about half the time, and that the lead will pass not infrequently from one player to the other. Imagine then a huge sample of records of ideal coin-tossing games, each consisting of exactly $2n$ trials. We pick one at random and observe the epoch of the last tie (in other words, the number of the last trial at which the accumulated numbers of heads and tails were equal). This number is even, and we denote it by $2k$ (so that $0 \le k \le n$). Frequent changes of the lead would imply that k is likely to be relatively close to n, but this is not so. Indeed, the next theorem reveals the amazing fact that the distribution of k is symmetric in the sense that any value k has exactly the same probability as $n - k$. This symmetry implies in particular that the inequalities $k > n/2$ and $k < n/2$ are equally likely.[11] *With probability $\frac{1}{2}$ no equalization occurred in the second half of the game, regardless of the length of the game.* Furthermore, the probabilities near the end points are *greatest*; the most probable values for k are the extremes 0 and n. These results show that intuition leads to an erroneous picture of the probable effects of chance fluctuations. A few numerical results may be illuminating.

---

[11] The symmetry of the distribution for k was found empirically by computers and verified theoretically without knowledge of the exact distribution (4.1). See D. Blackwell, P. Dewel, and D. Freedman, Ann. Math. Statist., vol. 35 (1964), p. 1344.

Examples. (*a*) Suppose that a great many coin-tossing games are conducted simultaneously at the rate of one per second, day and night, for a whole year. On the average, in one out of ten games the last equalization will occur before 9 days have passed, and the lead will not change during the following 356 days. In one out of twenty cases the last equalization takes place within $2\frac{1}{4}$ days, and in one out of a hundred cases it occurs within the first 2 hours and 10 minutes.

(*b*) Suppose that in a learning experiment lasting one year a child was consistently lagging except, perhaps, during the initial week. Another child was consistently ahead except, perhaps, during the last week. Would the two children be judged equal? Yet, let a group of 11 children be exposed to a similar learning experiment involving no intelligence but only chance. One among the 11 would appear as leader for all but one week, another as laggard for all but one week.

The exact probabilities for the possible values of k are given by

Theorem 1. (*Arc sine law for last visits.*) *The probability that up to and including epoch* $2n$ *the last visit to the origin occurs at epoch* $2k$ *is given by*

$$(4.1) \qquad\qquad \alpha_{2k,2n} = u_{2k}u_{2n-2k}, \qquad\qquad k = 0, 1, \ldots, n.$$

Proof. We are concerned with paths satisfying the conditions $S_{2k} = 0$ and $S_{2k+1} \neq 0, \ldots, S_{2n} \neq 0$. The first $2k$ vertices can be chosen in $2^{2k}u_{2k}$ different ways. Taking the point $(2k, 0)$ as new origin and using (3.1) we see that the next $(2n-2k)$ vertices can be chosen in $2^{2n-2k}u_{2n-2k}$ ways. Dividing by 2^{2n} we get (4.1). ▶

It follows from the theorem that the numbers (4.1) add to unity. The probability distribution which attaches weight $\alpha_{2k,2n}$ to the point $2k$ will be called *the discrete arc sine distribution of order* n, because the inverse sine function provides excellent numerical approximations. The distribution is symmetric in the sense that $\alpha_{2k,2n} = \alpha_{2n-2k,2n}$. For $n = 2$ the three values are $\frac{3}{8}, \frac{2}{8}, \frac{3}{8}$; for $n = 10$ see table 2. The central term is always smallest.

The main features of the arc sine distributions are best explained by

TABLE 2

DISCRETE ARC SINE DISTRIBUTION OF ORDER 10

	$k=0$ $k=10$	$k=1$ $k=9$	$k=2$ $k=8$	$k=3$ $k=7$	$k=4$ $k=6$	$k=5$
$\alpha_{2k,20}$	0.1762	0.0927	0.0736	0.0655	0.0617	0.0606

means of the graph of the function

$$(4.2) \qquad f(x) = \frac{1}{\pi\sqrt{x(1-x)}} \qquad 0 < x < 1.$$

Using Stirling's formula it is seen that u_{2n} is close to $1/\sqrt{\pi n}$, except when

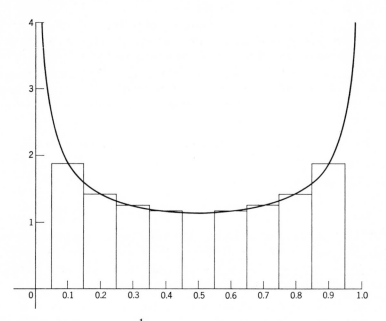

Figure 3. Graph of $f(x) = \dfrac{1}{\pi\sqrt{x(1-x)}}$. The construction explains the approximation (4.3).

n is very small. This yields the approximation

$$(4.3) \qquad \alpha_{2k,2n} \approx \frac{1}{n}f(x_k), \qquad where \quad x_k = \frac{k}{n} ;$$

the error committed is negligible except when k is extremely close to 0 or n. The right side equals the area of a rectangle with height $f(x_k)$ whose basis is the interval of length $1/n$ centered at x_k (see figure 3). For $0 < p < q < 1$ and large n the sum of the probabilities $\alpha_{2k,2n}$ with $pn < k < qn$ is therefore approximately equal to the area under the graph of f and above the interval $p < x < q$. This remains true also for $p = 0$ and $q = 1$ because the total area under the graph equals unity which is also true of the sum over all $\alpha_{2k,2n}$. Fortunately (4.2) can be integrated explicitly and we conclude that *for fixed* $0 < x < 1$ *and* n *sufficiently large*

$$(4.4) \qquad \sum_{k < xn} \alpha_{2k,2n} \approx \frac{2}{\pi} \arcsin \sqrt{x}$$

approximately. Note that the right side is independent of n which means

TABLE 3

THE CONTINUOUS ARC SINE DISTRIBUTION $A(x) = \dfrac{2}{\pi} \arcsin \sqrt{x}$

x	$A(x)$	x	$A(x)$	x	$A(x)$
0.00	0.000	0.20	0.295	0.40	0.436
0.01	0.064	0.21	0.303	0.41	0.442
0.02	0.090	0.22	0.311	0.42	0.449
0.03	0.111	0.23	0.318	0.43	0.455
0.04	0.128	0.24	0.326	0.44	0.462
0.05	0.144	0.25	0.333	0.45	0.468
0.06	0.158	0.26	0.341	0.46	0.474
0.07	0.171	0.27	0.348	0.47	0.481
0.08	0.183	0.28	0.355	0.48	0.487
0.09	0.194	0.29	0.362	0.49	0.494
				0.50	0.500
0.10	0.205	0.30	0.369		
0.11	0.215	0.31	0.376		
0.12	0.225	0.32	0.383		
0.13	0.235	0.33	0.390		
0.14	0.244	0.34	0.396		
0.15	0.253	0.35	0.403		
0.16	0.262	0.36	0.410		
0.17	0.271	0.37	0.416		
0.18	0.279	0.38	0.423		
0.19	0.287	0.39	0.429		

For $x > \frac{1}{2}$ use $A(1 - x) = 1 - A(x)$.

that table 3 suffices for all arc sine distributions of large order. (Actually the approximations are rather good even for relatively small values of n.)

We saw that, contrary to popular notions, it is quite likely that in a long coin-tossing game one of the players remains practically the whole time on the winning side, the other on the losing side. The next theorem elucidates the same phenomenon by an analysis of the fraction of the total time that the particle spends on the positive side. One feels intuitively that this fraction is most likely to be close to $\frac{1}{2}$, but the opposite is true: The possible values close to $\frac{1}{2}$ are least probable, whereas the extremes $k = 0$ and $k = n$ have the greatest probability. The analysis is facilitated by the fortunate circumstance that the theorem again involves the discrete arc sine distribution (4.1) (which will occur twice more in section 8).

Theorem 2. (*Discrete arc sine law for sojourn times.*) *The probability that in the time interval from* 0 *to* $2n$ *the particle spends* $2k$ *time units on the positive side and* $2n - 2k$ *time units on the negative side equals* $\alpha_{2k,2n}$.

(The total time spent on the positive side is necessarily even.)

Corollary.[12] *If* $0 < x < 1$, *the probability that* $\leq xn$ *time units are spent on the positive side and* $\geq (1 - x)n$ *on the negative side tends to* $\frac{2}{\pi}$ arc sin $\sqrt{x}$ *as* $n \to \infty$.

Examples. (*c*) From table 1 it is seen that the probability that in 20 tossings the lead never passes from one player to the other is about 0.352. The probability that the luckier player leads 16 times or more is about 0.685. (The approximation obtained from the corollary with $x = \frac{4}{5}$ is 0.590.) The probability that each player leads 10 times is only 0.06.

(*d*) Let n be large. With probability 0.20 the particle spends about 97.6 per cent of the time on the same side of the origin. In one out of ten cases the particle spends 99.4 per cent of the time on the same side.

(*e*) In example (*a*) a coin is tossed once per second for a total of 365 days. The accompanying table gives the times t_p such that with the stated

---

[12] Paul Lévy [*Sur certains processus stochastiques homogènes*, Compositia Mathematica, vol. 7 (1939), pp. 283–339] found this arc sine law for Brownian motion and referred to the connection with the coin-tossing game. A general arc sine limit law for the number of positive partial sums in a sequence of mutually independent random variables was proved by P. Erdös and M. Kac, *On the number of positive sums of independent random variables*, Bull. Amer. Math. Soc., vol. 53 (1947), pp. 1011–1020. The wide applicability of the arc sine limit law appeared at that time mysterious. The whole theory was profoundly reshaped when E. Sparre Andersen made the surprising discovery that many facets of the fluctuation theory of sums of independent random variables are of a purely combinatorial nature. [See Mathematica Scandinavica, vol. 1 (1953), pp. 263–285, and vol. 2 (1954), pp. 195–223.] The original proofs were exceedingly complicated, but they opened new avenues of research and are now greatly simplified. Theorem 2 was first proved by K. L. Chung and W. Feller by complicated methods. (See sections XII,5-6 of the first edition of this book.) Theorem 1 is new.

probability p the less fortunate player will be in the lead for a total time less than t_p.

p	t_p		p	t_p
0.9	153.95 days		0.3	19.89 days
0.8	126.10 days		0.2	8.93 days
0.7	99.65 days		0.1	2.24 days
0.6	75.23 days		0.05	13.5 hours
0.5	53.45 days		0.02	2.16 hours
0.4	34.85 days		0.01	32.4 minutes

▶

Proof of Theorem 2. Consider paths of the fixed length $2n$ and denote by $b_{2k,2n}$ the probability that exactly $2k$ sides lie above the t-axis. We have to prove that

(4.5) $$b_{2k,2v} = \alpha_{2k,2v}.$$

Now (3.4) asserts that $b_{2v,2v} = u_{2v}$ and for reasons of symmetry we have also $b_{0,2v} = u_{2v}$. It suffices therefore to prove (4.5) for $1 \leq k \leq v - 1$.

Assume then that exactly $2k$ out of the $2n$ time units are spent on the positive side, and $1 \leq k \leq v - 1$. In this case a first return to the origin must occur at some epoch $2r < 2n$, and two contingencies are possible. First, the $2r$ time units up to the first return may be spent on the positive side. In this case $r \leq k \leq n - 1$, and the section of the path beyond the vertex $(2r, 0)$ has exactly $2k - 2r$ sides above the axis. Obviously the number of such paths equals $\frac{1}{2} \cdot 2^{2r} f_{2r} \cdot 2^{2n-2r} b_{2k-2r,2n-2r}$. The other possibility is that the $2r$ time units up to the first return are spent on the negative side. In this case the section beyond the vertex $(2r, 0)$ has exactly $2k$ sides above the axis, whence $n - r \geq k$. The number of such paths equals $\frac{1}{2} \cdot 2^{2r} f_{2r} \cdot 2^{2n-2r} b_{2k,2n-2r}$. Accordingly, when $1 \leq k \leq n - 1$

(4.6) $$b_{2k,2n} = \frac{1}{2} \sum_{r=1}^{k} f_{2r} b_{2k-2r,2n-2r} + \frac{1}{2} \sum_{r=1}^{n-k} f_{2r} b_{2k,2n-2r}.$$

We now proceed by induction. The assertion (4.5) is trivially true for $v = 1$, and we assume it to be true for $v \leq n - 1$. Then (4.6) reduces to

(4.7) $$b_{2k,2n} = \frac{1}{2} u_{2n-2k} \sum_{r=1}^{k} f_{2r} u_{2k-2r} + \frac{1}{2} u_{2k} \sum_{r=1}^{n-k} f_{2r} u_{2n-2k-2r}.$$

In view of (2.6) the first sum equals u_{2k} while the second equals u_{2n-2k}. Hence (4.5) is true also for $v = n$. · ▶

[A paradoxical result connected with the arc sine law is contained in problem 4 of XIV,9.]

*5. CHANGES OF SIGN

The theoretical study of chance fluctuations confronts us with many paradoxes. For example, one should expect naively that in a prolonged coin-tossing game the observed number of changes of lead should increase roughly in proportion to the duration of the game. In a game that lasts twice as long, Peter should lead about twice as often. This intuitive reasoning is false. We shall show that, in a sense to be made precise, the number of changes of lead in n trials increases only as $\sqrt{n}$: in $100n$ trials one should expect only 10 times as many changes of lead as in n trials. This proves once more that the waiting times between successive equalizations are likely to be fantastically long.

We revert to random walk terminology. A *change of sign* is said to occur at epoch n if S_{n-1} and S_{n+1} are of opposite signs, that is, if the path crosses the axis. In this case $S_n = 0$, and hence n is necessarily an even (positive) integer.

Theorem 1.[13] *The probability $\xi_{r,2n+1}$ that up to epoch $2n + 1$ there occur exactly r changes of sign equals $2p_{2n+1,2r+1}$. In other words*

$$(5.1) \qquad \xi_{r,2n+1} = 2P\{S_{2n+1} = 2r + 1\}, \qquad r = 0, 1, \ldots.$$

Proof. We begin by rephrasing the theorem in a more convenient form. If the first step leads to the point $(1, 1)$ we take this point as the origin of a new coordinate system. To a crossing of the horizontal axis in the old system there now corresponds a crossing of the line below the new axis, that is, a crossing of the level -1. An analogous procedure is applicable when $S_1 = -1$, and it is thus seen that the theorem is fully equivalent to the following *proposition*: The probability that up to epoch $2n$ the level -1 is crossed exactly r times equals $2p_{2n+1,2r+1}$.

Consider first the case $r = 0$. To say that the level -1 has not been crossed amounts to saying that the level -2 has not been touched (or crossed). In this case S_{2n} is a non-negative even integer. For $k \geq 0$ we conclude from the basic reflection lemma of section 1 that the number of paths from $(0, 0)$ to $(2n, 2k)$ that do touch the level -2 equals the number of paths to $(2n, 2k + 4)$. The probability to reach the point

---

* This section is not used explicitly in the sequel.
[13] For an analogous theorem for the number of returns to the origin see problems 9-10. For an alternative proof see problem 11.

$(2n, 2k)$ without having touched the level -2 is therefore equal to $p_{2n,2k} - p_{2n,2k+4}$. The probability that the level -2 has not been touched equals the sum of the quantities for $k = 0, 1, 2, \ldots$. Most terms cancel, and we find that our probability equals $p_{2n,0} + p_{2n,2}$. This proves the assertion when $r = 0$ because

$$(5.2) \qquad p_{2n+1,1} = \tfrac{1}{2}(p_{2n,0}+p_{2n,2})$$

as is obvious from the fact that every path through $(2n + 1, 1)$ passes through either $(2n, 0)$ or $(2n, 2)$.

Next let $r = 1$. A path that crosses the level -1 at epoch $2\nu - 1$ may be decomposed into the section from $(0, 0)$ to $(2\nu, -2)$ and a path of length $2n - 2\nu$ starting at $(2\nu, -2)$. To the latter section we apply the result for $r = 0$ but interchanging the roles of plus and minus. We conclude that the number of paths of length $2n - 2\nu$ starting at $(2\nu, -2)$ and not crossing the level -1 equals the number of paths from $(2\nu, -2)$ to $(2n + 1, -3)$. But each path of this kind combines with the initial section to a path from $(0, 0)$ to $(2n + 1, -3)$. It follows that the number of paths of length $2n$ that cross the level -1 exactly once equals the number of paths from the origin to $(2n + 1, -3)$, that is, $2^{2n+1}p_{2n+1,3}$. This proves the assertion for $r = 1$.

The proposition with arbitrary r now follows by induction, the argument used in the second part of the proof requiring no change. (It was presented for the special case $r = 1$ only to avoid extra letters.) ▶

An amazing consequence of the theorem is that *the probability* $\xi_{r,n}$ *of r changes of sign in n trials decreases with r:*

$$(5.3) \qquad \xi_{0,n} \geq \xi_{1,n} > \xi_{2,n} > \cdots.$$

This means that regardless of the number of tosses, the event that the lead never changes is more probable than any preassigned number of changes.

Examples. (*a*) The probabilities x_r for exactly r changes of sign in 99 trials are as follows:

r	x_r	r	x_r
0	0.1592	7	0.0517
1	0.1529	8	0.0375
2	0.1412	9	0.0260
3	0.1252	10	0.0174
4	0.1066	11	0.0111
5	0.0873	12	0.0068
6	0.0686	13	0.0040

(*b*) The probability that in 10,000 trials no change of sign occurs is about 0.0160. The probabilities x_r for exactly r changes decrease very slowly; for $r = 10, 20, 30$ the values are $x_r = 0.0156, 0.0146,$ and 0.0130. The probability that in 10,000 trials the lead changes at most 10 times is about 0.0174; in other words, one out of six such series will show not more than 10 changes of lead. ▶

A pleasing property of the identity (5.1) is that it enables us to apply the normal approximation derived in section 2. Suppose that n is large and x a fixed positive number. The probability that fewer than $x\sqrt{n}$ changes of sign occur before epoch n is practically the same as $2\mathbf{P}\{S_n < 2x\sqrt{n}\}$, and according to (2.7) the last probability tends to $\mathfrak{N}(2x) - \frac{1}{2}$ as $n \to \infty$. We have thus

Theorem 2. (*Normal approximation.*) *The probability that fewer than $x\sqrt{n}$ changes of sign occur before epoch n tends to $2\mathfrak{N}(2x) - 1$ as $n \to \infty$.*

It follows that the *median* for the number of changes of sign is about $0.337\sqrt{n}$; this means that for n sufficiently large it is about as likely that there occur fewer than $0.337\sqrt{n}$ changes of sign than that occur more. With probability $\frac{1}{10}$ there will be fewer than $0.0628\sqrt{n}$ changes of sign, etc.[14]

6. AN EXPERIMENTAL ILLUSTRATION

Figure 4 represents the result of a computer experiment simulating 10,000 tosses of a coin; the same material is tabulated in example I, (6.c). The top line contains the graph of the first 550 trials; the next two lines represent the entire record of 10,000 trials the scale in the horizontal direction being changed in the ratio 1:10. The scale in the vertical direction is the same in the two graphs.

When looking at the graph most people feel surprised by the length of the intervals between successive crossings of the axis. As a matter of fact, the graph represents a rather mild case history and was chosen as the mildest among three available records. A more startling example is obtained by looking at the same graph in the *reverse* direction; that is, reversing the order in which the 10,000 trials actually occurred (see section 8). Theoretically, the series as graphed and the reversed series are equally legitimate as representative of an ideal random walk. The reversed random

---

[14] This approximation gives $\frac{1}{10}$ for the probability of at most 6 equalizations in 10,000 trials. This is an underestimate, the true value being about 0.112.

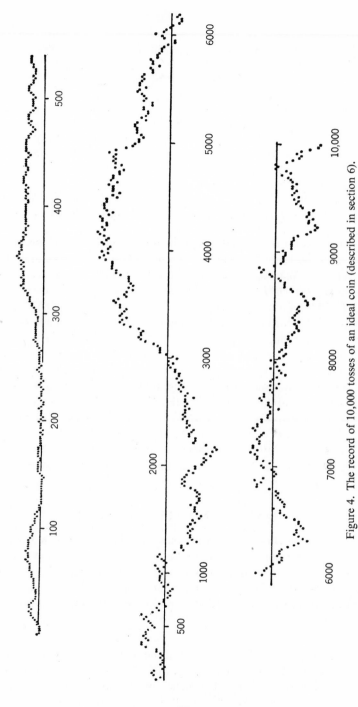

Figure 4. The record of 10,000 tosses of an ideal coin (described in section 6).

walk has the following characteristics. Starting from the origin

the path stays on the

negative side		positive side	
for the first	7804 *steps*	next	8 *steps*
next	2 *steps*	next	54 *steps*
next	30 *steps*	next	2 *steps*
next	48 *steps*	next	6 *steps*
next	2046 *steps*		

Total of 9930 steps   *Total of* 70 steps

Fraction of time: 0.993   *Fraction of time:* 0.007

This *looks* absurd, and yet the probability that in 10,000 tosses of a perfect coin the lead is at one side for more than 9930 trials and at the other for fewer than 70 exceeds $\frac{1}{10}$. In other words, on the average *one record out of ten will look worse than the one just described.* By contrast, the probability of a balance better than in the graph is only 0.072.

The original record of figure 4 contains 78 changes of sign and 64 other returns to the origin. The reversed series shows 8 changes of sign and 6 other returns to the origin. Sampling of expert opinion revealed that even trained statisticians expect much more than 78 changes of sign in 10,000 trials, and nobody counted on the possibility of only 8 changes of sign. Actually the probability of not more than 8 changes of sign exceeds 0.14, whereas the probability of more than 78 changes of sign is about 0.12. As far as the number of changes of sign is concerned the two records stand on a par and, theoretically, neither should cause surprise. If they seem startling, this is due to our faulty intuition and to our having been exposed to too many vague references to a mysterious "law of averages."

7. MAXIMA AND FIRST PASSAGES

Most of our conclusions so far are based on the basic lemma 3.1, which in turn is a simple corollary to the reflection principle. We now turn our attention to other interesting consequences of this principle.

Instead of paths that remain above the x-axis we consider paths that remain below the line $x = r$, that is, paths satisfying the condition

$$(7.1) \qquad\qquad \mathbf{S}_0 < r, \qquad \mathbf{S}_1 < r, \ldots, \mathbf{S}_n < r.$$

We say in this case that the *maximum* of the path is $< r$. (The maximum is ≥ 0 because $\mathbf{S}_0 = 0$.) Let $A = (n, k)$ be a point with ordinate $k \leq r$. A path from 0 to A touches or crosses the line $x = r$ if it violates the condition (7.1). By the reflection principle the number of such paths equals the number of paths from the origin to the point $A' = (n, 2r - k)$ which is the reflection of A on the line $x = r$. This proves

Lemma 1. *Let $k \leq r$. The probability that a path of length n leads to $A = (n, k)$ and has a maximum $\geq r$ equals $p_{n, 2r-k} = \mathbf{P}\{S_n = 2r - k\}$.*

The probability that the maximum equals r is given by the difference $p_{n, 2r-k} - p_{n, 2r+2-k}$. Summing over all $k \leq r$ we obtain the probability that an arbitrary path of length n has a maximum exactly equal to r. The sum is telescoping and reduces to $p_{n, r} + p_{n, r+1}$. Now $p_{n, r}$ vanishes unless n and r have the same parity, and in this case $p_{n, r+1} = 0$. We have thus

Theorem 1. *The probability that the maximum of a path of length n equals $r \geq 0$ coincides with the positive member of the pair $p_{n, r}$ and $p_{n, r+1}$.*

For $r = 0$ and even epochs the assertion reduces to

$$(7.2) \qquad \mathbf{P}\{S_1 \leq 0, S_2 \leq 0, \ldots, S_{2n} \leq 0\} = u_{2n}.$$

This, of course, is equivalent to the relation (3.4) which represents one version of the basic lemma. Accordingly, theorem 1 is a generalization of that lemma.

We next come to a notion that plays an important role in the general theory of stochastic processes. A *first passage through the point $r > 0$* is said to take place at epoch n if

$$(7.3) \qquad S_1 < r, \ldots, S_{n-1} < r, \qquad S_n = r.$$

In the present context it would be preferable to speak of a first *visit*, but the term first passage, which originates in the physical literature, is well established; furthermore, the term visit is not applicable to continuous processes.

Obviously a path satisfying (7.3) must pass through $(n - 1, r - 1)$ and its maximum up to epoch $n - 1$ must equal $r - 1$. We saw that the probability for this event equals $p_{n-1, r-1} - p_{n-1, r+1}$, and so we have

Theorem 2. *The probability $\varphi_{r, n}$ that the first passage through r occurs at epoch n is given by*

$$(7.4) \qquad \varphi_{r, n} = \tfrac{1}{2}[p_{n-1, r-1} - p_{n-1, r+1}].$$

A trite calculation shows that

$$(7.5) \qquad \varphi_{r, n} = \frac{r}{n} \binom{n}{\frac{n+r}{2}} 2^{-n}$$

[as always, the binomial coefficient is to be interpreted as zero if $(n+r)/2$ is not an integer]. For an alternative derivation see section 8.*b*.

The distribution (7.5) is most interesting when r is large. To obtain the probability that the first passage through r occurs before epoch N we must sum $\varphi_{r,n}$ over all $n \leq N$. It follows from the normal approximation (2.7) that only those terms will contribute significantly to the sum for which r^2/n is neither very large nor very close to 0. For such terms the estimates of VII, 2 provide the approximation

$$(7.6) \qquad \varphi_{r,n} \sim \sqrt{\frac{2}{\pi}} \frac{r}{\sqrt{n^3}} e^{-r^2/2n}.$$

In the summation it must be borne in mind that n must have the same parity as r. The sum is the Riemann sum to the integral in (7.7), and one is led to

Theorem 3. (*Limit theorem for first passages.*) *For fixed t the probability that the first passage through r occurs before epoch tr^2 tends to*[15]

$$(7.7) \qquad \sqrt{\frac{2}{\pi}} \int_{1/\sqrt{t}}^{\infty} e^{-\frac{1}{2}s^2} ds = 2\left[1 - \mathfrak{N}\left(\frac{1}{\sqrt{t}}\right)\right]$$

as $r \to \infty$, where $\mathfrak{N}$ is the normal distribution defined in VII,1.

It follows that, roughly speaking, the waiting time for the first passage through r increases with the *square* of r: the probability of a first passage after epoch $\frac{9}{4}r^2$ has a probability close to $\frac{1}{2}$. It follows that there must exist points $k < r$ such that the passage from k to $k + 1$ takes a time longer than it took to go from 0 to k.

The distribution of the first-passage times leads directly to the distribution of the epoch when the particle returns to the origin for the rth time.

Theorem 4. *The probability that the rth return to the origin occurs at epoch n is given by the quantity $\varphi_{r,n-r}$ of* (7.5).

In words: An rth return at epoch n has the same probability as a first passage through r at epoch $n - r$.

Proof.[16] Consider a path from the origin to $(n, 0)$ with all sides below the axis and exactly $r - 1$ interior vertices on the axis. For simplicity we shall call such a path representative. (Figure 5 shows such a path with $n = 20$ and $r = 5$.) A representative path consists of r sections with endpoints on the axis, and we may construct 2^r different paths by assigning different signs to the vertices in the several sections (that is, by mirroring sections on the axis). In this way we obtain all paths ending with an rth return, and thus there are exactly 2^r times as many paths ending with an rth return at epoch n as there are representative paths. The theorem may

---

[15] (7.7) defines the so-called positive stable distribution of order $\frac{1}{2}$. For a generalization of theorem 3 see problem 14 of XIV,9.

[16] For a proof in terms of generating functions see XI,(3.17).

be therefore restated as follows: There are exactly as many representative paths of length n as there are paths of length $n - r$ ending with a first passage through r. This is so, because if in a representative path we delete the r sides whose left endpoints are on the axis we get a path of length $n - r$ ending with a first passage through r. This procedure can be reversed by inserting r sides with negative slope starting at the origin and the $r - 1$ vertices marking the first passages through $1, 2, \ldots, r - 1$. (See figure 5.) ▶

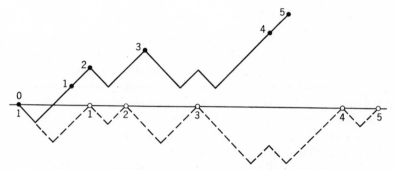

Figure 5. Illustrating first passages and returns to the origin.

It follows that the limit theorem for first returns is also applicable to rth returns as $r \to \infty$: *the probability that the rth return to the origin occurs before epoch tr^2 tends to the quantity* (7.7).

This result reveals another unexpected feature of the chance fluctuations in random walks. In the obvious sense the random walk starts from scratch every time when the particle returns to the origin. The epoch of the rth return is therefore the sum of r waiting times which can be interpreted as "measurements of the same physical quantity under identical conditions." It is generally believed that the average of r such observations is bound to converge to a "true value." But in the present case the sum is practically certain to be of the order of magnitude r^2, and so *the average increases roughly in proportion to r*. A closer analysis reveals that one among the r waiting times is likely to be of the same order of magnitude as the whole sum, namely r^2. In practice such a phenomenon would be attributed to an "experimental error" or be discarded as "outlier." It is difficult to see what one does not expect to see.

8. DUALITY. POSITION OF MAXIMA

Every path corresponds to a finite sequence of plus ones and minus ones, and reversing the order of the terms one obtains a new path. Geometrically the new path is obtained by rotating the given path through 180 degrees about its right endpoint, and taking the latter as origin of a new coordinate system. To every class of paths there corresponds in this way a new class of the same cardinality. If the steps of the original random walk are $X_1, X_2, \ldots, X_n$, then the steps of the new random walk are defined by

$$(8.1) \qquad X_1^* = X_n, \ldots, X_n^* = X_1.$$

The vertices of the new random walk are determined by the partial sums

$$(8.2) \qquad S_k^* = X_1^* + \cdots + X_k^* = S_n - S_{n-k}$$

(whence $S_0^* = 0$ and $S_n^* = S_n$). We shall refer to this as *the dual random walk*. To every event defined for the original random walk there corresponds an event of equal probability in the dual random walk, and in this way almost every probability relation has its dual. This simple method of deriving new relations is more useful than might appear at first sight. Its full power will be seen only in volume 2 in connection with general random walks and queuing theory, but even in the present context we can without effort derive some interesting new results.

To show this we shall review a few pairs of dual events, listing in each case the most noteworthy aspect. In the following list n is considered given and, to simplify language, the endpoint (n, S_n) of the path will be called *terminal point*. It is convenient to start from known events in the dual random walk.

(*a*) *First-passage times.* From (8.2) it is clear that the events defined, respectively, by

$$(8.3) \qquad\qquad S_j^* > 0, \qquad\qquad j = 1, 2, \ldots, n,$$

and

$$(8.4) \qquad\qquad S_n > S_j, \qquad\qquad j = 0, 1, \ldots, n - 1$$

are dual to each other. The second signifies that the terminal point was not visited before epoch n. We know from (3.2) that the first event has probability $\frac{1}{2}u_{2v}$ when $n = 2v > 0$ is even; for $n = 2v + 1$ the probability is the same because $S_{2v}^* > 0$ implies $S_{2v+1}^* > 0$. Accordingly, *the probability that a first passage through a positive point takes place at epoch n equals $\frac{1}{2}u_{2v}$ where $v = \frac{1}{2}n$ or $v = \frac{1}{2}(n-1)$.* (This is trivially true also for $n = 1$, but false for $n = 0$.) The duality principle leads us here to an interesting result which is not easy to verify directly.

(*b*) *Continuation.* In the preceding proposition the terminal point was not specified in advance. Prescribing the point r of the first passage means supplementing (8.4) by the condition $S_n = r$. The dual event consists of the path from the origin to (n, r) with all intermediate vertices above the axis. The number of such paths follows directly from the reflection lemma [with $A = (1, 1)$ and $B = (n, r)$], and we get thus a new proof for (7.4).

(c) *Maximum at the terminal point.* A new pair of dual events is defined when the strict inequalities $>$ in (8.3) and (8.4) are changed to $\geq$. The second event occurs whenever the term S_n is maximal even when this maximum was already attained at some previous epoch.[17] Referring to (3.4) one sees that *the probability of this event equals* u_{2v} where $v = \frac{1}{2}n$ or $v = \frac{1}{2}(n+1)$. It is noteworthy that the probabilities are twice the probabilities found under (a).

(d) The event that k returns to the origin have taken place is dual to the event that k visits to the terminal point occurred before epoch n. A similar statement applies to changes of sign. (For the probabilities see section 5 and problems 9–10.)

(e) *Arc sine law for the first visit to the terminal point.* Consider a randomly chosen path of length $n = 2v$. We saw under (a) that with probability $\frac{1}{2}u_{2v}$ the value S_{2v} is positive and such that no term of the sequence $S_0, S_1, \ldots, S_{2v-1}$ equals S_{2v}. The same is true for negative S_{2v}, and hence the probability that the value S_{2v} is not attained before epoch $2v$ equals u_{2v}; this is also the probability of the event that $S_{2v} = 0$ in which the terminal value is attained already at epoch 0. Consider now more generally the event that the first visit to the terminal point takes place at epoch $2k$ (in other words, we require that $S_{2k} = S_{2v}$ but $S_j \neq S_{2v}$ for $j < 2k$). This is the dual to the event that the last visit to the origin took place at epoch $2k$, and we saw in section 4 that such visits are governed by the discrete arc sine distribution. We have thus the unexpected result that *with probability* $\alpha_{2k,2v} = u_{2k}u_{2v-2k}$ *the first visit to the terminal point* S_{2v} *took place at epoch* $2v - 2k$ $(k = 0, 1, \ldots, v)$. It follows, in particular, that the epochs $2k$ and $2v - 2k$ are equally probable. Furthermore, very early and very late first visits are much more probable than first visits at other times.

(f) *Arc sine law for the position of the maxima.* As a last example of the usefulness of the duality principle we show that the results derived under (a) and (c) yield directly the probability distribution for the epochs at which the sequence $S_0, S_1, \ldots, S_n$ reaches its maximum value. Unfortunately the maximum value can be attained repeatedly, and so we must distinguish

---

[17] In the terminology used in chapter 12 of volume 2 we are considering a *weak ladder point* in contrast to the *strict* ladder points treated under (a).

between the first and the last maximum. The results are practically the same, however.

For simplicity let $n = 2v$ be even. The *first* maximum occurs at epoch k if

(8.5a) $$\mathbf{S}_0 < \mathbf{S}_k, \quad \ldots, \mathbf{S}_{k-1} < \mathbf{S}_k$$

(8.5b) $$\mathbf{S}_{k+1} \leq \mathbf{S}_k, \ldots \quad , \mathbf{S}_{2v} \leq \mathbf{S}_k.$$

Let us write k in the form $k = 2\rho$ or $k = 2\rho + 1$. According to (*a*) the probability of (8.5a) equals $\tfrac{1}{2}u_{2\rho}$, except when $\rho = 0$. The event (8.5b) involves only the section of the path following the epoch k and its probability obviously equals the probability that in a path of length $2v - k$ all vertices lie below or on the t-axis. It was shown under (*c*) that this probability equals $u_{2v-2\rho}$. Accordingly, *if $0 < k < 2v$ the probability that in the sequence $\mathbf{S}_0, \ldots, \mathbf{S}_{2v}$ the first maximum occurs at epochs $k = 2\rho$ or $k = 2\rho + 1$ is given by $\tfrac{1}{2}u_{2\rho}u_{2v-2\rho}$. For $k = 0$ and $k = 2v$ the probabilities are u_{2v} and $\tfrac{1}{2}u_{2v}$, respectively.*

(For the *last* maximum the probabilities for the epochs 0 and $2v$ are interchanged; the other probabilities remain unchanged provided k is written in the form $k = 2\rho$ or $k = 2\rho - 1$.)

We see that with a proper pairing of even and odd subscripts the position of the maxima becomes subject to the discrete arc sine distribution. Contrary to intuition the maximal accumulated gain is much more likely to occur towards the very beginning or the very end of a coin-tossing game than somewhere in the middle.

9. AN EQUIDISTRIBUTION THEOREM

We conclude this chapter by proving the theorem mentioned in connection with Galton's rank order test in example (1.*b*). It is instructive in that it shows how an innocuous variation in conditions can change the character of the result.

It was shown in section 4 that the number of sides lying above the x-axis is governed by the discrete arc sine distribution. We now consider the same problem but restricting our attention to paths leading from the origin to a point of the x-axis. The result is unexpected in itself and because of the striking contrast to the arc sine law.

Theorem. *The number of paths of length $2n$ such that $\mathbf{S}_{2n} = 0$ and exactly $2k$ of its sides lie above the axis is independent of k and equal to $2^{2n}u_{2n}/(n+1) = 2^{2n+1}f_{2n+2}$. (Here $k = 0, 1, \ldots, n$.)*

Proof. We consider the cases $k = 0$ and $k = n$ separately. The number of paths to $(2n, 0)$ with all sides above the x-axis equals the number of paths from $(1, 1)$ to $(2n, 0)$ which do not touch the line directly below the x-axis. By the reflection principle this number equals

$$(9.1) \qquad \binom{2n-1}{n} - \binom{2n-1}{n+1} = \frac{1}{n+1}\binom{2n}{n}.$$

This proves the assertion for $k = n$ and, by symmetry, also for $k = 0$.

For $1 \leq k \leq n - 1$ we use induction. The theorem is easily verified when $n = 1$, and we assume it correct for all paths of length less than $2n$. Denote by $2r$ the epoch of the first return. There are two possibilities. If the section of the path up to epoch $2r$ is on the positive side we must have $1 \leq r \leq k$ and the second section has exactly $2k - 2r$ sides above the axis. By the induction hypothesis a path satisfying these conditions can be chosen in

$$(9.2) \qquad 2^{2r-1}f_{2r} \cdot \frac{2^{2n-2r}}{n-r+1} u_{2n-2r} = \frac{2^{2n-2}}{r(n-r+1)} u_{2r-2}u_{2n-2r}$$

different ways. On the other hand, if the section up to the first return to the origin is on the negative side, then the terminal section of length $2n - 2r$ contains exactly $2k$ positive sides, and hence in this case $n - r \geq k$. For fixed r the number of paths satisfying these conditions is again given by (9.2). Thus the numbers of paths of the two types are obtained by summing (9.2) over $1 \leq r \leq k$ and $1 \leq r \leq n - k$, respectively. In the second sum change the summation index r to $\rho = n + 1 - r$. Then ρ runs from $k + 1$ to n, and the terms of the sum are identical with (9.2) when r is replaced by ρ. It follows that the number of paths with k positive sides is obtained by summing (9.2) over $1 \leq r \leq n$. Since k does not appear in (9.2) the sum is independent of k as asserted. Since the total number of paths is $2^{2n}u_{2n}$ this determines the number of paths in each category. (For a direct evaluation see problem 13.)   ▶

An analogous theorem holds also for the position of the maxima. (See problem 14.)

10. PROBLEMS FOR SOLUTION

1. (a) If $a > 0$ and $b > 0$, the number of paths $(s_1, s_2, \ldots, s_n)$ such that $s_1 > -b, \ldots, s_{n-1} > -b, s_n = a$ equals $N_{n,a} - N_{n,a+2b}$.

(b) If $b > a > 0$ there are $N_{n,a} - N_{n,2b-a}$ paths satisfying the conditions $s_1 < b, \ldots, s_{n-1} < b, s_n = a$.

2. Let $a > c > 0$ and $b > 0$. The number of paths which touch the line $x = a$ and then lead to (n, c) without having touched the line $x = -b$ equals

$N_{n,2a-c} - N_{n,2a+2b+c}$. (Note that this includes paths touching the line $x = -b$ *before* the line $x = a$.)

3. *Repeated reflections.* Let a and b be positive, and $-b < c < a$. The number of paths to the point (n, c) which meet neither the line $x = -b$ nor $x = a$ is given by the series

$$\sum (N_{n,2k(a+b)+c} - N_{n,2k(a+b)+2a-c}),$$

the series extending over all integers k from $-\infty$ to ∞, but having only finitely many non-zero terms.

Hint: Use and extend the method of the preceding problem.

Note. This is connected with the so-called *ruin problem* which arises in gambling when the two players have initial capitals a and b so that the game terminates when the accumulated gain reaches either a or $-b$. For the connection with statistical tests, see example (1.*c*).

(The method of repeated reflections will be used again in problem 17 of XIV,9 and in connection with diffusion theory in volume 2; X,5.)

4. From lemma 3.1 conclude (without calculations) that

$$u_0 u_{2n} + u_2 u_{2n-2} + \cdots + u_{2n} u_0 = 1.$$

5. Show that

$$u_{2n} = (-1)^n \binom{-\frac{1}{2}}{n} \qquad f_{2n} = (-1)^{n-1} \binom{\frac{1}{2}}{n}.$$

Derive the identity of the preceding problem as well as (2.6) from II, (12.9).

6. Prove geometrically that there are exactly as many paths ending at $(2n + 2, 0)$ and having all interior vertices strictly above the axis as there are paths ending at $(2n, 0)$ and having all vertices above or on the axis. Therefore $\mathbf{P}\{S_1 \geq 0, \ldots, S_{2n-1} \geq 0, S_{2n} = 0\} = 2f_{2n+2}$.

Hint: Refer to figure 1.

7. Prove lemma 3.1 geometrically by showing that the following construction establishes a one-to-one correspondence between the two classes of paths:

Given a path to $(2n, 0)$ denote its *leftmost* minimum point by $M = (k, m)$. Reflect the section from the origin to M on the vertical line $t = k$ and slide the reflected section to the endpoint $(2n, 0)$. If M is taken as origin of a new coordinate system the new path leads from the origin to $(2n, 2m)$ and has all vertices strictly above or on the axis. (This construction is due to E. Nelson.)

8. Prove formula (3.5) directly by considering the paths that never meet the line $x = -1$.

9. The probability that *before* epoch $2n$ there occur exactly r returns to the origin equals the probability that a return takes place at epoch $2n$ and is preceded by at least r returns. *Hint:* Use lemma 3.1.

10. *Continuation.* Denote by $z_{r,2n}$ the probability that exactly r returns to the origin occur up to and including epoch $2n$. Using the preceding problem show that $z_{r,2n} = p_{r,2n} + p_{r+1,2n} + \cdots$ where $p_{r,2n}$ is the probability that the rth return occurs at epoch $2n$. Using theorem 7.4 conclude that

$$z_{r,2n} = \frac{1}{2^{2n-r}} \cdot \binom{2n-r}{n}.$$

11. *Alternative derivation for the probabilities for the number of changes of sign.* Show that

$$\xi_{r,2n-1} = \frac{1}{2} \sum_{k=1}^{n-1} f_{2k}[\xi_{r-1,2n-1-2k} + \xi_{r,2n-1-2k}].$$

Assuming by induction that (5.1) holds for all epochs prior to $2n - 1$ show that this reduces to

$$\xi_{r,2n-1} = 2 \sum_{1}^{n-1} f_{2k} p_{2n-2k,2r}$$

which is the probability of reaching the point $(2n, 2r)$ after a return to the origin. Considering the first step and using the ballot theorem conclude that (5.1) holds.

12. The probability that $S_{2n} = 0$ and the maximum of $S_1, \ldots, S_{2n-1}$ equals k is the same as $P\{S_{2n} = 2k\} - P\{S_{2n} = 2k + 2\}$. Prove this by reflection.

13. In the proof of section 9 it was shown that

$$\sum_{r=1}^{n} \frac{1}{r(n-r+1)} u_{2r-2} u_{2n-2r} = \frac{1}{n+1} u_{2n}.$$

Show that this relation is equivalent to (2.6). *Hint:* Decompose the fraction.

14. Consider a path of length $2n$ with $S_{2n} = 0$. We order the sides in circular order by identifying 0 and $2n$ with the result that the first and the last side become adjacent. Applying a cyclical permutation amounts to viewing the same closed path with (k, S_k) as origin. Show that this preserves maxima, but moves them k steps ahead. Conclude that when all $2n$ cyclical permutations are applied the number of times that a maximum occurs at r is independent of r.

Consider now a randomly chosen path with $S_{2n} = 0$ and pick the place of the maximum if the latter is unique; if there are several maxima, pick one at random. This procedure leads to a number between 0 and $2n - 1$. Show that all possibilities are equally probable.

CHAPTER IV

Combination of Events

This chapter is concerned with events which are defined in terms of certain other events $A_1, A_2, \ldots, A_N$. For example, in bridge the event A, "at least one player has a complete suit," is the union of the four events A_k, "player number k has a complete suit" $(k = 1, 2, 3, 4)$. Of the events A_k one, two, or more can occur simultaneously, and, because of this overlap, the probability of A is not the sum of the four probabilities $\mathbf{P}\{A_k\}$. Given a set of events $A_1, \ldots, A_N$, we shall show how to compute the probabilities that $0, 1, 2, 3, \ldots$ among them occur.[1]

1. UNION OF EVENTS

If A_1 and A_2 are two events, then $A = A_1 \cup A_2$ denotes the event that either A_1 or A_2 or both occur. From I, (7.4) we know that

(1.1) $$\mathbf{P}\{A\} = \mathbf{P}\{A_1\} + \mathbf{P}\{A_2\} - \mathbf{P}\{A_1 A_2\}.$$

We want to generalize this formula to the case of N events $A_1, A_2, \ldots, A_N$; that is, we wish to compute the probability of the event that at least one among the A_k occurs. In symbols this event is

$$A = A_1 \cup A_2 \cup \cdots \cup A_N.$$

For our purpose it is not sufficient to know the probabilities of the individual events A_k, but we must be given complete information concerning all possible overlaps. This means that for every pair (i, j), every triple (i, j, k), etc., we must know the probability of A_i and A_j, or A_i, A_j, and

---

* The material of this chapter will not be used explicitly in the sequel. Only the first theorem is of considerable importance.

[1] For further information see M. Fréchet, *Les probabilités associées a un système d'événements compatibles et dépendants*, Actualités scientifiques et industrielles, nos. 859 and 942, Paris, 1940 and 1943.

A_k, etc., occurring simultaneously. For convenience of notation we shall denote these probabilities by the letter p with appropriate subscripts. Thus

$$(1.2) \qquad p_i = \mathbf{P}\{A_i\}, \qquad p_{ij} = \mathbf{P}\{A_i A_j\}, \qquad p_{ijk} = \mathbf{P}\{A_i A_j A_k\}, \ldots.$$

The order of the subscripts is irrelevant, but for uniqueness we shall always *write the subscripts in increasing order*; thus, we write $p_{3,7,11}$ and not $p_{7,3,11}$. Two subscripts are never equal. For the sum of all p's with r subscripts we shall write S_r, that is, we define

$$(1.3) \qquad S_1 = \sum p_i, \qquad S_2 = \sum p_{ij}, \qquad S_3 = \sum p_{ijk}, \ldots.$$

Here $i < j < k < \cdots \leq N$, so that in the sums each combination appears once and only once; hence S_r has $\binom{N}{r}$ terms. The last sum, S_N, reduces to the single term $p_{1,2,3,\ldots,N}$, which is the probability of the simultaneous realization of all N events. For $N = 2$ we have only the two terms S_1 and S_2, and (1.1) can be written

$$(1.4) \qquad \mathbf{P}\{A\} = S_1 - S_2.$$

The generalization to an arbitrary number N of events is given in the following

Theorem. *The probability P_1 of the realization of at least one among the events $A_1, A_2, \ldots, A_N$ is given by*

$$(1.5) \qquad P_1 = S_1 - S_2 + S_3 - S_4 + - \cdots \pm S_N.$$

Proof. We prove (1.5) by the so-called method of inclusion and exclusion (cf. problem 26). To compute P_1 we should add the probabilities of all sample points which are contained in at least one of the A_i, but each point should be taken only once. To proceed systematically we first take the points which are contained in only one A_i, then those contained in exactly two events A_i, and so forth, and finally the points (if any) contained in all A_i. Now let E be any sample point contained in exactly n among our N events A_i. Without loss of generality we may number the events so that E is contained in $A_1, A_2, \ldots, A_n$ but not contained in $A_{n+1}, A_{n+2}, \ldots, A_N$. Then $\mathbf{P}\{E\}$ appears as a contribution to those $p_i, p_{ij}, p_{ijk}, \ldots$ whose subscripts range from 1 to n. Hence $\mathbf{P}\{E\}$ appears n times as a contribution to S_1, and $\binom{n}{2}$ times as a contribution to S_2, etc. In all, when the right-hand side of (1.5) is expressed in terms of the probabilities of sample points we find $\mathbf{P}\{E\}$ with the factor

(1.6) $$n - \binom{n}{2} + \binom{n}{3} - + \cdots \pm \binom{n}{n}.$$

It remains to show that this number equals 1. This follows at once on comparing (1.6) with the binomial expansion of $(1-1)^n$ [cf. II, (8.7)]. The latter starts with 1, and the terms of (1.6) follow with reversed sign. Hence for every $n \geq 1$ the expression (1.6) equals 1. ▶

Examples. (*a*) In a game of bridge let A_i be the event "player number i has a complete suit." Then $p_i = 4 / \binom{52}{13}$; the event that both player i and player j have complete suits can occur in $4 \cdot 3$ ways and has probability $p_{ij} = 12 / \binom{52}{13}\binom{39}{13}$; similarly we find

$$p_{ijk} = 24 / \binom{52}{13}\binom{39}{13}\binom{26}{13}.$$

Finally, $p_{1,2,3,4} = p_{1,2,3}$, since whenever three players have a complete suit so does the fourth. The probability that *some* player has a complete suit is therefore $P_1 = 4p_1 - 6p_{1,2} + 4p_{1,2,3} - p_{1,2,3,4}$. Using Stirling's formula, we see that $P_1 = \frac{1}{4} \cdot 10^{-10}$ approximately. In this particular case P_1 is very nearly the sum of the probabilities of A_i, but this is the exception rather than the rule.

(*b*) *Matches* (*coincidences*). The following problem with many variants and a surprising solution goes back to Montmort (1708). It has been generalized by Laplace and many other authors.

Two equivalent decks of N different cards each are put into random order and matched against each other. If a card occupies the same place in both decks, we speak of a *match* (*coincidence* or *rencontre*). Matches may occur at any of the N places and at several places simultaneously. This experiment may be described in more amusing forms. For example, the two decks may be represented by a set of N letters and their envelopes, and a capricious secretary may perform the random matching. Alternatively we may imagine the hats in a checkroom mixed and distributed at random to the guests. A match occurs if a person gets his own hat. It is instructive to venture guesses as to how the probability of a match depends on N: How does the probability of a match of hats in a diner with 8 guests compare with the corresponding probability at a gathering of 10,000 people? It seems surprising that the probability is practically independent of N and roughly $\frac{2}{3}$. (For less frivolous applications cf. problems 10 and 11.)

TABLE 2

Poisson Approximation (2.11) to the Probabilities of Finding Exactly m Empty Cells When r Balls Are Randomly Distributed in $n = 1000$ Cells

$$p(m; \lambda)$$

r	λ	$m=0$	$m=1$	$m=2$	$m=3$	$m=4$	$m=5$	$m=6$	$m=7$	$m=8$	$m=9$	$m=10$	$m=11$
5000	6.74	0.0012	0.0080	0.0269	0.0604	0.1017	0.1371	0.1540	0.1482	0.1249	0.0935	0.0630	0.0386
5500	4.09	0.0167	0.0685	0.1400	0.1909	0.1951	0.1596	0.1088	0.0636	0.0325	0.0148	0.0060	0.0023
6000	2.48	0.0838	0.2077	0.2575	0.2128	0.1320	0.0655	0.0271	0.0096	0.0030	0.0008	0.0002	
6500	1.50	0.2231	0.3347	0.2510	0.1255	0.0471	0.0141	0.0035	0.0008	0.0001			
7000	0.91	0.4027	0.3661	0.1666	0.0506	0.0115	0.0021	0.0003					
7500	0.55	0.5777	0.3163	0.0873	0.0162	0.0023	0.0003						
8000	0.34	0.7126	0.2406	0.0414	0.0049	0.0004							
8500	0.20	0.8187	0.1637	0.0164	0.0011	0.0001							
9000	0.12	0.8869	0.1064	0.0064	0.0003								

The probabilities of having exactly 0, 1, 2, 3, ... matches will be calculated in section 4. Here we shall derive only the probability P_1 of at least 1 match. For simplicity of expression let us renumber the cards $1, 2, \ldots, N$ in such a way that one deck appears in its natural order, and assume that each permutation of the second deck has probability $1/N!$. Let A_k be the event that a match occurs at the kth place. This means that card number k is at the kth place, and the remaining $N - 1$ cards may be in an arbitrary order. Clearly $p_k = (N-1)!/N! = 1/N$. Similarly, for every combination i, j we have $p_{ij} = (N-2)!/N! = 1/N(N-1)$, etc. The sum S_r contains $\binom{N}{r}$ terms, each of which equals $(N-r)!/N!$. Hence $S_r = 1/r!$, and from (1.5) we find the required probability to be

$$(1.7) \qquad P_1 = 1 - \frac{1}{2!} + \frac{1}{3!} - + \cdots \pm \frac{1}{N!}.$$

Note that $1 - P_1$ represents the first $N + 1$ terms in the expansion

$$(1.8) \qquad e^{-1} = 1 - 1 + \frac{1}{2!} - \frac{1}{3!} + \frac{1}{4!} - + \cdots,$$

and hence

$$(1.9) \qquad P_1 \approx 1 - e^{-1} = 0.63212\ldots,$$

approximately. The degree of approximation is shown in the following table of correct values of P_1:

$N =$	3	4	5	6	7
$P_1 =$	0.66667	0.62500	0.63333	0.63196	0.63214

2. APPLICATION TO THE CLASSICAL OCCUPANCY PROBLEM

We now return to the problem of a random distribution of r balls in n cells, assuming that each arrangement has probability n^{-r}. We seek the probability $p_m(r, n)$ of finding exactly m cells empty.[2]

Let A_k be the event that cell number k is empty $(k = 1, 2, \ldots, n)$. In this event all r balls are placed in the remaining $n - 1$ cells, and this can be done in $(n-1)^r$ different ways. Similarly, there are $(n-2)^r$

---

[2] This probability was derived, by an entirely different method, in problem 8 in II, 11. Compare also the concluding remark in section 3.

arrangements, leaving two preassigned cells empty, etc. Accordingly

$$(2.1) \qquad p_i = \left(1 - \frac{1}{n}\right)^r, \quad p_{ij} = \left(1 - \frac{2}{n}\right)^r, \quad p_{ijk} = \left(1 - \frac{3}{n}\right)^r, \ldots$$

and hence for every $v \leq n$

$$(2.2) \qquad S_v = \binom{n}{v}\left(1 - \frac{v}{n}\right)^r.$$

The probability that at least one cell is empty is given by (1.5), and hence we find for the *probability that all cells are occupied*

$$(2.3) \quad p_0(r, n) = 1 - S_1 + S_2 - + \cdots = \sum_{v=0}^{n}(-1)^v\binom{n}{v}\left(1 - \frac{v}{n}\right)^r.$$

Consider now a distribution in which exactly m cells are empty. These m cells can be chosen in $\binom{n}{m}$ ways. The r balls are distributed among the remaining $n - m$ cells so that each of these cells is occupied; the number of such distributions is $(n-m)^r p_0(r, n-m)$. Dividing by n^r we find for the *probability that exactly m cells remain empty*

$$(2.4) \qquad p_m(r, n) = \binom{n}{m}\left(1 - \frac{m}{n}\right)^r p_0(r, n-m) =$$

$$= \binom{n}{m}\sum_{v=0}^{n-m}(-1)^v\binom{n-m}{v}\left(1 - \frac{m+v}{n}\right)^r.$$

We have already used the model of r random digits to illustrate the random distribution of r things in $n = 10$ cells. Empty cells correspond in this case to missing digits: if m cells are empty, $10 - m$ different digits appear in the given sequence. Table 1 provides a numerical illustration.

It is clear that a direct numerical evaluation of (2.4) is limited to the case of relatively small n and r. On the other hand, the occupancy problem is of particular interest when n is large. If 10,000 balls are distributed in 1000 cells, is there any chance of finding an empty cell? In a group of 2000 people, is there any chance of finding a day in the year which is not a birthday? Fortunately, questions of this kind can be answered by means of a remarkably simple approximation with an error which tends to zero as $n \to \infty$. This approximation and the argument leading to it are typical of many *limit theorems* in probability.

Our purpose, then, is to discuss the limiting form of the formula (2.4) as $n \to \infty$ and $r \to \infty$. The relation between r and n is, in principle,

TABLE 1

PROBABILITIES $p_m(r, 10)$ ACCORDING TO (2.4)

m	$r = 10$	$r = 18$
0	0.000 363	0.134 673
1	0.016 330	0.385 289
2	0.136 080	0.342 987
3	0.355 622	0.119 425
4	0.345 144	0.016 736
5	0.128 596	0.000 876
6	0.017 189	0.000 014
7	0.000 672	0.000 000
8	0.000 005	0.000 000
9	0.000 000	0.000 000

$p_m(r, 10)$ is the probability that exactly m of the digits $0, 1, \ldots, 9$ will *not* appear in a sequence of r random digits.

arbitrary, but if the average number r/n of balls per cell is excessive large, then we cannot expect any empty cells; in this case $p_0(r, n)$ near unity and all $p_m(r, n)$ with $m \geq 1$ are small. On the other hand r/n tends to zero, then practically all cells must be empty, and in this $p_m(r, n) \to 0$ for every fixed m. Therefore only the intermediate case real interest.

We begin by estimating the quantity S_v of (2.2). Since

$$(n-v)^v < (n)_v < n^v$$

we have

$$(2.5) \qquad n^v\left(1 - \frac{v}{n}\right)^{v+r} < v!\, S_v < n^v\left(1 - \frac{v}{n}\right)^r.$$

For $0 < t < 1$ it is clear from the expansion II, (8.10) that lies between t and $t/(1-t)$. Therefore

$$(2.6) \qquad \{ne^{-(v+r)/(n-v)}\}^v < v!\, S_v < \{ne^{-r/n}\}^v.$$

Now put for abbreviation

$$(2.7) \qquad ne^{-r/n} = \lambda$$

and suppose that r and n increase in such a way that strained to a finite interval $0 < a < \lambda < b$. For each fix

the extreme members in (2.6) then tends to unity, and so

$$(2.8) \qquad 0 \leq \frac{\lambda^{\nu}}{\nu!} - S_{\nu} \to 0.$$

This relation holds trivially when $\lambda \to 0$, and hence (2.8) remains true whenever r and n increase in such way that λ remains bounded. Now

$$(2.9) \qquad e^{-\lambda} - p_0(r, n) = \sum_{\nu=0}^{\infty} (-1)^{\nu} \left\{ \frac{\lambda^{\nu}}{\nu!} - S_{\nu} \right\}$$

and (2.8) implies that the right side tends to zero. Furthermore, the factor of $p_0(r, n - m)$ in (2.4) may be rewritten as S_m, and we have therefore for each fixed m

$$(2.10) \qquad p_m(r, n) - e^{-\lambda} \frac{\lambda^m}{m!} \to 0.$$

This completes the proof of the

Theorem.[3] *If n and r tend to infinity so that $\lambda = ne^{-r/n}$ remains bounded, then* (2.10) *holds for each fixed m.*

The approximating expressions

$$(2.11) \qquad p(m; \lambda) = e^{-\lambda} \frac{\lambda^m}{m!}$$

define the so-called *Poisson distribution*, which is of great importance and describes a variety of phenomena; it will be studied in chapter VI.

In practice we may use $p(m; \lambda)$ as an approximation whenever n is great. For moderate values of n an estimate of the error is required, but we shall not enter into it.

Examples. (*a*) Table 2 gives the approximate probabilities of finding m cells empty when the number of cells is 1000 and the number of balls varies from 5000 to 9000. For $r = 5000$ the median value of the number of empty cells is six: seven or more empty cells are about as probable as six or fewer. Even with 9000 balls in 1000 cells we have about one chance in nine to find an empty cell.

(*b*) In birthday statistics [example II, (3.*d*)] $n = 365$, and r is the number of people. For $r = 1900$ we find $\lambda = 2$, approximately. *In a village of 1900 people the probabilities $P_{[m]}$ of finding m days of the year*

---

[3] Due (with a different proof) to R. von Mises, *Über Aufteilungs- und Besetzungs-wahrscheinlichkeiten*, Revue de la Faculté des Sciences de l'Université d'Istanbul, N.S., vol. 4 (1939), pp. 145–163.

which are not birthdays are approximately as follows:

$$P_{[0]} = 0.135, \qquad P_{[1]} = 0.271, \qquad P_{[2]} = 0.271, \qquad P_{[3]} = 0.180,$$

$$P_{[4]} = 0.090, \qquad P_{[5]} = 0.036, \qquad P_{[6]} = 0.012, \qquad P_{[7]} = 0.003.$$

(c) When $n \log n + an$ balls are placed into n cells and n is large, the probability of finding all cells occupied is $1 - e^{-a}$.   ▶

Instead of empty cells one may consider cells containing exactly k balls. The argument used above for the special case $k = 0$ applies with minor changes. As von Mises has shown, the probability of finding exactly m cells with k-tuple occupancy can again be approximated by the Poisson distribution (2.11), but this time λ must be defined as

$$(2.12) \qquad \lambda = n \frac{e^{-r/n}}{k!} \left(\frac{r}{n}\right)^k.$$

3. THE REALIZATION OF m AMONG N EVENTS

The theorem of section 1 can be strengthened as follows.

Theorem. *For any integer m with $1 \leq m \leq N$ the probability $P_{[m]}$ that exactly m among the N events $A_1, \ldots, A_N$ occur simultaneously is given by*

$$(3.1) \quad P_{[m]} = S_m - \binom{m+1}{m} S_{m+1} + \binom{m+2}{m} S_{m+2} - + \cdots \pm \binom{N}{m} S_N.$$

Note: According to (1.5), the probability $P_{[0]}$ that none among the A_j occurs is

$$(3.2) \qquad P_{[0]} = 1 - P_1 = 1 - S_1 + S_2 - S_3 \pm \cdots \mp S_N.$$

This shows that (3.1) gives the correct value also for $m = 0$ provided we put $S_0 = 1$.

Proof. We proceed as in the proof of (1.5). Let E be an arbitrary sample point, and suppose that it is contained in exactly n among the N events A_j. Then $\mathbf{P}\{E\}$ appears as a contribution to $P_{[m]}$ only if $n = m$. To investigate how $\mathbf{P}\{E\}$ contributes to the right side of (3.1), note that $\mathbf{P}\{E\}$ appears in the sums $S_1, S_2, \ldots, S_n$ but not in S_{n+1}, $\ldots, S_N$. It follows that $\mathbf{P}\{E\}$ does not contribute to the right side in (3.1) if $n < m$. If $n = m$, then $\mathbf{P}\{E\}$ appears in one and only one term of S_m. To complete the proof of the theorem it remains to show that for $n > m$ the contributions of $\mathbf{P}\{E\}$ to the terms $S_m, S_{m+1}, \ldots, S_n$ on the right in (3.1) cancel. Now $\mathbf{P}\{E\}$ appears in S_k with the factor $\binom{n}{k}$, namely the number of k-tuplets that can be formed out of the n events containing the point E. For $n > m$ the total contribution of $\mathbf{P}\{E\}$ to the right side in (3.1) is therefore

$$(3.3) \qquad \binom{n}{m} - \binom{m+1}{m}\binom{n}{m+1} + \binom{m+2}{m}\binom{n}{m+2} - + \cdots .$$

When the binomial coefficients are expressed in terms of factorials, it is seen that this expression reduces to

$$(3.4) \qquad \binom{n}{m}\left\{\binom{n-m}{0} - \binom{n-m}{1} + - \cdots \pm \binom{n-m}{n-m}\right\}.$$

Within the braces we have the binomial expansion of $(1-1)^{n-m}$ so that (3.3) vanishes, as asserted.   ▶

The reader is asked to verify that a substitution from formula (2.2) into (3.1) leads *directly* to (2.4).

4. APPLICATION TO MATCHING AND GUESSING

In example (1.*b*) we considered the matching of two decks of cards and found that $S_k = 1/k!$. Substituting into (3.1), we find the following result.

In a random matching of two equivalent decks of N distinct cards the probability $P_{[m]}$ of having exactly m matches is given by

$$P_{[0]} = 1 - 1 + \frac{1}{2!} - \frac{1}{3!} + - \cdots \pm \frac{1}{(N-2)!} \mp \frac{1}{(N-1)!} \pm \frac{1}{N!}$$

$$(4.1) \qquad P_{[1]} = 1 - 1 + \frac{1}{2!} - \frac{1}{3!} + - \cdots \pm \frac{1}{(N-2)!} \mp \frac{1}{(N-1)!}$$

$$P_{[2]} = \frac{1}{2!}\left\{1 - 1 + \frac{1}{2!} - \frac{1}{3!} + - \cdots \pm \frac{1}{(N-3)!} \mp \frac{1}{(N-2)!}\right\}$$

$$P_{[3]} = \frac{1}{3!}\left\{1 - 1 + \frac{1}{2!} - \frac{1}{3!} + - \cdots \pm \frac{1}{(N-3)!}\right\}$$

$$\cdots \cdots \cdots \cdots \cdots \cdots \cdots \cdots$$

$$\cdots \cdots \cdots \cdots \cdots \cdots \cdots \cdots$$

$$P_{[N-2]} = \frac{1}{(N-2)!}\left\{1 - 1 + \frac{1}{2!}\right\}$$

$$P_{[N-1]} = \frac{1}{(N-1)!}\{1 - 1\} = 0 \qquad P_{[N]} = \frac{1}{N!} .$$

TABLE 3

PROBABILITIES OF m CORRECT GUESSES IN CALLING A DECK OF N DISTINCT CARDS

	$N = 3$		$N = 4$		$N = 5$		$N = 6$		$N = 10$		
	$P_{[m]}$	b_m	$P_{[m]}$	b_m	$P_{[m]}$	b_m	$P_{[m]}$	b_m	$P_{[m]}$	b_m	p_m
0	0.333	0.296	0.375	0.316	0.367	0.328	0.368	0.335	0.36788	0.34868	0.367879
1	0.500	0.444	0.333	0.422	0.375	0.410	0.367	0.402	0.36788	0.38742	0.367879
2	...	0.222	0.250	0.211	0.167	0.205	0.187	0.201	0.18394	0.19371	0.183940
3	0.167	0.037	...	0.047	0.083	0.051	0.056	0.053	0.06131	0.05740	0.061313
4			0.042	0.004	...	0.006	0.021	0.008	0.01534	0.01116	0.015328
5					0.008	0.000	...	0.001	0.00306	0.00149	0.003066
6							0.001	0.000	0.00052	0.00014	0.000511
7									0.00007	0.00001	0.000073
8									0.00001	.....	0.000009
9									.....	.....	0.000001
10									.....	.....	0.000000

The $P_{[m]}$ are given by (4.1), the b_m by (4.4). The last column gives the Poisson limits (4..3)

The last relation is obvious. The vanishing of $P_{[N-1]}$ expresses the impossibility of having $N - 1$ matches without having all N cards in the same order.

The braces on the right in (4.1) contain the initial terms of the expansion of e^{-1}. *For large N we have therefore approximately*

$$(4.2) \qquad P_{[m]} \approx \frac{e^{-1}}{m!}$$

In table 3 the columns headed $P_{[m]}$ give the exact values of $P_{[m]}$ for $N = 3, 4, 5, 6, 10$. The last column gives the limiting values

$$(4.3) \qquad p_m = \frac{e^{-1}}{m!} .$$

The approximation of p_m to $P_{[m]}$ is rather good even for moderate values of N.

For the numbers p_m defined by (4.3) we have

$$\sum p_k = e^{-1}\left(1 + 1 + \frac{1}{2!} + \frac{1}{3!} + \cdots\right) = e^{-1}e = 1.$$

Accordingly, the p_k may be interpreted as probabilities. Note that (4.3) represents the special case $\lambda = 1$ of the *Poisson distribution* (2.11).

Example. *Testing guessing abilities.* In wine tasting, psychic experiments, etc., the subject is asked to call an unknown order of N things, say, cards. Any actual insight on the part of the subject will appear as a departure from randomness. To judge the amount of insight we must appraise the probability of turns of good luck. Now chance guesses can be made according to several systems among which we mention three extreme possibilities. (i) The subject sticks to one card and keeps calling it. With this system he is sure to have one, and only one, correct guess in each series; chance fluctuations are eliminated. (ii) The subject calls each card once so that each series of N guesses corresponds to a rearrangement of the deck. If this system is applied without insight, formulas (4.1) should apply. (iii) A third possibility is that N guesses are made absolutely independently of each other. There are N^N possible arrangements. It is true that every person has fixed mental habits and is prone to call certain patterns more frequently than others, but in first approximation we may assume all N^N arrangements to be equally probable. Since m correct and $N-m$ incorrect guesses can be arranged in $\binom{N}{m}(N-1)^{N-m}$ different ways, the probability of exactly m correct guesses is now

$$(4.4) \qquad b_m = \binom{N}{m}\frac{(N-1)^{N-m}}{N^N}.$$

[This is a special case of the binomial distribution and has been derived in example II, (4.c).]

Table 3 gives a comparison of the probabilities of success when guesses are made in accordance with system (ii) or (iii). To judge the merits of the two methods we require the theory of mean values and probable fluctuations. It turns out that the average number of correct chance guesses is one under all systems; the chance fluctuations are somewhat larger under system (ii) than (iii). A glance at table 3 will show that in practice the differences will not be excessive.   ▶

5. MISCELLANY

(a) The Realization of at Least m Events

With the notations of section 3 *the probability* P_m *that m or more of the events* $A_1, \ldots, A_N$ *occur simultaneously is given by*

$$(5.1) \qquad P_m = P_{[m]} + P_{[m+1]} + \cdots + P_{[N]}.$$

To find a formula for P_m in terms of S_k it is simplest to proceed by induction, starting with the expression (1.5) for P_1 and using the recurrence relation $P_{m+1} = P_m - P_{[m]}$. We get for $m \geq 1$

$$(5.2) \quad P_m = S_m - \binom{m}{m-1}S_{m+1} +$$

$$+ \binom{m+1}{m-1}S_{m+2} - \binom{m+2}{m-1}S_{m+3} + \cdots \pm \binom{N-1}{m-1}S_N.$$

It is also possible to derive (5.2) directly, using the argument which led to (3.1).

(b) Further Identities

The coefficients S_ν can be expressed in terms of either $P_{[k]}$ or P_k as follows

$$(5.3) \qquad S_\nu = \sum_{k=\nu}^{N} \binom{k}{\nu} P_{[k]}$$

and

$$(5.4) \qquad S_\nu = \sum_{k=\nu}^{N} \binom{k-1}{\nu-1} P_k.$$

Indication of proof. For given values of $P_{[m]}$ the equations (3.1) may be taken as linear equations in the unknowns S_ν, and we have to prove that (5.3) represents the unique solution. If (5.3) is introduced into the expression (3.1) for $P_{[m]}$, the coefficient of $P_{[k]}$ $(m \leq k \leq N)$ to the right is found to be

$$(5.5) \qquad \sum_{\nu=m}^{k} (-1)^{\nu-m} \binom{\nu}{m} \binom{k}{\nu} = \binom{k}{m} \sum_{\nu=m}^{k} (-1)^{\nu-m} \binom{k-m}{\nu-m}.$$

If $k = m$ this expression reduces to 1. If $k > m$ the sum is the binomial expansion of $(1-1)^{k-m}$ and therefore vanishes. Hence the substitution (5.3) reduces (3.1) to the identity $P_{[m]} = P_{[m]}$. The uniqueness of the solution of (3.1) follows from the fact that each equation introduces only one new unknown, so that the S_ν can be computed recursively. The truth of (5.4) can be proved in a similar way.

(c) Bonferroni's Inequalities

A string of inequalities both for $P_{[m]}$ and for P_m can be obtained in the following way. If in either (3.1) or (5.2) only the terms involving $S_m, S_{m+1}, \ldots, S_{m+r-1}$ are retained while the terms involving $S_{m+r}, S_{m+r+1}, \ldots, S_N$ are dropped, then the error (i.e., true value minus approximation) has the sign of the first omitted term [namely, $(-1)^r$], and is smaller in absolute value. Thus, for $r = 1$ and $r = 2$:

$$(5.6) \qquad S_m - (m+1)S_{m+1} \leq P_{[m]} \leq S_m$$

and

$$(5.7) \qquad S_m - mS_{m+1} \leq P_m \leq S_m.$$

Indication of Proof. The identity (3.1) for $P_{[m]}$ shows that the assertion (5.6) is equivalent to

$$(5.8) \qquad \sum_{\nu=t}^{N} (-1)^{\nu-t} \binom{\nu}{m} S_\nu \geq 0,$$

for every t. Now use (5.3) to write the left side as a linear combination of the $P_{[k]}$. For $t \leq k \leq N$ the coefficient of $P_{[k]}$ equals

$$\sum_{v=t}^{k} (-1)^{v-t} \binom{v}{m}\binom{k}{v} = \binom{k}{m} \sum_{v=t}^{k} (-1)^{v-t} \binom{k-m}{v-m}.$$

The last sum equals $\binom{k-m-1}{t-m-1}$ and is therefore positive (problem 13 of II, 12). For further inequalities the reader is referred to Fréchet's monograph cited at the beginning of the chapter.

6. PROBLEMS FOR SOLUTION

Note: *Assume in each case that all possible arrangements have the same probability.*

1. Ten pair of shoes are in a closet. Four shoes are selected at random. Find the probability that there will be at least one pair among the four shoes selected.

2. Five dice are thrown. Find the probability that at least three of them show the same face. (Verify by the methods of II, 5.)

3. Find the probability that in five tossings a coin falls heads at least three times in succession.

4. Solve problem 3 for a head-run of at least length five in ten tossings.

5. Solve problems 3 and 4 for ace runs when a die is used instead of a coin.

6. Two dice are thrown r times. Find the probability p_r that each of the six combinations $(1, 1), \ldots, (6, 6)$ appears at least once.

7. *Quadruples in a bridge hand.* By a quadruple we shall understand four cards of the same face value, so that a bridge hand of thirteen cards may contain 0, 1, 2, or 3 quadruples. Calculate the corresponding probabilities.

8. *Sampling with replacement.* A sample of size r is taken from a population of n people. Find the probability u_r that N given people will all be included in the sample. (This is problem 12 of II, 11.)

9. *Sampling without replacement.* Answer problem 8 for this case and show that $u_r \to p^N$. (This is problem 3 of II, 11, but the present method leads to a formally entirely different result. Prove their identity.)

10. In the general expansion of a determinant of order N the number of terms containing one or more diagonal elements is $N! P_1$ defined by (1.7).

11. The number of ways in which 8 rooks can be placed on a chessboard so that none can take another and that none stands on the white diagonal is $8! (1 - P_1)$, where P_1 is defined by (1.7) with $N = 8$.

12. *A sampling (coupon collector's) problem.* A pack of cards consists of s identical series, each containing n cards numbered $1, 2, \ldots, n$. A random sample of $r \geq n$ cards is drawn from the pack without replacement. Calculate the probability u_r that each number is represented in the sample. (Applied to a deck of bridge cards we get for $s = 4$, $n = 13$ the probability that a hand of r cards contains all 13 values; and for $s = 13$, $n = 4$ we get the probability that all four suits are represented.)

13. *Continuation.* Show that as $s \to \infty$ one has $u_r \to p_0(r, n)$ where the latter expression is defined in (2.3). This means that in the limit our sampling becomes random sampling with replacement from the population of the numbers $1, 2, \ldots, n$.

14. *Continuation.* From the result of problem 12 conclude that

$$\sum_{k=0}^{n} (-1)^k \binom{n}{k} (ns - ks)_r = 0$$

if $r < n$ and for $r = n$

$$\sum_{k=0}^{n} (-1)^k \binom{n}{k} (ns - ks)_n = s^n n!.$$

Verify this by evaluating the rth derivative, at $x = 0$, of

$$\frac{1}{(1-x)^{ns-r+1}} \{1 - (1-x)^s\}^n.$$

15. In the sampling problem 12 find the probability that it will take exactly r drawings to get a sample containing all numbers. Pass to the limit as $s \to \infty$.

16. A cell contains N chromosomes, between any two of which an interchange of parts may occur. If r interchanges occur (which can happen in $\binom{N}{2}^r$ distinct ways), find the probability that exactly m chromosomes will be involved.[4]

17. Find the probability that exactly k suits will be missing in a poker hand.

18. Find the probability that a hand of thirteen bridge cards contains the ace-king pairs of exactly k suits.

19. *Multiple matching.* Two similar decks of N distinct cards each are matched simultaneously against a similar target deck. Find the probability u_m of having exactly m double matches. Show that $u_0 \to 1$ as $N \to \infty$ (which implies that $u_m \to 0$ for $m \geq 1$).

20. *Multiple matching.* The procedure of the preceding problem is modified as follows. Out of the $2N$ cards N are chosen at random, and only these N are matched against the target deck. Find the probability of no match. Prove that it tends to $1/e$ as $N \to \infty$.

21. *Multiple matching.* Answer problem 20 if r decks are used instead of two.

22. In the classical occupancy problem, the probability $P_{[m]}(k)$ of finding exactly m cells occupied by exactly k things is

$$P_{[m]}(k) = \frac{(-1)^m n! \, r!}{m! \, n^r} \sum_{j} (-1)^j \frac{(n-j)^{r-jk}}{(j-m)! \, (n-j)! \, (r-jk)! \, (k!)^j}$$

the summation extending over those $j \geq m$ for which $j \leq n$ and $kj \leq r$.

[4] For $N = 6$ see D. G. Catcheside, D. E. Lea, and J. M. Thoday, *Types of chromosome structural change introduced by the irradiation* of tradescantia *microspores*, Journal of Genetics, vol. 47 (1945–46), pp. 113–149.

23. Prove the last statement of section 2 for the case $k = 1$.

24. Using (3.1), derive the probability of finding exactly m empty cells in the case of Bose-Einstein statistics.

25. Verify that the formula obtained in 24 checks with II, (11.14).

26. Prove (1.5) by induction on N.

CHAPTER V

Conditional Probability.
Stochastic Independence

With this chapter we resume the systematic exposition of the fundamentals of probability theory.

1. CONDITIONAL PROBABILITY

The notion of conditional probability is a basic tool of probability theory, and it is unfortunate that its great simplicity is somewhat obscured by a singularly clumsy terminology. The following considerations lead in a natural way to the formal definition.

Preparatory Examples

Suppose a population of N people includes N_A colorblind people and N_H females. Let the events that a person chosen at random is colorblind and a female be A and H, respectively. Then (cf. the definition of random choice, II, 2)

$$(1.1) \qquad \mathbf{P}\{A\} = \frac{N_A}{N}, \qquad \mathbf{P}\{H\} = \frac{N_H}{N}.$$

We may now restrict our attention to the subpopulation consisting of females. The probability that a person chosen at random from this subpopulation is colorblind equals N_{HA}/N_H, where N_{HA} is the number of colorblind females. We have here no new notion, but we need a new notation to designate which particular subpopulation is under investigation. The most widely adopted symbol is $\mathbf{P}\{A \mid H\}$; it may be read "the probability of the event A (colorblindness), assuming the event H (that the person chosen is female)." In symbols:

$$(1.2) \qquad \mathbf{P}\{A \mid H\} = \frac{N_{AH}}{N_H} = \frac{\mathbf{P}\{AH\}}{\mathbf{P}\{H\}}.$$

Obviously every subpopulation may be considered as a population in its own right; we speak of a subpopulation merely for convenience of language to indicate that we have a larger population in the back of our minds. An insurance company may be interested in the frequency of damages of a fixed amount caused by lightning (event A). Presumably this company has several categories of insured objects such as industrial, urban, rural, etc. Studying separately the damages to industrial objects means to study the event A only in conjunction with the event H—"Damage is to an industrial object." Formula (1.2) again applies in an obvious manner. Note, however, that for an insurance company specializing in industrial objects the category H coincides with the whole sample space, and $P\{A \mid H\}$ reduces to $P\{A\}$.

Finally consider the bridge player North. Once the cards are dealt, he knows his hand and is interested only in the distribution of the remaining 39 cards. It is legitimate to introduce the aggregate of all possible distributions of these 39 cards as a new sample space, but it is obviously more convenient to consider them in conjunction with the given distribution of the 13 cards in North's hand (event H) and to speak of the probability of an event A (say South's having two aces) assuming the event H. Formula (1.2) again applies.   ▶

By analogy with (1.2) we now introduce the formal

Definition. *Let H be an event with positive probability. For an arbitrary event A we shall write*

$$(1.3) \qquad\qquad P\{A \mid H\} = \frac{P\{AH\}}{P\{H\}}.$$

The quantity so defined will be called the conditional probability of A on the hypothesis H (or for given H). When all sample points have equal probabilities, $P\{A \mid H\}$ is the ratio N_{AH}/N_H of the number of sample points common to A and H, to the number of points in H.

Conditional probabilities remain undefined when the hypothesis has zero probability. This is of no consequence in the case of discrete sample spaces but is important in the general theory.

Though the symbol $P\{A \mid H\}$ itself is practical, its phrasing in words is so unwieldy that in practice less formal descriptions are used. Thus in our introductory example we referred to the probability that a female is colorblind instead of saying "the conditional probability that a randomly chosen person is colorblind given that this person is a female." Often the phrase "on the hypothesis H" is replaced by "if it is known that H

occurred." In short, our formulas and symbols are unequivocal, but phrasings in words are often informal and must be properly interpreted.

For stylistic clarity probabilities in the original sample space are sometimes called *absolute probabilities* in contradistinction to conditional ones. Strictly speaking, the adjective "absolute" is redundant and will be omitted.

Taking conditional probabilities of various events with respect to a particular hypothesis H amounts to choosing H as a new sample space with probabilities proportional to the original ones; the proportionality factor $\mathbf{P}\{H\}$ is necessary in order to reduce the total probability of the new sample space to unity. This formulation shows that *all general theorems on probabilities are valid also for conditional probabilities with respect to any particular hypothesis H*. For example, the fundamental relation for the probability of the occurrence of either A or B or both takes on the form

(1.4) $\mathbf{P}\{A \cup B \mid H\} = \mathbf{P}\{A \mid H\} + \mathbf{P}\{B \mid H\} - \mathbf{P}\{AB \mid H\}.$

Similarly, all theorems of chapter IV concerning probabilities of the realization of m among N events carry over to conditional probabilities, but we shall not need them.

Formula (1.3) is often used in the form

(1.5) $\mathbf{P}\{AH\} = \mathbf{P}\{A \mid H\} \cdot \mathbf{P}\{H\}.$

This is the so-called theorem on compound probabilities. To generalize it to three events A, B, C we first take $H = BC$ as hypothesis and then apply (1.5) once more; it follows that

(1.6) $\mathbf{P}\{ABC\} = \mathbf{P}\{A \mid BC\} \cdot \mathbf{P}\{B \mid C\} \cdot \mathbf{P}\{C\}.$

A further generalization to four or more events is straightforward.

We conclude with a simple formula which is frequently useful. Let $H_1, \ldots, H_n$ be a set of mutually exclusive events of which one necessarily occurs (that is, the union of $H_1, \ldots, H_n$ is the entire sample space). Then any event A can occur only in conjunction with some H_j, or in symbols,

(1.7) $A = AH_1 \cup AH_2 \cup \cdots \cup AH_n.$

Since the AH_j are mutually exclusive, their probabilities add. Applying (1.5) to $H = H_j$ and adding, we get

(1.8) $\mathbf{P}\{A\} = \sum \mathbf{P}\{A \mid H_j\} \cdot \mathbf{P}\{H_j\}.$

This formula is useful because an evaluation of the conditional probabilities $P\{A \mid H_j\}$ is frequently easier than a direct calculation of $P\{A\}$.

Examples. (*a*) *Sampling without replacement.* From a population of the n elements $1, 2, \ldots, n$ an ordered sample is taken. Let i and j be two different elements. Assuming that i is the first element drawn (event H), what is the probability that the second element is j (event A)? Clearly $P\{AH\} = 1/n(n-1)$ and $P\{A \mid H\} = 1/(n-1)$. This expresses the fact that the second choice refers to a population of $n - 1$ elements, each of which has the same probability of being chosen. In fact, the most natural *definition* of random sampling is: "*Whatever the first r choices, at the $(r+1)$st step each of the remaining $n - r$ elements has probability $1/(n-r)$ to be chosen.*" This definition is equivalent to that given in chapter II, but we could not have stated it earlier since it involves the notion of conditional probability.

(*b*) Four balls are placed successively into four cells, all 4^4 arrangements being equally probable. Given that the first two balls are in different cells (event H), what is the probability that one cell contains exactly three balls (event A)? Given H, the event A can occur in two ways, and so $P\{A \mid H\} = 2 \cdot 4^{-2} = \frac{1}{8}$. (It is easy to verify directly that the events H and AH contain $12 \cdot 4^2$ and $12 \cdot 2$ points, respectively.)

(*c*) *Distribution of sexes.* Consider families with exactly two children. Letting b and g stand for boy and girl, respectively, and the first letter for the older child, we have four possibilities: bb, bg, gb, gg. These are the four sample points, and we associate probability $\frac{1}{4}$ with each. Given that a family has a boy (event H), what is the probability that both children are boys (event A)? The event AH means bb, and H means bb, or bg, or gb. Therefore, $P\{A \mid H\} = \frac{1}{3}$; in about one-third of the families with the characteristic H we can expect that A also will occur. It is interesting that most people expect the answer to be $\frac{1}{2}$. This is the correct answer to a different question, namely: A boy is chosen at random and found to come from a family with two children; what is the probability that the other child is a boy? The difference may be explained empirically. With our original problem we might refer to a card file of families, with the second to a file of males. In the latter, each family with two boys will be represented twice, and this explains the difference between the two results.

(*d*) *Stratified populations.* Suppose a human population consists of subpopulations or strata $H_1, H_2, \ldots$. These may be races, age groups, professions, etc. Let p_j be the probability that an individual chosen at random belongs to H_j. Saying "q_j is the probability that an individual in H_j is left-handed" is short for "q_j is the conditional probability of the event A (left-handedness) on the hypothesis that an individual belongs to

H_j." The probability that an individual chosen at random is left-handed is $p_1q_1 + p_2q_2 + p_3q_3 + \cdots$, which is a special case of (1.8). Given that an individual is left-handed, the conditional probability of his belonging to stratum H_j is

$$(1.9) \qquad \mathbf{P}\{H_j \mid A\} = \frac{p_jq_j}{p_1q_1 + p_2q_2 + \cdots}. \qquad \blacktriangleright$$

2. PROBABILITIES DEFINED BY CONDITIONAL PROBABILITIES. URN MODELS

In the preceding section we have taken the probabilities in the sample space for granted and merely calculated a few conditional probabilities. In applications, many experiments are described by specifying certain conditional probabilities (although the adjective "conditional" is usually omitted). Theoretically this means that the probabilities in the sample space are to be derived from the given conditional probabilities. It has already been pointed out [example (1.a)] that sampling without replacement is best defined by saying that whatever the result of the r first selections, each of the remaining elements has the same probability of being selected at the $(r+1)$st step. Similarly, in example (1.d) our stratified population is completely described by stating the absolute probabilities p_j of the several strata, and the conditional probability q_j of the characteristic "left-handed" within each stratum. A few more examples will reveal the general scheme more effectively than a direct description could.

Examples. (a) We return to example I,(5.b) in which three players a, b, and c take turns at a game. The scheme (*) on p. 18 describes the points of the sample space, but we have not yet assigned probabilities to them. Suppose now that the game is such that at each trial each of the two partners has probability $\frac{1}{2}$ of winning. This statement does not contain the word "conditional probability" but refers to it nonetheless. For it says that if player a participates in the rth round (event H), his probability of winning that particular round is $\frac{1}{2}$. It follows from (1.5) that the probability of a winning at the first and second try is $\frac{1}{4}$; in symbols, $\mathbf{P}\{aa\} = \frac{1}{4}$. A repeated application of (1.5) shows that $\mathbf{P}\{acc\} = \frac{1}{8}$, $\mathbf{P}\{acbb\} = \frac{1}{16}$, etc.; that is, a sample point of the scheme (*) involving r letters has probability 2^{-r}. This is the assignment of probabilities used in problem 5 in Chapter I,8 but now the description is more intuitive. (Continued in problem 14.)

(b) *Families.* We want to interpret the following statement. "The probability of a family having exactly k children is p_k (where $\sum p_k = 1$). For any family size all sex distributions have equal probabilities." Letting

b stand for boy and g for girl, our sample space consists of the points 0 (no children), b, g, bb, bg, gb, gg, bbb, ... The second assumption in quotation marks can be stated more formally thus: If it is known that the family has exactly n children, each of the 2^n possible sex distributions has conditional probability 2^{-n}. The probability of the hypothesis is p_n, and we see from (1.5) that the absolute probability of any arrangement of n letters b and g is $p_n \cdot 2^{-n}$.

Note that this is an example of a *stratified population*, the families of size j forming the stratum H_j. As an exercise let A stand for the event "the family has boys but no girls." Its probability is obviously $\mathbf{P}\{A\} = = p_1 \cdot 2^{-1} + p_2 \cdot 2^{-2} + \cdots$ which is a special case of (1.8). The hypothesis H_j in this case is "family has j children." We now ask the question: If it is known that a family has no girls, what is the (conditional) probability that it has only one child? Here A is the hypothesis. Let H be the event "only one child." Then AH means "one child and no girl," and

$$(2.1) \qquad \mathbf{P}\{H \mid A\} = \frac{\mathbf{P}\{AH\}}{\mathbf{P}\{A\}} = \frac{p_1 2^{-1}}{p_1 2^{-1} + p_2 2^{-2} + p_3 2^{-3} + \cdots},$$

which is a special case of (1.9).

(*c*) *Urn models for aftereffect.* For the sake of definiteness consider an industrial plant liable to accidents. The occurrence of an accident might be pictured as the result of a superhuman game of chance: Fate has in storage an urn containing red and black balls; at regular time intervals a ball is drawn at random, a red ball signifying an accident. If the chance of an accident remains constant in time, the composition of the urn is always the same. But it is conceivable that each accident has an *aftereffect* in that it either increases or decreases the chance of new accidents. This corresponds to an urn whose composition changes according to certain rules that depend on the outcome of the successive drawings. It is easy to invent a variety of such rules to cover various situations, but we shall be content with a discussion of the following[1]

Urn model: An urn contains b black and r red balls. A ball is drawn at random. It is replaced and, moreover, c balls of the color drawn and d balls of the opposite color are added. A new random drawing is made from

---

[1] The idea to use urn models to describe aftereffects (contagious diseases) seems to be due to Polya. His scheme [first introduced in F. Eggenberger and G. Polya, *Über die Statistik verketteter Vorgänge*, Zeitschrift für Angewandte Mathematik and Mechanik, vol. 3 (1923), pp. 279–289] served as a prototype for many models discussed in the literature. The model described in the text and its three special cases were proposed by B. Friedman, *A simple urn model*, Communications on Pure and Applied Mathematics, vol. 2 (1949), pp. 59–70.

the urn (*now containing* $r + b + c + d$ *balls*), *and this procedure is repeated*. Here c and d are arbitrary integers. They may be chosen *negative*, except that in this case the procedure may terminate after finitely many drawings for lack of balls. In particular, choosing $c = -1$ and $d = 0$ we have the model of *random drawings without replacement* which terminates after $r + b$ steps.

To turn our picturesque description into mathematics, note that it specifies conditional probabilities from which certain basic probabilities are to be calculated. A typical point of the sample space corresponding to n drawings may be represented by a sequence of n letters B and R. The event "black at first drawing" (i.e., the aggregate of all sequences starting with B) has probability $b/(b+r)$. If the first ball is black, the (conditional) probability of a black ball at the second drawing is

$$(b+c)/(b+r+c+d).$$

The (absolute) probability of the sequence black, black (i.e., the aggregate of the sample points starting with BB) is therefore, by (1.5),

$$(2.2) \qquad \frac{b}{b+r} \cdot \frac{b+c}{b+r+c+d}.$$

The probability of the sequence black, black, black is (2.2) multiplied by $(b+2c)/(b+r+2c+2d)$, etc. In this way the probabilities of all sample points can be calculated. It is easily verified by induction that the probabilities of all sample points indeed add to unity.

Explicit expressions for the probabilities are not readily obtainable except in the most important and best-known special case, that of

Polya's urn scheme which is characterized by $d = 0, c > 0$. Here after each drawing the number of balls of the color drawn increases, whereas the balls of opposite color remain unchanged in number. In effect the drawing of either color increases the probability of the same color at the next drawing, and we have a rough model of phenomena such as *contagious diseases*, where each occurrence increases the probability of further occurrences. The probability that of $n = n_1 + n_2$ drawings the first n_1 ones result in black balls and the remaining n_2 ones in red balls is given by

$$(2.3) \qquad \frac{b(b+c)(b+2c) \cdots (b+n_1c-c) \cdot r(r+c) \cdots (r+n_2c-c)}{(b+r)(b+r+c)(b+r+2c) \cdots (b+r+nc-c)}.$$

Consider now any other ordering of n_1 black and n_2 red balls. In calculating the probability that n drawings result in this particular order of colors we encounter the same factors as in (2.3) but rearranged in a new order. It follows that all possible sequences of n_1 black and n_2 red balls have the same probability. The analytical simplicity (and hence the easy applicability) of Polya's urn scheme is due mainly to this characteristic property. To obtain the probability $p_{n_1,n}$ that n drawings result in n_1 black and n_2 red balls in any order we must multiply the quantity (2.3) by $\binom{n}{n_1}$, namely the number of possible orderings. The use of general binomial coefficients permits us to rewrite this probability in either of the following forms:

$$(2.4) \qquad p_{n_1,n} = \frac{\binom{n_1-1+b/c}{n_1}\binom{n_2-1+r/c}{n_2}}{\binom{n-1+(b+r)/c}{n}} = \frac{\binom{-b/c}{n_1}\binom{-r/c}{n_2}}{\binom{-(b+r)/c}{n}}.$$

(The discussion of the Polya scheme is continued in problems 18–24. See also problems 9 and 10 of XVII, 10.)

In addition to the Polya scheme our urn model contains another special case of interest, namely the

Ehrenfest model[2] *of heat exchange* between two isolated bodies. In the original description, as used by physicists, the Ehrenfest model envisages two containers I and II and k particles distributed in them. A particle is chosen at random and moved from its container into the other container. This procedure is repeated. What is the distribution of the particles after n steps? To reduce this to an urn model it suffices to call the particles in container I red, the others black. Then at each drawing the ball drawn is replaced by a ball of the opposite color, that is, we have $c = -1$, $d = 1$. It is clear that in this case the process can continue as long as we please (if there are no red balls, a black ball is drawn automatically and replaced by a red one). [We shall discuss the Ehrenfest model in another way in example XV, (2.e).]

The special case $c = 0$, $d > 0$ has been proposed by Friedman as a model of a *safety campaign*. Every time an accident occurs (i.e., a red ball is drawn), the safety campaign is pushed harder; whenever no accident occurs, the campaign slackens and the probability of an accident increases.

(d) *Urn models for stratification. Spurious contagion.* To continue in the vein of the preceding example, suppose that each person is liable to accidents and that their occurrence is determined by random drawings from

---

[2] P. and T. Ehrenfest, *Über zwei bekannte Einwände gegen das Boltzmannsche H-Theorem*, Physikalische Zeitschrift, vol. 8 (1907), pp. 311–314. For a mathematical discussion see M. Kac, *Random walk and the theory of Brownian motion*, Amer. Math. Monthly, vol. 54 (1947), pp. 369–391.

an urn. This time, however, we shall suppose that no aftereffect exists, so that the composition of the urn remains unchanged throughout the process. Now the chance of an accident or proneness to accidents may vary from person to person or from profession to profession, and we imagine that each person (or each profession) has his own urn. In order not to complicate matters unnecessarily, let us suppose that there are just two types of people (two professions) and that their numbers in the total population stand in the ratio 1:5. We consider then an urn I containing r_1 red and b_1 black balls, and an urn II containing r_2 red and b_2 black balls. The experiment "choose a person at random and observe how many accidents he has during n time units" has the following counterpart: *A die is thrown; if ace appears, choose urn* I, *otherwise urn* II. *In each case* n *random drawings with replacement are selected from the urn.* Our experiment describes the situation of an insurance company accepting a new subscriber.

By using (1.8) it is seen that the probability of red at the first drawing is

$$(2.5) \qquad \mathbf{P}\{R\} = \frac{1}{6} \cdot \frac{r_1}{b_1 + r_1} + \frac{5}{6} \cdot \frac{r_2}{b_2 + r_2}$$

and the probability of a sequence red, red

$$(2.6) \qquad \mathbf{P}\{RR\} = \frac{1}{6} \cdot \left(\frac{r_1}{b_1 + r_1}\right)^2 + \frac{5}{6} \cdot \left(\frac{r_2}{b_2 + r_2}\right)^2.$$

No mathematical problem is involved in our model, but it has an interesting feature which has caused great confusion in applications. Suppose our insurance company observes that a new subscriber has an accident during the first year, and is interested in the probability of a further accident during the second year. In other words, given that the first drawing resulted in red, we ask for the (conditional) probability of a sequence red, red. This is clearly the ratio $\mathbf{P}\{RR\}/\mathbf{P}\{R\}$ and is *different* from $\mathbf{P}\{R\}$. For the sake of illustration suppose that

$$r_1/(b_1+r_1) = 0.6 \qquad \text{and} \qquad r_2/(b_2+r_2) = 0.06.$$

The probability of red at any drawing is 0.15, but if the first drawing resulted in red, the chances that the next drawing also results in red are 0.42. Note that our model assumes *no aftereffect* in the total population, and yet the occurrence of an accident for a person chosen at random increases the odds that this same person will have a second accident. This is, however, merely an effect of sampling: The occurrence of an accident has no real effect on the future, but it does serve as an indication that the person involved has a relatively high proneness to accidents. Continued observations enable us for this reason to improve our predictions for the future even though in reality this future is not at all affected by the past.

In the statistical literature it has become customary to use the word *contagion* instead of aftereffect. The *apparent* aftereffect of sampling was at first misinterpreted as an effect of true contagion, and so statisticians now speak of contagion (or contagious probability distributions) in a vague and misleading manner. Take, for example, the ecologist searching for insects in a field. If after an unsuccessful period he finds an insect, it is quite likely that he has finally reached the proximity of a litter, and in this case he may reasonably expect increased success. In other words, in practice every success increases the probability for further success, but once more this is only a side effect of the increased amount of information provided by the sampling. No aftereffect is involved, and it is misleading when the statistician speaks of contagion.

(*e*) The following example is famous and illustrative, but somewhat artificial. Imagine a collection of $N + 1$ urns, each containing a total of N red and white balls; the urn number k contains k red and $N - k$ white balls ($k = 0, 1, 2, \ldots, N$). An urn is chosen at random and n random drawings are made from it, the ball drawn being replaced each time. Suppose that all n balls turn out to be red (event A). We seek the (conditional) probability that the next drawing will also yield a red ball (event B). If the first choice falls on urn number k, then the probability of extracting in succession n red balls is $(k/N)^n$. Hence, by (1.8),

$$(2.7) \qquad \mathbf{P}\{A\} = \frac{1^n + 2^n + \cdots + N^n}{N^n(N+1)}.$$

The event AB means that $n + 1$ drawings yield red balls, and therefore

$$(2.8) \qquad \mathbf{P}\{AB\} = \mathbf{P}\{B\} = \frac{1^{n+1} + 2^{n+1} + \cdots + N^{n+1}}{N^{n+1}(N+1)}.$$

The required probability is $\mathbf{P}\{B \mid A\} = \mathbf{P}\{B\}/\mathbf{P}\{A\}$.

When N is large the numerator in (2.7) differs relatively little from the area between the x-axis and the graph of x^n between 0 and N. We have then approximately

$$(2.9) \quad \mathbf{P}\{A\} \approx \frac{1}{N^n(N+1)} \int_0^N x^n \, dx = \frac{N}{N+1} \cdot \frac{1}{n+1} \approx \frac{1}{n+1}.$$

A similar calculation applies to (2.8) and we conclude that for large N approximately

$$(2.10) \qquad \mathbf{P}\{B \mid A\} \approx \frac{n+1}{n+2}.$$

This result can be interpreted roughly as follows: If all compositions of an urn are equally probable, and if n trials yielded red balls, the probability of a red ball at the next trial is $(n+1)/(n+2)$. This is the so-called law of succession of Laplace (1812).

Before the ascendance of the modern theory, the notion of equal probabilities was often used as synonymous for "no advance knowledge." Laplace himself has illustrated the use of (2.10) by computing the probability that the sun will rise tomorrow, given that it has risen daily for 5000 years or $n = 1,826,213$ days. It is said that Laplace was ready to bet 1,826,214 to 1 in favor of regular habits of the sun, and we should be in a position to better the odds since regular service has followed for another century. A historical study would be necessary to appreciate what Laplace had in mind and to understand his intentions. His successors, however, used similar arguments in routine work and recommended methods of this kind to physicists and engineers in cases where the formulas have no operational meaning. We should have to reject the method even if, for sake of argument, we were to concede that our universe was chosen at random from a collection in which all conceivable possibilities were equally likely. In fact, it pretends to judge the chances of the sun's rising tomorrow from the *assumed* risings in the past. But the assumed rising of the sun on February 5, 3123 B.C., is by no means more certain than that the sun will rise tomorrow. We believe in both for the same reasons. ▶

Note on Bayes's Rule. In (1.9) and (2.2) we have calculated certain conditional probabilities directly from the definition. The beginner is advised always to do so and not to memorize the formula (2.12), which we shall now derive. It retraces in a general way what we did in special cases, but it is only a way of rewriting (1.3). We had a collection of events $H_1, H_2, \ldots$ which are mutually exclusive and exhaustive, that is, every sample point belonging to one, and only one, among the H_j. We were interested in

$$(2.11) \qquad\qquad \mathbf{P}\{H_k \mid A\} = \frac{\mathbf{P}\{AH_k\}}{\mathbf{P}\{A\}}.$$

If (1.5) and (1.8) are introduced into (2.11), it takes the form

$$(2.12) \qquad\qquad \mathbf{P}\{H_k \mid A\} = \frac{\mathbf{P}\{A \mid H_k\}\mathbf{P}\{H_k\}}{\sum_j \mathbf{P}\{A \mid H_j\}\mathbf{P}\{H_j\}}.$$

If the events H_k are called causes, then (2.12) becomes "Bayes's rule for the probability of causes." Mathematically, (2.12) is a special way of writing (1.3) and nothing more. The formula is useful in many statistical applications of the type described in examples (b) and (d), and we have used it there. Unfortunately, Bayes's rule has been somewhat discredited by metaphysical applications of the type described in example (e). In routine practice this kind of argument can be dangerous. A quality control engineer is concerned with one particular machine and not with an infinite population of machines from which one was chosen at random. He has been advised to use Bayes's rule on the grounds that it is logically acceptable and corresponds to our way of thinking. Plato used this type of argument to prove the existence of Atlantis, and philosophers used it to prove the absurdity of Newton's mechanics. But for our engineer the argument overlooks the circumstance that he desires success and that he will do better by estimating and minimizing the sources of various types of errors in prediction and guessing. The modern method of statistical tests and estimation is less intuitive but more realistic. It may be not only defended but also applied.

3. STOCHASTIC INDEPENDENCE

In the examples above the conditional probability $\mathbf{P}\{A \mid H\}$ generally does not equal the absolute probability $\mathbf{P}\{A\}$. Popularly speaking, the information whether H has occurred changes our way of betting on the event A. Only when $\mathbf{P}\{A \mid H\} = \mathbf{P}\{A\}$ this information does not permit any inference about the occurrence of A. In this case we shall say that A is stochastically independent of H. Now (1.5) shows that the condition $\mathbf{P}\{A \mid H\} = \mathbf{P}\{A\}$ can be written in the form

$$(3.1) \qquad\qquad \mathbf{P}\{AH\} = \mathbf{P}\{A\} \cdot \mathbf{P}\{H\}.$$

This equation is symmetric in A and H and shows that whenever A is stochastically independent of H, so is H of A. It is therefore preferable to start from the following symmetric

Definition 1. *Two events A and H are said to be stochastically independent (or independent, for short) if equation* (3.1) *holds.* This definition is accepted also if $\mathbf{P}\{H\} = 0$, in which case $\mathbf{P}\{A \mid H\}$ is not defined. The term *statistically* independent is synonymous with stochastically independent.

In practice one usually has the correct feeling that certain events must be stochastically independent, or else the probabilistic model would be absurd. As the following examples will show, there exist nevertheless situations in which the stochastic independence can be discovered only by computation.

Examples. (*a*) A card is chosen at random from a deck of playing cards. For reasons of symmetry we expect the events "spade" and "ace" to be independent. As a matter of fact, their probabilities are $\frac{1}{4}$ and $\frac{1}{13}$, and the probability of their simultaneous realization is $\frac{1}{52}$.

(*b*) Two true dice are thrown. The events "ace with first die" and "even face with second" are independent since the probability of their simultaneous realization, $\frac{3}{36} = \frac{1}{12}$, is the product of their probabilities, namely $\frac{1}{6}$ and $\frac{1}{2}$.

(*c*) In a random permutation of the four letters (*a, b, c, d*) the events "*a* precedes *b*" and "*c* precedes *d*" are independent. This is intuitively clear and easily verified.

(*d*) *Sex distribution.* We return to example (1.*c*) but now consider families with three children. We assume that each of the eight possibilities *bbb, bbg, . . . , ggg* has probability $\frac{1}{8}$. Let *H* be the event "the family has children of both sexes," and *A* the event "there is at most one girl." Then $P\{H\} = \frac{6}{8}$, and $P\{A\} = \frac{4}{8}$. The simultaneous realization of *A* and *H* means one of the possibilities *bbg, bgb, gbb,* and therefore $P\{AH\} = = \frac{3}{8} = P\{A\} \cdot P\{H\}$. Thus in families with three children the two events are independent. Note that this is not true for families with two or four children. This shows that it is not always obvious whether or not we have independence.   ▶

If *H* occurs, the complementary event *H'* does not occur, and vice versa. Stochastic independence implies that no inference can be drawn from the occurrence of *H* to that of *A*; therefore stochastic independence of *A* and *H* should mean the same as independence of *A* and *H'* (and, because of symmetry, also of *A'* and *H*, and of *A'* and *H'*). This assertion is easily verified, using the relation $P\{H'\} = 1 - P\{H\}$. Indeed, if (3.1) holds, then (since $AH' = A - AH$)

$$(3.2) \qquad P\{AH'\} = P\{A\} - P\{AH\} = P\{A\} - P\{A\} \cdot P\{H\} = $$
$$= P\{A\} \cdot P\{H'\},$$

as expected.

Suppose now that three events *A, B,* and *C* are pairwise independent so that

$$P\{AB\} = P\{A\} \cdot P\{B\}$$
$$(3.3) \qquad P\{AC\} = P\{A\} \cdot P\{C\}$$
$$P\{BC\} = P\{B\} \cdot P\{C\}.$$

One might think that these three relations should imply that also

$$P\{ABC\} = P\{A\}P\{B\}P\{C\},$$

in other words, that the pairwise independence of the three events should imply that the two events *AB* and *C* are independent. This is almost always true, but in principle it is possible that (3.3) holds and yet

$$P\{ABC\} = 0.$$

Actually such occurrences are so rare that their possibility passed unnoticed until S. Bernstein constructed an artificial example. It still takes some search to find a plausible natural example.

Example. (*e*) Consider the six permutations of the letters a, b, c as well as the three triples (a, a, a), (b, b, b), and (c, c, c). We take these nine triples as points of a sample space and attribute probability $\frac{1}{9}$ to each. Denote by A_k the event that the kth place is occupied by the letter a. Obviously each of these three events has probability $\frac{1}{3}$ while

$$\mathbf{P}\{A_1 A_2\} = \mathbf{P}\{A_1 A_3\} = \mathbf{P}\{A_2 A_3\} = \tfrac{1}{9}.$$

The three events are therefore *pairwise independent*, but they are *not* mutually independent because also $\mathbf{P}\{A_1 A_2 A_3\} = \frac{1}{9}$. (The occurrence of A_1 and A_2 implies the occurrence of A_3, and so A_3 is not independent of $A_1 A_2$.)

We obtain further examples by considering also the events B_k and C_k consisting, respectively, in the occurrence of the letters b and c at the kth place. We have now nine events in all, each with probability $\frac{1}{3}$. Clearly $\mathbf{P}\{A_1 B_2\} = \frac{1}{9}$ and generally *any two events with different subscripts are independent.* On the other hand, the letters appearing at the first two places uniquely determine the letter at the third place, and so C_3 is not independent of any among the nine events $A_1 A_2, \ldots, C_1 C_2$ involving the first two places.[3] We shall return to this example at the end of IX, 1. A further example is contained in problem 26.   ▶

It is desirable to reserve the term stochastic independence for the case where not only (3.3) holds, but in addition

(3.4) $$\mathbf{P}\{ABC\} = \mathbf{P}\{A\}\mathbf{P}\{B\}\mathbf{P}\{C\}.$$

This equation ensures that A and BC are independent and also that the same is true of B and AC, and C and AB. Furthermore, it can now be proved also that $A \cup B$ and C are independent. In fact, by the fundamental relation I, (7.4) we have

(3.5) $$\mathbf{P}\{A \cup B)C\} = \mathbf{P}\{AC\} + \mathbf{P}\{BC\} - \mathbf{P}\{ABC\}.$$

Again applying (3.3) and (3.4) to the right side, we can factor out $\mathbf{P}\{C\}$. The other factor is $\mathbf{P}\{A\} + \mathbf{P}\{B\} - \mathbf{P}\{AB\} = \mathbf{P}\{A \cup B\}$ and so

(3.6) $$\mathbf{P}\{A \cup B)C\} = \mathbf{P}\{(A \cup B)\}\mathbf{P}\{C\}.$$

---

[3] The construction generalizes to r-tuples with $r > 3$. The sample space then contains $r! + r$ points, namely of the $r!$ permutations of the symbols $a_1, \ldots, a_r$ and of the r repetitions of the same symbol a_j. To each permutation we attribute probability $1/r^2(r - 2)!$, and to each repetition probability $1/r^2$. If A_k is the event that a_1 occurs at the kth place, then the events A_k are pairwise independent, but no three among them are mutually independent.

This makes it plausible that the conditions (3.3) and (3.4) together suffice to avoid embarrassment; any event expressible in terms of A and B will be independent of C.

Definition 2. *The events* A_1, A_2, ..., A_n *are called mutually independent if for all combinations* $1 \leq i < j < k < \cdots \leq n$ *the multiplication rules*

$$\mathbf{P}\{A_iA_j\} = \mathbf{P}\{A_i\}\,\mathbf{P}\{A_j\}$$

$$\mathbf{P}\{A_iA_jA_k\} = \mathbf{P}\{A_i\}\,\mathbf{P}\{A_j\}\,\mathbf{P}\{A_k\}$$

(3.7)   ·

· ·

$$\mathbf{P}\{A_1A_2\cdots A_n\} = \mathbf{P}\{A_1\}\,\mathbf{P}\{A_2\}\cdots\mathbf{P}\{A_n\}$$

apply

The first line stands for $\binom{n}{2}$ equations, the second for $\binom{n}{3}$, etc. We have, therefore,

$$\binom{n}{2} + \binom{n}{3} + \cdots + \binom{n}{n} = (1+1)^n - \binom{n}{1} - \binom{n}{0} = 2^n - n - 1$$

conditions which must be satisfied. On the other hand, the $\binom{n}{2}$ conditions stated in the first line suffice to insure *pairwise independence*. The whole system (3.7) looks like a complicated set of conditions, but it will soon become apparent that its validity is usually obvious and requires no checking. It is readily seen by induction [starting with $n = 2$ and (3.2)] that

> *In definition 2 the system* (3.7) *may be replaced by the system of the* 2^n *equations obtained from the last equation in* (3.7) *on replacing an arbitrary number of events* A_j *by their complements* A_j'.

4. PRODUCT SPACES. INDEPENDENT TRIALS

We are now finally in a position to introduce the mathematical counterpart of empirical procedures which are commonly described by phrases such as continued experimentation, repeated observation, merging of two samples, combining two experiments and treating them as parts of a whole, etc. Specifically, the notion of independent trials corresponds to the intuitive concept of "experiments repeated under identical conditions." This notion is basic for probability theory and will add more realism to the examples treated so far.

We first require a notion that is by no means specific for probability theory. The *combinatorial product* of two sets A and B is the set of all ordered pairs (a, b) of their elements. We shall denote[4] it by (A, B). The definition carries over trivially to triples (A, B, C), quadruples (A, B, C, D), and even to infinite sequences.

The notion of combinatorial product is so natural that we have used it implicitly several times. For example, the conceptual experiment of tossing a coin three times is described by a sample space of eight points, namely the triples that can be formed with two letters H and T. This amounts to saying that the sample space is the combinatorial product of three spaces, each of which consists of the two points (elements) H and T. More generally, when we speak of two successive trials we refer to a sample space $\mathfrak{S}$ whose points represent the pairs of possible outcomes, and so $\mathfrak{S}$ is the combinatorial product of the two sample spaces corresponding to the individual trials. Given any two conceptual experiments with sample spaces $\mathfrak{A}$ and $\mathfrak{B}$, it is possible to consider them simultaneously or in succession. This amounts to considering pairs of possible outcomes, that is, to introduce the combinatorial product $(\mathfrak{A}, \mathfrak{B})$ as a new sample space. The question then arises as to how probabilities should be defined in this new sample space. The answer varies with circumstances, but before considering this point we turn to two examples which will clarify ideas and explain the prevalent terminology.

Examples. (*a*) *Cartesian spaces.* When the points of the plane are represented by pairs (x, y) of real numbers, the plane becomes the combinatorial product of the two axes. (The fact that geometry in the plane can be studied without use of coordinates shows that the same space can be considered from different viewpoints.) The three-dimensional space with points (x, y, z) may be viewed either as the triple product of the three axes, or else as the product of the x,y-plane and the z-axis.

In the plane, the set of points satisfying the two conditions $0 < x < 1$ and $0 < y < 1$ is the combinatorial product of two unit intervals. Note, however, that such a description is not possible for arbitrary sets such as triangles and ellipses. Finally we note that in the (x, y, z)-space the set defined by the same two inequalities is an infinite cylinder with a square cross-section. More generally, when interpreted in space, any set whose definition involves only the x- and y-coordinates may be viewed as a cylinder with generators parallel to the z-axis.

(*b*) *Alphabets and words.* Let A consist of the 26 standard letters. The triple product (A, A, A) is then the aggregate of all triples of letters or, as

---

[4] Another commonly used notation is $A \times B$. The terms combinatorial product and Cartesian product are synonymous.

we shall say, all three-letter "words." This viewpoint is used in communication and coding theory, but then it is not natural to consider words of a fixed length. Indeed, a message of arbitrary length may be considered a "word" provided a new symbol for separation (a blank) is added to the alphabet. It is then no longer necessary to introduce any assumptions concerning the length of words: Any finite message may be considered as the beginning of a potentially unending message, just as any written word is potentially the first of a series. Incidentally, communication theory uses arbitrary codes, and under its influence it has become common usage to refer to arbitrary symbols as letters of an alphabet. In this sense one describes the outcome of n repeated trials as a "message" or "word" of length n.   ▶

If $\mathfrak{S}$ is an arbitrary sample space with points $E_1, E_2, \ldots$ the n-fold combinatorial product $(\mathfrak{S}, \mathfrak{S}, \ldots, \mathfrak{S})$ of $\mathfrak{S}$ with itself is referred to as sample space for a succession of n trials corresponding to $\mathfrak{S}$. It is convenient to describe its points generically by symbols such as $(x_1, \ldots, x_n)$ where each x_i stands for some point of $\mathfrak{S}$. By analogy with example (a) it is usual to refer to the x_i as *coordinates*. The terms set and event are, of course, interchangeable. What we describe as *an event that depends only on the outcome of the first two trials* is generally called a set depending only on the first two coordinates.[5]

As already mentioned, all these notions and notations carry over to infinite sequences. Conceptually these present no difficulties; after all, the decimal expansion 3.1415... represents the number π as a point in an infinite product space, except that one speaks of the nth decimal rather than of the nth coordinate. *Infinite product spaces are the natural habitat of probability theory*. It is undesirable to specify a fixed number of coin tossings or a fixed length for a random walk. The theory becomes more flexible and simpler if we conceive of potentially unending sequences of trials and then direct our attention to events depending only on the first few trials. This conceptually simpler and more satisfactory approach unfortunately requires the technical apparatus of measure theory. The plan of this volume is to present the basic ideas of probability theory unobscured by technical difficulties. For this reason we are restricted to discrete sample spaces and must be satisfied with the study of finitely many trials. This means dealing with unspecified or variable sample spaces as the price for technical simplicity. This solution is unsatisfactory theoretically, but has little practical effect.

---

[5] That is to say, if $(x_1, x_2, \ldots)$ is a point of this set so are all points $(x_1', x_2', \ldots)$ such that $x_1' = x_1$ and $x_2' = x_2$. By analogy with example (a), sets depending only on specified coordinates (in any number) are called *cylindrical*.

We turn to the assignment of probabilities in product spaces. The various urn models of section 2 can be rephrased in terms of repeated trials and we have seen that probabilities of different types can be defined by means of conditional probabilities. Intuitively speaking, various forms of dependence between successive trials can be imagined, but nothing surpasses in importance the notion of independent trials or, more generally, independent experiments.

To be specific, consider two sample spaces $\mathfrak{A}$ and $\mathfrak{B}$, with points $\alpha_1, \alpha_2, \ldots$ and $\beta_1, \beta_2, \ldots$ carrying probabilities $p_1, p_2, \ldots$ and $q_1, q_2, \ldots$, respectively. We interpret the product space $(\mathfrak{A}, \mathfrak{B})$ as the sample space describing the succession of the two experiments corresponding to $\mathfrak{A}$ and $\mathfrak{B}$. Saying that these two experiments are independent implies that the two events "first outcome is α_i" and "second outcome is β_k" are stochastically independent. But this is so only if probabilities in $(\mathfrak{A}, \mathfrak{B})$ are defined by the product rule

(4.1) $$\mathbf{P}\{(\alpha_i, \beta_k)\} = p_i q_k.$$

Such an assignment of probabilities is legitimate[6] because these probabilities add to unity. In fact, summation over all points leads to the double sum $\sum\sum p_i q_k$, which is the product of the two sums $\sum p_i$ and $\sum q_k$.

We now establish the convention that *the phrase "two independent experiments" refers to the combinatorial product of two sample spaces with probabilities defined by the product rule* (4.1). *This convention applies equally to the notion of n successive independent experiments.*

We speak of repeated independent trials if the component sample spaces (*and the probabilities in them*) *are identical.*

This convention enables us, for example, to speak of n independent coin tossings as an abbreviation of a sample space of 2^n points, each carrying probability 2^{-n}.

An intuitively obvious property of independent experiments deserves mention. Let A be an event in $\mathfrak{A}$ containing the points $\alpha_{s_1}, \alpha_{s_2}, \ldots$; let similarly B be an event in $\mathfrak{B}$ containing the points $\beta_{t_1}, \beta_{t_2}, \ldots$. Then (A, B) is the event in $(\mathfrak{A}, \mathfrak{B})$ which consists of all pairs $(\alpha_{s_i}, \beta_{t_k})$, and clearly

(4.2) $$\mathbf{P}\{(A, B)\} = \sum\sum p_{s_i} q_{t_k} = (\sum p_{s_i})(\sum q_{t_k}) = \mathbf{P}\{A\}\mathbf{P}\{B\}.$$

The multiplication rule thus extends to arbitrary events in the two component spaces. This argument applies equally to n independent experiments and shows that *if a system of n events $A_1, \ldots, A_n$ is such that*

---

[6] Measures defined similarly occur outside probability theory and are called *product measures*.

A_k depends exclusively on the kth experiment, then the events $A_1, \ldots, A_n$ are mutually independent.

The theory of independent experiments is the analytically simplest and most advanced part of probability theory. It is therefore desirable, when possible, to interpret complicated experiments as the result of a succession of simpler independent experiments. The following examples illustrate situations where this procedure is possible.

Examples. (c) *Permutations.* We have considered the $n!$ permutations of a_1, $a_2, \ldots, a_n$ as points of a sample space and attributed probability $1/n!$ to each. We may consider the *same sample space* as representing $n - 1$ successive independent experiments as follows. Begin by writing down a_1. The first experiment consists in putting a_2 either before or after a_1. This done, we have three places for a_3 and the second experiment consists of a choice among them, deciding on the relative order of a_1, a_2, and a_3. In general, when $a_1, \ldots, a_k$ are put into some relative order, we proceed with experiment number k, which consists in selecting one of the $k + 1$ places for a_{k+1}. In other words, we have a succession of $n - 1$ experiments of which the kth can result in k different choices (sample points), each having probability $1/k$. The experiments are independent, that is, the probabilities are multiplicative. Each permutation of the n elements has probability $\frac{1}{2} \cdot \frac{1}{3} \cdots 1/n$, in accordance with the original definition.

(d) *Sampling without replacement.* Let the population be $(a_1, \ldots, a_n)$. In sampling without replacement each choice removes an element. After k steps there remain $n - k$ elements, and the next choice can be described by specifying the number ν of the place of the element chosen ($\nu = 1, 2, \ldots, n - k$). In this way the taking of a sample of size r without replacement becomes a succession of r experiments where the first has n possible results, the second $n - 1$, the third $n - 2$, etc. We attribute equal probabilities to all results of the individual experiments and postulate that the r experiments are independent. This amounts to attributing probability $1/(n)_r$ to each sample in accordance with our definition of random samples. Note that for $n = 100$, $r = 3$, the sample (a_{13}, a_{40}, a_{81}) means choices number 13, 39, 79, respectively: At the third experiment the seventy-ninth element of the reduced population of $n - 2$ was chosen. (With the original numbering the outcomes of the third experiment would depend on the first two choices.) We see that the notion of repeated independent experiments permits us to study sampling as a succession of independent operations.

▶

*5. APPLICATIONS TO GENETICS

The theory of heredity, originated by G. Mendel (1822–1884), provides instructive illustrations for the applicability of simple probability models. We shall restrict ourselves to indications concerning the most elementary problems. In describing the biological background, we shall necessarily oversimplify and concentrate on such facts as are pertinent to the mathematical treatment.

Heritable characters depend on special carriers, called *genes*. All cells of the body, except the reproductive cells or gametes, carry exact replicas

---

* This section treats a special subject and may be omitted.

of the same gene structure. The salient fact is that genes appear in pairs. The reader may picture them as a vast collection of beads on short pieces of string, the chromosomes. These also appear in pairs, and paired genes occupy the same position on paired chromosomes. In the simplest case each gene of a particular pair can assume two forms (alleles), A and a. Then three different pairs can be formed, and, with respect to this particular pair, the organism belongs to one of the three *genotypes AA, Aa, aa* (there is no distinction between Aa and aA). For example, peas carry a pair of genes such that A causes red blossom color and a causes white. The three genotypes are in this case distinguishable as red, pink, and white. Each pair of genes determines one heritable factor, but the majority of observable properties of organisms depend on several factors. For some characteristics (e.g., eye color and left-handedness) the influence of one particular pair of genes is predominant, and in such cases the effects of Mendelian laws are readily observable. Other characteristics, such as height, can be understood as the cumulative effect of a very large number of genes [cf. example X, (5.c)]. Here we shall study genotypes and inheritance for only one particular pair of genes with respect to which we have the three genotypes AA, Aa, aa. Frequently there are N different forms $A_1, \ldots, A_N$ for the two genes and, accordingly, $N(N+1)/2$ genotypes $A_1 A_1, A_1 A_2, \ldots, A_N A_N$. The theory applies to this case with obvious modifications (cf. problem 27). The following calculations apply also to the case where A is *dominant* and a *recessive*. By this is meant that Aa-individuals have the same observable properties as AA, so that only the pure aa-type shows an observable influence of the a-gene. All shades of partial dominance appear in nature. Typical partially recessive properties are blue eyes, left-handedness, etc.

The reproductive cells, or gametes, are formed by a splitting process and receive *one* gene only. Organisms of the pure AA- and aa-genotypes (or homozygotes) produce therefore gametes of only one kind, but Aa-organisms (hybrids or heterozygotes) produce A- and a-gametes in equal numbers. New organisms are derived from two parental gametes from which they receive their genes. Therefore each pair includes a paternal and a maternal gene, and any gene can be traced back to one particular ancestor in any generation, however remote.

The genotypes of offspring depend on a chance process. At every occasion, each parental gene has probability $\frac{1}{2}$ to be transmitted, and the successive trials are independent. In other words, we conceive of the genotypes of n offspring as the result of n independent trials, each of which corresponds to the tossing of two coins. For example, the genotypes of descendants of an $Aa \times Aa$ pairing are AA, Aa, aa with respective probabilities $\frac{1}{4}, \frac{1}{2}, \frac{1}{4}$. An $AA \times aa$ union can have only Aa-offspring, etc.

Looking at the population as a whole, we conceive of the pairing of parents as the result of a second chance process. We shall investigate only the so-called *random mating*, which is defined by this condition: If r descendants in the first filial generation are chosen at random, then their parents form a random sample of size r, with possible repetitions, from the aggregate of all possible parental pairs. In other words, each descendant is to be regarded as the product of a random selection of parents, and all selections are mutually independent. Random mating is an idealized model of the conditions prevailing in many natural populations and in field experiments. However, if red peas are sown in one corner of the field and white peas in another, parents of like color will unite more often than under random mating. Preferential selectivity (such as blondes preferring blondes) also violates the condition of random mating. Extreme non-random mating is represented by self-fertilizing plants and artificial inbreeding. Some such assortative mating systems will be analyzed mathematically, but for the most part we shall restrict our attention to random mating.

The genotype of an offspring is the result of four independent random choices. The genotypes of the two parents can be selected in $3 \cdot 3$ ways, their genes in $2 \cdot 2$ ways. It is fortunately possible to combine two selections and describe the process as one of double selection thus: The paternal and maternal genes are each selected independently and at random from the population of all genes carried by males or females, respectively, of the parental population.

Suppose that the three genotypes AA, Aa, aa occur among males and females in the same ratios, $u:2v:w$. We shall suppose $u + 2v + w = 1$ and call $u, 2v, w$, the *genotype frequencies*. Put

$$(5.1) \qquad p = u + v, \qquad q = v + w.$$

Clearly the numbers of A- and a-genes are as $p:q$, and since $p + q = 1$ we shall call p and q the *gene frequencies* of A and a. In each of the two selections an A-gene is selected with probability p, and, because of the assumed independence, the probability of an offspring being AA is p^2. The genotype Aa can occur in two ways, and its probability is therefore $2pq$. Thus, under random mating conditions *an offspring belongs to the genotypes AA, Aa, or aa with probabilities*

$$(5.2) \qquad u_1 = p^2, \qquad 2v_1 = 2pq, \qquad w_1 = q^2.$$

Examples. (*a*) All parents are Aa (heterozygotes); then $u = w = 0$, $2v = 1$, and $p = q = \frac{1}{2}$. (*b*) AA- and aa-parents are mixed in equal proportions; then $u = w = \frac{1}{2}$, $v = 0$, and again $p = q = \frac{1}{2}$. (*c*)

Finally, $u = w = \frac{1}{4}$, $2v = \frac{1}{2}$; again $p = q = \frac{1}{2}$. In all three cases we have for the filial generation $u_1 = \frac{1}{4}$, $2v_1 = \frac{1}{2}$, $w_1 = \frac{1}{4}$.   ▶

For a better understanding of the implications of (5.2) let us fix the gene frequencies p and q $(p + q = 1)$ and consider all systems of genotype frequencies $u, 2v, w$ for which $u + v = p$ and $v + w = q$. They all lead to the same probabilities (5.2) for the first filial generation. Among them there is the particular distribution

$$(5.3) \qquad\qquad u = p^2, \qquad 2v = 2pq, \qquad w = q^2.$$

Consider now a population—as in example (c)—in which the frequencies u, v, w of the three genotypes are given by (5.3). In accordance with (5.2) these frequencies are then transmitted unchanged as genotype probabilities in the next generation. For this reason genotype distributions of the particular form (5.3) are called *stationary* or equilibrium distributions. To every ratio $p:q$ there corresponds such a distribution.

In a large population the actually observed frequencies of the three genotypes in the filial generation will be close to the theoretical probabilities as given by (5.2).[7] It is highly remarkable that this distribution is stationary irrespective of the distribution $u:2v:w$ in the parental generation. In other words, if the observed frequencies coincided exactly with the calculated probabilities, then the first filial generation would have a stationary genotype distribution which would perpetuate itself without change in all succeeding generations. In practice, deviations will be observed, but for large populations we can say: *Whatever the composition of the parent population may be, random mating will within one generation produce an approximately stationary genotype distribution with unchanged gene frequencies.* From the second generation on, there is no tendency toward a systematic change; a steady state is reached with the first filial generation. This was first noticed by G. H. Hardy,[8] who thus resolved assumed difficulties in Mendelian laws. It follows in particular that under conditions of random mating the frequencies of the three genotypes must stand in the ratios $p^2:2pq:q^2$. This can in turn be used to check the assumption of random mating.

---

[7] Without this our probability model would be void of operational meaning. The statement is made precise by the law of large numbers and the central limit theorem, which permit us to estimate the effect of chance fluctuations.

[8] G. H. Hardy, *Mendelian proportions in a mixed population, Letter to the Editor,* Science, N.S., vol. 28 (1908), pp. 49–50. Anticipating the language of chapters IX and XV, we can describe the situation as follows. The frequencies of the three genotypes in the nth generation are three random variables whose expected values are given by (5.2) and do not depend on n. Their actual values will vary from generation to generation and form a stochastic process of the Markov type.

Hardy also pointed out that emphasis must be put on the word "approximately." Even with a stationary distribution we must expect small changes from generation to generation, which leads us to the following picture. Starting from any parent population, random mating tends to establish the stationary distribution (5.3) within *one* generation. For a stationary distribution there is no tendency toward a systematic change of any kind, but chance fluctuations will change the gene frequencies p and q from generation to generation, and the genetic composition will slowly drift. There are no restoring forces seeking to re-establish original frequencies. On the contrary, our simplified model leads to the conclusion [cf. example XV, (2.i)] that, for a population bounded in size, one gene should ultimately die out, so that the population would eventually belong to one of the pure types, AA or aa. In nature this does not necessarily occur because of the creation of new genes by mutations, selections, and many other effects.

Hardy's theorem is frequently interpreted to imply a strict stability for all times. It is a common fallacy to believe that the law of large numbers acts as a force endowed with memory seeking a return to the original state, and many wrong conclusions have been drawn from this assumption. Note that Hardy's law does not apply to the distribution of two pairs of genes (e.g., eye color and left-handedness) with the nine genotypes $AABB$, $AABb$, . . . , $aabb$. There is still a tendency toward a stationary distribution, but equilibrium is not reached in the first generation (cf. problem 31).

*6. SEX-LINKED CHARACTERS

In the introduction to the preceding section it was mentioned that genes lie on chromosomes. These appear in pairs and are transmitted as units, so that all genes on a chromosome stick together.[9] Our scheme for the inheritance of genes therefore applies also to chromosomes as units. Sex is determined by two chromosomes; females are XX, males XY. The mother necessarily transmits an X-chromosome, and the sex of offspring depends on the chromosome transmitted by the father. Accordingly, male and female gametes are produced in equal numbers. The difference in birth rate for boys and girls is explained by variations in prenatal survival chances.

We said that both genes and chromosomes appear in pairs, but there is an exception inasmuch as the genes situated on the X-chromosome have

---

* This section treats a special topic and may be omitted.

[9] This picture is somewhat complicated by occasional breakings and recombinations of chromosomes (cf. problem 12 of II,10).

no corresponding gene on Y. Females have two X-chromosomes, and hence two of such X-linked genes; however, in males the X-genes appear as singles. Typical are two sex-linked genes causing colorblindness and haemophilia. With respect to each of them, females can still be classified into the three genotypes, AA, Aa, aa, but, having only *one* gene, males have only the two genotypes A and a. Note that a son always has the father's Y-chromosome so that a sex-linked character cannot be inherited from father to son. However, it can pass from father to daughter and from her to a grandson.

We now proceed to adapt the analysis of the preceding section to the present situation. Assume again random mating and let the frequencies of the genotypes AA, Aa, aa in the *female* population be u, $2v$, w, respectively. As before put $p = u + v$, $q = v + w$. The frequencies of the two *male* genotypes A and a will be denoted by p' and q' ($p' + q' = 1$). Then p and p' are the frequencies of the A-gene in the female and male populations, respectively. The probability for a female descendant to be of genotype AA, Aa, aa will be denoted by u_1, $2v_1$, w_1; the analogous probabilities for the male types A and a are p_1', q_1'. Now a male offspring receives his X-chromosome from the female parent, and hence

$$(6.1) \qquad\qquad p_1' = p, \qquad q_1' = q.$$

For the three female genotypes we find, as in section 5,

$$(6.2) \qquad u_1 = pp', \qquad 2v_1 = pq' + qp', \qquad w_1 = qq'.$$

Hence

$$(6.3) \qquad p_1 = u_1 + v_1 = \tfrac{1}{2}(p+p'), \qquad q_1 = v_1 + w_1 = \tfrac{1}{2}(q+q').$$

This means that among the male descendants the genes A and a appear approximately with the frequencies p, q of the maternal population; the gene frequencies among female descendants are approximately p_1 and q_1, or halfway between those of the paternal and maternal populations. We discern here a tendency toward equalization of the gene frequencies. In fact, from (6.1) and (6.3) we get

$$(6.4) \qquad p_1' - p_1 = \tfrac{1}{2}(p-p'), \qquad q_1' - q_1 = \tfrac{1}{2}(q-q'),$$

and so random mating will in one generation reduce approximately by one-half the differences between gene frequencies among males and females. However, it will not eliminate the differences, and a tendency toward further reduction will subsist. In contrast to Hardy's law, no stationary situation is reached after one generation. We can pursue the systematic component of the changes from generation to generation by neglecting chance fluctuations and identifying the theoretical probabilities (6.2) and (6.3) with corresponding actual frequencies in the first filial generation.[10] For the second generation we obtain by the same process

$$(6.5) \quad p_2 = \tfrac{1}{2}(p_1 + p_1') = \tfrac{3}{4}p + \tfrac{1}{4}p', \qquad q_2 = \tfrac{1}{2}(q_1 + q_1') = \tfrac{3}{4}q + \tfrac{1}{4}q',$$

and, of course, $p_2' = p_1$, $q_2' = q_1$. A few more trials will lead to the general expression for the probabilities p_n and q_n among females of the nth descendant generation. Put

$$(6.6) \qquad \alpha = \tfrac{1}{3}(2p + p'), \qquad \beta = \tfrac{1}{3}(2q + q').$$

Then

$$(6.7) \qquad \begin{aligned} p_n &= \frac{p_{n-1} + p_{n-1}'}{2} = \alpha + (-1)^n \frac{p - p'}{3 \cdot 2^n}, \\ q_n &= \frac{q_{n-1} + q_{n-1}'}{2} = \beta + (-1)^n \frac{q - q'}{3 \cdot 2^n}, \end{aligned}$$

and $p_n' = p_{n-1}$, $q_n' = q_{n-1}$. Hence

$$(6.8) \qquad p_n \to \alpha, \qquad p_n' \to \alpha, \qquad q_n \to \beta, \qquad q_n' \to \beta.$$

The genotype frequencies in the female population, as given by (6.2), are

$$(6.9) \quad u_n = p_{n-1}p_{n-1}', \quad 2v_n = p_{n-1}q_{n-1}' + q_{n-1}p_{n-1}', \quad w_n = q_{n-1}q_{n-1}'.$$

Hence

$$(6.10) \qquad u_n \to \alpha^2, \qquad 2v_n \to 2\alpha\beta, \qquad w_n \to \beta^2.$$

(Note that $\alpha + \beta = 1$.)

These formulas show that there is a strong systematic tendency, from generation to generation, toward a state where the genotypes A and a appear among males with frequencies α and β, and the female genotypes AA, Aa, aa have probabilities α^2, $2\alpha\beta$, β^2, respectively. In practice, an approximate equilibrium will be reached after three or four generations. To be sure, small chance fluctuations will be superimposed on the described changes, but the latter represent the prevailing systematic tendency.

Our main conclusion is that under random mating we can expect the sex-linked genotypes A and a among males, and AA, Aa, aa among

---

[10] In the terminology introduced in footnote 8, p_n and q_n are the expected values of the gene frequencies in the nth female generation. With this interpretation the formulas for p_n and q_n are no longer approximations but exact.

females to occur approximately with the frequencies α, β, α^2, $2\alpha\beta$, β^2, respectively, where $\alpha + \beta = 1$.

Application. Many sex-linked genes, like colorblindness, are *recessive* and cause defects. Let a be such a gene. Then all a-males and all aa-females show the defect. Females of Aa-type may transmit the defect to their offspring but are not themselves affected. Hence we expect that a *recessive sex-linked defect which occurs among males with frequency α occurs among females with frequency α^2.* If one man in 100 is colorblind, one woman in 10,000 should be affected.

*7. SELECTION

As a typical example of the influence of selection we shall investigate the case where aa-individuals cannot multiply. This happens when the a-gene is recessive and lethal, so that aa-individuals are born but cannot survive. Another case occurs when artificial interference by breeding or by laws prohibits mating of aa-individuals.

Assume random mating among AA- and Aa-individuals but no mating of aa-types. Let the frequencies with which the genotypes AA, Aa, aa appear in the *total* population be u, $2v$, w. The corresponding frequencies for *parents* are then

$$(7.1) \qquad u^* = \frac{u}{1 - w}, \qquad 2v^* = \frac{2v}{1 - w}, \qquad w^* = 0.$$

We can proceed as in section 5, but we must use the quantities (7.1) instead of u, $2v$, w. Hence, (5.1) is to be replaced by

$$(7.2) \qquad p = \frac{u + v}{1 - w}, \qquad q = \frac{v}{1 - w}.$$

The probabilities of the three genotypes in the first filial generation are again given by (5.2); that is, $u_1 = p^2$, $2v_1 = 2pq$, and $w_1 = q^2$.

As before, in order to investigate the systematic changes from generation to generation, we have to replace u, v, w by u_1, v_1, w_1 and thus obtain probabilities u_2, v_2, w_2 for the second descendant generation, etc. In general we get from (7.2)

$$(7.3) \qquad p_n = \frac{u_n + v_n}{1 - w_n}, \qquad q_n = \frac{v_n}{1 - w_n}$$

and

$$(7.4) \qquad u_{n+1} = p_n^2, \qquad 2v_{n+1} = 2p_n q_n, \qquad w_{n+1} = q_n^2.$$

---

* This section treats a special subject and may be omitted.

A comparison of (7.3) and (7.4) shows that

$$(7.5) \qquad p_{n+1} = \frac{u_{n+1} + v_{n+1}}{1 - w_{n+1}} = \frac{p_n}{1 - q_n^2} = \frac{1}{1 + q_n}$$

and similarly

$$(7.6) \qquad q_{n+1} = \frac{v_{n+1}}{1 - w_{n+1}} = \frac{q_n}{1 + q_n}.$$

From (7.6) we can calculate q_n explicitly. In fact, taking reciprocals we get

$$(7.7) \qquad q_{n+1}^{-1} = 1 + q_n^{-1}$$

whence successively

$$(7.8) \qquad q_1^{-1} = 1 + q^{-1}, \qquad q_2^{-1} = 2 + q^{-1},$$
$$q_3^{-1} = 3 + q^{-1}, \quad \ldots, \quad q_n^{-1} = n + q^{-1}$$

or

$$(7.9) \qquad q_n = \frac{q}{1 + nq}, \qquad w_{n+1} = \left(\frac{q}{1 + qn}\right)^2.$$

We see that the unproductive (or undesirable) genotype gradually drops out, but the process is extremely slow. For $q = 0.1$ it takes ten generations to reduce the frequency of a-genes by one-half; this reduces the frequency of the aa-type approximately from 1 to $\frac{1}{4}$ per cent. (If a is sex-linked, the elimination proceeds much faster; see problem 29. For a generalized selection scheme see problem 30.)[11]

8. PROBLEMS FOR SOLUTION

1. Three dice are rolled. If no two show the same face, what is the probability that one is an ace?

2. Given that a throw with ten dice produced at least one ace, what is the probability p of two or more aces?

3. *Bridge.* In a bridge party West has no ace. What probability should he attribute to the event of his partner having (*a*) no ace, (*b*) two or more aces? Verify the result by a direct argument.

4. *Bridge.* North and South have ten trumps between them (trumps being cards of a specified suit). (*a*) Find the probability that all three remaining trumps are in the same hand (that is, either East or West has no trumps). (*b*)

---

[11] For a further analysis of various eugenic effects (which are frequently different from the ideas of enthusiastic proponents of sterilization laws) see G. Dahlberg, *Mathematical methods for population genetics*, New York and Basel, 1948.

If it is known that the king of trumps is included among the three, what is the probability that he is "unguarded" (that is, one player has the king, the other the remaining two trumps)?

5. Discuss the key problem in example II, (7.b) in terms of conditional probabilities following the pattern of example (2.a).

6. In a bolt factory machines A, B, C manufacture, respectively, 25, 35, and 40 per cent of the total. Of their output 5, 4, and 2 per cent are defective bolts. A bolt is drawn at random from the produce and is found defective. What are the probabilities that it was manufactured by machines A, B, C?

7. Suppose that 5 men out of 100 and 25 women out of 10,000 are colorblind. A colorblind person is chosen at random. What is the probability of his being male? (Assume males and females to be in equal numbers.)

8. Seven balls are distributed randomly in seven cells. If exactly two cells are empty, show that the (conditional) probability of a triple occupancy of some cells equals $\frac{1}{4}$. Verify this numerically using table 1 of II, 5.

9. A die is thrown as long as necessary for an ace to turn up. Assuming that the ace does not turn up at the first throw, what is the probability that more than three throws will be necessary?

10. *Continuation.* Suppose that the number, n, of throws is even. What is the probability that $n = 2$?

11. Let[12] the probability p_n that a family has exactly n children be αp^n when $n \geq 1$, and $p_0 = 1 - \alpha p(1 + p + p^2 + \cdots)$. Suppose that all sex distributions of n children have the same probability. Show that for $k \geq 1$ the probability that a family has exactly k boys is $2\alpha p^k/(2-p)^{k+1}$.

12. *Continuation.* Given that a family includes at least one boy, what is the probability that there are two or more?

13. Die A has four red and two white faces, whereas die B has two red and four white faces. A coin is flipped *once*. If it falls heads, the game continues by throwing die A alone; if it falls tails, die B is to be used. (a) Show that the probability of red at any throw is $\frac{1}{2}$. (b) If the first two throws resulted in red, what is the probability of red at the third throw? (c) If red turns up at the first n throws, what is the probability that die A is being used? (d) To which urn model is this game equivalent?

14. In example (2.a) let x_n be the conditional probability that the winner of the nth trial wins the entire game given that the game does not terminate at the nth trial; let y_n and z_n be the corresponding probabilities of victory for the losing and the pausing player, respectively, of the nth trial. (a) Show that

$$(*) \qquad x_n = \tfrac{1}{2} + \tfrac{1}{2}y_{n+1}, \qquad y_n = \tfrac{1}{2}z_{n+1}, \qquad z_n = \tfrac{1}{2}x_{n+1}.$$

(b) Show by a direct simple argument that in reality $x_n = x$, $y_n = y$, $z_n = z$ are independent of n. (c) Conclude that the probability that player a wins the game is $\tfrac{5}{14}$ (in agreement with problem 5 in I, 8). (d) Show that $x_n = \tfrac{4}{7}$, $y_n = \tfrac{1}{7}$, $z_n = \tfrac{2}{7}$ is the only bounded solution of $(*)$.

---

[12] According to A. J. Lotka, American family statistics satisfies our hypothesis with $p = 0.7358$. See *Théorie analytique des associations biologiques II*, Actualités scientifiques et industrielles, no. 780, Paris, 1939.

15. Let the events $A_1, A_2, \ldots, A_n$ be independent and $\mathbf{P}\{A_k\} = p_k$. Find the probability p that none of the events occurs.

16. *Continuation.* Show that always $p \leq e^{-\Sigma p_k}$.

17. *Continuation.* From Bonferroni's inequality IV, (5.7) deduce that the probability of k or more of the events $A_1, \ldots, A_n$ occurring simultaneously is less than $(p_1 + \cdots + p_n)^k/k!$.

18. *To Polya's urn scheme, example* (2.c). Given that the second ball was black, what is the probability that the first was black?

19. *To Polya's urn scheme, example* (2.c). Show by induction that the probability of a black ball at any trial is $b/(b+r)$.

20. *Continuation.* Prove by induction: for any $m < n$ the probabilities that the mth and the nth drawings produce (black, black) or (black, red) are

$$\frac{b(b+c)}{(b+r)(b+r+c)}, \qquad \frac{br}{(b+r)(b+r+c)},$$

respectively. Generalize to more than two drawings.

21. *Time symmetry of Polya's scheme.* Let A and B stand for either black or red (so that AB can be any of the four combinations). Show that the probability of A at the nth drawing, given that the mth drawing yields B, is the same as the probability of A at the mth drawing when the nth drawing yields B.

22. In Polya scheme let $p_k(n)$ be the probability of k black balls in the first n drawings. Prove the recurrence relation

$$p_k(n+1) = p_k(n)\frac{r + (n-k)c}{b + r + nc} + p_{k-1}(n)\frac{b + (k-1)c}{b - r + nc}$$

where $p_{-1}(n)$ is to be interpreted as 0. Use this relation for a new proof of (2.3).

23. *The Polya distribution.* In (2.4) set

(8.1) $$\frac{b}{b + r} = p, \qquad \frac{r}{b + r} = q, \qquad \frac{c}{b + r} = \gamma.$$

Show that

(8.2) $$p_{n_1, n} = \frac{\binom{-p/\gamma}{n_1}\binom{-q/\gamma}{n_2}}{\binom{-1/\gamma}{n}},$$

remains meaningful for arbitrary (not necessarily rational) constants $p > 0$, $q > 0$, $\gamma > 0$ such that $p + q = 1$. Verify that $p_{n_1, n} > 0$ and

$$\sum_{v=0}^{n} p_{v, n} = 1.$$

In other words, (8.2) defines a probability distribution on the integers $0, 1, \ldots, n$. It is called the Polya distribution.

24. *Limiting form of the Polya distribution.* If $n \to \infty$, $p \to 0$, $\gamma \to 0$ so that $np \to \lambda$, $n\gamma \to \rho^{-1}$, then for fixed n_1

$$p_{n_1,n} \to \binom{\lambda\rho + n_1 - 1}{n_1} \left(\frac{\rho}{1+\rho}\right)^{\lambda\rho} \left(\frac{1}{1+\rho}\right)^{n_1}.$$

Verify this and show that for fixed λ, ρ the terms on the right add to unity. (The right side represents the so-called *negative binomial distribution;* cf. VI, 8, and problem 37 in VI, 9.)

25. Interpret II, (11.8) in terms of conditional probabilities.

26. *Pairwise but not totally independent events.* Two dice are thrown and three events are defined as follows: A means "odd face with first die"; B means "odd face with second die"; finally, C means "odd sum" (one face even, the other odd). If each of the 36 sample points has probability $\frac{1}{36}$, then any two of the events are independent. The probability of each is $\frac{1}{2}$. Nevertheless, the three events cannot occur simultaneously.

Applications in Biology

27. Generalize the results of section 5 to the case where each gene can have any of the forms $A_1, A_2, \ldots, A_k$, so that there are $k(k+1)/2$ genotypes instead of three (multiple alleles).

28. *Brother-sister mating.* Two parents are selected at random from a population in which the genotypes AA, Aa, aa occur with frequencies u, $2v$, w. This process is repeated in their progeny. Find the probabilities that both parents of the first, second, third filial generation belong to AA [cf. examples XV, (2.j) and XVI, (4.b)].

29. *Selection.* Let a be a recessive sex-linked gene, and suppose that a selection process makes mating of a-males impossible. If the genotypes AA, Aa, aa appear among females with frequencies u, $2v$, w, show that for female descendants of the first generation $u_1 = u + v$, $2v_1 = v + w$, $w_1 = 0$, and hence $p_1 = p + \frac{1}{2}q$, $q_1 = \frac{1}{2}q$. That is to say, the frequency of the a-gene among females is reduced to one-half.

30. The selection problem of section 7 can be generalized by assuming that only the fraction λ $(0 < \lambda \leq 1)$ of the aa-class is eliminated. Show that

$$p = \frac{u+v}{1-\lambda w}, \qquad q = \frac{v+(1-\lambda)w}{1-\lambda w}.$$

More generally, (7.3) is to be replaced by

$$p_{n+1} = \frac{p_n}{1-\lambda q_n^2}, \qquad q_{n+1} = \frac{1-\lambda q_n}{1-\lambda q_n^2} q_n.$$

(The general solution of these equations appears to be unknown.)

31. Consider simultaneously two pairs of genes with possible forms (A, a) and (B, b), respectively. Any person transmits to each descendant one gene of each pair, and we shall suppose that each of the four possible combinations has probability $\frac{1}{4}$. (This is the case if the genes are on separate chromosomes; otherwise there is dependence.) There exist nine genotypes, and we assume that

their frequencies in the parent population are U_{AABB}, U_{aaBB}, U_{AAbb}, U_{aabb}, $2U_{AaBB}$, $2U_{Aabb}$, $2U_{AABb}$, $2U_{aaBb}$, $4U_{AaBb}$. Put

$$p_{AB} = U_{AABB} + U_{AABb} + U_{AaBB} + U_{AaBb},$$

$$p_{Ab} = U_{AAbb} + U_{Aabb} + U_{AABb} + U_{AaBb},$$

$$p_{aB} = U_{aaBB} + U_{aaBb} + U_{AaBB} + U_{AaBb},$$

$$p_{ab} = U_{aabb} + U_{Aabb} + U_{aaBb} + U_{AaBb}.$$

Compute the corresponding quantities for the first descendant generation. Show that for it

$$p_{AB}^{(1)} = p_{AB} - \delta, \qquad p_{Ab}^{(1)} = p_{Ab} + \delta,$$

$$p_{aB}^{(1)} = p_{aB} + \delta, \qquad p_{ab}^{(1)} = p_{ab} - \delta$$

with $2\delta = p_{AB}p_{ab} - p_{Ab}p_{aB}$. The stationary distribution is given by

$$p_{AB} - 2\delta = p_{Ab} + 2\delta, \text{ etc.}$$

(Notice that Hardy's law does *not* apply; the composition changes from generation to generation.)

32. Assume that the genotype frequencies in a population are $u = p^2$, $2v = 2pq$, $w = q^2$. Given that a man is of genotype Aa, the probability that his brother is of the same genotype is $(1 + pq)/2$.

Note: *The following problems are on family relations and give a meaning to the notion of degree of relationship. Each problem is a continuation of the preceding one. Random mating and the notations of section 5 are assumed. We are here concerned with a special case of Markov chains (cf. chapter XV). Matrix algebra simplifies the writing.*

33. Number the genotypes AA, Aa, aa by 1, 2, 3, respectively, and let p_{ik} ($i, k = 1, 2, 3$) be the conditional probability that an offspring is of genotype k if it is known that the male (or female) parent is of genotype i. Compute the nine probabilities p_{ik}, assuming that the probabilities for the other parent to be of genotype 1, 2, 3 are p^2, $2pq$, q^2, respectively.

34. Show that p_{ik} is also the conditional probability that the parent is of genotype k if it is known that the first offspring is of genotype i.

35. Prove that the conditional probability of a grandson (grandfather) to be of genotype k if it is known that the grandfather (grandson) is of genotype i is given by

$$p_{ik}^{(2)} = p_{i1}p_{1k} + p_{i2}p_{2k} + p_{i3}p_{3k}.$$

[The matrix $(p_{ik}^{(2)})$ is the square of the matrix (p_{ik}).]

36.[13] Show that $p_{ik}^{(2)}$ is also the conditional probability that a man is of genotype k if it is known that a specified half-brother is of genotype i.

---

[13] The first edition contained an error since the word brother (two common parents) was used where a *half*-brother was meant. This is pointed out in C. C. Li and Louis Sacks, Biometrika, vol. 40 (1954), pp. 347–360.

37. Show that the conditional probability of a man to be of genotype k when it is known that a specified great-grandfather (or great-grandson) is of genotype i is given by

$$p_{ik}^{(3)} = p_{i1}^{(2)}p_{1k} + p_{i2}^{(2)}p_{2k} + p_{i3}^{(2)}p_{3k} = p_{i1}p_{1k}^{(2)} + p_{i2}p_{2k}^{(2)} + p_{i3}p_{3k}^{(2)}.$$

[The matrix $(p_{ik}^{(3)})$ is the third power of the matrix (p_{ik}). This procedure gives a precise meaning to the notion of the degree of family relationship.]

38. More generally, define probabilities $p_{ik}^{(n)}$ that a descendant of the nth generation is of genotype k if a specified ancestor was of genotype i. Prove by induction that the $p_{ik}^{(n)}$ are given by the elements of the following matrix:

$$\begin{pmatrix} p^2 + pq/2^{n-1} & 2pq + q(q-p)/2^{n-1} & q^2 - q^2/2^{n-1} \\ p^2 + p(q-p)/2^n & 2pq + (1-4pq)/2^n & q^2 + q(p-q)/2^n \\ p^2 - p^2/2^{n-1} & 2pq + p(p-q)/2^{n-1} & q^2 + pq/2^{n-1} \end{pmatrix}.$$

(This shows that the influence of an ancestor decreases from generation to generation by the factor $\frac{1}{2}$.)

39. Consider the problem 36 for a *full* brother instead of a half-brother. Show that the corresponding matrix is

$$\begin{pmatrix} \frac{1}{4}(1+p)^2 & \frac{1}{2}q(1+p) & \frac{1}{4}q^2 \\ \frac{1}{4}p(1+p) & \frac{1}{4}(1+pq) & \frac{1}{4}q(1+q) \\ \frac{1}{4}p^2 & \frac{1}{2}p(1+q) & \frac{1}{4}(1+q)^2 \end{pmatrix}.$$

40. Show that the degree of relationship between uncle and nephew is the same as between grandfather and grandson.

CHAPTER VI

The Binomial
and the Poisson Distributions

1. BERNOULLI TRIALS[1]

Repeated independent trials are called Bernoulli trials if there are only two possible outcomes for each trial and their probabilities remain the same throughout the trials. It is usual to denote the two probabilities by p and q, and to refer to the outcome with probability p as *"success,"* S, and to the other as *"failure,"* F. Clearly, p and q must be non-negative, and

$$(1.1) \qquad\qquad p + q = 1.$$

The sample space of each individual trial is formed by the two points S and F. The sample space of n Bernoulli trials contains 2^n points or successions of n symbols S and F, each point representing one possible outcome of the compound experiment. Since the trials are independent, the probabilities multiply. In other words, *the probability of any specified sequence is the product obtained on replacing the symbols S and F by p and q, respectively.* Thus $\mathbf{P}\{(SSFSF \cdots FFS)\} = ppqpq \cdots qqp.$

Examples. The most familiar example of Bernoulli trials is provided by successive tosses of a true or symmetric coin; here $p = q = \frac{1}{2}$. If the coin is unbalanced, we still assume that the successive tosses are independent so that we have a model of Bernoulli trials in which the probability p for success can have an arbitrary value. Repeated random drawings from an urn of constant composition represent Bernoulli trials. Such trials arise also from more complicated experiments if we decide not to distinguish among several outcomes and describe any result simply as A or non-A. Thus with good dice the distinction between ace (S) and non-ace (F) leads

---

[1] James Bernoulli (1654–1705). His main work, the *Ars conjectandi*, was published in 1713.

to Bernoulli trials with $p = \frac{1}{6}$, whereas distinguishing between even or odd leads to Bernoulli trials with $p = \frac{1}{2}$. If the die is unbalanced, the successive throws still form Bernoulli trials, but the corresponding probabilities p are different. Royal flush in poker or double ace in rolling dice may represent success; calling all other outcomes failure, we have Bernoulli trials with $p = \dfrac{1}{649,740}$ and $p = \frac{1}{36}$, respectively. Reductions of this type are usual in statistical applications. For example, washers produced in mass production may vary in thickness, but, on inspection, they are classified as conforming (S) or defective (F) according as their thickness is, or is not, within prescribed limits. ▶

The Bernoulli scheme of trials is a theoretical model, and only experience can show whether it is suitable for the description of specified observations. Our knowledge that successive tossings of physical coins conform to the Bernoulli scheme is derived from experimental evidence. The man in the street, and also the philosopher K. Marbe,[2] believe that after a run of seventeen heads tail becomes more probable. This argument has nothing to do with imperfections of physical coins; it endows nature with memory, or, in our terminology, it denies the stochastic independence of successive trials. Marbe's theory cannot be refuted by logic but is rejected because of lack of empirical support.

In sampling practice, industrial quality control, etc., the scheme of Bernoulli trials provides an ideal standard even though it can never be fully attained. Thus, in the above example of the production of washers, there are many reasons why the output cannot conform to the Bernoulli scheme. The machines are subject to changes, and hence the probabilities do not remain constant; there is a persistence in the action of machines, and therefore long runs of deviations of like kind are more probable than they would be if the trials were truly independent. From the point of view of quality control, however, it is desirable that the process conform to the Bernoulli scheme, and it is an important discovery that, within certain limits, production can be made to behave in this way. The purpose of continuous control is then to discover at an early stage flagrant departures from the ideal scheme and to use them as an indication of impending trouble.

2. THE BINOMIAL DISTRIBUTION

Frequently we are interested only in the total number of successes produced in a succession of n Bernoulli trials but not in their order.

---

[2] *Die Gleichförmigkeit in der Welt*, Munich, 1916. Marbe's theory found wide acceptance; its most prominent opponent was von Mises.

The number of successes can be $0, 1, \ldots, n$, and our first problem is to determine the corresponding probabilities. Now the event "n trials result in k successes and $n - k$ failures" can happen in as many ways as k letters S can be distributed among n places. In other words, our event contains $\binom{n}{k}$ points, and, by definition, each point has the probability $p^k q^{n-k}$. This proves the

Theorem. *Let* $b(k; n, p)$ *be the probability that* n *Bernoulli trials with probabilities* p *for success and* $q = 1 - p$ *for failure result in* k *successes and* $n - k$ *failures. Then*

$$(2.1) \qquad\qquad b(k; n, p) = \binom{n}{k} p^k q^{n-k}.$$

In particular, the probability of no success is q^n, and the probability of at least one success is $1 - q^n$. ▶

We shall treat p as a constant and denote the number of successes in n trials by $\mathbf{S}_n$; then $b(k; n, p) = \mathbf{P}\{\mathbf{S}_n = k\}$. In the general terminology $\mathbf{S}_n$ is a *random variable*, and the function (2.1) is the "distribution" of this random variable; we shall refer to it as the *binomial distribution*. The attribute "binomial" refers to the fact that (2.1) represents the kth term of the binomial expansion of $(q+p)^n$. This remark shows also that

$$b(0; n, p) + b(1; n, p) + \cdots + b(n; n, p) = (q+p)^n = 1,$$

as is required by the notion of probability. The binomial distribution has been tabulated.[3]

Examples. (*a*) *Weldon's dice data.* Let an experiment consist in throwing twelve dice and let us count fives and sixes as "success." With perfect dice the probability of success is $p = \frac{1}{3}$ and the number of successes should follow the binomial distribution $b(k; 12, \frac{1}{3})$. Table 1 gives these probabilities, together with the corresponding observed average frequencies in 26,306 actual experiments. The agreement looks good, but for such extensive data it is really very bad. Statisticians usually judge closeness of fit by the chi-square criterion. According to it, deviations as large as those observed would happen with true dice only once in 10,000 times.

---

[3] For $n \leq 50$, see National Bureau of Standards, *Tables of the binomial probability distribution*, Applied Mathematics Series, vol. 6 (1950). For $50 \leq n \leq 100$, see H. C. Romig, *50–100 Binomial tables*, New York (John Wiley and Sons), 1953. For a wider range see *Tables of the cumulative binomial probability distribution*, by the Harvard Computation Laboratory, 1955, and *Tables of the cumulative binomial probabilities*, by the Ordnance Corps, ORDP 20-11 (1952).

TABLE 1
WELDON'S DICE DATA

k	$b(k; 12, \frac{1}{3})$	Observed frequency	$b(k; 12, 0.3377)$
0	0.007 707	0.007 033	0.007 123
1	0.046 244	0.043 678	0.043 584
2	0.127 171	0.124 116	0.122 225
3	0.211 952	0.208 127	0.207 736
4	0.238 446	0.232 418	0.238 324
5	0.190 757	0.197 445	0.194 429
6	0.111 275	0.116 589	0.115 660
7	0.047 689	0.050 597	0.050 549
8	0.014 903	0.015 320	0.016 109
9	0.003 312	0.003 991	0.003 650
10	0.000 497	0.000 532	0.000 558
11	0.000 045	0.000 152	0.000 052
12	0.000 002	0.000 000	0.000 002

It is, therefore, reasonable to assume that the dice were biased. A bias with probability of success $p = 0.3377$ would fit the observations.[4]

(b) In IV, 4, we have encountered the binomial distribution in connection with a card-guessing problem, and the columns b_m of table 3 exhibit the terms of the distribution for $n = 3, 4, 5, 6, 10$ and $p = n^{-1}$. In the occupancy problem II, (4.c) we found another special case of the binomial distribution with $p = n^{-1}$.

(c) How many trials with $p = 0.01$ must be performed to ensure that the probability for at least one success be $\frac{1}{2}$ or greater? Here we seek the smallest integer n for which $1 - (0.99)^n \geq \frac{1}{2}$, or $-n \log (0.99) \geq \log 2$; therefore $n \geq 70$.

(d) A power supply problem. Suppose that $n = 10$ workers are to use electric power intermittently, and we are interested in estimating the total load to be expected. For a crude approximation imagine that at any given time each worker has the same probability p of requiring a unit of power. If they work independently, the probability of exactly k workers requiring power at the same time should be $b(k; n, p)$. If, on the average, a worker uses power for 12 minutes per hour, we would put $p = \frac{1}{5}$. The probability of seven or more workers requiring current at the same time is then

---

[4] R. A. Fisher, *Statistical methods for research workers*, Edinburgh-London, 1932, p. 66.

$b(7; 10, 0.2) + \cdots + b(10; 10, 0.2) = 0.0008643584$. In other words, if the supply is adjusted to six power units, an overload has probability $0.00086\ldots$ and should be expected for about one minute in 1157, that is, about one minute in twenty hours. The probability of eight or more workers requiring current at the same time is only 0.0000779264 or about eleven times less.

(e) *Testing sera or vaccines.*[5] Suppose that the normal rate of infection of a certain disease in cattle is 25 per cent. To test a newly discovered serum n healthy animals are injected with it. How are we to evaluate the result of the experiment? For an absolutely worthless serum the probability that exactly k of the n test animals remain free from infection may be equated to $b(k; n, 0.75)$. For $k = n = 10$ this probability is about 0.056, and for $k = n = 12$ only 0.032. Thus, if out of ten or twelve test animals none catches infection, this may be taken as an indication that the serum has had an effect, although it is not a conclusive proof. Note that, without serum, the probability that out of seventeen animals at most one catches infection is about 0.0501. It is therefore *stronger evidence* in favor of the serum if out of seventeen test animals only one gets infected than if out of ten all remain healthy. For $n = 23$ the probability of at most two animals catching infection is about 0.0492, and thus two failures out of twenty-three is again better evidence for the serum than one out of seventeen or none out of ten.

(f) *Another statistical test.* Suppose n people have their blood pressure measured with and without a certain drug. Let the observations be $x_1, \ldots, x_n$ and $x_1', \ldots, x_n'$. We say that the ith trial resulted in success if $x_i < x_i'$, and in failure if $x_i > x_i'$. (For simplicity we may assume that no two measurements lead to *exactly* the same result.) If the drug has no effect, then our observation should correspond to n Bernoulli trials with $p = \frac{1}{2}$, and an excessive number of successes is to be taken as evidence that the drug has an effect.   ▶

3. THE CENTRAL TERM AND THE TAILS

From (2.1) we see that

(3.1) $$\frac{b(k; n, p)}{b(k-1; n, p)} = \frac{(n-k+1)p}{kq} = 1 + \frac{(n+1)p - k}{kq}.$$

Accordingly, the term $b(k; n, p)$ is greater than the preceding one for $k < (n+1)p$ and is smaller for $k > (n+1)p$. If $(n+1)p = m$ happens

[5] P. V. Sukhatme and V. G. Panse, *Size of experiments for testing sera or vaccines,* Indian Journal of Veterinary Science and Animal Husbandry, vol. 13 (1943), pp. 75–82.

to be an integer, then $b(m; n, p) = b(m - 1; n, p)$. There exists exactly one integer m such that

$$(3.2) \qquad (n+1)p - 1 < m \leq (n+1)p,$$

and we have the

Theorem. *As k goes from 0 to n, the terms $b(k; n, p)$ first increase monotonically, then decrease monotonically, reaching their greatest value when $k = m$, except that $b(m-1; n, p) = b(m; n, p)$ when $m = (n+1)p$.*

We shall call $b(m; n, p)$ the *central* term. Often m is called "the most probable number of successes," but it must be understood that for large values of n *all* terms $b(k; n, p)$ are small. In 100 tossings of a true coin the most probable number of heads is 50, but its probability is less than 0.08. In the next chapter we shall find that $b(m; n, p)$ is approximately $1/\sqrt{2\pi npq}$.

The probability of having exactly r successes is less interesting than the probability of at least r successes; that is,

$$(3.3) \qquad \mathbf{P}\{S_n \geq r\} = \sum_{v=0}^{\infty} b(r+v; n, p)$$

(The series is only formally infinite since the terms with $v > n-r$ vanish.) We shall now derive an upper bound for this probability which is useful even though more sophisticated estimates will be found in the next chapter. Suppose $r > np$. It is obvious from (3.1) that the terms of the series in (3.3) decrease faster than the terms of a geometric series with ratio $1 - (r-np)/rq$, and so

$$(3.4) \qquad \mathbf{P}\{S_n \geq r\} \leq b(r; n, p) \frac{rq}{r - np}.$$

On the other hand, there are more than $r - np$ integers k such that $m \leq k \leq r$. The corresponding terms of the binomial distribution add to less than unity, and none is smaller than $b(r; n, p)$. It follows that this quantity is at most $(r-np)^{-1}$, and hence

$$(3.5) \qquad \mathbf{P}\{S_n \geq r\} \leq \frac{rq}{(r-np)^2} \qquad \text{if } r > np.$$

The same argument could be applied to the left tail, but no calculations are necessary. In fact, saying that there are at most r successes amounts to saying that there are at least $n - r$ failures; applying the equivalent of (3.5) for failures we see that

$$(3.6) \qquad \mathbf{P}\{S_n \leq r\} \leq \frac{(n-r)p}{(np-r)^2} \qquad \text{if } r < np.$$

The next section will illustrate the usefulness of these inequalities for estimating the probability of large deviations from the most probable value m.

4. THE LAW OF LARGE NUMBERS

On several occasions we have mentioned that our *intuitive notion of probability* is based on the following assumption. If in n identical trials A occurs ν times, and if n is very large, then ν/n should be near the probability p of A. Clearly, a formal mathematical theory can never refer directly to real life, but it should at least provide theoretical counterparts to the phenomena which it tries to explain. Accordingly, we require that the vague introductory remark be made precise in the form of a theorem. For this purpose we translate "identical trials" as "Bernoulli trials" with probability p for success. If $\mathbf{S}_n$ is the number of successes in n trials, then $\mathbf{S}_n/n$ is the average number of successes and should be near p. It is now easy to give a precise meaning to this. Consider, for example, the probability that $\mathbf{S}_n/n$ exceeds $p + \epsilon$, where $\epsilon > 0$ is arbitrarily small but fixed. This probability is the same as $\mathbf{P}\{\mathbf{S}_n > n(p+\epsilon)\}$, and by (3.5) this is greater than $1/(n\epsilon^2)$. It follows that as n increases,

$$\mathbf{P}\{\mathbf{S}_n > n(p+\epsilon)\} \to 0.$$

We see in the same way that $\mathbf{P}\{\mathbf{S}_n < n(p-\epsilon)\} \to 0$, and thus

$$(4.1) \qquad \mathbf{P}\left\{\left|\frac{\mathbf{S}_n}{n} - p\right| < \epsilon\right\} \to 1.$$

In words: As n increases, the probability that the average number of successes deviates from p by more than any preassigned ϵ tends to zero. This is one form of the *law of large numbers* and serves as a basis for the intuitive notion of probability as a measure of relative frequencies. For practical applications it must be supplemented by a more precise estimate of the probability on the left side in (4.1); such an estimate is provided by the normal approximation to the binomial distribution [cf. the typical example VII, (4.h)]. Actually (4.1) is a simple consequence of the latter (problem 12 of VII, 7).

The assertion (4.1) is the classical law of large numbers. It is of very limited interest and should be replaced by the more precise and more useful *strong law of large numbers* (see VIII, 4).

Warning. It is usual to read into the law of large numbers things which it definitely does not imply. If Peter and Paul toss a perfect coin 10,000 times, it is customary to expect that Peter will be in the lead roughly half the time. *This is not true.* In a large number of *different* coin-tossing games it is reasonable to expect that at any *fixed* moment heads will be in the lead in roughly half of all cases. But it is quite likely that the player who ends at the winning side has been in the lead for practically the whole duration of the game. Thus, contrary to widespread belief, the time average for any individual game has nothing to do with the ensemble average at any given moment. For closer study of other unexpected and paradoxical properties of chance fluctuations the reader is referred to chapter III, in particular to the discussion of the arc sine laws.

5. THE POISSON APPROXIMATION[6]

In many applications we deal with Bernoulli trials where, comparatively speaking, n is large and p is small, whereas the product

$$(5.1) \qquad \lambda = np \qquad p = \frac{\lambda}{n}$$

is of moderate magnitude. In such cases it is convenient to use an approximation to $b(k; n, p)$ which is due to Poisson and which we proceed to derive. For $k = 0$ we have

$$(5.2) \qquad b(0; n, p) = (1-p)^n = \left(1 - \frac{\lambda}{n}\right)^n.$$

Passing to logarithms and using the Taylor expansion II, (8.10), we find

$$(5.3) \qquad \log b(0; n, p) = n \log \left(1 - \frac{\lambda}{n}\right) = -\lambda - \frac{\lambda^2}{2n} - \cdots$$

so that for large n

$$(5.4) \qquad b(0; n, p) \approx e^{-\lambda},$$

where the sign $\approx$ is used to indicate approximate equality (in the present case up to terms of order of magnitude n^{-1}). Furthermore, from (3.1) it is seen that for any fixed k and sufficiently large n

$$(5.5) \qquad \frac{b(k; n, p)}{b(k-1; n, p)} = \frac{\lambda - (k-1)p}{kq} \approx \frac{\lambda}{k}.$$

From this we conclude successively that

$$b(1; n, p) \approx \lambda \cdot b(0; n, p) \approx \lambda e^{-\lambda},$$

$$b(2; n, p) \approx \tfrac{1}{2}\lambda \cdot b(1; n, p) \approx \tfrac{1}{2}\lambda^2 e^{-\lambda},$$

[6] Siméon D. Poisson (1781–1840). His book, *Recherches sur la probabilité des jugements en matière criminelle et en matière civile, précédées des règles générales du calcul des probabilités*, appeared in 1837.

and generally by induction

(5.6) $$b(k; n, p) \approx \frac{\lambda^k}{k!} e^{-\lambda}.$$

This is the classical *Poisson approximation to the binomial distribution.*[7] In view of its great importance we introduce the notation

(5.7) $$p(k; \lambda) = e^{-\lambda} \frac{\lambda^k}{k!}.$$

With this notation $p(k; \lambda)$ should be an approximation to $b(k; n, \lambda/n)$ when n is sufficiently large.

Examples. (*a*) Table 3 of IV,4 tabulates the Poisson probabilities (5.7) with $\lambda = 1$ and, for comparison, the binomial distributions with $p = 1/n$ and $n = 3, 4, 5, 6, 10$. It will be seen that the agreement is surprisingly good despite the small values of n.

(*b*) *An empirical illustration.* The occurrence of the pair (7, 7) among 100 pairs of random digits should follow the binomial distribution with $n = 100$ and $p = 0.01$. The accompanying table 2 shows actual counts, N_k, in 100 batches of 100 pairs of random digits.[8] The ratios $N_k/100$ are

TABLE 2
AN EXAMPLE OF THE POISSON APPROXIMATION

k	$b(k; 100, 0.01)$	$p(k; 1)$	N_k
0	0.366 032	0.367 879	41
1	0.369 730	0.367 879	34
2	0.184 865	0.183 940	16
3	0.060 999	0.061 313	8
4	0.014 942	0.015 328	0
5	0.002 898	0.003 066	1
6	0.000 463	0.000 511	0
7	0.000 063	0.000 073	0
8	0.000 007	0.000 009	0
9	0.000 001	0.000 001	0

The first columns illustrate the Poisson approximation to the binomial distribution. The last column records the number of batches of 100 pairs of random digits each in which the combination (7, 7) appears exactly k times.

---

[7] For the degree of approximation see problems 33 and 34.

[8] M. G. Kendall and Babington Smith, *Tables of random sampling numbers*, Tracts for Computers No. 24, Cambridge, 1940.

compared with the theoretical binomial probabilities as well as with the corresponding Poisson approximations. The observed frequencies agree reasonably with the theoretical probabilities. (As judged by the χ^2-criterion, chance fluctuations should, in about 75 out of 100 similar cases, produce large deviations of observed frequencies from the theoretical probabilities.)

(c) *Birthdays.* What is the probability, p_k, that in a company of 500 people exactly k will have birthdays on New Year's Day? If the 500 people are chosen at random, we may apply the scheme of 500 Bernoulli trials with probability of success $p = \frac{1}{365}$. For the Poisson approximation we put $\lambda = \frac{500}{365} = 1.3699 \ldots$.

The correct probabilities and their Poisson approximations are as follows:

k	0	1	2	3	4	5	6
Binomial	0.2537	0.3484	0.2388	0.1089	0.0372	0.0101	0.0023
Poisson	0.2541	0.3481	0.2385	0.1089	0.0373	0.0102	0.0023

(d) *Defective items.* Suppose that screws are produced under statistical quality control so that it is legitimate to apply the Bernoulli scheme of trials. If the probability of a screw being defective is $p = 0.015$, then the probability that a box of 100 screws does not contain a defective one is $(0.985)^{100} = 0.22061$. The corresponding Poisson approximation is $e^{-1.5} = 0.22313\ldots$, which should be close enough for most practical purposes. We now ask: How many screws should a box contain in order that the probability of finding at least 100 conforming screws be 0.8 or better? If $100 + x$ is the required number, then x is a small integer. To apply the Poisson approximation for $n = 100 + x$ trials we should put $\lambda = np$, but np is approximately $100p = 1.5$. We then require the smallest integer x for which

$$(5.8) \qquad e^{-1.5}\left\{1 + \frac{1.5}{1} + \cdots + \frac{(1.5)^x}{x!}\right\} \geq 0.8.$$

In tables[9] we find that for $x = 1$ the left side is approximately 0.56, and for $x = 2$ it is 0.809. Thus the Poisson approximation would lead to the conclusion that 102 screws are required. Actually the probability of finding at least 100 conforming screws in a box of 102 is $0.8022\ldots$.

---

[9] E. C. Molina, *Poisson's exponential binomial limit*, New York (Van Nostrand), 1942. [These are tables giving $p(k; \lambda)$ and $p(k; \lambda) + p(k+1; \lambda) + \cdots$ for k ranging from 0 to 100.]

(e) *Centenarians.* At birth any particular person has a small chance of living 100 years, and in a large community the number of yearly births is large. Owing to wars, epidemics, etc., different lives are not stochastically independent, but as a first approximation we may compare n births to n Bernoulli trials with death after 100 years as success. In a stable community, where neither size nor mortality rate changes appreciably, it is reasonable to expect that the frequency of years in which exactly k centenarians die is approximately $p(k; \lambda)$, with λ depending on the size and health of the community. Records of Switzerland confirm this conclusion.[10]

(f) *Misprints, raisins, etc.* If in printing a book there is a constant probability of any letter being misprinted, and if the conditions of printing remain unchanged, then we have as many Bernoulli trials as there are letters. The frequency of pages containing exactly k misprints will then be approximately $p(k; \lambda)$, where λ is a characteristic of the printer. Occasional fatigue of the printer, difficult passages, etc., will increase the chances of errors and may produce clusters of misprints. Thus the Poisson formula may be used to discover radical departures from uniformity or from the state of statistical control. A similar argument applies in many cases. For example, if many raisins are distributed in the dough, we should expect that thorough mixing will result in the frequency of loaves with exactly k raisins to be approximately $p(k; \lambda)$ with λ a measure of the density of raisins in the dough.   ▶

6. THE POISSON DISTRIBUTION

In the preceding section the Poisson probabilities (5.7) appear merely as a convenient approximation to the binomial distribution in the case of large n and small p. In connection with the matching and occupancy problems of chapter IV we have studied different probability distributions, which have also led to the Poisson expressions $p(k; \lambda)$ as a limiting form. We have here a special case of the remarkable fact that there exist a few distributions of great universality which occur in a surprisingly great variety of problems. The three principal distributions, with ramifications throughout probability theory, are the binomial distribution, the normal distribution (to be introduced in the following chapter), and the *Poisson distribution*

$$(6.1) \qquad\qquad p(k; \lambda) = e^{-\lambda} \frac{\lambda^k}{k!},$$

which we shall now consider on its own merits.

---

[10] E. J. Gumbel, *Les centenaires*, Aktuárske Vedy, Prague, vol. 7 (1937), pp. 1–8.

We note first that on adding the quantities (6.1) for $k = 0, 1, 2, \ldots$ we get on the right side $e^{-\lambda}$ times the Taylor series for e^{λ}. Hence for any fixed λ the quantities $p(k; \lambda)$ add to unity, and therefore it is possible to conceive of an ideal experiment in which $p(k; \lambda)$ is the probability of exactly k successes. We shall now indicate why many physical experiments and statistical observations actually lead to such an interpretation of (6.1). The examples of the next section will illustrate the wide range and the importance of various applications of (6.1). The true nature of the Poisson distribution will become apparent only in connection with the theory of stochastic processes (cf. the new approaches in XII,2 and XVII,2).

Consider a sequence of random events occurring in time, such as radioactive disintegrations, or incoming calls at a telephone exchange. Each event is represented by a point on the time axis, and we are concerned with chance distributions of points. There exist many different types of such distributions, but their study belongs to the domain of continuous probabilities which we have postponed to the second volume. Here we shall be content to show that the simplest physical assumptions lead to $p(k; \lambda)$ as the probability of finding exactly k points (events) within a fixed interval of specified length. Our methods are necessarily crude, and we shall return to the same problem with more adequate methods in chapters XII and XVII.

The physical assumptions which we want to express mathematically are that the conditions of the experiment remain constant in time, and that non-overlapping time intervals are stochastically independent in the sense that information concerning the number of events in one interval reveals nothing about the other. The theory of probabilities in a continuum makes it possible to express these statements directly, but being restricted to discrete probabilities, we have to use an approximate finite model and pass to the limit.

Imagine a unit time interval partitioned into n subintervals of length $1/n$. A given collection of finitely many points in the interval may be regarded as the result of a chance process such that each subinterval has the same probability p_n to contain one or more points of the collection. A subinterval is then either occupied or empty, and the assumed independence of non-overlapping time intervals implies that we are dealing with Bernoulli trials: We assume that the probability for exactly k occupied subintervals is given by $b(k; n, p_n)$. We now refine this discrete model indefinitely by letting $n \to \infty$. The probability that the whole interval contains no point of the collection must tend to a finite limit. But this is the event that no cell is occupied, and its probability is $(1-p_n)^n$. Passing to logarithms it is seen that this quantity approaches a limit only if np_n

does. The contingency $np_n \to \infty$ is excluded because it would imply infinitely many points of the collection in even the smallest interval. Accordingly our model requires that there exists a number λ such that $np_n \to \lambda$. In this case the probability of exactly k occupied subintervals tends to $p(k; \lambda)$, and since we are dealing with individual points, the number of occupied cells agrees in the limit with the number of points of the collection contained in our unit time interval.[11]

In applications it is necessary to replace the unit time interval by an interval of arbitrary length t. If we divide it again into subintervals of length $1/n$ then the probabilities p_n remain unchanged, but the number of subintervals is given by the integer nearest to nt. The passage to the limit is the same except that λ is replaced by λt. This leads us to consider

$$(6.2) \qquad p(k; \lambda t) = e^{-\lambda t} \frac{(\lambda t)^k}{k!}$$

as the probability of finding exactly k points in a fixed interval of length t. In particular, the probability of no point in an interval of length t is

$$(6.3) \qquad p(0; \lambda t) = e^{-\lambda t},$$

and the probability of one or more points is therefore $1 - e^{-\lambda t}$.

The parameter λ is a physical constant which determines the density of points on the t-axis. The larger λ is, the smaller is the probability (6.3) of finding no point. Suppose that a physical experiment is repeated a great number N of times, and that each time we count the number of events in an interval of fixed length t. Let N_k be the number of times that exactly k events are observed. Then

$$(6.4) \qquad N_0 + N_1 + N_2 + \cdots = N.$$

The total number of points observed in the N experiments is

$$(6.5) \qquad N_1 + 2N_2 + 3N_3 + \cdots = T,$$

and T/N is the average. If N is large, we expect that

$$(6.6) \qquad N_k \approx Np(k; \lambda t)$$

---

[11] Other possibilities are conceivable. Our model may be a reasonable approximation in the study of automobile accidents, but it does not apply when one counts the number of cars smashed rather than the number of accidents as such. This is so because some accidents involve more than one car, and so it is necessary to consider single points, doublets, triplets, etc. In the limit we are lead to the compound Poisson distribution of XII,2. From the point of view of more general processes one could say that we are counting only the number of jumps, but leave their magnitude out of consideration.

(this lies at the root of all applications of probability and will be justified and made more precise by the law of large numbers in chapter X). Substituting from (6.6) into (6.5), we find

$$(6.7) \quad T \approx N\{p(1; \lambda t)+2p(2; \lambda t)+3p(3; \lambda t)+ \cdots\} =$$
$$= Ne^{-\lambda t}\lambda t\left\{1+\frac{\lambda t}{1}+\frac{(\lambda t)^2}{2!} + \cdots\right\} = N\lambda t$$

and hence

$$(6.8) \qquad\qquad \lambda t \approx T/N.$$

This relation gives us a means of estimating λ from observations and of comparing theory with experiments. The examples of the next section will illustrate this point.

Spatial Distributions

We have considered the distribution of random events or points along the t-axis, but the same argument applies to the distribution of points in plane or space. Instead of intervals of length t we have domains of area or volume t, and the fundamental assumption is that the probability of finding k points in any specified domain depends only on the area or volume of the domain but not on its shape. Otherwise we have the same assumptions as before: (1) if t is small, the probability of finding more than one point in a domain of volume t is small as compared to t; (2) non-overlapping domains are mutually independent. To find the probability that a domain of volume t contains exactly k random points, we subdivide it into n subdomains and approximate the required probability by the probability of k successes in n trials. This means neglecting the possibility of finding more than one point in the same subdomain, but our assumption (1) implies that the error tends to zero as $n \to \infty$. In the limit we get again the Poisson distribution (6.2). Stars in space, raisins in cake, weed seeds among grass seeds, flaws in materials, animal litters in fields are distributed in accordance with the Poisson law. See examples (7.b) and (7.e).

7. OBSERVATIONS FITTING THE POISSON DISTRIBUTION[12]

(a) *Radioactive disintegrations.* A radioactive substance emits α-particles; the number of particles reaching a given portion of space during

---

[12] The Poisson distribution has become known as the law of small numbers or of rare events. These are misnomers which proved detrimental to the realization of the fundamental role of the Poisson distribution. The following examples will show how misleading the two names are.

time t is the best-known example of random events obeying the Poisson law. Of course, the substance continues to decay, and in the long run the density of α-particles will decline. However, with radium it takes years before a decrease of matter can be detected; for relatively short periods the conditions may be considered constant, and we have an ideal realization of the hypotheses which led to the Poisson distribution.

In a famous experiment[13] a radioactive substance was observed during $N = 2608$ time intervals of 7.5 seconds each; the number of particles reaching a counter was obtained for each period. Table 3 records the

TABLE 3
EXAMPLE (a): RADIOACTIVE DISINTEGRATIONS

k	N_k	$Np(k; 3.870)$	k	N_k	$Np(k; 3.870)$
0	57	54.399	5	408	393.515
1	203	210.523	6	273	253.817
2	383	407.361	7	139	140.325
3	525	525.496	8	45	67.882
4	532	508.418	9	27	29.189
			$k \geq 10$	16	17.075
			Total	2608	2608.000

number N_k of periods with exactly k particles. The total number of particles is $T = \sum k N_k = 10,094$, the average $T/N = 3.870$. The theoretical values $Np(k; 3.870)$ are seen to be rather close to the observed numbers N_k. To judge the closeness of fit, an estimate of the probable magnitude of chance fluctuations is required. Statisticians judge the closeness of fit by the χ^2-criterion. Measuring by this standard, we should expect that under ideal conditions about 17 out of 100 comparable cases would show worse agreement than exhibited in table 3.

(b) *Flying-bomb hits on London.* As an example of a spatial distribution of random points consider the statistics of flying-bomb hits in the south of London during World War II. The entire area is divided into $N = 576$ small areas of $t = \frac{1}{4}$ square kilometers each, and table 4 records the number N_k of areas with exactly k hits.[14] The total number of hits is $T = \sum k N_k = 537$, the average $\lambda t = T/N = 0.9323 \ldots$. The fit of the

---

[13] Rutherford, Chadwick, and Ellis, *Radiations from radioactive substances*, Cambridge, 1920, p. 172. Table 3 and the χ^2-estimate of the text are taken from H. Cramér *Mathematical methods of statistics*, Uppsala and Princeton, 1945, p. 436.

[14] The figures are taken from R. D. Clarke, *An application of the Poisson distribution*, Journal of the Institute of Actuaries, vol. 72 (1946), p. 48.

Poisson distribution is surprisingly good; as judged by the χ^2-criterion, under ideal conditions some 88 per cent of comparable observations should show a worse agreement. It is interesting to note that most people believed in a tendency of the points of impact to cluster. If this were true, there would be a higher frequency of areas with either many hits or no hit and a deficiency in the intermediate classes. Table 4 indicates perfect randomness and homogeneity of the area; we have here an instructive illustration of the established fact that to the untrained eye randomness appears as regularity or tendency to cluster.

TABLE 4

EXAMPLE (b): FLYING-BOMB HITS ON LONDON

k	0	1	2	3	4	5 and over
N_k	229	211	93	35	7	1
$Np(k; 0.9323)$	226.74	211.39	98.54	30.62	7.14	1.57

(c) *Chromosome interchanges in cells.* Irradiation by X-rays produces certain processes in organic cells which we call chromosome interchanges. As long as radiation continues, the probability of such interchanges remains constant, and, according to theory, the numbers N_k of cells with exactly k interchanges should follow a Poisson distribution. The theory is also able to predict the dependence of the parameter λ on the intensity of radiation, the temperature, etc., but we shall not enter into these details. Table 5 records the result of eleven different series of experiments.[15] These are arranged according to goodness of fit. The last column indicates the approximate percentage of ideal cases in which chance fluctuations would produce a worse agreement (as judged by the χ^2-standard). The agreement between theory and observation is striking.

(d) *Connections to wrong number.* Table 6 shows statistics of telephone connections to a wrong number.[16] A total of $N = 267$ numbers was observed; N_k indicates how many numbers had exactly k wrong connections. The Poisson distribution $p(k; 8.74)$ shows again an excellent fit. (As judged by the χ^2-criterion the deviations are near the median value.) In Thorndike's paper the reader will find other telephone statistics

---

[15] D. G. Catcheside, D. E. Lea, and J. M. Thoday, *Types of chromosome structural change induced by the irradiation* of Tradescantia *microspores*, Journal of Genetics, vol. 47 (1945–46), pp. 113–136. Our table is table IX of this paper, except that the χ^2-levels were recomputed, using a single degree of freedom.

[16] The observations are taken from F. Thorndike, *Applications of Poisson's probability summation*, The Bell System Technical Journal, vol. 5 (1926), pp. 604–624. This paper contains a graphical analysis of 32 different statistics.

TABLE 5

EXAMPLE (c): CHROMOSOME INTERCHANGES INDUCED BY X-RAY
IRRADIATION

Experiment number		Cells with k interchanges				Total N	χ^2-level in per cent
		0	1	2	≥ 3		
1	Observed N_k	753	266	49	5	1073	95
	$Np(k; 0.35508)$	752.3	267.1	47.4	6.2		
2	Observed N_k	434	195	44	9	682	85
	$Np(k; 0.45601)$	432.3	197.1	44.9	7.7		
3	Observed N_k	280	75	12	1	368	65
	$Np(k; 0.27717)$	278.9	77.3	10.7	1.1		
4	Observed N_k	2278	273	15	0	2566	65
	$Np(k; 0.11808)$	2280.2	269.2	15.9	0.7		
5	Observed N_k	593	143	20	3	759	45
	$Np(k; 0.25296)$	589.4	149.1	18.8	1.7		
6	Observed N_k	639	141	13	0	793	45
	$Np(k; 0.21059)$	642.4	135.3	14.2	1.1		
7	Observed N_k	359	109	13	1	482	40
	$Np(k; 0.28631)$	362.0	103.6	14.9	1.5		
8	Observed N_k	493	176	26	2	697	35
	$Np(k; 0.33572)$	498.2	167.3	28.1	3.4		
9	Observed N_k	793	339	62	5	1199	20
	$Np(k; 0.39867)$	804.8	320.8	64.0	9.4		
10	Observed N_k	579	254	47	3	883	20
	$Np(k; 0.40544)$	588.7	238.7	48.4	7.2		
11	Observed N_k	444	252	59	1	756	5
	$Np(k; 0.49339)$	461.6	227.7	56.2	10.5		

TABLE 6
EXAMPLE (*d*): CONNECTIONS TO WRONG NUMBER

k	N_k	$Np(k;\ 8.74)$	k	N_k	$Np(k;\ 8.74)$
0–2	1	2.05	11	20	24.34
3	5	4.76	12	18	17.72
4	11	10.39	13	12	11.92
5	14	18.16	14	7	7.44
6	22	26.45	15	6	4.33
7	43	33.03	≥16	2	4.65
8	31	36.09		267	267.00
9	40	35.04			
10	35	30.63			

following the Poisson law. Sometimes (as with party lines, calls from groups of coin boxes, etc.) there is an obvious interdependence among the events, and the Poisson distribution no longer fits.

(*e*) *Bacteria and blood counts.* Figure 1 reproduces a photograph of a Petri plate with bacterial colonies, which are visible under the microscope as dark spots. The plate is divided into small squares. Table 7 reproduces the observed numbers of squares with exactly k dark spots in eight experiments with as many different kinds of bacteria.[17] We have here a

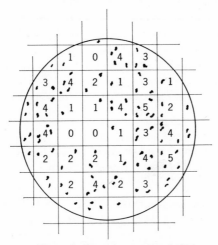

Figure 1. Bacteria on a Petri plate.

[17] The table is taken from J. Neyman, *Lectures and conferences on mathematical statistics* (mimeographed), Dept. of Agriculture, Washington, 1938.

TABLE 7
EXAMPLE (*e*): COUNTS OF BACTERIA

k	0	1	2	3	4	5	6	7	χ^2- Level
Observed N_k	5	19	26	26	21	13	8		97
Poisson theor.	6.1	18.0	26.7	26.4	19.6	11.7	9.5		
Observed N_k	26	40	38	17	7				66
Poisson theor.	27.5	42.2	32.5	16.7	9.1				
Observed N_k	59	86	49	30	20				26
Poisson theor.	55.6	82.2	60.8	30.0	15.4				
Observed N_k	83	134	135	101	40	16	7		63
Poisson theor.	75.0	144.5	139.4	89.7	43.3	16.7	7.4		
Observed N_k	8	16	18	15	9	7			97
Poisson theor.	6.8	16.2	19.2	15.1	9.0	6.7			
Observed N_k	7	11	11	11	7	8			53
Poisson theor.	3.9	10.4	13.7	12.0	7.9	7.1			
Observed N_k	3	7	14	21	20	19	7	9	85
Poisson theor.	2.1	8.2	15.8	20.2	19.5	15	9.6	9.6	
Observed N_k	60	80	45	16	9				78
Poisson theor.	62.6	75.8	45.8	18.5	7.3				

The last entry in each row includes the figures for higher classes and should be labeled "k" or more."

representative of an important practical application of the Poisson distribution to spatial distributions of random points.   ▶

8. WAITING TIMES. THE NEGATIVE BINOMIAL DISTRIBUTION

Consider a succession of n Bernoulli trials and let us inquire how long it will take for the rth success to turn up. Here r is a fixed positive integer. The total number of successes in n trials may, of course, fall short of r, but the probability that the rth success occurs at the trial number $v \leq n$

is clearly independent of n and depends only on ν, r, and p. Since necessarily $\nu \geq r$, it is preferable to write $\nu = k + r$. *The probability that the rth success occurs at the trial number* $r + k$ (*where* $k = 0, 1, \ldots$) *will be denoted by* $f(k; r, p)$. It equals *the probability that exactly* k *failures precede the rth success.* This event occurs if, and only if, among the $r + k - 1$ trials there are exactly k failures and the following, or $(r+k)$th, trial results in success; the corresponding probabilities are $\binom{r+k-1}{k} \cdot p^{r-1}q^{k}$ and p, whence

$$(8.1) \qquad f(k; r, p) = \binom{r+k-1}{k} \cdot p^{r}q^{k}.$$

Rewriting the binomial coefficient in accordance with II,(12.4), we find the alternative form

$$(8.2) \qquad f(k; r, p) = \binom{-r}{k}p^{r}(-q)^{k}, \qquad k = 0, 1, 2, \ldots.$$

Suppose now that *Bernoulli trials are continued as long as necessary for* r *successes to turn up.* A typical sample point is represented by a sequence containing an arbitrary number, k, of letters F and exactly r letters S, the sequence terminating by an S; the probability of such a point is, by definition, $p^{r}q^{k}$. We must ask, however, whether it is possible that the trials *never* end, that is, whether an infinite sequence of trials may produce fewer than r successes. Now $\sum_{k=0}^{\infty} f(k; r, p)$ is the probability that the rth success occurs after finitely many trials; accordingly, the possibility of an infinite sequence with fewer than r successes can be discounted if, and only if,

$$(8.3) \qquad \sum_{k=0}^{\infty} f(k; r, p) = 1.$$

This is so because by the binomial theorem

$$(8.4) \qquad \sum_{k=0}^{\infty} \binom{-r}{k}(-q)^{k} = (1-q)^{-r} = p^{-r}.$$

Multiplying (8.4) by p^{r} we get (8.3).

In our waiting time problem r is necessarily a positive integer, but the quantity defined by either (8.1) or (8.2) is non-negative and (8.3) holds for any positive r. *For arbitrary fixed real* $r > 0$ *and* $0 < p < 1$ *the sequence* $\{f(k; r, p)\}$ *is called a negative binomial distribution.* It occurs in many applications (and we have encountered it in problem 24 of V, as

TABLE 8

THE PROBABILITIES (8.5) IN THE MATCH BOX PROBLEM

r	u_r	U_r	r	u_r	U_r
0	0.079 589	0.079 589	15	0.023 171	0.917 941
1	0.079 589	0.159 178	16	0.019 081	0.937 022
2	0.078 785	0.237 963	17	0.015 447	0.952 469
3	0.077 177	0.315 140	18	0.012 283	0.964 752
4	0.074 790	0.389 931	19	0.009 587	0.974 338
5	0.071 674	0.461 605	20	0.007 338	0.981 676
6	0.067 902	0.529 506	21	0.005 504	0.987 180
7	0.063 568	0.593 073	22	0.004 041	0.991 220
8	0.058 783	0.651 855	23	0.002 901	0.944 121
9	0.053 671	0.705 527	24	0.002 034	0.996 155
10	0.048 363	0.753 890	25	0.001 392	0.997 547
11	0.042 989	0.796 879	26	0.000 928	0.998 475
12	0.037 676	0.834 555	27	0.000 602	0.999 077
13	0.032 538	0.867 094	28	0.000 379	0.999 456
14	0.027 676	0.894 770	29	0.000 232	0.999 688

u_r is the probability that, at the moment for the first time a match box is found empty, the other contains exactly r matches, assuming that initially each box contained 50 matches. $U_r = u_0 + u_1 + \cdots + u_r$ is the corresponding probability of having not more than r matches.

the limiting form of the Polya distribution). When r is a positive integer, $\{f(k; r, p)\}$ may be interpreted as the *probability distribution for the waiting time to the rth success;* as such it is also called the *Pascal* distribution. For $r = 1$ it reduces to the *geometric distribution* $\{pq^k\}$.

Examples. (a) *The problem of Banach's match boxes.*[18] A certain mathematician always carries one match box in his right pocket and one in his left. When he wants a match, he selects a pocket at random, the successive choices thus constituting Bernoulli trials with $p = \frac{1}{2}$. Suppose that initially each box contained exactly N matches and consider the moment when, for the first time, our mathematician *discovers* that a box is empty.

[18] This example was inspired by a humorous reference to Banach's smoking habits made by H. Steinhaus in an address honoring Banach. It became unexpectedly popular in the literature and for this reason I leave the name unchanged. References to Banach's *Oeuvres complètes* are, of course, spurious.

At that moment the other box may contain $0, 1, 2, \ldots, N$ matches, and we denote the corresponding probabilities by u_r. Let us identify "success" with choice of the left pocket. The left pocket will be found empty at a moment when the right pocket contains exactly r matches if, and only if, exactly $N - r$ failures precede the $(N+1)$st success. The probability of this event is $f(N-r; N+1, \frac{1}{2})$. The same argument applies to the right pocket and therefore the required probability is

$$(8.5) \qquad u_r = 2f(N-r; N+1, \tfrac{1}{2}) = \binom{2N-r}{N} 2^{-2N+r}.$$

Numerical values for the case $N = 50$ are given in table 8. (Cf. problems 21, and 22, and problem 11 of IX,9).

(b) *Generalization: Table tennis.* The nature of the preceding problem becomes clearer when one attributes different probabilities to the two boxes. For a change we interpret this variant differently. Suppose that Peter and Paul play a game which may be treated as a sequence of Bernoulli trials in which the probabilities p and q serve as measures for the players' skill. In ordinary table tennis the player who first accumulates 21 individual victories wins the whole game. For comparison with the preceding example we consider the general situation where $2\nu + 1$ individual successes are required. The game lasts at least $2\nu + 1$ and at most $4\nu + 1$ trials. Denote by a_r the probability that Peter wins at the trial number $4\nu + 1 - r$. This event occurs if, and only if, in the first $4\nu - r$ trials Peter has scored 2ν successes and thereafter wins the $(2\nu+1)$st trial. Thus

$$(8.6) \qquad a_r = \binom{4\nu - r}{2\nu} p^{2\nu+1} q^{2\nu-r}.$$

In our game $a_0 + \cdots + a_{2N}$ is the probability that Peter wins. The probability that the game ends exactly at the trial number $4\nu + 1 - r$ is given by $a_r + b_r$, where b_r is defined by (8.6) with p and q interchanged.

If we put $2\nu = N$ and $p = q = \frac{1}{2}$, the probabilities $a_r + b_r$ reduce to the probabilities u_r of the preceding example. ▶

9. THE MULTINOMIAL DISTRIBUTION

The binomial distribution can easily be generalized to the case of n repeated independent trials where each trial can have one of several outcomes. Denote the possible outcomes of each trial by $E_1, \ldots, E_r$, and suppose that the probability of the realization of E_i in each trial is

p_i $(i = 1, \ldots, r)$. For $r = 2$ we have Bernoulli trials; in general, the numbers p_i are subject only to the condition

$$(9.1) \qquad\qquad p_1 + \cdots + p_r = 1, \qquad\qquad p_i \geq 0.$$

The result of n trials is a succession like $E_3 E_1 E_2 \ldots$. *The probability that in* n *trials* E_1 *occurs* k_1 *times,* E_2 *occurs* k_2 *times, etc., is*

$$(9.2) \qquad\qquad \frac{n!}{k_1! \, k_2! \cdots k_r!} \, p_1^{k_1} p_2^{k_2} p_3^{k_3} \cdots p_r^{k_r};$$

here the k_i *are arbitrary non-negative integers subject to the obvious condition*

$$(9.3) \qquad\qquad k_1 + k_1 + \cdots + k_r = n.$$

If $r = 2$, then (9.2) reduces to the binomial distribution with $p_1 = p$, $p_2 = q$, $k_1 = k$, $k_2 = n - k$. The proof in the general case proceeds along the same lines, starting with II, (4.7).

Formula (9.2) is called the *multinomial distribution* because the right-hand member is the general term of the *multinomial* expansion of $(p_1 + \cdots + p_r)^n$. Its main application is to *sampling with replacement* when the individuals are classified into more than two categories (e.g., according to professions).

Examples. (*a*) In rolling twelve dice, what is the probability of getting each face twice? Here $E_1, \ldots, E_6$ represent the six faces, all k_i equal 2, and all p_i equal $\frac{1}{6}$. Therefore, the answer is $12! \, 2^{-6} 6^{-12} = 0.0034 \ldots$.

(*b*) *Sampling.* Let a population of N elements be divided into subclasses $E_1, \ldots, E_r$ of sizes $Np_1, \ldots, Np_r$. The multinomial distribution gives the probabilities of the several possible compositions of a random sample with replacement of size n taken from this population.

(*c*) *Multiple Bernoulli trials.* Two sequences of Bernoulli trials with probabilities of success and failure p_1, q_1, and p_2, q_2, respectively, may be considered one compound experiment with four possible outcomes in each trial, namely, the combinations (S, S), (S, F), (F, S), (F, F). The assumption that the two original sequences are independent is translated into the statement that the probabilities of the four outcomes are $p_1 p_2$, $p_1 q_2$, $q_1 p_2$, $q_1 q_2$, respectively. If k_1, k_2, k_3, k_4 are four integers adding to n, the probability that in n trials SS will appear k_1 times, SF k_2 times, etc., is

$$(9.4) \qquad\qquad \frac{n!}{k_1! \, k_2! \, k_3! \, k_4!} \, p_1^{k_1+k_2} q_1^{k_3+k_4} p_2^{k_1+k_3} q_2^{k_2+k_4}.$$

A special case occurs in *sampling inspection*. An item is conforming or defective with probabilities p and q. It may or may not be inspected with corresponding probabilities p' and q'. The decision of whether an item is inspected is made without knowledge of its quality, so that we have independent trials. (Cf. problems 25 and 26, and problem 12 of IX, 9.)

10. PROBLEMS FOR SOLUTION

1. Assuming all sex distributions to be equally probable, what proportion of families with exactly six children should be expected to have three boys and three girls?

2. A bridge player had no ace in three consecutive hands. Did he have reason to complain of ill luck?

3. How long has a series of random digits to be in order for the probability of the digit 7 appearing to be at least $\frac{9}{10}$?

4. How many independent bridge dealings are required in order for the probability of a preassigned player having four aces at least once to be $\frac{1}{2}$ or better? Solve again for some player instead of a given one.

5. If the probability of hitting a target is $\frac{1}{5}$ and ten shots are fired independently, what is the probability of the target being hit at least twice?

6. In problem 5, find the conditional probability that the target is hit at least twice, assuming that at least one hit is scored.

7. Find the probability that a hand of thirteen bridge cards selected at random contains exactly two red cards. Compare it with the corresponding probability in Bernoulli trials with $p = \frac{1}{2}$. (For a definition of bridge see footnote 1, in I, 1.)

8. What is the probability that the birthdays of six people fall in two calendar months leaving exactly ten months free? (Assume independence and equal probabilities for all months.)

9. In rolling six true dice, find the probability of obtaining (*a*) at least one, (*b*) exactly one, (*c*) exactly two, aces. Compare with the Poisson approximations.

10. If there are on the average 1 per cent left-handers, estimate the chances of having at least four left-handers among 200 people.

11. A book of 500 pages contains 500 misprints. Estimate the chances that a given page contains at least three misprints.

12. Colorblindness appears in 1 per cent of the people in a certain population. How large must a random sample (with replacements) be if the probability of its containing a colorblind person is to be 0.95 or more?

13. In the preceding exercise, what is the probability that a sample of 100 will contain (*a*) no, (*b*) two or more, colorblind people?

14. Estimate the number of raisins which a cookie should contain on the average if it is desired that not more than one cookie out of a hundred should be without raisin.

15. The probability of a royal flush in poker is $p = \dfrac{1}{649,740}$. How large has n to be to render the probability of no royal flush in n hands smaller than $1/e \approx \frac{1}{3}$? (*Note:* No calculations are necessary for the solution.)

16. A book of n pages contains on the average λ misprints per page. Estimate the probability that at least one page will contain more than k misprints.

17. Suppose that there exist two kinds of stars (or raisins in a cake, or flaws in a material). The probability that a given volume contains j stars of the first kind is $p(j; a)$, and the probability that it contains k stars of the second kind is $p(k; b)$; the two events are assumed to be independent. Prove that the probability that the volume contains a total of n stars is $p(n; a+b)$. (Interpret the assertion and the assumptions abstractly.)

18. *A traffic problem.* The flow of traffic at a certain street crossing is described by saying that the probability of a car passing during any given second is a constant p; and that there is no interaction between the passing of cars at different seconds. Treating seconds as indivisible time units, the model of Bernoulli trials applies. Suppose that a pedestrian can cross the street only if no car is to pass during the next three seconds. Find the probability that the pedestrian has to wait for exactly $k = 0, 1, 2, 3, 4$ seconds. (The corresponding general formulas are not obvious and will be derived in connection with the theory of success runs in XIII, 7.)

19. Two people toss a true coin n times each. Find the probability that they will score the same number of heads.

20. In a sequence of Bernoulli trials with probability p for success, find the probability that a successes will occur before b failures. (*Note:* The issue is decided after at most $a + b - 1$ trials. This problem played a role in the classical theory of games in connection with the question of how to divide the pot when the game is interrupted at a moment when one player lacks a points to victory, the other b points.)

21. In *Banach's match box problem* [example (8.a)] find the probability that at the moment when the first box is emptied (not found empty) the other contains exactly r matches (where $r = 1, 2, \ldots, N$).

22. *Continuation.* Using the preceding result, find the probability x that the box first emptied is not the one first found to be empty. Show that the expression thus obtained reduces to $x = \binom{2N}{N} 2^{-2N-1}$ or $\frac{1}{2}(N\pi)^{-\frac{1}{2}}$, approximately.

23. Proofs of a certain book were read independently by two proofreaders who found, respectively, k_1 and k_2 misprints; k_{12} misprints were found by both. Give a reasonable estimate of the unknown number, n, of misprints in the proofs. (Assume that proofreading corresponds to Bernoulli trials in which the two proofreaders have, respectively, probabilities p_1 and p_2 of catching a misprint. Use the law of large numbers.)

Note: The problem describes in simple terms an experimental setup used by Rutherford for the count of scintillations.

24. To estimate the size of an animal population by trapping,[19] traps are set r times in succession. Assuming that each animal has the same probability q of being trapped; that originally there were n animals in all; and that the only changes in the situation between the successive settings of traps are that

---

[19] P. A. P. Moran, *A mathematical theory of animal trapping*, Biometrika, vol. 38 (1951), pp. 307–311.

animals have been trapped (and thus removed); find the probability that the r trappings yield, respectively, $n_1, n_2, \ldots, n_r$ animals.

25. *Multiple Bernoulli trials.* In example (9.c) find the conditional probabilities p and q of (S, F) and (F, S), respectively, assuming that one of these combinations has occurred. Show that $p > \frac{1}{2}$ or $p < \frac{1}{2}$, according as $p_1 > p_2$ or $p_2 > p_1$.

26. *Continuation.*[20] If in n pairs of trials exactly m resulted in one of the combinations (S, F) or (F, S), show that the probability that (S, F) has occurred exactly k times is $b(k; m, p)$.

27. *Combination of the binomial and Poisson distributions.* Suppose that the probability of an insect laying r eggs is $p(r; \lambda)$ and that the probability of an egg developing is p. Assuming mutual independence of the eggs, show that the probability of a total of k survivors is given by the Poisson distribution with parameter λp.

Note: Another example for the same situation: the probability of k chromosome breakages is $p(k; \lambda)$, and the probability of a breakage healing is p. [For additional examples of a similar nature see IX, (1.d) and XII, 1.]

---

28. Prove the *theorem:*[21] The maximal term of the multinomial distribution (9.2) satisfies the inequalities

$$(10.1) \qquad np_i - 1 < k_i \leq (n+r-1)p_i, \qquad\qquad i = 1, 2, \ldots, r.$$

Hint: Prove first that the term is maximal if, and only if, $p_i k_j \leq p_j(k_i+1)$ for each pair (i, j). Add these inequalities for all j, and also for all $i \neq j$.

29. The terms $p(k; \lambda)$ of the Poisson distribution reach their maximum when k is the largest integer not exceding λ.

Note: *Problems 30–34 refer to the Poisson approximation of the binomial distribution. It is understood that $\lambda = np$.*

30. Show that as k goes from 0 to ∞ the ratios $a_k = b(k; n, p)/p(k; \lambda)$ first increase, then decrease, reaching their maximum when k is the largest integer not exceeding $\lambda + 1$.

31. As k increases, the terms $b(k; n, p)$ are first smaller, then larger, and then again smaller than $p(k; \lambda)$.

32. If $n \to \infty$ and $p \to 0$ so that $np = \lambda$ remains constant, then

$$b(k; n, p) \to p(k; \lambda)$$

uniformly for all k.

---

[20] A. Wald, *Sequential tests of statistical hypotheses*, Ann. Math. Statist., vol. 16 1945), p. 166. Wald uses the results given above to devise a practical method of comparing two empirically given sequences of trials (say, the output of two machines), with a view of selecting the one with the greater probability of success. He reduces this problem to the simpler one of finding whether in a sequence of Bernoulli trials the frequency of success differs significantly from $\frac{1}{2}$.

[21] In the first edition it was only asserted that $|k_i - np_i| \leq r$. The present improvement and its elegant proof are due to P. A. P. Moran.

33. Show that

(10.2)
$$\frac{\lambda^k}{k!}\left(1 - \frac{\lambda}{n}\right)^{n-k} \geq b(k; n, p) \geq \frac{\lambda^k}{k!}\left(1 - \frac{k}{n}\right)^k\left(1 - \frac{\lambda}{n}\right)^{n-k}.$$

34. Conclude from (10.2) that

(10.3)
$$p(k; \lambda)e^{k\lambda/n} > b(k; n, p) > p(k; \lambda)e^{-k^2/(n-k)-\lambda^2/(n-\lambda)}.$$

Hint: Use II, (12.26).

Note: Although (10.2) is very crude, the inequalities (10.3) provide excellent error estimates. It is easy to improve on (10.3) by calculations similar to those used in II, 9. Incidentally, using the result of problem 30, it is obvious that the exponent on the left in (10.3) may be replaced by $m\lambda/n$ which is $\leq(p+n^{-1})\lambda$.

Further Limit Theorems

35. *Binomial approximation to the hypergeometric distribution.* A population of N elements is divided into red and black elements in the proportion $p:q$ (where $p + q = 1$). A sample of size n is taken without replacement. The probability that it contains exactly k red elements is given by the hypergeometric distribution of II, 6. Show that as $N \to \infty$ this probability approaches $b(k; n, p)$.

36. In the preceding problem let p be small, n large, and $\lambda = np$ of moderate magnitude. The hypergeometric distribution can then be approximated by the Poisson distribution $p(k; \lambda)$. Verify this directly without using the binomial approximation.

37. In the *negative binomial distribution* $\{f(k; r, p)\}$ of section 8 let $q \to 0$ and $r \to \infty$ in such a way that $rq = \lambda$ remains fixed. Show that

$$f(k; r, p) \to p(k; \lambda).$$

(*Note:* This provides a limit theorem for the *Polya distribution:* cf. problem 24 of V, 8.)

38. *Multiple Poisson distribution.* When n is large and $np_j = \lambda_j$ is moderate for $j = 1, \ldots, r - 1$, the multinomial distribution (9.2) can be approximated by

$$e^{-(\lambda_1+\cdots+\lambda_{r-1})} \frac{\lambda_1^{k_1}\lambda_2^{k_2} \cdots \lambda_{r-1}^{k_{r-}}}{k_1! \, k_2! \cdots k_{r-1}!}.$$

Prove also that the terms of this distribution add to unity. (Note that problem 17 refers to a double Poisson distribution.)

39. (*a*) Derive (3.6) directly from (3.5) using the obvious relation

$$b(k; n, p) = b(n-k; n, q).$$

(*b*) Deduce the binomial distribution both by induction and from the general summation formula IV, (3.1).

40. Prove $\sum kb(k; n, p) = np$, and $\sum k^2 b(k; n, p) = n^2 p^2 + npq$.

41. Prove $\sum k^2 p(k; \lambda) = \lambda^2 + \lambda$.

42. Verify the identity

(10.4) $$\sum_{v=0}^{k} b(v; n_1, p)b(k-v; n_2, p) = b(k; n_1+n_2, p)$$

and interpret it probabilistically. *Hint:* Use II, (6.4).

Note: Relation (10.4) is a special case of *convolutions*, to be introduced in chapter XI; another example is (10.5).

43. Verify the identity

(10.5) $$\sum_{v=0}^{k} p(v; \lambda_1)p(k-v; \lambda_2) = p(k; \lambda_1+\lambda_2)$$

44. Let

(10.6) $$B(k; n, p) = \sum_{v=0}^{k} b(v; n, p)$$

be the probability of at most k successes in n trials. Then

(10.7) $$B(k; n+1, p) = B(k; n, p) - pb(k; n, p),$$

$$B(k+1; n+1, p) = B(k; n, p) + qb(k+1; n, p).$$

Verify this (*a*) from the definition, (*b*) analytically.

45. With the same notation[22]

(10.8) $$B(k; n, p) = (n-k)\binom{n}{k}\int_0^q t^{n-k-1}(1-t)^k \, dt$$

and

(10.9) $$1 - B(k; n, p) = n\binom{n-1}{k}\int_0^p t^k(1-t)^{n-k-1} \, dt.$$

Hint: Integrate by parts or differentiate both sides with respect to p. Deduce one formula from the other.

46. Prove

(10.10) $$p(0; \lambda) + \cdots + p(n; \lambda) = \frac{1}{n!}\int_\lambda^\infty e^{-x}x^n \, dx.$$

---

[22] The integral in (10.9) is the *incomplete beta function*. Tables of $1 - B(k; n, p)$ to 7 decimals for k and n up to 50 and $p = 0.01, 0.02, 0.03, \ldots$ are given in K. Pearson, *Tables of the incomplete beta function*, London (Biometrika Office), 1934.

CHAPTER VII

The Normal Approximation
to the Binomial Distribution

The normal approximation to the binomial distribution is of considerable theoretical and practical value. It played an important role in the development of probability theory because it lead to the first limit theorem. From a modern point of view it is only a special case of *the central limit theorem* to which we shall return in chapter X, but whose full treatment must be postponed to volume 2.

The special case $p = \frac{1}{2}$ was used in chapter III to obtain limit theorems for first passages, the number of changes of sign, etc. This special case is particularly simple, and is therefore treated separately in section 2.

1. THE NORMAL DISTRIBUTION

In order to avoid later interruptions we pause here to introduce two functions of great importance.

Definition. *The function defined by*

$$(1.1) \qquad \mathfrak{n}(x) = \frac{1}{\sqrt{2\pi}} e^{-\frac{1}{2}x^2}$$

is called the normal density function; its integral

$$(1.2) \qquad \mathfrak{N}(x) = \frac{1}{\sqrt{2\pi}} \int_{-\infty}^{x} e^{-\frac{1}{2}y^2} \, dy$$

is the normal distribution function.

The graph of $\mathfrak{n}(x)$ is the symmetric, bell-shaped curve shown in figure 1. Note that different units are used along the two axes: The maximum of $\mathfrak{n}(x)$ is $1/\sqrt{2\pi} = 0.399$, approximately, so that in an ordinary Cartesian system the curve $y = \mathfrak{n}(x)$ would be much flatter. [The notations $\mathfrak{n}$ and $\mathfrak{N}$ are not standard. In the first two editions the more customary ϕ and Φ were used, but in volume 2 consistency required that we reserve these letters for other purposes.]

Lemma 1. *The domain bounded by the graph of* $\mathfrak{n}(x)$ *and the x-axis has unit area, that is,*

$$(1.3) \qquad\qquad \int_{-\infty}^{+\infty} \mathfrak{n}(x)\, dx = 1.$$

Proof. We have

$$(1.4) \qquad \left\{\int_{-\infty}^{+\infty} \mathfrak{n}(x)\, dx\right\}^2 = \int_{-\infty}^{+\infty}\int_{-\infty}^{+\infty} \mathfrak{n}(x)\mathfrak{n}(y)\, dx\, dy =$$

$$= \frac{1}{2\pi} \int_{-\infty}^{+\infty}\int_{-\infty}^{+\infty} e^{-\frac{1}{2}(x^2+y^2)}\, dx\, dy.$$

This double integral can be expressed in polar coordinates thus:

$$(1.5) \qquad \frac{1}{2\pi} \int_0^{2\pi} d\theta \int_0^{\infty} e^{-\frac{1}{2}r^2} r\, dr = \int_0^{\infty} e^{-\frac{1}{2}r^2} r\, dr = -e^{-\frac{1}{2}r^2}\bigg|_0^{\infty} = 1$$

which proves the assertion. ▶

It follows from the definition and the lemma that $\mathfrak{N}(x)$ *increases steadily from* 0 *to* 1. Its graph (figure 2) is an S-shaped curve with

$$(1.6) \qquad\qquad \mathfrak{N}(-x) = 1 - \mathfrak{N}(x).$$

Table 1 gives the values[1] of $\mathfrak{N}(x)$ for positive x, and from (1.6) we get $\mathfrak{N}(-x)$.

For many purposes it is convenient to have an elementary estimate of the "tail," $1 - \mathfrak{N}(x)$, for large x. Such an estimate is given by

Lemma 2. *As* $x \to \infty$

$$(1.7) \qquad\qquad 1 - \mathfrak{N}(x) \sim x^{-1}\mathfrak{n}(x);$$

more precisely, the double inequality

$$(1.8) \qquad\qquad [x^{-1}-x^{-3}]\mathfrak{n}(x) < 1 - \mathfrak{N}(x) < x^{-1}\mathfrak{n}(x)$$

holds for every $x > 0$. (See problem 1.)

---

[1] For larger tables cf. *Tables of probability functions*, vol. 2, National Bureau of Standards, New York, 1942. There $\mathfrak{n}(x)$ and $\mathfrak{N}(x) - \mathfrak{N}(-x)$ are given to 15 decimals for x from 0 to 1 in steps of 0.0001 and for $x > 1$ in steps of 0.001.

[2] Here and in the sequel the sign $\sim$ is used to indicate that the *ratio* of the two sides tends to one.

TABLE 1. NORMAL DISTRIBUTION FUNCTION $\mathfrak{N}(x)$

	0.00	0.01	0.02	0.03	0.04	0.05	0.06	0.07	0.08	0.09
0.0	0.5000	0.5040	0.5080	0.5120	0.5159	0.5199	0.5239	0.5279	0.5319	0.5359
0.1	0.5398	0.5438	0.5478	0.5517	0.5557	0.5596	0.5636	0.5675	0.5714	0.5753
0.2	0.5793	0.5832	0.5871	0.5910	0.5948	0.5987	0.6026	0.6064	0.6103	0.6141
0.3	0.6179	0.6217	0.6255	0.6293	0.6331	0.6368	0.6406	0.6443	0.6480	0.6517
0.4	0.6554	0.6591	0.6628	0.6664	0.6700	0.6736	0.6772	0.6808	0.6844	0.6879
0.5	0.6915	0.6950	0.6985	0.7019	0.7054	0.7088	0.7123	0.7157	0.7190	0.7224
0.6	0.7257	0.7291	0.7324	0.7357	0.7389	0.7422	0.7454	0.7486	0.7518	0.7549
0.7	0.7580	0.7612	0.7642	0.7673	0.7704	0.7734	0.7764	0.7794	0.7823	0.7852
0.8	0.7881	0.7910	0.7939	0.7967	0.7995	0.8023	0.8051	0.8078	0.8016	0.8133
0.9	0.8159	0.8186	0.8212	0.8238	0.8264	0.8289	0.8315	0.8340	0.8365	0.8380
1.0	0.8413	0.8438	0.8461	0.8485	0.8508	0.8531	0.8554	0.8577	0.8599	0.8621
1.1	0.8643	0.8665	0.8686	0.8718	0.8729	0.8749	0.8770	0.8790	0.8810	0.8836
1.2	0.8849	0.8869	0.8888	0.8907	0.8925	0.8944	0.8962	0.8980	0.8997	0.9015
1.3	0.9032	0.9049	0.9066	0.9083	9.9099	0.9115	0.9131	0.9147	0.9162	0.9177
1.4	0.9192	0.9207	0.9222	0.9236	0.9251	0.9265	0.9279	0.9292	0.9306	0.9319

x										
1.5	0.9332	0.9345	0.9357	0.9370	0.9382	0.9394	0.9406	0.9418	0.9430	0.9441
1.6	0.9452	0.9463	0.9474	0.9485	0.9495	0.9505	0.9515	0.9525	0.9535	0.9545
1.7	0.9554	0.9564	0.9573	0.9582	0.9591	0.9599	0.9608	0.9616	0.9625	0.9633
1.8	0.9641	0.9649	0.9656	0.9664	0.9671	0.9678	0.9686	0.9693	0.9699	0.9706
1.9	0.9713	0.9719	0.9726	0.9732	0.9738	0.9744	0.9750	0.9758	0.9762	0.9767
2.0	0.9773	0.9778	0.9783	0.9788	0.9793	0.9798	0.9803	0.9808	0.9812	0.9817
2.1	0.9821	0.9826	0.9830	0.9834	0.9838	0.9842	0.9846	0.9850	0.9854	0.9857
2.2	0.9861	0.9865	0.9868	0.9871	0.9875	0.9878	0.9881	0.9884	0.9887	0.9890
2.3	0.9893	0.9896	0.9898	0.9901	0.9904	0.9906	0.9909	0.9911	0.9913	0.9916
2.4	0.9918	0.9920	0.9922	0.9925	0.9927	0.9929	0.9931	0.9932	0.9934	0.9936
2.5	0.9938	0.9940	0.9941	0.9943	0.9945	0.9946	0.9948	0.9949	0.9951	0.9952
2.6	0.9953	0.9955	0.9956	0.9957	0.9959	0.9960	0.9961	0.9962	0.9963	0.9964
2.7	0.9965	0.9966	0.9967	0.9968	0.9969	0.9970	0.9971	0.9972	0.9973	0.9974
2.8	0.9974	0.9975	0.9976	0.9977	0.9977	0.9978	0.9979	0.9980	0.9980	0.9981
2.9	0.9981	0.9982	0.9983	0.9984	0.9984	0.9984	0.9985	0.9985	0.9986	0.9986
3.0	0.9986	0.9987	0.9987	0.9988	0.9988	0.9988	0.9989	0.9989	0.9989	0.9990
3.1	0.9990	0.9991	0.9991	0.9991	0.9992	0.9992	0.9992	0.9992	0.9993	0.9993
3.2	0.9993	0.9993	0.9993	0.9994	0.9994	0.9994	0.9994	0.9994	0.9995	0.9995

For $x < 0$ use the relation $\mathfrak{N}(-x) = 1 - \mathfrak{N}(x)$.

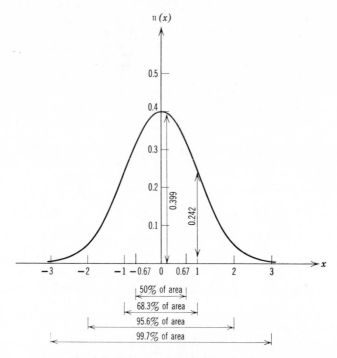

Figure 1. The normal density function ɳ.

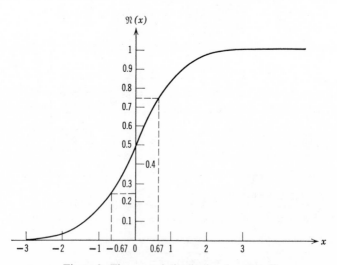

Figure 2. The normal distribution function 𝕹.

Proof. Obviously

(1.9) $$[1-3x^{-4}]\mathfrak{n}(x) < \mathfrak{n}(x) < [1+x^{-2}]\mathfrak{n}(x).$$

The members are the negatives of the derivatives of those in (1.8), and so (1.8) follows by integration between x and ∞. ▶

Note on Terminology. The term *distribution function* is used in the mathematical literature for never-decreasing functions of x which tend to 0 as $x \to -\infty$, and to 1 as $x \to \infty$. Statisticians currently prefer the term *cumulative distribution function*, but the adjective "cumulative" is redundant. A *density function* is a non-negative function $f(x)$ whose integral, extended over the entire x-axis, is unity. The integral from $-\infty$ to x of any density function is a distribution function. The older term *frequency function* is a synonym for density function.

The normal distribution function is often called the *Gaussian distribution*, but it was used in probability theory earlier by DeMoivre and Laplace. If the origin and the unit of measurement are changed, then $\mathfrak{N}(x)$ is transformed into $\mathfrak{N}((x-a)/b)$; this function is called the normal distribution function with mean a and variance b^2 (or standard deviation $|b|$). The function $2\mathfrak{N}(x\sqrt{2}) - 1$ is often called *error function*.

2. ORIENTATION: SYMMETRIC DISTRIBUTIONS

We proceed to explain the use of the normal distribution as an approximation to the binomial with $p = \frac{1}{2}$.

There are two reasons for treating the special case $p = \frac{1}{2}$ separately. First, the calculations are much simpler and therefore convey a better idea of how the normal distribution enters the problem. Second, this special case was used in connection with random walks (see III,2), and it is therefore desirable to supply a proof which is not obscured by the technicalities required for unsymmetric distributions.

For definiteness we take $n = 2\nu$ even, and to simplify notations we put

(2.1) $$a_k = b(\nu+k;\ 2\nu, \tfrac{1}{2});$$

that is, the a_k are the terms of the symmetric binomial distribution renumbered so as to indicate the distance from the central term; a_0 is the central term, and k runs from $-\nu$ to ν. Since $a_{-k} = a_k$ we shall consider only $k \geq 0$.

(*In the notation of chapter* III *we have* $a_k = p_{2\nu,2k}$; the following proof does not depend on notions developed after III,2 and could be inserted there.)

To get an idea concerning the behavior of the sequence $a_0, a_1, a_2, \ldots$ we shall compare its general term with a_0 using the relation

(2.2) $$a_k = a_0 \cdot \frac{\nu(\nu-1)\cdots(\nu-k+1)}{(\nu+1)(\nu+2)\cdots(\nu+k)}$$

which follows trivially from the definition.

We are interested only in large values of ν, and it will turn out that we need consider only values k such that k/ν is small, because for other k the terms a_k will be negligible. On dividing numerator and denominator by ν^k the individual factors take on the form $1 + j/\nu$ with j running from $-(k-1)$ to k. Now

$$(2.3) \qquad\qquad 1 + \frac{j}{\nu} = e^{j/\nu + \cdots}$$

where the dots indicate terms which add to less than $(j/\nu)^2$. Within this approximation the fraction in (2.2) reduces to an exponential with exponent

$$-\frac{2}{\nu}[1 + \cdots + (k-1)] - \frac{k}{\nu} = -\frac{k^2}{\nu},$$

and the error is less than k^3/ν^2. Accordingly, if $\nu \to \infty$ and k varies within a range $0 < k < K_\nu$ such that

$$(2.4) \qquad\qquad K_\nu^3/\nu^2 \to 0$$

we have the approximation

$$(2.5) \qquad\qquad a_k \sim a_0 e^{-k^2/\nu}.$$

When the binomial coefficient is expressed in terms of factorials it is seen from Stirling's formula[3] II,(9.1) that

$$(2.6) \qquad\qquad a_0 = \binom{2\nu}{\nu} 2^{-2\nu} \sim \frac{1}{\sqrt{\pi\nu}}.$$

Substituting into (2.5) we get

$$(2.7) \qquad\qquad a_k \sim h\mathfrak{n}(kh) \qquad\qquad \text{where} \quad h = \sqrt{2/\nu} = 2/\sqrt{n}.$$

---

[3] *Note on the constant in Stirling's formula.* It will be recalled from II,9 that we have not yet proved that the constant in Stirling's formula coincides with $\sqrt{2\pi}$. We now fill this gap as follows. The constant π in (2.6) must be replaced by an unknown constant; this does not affect the approximation theorem except that the right side in (2.10) must be multiplied by an unknown constant c, and we have to prove that $c = 1$. We use the amended form with $z_1 = 0$. The ratio of the two sides tends to 1 as $n \to \infty$. But the tail estimate VI,(3.5) shows that the left side lies between $\frac{1}{2}$ and $\frac{1}{2} - 4z_2^{-2}$, whereas for the right side (1.8) yields the double inequality

$$c > c[\mathfrak{N}(z_2) - \tfrac{1}{2}] = \tfrac{1}{2}c - c[1 - \mathfrak{N}(z_2)] > \tfrac{1}{2}c - c\mathfrak{n}(z_2)/z_2.$$

For z_2 sufficiently large the two sides are arbitrarily close to $\frac{1}{2}$ and to $\frac{1}{2}c$, respectively, and hence $c = 1$ as asserted.

This basic relation is valid when $\nu \to \infty$ *and* k *is restricted to values* $k < K_\nu$ *satisfying* (2.4). We shall use (2.7) principally for values k of the order of magnitude of $\sqrt{\nu}$, and then (2.4) is trivially satisfied.

In practice we require approximations for the probabilities carried by various intervals, that is, to partial sums of the form[4]

$$(2.8) \qquad A(x_1, x_2) = \sum_{x_1 \leq k \leq x_2} a_k$$

the summation extending over all integers between 0 and x, inclusive. We now show how $A(x)$ can be approximated by an area under the graph of $\mathfrak{n}$ which, in turn, can be expressed in terms of the integral $\mathfrak{N}$. Because of the monotone character of $\mathfrak{n}$ it is clear that the area under the graph of $\mathfrak{n}$ between kh and $(k+1)h$ is smaller than $h\mathfrak{n}(kh)$, but larger than $h\mathfrak{n}((k+1)h)$. It follows that

$$(2.9) \qquad \int_{x_1 h}^{x_2 h + h} \mathfrak{n}(s) \, ds < \sum_{x_1 \leq k \leq x_2} h\mathfrak{n}(kh) < \int_{x_1 h - h}^{x_2 h} \mathfrak{n}(s) \, ds.$$

In view of (2.9) the middle term is an approximation to $A(x_1, x_2)$; it is good when ν is large and k^2/ν moderate, that is, when h is small and xh moderate. The two extreme members in (2.9) equal $\mathfrak{N}(x_2 h + h) - \mathfrak{N}(x_1 h)$ and $\mathfrak{N}(x_2 h) - \mathfrak{N}(x_1 h - h)$, respectively; their difference tends to 0 with h, and so we can replace them by $\mathfrak{N}(x_2 h) - \mathfrak{N}(x_1 h)$.

We express this result in the form of a limit theorem, but replace the variable x by $z = xh$.

Approximation Theorem. *For fixed* $z_1 < z_2$

$$(2.10) \qquad \sum_{\frac{1}{2} z_1 \sqrt{n} \leq k \leq \frac{1}{2} z_2 \sqrt{n}} a_k \to \mathfrak{N}(z_2) - \mathfrak{N}(z_1).$$

We shall see presently that this result extends meaningfully to certain situations in which z_1 and z_2 are allowed to vary with n without remaining bounded. Note that the limit theorem of III, (2.7) is contained in (2.10), and that this is only a special case of the general theorem of the next section.

Bounds for the Error. We need not concern ourselves with the error committed in replacing the sum by an integral because (2.9) contains upper and lower bounds.

---

[4] We refrain from referring to $\mathbf{S}_n$ because this letter appears in different meanings in chapters III and VI. In the terminology of random walks $A(x_1, x_2)$ is the probability that at epoch $n = 2\nu$ the particle is between $2x_1$ and $2x_2$; in the present terminology $A(x_1, x_2)$ is the probability that $n = 2\nu$; trials yield a number of successes between $\nu + x_1$ and $\nu + x_2$. In the next section this number will be again denoted by S_n.

To estimate the error in the approximation (2.7) we put

$$(2.11) \qquad a_k = a_0 e^{-k^2/\nu + \epsilon_1} = \hbar(kh)e^{\epsilon_1 - \epsilon_2}$$

so that ϵ_1 represents the error committed by dropping the higher-order terms in (2.3) while ϵ_2 derives from (2.6). From our derivation it is clear that

$$(2.12) \qquad \epsilon_1 = \sum_{j=1}^{k-1} \left(\log \frac{1 + j/\nu}{1 - j/\nu} - \frac{2j}{\nu} \right) + \left(\log \left(1 + \frac{k}{\nu} \right) - \frac{k}{\nu} \right).$$

The error estimates are most interesting for relatively small ν, and to cover such cases we shall assume only that $k < \frac{1}{3}\nu$. Comparing the expansion II, (8.11) with a geometric series with ratio 1/3 it is seen that the general term in the series in (2.12) is positive and is less than $(j/\nu)^3$. The whole series is therefore positive and less than $k^4/(4\nu^3)$. From II,(8.9) it is similarly seen that the last term is negative and greater than $-3k^2/(4\nu^2)$. Thus

$$(2.13) \qquad -\frac{3k^2}{n^2} < \epsilon_1 < \frac{2k^4}{n^3}, \qquad\qquad \text{provided} \quad k < \tfrac{1}{6}n.$$

In most applications k and $\sqrt{n}$ are of comparable magnitude, and the condition $k < n/6$ is then trivially satisfied. Under such circumstances (2.13) is rather sharp.

As for (2.6), it follows from the improved version of Stirling's formula II,(9.15) that a better approximation for a_0 is obtained on multiplying the right side by $e^{1/(4n)}$, and that under any circumstances

$$(2.14) \qquad \frac{1}{4n} - \frac{1}{20n^3} < \epsilon_2 < \frac{1}{4n} + \frac{1}{360n^3}.$$

We have thus found *precise bounds for the error in the approximations* (2.7) *and* (2.10). These estimates are applicable even for relatively small values of n.

The main result of this investigation is that *the percentage error in* (2.7) *is of the order* k^2/n^2 *or* k^4/n^3, whichever is larger. In practice the estimate is usually applied when k^2/n is large, and in this case the relative error is of the order k^4/n^3. Our estimates also point the way how to improve the approximation by appropriate correction terms (problem 14).

3. THE DEMOIVRE-LAPLACE LIMIT THEOREM

We proceed to show how our approximations can be extended to the general binomial distribution with $p \neq \frac{1}{2}$. The procedure is the same, but the calculations are more involved. The first complication arises in connection with the central term of the distribution. As we saw in VI, (3.2), the index m of the central term is the unique integer of the form

$$(3.1) \qquad m = np + \delta \qquad\qquad \text{with} \quad -q < \delta \leq p.$$

The quantity δ will be ultimately neglected, but it occurs in the calculations. (In the case $p = \frac{1}{2}$ this was avoided by assuming $n = 2\nu$ even.)

As in the preceding section we now renumber the terms of the binomial distribution and write

$$(3.2) \qquad a_k = b(m+k; n, p) = \binom{n}{m+k} p^{m+k} q^{n-m-k}.$$

For definiteness we consider $k > 0$, but the same argument applies to $k < 0$. (Alternatively, the range $k < 0$ is covered by interchanging p and q.) In analogy with (2.2) we have now

$$(3.3) \qquad a_k = a_0 \frac{(n-m)(n-m-1)\cdots(n-m-k+1)p^k}{(m+1)(m+2)\cdots(m+k)q^k}.$$

This can be rewritten in the form

$$(3.4) \qquad a_k = a_0 \frac{(1-pt_0)(1-pt_1)\cdots(1-pt_{k-1})}{(1+qt_0)(1+qt_1)\cdots(1+qt_{k-1})}$$

where we put for abbreviation

$$(3.5) \qquad t_j = \frac{j + \delta + q}{(n+1)pq}.$$

We shall use (3.4) only for values of k for which t_k is small, say $t_k < \frac{1}{2}$. From the Taylor expansion II,(8.9) for the logarithm it is then clear that

$$(3.6) \qquad \frac{1 - pt_j}{1 + qt_j} = e^{-t_j + \cdots}$$

where the omitted quantity is in absolute value less than t_j^2. Thus

$$(3.7) \qquad a_k = a_0 e^{-(t_0 + \cdots + t_{k-1}) + \cdots}$$

where the dots indicate a quantity that is in absolute value less than[5] $kt_{k-1}^2 < k^3/(npq)^2$. Now

$$(3.8) \qquad t_0 + t_1 + \cdots + t_{k-1} = \frac{\frac{1}{2}k(k-1) + k(\delta+q)}{(n+1)pq}.$$

For simplicity we replace the right side by $k^2/(2npq)$ thereby committing an error less than $2k/(npq)$. Thus, if we write

$$(3.9) \qquad a_k = a_0 e^{-k^2/(2npq) + \rho_k},$$

---

[5] We shall be satisfied with very rough bounds for the error term.

the error term ρ_k satisfies the inequality

(3.10) $$|\rho_k| < \frac{k^3}{(npq)^2} + \frac{2k}{npq}.$$

We next show that

(3.11) $$a_0 = \frac{n!}{m!\,(n-m)!}\,p^m q^{n-m} \sim \frac{1}{\sqrt{2\pi npq}},$$

which generalizes the analogous relation (2.6) in the symmetric case. In the ideal case where $p = m/n$ the estimate (3.11) is an immediate consequence of Stirling's formula II,(9.1). A straightforward differentiation shows that the middle term in (3.11) assumes its maximum when $p = m/n$. For given m we need consider only values of p such that (3.1) holds, and the minimum of a_0 is then assumed at one of the endpoints, that is, for $p = m/(n+1)$ or $p = (m+1)/(n+1)$. With these values for p a direct application of Stirling's formula again leads to (3.11) except that n is replaced by $n + 1$. It follows that (3.11) holds for all possible values of p. If we put for abbreviation

(3.12) $$h = \frac{1}{\sqrt{npq}}$$

then (3.9) shows that

(3.13) $$a_k \sim h\mathfrak{n}(kh)$$

provided only that k varies with n in such a way that $\rho_k \to 0$. We have thus proved

Theorem 1. *If $n \to \infty$ and k is constrained to an interval $k < K_n$ such that $K_n^3/n^2 \to 0$, then (3.13) holds[6] uniformly in k; that is, for every $\epsilon > 0$ and n sufficiently large*

(3.14) $$1 - \epsilon < \frac{a_k}{h\mathfrak{n}(kh)} < 1 + \epsilon.$$

Example. Figure 3 illustrates the case $n = 10$ and $p = \frac{1}{5}$ where $npq = 1.6$. Considering that n is extremely small the approximation seems surprisingly good. For $k = 0, \ldots, 6$ the probabilities $b(k; n, p)$ are 0.1074, 0.2684, 0.3020, 0.2013, 0.0880, 0.0264, 0.0055. The corresponding approximations (3.13) are 0.0904, 0.2307, 0.3154, 0.2307, 0.0904, 0.0189, 0.0021.   ▶

---

[6] When k varies with n in such a way that $k^3/n^2 \to \infty$ the normal approximation is replaced by a limit theorem of a different type; see problems 13 and 15.

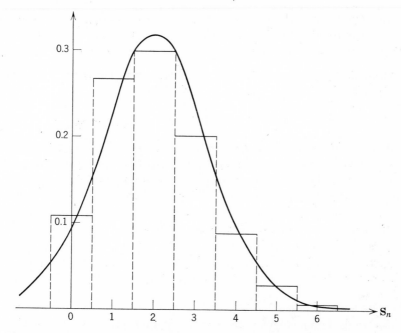

Figure 3. The normal approximation to the binomial distribution. The step function gives the probabilities $b(k; 10, \frac{1}{5})$ of k successes in ten Bernoulli trials with $p = \frac{1}{5}$. The continuous curve gives for each integer k the corresponding normal approximation.

The main application of theorem 1 is to obtain approximations to probabilities of the form

$$(3.15) \qquad \mathbf{P}\{\alpha \leq \mathbf{S}_n \leq \beta\} = \sum_{\nu=\alpha}^{\beta} b(\nu; n, p) = \sum_{k=\alpha-m}^{\beta-m} a_k.$$

Within the range of applicability of theorem 1 we obtain a good approximation when we replace a_k by $h\mathfrak{n}(kh)$. This quantity may be interpreted as the area of a rectangle with height $\mathfrak{n}(kh)$ whose basis is an interval of length h centered at kh (see figure 3). As usual we replace the area of the rectangle by the corresponding area between the x-axis and the graph of $\mathfrak{n}$; as is well known, the error thus committed is negligible in the limit when $h \to 0$. When α and β are integers we arrive thus at the approximation

$$(3.16) \qquad \mathbf{P}\{\alpha \leq \mathbf{S}_n \leq \beta\} \approx \mathfrak{N}((\alpha-m+\tfrac{1}{2})h) - \mathfrak{N}((\beta-m-\tfrac{1}{2})h).$$

It is advisable to use the normal approximation in this form when h is only moderately small and the greatest possible accuracy is desired. For the final formulation, however, it is preferable to replace the arguments on the right by the simpler expressions $z_1 = (\alpha - np)h$ and $z_2 = (\beta - np)h$; the error introduced by this simplification obviously tends to zero with h. We have thus proved the fundamental

Theorem 2. (*DeMoivre-Laplace limit theorem.*) *For fixed*[7] z_1 *and* z_2 *as* $n \to \infty$

$$(3.17) \qquad \mathbf{P}\{np + z_1\sqrt{npq} \leq \mathbf{S}_n \leq np + z_2\sqrt{nqp}\} \to \mathfrak{N}(z_2) - \mathfrak{N}(z_1).$$

Besides being of theoretical importance this theorem justifies the use of the right side as an approximation to the left.   From (3.10) it is easy to obtain good estimates of the error, but we shall not dwell on this point. Practical examples will be found in the next section.

The limit relation (3.17) takes on a more pleasing form if $\mathbf{S}_n$ is replaced by the reduced number of successes $\mathbf{S}_n^*$ defined by

$$(3.18) \qquad\qquad \mathbf{S}_n^* = \frac{\mathbf{S}_n - np}{\sqrt{npq}}.$$

This amounts to measuring the deviations of $\mathbf{S}_n$ from np in units of $\sqrt{npq}$. In the terminology of random variables (chapter IX) np would be called *the expectation*, and npq *the variance* of $\mathbf{S}_n$. (The square root $\sqrt{npq}$ is the standard deviation.)   The inequality on the left side in (3.17) is the same as $z_1 \leq \mathbf{S}_n^* \leq z_2$ and hence we can *restate* (3.17) *in the form*

$$(3.19) \qquad\qquad \mathbf{P}\{z_1 \leq \mathbf{S}_n^* \leq z_2\} \to \mathfrak{N}(z_2) - \mathfrak{N}(z_1).$$

In most cases we shall refer to the limit theorem in this form. It shows, in particular, that for large n the probability on the left is practically independent of p. This permits us to compare fluctuations in different series of Bernoulli trials simply by referring to our standard units.

Note on Optional Stopping

It is essential to note that our approximation theorems are valid only if the number n of trials is fixed in advance independently of the outcome of the trials. If a gambler has the privilege of stopping at a moment favorable to him, his ultimate gain cannot be judged from the normal approximation, for now the duration of the game depends on chance. For every fixed n it is very improbable that $\mathbf{S}_n^*$ is large, but, in the long run, even the most improbable thing is bound to happen, and we shall see that in a continued game $\mathbf{S}_n^*$ is practically certain to have a sequence of maxima of the order of magnitude $\sqrt{2 \log \log n}$ (this is the law of the iterated logarithm of VIII, 5).

---

[7] It is obvious from theorem 1 that this condition can be weakened. See also section 6 as well as problems 14 and 16.

4. EXAMPLES

(a) Let $p = \frac{1}{2}$ and $n = 200$. We consider $\mathbf{P}\{95 \leq \mathbf{S}_n \leq 105\}$, which is the probability that in 200 tosses of a coin the number of heads deviates from 100 by at most 5. Here $h = 1/\sqrt{50} = 0.141421 \cdots$ is relatively large, and it pays to be careful about the limits of the interval. The use of (3.16) leads us to the approximation

$$\mathbf{P}\{95 \leq \mathbf{S}_n \leq 105\} \approx \mathfrak{N}(5.5h) - \mathfrak{N}(-5.5h) =$$
$$= 2\mathfrak{N}(0.7778 \cdots) - 1 = 0.56331.$$

The true value is $0.56325 \ldots$ The smallness of the error is due largely to the symmetry of the distribution.

(b) Let $p = \frac{1}{10}$ and $n = 500$. Here $h = 1/\sqrt{45} = 0.14907 \ldots$ Proceeding as before we get

$$\mathbf{P}\{50 \leq \mathbf{S}_n \leq 55\} \approx \mathfrak{N}(5.5h) - \mathfrak{N}(-0.5h) =$$
$$= \mathfrak{N}(5.5h) + \mathfrak{N}(0.5h) - 1 = 0.3235 \cdots$$

against the correct value $0.3176 \ldots$ The error is about 2 per cent.

(c) The probability that $\mathbf{S}_n$ lies within the limits $np \pm 2\sqrt{npq}$ is about $\mathfrak{N}(2) - \mathfrak{N}(-2) = 0.9545$; for $np \pm 3\sqrt{npq}$ the probability is about 0.9973. It is surprising within how narrow limits the chance fluctuations are likely to lie. For example in 10^6 tosses of a coin the probability that the number of heads deviates from the mean 500000 by more than 1000 is less than 0.0455.

(d) Let $n = 100$, $p = 0.3$. Table 2 shows in a typical example (for relatively small n) how the normal approximation deteriorates as the interval (α, β) moves away from the central term.

(e) Let us find a number a such that, for large n, the inequality $|\mathbf{S}_n^*| > a$ has a probability near $\frac{1}{2}$. For this it is necessary that

$$\mathfrak{N}(a) - \mathfrak{N}(-a) = \tfrac{1}{2}$$

or $\mathfrak{N}(a) = \frac{3}{4}$. From tables of the normal distribution we find that $a = 0.6745$, and hence the two inequalities

(4.1) $|\mathbf{S}_n - np| < 0.6745\sqrt{npq}$ and $|\mathbf{S}_n - np| > 0.6745\sqrt{npq}$

are about equally probable. In particular, the probability is about $\frac{1}{2}$ that in n tossings of a coin the number of heads lies within the limits $\frac{1}{2}n \pm 0.337\sqrt{n}$, and, similarly, that in n throws of a die the number of aces lies within the interval $\frac{1}{6}n \pm 0.251\sqrt{n}$.

TABLE 2
COMPARISON OF THE BINOMIAL DISTRIBUTION FOR $n = 100$,
$p = 0.3$ AND THE NORMAL APPROXIMATION

Number of successes	Probability	Normal approximation	Percentage error
$9 \leq S_n \leq 11$	0.000 006	0.000 03	+400
$12 \leq S_n \leq 14$	0.000 15	0.000 33	+100
$15 \leq S_n \leq 17$	0.002 01	0.002 83	+40
$18 \leq S_n \leq 20$	0.014 30	0.015 99	+12
$21 \leq S_n \leq 23$	0.059 07	0.058 95	0
$24 \leq S_n \leq 26$	0.148 87	0.144 47	−3
$27 \leq S_n \leq 29$	0.237 94	0.234 05	−2
$31 \leq S_n \leq 33$	0.230 13	0.234 05	+2
$34 \leq S_n \leq 36$	0.140 86	0.144 47	+3
$37 \leq S_n \leq 39$	0.058 89	0.058 95	0
$40 \leq S_n \leq 42$	0.017 02	0.015 99	−6
$43 \leq S_n \leq 45$	0.003 43	0.002 83	−18
$46 \leq S_n \leq 48$	0.000 49	0.000 33	−33
$49 \leq S_n \leq 51$	0.000 05	0.000 03	−40

(*f*) *A competition problem.* This example illustrates practical applications of formula (3.17). Two competing railroads operate one train each between Chicago and Los Angeles; the two trains leave and arrive simultaneously and have comparable equipment. We suppose that n passengers select trains independently and at random so that the number of passengers in each train is the outcome of n Bernoulli trials with $p = \frac{1}{2}$. If a train carries $s < n$ seats, then there is a positive probability $f(s)$ that more than s passengers will turn up, in which case not all patrons can be accommodated. Using the approximation (3.17), we find

$$(4.2) \qquad\qquad f(s) \approx 1 - \Re\left(\frac{2s - n}{\sqrt{n}}\right).$$

If s is so large that $f(s) < 0.01$, then the number of seats will be sufficient in 99 out of 100 cases. More generally, the company may decide on an arbitrary risk level α and determine s so that $f(s) < \alpha$. For that purpose it suffices to put

$$(4.3) \qquad\qquad s \geq \tfrac{1}{2}(n + t_\alpha\sqrt{n}),$$

where t_α is the root of the equation $\alpha = 1 - \mathfrak{N}(t_\alpha)$, which can be found from tables. For example, if $n = 1000$ and $\alpha = 0.01$, then $t_\alpha \approx 2.33$ and $s = 537$ seats should suffice. If both railroads accept the risk level $\alpha = 0.01$, the two trains will carry a total of 1074 seats of which 74 will be empty. The loss from competition (or chance fluctuations) is remarkably small. In the same way, 514 seats should suffice in about 80 per cent of all cases, and 549 seats in 999 out of 1000 cases.

Similar considerations apply in other competitive supply problems. For example, if m movies compete for the same n patrons, each movie will put for its probability of success $p = 1/m$, and (4.3) is to be replaced by $s \geq m^{-1}[n + t_\alpha\sqrt{n(m-1)}]$. The total number of empty seats under this system is $ms - n \approx t_\alpha\sqrt{n(m-1)}$. For $\alpha = 0.01$, $n = 1000$, and $m = 2$, 3, 4, 5 this number is about 74, 105, 126, and 147, respectively. The loss of efficiency because of competition is again small.

(g) *Random digits.* In example II, (3.a) we considered $n = 1200$ trials with $p = 0.3024$ and an average of 0.3142 successes per trial. The discrepancy is $\epsilon = 0.0118$. Here

$$\mathbf{P}\left\{\left|\frac{\mathbf{S}_n}{n} - p\right| > \epsilon\right\} = \mathbf{P}\{|S_n - np| > \epsilon n\} \approx$$

$$\approx \mathbf{P}\{|\mathbf{S}_n - np| > 0.880\sqrt{npq}\} \approx 2(1 - \mathfrak{N}(0.88)) \approx 0.379.$$

This means that in about 38 out of 100 similar experiments the average number of successes should deviate from p by more than it does in our material.

(h) *Sampling.* An unknown fraction p of a certain population are smokers, and random sampling with replacement is to be used to determine p. It is desired to find p with an error not exceeding 0.005. How large should the sample size n be?

Denote the fraction of smokers in the sample by p'. Clearly no sample size can give absolute guarantee that $|p' - p| < 0.005$ because it is conceivable that by chance the sample contains only smokers. The best we can do is to render an error exceeding the preassigned bound 0.005 very improbable. For this purpose we settle for an arbitrary confidence level α, say $\alpha = 0.95$, and choose n so large that the event $|p' - p| < < 0.005$ will have a probability $\geq \alpha$. Since np' can be interpreted as the number of successes in n trials we have

$$(4.4) \qquad \mathbf{P}\{|p' - p| < 0.005\} = \mathbf{P}\{|\mathbf{S}_n - np| < 0.005n\}$$

and we wish to choose n so large that this probability is $\geq \alpha$. From the tables we first find the number z_α for which $\mathfrak{N}(z_\alpha) - \mathfrak{N}(-z_\alpha) = \alpha$. Relying on the normal approximation it is then necessary to choose n so large that $\dfrac{0.005\sqrt{n}}{\sqrt{pq}} \geq z_\alpha$, or $n \geq 40{,}000 pq z_\alpha^2$. This involves the unknown probability p, but we have under any circumstances $pq \leq \tfrac{1}{4}$, and so *a sample size* $n \geq 10{,}000 z_\alpha^2$ *should suffice.*

For the confidence level $\alpha = 0.95$ we find $z_\alpha = 1.960$ and hence a sample size of $n = 40{,}000$ would certainly suffice. A sample of this size would be costly, but the requirement that $|p' - p| < 0.005$ is exceedingly stringent. If it is only required that $|p' - p| < 0.01$, a sample size of 10,000 will suffice (on the same confidence level). The so-called accuracy to four percentage points means the event $|p' - p| < 0.045$ and requires only a sample size of 475: On the average only five out of one hundred random samples of this size will result in an estimate with a greater error. (The practical difficulty is usually to obtain a representative sample of any size.)

▶

5. RELATION TO THE POISSON APPROXIMATION

The error of the normal approximation will be small if npq is large. On the other hand, if n is large and p small, the terms $b(k; n, p)$ will be found to be near the Poisson probabilities $p(k; \lambda)$ with $\lambda = np$. For small λ only the Poisson approximation can be used, but for large λ we can use either the normal or the Poisson approximation. This implies that for large values of λ it must be possible to approximate the Poisson distribution by the normal distribution, and in example X, (1.c) we shall see that this is indeed so (cf. also problem 9). Here we shall be content to illustrate the point by a numerical and a practical example.

Examples. (a) The Poisson distribution with $\lambda = 100$ attributes to the set of integers $a, a + 1, \ldots, b$ the probability

$$P(a, b) = p(a; 100) + p(a+1; 100) + \cdots + p(b; 100).$$

This Poisson distribution may be considered as an approximation to the binomial distribution with $n = 100{,}000{,}000$ and $p = 10^{-6}$. Then $npq \approx 100$ and so it is not far-fetched to approximate this binomial distribution by the normal, at least for values close to the central term 100. But this means that $P(a, b)$ is being approximated by

$$\mathfrak{N}((b-99.5)/10) - \mathfrak{N}((a-100.5)/10).$$

The following sample gives an idea of the degree of approximation.

	Correct values	Normal approximation
$P(85, 90)$	0.113 84	0.110 49
$P(90, 95)$	0.184 85	0.179 50
$P(95, 105)$	0.417 63	0.417 68
$P(90, 110)$	0.706 52	0.706 28
$P(110, 115)$	0.107 38	0.110 49
$P(115, 120)$	0.053 23	0.053 35

(b) *A telephone trunking problem.* The following problem is, with some simplifications, taken from actual practice.[8] A telephone exchange A is to serve 2000 subscribers in a nearby exchange B. It would be too expensive and extravagant to install 2000 trunklines from A to B. It suffices to make the number N of lines so large that, under ordinary conditions, only one out of every hundred calls will fail to find an idle trunkline immediately at its disposal. Suppose that during the busy hour of the day each subscriber requires a trunkline to B for an average of 2 minutes. At a fixed moment of the busy hour we compare the situation to a set of 2000 trials with a probability $p = \frac{1}{30}$ in each that a line will be required. Under ordinary conditions these trials can be assumed to be independent (although this is not true when events like unexpected showers or earthquakes cause many people to call for taxicabs or the local newspaper; the theory no longer applies, and the trunks will be "jammed"). We have, then, 2000 Bernoulli trials with $p = \frac{1}{30}$, and the smallest number N is required such that the probability of more than N "successes" will be smaller than 0.01; in symbols $P\{S_{2000} \geq N\} < 0.01$.

For the *Poisson approximation* we should take $\lambda = \frac{2000}{30} \approx 66.67$. From the tables we find that the probability of 87 or more successes is about 0.0097, whereas the probability of 86 or more successes is about 0.013. This would indicate that 87 *trunklines should suffice.* For the *normal approximation* we first find from tables the root x of $1 - \mathfrak{N}(x) = 0.01$, which is $x = 2.327$. Then it is required that

$$(N - \tfrac{1}{2} - np)/\sqrt{npq} \geq 2.327.$$

Since $n = 2000$, $p = \frac{1}{30}$, this means $N \geq 67.17 + (2.327)(8.027) \approx 85.8$. Hence the normal approximation would indicate that 86 *trunklines should suffice.*

---

[8] E. C. Molina, *Probability in engineering*, Electrical Engineering, vol. 54 (1935), pp. 423–427, or *Bell Telephone System Technical Publications Monograph* B-854. There the problem is treated by the Poisson method given in the text, which is preferable from the engineer's point of view.

For practical purposes the two solutions agree. They yield further useful information. For example, it is conceivable that the installation might be cheaper if the 2000 subscribers were divided into two groups of 1000 each, and two separate groups of trunklines from A to B were installed. Using the method above, we find that actually some ten additional trunklines would be required so that the first arrangement is preferable. ▶

*6. LARGE DEVIATIONS

The DeMoivre-Laplace theorem describes the asymptotic behavior of $\mathbf{P}\{z_1 < \mathbf{S}_n^* < z_2\}$ for fixed z_1 and z_2. From its derivation it is clear that the theorem applies also when z_1 and z_2 are permitted to vary with n in such a way that $z_1 \to \infty$, provided that the growth is sufficiently slow. In this case both sides in (3.17) tend to 0, and the theorem is meaningful only if the *ratio* of the two sides tends to unity. The next theorem shows to what extent this is true. To simplify the formulation the double inequality $z_1 < \mathbf{S}_n^* < z_2$ is replaced by $\mathbf{S}_n^* > z_1$. This is justified by the following lemma, which shows that when $z_1 \to \infty$ the upper limit z_2 plays no role.

Lemma. *If $x_n \to \infty$ then for every fixed[9] $\eta > 0$*

$$(6.1) \qquad \frac{\mathbf{P}\{\mathbf{S}_n^* > x_n + \eta\}}{\mathbf{P}\{\mathbf{S}_n^* > x_n\}} \to 0,$$

that is,

$$(6.2) \qquad \mathbf{P}\{x_n < \mathbf{S}_n^* \leq x_n + \eta\} \sim \mathbf{P}\{\mathbf{S}_n^* > x_n\}.$$

In other words: When $\mathbf{S}_n^*$ exceeds x_n it is likely to be very close to x_n, and larger values play no role in the limit.

Proof. With the notation (3.2) for the binomial distribution we have

$$(6.3) \qquad \mathbf{P}\{\mathbf{S}_n^* > x_n\} = \sum_{\nu=0}^{\infty} a_{r_n+\nu}, \qquad \mathbf{P}\{\mathbf{S}_n^* > x_n + \eta\} = \sum_{\nu=0}^{\infty} a_{s_n+\nu},$$

where r_n and s_n are integers that differ at most by one unit from $x_n\sqrt{npq}$ and $(x_n+\eta)\sqrt{npq}$, respectively. Now it is obvious from (3.4)

---

* The theorem of this section is in general use, but in this volume it will be applied only in VII, 4 and VIII, 5.

[9] The proof will show that it suffices that $x_n\eta \to \infty$. For a stronger and more interesting version see problem 18.

that for large n

(6.4) $$\frac{a_{k+1}}{a_k} < 1 - pt_k < 1 - \frac{k}{n} < e^{-k/n},$$

and hence

(6.5) $$\frac{a_{s_n+v}}{a_{r_n+v}} < e^{-(s_n-r_n)r_n/n} < e^{-\frac{1}{2}\eta x_n pq}.$$

By assumption $x_n \to \infty$, and so the terms of the second series in (6.3) tend to become negligible in comparison with the corresponding terms of the first series. ▶

We are now in a position to extend the limit theorem as follows.

Theorem. *If $x_n \to \infty$ in such a way that $x_n^3/\sqrt{n} \to 0$, then*

(6.6) $$P\{S_n^* > x_n\} \sim 1 - \mathfrak{N}(x_n).$$

In view of (1.7) the asymptotic relation (6.6) *is fully equivalent to*

(6.7) $$P\{S_n^* > x_n\} \sim \frac{1}{\sqrt{2\pi}} \cdot \frac{1}{x_n} e^{-\frac{1}{2}x_n^2}.$$

Proof. In view of the preceding lemma and theorem 3.1

(6.8) $$P\{S_n^* > x_n\} \sim \sum_{k=r_n}^{\infty} h\mathfrak{n}(kh)$$

where r_n is an integer such that $|r_n h - x_n| < h$. The sum on the right therefore lies between $1 - \mathfrak{N}(x_n - 2h)$ and $1 - \mathfrak{N}(x_n + 2h)$. For the difference of these two quantities we get, using (1.7),

(6.9) $$\mathfrak{N}(x_n + 2h) - \mathfrak{N}(x_n - 2h) < 4h\mathfrak{n}(x_n - 2h) \to 0,$$

and so the sum in (6.8) is $\sim 1 - \mathfrak{N}(x_n)$, as asserted. ▶

For generalizations see problems 14 and 16.

7. PROBLEMS FOR SOLUTION

1. Generalizing (1.7), prove that

(7.1) $$1 - \mathfrak{N}(x) \sim \frac{1}{\sqrt{2\pi}} e^{-\frac{1}{2}x^2} \left\{ \frac{1}{x} - \frac{1}{x^3} + \frac{1 \cdot 3}{x^5} - \frac{1 \cdot 3 \cdot 5}{x^7} + - \cdots + \right.$$
$$\left. + (-1)^k \frac{1 \cdot 3 \cdots (2k-1)}{x^{2k+1}} \right\}$$

and that for $x > 0$ the right side *overestimates* $1 - \mathfrak{N}(x)$ if k is even, and *underestimates* if k is odd.

2. For every constant $a > 0$

$$(7.2) \qquad \frac{1 - \mathfrak{N}(x+a/x)}{1 - \mathfrak{N}(x)} \to e^{-a}$$

as $x \to \infty$.

3. Find the probability that among 10,000 random digits the digit 7 appears not more than 968 times.

4. Find an approximation to the probability that the number of aces obtained in 12,000 rollings of a die is between 1900 and 2150.

5. Find a number k such that the probability is about 0.5 that the number of heads obtained in 1000 tossings of a coin will be between 490 and k.

6. A sample is taken in order to find the fraction f of females in a population. Find a sample size such that the probability of a sampling error less than 0.005 will be 0.99 or greater.

7. In 10,000 tossings, a coin fell heads 5400 times. Is it reasonable to assume that the coin is skew?

_____

8. Find an approximation to the maximal term of the trinomial distribution

$$\frac{n!}{k!\, r!\, (n-k-r)!}\; p_1^k p_2^r (1-p_1-p_2)^{n-k-r}$$

9. *Normal approximation to the Poisson distribution.* Using Stirling's formula, show that, if $\lambda \to \infty$, then for fixed $\alpha < \beta$

$$(7.3) \qquad \sum_{\lambda+\alpha\sqrt{\lambda}<k<\lambda+\beta\sqrt{\lambda}} p(k;\lambda) \to \mathfrak{N}(\beta) - \mathfrak{N}(\alpha).$$

10. *Normal approximation to the hypergeometric distribution.* Let n, m, k be positive integers and suppose that they tend to infinity in such a way that

$$(7.4) \qquad \frac{r}{n+m} \to t, \quad \frac{n}{n+m} \to p, \quad \frac{m}{n+m} \to q, \quad h\{k-rp\} \to x$$

where $h = 1/\sqrt{(n+m)pqt(1-t)}$. Prove that

$$(7.5) \qquad \binom{n}{k}\binom{m}{r-k}\bigg/\binom{n+m}{r} \sim h\mathfrak{n}(x).$$

Hint: Use the normal approximation to the binomial distribution rather than Stirling's formula.

11. *Normal distribution and combinatorial runs.*[10] In II, (11.19) we found that in an arrangement of n alphas and m betas the probability of having exactly

_____

[10] A. Wald and J. Wolfowitz, *On a test whether two samples are from the same population*, Ann. Math. Statist., vol. 11 (1940), pp. 147–162. For more general results, see A. M. Mood, *The distribution theory of runs, ibid.*, pp. 367–392.

k runs of alphas is

(7.6) $$\pi_k = \binom{n-1}{k-1}\binom{m+1}{k} \bigg/ \binom{n+m}{n}.$$

Let $n \to \infty$, $m \to \infty$ so that (7.4) holds. For fixed $\alpha < \beta$ the probability that the number of alpha runs lies between $nq + \alpha q \sqrt{pn}$ and $nq + \beta q \sqrt{pn}$ tends to $\mathfrak{N}(\beta) - \mathfrak{N}(\alpha)$.

12. *A new derivation of the law of large numbers.* Derive the law of large numbers of VI, 4 from the de Moivre-Laplace limit theorem.

Limit Theorems for Large Deviations

13. Using the notations of section 3 show that if k varies with n in such a way that $k^4/n^3 \to 0$, then

(7.7) $$a_k = b(k+m\,;\,n,p) \sim h\mathfrak{n}(kh) \cdot e^{-(p-q)k^3h^4/6}, \qquad h = \frac{1}{\sqrt{npq}}.$$

This generalizes theorem 3.1.

14. Using the preceding problem and the lemma of section 6 prove the following

Theorem. *If x_n varies with n in such a way that $x_n^4/n \to 0$ but $x_n \to \infty$, then*

(7.8) $$\mathbf{P}\{S_n^* > x_n\} \sim [1 - \mathfrak{N}(x_n)]e^{-(p-q)x_n^3/(\sqrt{npq})}.$$

15. *Generalization of problem* 13. Put

(7.9) $$f(x) = \sum_{\nu=3}^{\infty} \frac{p^{\nu-1}(-q)^{\nu-1}}{\nu(\nu-1)} h^{\nu-2}x^\nu = \frac{p-q}{6} x^3 h + \frac{p^3+q^3}{12} x^4 h^2 + \cdots$$

where $h = 1/\sqrt{npq}$. If k varies with n in such a way that $k/n \to 0$ then

(7.10) $$a_k \sim h\mathfrak{n}(kh) \cdot e^{-f(kh)}.$$

[When $k^3/n^2 \to 0$ this reduces to theorem 3.1; when $k^4/n^3 \to 0$ we get (7.7); when $k^5/n^4 \to 0$ we get (7.7) with a fourth-degree term added in the exponent, etc.]

16. *Generalization of problem* 14. If x_n varies with n in such a way that $x_n \to \infty$ but $x_n/\sqrt{n} \to 0$, then

(7.11) $$\mathbf{P}\{S_n^* > x_n\} \sim [1 - \mathfrak{N}(x_n)]e^{-f(x_n)}.$$

When $x_n^4/n \to 0$ this reduces to (7.8). When x_n^5/n^3 one may replace $f(x_n^{\frac{3}{2}})$ by the fourth-degree polynomial appearing on the right in (7.9), etc.

17. If $p > q$ then $\mathbf{P}\{S_n^* > x\} > \mathbf{P}\{S_n^* < -x\}$ for all large x. *Hint:* Use problem 15.

18. If $x_n \to \infty$ and $x_n/\sqrt{n} \to 0$ show that

(7.12) $$\mathbf{P}\{x_n < S_n^* < x_n + a/x_n\} \sim (1-e^{-a})\mathbf{P}\{S_n^* > x_n\}.$$

In words: The conditional probability of the event $\{S_n^* \geq x_n + a/x_n\}$ given that $S_n^* > x_n$ tends to e^{-a}. (A weaker version of this theorem was proved by Khintchine.)

CHAPTER VIII*

Unlimited Sequences
of Bernoulli Trials

This chapter discusses certain properties of randomness and the important law of the iterated logarithm for Bernoulli trials. A different aspect of the fluctuation theory of Bernoulli trials (at least for $p = \frac{1}{2}$) is covered in chapter III.

1. INFINITE SEQUENCES OF TRIALS

In the preceding chapter we have dealt with probabilities connected with n Bernoulli trials and have studied their asymptotic behavior as $n \to \infty$. We turn now to a more general type of problem where the events themselves cannot be defined in a finite sample space.

Example. *A problem in runs.* Let α and β be positive integers, and consider a potentially unlimited sequence of Bernoulli trials, such as tossing a coin or throwing dice. Suppose that Paul bets Peter that a run of α consecutive successes will occur before a run of β consecutive failures. It has an intuitive meaning to speak of the event that Paul wins, but it must be remembered that in the mathematical theory the term event stands for "aggregate of sample points" and is meaningless unless an appropriate sample space has been defined. The model of a finite number of trials is insufficient for our present purpose, but the difficulty is solved by a simple passage to the limit. In n trials Peter wins or loses, or the game remains undecided. Let the corresponding probabilities be x_n, y_n, z_n ($x_n + y_n + z_n = 1$). As the number n of trials increases, the probability z_n of a tie can only decrease, and both x_n and y_n necessarily increase. Hence $x = \lim x_n$, $y = \lim y_n$, and $z = \lim z_n$ exist. Nobody would

---

* This chapter is not directly connected with the material covered in subsequent chapters and may be omitted at first reading.

hesitate to call them the probabilities of Peter's ultimate gain or loss or of a tie. However, the corresponding three events are defined only in the sample space of infinite sequences of trials, and this space is not discrete.

The example was introduced for illustration only, and the numerical values of x_n, y_n, z_n are not our immediate concern. We shall return to their calculation in example XIII, (8.b). The limits x, y, z may be obtained by a simpler method which is applicable to more general cases. We indicate it here because of its importance and intrinsic interest.

Let A be the event that *a run of* α *consecutive successes occurs before a run of* β *consecutive failures*. In the event A Paul wins and $x = \mathbf{P}\{A\}$. If u and v are the conditional probabilities of A under the hypotheses, respectively, that the first trial results in success or failure, then $x = pu + qv$ [see V, (1.8)]. Suppose first that the first trial results in success. In this case the event A can occur in α mutually exclusive ways: (1) The following $\alpha - 1$ trials result in successes; the probability for this is $p^{\alpha-1}$. (2) The first failure occurs at the νth trial where $2 \leq \nu \leq \alpha$. Let this event be H_ν. Then $\mathbf{P}\{H_\nu\} = p^{\nu-2}q$, and $\mathbf{P}\{A \mid H_\nu\} = v$. Hence (using once more the formula for compound probabilities)

(1.1) $$u = p^{\alpha-1} + qv(1+p+ \cdots +p^{\alpha-2}) = p^{\alpha-1} + v(1-p^{\alpha-1}).$$

If the first trial results in failure, a similar argument leads to

(1.2) $$v = pu(1+q+ \cdots +q^{\beta-2}) = u(1-q^{\beta-1}).$$

We have thus two equations for the two unknowns u and v and find for $x = pu + qv$

(1.3) $$x = p^{\alpha-1} \frac{1 - q^\beta}{p^{\alpha-1} + q^{\beta-1} - p^{\alpha-1}q^{\beta-1}} .$$

To obtain y we have only to interchange p and q, and α and β. Thus

(1.4) $$y = q^{\beta-1} \frac{1 - p^\alpha}{p^{\alpha-1} + q^{\beta-1} - p^{\alpha-1}q^{\beta-1}} .$$

Since $x + y = 1$, we have $z = 0$; *the probability of a tie is zero*.

For example, in tossing a coin $(p = \frac{1}{2})$ the probability that a run of two heads appears before a run of three tails is 0.7; for two consecutive heads before four consecutive tails the probability is $\frac{5}{8}$, for three consecutive heads before four consecutive tails $\frac{15}{22}$. In rolling dice there is probability 0.1753 that two consecutive aces will appear before five consecutive non-aces, etc.   ▶

In the present volume we are confined to the theory of discrete sample spaces, and this means a considerable loss of mathematical elegance. The general theory considers n Bernoulli trials only as the beginning of an infinite sequence of trials. A sample point is then represented by an infinite sequence of letters S and F, and the sample space is the aggregate of all such sequences. A finite sequence, like $SSFS$, stands for the aggregate of all points with this beginning, that is, for the compound event that in an infinite sequence of trials the first four result in S, S, F, S, respectively. In the infinite sample space the game of our example can be interpreted without a limiting process. Take any point, that is, a sequence *SSFSFF*. . . . In it a run of α consecutive *S*'s may or may not occur. If it does, it may or may not be preceded by a run of β consecutive *F*'s. In this way we get a classification of all sample points into three classes, representing the events "Peter wins," "Peter loses," "no decision." Their probabilities are the numbers x, y, z, computed above. The only trouble with this sample space is that it is not discrete, and we have not yet defined probabilities in general sample spaces.

Note that we are discussing a question of terminology rather than a genuine difficulty. In our example there was no question about the proper definition or interpretation of the number x. The trouble is only that for consistency we must either decide to refer to the number x as "the limit of the probability x_n that Peter wins in n trials" or else talk of the event "that Peter wins," which means referring to a non-discrete sample space. We propose to do both. For simplicity of language we shall refer to events even when they are defined in the infinite sample space; for precision, the theorems will also be formulated in terms of finite sample spaces and passages to the limit. The events to be studied in this chapter share the following salient feature of our example. The event "Peter wins," although defined in an infinite space, is the union of the events "Peter wins at the nth trial" ($n = 1, 2, \ldots$), each of which depends only on a finite number of trials. The required probability x is the limit of a monotonic sequence of probabilities x_n which depend only on finitely many trials. We require no theory going beyond the model of n Bernoulli trials; we merely take the liberty of simplifying clumsy expressions[1] by calling certain numbers probabilities instead of using the term "limits of probabilities."

2. SYSTEMS OF GAMBLING

The painful experience of many gamblers has taught us the lesson that no system of betting is successful in improving the gambler's chances. If the theory of probability is true to life, this experience must correspond to a provable statement.

For orientation let us consider a potentially unlimited sequence of Bernoulli trials and suppose that at each trial the bettor has the free choice

---

[1] For the reader familiar with general measure theory the situation may be described as follows. We consider only events which either depend on a finite number of trials or are limits of *monotonic* sequences of such events. We calculate the obvious limits of probabilities and clearly require no measure theory for that purpose. But only general measure theory shows that our limits are independent of the particular passage to the limit and are completely additive.

of whether or not to bet. A "system" consists in fixed rules selecting those trials on which the player is to bet. For example, the bettor may make up his mind to bet at every seventh trial or to wait as long as necessary for seven heads to occur between two bets. He may bet only following a head run of length 13, or bet for the first time after the first head, for the second time after the first run of two consecutive heads, and generally, for the kth time, just after k heads have appeared in succession. In the latter case he would bet less and less frequently. We need not consider the stakes at the individual trials; we want to show that no "system" changes the bettor's situation and that he can achieve the same result by betting every time. It goes without saying that this statement can be proved only for systems in the ordinary meaning where the bettor does not know the future (the existence or non-existence of genuine prescience is not our concern). It must also be admitted that the rule "go home after losing three times" does change the situation, but we shall rule out such uninteresting systems.

We define a system as a set of fixed rules which for every trial uniquely determine whether or not the bettor is to bet; at the kth trial the decision may depend on the outcomes of the first $k - 1$ trials, but not on the outcome of trials number k, $k + 1$, $k + 2$, . . . ; finally the rules must be such as to ensure an indefinite continuation of the game. Since the set of rules is fixed, the event "in n trials the bettor bets more than r times" is well defined and its probability calculable. The last condition requires that for every r, as $n \to \infty$, this probability tends to 1.

We now formulate our fundamental theorem to the effect that *under any system the successive bets form a sequence of Bernoulli trials with unchanged probability for success.* With an appropriate change of phrasing this theorem holds for all kinds of independent trials; the successive bets form in each case an exact replica of the original trials, so that no system can affect the bettor's fortunes. The importance of this statement was first recognized by von Mises, who introduced the impossibility of a successful gambling system as a fundamental axiom. The present formulation and proof follow Doob.[2] For simplicity we assume that $p = \frac{1}{2}$.

Let A_k be the event "first bet occurs at the kth trial." Our definition of system requires that as $n \to \infty$ the probability that the first bet has occurred before the nth trial tends to 1. This means that

$$\mathbf{P}\{A_1\} + \mathbf{P}\{A_2\} + \cdots + \mathbf{P}\{A_n\} \to 1,$$

or

(2.1) $$\sum \mathbf{P}\{A_k\} = 1.$$

Next, let B_k be the event "head at kth trial" and B the event "the trial

---

[2] J. L. Doob, *Note on probability*, Annals of Mathematics, vol. 37 (1936), pp. 363–367.

of the first bet results in heads." Then the event B is the union of the events A_1B_1, A_2B_2, A_3B_3, ... which are mutually exclusive. Now A_k depends only on the outcome of the first $k-1$ trials, and B_k only on the trial number k. Hence A_k and B_k are independent and $\mathbf{P}\{A_kB_k\} =$ $= \mathbf{P}\{A_k\}\mathbf{P}\{B_k\} = \frac{1}{2}\mathbf{P}\{A_k\}$. Thus $\mathbf{P}\{B\} = \sum \mathbf{P}\{A_kB_k\} = \frac{1}{2}\sum \mathbf{P}\{A_k\} = \frac{1}{2}$. This shows that under this system the probability of heads at the first bet is $\frac{1}{2}$, and the same statement holds for all subsequent bets.

It remains to show that the bets are stochastically independent. This means that the probability that the coin falls heads at both the first and the second bet should be $\frac{1}{4}$ (and similarly for all other combinations and for the subsequent trials). To verify this statement let A_k^* be the event that the second bet occurs at the kth trial. Let E represent the event "heads at the first two bets"; it is the union of all events $A_jB_jA_k^*B_k$ where $j < k$ (if $j \geq k$, then A_j and A_k^* are mutually exclusive and $A_jA_k^* = 0$). Therefore

$$(2.2) \qquad \mathbf{P}\{E\} = \sum_{j=1}^{\infty} \sum_{k=j+1}^{\infty} \mathbf{P}\{A_jB_jA_k^*B_k\}.$$

As before, we see that for fixed j and $k > j$, the event B_k (heads at kth trial) is independent of the event $A_jB_jA_k^*$ (which depends only on the outcomes of the first $k-1$ trials). Hence

$$(2.3) \qquad \mathbf{P}\{E\} = \frac{1}{2}\sum_{j=1}^{\infty} \sum_{k=j+1}^{\infty} \mathbf{P}\{A_jB_jA_k^*\} =$$

$$= \frac{1}{2}\sum_{j=1}^{\infty} \mathbf{P}\{A_jB_j\} \sum_{k=j+1}^{\infty} \mathbf{P}\{A_k^* \mid A_jB_j\}$$

[cf. V, (1.8)]. Now, whenever the first bet occurs and whatever its outcome, the game is sure to continue, that is, the second bet occurs sooner or later. This means that for given A_jB_j with $\mathbf{P}\{A_jB_j\} > 0$ the conditional probabilities that the second bet occurs at the kth trial must add to unity. The second series in (2.3) is therefore unity, and we have already seen that $\sum \mathbf{P}\{A_jB_j\} = \frac{1}{2}$. Hence $\mathbf{P}\{E\} = \frac{1}{4}$ as contended. A similar argument holds for any combination of trials.   ▶

Note that the situation is different when the player is permitted to vary his stakes. In this case there exist advantageous strategies, and the game depends on the strategy. We shall return to this point in XIV, 2.

3. THE BOREL-CANTELLI LEMMAS

Two simple lemmas concerning infinite sequences of trials are used so frequently that they deserve special attention. We formulate them for Bernoulli trials, but they apply to more general cases.

We refer again to an infinite sequence of Bernoulli trials. Let $A_1, A_2, \ldots$ be an infinite sequence of events each of which depends only on a finite number of trials; in other words, we suppose that there exists an integer n_k such that A_k is an event in the sample space of the first n_k Bernoulli trials. Put

$$(3.1) \qquad a_k = \mathbf{P}\{A_k\}.$$

(For example, A_k may be the event that the $2k$th trial concludes a run of at least k consecutive successes. Then $n_k = 2k$ and $a_k = p^k$.)

For every infinite sequence of letters S and F it is possible to establish whether it belongs to $0, 1, 2, \ldots$ or infinitely many among the $\{A_k\}$. This means that we can speak of the event U_r, that an unending sequence of trials produces more than r among the events $\{A_k\}$, and also of the event U_∞, that infinitely many among the $\{A_k\}$ occur. The event U_r is defined only in the infinite sample space, and its probability is the limit of $\mathbf{P}\{U_{n,r}\}$, the probability that n trials produce more than r among the events $\{A_k\}$. Finally, $\mathbf{P}\{U_\infty\} = \lim \mathbf{P}\{U_r\}$; this limit exists since $\mathbf{P}\{U_r\}$ decreases as r increases.

Lemma 1. *If $\sum a_k$ converges, then with probability one only finitely many events A_k occur.* More precisely, it is claimed that for r sufficiently large, $\mathbf{P}\{U_r\} < \epsilon$ or: *to every $\epsilon > 0$ it is possible to find an integer r such that the probability that n trials produce one or more among the events $A_{r+1}, A_{r+2}, \ldots$ is less than ϵ for all n.*

Proof. Determine r so that $a_{r+1} + a_{r+2} + \cdots \leq \epsilon$; this is possible since $\sum a_k$ converges. Without loss of generality we may suppose that the A_k are ordered in such a way that $n_1 \leq n_2 \leq n_3 \leq \ldots$. Let N be the last subscript for which $n_N \leq n$. Then $A_1, \ldots, A_N$ are defined in the space of n trials, and the lemma asserts that the probability that one or more among the events $A_{r+1}, A_{r+2}, \ldots, A_N$ occur is less than ϵ. This is true, since by the fundamental inequality I, (7.6) we have

$$(3.2) \quad \mathbf{P}\{A_{r+1} \cup A_{r+2} \cup \cdots \cup A_N\} \leq a_{r+1} + a_{r+2} + \cdots + a_N \leq \epsilon,$$

as contended.   ▶

A satisfactory converse to the lemma is known only for the special case of mutually independent A_k. This situation occurs when the trials are divided into non-overlapping blocks and A_k depends only on the trials in the kth block (for example, A_k may be the event that the kth thousand of trials produces more than 600 successes).

Lemma 2. *If the events A_k are mutually independent, and if $\sum a_k$ diverges, then with probability one infinitely many A_k occur.* In other words, it is claimed that for every r the probability that n trials produce more than r among the events A_k tends to 1 as $n \to \infty$.

Proof. Assume the contrary. There exists then an n such that with positive probability u no event A_k with $k > n$ is realized. But

$$(3.3) \qquad u \leq (1-a_n)(1-a_{n+1}) \cdots (1-a_{n+r})$$

because the product on the right is the probability that no A_k with $n \leq k \leq n + r$ occurs. Since $1 - x \leq e^{-x}$ the product on the right is $\leq e^{-(a_n + \cdots + a_{n+r})}$, and the sum in the exponent can be made arbitrarily large by choosing r sufficiently large. Thus $u = 0$ against the hypothesis. ▶

Examples. (*a*) What is the probability that in a sequence of Bernoulli trials the pattern *SFS* appears infinitely often? Let A_k be the event that the trials number k, $k + 1$, and $k + 2$ produce the sequence *SFS*. The events A_k are not mutually independent, but the sequence A_1, A_4, A_7, A_{10}, ... contains only mutually independent events (since no two depend on the outcome of the same trials). Since $a_k = p^2q$ is independent of k, the series $a_1 + a_4 + a_7 + \cdots$ diverges, and hence with probability one the pattern *SFS* occurs infinitely often. A similar argument obviously applies for arbitrary patterns of any length.

(*b*) *Books produced by coin tossing.* Consider a message such as PROB-ABILITY IS FUN written in the Morse code as a finite sequence of dots and dashes. When we write H for dot and T for dash this message will appear as a finite succession of heads and tails. It follows from the preceding example that a prolonged tossing of a coin is certain sooner or later to produce the given message and to repeat it infinitely often. By the same token the record of a prolonged coin-tossing game is bound to contain every conceivable book in the Morse code, from *Hamlet* to eight-place logarithmic tables. It has been suggested that an army of monkeys might be trained to pound typewriters at random in the hope that ultimately great works of literature would be produced. Using a coin for the same purpose may save feeding and training expenses and free the monkeys for other monkey business. ▶

4. THE STRONG LAW OF LARGE NUMBERS

The intuitive notion of probability is based on the expectation that the following is true: If S_n is the number of successes in the first n trials of a sequence of Bernoulli trials, then

$$(4.1) \qquad \frac{S_n}{n} \to p.$$

In the abstract theory this cannot be true for *every* sequence of trials; in fact, our sample space contains a point representing the conceptual possibility of an infinite sequence of uninterrupted successes, and for it $S_n/n = 1$. However, it is demonstrable that (4.1) holds with probability one, so that the cases where (4.1) does not hold form a negligible exception.

Note that we deal with a statement much stronger than the weak law of large numbers [VI, (4.1)]. The latter says that for every sufficiently large *fixed* n the average S_n/n is likely to be near p, but it does not say that S_n/n is bound to stay near p if the number of trials is increased. It leaves open the possibility that in n additional trials there occurs at least one among the events $k^{-1}S_k < p - \epsilon$ with $n < k \leq 2n$. The probability for this is the sum of a large number of probabilities of which we know only that they are individually small. We shall now prove that with probability one $S_n/n - p$ becomes *and remains* small.

Strong Law of Large Numbers. *For every $\epsilon > 0$ with probability one there occur only finitely many of the events*

$$(4.2) \qquad \left| \frac{S_n}{n} - p \right| > \epsilon.$$

This implies that (4.1) holds with probability one. In terms of finite sample spaces, it is asserted that to every $\epsilon > 0$, $\delta > 0$ there corresponds an r such that for all ν the probability of the simultaneous realization of the ν inequalities

$$(4.3) \qquad \left| \frac{S_{r+k}}{r + k} - p \right| < \epsilon, \qquad\qquad k = 1, 2, \ldots, \nu,$$

is greater than $1 - \delta$.

Proof. We shall prove a much stronger statement. Let A_k be the event

$$(4.4) \qquad \left| S_k^* \right| = \left| \frac{S_k - kp}{\sqrt{kpq}} \right| \geq \sqrt{2a \log k},$$

where $a > 1$. It is then obvious from VII, (6.7) that, at least for all k sufficiently large,

$$(4.5) \qquad P\{A_k\} < e^{-a \log k} = \frac{1}{k^a}.$$

Hence $\sum P\{A_k\}$ converges, and lemma 1 of the preceding section ensures that *with probability one only finitely many inequalities* (4.4) *hold.* On the other hand, if (4.2) holds, then

$$(4.6) \qquad \left| \frac{S_n - np}{\sqrt{npq}} \right| > \frac{\epsilon}{\sqrt{pq}} \cdot \sqrt{n}$$

and for large n the right side is larger than $\sqrt{2a \log n}$. Hence, the realization of infinitely many inequalities (4.2) implies the realization of infinitely many A_k and has therefore probability zero.   ▶

The strong law of large numbers was first formulated by Cantelli (1917), after Borel and Hausdorff had discussed certain special cases. Like the weak law, it is only a very special case of a general theorem on random variables. Taken in conjunction with our theorem on the impossibility of gambling systems, the law of large numbers implies the existence of the limit (4.1) not only for the original sequence of trials but also for all subsequences obtained in accordance with the rules of section 2. *Thus the two theorems together describe the fundamental properties of randomness which are inherent in the intuitive notion of probability* and whose importance was stressed with special emphasis by von Mises.

5. THE LAW OF THE ITERATED LOGARITHM

As in chapter VII let us again introduce the reduced number of successes in n trials

$$(5.1) \qquad S_n^* = \frac{S_n - np}{\sqrt{npq}}.$$

The Laplace limit theorem asserts that $P\{S_n^* > x\} \sim 1 - \mathfrak{N}(x)$. Thus, for every particular value of n it is improbable to have a large S_n^*, but it is intuitively clear that in a prolonged sequence of trials S_n^* will sooner or later take on arbitrarily large values. Moderate values of S_n^* are most probable, but the maxima will slowly increase. How fast? In the course of the proof of the strong law of large numbers we have concluded from (4.5) that with probability one the inequality $S_n^* < \sqrt{2a \log n}$ holds for each $a > 1$ and all sufficiently large n. This provides us with an upper bound for the fluctuations of S_n^*, but this bound is bad. To see this, let us apply the same argument to the subsequence $S_2^*, S_4^*, S_8^*, S_{16}^*, \ldots$; that is, let us define the event A_k by $S_{2^k}^* \geq \sqrt{2a \log k}$. The inequality (4.5) implies that $S_{2^k}^* < \sqrt{2a \log k}$ holds for $a > 1$ and all sufficiently large k. But for $n = 2^k$ we have $\log k \sim \log \log n$, and we conclude that for each $a > 1$ and all n of the form $n = 2^k$ the inequality

$$(5.2) \qquad S_n^* < \sqrt{2a \log \log n}$$

will hold from some k onward. It is now a fair guess that in reality (5.2) holds for *all* n sufficiently large and, in fact, this is one part of the law of the iterated logarithm. This remarkable theorem[3] asserts that $\sqrt{2 \log \log n}$ is the *precise* upper bound in the sense that for each $a < 1$ the reverse of the inequality (5.2) will hold for infinitely many n.

Theorem.   *With probability one we have*

$$(5.3) \qquad \limsup_{n \to \infty} \frac{S_n^*}{\sqrt{2 \log \log n}} = 1.$$

This means: For $\lambda > 1$ with probability one only finitely many of the events

$$(5.4) \qquad S_n > np + \lambda \sqrt{2npq \log \log n}$$

occur; for $\lambda < 1$ with probability one (5.4) *holds for infinitely many n.*
For reasons of symmetry (5.3) implies that

$$(5.3a) \qquad \liminf_{n \to \infty} \frac{S_n^*}{\sqrt{2 \log \log n}} = -1.$$

Proof.   We start with two preliminary remarks.

(1) There exists a constant $c > 0$ which depends on p, but not on n, such that

$$(5.5) \qquad \mathbf{P}\{S_n > np\} > c$$

for all n. In fact, an inspection of the binomial distribution shows that the left side in (5.5) is never zero, and the Laplace limit theorem shows that it tends to $\frac{1}{2}$ as $n \to \infty$. Accordingly, the left side is bounded away from zero, as asserted.

(2) We require the following *lemma*: Let x be fixed, and let A be the event that for at least one k with $k \leq n$

$$(5.6) \qquad S_k - kp > x.$$

Then

$$(5.7) \qquad \mathbf{P}\{A\} \leq c^{-1}\mathbf{P}\{S_n - np > x\}.$$

---

[3] A. Khintchine, *Über einen Satz der Wahrscheinlichkeitsrechnung*, Fundamenta Mathematicae, vol. 6 (1924), pp. 9–20. The discovery was preceded by partial results due to other authors. The present proof is arranged so as to permit straightforward generalization to more general random variables.

For a proof of the lemma let A_ν be the event that (5.6) holds for $k = \nu$ but not for $k = 1, 2, \ldots, \nu - 1$ (here $1 \leq \nu \leq n$). The events $A_1, A_2, \ldots, A_n$ are mutually exclusive, and A is their union. Hence

$$(5.8) \qquad \mathbf{P}\{A\} = \mathbf{P}\{A_1\} + \cdots + \mathbf{P}\{A_n\}.$$

Next, for $\nu < n$ let U_ν be the event that the total number of successes in the trials number $\nu + 1, \nu + 2, \ldots, n$ exceeds $(n-\nu)p$. If both A_ν and U_ν occur, then $\mathbf{S}_n > \mathbf{S}_\nu + (n-\nu)p > np + x$, and since the $A_\nu U_\nu$ are mutually exclusive, this implies

$$(5.9) \qquad \mathbf{P}\{\mathbf{S}_n - np > x\} \geq \mathbf{P}\{A_1 U_1\} + \cdots + \mathbf{P}\{A_{n-1} U_{n-1}\} + \mathbf{P}\{A_n\}.$$

Now A_ν depends only on the first ν trials and U_ν only on the following $n - \nu$ trials. Hence A_ν and U_ν are independent, and $\mathbf{P}\{A_\nu U_\nu\} = = \mathbf{P}\{A_\nu\}\mathbf{P}\{U_\nu\}$. From the preliminary remark (5.5) we know that $\mathbf{P}\{U_\nu\} > c > 0$, and so we get from (5.9) and (5.8)

$$(5.10) \qquad \mathbf{P}\{\mathbf{S}_n - np > x\} \geq c \sum \mathbf{P}\{A_\nu\} = c\mathbf{P}\{A\}.$$

This proves (5.7).

(3) We now prove the part of the theorem relating to (5.4) with $\lambda > 1$. Let γ be a number such that

$$(5.11) \qquad 1 < \gamma < \lambda$$

and let n_r be the integer nearest to γ^r. Let B_r be the event that the inequality

$$(5.12) \qquad \mathbf{S}_n - np > \lambda\sqrt{2n_r pq \log\log n_r}$$

holds for at least one n with $n_r \leq n < n_{r+1}$. Obviously (5.4) can hold for infinitely many n only if infinitely many B_r occur. Using the first Borel-Cantelli lemma, we see therefore that it suffices to prove that

$$(5.13) \qquad \sum \mathbf{P}\{B_r\} \quad \text{converges.}$$

By the inequality (5.7)

$$(5.14) \qquad \begin{aligned} \mathbf{P}\{B_r\} &\leq c^{-1}\mathbf{P}\{\mathbf{S}_{n_{r+1}} - n_{r+1}p > \lambda\sqrt{2n_r pq \log\log n_r}\} = \\ &= c^{-1}\mathbf{P}\left\{\mathbf{S}^*_{n_{r+1}} > \lambda\sqrt{2\frac{n_r}{n_{r+1}}\log\log n_r}\right\}. \end{aligned}$$

Now $n_{r+1}/n_r \sim \gamma < \lambda$, and hence for sufficiently large r

$$(5.15) \qquad \mathbf{P}\{B_r\} \leq c^{-1}\mathbf{P}\{\mathbf{S}^*_{n_{r+1}} > \sqrt{2\lambda \log\log n_r}\}.$$

From VII, (5.2) we get, therefore, for large r,

$$(5.16) \qquad \mathbf{P}\{B_r\} \leq c^{-1}e^{-\lambda \log \log n_r} = \frac{1}{c(\log n_r)^\lambda} \sim \frac{1}{c(r \log \gamma)^\lambda}.$$

Since $\lambda > 1$, the assertion (5.13) is proved.

(4) Finally, we prove the assertion concerning (5.4) with $\lambda < 1$. This time we choose for γ an integer so large that

$$(5.17) \qquad \frac{\gamma - 1}{\gamma} > \eta > \lambda$$

where η is a constant to be determined later, and put $n_r = \gamma^r$. The second Borel-Cantelli lemma applies only to independent events, and for this reason we introduce

$$(5.18) \qquad \mathbf{D}_r = \mathbf{S}_{n_r} - \mathbf{S}_{n_{r-1}};$$

$\mathbf{D}_r$ is the total number of successes following trial number n_{r-1} and up to and including trial n_r; for it we have the binomial distribution $b(k; n, p)$ with $n = n_r - n_{r-1}$. Let A_r be the event

$$(5.19) \qquad \mathbf{D}_r - (n_r - n_{r-1})p > \eta\sqrt{2pqn_r \log \log n_r}.$$

We claim that *with probability one infinitely many A_r occur.* Since the various A_r depend on non-overlapping blocks of trials (namely, $n_{r-1} < n \leq n_r$), they are mutually independent, and, according to the second Borel-Cantelli lemma, it suffices to prove that $\sum \mathbf{P}\{A_r\}$ diverges. Now

$$(5.20) \quad \mathbf{P}\{A_r\} = \mathbf{P}\left\{\frac{\mathbf{D}_r - (n_r - n_{r-1})p}{\sqrt{(n_r - n_{r-1})pq}} > \eta\sqrt{2\frac{n_r}{n_r - n_{r-1}} \log \log n_r}\right\}.$$

Here $n_r/(n_r - n_{r-1}) = \gamma/(\gamma - 1) < \eta^{-1}$, by (5.17). Hence

$$(5.21) \qquad \mathbf{P}\{A_r\} \geq \mathbf{P}\left\{\frac{\mathbf{D}_r - (n_r - n_{r-1})p}{\sqrt{(n_r - n_{r-1})pq}} > \sqrt{2\eta \log \log n_r}\right\}.$$

Using again the estimate VII, (6.7) we find for large r

$$(5.22) \qquad \mathbf{P}\{A_r\} > \frac{1}{\log \log n_r}e^{-\eta \log \log n_r} = \frac{1}{(\log \log n_r)(\log n_r)^\eta}.$$

Since $n_r = \gamma^r$ and $\eta < 1$, we find that for large r we have $\mathbf{P}\{A_r\} > 1/r$, which proves the divergence of $\sum \mathbf{P}\{A_r\}$.

The last step of the proof consists in showing that $S_{n_{r-1}}$ in (5.18) can be neglected. From the first part of the theorem, which has already been proved, we know that to every $\epsilon > 0$ we can find an N so that, with probability $1 - \epsilon$ or better, for all $r > N$,

$$(5.23) \qquad |S_{n_{r-1}} - n_{r-1}p| < 2\sqrt{2pqn_{r-1}\log\log n_{r-1}}\,.$$

Now suppose that η is chosen so close to 1 that

$$(5.24) \qquad 1 - \eta < \left(\frac{\eta - \lambda}{2}\right)^2.$$

Then from (5.17)

$$(5.25) \qquad 4n_{r-1} = 4n_r\,\gamma^{-1} < n_r(\eta - \lambda)^2$$

and hence (5.23) implies

$$(5.26) \qquad S_{n_{r-1}} - n_{r-1}p > -(\eta - \lambda)\sqrt{2pqn_r\log\log n_r}\,.$$

Adding (5.26) to (5.19), we obtain (5.4) with $n = n_r$. It follows that, with probability $1 - \epsilon$ or better, this inequality holds for infinitely many r, and this accomplishes the proof. $\qquad\blacktriangleright$

The law of the iterated logarithm for Bernoulli trials is a special case of a more general theorem first formulated by Kolmogorov.[4] At present it is possible to formulate stronger theorems (cf. problems 7 and 8).

6. INTERPRETATION IN NUMBER THEORY LANGUAGE

Let x be a real number in the interval $0 \leq x < 1$, and let

$$(6.1) \qquad x = .a_1a_2a_3\cdots$$

be its decimal expansion (so that each a_j stands for one of the digits $0, 1, \ldots, 9$). This expansion is unique except for numbers of the form $a/10^n$ (where a is an integer), which can be written either by means of an expansion containing infinitely many zeros or by means of an expansion containing infinitely many nines. To avoid ambiguities we now agree not to use the latter form.

The decimal expansions are connected with Bernoulli trials with $p = \frac{1}{10}$, the digit 0 representing success and all other digits failure. If we replace in

---

[4] A. Kolmogoroff, *Das Gesetz des iterierten Logarithmus*, Mathematische Annalen, vol. 101 (1929), pp. 126–135.

(6.1) all zeros by the letter S and all other digits by F, then (6.1) represents a possible outcome of an infinite sequence of Bernoulli trials with $p = \frac{1}{10}$. Conversely, an arbitrary sequence of letters S and F can be obtained in the described manner from the expansion of certain numbers x. In this way every event in the sample space of Bernoulli trials is represented by a certain aggregate of numbers x. For example, the event "success at the nth trial" is represented by all those x whose nth decimal is zero. This is an aggregate of 10^{n-1} intervals each of length 10^{-n}, and the total length of these intervals equals $\frac{1}{10}$, which is the probability of our event. Every particular finite sample sequence of length n corresponds to an aggregate of certain intervals; for example, the sequence SFS is represented by the nine intervals $0.01 \leq x < 0.011, 0.02 \leq x < 0.021, \ldots,$ $0.09 \leq x < 0.091$. The probability of each such sample sequence equals the total length of the corresponding intervals on the x-axis. Probabilities of more complicated events are always expressed in terms of probabilities of finite sample sequences, and the calculation proceeds according to the same addition rule that is valid for the familiar Lebesgue measure on the x-axis. Accordingly, our probabilities will always coincide with the measure of the corresponding aggregate of points on the x-axis. We have thus a means of translating all limit theorems for Bernoulli trials with $p = \frac{1}{10}$ into theorems concerning decimal expansions. The phrase "with probability one" is equivalent to "for almost all x" or "almost everywhere."

We have considered the random variable $\mathbf{S}_n$ which gives the number of successes in n trials. Here it is more convenient to emphasize the fact that $\mathbf{S}_n$ is a function of the sample point, and we write $\mathbf{S}_n(x)$ *for the number of zeros among the first n decimals of x.* Obviously the graph of $\mathbf{S}_n(x)$ is a step polygon whose discontinuities are necessarily points of the form $a/10^n$, where a is an integer. The ratio $\mathbf{S}_n(x)/n$ is called the *frequency of zeros* among the first n decimals of x.

In the language of ordinary measure theory the weak law of large numbers asserts that $\mathbf{S}_n(x)/n \to \frac{1}{10}$ in measure, whereas the strong law states that $\mathbf{S}_n(x)/n \to \frac{1}{10}$ almost everywhere. Khintchine's law of the iterated logarithm shows that

$$(6.2) \qquad \limsup \frac{\mathbf{S}_n(x) - n/10}{\sqrt{n \log \log n}} = 0.3\sqrt{2}$$

for almost all x. It gives an answer to a problem treated in a series of papers initiated by Hausdorff[5] (1913) and Hardy and Littlewood[6] (1914). For a further improvement of this result see problems 7 and 8.

[5] F. Hausdorff, *Grundzüge der Mengenlehre*, Leipzig, 1913.

[6] Hardy and Littlewood, *Some problems of Diophantine approximation*, Acta Mathematica. vol. 37 (1914), pp. 155–239.

Instead of the digit zero we may consider any other digit and can formulate the strong law of large numbers to the effect that the frequency of each of the ten digits tends to $\frac{1}{10}$ for almost all x. A similar theorem holds if the base 10 of the decimal system is replaced by any other base. This fact was discovered by Borel (1909) and is usually expressed by saying that almost all numbers are "normal."

7. PROBLEMS FOR SOLUTION

1. Find an integer β such that in rolling dice there are about even chances that a run of three consecutive aces appears before a non-ace run of length β.

2. Consider repeated independent trials with three possible outcomes A, B, C and corresponding probabilities p, q, r $(p + q + r = 1)$. Find the probability that a run of α consecutive A's will occur before a B-run of length β.

3. *Continuation.* Find the probability that an A-run of length α will occur before either a B-run of length β or a C-run of length γ.

4. In a sequence of Bernoulli trials let A_n be the event that a run of n consecutive successes occurs between the 2^nth and the 2^{n+1}st trial. If $p \geq \frac{1}{2}$, there is probability one that infinitely many A_n occur; if $p < \frac{1}{2}$, then with probability one only finitely many A_n occur.

5.[7] Denote by $\mathbf{N}_n$ the length of the success run beginning at the nth trial (i.e., $\mathbf{N}_n = 0$ if the nth trial results in F, etc.). Prove that with probability one

$$(7.1) \qquad \qquad \limsup \frac{\mathbf{N}_n}{\mathrm{Log}\, n} = 1$$

where Log denotes the logarithm to the basis $1/p$.

Hint: Consider the event A_n that the nth trial is followed by a run of more than $a \, \mathrm{Log}\, n$ successes. For $a > 1$ the calculation is straightforward. For $a < 1$ consider the subsequence of trials number $a_1, a_2, \ldots$ where a_n is an integer very close to $n \, \mathrm{Log}\, n$.

6. From the law of the iterated logarithm conclude: With probability one it will happen for infinitely many n that all $\mathbf{S}_k^*$ with $n < k < 17n$ are positive. (*Note:* Considerably stronger statements can be proved using the results of chapter III.)

7. Let $\phi(t)$ be a positive monotonically increasing function, and let n_r be the nearest integer to $e^{r/\log r}$. If

$$(7.2) \qquad \qquad \sum \frac{1}{\phi(n_r)} e^{-\frac{1}{2}\phi^2(n_r)}$$

converges, then with probability one, the inequality

$$(7.3) \qquad \qquad \mathbf{S}_n > np + \sqrt{npq}\ \phi(n)$$

---

[7] Suggested by a communication from D. J. Newman.

takes place only for infinitely many n. Note that without loss of generality we may suppose that $\phi(n) < 10\sqrt{\log \log n}$; the law of the iterated logarithm takes care of the larger $\phi(n)$.

8. Prove[8] that the series (7.2) converges if, and only if,

$$(7.4) \qquad\qquad \sum \frac{\phi(n)}{n} e^{-\frac{1}{2}\phi^2(n)}$$

converges. *Hint:* Collect the terms for which $n_{r-1} < n < n_r$ and note that $n_r - n_{r-1} \sim n_r(1 - 1/\log r)$; furthermore, (7.4) can converge only if $\phi^2(n) > 2 \log \log n$.

9. From the preceding problem conclude that with probability one

$$(7.5) \qquad \limsup [S_n^* - \sqrt{2 \log \log n}\,] \frac{\sqrt{2 \log \log n}}{\log \log \log n} = \frac{3}{2}.$$

---

[8] Problems 7 and 8 together show that in case of convergence of (7.4) the inequality (7.3) holds with probability one only for finitely many n. Conversely, if (7.4) diverges, the inequality (7.3) holds with probability one for infinitely many n. This converse is much more difficult to prove; cf. W. Feller, *The general form of the so-called law of the iterated logarithm*, Trans. Amer. Math. Soc., vol. 54 (1943), pp. 373–402, where more general theorems are proved for arbitrary random variables. For the special case of Bernoulli trials with $p = \frac{1}{2}$ cf. P. Erdös, *On the law of the iterated logarithm*, Ann. of Math. (2), vol. 43 (1942), pp. 419–436. The law of the iterated logarithm follows from the particular case $\phi(t) = \lambda\sqrt{2 \log \log t}$.

CHAPTER IX

Random Variables; Expectation

1. RANDOM VARIABLES

According to the definition given in calculus textbooks, the quantity y is called a *function* of the real number x if to every x there corresponds a value y. This definition can be extended to cases where the independent variable is not a real number. Thus the distance is a function of a pair of points; the perimeter of a triangle is a function defined on the set of triangles; a sequence $\{a_n\}$ is a function defined for all positive integers; the binomial coefficient $\binom{x}{k}$ is a function defined for pairs of numbers (x, k) of which the second is a non-negative integer. In the same sense we can say that the number S_n of successes in n Bernoulli trials is a function defined on the sample space; to each of the 2^n points in this space there corresponds a number S_n.

A function defined on a sample space is called a random variable. Throughout the preceding chapters we have been concerned with random variables without using this term. Typical random variables are the number of aces in a hand at bridge, of multiple birthdays in a company of n people, of success runs in n Bernoulli trials. In each case there is a unique rule which associates a number X with any sample point. The classical theory of probability was devoted mainly to a study of the gambler's gain, which is again a random variable; in fact, every random variable can be interpreted as the gain of a real or imaginary gambler in a suitable game. The position of a particle under diffusion, the energy, temperature, etc., of physical systems are random variables; but they are defined in non-discrete sample spaces, and their study is therefore deferred. In the case of a discrete sample space we can theoretically tabulate any random variable X by enumerating in some order all points of the space and associating with each the corresponding value of X.

The term random variable is somewhat confusing; random function would be more appropriate (the independent variable being a point in sample space, that is, the outcome of an experiment).

Let **X** be a random variable and let $x_1, x_2, \ldots$ be the values which it assumes;[1] in most of what follows the x_j will be integers. The aggregate of all sample points on which **X** assumes the fixed value x_j forms the event that $X = x_j$; its probability is denoted by $\mathbf{P}\{X = x_j\}$. *The function*

$$(1.1) \qquad\qquad \mathbf{P}\{X = x_j\} = f(x_j) \qquad\qquad (j = 1, 2, \ldots)$$

is called the (*probability*) *distribution*[2] *of the random variable* **X**. Clearly

$$(1.2) \qquad\qquad f(x_j) \geq 0, \qquad \sum f(x_j) = 1.$$

With this terminology we can say that in Bernoulli trials the number of successes $\mathbf{S}_n$ is a random variable with probability distribution $\{b(k; n, p)\}$, whereas the number of trials up to and including the first success is a random variable with the distribution $\{q^{k-1}p\}$.

Consider now two random variables **X** and **Y** defined on the same sample space, and denote the values which they assume, respectively, by $x_1, x_2, \ldots,$ and $y_1, y_2, \ldots$; let the corresponding probability distributions be $\{f(x_j)\}$ and $\{g(y_k)\}$. The aggregate of points in which the two conditions $X = x_j$ and $Y = y_k$ are satisfied forms an event whose probability will be denoted by $\mathbf{P}\{X = x_j, Y = y_k\}$. *The function*

$$(1.3) \qquad\qquad \mathbf{P}\{X = x_j, Y = y_k\} = p(x_j, y_k) \qquad (j, k = 1, 2, \ldots)$$

is called the joint probability distribution of **X** *and* **Y**. It is best exhibited in the form of a double-entry table as exemplified in tables 1 and 2. Clearly

$$(1.4) \qquad\qquad p(x_j, y_k) \geq 0, \qquad \sum_{j,k} p(x_j, y_k) = 1.$$

---

[1] In the standard mathematical terminology the set of values $x_1, x_2, \ldots$ should be called *the range of* **X**. Unfortunately the statistical literature uses the term range for the difference between the maximum and the minimum of **X**.

[2] For a discrete variable **X** the probability distribution is the function $f(x_j)$ defined on the aggregate of values x_j assumed by **X**. This term must be distinguished from the term "distribution function," which applies to non-decreasing functions which tend to 0 as $x \to -\infty$ and to 1 as $x \to \infty$. The distribution function $F(x)$ of **X** is defined by

$$F(x) = \mathbf{P}\{X \leq x\} = \sum_{x_j \leq x} f(x_j),$$

the last sum extending over all those x_j which do not exceed x. Thus the distribution function of a variable can be calculated from its probability distribution and vice versa. In this volume we shall not be concerned with distribution functions in general.

TABLE 1
JOINT DISTRIBUTION OF (N, X_1) IN EXAMPLE (a)

N \ X_1	0	1	2	3	Distribution of N
1	2/27	0	0	1/27	1/9
2	6/27	6/27	6/27	0	2/3
3	0	6/27	0	0	2/9
Distribution of X_1	8/27	12/27	6/27	1/27	

$$E(N) = 19/9, \quad E(N^2) = 129/27, \quad \text{Var}(N) = 26/81$$
$$E(X_1) = 1, \quad E(X_1^2) = 45/27, \quad \text{Var}(X_1) = 2/3$$
$$E(NX_1) = 19/9, \quad \text{Cov}(N, X_1) = 0.$$

N is the number of occupied cells, X_1 the number of balls in the first cell when 3 balls are distributed randomly in 3 cells.

TABLE 2
JOINT DISTRIBUTION OF (X_1, X_2) IN EXAMPLE (a)

X_2 \ X_1	0	1	2	3	Distribution of X_2
0	1/27	3/27	3/27	1/27	8/27
1	3/27	6/27	3/27	0	12/27
2	3/27	3/27	0	0	6/27
3	1/27	0	0	0	1/27
Distribution of X_1	8/27	12/27	6/27	1/27	

$$E(X_i) = 1, \quad E(X_i^2) = 45/27, \quad \text{Var}(X_i) = 2/3$$
$$E(X_1 X_2) = 2/3, \quad \text{Cov}(X_1, X_2) = -1/3.$$

X_i is the number of balls in the ith cell when 3 balls are distributed randomly in 3 cells.

Moreover, for every fixed j

(1.5) $p(x_j, y_1) + p(x_j, y_2) + p(x_j, y_3) + \cdots = \mathbf{P}\{X = x_j\} = f(x_j)$

and for every fixed k

(1.6) $p(x_1, y_k) + p(x_2, y_k) + p(x_3, y_k) + \cdots = \mathbf{P}\{Y = y_k\} = g(y_k).$

In other words, by adding the probabilities in individual rows and columns, we obtain the probability distributions of $\mathbf{X}$ and $\mathbf{Y}$. They may be exhibited as shown in tables 1 and 2 and are then called *marginal distributions*. The adjective "marginal" refers to the outer appearance in the double-entry table and is also used for stylistic clarity when the joint distribution of two variables as well as their individual (marginal) distributions appear in the same context. Strictly speaking, the adjective "marginal" is redundant.

The notion of joint distribution carries over to *systems of more than two random variables.*

Examples. (*a*) *Random placements of* 3 *balls into* 3 *cells.* We refer to the sample space of 27 points defined formally in table 1 accompanying example I, (2.*a*); to each point we attach probability $\frac{1}{27}$. Let $\mathbf{N}$ denote the number of occupied cells, and for $i = 1, 2, 3$ let $\mathbf{X}_i$ denote the number of balls in the cell number i. These are picturesque descriptions. Formally $\mathbf{N}$ is the function assuming the value 1 on the sample points number 1–3; the value 2 on the points number 4–21; and the value 3 on the points number 22–27. Accordingly, the probability distribution of $\mathbf{N}$ is defined by $\mathbf{P}\{N=1\} = \frac{1}{9}$, $\mathbf{P}\{N=2\} = \frac{2}{3}$, $\mathbf{P}\{N=3\} = \frac{2}{9}$. The joint distributions of $(\mathbf{N}, \mathbf{X}_1)$ and of $(\mathbf{X}_1, \mathbf{X}_2)$ are given in tables 1 and 2.

(*b*) *Multinomial distribution.* There are many situations in which the joint distribution of three random variables is given by the multinomial distribution (see VI, 9), that is,

(1.7)

$$\mathbf{P}\{X_1 = k_1, X_2 = k_2, X_3 = k_3\} = \frac{n!\, p_1^{k_1} p_2^{k_2} p_3^{k_3} (1 - p_1 - p_2 - p_3)^{n - k_1 - k_2 - k_3}}{k_1!\, k_2!\, k_3!\, (n - k_1 - k_2 - k_3)!}\,;$$

here $k_1, k_2,$ and k_3 are non-negative integers such that $k_1 + k_2 + k_3 \leq n$. For example if $\mathbf{X}_1$, $\mathbf{X}_2$, and $\mathbf{X}_3$ represent the numbers of ones, twos, and threes scored in n throws of an ideal die, then their joint distribution is given by (1.7) with $p_1 = p_2 = p_3 = \frac{1}{6}$. Again, suppose a sample with replacement is taken from a population consisting of several subpopulations or strata. If $\mathbf{X}_j$ stands for the number of elements in the sample that belong to the jth subpopulation, then the joint distribution of $(\mathbf{X}_1, \mathbf{X}_2, \mathbf{X}_3)$ is of the form (1.7).

To obtain the (marginal) distribution of (X_1, X_2) we have to keep k_1 and k_2 fixed and sum (1.7) over all possible values of k_3, that is, $k_3 = 0, \ldots, n - k_1 - k_2$. Using the binomial theorem we get the trinomial distribution

$$(1.8) \qquad \mathbf{P}\{X_1 = k_1, X_2 = k_2\} = \frac{n! \; p_1^{k_1} p_2^{k_2} (1 - p_1 - p_2)^{n - k_1 - k_2}}{k_1! \; k_2! \; (n - k_1 - k_2)!}.$$

Summing over $k_2 = 0, \ldots, n - k$, we get the distribution of X_1 alone: It reduces to the binomial distribution with $p = p_1$.

(c) *Geometric distributions.* Consider a sequence of Bernoulli trials continued at least as long as necessary to obtain two successes. Let X_1 be the number of failures preceding the first success, and X_2 the number of failures between the first two successes. The joint distribution of (X_1, X_2) is given by

$$(1.9) \qquad \qquad \mathbf{P}\{X_1 = j, X_2 = k\} = q^{j+k} p^2$$

(see VI, 8). Summing over k we get the obvious geometric distribution for X_1. (This example shows incidentally how the use of random variable avoids difficulties connected with non-denumerable sample spaces.)

(d) *Randomized sampling.* A somewhat surprising result is obtained from a variant of example (b). Suppose that the number of trials is not fixed in advance but depends on the outcome of a chance experiment in such a way that the probability of having exactly n trials equals $e^{-\lambda} \lambda^n / n!$. In other words, the number of trials itself is now a random variable with the Poisson distribution $\{e^{-\lambda} \lambda^n / n!\}$. Given the number n of trials, the event $\{X_1 = k_1, X_2 = k_2, X_3 = k_3\}$ has the (conditional) probability given by the right side in (1.7). To obtain the absolute probability of this event we must multiply the right side in (1.7) by $e^{-\lambda} \lambda^n / n!$ and sum over all possible n. For given k_j it is, of course, necessary that

$$n \geq k_1 + k_2 + k_3.$$

Introducing the difference r as a new summation index we get

$$(1.10) \quad \mathbf{P}\{X_1 = k_1, X_2 = k_2, X_3 = k_3\} =$$

$$= e^{-\lambda} \frac{(\lambda p_1)^{k_1} (\lambda p_2)^{k_2} (\lambda p_3)^{k_3}}{k_1! \; k_2! \; k_3!} \sum_{r=0}^{\infty} \frac{\lambda^r (1 - p_1 - p_2 - p_3)^r}{r!}.$$

On the right we recognize the exponential series and we can write the final result in the form

$$(1.11) \quad \mathbf{P}\{X_1 = k_1, X_2 = k_2, X_3 = k_3\} =$$

$$= e^{-\lambda p_1} \frac{(\lambda p_1)^{k_1}}{k_1!} \cdot e^{-\lambda p_2} \frac{(\lambda p_2)^{k_2}}{k_2!} \cdot e^{-\lambda p_3} \frac{(\lambda p_3)^{k_3}}{k_3!}.$$

Summation over k_2 and k_3 eliminates the second and third factors, and we see that $\mathbf{X}_1$ itself has a Poisson distribution. The curious fact is that the joint distribution assumes the form of a multiplication table; this will be described by saying that *the three variables* $\mathbf{X}_j$ *are mutually independent.* (This example is essentially a reformulation of problem 27 in VI, 10.) ▶

With the notation (1.3) the conditional probability of the event $\mathbf{Y} = y_k$, given that $\mathbf{X} = x_j$ [with $f(x_j) > 0$], becomes

$$(1.12) \qquad\qquad \mathbf{P}\{\mathbf{Y} = y_k \,|\, \mathbf{X} = x_j\} = \frac{p(x_j, y_k)}{f(x_j)}.$$

In this way a number is associated with every value of $\mathbf{X}$, and so (1.12) defines a function of $\mathbf{X}$. It is called the *conditional distribution of* $\mathbf{Y}$ *for given* $\mathbf{X}$, and is denoted by $\mathbf{P}\{\mathbf{Y} = y_k \,|\, \mathbf{X}\}$. A glance at tables 1 and 2 shows that the conditional probability (1.12) is in general different from $g(y_k)$. This indicates that inference can be drawn from the values of $\mathbf{X}$ to those of $\mathbf{Y}$ and vice versa; the two variables are (stochastically) *dependent*. The strongest degree of dependence exists when $\mathbf{Y}$ is a function of $\mathbf{X}$, that is, when the value of $\mathbf{X}$ uniquely determines $\mathbf{Y}$. For example, if a coin is tossed n times and $\mathbf{X}$ and $\mathbf{Y}$ are the numbers of heads and tails, then $\mathbf{Y} = n - \mathbf{X}$. Similarly, when $\mathbf{Y} = \mathbf{X}^2$, we can compute $\mathbf{Y}$ from $\mathbf{X}$. In the joint distribution this means that in each row all entries but one are zero. If, on the other hand, $p(x_j, y_k) = f(x_j)g(y_k)$ for all combinations of x_j, y_k, then the events $\mathbf{X} = x_j$ and $\mathbf{Y} = y_k$ are independent; the joint distribution assumes the form of a multiplication table. In this case we speak of *independent* random variables. They occur in particular in connection with independent trials; for example, the numbers scored in two throws of a die are independent. An example of a different nature is found in example (*d*).

Note that the joint distribution of $\mathbf{X}$ and $\mathbf{Y}$ determines the distributions of $\mathbf{X}$ and $\mathbf{Y}$, but that we cannot calculate the joint distribution of $\mathbf{X}$ and $\mathbf{Y}$ from their marginal distributions. If two variables $\mathbf{X}$ and $\mathbf{Y}$ have the same distribution, they may or may not be independent. For example, the two variables $\mathbf{X}_1$ and $\mathbf{X}_2$ in table 2 have the same distribution and are dependent.

All our notions apply also to the case of more than two variables. We recapitulate in the formal

Definition. *A random variable* $\mathbf{X}$ *is a function defined on a given sample space, that is, an assignment of a real number to each sample point. The probability distribution of* $\mathbf{X}$ *is the function defined in* (1.1). *If two random variables* $\mathbf{X}$ *and* $\mathbf{Y}$ *are defined on the same sample space, their joint distribution is given by* (1.3) *and assigns probabilities to all combinations*

(x_j, y_k) *of values assumed by* $\mathbf{X}$ *and* $\mathbf{Y}$. *This notion carries over, in an obvious manner, to any finite set of variables* $\mathbf{X}, \mathbf{Y}, \ldots, \mathbf{W}$ *defined on the same sample space. These variables are called mutually independent if, for any combination of values* $(x, y, \ldots, w)$ *assumed by them,*

$$(1.13) \quad \mathbf{P}\{\mathbf{X} = x, \mathbf{Y} = y, \ldots, \mathbf{W} = w\} =$$
$$= \mathbf{P}\{\mathbf{X} = x\}\,\mathbf{P}\{\mathbf{Y} = y\} \cdots \mathbf{P}\{\mathbf{W} = w\}.$$

In V, 4 we have defined the sample space corresponding to n mutually independent trials. Comparing this definition to (1.13), we see that *if* $\mathbf{X}_k$ *depends only on the outcome of the kth trial, then the variables* $\mathbf{X}_1, \ldots, \mathbf{X}_n$ *are mutually independent.* More generally, if a random variable $\mathbf{U}$ depends only on the outcomes of the first k trials, and another variable $\mathbf{V}$ depends only on the outcomes of the last $n-k$ trials, then $\mathbf{U}$ and $\mathbf{V}$ are independent (cf. problem 39).

We may conceive of a random variable as a labeling of the points of the sample space. This procedure is familiar from dice, where the faces are numbered, and we speak of numbers as the possible outcomes of individual trials. In conventional mathematical terminology we could say that a random variable $\mathbf{X}$ is a mapping of the original sample space onto a new space whose points are $x_1, x_2, \ldots$. Therefore:

Whenever $\{f(x_j)\}$ *satisfies the obvious conditions* (1.2) *it is legitimate to talk of a random variable* $\mathbf{X}$, *assuming the values* $x_1, x_2, \ldots$ *with probabilities* $f(x_1), f(x_2), \ldots$ *without further reference to the old sample space; a new one is formed by the sample points* $x_1, x_2, \ldots$ *Specifying a probability distribution is equivalent to specifying a sample space whose points are real numbers. Speaking of two independent random variables* $\mathbf{X}$ *and* $\mathbf{Y}$ *with distributions* $\{f(x_j)\}$ *and* $\{g(y_k)\}$ *is equivalent to referring to a sample space whose points are pairs of numbers* (x_j, y_k) *to which probabilities are assigned by the rule* $\mathbf{P}\{(x_j, y_k)\} = f(x_j)g(y_k)$. *Similarly, for the sample space corresponding to a set of* n *random variables* $(\mathbf{X}, \mathbf{Y}, \ldots, \mathbf{W})$ *we can take an aggregate of points* $(x, y, \ldots, w)$ *in the n-dimensional space to which probabilities are assigned by the joint distribution. The variables are mutually independent if their joint distribution is given by* (1.13).

Example. (*e*) *Bernoulli trials with variable probabilities.* Consider n *independent* trials, each of which has only two possible outcomes, S and F. The probability of S at the kth trial is p_k, that of F is $q_k = 1 - p_k$. If $p_k = p$, this scheme reduces to Bernoulli trials. The simplest way of describing it is to attribute the values 1 and 0 to S and F. The model is then completely described by saying that we have n mutually independent random variables $\mathbf{X}_k$ with distributions $\mathbf{P}\{\mathbf{X}_k = 1\} = p_k$, $\mathbf{P}\{\mathbf{X}_k = 0\} = q_k$. This scheme is known under the confusing name of "*Poisson trials.*" [See examples (5.*b*) and XI, (6.*b*).]   ▶

It is clear that the same distribution can occur in conjunction with different sample spaces. If we say that the random variable X assumes the values 0 and 1 with probabilities $\frac{1}{2}$, then we refer tacitly to a sample space consisting of the two points 0 and 1. But the variable X might have been defined by stipulating that it equals 0 or 1 according as the tenth tossing of a coin produces heads or tails; in this case X is defined in a sample space of sequences $(HHT\ldots)$, and this sample space has 2^{10} points.

In principle, it is possible to restrict the theory of probability to sample spaces defined in terms of probability distributions of random variables. This procedure avoids references to abstract sample spaces and also to terms like "trials" and "outcomes of experiments." The reduction of probability theory to random variables is a short-cut to the use of analysis and simplifies the theory in many ways. However, it also has the drawback of obscuring the probability background. The notion of random variable easily remains vague as "something that takes on different values with different probabilities." But random variables are ordinary functions, and this notion is by no means peculiar to probability theory.

Example. (f) Let X be a random variable with possible values $x_1, x_2, \ldots$ and corresponding probabilities $f(x_1), f(x_2), \ldots$. If it helps the reader's imagination, he may always construct a conceptual experiment leading to X. For example, subdivide a roulette wheel into arcs $l_1, l_2, \ldots$ whose lengths are as $f(x_1):f(x_2):\ldots$. Imagine a gambler receiving the (positive or negative) amount x_j if the roulette comes to rest at a point of l_j. Then X is the gambler's gain. In n trials, the gains are assumed to be n independent variables with the common distribution $\{f(x_j)\}$. To obtain two variables with a given joint distribution $\{p(x_j, y_k)\}$ let an arc correspond to each combination (x_j, y_k) and think of two gamblers receiving the amounts x_j and y_k, respectively. ▶

If $X, Y, Z, \ldots$ are random variables defined on the same sample space, then any function $F(X, Y, Z, \ldots)$ is again a random variable. Its distribution can be obtained from the joint distribution of $X, Y, Z, \ldots$ simply by collecting the terms which correspond to combinations of $(X, Y, Z, \ldots)$ giving the same value of $F(X, Y, Z, \ldots)$.

Example. (g) In the example illustrated by table 2 the sum $X_1 + X_2$ is a random variable assuming the values 0, 1, 2, 3 with probabilities $\frac{1}{27}, \frac{6}{27}, \frac{12}{27},$ and $\frac{8}{27}$. The product $X_1 X_2$ assumes the values 0, 1, and 2 with probabilities $\frac{15}{27}, \frac{6}{27},$ and $\frac{6}{27}$.

(h) We return to example (c) and consider various functions of X_1 and X_2. Most interesting is the sum $S = X_1 + X_2$. To obtain $P\{S = \nu\}$ we have to sum (1.9) over all values j, k such that $j + k = \nu$. There are

$\nu + 1$ such pairs, and in this special case they all have the same probability $p^\nu q^2$. Thus $P\{X = \nu\} = (\nu+1)q^kp^\nu$, which is a special case of VI, (8.1).

Next let U be defined as the smaller of the two variables X_1, X_2; in other words, $U = X_1$ if $X_2 \geq X_1$ and $U = X_2$ if $X_2 \leq X_1$. To obtain $P\{U = \nu\}$ we have to sum (1.9) over all pairs (j, k) such that $j = \nu$ and $k \geq \nu$, or else $j > \nu$ and $k = \nu$. This leads to two geometric series and

$$(1.14) \qquad P\{U = \nu\} = \frac{q^{2\nu}p^2}{1 - q} + \frac{q^{2\nu+1}p^2}{1 - q} = q^{2\nu}(1+q)p.$$

Here $\nu = 0, 1, \ldots$.

A similar calculation shows that

$$(1.15) \qquad\qquad P\{X_1 - X_2 = \nu\} = \frac{q^{|\nu|}p}{1 + q}, \quad \nu = 0, \pm 1, \pm 2, \ldots .$$

▶

Note on pairwise independence. As a matter of curiosity we have shown in example V,(3.e) that three events can be pairwise independent without being mutually independent. To formulate an analogous result for random variables we consider the simplest case, namely a sample space consisting of nine points, each carrying probability $\frac{1}{9}$. Six of these points we identify with the various permutations of the numbers 1, 2, 3 while the remaining three points stand for the triples $(1, 1, 1)$, $(2, 2, 2)$, and $(3, 3, 3)$. We now introduce three random variables X_1, X_2, X_3 such that X_k equals the number appearing at the kth place. The possible values of these variables are 1, 2, 3 and it is easily verified that their distributions and joint distributions are given by

$$(1.16) \qquad\qquad P\{X_j = r\} = \tfrac{1}{3}, \qquad P\{X_j = r, X_k = s\} = \tfrac{1}{9}.$$

[This differs only notationally from the conclusions in example V, (3.e).] It follows that our three random variables are pairwise independent. On the other hand, the knowledge of X_1 and X_2 uniquely determines X_3, and so the variables are not mutually independent.

To go a step further, define a triple (X_4, X_5, X_6) exactly as the triple (X_1, X_2, X_3) but independent of it. In this way we obtain six pairwise independent variables satisfying (1.16). Continuing in like manner we obtain *a sequence of variables* $X_1, X_2, \ldots, X_n, \ldots$ *satisfying* (1.16) *and such that the* X_k *are pairwise independent without being mutually independent*.[3] We shall return to this example in XV, (13.f).

2. EXPECTATIONS

To achieve reasonable simplicity it is often necessary to describe probability distributions rather summarily by a few "typical values." An example is provided by the median used in the waiting-time problems of

---

[3] The same construction leads to examples in which no three consecutive variables are independent. Further modifications lead to various counterexamples in the theory of stochastic processes. See W. Feller, *Non-Markovian processes with the semi-group property*, Ann. Math. Statist., vol. 30 (1959), pp. 1252–1253.

II, 7, and the central term of the binomial distribution. Among the typical values the expectation, or mean, is by far the most important. It lends itself best to analytical manipulations, and it is preferred by statisticians because of a property known as sampling stability. Its definition follows the customary notion of an average. If in a certain population n_k families have exactly k children, the total number of families is $n =$ $= n_0 + n_1 + n_2 + \cdots$ and the total number of children

$$m = n_1 + 2n_2 + 3n_3 + \cdots .$$

The average number of children per family is m/n. The analogy between probabilities and frequencies suggests the following

Definition. *Let* **X** *be a random variable assuming the values* $x_1, x_2, \ldots$ *with corresponding probabilities* $f(x_1), f(x_2), \ldots$ *The mean or expected value of* **X** *is defined by*

(2.1) $$\mathbf{E(X)} = \sum x_k f(x_k)$$

provided that the series converges absolutely. In this case we say that **X** *has a finite expectation. If* $\sum |x_k| f(x_k)$ *diverges, then we say that* **X** *has no finite expectation.*

It is sometimes convenient to think of probabilities intuitively as limits of observable frequencies in repeated experiments. This would lead to the following intuitive interpretation of the expectation. Let an experiment be repeated n times "under identical conditions," and denote by $\mathbf{X}_1, \ldots, \mathbf{X}_n$ the values of **X** that were actually observed. For large n the average $(\mathbf{X}_1 + \cdots + \mathbf{X}_n)/n$ should be close to $\mathbf{E(X)}$. The laws of large numbers give substance and precision to this vague intuitive description.

It goes without saying that the most common random variables have finite expectations; otherwise the concept would be impractical. However, variables without finite expectations occur in connection with important recurrence problems in physics. The terms *mean*, *average*, and *mathematical expectation* are synonymous. We also speak of the *mean of a distribution* instead of referring to a corresponding random variable. The notation $\mathbf{E(X)}$ is generally accepted in mathematics and statistics. In physics $\bar{\mathbf{X}}$, $\langle \mathbf{X} \rangle$, and $\langle \mathbf{X} \rangle_{Av}$ are common substitutes for $\mathbf{E(X)}$.

We wish to calculate expectations of functions such as $\mathbf{X}^2$. This function is a new random variable assuming the values x_k^2; in general, the probability of $\mathbf{X}^2 = x_k^2$ is not $f(x_k)$ but $f(x_k) + f(-x_k)$ and $\mathbf{E(X^2)}$ is defined as the sum of $x_k^2 \{ f(x_k) + f(-x_k) \}$. Obviously under all circumstances

(2.2) $$\mathbf{E(X^2)} = \sum x_k^2 f(x_k)$$

provided the series converges. The same procedure leads to the general

Theorem 1. *Any function* $\phi(x)$ *defines a new random variable* $\phi(\mathbf{X})$. *If* $\phi(\mathbf{X})$ *has finite expectation, then*

$$(2.3) \qquad \mathbf{E}(\phi(\mathbf{X})) = \sum \phi(x_k) f(x_k);$$

the series converges absolutely if, and only if, $\mathbf{E}(\phi(\mathbf{X}))$ *exists. For any constant* a *we have* $\mathbf{E}(a\mathbf{X}) = a\mathbf{E}(\mathbf{X})$.

If several random variables $\mathbf{X}_1, \ldots, \mathbf{X}_n$ are defined on the same sample space, then their sum $\mathbf{X}_1 + \cdots + \mathbf{X}_n$ is a new random variable. Its possible values and the corresponding probabilities can be readily found from the joint distribution of the $\mathbf{X}_\nu$ and thus $\mathbf{E}(\mathbf{X}_1 + \cdots + \mathbf{X}_n)$ can be calculated. A simpler procedure is furnished by the following important

Theorem 2. *If* $\mathbf{X}_1, \mathbf{X}_2, \ldots, \mathbf{X}_n$ *are random variables with expectations, then the expectation of their sum exists and is the sum of their expectations:*

$$(2.4) \qquad \mathbf{E}(\mathbf{X}_1 + \cdots + \mathbf{X}_n) = \mathbf{E}(\mathbf{X}_1) + \cdots + \mathbf{E}(\mathbf{X}_n).$$

Proof. It suffices to prove (2.4) for two variables $\mathbf{X}$ and $\mathbf{Y}$. Using the notation (1.3), we can write

$$(2.5) \qquad \mathbf{E}(\mathbf{X}) + \mathbf{E}(\mathbf{Y}) = \sum_{j,k} x_j p(x_j, y_k) + \sum_{j,k} y_k p(x_j, y_k),$$

the summation extending over all possible values x_j, y_k (which need not be all different). The two series converge absolutely; their sum can therefore be rearranged to give $\sum_{j,k} (x_j + y_k) p(x_j, y_k)$, which is by definition the expectation of $\mathbf{X} + \mathbf{Y}$. This accomplishes the proof. ▶

Clearly, no corresponding general theorem holds for products; for example, $\mathbf{E}(\mathbf{X}^2)$ is generally different from $(\mathbf{E}(\mathbf{X}))^2$. Thus, if $\mathbf{X}$ is the number scored with a balanced die,

$$\mathbf{E}(\mathbf{X}) = \tfrac{7}{2}, \quad \text{but} \quad \mathbf{E}(\mathbf{X}^2) = (1+4+9+16+25+36)/6 = 91/6.$$

However, the simple multiplication rule holds for mutually independent variables.

Theorem 3. *If* $\mathbf{X}$ *and* $\mathbf{Y}$ *are mutually independent random variables with finite expectations, then their product is a random variable with finite expectation and*

$$(2.6) \qquad \mathbf{E}(\mathbf{XY}) = \mathbf{E}(\mathbf{X})\mathbf{E}(\mathbf{Y}).$$

Proof. To calculate $E(XY)$ we must multiply each possible value $x_j y_k$ with the corresponding probability. Hence

$$(2.7) \qquad E(XY) = \sum_{j,k} x_j y_k f(x_j) g(y_k) = \left\{ \sum_j x_j f(x_j) \right\} \left\{ \sum_k y_k g(y_k) \right\},$$

the rearrangement being justified since the series converge absolutely. ▶

By induction the same multiplication rule holds for any number of mutually independent random variables.

It is convenient to have a notation also for the expectation of a conditional probability distribution. If X and Y are two random variables with the joint distribution (1.3), the *conditional expectation* $E(Y \mid X)$ *of Y for given X is the function which at the place x_j assumes the value*

$$(2.8) \qquad \sum_k y_k P\{Y = y_k \mid X = x_j\} = \frac{\sum_k y_k p(x_j, y_k)}{f(x_j)} \; ;$$

this definition is meaningful only if the series converges absolutely and $f(x_j) > 0$ for all j.

The conditional expectation $E(Y \mid X)$ is a new random variable. To calculate its expectation we have to multiply (2.8) by $f(x_j)$ and sum over x_j. The result is

$$(2.9) \qquad E(E(Y \mid X)) = E(Y).$$

3. EXAMPLES AND APPLICATIONS

(a) *Binomial distribution.* Let S_n be the number of successes in n Bernoulli trials with probability p for success. We know that S_n has the binomial distribution $\{b(k; n, p)\}$, whence $E(S_n) = \sum k b(k; n, p) = np \sum b(k-1; n-1, p)$. The last sum includes all terms of the binomial distribution for $n - 1$ and hence equals 1. Therefore *the mean of the binomial distribution* is

$$(3.1) \qquad E(S_n) = np.$$

The same result could have been obtained without calculation by a method which is often expedient. Let X_k be the number of successes scored at the kth trial. This random variable assumes only the values 0 and 1 with corresponding probabilities q and p. Hence

$$E(X_k) = 0 \cdot q + 1 \cdot p = p,$$

and since

(3.2) $S_n = X_1 + X_2 + \cdots + X_n$,

we get (3.1) directly from (2.4).

(b) *Poisson distribution.* If X has the Poisson distribution $p(k; \lambda) = e^{-\lambda}\lambda^k/k!$ (where $k = 0, 1, \ldots$) then

$$E(X) = \sum kp(k; \lambda) = \lambda \sum p(k-1; \lambda).$$

The last series contains all terms of the distribution and therefore adds to unity. Accordingly, *the Poisson distribution* $\{e^{-\lambda}\lambda^k/k!\}$ *has the mean* λ.

(c) *Negative binomial distribution.* Let X be a variable with the geometric distribution $P\{X = k\} = q^k p$ where $k = 0, 1, 2, \ldots$. Then $E(X) = qp(1+2q+3q^2+\cdots)$. On the right we have the derivative of a geometric series so that $E(X) = qp(1-q)^{-2} = q/p$. We have seen in VI, 8, that X may be interpreted as the number of failures preceding the first success in a sequence of Bernoulli trials. More generally, we have studied the sample space corresponding to Bernoulli trials which are continued until the nth success. For $r < n$, let $X_1 = X$, and let X_r be the number of failures between the $(r-1)$st and the rth success. Then each X_v has the geometric distribution $\{q^k p\}$, and $E(X_v) = q/p$. The sum

$$Y_r = X_1 + \cdots + X_r$$

is the number of failures preceding the rth success. In other words, Y_r is a random variable whose distribution is the negative binomial defined by either of the two equivalent formulas VI, (8.1) or VI, (8.2). It follows that *the mean of this negative binomial is* rq/p. This can be verified by direct computation. From VI, (8.2) it is clear that

$$kf(k; r, p) = rp^{-1}qf(k-1; r+1, p),$$

and the terms of the distribution $\{f(k-1; r+1, p)\}$ add to unity. This direct calculation has the advantage that it applies also to *non-integral* r. On the other hand, the first argument leads to the result without requiring knowledge of the explicit form of the distribution of $X_1 + \cdots + X_r$.

(d) *Waiting times in sampling.* A population of N distinct elements is sampled with replacement. Because of repetitions a random sample of size r will in general contain fewer than r distinct elements. As the sample size increases, new elements will enter the sample more and more rarely. We are interested in the sample size S_r necessary for the acquisition of r distinct elements. (As a special case, consider the population of $N = 365$ possible birthdays; here S_r represents the number of people sampled up to the moment where the sample contains r different birthdays. A similar interpretation is possible with random placements of balls into cells. Our problem is of particular interest to collectors of coupons and other items where the acquisition can be compared to random sampling.[4])

To simplify language let us call a drawing successful if it results in adding a new element to the sample. Then S_r is the number of drawings up to and including the rth success. Put $X_k = S_{k+1} - S_k$. Then $X_k - 1$ is the number of unsuccessful drawings between the kth and $(k+1)$st success. During these drawings the population contains $N - k$ elements that have not yet entered the sample, and so $X_k - 1$ is the number of failures preceding the first success in Bernoulli trials with $p = (N-k)/N$. In accordance with example (c) therefore $E(X_k) = 1 + q/p = N/(N-k)$. Since $S_r = 1 + X_1 + \cdots + X_r$ we get finally

$$(3.3) \qquad E(S_r) = N\left\{\frac{1}{N} + \frac{1}{N-1} + \cdots + \frac{1}{N-r+1}\right\}.$$

In particular, $E(S_N)$ is the expected number of drawings necessary to exhaust the entire population. For $N = 10$ we have $E(S_5) \approx 6.5$ and $E(S_{10}) \approx 29.3$. This means that, on the average, seven drawings suffice to cover the first half of a population of 10, but the second half will require an average of some 23 drawings.

To obtain an approximation to (3.3) we interpret $(N-k)^{-1}$ as area of a rectangle whose basis is a unit interval centered at $N - k$, and whose height is the ordinate of x^{-1} at that point. Replacing the area of this rectangle by the area under the graph of x^{-1} we get the approximation

$$(3.4) \qquad E(S_r) \approx N\int_{N-r+\frac{1}{2}}^{N+\frac{1}{2}} x^{-1}\,dx = N\log\frac{N+\frac{1}{2}}{N-r+\frac{1}{2}}.$$

As an application choose $\alpha < 1$ arbitrary and consider the *expected number of drawings to obtain a sample containing the fraction α of the entire population*. This equals $E(S_r)$ when r is the smallest integer $\geq \alpha N$. When $N \to \infty$ the error committed in (3.4) tends to 0, and we find for the desired expectation in the limit $N\log(1-\alpha)^{-1}$. Note that all these results are obtained without use of the probability distribution itself. [The latter can be derived easily from the occupancy probabilities found in IV, (2.3).]

---

[4] G. Polya, *Eine Wahrscheinlichkeitsaufgabe zur Kundenwerbung*, Zeitschrift für Angewandte Mathematik und Mechanik, vol. 10 (1930), pp. 96–97. Polya treats a slightly more general problem with different methods. There exists a huge literature treating variants of the coupon collector's problem. (Cf. problems 24, 25; problems 12–14 in XI,7; and 12 in II,11.)

(e) *An estimation problem.* An urn contains balls numbered 1 to N. Let X *be the largest number drawn in* n drawings when random sampling with replacement is used. The event $X \leq k$ means that each of n numbers drawn is less than or equal to k and therefore $P\{X \leq k\} = (k/N)^n$. Hence the probability distribution of X is given by

(3.5) $p_k = P\{X = k\} = P\{X \leq k\} - P\{X \leq k - 1\} =$

$$= \{k^n - (k-1)^n\}N^{-n}.$$

It follows that

(3.6) $E(X) = \sum_{k=1}^{N} kp_k = N^{-n} \sum_{k=1}^{N} \{k^{n+1} - (k-1)^{n+1} - (k-1)^n\} =$

$$= N^{-n} \left\{ N^{n+1} - \sum_{k=1}^{N} (k-1)^n \right\}.$$

For large N the last sum is approximately the area under the curve $y = x^n$ from $x = 0$ to $x = N$, that is, $N^{n+1}/(n+1)$. It follows that for large N

(3.7) $$E(X) \approx \frac{n}{n+1} N.$$

If a town has $N = 1000$ cars and a sample of $n = 10$ is observed, the expected number of the highest observed license plate (assuming randomness) is about 910. The practical statistician uses the observed maximum in a sample to estimate the unknown true number N. This method was used during the last war to estimate enemy production (cf. problems 8–9.)

(f) *Application to a statistical test.* This example[5] illustrates the practical use of expectations to avoid cumbersome calculations of probability distributions.

Spores of the fungus Sordaria are produced in chains of eight. The chain may break into several parts, and ultimately the spores escape in projectiles containing from 1 to 8 spores. There are reasons to suppose that the breakages at the seven links are stochastically independent and that the links have the same probability p to break. Under this hypothesis it is theoretically possible to calculate the joint distribution of singlets, doublets, etc., but this would involve tedious calculations. On the other hand, for an empirical test of the hypothesis it suffices to know the expected numbers of singlets, doublets, etc., and these are easily found.

---

[5] Taken from the Inaugural Address of D. R. Cox at Birbeck College (London) 1961. Cox refers to C. T. Ingold and S. A. Hadland, New Phytologist, vol. 58 (1959), pp. 46–57.

For example, the spores located at the ends of the chain have probability p to become singlets whereas for all other spores this probability equals p^2. By the addition rule therefore the expected number of singlets arising from one chain is given by $\epsilon_1 = 2p + 6p^2$. A similar argument shows that the expected number of doublets is $\epsilon_2 = 2qp + 5qp^2$ where $q = 1 - p$. In like manner $\epsilon_3 = 2q^2p + 4q^2p^2, \ldots, \epsilon_8 = q^7$. The expected number of projectiles is $\epsilon_1 + \cdots + \epsilon_8 = 1 + 7p$. (This is obvious without calculations because the expected number of breaks equals $7p$, and each break increases the number of projectiles by 1.)

TABLE 3
OBSERVED NUMBERS f_k AND EXPECTED NUMBERS $N\epsilon_k$
OF PROJECTILES OF SIZE k IN EXAMPLE (f)

k	f_k	$N\epsilon_k$	k	f_k	$N\epsilon_k$
1	490	458.3	5	200	170.6
2	343	360.8	6	134	131.7
3	265	281.8	7	72	101.1
4	199	219.7	8	272	250.3

In an actual field observation a total of 7251 spores were counted, apparently coming from a total of $N = 907$ chains (with 5 spores undetected). If our probabilistic model is applicable we should have approximately $(1+7p)N = 7251$, or $p = 0.168$. (This argument depends on the intuitive meaning of expectation, to be justified by the weak law of large numbers.) The observed number f_k of projectiles should be close to the expected number $N\epsilon_k$. As table 3 shows, the discrepancies were not startling and there is no reason to reject the model. ▶

4. THE VARIANCE

Let X be a random variable with distribution $\{f(x_j)\}$, and let $r \geq 0$ be an integer. *If the expectation of the random variable X^r, that is,*

$$(4.1) \qquad E(X^r) = \sum x_j^r f(x_j),$$

exists, then it is called the rth moment of X about the origin. If the series does not converge absolutely, we say that the rth moment does not exist. Since $|X|^{r-1} \leq |X|^r + 1$, it follows that *whenever the rth moment exists so does the $(r-1)$st, and hence all preceding moments.*

Moments play an important role in the general theory, but in the present volume we shall use only the second moment. If it exists, so does the mean

$$(4.2) \qquad \mu = E(X).$$

It is then natural to replace the random variable X by its *deviation from the mean*, $X - \mu$. Since $(x-\mu)^2 \leq 2(x^2+\mu^2)$ the second moment of $X - \mu$ exists whenever $E(X^2)$ exists. It is given by

$$(4.3) \qquad E((X-\mu)^2) = \sum_j (x_j^2 - 2\mu x_j + \mu^2) f(x_j).$$

Splitting the right side into three individual sums, we find it equal to $E(X^2) - 2\mu E(X) + \mu^2 = E(X^2) - \mu^2$.

Definition. *Let X be a random variable with second moment $E(X^2)$ and let $\mu = E(X)$ be its mean. We define a number called the variance of X by*

$$(4.4) \qquad \mathrm{Var}\,(X) = E((X-\mu)^2) = E(X^2) - \mu^2.$$

Its positive square root (or zero) is called the standard deviation of X.

For simplicity we often speak of the variance of a distribution without mentioning the random variable. "Dispersion" is a synonym for the now generally accepted term "variance."

Examples. (*a*) If X assumes the values $\pm c$, each with probability $\frac{1}{2}$, then $\mathrm{Var}\,(X) = c^2$.

(*b*) If X is the number of points scored with a symmetric die, then $\mathrm{Var}\,(X) = \frac{1}{6}(1^2+2^2+\cdots+6^2) - (\frac{7}{2})^2 = \frac{35}{12}$.

(*c*) For the *Poisson distribution* $p(k;\lambda)$ the mean is λ [cf. example (3.*b*)] and hence the variance $\sum k^2 p(k;\lambda) - \lambda^2 = \lambda \sum kp(k-1;\lambda) - \lambda^2 = \lambda \sum (k-1)p(k-1;\lambda) + \lambda \sum p(k-1;\lambda) - \lambda^2 = \lambda^2 + \lambda - \lambda^2 = \lambda$. In this case mean and variance are equal.

(*d*) For the *binomial distribution* [cf. example (3.*a*)] a similar computation shows that the variance is

$$\sum k^2 b(k;n,p) - (np)^2 = np \sum kb(k-1;n-1,p) - (np)^2 =$$
$$= np\{(n-1)p + 1\} - (np)^2 = npq. \quad \blacktriangleright$$

The usefulness of the notion of variance will appear only gradually, in particular, in connection with limit theorems of chapter X. Here we observe that the variance is a rough *measure of spread*. In fact, if $\mathrm{Var}\,(X) = \sum (x_j-\mu)^2 f(x_j)$ is small, then each term in the sum is small. A value x_j for which $|x_j - \mu|$ is large must therefore have a small probability $f(x_j)$. In other words, in case of small variance large deviations of X from the mean μ are improbable. Conversely, a large variance indicates that not all values assumed by X lie near the mean.

Some readers may be helped by the following interpretation in mechanics. Suppose that a unit mass is distributed on the x-axis so that the mass $f(x_j)$ is concentrated at the point x_j. Then the mean μ is the abscissa of the *center of gravity*, and the variance is the *moment of inertia*. Clearly different mass distributions may have the same center of gravity and the same moment of inertia, but it is well known that some important mechanical properties can be described in terms of these two quantities.

If **X** represents a measurable quantity like length or temperature, then its numerical values depend on the origin and the unit of measurement. A change of the latter means passing from **X** to a new variable $a\mathbf{X} + b$, where a and b are constants. Clearly $\mathrm{Var}\,(\mathbf{X}+b) = \mathrm{Var}\,(\mathbf{X})$, and hence

$$(4.5) \qquad \mathrm{Var}\,(a\mathbf{X}+b) = a^2\,\mathrm{Var}\,(\mathbf{X}).$$

The choice of the origin and unit of measurement is to a large degree arbitrary, and often it is most convenient to take the mean as origin and the standard deviation as unit. We have done so in VII, 3 when we introduced the normalized number of successes $\mathbf{S}_n^* = (\mathbf{S}_n - np)/\sqrt{npq}$. In general, if **X** has mean μ and variance σ^2, then $\mathbf{X} - \mu$ has mean zero and variance σ^2, and hence *the variable*

$$(4.6) \qquad \mathbf{X}^* = (\mathbf{X}-\mu)/\sigma \qquad\qquad (\sigma > 0)$$

has mean 0 *and variance* 1. *It is called the normalized variable corresponding to* **X**. In the physicist's language, the passage from **X** to **X*** would be interpreted as the introduction of dimensionless quantities.

5. COVARIANCE; VARIANCE OF A SUM

Let **X** and **Y** be two random variables on the same sample space. Then **X** + **Y** and **XY** are again random variables, and their distributions can be obtained by a simple rearrangement of the joint distribution of **X** and **Y**. Our aim now is to calculate $\mathrm{Var}\,(\mathbf{X}+\mathbf{Y})$. For that purpose we introduce the notion of covariance, which will be analyzed in greater detail in section 8. If the joint distribution of **X** and **Y** is $\{p(x_j, y_k)\}$, then the expectation of **XY** is given by

$$(5.1) \qquad \mathbf{E}(\mathbf{XY}) = \sum x_j y_k p(x_j, y_k),$$

provided, of course, that the series converges absolutely. Now $|x_j y_k| \leq \leq (x_j^2 + y_k^2)/2$ and therefore $\mathbf{E}(\mathbf{XY})$ certainly exists if $\mathbf{E}(\mathbf{X}^2)$ and $\mathbf{E}(\mathbf{Y}^2)$ exist. In this case there exist also the expectations

$$(5.2) \qquad \mu_x = \mathbf{E}(\mathbf{X}), \qquad \mu_y = \mathbf{E}(\mathbf{Y}),$$

and the variables $\mathbf{X} - \mu_x$ and $\mathbf{Y} - \mu_y$ have means zero. For their product we have from the addition rule of section 2

$$(5.3) \quad \mathbf{E}((\mathbf{X}-\mu_x)(\mathbf{Y}-\mu_y)) = \mathbf{E}(\mathbf{XY}) - \mu_x\mathbf{E}(\mathbf{Y}) - \mu_y\mathbf{E}(\mathbf{X}) + \mu_x\mu_y =$$
$$= \mathbf{E}(\mathbf{XY}) - \mu_x\mu_y.$$

Definition. *The covariance of* X *and* Y *is defined by*

$$(5.4) \qquad \text{Cov}(X, Y) = E((X-\mu_x)(Y-\mu_y)) = E(XY) - \mu_x\mu_y.$$

This definition is meaningful whenever X *and* Y *have finite variances.*

We know from section 2 that for independent variables $E(XY) = E(X)E(Y)$. Hence from (5.4) we have

Theorem 1. *If* X *and* Y *are independent, then* $\text{Cov}(X, Y) = 0$.

Note that *the converse is not true*. For example, a glance at table 1 shows that the two variables are dependent, but their covariance vanishes nevertheless. We shall return to this point in section 8. The next theorem is important, and the addition rule (5.6) for independent variables is constantly applied.

Theorem 2. *If* $X_1, \ldots, X_n$ *are random variables with finite variances* $\sigma_1^2, \ldots, \sigma_n^2$, *and* $S_n = X_1 + \cdots + X_n$, *then*

$$(5.5) \qquad \text{Var}(S_n) = \sum_{k=1}^{n} \sigma_k^2 + 2 \sum_{j,k} \text{Cov}(X_j, X_k)$$

the last sum extending over each of the $\binom{n}{2}$ *pairs* (X_j, X_k) *with* $j < k$.

In particular, if the X_j *are mutually independent,*

$$(5.6) \qquad \text{Var}(S_n) = \sigma_1^2 + \sigma_2^2 + \cdots + \sigma_n^2.$$

Proof. Put $\mu_k = E(X_k)$ and $m_n = \mu_1 + \cdots + \mu_n = E(S_n)$. Then $S_n - m_n = \sum (X_k - \mu_k)$ and

$$(5.7) \qquad (S_n - m_n)^2 = \sum (X_k - \mu_k)^2 + 2 \sum (X_j - \mu_j)(X_k - \mu_k).$$

Taking expectations, we get (5.5).   ▶

Examples. (*a*) *Binomial distribution* $\{b(k; n, p)\}$. In example (3.*a*), the variables X_k are mutually independent. We have

$$E(X_k^2) = 0^2 \cdot q + 1^2 \cdot p = p,$$

and $E(X_k) = p$. Hence $\sigma_k^2 = p - p^2 = pq$, and from (5.6) we see that *the variance of the binomial distribution* is npq. The same result was derived by direct computation in example (4.*d*).

(*b*) *Bernoulli trials with variable probabilities.* Let $X_1, \ldots, X_n$ be mutually independent random variables such that X_k assumes the values 1 and 0 with probabilities p_k and $q_k = 1 - p_k$ respectively. Then

$E(X_k) = p_k$ and $Var(X_k) = p_k - p_k^2 = p_k q_k$. Putting again

$$S_n = X_1 + \cdots + X_n$$

we have from (5.6)

(5.8) $$Var(S_n) = \sum_{k=1}^{n} p_k q_k.$$

As in example (1.e) the variable S_n may be interpreted as the total number of successes in n independent trials, each of which results in success or failure. Then $p = (p_1 + \cdots + p_n)/n$ is the average probability of success, and it seems natural to compare the present situation to Bernoulli trials with the constant probability of success p. Such a comparison leads us to a striking result. We may rewrite (5.8) in the form

$$Var(S_n) = np - \sum p_k^2.$$

Next, it is easily seen (by elementary calculus or induction) that among all combinations $\{p_k\}$ such that $\sum p_k = np$ the sum $\sum p_k^2$ assumes its minimum value when all p_k are equal. It follows that, if the average probability of success p is kept constant, $Var(S_n)$ *assumes its maximum value when* $p_1 = \cdots = p_n = p$. We have thus the surprising result that the *variability of* p_k, *or lack of uniformity, decreases the magnitude of chance fluctuations* as measured by the variance.[6] For example, the number of annual fires in a community may be treated as a random variable; for a given average number, the variability is *maximal* if all households have the *same* probability of fire. Given a certain average quality p of n machines, the *output will be least uniform if all machines are equal.* (An application to modern education is obvious but hopeless.)

(c) *Card matching.* A deck of n numbered cards is put into random order so that all $n!$ arrangements have equal probabilities. The number of matches (cards in their natural place) is a random variable S_n which assumes the values $0, 1, \ldots, n$. Its probability distribution was derived in IV, 4. From it the mean and variance could be obtained, but the following way is simpler and more instructive.

Define a random variable X_k which is either 1 or 0, according as card number k is or is not at the kth place. Then $S_n = X_1 + \cdots + X_n$. Now each card has probability $1/n$ to appear at the kth place. Hence $P\{X_k = 1\} = 1/n$ and $P\{X_k = 0\} = (n-1)/n$. Therefore $E(X_k) = 1/n$, and it follows that $E(S_n) = 1$: the average is one match per deck. To

---

[6] For stronger results in the same direction see W. Hoeffding, *On the distribution of the number of successes in independent trials*, Ann. Math. Statist., vol. 27 (1956), pp. 713–721. For an approximation by Poisson distributions see example XI, (6.b).

find $\text{Var}\,(\mathbf{S}_n)$ we first calculate the variance σ_k^2 of $\mathbf{X}_k$:

$$(5.9) \qquad \sigma_k^2 = \frac{1}{n} - \left(\frac{1}{n}\right)^2 = \frac{n-1}{n^2}\,.$$

Next we calculate $\mathbf{E}(\mathbf{X}_j\mathbf{X}_k)$. The product $\mathbf{X}_j\mathbf{X}_k$ is 0 or 1; the latter is true if both card number j and card number k are at their proper places, and the probability for that is $1/n(n-1)$. Hence

$$(5.10) \qquad \mathbf{E}(\mathbf{X}_j\mathbf{X}_k) = \frac{1}{n(n-1)}\,,$$

$$\text{Cov}\,(\mathbf{X}_j, \mathbf{X}_k) = \frac{1}{n(n-1)} - \frac{1}{n^2} = \frac{1}{n^2(n-1)}\,.$$

Thus finally

$$(5.11) \qquad \text{Var}\,(\mathbf{S}_n) = n\,\frac{n-1}{n^2} + 2\binom{n}{2}\frac{1}{n^2(n-1)} = 1.$$

We see that both mean and variance of the number of matches are equal to one. This result may be applied to the problem of *card guessing* discussed in IV, 4. There we considered three methods of guessing, one of which corresponds to card matching. The second can be described as a sequence of n Bernoulli trials with probability $p = 1/n$, in which case the expected number of correct guesses is $np = 1$ and the variance $npq = (n-1)/n$. The expected numbers are the same in both cases, but the larger variance with the first method indicates greater chance fluctuations about the mean and thus promises a slightly more exciting game. (With more complicated decks of cards the difference between the two variances is somewhat larger but never really big.) With the last mode of guessing the subject keeps calling the same card; the number of correct guesses is necessarily one, and chance fluctuations are completely eliminated (variance 0). We see that the strategy of calling cannot influence the expected number of correct guesses but has some influence on the magnitude of chance fluctuations.

(*d*) *Sampling without replacement.* Suppose that a population consists of b black and g green elements, and that a random sample of size r is taken (without repetitions). The number $\mathbf{S}_k$ of black elements in the sample is a random variable with the *hypergeometric distribution* (see II, 6) from which the mean and the variance can be obtained by direct computation. However, the following method is preferable. Define the random variable $\mathbf{X}_k$ to assume the values 1 or 0 according as the kth element in the sample is or is not black ($k \leq r$). For reasons of symmetry the probability that $X_k = 1$ is $b/(b+g)$, and hence

$$(5.12) \qquad E(X_k) = \frac{b}{b+g}, \qquad \text{Var}(X_k) = \frac{bg}{(b+g)^2}.$$

Next, if $j \neq k$, then $X_j X_k = 1$ if the jth and kth elements of the sample are black, and otherwise $X_j X_k = 0$. The probability of $X_j X_k = 1$ is $b(b-1)/(b+g)(b+g-1)$, and therefore

$$(5.13) \qquad E(X_j X_k) = \frac{b(b-1)}{(b+g)(b+g-1)},$$

$$\text{Cov}(X_j X_k) = \frac{-bg}{(b+g)^2(b+g-1)}.$$

Thus

$$(5.14) \qquad E(S_r) = \frac{rb}{b+g}, \qquad \text{Var}(S_r) = \frac{rbg}{(b+g)^2}\left\{1 - \frac{r-1}{b+g-1}\right\}.$$

In sampling with replacement we would have the same mean, but the variance would be slightly larger, namely, $rbg/(b+g)^2$. ▶

6. CHEBYSHEV'S INEQUALITY[7]

We saw that a small variance indicates that large deviations from the mean are improbable. This statement is made more precisely by Chebyshev's inequality, which is an exceedingly useful tool. It presupposes the existence of a second moment.

Theorem. *For any* $t > 0$

$$(6.1) \qquad P\{|X| \geq t\} \leq t^{-2} E(X^2).$$

In particular, if $E(X) = \mu$ *then*

$$(6.2) \qquad P\{|X - \mu| \geq t\} \leq t^{-2} \text{Var}(X).$$

Proof. The second inequality is obtained by applying the first to the variable $X - \mu$. Using the notations of section 4 we have

$$(6.3) \qquad P\{|X| > t\} = \sum_{|x_j| \geq t} f(x_j) \leq t^{-2} \sum_{|x_j| \geq t} x_j^2 f(x_j)$$

the sums extending over those x_j that exceed t in absolute value. The last sum is $\leq E(X^2)$, and so (6.1) is true. ▶

---

[7] P. L. Chebyshev (1821–1894).

Chebyshev's inequality must be regarded as a theoretical tool rather than a practical method of estimation. Its importance is due to its universality, but no statement of great generality can be expected to yield sharp results in individual cases.

Examples. (a) If X is the number scored in a throw of a true die, then [cf. example (4.b)], $\mu = \frac{7}{2}$, $\sigma^2 = \frac{35}{12}$. The maximum deviation of X from μ is $2.5 \approx 3\sigma/2$. The probability of greater deviations is zero, whereas Chebyshev's inequality only asserts that this probability is smaller than 0.47.

(b) For the binomial distribution $\{b(k; n, p)\}$ we have [cf. example (5.a)] $\mu = np$, $\sigma^2 = npq$. For large n we know that

$$(6.4) \qquad \mathbf{P}\{|S_n - np| > x\sqrt{npq}\} \approx 1 - \mathfrak{N}(x) + \mathfrak{N}(-x).$$

Chebyshev's inequality states only that the left side is less than x^{-2}; this is obviously a much poorer estimate than (6.4).

*7. KOLMOGOROV'S INEQUALITY

As an example of more refined methods we prove:

Let $X_1, \ldots, X_n$ *be mutually independent variables with expectations* $\mu_k = E(X_k)$ *and variances* σ_k^2. *Put*

$$(7.1) \qquad\qquad S_k = X_1 + \cdots + X_k$$

$$(7.2) \qquad\qquad m_k = E(S_k) = \mu_1 + \cdots + \mu_k,$$

$$s_k^2 = \mathrm{Var}\,(S_k) = \sigma_1^2 + \cdots + \sigma_k^2.$$

For every $t > 0$ *the probability of the simultaneous realization of the* n *inequalities*

$$(7.3) \qquad\qquad |S_k - m_k| < ts_n, \qquad\qquad k = 1, 2, \ldots, n,$$

is at least $1 - t^{-2}$.

For $n = 1$ this theorem reduces to Chebyshev's inequality. For $n > 1$ Chebyshev's inequality gives the same bound for the probability of the single relation $|S_n - m_n| < ts_n$, so that Kolmogorov's inequality is considerably stronger.

Proof. We want to estimate the probability x that at least one of the inequalities (7.3) does not hold. The theorem asserts that $x \le t^{-2}$.

---

* This section treats a special topic and should be omitted at first reading.

Define n random variables $\mathbf{Y}_v$ as follows: $\mathbf{Y}_v = 1$ if

(7.4) $$|\mathbf{S}_v - m_v| \geq ts_n$$

but

(7.5) $$|\mathbf{S}_k - m_k| < ts_n \quad \text{for} \quad k = 1, 2, \ldots, v-1;$$

$\mathbf{Y}_v = 0$ for all other sample points. In words, $\mathbf{Y}_v$ equals 1 at those points in which the vth of the inequalities (7.3) is the *first* to be violated. Then at any particular sample point at most one among the $\mathbf{Y}_k$ is 1, and the sum $\mathbf{Y}_1 + \mathbf{Y}_2 + \cdots + \mathbf{Y}_n$ can assume only the values 0 or 1; it is 1 if, and only if, at least one of the inequalities (7.3) is violated, and therefore

(7.6) $$x = \mathbf{P}\{\mathbf{Y}_1 + \cdots + \mathbf{Y}_n = 1\}.$$

Since $\mathbf{Y}_1 + \cdots + \mathbf{Y}_n$ is 0 or 1, we have $\sum \mathbf{Y}_k \leq 1$. Multiplying by $(\mathbf{S}_n - m_n)^2$ and taking expectations, we get

(7.7) $$\sum_{k=1}^{n} \mathbf{E}(\mathbf{Y}_k(\mathbf{S}_n - m_n)^2) \leq s_n^2.$$

For an evaluation of the terms on the left we put

(7.8) $$\mathbf{U}_k = (\mathbf{S}_n - m_n) - (\mathbf{S}_k - m_k) = \sum_{v=k+1}^{n} (\mathbf{X}_v - \mu_v).$$

Then

(7.9) $$\mathbf{E}(\mathbf{Y}_k(\mathbf{S}_n - m_n)^2) = \mathbf{E}(\mathbf{Y}_k(\mathbf{S}_k - m_k)^2) + 2\mathbf{E}(\mathbf{Y}_k\mathbf{U}_k(\mathbf{S}_k - m_k)) + \mathbf{E}(\mathbf{Y}_k\mathbf{U}_k^2).$$

Now, $\mathbf{U}_k$ depends only on $\mathbf{X}_{k+1}, \ldots, \mathbf{X}_n$ while $\mathbf{Y}_k$ and $\mathbf{S}_k$ depend only on $\mathbf{X}_1, \ldots, \mathbf{X}_k$. Hence $\mathbf{U}_k$ is independent of $\mathbf{Y}_k(\mathbf{S}_k - m_k)$ and therefore $\mathbf{E}(\mathbf{Y}_k\mathbf{U}_k(\mathbf{S}_k - m_k)) = \mathbf{E}(\mathbf{Y}_k(\mathbf{S}_k - m_k))\mathbf{E}(\mathbf{U}_k) = 0$, since $\mathbf{E}(\mathbf{U}_k) = 0$. Thus from (7.9)

(7.10) $$\mathbf{E}(\mathbf{Y}_k(\mathbf{S}_n - m_n)^2) \geq \mathbf{E}(\mathbf{Y}_k(\mathbf{S}_k - m_k)^2).$$

But $\mathbf{Y}_k \neq 0$ only if $|\mathbf{S}_k - m_k| \geq ts_n$, so that $\mathbf{Y}_k(\mathbf{S}_k - m_k)^2 \geq t^2 s_n^2 \mathbf{Y}_k$. Combining (7.7) and (7.10), we get therefore

(7.11) $$s_n^2 \geq t^2 s_n^2 \mathbf{E}(\mathbf{Y}_1 + \cdots + \mathbf{Y}_n).$$

Since $\mathbf{Y}_1 + \cdots + \mathbf{Y}_n$ equals either 0 or 1, the expectation to the right equals the probability x defined in (7.6). Thus $xt^2 \leq 1$ as asserted. ▶

*8. THE CORRELATION COEFFICIENT

Let X and Y be any two random variables with means μ_x and μ_y and positive variances σ_x^2 and σ_y^2. We introduce the corresponding normalized variables X^* and Y^* defined by (4.6). Their covariance is called *the correlation coefficient of* X, Y *and is denoted by* $\rho(X, Y)$. Thus, using (5.4),

$$(8.1) \qquad \rho(X, Y) = \text{Cov}(X^*, Y^*) = \frac{\text{Cov}(X, Y)}{\sigma_x \sigma_y}.$$

Clearly this correlation coefficient is independent of the origins and units of measurements, that is, for any constants a_1, a_2, b_1, b_2, with $a_1 > 0$, $a_2 > 0$, we have $\rho(a_1 X + b_1, a_2 Y + b_2) = \rho(X, Y)$.

The use of the correlation coefficient amounts to a fancy way of writing the covariance.[8] Unfortunately, the term correlation is suggestive of implications which are not inherent in it. We know from section 5 that $\rho(X, Y) = 0$ whenever X and Y are independent. It is important to realize that the converse is not true. In fact, *the correlation coefficient* $\rho(X, Y)$ *can vanish even if* Y *is a function of* X.

Examples. (*a*) Let X assume the values ± 1, ± 2 each with probability $\frac{1}{4}$. Let $Y = X^2$. The joint distribution is given by $p(-1, 1) = p(1, 1) = = p(2, 4) = p(-2, 4) = \frac{1}{4}$. For reasons of symmetry $\rho(X, Y) = 0$ even though we have a direct functional dependence of Y on X.

(*b*) Let U and V have the same distribution, and let $X = U + V$, $Y = U - V$. Then $E(XY) = E(U^2) - E(V^2) = 0$ and $E(Y) = 0$. Hence $\text{Cov}(X, Y) = 0$ and therefore also $\rho(X, Y) = 0$. For example, X and Y may be the sum and difference of points on two dice. Then X and Y are either both odd or both even and therefore dependent.   ▶

It follows that the correlation coefficient is by no means a general measure of dependence between X and Y. However, $\rho(X, Y)$ is connected with the *linear* dependence of X and Y.

Theorem. *We have always* $|\rho(X, Y)| \leq 1$; *furthermore,* $\rho(X, Y) = = \pm 1$ *only if there exist constants a and b such that* $Y = aX + b$, *except, perhaps, for values of* X *with zero probability.*

Proof. Let X^* and Y^* be the normalized variables. Then

$$(8.2) \quad \text{Var}(X^* \pm Y^*) = \text{Var}(X^*) \pm 2\,\text{Cov}(X^*, Y^*) + \text{Var}(Y^*) = = 2(1 \pm \rho(X, Y)).$$

---

* This section treats a special topic and may be omitted at first reading.

[8] The physicist would define the correlation coefficient as "dimensionless covariance."

The left side cannot be negative; hence $|\rho(\mathbf{X}, \mathbf{Y})| \leq 1$. For $\rho(\mathbf{X}, \mathbf{Y}) = 1$ it is necessary that $\mathrm{Var}\,(\mathbf{X}^* - \mathbf{Y}^*) = 0$ which means that with unit probability the variable $\mathbf{X}^* - \mathbf{Y}^*$ assumes only one value. In this case $\mathbf{X}^* - \mathbf{Y}^* = \mathrm{const.}$, and hence $\mathbf{Y} = a\mathbf{X} + \mathrm{const.}$ with $a = \sigma_y/\sigma_x$. A similar argument applies to the case $\rho(\mathbf{X}, \mathbf{Y}) = -1$. ▶

9. PROBLEMS FOR SOLUTION

1. Seven balls are distributed randomly in seven cells. Let $\mathbf{X}_i$ be the number of cells containing exactly i balls. Using the probabilities tabulated in II, 5, write down the joint distribution of $(\mathbf{X}_2, \mathbf{X}_3)$.

2. Two ideal dice are thrown. Let $\mathbf{X}$ be the score on the first die and $\mathbf{Y}$ be the larger of two scores. (a) Write down the joint distribution of $\mathbf{X}$ and $\mathbf{Y}$. (b) Find the means, the variances, and the covariance.

3. In five tosses of a coin let $\mathbf{X}, \mathbf{Y}, \mathbf{Z}$ be, respectively, the number of heads, the number of head runs, the length of the largest head run. Tabulate the 32 sample points together with the corresponding values of $\mathbf{X}, \mathbf{Y}$, and $\mathbf{Z}$. By simple counting derive the joint distributions of the pairs $(\mathbf{X}, \mathbf{Y})$, $(\mathbf{X}, \mathbf{Z})$, $(\mathbf{Y}, \mathbf{Z})$ and the distributions of $\mathbf{X} + \mathbf{Y}$ and $\mathbf{X}\mathbf{Y}$. Find the means, variances, covariances of the variables.

4. Let $\mathbf{X}, \mathbf{Y}$, and $\mathbf{Z}$ be independent random variables with the same geometric distribution $\{q^k p\}$. Find (a) $\mathbf{P}\{\mathbf{X} = \mathbf{Y}\}$; (b) $\mathbf{P}\{\mathbf{X} \geq 2\mathbf{Y}\}$; and (c) $\mathbf{P}\{\mathbf{X} + \mathbf{Y} \leq \mathbf{Z}\}$.

5. *Continuation.* Let $\mathbf{U}$ be the smaller of $\mathbf{X}$ and $\mathbf{Y}$, and put $\mathbf{V} = \mathbf{X} - \mathbf{Y}$. Show that $\mathbf{U}$ and $\mathbf{V}$ are independent.[9]

6. Let $\mathbf{X}_1$ and $\mathbf{X}_2$ be independent random variables with Poisson distributions $\{p(k; \lambda_1)\}$ and $\{p(k; \lambda_2)\}$.
(a) Prove that $\mathbf{X}_1 + \mathbf{X}_2$ has the Poisson distribution $\{p(k; \lambda_1 + \lambda_2)\}$.
(b) Show that the *conditional distribution of* $\mathbf{X}_1$ *given* $\mathbf{X}_1 + \mathbf{X}_2$ *is binomial*, namely

$$(9.1) \qquad \mathbf{P}\{\mathbf{X}_1 = k \mid \mathbf{X}_1 + \mathbf{X}_2 = n\} = b\left(k; n, \frac{\lambda_1}{\lambda_1 + \lambda_2}\right).$$

7. Let $\mathbf{X}_1$ and $\mathbf{X}_2$ be independent and have the common geometric distribution $\{q^k p\}$ (as in problem 4). Show without calculations that the *conditional distribution of* $\mathbf{X}_1$ *given* $\mathbf{X}_1 + \mathbf{X}_2$ *is uniform*, that is,

$$(9.2) \qquad \mathbf{P}\{\mathbf{X}_1 = k \mid \mathbf{X}_1 + \mathbf{X}_2 = n\} = \frac{1}{n+1}, \qquad k = 0, \ldots, n.$$

8. Let $\mathbf{X}_1, \ldots, \mathbf{X}_r$ be mutually independent random variables, each having the *uniform distribution* $\mathbf{P}\{\mathbf{X}_i = k\} = 1/N$ for $k = 1, 2, \ldots, N$. Let $\mathbf{U}_n$ be the smallest among the $\mathbf{X}_1, \ldots, \mathbf{X}_n$ and $\mathbf{V}_n$ the largest. Find the distributions of $\mathbf{U}_n$ and $\mathbf{V}_n$. What is the connection with the *estimation problem* (3.e)?

---

[9] The geometric distribution is the only probability distribution on the integers for which this is true. See T. S. Ferguson, *A characterization of the geometric distribution*, Amer. Math. Monthly, vol. 72 (1965), pp. 256–260.

9. *Continuation to the estimation problem in example* (3.*e*). (*a*) Find the joint distribution of the largest and the smallest observation. Specialize to $n = 2$. (*Hint:* Calculate first $\mathbf{P}\{X \leq r, Y \geq s\}$.)

(*b*) Find the conditional probability that the first two observations are j and k, given that $X = r$.

(*c*) Find $E(X^2)$ and hence an asymptotic expression for Var (X) as $N \to \infty$ (with n fixed).

10. *Simulating a perfect coin*. Given a biased coin such that the probability of heads is α, we simulate a perfect coin as follows. Throw the biased coin twice. Interpret *HT* as success and *TH* as failure; if neither event occurs repeat the throws until a decision is reached. (*a*) Show that this model leads to Bernoulli trials with $p = \frac{1}{2}$. (*b*) Find the distribution and the expectation of the number of throws required to reach a decision.

11. *The problem of Banach's match boxes*, *example* VI,(8.*a*). Show that the expectation of the distribution $\{u_r\}$ is given by $\mu = (2N+1)u_0 - 1$. Using Stirling's formula show that this is approximately $2\sqrt{N/\pi} - 1$. (For $N = 50$ the mean is about 7.04.)

Hint: Start from the relation

$$(N-r)u_r = \tfrac{1}{2}(2N+1)u_{r+1} - \tfrac{1}{2}(r+1)u_{r+1}.$$

Use the fact[10] that $\sum u_r = 1$.

12. *Sampling inspection*. Suppose that items with a probability p of being acceptable are subjected to inspection in such a way that the probability of an item being inspected is p'. We have four classes, namely, "acceptable and inspected," "acceptable but not inspected," etc. with corresponding probabilities pp', pq', $p'q$, qq' where $q = 1 - p$, $q' = 1 - p'$. We are concerned with double Bernoulli trials [see example VI,(9.*c*)]. Let N be the number of items passing the inspection desk (both inspected and uninspected) before the first defective is found, and let K be the (undiscovered) number of defectives among them. Find the joint distributions of N and K and the marginal distributions.

13. *Continuation*. Find $E\left(\dfrac{K}{N+1}\right)$ and Cov (K, N). $\Big[$In industrial practice the discovered defective item is replaced by an acceptable one so that $K/(N+1)$ is the fraction of defectives and measures the quality of the lot. Note that $E\left(\dfrac{K}{N+1}\right)$ is not $E(K)/E(N+1)$.$\Big]$

14. In a sequence of Bernoulli trials let X be the length of the run (of either successes or failures) started by the first trial. (*a*) Find the distribution of X, $E(X)$, Var (X). (*b*) Let Y be the length of the *second* run. Find the distribution of Y, $E(Y)$, Var (Y), and the joint distribution of X, Y.

15. Let X and Y have a common negative binomial distribution. Find the conditional probability $\mathbf{P}\{X = j \mid X + Y = k\}$ and show that the identity II, (12.16) now becomes obvious without any calculations.[11]

---

[10] This fact is not obvious analytically; it may be verified by induction on N.

[11] This derivation permits generalizations to more than two factors. It is due to T. K. M. Wisniewski, Amer. Statistician, vol. 20 (1966), p. 25.

16. If two random variables **X** and **Y** assume only two values each, and if Cov $(\mathbf{X}, \mathbf{Y}) = 0$, then **X** and **Y** are independent.

17. *Birthdays.* For a group of n people find the expected number of days of the year which are birthdays of exactly k people. (Assume 365 days and that all arrangements are equally probable.)

18. *Continuation.* Find the expected number of multiple birthdays. How large should n be to make this expectation exceed 1?

19. A man with n keys wants to open his door and tries the keys independently and at random. Find the mean and variance of the number of trials (a) if unsuccessful keys are not eliminated from further selections; (b) if they are. (Assume that only one key fits the door. The exact distributions are given in II, 7, but are not required for the present problem.)

20. Let $(\mathbf{X}, \mathbf{Y})$ be random variables whose joint distribution is the trinomial defined by (1.8). Find $E(\mathbf{X})$, Var $(\mathbf{X})$, and Cov $(\mathbf{X}, \mathbf{Y})$ (a) by direct computation, (b) by representing **X** and **Y** as sums of n variables each and using the methods of section 5.

21. Find the covariance of the number of ones and sixes in n throws of a die.

22. In the animal trapping problem 24 of VI, 10, prove that the expected number of animals trapped at the νth trapping is $nqp^{\nu-1}$.

23. If **X** has the *geometric* distribution $P\{\mathbf{X} = k\} = q^k p$ (where $k = 0, 1, \ldots$), show that Var $(\mathbf{X}) = qp^{-2}$. Conclude that the *negative* binomial distribution $\{f(k; r, p)\}$ has variance rqp^{-2} provided r is a positive integer. Prove by direct calculation that the statement remains true for all $r > 0$.

24. In the *waiting time problem* (3.d) prove that

$$\text{Var} \, (\mathbf{S}_r) = N \left\{ \frac{1}{(N-1)^2} + \frac{2}{(N-2)^2} + \cdots + \frac{r-1}{(N-r+1)^2} \right\}.$$

Conclude that $N^{-2}E(\mathbf{S}_N) \sim \sum k^{-2}$. (Incidentally, the value of this series is $\pi^2/6$.) *Hint:* Use the variance of the geometric distribution found in the preceding problem.

25. *Continuation.* Let $\mathbf{Y}_r$ be the number of drawings required to include r preassigned elements (instead of any r different elements as in the text). Find $E(\mathbf{Y}_r)$ and Var $(\mathbf{Y}_r)$. (*Note:* The exact distribution of $\mathbf{Y}_r$ was found in problem 12 of II, 11 but is not required for the present purpose.)

26. *The blood-testing problem.*[12] A large number, N, of people are subject to a blood test. This can be administered in two ways. (i) Each person can be

---

[12] This problem is based on a technique developed during World War II by R. Dorfman. In army practice Dorfman achieved savings up to 80 per cent. When the problem appeared in the first edition it caught widespread attention and led to various generalizations as well as to new industrial and biological applications. The main improvement consists in introducing more than two stages. See, for example, M. Sobel and P. A. Groll, *Group testing to eliminate efficiently all defectives in a binomial sample,* The Bell System Journal, vol. 38 (1959), pp. 1179–1252; G. S. Watson, *A study of the group screening method,* Technometrics, vol. 3 (1961), pp. 371–388; H. M. Finucan, *The blood-testing problem,* Applied Statistics, vol. 13 (1964), pp. 43–50.

tested separately. In this case N tests are required. (ii) The blood samples of k people can be pooled and analyzed together. If the test is *negative*, this *one* test suffices for the k people. If the test is *positive*, each of the k persons must be tested separately, and in all $k + 1$ tests are required for the k people.

Assume the probability p that the test is positive is the same for all people and that people are stochastically independent.

(a) What is the probability that the test for a pooled sample of k people will be positive?

(b) What is the expected value of the number, X, of tests necessary under plan (ii)?

(c) Find an equation for the value of k which will minimize the expected number of tests under the second plan. (Do not try numerical solutions.)

(d) Show that this k is close to $1/\sqrt{p}$, and hence that the minimum expected number of tests is about $2N\sqrt{p}$. (This remark is due to M. S. Raff.)

27. *Sample structure.* A population consists of r classes whose sizes are in the proportion $p_1:p_2:\cdots:p_r$. A random sample of size n is taken with replacement. Find the expected number of classes *not* represented in the sample.

28. Let X be the number of α runs in a random arrangement of r_1 alphas and r_2 betas. The distribution of X is given in problem 23 of II, 11. Find $E(X)$ and $\text{Var}(X)$.

29. In *Polya's urn scheme* [V,(2.c)] let X_n be one or zero according as the nth trial results in black or red. Prove $\rho(X_n, X_m) = c/(b+r+c)$ for $n \neq m$.

30. *Continuation.* Let S_n be the total number of black balls extracted in the first n drawings (that is, $S_n = X_1 + \cdots + X_n$). Find $E(S_n)$ and $\text{Var}(S_n)$. Verify the result by means of the recursion formula in problem 22 of V, 8. *Hint:* Use problems 19, 20 of V, 8.

31. *Stratified sampling.* A city has n blocks of which n_j have x_j inhabitants each $(n_1 + n_2 + \cdots = n)$. Let $m = \Sigma n_j x_j/n$ be the mean number of inhabitants per block and put $a^2 = n^{-1} \Sigma n_j x_j^2 - m^2$. In sampling without replacement r blocks are selected at random, and in each the inhabitants are counted. Let $X_1, \ldots, X_r$ be the respective number of inhabitants. Show that

$$E(X_1 + \cdots + X_r) = mr \qquad \text{Var}(X_1 + \cdots + X_r) = \frac{a^2 r(n-r)}{n-1}.$$

(In sampling with replacement the variance would be larger, namely, $a^2 r$.)

32. *Length of random chains.*[13] A chain in the x,y-plane consists of n links, each of unit length. The angle between two consecutive links is $\pm \alpha$ where α is a positive constant; each possibility has probability $\frac{1}{2}$, and the successive angles are mutually independent. The distance L_n from the beginning to the end of the chain is a random variable, and we wish to prove that

$$(9.3) \qquad E(L_n^2) = n \frac{1 + \cos \alpha}{1 - \cos \alpha} - 2 \cos \alpha \frac{1 - \cos^n \alpha}{(1 - \cos \alpha)^2}.$$

Without loss of generality the first link may be assumed to lie in the direction of the positive x-axis. The angle between the kth link and the positive x-axis

---

[13] This is the two-dimensional analogue to the problem of length of *long polymer molecules* in chemistry. The problem illustrates applications to random variables which are not expressible as sums of simple variables.

is a random variable S_{k-1} where $S_0 = 0$, $S_k = S_{k-1} + X_k\alpha$ and the X_k are mutually independent variables, assuming the values ± 1 with probability $\frac{1}{2}$. The projections on the two axes of the kth link are $\cos S_{k-1}$ and $\sin S_{k-1}$. Hence for $n \geq 1$

$$(9.4) \qquad L_n^2 = \left(\sum_{k=0}^{n-1} \cos S_k\right)^2 + \left(\sum_{k=0}^{n-1} \sin S_k\right)^2.$$

Prove by induction successively for $m < n$

$$(9.5) \qquad E(\cos S_n) = \cos^n \alpha, \qquad E(\sin S_n) = 0;$$

$$(9.6) \qquad E((\cos S_m) \cdot (\cos S_n)) = \cos^{n-m}\alpha \cdot E(\cos^2 S_m)$$

$$(9.7) \qquad E((\sin S_m) \cdot (\sin S_n)) = \cos^{n-m} \alpha \cdot E(\sin^2 S_m)$$

$$(9.8) \qquad E(L_n^2) - E(L_{n-1}^2) = 1 + 2 \cos \alpha \cdot \frac{1 - \cos^{n-1} \alpha}{1 - \cos \alpha}$$

(with $L_0 = 0$) and hence finally (9.3).

---

33. A sequence of Bernoulli trials is continued as long as necessary to obtain r successes, where r is a fixed integer. Let X be the number of trials required. Find[14] $E(r/X)$. (The definition leads to infinite series for which a finite expression can be obtained.)

34. In a random placement of r balls into n cells the probability of finding exactly m cells empty satisfies the recursion formula II,(11.8). Let m_r be the expected number of empty cells. *From the recursion formula* prove that

$$m_{r+1} = (1 - n^{-1})m_r, \qquad \text{and conclude} \qquad m_r = n \left(1 - \frac{1}{n}\right)^r.$$

35. Let S_n be the number of successes in n Bernoulli trials. Prove

$$E(|S_n - np|) = 2vqb(v; n, p)$$

where v is the integer such that $np < v \leq np + 1$.

Hint: The left side $= \sum_{k=0}^{v=1} (np - k)\binom{n}{k} p^k q^{n-k}$. Alternatively, use VI, (10.7).

36. Let $\{X_k\}$ be a sequence of mutually independent random variables with a common distribution. Suppose that the X_k assume only positive values and that $E(X_k) = a$ and $E(X_k^{-1}) = b$ exist. Let $S_n = X_1 + \cdots + X_n$. Prove that $E(S_n^{-1})$ is finite and that $E(X_k S_n^{-1}) = n^{-1}$ for $k = 1, 2, \ldots, n$.

---

[14] This example illustrates the effect of *optional stopping*. When the number n of trials is fixed, the ratio of the number N of successes to the number n of trials is a random variable whose expectation is p. It is often erroneously assumed that the same is true in our example where the number r of successes is fixed and the number of trials depends on chance. If $p = \frac{1}{2}$ and $r = 2$, then $E(2/X) = 0.614$ instead of 0.5; for $r = 3$ we find $E(3/X) = 0.579$.

37. *Continuation.*[15] Prove that

$$E\left(\frac{S_m}{S_n}\right) = \frac{m}{n}, \qquad \text{if } m \leq n$$

$$E\left(\frac{S_m}{S_n}\right) = 1 + (m-n)aE(S_n^{-1}), \qquad \text{if } m \geq n.$$

38. Let $X_1, \ldots, X_n$ be mutually independent random variables with a common distribution; let its mean be m, its variance σ^2. Let $\overline{X} = (X_1 + \cdots + X_n)/n$. Prove that[16]

$$\frac{1}{n-1} E\left(\sum_{k=1}^{n} (X_k - \overline{X})^2\right) = \sigma^2.$$

39. Let $X_1, \ldots, X_n$ be mutually independent random variables. Let U be a function of $X_1, \ldots, X_k$ and V a function of $X_{k+1}, \ldots, X_n$. Prove that U and V are mutually independent random variables.

---

40. *Generalized Chebyshev inequality.* Let $\phi(x) > 0$ for $x > 0$ be monotonically increasing and suppose that $E(\phi(|X|)) = M$ exists. Prove that

$$P\{|X| \geq t\} \leq \frac{M}{\phi(t)}.$$

41. *Schwarz inequality.* For any two random variables with finite variances one has $E^2(XY) \leq E(X^2)E(Y^2)$. Prove this from the fact that the quadratic polynomial $E((tX+Y)^2)$ is non-negative.

---

[15] The observation that problem 37 can be derived from 36 is due to K. L. Chung.
[16] This can be expressed by saying that $\sum(X_k - \overline{X})^2/(n-1)$ is an *unbiased estimator* of σ^2.

CHAPTER X

Law of Large Numbers

1. IDENTICALLY DISTRIBUTED VARIABLES

The limit theorems for Bernoulli trials derived in chapters VII and VIII are special cases of general limit theorems which cannot be treated in this volume. However, we shall here discuss at least some cases of the law of large numbers in order to reveal a new aspect of the expectation of a random variable.

The connection between Bernoulli trials and the theory of random variables becomes clearer when we consider the dependence of the number S_n of successes on the number n of trials. With each trial S_n increases by 1 or 0, and we can write

$$(1.1) \qquad S_n = X_1 + \cdots + X_n,$$

where the random variable X_k equals 1 if the kth trial results in success and zero otherwise. Thus S_n is a sum of n mutually independent random variables, each of which assumes the values 1 and 0 with probabilities p and q. From this it is only one step to consider sums of the form (1.1) where the X_k are mutually independent variables with an arbitrary distribution. The (weak) law of large numbers of VI,4, states that for large n the average proportion of successes S_n/n is likely to lie near p. This is a special case of the following

Law of Large Numbers. *Let* $\{X_k\}$ *be a sequence of mutually independent random variables with a common distribution. If the expectation* $\mu = E(X_k)$ *exists, then for every* $\epsilon > 0$ *as* $n \to \infty$

$$(1.2) \qquad P\left\{ \left| \frac{X_1 + \cdots + X_n}{n} - \mu \right| > \epsilon \right\} \to 0;$$

in words, the probability that the average S_n/n will differ from the expectation by less than an arbitrarily prescribed ϵ tends to one.

In this generality the theorem was first proved by Khintchine.[1] Older proofs had to introduce the unnecessary restriction that the variance Var $(\mathbf{X}_k)$ should also be finite.[2] For this case, however, there exists a much more precise result which generalizes the DeMoivre-Laplace limit theorem for Bernoulli trials, namely the

Central Limit Theorem. *Let* $\{\mathbf{X}_k\}$ *be a sequence of mutually independent random variables with a common distribution. Suppose that* $\mu = \mathbf{E}(\mathbf{X}_k)$ *and* $\sigma^2 = $ Var $(\mathbf{X}_k)$ *exist and let* $\mathbf{S}_n = \mathbf{X}_1 + \cdots + \mathbf{X}_n$. *Then for every fixed* β

(1.3) $$\mathbf{P}\left\{\frac{\mathbf{S}_n - n\mu}{\sigma\sqrt{n}} < \beta\right\} \to \mathfrak{N}(\beta)$$

where $\mathfrak{N}(x)$ is the normal distribution introduced in VII,1. This theorem is due to Lindeberg[3]; Ljapunov and other authors had previously proved it under more restrictive conditions. It must be understood that this theorem is only a special case of a much more general theorem whose formulation and proof are deferred to the second volume. Here we note that (1.3) is stronger than (1.2), since it gives an estimate for the probability that the discrepancy $|n^{-1}\mathbf{S}_n - \mu|$ is larger than $\sigma/\sqrt{n}$. On the other hand, the law of large numbers (1.2) holds even when the random variables $\mathbf{X}_k$ have no finite variance so that it is more general than the central limit theorem. For this reason we shall give an independent proof of the law of large numbers, but first we illustrate the two limit theorems.

Examples. (*a*) In a sequence of independent throws of a symmetric die let $\mathbf{X}_k$ be the number scored at the kth throw. Then

$$\mathbf{E}(\mathbf{X}_k) = (1+2+3+4+5+6)/6 = 3.5,$$

and Var $(\mathbf{X}_k) = (1^2+2^2+3^2+4^2+5^2+6^2)/6 - (3.5)^2 = \frac{35}{12}$. The law of large numbers states that for large n the average score $\mathbf{S}_n/n$ is likely to be near 3.5. The central limit theorem states that

(1.4) $$\mathbf{P}\{|\mathbf{S}_n - 3.5n| < \alpha\sqrt{35n/12}\} \approx \mathfrak{N}(\alpha) - \mathfrak{N}(-\alpha).$$

For $n = 1000$ and $\alpha = 1$ this reduces to $\mathbf{P}\{3450 < \mathbf{S}_n < 3550\} \approx 0.68$. For $\alpha = 0.6744 \cdots$ the right side in (1.4) equals $\frac{1}{2}$, and so there are

---

[1] A. Khintchine, Comptes rendus de l'Académie des Sciences, Paris, vol. 189 (1929), pp. 477–479. Incidentally, the reader should observe the warning given in connection with the law of large numbers for Bernoulli trials at the end of VI,4.

[2] A. Markov showed that the existence of $\mathbf{E}(|\mathbf{X}_k|^{1+a})$ for some $a > 0$ suffices.

[3] J. W. Lindeberg, *Eine neue Herleitung des Exponentialgesetzes in der Wahrscheinlichkeitsrechnung*, Mathematische Zeitschrift, vol. 15 (1922), pp. 211–225.

roughly equal chances that S_n lies within or without the interval 3500 ± 36.

(b) *Sampling.* Suppose that in a population of N families there are N_k families with exactly k children $(k = 0, 1, \ldots; \sum N_k = N)$. For a family chosen at random, the number of children is a random variable which assumes the value v with probability $p_v = N_v/N$. A sample of size n with replacement represents n independent random variables or "observations" $X_1, \ldots, X_n$, each with the same distribution; S_n/n is the *sample average.* The law of large numbers tells us that for sufficiently large random samples the sample average is likely to be near $\mu = \sum v p_v = \sum v N_v/N$, namely the population average. The central limit theorem permits us to estimate the probable magnitude of the discrepancy and to determine the sample size necessary for reliable estimates. In practice both μ and σ^2 are unknown, but it is usually easy to obtain a preliminary estimate of σ^2, and it is always possible to keep to the safe side. If it is desired that there be probability 0.99 or better that the sample average S_n/n differ from the unknown population mean μ by less than $\frac{1}{10}$, then the sample size should be such that

$$(1.5) \qquad \mathbf{P}\left\{\left|\frac{S_n - n\mu}{n}\right| < \frac{1}{10}\right\} \geq 0.99.$$

The root of $\mathfrak{N}(x) - \mathfrak{N}(-x) = 0.99$ is $x = 2.57\ldots$, and hence n should satisfy $\sqrt{n}/10\sigma \geq 2.57$ or $n \geq 660\sigma^2$. A cautious preliminary estimate of σ^2 gives us an idea of the required sample size. Similar situations occur frequently. Thus when the experimenter takes the mean of n measurements he, too, relies on the law of large numbers and uses a sample mean as an estimate for an unknown theoretical expectation. The reliability of this estimate can be judged only in terms of σ^2, and usually one is compelled to use rather crude estimates for σ^2.

(c) *The Poisson distribution.* In VII,5, we found that for large λ the Poisson distribution $\{p(k; \lambda)\}$ can be approximated by the normal distribution. This is really a direct consequence of the central limit theorem. Suppose that the variables X_k have a Poisson distribution $\{p(k; \gamma)\}$. Then S_n has a Poisson distribution $\{p(k; n\gamma)\}$ with mean and variance equal to $n\gamma$. Writing λ for $n\gamma$, we conclude that as $n \to \infty$

$$(1.6) \qquad \sum_{k < \lambda + \beta\sqrt{\lambda}} e^{-\lambda}\lambda^k/k! \to \mathfrak{N}(\beta)$$

the summation extending over all k up to $\lambda + \beta\sqrt{\lambda}$. It is now obvious that (1.6) holds also when λ approaches ∞ in an arbitrary manner. This theorem is used in the theory of summability of divergent series and is of general interest; estimates of the difference of the two sides in (1.6) are available from the general theory.   ▶

Note on Variables without Expectation

Both the law of large numbers and the central limit theorem become meaningless if the expectation μ does not exist, but they can be replaced by more general theorems supplying the same sort of information. In the modern theory variables without expectation play an important role and many waiting and recurrence times in physics turn out to be of this type. This is true even of the simple coin-tossing game.

Suppose that n coins are tossed one by one. For the kth coin let $\mathbf{X}_k$ be the waiting time up to the first equalization of the accumulated numbers of heads and tails. The $\mathbf{X}_k$ are mutually independent random variables with a common distribution: each $\mathbf{X}_k$ assumes only even positive values and $\mathbf{P}\{\mathbf{X}_k = 2r\} = f_{2r}$ with the probability distribution $\{f_{2r}\}$ defined in III,(3.7). The sum $\mathbf{S}_n = \mathbf{X}_1 + \cdots + \mathbf{X}_n$ has the same distribution as the waiting time to the nth equalization of the accumulated numbers of heads and tails or, what amounts to the same, the epoch of the nth return to the origin in a symmetric random walk. The distribution of $\mathbf{S}_n$ was found in theorem 4 of III,7, and it was shown that

$$(1.7) \qquad \mathbf{P}\{\mathbf{S}_n < n^2 x\} \to 2[1 - \mathfrak{N}(1/\sqrt{x}\,)].$$

We have here a limit theorem of the same character as the central limit theorem with the remarkable difference that this time *the variable* $\mathbf{S}_n/n^2$ *rather than* $\mathbf{S}_n/n$ *possesses a limit distribution*. In the physicist's language the $\mathbf{X}_k$ stand for independent measurements of the same physical quantity, and the theorem asserts that, in probability, *the average*

$$(\mathbf{X}_1 + \cdots + \mathbf{X}_n)/n$$

increases linearly with n. This paradoxical result cannot be shrugged off as representing a pathological case because it turns out that our $\mathbf{X}_k$ are typical of the waiting times occurring in many physical and economical processes. The limit theorem (1.7) is also typical of many modern limit theorems for variables without expectation.[4]

*2. PROOF OF THE LAW OF LARGE NUMBERS

There is no loss of generality in assuming that $\mu = \mathbf{E}(\mathbf{X}_k) = 0$, for otherwise we would replace $\mathbf{X}_k$ by $\mathbf{X}_k - \mu$, and this involves merely a

---

[4] For an analogue to the law of large numbers for variables without expectation see section 4 and problem 13. The surprising consequences of (1.7) were discussed at length in chapter III.

* This section should be omitted at first reading.

change of notation. In the special case where $\sigma^2 = \mathrm{Var}\,(\mathbf{X}_k)$ exists the law of large numbers is a trivial consequence of Chebyshev's inequality IX,(6.2) according to which

$$(2.1) \qquad P\{|\mathbf{S}_n| > t\} \le \frac{n\sigma^2}{t^2}.$$

For $t = \epsilon n$ the right side tends to 0, and so (1.2) is true.

The case where the second moment does not exist is more difficult. The proof depends on the versatile *method of truncation* which is a standard tool in deriving various limit theorems. Let δ be a positive constant to be determined later. For each n we define n pairs of random variables as follows.

$$(2.2) \qquad \begin{array}{llll} \mathbf{U}_k = \mathbf{X}_k, & \mathbf{V}_k = 0 & \textit{if} & |\mathbf{X}_k| \le \delta n, \\ \mathbf{U}_k = 0, & \mathbf{V}_k = \mathbf{X}_k & \textit{if} & |\mathbf{X}_k| > \delta n. \end{array}$$

Here $k = 1, \ldots, n$ and the dependence of the $\mathbf{U}_k$ and $\mathbf{V}_k$ on n must be borne in mind. By this definition

$$(2.3) \qquad \mathbf{X}_k = \mathbf{U}_k + \mathbf{V}_k$$

and to prove the law of large numbers it suffices to show that for given $\epsilon > 0$ the constant δ can be chosen so that as $n \to \infty$

$$(2.4) \qquad P\{|\mathbf{U}_1 + \cdots + \mathbf{U}_n| > \tfrac{1}{2}\epsilon n\} \to 0$$

and

$$(2.5) \qquad P\{|\mathbf{V}_1 + \cdots + \mathbf{V}_n| > \tfrac{1}{2}\epsilon n\} \to 0.$$

For the proof denote the possible values of the $\mathbf{X}_j$ by $x_1, x_2, \ldots$ and their probabilities by $f(x_j)$. Put $a = E(|\mathbf{X}_j|)$, that is,

$$(2.6) \qquad a = \sum_j |x_j|\,f(x_j).$$

The variable $\mathbf{U}_1$ is bounded by δn and hence clearly

$$(2.7) \qquad E(\mathbf{U}_1^2) < a\,\delta n.$$

The variables $\mathbf{U}_1, \ldots, \mathbf{U}_n$ have the same distribution and are mutually independent. Therefore

$$(2.8) \qquad \mathrm{Var}\,(\mathbf{U}_1 + \cdots + \mathbf{U}_n) = n\,\mathrm{Var}\,(\mathbf{U}_1) \le n E(\mathbf{U}_1^2) \le a\,\delta n^2.$$

On the other hand, by the very definition of the $\mathbf{U}_k$ as $n \to \infty$

$$(2.9) \qquad E(\mathbf{U}_1) \to E(\mathbf{X}_1) = 0.$$

It follows that for n sufficiently large

(2.10) $$\mathbf{E}((\mathbf{U}_1 + \cdots + \mathbf{U}_n)^2) \leq 2a\,\delta n^2.$$

The relation (2.4) is now an immediate consequence of Chebyshev's inequality IX,(6.1) according to which

(2.11) $$\mathbf{P}\{|\mathbf{U}_1 + \cdots + \mathbf{U}_n| > \tfrac{1}{2}\epsilon n\} \geq \frac{8a\,\delta}{\epsilon^2}.$$

By choosing δ small enough we can make the right side as small as we please, and so (2.4) is true.

As for (2.5), note that

(2.12) $$\mathbf{P}\{\mathbf{V}_1 + \cdots + \mathbf{V}_n \neq 0\} \leq n\mathbf{P}\{\mathbf{V}_1 \neq 0\}$$

by the basic inequality I,(7.6). For arbitrary $\delta > 0$ we have

(2.13)
$$\mathbf{P}\{\mathbf{V}_1 \neq 0\} = \mathbf{P}\{|\mathbf{X}_1| > \delta n\} = \sum_{|x_j| > \delta n} f(x_j)$$
$$\leq \frac{1}{\delta n} \sum_{|x_j| > \delta n} |x_j|\, f(x_j).$$

The last sum tends to 0 as $n \to \infty$. Therefore also the left side in (2.12) tends to 0. This statement is stronger than (2.5) and completes the proof.   ▶

3. THE THEORY OF "FAIR" GAMES

For a further analysis of the implications of the law of large numbers we shall use the time-honored terminology of gamblers, but our discussion bears equally on less frivolous applications, and our two basic assumptions are more realistic in statistics and physics than in gambling halls. First, we shall assume that our gambler possesses an *unlimited capital* so that no loss can force a termination of the game. (Dropping this assumption leads to the problem of the gambler's *ruin*, which from the very beginning has intrigued students of probability. It is of importance in Wald's sequential analysis and in the theory of stochastic processes, and will be taken up in chapter XIV.) Second, we shall assume that the gambler *does not have the privilege of optional stopping; the number n of trials must be fixed in advance* independently of the development of the game. (In reality a player blessed with an unlimited capital can wait for a run of good luck and quit at an opportune moment. He is not interested in the probable state at a prescribed moment, but only in the maximal fluctuations likely to occur in the long run. Light is shed on this problem by the law of the iterated logarithm rather than by the law of large numbers (see VIII,5).)

The random variable X_k will be interpreted as the (positive or negative) gain at the kth trial of a player who keeps playing the same type of game of chance. The sum $S_n = X_1 + \cdots + X_n$ is the accumulated gain in n independent trials. If the player pays for each trial an entrance fee μ' (not necessarily positive), then $n\mu'$ represents the accumulated entrance fees, and $S_n - n\mu'$ the *accumulated net gain*. The law of large numbers applies when $\mu = E(X_k)$ exists. It says roughly that for sufficiently large n the difference $S_n - n\mu$ is likely to be small in comparison to n. Therefore, if the entrance fee μ' is smaller than μ, then, for large n, the player is likely to have a positive gain of the order of magnitude $n(\mu - \mu')$. For the same reason an entrance fee $\mu' > \mu$ is practically sure to lead to a loss. In short, the case $\mu' < \mu$ is *favorable* to the player, while $\mu' > \mu$ is *unfavorable*.

Note that nothing is said about the case $\mu' = \mu$. The *only* possible conclusion in this case is that, for n sufficiently large, the accumulated gain or loss $S_n - n\mu$ will with overwhelming probability be small in comparison with n. It is not stated whether $S_n - n\mu$ is likely to be positive or negative, that is, whether the game is favorable or unfavorable. This was overlooked in the classical theory which called $\mu' = \mu$ a "fair" price and a game with $\mu' = \mu$ "*fair*." Much harm was done by the misleading suggestive power of this name. It must be understood that *a "fair" game may be distinctly unfavorable to the player.*   ▶

In applications to gambling and in other simple situations where the variables X_k have a finite second moment the notion of "fairness" can be justified, but when the variance is infinite, the term "fair game" becomes an absolute misnomer. There is no reason to believe that the accumulated net gain $S_n - n\mu'$ fluctuates around zero. In fact, *there exist examples of "fair" games*[5] *where the probability tends to one that the player will have sustained a net loss.* The law of large numbers asserts that this net loss is likely to be of smaller order of magnitude than n. However, nothing more can be asserted. If a_n is an arbitrary sequence such that $a_n/n \to 0$, it is possible to construct a "fair" game where the probability tends to one that at the nth trial the accumulated net loss exceeds a_n. Problem 15 contains an example where the player has a practical assurance that his loss will exceed $n/\log n$. This game is "fair," and the entrance fee is unity. It is difficult to imagine that a player will find it "fair" if he is practically sure to sustain a steadily increasing loss.

---

[5] W. Feller, *Note on the law of large numbers and "fair" games*, Ann. Math. Statist., vol. 16 (1945), pp. 301–304.

It would be a mistake to dismiss such phenomena as pathological or as being without practical importance. The neglect of random variables without expectations has done much harm in applications because such variables play an essential role even in the simplest stochastic processes. For example, the simple random walk (or coin-tossing game) discussed in chapter III serves as prototype for many stochastic processes in physics and economics. As was shown in chapter III, the waiting and first-passage times in this random walk do not have expectations, and they are therefore subject to chance fluctuations that appear paradoxical and do not accord with our intuition. This faulty intuition as well as many modern applications of probability theory are under the strong influence of traditional misconceptions concerning the meaning of the law of large numbers and of a popular mystique concerning a so-called law of averages. These are inherited from the classical theory in which mathematical analysis was inevitably interwoven with empirical and metaphysical considerations, and in which something mystical adhered to the various limit theorems.[6]

Let us return to the "normal" situations where not only $E(X_k)$ but also $Var(X_k)$ exists. In this case the law of large numbers is supplemented by the central limit theorem, and the latter tells us that, with a "fair" game, the long-run net gain $S_n - n\mu$ is likely to be of the order of magnitude $\sqrt{n}$ and that for large n there are about equal odds for this net gain to be positive or negative. Thus, when the central limit theorem applies, the term "fair" appears justified, but even in this case we deal with a limit theorem with emphasis on the words "long run."

For illustration, consider a slot machine where the player has a probability of 10^{-6} to win $10^6 - 1$ dollars, and the alternative of losing the entrance fee $\mu' = 1$. Here we have Bernoulli trials, and the game is "fair." In a million trials the player pays as many dollars in entrance fees. He may hit the jackpot $0, 1, 2, \ldots$ times. We know from the Poisson approximation to the binomial distribution that, with an accuracy to several decimal places, the probability of hitting the jackpot exactly k times is $e^{-1}/k!$. Thus the player has probability $0.368 \ldots$ to lose a million, and the same probability of barely recovering his expenses; he has probability $0.184 \ldots$ to gain exactly one million, etc. Here 10^6 trials are equivalent to one single trial in a game with the gain distributed according to a Poisson distribution. Such a game can be realized, for example, by matching two large decks of cards as described in IV,4. Nobody would expect the law of large numbers to become operative in practice after three

---

[6] The student of modern probability theory may be astonished to hear that as late as 1934 leading experts could question the possibility of formulating the basic limit theorems of probability in purely analytic terms.

or four matchings. By the same token, when applied to our slot machine the law of large numbers is operationally meaningless unless many millions of trials are involved. Now all fire, automobile, and similar insurance is of the described type; the risk involves a huge sum, but the corresponding probability is very small. Moreover, the insured plays ordinarily only one trial per year, so that the number n of trials never grows large. For him the game is necessarily "unfair," and yet it is usually economically advantageous; the law of large numbers is of no relevance to him. As for the company, it plays a large number of games, but because of the large variance the chance fluctuations are pronounced. The premiums must be fixed so as to preclude a huge loss in any specific year, and hence the company is concerned with the ruin problem rather than the law of large numbers.

*4. THE PETERSBURG GAME

In the classical theory the notion of expectation was not clearly disassociated from the definition of probability, and no mathematical formalism existed to handle it. Random variables with infinite expectations therefore produced insurmountable difficulties, and even quite recent discussions appear strange to the student of modern probability. The importance of variables without expectation has been stressed in the preceding sections, and it seems appropriate here to give an example for the analogue of the law of large numbers in the case of such variables. For that purpose we use the time-honored so-called Petersburg paradox.[7]

A single trial in the Petersburg game consists in tossing a true coin until it falls heads; if this occurs at the rth throw the player receives 2^r dollars. In other words, we are dealing with independent random variables assuming the values 2^1, 2^2, 2^3, ... with corresponding probabilities 2^{-1}, 2^{-2}, 2^{-3}, ... Their expectation is formally defined by $\sum x_r f(x_r)$ with $x_r = 2^r$ and $f(x_r) = 2^{-r}$, so that each term of the series equals 1. Thus the gain has no finite expectation, and the law of large numbers is inapplicable. Now the game becomes less favorable to the player when amended by the rule that he receives nothing if no decision is reached in N tosses (that is, if the coin falls tails N times in succession). The gain in this less favorable game has the finite expectation N, and the law of large numbers applies. It follows that the original game will be "favorable" to the player even if he pays the entrance fee N for each trial. This is true for every N, but the larger N the longer will it take to render a positive gain probable, and so it is

---

* This section should be omitted at first reading.
[7] This paradox was discussed by Daniel Bernoulli (1700–1782). Note that Bernoulli trials are named after James Bernoulli.

meaningless to speak of a "favorable" game. The classical theory concluded that $\mu' = \infty$ is a "fair" entrance fee, but the modern student will hardly understand the mysterious discussions of this "paradox."

It is perfectly possible to determine entrance fees with which the Petersburg game will have all properties of a "fair" game in the classical sense, except that these entrance fees will depend on the number of trials instead of remaining constant. Variable entrance fees are undesirable in gambling halls, but there the Petersburg game is impossible anyway because of limited resources. In the case of a finite expectation $\mu = \mathbf{E}(\mathbf{X}_k) > 0$, a game is called "fair" if for large n the ratio of the accumulated gain $\mathbf{S}_n$ to the accumulated entrance fees e_n is likely to be near 1 (that is, if the difference $\mathbf{S}_n - e_n$ is likely to be of smaller order of magnitude than e_n). If $\mathbf{E}(\mathbf{X}_k)$ does not exist, we cannot keep the entrance fees constant, but must determine e_n in another way. We shall say that a *game with accumulated entrance fees* e_n *is fair in the classical sense if for every* $\epsilon > 0$

(4.1)
$$\mathbf{P}\left\{\left|\frac{\mathbf{S}_n}{e_n} - 1\right| > \epsilon\right\} \to 0.$$

This is the complete analogue of the law of large numbers where $e_n = n\mu'$. The latter is interpreted by the physicist to the effect that the average of n independent measurements is bound to be near μ. In the present instance the average of n measurements is bound to be near e_n/n. Our limit theorem (4.1), when it applies, has a mathematical and operational meaning which does not differ from the law of large numbers.

We shall now show[8] that the *Petersburg game becomes "fair" in the classical sense if we put* $e_n = n \operatorname{Log} n$, where $\operatorname{Log} n$ is the logarithm to the base 2, that is, $2^{\operatorname{Log} n} = n$.

Proof. We use the method of truncation of section 2, this time defining the variables $\mathbf{U}_k$ and $\mathbf{V}_k$ $(k = 1, 2, \ldots, n)$ by

(4.2)
$$\mathbf{U}_k = \mathbf{X}_k, \qquad \mathbf{V}_k = 0 \qquad \text{if} \quad \mathbf{X}_k \leq n \operatorname{Log} n;$$
$$\mathbf{U}_k = 0, \qquad \mathbf{V}_k = \mathbf{X}_k \qquad \text{if} \quad \mathbf{X}_k > n \operatorname{Log} n.$$

Then

(4.3) $\quad \mathbf{P}\{|e_n^{-1}\mathbf{S}_n - 1| > \epsilon\} \leq \mathbf{P}\{|\mathbf{U}_1 + \cdots + \mathbf{U}_n - e_n| > \epsilon e_n\}$
$$+ \mathbf{P}\{\mathbf{V}_1 + \cdots + \mathbf{V}_n \neq 0\}$$

because the event on the left cannot occur unless at least one of the events

---

[8] This is a special case of a generalized law of large numbers from which necessary and sufficient conditions for (4.1) can easily be derived; cf. W. Feller, Acta Scientiarum Litterarum Univ. Szeged, vol. 8 (1937), pp. 191–201.

on the right is realized. Now

$$(4.4) \quad \mathbf{P}\{\mathbf{V}_1 + \cdots + \mathbf{V}_n \neq 0\} \leq n\mathbf{P}\{\mathbf{X}_1 > n \operatorname{Log} n\} \leq \frac{2}{\operatorname{Log} n} \to 0.$$

To verify (4.3) it suffices therefore to prove that

$$(4.5) \qquad \mathbf{P}\{\, |\mathbf{U}_1 + \cdots + \mathbf{U}_n - n \operatorname{Log} n| > \epsilon n \operatorname{Log} n\} \to 0.$$

Put $\mu_n = \mathbf{E}(\mathbf{U}_k)$ and $\sigma_n^2 = \operatorname{Var}(\mathbf{U}_k)$; these quantities depend on n, but are common to $\mathbf{U}_1, \mathbf{U}_2, \ldots, \mathbf{U}_n$. If r is the largest integer such that $2^r \leq n \operatorname{Log} n$, then $\mu_n = r$ and hence for sufficiently large n

$$(4.6) \qquad\qquad \operatorname{Log} n < \mu_n \leq \operatorname{Log} n + \operatorname{Log} \operatorname{Log} n.$$

Similarly

$$(4.7) \quad \sigma_n^2 < \mathbf{E}(\mathbf{U}_k^2) = 2 + 2^2 + \cdots + 2^r < 2^{r+1} \leq 2n \operatorname{Log} n.$$

Since the sum $\mathbf{U}_1 + \cdots + \mathbf{U}_n$ has mean $n\mu_n$ and variance $n\sigma_n^2$, we have by Chebyshev's inequality

$$(4.8) \quad \mathbf{P}\{|\mathbf{U}_1 + \cdots + \mathbf{U}_n - n\mu_n| > \epsilon n\mu_n\} \leq \frac{n\sigma_n^2}{\epsilon^2 n^2 \mu_n^2} < \frac{2}{\epsilon^2 \operatorname{Log} n} \to 0.$$

Now by (4.6) $\mu_n \sim \operatorname{Log} n$, and hence (4.8) is equivalent to (4.5). ▶

5. VARIABLE DISTRIBUTIONS

Up to now we have considered only variables $\mathbf{X}_k$ having the same distribution. This situation corresponds to a repetition of the same game of chance, but it is more interesting to see what happens if the type of game changes at each step. It is not necessary to think of gambling places; the statistician who applies statistical tests is engaged in a dignified sort of gambling, and in his case the distribution of the random variables changes from occasion to occasion.

To fix ideas we shall imagine that an infinite sequence of probability distributions is given so that for each n we have n mutually independent variables $\mathbf{X}_1, \ldots, \mathbf{X}_n$ with the prescribed distributions. We assume that the means and variances exist and put

$$(5.1) \qquad\qquad \mu_k = \mathbf{E}(\mathbf{X}_k), \qquad \sigma_k^2 = \operatorname{Var}(\mathbf{X}_k).$$

The sum $\mathbf{S}_n = \mathbf{X}_1 + \cdots + \mathbf{X}_n$ has mean m_n and variance s_n^2 given by

$$(5.2) \qquad\qquad m_n = \mu_1 + \cdots + \mu_n, \qquad s_n^2 = \sigma_1^2 + \cdots + \sigma_n^2$$

[cf. IX,(2.4) and IX,(5.6)]. In the special case of identical distributions we had $m_n = n\mu$, $s_n^2 = n\sigma^2$.

The (weak) *law of large numbers is said to hold for the sequence* $\{X_k\}$ *if for every* $\epsilon > 0$

$$(5.3) \qquad \mathbf{P}\left\{\frac{|\mathbf{S}_n - m_n|}{n} > \epsilon\right\} \to 0.$$

The sequence $\{X_k\}$ *is said to obey the central limit theorem if for every fixed* $\alpha < \beta$

$$(5.4) \qquad \mathbf{P}\left\{\alpha < \frac{\mathbf{S}_n - m_n}{s_n} < \beta\right\} \to \mathfrak{N}(\beta) - \mathfrak{N}(\alpha).$$

It is one of the salient features of probability theory that both the law of large numbers and the central limit theorem hold for a surprisingly large class of sequences $\{X_k\}$. In particular, *the law of large numbers holds whenever the* X_k *are uniformly bounded*, that is, whenever there exists a constant A such that $|X_k| < A$ for all k. More generally, *a sufficient condition for the law of large numbers to hold is that*

$$(5.5) \qquad \frac{s_n}{n} \to 0.$$

This is a direct consequence of the Chebyshev inequality, and the proof given in the opening passage of section 2 applies. Note, however, that the condition (5.5) is not necessary (cf. problem 14).

Various sufficient conditions for the central limit theorem have been discovered, but all were superseded by the *Lindeberg*[9] *theorem according to which the central limit theorem holds whenever for every* $\epsilon > 0$ *the truncated variables* $\mathbf{U}_k$ *defined by*

$$(5.6) \qquad \begin{aligned} \mathbf{U}_k &= \mathbf{X}_k - \mu_k & \text{if } \ |\mathbf{X}_k - \mu_k| \leq \epsilon s_n, \\ \mathbf{U}_k &= 0 & \text{if } \ |\mathbf{X}_k - \mu_k| > \epsilon s_n, \end{aligned}$$

satisfy the conditions $s_n \to \infty$ *and*

$$(5.7) \qquad \frac{1}{s_n^2}\sum_{k=1}^{n}\mathbf{E}(\mathbf{U}_k^2) \to 1.$$

If the $\mathbf{X}_k$ are uniformly bounded, that is, if $|\mathbf{X}_k| < A$, then $\mathbf{U}_k = = \mathbf{X}_k - \mu_k$ for all n which are so large that $s_n > 2A\epsilon^{-1}$. The left side in (5.7) then equals 1. Therefore the Lindeberg theorem implies that *every uniformly bounded sequence* $\{X_k\}$ *of mutually independent random variables*

---

[9] J. W. Lindeberg, *loc. cit.* (footnote 3).

obeys the central limit theorem, provided, of course, that $s_n \to \infty$. It was found that the Lindeberg conditions are also necessary for (5.4) to hold.[10] The proof is deferred to the second volume, where we shall also give estimates for the difference between the two sides in (5.4).

When variables X_k have a common distribution we found the central limit theorem to be stronger than the law of large numbers. This is not so in general, and we shall see that the central limit theorem may apply to sequences which do not obey the law of large numbers.

Examples. (*a*) Let $\lambda > 0$ be fixed, and let $X_k = \pm k^\lambda$, each with probability $\frac{1}{2}$ (e.g., a coin is tossed, and at the kth throw the stakes are $\pm k^\lambda$). Here $\mu_k = 0$, $\sigma_k^2 = k^{2\lambda}$, and

$$(5.8) \qquad s_n^2 = 1^{2\lambda} + 2^{2\lambda} + 3^{2\lambda} + \cdots + n^{2\lambda} \sim \frac{n^{2\lambda+1}}{2\lambda + 1}.$$

The condition (5.5) is satisfied if $\lambda < \frac{1}{2}$. Therefore the law of large numbers holds if $\lambda < \frac{1}{2}$; we proceed to show that it does not hold if $\lambda \geq \frac{1}{2}$.

For $k = 1, 2, \ldots, n$ we have $|X_k| = k^\lambda \leq n^\lambda$, so that for $n > (2\lambda+1)\epsilon^{-2}$ the truncated variables U_k are identical with the X_k. Hence the Lindeberg condition holds, and so

$$(5.9) \qquad \mathbf{P}\left\{ \alpha < \sqrt{\frac{2\lambda + 1}{n^{2\lambda+1}}}\, \mathbf{S}_n < \beta \right\} \to \mathfrak{N}(\beta) - \mathfrak{N}(\alpha).$$

It follows that $\mathbf{S}_n$ is likely to be of the order of magnitude $n^{\lambda+\frac{1}{2}}$, so that the law of large numbers cannot apply for $\lambda \geq \frac{1}{2}$. We see that in this example *the central limit theorem applies for all $\lambda > 0$, but the law of large numbers only if $\lambda < \frac{1}{2}$.*

(*b*) Consider two independent sequences of 1000 tossings of a coin (or emptying two bags of 1000 coins each), and let us examine the *difference* **D** of the number of heads. Let the tossings of the two sequences be numbered from 1 to 1000 and from 1001 to 2000, respectively and define 2000 random variables X_k as follows: If the kth coin falls tails, then $X_k = 0$. If it falls heads, we put $X_k = 1$ for $k \leq 1000$ and $X_k = -1$, for $k > 1000$. Then $\mathbf{D} = X_1 + \cdots + X_{2000}$. The variables X_k have mean $\mu_k = \pm\frac{1}{2}$ and variance $\sigma_k^2 = \frac{1}{4}$, and hence $\mathbf{E}(\mathbf{D}) = 0$ and $\mathrm{Var}(\mathbf{D}) = 500$. Thus the probability that the difference **D** will lie within

---

[10] W. Feller, *Über den zentralen Grenzwertsatz der Wahrscheinlichkeitsrechnung* Mathematische Zeitschrift, vol. 40 (1935), pp. 521–559. There also a generalized central limit theorem is derived which may apply to variables without expectations. Note that we are here considering only independent variables; for dependent variables the Lindeberg condition is neither necessary nor sufficient.

the limits $\pm\sqrt{500}\alpha$ is $\mathfrak{N}(\alpha) - \mathfrak{N}(-\alpha)$, approximately, and $\mathbf{D}$ is comparable to the deviation $\mathbf{S}_{2000} - 1000$ of the number of heads in 2000 tossings from its expected number 1000.

(c) An application to the *theory of inheritance* will illustrate the great variety of conclusions based on the central limit theorem. In V,5, we studied traits which depend essentially only on one pair of genes (alleles). We conceive of other characters (like height) as the cumulative effect of many pairs of genes. For simplicity, suppose that for each particular pair of genes there exist three genotypes AA, Aa, or aa. Let x_1, x_2, and x_3 be the corresponding contributions. The genotype of an individual is a random event, and the contribution of a particular pair of genes to the height is a random variable $\mathbf{X}$, assuming the three values x_1, x_2, x_3 with certain probabilities. The height is the cumulative effect of many such random variables $\mathbf{X}_1, \mathbf{X}_2, \ldots, \mathbf{X}_n$, and since the contribution of each is small, we may in first approximation assume that the height is the *sum* $\mathbf{X}_1 + \cdots + \mathbf{X}_n$. It is true that not *all* the $\mathbf{X}_k$ are mutually independent. But the central limit theorem holds also for large classes of dependent variables, and, besides, it is plausible that the great majority of the $\mathbf{X}_k$ can be treated as independent. These considerations can be rendered more precise; here they serve only as indication of how the central limit theorem explains why many biometric characters, like height, exhibit an empirical distribution close to the normal distribution. This theory permits also the prediction of properties of inheritance, e.g., the dependence of the mean height of children on the height of their parents. Such biometric investigations were initiated by F. Galton and Karl Pearson.[11]   ▶

*6. APPLICATIONS TO COMBINATORIAL ANALYSIS

We shall give two examples of applications of the central limit theorem to problems not directly connected with probability theory. Both relate to the $n!$ permutations of the n elements $a_1, a_2, \ldots, a_n$, to each of which we attribute probability $1/n!$.

(a) **Inversions.** In a given permutation the element a_k is said to induce r inversions if it precedes exactly r elements with smaller index (i.e., elements which precede a_k in the natural order). For example, in $(a_3 a_6 a_1 a_5 a_2 a_4)$ the elements a_1 and a_2 induce no inversion, a_3 induces two, a_4 none, a_5 two, and a_6 four. In $(a_6 a_5 a_4 a_3 a_2 a_1)$ the element a_k induces $k - 1$ inversions and there are fifteen inversions in all. The

---

[11] Sir Francis Galton (1822–1911); Karl Pearson (1857–1936).

* This section treats a special topic and may be omitted.

number $\mathbf{X}_k$ of inversions induced by a_k is a random variable, and $\mathbf{S}_n = \mathbf{X}_1 + \cdots + \mathbf{X}_n$ is the total number of inversions. Here $\mathbf{X}_k$ assumes the values $0, 1, \ldots, k-1$, each with probability $1/k$, and therefore

$$\mu_k = \frac{k-1}{2},$$

(6.1)

$$\sigma_k^2 = \frac{1 + 2^2 + \cdots + (k-1)^2}{k} - \left(\frac{k-1}{2}\right)^2 = \frac{k^2-1}{12}.$$

The number of inversions produced by a_k does not depend on the relative order of $a_1, a_2, \ldots, a_{k-1}$, and the $\mathbf{X}_k$ are therefore mutually independent. From (6.1) we get

(6.2) $$m_n = \frac{1 + 2 + \cdots + (n-1)}{2} = \frac{n(n-1)}{4} \sim \frac{n^2}{4}$$

and

(6.3) $$s_n^2 = \frac{1}{12} \sum_{k=1}^{n}(k^2-1) = \frac{2n^3 + 3n^2 - 5n}{72} \sim \frac{n^3}{36}.$$

For large n we have $\epsilon s_n > n \geq \mathbf{U}_k$, and hence the variables $\mathbf{U}_k$ of the Lindeberg condition are identical with $\mathbf{X}_k$. Therefore the central limit theorem applies, and we conclude that the *number $\mathbf{N}_n$ of permutations for which the number of inversions lies between the limits* $\frac{n^2}{4} \pm \frac{\alpha}{6}\sqrt{n^3}$ *is, asymptotically, given by* $n!\{\mathfrak{N}(\alpha) - \mathfrak{N}(-\alpha)\}$. In particular, for about one-half of all permutations the number of inversions lies between the limits $\frac{1}{4}n^2 \pm 0.11\sqrt{n^3}$.

(b) Cycles. Every permutation can be broken down into cycles, that is, groups of elements permuted among themselves. Thus in $(a_3a_6a_1a_5a_2a_4)$ we find that a_1 and a_3 are interchanged, and that the remaining four elements are permuted among themselves; this permutation contains two cycles. If an element is in its natural place, it forms a cycle so that the identity permutation $(a_1, a_2, \ldots, a_n)$ contains as many cycles as elements. On the other hand, the cyclical permutations $(a_2, a_3, \ldots, a_n, a_1)$, $(a_3, a_4, \ldots, a_n, a_1, a_2)$, etc., contain a single cycle each. For the study of cycles it is convenient to describe the pemutation by means of arrows indicating the places occupied by the several elements. For example, $1 \to 3 \to 4 \to 1$ indicates that a_1 is at the third place, a_3 at the fourth, and a_4 at the first, the third step thus completing the cycle. This description continues with a_2, which is the next element in the natural order. In this notation the permutation $(a_4, a_8, a_1, a_3, a_2, a_5, a_7, a_6)$ is described by: $1\to3\to4\to1$; $2\to5\to6\to8\to2$; $7\to7$. In other words, we construct a permutation $(a_1, \ldots, a_n)$ by a succession of n decisions. First we choose the place i to be occupied by a_1, next the place to be occupied by a_i, and so forth. At the 1st, 2nd, $\ldots$, nth step we have $n, n-1, \ldots, 1$ choices and exactly one among them completes a cycle.

Let X_k equal 1 if a cycle is completed at the kth step in this build-up; otherwise let $X_k = 0$. (In the last example $X_3 = X_7 = X_8 = 1$ and $X_1 = X_2 = X_4 = X_5 = X_6 = 0$.) Clearly $X_1 = 1$ if, and only if, a_1 is at the first place. From our construction it follows that $P\{X_k = 1\} =$

$$= \frac{1}{n-k+1} \quad \text{and} \quad P\{X_k = 0\} = \frac{n-k}{n-k+1}, \quad \text{and that the variables } X_k$$

are mutually independent.[12] Their means and variances are

$$(6.4) \qquad \mu_k = \frac{1}{n-k+1}, \qquad \sigma_k^2 = \frac{n-k}{(n-k+1)^2}$$

whence

$$(6.5) \qquad m_n = 1 + \frac{1}{2} + \frac{1}{3} + \cdots + \frac{1}{n} \sim \log n$$

and

$$(6.6) \qquad s_n^2 = \sum_{k=1}^{n} \frac{n-k}{(n-k+1)^2} \sim \log n.$$

$S_n = X_1 + \cdots + X_n$ is the total number of cycles. *Its average is m_n; and the number of permutations with cycles between $\log n + \alpha\sqrt{\log n}$ and $\log n + \beta\sqrt{\log n}$ is given by $n!\{\mathfrak{N}(\beta)-\mathfrak{N}(\alpha)\}$, approximately.* The refined forms of the central limit theorem give more precise estimates.[13]

*7. THE STRONG LAW OF LARGE NUMBERS

The (weak) law of large numbers (5.3) asserts that for every particular sufficiently large n the deviation $|S_n - m_n|$ is likely to be small in comparison to n. It has been pointed out in connection with Bernoulli trials

---

[12] Formally, the distribution of X_k depends not only on k but also on n. It suffices to reorder the X_k, starting from $k = n$ down to $k = 1$, to have the distribution depend only on the subscript. [See also example XI, (2.e).]

[13] A great variety of asymptotic estimates in combinatorial analysis were derived by other methods by V. Gončarov, *Du domaine d'analyse combinatoire*, Bulletin de l'Académie Sciences URSS, Sér. Math. (in Russian, French summary), vol. 8 (1944), pp. 3–48. The present method is simpler but more restricted in scope; cf. W. Feller, *The fundamental limit theorems in probability*, Bull. Amer. Math. Soc., vol. 51 (1945), pp. 800–832.

* This section treats a special topic and may be omitted.

(chapter VIII) that this does not imply that $|S_n - m_n|/n$ remains small for all large n; it can happen that the law of large numbers applies but that $|S_n - m_n|/n$ continues to fluctuate between finite or infinite limits. The law of large numbers permits only the conclusion that large values of $|S_n - m_n|/n$ occur at infrequent moments.

We say that the sequence X_k *obeys the strong law of large numbers if to every pair* $\epsilon > 0$, $\delta > 0$, *there corresponds an* N *such that there is probability* $1 - \delta$ *or better that for every* $r > 0$ *all* $r + 1$ *inequalities*

(7.1)
$$\frac{|S_n - m_n|}{n} < \epsilon, \qquad n = N, N + 1, \ldots, N + r$$

will be satisfied.

We can interpret (7.1) roughly by saying that with an overwhelming probability $|S_n - m_n|/n$ remains small[14] for all $n > N$.

The Kolmogorov Criterion. *The convergence of the series*

(7.2)
$$\sum \sigma_k^2/k^2$$

is a sufficient condition for the strong law of large numbers to apply to the sequence of mutually independent random variables X_k *with variances* σ_k^2.

Proof. Let A_ν be the event that for at least one n with $2^{\nu-1} < n \leq 2^\nu$ the inequality (7.1) does *not* hold. Obviously it suffices to prove that for all ν sufficiently large and all r

$$P\{A_\nu\} + P\{A_{\nu+1}\} + \cdots + P\{A_{\nu+r}\} < \delta,$$

that is, that the series $\sum P\{A_\nu\}$ converges. Now the event A_ν implies that for some n with $2^{\nu-1} < n \leq 2^\nu$

(7.3)
$$|S_n - m_n| \geq \epsilon \cdot 2^{\nu-1}$$

and by Kolmogorov's inequality of IX,7

(7.4)
$$P\{A_\nu\} \leq 4\epsilon^{-2} \cdot s_{2^\nu}^2 \cdot 2^{-2\nu}.$$

Hence

(7.5)
$$\sum_{\nu=1}^{\infty} P\{A_\nu\} \leq 4\epsilon^{-2} \sum_{\nu=1}^{\infty} 2^{-2\nu} \sum_{k=1}^{2^\nu} \sigma_k^2 = 4\epsilon^{-2} \sum_{k=1}^{\infty} \sigma_k^2 \sum_{2^\nu \geq k} 2^{-2\nu} \leq 8\epsilon^{-2} \sum_{k=1}^{\infty} \frac{\sigma_k^2}{k^2}$$

which accomplishes the proof.   ▶

----

[14] The general theory introduces a sample space corresponding to the infinite sequence $\{X_k\}$. The strong law then states that with probability one $|S_n - m_n|/n$ tends to zero. In real variable terminology the strong law asserts convergence almost everywhere, and the weak law is equivalent to convergence in measure.

As a typical application we prove the

Theorem. *If the mutually independent random variables* $\mathbf{X}_k$ *have a common distribution* $\{f(x_j)\}$ *and if* $\mu = \mathbf{E}(\mathbf{X}_k)$ *exists, then the strong law of large numbers applies to the sequence* $\{\mathbf{X}_k\}$.

This theorem is, of course, stronger than the weak law of section 1. The two theorems are treated independently because of the methodological interest of the proofs. For a converse cf. problems 17 and 18.

Proof. We again use the method of truncation. Two new sequences of random variables are introduced by

(7.6)
$$\mathbf{U}_k = \mathbf{X}_k, \qquad \mathbf{V}_k = 0 \qquad\quad if \;\; |\mathbf{X}_k| < k,$$
$$\mathbf{U}_k = 0, \qquad\;\; \mathbf{V}_k = \mathbf{X}_k \qquad\;\; if \;\; |\mathbf{X}_k| \geq k.$$

The $\mathbf{U}_k$ are mutually independent, and we proceed to show that they satisfy Kolmogorov's criterion. For $\sigma_k^2 = \mathrm{Var}(\mathbf{U}_k)$ we get

(7.7)
$$\sigma_k^2 \leq \mathbf{E}(\mathbf{U}_k^2) = \sum_{|x_j| < k} x_j^2 f(x_j).$$

Put for abbreviation

(7.8)
$$a_v = \sum_{v-1 \leq |x_j| < v} |x_j|\, f(x_j).$$

Then the series $\sum a_v$ converges since $\mathbf{E}(\mathbf{X}_k)$ exists. Moreover, from (7.7),

(7.9)
$$\sigma_k^2 \leq a_1 + 2a_2 + 3a_3 + \cdots + ka_k$$
and

(7.10)
$$\sum_{k=1}^{\infty} \frac{\sigma_k^2}{k^2} \leq \sum_{k=1}^{\infty} \frac{1}{k^2} \sum_{v=1}^{k} v a_v = \sum_{v=1}^{\infty} v a_v \sum_{k=v}^{\infty} \frac{1}{k^2} < 2 \sum_{v=1}^{\infty} a_v < \infty.$$

Thus the criterion (7.2) holds for $\{\mathbf{U}_k\}$. Now

(7.11)
$$\mathbf{E}(\mathbf{U}_k) = \mu_k = \sum_{|x_j| < k} x_j f(x_j)$$

so that $\mu_k \to \mu$ and hence $(\mu_1 + \mu_2 + \cdots + \mu_n)/n \to \mu$. From the strong law of large numbers for $\{\mathbf{U}_k\}$ we conclude therefore that with probability $1 - \delta$ or better

(7.12)
$$\left| n^{-1} \sum_{k=1}^{n} \mathbf{U}_k - \mu \right| < \epsilon$$

for *all* $n > N$ provided N is chosen sufficiently large. It remains to prove that the same assertion holds true when the $\mathbf{U}_k$ are replaced by

$\mathbf{X}_k$. It suffices obviously to show that N can be chosen so large that with a probability arbitrarily close to unity the event $\mathbf{U}_k = \mathbf{X}_k$ occurs for all $k > N$. This amounts to saying that with probability one only finitely many among the variables $\mathbf{V}_k$ are different from zero. By the first Borel-Cantelli lemma of VIII,3 this is the case whenever the series $\sum \mathbf{P}\{\mathbf{V}_k \neq 0\}$ converges, and we now complete the proof by establishing the convergence of this series. Obviously

$$(7.13) \quad \mathbf{P}\{\mathbf{V}_n \neq 0\} = \sum_{|x_j| \geq n} f(x_j) \leq \frac{a_{n+1}}{n} + \frac{a_{n+2}}{n+1} + \frac{a_{n+3}}{n+2} + \cdots$$

and hence

$$(7.14) \quad \sum \mathbf{P}\{\mathbf{V}_n \neq 0\} \leq \sum_{n=1}^{\infty} \sum_{\nu=n}^{\infty} \frac{a_{\nu+1}}{\nu} = \sum_{\nu=1}^{\infty} \frac{a_{\nu+1}}{\nu} \sum_{n=1}^{\nu} 1 = \sum_{\nu} a_{\nu+1} < \infty,$$

as asserted.

8. PROBLEMS FOR SOLUTION

1. Prove that the law of large numbers applies in example (5.a) also when $\lambda \leq 0$. The central limit theorem holds if $\lambda \geq -\frac{1}{2}$.

2. Decide whether the law of large numbers and the central limit theorem hold for the sequences of mutually independent variables $\mathbf{X}_k$ with distributions defined as follows $(k \geq 1)$:

(a) $\mathbf{P}\{\mathbf{X}_k = \pm 2^k\} = \frac{1}{2}$;

(b) $\mathbf{P}\{\mathbf{X}_k = \pm 2^k\} = 2^{-(2k+1)}$, $\mathbf{P}\{\mathbf{X}_k = 0\} = 1 - 2^{-2k}$;

(c) $\mathbf{P}\{\mathbf{X}_k = \pm k\} = 1/(2\sqrt{k})$, $\mathbf{P}\{\mathbf{X}_k = 0\} = 1 - 1/\sqrt{k}$.

3. *Ljapunov's condition* (1901). Show that Lindeberg's condition is satisfied if for some $\delta > 0$

$$\frac{1}{s_m^{2+\delta}} \sum_{k=1}^{n} \mathbf{E}|(\mathbf{X}_k|^{2+\delta}) \to 0.$$

4. Let the $\mathbf{X}_k$ be mutually independent random variables such that $\mathbf{X}_k$ assumes the $2k + 1$ values $0, \pm L_k, \pm 2L_k, \ldots, \pm kL_k$, each with probability $1/(2k+1)$. Find conditions on the constants L_k which will ensure that the law of large numbers and/or the central limit theorem holds for $\{\mathbf{X}_k\}$.

5. Do the same problem if $\mathbf{X}_k$ assumes the values a_k, $-a_k$, and 0 with probabilities p_k, p_k and $1 - 2p_k$.

Note: *The following seven problems treat the weak law of large numbers for dependent variables.*

6. In problem 13 of V, 8 let $\mathbf{X}_k = 1$ if the kth throw results in red, and $\mathbf{X}_k = 0$ otherwise. Show that the law of large numbers does not apply.

7. Let the $\{\mathbf{X}_k\}$ be mutually independent and have a common distribution with mean μ and finite variance. If $\mathbf{S}_n = \mathbf{X}_1 + \cdots + \mathbf{X}_n$, prove that the law

of large numbers does not hold for the sequence $\{S_n\}$ but holds for $a_n S_n$ if $na_n \to 0$. *Hint:* Calculate $\text{Var}(S_1, \ldots, S_n)/n$.

8. Let $\{X_k\}$ be a sequence of random variables such that X_k may depend on X_{k-1} and X_{k+1} but is independent of all other X_j. Show that the law of large numbers holds, provided the X_k have bounded variances.

9. If the joint distribution of $(X_1, \ldots, X_n)$ is defined for every n so that the variances are bounded and all covariances are negative, the law of large numbers applies.

10. *Continuation.* Replace the condition $\text{Cov}(X_j, X_k) \leq 0$ by the assumption that $\text{Cov}(X_j, X_k) \to 0$ uniformly as $|j - k| \to \infty$. Prove that the law of large numbers holds.

11. If $|S_n| < cn$ and $\text{Var}(S_n) > \alpha n^2$, then the law of large numbers does not apply to $\{X_k\}$.

12. In the Polya urn scheme [example V, $(2.c)$] let X_k equal 1 or 0 according to whether the kth ball drawn is black or red. Then S_n is the number of black balls in n drawings. Prove that the law of large numbers does not apply to $\{X_k\}$. *Hint:* Use the preceding problem and problem 30 of IX, 9.

---

13. The mutually independent random variables X_k assume the values $r = 2, 3, 4, \ldots$ with probability $p_r = c/(r^2 \log r)$ where c is a constant such that $\sum p_r = 1$. Show that the generalized law of large numbers (4.1) holds if we put $e_n = c \cdot n \log \log n$.

14. Let $\{X_n\}$ be a sequence of mutually independent random variables such that $X_n = \pm 1$ with probability $(1 - 2^{-n})/2$ and $X_n = \pm 2^n$ with probability 2^{-n-1}. Prove that both the weak and the strong law of large numbers apply to $\{X_k\}$. [*Note:* This shows that the condition (5.5) is not necessary.]

15. *Example of an unfavorable "fair" game.* Let the possible values of the gain at each trial be $0, 2, 2^2, 2^3, \ldots$; the probability of the gain being 2^k is

(8.1)
$$p_k = \frac{1}{2^k k(k+1)},$$

and the probability of 0 is $p_0 = 1 - (p_1 + p_2 + \cdots)$. The expected gain is

(8.2) $\mu = \sum 2^k p_k = (1 - \tfrac{1}{2}) + (\tfrac{1}{2} - \tfrac{1}{3}) + (\tfrac{1}{3} - \tfrac{1}{4}) + \cdots = 1.$

Assume that at each trial the player pays a unit amount as entrance fee, so that after n trials his net gain (or loss) is $S_n - n$. Show that for every $\epsilon > 0$ *the probability approaches unity that in n trials the player will have sustained a loss greater than* $(1 - \epsilon)n/\text{Log}_2 n$, where $\text{Log}_2 n$ denotes the logarithm to the base 2. In symbols, prove that

(8.3) $\mathbf{P}\left\{ S_n - n < -\frac{(1-\epsilon)n}{\text{Log}_2 n} \right\} \to 1,$

Hint: Use the truncation method of section 4, but replace the bound $n \text{ Log } n$ of (4.2) by $n/\text{Log}_2 n$. Show that the probability that $U_k = X_k$ for all $k \leq n$

tends to 1 and prove that

(8.4) $$\mathbf{P}\left\{|\mathbf{U}_1 + \cdots + \mathbf{U}_n - n\mathbf{E}(\mathbf{U}_1)| < \frac{\epsilon n}{\mathrm{Log}_2\, n}\right\} \to 1.$$

(8.5) $$1 - \frac{1}{\mathrm{Log}_2\, n} \geq \mathbf{E}(\mathbf{U}_1) \geq 1 - \frac{1 + \epsilon}{\mathrm{Log}_2\, n}\,.$$

For details see the paper cited in footnote 5.

16. Let $\{\mathbf{X}_n\}$ be a sequence of mutually independent random variables with a common distribution. Suppose that the $\mathbf{X}_n$ do not have a finite expectation and let A be a positive constant. The probability is one that infinitely many among the events $|\mathbf{X}_n| > An$ occur.

17. *Converse to the strong law of large numbers.* Under the assumption of problem 16 there is probability one that $|\mathbf{S}_n| > An$ for infinitely many n.

18. *A converse to Kolmogorov's criterion.* If $\sum \sigma_k^2/k^2$ diverges, then there exists a sequence $\{\mathbf{X}_k\}$ of mutually independent random variables with Var $\{\mathbf{X}_k\} = \sigma_k^2$ for which the strong law of large numbers does not apply. *Hint:* Prove first that the convergence of $\sum \mathbf{P}\{|\mathbf{X}_n| > \epsilon n\}$ is a necessary condition for the strong law to apply.

CHAPTER XI

Integral-Valued Variables.
Generating Functions

1. GENERALITIES

Among discrete random variables those assuming only the integral values $k = 0, 1, 2, \ldots$ are of special importance. Their study is facilitated by the powerful method of generating functions which will later be recognized as a special case of the method of characteristic functions on which the theory of probability depends to a large extent. More generally, the subject of generating functions belongs to the domain of operational methods which are widely used in the theory of differential and integral equations. In the theory of probability generating functions have been used since DeMoivre and Laplace, but the power and the possibilities of the method are rarely fully utilized.

Definition. *Let $a_0, a_1, a_2, \ldots$ be a sequence of real numbers. If*

$$(1.1) \qquad A(s) = a_0 + a_1 s + a_2 s^2 + \cdots$$

converges in some interval $-s_0 < s < s_0$, then $A(s)$ is called the generating function of the sequence $\{a_j\}$.

The variable s itself has no significance. If the sequence $\{a_j\}$ is bounded, then a comparison with the geometric series shows that (1.1) converges at least for $|s| < 1$.

Examples. If $a_j = 1$ for all j, then $A(s) = 1/(1-s)$. The generating function of the sequence $(0, 0, 1, 1, 1, \ldots)$ is $s^2/(1-s)$. The sequence $a_j = 1/j!$ has the generating function e^s. For fixed n the sequence $a_j = \binom{n}{j}$ has the generating function $(1+s)^n$. If $\mathbf{X}$ is the number scored in a throw of a perfect die, the probability distribution of $\mathbf{X}$ has the generating function $(s+s^2+s^3+s^4+s^5+s^6)/6$. ▶

264

Let X be a random variable assuming the values $0, 1, 2, \ldots$. It will be convenient to have a notation both for the distribution of X and for its tails, and we shall write

(1.2) $$P\{X = j\} = p_j, \qquad P\{X > j\} = q_j.$$

Then

(1.3) $$q_k = p_{k+1} + p_{k+2} + \cdots \qquad\qquad k \geq 0.$$

The generating functions of the sequences $\{p_j\}$ and $\{q_k\}$ are

(1.4) $$P(s) = p_0 + p_1 s + p_2 s^2 + p_3 s^3 + \cdots$$

(1.5) $$Q(s) = q_0 + q_1 s + q_2 s^2 + q_3 s^3 + \cdots .$$

As $P(1) = 1$, *the series for* $P(s)$ *converges absolutely at least for* $-1 \leq s \leq 1$. The coefficients of $Q(s)$ are less than unity, and so *the series for* $Q(s)$ *converges at least in the open interval* $-1 < s < 1$.

Theorem 1. *For* $-1 < s < 1$

(1.6) $$Q(s) = \frac{1 - P(s)}{1 - s}.$$

Proof. The coefficient of s^n in $(1-s) \cdot Q(s)$ equals $q_n - q_{n-1} = -p_n$ when $n \geq 1$, and equals $q_0 = p_1 + p_2 + \cdots = 1 - p_0$ when $n = 0$. Therefore $(1-s) \cdot Q(s) = 1 - P(s)$ as asserted. ▶

Next we examine the derivative

(1.7) $$P'(s) = \sum_{k=1}^{\infty} k p_k s^{k-1}.$$

The series converges at least for $-1 < s < 1$. For $s = 1$ the right side reduces formally to $\sum k p_k = E(X)$. Whenever this expectation exists, the derivative $P'(s)$ will be continuous in the closed interval $-1 \leq s \leq 1$. If $\sum k p_k$ diverges, then $P'(s) \to \infty$ as $s \to 1$. In this case we say that X *has an infinite expectation* and write $P'(1) = E(X) = \infty$. (All quantities being positive, there is no danger in the use of the symbol ∞.) Applying the mean value theorem to the numerator in (1.6), we see that $Q(s) = P'(\sigma)$ where σ is a point lying between s and 1. Since both functions are monotone this implies that $P'(s)$ and $Q(s)$ have the same finite or infinite limit which we denote by $P'(1)$ or $Q(1)$. This proves

Theorem 2. *The expectation* $E(X)$ *satisfies the relations*

(1.8) $$E(X) = \sum_{j=1}^{\infty} j p_j = \sum_{k=0}^{\infty} q_k,$$

or in terms of the generating functions,

(1.9) $$E(X) = P'(1) = Q(1).$$

By differentiation of (1.7) and of the relation $P'(s) = Q(s) - (1-s)Q'(s)$ we find in the same way

(1.10) $$E(X(X-1)) = \sum k(k-1)p_k = P''(1) = 2Q'(1).$$

To obtain the variance of X we have to add $E(X) - E^2(X)$ which leads us to

Theorem 3. *We have*

(1.11) $$\text{Var}(X) = P''(1) + P'(1) - P'^2(1) =$$
$$= 2Q'(1) + Q(1) - Q^2(1).$$

In the case of an infinite variance $P''(s) \to \infty$ as $s \to 1$.

The realtions (1.9) and (1.11) frequently provide the simplest means to calculate $E(X)$ and $\text{Var}(X)$.

2. CONVOLUTIONS

If a random variable X assumes only non-negative integral values, then s^X is a well-defined new random variable, and the generating function of the distribution of X can be written in the compact form $E(s^X)$. If X and Y are independent, so are s^X and s^Y, and hence

$$E(s^{X+Y}) = E(s^X)E(s^Y).$$

We proceed to give a different proof for this important result because it will lead us to a useful generalization.

Let X and Y be non-negative independent integral-valued random variables with probability distributions $P\{X = j\} = a_j$ and $P\{Y = j\} = b_j$. The event $(X = j, Y = k)$ has probability $a_j b_k$. The sum $S = X + Y$ is a new random variable, and the event $S = r$ is the union of the mutually exclusive events

$$(X = 0, Y = r), \quad (X = 1, Y = r - 1), \ldots, (X = r, Y = 0).$$

Therefore the distribution $c_r = P\{S = r\}$ is given by

(2.1) $$c_r = a_0 b_r + a_1 b_{r-1} + a_2 b_{r-2} + \cdots + a_{r-1} b_1 + a_r b_0.$$

The operation (2.1), leading from the two sequences $\{a_k\}$ and $\{b_k\}$ to a new sequence $\{c_k\}$, occurs so frequently that it is convenient to introduce a special name and notation for it.

Definition. *Let* $\{a_k\}$ *and* $\{b_k\}$ *be any two numerical sequences (not necessarily probability distributions). The new sequence* $\{c_r\}$ *defined by* (2.1) *is called the convolution[1] of* $\{a_k\}$ *and* $\{b_k\}$ *and will be denoted by*

$$(2.2) \qquad \{c_k\} = \{a_k\} * \{b_k\}.$$

Examples. (*a*) If $a_k = b_k = 1$ for all $k \geq 0$, then $c_k = k + 1$. If $a_k = k$, $b_k = 1$, then $c_k = 1 + 2 + \cdots + k = k(k+1)/2$. Finally, if $a_0 = a_1 = \frac{1}{2}$, $a_k = 0$ for $k \geq 2$, then $c_k = (b_k + b_{k-1})/2$, etc. ▶

The sequences $\{a_k\}$ and $\{b_k\}$ have generating functions $A(s) = \sum a_k s^k$ and $B(s) = \sum b_k s^k$. The product $A(s)B(s)$ can be obtained by termwise multiplication of the power series for $A(s)$ and $B(s)$. Collecting terms with equal powers of s, we find that the coefficient c_r of s^r in the expansion of $A(s)B(s)$ is given by (2.1). We have thus the

Theorem. *If* $\{a_k\}$ *and* $\{b_k\}$ *are sequences with generating functions* $A(s)$ *and* $B(s)$, *and* $\{c_k\}$ *is their convolution, then the generating function* $C(s) = \sum c_k s^k$ *is the product*

$$(2.3) \qquad C(s) = A(s)B(s).$$

If **X** *and* **Y** *are non-negative integral-valued mutually independent random variables with generating functions* $A(s)$ *and* $B(s)$, *then their sum* **X** + **Y** *has the generating function* $A(s)B(s)$.

Let now $\{a_k\}$, $\{b_k\}$, $\{c_k\}$, $\{d_k\}$, . . . be any sequences. We can form the convolution $\{a_k\} * \{b_k\}$, and then the convolution of this new sequence with $\{c_k\}$, etc. The generating function of $\{a_k\} * \{b_k\} * \{c_k\} * \{d_k\}$ is $A(s)B(s)C(s)D(s)$, and this fact shows that the order in which the convolutions are performed is immaterial. For example, $\{a_k\} * \{b_k\} * \{c_k\} = \{c_k\} * \{b_k\} * \{a_k\}$, etc. *Thus the convolution is an associative and commutative operation* (exactly as the summation of random variables).

In the study of sums of independent random variables $\mathbf{X}_n$ the special case where the $\mathbf{X}_n$ have a common distribution is of particular interest. *If* $\{a_j\}$ *is the common probability distribution of the* $\mathbf{X}_n$, *then the distribution of* $\mathbf{S}_n = \mathbf{X}_1 + \cdots + \mathbf{X}_n$ *will be denoted by* $\{a_j\}^{n*}$. Thus

$$(2.4) \qquad \{a_j\}^{2*} = \{a_j\} * \{a_j\}, \qquad \{a_j\}^{3*} = \{a_j\}^{2*} * \{a_j\}, \ldots$$

and generally

$$(2.5) \qquad \{a_j\}^{n*} = \{a_j\}^{(n-1)*} * \{a_j\}.$$

---

[1] Some writers prefer the German word *faltung*. The French equivalent is *composition*.

In words, $\{a_j\}^{n*}$ is the sequence of numbers whose generating function is $A^n(s)$. In particular, $\{a_j\}^{1*}$ is the same as $\{a_j\}$, and $\{a_j\}^{0*}$ is defined as the sequence whose generating function is $A^0(s) = 1$, that is, the sequence $(1, 0, 0, 0, \ldots)$.

Examples. (b) *Binomial distribution.* The generating function of the binomial distribution with terms $b(k; n, p) = \binom{n}{k} p^k q^{n-k}$ is

$$(2.6) \qquad \sum_{k=0}^{n} \binom{n}{k} (ps)^k q^{n-k} = (q + ps)^n.$$

The fact that this generating function is the nth power of $q + ps$ shows that $\{b(k; n, p)\}$ is the distribution of a sum $\mathbf{S}_n = \mathbf{X}_1 + \cdots + \mathbf{X}_n$ of n independent random variables with the common generating function $q + ps$; each variable $\mathbf{X}_j$ assumes the value 0 with probability q and the value 1 with probability p. Thus

$$(2.7) \qquad \{b(k; n, p)\} = \{b(k; 1, p)\}^{n*}.$$

The representation $\mathbf{S}_n = \mathbf{X}_1 + \cdots + \mathbf{X}_n$ has already been used [e.g., in examples IX,(3.a) and IX, (5.a)]. The preceding argument may be reversed to obtain a new derivation of the binomial distribution. The mutliplicative property $(q+ps)^m(q+ps)^n = (q+ps)^{m+n}$ shows also that

$$(2.8) \qquad \{b(k; m, p)\} * \{b(k; n, p)\} = \{b(k; m+n, p)\}$$

which is the same as VI,(10.4). Differentiation of $(q+ps)^n$ leads also to a simple proof that $\mathbf{E}(\mathbf{S}_n) = np$ and $\mathrm{Var}\,(\mathbf{S}_n) = npq$.

(c) *Poisson distribution.* The generating function of the distribution $p(k; \lambda) = e^{-\lambda} \lambda^k / k!$ is

$$(2.9) \qquad \sum_{k=0}^{\infty} e^{-\lambda} \frac{(\lambda s)^k}{k!} = e^{-\lambda + \lambda s}.$$

It follows that

$$(2.10) \qquad \{p(k; \lambda)\} * \{p(k; \mu)\} = \{p(k; \lambda+\mu)\},$$

which is the same as VI,(10.5). By differentiation we find again that both mean and variance of the Poisson distribution equal λ [cf. example IX,(4.c)].

(d) *Geometric and negative binomial distributions.* Let $\mathbf{X}$ be a random variable with the geometric distribution

$$(2.11) \qquad \mathbf{P}\{\mathbf{X} = k\} = q^k p, \qquad\qquad k = 0, 1, 2, \ldots$$

where p and q are positive constants with $p + q = 1$. The corresponding *generating function is*

$$(2.12) \qquad p \sum_{k=0}^{\infty} (qs)^k = \frac{p}{1 - qs}.$$

Using the results of section 1 we find easily $E(X) = q/p$ and $Var(X) = q/p^2$, in agreement with the findings in example IX,(3.c).

In a sequence of Bernoulli trials the probability that the *first success* occurs after exactly k failures [i.e., at the $(k+1)$st trial] is $q^k p$, and so X may be interpreted as the *waiting time for the first success*. Strictly speaking, such an interpretation refers to an infinite sample space, and the advantage of the formal definition (2.11) and the terminology of random variables is that we need not worry about the structure of the original sample space. The same is true of *the waiting time for the rth success*. If X_k denotes the number of failures following the $(k-1)$st and preceding the kth success, then $S_r = X_1 + X_2, + \cdots + X_r$ is the total number of failures preceding the rth success (and $S_r + r$ is the number of trials up to and including the rth success). The notion of Bernoulli trials requires that the X_k should be mutually independent with the same distribution (2.11), and we can *define* the X_k by this property. Then S_r has the generating function

$$(2.13) \qquad \left(\frac{p}{1 - qs}\right)^r.$$

and the binomial expansion II,(8.7) shows at once that the coefficient of s^k equals

$$(2.14) \qquad f(k; r, p) = \binom{-r}{k} p^r (-q)^k, \qquad k = 0, 1, 2, \ldots.$$

It follows that $P\{S_r = k\} = f(k; r, p)$, in agreement with the distribution for the number of failures preceding the rth success derived in VI,8. We can restate this result by saying that *the distribution* $\{f(k; r, p)\}$ *is the r-fold convolution of the geometric distribution with itself*, in symbols

$$(2.15) \qquad \{f(k; r, p)\} = \{q^k p\}^{r*}.$$

So far we have considered r as an integer, but it will be recalled from VI,8, that $\{f(k; r, p)\}$ defines the *negative binomial distribution* also when $r > 0$ is not an integer. The generating function is still defined by (2.13) and we see that for arbitrary $r > 0$ the *mean and variance of the negative binomial distribution are* rq/p *and* rq/p^2 *and that*

$$(2.16) \qquad \{f(k; r_1, p)\} * \{f(k; r_2, p)\} = \{f(k; r_1 + r_2, p)\}.$$

(e) *Cycles.* In X,(6.b) we studied the number S_n of cycles in a random permutation of n elements. It was shown that it is possible to represent this random variable as the sum $S_n = X_1 + \cdots + X_n$ of n independent variables such that X_k assumes the two values 1 and 0 with probabilities $(n-k+1)^{-1}$ and $(n-k)(n-k+1)^{-1}$, respectively. It follows immediately that the generating function of S_n is given by the product

$$(2.17) \qquad \frac{n-1+s}{n} \cdot \frac{n-2+s}{n-1} \cdots \frac{1+s}{2} \cdot \frac{s}{1} = (-1)^n \binom{-s}{n}.$$

The coefficients of this polynomial determine the probability distribution of S_n, but an explicit representation requires knowledge of the Stirling numbers. We have here an example of a very usual situation, namely that the generating function is simpler than the probability distribution itself. It is therefore fortunate that much information can be extracted from the generating function.   ▶

3. EQUALIZATIONS AND WAITING TIMES IN BERNOULLI TRIALS

We pause here to illustrate the power and the flexibility of the method of generating functions by a discussion of a few important problems of methodological interest. The results play a prominent role in the theory of random walks and may be considered the prototypes of related results in diffusion theory. They will be derived by different methods in chapter XIV (see, in particular, sections 4 and 9). In the special case $p = \frac{1}{2}$ the results were derived in a different form by combinatorial methods in chapter III. A comparison of the methods should prove illuminating.[2]

In the following we consider Bernoulli trials with probability p for success. We put $X_k = +1$ if the kth trial results in success, and $X_k = -1$ otherwise. In other words, the object of our investigation is a sequence of mutually independent random variables assuming the values $+1$ and -1, with probabilities p and q, respectively. This description is simplest and most natural, but since it refers to an unending sequence of trials it leads formally to nondenumerable sample spaces. Actually we shall only calculate certain probabilities involving a specified finite number of trials, and so there arise no problems of principle. We could speak of a fixed number N of trials and let $N \to \infty$, but this would be unnecessary pedantry and harmful to probabilistic intuition.

As usual we put

$$(3.1) \qquad S_n = X_1 + \cdots + X_n, \qquad S_0 = 0.$$

---

[2] It should be clear from this account that the present section is inserted for purposes of illustration as well as for its intrinsic interest, but that it is not a prerequisite for the remainder of this book.

In the time-honored gambling terminology Peter and Paul are playing for unit stakes and S_n represents Peter's accumulated gain at the conclusion of the nth trial. In random walk terminology S_n is the position of a "particle" which at regular time intervals takes a unit step to the right or to the left. The random walk is unsymmetric if $p \neq \frac{1}{2}$.

(a) **Waiting Time for a Gain.** The event

$$(3.2) \qquad S_1 \leq 0, \ldots, S_{n-1} \leq 0, \qquad S_n = 1$$

signifies in gambling terminology that the nth trial is the first to render Peter's accumulated gain positive. In random walk terminology *the first visit to* $+1$ takes place at the nth step; a more usual description employs the language of physical diffusion theory and calls (3.2) a *first passage* through 1. We seek the probability ϕ_n of this event. More precisely, we seek their generating function

$$(3.3) \qquad \Phi(s) = \sum_{n=0}^{\infty} \phi_n s^n$$

where we put $\phi_0 = 0$ for convenience.[3] By definition $\phi_1 = p$. If (3.2) holds for some $n > 1$ then $S_1 = -1$ and there exists a *smallest* subscript $\nu < n$ such that $S_\nu = 0$. The outcome of the first n trials may now be described in gambling terminology as follows. (1) At the first trial Peter loses a unit amount. (2) It takes exactly $\nu - 1$ further trials for Peter to reestablish the initial situation. (3) It takes exactly $n - \nu$ further trials for Peter to attain a positive net gain. These three events depend on non-overlapping blocks of trials and are therefore mutually independent. From the definition it is clear that the events (2) and (3) have probabilities $\phi_{\nu-1}$ and $\phi_{n-\nu}$, respectively, and so the probability of the simultaneous realization of all three events is given by the product $q\phi_{\nu-1}\phi_{n-\nu}$. Now the event (3.2) occurs if, and only if, the events (1)–(3) occur for some $\nu < n$. Summing over all possible ν we get

$$(3.4) \qquad \phi_n = q(\phi_1\phi_{n-2} + \phi_2\phi_{n-3} + \cdots + \phi_{n-2}\phi_1).$$

It must be remembered that this relation is valid only for $n > 1$ and that $\phi_1 = p$ and $\phi_0 = 0$. Multiplying (3.4) by s^n and summing over $n = 2, 3, \ldots$ we get therefore on the left $\Phi(s) - ps$. The quantity within the parenthesis is the $(n-1)$st term of the convolution $\{\phi_n\} * \{\phi_n\}$, and

---

[3] As will be seen later on, the generating function Φ can be obtained directly by a simple probabilistic argument. The following less elegant derivation is given because it provides a good exercise in handling convolution equations, which also appear in various contexts outside probability theory. (See, for example, problem 6.)

so the right side leads to $qs \cdot \Phi^2(s)$ by the theorem of section 2. We see thus that *the generating function Φ satisfies the quadratic equation*

$$(3.5) \qquad \Phi(s) - ps = qs\Phi^2(s).$$

Of the two roots one is unbounded near $s = 0$, and our generating function is given by the unique bounded solution

$$(3.6) \qquad \Phi(s) = \frac{1 - \sqrt{1 - 4pqs^2}}{2qs},$$

where $\sqrt{}$ denotes the positive root. The binomial expansion II,(8.7) enables us to write down the coefficients in the form

$$(3.7) \qquad \phi_{2k-1} = \frac{(-1)^{k-1}}{2q}\binom{\frac{1}{2}}{k}(4pq)^k, \qquad \phi_{2k} = 0.$$

We are thus in the possession of explicit expressions for the required probabilities ϕ_k, but they are of secondary interest; it is more instructive to extract the relevant information directly from the generating function.

First we note that the sum $\sum \phi_n$ is given by

$$(3.8) \qquad \Phi(1) = \frac{1 - |p - q|}{2q},$$

and so

$$(3.9) \qquad \sum \phi_n = \begin{array}{ll} p/q & \text{if } p < q \\ 1 & \text{if } p \geq q. \end{array}$$

In other words: *If $p \leq q$ the probability that the sums S_n remain negative forever equals $(q-p)/q$.* If $p \geq q$ this probability is zero so that with probability one S_n will sooner or later become positive. How long will it take? An easy calculation shows that $\Phi'(1) = (p-q)^{-1}$ if $p > q$ and $\Phi'(1) = \infty$ if $p = q = \frac{1}{2}$. We conclude that *when $p = \frac{1}{2}$ the number of trials preceding the first positive sum S_n has infinite expectation.*

It is worthwhile to restate this noteworthy result in gambling terminology. It implies that in an ideal coin-tossing game Peter is theoretically sure sooner or later to attain a positive net gain, but the expected number of trials required to achieve this goal is infinite. A player with finite capital is therefore by no means certain of ever reaching a positive net gain. We shall return to this question in connection with the ruin problem in chapter XIV.

The derivation of the quadratic equation (3.5) for Φ may be described more concisely in probabilistic terms as follows. Denote by N the first subscript for which $S_N > 0$. Then N is a random variable in the slightly generalized sense that it is not defined in the event that $S_n \leq 0$ for *all* n. (In the terminology of chapter XIII we should call N a *defective variable*.) The generating function Φ can now be written in the form $\Phi(s) = E(s^N)$. If $X_1 = -1$ we have $N = 1 + N_1 + N_2$, where N_1 is the number of trials required to increase the partial sums S_k from -1 to 0, and N_2 is the number of subsequent trials required for the increase from 0 to 1. These variables are independent and have the same distribution as N. For the conditional expectation of s^N we get therefore

$$E(s^N \mid X_1 = -1) = E(s^{1+N_1+N_2} \mid X_1 = -1) = s\Phi^2(s),$$

$$E(s^N \mid X_1 = 1) = s.$$

But

(3.10) $$E(s^N) = pE(s^N \mid X_1 = 1) + qE(s^N \mid X_1 = -1),$$

which reduces to the quadratic equation (3.5) for $\Phi(s) = E(s^N)$.

(b) Returns to Equilibrium. An equalization of the accumulated numbers of successes and failures occurs at the kth trial if $S_k = 0$. Borrowing a term from diffusion theory, we describe this event as a return to equilibrium. The number of trials is necessarily even, and the probability of a return at the $2n$th trial is given by

(3.11) $$u_{2n} = \binom{2n}{n} p^n q^n = (-1)^n \binom{-\frac{1}{2}}{n} (4pq)^n.$$

From the binomial expansion II,(8.7) we get for the generating function

(3.12) $$U(s) = \sum_{n=0}^{\infty} u_{2n} s^{2n} = \frac{1}{\sqrt{1 - 4pqs^2}}.$$

Note that $\{u_n\}$ is *not* a probability distribution because returns to equilibrium can occur repeatedly.

(c) The First Return to Equilibrium occurs at the $2n$th trial if $S_{2n} = 0$ but $S_k \neq 0$ for $k = 1, \ldots, 2n - 1$. Denote the probability of this event by f_{2n}. (Of course, $f_{2n-1} = 0$.) We consider separately the two subevents with $X_1 = 1$ and $X_1 = -1$ and denote their probabilities by f_{2n}^+ and f_{2n}^-. From what was said under (*a*) it is clear that $f_{2n}^- = q\phi_{2n-1}$ because the first $2n - 2$ partial sums $X_2 + X_3 + \cdots + X_k$ are ≤ 0, but the next is positive. Using (3.6) we get therefore

(3.13) $$F^-(s) = \sum_{n=1}^{\infty} f_{2n}^- s^{2n} = qs\Phi(s) = \frac{1 - \sqrt{1-4pqs^2}}{2}.$$

For reasons of symmetry the generating function of $\{f_n^+\}$ is obtained by interchanging p and q. It follows that $F^+ = F^-$ and so finally[4]

(3.14) $$F(s) = \sum_{n=1}^{\infty} f_n s^n = 1 - \sqrt{1 - 4pqs^2}.$$

---

[4] An alternative derivation will be found in example XIII,(4.*b*).

Interesting conclusions can be drawn from this without using an explicit form for the coefficients f_n. Clearly $F(1)$ equals the probability that a return to equilibrium occurs sooner or later. Now $F(1) = 1 - |p - q|$ and so $|p - q|$ *is the probability that no return to equilibrium ever occurs. that is,* $S_k \neq 0$ *for all* $k > 0$. Only in the symmetric case $p = \frac{1}{2}$ is a return to equilibrium certain. In this case $\{f_n\}$ represents the probability distribution for the waiting time for the first return. This waiting time has *infinite expectation.*

In the symmetric case $p = \frac{1}{2}$ we have

$$(3.15) \qquad\qquad U(s) = \frac{1 - F(s)}{1 - s^2} .$$

Since both U and F are power series in s^2 this relation differs only notationally from (1.6), and by theorem 1.1

$$(3.16) \qquad\qquad u_{2n} = f_{2n+2} + f_{2n+4} + \cdots .$$

In words, *when* $p = \frac{1}{2}$ *the probability that* $S_{2n} = 0$ *equals the probability that the* $2n$ *sums* $S_1, \ldots, S_{2n}$ *are different from zero.* This result was derived by different methods in III,3 and played a basic role in the analysis of the paradoxical nature of the fluctuations in coin-tossing games.

(d) First Passages and Later Returns.   We say that a *first passage through* $r > 0$ *occurs at the* nth *trial if* $S_n = r$ *but* $S_k < r$ *for all* $k < n$. The probability for this will be denoted by $\phi_n^{(r)}$. The trials following the first passage through $\nu > 0$ form a probabilistic replica of the whole sequence and hence the number of trials following the first passage through ν up to and including the first passage through $\nu + 1$ has the same distribution $\{\phi_n\}$ as the number of trials up to the first passage through 1. When $p < q$ the ϕ_n do not add to unity, but it still makes sense to say that the waiting time for the first passage is a random variable with the (possibly defective) distribution $\{\phi_n\}$. The waiting times between the successive first passages are mutually independent, and so the total waiting time for the first passage through r is the sum of r independent variables with the common distribution $\{\phi_n\}$. *The generating function of the first-passage probabilities* $\phi_n^{(r)}$ *is therefore given by the* rth *power of* Φ. [Beginners should verify this statement directly by deriving for $\phi_n^{(2)}$ a convolution equation similar to (2.4) and proceeding by induction.]

A similar argument holds for the probability $f_n^{(r)}$ that *the* rth *return to equilibrium occurs at the* nth *trial. The generating function of* $\{f_n^{(r)}\}$ *is given by the* rth *power* F^r. Comparing (3.6) and (3.14) one sees immediately that

(3.17) $$f_n^{(r)} = (2q)^r \phi_{n-r}^{(r)}.$$

In the special case $p = q = \frac{1}{2}$ this result is contained in theorem 4 of III,7.

From the generating functions it is easy to derive approximations and limit theorems, but this depends on the use of Laplace transforms which will be treated only in chapter XIII of volume 2. There is no systematic way to derive an explicit expression for $f_n^{(r)}$ from the generating function F^r, but a good guess is easily verified from the form of the generating function. From theorem 4 of III, 7 one can guess that

(3.18) $$f_{2n}^{(r)} = \frac{r}{2n-r}\binom{2n-r}{n}2^r(pq)^n.$$

To verify this conjecture it suffices to note that the identity

$$F^r(s) = 2F^{r-1}(s) - 4pqs^2F^{r-2}(s)$$

implies the recursion relation

(3.19) $$f_{2n}^{(r)} = 2f_{2n}^{(r-1)} - 4pq f_{2n-2}^{(r-2)},$$

which is also satisfied by the right side in (3.18). The truth of (3.18) therefore follows by induction. For an equivalent expression of a different outer appearance see problem 13 of XIV, 9.

4. PARTIAL FRACTION EXPANSIONS

Given a generating function $P(s) = \sum p_k s^k$ the coefficients p_k can be found by differentiations from the obvious formula $p_k = P^{(k)}(0)/k!$. In practice it may be impossible to obtain explicit expressions and, anyhow, such expressions are frequently so complicated that reasonable approximations are preferable. The most common method for obtaining such approximations is based on partial fraction expansions. It is known from the theory of complex variables that a large class of functions admits of such expansions, but we shall limit our exposition to the simple case of *rational functions*.

Suppose then that the generating function is of the form

(4.1) $$P(s) = \frac{U(s)}{V(s)}$$

where U and V are polynomials without common roots. For simplicity let us first assume that the degree of U is lower than the degree of V, say m. Moreover, suppose that the equation $V(s) = 0$ has m distinct (real or imaginary) roots $s_1, s_2, \ldots, s_m$. Then

(4.2) $$V(s) = (s-s_1)(s-s_2) \cdots (s-s_m),$$

and it is known from algebra that $P(s)$ can be decomposed into *partial fractions*

$$(4.3) \qquad P(s) = \frac{\rho_1}{s_1 - s} + \frac{\rho_2}{s_2 - s} + \cdots + \frac{\rho_m}{s_m - s}$$

where $\rho_1, \rho_2, \ldots, \rho_m$ are constants. To find ρ_1 multiply (4.3) by $s_1 - s$; as $s \to s_1$ the product $(s_1 - s)P(s)$ tends to ρ_1. On the other hand, from (4.1) and (4.2) we get

$$(4.4) \qquad (s_1 - s)P(s) = \frac{-U(s)}{(s - s_2)(s - s_3) \cdots (s - s_m)}.$$

As $s \to s_1$ the numerator tends to $-U(s_1)$ and the denominator to $(s_1 - s_2)(s_1 - s_3) \cdots (s_1 - s_m)$, which is the same as $V'(s_1)$. Thus $\rho_1 = -U(s_1)/V'(s_1)$. The same argument applies to all roots, so that for $k \leq m$

$$(4.5) \qquad \rho_k = \frac{-U(s_k)}{V'(s_k)}.$$

Given the ρ_k, we can easily derive an exact expression for the coefficient of s^n in $P(s)$. Write

$$(4.6) \qquad \frac{1}{s_k - s} = \frac{1}{s_k} \cdot \frac{1}{1 - s/s_k}.$$

For $|s| < |s_k|$ we expand the last fraction into a geometric series

$$(4.7) \qquad \frac{1}{1 - s/s_k} = 1 + \frac{s}{s_k} + \left(\frac{s}{s_k}\right)^2 + \left(\frac{s}{s_k}\right)^3 + \cdots.$$

Introducing these expressions into (4.3), we find for the *coefficient p_n of s^n*

$$(4.8) \qquad p_n = \frac{\rho_1}{s_1^{n+1}} + \frac{\rho_2}{s_2^{n+1}} + \cdots + \frac{\rho_m}{s_m^{n+1}}.$$

Thus, to get p_n we have first to find the roots $s_1, \ldots, s_m$ of the denominator and then to determine the coefficients $\rho_1, \ldots, \rho_m$ from (4.5).

In (4.8) we have an *exact* expression for the probability p_n. The labor involved in calculating all m roots is usually prohibitive, and therefore formula (4.8) is primarily of theoretical interest. Fortunately a single term in (4.8) almost always provides a satisfactory approximation. In fact, suppose that s_1 is a root which is *smaller* in absolute value than all other roots. Then the first denominator in (4.8) is smallest. Clearly, as n increases, the proportionate contributions of the other terms decrease and the first term preponderates. In other words, *if s_1 is a root of $V(s) = 0$ which is smaller in absolute value than all other roots, then, as $n \to \infty$,*

$$(4.9) \qquad p_n \sim \frac{\rho_1}{s_1^{n+1}}$$

(the sign $\sim$ indicating that the ratio of the two sides tends to 1). Usually this formula provides surprisingly good approximations even for relatively small values of n. The main advantage of (4.9) lies in the fact that it requires the computation of only one root of an algebraic equation.

It is easy to remove the restrictions under which we have derived the asymptotic formula (4.9). To begin with, the degree of the numerator in (4.1) may exceed the degree m of the denominator. Let $U(s)$ be of degree $m + r$ ($r \geq 0$); a division reduces $P(s)$ to a polynomial of degree r plus a fraction $U_1(s)/V(s)$ in which $U_1(s)$ is a polynomial of a degree lower than m. The polynomial affects only the first $r + 1$ terms of the distribution $\{p_n\}$, and $U_1(s)/V(s)$ can be expanded into partial fractions as explained above. Thus (4.9) remains true. Secondly, the restriction that $V(s)$ should have only simple roots is unnecessary. It is known from algebra that every rational function admits of an expansion into partial fractions. If s_k is a double root of $V(s)$, then the partial fraction expansion (4.3) will contain an additional term of the form $a/(s-s_k)^2$, and this will contribute a term of the form $a(n+1)s_k^{-(n+2)}$ to the exact expression (4.8) for p_n. However, this does not affect the asymptotic expansion (4.9), provided only that s_1 is a simple root. We note this result for future reference as a

Theorem. *If $P(s)$ is a rational function with a simple root s_1 of the denominator which is smaller in absolute value than all other roots, then the coefficient p_n of s^n is given asymptotically by $p_n \sim \rho_1 s_1^{-(n+1)}$, where ρ_1 is defined in* (4.5).

A similar asymptotic expansion exists also in the case where s_1 is a multiple root. (See problem 25.)

Examples.[5] (*a*) Let a_n be the probability that n Bernoulli trials result in an *even number of successes*. This event occurs if an initial failure at the first trial is followed by an even number of successes or if an initial success is followed by an odd number. Therefore for $n \geq 1$

$$(4.10) \qquad a_n = q a_{n-1} + p(1 - a_{n-1}), \qquad a_0 = 1.$$

---

[5] A good illustration for the use of partial fractions for numerical approximations is provided by the theory of success runs in XIII, 7. The explicit expressions for the ruin probabilities in XIV, 5 and for the transition probabilities in XVI, 1 also depend on the method of partial fractions.

Multiplying by s^n and adding over $n = 1, 2, \ldots$ we get for the generating function the relation

$$A(s) - 1 = qsA(s) + ps(1-s)^{-1} - psA(s)$$

or

$$2A(s) = [1-s]^{-1} + [1-(q-p)s]^{-1}.$$

Expanding into geometric series we get finally a_n explicitly in the form

(4.11) $$2a_n = 1 + (q-p)^n,$$

which is in every way preferable to the obvious answer

$$a_n = b(0; n, p) + b(2; n, p) + \cdots.$$

(b) Let q_n be the probability that in n tosses of an ideal coin no run of three consecutive heads appears. (Note that $\{q_n\}$ is not a probability distribution; if p_n is the probability that the first run of three consecutive heads ends at the nth trial, then $\{p_n\}$ is a probability distribution, and q_n represents its "tails," $q_n = p_{n+1} + p_{n+2} + \cdots$.)

We can easily show that q_n satisfies the recurrence formula

(4.12) $$q_n = \tfrac{1}{2}q_{n-1} + \tfrac{1}{4}q_{n-2} + \tfrac{1}{8}q_{n-3}, \qquad n \geq 3.$$

In fact, the event that n trials produce no sequence HHH can occur only when the trials begin with T, HT, or HHT. The probabilities that the following trials lead to no run HHH are q_{n-1}, q_{n-2}, and q_{n-3}, respectively, and the right side of (4.12) therefore contains the probabilities of the three mutually exclusive ways in which the event "no run HHH" can occur.

Evidently $q_0 = q_1 = q_2 = 1$, and hence the q_n can be calculated recursively from (4.12). To obtain the generating function $Q(s) = \sum q_n s^n$ we multiply both sides by s^n and add over $n \geq 3$. The result is

$$Q(s) - 1 - s - s^2 = \tfrac{1}{2}s\{Q(s)-1-s\} + \tfrac{1}{4}s^2\{Q(s)-1\} + \tfrac{1}{8}s^3Q(s)$$

or

(4.13) $$Q(s) = \frac{2s^2 + 4s + 8}{8 - 4s - 2s^2 - s^3}.$$

The denominator has the root $s_1 = 1.0873778 \ldots$ and two complex roots. For $|s| < s_1$ we have $|4s + 2s^2 + s^3| < 4s_1 + 2s_1^2 + s_1^3 = 8$, and the same inequality holds also when $|s| = s_1$ unless $s = s_1$. Hence the other two roots exceed s_1 in absolute value. Thus, from (4.9)

(4.14) $$q_n \sim \frac{1.236840}{(1.0873778)^{n+1}},$$

where the numerator equals $(2s_1^2+4s_1+8)/(4+4s_1+3s_1^2)$. This is a remarkably good approximation even for small values of n. It approximates $q_3 = 0.875$ by 0.8847 and $q_4 = 0.8125$ by 0.81360. The percentage error decreases steadily, and $q_{12} = 0.41626\ldots$ is given correct to five decimal places.   ▶

5. BIVARIATE GENERATING FUNCTIONS

For a pair of integral-valued random variables $\mathbf{X}, \mathbf{Y}$ with a joint distribution of the form

$$(5.1) \qquad \mathbf{P}\{\mathbf{X} = j, \mathbf{Y} = k\} = p_{jk} \qquad j, k = 0, 1, \ldots$$

we define a generating function depending on two variables

$$(5.2) \qquad P(s_1, s_2) = \sum_{j,k} p_{jk} s_1^j s_2^k.$$

Such generating functions will be called bivariate for short.

The considerations of the first two sections apply without essential modifications, and it will suffice to point out three properties evident from (5.2):

(a) *The generating function of the marginal distributions* $\mathbf{P}\{\mathbf{X} = j\}$ *and* $\mathbf{P}\{\mathbf{Y} = k\}$ *are* $A(s) = P(s, 1)$ *and* $B(s) = P(1, s)$.

(b) *The generating function of* $\mathbf{X} + \mathbf{Y}$ *is* $P(s, s)$.

(c) *The variables* $\mathbf{X}$ *and* $\mathbf{Y}$ *are independent if, and only if,* $P(s_1, s_2) = A(s_1)B(s_2)$ *for all* s_1, s_2.

Examples. (a) *Bivariate Poisson distribution.* It is obvious that

$$(5.3) \qquad P(s_1, s_2) = e^{-a_1-a_2-b+a_1s_1+a_2s_2+bs_1s_2}, \qquad a_i > 0, b > 0$$

has a power-series expansion with positive coefficients adding up to unity. Accordingly $P(s_1, s_2)$ represents the generating function of a bivariate probability distribution. The marginal distributions are Poisson distributions with mean $a_1 + b$ and $a_2 + b$, respectively, but the sum $\mathbf{X} + \mathbf{Y}$ has the generating function $e^{-a_1-a_2-b+(a_1+a_2)s+bs^2}$ and is *not* a Poisson variable. (It is a compound Poisson distribution; see XII, 2.)

(b) *Multinomial distributions.* Consider a sequence of n independent trials, each of which results in E_0, E_1, or E_2 with respective probabilities p_0, p_1, p_2. If $\mathbf{X}_i$ is the number of occurrences of E_i, then $(\mathbf{X}_1, \mathbf{X}_2)$ has a trinomial distribution with generating function $(p_0+p_1s_1+p_2s_2)^n$.   ▶

*6. THE CONTINUITY THEOREM

We know from chapter VI that the Poisson distribution $\{e^{-\lambda}\lambda^k/k!\}$ is the limiting form of the binomial distribution with the probability p depending on n in such a way that $np \to \lambda$ as $n \to \infty$. Then

$$b(k; n, p) \to e^{-\lambda}\lambda^k/k!.$$

The generating function of $\{b(k; n, p)\}$ is $(q+ps)^n = \{1 - \lambda(1-s)/n\}^n$. Taking logarithms, we see directly that this generating function tends to $e^{-\lambda(1-s)}$, which is the generating function of the Poisson distribution. We shall show that this situation prevails in general; a sequence of probability distributions converges to a limiting distribution if and only if the corresponding generating functions converge. Unfortunately, this theorem is of limited applicability, since the most interesting limiting forms of discrete distributions are continuous distributions (for example, the normal distribution appears as a limiting form of the binomial distribution).

Continuity Theorem. *Suppose that for every fixed n the sequence $a_{0,n}, a_{1,n}, a_{2,n}, \ldots$ is a probability distribution, that is,*

$$(6.1) \qquad a_{k,n} \geq 0, \qquad \sum_{k=0}^{\infty} a_{k,n} = 1.$$

In order that a limit

$$(6.2) \qquad a_k = \lim_{n \to \infty} a_{k,n}$$

exists for every $k \geq 0$ it is necessary and sufficient that the limit

$$(6.3) \qquad A(s) = \lim_{n \to \infty} \sum_{k=0}^{\infty} a_{k,n} s^k$$

exists for each s in the open interval $0 < s < 1$. In this case automatically

$$(6.4) \qquad A(s) = \sum_{k=0}^{\infty} a_k s^k.$$

It is obvious that $a_k \geq 0$ and that $\sum a_k \leq 1$. Note, however, that the sum may be strictly less than 1. For example, if $a_{k,n} = f_{k+n}$ then $a_k = 0$ for all k.

---

* The continuity theorem will be used only in the derivation of the general form for infinitely divisible distributions in XII, 2 and for the total progeny in branching processes in XII, 5.

Proof.[6] Let $A_n(s)$ stand for the series on the right side in (6.3).

(i) Assume (6.2) and define $A(s)$ by (6.4). Since $|a_{k,n} - a_k| \leq 1$ we have for $0 < s < 1$

$$(6.5) \qquad |A_n(s) - A(s)| \leq \sum_{k=0}^{r} |a_{k,n} - a_k| + \frac{s^r}{1-s}.$$

If we choose r so large that $s^r < \epsilon(1-s)$, the right side will be less than 2ϵ for all n sufficiently large. Thus the left side can be made as small as we please, and so (6.3) is true.

(ii) Assume (6.3). Clearly $A(s)$ depends monotonically on s, and so $A(0)$ exists as the limit of $A(s)$ as $s \to 0$. Now

$$(6.6) \qquad a_{0,n} \leq A_n(s) \leq a_{0,n} + s/(1-s).$$

It follows that as $n \to \infty$ all limit values of $a_{0,n}$ lie between $A(0)$ and $A(s) - s/(1-s)$. Letting $s \to 0$ we see that $a_{0,n} \to A(0)$, and so (6.2) holds when $k = 0$.

This argument extends successively to all k. Indeed, for $0 < s < 1$

$$(6.7) \qquad \frac{A_n(s) - a_{0,n}}{s} \to \frac{A(s) - A(0)}{s}.$$

On the left we have a power series with nonnegative coefficients, and (6.7) is in every way analogous to (6.3). Arguing as before we find first that the derivative $A'(0)$ exists, and then that $a_{1,n} \to A'(0)$. By induction we get (6.2) for all k. ▶

Examples. (a) *The negative binomial distribution.* We saw in example (2.d) that the generating function of the distribution $\{f(k; r, p)\}$ is $p^r(1-qs)^{-r}$. Now let λ be fixed, and let $p \to 1$, $q \to 0$, and $r \to \infty$ so that $q \sim \lambda/r$. Then

$$(6.8) \qquad \left(\frac{p}{1-qs}\right)^r = \left(\frac{1 - \lambda/r}{1 - \lambda s/r}\right)^r.$$

Passing to logarithms, we see that the right side tends to $e^{-\lambda + \lambda s}$, which is the generating function of the Poisson distribution $\{e^{-\lambda}\lambda^k/k!\}$. Hence *if $r \to \infty$ and $rq \to \lambda$, then*

$$(6.9) \qquad f(k; r, p) \to e^{-\lambda} \frac{\lambda^k}{k!}.$$

---

[6] The theorem is a special case of the continuity theorem for Laplace-Stieltjes transforms, and the proof follows the general pattern. In the literature the continuity theorem for generating functions is usually stated and proved under unnecessary restrictions.

(b) *Bernoulli trials with variable probabilities.*[7] Consider n independent trials such that the kth trial results in success with probability p_k and in failure with probability $q_k = 1 - p_k$. The number $\mathbf{S}_n$ of successes can be written as the sum $\mathbf{S}_n = \mathbf{X}_1 + \cdots + \mathbf{X}_n$ of n mutually independent random variables $\mathbf{X}_k$ with the distributions $\mathbf{P}\{\mathbf{X}_k = 0\} = q_k$,

$$\mathbf{P}\{\mathbf{X}_k = 1\} = p_k.$$

The generating function of $\mathbf{X}_k$ is $q_k + p_k s$, and hence the generating function of $\mathbf{S}_n$

(6.10) $$P(s) = (q_1+p_1s)(q_2+p_2s) \cdots (q_n+p_ns).$$

As an application of this scheme let us assume that each house in a city has a small probability p_k of burning on a given day.   The sum $p_1 + \cdots + p_n$ is the expected number of fires in the city, n being the number of houses. We have seen in chapter VI that if all p_k are equal and if the houses are stochastically independent, then the number of fires is a random variable whose distribution is near the Poisson distribution. We show now that this conclusion remains valid also under the more realistic assumption that the probabilities p_k are not equal. This result should increase our confidence in the Poisson distribution as an adequate description of phenomena which are the cumulative effect of many improbable events ("successes"). Accidents and telephone calls are typical examples.

We use the now familiar model of an increasing number n of variables where the probabilities p_k depend on n in such a way that the largest p_k tends to zero, but the sum $p_1 + p_2 + \cdots + p_n = \lambda$ remains constant. Then from (6.10)

(6.11) $$\log P(s) = \sum_{k=1}^{n} \log \{1 - p_k(1-s)\}.$$

Since $p_k \to 0$, we can use the fact that $\log(1-x) = -x - \theta x$, where $\theta \to 0$ as $x \to 0$. It follows that

(6.12) $$\log P(s) = -(1-s)\left\{\sum_{k=1}^{n}(p_k+\theta_k p_k)\right\} \to -\lambda(1-s),$$

so that $P(s)$ tends to the generating function of the Poisson distribution. Hence, $\mathbf{S}_n$ *has in the limit a Poisson distribution.* We conclude that for large n and moderate values of $\lambda = p_1 + p_2 + \cdots + p_n$ the distribution of $\mathbf{S}_n$ can be approximated by a Poisson distribution.   ▶

---

[7] See also examples IX, (1.e) and IX, (5.b).

EMS FOR SOLUTION

iable with generating function $P(s)$. Find the
and 2X.

ns of (a) $\mathbf{P}\{X \leq n\}$, (b) $\mathbf{P}\{X < n\}$, (c) $\mathbf{P}\{X \geq n\}$,
2n\}.

i trials let u_n be the probability that the com-
t time at trials number $n - 1$ and n. Find the
variance.

ulas of II, 12, represent convolutions and where
used.

ways in which the score n can be obtained by
times. Show that the generating function of
$s^6\}^{-1} - 1$.

ways in which a convex polygon $P_0 P_1 \cdots P_n$
ioned into triangles by drawing $n - 2$ (non-
$= 1$. Show that for $n \geq 2$

$+ a_2 a_{n-2} + \cdots + a_{n-1} a_1$.

d an explicit expression for a_n.

Hint: Assume that one of the diagonals passes through P_0 and let k be the smallest subscript such that $P_0 P_k$ appears among the diagonals.

Note: *Problems 7–11 refer to section 3. The generating functions* Φ, *U*, *and F refer respectively to first passages through* 1, *returns to equilibrium, and first returns; see* (3.6), (3.12), *and* (3.14). *No calculations are necessary.*

7. (a) The probability that a return to equilibrium occurs at or before the nth trial is given by $(1-s)^{-1}F(s)$.

(b) Conclude: The generating function for the probability that $S_j \neq 0$ for $j = 1, \ldots, n$ is given by $\sqrt{\dfrac{1+s}{1-s}} = (1+s)U(s)$.

(c) Show that this is equivalent to the proposition following (3.16).

8. The generating function for the probabilities that no return to equilibrium occurs after the nth trial (exclusive) is given by $(1-s)^{-1}U(s)|p - q|$.

9. (a) The generating function for $\mathbf{P}\{S_n = r\}$ (with $r > 0$ fixed) is given by $\Phi^r(s)U(s)$.

(b) When $p = \frac{1}{2}$ this is also the generating function for the probability that $S_k = r$ for exactly one subscript $k \leq n$.

10. (a) Find the generating function for the probabilities that the event $S_n = r$ will occur exactly k times ($r > 0$ and $k > 0$ fixed).

(b) Do the same problem with "exactly" replaced by "at most."

11. (a) Find the generating function for the probability that the first return to equilibrium following a first passage through $r > 0$ occurs at trial number r.

(b) Do the same problem with the words "the first" omitted.

---

[8] The problem appears in G. Polya, *Mathematics of plausible reasoning*, Princeton (Princeton University Press), 1954, p. 102.

12. In the *waiting time example* IX, (3.d) find the generating function of S_r (for r fixed). Verify formula IX, (3.3) for the mean and calculate the variance.

13. *Continuation.* The following is an alternative method for deriving the same result. Let $p_n(r) = P\{S_r = n\}$. Prove the recursion formula

(7.1) $$p_{n+1}(r) = \frac{r-1}{N} p_n(r) + \frac{N-r+1}{N} p_n(r-1).$$

Derive the generating function directly from (7.1).

14. Solve the two preceding problems for r preassigned elements (instead of r arbitrary ones).

15.[9] Let the sequence of Bernoulli trials up to the first failure be called a *turn*. Find the generating function and the probabiity distribution of the accumulated numbers S_r of successes in r turns.

16. *Continuation.* (*a*) Let **R** be the number of successive turns up to the νth success (that is, the νth success occurs during the **R**th turn). Find **E(R)** and Var **(R)**. Prove that

$$P\{R = r\} = p^\nu q^{r-1} \binom{r+\nu-2}{\nu-1}.$$

(*b*) Consider *two* sequences of Bernoulli trials with probabilities p_1, q_1, and p_2, q_2, respectively. Find the probability that the same number of turns will lead to the Nth success.

---

17. Let **X** assume the values $0, 1, \ldots, r-1$ each with the same probability $1/r$. When r is a composite number, say $r = ab$, it is possible to represent **X** as the sum of two independent integral-valued random variables.

18. Let $S_n = X_1 + \cdots + X_n$ be the sum of mutually independent variables each assuming the values $1, 2, \ldots, a$ with probability $1/a$. Show that the generating function is given by

$$P(s) = \left\{ \frac{s(1-s^a)}{a(1-s)} \right\}^n$$

whence for $j \geq n$

$$P\{S_n = j\} = a^{-n} \sum_{\nu=0}^{\infty} (-1)^{\nu+j-n-a\nu} \binom{n}{\nu} \binom{-n}{j-n-a\nu}$$
$$= a^{-n} \sum_{\nu=0}^{\infty} (-1)^\nu \binom{n}{\nu} \binom{j-a\nu-1}{n-1}.$$

(Only finitely many terms in the sum are different from zero.)

---

[9] Problems 15–16 have a direct bearing on the *game of billiards*. The probability p of success is a measure of the player's skill. The player continues to play until he fails. Hence the number of successes he accumulates is the length of his "turn." The game continues until one player has scored N successes. Problem 15 therefore gives the probability distribution of the number of turns one player needs to score k successes, problem 16 the average duration and the probability of a tie between two players. For further details cf. O. Bottema and S. C. Van Veen, *Kansberekningen bij het biljartspel*, Nieuw Archief voor Wiskunde (in Dutch), vol. 22 (1943), pp. 16–33 and 123–158.

Note: For $a = 6$ we get the probability of scoring the sum $j + n$ in a throw with n dice. The solution goes back to De Moivre.

19. *Continuation.* The probability $\mathbf{P}\{\mathbf{S}_n \leq j\}$ has the generating function $P(s)/(1-s)$ and hence

$$\mathbf{P}\{\mathbf{S}_n \leq j\} = \frac{1}{a^n} \sum_\nu (-1)^\nu \binom{n}{\nu} \binom{j-a\nu}{n}.$$

20. *Continuation: the limiting form.* If $a \to \infty$ and $j \to \infty$, so that $j/a \to x$, then

$$\mathbf{P}\{\mathbf{S}_n \leq j\} \to \frac{1}{n!} \sum_\nu (-1)^\nu \binom{n}{\nu} (x-\nu)^n,$$

the summation extending over all ν with $0 \leq \nu < x$.

Note: This result is due to Lagrange. In the theory of geometric probabilities the right-hand side represents the distribution function of the sum of n independent random variables with "uniform" distribution in the interval $(0, 1)$.

21. Let u_n be the probability that the number of successes in n Bernoulli trials is divisible by 3. Find a recursive relation for u_n and hence the generating function.

22. *Continuation: alternative method.* Let v_n and w_n be the probabilities that $\mathbf{S}_n$ is of the form $3v + 1$ and $3v + 2$, respectively (so that $u_n + v_n + w_n = 1$). Find three simultaneous recursive relations and hence three equations for the generating functions.

23. Let $\mathbf{X}$ and $\mathbf{Y}$ be independent variables with generating functions $U(s)$ and $V(s)$. Show that $\mathbf{P}\{\mathbf{X} - \mathbf{Y} = j\}$ is the coefficient of s^j in $U(s) V(1/s)$, where $j = 0, \pm 1, \pm 2, \ldots$.

24. *Moment generating functions.* Let $\mathbf{X}$ be a random variable with generating function $P(s)$, and suppose that $\sum p_n s^n$ converges for some $s_0 > 1$. Then all moments $m_r = \mathbf{E}(\mathbf{X}^r)$ exist, and the generating function $F(s)$ of the sequence $m_r/r!$ converges at least for $|s| < \log s_0$. Moreover

$$F(s) = \sum_{r=0}^\infty \frac{m_r}{r!} s^r = P(e^s).$$

Note: $F(s)$ is usually called the *moment generating function*, although in reality it generates $m_r/r!$.

25. Suppose that $A(s) = \sum a_n s^n$ is a rational function $U(s)/V(s)$ and that s_1 is a root of $V(s)$, which is smaller in absolute value than all other roots. If s_1 is of multiplicity r, show that

$$a_n \sim \frac{\rho_1}{s_1^{n+r}} \binom{n+r-1}{r-1}$$

where $\rho_1 = (-1)^r r! \, U(s_1)/V^{(r)}(s_1)$.

26. *Bivariate negative binomial distributions.* Show that for positive values of the parameters $p_0^a \{1 - p_1 s_1 - p_2 s_2\}^{-a}$ is the generating function of the distribution, of a pair $(\mathbf{X}, \mathbf{Y})$ such that the marginal distributions of $\mathbf{X}, \mathbf{Y}$, and $\mathbf{X} + \mathbf{Y}$ are negative binomial distributions.[10]

---

[10] Distributions of this type were used by G. E. Bates and J. Neyman in investigations of accident proneness. See University of California Publications in Statistics, vol. 1, 1952.

CHAPTER XII*

Compound Distributions. Branching Processes

A substantial part of probability theory is connected with sums of independent random variables, and in many situations the number of terms in such sums is itself a random variable. We consider here this situation for the special case of integral-valued random variables, partly to illustrate the use of generating functions, partly as a preparation for the study of infinitely divisible distributions and of processes with independent increments in volume 2.

As a particularly enticing application we describe the elements of the beautiful theory of branching processes.

1. SUMS OF A RANDOM NUMBER OF VARIABLES

Let $\{\mathbf{X}_k\}$ be a sequence of mutually independent random variables with the common distribution $\mathbf{P}\{\mathbf{X}_k = j\} = f_j$ and generating function $f(s) = \Sigma f_i s^i$. We are often interested in sums

$$\mathbf{S_N} = \mathbf{X}_1 + \mathbf{X}_2 + \cdots + \mathbf{X_N},$$

where the number $\mathbf{N}$ of terms is a random variable independent of the $\mathbf{X}_j$. Let $\mathbf{P}\{\mathbf{N} = n\} = g_n$ be the distribution of $\mathbf{N}$ and $g(s) = \Sigma g_n s^n$ its generating function. For the distribution $\{h_j\}$ of $\mathbf{S_N}$ we get from the fundamental formula for conditional probabilities

$$(1.1) \qquad h_j = \mathbf{P}\{\mathbf{S_N} = j\} = \sum_{n=0}^{\infty} \mathbf{P}\{\mathbf{N} = n\}\mathbf{P}\{\mathbf{X}_1 + \cdots + \mathbf{X}_n = j\}.$$

If $\mathbf{N}$ assumes only finitely many values, the random variable $\mathbf{S_N}$ is defined on the sample space of finitely many $\mathbf{X}_k$. Otherwise the probabilistic definition of $\mathbf{S_N}$ as a sum involves the sample space of an infinite

---

* The contents of this chapter will not be used in the sequel.

sequence $\{X_k\}$, but we shall be dealing only with the distribution function of S_N: for our purposes we take the distribution (1.1) as definition of the variable S_N on the sample space with points $0, 1, 2, \ldots$.

For a fixed n the distribution of $X_1 + X_2 + \cdots + X_n$ is given by the n-fold convolution of $\{f_i\}$ with itself, and therefore (1.1) can be written in the compact form

$$(1.2) \qquad \{h_j\} = \sum_{n=0}^{\infty} g_n \{f_j\}^{n*}.$$

This formula can be simplified by the use of generating functions. The generating function of $\{f_j\}^{n*}$ is $f^n(s)$ and it is obvious from (1.2) that the generating function of the sum S_N is given by

$$(1.3) \qquad h(s) = \sum_{j=0}^{\infty} h_j s^j = \sum_{n=0}^{\infty} g_n f^n(s).$$

The right side is the power series for $g(s)$ with s replaced by $f(s)$; hence it equals $g(f(s))$. This proves the

Theorem. *The generating function of the sum* $S_N = X_1 + \cdots + X_N$ *is the compound function* $g(f(s))$.

The proof can be reformulated in terms of conditional expectations. By definition

$$(1.4) \qquad E(s^{S_N} \mid N = n) = f^n(s),$$

and to obtain $h(s) = E(s^{S_N})$ we have to multiply this quantity by $P\{N = n\}$ and sum over n [see IX,(2.9)].

Two special cases are of interest.

(a) If the X_i are Bernoulli variables with $P\{X_i = 1\} = p$ and $P\{X_i = 0\} = q$, then $f(s) = q + ps$ and therefore $h(s) = g(q+ps)$.

(b) If N has a Poisson distribution with mean t then $h(s) = e^{-t+tf(s)}$. The distribution with this generating function will be called the *compound Poisson distribution*. In particular, if the X_i are Bernoulli variables *and* N has a Poisson distribution, then $h(s) = e^{-tp+tps}$; the *sum* S_N *has a Poisson distribution with mean* tp.

Examples. (a) We saw in example VI, (7.c) that X-rays produce chromosome breakages in cells; for a given dosage and time of exposure the number N of breakages in individual cells has a Poisson distribution. Each breakage has a fixed probability q of healing whereas with probability $p = 1 - q$ the cell dies. Here S_N is the number of *observable* breakages[1] and has a Poisson distribution with mean tp.

---

[1] See D. G. Catcheside, Genetic effects of radiations, *Advances in Genetics*, edited by M. Demerec, vol. 2, Academic Press, New York, 1948, pp. 271–358, in particular p. 339.

(b) In animal-trapping experiments[2] g_n represents the probability that a species is of size n. If all animals have the same probability p of being trapped, then (assuming stochastic independence) the number of trapped representatives of one species in the sample is a variable S_N with generating function $g(q+ps)$. This description can be varied in many ways. For example, let g_n be the probability of an insect laying n eggs, and p the probability of survival of an egg. Then S_N is the number of surviving eggs. Again, let g_n be the probability of a family having n children and let the sex ratio of boys to girls be $p:q$. Then S_N represents the number of boys in a family.

(c) Each plant has a large number of seeds, but each seed has only a small probability of survival, and it is therefore reasonable to assume that the number of survivors of an individual plant has a Poisson distribution. If $\{g_n\}$ represents the distribution of the number of parent plants, $g(e^{-\lambda+\lambda s})$ is the generating function of the number of surviving seeds.

(d) *Required service time.* Consider a telephone trunkline, a counter, or any other server with the property that the service times required by the successive customers may be regarded as independent random variables $X_1, X_2, \ldots$ with a common distribution. The number of customers (or calls) arriving during a day is itself a random variable N, and the total service time required by them is therefore a random sum $X_1 + \cdots + X_N$.

2. THE COMPOUND POISSON DISTRIBUTION

Among the random sums $S_N = X_1 + \cdots + X_N$ by far the most important are those for which N has a Poisson distribution. For reasons that will presently become apparent we denote the expectation of N by λt. If the X_j have the common distribution $\{f_i\}$ then S_N has *the compound Poisson distribution*

$$(2.1) \qquad \{h_i\}_t = e^{-\lambda t} \sum_{n=0}^{\infty} \frac{(\lambda t)^n}{n!} \{f_i\}^{n*}$$

with the generating function

$$(2.2) \qquad h_t(s) = e^{-\lambda t + \lambda t f(s)}.$$

Examples. (a) *Accumulated damage.* Suppose that the number of hits by lightning during any time interval of duration t is a Poisson variable with expectation λt. If $\{f_n\}$ is the probability distribution of the damage

---

[2] D. G. Kendall, *On some modes of population growth leading to R. A. Fisher's logarithmic series distribution*, Biometrika, vol. 35 (1948), pp. 6–15.

caused by an individual hit by lightning, then (assuming stochastic independence) the total damage during time t has the compound Poisson distribution (2.1).

(b) *Cosmic ray showers.* It is generally supposed that the number N of cosmic ray showers during a time interval of length t has a Poisson distribution with expectation λt. For any given counter, the number of registrations caused by a shower is a random variable with a distribution $\{f_i\}$. The total number of registrations during a time t is again a random sum S_N with the compound Poisson distribution (2.1).

(c) *In ecology* it is assumed that the number of animal litters in a plot has a Poisson distribution with expectation proportional to the area t of the plot. Let $\{f_k\}$ be the distribution of the number of animals in a litter and assume that the litters are independent. Under these conditions the number of animals in the plot is subject to the compound Poisson distribution (2.1). This model is widely used in practice.   ▶

It will be noticed that all three examples are closely related to the phenomena discussed in VI,6 in connection with the Poisson distribution. In the first two examples a variable S_N is associated with every time interval. [The same is true of example (c) if we agree to treat the area as operational time.] It is implicit in the model that when an interval is partitioned into two non-overlapping intervals their contributions are stochastically independent and add to S_N. In terms of the generating function (2.2) this means that

$$(2.3) \qquad\qquad h_{t+\tau}(s) = h_t(s)h_\tau(s).$$

Every compound Poisson generating function (2.2) satisfies (2.3). We shall now show that also the converse is true: A family of probability generating functions h_t satisfying (2.3) is necessarily of the form (2.2). [It must be understood that this statement is true only for integral-valued random variables. The notion of a compound Poisson distribution remains meaningful even when the X_j have an arbitrary distribution while an analogue to (2.3) plays an important role in the general theory of stochastic processes with independent increments. Such processes, however, are not necessarily subject to compound Poisson distributions.] The following definition and theorem really refer to probability distributions on the integers $0, 1, \ldots$, but for simplicity they are formulated in terms of the corresponding generating functions.

Definition. *A probability generating function h is called infinitely divisible if for each positive integer n the nth root $\sqrt[n]{h}$ is again a probability generating function.*

It follows from the next theorem that the statement remains true even if $n > 0$ is not an integer. If a family of probability generating functions satisfy (2.3) then $\sqrt[n]{h_t} = h_{t/n}$, and so h_t is infinitely divisible. The converse to this statement is contained in

Theorem.[3]   *The only infinitely divisible probability generating functions are those of the form* (2.2) *with* $\{f_i\}$ *a probability distribution on* $0, 1, \ldots$.

Proof.   Put $h(s) = \sum h_k s^k$ and suppose that $\sqrt[n]{h}$ is a probability generating function for each $n \geq 1$. Then $h_0 > 0$, for otherwise the absolute term in the power series for $\sqrt[n]{h}$ would vanish, and this in turn would imply that $h_0 = h_1 = \cdots = h_{n-1} = 0$. It follows that $\sqrt[n]{h(s)} \to 1$ for every $0 \leq s \leq 1$ and so

$$(2.4) \quad \log \sqrt[n]{h(s)/h_0} = \log\left[1 + (\sqrt[n]{h(s)/h_0} - 1)\right] \sim \sqrt[n]{h(s)/h_0} - 1,$$

where the sign $\sim$ indicates that the ratio of the two sides tends to unity. Combining this relation with its special case for $s = 1$ we get [since $h(1) = 1$]

$$(2.5) \quad \frac{\log h(s) - \log h_0}{-\log h_0} = \frac{\log \sqrt[n]{h(s)/h_0}}{\log \sqrt[n]{1/h_0}} \sim \frac{\sqrt[n]{h(s)} - \sqrt[n]{h_0}}{1 - \sqrt[n]{h_0}}.$$

The right side is a power series with positive coefficients and for $s = 1$ it is seen that these coefficients add to unity. Thus for each n the right side represents a probability generating function and so the left side is the limit of a sequence of probability generating functions. By the continuity theorem of XI,6 this implies that the left side itself is the generating function of a non-negative sequence $\{f_j\}$. Letting $s = 1$ we see that $\sum f_j = 1$. This means that h is of the form (2.2) with $\lambda t = -\log h_0$.   ▶

The theorem may be restated in the form of the

Criterion.   *A function* h *is an infinitely divisible probability generating function if, and only if,* $h(1) = 1$ *and*

$$(2.6) \quad \log \frac{h(s)}{h(0)} = \sum_{k=1}^{\infty} a_k s^k \qquad \text{where} \quad a_k \geq 0, \quad \sum a_k = \lambda < \infty.$$

Indeed, in (2.6) it suffices to put $f_k = a_k/\lambda$ to reduce h to the canonical form (2.2) (with $t = 1$), and this in turn is the generating function of the compound Poisson distribution defined in (2.1).

---

[3] This is a simple special case of an important theorem of P. Lévy.

Examples. (*d*) Comparing (2.2) with the theorem of the preceding section we see that if the distribution of **N** is infinitely divisible, the same is true of the distribution of the random sum S_N.

(*e*) *The negative binomial* distribution with generating function

$$(2.7) \qquad\qquad h_t(s) = \left(\frac{p}{1 - qs}\right)^t, \qquad\qquad p + q = 1,$$

has the property (2.3) and is therefore infinitely divisible. Passing to logarithms one sees immediately that it is indeed of the form (2.2) with

$$(2.8) \qquad\qquad f_n = q^n/\lambda n, \qquad \lambda = \log p^{-1}.$$

$\{f_n\}$ is known as the *logarithmic distribution* and is used by statisticians in various contexts.

(*f*) From the expansions II,(8.9) and (8.10) it is obvious that when $q = 1 - p > p$ the functions

$$(2.9) \qquad f(s) = \sqrt{q - p}\ \sqrt{\frac{q + ps}{q - ps}}, \qquad g(s) = \frac{\sqrt{q - p}}{\sqrt{q^2 - p^2 s^2}}$$

satisfy the condition (2.6), and so both *f and g are infinitely divisible probability generating functions.* It is interesting to note that

$$(2.10) \qquad\qquad f(s) = g(s)(q+ps).$$

We have here *a factorization of the infinitely divisible f into two generating functions, of which only one is infinitely divisible.* The possibility of such factorizations came originally as a great surprise and for a while the topic attracted much attention.   ▶

A remarkable property of the compound Poisson distribution has been the object of some curious speculations. If we put for abbreviation $\lambda_i = \lambda f_i$ the generating function h_t of (2.2) can be factored in the form

$$(2.11) \qquad h_t(s) = e^{\lambda_1 t(s-1)} \cdot e^{\lambda_2 t(s^2-1)} \cdot e^{\lambda_3 t(s^3-1)} \cdots.$$

The product can be infinite, but this has no bearing on our discussion and we may suppose that only finitely many λ_i are positive. The first factor is the generating function of an ordinary Poisson distribution with expectation $\lambda_1 t$. The second factor is the generating function for two times a Poisson variable, that is, the familiar probability $e^{-\lambda_2 t}(\lambda_2 t)^n/n!$ is carried by the point $2n$ rather than n. In like manner the kth factor corresponds to a Poisson distribution attributing probabilities to the multiples of k. Thus (2.11) gives a new representation of S_N as the sum of independent variables $Y_1, Y_2, \ldots$ such that Y_k takes on only the values $0, k, 2k, \ldots$ but has otherwise a Poisson distribution. The content of (2.11) may be described as follows. Let N_j stand for the number of those variables among $X_1, \ldots, X_N$ that are equal to j. Then $N = N_1 + N_2 + \cdots$ and (2.11) states that the variables N_k *are mutually independent and subject to Poisson distributions.*

Example. (g) *Automobile accidents.* Interpret X_n as the number of automobiles involved in the nth accident. Under the standard assumption that the X_n are independent and that the number N of accidents has a Poisson distribution, the total number of cars involved in the accidents is given by $X_1 + \cdots + X_N$ and has the compound Poisson distribution (2.1). We may now consider separately the number N_k of accidents involving exactly k cars. According to (2.11) the variables N_k are mutually independent and have Poisson distributions. The practical implications of this result require no comment.   ▶

[For a generalization of the compound Poisson distribution see example XVII,(9.*a*).]

2a. Processes with independent increments

The preceding results gain in interest through their intimate connections with an important class of stochastic processes. These will now be indicated informally even though the theory lies beyond the scope of the present book.

To begin with the simplest example consider the number of incoming calls at a telephone exchange as a function of time. The development at an individual exchange is described by recording for each t the number $Z(t)$ of calls that arrived between 0 and t. If the successive calls arrived at $t_1, t_2, \ldots$, then $Z(t) = 0$ for $0 < t < t_1$, and generally $Z(t) = k$ for $t_k < t < t_{k+1}$. Conversely, every non-decreasing function assuming only the values $0, 1, 2, \ldots$ represents a possible development at a telephone exchange. A probabilistic model must therefore be based on a sample space whose individual points represent functions $Z(t)$ (rather than sequences as in the case of discrete trials). Probabilities must be assigned in a manner enabling us to deal with intricate events such as the event that $Z(t+1) - Z(t)$ will ever exceed 17 or that $Z(t)$ will at some time exceed $at + b$ (the latter event is the main object of the ruin problem in the collective theory of risk). In the following we shall take it for granted that such an assignment is indeed possible; our aim is to show that simple and natural assumptions concerning the nature of the process imply that for every fixed t the random variable $Z(t)$ must have a compound Poisson distribution.

Similar considerations apply to a great variety of empirical phenomena. Instead of the number of telephone ca: ls the variable $Z(t)$ may represent the accumulated length (or cost) of the ensuing conversations, or the number of cars involved in accidents, the accumulated damage due to lightning, the total consumption of electricity, the accumulated rainfall, etc. Within the framework of the present chapter we must assume that the variables $Z(t)$ assume only non-negative integral values, but the theory can be generalized to arbitrary random variables. We focus our attention on processes satisfying the following two basic assumptions, which seem natural in many applications.

(a) The process is *time-homogeneous*, that is, the distributions of increments $\mathbf{Z}(t+h) - \mathbf{Z}(t)$ depend only on the length of the time interval, but not on its position.[4]

(b) The increments $\mathbf{Z}(t_2) - \mathbf{Z}(t_1)$ and $\mathbf{Z}(t_1) - \mathbf{Z}(t_0)$ over contiguous time intervals are mutually independent. The results of the preceding section may now be restated as follows: *If* there exists a process satisfying the postulates (a) and (b), then its increments $\mathbf{Z}(t+h) - \mathbf{Z}(t)$ have compound Poisson distributions. In particular, when $\mathbf{Z}(t)$ changes only by unit amounts the variables have simple Poisson distributions. [Cf. (2.11).]

We have thus found a characterization of the simple and compound Poisson distributions by intrinsic properties; by contrast to the derivation in chapter VI the Poisson distribution no longer appears as an approximation, but stands on its own rights (one might say: as an expression of a natural law). Of course, we are now faced with the converse problem to see whether any family of compound Poisson distributions really corresponds to a stochastic process. The answer is affirmative, but it turns out (somewhat surprisingly) that our two postulates do not suffice to describe a *unique* process. For a unique description of an interesting class of processes it is necessary to strengthen the postulate (b) by requiring that for any n the n increments corresponding to a finite partition $t_0 < t_1 < \cdots < t_n$ be mutually independent. This is the defining property of *processes with independent increments*. Any family of compound Poisson distributions determines uniquely a process with independent increments, and so no theoretical difficulties arise. But we have assumed the independence property only for two intervals. This restricted postulate suffices to determine the form of the distributions of the increments, but it is possible to construct rather pathological processes with this property.[5] This example illustrates the difficulties inherent in the construction of a complete model of a stochastic process.

3. EXAMPLES FOR BRANCHING PROCESSES

We shall describe a chance process which serves as a simplified model of many empirical processes and also illustrates the usefulness of generating functions. In words the process may be described as follows.

We consider particles which are able to produce new particles of like kind. A single particle forms the original, or zero, generation. Every particle has probability p_k $(k = 0, 1, 2, \ldots)$ of creating exactly k new particles; the direct descendants of the nth generation form the $(n+1)$st generation. The particles of each generation act independently of each other. We are interested in the size of the successive generations.

---

[4] This condition is less restrictive than might appear at first sight. For example, in a telephone exchange incoming calls are more frequent during the busiest hour of the day than, say, between midnight and 1 A.M.; the process is therefore not homogeneous in time. However, for obvious reasons telephone engineers are concerned mainly with the "busy hour" of the day, and for that period the process can be considered homogeneous. Experience shows also that during the busy hour the incoming traffic follows the Poisson distribution with surprising accuracy.

[5] In such a process the increment $\mathbf{Z}(t_3) - \mathbf{Z}(t_2)$ is independent of $\mathbf{Z}(t_2) - \mathbf{Z}(t_1)$ as well as of $\mathbf{Z}(t_1) - \mathbf{Z}(t_0)$, and yet may be completely determined by the latter pair. See W. Feller, *Non-Markovian processes with the semi-group property*, Ann. Math. Statist., vol. 30 (1959), pp. 1252–1253.

A few illustrations may precede a rigorous formulation in terms of random variables.

(a) *Nuclear chain reactions.* This application became familiar in connection with the atomic bomb.[6] The particles are neutrons, which are subject to chance hits by other particles. Let p be the probability that the particle sooner or later scores a hit, thus creating m particles; then $q = 1 - p$ is the probability that the particle has no descendants; that is, it remains inactive (is removed or absorbed in a different way). In this scheme the only possible numbers of descendants are 0 and m, and the corresponding probabilities are q and p (i.e., $p_0 = q$, $p_m = p$, $p_j = 0$ for all other j). At worst, the first particle remains inactive and the process never starts. At best, there will be m particles of the first generation, m^2 of the second, and so on. If p is near one, the number of particles is likely to increase very rapidly. Mathematically, this number may increase indefinitely. Physically speaking, for very large numbers of particles the probabilities of fission cannot remain constant, and also stochastic independence is impossible. However, for ordinary chain reactions, the mathematical description "indefinitely increasing number of particles" may be translated by "explosion."

(b) *Survival of family names.* Here (as often in life), only male descendants count; they play the role of particles, and p_k is the probability for a newborn boy to become the progenitor of exactly k boys. Our scheme introduces two artificial simplifications. Fertility is subject to secular trends, and therefore the distribution $\{p_k\}$ in reality changes from generation to generation. Moreover, common inheritance and common environment are bound to produce similarities among brothers which is contrary to our assumption of stochastic independence. Our model can be refined to take care of these objections, but the essential features remain unaffected. We shall derive the probability of finding k carriers of the family name in the nth generation and, in particular, the probability of an extinction of the line. Survival of family names appears to have been the first chain reaction studied by probability methods. The problem was first treated by F. Galton (1889); for a detailed account the reader is referred to A. Lotka's book.[7] Lotka shows that American experience is reasonably well described by the distribution $p_0 = 0.4825$, $p_k = (0.2126)(0.5893)^{k-1}$ ($k \geq 1$), which, except for the first term, is a geometric distribution.

---

[6] The following description follows E. Schroedinger, *Probability problems in nuclear chemistry*, Proceedings of the Royal Irish Academy, vol. 51, sect. A, No. 1 (December 1945). There the assumption of spatial homogeneity is removed.

[7] *Théorie analytique des associations biologiques*, vol. 2, *Actualités scientifiques et industrielles*, No. 780 (1939), pp. 123–136, Hermann et Cie, Paris.

(c) *Genes and mutations.* Every gene of a given organism (V,5) has a chance to reappear in 1, 2, 3, . . . direct descendants, and our scheme describes the process, neglecting, of course, variations within the population and with time. This scheme is of particular use in the study of mutations, or changes of form in a gene. A spontaneous mutation produces a single gene of the new kind, which plays the role of a zero-generation particle. The theory leads to estimates of the chances of survival and of the spread of the mutant gene. To fix ideas, consider (following R. A. Fisher) a corn plant which is father to some 100 seeds and mother to an equal number. If the population size remains constant, an average of two among these 200 seeds will develop to a plant. Each seed has probability $\frac{1}{2}$ to receive a particular gene. The probability of a mutant gene being represented in exactly k new plants is therefore comparable to the probability of exactly k successes in 200 Bernoulli trials with probability $p = \frac{1}{200}$, and it appears reasonable to assume that $\{p_k\}$ is, approximately, a Poisson distribution with mean 1. If the gene carries a biological advantage, we get a Poisson distribution with mean $\lambda > 1$.

(d) *Waiting lines.*[8] Interesting applications of branching processes occur in queuing theory. Roughly speaking, a customer arriving at an empty server and receiving immediate service is termed ancestor; his direct descendants are the customers arriving during his service time and forming a waiting line. This process continues as long as the queue lasts. We shall return to it in greater detail in example (5.b), and to an even more interesting variant in example (5.c).   ▶

4. EXTINCTION PROBABILITIES IN BRANCHING PROCESSES

Denote by Z_n the size of the nth generation, and by P_n the generating function of its probability distribution. By assumption $Z_0 = 1$ and

$$(4.1) \qquad P_1(s) = P(s) = \sum_{k=0}^{\infty} p_k s^k.$$

The nth generation can be divided into Z_1 clans according to the ancestor in the first generation. This means that Z_n is the sum of Z_1 random variables $Z_n^{(k)}$, each representing the size of the offspring of one member of the first generation. By assumption each $Z_n^{(k)}$ has the same probability distribution as Z_{n-1} and (for fixed n) the variables $Z_n^{(k)}$ are mutually

---

[8] D.G. Kendall, *Some problems in the theory of queues*, J. Roy. Statist. Soc. (Series B), vol. 13 (1951), pp. 151–173, and discussion 173–185.

independent. The generating function P_n is therefore given by the compound function

(4.2) $P_n(s) = P(P_{n-1}(s))$.

This result enables us to calculate recursively all the generating functions. In view of (4.2) we have $P_2(s) = P(P(s))$, then $P_3(s) = P(P_2(s))$, etc. The calculations are straightforward, though explicit expressions for P_n are usually hard to come by. We shall see presently that it is nevertheless possible to draw important conclusions from (4.2).

Example. (*a*) Suppose that the number of direct descendants is subject to the geometric distribution $\{qp^k\}$ where $p \neq q$. Then $P(s) = q/(1-ps)$ and an explicit calculation of P_2, P_3, etc., leads us (with some patience) to the general formula

(4.3) $P_n(s) = q \cdot \dfrac{p^n - q^n - (p^{n-1}-q^{n-1})ps}{p^{n+1} - q^{n+1} - (p^n-q^n)ps}$.

It is easy to verify that (4.3) indeed satisfies (4.2).

If $p = q$, we get, letting $p \to \frac{1}{2}$,

(4.4) $P_n(s) = \dfrac{n - (n-1)s}{n + 1 - ns}$.

Note that $P_n(0) \to q/p$ if $p > q$, but $P_n(0) \to 1$ if $p \leq q$. We shall now interpret this result and find its analogue for arbitrary distributions $\{p_k\}$.   ▶

The first question concerning our branching process is whether it will continue forever or whether the progeny will die out after finitely many generations. Put

(4.5) $x_n = \mathbf{P}\{\mathbf{Z}_n = 0\} = P_n(0)$.

This is the probability that the process terminates at or before the nth generation. By definition $x_1 = p_0$ and from (4.2) it is clear that

(4.6) $x_n = P(x_{n-1})$.

The extreme cases $p_0 = 0$ and $p_0 = 1$ being trivial, we now suppose that $0 < p_0 < 1$. From the monotone character of P we conclude then that $x_2 = P(p_0) > P(0) = x_1$, and hence by induction that $x_1 < x_2 < x_3 < \cdots$. It follows that there exists a limit $x \leq 1$, and from (4.6) it is clear that

(4.7) $x = P(x)$.

For $0 \leq s \leq 1$ the graph of $P(s)$ is a *convex* curve starting at the point $(0, p_0)$ above the bisector and ending at the point $(1, 1)$ on the bisector. Accordingly only two situations are possible:

Case (i).   The graph is entirely above the bisector. In this case $x = 1$ is the unique root of the equation (4.7), and so $x_n \to 1$. Furthermore, in this case $1 - P(s) \le 1 - s$ for all s, and letting $s \to 1$ we see that the derivative $P'(1)$ satisfies the inequality $P'(1) \le 1$.

Case (ii).   The graph of P intersects the bisector at some point $\sigma < 1$. Since a convex curve intersects a straight line in at most two points, in this case $P(s) > s$ for $s < \sigma$ but $P(s) < s$ for $\sigma < s < 1$. Then $x_1 = P(0) < P(\sigma) = \sigma$, and by induction $x_n = P(x_{n-1}) < P(\sigma) = \sigma$. It follows that $x_n \to \sigma$ and so $x = \sigma$. On the other hand, by the mean value theorem there exists a point between σ and 1 at which the derivative P' equals one. This derivative being monotone, it follows that $P'(1) > 1$.

We see thus that the two cases are characterized by $P'(1) \le 1$ and $P'(1) > 1$, respectively. But

$$(4.8) \qquad \mu = P'(1) = \sum_{k=0}^{\infty} k p_k \le \infty$$

is *the expected number of direct descendants,* and we have proved the interesting

Theorem. *If $\mu \le 1$ the process dies out with probability one. If, however, $\mu > 1$ the probability x_n that the process terminates at or before the nth generation tends to the unique root $x < 1$ of the equation* (4.7).

In practice the convergence $x_n \to x$ is usually rapid and so with a great probability the process either stops rather soon, or else it continues forever. The expected size of the nth generation is given by $\mathbf{E}(\mathbf{Z}_n) = P'_n(1)$. From (4.2) we get by the chain rule $P'_n(1) = P'(1)P'_{n-1}(1) = \mu \mathbf{E}(\mathbf{X}_{n-1})$, and hence[9]

$$(4.9) \qquad\qquad \mathbf{E}(\mathbf{X}_n) = \mu^n.$$

It is not surprising that the process is bound for extinction when $\mu < 1$, but it was not clear a priori that a stable situation is impossible even when $\mu = 1$. When $\mu > 1$ one should expect a geometric growth in accordance with (4.9). This is true in some average sense, but no matter how large μ there is a finite probability of extinction. It is easily seen that $P_n(s) \to x$ for all $s < 1$ and this means that the coefficients of s, s^2, s^3, etc., all tend to 0. After *a sufficient number of generations it is therefore likely that there*

---

[9] For further details see the comprehensive treatise by T. E. Harris, *The theory of branching processes*, Berlin (Springer), 1963.

are either no descendants or else a great many descendants (the corresponding probabilities being x and $1 - x$).

5. THE TOTAL PROGENY IN BRANCHING PROCESSES

We now turn our attention to the random variable[10]

(5.1) $$Y_n = 1 + Z_1 + \cdots + Z_n$$

which equals the total number of descendants up to and including the nth generation and also including the ancestor (zero generation). Letting $n \to \infty$ we get the size of the total progeny which may be finite or infinite. Clearly, for each n the random variable Y_n is well defined and we denote by R_n the generating function of its probability distribution. Since $Y_1 = 1 + Z_1$ we have $R_1(s) = sP(s)$. A recursion formula for R_n can be derived by the argument of the preceding section, the only difference being that to obtain Y_n we must add the progenitor to the sum of the progenies of the Z_1 members of the first generation. Accordingly

(5.2) $$R_n(s) = sP(R_{n-1}(s)).$$

From this recursion formula it is theoretically possible to calculate successively $R_1, R_2, \ldots$, but the labor is prohibitive. Fortunately it is possible to discuss the asymptotic behavior of R_n by the geometric argument used in the preceding section to derive the extinction probability x.

First we note that for each $s < 1$

(5.3) $$R_2(s) = sP(R_1(s)) < sP(s) = R_1(s)$$

and by induction it follows that $R_n(s) < R_{n-1}(s)$. Accordingly $R_n(s)$ decreases monotonically to a limit $\rho(s)$, and the latter satisfies

(5.4) $$\rho(s) = sP(\rho(s)) \qquad\qquad 0 < s < 1.$$

From the continuity theorem of XI,6 we know that as limit of probability generating functions ρ is the generating function of a sequence of non-negative numbers ρ_k such that $\sum \rho_k \leq 1$.

It follows from (5.4) that for fixed $s < 1$ the value $\rho(s)$ is a root of the equation

(5.5) $$t = sP(t).$$

---

[10] This section was inspired by I. J. Good, *The number of individuals in a cascade process*, Proc. Cambridge Philos. Soc., vol. 45 (1949), pp. 360–363.

We show that this root is unique. For that purpose we denote again by x the smallest positive root of $x = P(x)$ (so that $x \leq 1$). We observe that $y = sP(t)$ (with s fixed) is a convex function of t and so its graph intersects the line $y = t$ in at most two points. But for $t = 0$ the right side in (5.5) is greater than the left, whereas the inequality is reversed when $t = x$, and also when $t = 1$; thus (5.5) has exactly one root between 0 and x, and no root between x and 1. Accordingly, $\rho(s)$ is uniquely characterized as this root, and we see furthermore that $\rho(s) < x$. But $\rho(1)$ is obviously a root of $t = P(t)$, and since x is the smallest root of this equation it is clear that $\rho(1) = x$. In other words, ρ is an honest probability generating function if, and only if, $x = 1$. We can summarize these findings as follows.

Let ρ_k be the probability that the total progeny consists of k elements.
(a) $\sum \rho_k$ equals the extinction probability x (and $1 - x$ equals the probability of an infinite progeny).
(b) The generating function $\rho(s) = \sum \rho_k s^k$ is given by the unique positive root of (5.5), and $\rho(s) \leq x$.

We know already that with probability one the total progeny is finite whenever $\mu \leq 1$. By differentiation of (5.4) it is now seen that its expectation equals $1/(1 - \mu)$ when $\mu < 1$ and is infinite when $\mu = 1$.

Examples. (a) In example (4.a) we had $P(s) = q/(1 - ps)$, and (5.5) reduces to the quadratic equation $pt^2 - t + qs = 0$ from which we conclude that

(5.6)
$$\rho(s) = \frac{1 - \sqrt{1 - 4pqs}}{2p} .$$

(This generating function occurred also in connection with the first-passage times in XI,3.)

(b) *Busy periods.* We turn to a more detailed analysis of the queuing problem mentioned in example (3.d). Suppose for simplicity that customers can arrive only one at a time and only at integral-valued epochs.[11] We assume that the arrivals are regulated by Bernoulli trials in such a way that at epoch n a customer arrives with probability p, while with probability $q = 1 - p$ no arrival takes place. A customer arriving when the server is free is served immediately, and otherwise he joins the queue (waiting line). The server continues service without interruption as long as there are customers in the queue requiring service. We suppose finally that the

---

[11] Following a practice introduced by J. Riordan we use the term epoch for points on the time axis because the alternative terms such as time, moment, etc., are overburdened with other meanings.

successive service times are independent (integral-valued) random variables with a common distribution $\{\beta_k\}$ and generating function $\beta(s) =$ $= \sum \beta_k s^k$.

Suppose then that a customer arrives at epoch 0 and finds the server free. His service time starts immediately. If it has duration n, the counter becomes free at epoch n provided that no new customer arrives at epochs $1, 2, \ldots, n$. Otherwise the service continues without interruption. By *busy period* is meant the duration of uninterrupted service commencing at epoch 0. We show how the theory of branching process may be used to analyze the duration of the busy period.

The customer arriving at epoch 0 initiates the busy period and will be called ancestor. The first generation consists of the customers arriving prior to or at the epoch of the termination of the ancestor's service time. If there are no such direct descendants the process stops. Otherwise the direct descendants are served successively, and during their service times their direct descendants join the queue. We have here a branching process such that *the probability* x *of extinction equals the probability of a termination of the busy period, and the total progeny consists of all customers* (*including the ancestor*) *arriving during the busy period*. Needless to say, only queues with $x = 1$ are feasible in practice.

To apply our results we require the generating function $P(s)$ for the number of direct descendants. By definition this number is determined by the random sum $\mathbf{X}_1 + \cdots + \mathbf{X}_N$ where the $\mathbf{X}_j$ are mutually independent and assume the values 1 and 0 with probabilities p and q, while $\mathbf{N}$ is the length of the ancestor's service time. Thus in the present situation $P(s) = \beta(ps+q)$, and hence $\mu = p\sigma$ where $\sigma = \beta'(1)$ is the expected duration of the service time. It follows that *the busy period is certain to terminate only if* $p\sigma \le 1$. *The expected number of customers during a busy period is finite only if* $p\sigma < 1$. In other words, congestion is guaranteed when $p\sigma = 1$, and long queues must be the order of the day unless $p\sigma$ is substantially less than 1.

(c) *Duration of the busy period.* The preceding example treats the number of customers during a busy period, but the actual duration of the busy period is of greater practical interest. It can be obtained by the elegant device[12] of considering time units as elements of a branching process. We say that the epoch n has no descendants if no customer arrives at epoch n. If such a customer arrives and his service time lasts r time units, then the epochs $n + 1, \ldots, n + r$ are counted as direct descendants of the epoch. Suppose that at epoch 0 the server is free. A little reflection now shows that

---

[12] It is due to I. J. Good. See the discussion following Kendall's paper quoted in example (3.d).

the branching process originated by the epoch 0 either does not come off at all or else lasts exactly for the duration of the uninterrupted service time initiated by a new customer. The generating function for the number of direct descendants is given by

$$(5.7) \qquad P(s) = q + p\beta(s).$$

The root x gives the probability of a termination of the busy period. The total progeny equals 1 with probability q while with probability p it equals the duration of the busy period commencing at epoch 0. The duration of the busy period itself has obviously the generating function given by $\beta(\rho(s))$. ▶

6. PROBLEMS FOR SOLUTION

1. The distribution (1.1) of the random sum S_N has mean $E(N)E(X)$ and variance $E(N) \operatorname{Var}(X) + \operatorname{Var}(N)E^2(X)$. Verify this (*a*) using the generating function, (*b*) directly from the definition and the notion of conditional expectations.

2. *Animal trapping* [example (1.*b*)]. If $\{g_n\}$ is a geometric distribution, so is the resulting distribution. If $\{g_n\}$ is a logarithmic distribution [cf. (2.8)], there results a logarithmic distribution with an added term.

3. In N Bernoulli trials, where N is a random variable with a Poisson distribution, the numbers of successes and failures are stochastically independent variables. Generalize this to the multinomial distribution (*a*) directly, (*b*) using multivariate generating functions. [Cf. example IX,(1.*d*).]

4. *Randomization.* Let N have a Poisson distribution with mean λ, and let N balls be placed randomly into n cells. Show without calculation that the probability of finding exactly m cells empty is $\binom{n}{m} e^{-\lambda m/n}[1 - e^{-\lambda/n}]^{n-m}$.

5. *Continuation.*[13] Show that when a fixed number r of balls is placed randomly into n cells the probability of finding exactly m cells empty equals the coefficient of $e^{-\lambda} \lambda^r/r!$ in the expression above. (*a*) Discuss the connection with moment generating functions (problem 24 of XI, 7). (*b*) Use the result for an effortless derivation of II,(11.7).

6. *Mixtures of probability distributions.* Let $\{f_i\}$ and $\{g_i\}$ be two probability distributions, $\alpha > 0$, $\beta > 0$, $\alpha + \beta = 1$. Then $\{\alpha f_i + \beta g_i\}$ is again a probability distribution. Discuss its meaning and the connection with the urn models of V,2. Generalize to more than two distributions. Show that such a mixture can be a compound Poisson distribution.

7. Using generating functions show that in the branching process $\operatorname{Var}(X_{n+1}) = \mu \operatorname{Var}(X_n) + \mu^{2n}\sigma^2$. Using conditional expectations prove the equivalent

---

[13] This elegant derivation of various combinatorial formulas by randomizing a parameter is due to C. Domb, *On the use of a random parameter in combinatorial problems*, Proceedings Physical Society, Sec. A., vol. 65 (1952), pp. 305–309.

relation $\text{Var}(\mathbf{X}_{n+1}) = \mu^2 \text{Var}(\mathbf{X}_n) + \mu^n \sigma^2$. Conclude from either form that $\text{Var}(\mathbf{X}_n) = \sigma^2(\mu^{2n-2} + \mu^{2n-3} + \cdots + \mu^{n-1})$.

8. *Continuation.* If $n > m$ show that $\mathbf{E}(\mathbf{X}_n \mathbf{X}_m) = \mu^{n-m} \mathbf{E}(\mathbf{X}_m^2)$.

9. *Continuation.* Show that the bivariate generating function of $(\mathbf{X}_m, \mathbf{X}_n)$ is $P_m(s_1 P_{n-m}(s_2))$. Use this to verify the assertion in problem 8.

10. *Branching processes with two types of individuals.* Assume that each individual can have descendants of either kind; the numbers of descendants of the two types are regulated by two bivariate generating functions $P_1(s_1, s_2)$ and $P_2(s_1, s_2)$. We have now two extinction probabilities x, y depending on the type of the ancestor. Show that the pair (x, y) satisfies the equations

(6.1) $$x = P_1(x, y), \qquad y = P_2(x, y).$$

Prove that these equations have at most one solution $0 \le x \le 1$, $0 \le y \le 1$ different from $(1, 1)$. The solution $(1, 1)$ is unique if, and only if, $\mu_{11} \le 1$, $\mu_{22} \le 1$ and $(1 - \mu_{11})(1 - \mu_{22}) \ge \mu_{12}\mu_{21}$ where $\mu_{ij} = \dfrac{\partial P_i(1, 1)}{\partial s_j}$.

CHAPTER XIII

Recurrent Events.
Renewal Theory

1. INFORMAL PREPARATIONS AND EXAMPLES

We shall be concerned with certain repetitive, or recurrent, patterns connected with repeated trials. Roughly speaking, a pattern $\mathcal{E}$ qualifies for the following theory if after each occurrence of $\mathcal{E}$ the trials start from scratch in the sense that the trials following an occurrence of $\mathcal{E}$ form a replica of the whole experiment. The waiting times between successive occurrences of $\mathcal{E}$ are mutually independent random variables having the same distribution.

The simplest special case arises when $\mathcal{E}$ stands as abbreviation for "a success occurs" in a sequence of Bernoulli trials. The waiting time up to the first success has a geometric distribution; when the first success occurs, the trials start anew, and the number of trials between the rth and the $(r+1)$st success has the same geometric distribution. The waiting time up to the rth success is the sum of r independent variables [example IX,(3.c)]. This situation prevails also when $\mathcal{E}$ stands for "a success followed by failure": The occurrence of the pattern SF reestablishes the initial situation, and the waiting time for the next occurrence of SF is independent of the preceding trials. By contrast, suppose that people are sampled one by one and let $\mathcal{E}$ stand for "two people in the sample have the same birthday." This $\mathcal{E}$ is not repetitive because after its first realization $\mathcal{E}$ persists forever. If we change the definition to "$\mathcal{E}$ occurs whenever the birthday of the newly added person is already present in the sample," then $\mathcal{E}$ can occur any number of times, but after an occurrence of $\mathcal{E}$ the process does *not* start from scratch. This is so because the increasing sample size makes duplications of birthdays more likely; a long waiting time for the first double birthday promises therefore a shorter waiting time for the second duplication, and so the consecutive waiting times are neither independent nor subject to a common distribution.

The importance of the theory of recurrent patterns is due to the fact that such patterns occur frequently in connection with various sequences of variables (stochastic processes). The laws governing a sequence of random variables may be so intricate as to preclude a complete analysis but the existence of a repetitive pattern makes it always possible to discuss essential features of the sequence, to prove the existence of certain limits, etc. This approach contributes greatly to the simplification and unification of many theories.

We proceed to review a few typical examples, some of which are of intrinsic interest. The first examples refer to the familiar Bernoulli trials, but the last three involve more complicated schemes. In their description we use terms such as "server" and "customer," but in each case we give a mathematical definition of a sequence of random variables which is complete in the sense that it uniquely determines the probabilities of all possible events. In practice, not even the basic probabilities can be calculated explicitly, but it will turn out that the theory of repetitive patterns nevertheless leads to significant results.

Examples. (a) *Return to equilibrium.* In a sequence of Bernoulli trials let $\mathcal{E}$ stand as abbreviation for "the accumulated numbers of successes and failures are equal." As we have done before, we describe the trials in terms of mutually independent random variables $X_1, X_2, \ldots$ assuming the values 1 and -1 with probabilities p and q, respectively. As usual, we put

$$(1.1) \qquad S_0 = 0, \qquad S_n = X_1 + \cdots + X_n.$$

Then S_n is the accumulated excess of heads over tails, and $\mathcal{E}$ *occurs if, and only if,* $S_n = 0$. It goes without saying that the occurrence of this event reestablishes the initial situation in the sense that the subsequent partial sums $S_{n+1}, S_{n+2}, \ldots$ form a probabilistic replica of the whole sequence $S_1, S_2, \ldots$. [Continued in example (4.b).]

(b) *Return to equilibrium through negative values.* We modify the last example by stipulating that $\mathcal{E}$ occurs at the nth trial if

$$(1.2) \qquad S_n = 0, \quad but \quad S_1 < 0, \ldots, S_{n-1} < 0.$$

Again, it is clear that the occurrence of $\mathcal{E}$ implies that we start from scratch. [Continued in example (4.c).]

(c) Another variant of example (a) is the event $\mathcal{E}$ that the accumulated number of successes equals λ times the accumulated number of failures (where $\lambda > 0$ is an arbitrary, but fixed, number). If $\mathcal{E}$ occurs at the nth trial, it occurs again at the $(n+m)$th trial only if among the trials number $n + 1, \ldots, n + m$ there occur exactly λ times as many successes as failures. The waiting times between successive occurrences of $\mathscr{E}$ are therefore independent and identically distributed. As a special case consider the event that $6n$ throws of a perfect die yield exactly n aces. (Continued in problems 4–5.)

(*d*) *Ladder variables.* Adhering to the notations of example (*a*) we define a new repetitive pattern $\mathscr{E}$ by stipulating that $\mathscr{E}$ *occurs at the nth trial if* S_n *exceeds all preceding sums*, that is, if

$$(1.3) \qquad\qquad S_n > 0, \qquad S_n > S_1, \ldots, S_n > S_{n-1}.$$

If $\mathscr{E}$ occurs at the *n*th trial the process starts from scratch in the following sense. Assuming (1.3) to hold, $\mathscr{E}$ occurs at the $(n+m)$th trial if, and only if,

$$(1.4) \qquad\qquad S_{n+m} > S_n, \ldots, S_{n+m} > S_{n+m-1}.$$

But the differences $S_{n+k} - S_n$ are simply the partial sums of the residual sequence $X_{n+1}, X_{n+2}, \ldots$ and so the reoccurrence of $\mathscr{E}$ is defined in terms of this residual sequence exactly as $\mathscr{E}$ is defined for the whole sequence. In other words, for the study of $\mathscr{E}$ the whole past becomes irrelevant every time $\mathscr{E}$ occurs. [Continued in example (4.*d*).]

(*e*) *Success runs in Bernoulli trials.* In the preceding examples the definition of $\mathscr{E}$ was straightforward, but we turn now to a situation in which a judicious definition is necessary to make the theory of recurrent patterns applicable. In the classical literature a "success run of length *r*" meant an uninterrupted sequence of either exactly *r*, or of at least *r*, successes. Neither convention leads to a recurrent pattern. Indeed, if exactly *r* successes are required, then a success at the $(n+1)$st trial may undo the run completed at the *n*th trial. On the other hand, if at least *r* successes are required, then every run may be prolonged indefinitely and it is clear that the occurrence of a run does not reestablish the initial situation. The classical theory of runs was rather messy, and a more systematic approach is possible by defining a run of length *r* in such a way that it becomes a recurrent pattern. A *first* run of length *r* is uniquely defined, and we now agree to start counting from scratch every time a run occurs. With this convention the sequence $SSS \mid SFSSS \mid SSS \mid F$ contains three success runs of length three (occurring at trials number 3, 8, and 11). It contains five runs of length two (trials number 2, 4, 7, 9, 11). The formal definition is as follows: *A sequence of n letters S and F contains as many S-runs of length r as there are non-overlapping uninterrupted blocks containing exactly r letters S each.* With this convention we say that $\mathscr{E}$ occurs at the *n*th trial if a new run of length *r* is added to the sequence. This defines a recurrent pattern and greatly simplifies the theory without affecting its basic features. (Continued in section 7.)

(*f*) *Continuation: Related patterns.* It is obvious that the considerations of the preceding example apply to more general patterns, such as the occurrence of the succession *SFSF*. More interesting is that no limitation to a fixed pattern is necessary. Thus the occurrence of "*two successes and three failures*" defines a repetitive pattern, and the same is true of "either a success run of length r or a failure run of length ρ." (Continued in section 8.)

(*g*) *Geiger counters.* Counters of the type used for cosmic rays and α-particles may be described by the following simplified model.[1] Bernoulli trials are performed at a uniform rate. A counter is meant to register successes, but the mechanism is locked for exactly $r-1$ trials following each registration. In other words, a success at the nth trial is registered if, and only if, no registration has occurred in the preceding $r-1$ trials. The counter is then locked at the conclusion of trials number $n, \ldots, n + r - 1$, and is freed at the conclusion of the $(n+r)$th trial provided this trial results in failure. The output of the counter represents dependent trials. Each registration has an aftereffect, but, whenever the counter is free (not locked) the situation is exactly the same, and the trials start from scratch. Letting $\mathcal{E}$ stand for "at the conclusion of the trial the counter is free," we have a typical recurrent pattern. [Continued in example (4.*e*).]

(*h*) *The simplest queuing process* is defined in terms of a sequence of Bernoulli trials and a sequence of random variables $X_1, X_2, \ldots$ assuming only positive integral values. The X_k have a common distribution $\{\beta_k\}$ and are independent of each other and of the Bernoulli trials. We interpret success at the nth trial as the arrival at epoch[2] n of a customer at a server (or a call at a telephone trunk line). The variable X_n represents the service time of the nth customer arriving at the server. At any epoch the server is either "free" or "busy" and the process proceeds according to the following rules. Initially (at epoch 0) the server is free. A customer arriving when the counter is free is served immediately, but following his arrival the server is busy for the duration of the service time. Customers arriving when the server is busy form a waiting line (queue). The server serves customers without interruption as long as there is a demand.

These rules determine the process uniquely, for given a sample sequence $(S, F, S, S, S, F, F, \ldots)$ for the arrival process and a sample sequence $(3, 1, 17, 2, \ldots)$ for the successive service times, it is not difficult to find

---

[1] This is the discrete analogue of the so-called counters of type I. Type II is described in problem 8.

[2] We use the term *epoch* to denote points on the time axis. Terms such as waiting time will refer to durations. This practice was introduced by J. Riordan because in queuing theory the several meanings of words like time, moment, etc., are apt to cause confusion.

the size of the queue at any epoch, and the waiting time of the nth customer. In principle, therefore, we should be able to calculate all pertinent probabilities, but it is not easy to find practicable methods. Now it is clear that every time the server is free the situation is exactly the same as it is at epoch 0. In our terminology therefore the contingency "the server is free" constitutes a recurrent pattern. We shall see that the very existence of such a recurrent pattern has important consequences; for example, it implies that the probability distributions for the size of the queue at epoch n, for the waiting time of the nth customer, and for similar random variables tend to definite limits when $n \to \infty$ (theorem 5.2). In other words, the existence of a recurrent pattern enables us to prove the existence of a steady state and to analyze its dominant features.

(*i*) *Servicing of machines.* The scope of the method of recurrent patterns may be illustrated by a variant of the preceding example in which the arrivals are no longer regulated by Bernoulli trials. To fix ideas, let us interpret the "customers" as identical machines subject to occasional breakdowns, and the "server" as a repairman. We adhere to the same conventions concerning servicing and the formation of queues, but introduce a new chance mechanism for the "arrivals," that is, for the breakdowns. Suppose there are N machines in all, and consider two extreme cases.

(*a*) Suppose first that as long as a machine is in working condition it has a fixed probability p to break down at the next epoch; when it breaks down it is replaced by an identical new machine, and the serving time is interpreted as the time required for the installation of a new machine. We treat the machines as independent, and the breakdowns are regulated by N independent sequences of Bernoulli trials. Note that the more machines are in the queue, the fewer machines are in working condition, and hence the length of the queue at any epoch influences the probability of new arrivals (or service calls). This is in marked contrast to the preceding example, but the contingency "server is idle" constitutes nevertheless a recurrent pattern because we are confronted with precisely the same situation whenever it occurs.

(*b*) Suppose now that every repair has an aftereffect in that it increases the probabilities of further breakdowns. This implies that the machines deteriorate steadily and so once a machine breaks down it is impossible that the favorable initial situation should be repeated. In this case there is no recurrent pattern to help the analysis.   ▶

2. DEFINITIONS

We consider a sequence of repeated trials with possible outcomes E_j $(j = 1, 2, \ldots)$. They need not be independent (applications to Markov chains being of special interest). As usual, we suppose that it is in principle possible to continue the trials indefinitely, the probabilities $\mathbf{P}\{E_{j_1}, E_{j_2}, \ldots, E_{j_n}\}$ being defined consistently for all finite sequences. Let $\mathcal{E}$ be an attribute of finite sequences; that is, we suppose that it is uniquely determined whether a sequence $(E_{j_1}, \ldots, E_{j_n})$ has, or has not, the characteristic $\mathcal{E}$. We agree that the expression "$\mathcal{E}$ occurs at the nth place in the (finite or infinite) sequence $E_{j_1}, E_{j_2}, \ldots$" is an abbreviation for "The subsequence $E_{j_1}, E_{j_2}, \ldots, E_{j_n}$ has the attribute $\mathcal{E}$." This convention implies that the occurrence of $\mathcal{E}$ at the nth trial depends soley on the outcome of the first n trials. It is also understood that *when speaking of a "recurrent event $\mathcal{E}$," we are really referring to a class of events* defined by the property that $\mathcal{E}$ occurs. Clearly $\mathcal{E}$ itself is a label rather than an event. We are here abusing the language in the same way as is generally accepted in terms such as "a two-dimensional problem"; the problem itself is dimensionless.

Definition 1. *The attribute $\mathcal{E}$ defines a recurrent event if*:
(a) *In order that $\mathcal{E}$ occurs at the nth and the $(n+m)$th place of the sequence $(E_{j_1}, E_{j_2}, \ldots, E_{j_{n+m}})$ it is necessary and sufficient that $\mathcal{E}$ occurs at the last place in each of the two subsequences $(E_{j_1}, E_{j_2}, \ldots, E_{j_n})$ and $(E_{j_{n+1}}, E_{j_{n+2}}, \ldots, E_{j_{n+m}})$.*
(b) *If $\mathcal{E}$ occurs at the nth place then identically*

$$\mathbf{P}\{E_{j_1}, \ldots, E_{j_{n+m}}\} = \mathbf{P}\{E_{j_1}, \ldots, E_{j_n}\}\, \mathbf{P}\{E_{j_{n+1}}, \ldots, E_{j_{n+m}}\}.$$

It has now an obvious meaning to say that $\mathcal{E}$ occurs in the sequence $(E_{j_1}, E_{j_2}, \ldots)$ *for the first time* at the nth place, etc. It is also clear that with each recurrent event $\mathcal{E}$ there are associated the two sequences of numbers defined for $n = 1, 2, \ldots$ as follows

(2.1)
$$u_n = \mathbf{P}\{\mathcal{E} \text{ occurs at the } n\text{th trial}\},$$
$$f_n = \mathbf{P}\{\mathcal{E} \text{ occurs for the first time at the } n\text{th trial}\}.$$

It will be convenient to define

(2.2)
$$f_0 = 0, \qquad u_0 = 1,$$

and to introduce the generating functions

(2.3)
$$F(s) = \sum_{k=1}^{\infty} f_k s^k, \qquad U(s) = \sum_{k=0}^{\infty} u_k s^k.$$

Observe that $\{u_k\}$ is not a probability distribution; in fact, in representative cases we shall have $\sum u_k = \infty$. However, the events "$\mathcal{E}$ occurs for the first time at the nth trial" are mutually exclusive, and therefore

$$(2.4) \qquad f = F(1) = \sum_{n=1}^{\infty} f_n \le 1.$$

It is clear that $1 - f$ should be interpreted as *the probaiblity that $\mathcal{E}$ does not occur in an indefinitely prolonged sequence of trials.* If $f = 1$ we may introduce a random variable $\mathbf{T}$ with distribution

$$(2.5) \qquad \mathbf{P}\{\mathbf{T} = n\} = f_n.$$

We shall use the same notation (2.5) even if $f < 1$. Then $\mathbf{T}$ *is an improper, or defective, random variable, which with probability* $1 - f$ *does not assume a numerical value.* (For our purposes we could assign to $\mathbf{T}$ the symbol ∞, and it should be clear that no new rules are required.)

The *waiting time for* $\mathcal{E}$, that is, the number of trials up to and including the first occurrence of $\mathcal{E}$, is a random variable with the distribution (2.5); however, this random variable is really defined only in the space of infinite sequences $(E_{j_1}, E_{j_2}, \ldots)$.

By the definition of recurrent events the probability that $\mathcal{E}$ occurs for the first time at trial number k and for the *second* time at the nth trial equals $f_k f_{n-k}$. Therefore the probability $f_n^{(2)}$ that $\mathcal{E}$ occurs for the second time at the nth trial equals

$$(2.6) \qquad f_n^{(2)} = f_1 f_{n-1} + f_2 f_{n-2} + \cdots + f_{n-1} f_1.$$

The right side is the convolution of $\{f_n\}$ with itself and therefore $\{f_n^{(2)}\}$ represents the probability distribution of the sum of two independent random variables each having the distribution (2.5). More generally, if $f_n^{(r)}$ is the probability that the rth occurrence of $\mathcal{E}$ takes place at the nth trial we have

$$(2.7) \qquad f_n^{(r)} = f_1 f_{n-1}^{(r-1)} + f_2 f_{n-2}^{(r-1)} + \cdots + f_{n-1} f_1^{(r-1)}.$$

This simple fact is expressed in the

Theorem. *Let $f_n^{(r)}$ be the probability that the rth occurrence of $\mathcal{E}$ takes place at the nth trial. Then $\{f_n^{(r)}\}$ is the probability distribution of the sum*

$$(2.8) \qquad \mathbf{T}^{(r)} = \mathbf{T}_1 + \mathbf{T}_2 + \cdots + \mathbf{T}_r$$

of r independent random variables $\mathbf{T}_1, \ldots, \mathbf{T}_r$ *each having the distribution* (2.5). *In other words: For fixed r the sequence $\{f_n^{(r)}\}$ has the generating function* $F^r(s)$.

It follows in particular that

$$(2.9) \qquad \sum_{n=1}^{\infty} f_n^{(r)} = F^r(1) = f^r.$$

In words: *the probability that* $\mathcal{E}$ *occurs at least* r *times equals* f^r (a fact which could have been anticipated). We now introduce

Definition 2. *A recurrent event* $\mathcal{E}$ *will be called persistent*[3] *if* $f = 1$ *and transient if* $f < 1$.

For a transient $\mathcal{E}$ the probability f^r that it occurs at least r times tends to zero, whereas for a persistent $\mathcal{E}$ this probability remains unity. This can be described by saying *with probability one a persistent* $\mathcal{E}$ *is bound to occur infinitely often whereas a transient* $\mathcal{E}$ *occurs only a finite number of times.* (This statement not only is a description but is formally correct if interpreted in the sample space of infinite sequences $E_{j_1}, E_{j_2}, \ldots$.)

We require one more definition. In Bernoulli trials a return to equilibrium [example (1.a)] can occur only at an *even*-numbered trial. In this case $f_{2n+1} = u_{2n+1} = 0$, and the generating functions $F(s)$ and $U(s)$ are power series in s^2 rather than s. Similarly, in example (1.c) if λ is an integer, $\mathcal{E}$ can occur at the nth trial only if n is a multiple of $\lambda + 1$. We express this by saying that $\mathcal{E}$ is periodic. In essence periodic recurrent events differ only notationally from non-periodic ones, but every theorem requires a special mention of the exceptional periodic case. In other words, periodic recurrent events are a great nuisance without redeeming features of interest.

Definition 3. *The recurrent event* $\mathcal{E}$ *is called periodic if there exists an integer* $\lambda > 1$ *such that* $\mathcal{E}$ *can occur only at trials number* $\lambda, 2\lambda, 3\lambda, \ldots$ (*i.e.,* $u_n = 0$ *whenever* n *is not divisible by* λ). *The greatest* λ *with this property is called the period of* $\mathcal{E}$.

In conclusion let us remark that in the sample space of infinite sequences $E_{j_1}, E_{j_2}, \ldots$ the number of trials between the $(r-1)$st and the rth occurrence of $\mathcal{E}$ is a well-defined random variable (possibly a defective one), having the probability distribution of our $\mathbf{T}_r$. In other words, our variables $\mathbf{T}_r$ really stand for the *waiting times between the successive occurrences of* $\mathcal{E}$ (*the recurrence times*). We have defined the $\mathbf{T}_r$ analytically in order not to refer to sample spaces beyond the scope of this volume, but it is hoped that the probabilistic background appears in all its intuitive simplicity. The notion of recurrent events is designed to

---

[3] In the first edition the terms certain and uncertain were used, but the present terminology is preferable in applications to Markov chains.

reduce a fairly general situation to sums of independent random variables. Conversely, *an arbitrary probability distribution* $\{f_n\}$, $n = 1, 2, \ldots$ *may be used to define a recurrent event.* We prove this assertion by the

Example. *Self-renewing aggregates.* Consider an electric bulb, fuse, or other piece of equipment with a finite life span. As soon as the piece fails, it is replaced by a new piece of like kind, which in due time is replaced by a third piece, and so on. We assume that the life span is a random variable which ranges only over multiples of a unit time interval (year, day, or second). Each time unit then represents a trial with possible outcomes "replacement" and "no replacement." The successive replacements may be treated as recurrent events. If f_n is the probability that a new piece will serve for exactly n time units, then $\{f_n\}$ is the distribution of the recurrence times. When it is certain that the life span is finite, then $\sum f_n = 1$ and the recurrent event is persistent. Usually it is known that the life span cannot exceed a fixed number m, in which case the generating function $F(s)$ is a polynomial of a degree not exceeding m. In applications we desire the probability u_n that a replacement takes place at time n. This u_n may be calculated from (3.1). Here we have a class of recurrent events defined solely in terms of an arbitrary distribution $\{f_n\}$. The case $f < 1$ is not excluded, $1 - f$ being the probability of an eternal life of our piece of equipment. ▶

3. THE BASIC RELATIONS

We adhere to the notations (2.1)–(2.4) and propose to investigate the connection between the $\{f_n\}$ and the $\{u_n\}$. The probability that $\mathcal{E}$ occurs for the first time at trial number ν and then again at a later trial $n > \nu$ is, by definition, $f_\nu u_{n-\nu}$. The probability that $\mathcal{E}$ occurs at the nth trial for the first time is $f_n = f_n u_0$. Since these cases are mutually exclusive we have

$$(3.1) \qquad u_n = f_1 u_{n-1} + f_2 u_{n-2} + \cdots + f_n u_0, \qquad n \geq 1.$$

At the right we recognize the convolution $\{f_k\} * \{u_k\}$ with the generating function $F(s) U(s)$. At the left we find the sequence $\{u_n\}$ with the term u_0 missing, so that its generating function is $U(s) - 1$. Thus $U(s) - 1 = = F(s) U(s)$, and we have proved

Theorem 1. *The generating functions of* $\{u_n\}$ *and* $\{f_n\}$ *are related by*

$$(3.2) \qquad U(s) = \frac{1}{1 - F(s)}.$$

Note. The right side in (3.2) can be expanded into a geometric series $\sum F^r(s)$ converging for $|s| < 1$. The coefficient $f_n^{(r)}$ of s^n in $F^r(s)$ being the probability that the rth occurrence of $\mathcal{E}$ takes place at the nth trial, (3.2) is equivalent to

$$(3.3) \qquad \qquad \dot{u}_n = f_n^{(1)} + f_n^{(2)} + \cdots ;$$

this expresses the obvious fact that if $\mathcal{E}$ occurs at the nth trial, it has previously occurred $0, 1, 2, \ldots, n - 1$ times. (Clearly $f_n^{(r)} = 0$ for $r > n$.)

Theorem 2. *For $\mathcal{E}$ to be transient, it is necessary and sufficient that*

$$(3.4) \qquad \qquad u = \sum_{j=0}^{\infty} u_j$$

is finite. In this case the probability f that $\mathcal{E}$ ever occurs is given by

$$(3.5) \qquad \qquad f = \frac{u - 1}{u}.$$

Note. We can interpret u_j as the expectation of a random variable which equals 1 or 0 according to whether $\mathcal{E}$ does or does not occur at the jth trial. Hence $u_1 + u_2 + \cdots + u_n$ *is the expected number of occurrences of $\mathcal{E}$ in n trials,* and $u - 1$ can be interpreted as the expected number of occurrences of $\mathcal{E}$ in infinitely many trials.

Proof. The coefficients u_k being non-negative, it is clear that $U(s)$ increases monotonically as $s \to 1$ and that for each N

$$\sum_{n=0}^{N} u_n \le \lim_{s \to 1} U(s) \le \sum_{n=0}^{\infty} u_n = u.$$

Since $U(s) \to (1 - f)^{-1}$ when $f < 1$ and $U(s) \to \infty$ when $f = 1$, the theorem follows. ▶

The next theorem is of particular importance.[4] The proof is of an

---

[4] Special cases are easily proved (see problem 1) and were known for a long time. A huge literature tried to improve on the conditions, but it was generally believed that some restrictions were necessary. In full generality theorem 3 was proved by P. Erdös, W. Feller, and H. Pollard, A theorem on power series, Bull. Amer. Math. Soc. vol. 55 (1949), pp. 201–204. After the appearance of the first edition it was observed by K. L. Chung that the theorem could be derived from Kolmogorov's results about the asymptotic behavior of Markov chains. Many prominent mathematicians proved various extensions of the theorem to different classes of probability distributions. These investigations contributed to the methodology of modern probability theory. Eventually it turned out that an analogue to theorem 3 holds for arbitrary probability distributions. For an elementary (if not simple) proof see XI,9 of volume 2.

elementary nature, but since it does not contribute to a probabilistic understanding we defer it to the end of the chapter.

Theorem 3. *Let $\mathcal{E}$ be persistent and not periodic and denote by μ the mean of the recurrence times $\mathbf{T}_v$, that is,*

$$(3.6) \qquad\qquad \mu = \sum jf_j = F'(1)$$

(possibly $\mu = \infty$). Then

$$(3.7) \qquad\qquad u_n \to \mu^{-1}$$

as $n \to \infty$ $(u_n \to 0$ if the mean recurrence time is infinite).

The restriction to non-periodic $\mathcal{E}$ is easily removed. In fact, when $\mathcal{E}$ has period λ the series $\sum f_n s^n$ contains only powers of s^λ. Let us call a power series honest if this is not the case for any integer $\lambda > 1$. Theorem 3 may then be restated to the effect, that *if F is an honest probability generating function and U is defined by* (3.2), *then $u_n \to 1/F'(1)$.* Now if $\mathcal{E}$ has period λ then $F(s^{1/\lambda})$ is an honest probability generating function, and hence the coefficients of $U(s^{1/\lambda})$ converge to $\lambda/F'(1)$. We have thus

Theorem 4. *If $\mathcal{E}$ is persistent and has period λ then*

$$(3.8) \qquad\qquad u_{n\lambda} \to \lambda/\mu$$

while $u_k = 0$ for every k not divisible by λ.

4. EXAMPLES

(a) *Successes in Bernoulli trials.* For a trite example let $\mathcal{E}$ stand for "success" in a sequence of Bernoulli trials. Then $u_n = p$ for $n \geq 1$, whence

$$(4.1) \qquad U(s) = \frac{1 - qs}{1 - s} \quad\text{and therefore}\quad F(s) = \frac{ps}{1 - qs}$$

by virtue of (3.2). In this special case theorem 2 merely confirms the obvious fact that the waiting times between consecutive successes have a geometric distribution with expectation $1/p$.

(b) *Returns to equilibrium [example (1.a)].* At the kth trial the accumulated numbers of heads and tails can be equal only if $k = 2n$ is even, and in this case the probability of an equalization equals

$$(4.2) \qquad u_{2n} = \binom{2n}{n} p^n q^n = \binom{-\frac{1}{2}}{n}(-4pq)^n.$$

From the binomial expansion II, (8.7) it follows therefore that

$$(4.3) \qquad U(s) = \frac{1}{\sqrt{1 - 4pqs^2}}$$

and hence from (3.2)

$$(4.4) \qquad F(s) = 1 - \sqrt{1 - 4pqs^2}.$$

A second application of the binomial expansion leads to an explicit expression for f_{2n}. (Explicit expressions for u_{2n} and f_{2n} when $p = \frac{1}{2}$ were derived by combinatorial methods in III, 2–3; the generating functions U and F were found by other methods in XI,3. It will be noticed that only the present method requires no artifice.)

For $s = 1$ the square root in (4.4) equals $|p - q|$ and so

$$(4.5) \qquad f = 1 - |p - q|.$$

Thus *returns to equilibrium represent a recurrent event with period* 2 *which is transient when $p \neq q$, and persistent in the symmetric case $p = q$.* The probability of at least r returns to equilibrium equals f^r.

When $p = q = \frac{1}{2}$ the waiting time for the first return to equilibrium is a proper random variable, but $F'(1) = \infty$ and so *the mean recurrence time μ is infinite.* (This follows also from theorem 4 and the fact that $u_n \to 0$.) The fact that the mean recurrence time is infinite implies that the chance fluctuations in an individual prolonged coin-tossing game are far removed from the familiar pattern governed by the normal distribution. The rather paradoxical true nature of these fluctuations was discussed in chapter III.

(*c*) *Return to equilibrium through negative values.* In example (1.*b*) the return to equilibrium was subject to the restriction that no preceding partial sum $\mathbf{S}_j$ was positive. The distribution of the recurrence times for this recurrent event is defined by

$$(4.6) \qquad f_{2n}^- = \mathbf{P}\{\mathbf{S}_{2n} = 0, \mathbf{S}_1 < 0, \ldots, \mathbf{S}_{2n-1} < 0\}$$

and, of course, $f_{2n-1}^- = 0$. It does not seem possible to find these probabilities by a direct argument, but they follow easily from the preceding example. Indeed, a sample sequence $(\mathbf{X}_1, \ldots, \mathbf{X}_{2n})$ satisfying the condition in (4.6) contains n plus ones and n minus ones, and hence it has the same probability as $(-\mathbf{X}_1, \ldots, -\mathbf{X}_{2n})$. Now a *first* return to equilibrium occurs either through positive or through negative values, and we conclude that these two contingencies have the same probability. Thus $f_{2n}^- = \frac{1}{2}f_{2n}$ where $\{f_n\}$ is the distribution for the returns to equilibrium found in the preceding example. The generating function for our recurrence times is therefore given by

(4.7) $$F^-(s) = \tfrac{1}{2} - \tfrac{1}{2}\sqrt{1 - 4pqs^2},$$

and hence

(4.8) $$U^-(s) = \frac{2}{1 + \sqrt{1 - 4pqs^2}} = \frac{1 - \sqrt{1 - 4pqs^2}}{2pqs^2}.$$

The event $\mathcal{E}$ is transient, the probability that it ever occurs being $\tfrac{1}{2} - \tfrac{1}{2}|p - q|$.

(d) *Ladder variables.* The first positive partial sum can occur at the kth trial only if $k = 2n + 1$ is odd. For the corresponding probabilities we write

(4.9) $$\phi_{2n+1} = \mathbf{P}\{S_1 < 0, \ldots, S_{2n} = 0, S_{2n+1} = 1\}.$$

Thus $\{\phi_k\}$ is the distribution of the recurrent event of example (1.d). Now the condition in (4.9) requires that $X_{2n+1} = +1$, and that the recurrent event of the preceding example occurs at the $2n$th trial. It follows that $\phi_{2n+1} = p \cdot u_{2n}^-$. With obvious notations therefore

(4.10) $$\Phi(s) = psU^-(s) = \frac{1 - \sqrt{1 - 4pqs^2}}{2qs}.$$

This is the generating function for the first-passage times found in XI,(3.6). An explicit expression for ϕ_{2n+1} follows from (4.10) using the binomial expansion II,(8.7). This expression for ϕ_{2n+1} agrees with that found by combinatorial methods in theorem 2 of III,7.

(e) *Geiger counters.* In example (1.g) the counter remains free if no registration takes place at epoch 1. Otherwise it becomes locked and is freed again at epoch $r + 1$ if no particle arrives at that epoch; the counter is freed at epoch $2r + 1$ if a particle appears at epoch $r + 1$, but none at epoch $2r + 1$, and so on. The generating function of the recurrence times is therefore given by

(4.11) $$qs + qps^{r+1} + qp^2s^{2r+1} + \cdots = \frac{qs}{1 - ps^r}.$$

(See also problems 7–9.)

(f) *The simplest queuing problem* [example (1.h)]. Here the server remains free if no customer arrives at epoch 1. If a customer arrives there follows a so-called "busy period" which terminates at the epoch when the counter first becomes free. The generating function $\rho(s)$ for the busy period was derived in example XII,(5.c) using the methods of branching processes.

It follows that in the present case the generating function of the recurrence times is given by $qs + ps\rho(s)$, in agreement with XII,(5.7).

(g) *Ties in multiple coin games.* We conclude with a simple example showing the possibility of certain conclusions without explicit knowledge of the generating functions. Let $r \geq 2$ be an arbitrary integer and consider a sequence of simultaneous independent tosses of r coins. Let $\mathcal{E}$ stand for the recurrent event that *all r coins are in the same phase* (that is, the accumulated numbers of heads are the same for all r coins). The probability that this occurs at the nth trial is

$$(4.12) \qquad u_n = 2^{-rn}\left[\binom{n}{0}^r + \binom{n}{1}^r + \cdots + \binom{n}{n}^r \right].$$

On the right we recognize the terms of the binomial distribution with $p = \frac{1}{2}$, and from the normal approximation to the latter we conclude easily that for each fixed r as $n \to \infty$

$$(4.13) \qquad u_n \sim \left(\frac{2}{\pi n}\right)^{\frac{1}{2}r} \sum_j e^{-2rj^2/n}$$

(the summation extending over all integers j between $-\frac{1}{2}n$ and $\frac{1}{2}n$). But by the very definition of the integral

$$(4.14) \qquad 2\sqrt{\frac{r}{n}} \sum_j e^{-2rj^2/n} \to \int_{-\infty}^{+\infty} e^{-\frac{1}{2}x^2}\, dx = \sqrt{2\pi}$$

and hence we conclude that

$$(4.15) \qquad u_n \sim \frac{1}{\sqrt{r}}\left(\frac{2}{\pi n}\right)^{\frac{1}{2}(r-1)}.$$

This implies that $\sum u_n$ diverges when $r \leq 3$, but converges when $r \geq 4$. It follows that $\mathcal{E}$ *is persistent when $r \leq 3$ but transient if $r \geq 4$.* Since $u_n \to 0$ the mean recurrence time is infinite when $r \leq 3$. (Compare problems 2 and 3.)   ▶

5. DELAYED RECURRENT EVENTS. A GENERAL LIMIT THEOREM

We shall now introduce a slight extension of the notion of recurrent events which is so obvious that it could pass without special mention, except that it is convenient to have a term for it and to have the basic equations on record.

Perhaps the best informal description of delayed recurrent events is to say that they refer to trials where we have "missed the beginning and start in the middle." The waiting time up to the *first* occurrence of $\mathcal{E}$ has a distribution $\{b_n\}$ different from the distribution $\{f_n\}$ of the recurrence times between the following occurrences of $\mathcal{E}$. The theory applies without change except that the trials following each occurrence of $\mathcal{E}$ are exact replicas of a fixed sample space which is not identical with the original one.

The situation being so simple, we shall forego formalities and agree to speak of a *delayed recurrent $\mathcal{E}$ when the definition of recurrent events applies only if the trials leading up to the first occurrence of $\mathcal{E}$ are disregarded; it is understood that the waiting time up to the first appearance of $\mathcal{E}$ is a random variable independent of the following recurrence times, although its distribution $\{b_n\}$ may be different from the common distribution $\{f_n\}$ of the recurrence times.*

We denote by v_n the *probability of the occurrence of $\mathcal{E}$ at the nth trial.* To derive an expression for v_n we argue as follows. Suppose that $\mathcal{E}$ occurs at trial number $k < n$. Relative to the subsequent trials $\mathcal{E}$ becomes an ordinary recurrent event and so the (conditional) probability of a renewed occurrence at the nth trial equals u_{n-k}. Now if $\mathcal{E}$ occurs at the nth trial this is either its first occurrence, or else the first occurrence took place at the kth trial for some $k < n$. Summing over all possibilities we get

$$(5.1) \qquad v_n = b_n + b_{n-1}u_1 + b_{n-2}u_2 + \cdots + b_1 u_{n-1} + b_0 u_n.$$

We are thus in possession of an explicit expression for v_n. [For an alternative proof see example (10.a).] The relations (5.1) may be rewritten in the compact form of a convolution equation:

$$(5.2) \qquad \{v_n\} = \{b_n\} * \{u_n\}.$$

This implies that the corresponding generating functions satisfy the identity

$$(5.3) \qquad V(s) = B(s)U(s) = \frac{B(s)}{1 - F(s)} .$$

Example. (a) In the Bernoulli trials considered in examples (4.a)–(4.d) the event $\mathbf{S}_n = 1$ is a delayed recurrent event. The waiting time for its first occurrence has the generating function Φ of (4.10); the recurrence times between successive occurrences of $\{\mathbf{S}_n = 1\}$ have the generating function F of the returns to equilibrium [see (4.4)]. Thus in the present case $V = \Phi/(1-F)$. ▶

It is easy to show that the asymptotic behavior of the probabilities v_n is essentially the same as that of u_n. To avoid trivialities we assume that $\mathscr{E}$ is not periodic.[5] We know from section 3 that in this case u_n approaches a finite limit, and that $\sum u_n < \infty$ if, and only if, $\mathscr{E}$ is transient.

Theorem 1. *If* $u_n \to \omega$ *then*

$$(5.4) \qquad\qquad v_n \to b\omega \qquad where \quad b = \sum b_k = B(1).$$

If $\sum u_n = u < \infty$ *then*

$$(5.5) \qquad\qquad \sum v_n = bu.$$

In particular, $v_n \to \mu^{-1}$ *if* $\mathscr{E}$ *is persistent.*

Proof. Let $r_k = b_{k+1} + b_{k+2} + \cdots$. Since $u_n \leq 1$ it is obvious from (5.1) that for $n > k$

$$(5.6) \quad b_0 u_n + \cdots + b_k u_{n-k} \leq v_n \leq b_0 u_n + \cdots + b_k u_{n-k} + r_k.$$

Choose k so large that $r_k < \epsilon$. For n sufficiently large the leftmost member in (5.6) is then greater than $b\omega - 2\epsilon$, whereas the rightmost member is less than $b\omega + 2\epsilon$. Thus (5.4) is true. The assertion (5.5) follows either by summing (5.1) over n, or else from (5.3) on letting $s = 1$.

▶

We turn to a general limit theorem of wide applicability. Suppose that there are denumerably many possible states $E_0, E_1, \ldots$ for a certain system, and that the transitions from one state to another depend on a chance mechanism of some sort. For example, in the simple queuing process (1.h) we say that the system is in state E_k if there are k customers in the queue, including the customer being served. A problem involving seventeen servers may require eighteen numbers to specify the state of the system, but all imaginable states can still be ordered in a sequence $E_0, E_1, \ldots$. We need not consider how this is best done, because the following theorem does not lead to practical methods for evaluating probabilities. It is a pure existence theorem showing that a steady state exists under most circumstances encountered in practice. This is of conceptual interest, but also of practical value because, as a rule, mathematical analysis of a steady state is much simpler than the study of the time-dependent process.

We suppose that for $n = 1, 2, \ldots$ and every n-tuple $(r_1, \ldots, r_n)$ there exists a well-defined probability that the states of the system at epochs

---

[5] Periodic recurrent events are covered by theorem 10.2. For a different proof of theorem 1 see example (10.a).

$0, 1, \ldots, n - 1$ are represented by $(E_{r_1}, \ldots, E_{r_n})$. We shall not introduce any particular assumptions concerning the mutual dependence of these events or the probabilities for the transitions from one state to another. For simplicity we consider only *the probabilities $p_n^{(r)}$ that at epoch n the system is in state E_r*. (It will be obvious how the theorem generalizes to pairs, triples, etc.) The crucial assumption is that there exists some recurrent event $\mathcal{E}$ connected with our process. For example, in the queuing process $(1.h)$ the state E_0 represents such a recurrent event. In this case, if $\mathcal{E}$ were transient there would exist a positive probability that the queue does not terminate. This would imply that sooner or later we would encounter an unending queue, that is, a queue of indefinitely increasing size. This is a limit theorem of some sort showing that such servers are impossible in practice. This example should explain the role of the condition that $\mathcal{E}$ be persistent. (The non-periodicity is introduced only to avoid trivialities).

Theorem 2. *Assume that there exists a non-periodic persistent (possibly delayed) recurrent event $\mathcal{E}$ associated with our process. Then as $n \to \infty$*

$$(5.7) \qquad\qquad p_n^{(r)} \to p^{(r)}$$

where

$$(5.8) \qquad\qquad \sum p^{(r)} = 1$$

if the mean recurrence time μ is finite, and $p^{(r)} = 0$ otherwise.

Proof. Every time when $\mathcal{E}$ occurs the process starts from scratch. There exists therefore a well-defined conditional probability $g_n^{(r)}$ that if $\mathcal{E}$ occurs at some epoch, the state E_r occurs n time units later and *before* the next occurrence of $\mathcal{E}$ (here $n = 0, 1, \ldots$). For delayed recurrent events we require also the probability $\gamma_n^{(r)}$ that E_r occurs at epoch n *before* the first occurrence of $\mathcal{E}$. (Clearly $\gamma_n^{(r)} = g_n^{(r)}$ if $\mathcal{E}$ is not delayed.)

Let us now classify the ways in which E_r can occur at epoch n according to the last occurrence of $\mathcal{E}$ before epoch n. First, it is possible that $\mathcal{E}$ did not yet occur. The probability for this is $\gamma_n^{(r)}$. Or else there exists a $k \le n$ such that $\mathcal{E}$ occurred at epoch k but not between k and n. The probability for this is $v_k g_{n-k}^{(r)}$. Summing over all mutually exclusive cases we find

$$(5.9) \qquad p_n^{(r)} = \gamma_n^{(r)} + g_{n-1}^{(r)} v_1 + g_{n-2}^{(r)} v_2 + \cdots + g_0^{(r)} v_n.$$

(Here we adhere to the notations of theorem 1. For delayed events $v_0 = 0$; for non-delayed events $v_k = u_k$ and $\gamma_n^{(r)} = g_n^{(r)}$.)

The relation (5.9) is analogous to (5.1) except for the appearance of the term $\gamma_n^{(r)}$ on the right. This quantity is obviously smaller than the probability that $\mathcal{E}$ did not occur before epoch n, and $\mathcal{E}$ being persistent it follows that $\gamma_n^{(r)} \to 0$ as $n \to \infty$. For the remaining terms we can apply theorem 1 with the notational change that u_k is replaced by v_k and b_k by $g_n^{(r)}$. Since $\mathcal{E}$ is persistent $v_n \to \mu^{-1}$ and it follows that

(5.10) $$p_n^{(r)} \to \mu^{-1} \sum_{k=0}^{\infty} g_k^{(r)}.$$

This proves the existence of the limits (5.7). To prove that they add to unity note that at any epoch the system is in some state and hence

(5.11) $$\sum_{r=0}^{\infty} g_n^{(r)} = g_n$$

is the probability that a recurrence time is $\geq n$, that is,

$$g_n = f_n + f_{n+1} + \cdots.$$

Thus

(5.12) $$\sum_{r=0}^{\infty} p^{(r)} = \frac{1}{\mu} \sum_{n=0}^{\infty} g_n = 1$$

by XI, (1.8).   ▶

[The limit theorem in example (10.b) may be treated as a special case of the present theorem.]

6. THE NUMBER OF OCCURRENCES OF $\mathcal{E}$

Up to now we have studied a recurrent event $\mathcal{E}$ in terms of the waiting times between its successive occurrences. Often it is preferable to consider the number n of trials as given and to take *the number $\mathbf{N}_n$ of occurrences of $\mathcal{E}$* in the first n trials as basic variable. We shall now investigate the asymptotic behavior of the distribution of $\mathbf{N}_n$ for large n. For simplicity we assume that $\mathcal{E}$ is not delayed.

As in (2.8) let $\mathbf{T}^{(r)}$ stand for the number of trials up to and including the rth occurrence of $\mathcal{E}$. The probability distributions of $\mathbf{T}^{(r)}$ and $\mathbf{N}_n$ are related by the obvious identity

(6.1) $$\mathbf{P}\{\mathbf{N}_n \geq r\} = \mathbf{P}\{\mathbf{T}^{(r)} \leq n\}.$$

We begin with the simple case where $\mathcal{E}$ is persistent and the distribution $\{f_n\}$ of its recurrence times has finite mean μ and variance σ^2. Since $\mathbf{T}^{(r)}$ is the sum of r independent variables, the central limit theorem of

X,1 asserts that for each fixed x as $r \to \infty$

(6.2) $$\mathbf{P}\left\{\frac{\mathbf{T}^{(r)} - r\mu}{\sigma\sqrt{r}} < x\right\} \to \mathfrak{N}(x)$$

where $\mathfrak{N}(x)$ is the normal distribution function. Now let $n \to \infty$ and $r \to \infty$ in such a way that

(6.3) $$\frac{n - r\mu}{\sigma\sqrt{r}} \to x;$$

then (6.1) and (6.2) together lead to

(6.4) $$\mathbf{P}\{\mathbf{N}_n \geq r\} \to \mathfrak{N}(x).$$

To write this relation in a more familiar form we introduce the *reduced variable*

(6.5) $$\mathbf{N}_n^* = (\mu\mathbf{N}_n - n)\sqrt{\frac{\mu}{\sigma^2 n}}.$$

The inequality $\mathbf{N}_n \geq r$ is identical with

(6.6) $$\mathbf{N}_n^* \geq \frac{r\mu - n}{\sigma\sqrt{r}} \cdot \sqrt{\frac{r\mu}{n}} = -x\sqrt{\frac{r\mu}{n}}.$$

On dividing (6.3) by r it is seen that $n/r \to \mu$, and hence the right side in (6.6) tends to $-x$. Since $\mathfrak{N}(-x) = 1 - \mathfrak{N}(x)$ it follows that

(6.7) $\mathbf{P}\{\mathbf{N}_n^* \geq -x\} \to \mathfrak{N}(x)$ *or* $\mathbf{P}\{\mathbf{N}_n^* < -x\} \to 1 - \mathfrak{N}(x),$

and we have proved the

Theorem. *Normal approximation. If the recurrent event $\mathcal{E}$ is persistent and its recurrence times have finite mean μ and variance σ^2, then both the number $\mathbf{T}^{(r)}$ of trials up to the rth occurrence of $\mathcal{E}$ and the number $\mathbf{N}_n$ of occurrences of $\mathcal{E}$ in the first n trials are asymptotically normally distributed as indicated in* (6.2) *and* (6.7).

Note that in (6.7) we have the central limit theorem applied to a sequence of *dependent* variables $\mathbf{N}_n$. Its usefulness will be illustrated in the next section by an application to the theory of runs.

The relations (6.7) make it plausible that

(6.8) $$\mathbf{E}(\mathbf{N}_n) \sim n/\mu, \qquad \mathrm{Var}\,(\mathbf{N}_n) \sim n\sigma^2/\mu^3$$

where the sign $\sim$ indicates that the ratio of the two sides tends to unity. To prove (6.8) we note that $\mathbf{N}_n$ is the sum of n (dependent) variables $\mathbf{Y}_k$

such that Y_k equals one or zero according as $\mathcal{E}$ does or does not occur at the kth trial. Thus $E(Y_k) = u_k$ and

$$(6.9) \qquad\qquad E(N_n) = u_1 + u_2 + \cdots + u_n.$$

Since $u_n \to \mu^{-1}$ this implies the first relation in (6.8). The second follows by a similar argument (see problem 20).

Unfortunately surprisingly many recurrence times occurring in various stochastic processes and in applications have *infinite expectations*. In such cases the normal approximation is replaced by more general limit theorems of an entirely different character,[6] and the chance fluctuations exhibit unexpected features. For example, one expects intuitively that $E(N_n)$ should increase linearly with n "because on the average $\mathcal{E}$ must occur twice as often in twice as many trials." Yet *this is not so*. An infinite mean recurrence time implies that $u_n \to 0$, and then $E(N_n)/n \to 0$ by virtue of (6.9). This means that in the long run the occurrences of $\mathcal{E}$ become rarer and rarer, and this is possible only if some recurrence times are fantastically large. Two examples may show how pronounced this phenomenon is apt to be.

Examples. (*a*) When $\mathcal{E}$ stands for a return to equilibrium in a coin-tossing game [example (4.*b*) with $p = \frac{1}{2}$] we have $u_{2n} \sim 1/\sqrt{\pi n}$, and (6.9) approximates an integral for $(\pi x)^{-\frac{1}{2}}$; this implies $E(N_{2n}) \sim 2\sqrt{n/\pi}$. Thus the *average* recurrence time up to epoch n is likely to increase as $\sqrt{n}$. The curious consequences of this were discussed at length in chapter III.

(*b*) Returning to example (4.*g*) consider repeated tosses of $r = 3$ dice and let $\mathcal{E}$ stand for the event that all three coins are in the same phase. We saw that $\mathcal{E}$ is a persistent recurrent event, and that $u_n \sim \dfrac{2}{\sqrt{3} \cdot \pi n}$.

Thus $E(N_n)$ *increases roughly* as $\log n$ and so the *average* of the recurrence times up to epoch n is likely to be of the fantastic magnitude $n/\log n$. ▶

*7. APPLICATION TO THE THEORY OF SUCCESS RUNS

In the sequel r will denote a fixed positive integer and $\mathcal{E}$ will stand for the occurrence of a success run of length r in a sequence of Bernoulli trials. It is important that the length of a run be defined as stated in

---

* Sections 7 and 8 treat a special topic and may be omitted.
[6] W. Feller, *Fluctuation theory of recurrent events*, Trans. Amer. Math. Soc., vol. 67 (1949), pp. 98–119.

example (1.e), for otherwise runs are not recurrent events, and the calculations become more involved. As in (2.1) and (2.2), u_n *is the probability of ε at the nth trial, and f_n is the probability that the first run of length r occurs at the nth trial.*

The probability that the r trials number $n, n - 1, n - 2, \ldots, n - r + 1$ result in success is obviously p^r. In this case ε occurs at one among these r trials; the probability that ε occurs at the trial number $n - k$ ($k = 0, 1, \ldots, r - 1$) and the following k trials result in k successes equals $u_{n-k} p^k$. Since these r possibilities are mutually exclusive, we get the recurrence relation[7]

$$(7.1) \qquad u_n + u_{n-1} p + \cdots + u_{n-r+1} p^{r-1} = p^r$$

valid for $n \geq r$. Clearly

$$(7.2) \qquad u_1 = u_2 = \cdots = u_{r-1} = 0, \qquad u_0 = 1.$$

On multiplying (7.1) by s^n and summing over $n = r, r+1, r+2, \ldots,$ we get on the left side

$$(7.3) \qquad \{U(s) - 1\}(1 + ps + p^2 s^2 + \cdots + p^{r-1} s^{r-1})$$

and on the right side $p^r(s^r + s^{r+1} + \cdots)$. The two series are geometric, and we find that

$$(7.4) \qquad \{U(s) - 1\} \cdot \frac{1 - (ps)^r}{1 - ps} = \frac{p^r s^r}{1 - s}$$

or

$$(7.5) \qquad U(s) = \frac{1 - s + q p^r s^{r+1}}{(1-s)(1 - p^r s^r)} .$$

From (3.2), we get now *the generating function of the recurrence times:*

$$(7.6) \quad F(s) = \frac{p^r s^r (1 - ps)}{1 - s + q p^r s^{r+1}} = \frac{p^r s^r}{1 - qs(1 + ps + \cdots + p^{r-1} s^{r-1})} .$$

The fact that $F(1) = 1$ shows that in a prolonged sequence of trials the number of runs of any length is certain to increase over all bounds. The mean recurrence time μ could be obtained directly from (7.1) since we know that $u_n \to \mu^{-1}$. Since we require also the variance, it is preferable

---

[7] The classical approach consists in deriving a recurrence relation for f_n. This method is more complicated and does not apply to, say, runs of either kind or patterns like *SSFFSS*, to which our method applies without change [cf. example (8.c)].

to calculate the derivatives of $F(s)$. This is best done by implicit differentiation after clearing (7.6) of the denominator. An easy calculation then shows that *the mean and variance of the recurrence times of runs of length r are*

$$(7.7) \qquad \mu = \frac{1 - p^r}{qp^r}, \qquad \sigma^2 = \frac{1}{(qp^r)^2} - \frac{2r + 1}{qp^r} - \frac{p}{q^2},$$

respectively. By the theorem of the last section for large n *the number N_n of runs of length r produced in n trials is approximately normally*

TABLE 2

MEAN RECURRENCE TIMES FOR SUCCESS RUNS IF TRIALS
ARE PERFORMED AT THE RATE OF ONE PER SECOND

Length of Run	$p = 0.6$	$p = 0.5$ (Coins)	$p = \frac{1}{6}$ (Dice)
$r = 5$	30.7 seconds	1 minute	2.6 hours
10	6.9 minutes	34.1 minutes	28.0 months
15	1.5 hours	18.2 hours	18,098 years
20	19 hours	24.3 days	140.7 million years

distributed, that is, for fixed $\alpha < \beta$ the probability that

$$(7.8) \qquad \frac{n}{\mu} + \alpha\sigma\sqrt{\frac{n}{\mu^3}} < N_n < \frac{n}{\mu} + \beta\sigma\sqrt{\frac{n}{\mu^3}}$$

tends to $\mathfrak{N}(\beta) - \mathfrak{N}(\alpha)$. This fact was first proved by von Mises, by rather lengthy calculations. Table 2 gives a few typical means of recurrence times.

The method of partial fractions of XI, 4, permits us to derive excellent approximations. The second representation in (7.6) shows clearly that the denominator has a unique *positive root* $s = x$. For every real or complex number s with $|s| \leq x$ we have

$$(7.9) \quad |qs(1+ps+ \cdots +p^{r-1}s^{r-1})| \leq qx(1+px+ \cdots +p^{r-1}x^{r-1}) = 1$$

where the equality sign is possible only if all terms on the left have the same argument, that is, if $s = x$. Hence x is smaller in absolute value than any other root of the denominator in (7.6). We can, therefore, apply formulas (4.5) and (4.9) of chapter XI with $s_1 = x$, letting $U(s) = = p^r s^r(1-ps)$ and $V(s) = 1 - s + qp^r s^{r+1}$. We find, using that $V(x) = 0$,

$$(7.10) \qquad f_n \sim \frac{(x-1)(1-px)}{(r+1-rx)q} \cdot \frac{1}{x^{n+1}}.$$

The probability of no run in n trials is $q_n = f_{n+1} + f_{n+2} + f_{n+3} + \cdots$
and summing the geometric series in (7.10) we get

$$(7.11) \qquad q_n \sim \frac{1-px}{(r+1-rx)q} \cdot \frac{1}{x^{n+1}}.$$

We have thus found that *the probability of no success run of length* r
in n *trials satisfies* (7.11). Table 3 shows that the right side gives surprisingly good approximations even for very small n, and the approximation improves rapidly with n. This illustrates the power of the method
of generating function and partial fractions.

TABLE 3

PROBABILITY OF HAVING NO SUCCESS RUN OF LENGTH
$r = 2$ IN n TRIALS WITH $p = \frac{1}{2}$

n	q_n Exact	From (7.11)	Error
2	0.75	0.76631	0.0163
3	0.625	0.61996	0.0080
4	0.500	0.50156	0.0016
5	0.40625	0.40577	0.0005

Numerical Calculations. For the benefit of the practical-minded reader we use this
occasion to show that the numerical calculations involved in partial fraction expansions
are often less formidable than they appear at first sight, and that excellent estimates of
the error can be obtained.

The asymptotic expansion (7.11) raises two questions: First, the contribution of
the $r - 1$ neglected roots must be estimated, and second, the dominant root x must
be evaluated.

The first representation in (7.6) shows that all roots of the denominator of $F(s)$
satisfy the equation

$$(7.12) \qquad s = 1 + qp^r s^{r+1},$$

but (7.12) has the additional extraneous root $s = p^{-1}$. For positive s the graph of
$f(s) = 1 + qp^r s^{r+1}$ is convex; it intersects the bisector $y = s$ at x and p^{-1} and in
the interval between x and p^{-1} the graph lies *below* the bisector. Furthermore,
$f'(p^{-1}) = (r+1)q$. If this quantity exceeds unity, the graph of $f(s)$ crosses the bisector
at $s = p$ from below, and hence $p^{-1} > x$. To fix ideas we shall assume that

$$(7.13) \qquad (r+1)q > 1;$$

in this case $x < p^{-1}$, and $f(s) < s$ for $x < s < p^{-1}$. It follows that for all complex
numbers s such that $x < |s| < p^{-1}$ we have $|f(s)| \leq f(|s|) < |s|$ so that no root s_k
can lie in the annulus $x < |s| < p^{-1}$. Since x was chosen as the root smallest in

absolute value, this implies that

(7.14) $$|s_k| > p^{-1} \qquad\qquad when \quad s_k \neq x.$$

By differentiation of (7.12) it is now seen that all roots are simple.

   The contribution of each root to q_n is of the same form as the contribution (7.11) of the dominant root x, and therefore the $r - 1$ terms neglected in (7.11) are of the form

(7.15) $$A_k = \frac{ps_k - 1}{rs_k - (r + 1)} \cdot \frac{1}{qs_k^{n+1}}.$$

We require an upper bound for the first fraction on the right. For that purpose note that for fixed $s > p^{-1} > (r + 1)r^{-1}$

(7.16) $$\left| \frac{pse^{i\theta} - 1}{rse^{i\theta} - (r + 1)} \right| \leq \frac{ps + 1}{rs + r + 1};$$

in fact, the quantity on the left obviously assumes its maximum and minimum for $\theta = 0$ and $\theta = \pi$, and a direct substitution shows that 0 corresponds to a minimum, π to a maximum. In view of (7.13) and (7.14) we have then

(7.17) $$|A_k| < \frac{2p^{n+1}}{(r + 1 + rp^{-1})q} < \frac{2p^{n+2}}{rq(1 + p)}.$$

We conclude that in (7.11) *the error committed by neglecting the $r - 1$ roots different from x is less in absolute value than*

(7.18) $$\frac{2(r - 1)p}{rq(1 + p)}.$$

   The root x is easily calculated from (7.12) by successive approximations putting $x_0 = 1$ and $x_{v+1} = f(x_v)$. The sequence will converge monotonically to x, and each term provides a lower bound for x, whereas any value s such that $s > f(s)$ provides an upper bound. It is easily seen that

(7.19) $$x = 1 + qp^r + (r + 1)(qp^r)^2 + \cdots.$$

*8. MORE GENERAL PATTERNS

   Our method is applicable to more general problems which have been considered as considerably more difficult than simple runs.

   Examples. (*a*) *Runs of either kind.* Let $\mathcal{E}$ stand for "*either a success run of length r or a failure run of length ρ*" [see example (1.*f*)]. We are dealing with *two* recurrent events $\mathcal{E}_1$ and $\mathcal{E}_2$, where $\mathcal{E}_1$ stands for "success run of length r" and $\mathcal{E}_2$ for "failure run of length ρ" and $\mathcal{E}$ means "either $\mathcal{E}_1$ or $\mathcal{E}_2$." To $\mathcal{E}_1$ there corresponds the generating function (7.5) which will now be denoted by $U_1(s)$. The corresponding generating function

---

   * This section treats a special topic and may be omitted.

$U_2(s)$ for $\mathcal{E}_2$ is obtained from (7.5) by interchanging p and q and replacing r by ρ. The probability u_n that $\mathcal{E}$ occurs at the nth trial is the sum of the corresponding probabilities for $\mathcal{E}_1$ and $\mathcal{E}_2$, except that $u_0 = 1$. It follows that

$$(8.1) \qquad U(s) = U_1(s) + U_2(s) - 1.$$

The generating function $F(s)$ of the recurrence times of $\mathcal{E}$ is again $F(s) = 1 - U^{-1}(s)$ or

$$(8.2) \qquad F(s) = \frac{(1-ps)p^r s^r(1-q^\rho s^\rho) + (1-qs)q^\rho s^\rho(1-p^r s^r)}{1 - s + qp^r s^{r+1} + pq^\rho s^{\rho+1} - p^r q^\rho s^{r+\rho}}.$$

The *mean recurrence time* follows by differentiation

$$(8.3) \qquad \mu = \frac{(1-p^r)(1-q^\rho)}{qp^r + pq^\rho - p^r q^\rho}.$$

As $\rho \to \infty$, this expression tends to the mean recurrence time of success runs as given in (7.7).

(*b*) In VIII,1, we calculated the probability x that a *success run of length r occurs before a failure run of length ρ*. Define two recurrent events $\mathcal{E}_1$ and $\mathcal{E}_2$ as in example (*a*). Let x_n = probability that $\mathcal{E}_1$ occurs for the first time at the nth trial and no $\mathcal{E}_2$ precedes it; f_n = probability that $\mathcal{E}_1$ occurs for the first time at the nth trial (with no condition on $\mathcal{E}_2$). Define y_n and g_n as x_n and f_n, respectively, but with $\mathcal{E}_1$ and $\mathcal{E}_2$ interchanged.

The generating function for f_n is given in (7.6), and $G(s)$ is obtained by interchanging p and q and replacing r by ρ. For x_n and y_n we have the obvious recurrence relations

$$(8.4) \qquad x_n = f_n - (y_1 f_{n-1} + y_2 f_{n-2} + \cdots + y_{n-1} f_1)$$

$$y_n = g_n - (x_1 g_{n-1} + x_2 g_{n-2} + \cdots + x_{n-1} g_1).$$

They are of the convolution type, and for the corresponding generating functions we have, therefore,

$$(8.5) \qquad X(s) = F(s) - Y(s)F(s)$$

$$Y(s) = G(s) - X(s)G(s).$$

From these two linear equations we get

$$(8.6) \qquad X(s) = \frac{F(s)\{1 - G(s)\}}{1 - F(s)G(s)}, \qquad Y(s) = \frac{G(s)\{1 - F(s)\}}{1 - F(s)G(s)}.$$

Expressions for x_n and y_n can again be obtained by the method of partial fractions. For $s = 1$ we get $X(1) = \sum x_n = x$, the probability of $\mathcal{E}_1$ occurring before $\mathcal{E}_2$. Both numerator and denominator vanish, and $X(1)$ is obtained from L'Hospital's rule differentiating numerator and denominator: $X(1) = G'(1)/\{F'(1) + G'(1)\}$. Using the values $F'(1) = (1-p^r)/qp^r$ and $G'(1) = (1-q^\rho)/pq^\rho$ from (7.7), we find $X(1)$ as given in VIII,(1.3).

(c) Consider the recurrent event defined by the pattern $SSFFSS$. Repeating the argument of section 7, we easily find that

$$(8.7) \qquad p^4 q^2 = u_n + p^2 q^2 u_{n-4} + p^3 q^2 u_{n-5}.$$

Since we know that $u_n \to \mu^{-1}$ we get for the mean recurrence time $\mu = p^{-4} q^{-2} + p^{-2} + p^{-1}$. For $p = q = \frac{1}{2}$ we find $\mu = 70$, whereas the mean recurrence time for a success run of length 6 is 126. This shows that, contrary to expectation, *there is an essential difference in coin tossing between head runs and other patterns of the same length.*   ▶

9. LACK OF MEMORY OF GEOMETRIC WAITING TIMES

The geometric distribution for waiting times has an interesting and important property not shared by any other distribution. Consider a sequence of Bernoulli trials and let **T** be the number of trials up to and including the first success. Then $\mathbf{P}\{\mathbf{T} > k\} = q^k$. Suppose we know that no success has occurred during the first m trials; the waiting time **T** from this mth failure to the first success has exactly the same distribution $\{q^k\}$ and is independent of the number of preceding failures. In other words, the probability that the waiting time will be prolonged by k always equals the initial probability of the total length exceeding k. If the life span of an atom or a piece of equipment has a geometric distribution, then *no aging* takes place; as long as it lives, the atom has the same probability of decaying at the next trial. Radioactive atoms actually have this property (except that in the case of a continuous time the exponential distribution plays the role of the geometric distribution). Conversely, if it is known that a phenomenon is characterized by a complete lack of memory or aging, then the probability distribution of the duration must be geometric or exponential. Typical is a well-known type of telephone conversation often cited as the model of incoherence and depending entirely on momentary impulses; a possible termination is an instantaneous chance effect without relation to the past chatter. By contrast, the knowledge that no streetcar has passed for five minutes increases our expectation that it will come soon. In coin tossing, the probability that the cumulative numbers of heads and tails will equalize at the second trial is $\frac{1}{2}$. However, given that they did not, the probability that they equalize after two additional trials is only $\frac{1}{4}$. These are examples for aftereffect.

For a rigorous formulation of the assertion, suppose that a waiting time $\mathbf{T}$ assumes the values $0, 1, 2, \ldots$ with probabilities $p_0, p_1, p_2, \ldots$. Let the distribution of $\mathbf{T}$ have the following property: *The conditional probability that the waiting time terminates at the kth trial, assuming that it has not terminated before, equals* p_0 *(the probability at the first trial). We claim that* $p_k = (1-p_0)^k p_0$, *so that* $\mathbf{T}$ *has a geometric distribution.*

For a proof we introduce again the "tails"

$$q_k = p_{k+1} + p_{k+2} + p_{k+3} + \cdots = \mathbf{P}\{\mathbf{T} > k\}.$$

Our hypothesis is $\mathbf{T} > k - 1$, and its probability is q_{k-1}. The conditional probability of $\mathbf{T} = k$ is therefore p_k/q_{k-1}, and the assumption is that for all $k \geq 1$

$$(9.1) \qquad \frac{p_k}{q_{k-1}} = p_0.$$

Now $p_k = q_{k-1} - q_k$, and hence (9.1) reduces to

$$(9.2) \qquad \frac{q_k}{q_{k-1}} = 1 - p_0.$$

Since $q_0 = p_1 + p_2 + \cdots = 1 - p_0$, it follows that $q_k = (1-p_0)^{k+1}$, and hence $p_k = q_{k-1} - q_k = (1 - p_0)^k p_0$, as asserted. ▶

In the theory of stochastic processes the described lack of memory is connected with the *Markovian property;* we shall return to it in XV,13.

10. RENEWAL THEORY

The convolution equations which served as a basis for the theory of recurrent events are of much wider applicability than appears in the foregoing sections. We shall therefore restate their analytic content in somewhat greater generality and describe the typical probabilistic renewal argument as well as applications to the study of populations of various sorts.

We start from two arbitrary sequences[8] $f_1, f_2, \ldots$ and $b_0, b_1, \ldots$ of real numbers. A new sequence $v_0, v_1, \ldots$ may then be defined by the

---

[8] We put $f_0 = 0$. It is clear from (10.1) that the case $0 < f_0 < 1$ involves only the change of notations, replacing f_k by $f_k \mid (1 - f_0)$ and b_k by $b_k \mid (1 - f_0)$.

convolution equations

(10.1) $$v_n = b_n + f_1 v_{n-1} + f_2 v_{n-2} + \cdots + f_n v_0.$$

These define recursively $v_0, v_1, v_2, \ldots$ and so the v_n are uniquely defined under any circumstances. We shall, however, consider only sequences satisfying the conditions[9]

(10.2) $$f_n \geq 0, \qquad f = \sum_{n=1}^{\infty} f_n < \infty; \qquad b_n \geq 0, \qquad b = \sum_{n=0}^{\infty} b_n < \infty.$$

In this case the v_n are non-negative and the corresponding generating functions must satisfy the identity

(10.3) $$V(s) = \frac{B(s)}{1 - F(s)}.$$

The generating functions F and B converge at least for $0 \leq s < 1$, and so (10.3) defines a power series converging as long as $F(s) < 1$. Relations (10.1) and (10.3) are fully equivalent. In section 3 we considered the special case $B(s) = 1$ (with $v_n = u_n$ for all n). Section 5 covered the general situation under the restriction $f \leq 1$. In view of applications to population theory we shall now permit that $f > 1$; fortunately this case is easily reduced to the standard case $f = 1$.

We shall say that *the sequence* $\{f_n\}$ *has period* $\lambda > 1$ if $f_n = 0$ except when $n = k\lambda$ is a multiple of λ, and λ is the greatest integer with this property. This amounts to saying that $F(s) = F_1(s^\lambda)$ is a power series in s^λ, but not in $s^{r\lambda}$ for any $r > 1$. We put again

(10.4) $$\mu = \sum n f_n \leq \infty$$

and adhere to the convention that μ^{-1} is to be interpreted as 0 if $\mu = \infty$.

Theorem 1. (*Renewal theorem.*) *Suppose* (10.2) *and that* $\{f_n\}$ *is not periodic.*

(i) *If* $f < 1$ *then* $v_n \to 0$ *and*

(10.5) $$\sum_{n=0}^{\infty} v_n = \frac{b}{1-f}.$$

(ii) *If* $f = 1$

(10.6) $$v_n \to b\mu^{-1}.$$

---

[9] The positivity of f_n is essential, but the convergence of the two series is imposed only for convenience. No general conclusion can be drawn if $b = \infty$ *and* $f = \infty$. The assertion (10.7) remains true when $f = \infty$ except that in this case $F'(\xi)$ is not necessarily finite, and (10.7) is meaningless if $b = \infty$ *and* $F'(\xi) = \infty$.

(iii) *If $f > 1$ there exists a unique positive root of the equation $F(\xi) = 1$,* and

$$(10.7) \qquad\qquad \xi^n v_n \to \frac{B(\xi)}{\xi F'(\xi)}.$$

Obviously $\xi < 1$ and hence the derivative $F'(\xi)$ is finite; (10.7) shows that the sequence $\{v_n\}$ behaves ultimately like a geometric sequence with ratio $\xi^{-1} > 1$.

Proof. The assertions (i) and (ii) were proved in section 5. To prove (iii) it suffices to apply the result (ii) to the sequences $\{f_n\xi^n\}$, $\{b_n\xi^n\}$, and $\{v_n\xi^n\}$ with generating functions given by $F(\xi s)$, $B(\xi s)$, and $V(\xi s)$, respectively. ▶

We have excluded periodic sequences $\{f_n\}$ because they are of secondary interest. Actually they present nothing new. Indeed, if $\{b_n\}$ and $\{f_n\}$ have the same period λ then both $B(s)$ and $F(s)$ are power series in s^λ, and hence the same is true of $V(s)$. Theorem 1 then applies to the sequences $\{f_{n\lambda}\}$, $\{b_{n\lambda}\}$, and $\{v_{n\lambda}\}$ with generating functions $F(s^{1/\lambda})$, $B(s^{1/\lambda})$, and $V(s^{1/\lambda})$. When $F(1) = 1$ it follows that $v_{n\lambda} \to b\lambda/\mu$. Now the most general power series B can be written as a linear combination

$$(10.8) \qquad\qquad B(s) = B_0(s) + sB_1(s) + \cdots + s^{\lambda-1}B_{\lambda-1}(s)$$

of λ power series B_j each of which involves only powers of s^λ. Introducing this into (10.3) and applying the result just stated shows the validity of

Theorem 2. *Let* (10.2) *hold and suppose that* $\{f_n\}$ *has period* $\lambda > 1$.

(i) *If $f < 1$ then* (10.5) *holds.*
(ii) *If $f = 1$ then for $j = 0, 1, \ldots, \lambda - 1$ as $n \to \infty$*

$$(10.9) \qquad\qquad u_{n\lambda+j} \to \lambda B_j(1)/\mu.$$

(iii) *If $f > 1$ then for $j = 0, 1, \ldots, \lambda - 1$ as $n \to \infty$*

$$(10.10) \qquad\qquad \xi^{n\lambda} u_{n\lambda+j} \to \lambda B_j(\xi)/(\xi\mu).$$

In a great variety of stochastic processes it is possible to adapt the argument used for recurrent events to show that certain probabilities satisfy an equation of the convolution type like (10.1). Many important limit theorems appear in this way as simple corollaries of theorem 1. This approach has now generally supplanted clumsier older methods and has become known as *renewal argument*. Its full power appears only when used for processes with a continuous time parameter, but the first two examples may serve as an illustration. For further examples see problems 8–9. An application of theorem 1 to a non-probabilistic limit theorem is contained in example (*c*). The last two examples are devoted to practical applications.

Examples. (*a*) *Delayed recurrent events.* We give a new derivation of the result in section 5 for a delayed recurrent event $\mathcal{E}$ with the distribution $\{f_j\}$ for the recurrence times, and the distribution $\{b_j\}$ for the *first* occurrence of $\mathcal{E}$. Let v_n stand for the probability that $\mathcal{E}$ occurs at the *n*th trial. We show that (10.1) holds. There are two ways in which $\mathcal{E}$ can occur at the *n*th trial. The occurrence may be the first, and the probability for this is b_n. Otherwise there was a last occurrence of $\mathcal{E}$ before the *n*th trial, and so there exists a number $1 \leq j < n$ such that $\mathcal{E}$ did occur at the *j*th trial and the *next* time at the *n*th trial. The probability for this is $v_j f_{n-j}$. The cases are mutually exclusive, and so

$$(10.11) \qquad v_n = b_n + v_1 f_{n-1} + v_2 f_{n-2} + \cdots + v_{n-1} f_1,$$

which is the same as (10.1). The generating function V is therefore given by (10.3) in agreement with the result in section 5. (Though the results agree even formally, the arguments are different: in section 5 the enumeration proceeded according to the first appearance of $\mathcal{E}$ whereas the present argument uses the last appearance. Both procedures are used in other circumstances and sometimes lead to formally different equations.)

(*b*) *Hitting probabilities.* Consider a sequence of trials with a proper (not delayed) persistent recurrent event $\mathcal{E}$. Let $v \geq 0$ be an integer. Suppose that we start to observe the process only after the *v*th trial and that we are interested in the waiting time for the next occurrence of $\mathcal{E}$. More formally, for $r = 1, 2, \ldots$ denote by $w_v(r)$ the probability that *the first occurrence of $\mathcal{E}$ after the *v*th trial* takes place at the $(v+r)$th trial. Thus $w_0(r) = f_r$ and $w_v(0) = 0$. [The $w_v(r)$ are called hitting probabilities because of their meaning in random walks. In other contexts it is more natural to speak of the distribution of the residual waiting time commencing at the *v*th trial. Cf. example XV,(2.k).]

To determine these probabilities we use the standard renewal argument as follows. It is possible that $\mathcal{E}$ occurs for the very first time at the $(v+r)$th trial. The probability for this is f_{v+r}. Otherwise there exists an integer $k \leq v$ such that $\mathcal{E}$ occurred for the first time at the *k*th trial. The continuation of the process after the *k*th trial is a probabilistic replica of the whole process, except that the original *v*th trial now becomes the $(v-k)$th trial. The probability of our event is therefore $f_k w_{v-k}(r)$, and hence for each $r > 0$

$$(10.12) \qquad w_v(r) = f_{v+r} + \sum_{k=1}^{v} f_k w_{v-k}(r).$$

This equation is of the standard type (10.1) with $b_n = f_{n+r}$. We are not interested in the generating function but wish to describe the asymptotic behavior of the hitting probabilities for very large v. This is achieved by theorem 1. Put

(10.13) $\rho_k = f_{k+1} + f_{k+2} + \cdots$

and recall from XI,(1.8) that the mean recurrence time satisfies

(10.14) $\mu = \rho_1 + \rho_2 + \cdots.$

If $\mathcal{E}$ is not periodic we conclude from theorem 1 that as $\nu \to \infty$

$$
\text{(10.15)} \qquad w_\nu(r) \to
\begin{array}{ll}
\rho_r/\mu & \text{if } \mu < \infty \\[2mm]
0 & \text{if } \mu = \infty.
\end{array}
$$

This result is of great interest. In the case of a finite mean recurrence time it implies that $\{\rho_r/\mu\}$ is a probability distribution, and hence we have a limit theorem of a standard type. If, however, $\mu = \infty$ *the probability tends to* 1 *that the waiting time will exceed any given integer* r. In other words, our waiting times behave much worse than the recurrence times themselves. This unexpected phenomenon has significant consequences discussed in detail in volume 2. (See also problem 10.)

(c) *Repeated averaging.* The following problem is of an analytic character and was treated in various contexts by much more intricate methods. Suppose that $f_1 + \cdots + f_r = 1$ with $f_j \geq 0$. Given any r numbers $v_1, \ldots, v_r$ we define $f_1 v_r + \cdots + f_r v_1$ as their *weighted average*. We now define an infinite sequence $v_1, v_2, \ldots$ starting with the given r-tuple and defining v_n as the weighted average of the preceding r terms. In other words, for $n > r$ we define

(10.16) $v_n = f_1 v_{n-1} + \cdots + f_r v_{n-r}.$

Since the sequence $f_1, f_2, \ldots$ terminates with the rth term these equations are of the form (10.1). We now define the b_k so that (10.1) will be true for all n. This means that we put $b_0 = v_0 = 0$ and

(10.17) $b_k = v_k - f_1 v_{k-1} - \cdots - f_{k-1} v_1$ $k \leq r.$

(For $k > r$, by definition $b_k = 0$.) Without any calculations it follows from theorem 1 that with this repeated averaging the v_n *tend to a finite limit.* To calculate the limit we have to evaluate $b = b_1 + \cdots + b_r$. With the notation (10.13) for the remainders of $\sum f_k$ it is obvious from (10.17) and (10.6) that

$$
\text{(10.18)} \qquad v_n \to \frac{v_1 \rho_{r-1} + \cdots + v_r \rho_0}{f_1 + 2f_2 + \cdots + rf_r}.
$$

For example, if $r = 3$ and one takes *arithmetic means*, then $f_1 = f_2 = = f_3 = \frac{1}{3}$ and

(10.19) $v_n \to \frac{1}{6}(v_1 + 2v_2 + 3v_3)$.

The ease with which we derived this result should not obscure the fact that the problem is difficult when taken out of the present context. (For an alternative treatment see problem 15 of XV,14.)

TABLE 1

ILLUSTRATING THE DEVELOPMENT OF THE AGE DISTRIBUTION
IN A POPULATION DESCRIBED IN EXAMPLE (10.d)

n:	0	1	2	3	4	5	6	7	∞
$k = 0$	500	397	411.4	412	423.8	414.3	417.0	416.0	416.7
1	320	400	317.6	329.1	329.6	339.0	331.5	333.6	333.3
2	74	148	185	146.9	152.2	152.4	156.8	153.3	154.2
3	100	40	80	100	79.4	82.3	82.4	84.8	83.3
4	6	15	6	12	15	11.9	12.3	12.4	12.5

The columns give the age distribution of a population of $N = 1000$ elements at epochs $n = 0, 1, \ldots, 7$ together with the limiting distribution. The assumed mortalities are[10]

$$f_1 = 0.20; \quad f_2 = 0.43; \quad f_3 = 0.17; \quad f_4 = 0.17; \quad f_5 = 0.03,$$

so that no piece effectively attains age 5.

(*d*) *Self-renewing aggregates.* We return to the example of section 2 where a piece of equipment installed at epoch n has a lifetime with probability distribution $\{f_n\}$. When it expires it is immediately replaced by a new piece of the same character, and so the successive replacements constitute a persistent recurrent event in a sequence of dependent trials (whose outcomes decide whether or not a replacement takes place).

Suppose now that the piece of equipment installed at epoch 0 has an age k rather than being new. This affects only the first waiting time, and so $\mathcal{E}$ becomes a *delayed* recurrent event. To obtain the distribution $\{b_n\}$ of the first waiting time note that b_n is the (conditional) expectation that a piece will expire at age $n + k$ given that it has attained age k. Thus for $k \geq 1$

(10.20) $b_n = f_{n+k}/r_k \qquad where \quad r_k = f_{k+1} + f_{k+2} + \cdots.$

In practice one is not interested in a single piece of equipment but in a whole population (say the street lamps in a town). Suppose then that *the initial population* (at epoch 0) *consists of* N *pieces, among which* β_k *have*

---

[10] The roots of the equation $1 - F(s) = 0$ are 1, $-\frac{5}{3}$, -5, and $\pm 2i$. The mean recurrence time is 2.40.

age k (where $\sum \beta_k = N$). Each piece originates a line of descendants which may require a replacement at epoch n. *The expected number* v_n *of all replacements at epoch* n *obviously satisfies the basic equations* (10.1) *with*

$$(10.21) \qquad b_n = \sum \beta_k f_{n+k}/r_k.$$

We have here the first example where v_n is an *expectation* rather than a probability; we know only that $v_n < N$.

An easy calculation shows that $b = \sum b_n = N$, and so theorem 1 shows that $v_n \to N/\mu$ provided that the replacements are not periodic. This result implies the existence of a *stable limit for the age distribution*. In fact, for a piece to be of age k at epoch n it is necessary and sufficient that it was installed at epoch $n - k$ and that it survived age k. The expected number of such pieces is therefore $v_{n-k}r_k$ and tends to Nr_k/μ as $n \to \infty$. In other words, as time goes on the *fraction of the population of age* k *tends to* r_k/μ. Thus *the limiting age distribution is independent of the initial age distribution* and depends only on the mortalities f_n. A similar result holds under much wider conditions. For a numerical illustration see table 1. It reveals the noteworthy fact that the approach to the limit is not monotone. (See also problems 16–18.)

(*e*) *Human populations.* For an example where $f = \sum f_n > 1$ we use the simplest model of a human population. It is analogous to the model in the preceding example except that the population size is now variable and female births take over the role of replacements. The novel feature is that a mother may have any number of daughters, and hence her line may become extinct, but it may also increase in numbers. We now define f_n the probability, at birth, that a mother will (survive and) at age n give birth to a female child. (The dependence on the number and the ages of previous children is neglected.) Then $f = \sum f_n$ is the expected number of daughters and so in a healthy population $f > 1$. Theorem 1 then promises a population size that increases roughly at the constant rate ξ, and the age distribution of the population tends to a limit as described in the preceding example. The model is admittedly crude but presents nevertheless some practical interest. The curious dependence of the limiting behavior ξ was certainly not predictable without a proper mathematical analysis.   ▶

*11. PROOF OF THE BASIC LIMIT THEOREM

In section 3 we omitted the proof of theorem 3 which we now restate as follows: *Let* $f_1, f_2, \ldots$ *be a sequence of numbers* $f_n \geq 0$ *such that*

---

* This section is not used in the sequel.

$\sum f_n = 1$ *and* 1 *is the greatest common divisor of those* n *for which* $f_n > 0$. *Let* $u_0 = 1$ *and*

(11.1) $u_n = f_1 u_{n-1} + f_2 u_{n-2} + \cdots + f_n u_0,$ $n \geq 1.$

Then

(11.2) $u_n \to \mu^{-1}$ *where* $\mu = \sum_{n=1}^{\infty} n f_n$

(μ^{-1} *being interpreted as* 0 *when* $\mu = \infty$).

In order not to interrupt the argument we preface the proof by two well-known lemmas that are widely used outside probability.

Let A be the set of all integers n for which $f_n > 0$, and denote by A^+ the set of all positive linear combinations

(11.3) $p_1 a_1 + \cdots + p_r a_r$

of numbers $a_1, \ldots, a_r$ in A (the p_j are positive integers).

Lemma 1. *There exists an integer* N *such that* A^+ *contains all integers* $n > N$.

Proof. As is known from Euclid, the fact that 1 is the greatest common divisor of the numbers in A means that it is possible to choose integers $a_1, \ldots, a_r$ in A and (not necessarily positive) integers c_j such that

(11.4) $c_1 a_1 + \cdots + c_r a_r = 1.$

Put $s = a_1 + \cdots + a_r$. *Every* integer n admits of a unique representation $n = xs + y$ where x and y are integers and $0 \leq y < s$. Then

(11.5) $n = \sum_{k=1}^{r} (x + c_k y) a_k$

and all the coefficients will be positive as soon as x exceeds y times the largest among the numbers $|c_k|$.   ▶

Lemma 2. (*Selection principle.*) *Suppose that for every integer* $\nu > 0$ *we are given a sequence of numbers* $z_1^{(\nu)}, z_2^{(\nu)}, \ldots$ *such that* $0 \leq z_k^{(\nu)} \leq 1$. *Then there exists a sequence* $\nu^{(1)}, \nu^{(2)}, \ldots \to \infty$ *such that as* ν *runs through it,* $z_k^{(\nu)}$ *tends to a limit for every fixed* k.

Proof[11] Choose an increasing sequence $\nu_1^{(1)}, \nu_1^{(1)}, \ldots$ such that as ν runs through it $z_1^{(\nu)}$ converges to a limit z_1. Out of this sequence choose

---

[11] The proof is based on the so-called *diagonal method* due to G. Cantor (1845–1918). It has become a standard tool but was shockingly new in Cantor's time.

a *subsequence* $v_1^{(2)}, v_2^{(2)}, \ldots$ such that as v runs through it $z_2^{(v)} \to z_2$. Continuing in this way we get for each n a sequence of integers $v_j^{(n)} \to \infty$ such that as v runs through it $z_n^{(v)} \to z_n$, and each $v_j^{(n)}$ is an element of the preceding sequence $\{v_j^{(n-1)}\}$. Finally, put $v^{(r)} = v_r^{(r)}$. Let $r > n$. Except for the first n terms every element $v^{(r)}$ appears in the sequence $v_1^{(n)}, v_2^{(n)}, \ldots$, and hence $z_n^{(v)} \to z_n$ as v runs through the sequence $v^{(1)}, v^{(2)}, \ldots$.   ▶

Lemma 3. *Let* $\{w_n\}$ $(n = 0, \pm 1, \pm 2, \ldots)$ *be a doubly infinite sequence of numbers such that* $0 \leq w_n \leq 1$ *and*

$$(11.6) \qquad w_n = \sum_{k=1}^{\infty} f_k w_{n-k}$$

for each n. *If* $w_0 = 1$ *then* $w_n = 1$ *for all* n.

Proof. Since

$$(11.7) \qquad w_0 = \sum_{k=1}^{\infty} f_k w_{-k} \leq \sum_{k=1}^{\infty} f_k = 1$$

the condition $w_0 = 1$ requires that the two series agree termwise, and so for each k either $f_k = 0$ or else $w_{-k} = 1$. This means that $w_{-a} = 1$ for every integer a of A. But then the argument used for $n = 0$ applies also with $n = -a$, and we conclude that $w_{-a-b} = 1$ whenever the integers a and b are in A. Proceeding by induction we conclude that $w_{-m} = 1$ for every integer in A^+, and hence $w_{-m} = 1$ for every $m > N$. But this implies that for $n = -N$ the right side in (11.6) equals 1 and so $w_{-N} = 1$. Letting $n = -N + 1$ we find in like manner $w_{-N+1} = 1$, and proceeding in this way we find by induction that $w_n = 1$ for all n.   ▶

Proof of the theorem. Let

$$(11.8) \qquad \eta = \limsup_{n \to \infty} u_n.$$

It is obvious from (11.1) that $0 \leq \eta \leq 1$, and there exists a sequence $r_1, r_2, \ldots$ tending to infinity such that as $v \to \infty$

$$(11.9) \qquad u_{r_v} \to \eta.$$

For each positive integer v we define a doubly infinite sequence $\{u_n^{(v)}\}$ by

$$(11.10) \qquad u_n^{(v)} = \begin{cases} u_{r_v + n} & \text{for} \quad n \geq -r_v \\ 0 & \text{for} \quad n < -r_v. \end{cases}$$

For simplicity of expression lemma 2 was formulated for simple sequences, but it obviously applies to double sequences also. Accordingly, it is possible to choose an increasing sequence of integers $v_1, v_2, \ldots$ such that when v runs through it $u_n^{(v)}$ tends to a limit w_n for each n. From the construction $0 \leq w_n \leq \eta$ and $w_0 = \eta$. Furthermore, for each v and $n > -v$ the definition (11.1) reads

$$(11.11) \qquad u_n^{(v)} = \sum_{k=1}^{\infty} f_k u_{n-k}^{(v)},$$

and in the limit we find the relation (11.6). By lemma 3 therefore $w_n = \eta$ for all n.

We are now ready for the final argument. As before we put

$$(11.12) \qquad \rho_k = f_{k+1} + f_{k+2} + \cdots$$

so that $r_0 = 1$ and $\sum \rho_k = \mu$ [see XI, (1.8)]. Summing the defining relations (11.1) over $n = 1, 2, \ldots, N$ and collecting terms we get the identity

$$(11.13) \qquad \rho_0 u_N + \rho_1 u_{N-1} + \cdots + \rho_N u_0 = 1.$$

We use this relation successively for $N = v_1, v_2, \ldots$. As N runs through this sequence $u_{N-k} \to w_{-k} = \eta$ for each k. If $\sum \rho_k = \infty$ it follows that $\eta = 0$ and so $u_n \to 0$ as asserted. When $\mu = \sum \rho_k < \infty$ it follows that $\eta = \mu^{-1}$, and it remains to show that this implies $u_N \to \eta$ for any approach $N \to \infty$. By the definition of the upper limit we have $u_{N-k} < \eta + \epsilon$ for each fixed k and N sufficiently large. Furthermore $u_n \leq 1$ for all n. Suppose then that N approaches infinity in such a manner that $u_N \to \eta_0$. From (11.13) it is clear that ultimately

$$(11.14) \quad \rho_0 \eta_0 + (\rho_1 + \cdots + \rho_r)(\eta + \epsilon) + (\rho_{r+1} + \rho_{r+2} + \cdots) \geq 1,$$

and hence

$$(11.15) \qquad \rho_0(\eta_0 - \eta) + \mu(\eta + \epsilon) \geq 1.$$

But $\mu\eta = 1$ and $\eta_0 \leq \eta$ by the definition of η. Since (11.15) is true for arbitrary $\epsilon > 0$ it follows that $\eta_0 = \eta$ and so $u_N \to \mu^{-1}$ for any approach $N \to \infty$. ▶

12. PROBLEMS FOR SOLUTION

1. Suppose that $F(s)$ is a polynomial. Prove for this case all theorems of section 3, using the partial fraction method of XI, 4.

2. Let r coins be tossed repeatedly and let $\mathcal{E}$ be the recurrent event that for each of the r coins the accumulated number of heads and tails are equal. Is $\mathcal{E}$ persistent or transient? For the smallest r for which $\mathcal{E}$ is transient, estimate the probability that $\mathcal{E}$ ever occurs.

3. In a sequence of independent throws of a perfect die let $\mathcal{E}$ stand for the event that the accumulated numbers of ones, twos, . . . , sixes are equal. Show that $\mathcal{E}$ is a transient (periodic) recurrent event and estimate the probability f that $\mathcal{E}$ will ever occur.

4. In a sequence of Bernoulli trials let $\mathcal{E}$ occur when the accumulated number of successes equals λ times the accumulated number of failures; here λ is a positive integer. [See example (1.c).] Show that $\mathcal{E}$ is persistent if, and only if, $p/q = \lambda$, that is, $p = \lambda/(\lambda+1)$. *Hint:* Use the normal approximation.

5. In a sequence of Bernoulli trials we say that $\mathcal{E}$ occurs when the accumulated number of successes is twice the accumulated number of failures and the ratio has never exceeded 2. Show that $\mathcal{E}$ is transient and periodic. The generating function is determined by the cubic equation $F(s) = qs(U(s)ps)^2$. (*Hint:* $U(s)ps$ is the generating function for the waiting time for the number of successes to *exceed* twice the number of failures.)

6. Let the $\mathbf{X}_j$ be independent integral-valued random variables with a common distribution. Assume that these variables assume both positive and negative values. Prove that the event defined by $\mathbf{S}_n = 0, \mathbf{S}_1 \leq 0, \ldots, \mathbf{S}_{n-1} \leq 0$ is recurrent and transient.

7. *Geiger counters.* [See examples (1.g) and (4.e).] Denote by $\mathbf{N}_n$ and $\mathbf{Z}_n$, respectively, the number of occurrences of $\mathcal{E}$ and the number of registrations up to and including epoch n. Discuss the relationship between these variables and find asymptotic expressions for $\mathbf{E}(\mathbf{Z}_n)$ and $\mathrm{Var}\,(\mathbf{Z}_n)$.

8. In *Geiger counters of type* II every arriving particle (whether registered or not) locks the counter for exactly r time units (that is, at the $r - 1$ trials following the arrival). The duration of the locked time following a registration is therefore a random variable. Find its generating function G. If $\mathcal{E}$ is again the recurrent event that the counter is free, express the generating function F of the recurrence times in terms of G. Finally, find the mean recurrence time.

9. *A more general type of Geiger counters.* As in problem 8 we assume that every arriving particle completely obliterates the effect of the preceding ones, but we assume now that the time for which a particle locks the counter is a random variable with a given generating function $B(s)$. [In the preceding problem $B(s) = s^r$.] Do problem 8 under these more general conditions.

10. For a delayed recurrent event $\mathcal{E}$ the probabilities v_n are constant only when the generating function of the first occurrence of $\mathcal{E}$ is given by $B(s) = [1-F(s)]/\mu(1-s)$, that is, when $b_n = f_{n+1} + f_{n+2} + \cdots$. Discuss the relation with the limit theorem for hitting probabilities in example (10.b).

11. Find an approximation to the probability that in 10,000 tossings of a coin the number of head runs of length 3 will lie between 700 and 730.

12. In a sequence of tossings of a coin let $\mathcal{E}$ stand for the pattern HTH. Let r_n be the probability that $\mathcal{E}$ does not occur in n trials. Find the generating function and use the partial fraction method to obtain an asymptotic expansion.

13. In example (8.a) the expected duration of the game is

$$\mu_1\mu_2/(\mu_1+\mu_2),$$

where μ_1 and μ_2 are the mean recurrence times for success runs of length r and failure runs of length ρ, respectively.

14. The possible outcomes of each trial are A, B, and C; the corresponding probabilities are α, β, γ ($\alpha + \beta + \gamma = 1$). Find the generating function of the probability that in n trials there is no run of length r: (a) of A's, (b) of A's or B's, (c) of any kind.

15. *Continuation.* Find the probability that the first A-run of length r precedes the first B-run of length ρ and terminates at the nth trial. (*Hint:* The generating function is of the form $\mathfrak{X}(s)$ in (8.6) except that ρ is replaced by α in the expression for F, and by β in $\mathfrak{G}$.)

16. *Self-renewing aggregates.* In example (10.d) find the limiting age distribution assuming that the lifetime distribution is geometric: $f_k = q^{k-1}p$.

17. *Continuation.* The initial *age distribution* $\{\beta_k\}$ is called *stationary* if it perpetuates itself for all times. Show (without computation) that this is the case only when $\beta_k = r_k/\mu$.

18. *Continuation.* Denote by $w_k(n)$ the expected number of elements at epoch n that are of age k. Find the determining equations and verify from them that the population size remains constant. Furthermore, show that the expected number $w_0(n)$ satisfies

$$w_0(n) = w_0(n-1)f_1/r_0 + w_1(n-1)f_2/r_1 + \cdots.$$

---

19. Let $\mathcal{E}$ be a persistent aperiodic recurrent event. Assume that the recurrence time has finite mean μ and variance σ^2. Put $q_n = f_{n+1} + f_{n+2} + \cdots$ and $r_n = q_{n+1} + q_{n+2} + \cdots$. Show that the generating functions $Q(s)$ and $R(s)$ converge for $s = 1$. Prove that

$$(12.1) \qquad u_0 + \sum_{n=1}^{\infty} \left(u_n - \frac{1}{\mu} \right) s^n = \frac{R(s)}{\mu Q(s)}$$

and hence that

$$(12.2) \qquad u_0 + \sum_{n=1}^{\infty} \left(u_n - \frac{1}{\mu} \right) = \frac{\sigma^2 - \mu + \mu^2}{2\mu^2}.$$

20. Let $\mathcal{E}$ be a persistent recurrent event and N_r the number of occurrences of $\mathcal{E}$ in r trials. Prove that

$$(12.3) \qquad E(N_r^2) = u_1 + \cdots + u_r + 2\sum_{j=1}^{r-1} u_j(u_1 + \cdots + u_{r-j})$$

and hence that $E(N_r^2)$ is the coefficient of s^r in

$$(12.4) \qquad \frac{F^2(s) + F(s)}{(1-s)\{1-F(s)\}^2}$$

(Note that this may be reformulated more elegantly using bivariate generating functions.)

21. Let $q_{k,n} = P\{N_k = n\}$. Show that $q_{k,n}$ is the coefficient of s^k in

$$(12.5) \qquad F^n(s) \frac{\{1-F(s)\}}{1-s}.$$

Deduce that $E(N_r)$ and $E(N_r^2)$ are the coefficients of s^r in

(12.6)
$$\frac{F(s)}{(1-s)\{1-F(s)\}}$$

and (12.4), respectively.

22. Using the notations of problem 19, show that

(12.7)
$$\frac{F(s)}{(1-s)\{1-F(s)\}} = -\frac{1}{1-s} + \frac{1}{\mu(1-s)^2} + \frac{R(s)}{\mu\{1-F(s)\}} \,.$$

Hence, using the last problem, conclude that

(12.8)
$$E(N_r) = \frac{r}{\mu} + \frac{\sigma^2 + \mu - \mu^2}{2\mu^2} + \epsilon_r$$

with $\epsilon_r \to 0$.

23. *Continuation.* Using a similar argument, show that

(12.9)
$$E(N_r^2) = \frac{r^2}{\mu^2} + \frac{2\sigma^2 + \mu - \mu^2}{\mu^3} r + \alpha_r,$$

where $\alpha_r/r \to 0$. Hence

(12.10)
$$\text{Var}\,(N_r) \sim \frac{\sigma^2}{\mu^3} r.$$

(*Hint:* Decompose the difference of (12.4) and (12.7) into three fractions with denominators containing the factor $(1-s)^k$, $k = 1, 2, 3$.)

24. In a sequence of Bernoulli trials let $q_{k,n}$ be the probability that exactly n success runs of length r occur in k trials. Using problem 21, show that the generating function $Q_k(x) = \sum q_{k,n} x^n$ is the coefficient of s^k in

$$\frac{1 - p^r s^r}{1 - s + qp^r s^{r+1} - (1-ps)p^r s^r x} \,.$$

Show, furthermore, that the root of the denominator which is smallest in absolute value is $s_1 \approx 1 + qp^r(1-x)$.

25. *Continuation. The Poisson distribution of long runs.*[12] If the number k of trials and the length r of runs both tend to infinity, so that $kqp^r \to \lambda$, then the probability of having exactly n runs of length r tends to $e^{-\lambda}\lambda^n/n!$.

Hint: Using the preceding problem, show that the generating function is asymptotically $\{1 + qp^r(1-x)\}^{-k} \sim e^{-\lambda(1-x)}$. Use the *continuity theorem* of XI, 6.

---

[12] The theorem was proved by von Mises, but the present method is considerably simpler.

CHAPTER XIV

Random Walk and Ruin Problems

1. GENERAL ORIENTATION

The first part of this chapter is devoted to Bernoulli trials, and once more the picturesque language of betting and random walks is used to simplify and enliven the formulations.

Consider the familiar gambler who wins or loses a dollar with probabilities p and q, respectively. Let his initial capital be z and let him play against an adversary with initial capital $a - z$, so that the combined capital is a. The game continues until the gambler's capital either is reduced to zero or has increased to a, that is, until one of the two players is ruined. We are interested in the probability of the gambler's ruin and the probability distribution of the duration of the game. This is *the classical ruin problem*.

Physical applications and analogies suggest the more flexible interpretation in terms of the notion of a variable point or "*particle*" on the x-axis. This particle starts from the *initial position* z, and moves at regular time intervals a unit step in the positive or negative direction, depending on whether the corresponding trial resulted in success or failure. The position of the particle after n steps represents the gambler's capital at the conclusion of the nth trial. The trials terminate when the particle for the first time reaches either 0 or a, and we describe this by saying that the particle performs *a random walk with absorbing barriers at* 0 *and a*. This random walk is *restricted* to the possible positions $1, 2, \ldots, a - 1$; in the absence of absorbing barriers the random walk is called *unrestricted*. Physicists use the random-walk model as a crude approximation to one-dimensional diffusion or Brownian motion, where a physical particle is exposed to a great number of molecular collisions which impart to it a random motion. The case $p > q$ corresponds to a *drift* to the right when shocks from the left are more probable; when $p = q = \frac{1}{2}$, the random walk is called *symmetric*.

342

In the limiting case $a \to \infty$ we get a random walk on a semi-infinite line: A particle starting at $z > 0$ performs a random walk up to the moment when it for the first time reaches the origin. In this formulation we recognize the *first-passage time problem;* it was solved by elementary methods in chapter III (at least for the symmetric case) and by the use of generating functions in XI,3. We shall encounter formulas previously obtained, but the present derivation is self-contained.

In this chapter we shall use the method of *difference equations* which serves as an introduction to the differential equations of diffusion theory. This analogy leads in a natural way to various modifications and generalizations of the classical ruin problem, a typical and instructive example being the replacing of absorbing barriers by *reflecting* and *elastic* barriers. To describe a reflecting barrier, consider a random walk in a finite interval as defined before except that whenever the particle is at point 1 it has probability p of moving to position 2 and probability q to stay at 1. In gambling terminology this corresponds to a convention that whenever the gambler loses his last dollar it is generously replaced by his adversary so that the game can continue. The physicist imagines a wall placed at the point $\frac{1}{2}$ of the x-axis with the property that a particle moving from 1 toward 0 is reflected at the wall and returns to 1 instead of reaching 0. Both the absorbing and the reflecting barriers are special cases of the so-called elastic barrier. We define an *elastic barrier at the origin by the rule that from position 1 the particle moves with probability p to position 2; with probability δq it stays at 1; and with probability $(1-\delta)q$ it moves to 0 and is absorbed* (i.e., the process terminates). For $\delta = 0$ we have the classical ruin problem or absorbing barriers, for $\delta = 1$ reflecting barriers. As δ runs from 0 to 1 we have a family of intermediate cases. The greater δ is, the more likely is the process to continue, and with two reflecting barriers the process can never terminate.

Sections 2 and 3 are devoted to an elementary discussion of the classical ruin problem and its implications. The next three sections are more technical (and may be omitted); in 4 and 5 we derive the relevant generating functions and from them explicit expressions for the distribution of the duration of the game, etc. Section 6 contains an outline of the passage to the limit to the diffusion equation (the formal solutions of the latter being the limiting distributions for the random walk).

In section 7 the discussion again turns elementary and is devoted to *random walks in two or more dimensions* where new phenomena are encountered. Section 8 treats a generalization of an entirely different type, namely a random walk in one dimension where the particle is no longer restricted to move in unit steps but is permitted to change its position in jumps which are arbitrary multiples of unity. Such generalized random walks have attracted widespread interest in connection with Wald's theory of *sequential sampling.*

The problem section contains essential complements to the text and outlines of alternative approaches. It is hoped that a comparison of the methods used will prove highly instructive.

In conclusion it must be emphasized that each random walk represents a special Markov chain, and so the present chapter serves partly as an introduction to the next where several random-walk problems (e.g., elastic barriers) will be reformulated.

2. THE CLASSICAL RUIN PROBLEM

We shall consider the problem stated at the opening of the present chapter. Let q_z be the probability of the gambler's ultimate[1] ruin and p_z the probability of his winning. In random-walk terminology q_z and p_z are the probabilities that a particle starting at z will be absorbed at 0 and a, respectively. We shall show that $p_z + q_z = 1$, so that we need not consider the possibility of an unending game.

After the first trial the gambler's fortune is either $z - 1$ or $z + 1$, and therefore we must have

$$(2.1) \qquad\qquad q_z = pq_{z+1} + qq_{z-1}$$

provided $1 < z < a - 1$. For $z = 1$ the first trial may lead to ruin, and (2.1) is to be replaced by $q_1 = pq_2 + q$. Similarly, for $z = a - 1$ the first trial may result in victory, and therefore $q_{a-1} = qq_{a-2}$. To unify our equations we define

$$(2.2) \qquad\qquad q_0 = 1, \qquad q_a = 0.$$

With this convention the probability q_z of ruin satisfies (2.1) for $z = = 1, 2, \ldots, a - 1$.

Systems of the form (2.1) are known as *difference equations,* and (2.2) represents the *boundary conditions* on q_z. We shall derive an explicit expression for q_z by the *method of particular solutions,* which will also be used in more general cases.

Suppose first that $p \neq q$. It is easily verified that the difference

---

[1] Strictly speaking, the probability of ruin is defined in a sample space of infinitely prolonged games, but we can work with the sample space of n trials. The probability of ruin in less than n trials increases with n and has therefore a limit. We call this *limit* "the probability of ruin." All probabilities in this chapter may be interpreted in this way without reference to infinite spaces (cf. VIII,1).

equations (2.1) admit of the two particular solutions $q_z = 1$ and $q_z = (q/p)^z$. It follows that for arbitrary constants A and B the sequence

$$(2.3) \qquad q_z = A + B\left(\frac{q}{p}\right)^z$$

represents a formal solution of (2.1). The boundary conditions (2.2) will hold if, and only if, A and B satisfy the two linear equations $A + B = 1$ and $A + B(q/p)^a = 0$. Thus

$$(2.4) \qquad q_z = \frac{(q/p)^a - (q/p)^z}{(q/p)^a - 1}$$

is a formal solution of the difference equation (2.1), satisfying the boundary conditions (2.2). In order to prove that (2.4) is the required probability of ruin it remains to show that the solution is unique, that is, that *all* solutions of (2.1) are of the form (2.3). Now, given an arbitrary solution of (2.1), the two constants A and B can be chosen so that (2.3) will agree with it for $z = 0$ and $z = 1$. From these two values all other values can be found by substituting in (2.1) successively $z = 1, 2, 3, \ldots$. Therefore two solutions which agree for $z = 0$ and $z = 1$ are identical, and hence every solution is of the form (2.3).

Our argument breaks down if $p = q = \frac{1}{2}$, for then (2.4) is meaningless because in this case the two formal particular solutions $q_z = 1$ and $q_z = (q/p)^z$ are identical. However, when $p = q = \frac{1}{2}$ we have a formal solution in $q_z = z$, and therefore $q_z = A + Bz$ is a solution of (2.1) depending on two constants. In order to satisfy the boundary conditions (2.2) we must put $A = 1$ and $A + Ba = 0$. Hence

$$(2.5) \qquad q_z = 1 - \frac{z}{a}.$$

(The same numerical value can be obtained formally from (2.4) by finding the limit as $p \to \frac{1}{2}$, using L'Hospital's rule.)

We have thus proved that the required *probability of the gambler's ruin is given by* (2.4) *if* $p \neq q$, *and by* (2.5) *if* $p = q = \frac{1}{2}$. The probability p_z of the gambler's winning the game equals the probability of his adversary's ruin and is therefore obtained from our formulas on replacing p, q, and z by q, p, and $a - z$, respectively. It is readily seen that $p_z + q_z = 1$, as stated previously.

We can reformulate our result as follows: *Let a gambler with an initial capital z play against an infinitely rich adversary who is always willing to play, although the gambler has the privilege of stopping at his pleasure. The gambler adopts the strategy of playing until he either loses his capital or* *increases it to* a (*with a net gain* $a - z$). *Then* q_z *is the probability of his losing and* $1 - q_z$ *the probability of his winning.*

Under this system the gambler's ultimate gain or loss is a random variable **G** which assumes the values $a - z$ and $-z$ with probabilities $1 - q_z$ and q_z, respectively. The expected gain is

(2.6) $$E(G) = a(1 - q_z) - z.$$

Clearly $E(G) = 0$ if, and only if, $p = q$. This means that, with the system described, *a "fair" game remains fair, and no "unfair" game can be changed into a "fair" one.*

From (2.5) we see that in the case $p = q$ a player with initial capital $z = 999$ has a probability 0.999 to win a dollar before losing his capital. With $q = 0.6$, $p = 0.4$ the game is unfavorable indeed, but still the probability (2.4) of winning a dollar before losing the capital is about $\frac{2}{3}$. In general, a gambler with a relatively large initial capital z has a reasonable chance to win a small amount $a - z$ before being ruined.[2]

[For a surprising consequence of our result see problem 4.]

Let us now investigate the effect of *changing stakes*. Changing the unit from a dollar to a half-dollar is equivalent to doubling the initial capitals. The corresponding probability of ruin q_z^* is obtained from (2.4) on replacing z by $2z$ and a by $2a$:

(2.7) $$q_z^* = \frac{(q/p)^{2a} - (q/p)^{2z}}{(q/p)^{2a} - 1} = q_z \cdot \frac{(q/p)^a + (q/p)^z}{(q/p)^a + 1}.$$

For $q > p$ the last fraction is greater than unity and $q_z^* > q_z$. We restate this conclusion as follows: *if the stakes are doubled while the initial capitals remain unchanged, the probability of ruin decreases for the player whose probability of success is* $p < \frac{1}{2}$ *and increases for the adversary (for whom the game is advantageous).*[3] Suppose, for example, that Peter owns 90 dollars and Paul 10, and let $p = 0.45$, the game being unfavorable to Peter. If at each trial the stake is one dollar, table 1 shows the probability

---

[2] A certain man used to visit Monte Carlo year after year and was always successful in recovering the cost of his vacations. He firmly believed in a magic power over chance. Actually his experience is not surprising. Assuming that he started with ten times the ultimate gain, the chances of success in any year are nearly 0.9. The probability of an unbroken sequence of ten successes is about $(1 - \frac{1}{10})^{10} \approx e^{-1} \approx 0.37$. Thus continued success is by no means improbable. Moreover, *one* failure would, of course, be blamed on an oversight or momentary indisposition.

[3] A detailed analysis of other possible strategies will be found in the (not elementary) book by L. E. Dubbins and L. J. Savage, *How to gamble if you must* (which has a more informative subtitle: *Inequalities for stochastic processes*), New York (McGraw-Hill), 1965.

of Peter's ruin to be 0.866, approximately. If the same game is played for a stake of 10 dollars, the probability of Peter's ruin drops to less than one fourth, namely about 0.210. Thus the effect of increasing stakes is more pronounced than might be expected. In general, if k dollars are staked at each trial, we find the probability of ruin from (2.4), replacing z by z/k and a by a/k; the probability of ruin decreases as k increases. In a game with constant stakes the unfavored gambler minimizes the probability of ruin by selecting the stake as large as consistent with his goal of gaining an amount fixed in advance. The empirical validity of this conclusion has

TABLE 1

ILLUSTRATING THE CLASSICAL RUIN PROBLEM

p	q	z	a	Probability of Ruin	Probability of Success	Expected Gain	Expected Duration
0.5	0.5	9	10	0.1	0.9	0	9
0.5	0.5	90	100	0.1	0.9	0	900
0.5	0.5	900	1,000	0.1	0.9	0	90,000
0.5	0.5	950	1,000	0.05	0.95	0	47,500
0.5	0.5	8,000	10,000	0.2	0.8	0	16,000,000
0.45	0.55	9	10	0.210	0.790	−1.1	11
0.45	0.55	90	100	0.866	0.134	−76.6	765.6
0.45	0.55	99	100	0.182	0.818	−17.2	171.8
0.4	0.6	90	100	0.983	0.017	−88.3	441.3
0.4	0.6	99	100	0.333	0.667	−32.3	161.7

The initial capital is z. The game terminates with ruin (loss z) or capital a (gain $a - z$).

been challenged, usually by people who contended that every "unfair" bet is unreasonable. If this were to be taken seriously, it would mean the end of all insurance business, for the careful driver who insures against liability obviously plays a game that is technically "unfair." Actually, there exists no theorem in probability to discourage such a driver from taking insurance.

The limiting case $a = \infty$ corresponds to a game against an infinitely rich adversary. Letting $a \to \infty$ in (2.4) and (2.5) we get

$$(2.8) \qquad q_z = \begin{cases} 1 & \text{if } p \leq q \\ (q/p)^z & \text{if } p > q. \end{cases}$$

We interpret q_z *as the probability of ultimate ruin of a gambler with initial capital z playing against an infinitely rich adversary.*[4] In random walk

---

[4] It is easily seen that the q_z represent a solution of the difference equations (2.1) satisfying the (now unique) boundary condition $q_0 = 1$. When $p > q$ the solution is not unique. Actually our result is contained in XI,(3.9) and will be derived independently (in a strengthened form) in section 4.

terminology q_z is the probability that a particle starting at $z > 0$ will ever reach the origin. It is more natural to rephrase this result as follows: *In a random walk starting at the origin the probability of ever reaching the position $z > 0$ equals 1 if $p \geq q$ and equals $(p/q)^z$ when $p < q$.*

3. EXPECTED DURATION OF THE GAME

The probability distribution of the duration of the game will be deduced in the following sections. However, its expected value can be derived by a much simpler method which is of such wide applicability that it will now be explained at the cost of a slight duplication.

We are still concerned with the classical ruin problem formulated at the beginning of this chapter. We shall assume as known the fact that the duration of the game has a finite expectation D_z. A rigorous proof will be given in the next section.

If the first trial results in success the game continues as if the initial position had been $z + 1$. The conditional expectation of the duration assuming success at the first trial is therefore $D_{z+1} + 1$. This argument shows that the expected duration D_z satisfies the difference equation

$$(3.1) \qquad D_z = pD_{z+1} + qD_{z-1} + 1, \qquad 0 < z < a$$

with the boundary conditions

$$(3.2) \qquad D_0 = 0, \qquad D_a = 0.$$

The appearance of the term 1 makes the difference equation (3.1) non-homogeneous. If $p \neq q$, then $D_z = z/(q-p)$ is a formal solution of (3.1). The difference Δ_z of any two solutions of (3.1) satisfies the homogeneous equations $\Delta_z = p\Delta_{z+1} + q\Delta_{z-1}$, and we know already that all solutions of this equation are of the form $A + B(q/p)^z$. It follows that when $p \neq q$ all solutions of (3.1) are of the form

$$(3.3) \qquad D_z = \frac{z}{q - p} + A + B\left(\frac{q}{p}\right)^z.$$

The boundary conditions (3.2) require that

$$A + B = 0, \qquad A + B(q/p)^a = -a/(q-p).$$

Solving for A and B, we find

$$(3.4) \qquad D_z = \frac{z}{q - p} - \frac{a}{q - p} \cdot \frac{1 - (q/p)^z}{1 - (q/p)^a}.$$

Again the method breaks down if $q = p = \frac{1}{2}$. In this case we replace $z/(q-p)$ by $-z^2$, which is now a solution of (3.1). It follows that when $p = q = \frac{1}{2}$ all solutions of (3.1) are of the form $D_z = -z^2 + A + Bz$. The required solution D_z satisfying the boundary conditions (3.2) is

$$(3.5) \qquad\qquad D_z = z(a-z).$$

The expected duration of the game in the classical ruin problem is given by (3.4) or (3.5), according as $p \neq q$ or $p = q = \frac{1}{2}$.

It should be noted that this duration is considerably longer than we would naively expect. If two players with 500 dollars each toss a coin until one is ruined, the average duration of the game is 250,000 trials. If a gambler has only one dollar and his adversary 1000, the average duration is 1000 trials. Further examples are found in table 1.

As indicated at the end of the preceding section, we may pass to the limit $a \to \infty$ and consider a game against an infinitely rich adversary. When $p > q$ the game may go on forever, and in this case it makes no sense to talk about its expected duration. When $p < q$ we get for the expected duration $z(q-p)^{-1}$, but when $p = q$ the expected duration is infinite. (The same result was established in XI,3 and will be proved independently in the next section.)

*4. GENERATING FUNCTIONS FOR THE DURATION OF THE GAME AND FOR THE FIRST-PASSAGE TIMES

We shall use the method of generating functions to study the duration of the game in the classical ruin problem, that is, the restricted random walk with absorbing barriers at 0 and a. The initial position is z (with $0 < z < a$). Let $u_{z,n}$ denote the probability that the process ends with the nth step at the barrier 0 (gambler's ruin at the nth trial). After the first step the position is $z + 1$ or $z - 1$, and we conclude that for $1 < z < a - 1$ and $n \geq 1$

$$(4.1) \qquad\qquad u_{z,n+1} = pu_{z+1,n} + qu_{z-1,n}.$$

This is a difference equation analogous to (2.1), but depending on the two variables z and n. In analogy with the procedure of section 2 we wish to define boundary values $u_{0,n}$, $u_{a,n}$, and $u_{z,0}$ so that (4.1) becomes valid also for $z = 1$, $z = a - 1$, and $n = 0$. For this purpose we put

$$(4.2) \qquad\qquad u_{0,n} = u_{a,n} = 0 \qquad\qquad when \quad n \geq 1$$

---

* This section together with the related section 5 may be omitted at first reading.

and

(4.3) $$u_{0,0} = 1, \qquad u_{z,0} = 0 \qquad when \quad 0 < z \leq a.$$

Then (4.1) holds for all z with $0 < z < a$ and all $n \geq 0$.

We now introduce the generating functions

(4.4) $$U_z(s) = \sum_{n=0}^{\infty} u_{z,n} s^n.$$

Multiplying (4.1) by s^{n+1} and adding for $n = 0, 1, 2, \ldots$, we find

(4.5) $$U_z(s) = psU_{z+1}(s) + qsU_{z-1}(s), \qquad 0 < z < a;$$

the boundary conditions (4.2) and (4.3) lead to

(4.6) $$U_0(s) = 1, \qquad U_a(s) = 0.$$

The system (4.5) represents difference equations analogous to (2.1), and the boundary conditions (4.6) correspond to (2.2). The novelty lies in the circumstance that the coefficients and the unknown $U_z(s)$ now depend on the variable s, but as far as the difference equation is concerned, s is merely an arbitrary constant. We can again apply the method of section 2 provided we succeed in finding two particular solutions of (4.5). It is natural to inquire whether there exist two solutions $U_z(s)$ of the form $U_z(s) = \lambda^z(s)$. Substituting this expression into (4.5), we find that $\lambda(s)$ must satisfy the quadratic equation

(4.7) $$\lambda(s) = ps\lambda^2(s) + qs,$$

which has the two roots

(4.8) $$\lambda_1(s) = \frac{1 + \sqrt{1-4pqs^2}}{2ps}, \qquad \lambda_2(s) = \frac{1 - \sqrt{1-4pqs^2}}{2ps}$$

(we take $0 < s < 1$ and the positive square root).

We are now in possession of two particular solutions of (4.5) and conclude as in section 2 that every solution is of the form

(4.9) $$U_z(s) = A(s)\lambda_1^z(s) + B(s)\lambda_2^z(s)$$

with $A(s)$ and $B(s)$ arbitrary. To satisfy the boundary conditions (4.6), we must have $A(s) + B(s) = 1$ and $A(s)\lambda_1^a(s) + B(s)\lambda_2^a(s) = 0$, whence

(4.10) $$U_z(s) = \frac{\lambda_1^a(s)\lambda_2^z(s) - \lambda_1^z(s)\lambda_2^a(s)}{\lambda_1^a(s) - \lambda_2^a(s)}.$$

Using the obvious relation $\lambda_1(s)\lambda_2(s) = q/p$, this simplifies to

$$(4.11) \qquad U_z(s) = \left(\frac{q}{p}\right)^z \frac{\lambda_1^{a-z}(s) - \lambda_2^{a-z}(s)}{\lambda_1^a(s) - \lambda_2^a(s)}.$$

This is *the required generating function of the probability of ruin (absorption at 0) at the nth trial.* The same method shows that the generating function for the probabilities of absorption at a is given by

$$(4.12) \qquad \frac{\lambda_1^z(s) - \lambda_2^z(s)}{\lambda_1^a(s) - \lambda_2^a(s)}.$$

The generating function for *the duration of the game* is, of course, the sum of the generating functions (4.11) and (4.12).

Infinite Intervals and First Passages

The preceding considerations apply equally to random walks on the interval $(0, \infty)$ with an absorbing barrier at 0. A particle starting from the position $z > 0$ is eventually absorbed at the origin or else the random walk continues forever. Absorption corresponds to the ruin of a gambler with initial capital z playing against an infinitely rich adversary. The generating function $U_z(s)$ of the probabilities $u_{z,n}$ that absorption takes place exactly at the nth trial satisfies again the difference equations (4.5) and is therefore of the form (4.9), but this solution is unbounded at infinity unless $A(s) = 0$. The other boundary condition is now $U_0(s) = 1$, and hence $B(s) = 1$ or

$$(4.13) \qquad U_z(s) = \lambda_2^z(s).$$

[The same result can be obtained by letting $a \to \infty$ in (4.11), and remembering that $\lambda_1(s)\lambda_2(s) = q/p$.]

It follows from (4.13) for $s = 1$ that an ultimate absorption is certain if $p \le q$, and has probability $(q/p)^z$ otherwise. The same conclusion was reached in section 2.

Our absorption at the origin admits of an important alternative interpretation as a first passage in an *unrestricted* random walk. Indeed, on moving the origin to the position z it is seen that in a random walk on the entire line and starting from the origin $u_{z,n}$ *is the probability that the first visit to the point* $-z < 0$ *takes place at the nth trial.* That the corresponding generating function (4.13) is the zth power of λ_2 reflects the obvious fact that the waiting time for the first passage through $-z$ is the sum of z independent waiting times between the successive first passages through $-1, -2, \ldots, -z$.

An explicit formula for $u_{z,n}$ in the special case $p = \frac{1}{2}$ was derived by elementary methods in III,(7.5). Considering that $(n+z)/2$ steps must lead to the left, and $(n-z)/2$ to the right, one concludes easily that in general the same formula holds except that the individual paths have now probability $p^{(n-z)/2}q^{(n+z)/2}$ rather than 2^{-n}. Thus

$$(4.14) \qquad u_{z,n} = \frac{z}{n}\binom{n}{(n+z)/2} p^{(n-z)/2}q^{(n+z)/2},$$

where the binomial coefficient is to be interpreted as zero if n and z are not of the same parity. (Concerning the derivation of this formula from the generating function see the end of XI,3. An alternative explicit formula of an entirely different appearance is contained in problem 13.)

*5. EXPLICIT EXPRESSIONS

The generating function U_z of (4.11) depends formally on a square root but is actually a rational function. In fact, an application of the binomial theorem reduces the denominator to the form

$$(5.1) \qquad \lambda_1^a(s) - \lambda_2^a(s) = s^{-a}\sqrt{1-4pqs^2}\; P_a(s)$$

where P_a is an even polynomial of degree $a - 1$ when a is odd, and of degree $a - 2$ when a is even. The numerator is of the same form except that a is replaced by $a - z$. Thus U_z is the ratio of two polynomials whose degrees differ at most by 1. Consequently it is possible to derive an explicit expression for the ruin probabilities $u_{z,n}$ by the method of partial fractions described in XI,4. The result is interesting because of its connection with diffusion theory, and the derivation as such provides an excellent illustration for the techniques involved in the practical use of partial fractions.

The calculations simplify greatly by the use of an auxiliary variable ϕ defined by

$$(5.2) \qquad \cos \phi = \frac{1}{2\sqrt{pq}\cdot s}.$$

(To $0 < s < 1$ there correspond complex values of ϕ, but this has no effect on the formal calculations.) From (4.8)

$$(5.3) \qquad \lambda_1(s) = \sqrt{q/p}\,[\cos \phi + i \sin \phi] = \sqrt{q/p}\; e^{i\phi}$$

while $\lambda_2(s)$ equals the right side with i replaced by $-i$. Accordingly

$$(5.4) \qquad U_z(s) = (\sqrt{q/p})^z\, \frac{\sin (a-z)\phi}{\sin a\phi}.$$

The roots $s_1, s_2, \ldots$ of the denominator are simple and hence there exists a partial fraction expansion of the form

$$(5.5) \quad \left(\sqrt{q/p}\right)^z \cdot \frac{\sin(a-z)\phi}{\sin a\phi} = A + Bs + \frac{\rho_1}{s_1 - s} + \cdots + \frac{\rho_{a-1}}{s_{a-1} - s}.$$

In principle we should consider only the roots s_ν which are not roots of the numerator also, but if s_ν is such a root then $U_z(s)$ is continuous at $s = s_\nu$ and hence $\rho_\nu = 0$. Such canceling roots therefore do not contribute to the right side and hence it is not necessary to treat them separately.

The roots $s_1, \ldots, s_{a-1}$ correspond obviously to $\phi_\nu = \pi\nu/a$ with $\nu = 1, \ldots, a - 1$, and so

$$(5.6) \qquad\qquad s_\nu = \frac{1}{2\sqrt{pq}\,\cos \pi\nu/a}.$$

This expression makes no sense when $\nu = a/2$ and a is even, but then ϕ_ν is a root of the numerator also and this root should be discarded. The corresponding term in the final result vanishes, as is proper.

To calculate ρ_ν we multiply both sides in (5.5) by $s_\nu - s$ and let $s \to s_\nu$. Remembering that $\sin a\phi_\nu = 0$ and $\cos a\phi_\nu = 1$ we get

$$\rho_\nu = \left(\sqrt{q/p}\right)^z \sin z\phi_\nu \cdot \lim_{s \to s_\nu} \frac{s - s_\nu}{\sin a\phi}.$$

The last limit is determined by L'Hospital's rule using implicit differentiation in (5.2). The result is

$$\rho_\nu = a^{-1} \cdot 2\sqrt{pq}\,\left(\sqrt{q/p}\right)^z \sin z\phi_\nu \cdot \sin \phi_\nu \cdot s_\nu^2.$$

From the expansion of the right side in (5.5) into geometric series we get for $n > 1$

$$u_{z,n} = \sum_{\nu=1}^{a-1} \rho_\nu s_\nu^{-n-1} = a^{-1} 2\sqrt{pq}\,\left(\sqrt{q/p}\right)^z \sum_{\nu=1}^{a-1} s_\nu^{-n+1} \cdot \sin \phi_\nu \cdot \sin z\phi_\nu$$

and hence finally

$$(5.7) \qquad u_{z,n} = a^{-1} 2^n p^{(n-z)/2} q^{(n+z)/2} \sum_{\nu=1}^{a-1} \cos^{n-1}\frac{\pi\nu}{a} \sin \frac{\pi\nu}{a} \sin \frac{\pi z\nu}{a}.$$

This, then, is an explicit formula for *the probability of ruin at the nth trial*. It goes back to Lagrange and has been derived by classical authors in various ways,[5] but it continues to be rediscovered in the modern literature.

---

[5] For an elementary derivation based on trigonometric interpolation see R. E. Ellis, Cambridge Math. J., vol. 4 (1844), or his *Collected works*, Cambridge and London 1863.

It is interesting that the method of images (or of repeated reflections) leads to another explicit expression for $u_{z,n}$ in terms of binomial coefficients (problem 21). An alternative method for deriving (5.7) is described in XVI,3.

Passing to the limit as $a \to \infty$ we get the probability that in a game against an infinitely rich adversary a player with initial capital z will be ruined at the nth trial. (See problem 13.)

A glance at the sum in (5.7) shows that the terms corresponding to the summation indices $v = k$ and $v = a - k$ are of the same absolute value; they are of the same sign when n and z are of the same parity and cancel otherwise. Accordingly $u_{z,n} = 0$ *when* $n - z$ *is odd while for even* $n - z$ *and* $n > 1$

$$(5.8) \qquad u_{z,n} = a^{-1} 2^{n+1} p^{(n-z)/2} q^{(n+z)/2} \sum_{v < a/2} \cos^{n-1} \frac{\pi v}{a} \sin \frac{\pi v}{a} \sin \frac{\pi z v}{a}$$

the summation extending over the positive integers $< a/2$. This form is more natural than (5.7) because now the coefficients $\cos \pi v/a$ form a decreasing sequence and so for large n it is essentially only the first term that counts.

*6. CONNECTION WITH DIFFUSION PROCESSES

This section is devoted to an informal discussion of random walks in which the length δ of the individual steps is small but the steps are spaced so close in time that the resultant change appears practically as a continuous motion. A passage to the limit leads to the Wiener process (Brownian motion) and other diffusion processes. The intimate connection between such processes and random walks greatly contributes to the understanding of both.[6] The problem may be formulated in mathematical as well as in physical terms.

It is best to begin with an *unrestricted random walk* starting at the origin. The nth step takes the particle to the position $\mathbf{S}_n$ where $\mathbf{S}_n = \mathbf{X}_1 + \cdots + \mathbf{X}_n$ is the sum of n independent random variables each assuming the values $+1$ and -1 with probabilities p and q, respectively. Thus

$$(6.1) \qquad E(\mathbf{S}_n) = (p-q)n, \qquad \text{Var}(\mathbf{S}_n) = 4pqn.$$

Figure 4 of III,6 presents the first 10,000 steps of such a random walk with $p = q = \frac{1}{2}$; to fit the graph to a printed page it was necessary to choose

---

[6] This approach was also fruitful historically. It was fully exploited (though in a heuristic manner) by L. Bachelier, whose work has inspired A. Kolmogorov to develop the formal foundations of Markov processes. See, in particular, L. Bachelier, *Calcul des probabilités*, Paris (Gauthier-Villars), 1912.

appropriate scales for the two axes. Let us now go a step further and contemplate a motion picture of the random walk. Suppose that it is to take 1000 seconds (between 16 and 17 minutes). To present one million steps it is necessary that the random walk proceeds at the rate of one step per millisecond, and this fixes the time scale. What units are we to choose to be reasonably sure that the record will fit a screen of a given height? For this question we use a fixed unit of measurement, say inches or feet, both for the screen and the length of the individual steps. We are then no longer concerned with the variables S_n, but with δS_n, where δ stands for the length of the individual steps. Now

$$(6.2) \qquad E(\delta S_n) = (p-q)\,\delta n, \qquad \text{Var}\,(\delta S_n) = 4pq\,\delta^2 n,$$

and it is clear from the central limit theorem that the contemplated film is possible only if for $n = 1,000,000$ both quantities in (6.2) are smaller than the width of the screen. But if $p \neq q$ and δn is comparable to the width of the screen, $\delta^2 n$ will be indistinguishable from 0 and the film will show linear motion without visible chance fluctuations. The character of the random walk can be discerned only when $\delta^2 n$ is of a moderate positive magnitude, and this is possible only when $p - q$ is of a magnitude comparable to δ.

If the question were purely mathematical we should conclude that the desired graphical presentation is impossible unless $p = q$, but the situation is entirely different when viewed from a physical point of view. In Brownian motion we see particles suspended in a liquid moving in random fashion, and the question arises naturally whether the motion can be interpreted as the result of a tremendous number of collisions with smaller particles in the liquid. It is, of course, an over-simplification to assume that the collisions are spaced uniformly in time and that each collision causes a displacement precisely equal to $\pm\delta$. Anyhow, for a first orientation we treat the impacts as governed by Bernoulli trials and ask whether the observed motion of the particles is compatible with this picture. From actual observations we find the average displacement c and the variance D for a unit time interval. Denote by r the (unknown) number of collisions per time unit. Then we must have, approximately,

$$(6.3) \qquad (p-q)\,\delta r = c, \qquad 4pq\,\delta^2 r = D.$$

In a simulated experiment no chance fluctuations would be observable unless the two conditions (6.3) are satisfied with $D > 0$. An experiment with $p = 0.6$ and $\delta r = 1$ is imaginable, but in it the variance would be so small that the motion would appear deterministic: A clump of particles initially close together would remain together as if it were a rigid body.

Essentially the same consideration applies to many other phenomena in physics, economics, learning theory, evolution theory, etc., when slow fluctuations of the state of a system are interpreted as the result of a huge number of successive small changes due to random impacts. The simple random-walk model does not appear realistic in any particular case, but fortunately the situation is similar to that in the central limit theorem. Under surprisingly mild conditions the nature of the individual changes is not important, because the observable effect depends only on their expectation and variance. In such circumstances it is natural to take the simple random-walk model as universal prototype.

To summarize, as a preparation for a more profound study of various stochastic processes it is natural to consider random walks in which the length δ of the individual steps is small, the number r of steps per time unit is large, and $p - q$ is small, the balance being such that (6.3) holds (where c and $D > 0$ are given constants). The words large and small are vague and must remain flexible for practical applications.[7]

The analytical formulation of the problem is as follows. To every choice of δ, r, and p there corresponds a random walk. *We ask what happens in the limit when $\delta \to 0$, $r \to \infty$, and $p \to \frac{1}{2}$ in such a manner that*

$$(6.4) \qquad (p-q)\delta r \to c, \qquad 4pq\delta^2 r \to D.$$

Two procedures are available. Whenever we are in possession of an explicit expression for relevant probabilities we can pass to the limit directly. We shall illustrate this method because it sheds new light on the normal approximation and the limit theorems derived in chapter III. This method is of limited scope, however, because it does not lend itself to generalizations. More fruitful is the start from the difference equations governing the random walks and the derivation of the limiting differential equations. It turns out that these differential equations govern well defined stochastic processes depending on a continuous time parameter. The same is true of various obvious generalizations of these differential equations, and so the second method leads to the important general class of diffusion processes.

---

[7] The number of molecular shocks per time unit is beyond imagination. At the other extreme, in evolution theory one considers small changes from one generation to the next, and the time separating two generations is not small by everyday standards. The number of generations considered is not fantastic either, but may go into many thousands. The point is that the process proceeds on a scale where the changes appear in practice continuous and a diffusion model with continuous time is preferable to the random-walk model.

To describe the direct method in the simplest case we continue to denote by $\{S_n\}$ the standard random walk with unit steps and put

(6.5) $$v_{k,n} = \mathbf{P}\{S_n = k\}.$$

In our accelerated random walk the nth step takes place at epoch n/r, and the position is $S_n \delta = k\delta$. We are interested in the probability of finding the particle at a given epoch t in the neighborhood of a given point x, and so we must investigate the asymptotic behavior of $v_{k,n}$ when $k \to \infty$ and $n \to \infty$ in such a manner that $n/r \to t$ and $k\delta \to x$. The event $\{S_n = k\}$ requires that n and k be of the same parity and takes place when exactly $(n+k)/2$ among the first n steps lead to the right. From the de Moivre-Laplace approximation we conclude therefore that in our passage to the limit

(6.6) $$v_{k,n} \sim \frac{1}{\sqrt{2\pi npq}} e^{-[\frac{1}{2}(n+k)-np]^2/(2npq)} = \frac{1}{\sqrt{2\pi npq}} e^{-[k-n(p-q)]^2/(8npq)}$$

$$\sim \frac{2\delta}{\sqrt{2\pi Dt}} e^{-(x-ct)^2/(2Dt)}$$

where the sign $\sim$ indicates that the ratio of the two sides tends to unity. Now $v_{k,n}$ is the probability of finding $S_n \delta$ between $k\delta$ and $(k+2)\delta$, and since this interval has length 2δ we can say that the ratio $v_{k,n}/(2\delta)$ measures locally the probability per unit length, that is the probability *density*. The last relation in (6.6) implies that the ratio $v_{k,n}/(2\delta)$ tends to

(6.7) $$v(t, x) = \frac{1}{\sqrt{2\pi Dt}} e^{-\frac{1}{2}(x-ct)^2/Dt}.$$

It follows that sums of the probabilities $v_{k,n}$ can be approximated by integrals over $v(t, x)$, and our result may be restated to the effect that with our passage to the limit

(6.8) $$\mathbf{P}\{\alpha < S_n \delta < \beta\} \to \frac{1}{\sqrt{2\pi Dt}} \int_\alpha^\beta e^{-\frac{1}{2}(x-ct)^2/Dt} \, dx.$$

The integral on the right can be expressed in terms of the normal distribution function $\mathfrak{N}$ and (6.8) is in fact only a notational variant of the de Moivre-Laplace limit theorem for the binomial distribution.

The approach based on the appropriate difference equations is more interesting. Considering the position of the particle at the nth and the $(n+1)$st trial it is obvious that the probabilities $v_{k,n}$ satisfy the difference equations

(6.9) $$v_{k,n+1} = pv_{k-1,n} + qv_{k+1,n}.$$

On multiplying by 2δ it follows from our preceding result that the limit $v(t, x)$ should be an *approximate* solution of the difference equation

$$(6.10) \qquad v(t+r^{-1}, x) = pv(t, x-\delta) + qv(t, x+\delta).$$

Since v has continuous derivatives we can expand the terms according to Taylor's theorem. Using the first-order approximation on the left and second-order approximation on the right we get (after canceling the leading terms)

$$(6.11) \qquad \frac{\partial v(t, x)}{\partial t} = (q-p)\, \delta r \cdot \frac{\partial v(t, x)}{\partial x} + \frac{1}{2}\, \delta^2 r \frac{\partial^2 v(t, x)}{\partial x^2} + \cdots.$$

In our passage to the limit the omitted terms tend to zero and (6.11) becomes in the limit

$$(6.12) \qquad \frac{\partial v(t, x)}{\partial t} = -c\, \frac{\partial v(t, x)}{\partial x} + \frac{1}{2}\, D\, \frac{\partial^2 v(t, x)}{\partial x^2}.$$

This is a special *diffusion equation* also known as the *Fokker-Planck* equation for diffusion. Our calculations were purely formal and heuristic, but it will not come as a surprise that the function v of (6.7) indeed satisfies the differential equation (6.12). Furthermore, it can be shown that (6.7) represents the only solution of the diffusion equation having the obvious properties required by the probabilistic interpretation.

The diffusion equation (6.12) can be generalized by permitting the coefficients c and D to depend on x and t. Furthermore, it possesses obvious analogues in higher dimensions, and all these generalizations can be derived directly from general probabilistic postulates. This topic will be taken up in chapter X of volume 2; here we must be satisfied by these brief and heuristic indications of the connections between random walks and general diffusion theory.

As a second example we take the ruin probabilities $u_{z,n}$ discussed in the preceding two sections. The underlying difference equations (4.1) differ from (6.9) in that the coefficients p and q are interchanged.[8] The formal calculations indicated in (6.11) now lead to a diffusion equation obtained from (6.12) on replacing $-c$ by c. Our limiting procedure leads from the probabilities $u_{z,n}$ to a function $u(t, \xi)$ which satisfies this modified diffusion equation and which has probabilistic significance

---

[8] The reason is that in $u_{z,n}$ the variable z stands for the *initial* position whereas the probability $v_{k,n}$ refers to the position at the running time. In the terminology to be introduced in volume 2, probabilities depending on the initial position satisfy *backward* (retrospective) equations, the others *forward* (or Fokker-Planck) equations. In physics the latter are sometimes called *continuity* equations. The same situation will be encountered in chapter XVII.

similar to $u_{z,n}$: In a diffusion process starting at the point $\xi > 0$ the probability that the particle reaches the origin *before* reaching the point $\alpha > \xi$ and that this event occurs in the time interval $t_1 < t < t_2$ is given by the integral of $u(t, \xi)$ over this interval.

The formal calculations are as follows. For $u_{z,n}$ we have the explicit expression (5.8). Since z and n must be of the same parity, $u_{z,n}$ corresponds to the interval between n/r and $(n+2)/r$, and we have to calculate the limit of the ratio $u_{z,n}r/2$ when $r \to \infty$ and $\delta \to 0$ in accordance with (6.4). The length a of the interval and the initial position z must be adjusted so as to obtain the limits α and ξ. Thus $z \sim \xi/\delta$ and $a \sim \alpha/\delta$. It is now easy to find the limits for the individual factors in (5.8).

From (6.4) we get $2p \sim 1 + c\delta/D$, and

$$2q \sim 1 - c\delta/D;$$

from the second relation in (6.4) we see that $\delta^2 r \to D$. Therefore

(6.13)
$$(4pq)^{\frac{1}{2}n}(q/p)^{\frac{1}{2}z} \sim (1-c^2\delta^2/D^2)^{\frac{1}{2}(rt)}(1-2c\delta/D)^{\frac{1}{2}\xi/\delta}$$
$$\sim e^{-\frac{1}{2}c^2t/D} \cdot e^{-c\xi/D}$$

Similarly for fixed ν

(6.14)
$$\left(\cos\frac{\nu\pi\delta}{\alpha}\right)^n \sim \left(1 - \frac{\nu^2\pi^2\delta^2}{2\alpha^2}\right)^{tr} \sim e^{-\frac{1}{2}\nu^2\pi^2Dt/\alpha^2}.$$

Finally $\sin \nu\pi\delta/\alpha \sim \nu\pi\delta/\alpha$. Substitution into (5.8) leads formally to

(6.15)
$$u(t, \xi) = \pi D\alpha^{-2}e^{-\frac{1}{2}(ct+2\xi)c/D}\sum_{\nu=1}^{\infty} \nu e^{-\frac{1}{2}\nu^2\pi^2Dt/\alpha^2} \sin\frac{\pi\xi\nu}{\alpha}.$$

(Since the series converges uniformly it is not difficult to justify the formal calculations.) In physical diffusion theory (6.15) is known as *Fürth's formula for first passages*. [For the limiting case $\alpha = \infty$ see problem 14. For an alternative form of (6.15) see problem 22.]

*7. RANDOM WALKS IN THE PLANE AND SPACE

In a two-dimensional random walk the particle moves in unit steps in one of the four directions parallel to the x- and y-axes. For a particle starting at the origin the possible positions are all points of the plane with integral-valued coordinates. Each position has four *neighbors*. Similarly, in three dimensions each position has six neighbors. The random walk is defined by specifying the corresponding four or six probabilities. For

---

* This section treats a special topic and may be omitted at first reading.

simplicity we shall consider only the *symmetric* case where all directions have the same probability. The complexity of problems is considerably greater than in one dimension, for now the domains to which the particle is restricted may have arbitrary shapes and complicated boundaries take the place of the single-point barriers in the one-dimensional case.

We begin with an interesting theorem due to Polya.[9]

Theorem. *In the symmetric random walks in one and two dimensions there is probability one that the particle will sooner or later (and therefore infinitely often) return to its initial position. In three dimensions, however, this probability is* <1. (It is about 0.35. The expected number of returns is then $0.65 \sum k(0.35)^k = 0.35/0.65 \approx 0.53$.)

Before proving the theorem let us give two alternative formulations, both due to Polya. First, it is almost obvious that the theorem implies that in *one and two dimensions there is probability* 1 *that the particle will pass infinitely often through every possible point*; in three dimensions this is not true, however. Thus the statement "all roads lead to Rome" is, in a way, justified in two dimensions.

Alternatively, consider *two* particles performing independent symmetric random walks, the steps occurring simultaneously. Will they ever meet? To simplify language let us define the *distance* of two possible positions as the smallest number of steps leading from one position to the other. (This distance equals the sum of absolute differences of the coordinates.) If the two particles move one step each, their mutual distance either remains the same or changes by two units, and so their distance either is even at all times or else is always odd. In the second case the two particles can never occupy the same position. In the first case it is readily seen that the probability of their meeting at the nth step equals the probability that the first particle reaches in $2n$ steps the initial position of the second particle. Hence our theorem states that in two, but not in three, dimensions the two particles are sure infinitely often to occupy the same position. If the initial distance of the two particles is odd, a similar argument shows that they will infinitely often occupy neighboring positions. If this is called meeting, then our theorem asserts that *in one and two dimensions the two particles are certain to meet infinitely often, but in three dimensions there is a positive probability that they never meet.*

---

[9] G. Polya, *Über eine Aufgabe der Wahrscheinlichkeitsrechnung betreffend die Irrfahrt im Strassennetz*, Mathematische Annalen, vol. 84 (1921), pp. 149–160. The numerical value 0.35 was calculated by W. H. McCrea and F. J. W. Whipple, *Random paths in two and three dimensions*, Proceedings of the Royal Society of Edinburgh, vol. 60 (1940), pp. 281–298.

Proof. For one dimension the theorem has been proved in example XIII,(4.b) by the method of recurrent events. The proof for two and three dimensions proceeds along the same lines. Let u_n be the probability that the nth trial takes the particle to the initial position. According to theorem 2 of XIII,3, we have to prove that in the case of two dimensions $\sum u_n$ diverges, whereas in the case of three dimensions $\sum u_n \approx 0.53$. In two dimensions a return to the initial position is possible only if the numbers of steps in the positive x- and y-directions equal those in the negative x- and y-directions, respectively. Hence $u_n = 0$ if n is odd and [using the multinomial distribution VI,(9.2)]

$$(7.1) \qquad u_{2n} = \frac{1}{4^{2n}} \sum_{k=0}^{n} \frac{(2n)!}{k!\, k!\, (n-k)!\, (n-k)!} = \frac{1}{4^{2n}} \binom{2n}{n} \sum_{k=0}^{n} \binom{n}{k}^2$$

By II,(12.11) the right side equals $4^{-2n}\binom{2n}{n}^2$. Stirling's formula now shows that u_{2n} is of the order of magnitude $1/n$, so that $\sum u_{2n}$ diverges as asserted.

In three dimensions we find similarly

$$(7.2) \qquad u_{2n} = 6^{-2n} \sum_{j,k} \frac{(2n)!}{j!\, j!\, k!\, k!\, (n-j-k)!\, (n-j-k)!},$$

the summation extending over all j, k with $j + k \leq n$. It is easily verified that

$$(7.3) \qquad u_{2n} = \frac{1}{2^{2n}} \binom{2n}{n} \sum_{j,k} \left\{ \frac{1}{3^n} \frac{n!}{j!\, k!\, (n-j-k)!} \right\}^2.$$

Within the braces we have the terms of a trinomial distribution, and we know that they add to unity. Hence the sum of the squares is smaller than the maximum term within braces, and the latter is attained when both j and k are about $n/3$. Stirling's formula shows that this maximum is of the order of magnitude n^{-1}, and therefore u_{2n} is of the magnitude $1/\sqrt{n^3}$ so that $\sum u_{2n}$ converges as asserted.   ▶

We conclude this section with another problem which generalizes the concept of *absorbing barriers*. Consider the case of two dimensions where instead of the interval $0 \leq x \leq a$ we have a plane domain D, that is, a collection of points with integral-valued coordinates. Each point has four neighbors, but for some points of D one or more of the neighbors lie outside D. Such points form the boundary of D, and all other points are called interior points. In the one-dimensional case the two barriers form the boundary, and our problem consisted in finding the probability that, starting from z, the particle will reach the boundary point 0 before reaching a. By analogy, we now ask for the probability that the particle will reach a certain section of the boundary before reaching any boundary point that is not in this section. This means that we divide all boundary points into two sets B' and B''. If (x, y) is an interior point, we seek the probability $u(x, y)$ that, starting from (x, y), the particle will reach a point of B' before reaching a point of B''. In particular, if B' consists of a single point, then $u(x, y)$ is the probability that the particle will, sooner or later, be absorbed at the particular point.

Let (x, y) be an interior point. The first step takes the particle from (x, y) to one of the four neighbors $(x \pm 1, y)$, $(x, y \pm 1)$, and if all four of them are interior points, we have obviously

$$(7.4) \quad u(x, y) = \tfrac{1}{4}[u(x+1, y) + u(x-1, y) + u(x, y+1) + u(x, y-1)].$$

This is a partial difference equation which takes the place of (2.1) (with $p = q = \tfrac{1}{2}$). If $(x+1, y)$ is a boundary point, then its contribution $u(x+1, y)$ must be replaced by 1 or 0, according to whether $(x+1, y)$ belongs to B' or B''. *Hence (7.4) will be valid for all interior points if we agree that for a boundary point (ξ, η) in B' we put $u(\xi, \eta) = 1$ whereas $u(\xi, \eta) = 0$ if (ξ, η) is in B''. This convention takes the place of the boundary conditions (2.2).*

In (7.4) we have a system of linear equations for the unknowns $u(x, y)$; to each interior point there correspond one unknown and one equation. The system is non-homogeneous, since in it there appears at least one boundary point (ξ, η) of B' and it gives rise to a contribution $\tfrac{1}{4}$ on the right side. If the domain D is finite, there are as many equations as unknowns, and it is well known that the system has a unique solution if, and only if, the corresponding homogeneous system (with $u(\xi, \eta) = 0$ for all boundary points) has no non-vanishing solution. Now $u(x, y)$ is the mean of the four neighboring values $u(x \pm 1, y)$, $u(x, y \pm 1)$ and cannot exceed all four. In other words, in the interior $u(x, y)$ has neither a maximum nor a minimum in the strict sense, and the greatest and the smallest value occur at boundary points. Hence, if all boundary values vanish, so does $u(x, y)$ at all interior points, which proves the existence and uniqueness of the solution of (7.4). Since the boundary values are 0 and 1, all values $u(x, y)$ lie between 0 and 1, as is required for probabilities. These statements are true also for the case of infinite domains, as can be seen from a general theorem on infinite Markov chains.[10]

---

[10] Explicit solutions are known in only a few cases and are always very complicated. Solutions for the case of rectangular domains, infinite strips, etc., will be found in the paper by McCrea and Whipple cited in the preceding footnote.

*8. THE GENERALIZED ONE-DIMENSIONAL RANDOM WALK (SEQUENTIAL SAMPLING)

We now return to one dimension but abandon the restriction that the particle moves in unit steps. Instead, *at each step the particle shall have probability p_k to move from any point x to $x + k$, where the integer k* may be zero, positive, or negative. We shall investigate the following *ruin problem: The particle starts from a position z such that $0 < z < a$; we seek the probability u_z that the particle will arrive at some position ≤ 0 before reaching any position $\geq a$.* In other words, the position of the particle following the nth trial is the point $z + \mathbf{X}_1 + \mathbf{X}_2 + \cdots + \mathbf{X}_n$ of the x-axis, where the $\{\mathbf{X}_k\}$ are mutually independent random variables with the common distribution $\{p_v\}$; the process stops when for the first time either $\mathbf{X}_1 + \cdots \mathbf{X}_n \leq -z$ or $\mathbf{X}_1 + \cdots \mathbf{X}_n \geq a - z$.

This problem has attracted widespread interest in connection with *sequential sampling.* There the $\mathbf{X}_k$ represent certain characteristics of samples or observations. Measurements are taken until a sum $\mathbf{X}_1 + + \cdots + \mathbf{X}_k$ falls outside two preassigned limits (our $-z$ and $a - z$). In the first case the procedure leads to what is technically known as *rejection,* in the second case to *acceptance.*[11]

Example. (*a*) As an illustration, take Bartky's double-sampling inspection scheme. To test a consignment of items, samples of size N are taken and subjected to complete inspection. It is assumed that the samples are stochastically independent and that the number of defectives in each has the same binomial distribution. Allowance is made for one defective item per sample, and so we let $\mathbf{X}_k + 1$ equal the number of defectives in the kth sample. Then for $k \geq 0$

$$p_k = \binom{N}{k+1} p^{k+1} q^{N-k-1}$$

and $p_{-1} = q^N$, $p_x = 0$ for $x < -1$. The procedural rule is as follows: A preliminary sample is drawn and, if it contains no defective, the whole consignment is accepted; if the number of defectives exceeds a, the whole lot is rejected. In either of these cases the process stops. If, however, the number z of defectives lies in the range $1 \leq z \leq a$, the sampling

---

* This section is not used later on.

[11] The general theory of sequential statistical procedures was developed by Abraham Wald during the Second World War in connection with important practical problems. Modern treatments can be found in many textbooks on mathematical statistics. Bartky's scheme described in the example dates from 1943 and seems to have been the very first sequential sampling procedure proposed in the literature.

continues in the described way as long as the sum is contained between 1 and a. Sooner or later it will become either 0, in which case the consignment is accepted, or $\geq a$, in which case the consignment is rejected. ▶

Without loss of generality we shall suppose that steps are possible in both the positive and negative directions. Otherwise we would have either $u_z = 0$ or $u_z = 1$ for all z. The probability of ruin at the *first* step is obviously

$$(8.1) \qquad r_z = p_{-z} + p_{-z-1} + p_{-z-2} + \cdots$$

(a quantity which may be zero). The random walk continues only if the particle moved to a position x with $0 < x < a$; the probability of a jump from z to x is p_{x-z}, and the probability of subsequent ruin is then u_x. Therefore

$$(8.2) \qquad u_z = \sum_{x=1}^{a-1} u_x p_{x-z} + r_z.$$

Once more we have here $a - 1$ linear equations for $a - 1$ unknowns u_z. The system is non-homogeneous, since at least for $z = 1$ the probability r_1 is different from zero (because steps in the negative direction are possible). To show that the linear system (8.2) possesses a unique solution we must show that the associated homogeneous system

$$(8.3) \qquad u_z = \sum_{x=1}^{a-1} u_x p_{x-z}$$

has no solution except zero. To reduce the number of subscripts appearing in the proof we assume that $p_{-1} \neq 0$ (but the argument applies equally to other positive terms with negative index). Suppose, then, that u_z satisfies (8.3) and denote by M the maximum of the values u_z. Let $u_r = M$. Since the coefficients p_{x-z} in (8.3) add to ≤ 1 this equation is possible for $z = r$ only if those u_x that actually appear on the right side (with positive coefficients) equal M and if their coefficients add to unity. Hence $u_{r-1} = M$ and, arguing in the same way, $u_{r-2} = u_{r-3} = \cdots = = u_1 = M$. However, for $z = 1$ the coefficients p_{x-r} in (8.3) add to less than unity, so that M must be zero.

It follows that (8.2) has a unique solution, and thus our problem is determined. Again we simplify the writing by introducing the boundary conditions

$$(8.4) \qquad \begin{array}{ll} u_x = 1 & \text{if } x \leq 0 \\[6pt] u_x = 0 & \text{if } x \geq a. \end{array}$$

Then (8.2) can be written in the form

$$(8.5) \qquad u_z = \sum u_x p_{x-z},$$

the summation now extending over all x [for $x \geq a$ we have no contribution owing to the second condition (8.4); the contributions for $x \leq 0$ add to r_z owing to the first condition].

For large a it is cumbersome to solve $a - 1$ linear equations directly, and it is preferable to use the *method of particular solutions* analogous to the procedure of section 2. It works whenever the probability distribution $\{p_k\}$ has relatively few positive terms. Suppose that only the p_k with $-\nu \leq k \leq \mu$ are different from zero, so that the largest possible jumps in the positive and negative directions are μ and ν, respectively. The *characteristic equation*

$$(8.6) \qquad \sum p_k \sigma^k = 1$$

is equivalent to an algebraic equation of degree $\nu + \mu$. If σ is a root of (8.6), then $u_z = \sigma^z$ is a formal solution of (8.5) for all z, but this solution does not satisfy the boundary conditions (8.4). If (8.6) has $\mu + \nu$ distinct roots $\sigma_1, \sigma_2, \ldots$, then the linear combination

$$(8.7) \qquad u_z = \sum A_k \sigma_k^z$$

is again a formal solution of (8.5) for all z, and we must adjust the constants A_k to satisfy the boundary conditions. Now for $0 < z < a$ only values x with $-\nu + 1 \leq x \leq a + \mu - 1$ appear in (8.5). It suffices therefore to satisfy the boundary conditions (8.4) for $x = 0, -1, -2, \ldots, -\nu + 1$, and $x = a, a + 1, \ldots, a + \mu - 1$, so that we have $\mu + \nu$ conditions in all. If σ_k is a double root of (8.6), we lose one constant, but in this case it is easily seen that $u_z = z\sigma_k^z$ is another formal solution. In every case the $\mu + \nu$ boundary conditions determine the $\mu + \nu$ arbitrary constants.

Example. (*b*) Suppose that each individual step takes the particle to one of the four nearest positions, and we let $p_{-2} = p_{-1} = p_1 = p_2 = \frac{1}{4}$. The characteristic equation (8.6) is $\sigma^{-2} + \sigma^{-1} + \sigma + \sigma^2 = 4$. To solve it we put $t = \sigma + \sigma^{-1}$: with this substitution our equation becomes $t^2 + t = 6$, which has the roots $t = 2, -3$. Solving $t = \sigma + \sigma^{-1}$ for σ we find the four roots

$$(8.8) \quad \sigma_1 = \sigma_2 = 1, \qquad \sigma_3 = \frac{-3 + \sqrt{5}}{2} = \sigma_4^{-1}, \qquad \sigma_4 = \frac{-3 - \sqrt{5}}{2} = \sigma_3^{-1}.$$

Since σ_1 is a double root, the general solution of (8.5) in our case is

$$(8.9) \qquad u_z = A_1 + A_2 z + A_3 \sigma_3^z + A_4 \sigma_4^z.$$

The boundary conditions $u_0 = u_{-1} = 1$ and $u_a = u_{a+1} = 0$ lead to four linear equations for the coefficients A_j and to the final solution

$$(8.10) \qquad u_z = 1 - \frac{z}{a} + \frac{(2z-a)(\sigma_3^a - \sigma_4^a) - a(\sigma_3^{2z-a} - \sigma_4^{2z-a})}{a\{(a+2)(\sigma_3^a - \sigma_4^a) - a(\sigma_3^{a+2} - \sigma_4^{a+2})\}}. \qquad \blacktriangleright$$

Numerical Approximations. Usually it is cumbersome to find all the roots, but rather satisfactory approximations can be obtained in a surprisingly simple way. Consider first the case where the probability distribution $\{p_k\}$ has mean zero. Then the characteristic equation (8.6) has a double root at $\sigma = 1$, and $A + Bz$ is a formal solution of (8.5). Of course, the two constants A and B do not suffice to satisfy the $\mu + \nu$ boundary conditions (8.4). However, if we determine A and B so that $A + Bz$ vanishes for $z = a + \mu - 1$ and equals 1 for $z = 0$, then $A + Bx \geq 1$ for $x \leq 0$ and $A + Bx \geq 0$ for $a \leq x < a + \mu$ so that $A + Bz$ satisfies the boundary conditions (8.4) with the equality sign replaced by $\geq$. Hence the difference $A + Bz - u_z$ is a formal solution of (8.5) with non-negative boundary values, and therefore $A + Bz - u_z \geq 0$. In like manner we can get a lower bound for u_z by determining A and B so that $A + Bz$ vanishes for $z = a$ and equals 1 for $z = -\nu + 1$. Hence

$$(8.11) \qquad \frac{a - z}{a + \nu - 1} \leq u_z \leq \frac{a + \mu - z - 1}{a + \mu - 1}.$$

This estimate is excellent when a is large as compared to $\mu + \nu$. [Of course, $u_z \approx (1 - z/a)$ is a better approximation but does not give precise bounds.]

Next, consider the general case where the mean of the distribution $\{p_k\}$ is not zero. The characteristic equation (8.6) has then a simple root at $\sigma = 1$. The left side of (8.6) approaches ∞ as $\sigma \to 0$ and as $\sigma \to \infty$. For positive σ the curve $y = \Sigma p_k \sigma^k$ is continuous and convex, and since it intersects the line $y = 1$ at $\sigma = 1$, there exists exactly one more intersection. Therefore, the characteristic equation (8.6) has exactly two positive roots, 1 and σ_1. As before, we see that $A + B\sigma_1^z$ is a formal solution of (8.5), and we can apply our previous argument to this solution instead of $A + Bz$. We find in this case

$$(8.12) \qquad \frac{\sigma_1^a - \sigma_1^z}{\sigma_1^a - \sigma_1^{-\nu+1}} \leq u_z \leq \frac{\sigma_1^{a+\mu-1} - \sigma_1^z}{\sigma_1^{a+\mu-1} - 1},$$

and have the

Theorem. *The solution of our ruin problem satisfies the inequalities* (8.11) *if* $\{p_k\}$ *has zero mean, and* (8.12) *otherwise. Here* σ_1 *is the unique positive root different from* 1 *of* (8.6), *and* μ *and* $-\nu$ *are defined, respectively, as the largest and smallest subscript for which* $p_k \neq 0$.

Let $m = \Sigma k p_k$ be the *expected gain* in a single trial (or expected length of a single step). It is easily seen from (8.6) that $\sigma_1 > 1$ or $\sigma_1 < 1$ according to whether $m < 0$ or $m > 0$. Letting $a \to \infty$, we conclude from our theorem that *in a game against an infinitely rich adversary the probability of an ultimate ruin is one if and only if* $m \leq 0$. The *duration of game* can be discussed by similar methods (cf. problem 9).

9. PROBLEMS FOR SOLUTION

Note: *Problems 1–4 refer only to section 2 and require no calculations.*

1. In a random walk starting at the origin find the probability that the point $a > 0$ will be reached before the point $-b < 0$.

2. Prove that with the notations of section 2:

(*a*) In a random walk starting at the origin the probability to reach the point $a > 0$ before returning to the origin equals $p(1 - q_1)$.

(*b*) In a random walk starting at $a > 0$ the probability to reach the origin before returning to the starting point equals qq_{a-1}.

3. If $q \geq p$, conclude from the preceding problem: In a random walk starting at the origin the number of visits to the point $a > 0$ that take place before the first return to the origin has a geometric distribution with ratio $1 - qq_{a-1}$. (Why is the condition $q \geq p$ necessary?)

4. Using the preceding two problems prove the theorem[12]: *The number of visits to the point $a > 0$ that take place prior to the first return to the origin has expectation* $(p/q)^a$ *when* $p < q$ *and* 1 *when* $p = q$.

5. Consider the ruin problem of sections 2 and 3 for the case of a modified random walk in which the particle moves a unit step to the right or left, or stays at its present position with probabilities α, β, γ, respectively ($\alpha + \beta + \gamma = 1$). (In gambling terminology, the bet may result in a tie.)

6. Consider the ruin problem of sections 2 and 3 for the case where the origin is an *elastic* barrier (as defined in section 1). The difference equations for the probability of ruin (absorption at the origin) and for the expected duration are the same, but with new boundary conditions.

7. A particle moves at each step *two* units to the right or *one* unit to the left, with corresponding probabilities p and q ($p + q = 1$). If the starting position is $z > 0$, find the probability q_z that the particle will ever reach the origin. (This is a ruin problem against an infinitely rich adversary.)

Hint: The analogue to (2.1) leads to a cubic equation with the particular solution $q_z = 1$ and two particular solutions of the form λ^z, where λ satisfies a quadratic equation.

8. *Continuation.*[13] Show that q_1 equals the probability that in a sequence of Bernoulli trials the accumulated number of failures will ever exceed twice the accumulated number of successes.

[When $p = q$ this probability equals $(\sqrt{5} - 1)/2$.]

---

[12] The truly amazing implications of this result appear best in the language of fair games. A perfect coin is tossed until the first equalization of the accumulated numbers of heads and tails. The gambler receives one penny for every time that the accumulated number of heads exceeds the accumulated number of tails by m. The "*fair entrance fee*" *equals* 1 *independently of* m.

For a different (elementary) proof see problems 1–2 of XII,10 in volume 2.

[13] This problem was formulated by D. J. Newman. That its solution is a simple corollary to the preceding problem (in the second edition) was observed by W. A. O'N. Waugh. The reader may try the same approach for the more general problem when the factor 2 is replaced by some other rational. A solution along different lines was devised by J. S. Frame. See *Solution to problem 4864*, Amer. Math. Monthly, vol. 67 (1960), pp. 700–702.

9. In the generalized random-walk problem of section 8 put [in analogy with (8.1)] $p_z = p_{a-z} + p_{a+1-z} + p_{a+2-z} + \cdots$, and let $d_{z,n}$ be the probability that the game lasts for exactly n steps. Show that for $n \geq 1$

$$d_{z,n+1} = \sum_{x=1}^{a-1} d_{x,n} p_{x-z}$$

with $d_{z,1} = r_z + p_z$. Hence prove that the generating function $d_z(\sigma) = \Sigma d_{z,n} \sigma^n$ is the solution of the system of linear equations

$$\sigma^{-1} d_z(\sigma) - \sum_{x=1}^{a-1} d_x(\sigma) p_{x-z} = r_z + p_z.$$

By differentiation it follows that the expected duration e_z is the solution of

$$e_z - \sum_{x=1}^{a-1} e_x p_{x-z} = 1.$$

10. In the random walk with *absorbing* barriers at the points 0 and a and with initial position z, let $w_{z,n}(x)$ be the probability that the nth step takes the particle to the position x. Find the difference equations and boundary conditions which determine $w_{z,n}(x)$.

11. *Continuation.* Modify the boundary conditions for the case of two *reflecting barriers* (i.e., elastic barriers with $\delta = 1$).

12. A symmetric random walk $(p = q)$ has possible positions $1, 2, \ldots, a - 1$. There is an absorbing barrier at the origin and a reflecting barrier at the other end. Find the generating function for the waiting time for absorption.

13. *An alternative form for the first-passage probabilities.* In the explicit formula (5.7) for the ruin probabilities let $a \to \infty$. Show that the result is

$$u_{z,n} = 2^n p^{(n-z)/2} q^{(n+z)/2} \int_0^1 \cos^{n-1} \pi x \cdot \sin \pi x \cdot \sin \pi x z \cdot dx.$$

Consequently, this formula must be equivalent to (4.14). Verify this by showing that the appropriate difference equations and boundary conditions are satisfied.

14. *Continuation: First passages in diffusion.* Show that the passage to the limit described in section 6 leads from the last formula to the expression

$$\frac{z}{\sqrt{2\pi Dt^3}} e^{-(z+ct)^2/(2Dt)}$$

for the probability density for the waiting time for absorption at the origin in a diffusion starting at the point $z > 0$. When $p = q$ this result is equivalent to the limit theorem 3 of III,7.

Note: *In the following problems $v_{x,n}$ is the probability* (6.1) *that in an un-restricted random walk starting at the origin the nth step takes the particle to the position x. The reflection principle of* III, 1 *leads to an alternative treatment.*

15. *Method of images.*[14] Let $p = q = \frac{1}{2}$. In a random walk in $(0, \infty)$ with an absorbing barrier at the origin and initial position at $z > 0$, let $u_{z,n}(x)$ be the probability that the nth step takes the particle to the position $x > 0$. Show that $u_{z,n}(x) = v_{x-z,n} - v_{x+z,n}$. [*Hint:* Show that a difference equation corresponding to (4.1) and the appropriate boundary conditions are satisfied.]

16. *Continuation.* If the origin is a *reflecting barrier*, then

$$u_{z,n}(x) = v_{x-z,n} + v_{x+z-1,n}.$$

17. *Continuation.* If the random walk is restricted to $(0, a)$ and both barriers are *absorbing*, then

(9.1) $$u_{z,n}(x) = \sum_k \{v_{x-z-2ka,n} - v_{x+z-2ka,n}\},$$

the summation extending over all k, positive or negative (only finitely many terms are different from zero). If both barriers are *reflecting*, equation (9.1) holds with *minus* replaced by *plus* and $x + z$ replaced by $x + z - 1$.

18. *Distribution of maxima.* In a symmetric unrestricted random walk starting at the origin let $\mathbf{M}_n$ be the maximum abscissa of the particle in n steps. Using problem 15, show that

(9.2) $$\mathbf{P}\{\mathbf{M}_n = z\} = v_{z,n} + v_{z+1,n}.$$

19. Let $V_x(s) = \sum v_{x,n}s^n$ (cf. the note preceding problem 15). Prove that $V_x(s) = V_0(s)\lambda_2^{-x}(s)$ when $x \leq 0$ and $V_x(s) = V_0(s)\lambda_1^{-x}(s)$ when $x \geq 0$, where $\lambda_1(s)$ and $\lambda_2(s)$ are defined in (4.8). Moreover, $V_0(s) = (1 - 4pqs^2)^{-\frac{1}{2}}$.

Note: These relations follow *directly* from the fact that $\lambda_1(s)$ and $\lambda_2(s)$ are generating functions of first-passage times as explained at the conclusion of section 4.

20. In a random walk in $(0, \infty)$ with an absorbing barrier at the origin and initial position at z, let $u_{z,n}(x)$ be the probability that the nth step takes the particle to the position x, and let

(9.3) $$U_z(s; x) = \sum_{n=0}^{\infty} u_{z,n}(x)s^n.$$

Using problem 19, show that $U_z(s; x) = V_{x-z}(s) - \lambda_2^z(s)V_x(s)$. Conclude

(9.4) $$u_{z,n}(x) = v_{x-z,n} - (q/p)^z \cdot v_{x+z,n}.$$

Compare with the result of problem 15 and derive (9.4) from the latter by combinatorial methods.

---

[14] Problems 15–17 are examples of the *method of images.* The term $v_{x-z,n}$ corresponds to a particle in an unrestricted random walk, and $v_{x+z,n}$ to an "image point." In (9.1) we find image points starting from various positions, obtained by repeated reflections at both boundaries. In problems 20–21 we get the general result for the unsymmetric random walk using generating functions. In the theory of differential equations the method of images is always ascribed to Lord Kelvin. In the probabilistic literature the equivalent reflection principle is usually attributed to D. André. See footnote 5 of III,1.

21. *Alternative formula for the probability of ruin* (5.7). Expanding (4.11) into a geometric series, prove that

$$u_{z,n} = \sum_{k=0}^{\infty} \left(\frac{p}{q}\right)^{ka} w_{z+2ka,n} - \sum_{k=1}^{\infty} \left(\frac{p}{q}\right)^{ka-z} w_{2ka-z,n}$$

where $w_{z,n}$ denotes the first-passage probability of (4.14).

22. If the passage to the limit of section 6 is applied to the expression for $u_{z,n}$ given in the preceding problem, show that the probability density of the absorption time equals[15]

$$\frac{1}{\sqrt{2\pi Dt^3}} e^{-(ct+2\xi)c/(2D)} \sum_{k=-\infty}^{\infty} (\xi + 2k\alpha)e^{-(\xi+2k\alpha)^2/(2Dt)}$$

(*Hint:* Apply the normal approximation to the binomial distribution.)

23. *Renewal method for the ruin problem.*[16] In the random walk with two absorbing barriers let $u_{z,n}$ and $u_{z,n}^*$ be, respectively, the probabilities of absorption at the left and the right barriers. By a proper interpretation prove the truth of the following two equations:

$$V_{-z}(s) = U_z(s)V_0(s) = U_z^*(s)V_{-a}(s),$$

$$V_{a-z}(s) = U_z(s)V_a(s) + U_z^*(s)V_0(s).$$

Derive (4.11) by solving this system for $U_z(s)$.

24. Let $u_{z,n}(x)$ be the probability that the particle, starting from z, will at the nth step be at x without having previously touched the absorbing barriers. Using the notations of problem 23, show that for the corresponding generating function $U_z(s; x) = \Sigma u_{z,n}(x)s^n$ we have

$$U_z(s; x) = V_{x-z}(s) - U_z(s)V_x(s) - U_z^*(s)V_{x-a}(s).$$

(No calculations are required.)

25. *Continuation.* The generating function $U_z(s; x)$ of the preceding problem can be obtained by putting $U_z(s; x) = V_{x-z}(s) - A\lambda_1^z(s) - B\lambda_2^z(s)$ and determining the constants so that the boundary conditions $U_z(s; x) = 0$ for $z = 0$ and $z = a$ are satisfied. With *reflecting barriers* the boundary conditions are $U_0(s; x) = U_1(s; x)$ and $U_a(s; x) = U_{a-1}(s; x)$.

26. Prove the formula

$$v_{x,n} = (2\pi)^{-1} 2^n p^{(n+x)/2} q^{(n-x)/2} \int_{-\pi}^{\pi} \cos^n t \cdot \cos tx \cdot dt$$

by showing that the appropriate difference equation is satisfied. Conclude that

$$V_x(s) = (2\pi)^{-1} \left(\frac{p}{q}\right)^{x/2} \int_{-\pi}^{\pi} \frac{\cos tx}{1 - 2\sqrt{pq} \cdot s \cdot \cos t} dt.$$

---

[15] The agreement of the new formula with the limiting form (6.15) is a well-known fact of the theory of theta functions. See XIX, (5.8) of volume 2.

[16] Problems 23–25 contain a new and independent derivation of the main results concerning random walks in one dimension.

27. In a three-dimensional symmetric random walk the particle has probability one to pass infinitely often through any particular line $x = m$, $y = n$. (*Hint:* Cf. problem 5.)

28. In a two-dimensional symmetric random walk starting at the origin the probability that the nth step takes the particle to (x, y) is

$$(2\pi)^{-2}2^{-n} \int_{-\pi}^{\pi} \int_{-\pi}^{\pi} (\cos \alpha + \cos \beta)^n \cdot \cos x\alpha \cdot \cos y\beta \cdot d\alpha \, d\beta.$$

Verify this formula and find the analogue for three dimensions. (*Hint:* Check that the expression satisfies the proper difference equation.)

29. In a two-dimensional symmetric random walk let $\mathbf{D}_n^2 = x^2 + y^2$ be the square of the distance of the particle from the origin at time n. Prove $\mathbf{E}(\mathbf{D}_n^2) = n$. [*Hint:* Calculate $\mathbf{E}(\mathbf{D}_{n-1}^2 - \mathbf{D}_n^2)$.]

30. In a symmetric random walk in d dimensions the particle has probability 1 to return infinitely often to a position already previously occupied. *Hint:* At each step the probability of moving to a new position is at most $(2d-1)/(2d)$.

31. Show that the method described in section 8 works also for the generating function $U_z(s)$ of the waiting time for ruin.

CHAPTER XV

Markov Chains

1. DEFINITION

Up to now we have been concerned mostly with independent trials which can be described as follows. A set of possible outcomes $E_1, E_2, \ldots$, (finite or infinite in number) is given, and with each there is associated a probability p_k; the probabilities of sample sequences are defined by the multiplicative property $\mathbf{P}\{(E_{j_0}, E_{j_1}, \ldots, E_{j_n})\} = p_{j_0} p_{j_1} \cdots p_{j_n}$. In the theory of Markov chains we consider the simplest generalization which consists in permitting the outcome of any trial to depend on the outcome of the directly preceding trial (and only on it). The outcome E_k is no longer associated with a fixed probability p_k, but to every pair (E_j, E_k) there corresponds a *conditional probability* p_{jk}; given that E_j has occurred at some trial, the probability of E_k at the next trial is p_{jk}. In addition to the p_{jk} we must be given the probability a_k of the outcome E_k at the *initial* trial. For p_{jk} to have the meaning attributed to them, the probabilities of sample sequences corresponding to two, three, or four trials must be defined by

$$\mathbf{P}\{(E_j, E_k)\} = a_j p_{jk}, \qquad \mathbf{P}\{(E_j, E_k, E_r)\} = a_j p_{jk} p_{kr},$$

$$\mathbf{P}\{(E_j, E_k, E_r, E_s)\} = a_j p_{jk} p_{kr} p_{rs},$$

and generally

(1.1) $\qquad \mathbf{P}\{(E_{j_0}, E_{j_1}, \ldots, E_{j_n})\} = a_{j_0} p_{j_0 j_1} p_{j_1 j_2} \cdots p_{j_{n-2} j_{n-1}} p_{j_{n-1} j_n}.$

Here the initial trial is numbered zero, so that trial number one is the second trial. (This convention is convenient and has been introduced tacitly in the preceding chapter.)

Several processes treated in the preceding chapters are Markov chains, but in special cases it is often preferable to use different notations and modes of description. The principal results of the present chapter concern the existence of certain limits and equilibrium distributions; they are, of course, independent of notations and apply to all Markov chains.

Examples. (*a*) *Random walks.* A random walk on the line is a Markov chain, but it is natural to order the possible positions in a doubly infinite sequence $\ldots, -2, -1, 0, 1, 0, \ldots$. With this order transitions are possibly only between neighboring positions, that is, $p_{jk} = 0$ unless $k = j \pm 1$. With our present notations we would be compelled to order the integers in a simple sequence, say $0, 1, -1, 2, -2, \ldots$ and this would lead to clumsy formulas for the probabilities p_{jk}. The same remark applies to random walks in higher dimensions: For actual calculations it is preferable to specify the points by their coordinates, but the symbolism of the present chapter can be used for theoretical purposes.

(*b*) *Branching processes.* Instead of saying that the nth trial results in E_k we said in XII,3 that the nth generation is of size k. Otherwise, we were concerned with a standard Markov chain whose transition probability p_{jk} is the coefficient of a s^k in the jth power $p^j(s)$ of the given generating function.

(*c*) *Urn models.* It is obvious that several urn models of V.2 represent Markov chains. Conversely, every Markov chain is equivalent to an urn model as follows. Each occurring subscript is represented by an urn, and each urn contains balls marked $E_1, E_2, \ldots$. The composition of the urns remains fixed, but varies from urn to urn; in the jth urn the probability to draw a ball marked E_k is p_{jk}. At the *initial*, or zero-th, trial an urn is chosen in accordance with the probability distribution $\{a_i\}$. From that urn a ball is drawn at random, and if it is marked E_j, the next drawing is made from the jth urn, etc. Obviously with this procedure the probability of a sequence $(E_{j_0}, \ldots, E_{j_n})$ is given by (1.1). We see that the notion of a Markov chain is not more general than urn models, but the new symbolism will prove more practical and more intuitive.   ▶

If a_k is the probability of E_k at the initial (or zero-th) trial, we must have $a_k \geq 0$ and $\sum a_k = 1$. Moreover, whenever E_j occurs it must be followed by some E_k, and it is therefore necessary that for all j and k

$$(1.2) \qquad p_{j1} + p_{j2} + p_{j3} + \cdots = 1, \qquad p_{jk} \geq 0.$$

We now show that for any numbers a_k and p_{jk} satisfying these conditions, the assignment (1.1) is a permissible definition of probabilities in the sample space corresponding to $n + 1$ trials. The numbers defined in (1.1) being non-negative, we need only prove that they add to unity. Fix first $j_0, j_1, \ldots, j_{n-1}$ and add the numbers (1.1) for all possible j_n. Using (1.2) with $j = j_{n-1}$, we see immediately that the sum equals $a_{j_0} p_{j_0 j_1} \cdots p_{j_{n-2} j_{n-1}}$. Thus the sum over all numbers (1.1) does not depend on n, and since $\sum a_{i_0} = 1$, the sum equals unity for all n.

The definition (1.1) depends formally on the number of trials, but our argument proves the mutual consistency of the definitions (1.1) for all n.

For example, to obtain the probability of the event "the first two trials result in (E_j, E_k)," we have to fix $j_0 = j$ and $j_1 = k$, and add the probabilities (1.1) for all possible $j_2, j_3, \ldots, j_n$. We have just shown that the sum is $a_j p_{jk}$ and is thus independent of n. This means that it is usually not necessary explicitly to refer to the number of trials; the event $(E_{j_0}, \ldots, E_{j_r})$ has the same probability in all sample spaces of more than r trials. In connection with independent trials it has been pointed out repeatedly that. from a mathematical point of view, it is most satisfactory to introduce only the unique sample space of unending sequences of trials and to consider the result of finitely many trials as the beginning of an infinite sequence. This statement holds true also for Markov chains. Unfortunately, sample spaces of infinitely many trials lead beyond the theory of discrete probabilities to which we are restricted in the present volume.

To summarize, our starting point is the following

Definition. *A sequence of trials with possible outcomes* $E_1, E_2, \ldots$ *is called a Markov chain[1] if the probabilities of sample sequences are defined by* (1.1) *in terms of a probability distribution* $\{a_k\}$ *for* E_k *at the initial (or zero-th) trial and fixed conditional probabilities* p_{jk} *of* E_k *given that* E_j *has occurred at the preceding trial.*

A slightly modified terminology is better adapted for applications of Markov chains. The possible outcomes E_k are usually referred to as possible *states of the system*; instead of saying that the nth trial results in E_k one says that the nth *step leads to* E_k, or that E_k is entered at the nth step. Finally, p_{jk} is called the probability of a *transition from* E_j *to* E_k. As usual we imagine the trials performed at a uniform rate so that the number of the step serves as time parameter.

The transition probabilities p_{jk} will be arranged in a *matrix of transition probabilities*

(1.3)
$$
P = \begin{bmatrix}
p_{11} & p_{12} & p_{13} & \cdots \\
p_{21} & p_{22} & p_{23} & \cdots \\
p_{31} & p_{32} & p_{33} & \cdots \\
\cdot & \cdot & \cdot & \cdots \\
\cdot & \cdot & \cdot & \cdots \\
\cdot & \cdot & \cdot & \cdots
\end{bmatrix}
$$

---

[1] This is not the standard terminology. We are here considering only a special class of Markov chains, and, strictly speaking, here and in the following sections the term Markov chain should always be qualified by adding the clause "with stationary transition probabilities." Actually, the general type of Markov chain is rarely studied. It will be defined in section 13, where the Markov property will be discussed in relation to general stochastic processes. There the reader will also find examples of dependent trials that do not form Markov chains.

where the first subscript stands for row, the second for column. Clearly
P is a square matrix with non-negative elements and unit row sums. Such
a matrix (finite or infinite) is called a *stochastic matrix*. *Any stochastic
matrix can serve as a matrix of transition probabilities; together with our
initial distribution* $\{a_k\}$ *it completely defines a Markov chain with states*
$E_1, E_2, \ldots$.

In some special cases it is convenient to number the states starting with
0 rather than with 1. A zero row and zero column are then to be added
to P.

Historical Note. Various problems treated in the classical literature by urn models
now appear as special Markov chains, but the original methods were entirely different.
Furthermore, many urn models are of a different character because they involve
aftereffects, and this essential difference was not properly understood. In fact, the
confusion persisted long after Markov's pioneer work. A. A. Markov (1856–1922)
laid the foundations of the theory of finite Markov chains, but concrete applications
remained confined largely to card-shuffling and linguistic problems. The theoretical
treatment was usually by algebraic methods related to those described in the next
chapter. This approach is outlined in M. Fréchet's monograph.[2]

The theory of chains with infinitely many states was introduced by A. Kolmogorov.[3]
The new approach in the first edition of this book made the theory accessible to a
wider public and drew attention to the variety of possible applications. Since then
Markov chains have become a standard topic in probability and a familiar tool in
many applications. For more recent theoretical developments see the notes to sections
11 and 12.

2. ILLUSTRATIVE EXAMPLES

(For applications to the classical problem of card-shuffling see section
10.)

(*a*) When there are only two possible states E_1 and E_2 the matrix of
transition probabilities is necessarily of the form

$$P = \begin{bmatrix} 1 - p & p \\ \alpha & 1 - \alpha \end{bmatrix}.$$

Such a chain could be realized by the following conceptual experiment. A
particle moves along the x-axis in such a way that its absolute speed remains constant but the direction of the motion can be reversed. The
system is said to be in state E_1 if the particle moves in the positive direction, and in state E_2 if the motion is to the left. Then p is the probability

---

[2] *Recherches théoriques modernes sur le calcul des probabilités*, vol. 2 (Théorie des
événements en chaine dans le cas d'un nombre fini d'états possibles), Paris, 1938.

[3] *Anfangsgründe der Theorie der Markoffschen Ketten mit unendlich vielen möglichen
Zuständen*, Matematičeskii Sbornik, N.S., vol. 1 (1936), pp. 607–610. This paper
contains no proofs. A complete exposition was given only in Russian, in Bulletin de
l'Université d'État à Moscou, Sect. A., vol. 1 (1937), pp. 1–15.

of a reversal when the particle moves to the right, and α the probability of a reversal when it moves to the left. [For a complete analysis of this chain see example XVI,(2.a).]

(b) *Random walk with absorbing barriers.* Let the possible states be $E_0, E_1, \ldots, E_\rho$ and consider the matrix of transition probabilities

$$P = \begin{bmatrix} 1 & 0 & 0 & 0 & \cdots & 0 & 0 & 0 \\ q & 0 & p & 0 & \cdots & 0 & 0 & 0 \\ 0 & q & 0 & p & \cdots & 0 & 0 & 0 \\ \cdot & \cdot & \cdot & \cdot & \cdots & \cdot & \cdot & \cdot \\ \cdot & \cdot & \cdot & \cdot & \cdots & \cdot & \cdot & \cdot \\ 0 & 0 & 0 & 0 & \cdots & q & 0 & p \\ 0 & 0 & 0 & 0 & \cdots & 0 & 0 & 1 \end{bmatrix}.$$

From each of the "interior" states $E_1, \ldots, E_{\rho-1}$ transitions are possible to the right and the left neighbors (with $p_{i,i+1} = p$ and $p_{i,i-1} = q$). However, no transition is possible from either E_0 or E_ρ to any other state; the system may move from one state to another, but once E_0 or E_ρ is reached, the system stays there fixed forever. Clearly this Markov chain differs only terminologically from the model of a random walk with absorbing barriers at 0 and ρ discussed in the last chapter. There the random walk started from a fixed point z of the interval. In Markov chain terminology this amounts to choosing the initial distribution so that $a_z = 1$ (and hence $a_x = 0$ for $x \neq z$). To a randomly chosen initial state there corresponds the initial distribution $a_k = 1/(\rho+1)$.

(c) *Reflecting barriers.* An interesting variant of the preceding example is represented by the chain with possible states $E_1, \ldots, E_\rho$ and transition probabilities

$$P = \begin{bmatrix} q & p & 0 & 0 & \cdots & 0 & 0 & 0 \\ q & 0 & p & 0 & \cdots & 0 & 0 & 0 \\ 0 & q & 0 & p & \cdots & 0 & 0 & 0 \\ \cdot & \cdot & \cdot & \cdot & \cdots & \cdot & \cdot & \cdot \\ \cdot & \cdot & \cdot & \cdot & \cdots & \cdot & \cdot & \cdot \\ \cdot & \cdot & \cdot & \cdot & \cdots & \cdot & \cdot & \cdot \\ 0 & 0 & 0 & 0 & \cdots & q & 0 & p \\ 0 & 0 & 0 & 0 & \cdots & 0 & q & p \end{bmatrix}$$

This chain may be interpreted in gambling language by considering two players playing for unit stakes with the agreement that every time a player loses his last dollar his adversay returns it so that the game can continue forever. We suppose that the players own between them $\rho + 1$ dollars and say that the system is in state E_k if the two capitals are k and $\rho - k + 1$, respectively. The transition probabilities are then given by our matrix P. In the terminology introduced in XIV,1 our chain represents a random walk with reflecting barriers at the points $\frac{1}{2}$ and $\rho + \frac{1}{2}$. Random walks with elastic barriers can be treated in the same way. A complete analysis of the reflecting barrier chain will be found in XVI,3. [See also example (7.c).]

(d) *Cyclical random walks.* Again let the possible states be $E_1, E_2, \ldots, E_\rho$ but order them cyclically so that E_ρ has the neighbors $E_{\rho-1}$ and E_1. If, as before, the system always passes either to the right or to the left neighbor, the rows of the matrix P are as in example (b), except that the first row is $(0, p, 0, 0, \ldots, 0, q)$ and the last $(p, 0, 0, 0, \ldots, 0, q, 0)$.

More generally, we may permit transitions between any two states. Let $q_0, q_1, \ldots, q_{\rho-1}$ be, respectively, the probability of staying fixed or moving $1, 2, \ldots, \rho - 1$ units to the right (where k units to the right is the same as $\rho - k$ units to the left). Then P is the cyclical matrix

$$
P = \begin{bmatrix}
q_0 & q_1 & q_2 & \cdots & q_{\rho-2} & q_{\rho-1} \\
q_{\rho-1} & q_0 & q_1 & \cdots & q_{\rho-3} & q_{\rho-2} \\
q_{\rho-2} & q_{\rho-1} & q_0 & \cdots & q_{\rho-4} & q_{\rho-3} \\
\cdot & \cdot & \cdot & \cdots & \cdot & \cdot \\
\cdot & \cdot & \cdot & \cdots & \cdot & \cdot \\
q_1 & q_2 & q_3 & \cdots & q_{\rho-1} & q_0
\end{bmatrix}.
$$

For an analysis of this chain see example XVI,(2.d).

(e) *The Ehrenfest model of diffusion.* Once more we consider a chain with the $\rho + 1$ states $E_0, E_1, \ldots, E_\rho$ and transitions possible only to the right and to the left neighbor; this time we put $p_{j,j+1} = 1 - j/\rho$ and $p_{j,j-1} = j/\rho$, so that

$$
P = \begin{bmatrix}
0 & 1 & 0 & 0 & \cdots & 0 & 0 \\
\rho^{-1} & 0 & 1 - \rho^{-1} & 0 & \cdots & 0 & 0 \\
0 & 2\rho^{-1} & 0 & 1 - 2\rho^{-1} & \cdots & 0 & 0 \\
\cdot & \cdot & \cdot & \cdot & \cdots & \cdot & \cdot \\
\cdot & \cdot & \cdot & \cdot & \cdots & \cdot & \cdot \\
0 & 0 & 0 & 0 & \cdots & 0 & \rho^{-1} \\
0 & 0 & 0 & 0 & \cdots & 1 & 0
\end{bmatrix}.
$$

This chain has two interesting physical interpretations. For a discussion of various recurrence problems in statistical mechanics, P. and T. Ehren-fest[4] described a conceptual urn experiment where ρ molecules are dis-tributed in two containers A and B. At each trial a molecule is chosen at random and moved from its container to the other. The state of the system is determined by the number of molecules in A. Suppose that at a certain moment there are exactly k molecules in the container A. At the next trial the system passes into E_{k-1} or E_{k+1} according to whether a molecule in A or B is chosen; the corresponding probabilities are k/ρ and $(\rho-k)/\rho$, and therefore our chain describes Ehrenfest's experiment. However, our chain can also be interpreted as *diffusion with a central force*, that is, a random walk in which the probability of a step to the right varies with the position. From $x = j$ the particle is more likely to move to the right or to the left according as $j < \rho/2$ or $j > \rho/2$; this means that the particle has a tendency to move toward $x = \rho/2$, which corresponds to an attractive elastic force increasing in direct proportion to the distance. [The Ehrenfest model has been described in example V(2.c); see also example (7.d) and problem 12.]

(*f*) *The Bernoulli-Laplace model of diffusion.*[5] A model similar to the Ehrenfest model was proposed by D. Bernoulli as a probabilistic analogue for the flow of two incompressible liquids between two containers. This time we have a total of 2ρ particles among which ρ are black and ρ white. Since these particles are supposed to represent incompressible liquids the densities must not change, and so the number ρ of particles in each urn remains constant. We say that the system is in state E_k ($k = 0$, $1, \ldots, \rho$) if the first urn contains k white particles. (This implies that it contains $\rho - k$ black particles while the second urn contains $\rho - k$ white and k black particles). At each trial one particle is chosen from each urn, and these two particles are interchanged. The transition probabilities are then given by

$$(2.1) \qquad p_{j,j-1} = \left(\frac{j}{\rho}\right)^2, \qquad p_{j,j+1} = \left(\frac{\rho-j}{\rho}\right)^2, \qquad p_{jj} = 2\,\frac{j(\rho-j)}{\rho^2}$$

---

[4] P. and T. Ehrenfest, *Über zwei bekannte Einwände gegen das Boltzmannsche H-Theorem*, Physikalische Zeitschrift, vol. 8 (1907), pp. 311–314. Ming Chen Wang and G. E. Uhlenbeck, *On the theory of the Brownian motion II*, Reviews of Modern Physics, vol. 17 (1945), pp. 323–342. For a more complete discussion see M. Kac, *Random walk and the theory of Brownian motion*, Amer. Math. Monthly, vol. 54 (1947), pp. 369–391. These authors do not mention Markov chains, but Kac uses methods closely related to those described in the next chapter. See also B. Friedman, *A simple urn model*, Communications on Pure and Applied Mathematics, vol. 2 (1949), pp. 59–70.

[5] In the form of an urn model this problem was treated by Daniel Bernoulli in 1769, criticized by Malfatti in 1782, and analyzed by Laplace in 1812. See I. Todhunter, *A history of the mathematical theory of probability*, Cambridge, 1865.

and $p_{jk} = 0$ whenever $|j - k| > 1$ (here $j = 0, \ldots, \rho$). [For the steady state distribution see example $(7.e)$; for a generalization of the model see problem 10.]

(g) *Random placements of balls.* Consider a sequence of independent trials each consisting in placing a ball at random in one of ρ given cells (or urns). We say that the system is in state E_k if exactly k cells are occupied. This determines a Markov chain with states $E_0, \ldots, E_\rho$ and transition probabilities such that

$$(2.2) \qquad\qquad p_{jj} = \frac{j}{\rho}, \qquad p_{j,j+1} = \frac{\rho - j}{\rho}$$

and, of course, $p_{jk} = 0$ for all other combinations of j and k. If initially all cells are empty, the distribution $\{a_k\}$ is determined by $a_0 = 1$ and $a_k = 0$ for $k > 0$. [This chain is further analyzed in example XVI,$(2.e)$. Random placements of balls were treated from different points of view in II,5 and IV,2.]

(h) *An example from cell genetics.*[6] A Markov chain with states E_0, $\ldots, E_N$ and transition probabilities

$$(2.3) \qquad\qquad p_{jk} = \binom{2j}{k} \binom{2N - 2j}{N - k} \Big/ \binom{2N}{N}$$

occurs in a biological problem which may be described roughly as follows. Each cell of a certain organism contains N particles, some of which are of type A, the others of type B. The cell is said to be in state E_j if it contains exactly j particles of type A. Daughter cells are formed by cell division, but prior to the division each particle replicates itself; the daughter cell inherits N particles chosen at random from the $2j$ particles of type A and $2N - 2j$ particles of type B present in the parental cell. The probability that a daughter cell is in state E_k is then given by the hypergeometric distribution (2.3).

It will be shown in example $(8.b)$ that *after sufficiently many generations the entire population will be* (*and remain*) *in one of the pure states E_0 or E_N*; the probabilities of these two contingencies are $1 - j/N$ and j/N, respectively, where E_j stands for the initial state.

---

[6] I. V. Schensted, *Model of subnuclear segregation in the macronucleus of ciliates*, The Amer. Naturalist, vol. 92 (1958), pp. 161–170. This author uses essentially the methods of chapter XVI, but does not mention Markov chains. Our formulation of the problem is mathematically equivalent, but oversimplified biologically.

(*i*) *Examples from population genetics.*[7] Consider the successive generations of a population (such as the plants in a corn field) which is kept constant in size by the selection of N individuals in each generation. A particular gene assuming the forms A and a has $2N$ representatives; if in the nth generation A occurs j times, then a occurs $2N - j$ times. In this case we say that the population is in state E_j $(0 \leq j \leq 2N)$. Assuming random mating, the composition of the following generation is determined by $2N$ Bernoulli trials in which the A-gene has probability $j/2N$. We have therefore a Markov chain with

$$(2.4) \qquad p_{jk} = \binom{2N}{k} \left(\frac{j}{2N}\right)^k \left(1 - \frac{j}{2N}\right)^{2N-k}.$$

In the states E_0 and E_{2N} all genes are of the same type, and no exit from these states is possible. (They are called homozygous.) It will be shown in example (8.*b*) that *ultimately the population will be fixed at one of the homozygous states* E_0 *or* E_{2N}. If the population starts from the initial state E_j the corresponding probabilities are $1 - j/(2N)$ and $j/(2N)$.

This model can be modified so as to take into account possible mutations and selective advantages of the genes.

(*j*) *A breeding problem.* In the so-called brother-sister mating two individuals are mated, and among their direct descendants two individuals of opposite sex are selected at random. These are again mated, and the process continues indefinitely. With three genotypes AA, Aa, aa for each parent, we have to distinguish six combinations of parents which we label as follows: $E_1 = AA \times AA$, $E_2 = AA \times Aa$, $E_3 = Aa \times Aa$, $E_4 = Aa \times aa$, $E_5 = aa \times aa$, $E_6 = AA \times aa$. Using the rules of V,5 it is easily seen that the matrix of transition probabilities is in this case

$$\begin{bmatrix} 1 & 0 & 0 & 0 & 0 & 0 \\ \frac{1}{4} & \frac{1}{2} & \frac{1}{4} & 0 & 0 & 0 \\ \frac{1}{16} & \frac{1}{4} & \frac{1}{4} & \frac{1}{4} & \frac{1}{16} & \frac{1}{8} \\ 0 & 0 & \frac{1}{4} & \frac{1}{2} & \frac{1}{4} & 0 \\ 0 & 0 & 0 & 0 & 1 & 0 \\ 0 & 0 & 1 & 0 & 0 & 0 \end{bmatrix}.$$

---

[7] This problem was discussed by different methods by R. A. Fisher and S. Wright. The formulation in terms of Markov chains is due to G. Malécot, *Sur un problème de probabilités en chaine que pose la génétique,* Comptes rendus de l'Académie des Sciences, vol. 219 (1944), pp. 379–381.

[The discussion is continued in problem 4; a complete treatment is given in example XVI,(4.*b*).]

(*k*) *Recurrent events and residual waiting times.* The chain with states E_0, $E_1, \ldots$ and transition probabilities

$$P = \begin{bmatrix} f_1 & f_2 & f_3 & f_4 & \cdots \\ 1 & 0 & 0 & 0 & \cdots \\ 0 & 1 & 0 & 0 & \cdots \\ 0 & 0 & 1 & 0 & \cdots \\ 0 & 0 & 0 & 1 & \cdots \\ \cdot & \cdot & \cdot & \cdot & \cdots \\ \cdot & \cdot & \cdot & \cdot & \cdots \end{bmatrix}$$

will be used repeatedly for purposes of illustration; the probabilities f_k are arbitrary except that they must add to unity. To visualize the process suppose that it starts from the initial state E_0. If the first step leads to E_{k-1} the system is bound to pass successively through $E_{k-2}, E_{k-3}, \ldots$, and at the *k*th step the system returns to E_0, whence the process starts from scratch. The successive returns to E_0 thus represent a persistent recurrent event $\mathcal{E}$ with the distribution $\{f_k\}$ for the recurrence times. The state of the system at any time is determined by the waiting time to the *next* passage through E_0. In most concrete realizations of recurrent events the waiting time for the next occurrence depends on future developments and our Markov chain is then without operational meaning. But the chain is meaningful when it is possible to imagine that simultaneously with each occurrence of $\mathcal{E}$ there occurs a random experiment whose outcome decides on the length of the next waiting time. Such situations occur in practice although they are the exception rather than the rule. For example, in the theory of self-renewing aggregates [example XIII,(10.*d*)] it is sometimes assumed that the lifetime of a newly installed piece of equipment depends on the choice of this piece but is completely determined once the choice is made. Again, in the theory of queues at servers or telephone trunk lines the successive departures of customers usually correspond to recurrent events. Suppose now that there are many types of customers but that each type requires service of a known duration. The waiting time between two successive departures is then uniquely determined from the moment when the corresponding customer joins the waiting line. [See example (7.*g*).]

(*l*) *Another chain connected with recurrent events.* Consider again a chain with possible states $E_0, E_1, \ldots$ and transition probabilities

$$
P = \begin{bmatrix}
q_1 & p_1 & 0 & 0 & 0 & \cdots \\
q_2 & 0 & p_2 & 0 & 0 & \cdots \\
q_3 & 0 & 0 & p_3 & 0 & \cdots \\
q_4 & 0 & 0 & 0 & p_4 & \cdots \\
\cdot & \cdot & \cdot & \cdot & \cdot & \cdots \\
\cdot & \cdot & \cdot & \cdot & \cdot & \cdots
\end{bmatrix}
$$

where $p_k + q_k = 1$. For a picturesque description we may interpret the state E_k as representing the "age" of the system. When the system reaches age k the aging process continues with probability p_{k+1}, but with probability q_{k+1} it rejuvenates and starts afresh with age zero. The successive passages through the state E_0 again represent a recurrent event and the probability that a recurrence time equals k is given by the product $p_1 p_2 \cdots p_{k-1} q_k$. It is possible to choose the p_k in such a way as to obtain a prescribed distribution $\{f_k\}$ for the recurrence times; it suffices to put $q_1 = f_1$, then $q_2 = f_2/p_1$, and so on. Generally

$$
(2.5) \qquad\qquad p_k = \frac{1 - f_1 - \cdots - f_k}{1 - f_1 - \cdots - f_{k-1}}.
$$

In this way an arbitrary recurrent event $\mathcal{E}$ with recurrence time distribution $\{f_k\}$ corresponds to a Markov chain with matrix P determined by (2.5). At the nth trial the system is in state E_k if, and only if, the trial number $n - k$ was the last at which $\mathcal{E}$ occurred (here $k = 0, 1, \ldots$). This state is frequently called "the spent waiting time." [The discussion is continued in examples (5.*b*), (7.*f*), and (8.*e*).]

(*m*) *Success runs.* As a special case of the preceding example consider a sequence of Bernoulli trials and let us agree that at the nth trial the system is in the state E_k if the last *failure* occurred at the trial number $n - k$. Here $k = 0, 1, \ldots$ and the zeroth trial counts as failure. In other words, the index k equals the length of the uninterrupted block of successes ending at the nth trial. The transition probabilities are those of the preceding example with $p_k = p$ and $q_k = q$ for all k.

3. HIGHER TRANSITION PROBABILITIES

We shall denote by $p_{jk}^{(n)}$ *the probability of a transition from E_j to E_k in exactly n steps.* In other words, $p_{jk}^{(n)}$ is the conditional probability of entering E_k at the nth step given the initial state E_j; this is the sum of the probabilities of all possible paths $E_j E_{j_1} \cdots E_{j_{n-1}} E_k$ of length n starting at E_j and ending at E_k. In particular $p_{jk}^{(1)} = p_{jk}$ and

(3.1) $$p_{jk}^{(2)} = \sum_v p_{jv} p_{vk}.$$

By induction we get *the general recursion formula*

(3.2) $$p_{jk}^{(n+1)} = \sum_v p_{jv} p_{vk}^{(n)};$$

a further induction on m leads to *the basic identity*

(3.3) $$p_{jk}^{(m+n)} = \sum_v p_{jv}^{(m)} p_{vk}^{(n)}$$

(which is a special case of the Chapman-Kolmogorov identity). It reflects the simple fact that the first m steps lead from E_j to some intermediate state E_v, and that the probability of a subsequent passage from E_v to E_k does not depend on the manner in which E_v was reached.[8]

In the same way as the p_{jk} form the matrix P, *we arrange the $p_{jk}^{(n)}$ in a matrix to be denoted by P^n*. Then (3.2) states that to obtain the element $p_{jk}^{(n+1)}$ of P^{n+1} we have to multiply the elements of the jth row of P by the corresponding elements of the kth column of P^n and add all products. This operation is called row-into-column multiplication of the matrices P and P^n and is expressed symbolically by the equation $P^{n+1} = PP^n$. This suggests calling P^n the nth power of P; equation (3.3) expresses the familiar law $P^{m+n} = P^m P^n$.

In order to have (3.3) true for all $n \geq 0$ we define $p_{jk}^{(0)}$ by $p_{jj}^{(0)} = 1$ and $p_{jk}^{(0)} = 0$ for $j \neq k$ as is natural.

Examples. (*a*) *Independent trials.* Explicit expressions for the higher-order transition probabilities are usually hard to come by, but fortunately they are only of minor interest. As an important, if trivial, exception we note the special case of independent trials. This case arises when all rows of P are identical with a given probability distribution, and it is clear without calculations that this implies $P^n = P$ for all n.

(*b*) *Success runs.* In example (2.*m*) it is easy to see [either from the recursion formula (3.2) or directly from the definition of the process] that

$$p_{jk}^{(n)} = \begin{cases} q p^k & \text{for} \quad k = 0, 1, \ldots, n-1 \\ p^k & \text{for} \quad k = n \\ 0 & \text{otherwise.} \end{cases}$$

---

[8] The latter property is characteristic of Markov processes to be defined in section 13. It has been assumed for a long time that (3.3) could be used for a definition of Markov chains but, surprisingly, this is not so [see example (13.*f*)].

In this case it is clear that P^n converges to a matrix such that all elements in the column number k equal qp^k. ▶

Absolute Probabilities

Let again a_j stand for the probability of the state E_j at the initial (or zeroth) trial. The (unconditional) probability of entering E_k at the nth step is then

$$(3.4) \qquad\qquad a_k^{(n)} = \sum_j a_j p_{jk}^{(n)}.$$

Usually we let the process start from a fixed state E_i, that is, we put $a_i = 1$. In this case $a_k^{(n)} = p_{ik}^{(n)}$.

We feel intuitively that the influence of the initial state should gradually wear off so that for large n the distribution (3.4) should be nearly independent of the initial distribution $\{a_j\}$. This is the case if (as in the last example) $p_{jk}^{(n)}$ converges to a limit independent of j, that is, if P^n converges to a matrix with identical rows. We shall see that this is usually so, but once more we shall have to take into account the annoying exception caused by periodicities.

4. CLOSURES AND CLOSED SETS

We shall say that E_k *can be reached from* E_j *if there exists some* $n \geq 0$ *such that* $p_{jk}^{(n)} > 0$ (i.e., if there is a positive probability of reaching E_k from E_j including the case $E_k = E_j$). For example, in an unrestricted random walk each state can be reached from every other state, but from an absorbing barrier no other state can be reached.

Definition. *A set* C *of states is closed if no state outside* C *can be reached from any state* E_j *in* C. *For an arbitrary set* C *of states the smallest closed set containing* C *is called the closure of* C.

A single state E_k *forming a closed set will be called absorbing.*

A Markov chain is irreducible if there exists no closed set other than the set of all states.

Clearly C is closed if, and only if, $p_{jk} = 0$ whenever j is in C and k outside C, for in this case we see from (3.2) that $p_{jk}^{(n)} = 0$ for every n. We have thus the obvious

Theorem. *If in the matrices* P^n *all rows and all columns corresponding to states outside the closed set* C *are deleted, there remain stochastic matrices for which the fundamental relations (3.2) and (3.3) again hold.*

This means that we have a Markov chain defined on C, and this *subchain can be studied independently of all other states.*

The state E_k is absorbing if, and only if, $p_{kk} = 1$; in this case the matrix of the last theorem reduces to a single element. In general it is clear that the totality of all states E_k that can be reached from a given state E_j forms a closed set. (Since the closure of E_j cannot be smaller it coincides with this set.) An irreducible chain contains no proper closed subsets, and so we have the simple but useful

Criterion. *A chain is irreducible if, and only if, every state can be reached from every other state.*

Examples. (*a*) In order to find all closed sets it suffices to know which p_{jk} vanish and which are positive. Accordingly, we use a $*$ to denote positive elements and consider a typical matrix, say

$$P = \begin{bmatrix}
0 & 0 & 0 & * & 0 & 0 & 0 & 0 & * \\
0 & * & * & 0 & * & 0 & 0 & 0 & * \\
0 & 0 & 0 & 0 & 0 & 0 & 0 & * & 0 \\
* & 0 & 0 & 0 & 0 & 0 & 0 & 0 & 0 \\
0 & 0 & 0 & 0 & * & 0 & 0 & 0 & 0 \\
0 & * & 0 & 0 & 0 & 0 & 0 & 0 & 0 \\
0 & * & 0 & 0 & 0 & * & * & 0 & 0 \\
0 & 0 & * & 0 & 0 & 0 & 0 & 0 & 0 \\
0 & 0 & 0 & * & 0 & 0 & 0 & 0 & *
\end{bmatrix}$$

We number the states from 1 to 9. In the fifth row a $*$ appears only at the fifth place, and therefore $p_{55} = 1$: the state E_5 is *absorbing*. The third and the eighth row contain only one positive element each, and it is clear that E_3 and E_8 form a *closed* set. From E_1 passages are possible into E_4 and E_9, and from there only to E_1, E_4, E_9. Accordingly the three states E_1, E_4, E_9 form another *closed* set.

From E_2 direct transitions are possible to itself and to E_3, E_5, and E_8. The pair (E_3, E_8) forms a closed set while E_5 is asorbing; accordingly, the closure of E_2 consists of the set E_2, E_3, E_5, E_8. The closures of the remaining states E_6 and E_7 are easily seen to consist of all nine states.

The appearance of our matrix and the determination of the closed sets can be simplified by renumbering the states in the order

$$E_5 E_3 E_8 E_1 E_4 E_9 E_2 E_6 E_7.$$

The closed sets then contain only adjacent states and a glance at the new matrix reveals the grouping of the states.

(b) In the matrix of example (2.*j*) the states E_1 and E_5 are absorbing and there exist no other closed sets.

(c) In the genetics example (2.*i*) the states E_0 and E_{2N} are absorbing. When $0 < j < 2N$ the closure of E_j contains all states. In example (2.*h*) the states E_0 and E_N are absorbing. ▶

Consider a chain with states $E_1, \ldots, E_\rho$ such that $E_1, \ldots, E_r$ form a closed set $(r < \rho)$. The r by r submatrix of P appearing in the left upper corner is then stochastic, and we can exhibit P in the form of a partitioned matrix

$$(4.1) \qquad\qquad P = \begin{bmatrix} Q & 0 \\ U & V \end{bmatrix}.$$

The matrix in the upper right corner has r rows and $\rho - r$ columns and only zero entries. Similarly, U stands for a matrix with $\rho - r$ rows and r columns while V is a square matrix. We shall use the symbolic partitioning (4.1) also when the closed set C and its complement C' contain infinitely many states; the partitioning indicates merely the grouping of the states and the fact that $p_{jk} = 0$ whenever E_j is in C and E_k in the complement C'. From the recursion formula (3.2) it is obvious that the higher-order transition probabilities admit of a similar partitioning:

$$(4.2) \qquad\qquad P^n = \begin{bmatrix} Q^n & 0 \\ U_n & V^n \end{bmatrix}.$$

We are not at present interested in the form of the elements of the matrix U_n appearing in the left lower corner. The point of interest is that (4.2) reveals three obvious, but important, facts. First, $p_{jk}^{(n)} = 0$ whenever $E_j \in C$ but $E_k \in C'$. Second, the appearance of the power Q^n indicates that when both E_j and E_k are in C the transition probabilities $p_{jk}^{(n)}$ are obtained from the recursion formula (3.2) with the summation restricted to the states of the closed set C. Finally, the appearance of V^n indicates that the last statement remains true when C is replaced by its complement C'. As a consequence it will be possible to simplify the further study of Markov chains by considering separately the states of the closed set C and those of the complement C'.

Note that we have not assumed Q to be irreducible. If C decomposes into several closed subsets then Q admits of a further partitioning. There exist chains with infinitely many closed subsets.

Example. (d) As was mentioned before, a random walk in the plane represents a special Markov chain even though an ordering of the states in a simple sequence would be inconvenient for practical purposes. Suppose now that we modify the random walk by the rule that on reaching the

x-axis the particle continues a random walk along this axis without ever leaving it. The points of the x-axis then form an infinite closed set. On the other hand, if we stipulate that on reaching the x-axis the particle remains forever fixed at the hitting point, then every point of the x-axis becomes an absorbing state.   ▶

5. CLASSIFICATION OF STATES

In a process starting from the initial state E_j the successive returns to E_j constitute a recurrent event, while the successive passages through any other state constitute a delayed recurrent event (as defined in XIII,5). The theory of Markov chains therefore boils down to a simultaneous study of many recurrent events. The general theory of recurrent events is applicable without modifications, but to avoid excessive references to chapter XIII we shall now restate the basic definitions. The present chapter thus becomes essentially self-contained and independent of chapter XIII except that the difficult proof of (5.8) will not be repeated in full.

The states of a Markov chain will be classified independently from two viewpoints. The classification into persistent and transient states is fundamental, whereas the classification into periodic and aperiodic states concerns a technical detail. It represents a nuisance in that it requires constant references to trivialities; the beginner should concentrate his attention on chains without periodic states. All definitions in this section involve only the matrix of transition probabilities and are independent of the initial distribution $\{a_j\}$.

Definition 1. *The state E_j has period $t > 1$ if $p_{jj}^{(n)} = 0$ unless $n = vt$ is a multiple of t, and t is the largest integer with this property. The state E_j is aperiodic if no such $t > 1$ exists.*[9]

To deal with a periodic E_j it suffices to consider the chain at the trials number $t, 2t, 3t, \ldots$. In this way we obtain a new Markov chain with transition probabilities $p_{ik}^{(t)}$, and in this new chain E_j is aperiodic. In this way results concerning aperiodic states can be transferred to periodic states. The details will be discussed in section 9 and (excepting the following example) we shall now concentrate our attention on aperiodic chains.

Example. (*a*) In an unrestricted random walk all states have period 2. In the random walk with absorbing barriers at 0 and ρ [example (2.*b*)] the interior states have period 2, but the absorbing states E_0 and E_ρ are, of course, aperiodic. If at least one of the barriers is made reflecting [example (2.*c*)], all states become aperiodic.   ▶

---

[9] A state E_j to which no return is possible (for which $p_{jj}^{(n)} = 0$ for all $n > 0$) will be considered aperiodic.

Notation. *Throughout this chapter $f_{jk}^{(n)}$ stands for the probability that in a process starting from E_j the first entry to E_k occurs at the nth step. We put $f_{jk}^{(0)} = 0$ and*

$$(5.1) \qquad\qquad f_{jk} = \sum_{n=1}^{\infty} f_{jk}^{(n)}$$

$$(5.2) \qquad\qquad \mu_j = \sum_{n=1}^{\infty} n f_{jj}^{(n)}.$$

Obviously f_{jk} is the probability that, starting from E_j, the system will ever pass through E_k. Thus $f_{jk} \leq 1$. When $f_{jk} = 1$ the $\{f_{jk}^{(n)}\}$ is a proper probability distribution and we shall refer to it as the *first-passage distribution for E_k*. In particular, $\{f_{jj}^{(n)}\}$ represents the distribution of *the recurrence times for E_j*. The definition (5.2) is meaningful only when $f_{jj} = 1$, that is, when a return to E_j is certain. In this case $\mu_j \leq \infty$ is the *mean recurrence time for E_j*.

No actual calculation of the probabilities $f_{jk}^{(n)}$ is required for our present purposes, but for conceptual clarity we indicate how the $f_{jk}^{(n)}$ can be determined (by the standard renewal argument). If the first passage through E_k occurs at the νth trial $(1 \leq \nu \leq n - 1)$ the (conditional) probability of E_k at the nth trial equals $p_{kk}^{(n-\nu)}$. Remembering the convention that $p_{kk}^{(0)} = 1$ we conclude that

$$(5.3) \qquad\qquad p_{jk}^{(n)} = \sum_{\nu=1}^{n} f_{jk}^{(\nu)} p_{kk}^{(n-\nu)}.$$

Letting successively $n = 1, 2, \ldots$ we get recursively $f_{jk}^{(1)}, f_{jk}^{(2)}, \ldots$. Conversely, if the $f_{jk}^{(n)}$ are known for the pair j, k then (5.3) determines all the transition probabilities $p_{jk}^{(n)}$.

The first question concerning any state E_j is whether a return to it is certain. If it is certain, the question arises whether the mean recurrence time μ_j is finite or infinite. The following definition agrees with the terminology of chapter XIII.

Definition 2. *The state E_j is persistent if $f_{jj} = 1$ and transient if $f_{jj} < 1$.*

A persistent state E_j is called null state if its mean recurrence time $\mu_j = \infty$.

This definition applies also to periodic states. It classifies all persistent states into null states and non-null states. The latter are of special interest, and since we usually focus our attention on aperiodic states it is convenient to use the term ergodic for aperiodic, persistent non-null states.[10] This leads us to

Definition 3. *An aperiodic persistent state E_j with $\mu_j < \infty$ is called ergodic.*

The next theorem expresses the conditions for the different types in terms of the transition probabilities $p_{jj}^{(n)}$. It is of great importance even though the criterion contained in it is usually too difficult to be useful. Better criteria will be found in sections 7 and 8, but unfortunately there exists no simple universal criterion.

Theorem. (i) *E_j is transient if, and only if,*

$$(5.4) \qquad \sum_{n=0}^{\infty} p_{jj}^{(n)} < \infty.$$

In this case

$$(5.5) \qquad \sum_{n=1}^{\infty} p_{ij}^{(n)} < \infty$$

for all i.

(ii) *E_j is a (persistent) null state if, and only if,*

$$(5.6) \qquad \sum_{n=0}^{\infty} p_{jj}^{(n)} = \infty, \quad but \quad p_{jj}^{(n)} \to 0$$

as $n \to \infty$. In this case

$$(5.7) \qquad p_{ij}^{(n)} \to 0$$

for all i.

(iii) *An aperiodic (persistent) state E_j is ergodic if, and only if, $\mu_j < \infty$. In this case as $n \to \infty$*

$$(5.8) \qquad p_{ij}^{(n)} \to f_{ij}\mu_j^{-1}.$$

Corollary. *If E_j is aperiodic, $p_{ij}^{(n)}$ tends either to 0 or to the limit given by (5.8).*

---

[10] Unfortunately this terminology is not generally accepted. In Kolmogorov's terminology transient states are called "*unessential*," but this chapter was meant to show that the theoretical and practical interest often centers on transient states. (Modern potential theory supports this view.) Ergodic states are sometimes called "*positive*," and sometimes the term "ergodic" is used in the sense of our persistent. (In the first edition of this book persistent E_j were regretably called recurrent.)

Proof. The assertion (5.4) is contained in theorem 2 of XIII,3. The assertion (5.5) is an immediate consequence of this and (5.3), but it is also contained in theorem 1 of XIII,5.

For an aperiodic persistent state E_j theorem 3 of XIII, 3 asserts that $p_{jj}^{(n)} \to \mu_j^{-1}$, where the right side is to be interpreted as zero if $\mu_j = \infty$. The assertions (5.7) and (5.8) follow again immediately from this and (5.3), or else from theorem 1 of XIII,5.

Let E_j be persistent and $\mu_j = \infty$. By theorem 4 of XIII,3 in this case $p_{jj}^{(n)} \to 0$, and this again implies (5.7). ▶

Examples. (*b*) Consider the state E_0 of the chain of example (2.*l*). The peculiar nature of the matrix of transition probabilities shows that a first return at the nth trial can occur only through the sequence

$$E_0 \to E_1 \to E_2 \to \cdots \to E_{n-1} \to E_0,$$

and so for $n \geq 1$

$$(5.9) \qquad f_{00}^{(n)} = p_1 p_2 \cdots p_{n-1} q_n$$

and $f_{00}^{(1)} = q_1$. In the special case that the p_k are defined by (2.5) this reduces to $f_{00}^{(n)} = f_n$. Thus E_0 is transient if $\sum f_n < 1$. For a persistent E_0 the mean recurrence time μ_0 of E_0 coincides with the expectation of the distribution $\{f_n\}$. Finally, if E_0 has period t then $f_n = 0$ except when n is a multiple of t. In short, as could be expected, E_0 is under any circumstances of the same type as the recurrent event $\mathcal{E}$ associated with our Markov chain.

(*c*) In example (4.*a*) no return to E_2 is possible once the system leaves this state, and so E_2 is transient. A slight refinement of this argument shows that E_6 and E_7 are transient. From theorem 6.4 it follows easily that all other states are ergodic. ▶

6. IRREDUCIBLE CHAINS. DECOMPOSITIONS

For brevity we say that *two states are of the same type* if they agree in all characteristics defined in the preceding section. In other words, two states of the same type have the same period or they are both aperiodic; both are transient or else both are persistent; in the latter case either both mean recurrence times are infinite, or else both are finite.

The usefulness of our classification depends largely on the fact that for all practical purposes it is always possible to restrict the attention to states of one particular type. The next theorem shows that this is strictly true for irreducible chains.

Theorem 1. *All states of an irreducible chain are of the same type*

Proof. Let E_j and E_k be two arbitrary states of an irreducible chain. In view of the criterion of section 4 every state can be reached from every other state, and so there exist integers r and s such that $p_{jk}^{(r)} = \alpha > 0$ and $p_{kj}^{(s)} = \beta > 0$. Obviously

(6.1) $$p_{jj}^{(n+r+s)} \geq p_{jk}^{(r)} p_{kk}^{(n)} p_{kj}^{(s)} = \alpha\beta p_{kk}^{(n)}.$$

Here j, k, r, and s are fixed while n is arbitrary. For a transient E_j the left side is the term of a convergent series, and therefore the same is true of $p_{kk}^{(n)}$. Furthermore, if $p_{jj}^{(n)} \to 0$ then also $p_{kk}^{(n)} \to 0$. The same statements remain true when the roles of j and k are interchanged, and so either both E_j and E_k are transient, or neither is; if one is a null state, so is the other.

Finally, suppose that E_j has period t. For $n = 0$ the right side in (6.1) is positive, and hence $r + s$ is a multiple of t. But then the left side vanishes unless n is a multiple of t, and so E_k has a period which is a multiple of t. Interchanging the roles of j and k we see that these states have the same period.   ▶

The importance of theorem 1 becomes apparent in conjunction with

Theorem 2. *For a persistent E_j there exists a unique irreducible closed set C containing E_j and such that for every pair E_i, E_k of states in C*

(6.2) $$f_{ik} = 1 \quad and \quad f_{ki} = 1.$$

In other words: Starting from an arbitrary state E_i in C the system is certain to pass through every other state of C; by the definition of closure no exit from C is possible.

Proof. Let E_k be a state that can be reached from E_j. It is then obviously possible to reach E_k without previously returning to E_j, and we denote the probability of this event by α. Once E_k is reached, the probability of never returning to E_j is $1 - f_{kj}$. The probability that, starting from E_j, the system never returns to E_j is therefore at least $\alpha(1 - f_{kj})$. But for a persistent E_j the probability of no return is zero, and so $f_{kj} = 1$ for every E_k that can be reached from E_j.

Denote by C the aggregate of all states that can be reached from E_j. If E_i and E_k are in C we saw that E_j can be reached from E_k, and hence also E_i can be reached from E_k. Thus every state in C can be reached from every other state in C, and so C is irreducible by the criterion of section 4. It follows that all states in C are persistent, and so every E_i can be assigned the role of E_j in the first part of the argument. This means that $f_{ki} = 1$ for all E_k in C, and so (6.2) is true.   ▶

The preceding theorem implies that the closure of a persistent state is irreducible. This is not necessarily true of transient states.

Example. Suppose that $p_{jk} = 0$ whenever $k \leq j$, but $p_{j,j+1} > 0$. Transitions take place only to higher states, and so no return to any state is possible. Every E_j is transient, and the closure of E_j consists of the states $E_j, E_{j+1}, E_{j+2}, \ldots$, but contains the closed subset obtained by deleting E_j. It follows that there exist no irreducible sets.   ▶

The last theorem implies in particular that no transient state can ever be reached from a persistent state. If the chain contains both types of states, this means that the matrix P can be partitioned symbolically in the form (4.1) where the matrix Q corresponds to the persistent states. Needless to say, Q may be further decomposable. But every persistent state belongs to a unique *irreducible* subset, and no transition between these subsets is possible. We recapitulate this in

Theorem 3. *The states of a Markov chain can be divided, in a unique manner, into non-overlapping sets T, C_1, $C_2, \ldots$ such that*

(i) *T consists of all transient states.*

(ii) *If E_j is in C_v then $f_{jk} = 1$ for all E_k in C_v while $f_{jk} = 0$ for all E_k outside C_v.*

This implies that C_v is irreducible and contains only persistent states of the same type. The example above shows that all states can be transient, while example (4.*d*) proves the possibility of infinitely many C_v.

We derive the following theorem as a simple corollary to theorem 2, but it can be proved in other simple ways (see problems 18–20).

Theorem 4. *In a finite chain there exist no null states, and it is impossible that all states are transient.*

Proof. The rows of the matrix P^n add to unity, and as they contain a fixed number of elements it is impossible that $p_{jk}^{(n)} \to 0$ for all pairs j, k. Thus not all states are transient. But a persistent state belongs to an irreducible set C. All states of C are of the same type. The fact that C contains a persistent state and at least one non-null state therefore implies that it contains no null state.   ▶

7. INVARIANT DISTRIBUTIONS

Since every persistent state belongs to an irreducible set whose asymptotic behavior can be studied independently of the remaining states, we shall now concentrate on irreducible chains. All states of such a chain are of the same type and we begin with the simplest case, namely chains with finite mean recurrence times μ_j. To avoid trivialities we postpone the discussion of periodic chains to section 9. In other words, we consider now chains whose states are ergodic (that is, they are aperiodic and persistent with finite mean recurrence times. See definition 5.3).

Theorem. *In an irreducible chain with only ergodic elements the limits*

$$(7.1) \qquad u_k = \lim_{n \to \infty} p_{jk}^{(n)}$$

exist and are independent of the initial state j. Furthermore $u_k > 0$,

$$(7.2) \qquad \sum u_k = 1$$

and[11]

$$(7.3) \qquad u_j = \sum_i u_i p_{ij}.$$

Conversely, suppose that the chain is irreducible and aperiodic, and that there exist numbers $u_k \geq 0$ satisfying (7.2)–(7.3). Then all states are ergodic, the u_k are given by (7.1), and

$$(7.4) \qquad u_k = 1/\mu_k$$

where μ_k is the mean recurrence time of E_k.

Proof. (*i*) Suppose the chain irreducible and ergodic, and define u_k by (7.4). Theorem 6.2 guarantees that $f_{ij} = 1$ for every pair of states, and so the assertion (7.1) reduces to (5.8). Now

$$(7.5) \qquad p_{ik}^{(n+1)} = \sum_j p_{ij}^{(n)} p_{jk}.$$

As $n \to \infty$ the left side approaches u_k, while the general term of the sum on the right tends to $u_j p_{jk}$. Taking only finitely many terms we infer that

$$(7.6) \qquad u_k \geq \sum_j u_j p_{jk}.$$

For fixed i and n the left sides in (7.5) add to unity, and hence

$$(7.7) \qquad s = \sum u_k \leq 1.$$

Summing over k in (7.6) we get the relation $s \geq s$ in which the inequality sign is impossible. We conclude that in (7.6) the equality sign holds for all k, and so the first part of the theorem is true.

---

[11] If we conceive of $\{u_j\}$ as a row vector, (7.3) can be written in the matrix form $u = uP$.

(ii) Assume $u_k \geq 0$ and (7.2)–(7.3). By induction

(7.8) $$u_k = \sum_i u_i p_{ik}^{(n)}$$

for every $n > 1$. Since the chain is assumed irreducible all states are of the same type. If they were transient or null states, the right side in (7.8) would tend to 0 as $n \to \infty$, and this cannot be true for all k because the u_k add to unity. Periodic chains being excluded, this means that the states are ergodic and so the first part of the theorem applies. Thus, letting $n \to \infty$,

(7.9) $$u_k = \sum_i u_i \mu_k^{-1}.$$

Accordingly, the probability distribution $\{u_k\}$ is proportional to the probability distribution $\{\mu_k^{-1}\}$, and so $u_k = \mu_k^{-1}$ as asserted. ▶

To appreciate the meaning of the theorem consider the development of the process from an initial distribution $\{a_j\}$. The probability of the state E_k at the nth step is given by

(7.10) $$a_k^{(n)} = \sum_j a_j p_{jk}^{(n)}$$

[see (3.4)]. In view of (7.1) therefore as $n \to \infty$

(7.11) $$a_k^{(n)} \to u_k.$$

In other words, whatever the initial distribution, the probability of E_k tends to u_k. On the other hand, when $\{u_k\}$ is the initial distribution (that is, when $a_k = u_k$), then (7.3) implies $a_k^{(1)} = u_k$, and by induction $a_k^{(n)} = u_k$ for all n. Thus an initial distribution satisfying (7.3) perpetuates itself for all times. For this reason it is called invariant.

Definition. *A probability distribution $\{u_k\}$ satisfying (7.3) is called invariant or stationary (for the given Markov chain).*

The main part of the preceding theorem may now be reformulated as follows.

An irreducible aperiodic chain possesses an invariant probability distribution $\{u_k\}$ if, and only if, it is ergodic. In this case $u_k > 0$ for all k, and the absolute probabilities $a_k^{(n)}$ tend to u_k irrespective of the initial distribution.

The physical significance of stationarity becomes apparent if we imagine a large number of processes going on simultaneously. To be specific, consider N particles performing independently the same type of random walk. At the nth step the expected number of particles in state E_k equals $Na_k^{(n)}$ which tends to Nu_k. After a sufficiently long time the distribution will be approximately invariant, and the physicist would say that he observes the particles in equilibrium. The distribution $\{u_k\}$ is therefore also called *equilibrium distribution*. Unfortunately this term distracts attention from the important circumstance that it refers to a so-called *macroscopic equilibrium*, that is, an equilibrium maintained by a large number of transitions in opposite directions. The individual particle exhibits no tendency to equilibrium, and our limit theorem has no implications for the individual process. Typical in this respect is the symmetric random walk discussed in chapter III. If a large number of particles perform independently such random walks starting at the origin, then at any time roughly half of them will be to the right, the other half to the left of the origin. But this does not mean that the majority of the particles spends half their time on the positive side. On the contrary, the arc sine laws show that the majority of the particles spend a disproportionately large part of their time on the same side of the origin, and in this sense *the majority is not representative of the ensemble*. This example is radical in that it involves infinite mean recurrence times. With ergodic chains the chance fluctuations are milder, but for practical purposes they will exhibit the same character whenever the recurrence times have very large (or infinite) variances. Many protracted discussions and erroneous conclusions could be avoided by a proper understanding of the statistical nature of the "tendency toward equilibrium."

In the preceding theorem we assumed the chain irreducible and aperiodic, and it is pertinent to ask to what extent these assumptions are essential. A perusal of the proof will show that we have really proved more than is stated in the theorem. In particular we have, in passing, obtained the following criterion applicable to arbitrary chains (including periodic and reducible chains).

Criterion. *If a chain possesses an invariant probability distribution* $\{u_k\}$, *then* $u_k = 0$ *for each* E_k *that is either transient or a persistent null state.*

In other words, $u_k > 0$ implies that E_k is persistent and has a finite mean recurrence time, but E_k may be periodic.

Proof. We saw that the stationarity of $\{u_k\}$ implies (7.8). If E_k is either transient or a null state, then $p_{jk}^{(n)} \to 0$ for all j, and so $u_k = 0$ as asserted.   ▶

As for periodic chains, we anticipate the result proved in section 9 that *a unique invariant probability distribution* $\{u_k\}$ *exists for every irreducible chain whose states have finite mean recurrence times.* Periodic chains were excluded from the theorems only because the simple limit relations (7.1) and (7.11) take on a less attractive form which detracts from the essential point without really affecting it.

Examples. (*a*) Chains with several irreducible components may admit of several stationary solutions. A trite, but typical, example is presented by the random walk with two absorbing states E_0 and E_ρ [example (2.*b*)]. Every probability distribution of the form $(\alpha, 0, 0, \ldots, 0, 1 - \alpha)$, attributing positive weights only to E_0 and E_ρ, is stationary.

(*b*) Given a matrix of transition probabilities p_{jk} it is not always easy to decide whether an invariant distribution $\{u_k\}$ exists. A notable exception occurs when

$$(7.12) \qquad p_{jk} = 0 \quad for \quad |k - j| > 1,$$

that is, when all non-zero elements of the matrix are on the main diagonal or on a line directly adjacent to it. With the states numbered starting with 0 the defining relations (7.3) take on the form

$$(7.13) \qquad \begin{aligned} u_0 &= p_{00}u_0 + p_{10}u_1 \\ u_1 &= p_{01}u_0 + p_{11}u_1 + p_{21}u_2, \end{aligned}$$

and so on. To avoid trivialities we assume that $p_{j,j+1} > 0$ and $p_{j,j-1} > 0$ for all j, but nothing is assumed about the diagonal elements p_{jj}. The equations (7.13) can be solved successively for $u_1, u_2, \ldots$. Remembering that the row sums of the matrix P add to unity we get

$$(7.14) \qquad u_1 = \frac{p_{01}}{p_{10}} u_0, \qquad u_2 = \frac{p_{01}p_{12}}{p_{10}p_{21}} u_0, \qquad u_3 = \frac{p_{01}p_{12}p_{23}}{p_{10}p_{21}p_{32}} u_0,$$

and so on. The resulting (finite or infinite) sequence $u_0, u_1, \ldots$ represents the unique solution of (7.13). To make it a probability distribution the norming factor u_0 must be chosen so that $\sum u_k = 1$. Such a choice is possible if, and only if,

$$(7.15) \qquad \sum \frac{p_{01}p_{12}p_{23} \cdots p_{k-1,k}}{p_{10}p_{21}p_{32} \cdots p_{k,k-1}} < \infty.$$

This, then, is the necessary and sufficient condition for the existence of an invariant probability distribution; if it exists, it is necessarily unique. [If (7.15) is false, (7.12) is a so-called invariant measure. See section 11.]

In example (8.*d*) we shall derive a similar criterion to test whether the states are persistent. The following three examples illustrate the applicability of our criterion.

(c) *Reflecting barriers.* The example (2.c) (with $\rho \leq \infty$) represents the special case of the preceding example with $p_{j,j+1} = p$ for all $j < \rho$ and $p_{j,j-1} = q$ for all $j > 1$. When the number of states is finite there exists an invariant distribution with u_k proportional to $(p/q)^k$. With infinitely many states the convergence of (7.15) requires that $p < q$, and in this case $u_k = (1 - p/q)(p/q)^k$. From the general theory of random walks it is clear that the states are transient when $p > q$, and persistent null states when $p = q$. This will follow also from the criterion in example (8.d).

(d) *The Ehrenfest model of diffusion.* For the matrix of example (2.e) the solution (7.14) reduces to

$$(7.16) \qquad\qquad u_k = \binom{\rho}{k} u_0, \qquad\qquad k = 0, \ldots, \rho.$$

The binomial coefficients are the terms in the binomial expansion for $(1+1)^\rho$, and to obtain a probability distribution we must therefore put $u_0 = 2^{-\rho}$. The chain has period 2, the states have finite mean recurrence times, and *the binomial distribution with $p = \frac{1}{2}$ is invariant.*

This result can be interpreted as follows: Whatever the initial number of molecules in the first container, after a long time the probability of finding k molecules in it is nearly the same as if the a molecules had been distributed at random, each molecule having probability $\frac{1}{2}$ to be in the first container. This is a typical example of how our result gains physical significance.

For large a the normal approximation to the binomial distribution shows that, once the limiting distribution is approximately established, we are practically certain to find about one-half the molecules in each container. To the physicist $a = 10^6$ is a small number, indeed. But even with $a = 10^6$ molecules the probability of finding more than 505,000 molecules in one container (density fluctuation of about 1 per cent) is of the order of magnitude 10^{-23}. With $a = 10^8$ a density fluctuation of one in a thousand has the same negligible probability. It is true that the system will occasionally pass into very improbable states, but their recurrence times are fantastically large as compared to the recurrence times of states near the equilibrium. Physical irreversibility manifests itself in the fact that, whenever the system is in a state far removed from equilibrium, it is much more likely to move toward equilibrium than in the opposite direction.

(e) *The Bernoulli-Laplace model of diffusion.* For the matrix with elements (2.1) we get from (7.14)

$$(7.17) \qquad\qquad u_k = \binom{\rho}{k}^2 u_0, \qquad\qquad k = 0, \ldots, \rho.$$

The binomial coefficients add to $\binom{2\rho}{\rho}$ [see II,(12.11)], and hence

(7.18) $$u_k = \binom{\rho}{k}^2 \bigg/ \binom{2\rho}{\rho}$$

represents *an invariant distribution*. It is a hypergeometric distribution (see II,6). This means that in the state of equilibrium the distribution of colors in each container is the same as if the ρ particles in it had been chosen at random from a collection of ρ black and ρ white particles.

(f) In example (2.l) the defining relations for an invariant probability distribution are

(7.19a) $$u_k = p_k u_{k-1} \qquad\qquad k = 1, 2, \ldots$$

(7.19b) $$u_0 = q_1 u_0 + q_2 u_1 + q_3 u_2 + \cdots.$$

From (7.19a) we get

(7.20) $$u_k = p_1 \cdots p_k u_0,$$

and it is now easily seen that the first k terms on the right in (7.19b) add to $u_0 - u_k$. Thus (7.19b) is automatically satisfied whenever $u_k \to 0$, and *an invariant probability distribution exists if, and only if,*

(7.21) $$\sum_k p_1 p_2 \cdots p_k < \infty.$$

[See also examples (8.e) and (11.c).]

(g) *Recurrent events.* In example (2.k) the conditions for an invariant probability distribution reduce to

(7.22) $$u_k = u_{k+1} + f_{k+1} u_0 \qquad\qquad k = 0, 1, \ldots.$$

Adding over $k = 0, 1, \ldots$ we get

(7.23) $$u_n = r_n u_0, \qquad where \quad r_n = f_{n+1} + f_{n+2} + \cdots.$$

Now $r_0 + r_1 \cdots = \mu$ is the expectation of the distributions. *An invariant probability distribution is given by* $u_n = r_n/\mu$ *if* $\mu < \infty$; no such probability distribution exists when $\mu = \infty$.

It will be recalled that our Markov chain is connected with a recurrent event $\mathcal{E}$ with recurrence time distribution $\{f_k\}$. In the special case $p_k = r_k/r_{k-1}$ the chain of the preceding example is connected with the same recurrent event $\mathcal{E}$ and in this case (7.20) and (7.23) are equivalent. Hence *the invariant distributions are the same.* In the language of queuing theory one should say that the *spent waiting time and the residual waiting time tend to the same distribution,* namely $\{r_n/\mu\}$.

We derived the basic limit theorems for Markov chains from the theory of recurrent events. We now see that, conversely, recurrent events could be treated as special Markov chains. [See also example (11.d).]

(*h*) *Doubly stochastic matrices.* A stochastic matrix P is called doubly stochastic if not only the row sums but also the column sums are unity. If such a chain contains only a finite number, a, of states then $u_k = a^{-1}$ represents an invariant distribution. This means that in macroscopic equilibrium all states are equally probable.   ▶

8. TRANSIENT STATES

We saw in section 6 that the persistent states of any Markov chain may be divided into non-overlapping closed irreducible sets $C_1, C_2, \ldots$. In general there exists also a non-empty class T of transient states. When the system starts from a transient state two contingencies arise: Either the system ultimately passes into one of the closed sets C_ν and stays there forever, or else the system remains forever in the transient set T. Our main problem consists in determining the corresponding probabilities. Its solution will supply a criterion for deciding whether a state is persistent or transient.

Examples. (*a*) *Martingales.* A chain is called a martingale if for every j the expectation of the probability distribution $\{p_{jk}\}$ equals j, that is, if

$$(8.1) \qquad \sum_k p_{jk} k = j.$$

Consider a finite chain with states $E_0, \ldots, E_a$. Letting $j = 0$ and $j = a$ in (8.1) we see that $p_{00} = p_{aa} = 1$, and so E_0 and E_a are absorbing. To avoid trivialities we assume that the chain contains no further closed sets. It follows that the interior states $E_1, \ldots, E_{a-1}$ are transient, and so the process will ultimately terminate either at E_0 or at E_a. From (8.1) we infer by induction that for all n

$$(8.2) \qquad \sum_{k=0}^{a} p_{ik}^{(n)} k = i.$$

But $p_{ik}^{(n)} \to 0$ for every transient E_k, and so (8.2) implies that for all $i > 0$

$$(8.3) \qquad p_{ia}^{(n)} \to i/a.$$

In other words, if the process starts with E_i *the probabilities of ultimate absorption at E_0 and E_a are $1 - i/a$ and i/a, respectively.*

(b) *Special cases.* The chains of the examples from genetics (2.*h*) and (2.*i*) are of the form discussed in the preceding example with $a = N$ and $a = 2N$, respectively. Given the initial state E_i, the probability of ultimate fixation at E_0 is therefore $1 - i/a$.

(c) Consider a chain with states E_0, E_1, ... such that E_0 is absorbing while from other states E_j transitions are possible to the right neighbor E_{j+1} and to E_0, but to no other state. For $j \geq 1$ we put

$$(8.4) \qquad\qquad p_{j0} = \epsilon_j, \qquad p_{j,j+1} = 1 - \epsilon_j$$

where $\epsilon_j > 0$. With the initial state E_j the probability of no absorption at E_0 in n trials equals

$$(8.5) \qquad\qquad (1 - \epsilon_j)(1 - \epsilon_{j+1}) \cdots (1 - \epsilon_{j+n-1}).$$

This product decreases with increasing n and hence it approaches a limit λ_j. We infer that the probability of ultimate absorption equals $1 - \lambda_j$ while with probability λ_j the system remains forever at transient states. In order that $\lambda_j > 0$ it is necessary and sufficient that $\sum \epsilon_k < \infty$. ▶

The study of the transient states depends on the submatrix of P obtained by deleting all rows and columns corresponding to persistent states and retaining only the elements p_{jk} for which both E_j and E_k are transient. The row sums of this submatrix are no longer unity, and it is convenient to introduce the

Definition. *A square matrix* Q *with elements* q_{ik} *is substochastic if* $q_{ik} \geq 0$ *and all row sums are* ≤ 1.

In the sense of this definition every stochastic matrix is substochastic and, conversely, every substochastic matrix can be enlarged to a stochastic matrix by adding an absorbing state E_0. (In other words, we add a top row $1, 0, 0, \ldots$ and a column whose elements are the defects of the rows of Q.) It is therefore obvious that what was said about stochastic matrices applies without essential change also to substochastic matrices. In particular, the recursion relation (3.2) defines the nth power Q^n as the matrix with elements

$$(8.6) \qquad\qquad q_{ik}^{(n+1)} = \sum_v q_{iv} q_{vk}^{(n)}.$$

Denote by $\sigma_i^{(n)}$ the sum of the elements in the ith row of Q^n. Then for $n \geq 1$

$$(8.7) \qquad\qquad \sigma_i^{(n+1)} = \sum_v q_{iv} \sigma_v^{(n)},$$

and this relation remains valid also for $n = 0$ provided we put $\sigma_v^{(0)} = 1$ for all v. The fact that Q is substochastic means that $\sigma_i^{(1)} \leq \sigma_i^{(0)}$, and from (8.7) we see now by induction that $\sigma_i^{(n+1)} \leq \sigma_i^{(n)}$. For fixed i therefore the sequence $\{\sigma_i^{(n)}\}$ decreases monotonically to a limit $\sigma_i \geq 0$, and clearly

$$(8.8) \qquad\qquad \sigma_i = \sum_v q_{iv}\sigma_v.$$

The whole theory of the transient states depends on the solutions of this system of equations. In some cases there exists no non-zero solution (that is, we have $\sigma_i = 0$ for all i). In others, there may exist infinitely many linearly independent solutions, that is, different sequences of numbers satisfying

$$(8.9) \qquad\qquad x_i = \sum_v q_{iv}x_v.$$

Our first problem is to characterize the particular solution $\{\sigma_i\}$. We are interested only in solutions $\{x_i\}$ such that $0 \leq x_i \leq 1$ for all i. This can be rewritten in the form $0 \leq x_i \leq \sigma_i^{(0)}$; comparing (8.9) with (8.7) we see inductively that $x_i \leq \sigma_i^{(n)}$ for all n, and so

$$(8.10) \qquad\qquad 0 \leq x_i \leq 1 \quad \textit{implies} \quad x_i \leq \sigma_i \leq 1.$$

The solution $\{\sigma_i\}$ will be called *maximal*, but it must be borne in mind that in many cases $\sigma_i = 0$ for all i. We summarize this result in the following

Lemma. *For a substochastic matrix Q the linear system* (8.9) *possesses a maximal solution* $\{\sigma_i\}$ *with the property* (8.10). *These* σ_i *represent the limits of the row sums of* Q^n.

We now identify Q with the submatrix of P obtained by retaining only the elements p_{jk} for which E_j and E_k are transient. The linear system (8.9) may then be written in the form

$$(8.11) \qquad\qquad x_i = \sum_T p_{iv}x_v, \qquad\qquad E_i \in T,$$

the summation extending only over those v for which E_v belongs to the class T of transient states. With this identification $\sigma_i^{(n)}$ is the probability that, with the initial state E_i, no transition to a persistent state occurs during the first n trials. Hence the limit σ_i equals the probability that no such transition ever occurs. We have thus

Theorem 1. *The probabilities x_i that, starting from E_i that the system stays forever among the transient states are given by the maximal solution of* (8.11).

The same argument leads to the

Criterion. *In an irreducible[12] Markov chain with states* $E_0, E_1, \ldots$
the state E_0 *is persistent if, and only if, the linear system*

$$(8.12) \qquad\qquad x_i = \sum_{v=1}^{\infty} p_{iv} x_v, \qquad\qquad i \geq 1$$

admits of no solution with $0 \leq x_i \leq 1$ *except* $x_i = 0$ *for all* i.

Proof. We identify the matrix Q of the lemma with the submatrix of P obtained by deleting the row and column corresponding to E_0. The argument used for theorem 1 shows that σ_i is the probability that (with E_i as initial state) the system remains forever among the states $E_1, E_2, \ldots$. But if E_0 is persistent the probability f_{i0} of reaching E_0 equals 1, and hence $\sigma_i = 0$ for all i. ▶

Examples. (*d*) As in example (7.*b*) we consider a chain with states $E_0, E_1, \ldots$ such that

$$(8.13) \qquad\qquad p_{jk} = 0 \qquad when \qquad |k - j| > 1.$$

To avoid trivialities we assume that $p_{j,j+1} \neq 0$ and $p_{j,j-1} \neq 0$. The chain is irreducible because every state can be reached from every other state. Thus all states are of the same type, and it suffices to test the character of E_0. The equations (8.12) reduce to the recursive system

$$(8.14) \qquad\qquad x_1 = p_{11} x_1 + p_{12} x_2$$
$$p_{j,j-1}(x_j - x_{j-1}) = p_{j,j+1}(x_{j+1} - x_j), \qquad\qquad j \geq 2.$$

Thus

$$(8.15) \qquad\qquad x_j - x_{j+1} = \frac{p_{21} p_{32} \cdots p_{j,j-1}}{p_{23} p_{34} \cdots p_{j,j+1}} (x_1 - x_2).$$

Since $p_{10} > 0$ we have $x_2 - x_1 > 0$, and so a bounded non-negative solution $\{x_j\}$ exists if, and only if,

$$(8.16) \qquad\qquad \sum \frac{p_{21} \cdots p_{j,j-1}}{p_{23} \cdots p_{j,j+1}} < \infty.$$

The chain is persistent if, and only if, the series diverges. In the special case of random walks we have $p_{j,j+1} = p$ and $p_{j,j-1} = q$ for all $j > 1$, and we see again that the states are persistent if, and only if, $p \leq q$.

---

[12] Irreducibility is assumed only to avoid notational complications. It represents no restriction because it suffices to consider the closure of E_0. Incidentally, the criterion applies also to periodic chains.

(This chain may be interpreted as a random walk on the line with probabilities varying from place to place.)

(e) For the matrix of example (2.l) the equations (8.12) reduce to

$$(8.17) \qquad x_j = p_{j+1}x_{j+1}$$

and a bounded positive solution exists if, and only if, the infinite product $p_1 p_2 \cdots$ converges. If the chain is associated with a recurrent event $\mathcal{E}$, the p_k are given by (2.5) and the product converges if, and only if, $\sum f_j < \infty$. Thus (as could be anticipated) the chain and $\mathcal{E}$ are either both transient, or both persistent. ▶

To answer the last question proposed at the beginning of this section, denote again by T the class of transient states and let C be any *closed* set of persistent states. (It is not required that C be irreducible.) Denote by y_i *the probability of ultimate absorption in* C, given the initial state E_i. We propose to show that the y_i satisfy the system of inhomogeneous equations

$$(8.18) \qquad y_i = \sum_T p_{iv}y_v + \sum_C p_{iv}, \qquad\qquad E_i \in T,$$

the summations extending over those v for which $E_v \in T$ and $E_v \in C$, respectively. The system (8.18) may admit of several independent solutions, but the following proof will show that among them there exists a *minimal* solution defined in the obvious manner by analogy with (8.10).

Theorem 2. *The probabilities* y_i *of ultimate absorption in the closed persistent set* C *are given by the minimal non-negative solution of* (8.18).

Proof. Denote by $y_i^{(n)}$ the probability that an absorption in C takes place at or before the nth step. Then for $n \geq 1$ clearly

$$(8.19) \qquad y_i^{(n+1)} = \sum_T p_{iv}y_v^{(n)} + \sum_C p_{iv}$$

and this is true also for $n = 0$ provided we put $y_v^{(0)} = 0$ for all v. For fixed i the sequence $\{y_i^{(n)}\}$ is non-decreasing, but it remains bounded by 1. The limits obviously satisfy (8.18). Conversely, if $\{y_i\}$ is any non-negative solution of (8.18) we have $y_i \geq y_i^{(1)}$ because the second sum in (8.18) equals $y_i^{(1)}$. By induction $y_i \geq y_i^{(n)}$ for all n, and so the limits of $y_i^{(n)}$ represent a minimal solution. ▶

For an illustration see example (c).

*9. PERIODIC CHAINS

Periodic chains present no difficulties and no unexpected new features. They were excluded in the formulation of the main theorem in section 7 only because they are of secondary interest and their description requires disproportionately many words. The discussion of this section is given for the sake of completeness rather than for its intrinsic interest. The results of this section will not be used in the sequel.

The simplest example of a chain with period 3 is a chain with three states in which only the transitions $E_1 \to E_2 \to E_3 \to E_1$ are possible. Then

$$P = \begin{pmatrix} 0 & 1 & 0 \\ 0 & 0 & 1 \\ 1 & 0 & 0 \end{pmatrix}, \qquad P^2 = \begin{pmatrix} 0 & 0 & 1 \\ 1 & 0 & 0 \\ 0 & 1 & 0 \end{pmatrix}, \qquad P^3 = \begin{pmatrix} 1 & 0 & 0 \\ 0 & 1 & 0 \\ 0 & 0 & 1 \end{pmatrix}.$$

We shall now show that this example is in many respects typical.

Consider an irreducible chain with finitely or infinitely many states $E_1, E_2, \ldots$. By theorem 6.1 all states have the same period t (we assume $t > 1$). Since in an irreducible chain every state can be reached from every other state there exist for every state E_k two integers a and b such that $p_{1k}^{(a)} > 0$ and $p_{k1}^{(b)} > 0$. But $p_{11}^{(a+b)} \geq p_{1k}^{(a)} p_{k1}^{(b)}$ and so $a + b$ must be divisible by the period t. Keeping b fixed we conclude that each integer a for which $p_{1k}^{(a)} > 0$ is of the form $\alpha + \nu t$ where α is a fixed integer with $0 \leq \alpha < t$. The integer α is characteristic of the state E_k and so all states can be divided into t mutually exclusive classes $G_0, \ldots, G_{t-1}$ such that

(9.1) $\qquad$ if $E_k \in G_\alpha$ then $p_{1k}^{(n)} = 0$ $\qquad$ unless $n = \alpha + \nu t$.

We imagine the classes $G_0, \ldots, G_{t-1}$ ordered cyclically so that G_{t-1} is the left neighbor of G_0.

It is now obvious that *one-step* transitions are possible only to a state in the neighboring class to the right, and hence a path of t steps leads always to a state of the same class. This implies that in the Markov chain with transition matrix P^t each class G_α forms a closed set.[13] This

---

[13] When $t = 3$ there are three classes and with the symbolic partitioning introduced in section 4 the matrix P takes on the form

$$\begin{pmatrix} 0 & A & 0 \\ 0 & 0 & B \\ C & 0 & 0 \end{pmatrix}$$

where A represents the matrix of transition probabilities from G_0 to G_1, and so on.

set is irreducible because in the original chain every state can be reached from any other state and within the same class the required number of steps is necessarily divisible by t. We have thus proved the

Theorem. *In an irreducible chain with period t the states can be divided into t mutually exclusive classes $G_0, \ldots, G_{t-1}$ such that* (9.1) *holds and a one-step transition always leads to a state in the right neighboring class* (*in particular, from G_{t-1} to G_0*). *In the chain with matrix P^t each class G_α corresponds to an irreducible closed set.*

Using this theorem it is now easy to describe the asymptotic behavior of the transition probabilities $p_{jk}^{(n)}$. We know that $p_{jk}^{(n)} \to 0$ if E_k is either transient or a persistent null state, and also that all states are of the same type (section 6). We need therefore consider only the case where each state E_k has a finite mean recurrence time μ_k. Relative to the chain with matrix P^t the state E_k has the mean recurrence time μ_k/t, and relative to this chain each class G_α is ergodic. Thus, if E_j belongs to G_α

$$(9.2) \qquad \lim_{n \to \infty} p_{jk}^{(nt)} = \begin{cases} t/\mu_k & \text{if } E_k \in G_\alpha \\ 0 & \text{otherwise} \end{cases}$$

and the weights t/μ_k define a probability distribution on the states of the class G_α (see the theorem of section 7). Since there are t such classes *the numbers $u_k = 1/\mu_k$ define a probability distribution on the integers* as was the case for aperiodic chains. We show that this distribution is invariant. For this purpose we need relations corresponding to (9.2) when the exponent is not divisible by the period t.

We start from the fundamental relation

$$(9.3) \qquad p_{jk}^{(nt+\beta)} = \sum_v p_{jv}^{(\beta)} p_{vk}^{(nt)}.$$

The factor $p_{jv}^{(\beta)}$ vanishes except when E_v is in $G_{\alpha+\beta}$. (When $\alpha + \beta \geq t$ read $G_{\alpha+\beta-t}$ for $G_{\alpha+\beta}$.) In this case $p_{vk}^{(nt)}$ vanishes unless E_k is in $G_{\alpha+\beta}$, and hence for fixed β and E_j in G_α

$$(9.4) \qquad \lim_{n \to \infty} p_{jk}^{(nt+\beta)} = \begin{cases} t/\mu_k & \text{if } E_k \in G_{\alpha+\beta} \\ 0 & \text{otherwise.} \end{cases}$$

We now rewrite (9.3) in the form

$$(9.5) \qquad p_{ik}^{(nt+1)} = \sum_v p_{iv}^{(nt)} p_{vk}.$$

Consider an arbitrary state E_k and let G_ρ be the class to which it belongs. Then $p_{vk} = 0$ unless $E_v \in G_{\rho-1}$, and so both sides in (9.5) vanish unless

$E_i \in G_{\rho-1}$. In this case $p_{ik}^{(nt+1)} \to tu_k$ whence

$$(9.6) \qquad\qquad u_k = \sum_v u_v p_{vk}.$$

Since E_k is an arbitrary state we have proved that *the probability distribution $\{u_k\}$ is invariant.*

10. APPLICATION TO CARD SHUFFLING

A deck of N cards numbered $1, 2, \ldots, N$ can be arranged in $N!$ different orders, and each represents a possible state of the system. Every particular shuffling operation effects a transition from the existing state into some other state. For example, "cutting" will change the order $(1, 2, \ldots, N)$ into one of the N cyclically equivalent orders $(r, r+1, \ldots, N, 1, 2, \ldots, r - 1)$. The same operation applied to the inverse order $(N, N - 1, \ldots, 1)$ will produce $(N - r + 1, N - r, \ldots, 1, N, N - 1, \ldots, N - r + 2)$. In other words, we conceive of each particular shuffling operation as a transformation $E_j \to E_k$. If *exactly* the same operation is repeated, the system will pass (starting from the given state E_j) through a well-defined succession of states, and after a finite number of steps the original order will be re-established. From then on the same succession of states will recur periodically. For most operations the period will be rather small, and in *no* case can all states be reached by this procedure.[14] For example, a perfect "lacing" would change a deck of $2m$ cards from $(1, \ldots, 2m)$ into $(1, m+1, 2, m+2, \ldots, m, 2m)$. With six cards four applications of this operation will re-establish the original order. With ten cards the initial order will reappear after six operations, so that repeated perfect lacing of a deck of ten cards can produce only six out of the $10! = 3,628,800$ possible orders.

In practice the player may wish to vary the operation, and at any rate, accidental variations will be introduced by chance. We shall assume that we can account for the player's habits and the influence of chance variations by assuming that every particular operation has a certain probability (possibly zero). We need assume nothing about the numerical values of these probabilities but shall suppose that the player operates without regard to the past and does not know the order of the cards.[15] This implies that the successive operations correspond to independent trials with fixed probabilities; for the actual deck of cards we then have a Markov chain.

---

[14] In the language of group theory this amounts to saying that the permutation group is not cyclic and can therefore not be generated by a single operation.

[15] This assumption corresponds to the usual situation at bridge. It is easy to devise more complicated shuffling techniques in which the operations depend on previous operations and the final outcome is not a Markov chain [cf. example (13.e)].

We now show that the matrix P of transition probabilities is *doubly stochastic* [example (7.h)]. In fact, if an operation changes a state (order of cards) E_j to E_k, then there exists another state E_r which it will change into E_j. This means that the elements of the jth column of P are identical with the elements of the jth row, except that they appear in a different order. All column sums are therefore unity.

It follows that no state can be transient. *If the chain is irreducible and aperiodic, then in the limit all states become equally probable.* In other words, *any* kind of shuffling will do, provided only that it produces an irreducible and aperiodic chain. It is safe to assume that this is usually the case. Suppose, however, that the deck contains an even number of cards and the procedure consists in dividing them equally into two parts and shuffling them separately by any method. If the two parts are put together in their original order, then the Markov chain is reducible (since not every state can be reached from every other state). If the order of the two parts is inverted, the chain will have period 2. Thus both contingencies can arise in theory, but hardly in practice, since chance precludes perfect regularity.

It is seen that continued shuffling may reasonably be expected to produce perfect "randomness" and to eliminate all traces of the original order. It should be noted, however, that the number of operations required for this purpose is extremely large.[16]

*11. INVARIANT MEASURES. RATIO LIMIT THEOREMS

In this section we consider an irreducible chain with persistent null states. Our main objective is to derive analogues to the results obtained in section 7 for chains whose states have finite mean recurrence times. An outstanding property of such chains is the existence of an invariant (or stationary) probability distribution defined by

$$(11.1) \qquad u_k = \sum_v u_v p_{vk}.$$

We know that no such invariant probability distribution exists when the mean recurrence times are infinite, but we shall show that the linear

---

* The next two sections treat topics playing an important role in contemporary research, but the results will not be used in this book.

[16] For an analysis of unbelievably poor results of shuffling in records of extrasensory perception experiments, see W. Feller, *Statistical aspects of ESP*, Journal of Parapsychology, vol. 4 (1940), pp. 271–298. In their amazing *A review of Dr. Feller's critique, ibid.*, pp. 299–319, J. A. Greenwood and C. E. Stuart try to show that these results are due to chance. Both their arithmetic and their experiments have a distinct tinge of the supernatural.

system (11.1) still admits of a positive solution $\{u_k\}$ such that $\sum u_k = \infty$. Such $\{u_k\}$ is called *an invariant (or stationary) measure*. If the chain is irreducible and persistent, the invariant measure is unique up to an arbitrary norming constant.

Examples. (*a*) Suppose that the matrix P of transition probabilities is doubly stochastic, that is, the column sums as well as the row sums are unity. Then (11.1) holds with $u_k = 1$ for all k. This fact is expressed by saying that the *uniform measure is invariant*.

(*b*) *Random walks.* An interesting special case is provided by the unrestricted random walk on the line. We number the states in their natural order from $-\infty$ to ∞. This precludes exhibiting the transition probabilities in the standard form of a matrix, but the necessary changes of notation are obvious. If the transitions to the right and left neighbors have probabilities p and q, respectively, the system (11.1) takes on the form

$$u_k = pu_{k-1} + qu_{k+1}, \qquad\qquad -\infty < k < \infty.$$

The states are persistent only if $p = q = \frac{1}{2}$, and in this case $u_k = 1$ represents the only positive solution. This solution remains valid if $p \neq q$, except that it is no longer unique; a second non-negative solution is represented by $u_k = (p/q)^k$. This example proves that an invariant measure may exist also for transient chains, but it need not be unique. We shall return to this interesting point in the next section.

The invariant $\{u_j\}$ measure can be interpreted intuitively if one considers simultaneously infinitely many processes subject to the same matrix P of transition probabilities. For each j define a random variable $\mathbf{N}_j$ with a Poisson distribution with mean u_j, and consider $\mathbf{N}_j$ independent processes starting from E_j. We do this simultaneously for all states, assuming that all these processes are mutually independent. It is not difficult to show that at any given time with probability one only finitely many processes will be found in any given state E_k. The number of processes found at the nth step in state E_k is therefore a random variable $\mathbf{X}_k^{(n)}$ and *the invariance of* $\{u_k\}$ *implies that* $\mathbf{E}\{\mathbf{X}_k^{(n)}\} = u_k$ *for all* n. (Cf. problem 29.)

(*c*) In example (7.*f*) we found that an invariant probability distribution exists only if the series (7.21) converges. In case of divergence (7.20) still represents an invariant measure provided only that $u_k \to 0$, which is the same as $p_1 p_2 \cdots p_k \to 0$. No invariant measure exists when the product $p_1 \cdots p_k$ remains bounded away from 0, for example, when $p_k = 1 - (k+1)^{-2}$. In this case the chain is transient.

(*d*) In example (7.*g*) the relations (7.23) define an invariant measure even when $\mu = \infty$.   ▶

In ergodic chains the probabilities $p_{jk}^{(n)}$ tend to the term u_k of the invariant probability distribution. For persistent null chains we shall prove a weaker version of this result, namely that as $N \to \infty$ for all E_α and E_β

$$(11.2) \qquad \frac{\sum\limits_{n=0}^{N} p_{\alpha i}^{(n)}}{\sum\limits_{n=0}^{N} p_{\beta j}^{(n)}} \to \frac{u_i}{u_j}.$$

The sums on the left represent the expected numbers of passages, in the first N trials, through E_i and E_j. Roughly speaking (11.2) states that these expectations are asymptotically independent of the initial states E_α and E_β, and stand in the same proportion as the corresponding terms of the invariant measures. Thus the salient facts are the same as in the case of ergodic chains, although the situation is more complicated. On the other hand, periodic chains now require no special consideration. [In fact (11.2) covers *all* persistent chains. For an ergodic chain the numerator on the left is $\sim N u_i$.]

Relations of the form (11.2) are called *ratio limit theorems*. We shall derive (11.2) from a stronger result which was until recently considered a more complicated refinement. Our proofs will be based on considering only paths avoiding a particular state E_r. Following Chung we call the forbidden state E_r *taboo*, and the transition probabilities to it are *taboo probabilities*.

Definition. *Let E_r be an arbitrary, but fixed, state. For $E_k \neq E_r$ and $n \geq 1$ we define $_r p_{jk}^{(n)}$ as the probability that, starting from E_j, the state E_k is entered at the nth step without a previous passage through E_r.*

Here E_j is allowed to coincide with E_r. We extend this definition to $E_k = E_r$ and $n = 0$ in the natural way by

$$(11.3) \qquad _r p_{jr}^{(n)} = 0 \qquad\qquad n \geq 1$$

and

$$(11.4) \qquad _r p_{jk}^{(0)} = \begin{cases} 1 & \text{if } E_j = E_k \\ 0 & \text{otherwise.} \end{cases}$$

In analytical terms we have for $n \geq 0$ and $E_k \neq E_r$

$$(11.5) \qquad _r p_{jk}^{(n+1)} = \sum_v {_r p_{jv}^{(n)}} p_{vk}.$$

In fact, for $n = 0$ the sum on the right reduces to a single term, namely p_{jk}. When $n \geq 1$ the term corresponding to $v = r$ vanishes by virtue of (11.3), and so (11.5) is equivalent to the original definition.

Introducing E_r as taboo state amounts to considering the original Markov process only until E_r is entered for the first time. In an irreducible persistent chain the state E_r is entered with probability one from any initial state E_j. It follows that in the chain with taboo E_r the successive passages through the initial state E_j form a *transient* recurrent event; and the passages through any other state $E_k \neq E_r$ form a delayed transient recurrent event. Thus for $E_k \neq E_r$

$$(11.6) \qquad \sum_{n=0}^{\infty} {}_r p_{jk}^{(n)} = {}_r \pi_{jk} < \infty$$

by the basic theorem 2 of XIII,3. For $E_k = E_r$ the summands with $n \geq 1$ vanish and the sum reduces to 1 or 0 according as $j = r$ or $j \neq r$.

We are now in a position to prove the existence of an invariant measure, that is, of numbers u_k satisfying (11.1). This will not be used in the proof of theorem 2.

Theorem 1. *If the chain is irreducible and persistent, the numbers*

$$(11.7) \qquad u_k = {}_r \pi_{rk}$$

represent an invariant measure; furthermore $u_k > 0$ for all k and $u_r = 1$.
Conversely, if $u_k \geq 0$ for all k and (11.1) holds, then there exists a constant λ such that $u_k = \lambda \cdot {}_r \pi_{rk}$.

Here E_r is arbitrary, but the asserted uniqueness implies that the sequences $\{u_k\}$ obtained by varying r differ only by proportionality factors. Note that the theorem and its proof cover also chains with finite mean recurrence times.

Proof. If $k \neq r$ we use (11.5) with $j = r$. Summing over $n = 0$, $1, \ldots$ we get

$$(11.8) \qquad {}_r \pi_{rk} = \sum_v {}_r \pi_{rv} p_{vk},$$

and so the numbers (11.7) satisfy the defining equations (11.1) at least when $k \neq r$. For $j = k = r$ it is clear that

$$(11.9) \qquad \sum_v {}_r p_{rv}^{(n)} p_{vr} = f_{rr}^{(n+1)}$$

equals the probability that (in the original chain) the first return to E_r occurs at the $(n+1)$st step. Since the chain is irreducible and persistent these probabilities add to unity. Summing (11.9) over $n = 0, 1, \ldots$ we get therefore

(11.10)
$$\sum_{v} {}_r\pi_{rv}p_{vr} = 1.$$

But by definition ${}_r\pi_{rr} = 1$, and so (11.8) is true also for $k = r$. Accordingly (11.7) represents an invariant measure.

Next consider an arbitrary non-negative invariant measure $\{u_k\}$. It is clear from the definition (11.1) that if $u_k = 0$ for some k, then $u_v = 0$ for all v such that $p_{vk} > 0$. By induction it follows that $u_v = 0$ for every v such that E_k can be reached from E_v. As the chain is irreducible this implies that $u_v = 0$ for all v. Thus an invariant measure is strictly positive (or identically zero).

For the converse part of the theorem we may therefore assume that the given invariant measure is normed by the condition $u_r = 1$ for some prescribed r. Then

(11.11)
$$u_k = p_{kr} + \sum_{j \neq r} u_j p_{jk}.$$

Suppose $k \neq r$. We express the u_j inside the sum by means of the defining relation (11.1) and separate again the term involving u_r in the double sum. The result is

(11.12)
$$u_k = p_{rk} + {}_r p_{rk}^{(2)} + \sum_{v \neq r} u_v \cdot {}_r p_{vk}^{(2)}.$$

Proceeding in like manner we get for every n

(11.13)
$$u_k = p_{rk} + {}_r p_{rk}^{(2)} + \cdots + {}_r p_{rk}^{(n)} + \sum_{v \neq r} u_v \cdot {}_r p_{vk}^{(n)}.$$

Letting $n \to \infty$ we see that $u_k \geq {}_r\pi_{rk}$. It follows that $\{u_k - {}_r\pi_{rk}\}$ defines an invariant measure vanishing for the particular value $k = r$. But such a measure vanishes identically, and so (11.7) is true. ▶

It will be seen presently that the following theorem represents a sharpening of the ratio limit theorem.

Theorem 2. *In an irreducible persistent chain*

(11.14)
$$0 \leq \sum_{n=0}^{N} p_{kk}^{(n)} - \sum_{n=0}^{N} p_{\alpha k}^{(n)} \leq {}_\alpha\pi_{kk}$$

and

(11.15)
$$-1 \leq \frac{1}{{}_j\pi_{ii}} \sum_{n=0}^{N} p_{ii}^{(n)} - \frac{1}{{}_i\pi_{jj}} \sum_{n=0}^{N} p_{jj}^{(n)} \leq 1$$

for all N.

Proof of (11.14). Consider the first entry to E_k; it is clear that for $\alpha \neq k$

$$(11.16) \qquad p_{\alpha k}^{(n)} = \sum_{\nu=1}^{n} f_{\alpha k}^{(\nu)} p_{kk}^{(n-\nu)}.$$

[This is the same as (5.3).] Summing over n we get

$$(11.17) \qquad \sum_{n=0}^{N} p_{\alpha k}^{(n)} \leq \sum_{n=0}^{N} p_{kk}^{(n)} \cdot \sum_{\nu=1}^{\infty} f_{\alpha k}^{(\nu)} = \sum_{n=0}^{N} p_{kk}^{(n)}$$

which proves the first inequality in (11.14).

Next we note that, starting from E_k, a return to E_k may occur without intermediate passage through E_α, or else, a first entry to E_α occurs at the νth step with $1 \leq \nu < n$. This means that

$$(11.18) \qquad p_{kk}^{(n)} = {}_\alpha p_{kk}^{(n)} + \sum_{\nu=1}^{n} f_{k\alpha}^{(\nu)} p_{\alpha k}^{(n-\nu)}.$$

Summation over n leads to the second inequality in (11.14).

Proof of (11.15). On account of the obvious symmetry in i and j it suffices to prove the second inequality. We start from the identity

$$(11.19) \qquad p_{ii}^{(n)} = {}_j p_{ii}^{(n)} + \sum_{\nu=1}^{n-1} p_{ij}^{(n-\nu)} \cdot {}_j p_{ji}^{(\nu)}$$

which expresses the fact that a return from E_i to E_i occurs either without intermediate passage through E_j, or else the *last* entry to E_j occurs at the $(n-\nu)$th step and the next ν steps lead from E_j to E_i without further return to E_j. Summing over n we get

$$(11.20) \qquad \begin{aligned} \sum_{n=0}^{N} p_{ii}^{(n)} &\leq {}_j\pi_{ii} + {}_j\pi_{ji} \sum_{n=0}^{N} p_{ij}^{(n)} \\ &\leq {}_j\pi_{ii} + {}_j\pi_{ji} \sum_{n=0}^{N} p_{jj}^{(n)} \end{aligned}$$

by virtue of (11.14). To put this inequality into the symmetric form of (11.15) it suffices to note that

$$(11.21) \qquad {}_j\pi_{ji} = \frac{{}_j\pi_{ii}}{{}_i\pi_{jj}}.$$

In fact, by analogy with (11.16) we have

$$(11.22) \qquad {}_j\pi_{ji} = {}_i f_{ji} \cdot {}_j\pi_{ii}$$

where $_jf_{ji}$ is the probability of reaching E_i from E_j without a previous return to E_j. The alternative to this event is that a return to E_j occurs before an entry to E_i, and hence

$$(11.23) \qquad _jf_{ji} = 1 - {}_if_{jj} = \frac{1}{_i\pi_{jj}}.$$

(The last equation is the basic identity for the transient recurrent event which consists in a return to E_j without an intermediate passage through E_i.) Substituting from (11.23) into (11.22) we get the assertion (11.21), and this accomplishes the proof. ▶

The relation (11.21) leads to the interesting

Corollary 1. *If $\{u_k\}$ is an invariant measure, then*

$$(11.24) \qquad \frac{_j\pi_{ii}}{_i\pi_{jj}} = \frac{u_i}{u_j}.$$

Proof. The invariant measure is determined up to a multiplicative constant, and so the right side in (11.24) is uniquely determined. We may therefore suppose that $\{u_k\}$ is the invariant measure defined by (11.7) when the taboo state E_r is identified with E_j. But then $u_j = 1$ and $_j\pi_{ji} = u_i$, and so (11.21) reduces to (11.24). ▶

Corollary 2. (*Ratio limit theorem.*) *In an irreducible persistent chain the ratio limit theorem* (11.2) *holds.*

Proof. The sums of theorem 2 tend to ∞ as $N \to \infty$. The ratio of the two sums in (11.14) therefore tends to unity, and so it suffices to prove (11.2) for the special choice $\alpha = i$ and $\beta = j$. But with this choice (11.2) is an immediate consequence of (11.15) and (11.24). ▶

The existence of an invariant measure for persistent chains was first proved by C. Derman (1954). The existence of a limit in (11.2) was demonstrated by A. Doblin (1938). Taboo probabilities as a powerful tool in the theory of Markov chains were introduced by Chung (1953). Further details are given in the first part of his basic treatise.[17] The boundedness of the partial sums $\sum_0^N (p_{kk}^{(n)} - p_{ii}^{(n)})$ was proved by S. Orey, who considered also the problem of convergence.[18]

---

[17] *Markov chains with stationary transition probabilities*, Berlin (Springer), 1960. A revised edition covering boundary theory is in preparation. (Our notations are not identical with his.)

[18] *Sums arising in the theory of Markov chains*, Proc. Amer. Math. Soc., vol. 12 (1961), pp. 847–856.

*12. REVERSED CHAINS. BOUNDARIES

When studying the development of a system we are usually interested in the probabilities of possible future events, but occasionally it is necessary to study the past. In the special case of a Markov chain we may ask for the (conditional) probability that at some time in the past the system was in state E_i given that the present state is E_j.

Consider first a chain with a strictly positive invariant probability distribution $\{u_k\}$; that is, we assume that $u_k > 0$ and $\sum u_k = 1$ where

$$(12.1) \qquad u_k = \sum_v u_v p_{vk}.$$

[Recall from the theorem in section 7 that the invariant probability distribution of an irreducible chain is automatically strictly positive.]

If the process starts from $\{u_k\}$ as initial distribution, the probability of finding the system at any time in state E_i equals u_i. Given this event, the conditional probability that n time units earlier the system was in state E_j equals

$$(12.2) \qquad q_{ij}^{(n)} = \frac{u_j p_{ji}^{(n)}}{u_i}.$$

For $n = 1$ we get

$$(12.3) \qquad q_{ij} = \frac{u_j p_{ji}}{u_i}.$$

In view of (12.1) it is clear that the q_{ij} are the elements of a *stochastic* matrix Q. Furthermore, the probabilities $q_{ij}^{(n)}$ are simply the elements of the nth power Q^n (in other words, the $q_{ij}^{(n)}$ can be calculated from the q_{ij} in the same manner as the $p_{ji}^{(n)}$ are calculated from the p_{ji}). It is now apparent that *the study of the past development of our Markov chain reduces to the study of a Markov chain with transition probabilities* q_{ij}. The absolute probabilities of the new chain coincide, of course, with the invariant probability distribution $\{u_k\}$. The probabilities q_{ij} are called *inverse probabilities* (relative to the original chain) and the procedure leading from one chain to the other is called *reversal of the time*. In the special case where $q_{ij} = p_{ij}$ one says that the chain is *reversible*; the probability relations for such a chain are symmetric in time.

We know that an irreducible chain possesses an invariant probability distribution only if the states have finite mean recurrence times. If the states are persistent null states there exists an invariant measure which is unique except for an arbitrary multiplicative constant. For a transient chain all contingencies are possible: some chains have no invariant measure, others infinitely many. [Examples (11.*b*) and (11.*c*).] Under these circumstances it is remarkable that the transformation (12.3) *defines a stochastic matrix* Q *whenever* $\{u_k\}$ *is a strictly positive invariant measure.* The powers of Q are given by (12.2). In this sense *every strictly positive invariant measure defines a reversed Markov chain.* Unfortunately the new transition probabilities q_{ij} cannot be interpreted directly as conditional probabilities in the old process.[19]

A glance at (12.3) shows that $\{u_j\}$ is an invariant measure also for the reversed chain. Furthermore it is clear from (12.2) that either both series $\sum_n q_{ij}^{(n)}$ and $\sum_n p_{ji}^{(n)}$ converge or both diverge. It follows that *the states of the two chains are of the same type*: if one chain is transient, or persistent, so is the other.

Examples. (*a*) The invariant probability distribution corresponding to the *Ehrenfest model* [example (2.*e*)] was found in (7.16). A simple calculation shows that *the Ehrenfest model is reversible* in the sense that $q_{ij} = p_{ij}$.

(*b*) In example (11.*b*) we found the invariant measures corresponding to a random walk on the line in which the transitions to the right and left neighbor have probabilities p and q, respectively. If we choose $u_k = 1$ for $k = 0, \pm 1, \pm 2, \ldots$, we get $q_{ij} = p_{ji}$, and we are led to a new random walk in which the roles of p and q are interchanged. On the other hand, the invariant measure with $u_k = (p/q)^k$ yields a reversed random walk identical with the original one.

(*c*) In examples (2.*k*) and (2.*l*) we introduced two Markov chains related to a recurrent event $\mathcal{E}$. For a persistent $\mathcal{E}$ with finite mean recurrence time μ we saw in example (7.*g*) that the two chains have the same invariant probability distribution defined by (7.23). When $\mu = \infty$ these relations define an invariant measure common to the two chains [see examples (11.*c*) and (11.*d*)]. A simple calculation now shows that *the two chains are obtained from each other by reversing the time.* This is not surprising seeing that the chain of (2.*k*) concerns the waiting time to the next occurrence of $\mathcal{E}$ while (2.*l*) refers to the time elapsed from the last occurrence. ▶

Consider now an arbitrary irreducible transient chain with an invariant measure $\{u_k\}$. The equations (12.1) defining an invariant measure may admit of other solutions, and the question of uniqueness is closely related

---

[19] For an operational interpretation of the q_{ij} it is necessary to consider infinitely many simultaneous processes, as indicated in example (11.*b*).

with the question of uniqueness of the adjoint system of linear equations,[20]

(12.4) $$\xi_i = \sum_v p_{iv}\xi_v,$$

which played an important role in section 8. This system admits of the trivial solution $\xi_i = c$ for all i. Any non-negative solution is automatically strictly positive. (Indeed, $\xi_i = 0$ would imply $\xi_v = 0$ for all v such that $p_{iv} > 0$. This in turn would imply $\xi_v = 0$ whenever $p_{iv}^{(2)} > 0$, and generally $\xi_v = 0$ for every state E_v that can be reached from E_i. Thus $\xi_v = 0$ for all v because the chain is irreducible.) If $\{\xi_i\}$ is a non-constant solution then a glance at (12.3) shows that

(12.5) $$v_i = u_i\xi_i$$

defines an invariant measure for the reverse matrix Q. Conversely, if $\{v_i\}$ stands for such a measure then (12.5) defines a positive solution of (12.4). In other words, *the positive solutions of* (12.4) *stand in one-to-one correspondence with the invariant measures of the reversed chain*[21] with matrix Q.

In the modern theory of Markov chains and potentials the positive solutions $\{\xi_i\}$ and $\{u_k\}$ are used to define boundaries. It is beyond the scope of this book to describe how this is done, but the following examples may give some idea of what is meant by an *exit boundary*.

Examples. (*a*) Consider a random walk on the infinite line such that from the position $j \neq 0$ the particle moves with probability p a unit step away from the origin, and with probability q a unit step toward the origin. From the origin the particle moves with equal probabilities to $+1$ or -1. We assume $p > q$.

---

[20] If ξ stands for the column vector with components ξ_i the system (12.4) reduces to the matrix equation $\xi = P\xi$. The system (12.1) corresponds to $u = uP$ where u is a row vector.

[21] For an irreducible persistent chain the invariant measure is unique up to a multiplicative constant. Since the chains with matrices P and Q are of the same type we have proved the

Theorem. *For an irreducible persistent chain the only non-negative solution of* (12.4) *is given by* $\xi_i = $ const.

This can be proved also by repeating almost verbatim the last part of the proof of theorem 11.1. Indeed, by induction we find that for arbitrary i, r, and n

$$\xi_i = [f_{ir}^{(1)} + \cdots + f_{ir}^{(n)}]\xi_r + \sum_v {}_r p_{iv}^{(n)}\xi_v.$$

For a persistent chain the expression within brackets tends to 1 while the series tends to 0. Hence $\xi_i = \xi_r$ as asserted.

In the Markov chain the states are numbered from $-\infty$ to ∞, and the equations (12.4) take on the form

$$\xi_i = p\xi_{i+1} + q\xi_{i-1} \qquad\qquad i > 0,$$

(12.6) $$\xi_0 = \tfrac{1}{2}\xi_1 + \tfrac{1}{2}\xi_{-1}$$

$$\xi_i = q\xi_{i+1} + p\xi_{i-1} \qquad\qquad i < 0.$$

Put

(12.7) $$\eta_i = 1 - \frac{1}{2}\left(\frac{q}{p}\right)^i \quad for \quad i \geq 0, \qquad \eta_i = \frac{1}{2}\left(\frac{q}{p}\right)^{-i} \quad for \quad i \leq 0.$$

It is easily seen that $\xi_i = \eta_i$ and $\xi_i = 1 - \eta_i$ defines two[22] non-trivial solutions of the system (12.6). It follows that our chain is transient, and so the position of the particle necessarily tends either to $+\infty$ or to $-\infty$.

This conclusion can be reached directly from the theory of random walks. In fact, we know from XIV,2 that when the particle starts from a position $i > 0$ the probability of ever reaching the origin equals $(q/p)^i$. For reasons of symmetry a particle starting from the origin has equal probabilities to drift toward $+\infty$ or $-\infty$, and so the probability of an ultimate drift to $-\infty$ equals $\tfrac{1}{2}(q/p)^i$. We conclude that η_i *is the probability that, starting from an arbitrary position* i, *the particle ultimately drifts to* $+\infty$. The drift to $-\infty$ has probability $1 - \eta_i$. In the modern theory the situation would be described by introducing the "exit boundary points" $+\infty$ and $-\infty$.

(*b*) The preceding example is somewhat misleading by its simplicity, and it may therefore be useful to have an example of *a boundary consisting of infinitely many points*. For this purpose we consider a random walk in the x,y-plane as follows. The x-coordinate performs an ordinary random walk in which the steps $+1$ and -1 have probabilities p and $q < p$. The y-coordinate remains fixed except when the x-coordinate is zero, in which case the y-coordinate decreases by 1. More explicitly, when $j \neq 0$ only the transitions $(j, k) \rightarrow (j + 1, k)$ and $(j-1, k)$ are possible, and they have probabilities p and $q < p$, respectively. From $(0, k)$ the particle moves with probability p to $(1, k-1)$ and with probability q to $(-1, k-1)$.

From the theory of random walks we know that the x-coordinate is bound to tend to $+\infty$, and that (with probability one) it will pass only finitely often through 0. It follows that (excepting an event of zero probability) the y-coordinate will change only finitely often. This means that

---

[22] The most general solution is given by $\xi_i = A + B\eta_i$ where A and B are arbitrary constants. Indeed, these constants can be chosen so as to yield prescribed values for ξ_1 and ξ_{-1}, and it is obvious from (12.6) that the values for ξ_1 and ξ_{-1} uniquely determine all ξ_i.

after finitely many changes of the y-coordinate the particle will remain on a line $y = r$. In this sense there are infinitely many "escape routes to infinity," and for each initial position (j, k) we may calculate[23] the probability $\xi_{j,k}^{(r)}$ that the particle ultimately settles on the line $y = r$. It is easily seen that for fixed r the probabilities $\xi_{j,k}^{(r)}$ represent a solution of the system corresponding to (12.4), and that the most general solution is a linear combination of these particular solutions. Furthermore, the particular solution $\xi_{j,k}^{(r)}$ is characterized by the intuitively obvious "boundary condition" that $\xi_{j,k}^{(r)} \to 0$ as $j \to \infty$ except when $k = r$, in which case $\xi_{j,r}^{(r)} \to 1$.   ▶

These examples are typical in the following sense. Given an irreducible transient Markov chain it is always possible to define a "boundary" such that with probability one the state of the system tends to some point of the boundary. Given a set Γ on the boundary we can ask for the probability η_i that, starting from the initial state E_i, the system converges to a point of Γ. We refer to $\{\eta_i\}$ as the *absorption probabilities for* Γ. It turns out that such absorption probabilities are always solutions of the linear system (12.4) and, conversely, that all bounded solutions of (12.4) are linear combinations of absorption probabilities. Furthermore, the absorption probabilities $\{\eta_i\}$ for Γ are given by the unique solution of (12.4) which assumes the boundary values 1 on Γ and the boundary values 0 on the complement of Γ on the boundary. We may now form a new stochastic matrix $\hat{P}$ with elements

$$(12.8) \qquad\qquad \hat{p}_{ik} = p_{ik} \frac{\eta_k}{\eta_i}.$$

This is the conditional probability of a transition from E_i to E_k given that the state ultimately tends to a point of Γ. The Markov process with matrix $\hat{P}$ may be described as obtained from the original process by conditioning on the hypothesis of an ultimate absorption in Γ. Since the

---

[23] An explicit expression for $\xi_{j,k}^{(r)}$ can be obtained from the results in XIV,2 concerning one-dimensional random walks. From an initial position $i \leq 0$ the probability that the origin will be touched exactly $\rho > 0$ times equals $(2q)^{\rho-1}(p-q)$; when $i \geq 0$ this probability equals $(q/p)^i(2q)^{\rho-1}(p-q)$. The probability that the origin is never touched equals 0 for $i \leq 0$ and $1 - (q/p)^i$ for $i \geq 0$. It follows easily that for $i \leq 0$

$$\xi_{i,k}^{(r)} = (2q)^{k-r-1}(p-q) \qquad\qquad\qquad k > r$$

while for $i > 0$

$$\xi_{i,k}^{(r)} = (q/p)^i(2q)^{k-r-1}(p-q) \qquad\qquad\qquad k > r$$

$$\xi_{i,r}^{(r)} = 1 - (q/p)^i$$

and, of course, $\xi_{i,r}^{(k)} = 0$ when $k < r$.

future development can never be known in advance such a conditioning appears at first sight meaningless. It is nevertheless a powerful analytic tool and has even an operational meaning for processes that have been going on for a very long time.

A boundary can be defined also for the matrix Q obtained by a reversal of the time. In general therefore there are two distinct boundaries corresponding to a given chain. They are called *exit* and *entrance* boundaries, respectively. Roughly speaking, the former refers to the remote future, the latter to the remote past.

Time-reversed Markov chains were first considered by A. Kolmogorov.[24] The role of the solutions of (12.4) was stressed in the earlier editions of this book. Exit and entrance boundaries were introduced by W. Feller.[25] His construction is satisfactory when there are only finitely many boundary points, but in general it is simpler to adapt the construction introduced by R. S. Martin in the theory of harmonic functions. This was pointed out by J. L. Doob.[26] The relativization (12.8) was introduced by Feller;[26] an analogous transformation in the theory of classical harmonic functions was defined at the same time by M. Brelot.[27]

13. THE GENERAL MARKOV PROCESS

In applications it is usually convenient to describe Markov chains in terms of random variables. This can be done by the simple device of replacing in the preceding sections the symbol E_k by the integer k. The state of the system at time n then is a random variable $\mathbf{X}^{(n)}$, which assumes the value k with probability $a_k^{(n)}$; the joint distribution of $\mathbf{X}^{(n)}$ and $\mathbf{X}^{(n+1)}$ is given by $\mathbf{P}\{\mathbf{X}^{(n)} = j, \mathbf{X}^{(n+1)} = k\} = a_j^{(n)} p_{jk}$, and the joint distribution of $(\mathbf{X}^{(0)}, \ldots, \mathbf{X}^{(n)})$ is given by (1.1). It is also possible, and sometimes preferable, to assign to E_k a numerical value e_k different from k. With this notation a Markov chain becomes a special stochastic process,[28] or in other words, a sequence of (dependent) random variables[29]

---

[24] *Zur Theorie der Markoffschen Ketten*, Mathematische Annalen, vol. 112(1935), pp. 155–160.

[25] *Boundaries induced by positive matrices*, Trans. Amer. Math. Soc., vol. 83(1956), pp. 19–54.

[26] *Discrete potential theory and boundaries*, J. Math. Mechanics, vol. 8(1959), pp. 433–458.

[27] *Le problème de Dirichlet. Axiomatique et frontière de Martin*, J. Math. Pures Appl., vol. 35(1956), pp. 297–335.

[28] The terms "stochastic process" and "random process" are synonyms and cover practically all the theory of probability from coin tossing to harmonic analysis. In practice, the term "stochastic process" is used mostly when a time parameter is introduced.

[29] This formulation refers to an infinite product space, but in reality we are concerned only with joint distributions of finite collections of the variables.

$(\mathbf{X}^{(0)}, \mathbf{X}^{(1)}, \ldots)$. The superscript n plays the role of time. In chapter XVII we shall get a glimpse of more general stochastic processes in which the time parameter is permitted to vary continuously. The term "Markov process" is applied to a very large and important class of stochastic processes (with both discrete and continuous time parameters). Even in the discrete case there exist more general Markov processes than the simple chains we have studied so far. It will, therefore, be useful to give a definition of the Markov property, to point out the special condition characterizing our Markov chains, and, finally, to give a few examples of non-Markovian processes.

Conceptually, a Markov process is the probabilistic analogue of the processes of classical mechanics, where the future development is completely determined by the present state and is independent of the way in which the present state has developed. These processes differ essentially from processes with aftereffect (or hereditary processes), such as occur in the theory of plasticity, where the whole past history of the system influences its future. In stochastic processes the future is not uniquely determined, but we have at least probability relations enabling us to make predictions. For the Markov chains studied in this chapter it is clear that probability relations relating to the future depend on the present state, but not on the manner in which the present state has emerged from the past. In other words, if two independent systems subject to the same transition probabilities happen to be in the same state, then all probabilities relating to their future developments are identical. This is a rather vague description which is formalized in the following

Definition. *A sequence of discrete-valued random variables is a Markov process if, corresponding to every finite collection of integers $n_1 < n_2 < \cdots < n_r < n$, the joint distribution of $(\mathbf{X}^{(n_1)}, \mathbf{X}^{(n_2)}, \ldots, \mathbf{X}^{(n_r)}, \mathbf{X}^{(n)})$ is defined in such a way that the conditional probability of the relation $\mathbf{X}^{(n)} = x$ on the hypothesis $\mathbf{X}^{(n_1)} = x_1, \ldots, \mathbf{X}^{(n_r)} = x_r$ is identical with the conditional probability of $\mathbf{X}^{(n)} = x$ on the single hypothesis $\mathbf{X}^{(n_r)} = x_r$. Here $x_1, \ldots, x_r$, are arbitrary numbers for which the hypothesis has a positive probability.*

Reduced to simpler terms, this definition states that, given the present state x_r, no additional data concerning states of the system in the past can alter the (conditional) probability of the state x at a future time.

The Markov chains studied so far in this chapter are obviously Markov processes, but they have the additional property that their *transition probabilities* $p_{jk} = \mathbf{P}\{\mathbf{X}^{(m+1)} = k \mid \mathbf{X}^{(m)} = j\}$ are independent of m. The more general transition probabilities

(13.1) $$p_{jk}^{(n-m)} = \mathbf{P}\{\mathbf{X}^{(n)} = k \mid \mathbf{X}^{(m)} = j\} \qquad (m < n)$$

then depend only on the difference $n - m$. Such transition probabilities are called *stationary* (*or time-homogeneous*). For a general integral-valued Markov chain the right side in (13.1) depends on m and n. We shall denote it by $p_{jk}(m, n)$ so that $p_{jk}(n, n + 1)$ define the one-step transition probabilities. Instead of (1.1) we get now for the probability of the path $(j_0, j_1, \ldots, j_n)$ the expression

(13.2) $$a^{(0)}_{j_0} p_{j_0 j_1}(0, 1) p_{j_1 j_2}(1, 2) \cdots p_{j_{n-1} j_n}(n-1, n).$$

The proper generalization of (3.3) is obviously the identity

(13.3) $$p_{jk}(m, n) = \sum_v p_{jv}(m, r) p_{vk}(r, n)$$

which is valid for all r with $m < r < n$. This identity follows directly from the definition of a Markov process and also from (13.2); it is called the *Chapman-Kolmogorov* equation. [Transition probabilities $p_{jk}(m, n)$ are defined also for non-Markovian discrete processes, but for them the factor $p_{vk}(r, n)$ in (13.3) must be replaced by an expression depending not only on v and k, but also on j.]

The Markov chains studied in this chapter represent the general time-homogeneous discrete Markov process. We shall not dwell on the time-inhomogeneous Markov process. The following examples may be helpful for an understanding of the Markov property and will illustrate situations when the Chapman-Kolmogorov equation (13.3) does not hold.

Examples of Non-Markovian Processes

(a) *The Polya urn scheme* [example V,(2.c)]. Let $X^{(n)}$ equal 1 or 0 according to whether the nth drawing results in a black or red ball. The sequence $\{X^{(n)}\}$ is *not* a Markov process. For example,

$$P\{X^{(3)} = 1 \mid X^{(2)} = 1\} = (b+c)/(b+r+c),$$

but

$$P\{X^{(3)} = 1 \mid X^{(2)} = 1, X^{(1)} = 1\} = (b+2c)/(b+r+2c).$$

(Cf. problems V, 19–20.) On the other hand, if $Y^{(n)}$ is the number of black balls in the urn a time n, then $\{Y^{(n)}\}$ is an ordinary Markov chain with constant transition probabilities.

(b) *Higher sums.* Let $Y_0, Y_1, \ldots$ be mutually independent random variables, and put $S_n = Y_0 + \cdots + Y_n$. The difference $S_n - S_m$ (with $m < n$) depends only on $Y_{m+1}, \ldots, Y_n$, and it is therefore easily seen that the sequence $\{S_n\}$ is a Markov process. Now let us go one step further and define a new sequence of random variables U_n by

$$U_n = S_0 + S_1 + \cdots + S_n = Y_n + 2Y_{n-1} + 3Y_{n-2} + \cdots + (n+1) Y_0.$$

The sequence $\{U_n\}$ forms a stochastic process whose probability relations can, in principle, be expressed in terms of the distributions of the Y_k. The $\{U_n\}$ process is in general not of the Markov type, since there is no reason why, for example, $P\{U_n = 0 \mid U_{n-1} = a\}$ should be the same as $P\{U_n = 0 \mid U_{n-1} = a, U_{n-2} = b\}$; the knowledge of U_{n-1} and U_{n-2} permits better predictions than the sole knowledge of U_{n-1}.

In the case of a continuous time parameter the preceding summations are replaced by integrations. In diffusion theory the Y_n play the role of accelerations; the S_n are then velocities, and the U_n positions. If only positions can be measured, we are compelled to study a non-Markovian process, even though it is indirectly defined in terms of a Markov process.

(c) *Moving averages.* Again let $\{Y_n\}$ be a sequence of mutually independent random variables. Moving averages of order r are defined by $X^{(n)} = (Y_n + Y_{n+1} + \cdots + Y_{n+r-1})/r$. It is easily seen that the $X^{(n)}$ are not a Markov process. Processes of this type are common in many applications (cf. problem 25).

(d) *A traffic problem.* For an empirical example of a non-Markovian process R. Fürth[30] made extensive observations on the number of pedestrians on a certain segment of a street. An idealized mathematical model of this process can be obtained in the following way. For simplicity we assume that all pedestrians have the same speed v and consider only pedestrians moving in one direction. We partition the x-axis into segments $I_1, I_2, \ldots$ of a fixed length d and observe the configuration of pedestrians regularly at moments d/v time units apart. Define the random variable Y_k as the number of pedestrians initially in I_k. At the nth observation these same pedestrians will be found in I_{k-n}, whereas the interval I_k will contain Y_{k+n} pedestrians. The total number of pedestrians within the interval $0 < x < Nd$ is therefore given by $X^{(n)} = Y_{n+1} + \cdots + Y_{n+N}$, and so our process is essentially a moving average process. The simplest model for the random variables Y_k is represented by Bernoulli trials. In the limit as $d \to 0$ they lead to a continuous model, in which a Poisson distribution takes over the role of the binomial distribution.

(e) *Superposition of Markov processes* (*composite shuffling*). There exist many technical devices (such as groups of selectors in telephone exchanges, counters, filters) whose action can be described as a superposition of two Markov processes with an output which is non-Markovian. A fair idea

---

[30] R. Fürth, *Schwankungserscheinungen in der Physik*, Sammlung Vieweg, Braunschweig, 1920, pp. 17ff. The original observations appeared in Physikalische Zeitschrift, vols. 19 (1918) and 20 (1919).

of such mechanisms may be obtained from the study of the following method of card shuffling.

In addition to the target deck of N cards we have an equivalent auxiliary deck, and the usual shuffling technique is applied to this auxiliary deck. If its cards appear in the order $(a_1, a_2, \ldots, a_N)$, we permute the cards of the target deck so that the first, second, . . . , Nth cards are transferred to the places number $a_1, a_2, \ldots, a_N$. Thus the shuffling of the auxiliary deck indirectly determines the successive orderings of the target deck. The latter form *a stochastic process which is not of the Markov type.* To prove this, it suffices to show that the knowledge of two successive orderings of the target deck conveys in general more clues to the future than the sole knowledge of the last ordering. We show this in a simple special case.

Let $N = 4$, and suppose that the auxiliary deck is initially in the order (2431). Suppose, furthermore, that the shuffling operation always consists of a true "cutting," that is, the ordering (a_1, a_2, a_3, a_4) is changed into one of the three orderings (a_2, a_3, a_4, a_1), (a_3, a_4, a_1, a_2), (a_4, a_1, a_2, a_3); we attribute to each of these three possibilities probability $\frac{1}{3}$. With these conventions the auxiliary deck will at any time be in one of the four orderings (2431), (4312), (3124), (1243). On the other hand, a little experimentation will show that the target deck will gradually pass through all 24 possible orderings and that each of them will appear in combination with each of the four possible orderings of the auxiliary deck. This means that the ordering (1234) of the target deck will recur infinitely often, and it will always be succeeded by one of the four orderings (4132), (3421), (2314), (1243). Now the auxiliary deck can never remain in the same ordering, and hence the target deck cannot twice in succession undergo the same permutation. Hence, if at trials number $n - 1$ and n the orderings are (1234) and (1243), respectively, then at the next trial the state (1234) is impossible. Thus two consecutive observations convey more information than does one single observation.

(f) A non-Markovian process satisfying the Chapman-Kolmogorov equation. The identity (3.3) was derived from the assumption that a transition from E_v to E_k does not depend on the manner in which the state E_v was reached. Originally it seemed therefore intuitively clear that no non-Markovian process should satisfy this identity; this conjecture seemed supported by the fact that the n-step transition probabilities of such a process must satisfy a host of curious identities. It turned out nevertheless that exceptions exist (at least in theory). In fact, in IX,1 we encountered an infinite sequence of pairwise independent identically distributed random variables assuming the values 1, 2, and 3 each with probability $\frac{1}{3}$. We have thus a process with possible states 1, 2, 3 and such that $p_{jk} = \frac{1}{3}$ for all combinations of j and k. The indentity (3.3) is therefore trivially satisfied with $p_{jk}^{(n)} = \frac{1}{3}$. The process is nonetheless non-Markovian. To see this suppose that the first step takes the system to the state 2. A transition to 3 at the next step is then possible if, and only if, the initial state was 1. Thus the transitions following the first step depend not only on the present state but also on the initial state. (For various modifications see the note and footnote 3 in IX,1.)

14. PROBLEMS FOR SOLUTION

1. In a sequence of Bernoulli trials we say that at time n the state E_1 is observed if the trials number $n-1$ and n resulted in SS. Similarly E_2, E_3, E_4 stand for SF, FS, FF. Find the matrix P and all its powers. Generalize the scheme.

2. Classify the states for the four chains whose matrices P have the rows given below. Find in each case P^2 and the asymptotic behavior of $p_{jk}^{(n)}$.

(a) $(0, \frac{1}{2}, \frac{1}{2})$, $(\frac{1}{2}, 0, \frac{1}{2})$, $(\frac{1}{2}, \frac{1}{2}, 0)$;

(b) $(0, 0, 0, 1)$, $(0, 0, 0, 1)$, $(\frac{1}{2}, \frac{1}{2}, 0, 0)$, $(0, 0, 1, 0)$;

(c) $(\frac{1}{2}, 0, \frac{1}{2}, 0, 0)$, $(\frac{1}{4}, \frac{1}{2}, \frac{1}{4}, 0, 0)$, $(\frac{1}{2}, 0, \frac{1}{2}, 0, 0)$, $(0, 0, 0, \frac{1}{2}, \frac{1}{2})$, $(0, 0, 0, \frac{1}{2}, \frac{1}{2})$;

(d) $(0, \frac{1}{2}, \frac{1}{2}, 0, 0, 0)$, $(0, 0, 0, \frac{1}{3}, \frac{1}{3}, \frac{1}{3})$, $(0, 0, 0, \frac{1}{3}, \frac{1}{3}, \frac{1}{3})$, $(1, 0, 0, 0, 0, 0)$, $(1, 0, 0, 0, 0, 0)$, $(1, 0, 0, 0, 0, 0)$.

3. We consider throws of a true die and agree to say that at epoch n the system is in state E_j if j is the highest number appearing in the first n throws. Find the matrix P^n and verify that (3.3) holds.

4. In example (2.j) find the (absorption) probabilities x_k and y_k that, starting from E_k, the system will end in E_1 or E_5, respectively ($k = 2, 3, 4, 6$). (Do this problem from the basic definitions without referring to section 8.)

5. Treat example I, (5.b) as a Markov chain. Calculate the probability of winning for each player.

6. Let E_0 be absorbing (that is, put $p_{00} = 1$). For $j > 0$ let $p_{jj} = p$ and $p_{j,j-1} = q$, where $p + q = 1$. Find the probability $f_{j0}^{(n)}$ that absorption at E_0 takes place exactly at the nth step. Find also the expectation of this distribution.

7. The first row of the matrix P is given by $v_0, v_1, \ldots$. For $j > 0$ we have (as in the preceding problem) $p_{jj} = p$ and $p_{j,j-1} = q$. Find the distribution of the recurrence time for E_0.

8. For $j = 0, 1, \ldots$ let $p_{j,j+2} = v_j$ and $p_{j0} = 1 - v_j$. Discuss the character of the states.

9. *Two reflecting barriers.* A chain with states $1, 2, \ldots, \rho$ has a matrix whose first and last rows are $(q, p, 0, \ldots, 0)$ and $(0, \ldots, 0, q, p)$. In all other rows $p_{k,k+1} = p, p_{k,k-1} = q$. Find the stationary distribution. Can the chain be periodic?

10. Generalize the *Bernoulli-Laplace model of diffusion* [example (2.f)] by assuming that there are $b \geq \rho$ black particles and $w = 2\rho - b$ white ones. The number of particles in each container remains $= \rho$.

11. A chain with states $E_0, E_1, \ldots$ has transition probabilities

$$p_{jk} = e^{-\lambda} \sum_{v=0}^{j} \binom{j}{v} p^v q^{j-v} \frac{\lambda^{k-v}}{(k-v)!}$$

where the terms in the sum should be replaced by zero if $v > k$. Show that

$$p_{jk}^{(n)} \to e^{-\lambda/q} \frac{(\lambda/q)^k}{k!}.$$

Note: This chain occurs in statistical mechanics[31] and can be interpreted as follows. The state of the system is defined by the number of particles in a certain region of space. During each time interval of unit length each particle has probability q to leave the volume, and the particles are stochastically independent. Moreover, new particles may enter the volume, and the probability of r entrants is given by the Poisson expression $e^{-\lambda}\lambda^r/r!$. The stationary distribution is then a Poisson distribution with parameter λ/q.

12. *Ehrenfest model.* In example (2.e) let there initially be j molecules in the first container, and let $\mathbf{X}^{(n)} = 2k - a$ if at the nth step the system is in state k (so that $\mathbf{X}^{(n)}$ is the difference of the number of molecules in the two containers). Let $e_n = \mathbf{E}(\mathbf{X}^{(n)})$. Prove that $e_{n+1} = (a-2)e_n/a$, whence $e_n = (1-2/a)^n(2j-a)$. (Note that $e_n \to 0$ as $n \to \infty$.)

13. Treat the counter problem, example XIII, (1.g), as a Markov chain.

14. *Plane random walk with reflecting barriers.* Consider a *symmetric* random walk in a bounded region of the plane. The boundary is reflecting in the sense that, whenever in a unrestricted random walk the particle would leave the region, it is forced to return to the last position. Show that, if every point of the region can be reached from every other point, there exists a stationary distribution and that $u_k = 1/a$, where a is the number of positions in the region. (If the region is unbounded the states are persistent null states and $u_k = 1$ represents an invariant measure.)

15. *Repeated averaging.* Let $\{x_1, x_2, \ldots\}$ be a bounded sequence of numbers and P the matrix of an ergodic chain. Prove that $\sum_j p_{ij}^{(n)}x_j \to \Sigma u_j x_j$. Show that the repeated averaging procedure of example XIII, (10.c) is a special case.

16. In the theory of *waiting lines* we ecounter the chain matrix

$$
\begin{bmatrix}
p_0 & p_1 & p_2 & p_3 & \cdots \\
p_0 & p_1 & p_2 & p_3 & \cdots \\
0 & p_0 & p_1 & p_2 & \cdots \\
0 & 0 & p_0 & p_1 & \cdots
\end{bmatrix}
$$

where $\{p_k\}$ is a probability distribution. Using generating functions, discuss the character of the states. Find the generating function of the stationary distribution, if any.

17. *Waiting time to absorption.* For transient E_j let $\mathbf{Y}_j$ be the time when the system for *the first time* passes into a persistent state. Assuming that the probability of staying forever in transient states is zero, prove that $d_j = \mathbf{E}(\mathbf{Y}_j)$ is uniquely determined as the solution of the system of linear equations

$$
d_j = \sum_T p_{j\nu}d_\nu + 1,
$$

the summation extending over all ν such that E_ν is transient. However, d_ν need not be finite.

---

[31] S. Chandrasekhar, *Stochastic problems in physics and astronomy*, Reviews of Modern Physics, vol. 15 (1943), pp. 1–89, in particular p. 45.

18. If the number of states is $a < \infty$ and if E_k can be reached from E_j, then it can be reached in $a - 1$ steps or less $(i \neq k)$.

19. Let the chain contain a states and let E_j be persistent. There exists a number $q < 1$ such that for $n \geq a$ the probability of the recurrence time of E_j exceeding n is smaller than q^n. (*Hint:* Use problem 18.)

20. In a finite chain E_j is transient if and only if there exists an E_k such that E_k can be reached from E_j but not E_j from E_k. (For infinite chains this is false, as shown by random walks.)

21. An irreducible chain for which *one* diagonal element p_{jj} is positive cannot be periodic.

22. A finite irreducible chain is non-periodic if and only if there exists an n such that $p_{jk}^{(n)} > 0$ for all j and k.

23. In a chain with a states let $(x_1, \ldots, x_a)$ be a solution of the system of linear equations $x_j = \Sigma p_{jv} x_v$. Prove: (*a*) If $x_j \leq 1$ for all j then the states for which $x_r = 1$ form a closed set. (*b*) If E_j and E_k belong to the same irreducible set then $x_j = x_k$. (*c*) In a finite irreducible chain the solution $\{x_j\}$ reduces to a constant. *Hint:* Consider the restriction of the equations to a closed set.

24. *Continuation.* If $(x_1, \ldots, x_a)$ is a (complex valued) solution of $x_j = = s\Sigma p_{jv} x_v$ with $|s| = 1$ but $s \neq 1$, then there exists an integer $t > 1$ such that $s^t = 1$. If the chain is irreducible, then the smallest integer of this kind is the period of the chain.
Hint: Without loss of generality assume $x_1 = 1 \geq |x_v|$. Consider successively the states reached in $1, 2, \ldots$ steps.

25. *Moving averages.* Let $\{Y_k\}$ be a sequence of mutually independent random variables, each assuming the values ± 1 with probability $\frac{1}{2}$. Put $X^{(n)} = (Y_n + Y_{n+1})/2$. Find the transition probabilities

$$p_{jk}(m, n) = P\{X^{(n)} = k \mid X^{(m)} = j\},$$

where $m < n$ and $j, k = -1, 0, 1$. Conclude that $\{X^{(n)}\}$ is not a Markov process and that (13.3) does not hold.

26. In a sequence of Bernoulli trials say that the state E_1 is observed at time n if the trials number $n - 1$ and n resulted in success; otherwise the system is in E_2. Find the n-step transition probabilities and discuss the non-Markovian character.
Note: This process is obtained from the chain of problem 1 by lumping together three states. Such a *grouping* can be applied to any Markov chain and destroys the Markovian character. Processes of this type were studied by Harris.[32]

27. *Mixing of Markov chains.* Given two Markov chains with the same number of states, and matrices P_1 and P_2. A new process is defined by an initial distribution and n-step transition probabilities $\frac{1}{2}P_1^n + \frac{1}{2}P_2^n$. Discuss the non-Markovian character and the relation to the urn models of V, 2.

---

[32] T. E. Harris, *On chains of infinite order*, Pacific Journal of Mathematics, vol. 5 (1955), Supplement 1, pp. 707–724.

28. Let N be a Poisson variable with expectation λ. Consider N independent Markov processes starting at E_0 and having the same matrix P. Denote by $Z_k^{(n)}$ the number among them after n steps are found in state E_k. Show that $Z_k^{(n)}$ has a Poisson distribution with expectation $\lambda \cdot p_{0k}^{(n)}$.

Hint: Use the result of example XII,(1.b).

29. Using the preceding problem show that the variable $X_k^{(n)}$ of example (11.b) has a Poisson distribution with expectation $\sum_j u_j p_{jk}^{(n)} = u_k$.

CHAPTER XVI *

Algebraic Treatment
of Finite Markov Chains

In this chapter we consider a Markov chain with finitely many states $E_1, \ldots, E_\rho$ and a given matrix of transition probabilities p_{jk}. Our main aim is to derive explicit formulas for the n-step transition probabilities $p_{jk}^{(n)}$. We shall not require the results of the preceding chapter, except the general concepts and notations of section 3.

We shall make use of the method of generating functions and shall obtain the desired results from the partial fraction expansions of XI,4. Our results can also be obtained directly from the theory of canonical decompositions of matrices (which in turn can be derived from our results). Moreover, for *finite* chains the ergodic properties proved in chapter XV follow from the results of the present chapter. However, for simplicity, we shall slightly restrict the generality and disregard exceptional cases which complicate the general theory and hardly occur in practical examples.

The general method is outlined in section 1 and illustrated in sections 2 and 3. In section 4 special attention is paid to transient states and absorption probabilities. In section 5 the theory is applied to finding the variances of the recurrence times of the states E_j.

1. GENERAL THEORY

For fixed j and k we introduce the generating function[1]

$$(1.1) \qquad P_{jk}(s) = \sum_{n=0}^{\infty} p_{jk}^{(n)} s^n.$$

---

* This chapter treats a special topic and may be omitted.

[1] Recall that $p_{jk}^{(0)}$ equals 0 or 1 according as $j \neq k$ or $j = k$. (The $p_{jk}^{(0)}$ are known as Kronecker symbols.)

Multiplying by sp_{ij} and adding over $j = 1, \ldots, \rho$ we get

$$(1.2) \qquad s\sum_{j=1}^{\rho} p_{ij}P_{jk}(s) = P_{ik}(s) - p_{ik}^{(0)}.$$

This means that for fixed k and s the quantities $z_j = P_{jk}(s)$ satisfy a system of a linear equations of the form

$$(1.3) \qquad z_i - s\sum_{j=1}^{\rho} p_{ij}z_j = b_i.$$

The solutions z_j of (1.3) are obviously rational functions of s with a common denominator $D(s)$, the determinant of the system. To conform with the standard notations of linear algebra we put $s = t^{-1}$. Then $t^{\rho}D(t^{-1})$ is a polynomial of degree ρ (called the characteristic polynomial of the matrix P of transition probabilities p_{jk}). Its roots $t_1, \ldots, t_{\rho}$ are called the *characteristic roots* (or eigenvalues) of the matrix P.

We now introduce the *simplifying assumptions that the characteristic roots $t_1, \ldots, t_{\rho}$ are simple* (distinct) *and*[2] $\neq 0$. This is a slight restriction of generality, but the theory will cover most cases of practical interest.

As already stated, for fixed k the ρ quantities $P_{jk}(s)$ are rational functions of s with the common denominator $D(s)$. The roots of $D(s)$ are given by the reciprocals of the non-vanishing characteristic roots t_{ν}. It follows therefore from the results of XI,4 that there exist constants $b_{jk}^{(\nu)}$ such that[3]

$$(1.4) \qquad P_{jk}(s) = \frac{b_{jk}^{(1)}}{1 - st_1} + \cdots + \frac{b_{jk}^{(\rho)}}{1 - st_{\rho}}.$$

Expanding the fractions into geometric series we get the equivalent relations

$$(1.5) \qquad p_{jk}^{(n)} = b_{jk}^{(1)}t_1^n + \cdots + b_{jk}^{(\rho)}t_{\rho}^n$$

valid for all integers $n \geq 0$. We proceed to show that the coefficients $b_{jk}^{(\nu)}$ are uniquely determined as solutions of certain systems of linear equations. The quantity $p_{ik}^{(n+1)}$ can be obtained from (1.5) by changing n into $n + 1$, but also by multiplying (1.5) by p_{ji} and summing over

---

[2] The condition $t_r \neq 0$ will be discarded presently. A chain with multiple roots is treated numerically in example (4.*b*).

[3] In theory we should omit those roots t_r that cancel against a root of the numerator. For such roots we put $b_{jk}^{(\nu)} = 0$ and so (1.4) and (1.5) remain valid under any circumstances.

$j = 1, \ldots, \rho$. Equating the two expressions we get an identity of the form

$$(1.6) \qquad C_1 t_1^n + \cdots + C_\rho t_\rho^n = 0$$

valid for all n. This is manifestly impossible unless all coefficients vanish, and we conclude that

$$(1.7) \qquad \sum_{j=1}^{\rho} p_{ij} b_{jk}^{(v)} = t_v b_{ik}^{(v)}$$

for all combinations i, k, and v. On multiplying (1.5) by p_{kr} and summing over k we get in like manner

$$(1.8) \qquad \sum_{k=1}^{\rho} b_{jk}^{(v)} p_{kr} = t_v b_{jr}^{(v)}.$$

Consider the ρ by ρ matrix $b^{(v)}$ with elements $b_{ik}^{(v)}$. The relations[4] (1.7) assert that its kth column represents a solution of the ρ linear equations

$$(1.9) \qquad \sum_{j=1}^{\rho} p_{ij} x_j - t x_i = 0$$

with $t = t_v$; similarly (1.8) states that the jth row satisfies

$$(1.10) \qquad \sum_{k=1}^{\rho} y_k p_{kr} - t y_r = 0$$

with $t = t_v$. The system (1.10) is obtained from (1.9) by interchanging rows and columns, and so the determinants are the same. The determinant of (1.9) vanishes only if t coincides with one of the distinct characteristic values $t_1, \ldots, t_\rho$. In other words, the two systems (1.9) and (1.10) admit of a non-trivial solution if, and only if, $t = t_v$ for some v. We denote a pair of corresponding solutions by $(x_1^{(v)}, \ldots, x_\rho^{(v)})$ and $(y_1^{(v)}, \ldots, y_\rho^{(v)})$. They are determined up to multiplicative constants, and so

$$(1.11) \qquad b_{jk}^{(v)} = c^{(v)} x_j^{(v)} y_k^{(v)},$$

where $c^{(v)}$ is a constant (independent of j and k). To find this unknown constant we note that (1.9) implies by induction that

$$(1.12) \qquad \sum_{j=1}^{\rho} p_{ij}^{(n)} x_j = t^n x_i$$

for all n. We use this relation for $t = t_\lambda$, where λ is an arbitrary integer between 1 and ρ. When $p_{ij}^{(n)}$ is expressed in accordance with (1.5) we

---

[4] The two systems (1.7) and (1.8) may be written in the compact matrix form $Pb^{(v)} = t_v b^{(v)}$ and $b^{(v)} P = t_v b^{(v)}$.

find

(1.13) $$t_\lambda^n x_i = t_1^n c^{(1)} x_i^{(1)} \sum_{k=1}^{\rho} y_k^{(1)} x_k^{(\lambda)} + \cdots + t_\rho^n c^{(\rho)} x_i^{(\rho)} \sum_{k=1}^{\rho} y_k^{(\rho)} x_k^{(\lambda)} .$$

This represents an identity of the form (1.6) which can hold only if all coefficients vanish. Equating the coefficients of t_λ^n on both sides we get finally[5]

(1.14) $$c^{(\lambda)} \sum_{k=1}^{\rho} y_k^{(\lambda)} x_k^{(\lambda)} = 1.$$

This relation determines the coefficient $b_{jk}^{(\lambda)}$ in (1.11). It is true that the $x_j^{(\lambda)}$ and $y_k^{(\lambda)}$ are determined only up to a multiplicative constant, but replacing $x_j^{(\lambda)}$ by $A x_j^{(\lambda)}$ and $y_k^{(\lambda)}$ by $B y_k^{(\lambda)}$ changes $c^{(\lambda)}$ into $c^{(\lambda)}/AB$, and the coefficient $b_{jk}^{(\lambda)}$ remains unchanged.

We summarize this result as follows. The two systems of linear equations (1.9) and (1.10) admit of non-trivial solutions only for at most ρ distinct values of t (the same for both systems). We suppose that there are exactly ρ such values $t_1, \ldots, t_\rho$, all different from 0. *To each t_λ choose a non-zero solution $(x_1^{(\lambda)}, \ldots, x_\rho^{(\lambda)})$ of (1.9) and a non-zero solution $(y_1^{(\lambda)}, \ldots, y_\rho^{(\lambda)})$ of (1.10). With $c^{(\lambda)}$ given by (1.14) we have then for $n = 0, 1, \ldots$*

(1.15) $$p_{jk}^{(n)} = \sum_{\lambda=1}^{\rho} c^{(\lambda)} x_j^{(\lambda)} y_k^{(\lambda)} t_\lambda^n .$$

We have thus found an explicit expression for all the transition probabilities.[6]

The assumption that the characteristic roots are distinct is satisfied in most practical cases, except for decomposable chains, and these require only minor changes in the setup (see section 4). Not infrequently, however, 0 is among the characteristic roots. In this case we put $t_\rho = 0$. The novel feature derives from the fact that the determinant $D(s)$ of the system (1.3) now has only the $\rho - 1$ roots $t_1^{-1}, \ldots, t_{\rho-1}^{-1}$, and so the generating function $P_{jk}(s)$ is the ratio of two polynomials of degree $\rho - 1$. The

---

[5] The vanishing of the other coefficients implies that $\sum_{k=1}^{\rho} y_k^{(\lambda)} x_k^{(\nu)} = 0$ whenever $\lambda \neq \nu$.

[6] The final formula (1.15) becomes more elegant in matrix form. Let $X^{(\lambda)}$ be the *column* vector (or ρ by 1 matrix) with elements $x_j^{(\lambda)}$, and $Y^{(\lambda)}$ the *row* vector (or 1 by ρ matrix) with elements $y_k^{(\lambda)}$. Then (1.15) takes on the form

$$P^n = \sum_{\lambda=1}^{\rho} c^{(\lambda)} X^{(\lambda)} Y^{(\lambda)} t_\lambda^n$$

and $c^{(\lambda)}$ is defined by the scalar equation $c^{(\lambda)} Y^{(\lambda)} X^{(\lambda)} = 1$.

partial fraction expansions require that the degree of the numerator be smaller than the degree of the denominator, and to achieve this we must first subtract an appropriate constant from $P_{jk}(s)$. In this way we obtain for $P_{jk}(s)$ a partial fraction expansion differing from (1.4) in that the last term is replaced by a constant. A glance at (1.15) shows that this affects the right side only when $n = 0$. In other words, *the explicit representation* (1.15) *of* $p_{jk}^{(n)}$ *remains valid for* $n \geq 1$ *even if* $t_\rho = 0$ (provided the roots $t_1, \ldots, t_{\rho-1}$ are distinct and different from zero).

The left side in (1.15) can remain bounded for all n only if $|t_\lambda| \leq 1$ for all λ. For $t = 1$ the equations (1.9) have the solution $x_j = 1$ and so one characteristic root equals 1. Without loss of generality we may put $t_1 = 1$. If the chain is aperiodic we have $|t_\lambda| < 1$ for all other roots and one sees from (1.15) that as $n \to \infty$

(1.16) $$p_{jk}^{(n)} \to c^{(1)} y_k^{(1)} .$$

In other words, *the invariant probability distribution is characterized as a solution of* (1.10) *with* $t = 1$.

2. EXAMPLES

(*a*) Consider first a chain with only two states. The matrix of transition probabilities assumes the simple form

$$P = \begin{pmatrix} 1-p & p \\ \alpha & 1-\alpha \end{pmatrix}$$

where $0 < p < 1$ and $0 < \alpha < 1$. The calculations are trivial since they involve only systems of two equations. The characteristic roots are $t_1 = 1$ and $t_2 = (1-\alpha-p)$. The explicit representation (1.15) for $p_{jk}^{(n)}$ may be exhibited in matrix form

$$P^n = \frac{1}{\alpha + p} \begin{pmatrix} \alpha & p \\ \alpha & p \end{pmatrix} + \frac{(1-\alpha-p)^n}{\alpha + p} \begin{pmatrix} p & -p \\ -\alpha & \alpha \end{pmatrix}$$

(where factors common to all four elements have been taken out as factors to the matrices). This formula is valid for $n \geq 0$.

(*b*) Let

(2.1) $$P = \begin{bmatrix} 0 & 0 & 0 & 1 \\ 0 & 0 & 0 & 1 \\ \frac{1}{2} & \frac{1}{2} & 0 & 0 \\ 0 & 0 & 1 & 0 \end{bmatrix}$$

[this is the matrix of problem (2.b) in XV,14]. The system (1.9) reduces to

$$(2.2) \qquad x_4 = tx_1, \qquad x_4 = tx_2, \qquad \tfrac{1}{2}(x_1+x_2) = tx_3, \qquad x_3 = tx_4.$$

To $t = 0$ there corresponds the solution $(1, -1, 0, 0)$, but we saw that the characteristic root 0 is not required for the explicit representation of $p_{jk}^{(n)}$ for $n \geq 1$. The standard procedure of eliminating variables shows that the other characteristic roots satisfy the cubic equation $t^3 = 1$. If we put for abbreviation

$$(2.3) \qquad \theta = e^{\frac{2}{3}\pi i} = \cos \tfrac{2}{3}\pi + i \sin \tfrac{2}{3}\pi$$

(where $i^2 = -1$) the three characteristic roots are $t_1 = 1$, $t_2 = \theta$, and $t_3 = \theta^2$ (which is the same as $t_3 = \theta^{-1}$). We have now to solve the systems (1.9) and (1.10) with these values for t. Since a multiplicative constant remains arbitrary we may put $x_1^{(v)} = y_1^{(v)} = 1$. The solutions then coincide, respectively, with the first columns and first rows of the three matrices in the final explicit representation

$$(2.4)$$

$$P^n = \frac{1}{6}\begin{bmatrix} 1 & 1 & 2 & 2 \\ 1 & 1 & 2 & 2 \\ 1 & 1 & 2 & 2 \\ 1 & 1 & 2 & 2 \end{bmatrix} + \frac{\theta^n}{6}\begin{bmatrix} 1 & 1 & 2\theta & 2\theta^2 \\ 1 & 1 & 2\theta & 2\theta^2 \\ \theta^2 & \theta^2 & 2 & 2\theta \\ \theta & \theta & 2\theta^2 & 2 \end{bmatrix} + \frac{\theta^{2n}}{6}\begin{bmatrix} 1 & 1 & 2\theta^2 & 2\theta \\ 1 & 1 & 2\theta^2 & 2\theta \\ \theta & \theta & 2 & 2\theta^2 \\ \theta^2 & \theta^2 & 2\theta & 2 \end{bmatrix}.$$

Since we have discarded the characteristic root $t = 0$ this formula is valid only for $n \geq 1$.

It is obvious from (2.4) that the chain has period 3. To see the asymptotic behavior of P^n we note that $1 + \theta + \theta^2 = 0$. Using this it is easily verified that when $n \to \infty$ through numbers of the form $n = 3k$ the rows of P^n tend to $(\tfrac{1}{2}, \tfrac{1}{2}, 0, 0)$. For $n = 3k + 1$ and $n = 3k + 2$ the corresponding limits are $(0, 0, 0, 1)$ and $(0, 0, 1, 0)$. It follows that the invariant probability distribution is given by $(\tfrac{1}{6}, \tfrac{1}{6}, \tfrac{1}{3}, \tfrac{1}{3})$.

(c) Let $p + q = 1$, and

$$(2.5) \qquad\qquad P = \begin{bmatrix} 0 & p & 0 & q \\ q & 0 & p & 0 \\ 0 & q & 0 & p \\ p & 0 & q & 0 \end{bmatrix}.$$

This chain represents a special case of the next example but is treated separately because of its simplicity. It is easily seen that the system (1.9) reduces to two linear equations for the two unknowns $x_1 + x_3$ and

$x_2 + x_4$, and hence that the four characteristic roots are given by

$$(2.6) \qquad t_1 = 1, \qquad t_2 = -1, \qquad t_3 = i(q-p), \qquad t_4 = -i(q-p).$$

The corresponding solutions are $(1, 1, 1, 1)$, $(-1, 1, -1, 1)$, $(-i, -1, i, 1)$, and $(i, -1, -i, 1)$. [It will be noted that they are of the form $(\theta, \theta^2, \theta^3, \theta^4)$ where θ is a fourth root of unity.] The system (1.10) differs from (1.9) only in that the roles of p and q are interchanged, and we get therefore without further calculations

$$(2.7) \qquad p_{jk}^{(n)} = \tfrac{1}{4}\{1 + (q-p)^n i^{j-k-n}\}\{1 + (-1)^{k+j-n}\}.$$

(d) In the *general cyclical random walk* of example XV, (2.d) the first row of the matrix P is given by $q_0, \ldots, q_{\rho-1}$ and the other rows are obtained by cyclical permutations. In the special case $\rho = 4$ it was shown in the preceding example that $x_j^{(\nu)}$ and $y_k^{(\nu)}$ are expressible as powers of the fourth roots of unity. It is therefore natural to try a similar procedure in terms of the ρth root of unity, namely

$$(2.8) \qquad \theta = e^{2i\pi/\rho}.$$

All ρth roots of unity are given by $1, \theta, \theta^2, \ldots, \theta^{\rho-1}$. For $r = 1, \ldots,$ we put

$$(2.9) \qquad t_r = \sum_{\nu=0}^{\rho-1} q_\nu \theta^{\nu r}$$

It is easily verified that for $t = t_r$ the systems (1.9) and (1.10) have the solutions

$$(2.10) \qquad x_j^{(r)} = \theta^{rj}, \qquad y_k^{(r)} = \theta^{-rk}$$

and for the corresponding coefficients $c^{(r)}$ we have in all cases $c^{(r)} = 1/\rho$. Thus finally[7]

$$(2.11) \qquad p_{jk}^{(n)} = \rho^{-1} \sum_{r=1}^{\rho-1} \theta^{r(j-k)} t_r^n.$$

---

[7] For $n = 0$ the right side in (2.11) is defined only when no t_r vanishes. Actually we have proved the validity of (2.11) for $n \geq 1$ assuming that the roots t_r are distinct, and this is not necessarily true in the present situation. For example, if $q_k = \rho^{-1}$ for all k then $t_0 = 1$, but $t_1 = \cdots = t_{\rho-1} = 0$. Even in this extreme case (2.11) remains valid since the right side yields for all j, k, and $n \geq 1$. Fortunately it is not difficult to verify (2.11) directly by induction on n. In particular, when $n = 1$ the factor of q_ν in (2.9) reduces to

$$\sum_{r=0}^{\rho-1} \theta^{r(j-k+\nu)}.$$

This sum is zero except when $j - k + \nu = 0$ or ρ, in which case each term equals one. Hence $p_{jk}^{(1)}$ reduces to q_{k-j} if $k \geq j$ and to $q_{\rho+k-j}$ if $k < j$, and this is the given matrix (p_{jk}).

(e) *The occupancy problem.* Example XV, (2.g) shows that the classical occupancy problem can be treated by the method of Markov chains. The system is in state j if there are j occupied and $\rho - j$ empty cells. If this is the initial situation and n additional balls are placed at random, then $p_{jk}^{(n)}$ is the probability that there will be k occupied and $\rho - k$ empty cells (so that $p_{jk}^{(n)} = 0$ if $k < j$). For $j = 0$ this probability follows from II, (11.7). We now derive a formula for $p_{jk}^{(n)}$, thus generalizing the result of chapter II.

Since $p_{jj} = j/\rho$ and $p_{j,j+1} = (\rho-j)/\rho$ the system (1.9) reduces to

$$(2.12) \qquad (\rho t - j)x_j = (\rho - j)x_{j+1}.$$

For $t = 1$ this implies $x_j = 1$ for all j. When $t \neq 1$ it is necessary that $x_\rho = 0$, and hence there exists some index r such that $x_{r+1} = 0$ but $x_r \neq 0$; from (2.12) it follows then that $\rho\,t = r$. The characteristic roots are therefore given by

$$(2.13) \qquad t_r = r/\rho, \qquad\qquad r = 1, \ldots, \rho.$$

The corresponding solutions of (2.12) are given by

$$(2.14) \qquad x_j^{(r)} = \binom{r}{j} \Big/ \binom{\rho}{j}$$

so that $x_j^{(r)} = 0$ when $j > r$. For $t = t_r$ the system (1.10) reduces to

$$(2.15) \qquad (r-j)y_j^{(r)} = (\rho-j+1)y_{j-1}^{(r)}$$

and has the solution

$$(2.16) \qquad y_j^{(r)} = \binom{\rho-r}{j-r}(-1)^{j-r}$$

where, of course, $y_j^{(r)} = 0$ if $j < r$. Since $x_j^{(r)} = 0$ for $j > r$ and $y_j^{(r)} = 0$ for $j < r$ we get

$$c^{(r)} = x_r^{(r)} y_r^{(r)} = \binom{\rho}{r}$$

and hence

$$(2.17) \qquad p_{jk}^{(n)} = \sum_{r=j}^{k} \left(\frac{r}{\rho}\right)^n \binom{\rho}{r}\binom{r}{j}\binom{\rho-r}{k-r}(-1)^{k-r} \Big/ \binom{\rho}{j}.$$

On expressing the binomial coefficients in terms of factorials, this formula simplifies to

$$(2.18) \qquad p_{jk}^{(n)} = \binom{\rho-j}{\rho-k} \sum_{v=0}^{k-j} \left(\frac{v+j}{\rho}\right)^n (-1)^{k-j-v}\binom{k-j}{v},$$

with $p_{jk}^{(n)} = 0$ if $k < j$.　　　　　　　　　　　　　　　　　　▶

[For a numerical illustration see example (4.b).]

3. RANDOM WALK WITH REFLECTING BARRIERS

The application of Markov chains will now be illustrated by a complete discussion of a random walk with states $1, 2, \ldots, \rho$ and two reflecting barriers.[8] The matrix P is displayed in example XV, (2.c). For $2 \leq k \leq$ $\leq \rho - 1$ we have $p_{k,k+1} = p$ and $p_{k,k-1} = q$; the first and the last rows are defined by $(q, p, 0, \ldots, 0)$ $(0, \ldots, 0, q, p)$.

For convenience of comparisons with the developments in chapter XIV we now discard the variable $t = s^{-1}$ and write the characteristic roots in the form s_r^{-1} (rather than t_r); it will be convenient to number them from 0 to $\rho - 1$. In terms of the variable s the linear system (1.9) becomes

$$x_1 = s(qx_1 + px_2)$$

(3.1) $$x_j = s(qx_{j-1} + px_{j+1}) \qquad (j = 2, 3, \ldots, \rho - 1)$$

$$x_\rho = s(qx_{\rho-1} + px_\rho).$$

This system admits the solution $x_j = 1$ corresponding to the root $s = 1$. To find all other solutions we apply the method of particular solutions (which we have used for similar equations in XIV, 4). The middle equation in (3.1) is satisfied by $x_j = \lambda^j$ provided that λ is a root of the quadratic equation $\lambda = qs + \lambda^2 ps$. The two roots of this equation are

$$(3.2) \qquad \lambda_1(s) = \frac{1 + \sqrt{1 - 4pqs^2}}{2ps}, \qquad \lambda_2(s) = \frac{1 - \sqrt{1 - 4pqs^2}}{2ps},$$

and the most general solution of the middle equation in (3.1) is therefore

$$(3.3) \qquad x_j = A(s)\lambda_1^j(s) + B(s)\lambda_2^j(s),$$

where $A(s)$ and $B(s)$ are arbitrary. The first and the last equation in (3.1) will be satisfied by (3.3) if, and only if, $x_0 = x_1$ and $x_\rho = x_{\rho+1}$. This requires that $A(s)$ and $B(s)$ satisfy the conditions

$$A(s)\{1 - \lambda_1(s)\} + B(s)\{1 - \lambda_2(s)\} = 0$$
(3.4)
$$A(s)\lambda_1^\rho(s)\{1 - \lambda_1(s)\} + B(s)\lambda_2^\rho(s)\{1 - \lambda_2(s)\} = 0.$$

Conversely, if these two equations hold for some value of s, then (3.3) represents a solution of the linear system (3.1) and this solution is identically zero only when $\lambda_1(s) = \lambda_2(s)$. Our problem is therefore to find the

---

[8] Part of what follows is a repetition of the theory of chapter XIV. Our quadratic equation occurs there as (4.7); the quantities $\lambda_1(s)$ and $\lambda_2(s)$ of the text were given in (4.8), and the general solution (3.3) appears in chapter XIV as (4.9). The two methods are related, but in many cases the computational details will differ radically.

values of s for which

$$(3.5) \qquad \lambda_1^\rho(s) = \lambda_2^\rho(s) \qquad but \qquad \lambda_1(s) \neq \lambda_2(s).$$

Since $\lambda_1(s)\lambda_2(s) = q/p$ the first relation implies that $\lambda_1(s)\sqrt{p/q}$ must be a (2ρ)th root of unity, that is, we must have

$$(3.6) \qquad \lambda_1(s) = \sqrt{q/p}\, e^{i\pi r/\rho}$$

where r is an integer such that $0 \leq r < 2\rho$. From the definition (3.2) it follows easily that (3.6) holds only when $s = s_r$ where

$$(3.7) \qquad s_r^{-1} = 2\sqrt{pq} \cdot \cos \pi r/\rho.$$

The value $s = s_\rho$ violates the second condition in (3.5); furthermore $s_r = s_{2\rho-r}$, and so ρ distinct characteristic values are given by (3.7) with $r = 0, 1, \ldots, \rho - 1$.

Solving (3.4) with $s = s_r$ and substituting into (3.3) we get

$$(3.8) \qquad x_j^{(r)} = \left(\frac{q}{p}\right)^{j/2} \sin \frac{\pi r j}{\rho} - \left(\frac{q}{p}\right)^{(j+1)/2} \sin \frac{\pi r(j-1)}{\rho}$$

for $r = 1, \ldots, \rho - 1$ whereas for $r = 0$

$$(3.9) \qquad x_j^{(0)} = 1.$$

The adjoint system (1.10) reduces to

$$
(3.10) \qquad
\begin{aligned}
y_1 &= sq(y_1 + y_2), \\
y_k &= s(py_{k-1} + qy_{k+1}), \qquad (k = 2, \ldots, \rho - 1) \\
y_\rho &= sp(y_{\rho-1} + y_\rho).
\end{aligned}
$$

The middle equation is the same as (3.1) with p and q interchanged, and its general solution is therefore obtained from (3.3) by interchanging p and q. The first and the last equations can be satisfied if $s = s_r$, and a simple calculation shows that for $r = 1, 2, \ldots, \rho-1$ the solution of (3.10) is

$$(3.11) \qquad y_k^{(r)} = \left(\frac{p}{q}\right)^{k/2} \sin \frac{\pi r k}{\rho} - \left(\frac{p}{q}\right)^{(k-1)/2} \sin \frac{\pi r(k-1)}{\rho}.$$

For $s_0 = 1$ we get similarly

$$(3.12) \qquad y_k^{(0)} = (p/q)^k.$$

It remains to find the coefficients $c^{(r)}$ defined by

(3.13)
$$c^{(r)} \sum_{k=0}^{\rho-1} x_k^{(r)} y_k^{(r)} = 1.$$

When $r = 0$ the kth term of the sum equals $(p/q)^k$ and so

(3.14)
$$c^{(0)} = \frac{q}{p} \cdot \frac{(p/q) - 1}{(p/q)^\rho - 1},$$

except when $p = q$, in which case $c_0 = 1/\rho$. When $r \geq 1$ an elementary, if tedious, calculation[9] leads to

(3.15)
$$c^{(r)} = \frac{2p}{\rho} \left\{ 1 - 2\sqrt{pq} \cos \frac{\pi r}{\rho} \right\}^{-1}.$$

Accordingly, the general representation (1.15) for the higher transition probabilities leads to the final result[10]

(3.16) $$p_{jk}^{(n)} = \frac{(p/q) - 1}{(p/q)^\rho - 1} \left(\frac{p}{q}\right)^{k-1} + \frac{2p}{\rho} \sum_{r=1}^{\rho-1} \frac{x_j^{(r)} y_k^{(r)} [2\sqrt{pq} \cos \pi r/\rho]^n}{1 - 2\sqrt{pq} \cos \pi r/\rho}$$

with $x_j^{(r)}$ and $y_k^{(r)}$ defined by (3.8) and (3.11). When $p = q$ the first term on the right is to be interpreted as $1/\rho$.

4. TRANSIENT STATES; ABSORPTION PROBABILITIES

The theorem of section 1 was derived under the assumption that the roots $t_1, t_2, \ldots$ are distinct. The presence of multiple roots does not require essential modifications, but we shall discuss only a particular

---

[9] The calculations simplify considerably in complex notation using the fact that $\sin v = [e^{iv} - e^{-iv}]/(2i)$. The sum in (3.13) reduces to a linear combination (with complex coefficients) of sums of the form

$$\sum_{j=0}^{\rho-1} e^{2j\pi i m/\rho}$$

where $m = 0$ or $m = \pm 1$. In the first case the sum equals ρ, in the second 0, and (3.15) follows trivially.

[10] For analogous formulas in the case of one reflecting and one absorbing barrier see M. Kac, *Random walk and the theory of Brownian motion*, Amer. Math. Monthly, vol. 54 (1947), pp. 369–391. The definition of the reflecting barrier is there modified so that the particle may reach 0; whenever this occurs, the next step takes it to 1. The explicit formulas are then more complicated. Kac's paper contains also formulas for $p_{jk}^{(n)}$ in the Ehrenfest model [example XV, (2.e)].

case of special importance. The root $t_1 = 1$ is multiple whenever the chain contains two or more closed subchains, and this is a frequent situation in problems connected with absorption probabilities. It is easy to adapt the method of section 1 to this case. For conciseness and clarity, we shall explain the procedure by means of examples which will reveal the main features of the general case.

Examples. (a) Consider the matrix of transition probabilities

$$(4.1) \qquad P = \begin{bmatrix} \frac{1}{3} & \frac{2}{3} & 0 & 0 & 0 & 0 \\ \frac{2}{3} & \frac{1}{3} & 0 & 0 & 0 & 0 \\ 0 & 0 & \frac{1}{4} & \frac{3}{4} & 0 & 0 \\ 0 & 0 & \frac{1}{5} & \frac{4}{5} & 0 & 0 \\ \frac{1}{4} & 0 & \frac{1}{4} & 0 & \frac{1}{4} & \frac{1}{4} \\ \frac{1}{6} & \frac{1}{6} & \frac{1}{6} & \frac{1}{6} & \frac{1}{6} & \frac{1}{6} \end{bmatrix}.$$

It is clear that E_1 and E_2 form a closed set (that is, no transition is possible to any of the remaining four states; compare XV, 4). Similarly E_3 and E_4 form another closed set. Finally, E_5 and E_6 are transient states. After finitely many steps the system passes into one of the two closed sets and remains there.

The matrix P has the form of a partitioned matrix

$$(4.2) \qquad P = \begin{bmatrix} A & 0 & 0 \\ 0 & B & 0 \\ U & V & T \end{bmatrix}$$

where each letter stands for a 2 by 2 matrix and each zero for a matrix with four zeros. For example, A has the rows $(\frac{1}{3}, \frac{2}{3})$ and $(\frac{2}{3}, \frac{1}{3})$; this is the matrix of transition probabilities corresponding to the chain formed by the two states E_1 and E_2. This matrix can be studied by itself, and the powers A^n can be obtained from example (2.a) with $p = \alpha = \frac{2}{3}$. When the powers $P^2, P^3, \ldots$ are calculated, it will be found that the first two rows are in no way affected by the remaining four rows. More precisely, P^n has the form

$$(4.3) \qquad P^n = \begin{bmatrix} A^n & 0 & 0 \\ 0 & B^n & 0 \\ U_n & V_n & T^n \end{bmatrix}$$

where A^n, B^n, T^n are the nth powers of A, B, and T, respectively, and can be calculated[11] by the method of section 1 [cf. example $(2.a)$ where all calculations are performed]. Instead of six equations with six unknowns we are confronted only with systems of two equations with two unknowns each.

It should be noted that the matrices U_n and V_n in (4.3) are not powers of U and V and cannot be obtained in the same simple way as A^n, B^n, and T^n. However, in the calculation of $P^2, P^3, \ldots$ the third and fourth columns never affect the remaining four columns. In other words, if in P^n the rows and columns corresponding to E_3 and E_4 are deleted, we get the matrix

$$(4.4) \qquad \begin{pmatrix} A^n & 0 \\ U_n & T^n \end{pmatrix}$$

which is the nth power of the corresponding submatrix in P, that is, of

$$(4.5) \qquad \begin{pmatrix} A & 0 \\ U & T \end{pmatrix} = \begin{bmatrix} \frac{1}{3} & \frac{2}{3} & 0 & 0 \\ \frac{2}{3} & \frac{1}{3} & 0 & 0 \\ \frac{1}{4} & 0 & \frac{1}{4} & \frac{1}{4} \\ \frac{1}{6} & \frac{1}{6} & \frac{1}{6} & \frac{1}{6} \end{bmatrix}.$$

Therefore matrix (4.4) can be calculated by the method of section 1, which in the present case simplifies considerably. The matrix V_n can be obtained in a similar way.

Usually the explicit forms of U_n and V_n are of interest only inasmuch as they are connected with *absorption probabilities*. If the system starts from, say, E_5, what is the *probability λ that it will eventually pass into the closed set formed by E_1 and E_2* (and not into the other closed set)? What is the *probability λ_n that this will occur exactly at the nth step*? Clearly $p_{51}^{(n)} + p_{52}^{(n)}$ is the probability that the considered event occurs at the nth step or before, that is,

$$p_{51}^{(n)} + p_{52}^{(n)} = \lambda_1 + \lambda_2 + \cdots + \lambda_n.$$

Letting $n \to \infty$, we get λ. A preferable way to calculate λ_n is as follows. The $(n-1)$st step must take the system to a state other than E_1 and E_2, that is, to either E_5 or E_6 (since from E_3 or E_4 no transition to E_1 and E_2 is possible). The nth step then takes the system to E_1 or E_2.

---

[11] In T the rows do not add to unity so that T is not a stochastic matrix. The matrix is substochastic in the sense of the definition in XV, 8. The method of section 1 applies without change, except that $t = 1$ is no longer a root (so that $T^n \to 0$).

Hence

$$\lambda_n = p_{55}^{(n-1)}(p_{51}+p_{52}) + p_{56}^{(n-1)}(p_{61}+p_{62}) = \tfrac{1}{4}p_{55}^{(n-1)} + \tfrac{1}{3}p_{56}^{(n-1)}.$$

It will be noted that λ_n is completely determined by the elements of T^{n-1}, and this matrix is easily calculated. In the present case

$$p_{55}^{(n)} = p_{56}^{(n)} = \tfrac{1}{4}(\tfrac{5}{12})^{n-1} \quad \text{and hence} \quad \lambda_n = \tfrac{7}{48}(\tfrac{5}{12})^{n-2}.$$

(b) *Brother-sister mating.* We conclude by a numerical treatment of the chain of example XV, $(2.j)$. The main point of the following discussion is to show that the canonical representation

(4.6)
$$p_{jk}^{(n)} = \sum_{r=1}^{6} t_r^n c^{(r)} x_j^{(r)} y_k^{(r)}$$

remains valid even though $t = 1$ is a *double root* of the characteristic equation.

The system (1.9) of linear equations takes on the form

(4.7) $x_1 = tx_1, \quad \tfrac{1}{4}x_1 + \tfrac{1}{2}x_2 + \tfrac{1}{4}x_3 = tx_2,$

$\tfrac{1}{16}x_1 + \tfrac{1}{4}x_2 + \tfrac{1}{4}x_3 + \tfrac{1}{4}x_4 + \tfrac{1}{16}x_5 + \tfrac{1}{8}x_6 = tx_3$

$\tfrac{1}{4}x_3 + \tfrac{1}{2}x_4 + \tfrac{1}{4}x_5 = tx_4, \quad x_5 = tx_5, \quad x_3 = tx_6,$

and these equations exhibit the form of the given matrix. From the first and fifth equations it is clear that $x_1 = x_5 = 0$ unless $t = 1$. For $t \neq 1$, therefore, the equations reduce effectively to four equations for four unknowns and the standard elimination of variables leads to a fourth-degree equation for t as a condition for the compatibility of the four equations. Since there are six characteristic roots in all it follows that $t = 1$ is a double root. It is not difficult to verify that the six characteristic roots are[12]

(4.8) $t_1 = t_2 = 1, \quad t_3 = \tfrac{1}{2}, \quad t_4 = \tfrac{1}{4}, \quad t_5 = \tfrac{1}{4} + \tfrac{1}{4}\sqrt{5}, \quad t_6 = \tfrac{1}{4} - \tfrac{1}{4}\sqrt{5}.$

The corresponding solutions $(x_1^{(r)}, \ldots, x_6^{(r)})$ of (4.7) can be chosen as follows:

(4.9) $(1, \tfrac{3}{4}, \tfrac{1}{2}, \tfrac{1}{4}, 0, \tfrac{1}{2}), \quad (0, \tfrac{1}{4}, \tfrac{1}{2}, \tfrac{3}{4}, 1, \tfrac{1}{2}), \quad (0, 1, 0, -1, 0, 0)$

$(0, 1, -1, 1, 0, -4), \quad (0, 1, -1+\sqrt{5}, 1, 0, 6-2\sqrt{5}),$

$(0, 1, -1-\sqrt{5}, 1, 0, \quad 6+2\sqrt{5}).$

---

[12] The root $t_3 = \tfrac{1}{2}$ can be found by inspection since it corresponds to the simple solution $x_2 = -x_4 = 1$ and $x_1 = x_3 = x_5 = x_6 = 0$. The cubic equation for the other roots is of a simple character.

The next problem is to find the corresponding solutions $(y_1^{(r)}, \ldots, y_6^{(r)})$ of the system obtained from (4.7) by interchanging rows and columns. For $r \geq 3$ this solution is determined up to a multiplicative constant, but corresponding to the double root $t_1 = t_2 = 1$ we have to choose among infinitely many solutions of the form $(a, 0, 0, 0, b, 0)$. The appropriate choice becomes obvious from the form of the desired representation (4.6). Indeed, a glance at (4.9) shows that $x_1^{(r)} = 0$ except for $r = 1$, and hence (4.6) yields $p_{1k}^{(n)} = c^{(1)} y_k^{(1)}$ for all k and n. But E_1 is an absorbing state and it is obvious that $p_{1k}^{(n)} = 0$ for all $k \neq 1$. It follows that for $r = 1$ we must choose a solution of the form $(a, 0, 0, 0, 0, 0)$, and for the same reason a solution corresponding to $r = 2$ is $(0, 0, 0, 0, b, 0)$. The solutions corresponding to the remaining characteristic values are easily found. (Those chosen in our calculations are exhibited by the second rows of the matrices below.) The norming constants $c^{(r)}$ are then determined by (1.14), and in this way we get all the qualities entering the representation formula (4.6).

In the display of the final result the matrices corresponding to $r = 1$ and $r = 2$ have been combined into one. Furthermore, the elements $c^{(r)} x_j^{(r)} y_k^{(r)}$ corresponding to $r = 5$ and $r = 6$ are of the form $a \pm b\sqrt{5}$. For typographical convenience and clarity it was necessary to regroup their contributions in the form $a[t_5^n + t_6^n]$ and $b\sqrt{5}[t_5^n - t_6^n]$.

$$
P^n = \begin{vmatrix} 1 & 0 & 0 & 0 & 0 & 0 \\ \frac{3}{4} & 0 & 0 & 0 & \frac{1}{4} & 0 \\ \frac{1}{2} & 0 & 0 & 0 & \frac{1}{2} & 0 \\ \frac{1}{4} & 0 & 0 & 0 & \frac{3}{4} & 0 \\ 0 & 0 & 0 & 0 & 1 & 0 \\ \frac{1}{2} & 0 & 0 & 0 & \frac{1}{2} & 0 \end{vmatrix} + \frac{2^{-n}}{4} \begin{vmatrix} 0 & 0 & 0 & 0 & 0 & 0 \\ -1 & 2 & 0 & -2 & 1 & 0 \\ 0 & 0 & 0 & 0 & 0 & 0 \\ 1 & -2 & 0 & 2 & -1 & 0 \\ 0 & 0 & 0 & 0 & 0 & 0 \\ 0 & 0 & 0 & 0 & 0 & 0 \end{vmatrix}
$$

$$
+ \frac{4^{-n}}{20} \begin{vmatrix} 0 & 0 & 0 & 0 & 0 & 0 \\ -1 & 4 & -4 & 4 & -1 & -2 \\ 1 & -4 & 4 & -4 & 1 & 2 \\ -1 & 4 & -4 & 4 & -1 & -2 \\ 0 & 0 & 0 & 0 & 0 & 0 \\ 4 & -16 & 16 & -16 & 4 & 8 \end{vmatrix} + \frac{t_5^n + t_6^n}{40} \begin{vmatrix} 0 & 0 & 0 & 0 & 0 & 0 \\ -9 & 6 & 4 & 6 & -9 & 2 \\ -11 & 4 & 16 & 4 & -11 & -2 \\ -9 & 6 & 4 & 6 & -9 & 2 \\ 0 & 0 & 0 & 0 & 0 & 0 \\ -14 & 16 & -16 & 16 & -14 & 12 \end{vmatrix}
$$

$$
+ \frac{t_5^n - t_6^n}{40} \sqrt{5} \begin{vmatrix} 0 & 0 & 0 & 0 & 0 & 0 \\ -4 & 2 & 4 & 2 & -4 & 0 \\ -5 & 4 & 0 & 4 & -5 & 2 \\ -4 & 2 & 4 & 2 & -4 & 0 \\ 0 & 0 & 0 & 0 & 0 & 0 \\ -6 & 0 & 16 & 0 & -6 & -4 \end{vmatrix}.
$$

It is easily verified that this formula is valid for $n = 0$. On the other hand, from the structure of the right side in (4.6) it is clear that if (4.6) holds for some n then it is valid also for $n + 1$. In this way the validity of (4.6) can be established without recourse to the general theory of section 1.

5. APPLICATION TO RECURRENCE TIMES

In problem 19 of XIII,12 it is shown how the mean μ and the variance σ^2 of the recurrence time of a recurrent event $\mathcal{E}$ can be calculated in terms of the probabilities u_n that $\mathcal{E}$ occurs at the nth trial. If $\mathcal{E}$ is not periodic, then

$$(5.1) \qquad u_n \to \frac{1}{\mu} \quad \text{and} \quad \sum_{n=0}^{\infty} \left(u_n - \frac{1}{\mu} \right) = \frac{\sigma^2 - \mu + \mu^2}{2\mu^2},$$

provided that σ^2 is finite.

If we identify $\mathcal{E}$ with a persistent state E_j, then $u_n = p_{jj}^{(n)}$ (and $u_0 = 1$). In a finite Markov chain all recurrence times have finite variance (cf. problem 19 of XV, 14), so that (5.1) applies. Suppose that E_j is not periodic and that formula (1.5) applies. Then $t_1 = 1$ and $|t_r| < 1$ for $r = 2, 3, \ldots$, so that $p_{jj}^{(n)} \to \rho_{jj}^{(1)} = \mu_j^{-1}$. To the term $u_n - \mu^{-1}$ of (5.1) there corresponds

$$(5.2) \qquad p_{jj}^{(n)} - \frac{1}{\mu_j} = \sum_{r=2}^{\rho} \rho_{jj}^{(r)} t_r^n.$$

This formula is valid for $n \geq 1$; summing the geometric series with ratio t_r, we find

$$(5.3) \qquad \sum_{n=1}^{\infty} \left(p_{jj}^{(n)} - \frac{1}{\mu_j} \right) = \sum_{r=2}^{\rho} \frac{\rho_{jj}^{(r)} t_r}{1 - t_r}.$$

Introducing this into (5.1), we find that if E_j is a *non-periodic persistent state, then its mean recurrence time is given by* $\mu_j = 1/\rho_{jj}^{(1)}$, *and the variance of its recurrence time is*

$$(5.4) \qquad \sigma_j^2 = \mu_j - \mu_j^2 + 2\mu_j^2 \sum_{r=2}^{\rho} \frac{\rho_{jj}^{(r)} t_r}{1 - t_r}$$

provided, of course, that formula (1.3) is applicable and $t_1 = 1$. The case of periodic states and the occurrence of double roots require only obvious modifications.

CHAPTER XVII

The Simplest Time-Dependent Stochastic Processes[1]

1. GENERAL ORIENTATION. MARKOV PROCESSES

The Markov chains of the preceding chapters may be described very roughly as stochastic processes in which the future development depends only on the present state, but not on the past history of the process or the manner in which the present state was reached. These processes involve only countably many states $E_1, E_2, \ldots$ and depend on a discrete time parameter, that is, changes occur only at fixed epochs[2] $t = 0, 1, \ldots$. In the present chapter we shall consider phenomena such as telephone calls, radioactive disintegrations, and chromosome breakages, where changes may occur at any time. Mathematically speaking, we shall be concerned with stochastic processes involving only countably many states but depending on a continuous time parameter. A complete description of such processes is not possible within the framework of discrete probabilities and, in fact, we are not in a position to delineate formally the class of Markov processes in which we are interested. Indeed, to describe the past history of the process we must specify the epochs at which changes have occurred, and this involves probabilities in a continuum. Saying that the future development is independent of the past history has an obvious intuitive meaning (at least by analogy with discrete Markov chains), but a formal definition involves conditional probabilities which are beyond the scope of this book. However, many problems connected with such

---

[1] This chapter is almost independent of chapters X–XVI. For the use of the term stochastic process see footnote 28 in XV, 13.

[2] As in the preceding chapters, when dealing with stochastic processes we use the term *epoch* to denote points on the time axis. In formal discussions the word *time* will refer to durations.

processes can be treated separately by quite elementary methods provided
it is taken for granted that the processes actually exist. We shall now proceed in this manner.

To the transition probability $p_{jk}^{(n)}$ of discrete Markov chains there
corresponds now the transition probability $P_{jk}(t)$, namely the conditional
probability of the state E_k at epoch $t+s$ given that at epoch $s < t+s$
the system was in state E_j. As the notation indicates, it is supposed that
this probability depends only on the duration t of the time interval, but
not on its position on the time axis. Such transition probabilities are
called *stationary* or time-homogeneous. (However, inhomogeneous
processes will be treated in section 9.) The analogue to the basic relations
XV,(3.3) is *the Chapman-Kolmogorov identity*

$$(1.1) \qquad\qquad P_{ik}(\tau+t) = \sum_j P_{ij}(\tau)P_{jk}(t),$$

which is based on the following reasoning. Suppose that at epoch 0 the
system is in state E_i. The jth term on the right then represents the probability of the compound event of finding the system at epoch τ in state
E_j, and at the later epoch $\tau+t$ in state E_k. But a transition from E_i at
epoch 0 to E_k at epoch $\tau+t$ necessarily occurs through some intermediary state E_j at epoch τ and summing over all possible E_j we
see that (1.1) must hold for arbitrary (fixed) $\tau > 0$ and $t > 0$.

In this chapter we shall study solutions of the basic identity (1.1). It will
be shown that simple postulates adapted to concrete situations lead to
systems of differential equations for the $P_{jk}(t)$, and interesting results can
be obtained from these differential equations even without solving them.
These results are meaningful because our solutions are actually the transition probabilities of a Markov process which is uniquely determined by
them and the initial state at epoch 0. This intuitively obvious fact[3] will
be taken for granted without proof.

For fixed j and t the transition probabilities $P_{jk}(t)$ define an ordinary
discrete probability distribution. It depends on the continuous parameter
t, but we have encountered many families of distributions involving continuous parameters. Technically the considerations of the following
sections remain within the framework of discrete probabilities, but this
artificial limitation is too rigid for many purposes. The Poisson distribu-
tion $\{e^{-\lambda t}(\lambda t)^n/n!\}$ may illustrate this point. Its zero term $e^{-\lambda t}$ may be

---

[3] It is noteworthy, however, that there may exist (rather pathological) non-Markovian
processes with the same transition probabilities. This point was discussed at length in
XII, 2.*a*, in connection with processes with independent increments (which are a special
class of Markov processes). See also the discussion in section 9, in particular footnote
18.

interpreted as probability that no telephone call arrives within a time interval of fixed length t. But then $e^{-\lambda t}$ is also the probability that the waiting time for the first call exceeds t, and so we are indirectly concerned with a continuous probability distribution on the time axis. We shall return to this point in section 6.

2. THE POISSON PROCESS

The basic Poisson process may be viewed from various angles, and here we shall consider it as the prototype for the processes of this chapter. The following derivation of the Poisson distribution lends itself best for our generalizations, but it is by no means the best in other contexts. It should be compared with the elementary derivation in VI, 6 and the treatment of the Poisson process in XII, (2.a) as the simplest process with independent increments.

For an empirical background take random events such as disintegrations of particles, incoming telephone calls, and chromosome breakages under harmful irradiation. All occurrences are assumed to be of the same kind, and we are concerned with the total number $\mathbf{Z}(t)$ of occurrences in an arbitrary time interval of length t. Each occurrence is represented by a point on the time axis, and hence we are really concerned with certain random placements of points on a line. The underlying physical assumption is that the forces and influences governing the process remain constant so that the probability of any particular event is the same for all time intervals of duration t, and is independent of the past development of the process. In mathematical terms this means that the process is a time-homogeneous Markov process in the sense described in the preceding section. As stated before, we do not aim at a full theory of such processes, but shall be content with deriving the basic probabilities

$$(2.1) \qquad P_n(t) = \mathbf{P}\{\mathbf{Z}(t) = n\}.$$

These can be derived rigorously from simple postulates without appeal to deeper theories.

To introduce notations appropriate for the other processes in this chapter we choose an origin of time measurement and say that *at epoch* $t > 0$ *the system is in state* E_n if exactly n jumps occurred between 0 and t. Then $P_n(t)$ equals the probability of the state E_n at epoch t, but $P_n(t)$ may be described also as the transition probability from an arbitrary state E_j at an arbitrary epoch s to the state E_{j+n} at epoch $s + t$. We now translate our informal description of the process into properties of the probabilities $P_n(t)$.

Let us partition a time interval of unit length into N subintervals of length $h = N^{-1}$. The probability of a jump within any one among these subintervals equals $1 - P_0(h)$, and so the expected number of subintervals containing a jump equals $h^{-1}[1-P_0(h)]$. One feels intuitively that as $h \to 0$ this number will converge to the expected number of jumps within any time interval of unit length, and it is therefore natural to assume[4] that there exists a number $\lambda > 0$ such that

(2.2) $h^{-1}[1-P_0(h)] \to \lambda.$

The physical picture of the process requires also that a jump always leads from a state E_j to the neighboring state E_{j+1}, and this implies that the expected number of subintervals (of length h) containing more than one jump should tend to 0. Accordingly, we shall assume that as $h \to 0$

(2.3) $h^{-1}[1-P_0(h)-P_1(h)] \to 0.$

For the final formulation of the postulates we write (2.2) in the form $P_0(h) = 1 - \lambda h + o(h)$ where (as usual) $o(h)$ denotes a quantity of smaller order of magnitude than h. (More precisely, $o(h)$ stands for a quantity such that $h^{-1}o(h) \to 0$ as $h \to 0$.) With this notation (2.3) is equivalent to $P_1(h) = \lambda h + o(h)$. We now formulate the

Postulates for the Poisson process.   *The process starts at epoch* 0 *from the state* E_0. (i) *Direct transitions from a state* E_j *are possible only to* E_{j+1}. (ii) *Whatever the state* E_j *at epoch* t, *the probability of a jump within an ensuing short time interval between* t *and* $t+h$ *equals* $\lambda h + o(h)$, *while the probability of more than one jump is* $o(h)$.

As explained in the preceding section, these conditions are weaker than our starting notion that the past history of the process in no way influences the future development. On the other hand, our postulates are of a purely analytic character, and they suffice to show that we must have

(2.4) $P_n(t) = \frac{(\lambda t)^n}{n!} e^{-\lambda t}.$

To prove this assume first $n \geq 1$ and consider the event that at epoch $t+h$ the system is in state E_n. The probability of this event equals $P_n(t+h)$, and the event can occur in three mutually exclusive ways. First, at epoch t the system may be in state E_n and no jump occurs between t and $t+h$. The probability of this contingency is

$$P_n(t)P_0(h) = P_n(t)[1-\lambda h] + o(h).$$

---

[4] The assumption (2.2) is introduced primarily because of its easy generalization to other processes. In the present case it would be more natural to observe that $P_0(t)$ must satisfy the functional equation $P_0(t+\tau) = P_0(t)P_0(\tau)$, which implies (2.2). (See section 6.)

The second possibility is that at epoch t the system is in state E_{n-1} and exactly one jump occurs between t and $t+h$. The probability for this is $P_{n-1}(t) \cdot \lambda h + o(h)$. Any other state at epoch t requires more than one jump between t and $t+h$, and the probability of such an event is $o(h)$. Accordingly we must have

$$(2.5) \qquad P_n(t+h) = P_n(t)(1-\lambda h) + P_{n-1}(t)\lambda h + o(h)$$

and this relation may be rewritten in the form

$$(2.6) \qquad \frac{P_n(t+h) - P_n(t)}{h} = -\lambda P_n(t) + \lambda P_{n-1}(t) + \frac{o(h)}{h}.$$

As $h \to 0$, the last term tends to zero; hence the limit[5] of the left side exists and

$$(2.7) \qquad P_n'(t) = -\lambda P_n(t) + \lambda P_{n-1}(t) \qquad\qquad (n \geq 1).$$

For $n = 0$ the second and third contingencies mentioned above do not arise, and therefore (2.7) is to be replaced by

$$(2.8) \qquad P_0(t+h) = P_0(t)(1-\lambda h) + o(h),$$

which leads to

$$(2.9) \qquad P_0'(t) = -\lambda P_0(t).$$

From this and $P_0(0) = 1$ we get $P_0(t) = e^{-\lambda t}$. Substituting this $P_0(t)$ into (2.7) with $n = 1$, we get an ordinary differential equation for $P_1(t)$. Since $P_1(0) = 0$, we find easily that $P_1(t) = \lambda t e^{-\lambda t}$, in agreement with (2.4). Proceeding in the same way, we find successively all terms of (2.4).

3. THE PURE BIRTH PROCESS

The simplest generalization of the Poisson process is obtained by permitting the probabilities of jumps to depend on the actual state of the system. This leads us to the following

Postulates. (i) *Direct transitions from a state E_j are possible only to E_{j+1}.* (ii) *If at epoch t the system is in state E_n the probability of a jump*

---

[5] Since we restricted h to positive values, $P_n'(t)$ in (2.7) should be interpreted as a right-hand derivative. It is really an ordinary two-sided derivative. In fact, the term $o(h)$ in (2.5) does not depend on t and therefore remains unchanged when t is replaced by $t - h$. Thus (2.5) implies continuity, and (2.6) implies differentiability in the ordinary sense. This remark applies throughout the chapter and will not be repeated.

within an ensuing short time interval between t *and* $t+h$ *equals* $\lambda_n h + o(h)$, *while the probability of more than one jump within this interval is* $o(h)$.

The salient feature of this assumption is that the time which the system spends in any particular state plays no role; there are sudden changes of state but no aging as long as the system remains within a single state.

Again let $P_n(t)$ be the probability that at epoch t the system is in state E_n. The functions $P_n(t)$ satisfy a system of differential equations which can be derived by the argument of the preceding section, with the only change that (2.5) is replaced by

$$(3.1) \qquad P_n(t+h) = P_n(t)(1 - \lambda_n h) + P_{n-1}(t)\lambda_{n-1}h + o(h).$$

In this way we get the *basic system of differential equations*

$$(3.2) \qquad \begin{aligned} P_n'(t) &= -\lambda_n P_n(t) + \lambda_{n-1}P_{n-1}(t) \qquad\qquad (n \geq 1), \\ P_0'(t) &= -\lambda_0 P_0(t). \end{aligned}$$

In the Poisson process it was natural to assume that the system starts from the initial state E_0 at epoch 0. We may now assume more generally that the system starts from an arbitrary initial state E_i. This implies that[6]

$$(3.3) \qquad\qquad P_i(0) = 1, \qquad P_n(0) = 0 \qquad\qquad for \quad n \neq i.$$

These *initial conditions* uniquely determine the solution $\{P_n(t)\}$ of (3.2). [In particular, $P_0(t) = P_1(t) = \cdots = P_{i-1}(t) = 0$.] Explicit formulas for $P_n(t)$ have been derived independently by many authors but are of no interest to us. It is easily verified that for arbitrarily prescribed λ_n the system $\{P_n(t)\}$ has all required properties, except that under certain conditions $\sum P_n(t) < 1$. This phenomenon will be discussed in section 4.

Examples. (a) *Radioactive transmutations.* A radioactive atom, say uranium, may by emission of particles or γ-rays change to an atom of a different kind. Each kind represents a possible state of the system, and as the process continues, we get a succession of transitions $E_0 \to E_1 \to E_2 \to \to \cdots \to E_m$. According to accepted physical theories, the probability of a transition $E_n \to E_{n+1}$ remains unchanged as long as the atom is in state E_n, and this hypothesis is expressed by our starting supposition. The differential equations (3.2) therefore describe the process (a fact well known to physicists). If E_m is the terminal state from which no further

---

[6] It will be noticed that $P_n(t)$ is the same as the transition probability $P_{in}(t)$ of section 1.

transitions are possible, then $\lambda_m = 0$ and the system (3.2) terminates with $n = m$. [For $n > m$ we get automatically $P_n(t) = 0$.]

(b) *The Yule process.* Consider a population of members which can (by splitting or otherwise) give birth to new members but cannot die. Assume that during any short time interval of length h each member has probability $\lambda h + o(h)$ to create a new one; the constant λ determines the rate of increase of the population. If there is no interaction among the members and at epoch t the population size is n, then the probability that an increase takes place at some time between t and $t+h$ equals $n\lambda h + o(h)$. The probability $P_n(t)$ that the population numbers exactly n elements therefore satisfies (3.2) with $\lambda_n = n\lambda$, that is,

$$(3.4) \qquad P'_n(t) = -n\lambda P_n(t) + (n-1)\lambda P_{n-1}(t) \qquad (n \geq 1).$$

$$P'_0(t) = 0.$$

Denote the initial population size by i. The initial conditions (3.3) apply and it is easily verified that for $n \geq i > 0$

$$(3.5) \qquad P_n(t) = \binom{n-1}{n-i} e^{-i\lambda t}(1-e^{-\lambda t})^{n-i}$$

and, of course, $P_n(t) = 0$ for $n < i$ and all t. Using the notation VI,(8.1) for the negative binomial distribution we may rewrite (3.5) as $P_n(t) = f(n - i;\ i,\ e^{-\lambda t})$. It follows [cf. example IX,(3.c)] that the population size at epoch t is the sum of i independent random variables each having the distribution obtained from (3.5) on replacing i by 1. These i variables represent the progenies of the i original members of our population.

This type of process was first studied by Yule[7] in connection with the mathematical theory of evolution. The population consists of the species within a genus, and the creation of a new element is due to mutations.

---

[7] G. Udny Yule, *A mathematical theory of evolution, based on the conclusions of Dr. J. C. Willis*, F.R.S., Philosophical Transactions of the Royal Society, London, Series B, vol. 213 (1924), pp. 21–87. Yule does not introduce the differential equations (3.4) but derives $P_n(t)$ by a limiting process similar to the one used in VI,5, for the Poisson process. Much more general, and more flexible, models of the same type were devised and applied to epidemics and population growth in an unpretentious and highly interesting paper by Lieutenant Colonel A. G. M'Kendrick, *Applications of mathematics to medical problems*, Proceedings Edinburgh Mathematical Society, vol. 44 (1925), pp. 1–34. It is unfortunate that this remarkable paper passed practically unnoticed. In particular, it was unknown to the present author when he introduced various stochastic models for population growth in *Die Grundlagen der Volterraschen Theorie des Kampfes ums Dasein in wahrscheinlichkeitstheoretischer Behandlung*, Acta Biotheoretica, vol. 5 (1939), pp. 11–40.

The assumption that each species has the same probability of throwing out a new species neglects the difference in species sizes. Since we have also neglected the possibility that a species may die out, (3.5) can be expected to give only a crude approximation.

Furry[8] used the same model to describe a process connected with cosmic rays, but again the approximation is rather crude. The differential equations (3.4) apply strictly to a population of particles which can split into exact replicas of themselves, provided, of course, that there is no interaction among particles.   ▶

*4. DIVERGENT BIRTH PROCESSES

The solution $\{P_n(t)\}$ of the infinite system of differential equations (3.2) subject to initial conditions (3.3) can be calculated inductively, starting from $P_i(t) = e^{-\lambda_i t}$. The distribution $\{P_n(t)\}$ is therefore uniquely determined. From the familiar formulas for solving linear differential equations it follows also that $P_n(t) \geq 0$. The only question left open is whether $\{P_n(t)\}$ is a proper probability distribution, that is, whether or not

$$(4.1) \qquad\qquad \sum P_n(t) = 1$$

for all t. We shall see that this is not always so: With rapidly increasing coefficients λ_n it may happen that

$$(4.2) \qquad\qquad \sum P_n(t) < 1.$$

When this possibility was discovered it appeared disturbing, but it finds a ready explanation. The left side in (4.2) may be interpreted as the probability that during a time interval of duration t only a *finite number* of jumps takes place. Accordingly, the difference between the two sides in (4.2) accounts for the possibility of infinitely many jumps, or a sort of explosion. For a better understanding of this phenomenon let us compare our probabilistic model of growth with the familiar deterministic approach.

The quantity λ_n in (3.2) could be called the average rate of growth of a population of size n. For example, in the special case (3.4) we have $\lambda_n = n\lambda$, so that the average rate of growth is proportional to the actual population size. If growth is not subject to chance fluctuations and has a rate of increase proportional to the instantaneous population size $x(t)$,

---

* This section treats a special topic and may be omitted.

[8] *On fluctuation phenomena in the passage of high-energy electrons through lead*, Physical Reviews, vol. 52 (1937), p. 569.

the latter varies in accordance with the deterministic differential equation

(4.3)
$$\frac{dx(t)}{dt} = \lambda x(t).$$

It implies that

(4.4)
$$x(t) = ie^{\lambda t},$$

where $i = x(0)$ is the initial population size. It is readily seen that the expectation $\sum n P_n(t)$ of the distribution (3.5) coincides with $x(t)$, and thus $x(t)$ describes not only a deterministic growth process, but also the expected population size in example (3.b).

Let us now consider a deterministic growth process where the rate of growth increases faster than the population size. To a rate of growth proportional to $x^2(t)$ there corresponds the differential equation

(4.5)
$$\frac{dx(t)}{dt} = \lambda x^2(t)$$

whose solution is

(4.6)
$$x(t) = \frac{i}{1 - \lambda it}.$$

Note that $x(t)$ increases beyond all bounds as $t \to 1/\lambda i$. In other words, the assumption that the rate of growth increases as the square of the population size implies an infinite growth within a finite time interval. Similarly, if in (3.4) the λ_n increase too fast, there is a finite probability that infinitely many changes take place in a finite time interval. A precise answer about the conditions when such a divergent growth occurs is given by the

Theorem. *In order that $\sum P_n(t) = 1$ for all t it is necessary and sufficient that the series $\sum \lambda_n^{-1}$ diverges.*[9]

Proof. Put

(4.7)
$$S_k(t) = P_0(t) + \cdots + P_k(t).$$

Because of the obvious monotonicity the limit

(4.8)
$$\mu(t) = \lim_{k \to \infty} [1 - S_k(t)]$$

exists. Summing the differential equations (3.2) over $n = 0, \ldots, k$ we get

(4.9)
$$S_k'(t) = -\lambda_k P_k(t).$$

---

[9] It is not difficult to see that the inequality $\sum P_n(t) < 1$ holds either for all $t > 0$, or else for no $t > 0$. See problem 22.

In view of the initial conditions (3.3) this implies for $k \geq i$

$$(4.10) \qquad\qquad 1 - S_k(t) = \lambda_k \int_0^t P_k(\tau) \, d\tau .$$

Because of (4.8) the left side lies between μ and 1, and hence

$$(4.11) \qquad\qquad \lambda_k^{-1} \mu(t) \leq \int_0^t P_k(s) \, ds \leq \lambda_k^{-1}.$$

Summing for $k = i, \ldots, n$ we get for $n \geq i$

$$(4.12) \quad \mu(t)[\lambda_i^{-1} + \cdots + \lambda_n^{-1}] \leq \int_0^t S_n(s) \, ds \leq \lambda_i^{-1} + \cdots + \lambda_n^{-1}.$$

When $\sum \lambda_n^{-1} < \infty$ the rightmost member remains bounded as $n \to \infty$, and hence it is impossible that the integrand tends to 1 for all t. Conversely, if $\sum \lambda_n^{-1} = \infty$ we conclude from the first inequality that $\mu(t) = 0$ for all t, and in view of (4.8) this implies that $S_n(t) \to 1$, as asserted. ▶

The criterion becomes plausible when interpreted probabilistically. The system spends some time at the initial state E_0, moves from there to E_1, stays for a while there, moves on to E_2, etc. The probability $P_0(t)$ that the sojourn time in E_0 exceeds t is obtained from (3.2) as $P_0(t) = e^{-\lambda_0 t}$. This sojourn time, T_0, is a random variable, but its range is the positive t-axis and therefore formally out of bounds for this book. However, the step from a geometric distribution to an exponential being trivial, we may with impunity trespass a trifle. An approximation to T_0 by a discrete random variable with a geometric distribution shows that it is natural to define the expected sojourn time at E_0 by

$$(4.13) \qquad\qquad \mathbf{E}(T_0) = \int_0^\infty t e^{-\lambda_0 t} \, \lambda_0 \, dt = \lambda_0^{-1}.$$

At the epoch when the system enters E_j, the state E_j takes over the role of the initial state and the same conclusion applies to the sojourn time T_j at E_j: The *expected sojourn time at E_j is $\mathbf{E}(T_j) = \lambda_j^{-1}$*. It follows that $\lambda_0^{-1} + \lambda_1^{-1} + \cdots + \lambda_n^{-1}$ is the expected duration of the time it takes the system to pass through $E_0, E_1, \ldots, E_n$, and we can restate the criterion of section 4 as follows:

In order that $\sum P_n(t) = 1$ for all t it is necessary and sufficient that

$$(4.14) \qquad\qquad \sum \mathbf{E}(T_j) = \sum \lambda_j^{-1} = \infty ;$$

that is, the total expected duration of the time spent at $E_0, E_1, E_2, \ldots$ must be infinite. Of course, $L_0(t) = 1 - \sum P_n(t)$ is the probability that the system has gone through *all* states before epoch t.

With this interpretation the possibility of the inequality (4.2) becomes understandable. If the expected sojourn time at E_j is 2^{-j}, the probability that the system has passed through all states within time $1 + 2^{-1} + 2^{-2} + \cdots = 2$ must be positive. Similarly, a particle moving along the x-axis at an exponentially increasing velocity traverses the entire axis in a finite time.

[We shall return to divergent birth process in example (9.b).]

5. THE BIRTH-AND-DEATH PROCESS

The pure birth process of section 3 provides a satisfactory description of radioactive transmutations, but it cannot serve as a realistic model for changes in the size of populations whose members can die (or drop out). This suggests generalizing the model by permitting transitions from the state E_n not only to the next higher state E_{n+1} but also to the next lower state E_{n-1}. (More general processes will be defined in section 9.) Accordingly we start from the following

Postulates. *The system changes only through transitions from states to their nearest neighbors (from E_n to E_{n+1} or E_{n-1} if $n \geq 1$, but from E_0 to E_1 only). If at epoch t the system is in state E_n, the probability that between t and $t+h$ the transition $E_n \to E_{n+1}$ occurs equals $\lambda_n h + o(h)$, and the probability of $E_n \to E_{n-1}$ (if $n \geq 1$) equals $\mu_n h + o(h)$. The probability that during $(t, t+h)$ more than one change occurs is $o(h)$.*

It is easy to adapt the method of section 2 to derive differential equations for the probabilities $P_n(t)$ of finding the system in state E_n. To calculate $P_n(t+h)$, note that the state E_n at epoch $t+h$ is possible only under one of the following conditions: (1) At epoch t the system is in E_n and between t and $t+h$ no change occurs; (2) at epoch t the system is in E_{n-1} and a transition to E_n occurs; (3) at epoch t the system is in E_{n+1} and a transition to E_n occurs; (4) between t and $t+h$ there occur two or more transitions. By assumption, the probability of the last event is $o(h)$. The first three contingencies are mutually exclusive and their probabilities add. Therefore

$$(5.1) \quad P_n(t+h) = P_n(t)\{1 - \lambda_n h - \mu_n h\} + \\ + \lambda_{n-1} h P_{n-1}(t) + \mu_{n+1} h P_{n+1}(t) + o(h).$$

Transposing the term $P_n(t)$ and dividing the equation by h we get on the left the difference ratio of $P_n(t)$, and in the limit as $h \to 0$

$$(5.2) \qquad P_n'(t) = -(\lambda_n + \mu_n)P_n(t) + \lambda_{n-1}P_{n-1}(t) + \mu_{n+1}P_{n+1}(t).$$

This equation holds for $n \geq 1$. For $n = 0$ in the same way

$$(5.3) \qquad\qquad P_0'(t) = -\lambda_0 P_0(t) + \mu_1 P_1(t).$$

If the initial state is E_i, the *initial conditions* are

$$(5.4) \qquad\qquad P_i(0) = 1, \qquad P_n(0) = 0 \qquad\qquad for \quad n \neq i.$$

The birth-and-death process is thus seen to depend on the infinite system of differential equations (5.2)–(5.3) together with the initial condition (5.4). The question of existence and of uniqueness of solutions is in this case by no means trivial. In a pure birth process the system (3.2) of differential equations was also infinite, but it had the form of recurrence relations; $P_0(t)$ was determined by the first equation and $P_n(t)$ could be calculated from $P_{n-1}(t)$. The new system (5.2) is not of this form, and all $P_n(t)$ must be found simultaneously. We shall here (and elsewhere in this chapter) state properties of the solutions without proof.[10]

For arbitrarily prescribed coefficients $\lambda_n \geq 0$, $\mu_n \geq 0$ *there always exists a positive solution* $\{P_n(t)\}$ *of* (5.2)–(5.4) *such that* $\sum P_n(t) \leq 1$. *If the coefficients are bounded* (*or increase sufficiently slowly*), *this solution is unique and satisfies the regularity condition* $\sum P_n(t) = 1$. However, it is possible to choose the coefficients in such a way that $\sum P_n(t) < 1$ and that there exist infinitely many solutions. In the latter case we encounter a phenomenon analogous to that studied in the preceding section for the pure birth process. This situation is of considerable theoretical interest, but the reader may safely assume that in all cases of practical significance the conditions of uniqueness are satisfied; in this case automatically $\sum P_n(t) = 1$ (see section 9).

When $\lambda_0 = 0$ the transition $E_0 \to E_1$ is impossible. In the terminology of Markov chains E_0 is an *absorbing state* from which no exit is possible; once the system is in E_0 it stays there. From (5.3) it follows that in this case $P_0'(t) \geq 0$, so that $P_0(t)$ increases monotonically. The limit $P_0(\infty)$ is the probability of *ultimate absorption*.

It can be shown (either from the explicit form of the solutions or from the general ergodic theorems for Markov processes) that under any circumstance *the limits*

$$(5.5) \qquad \lim_{t \to \infty} P_n(t) = p_n$$

exist and are independent of the initial conditions (5.4); they satisfy the system of linear equations obtained from (5.2)–(5.3) on replacing the derivatives on the left by zero.

The relations (5.5) resemble the limit theorems derived in XV,7 for ordinary Markov chains, and the resemblance is more than formal. Intuitively (5.5) becomes almost obvious by a comparison of our process

---

[10] The simplest existence proof and uniqueness criterion are obtained by specialization from the general theory developed by the author (see section 9). Solutions of the birth-and-death process such that $\sum P_n(t) < 1$ have recently attracted wide attention. For explicit treatments see W. Lederman and G. E. Reuter, *Spectral theory for the differential equations of simple birth and death processes*. Philosophical Transactions of the Royal Society, London, Series A, vol. 246 (1954), pp. 387–391; S. Karlin and J. L. McGregor, *The differential equations of birth-and-death processes and the Stieltjes moment problem*, Trans. Amer. Math. Soc., vol. 85 (1957), pp. 489–546, and *The classification of birth and death processes*, ibid. vol. 86 (1957), pp. 366–400. See also W. Feller, *The birth and death processes as diffusion processes*, Journal de Mathématiques Pures at Appliquées, vol. 38 (1959), pp. 301–345.

with a simple Markov chain with transition probabilities

$$(5.6) \qquad p_{n,n+1} = \frac{\lambda_n}{\lambda_n + \mu_n}, \qquad p_{n,n-1} = \frac{\mu_n}{\lambda_n + \mu_n}.$$

In this chain the only direct transitions are $E_n \to E_{n+1}$ and $E_n \to E_{n-1}$, and they have the same conditional probabilities as in our process; the difference between the chain and our process lies in the fact that, with the latter, changes can occur at arbitrary times, so that the number of transitions during a time interval of length t is a random variable. However, for large t this number is certain to be large, and hence it is plausible that for $t \to \infty$ the probabilities $P_n(t)$ behave as the corresponding probabilities of the simple chain.

If the simple chain with transition probabilities (5.6) is transient we have $p_n = 0$ for all n; if the chain is ergodic the p_n define a stationary probability distribution. In this case (5.5) is usually interpreted as a "tendency toward the steady state condition" and this suggestive name has caused much confusion. It must be understood that, except when E_0 is an absorbing state, the chance fluctuations continue forever unabated and (5.5) shows only that in the long run the influence of the initial condition disappears. The remarks made in XV, 7 concerning the statistical equilibria apply here without change.

The principal field of applications of the birth-and-death process is to problems of waiting times, trunking, etc.; see sections 6 and 7.

Examples. (*a*) *Linear growth.* Suppose that a population consists of elements which can split or die. During any short time interval of length h the probability for any living element to split into two is $\lambda h + o(h)$, whereas the corresponding probability of dying is $\mu h + o(h)$. Here λ and μ are two constants characteristic of the population. If there is no interaction among the elements, we are led to a birth and death process with $\lambda_n = n\lambda$, $\mu_n = n\mu$. The basic differential equations take on the form

$$(5.7) \quad \begin{aligned} P_0'(t) &= \mu P_1(t), \\ P_n'(t) &= -(\lambda+\mu)n P_n(t) + \lambda(n-1)P_{n-1}(t) + \mu(n+1)P_{n+1}(t). \end{aligned}$$

Explicit solutions can be found[11] (cf. problems 11–14), but we shall not

---

[11] A systematic way consists in deriving a partial differential equation for the generating function $\sum P_n(t)s^n$. A more general process where the coefficients λ and μ in (5.7) are permitted to depend on time is discussed in detail in David G. Kendall, *The generalized "birth and death" process*, Ann. Math. Statist., vol. 19 (1948), pp. 1–15. See also the same author's *Stochastic processes and population growth*, Journal of the Royal Statistical Society, B, vol. 11 (1949), pp. 230–265 where the theory is generalized to take account of the age distribution in biological populations.

discuss this aspect. The limits (5.5) exist and satisfy (5.7) with $P'_n(t) = 0$. From the first equation we find $p_1 = 0$, and we see by induction from the second equation that $p_n = 0$ for all $n \geq 1$. If $p_0 = 1$, we may say that the probability of ultimate extinction is 1. If $p_0 < 1$, the relations $p_1 = p_2 \cdots = 0$ imply that with probability $1 - p_0$ the population increases over all bounds; ultimately the population must either die out or increase indefinitely. To find the probability p_0 of extinction we compare the process to the related Markov chain. In our case the transition probabilities (5.6) are independent of n, and we have therefore an ordinary random walk in which the steps to the right and left have probabilities $p = \lambda/(\lambda+\mu)$ and $q = \mu/(\lambda+\mu)$, respectively. The state E_0 is absorbing. We know from the classical ruin problem (see XIV, 2) that the probability of extinction is 1 if $p \leq q$ and $(q/p)^i$ if $q < p$ and i is the initial state. We conclude that *in our process the probability $p_0 = \lim P_0(t)$ of ultimate extinction is 1 if $\lambda \leq \mu$, and $(\mu/\lambda)^i$ if $\lambda > \mu$.* (This is easily verified from the explicit solution; see problems 11–14.)

As in many similar cases, the explicit solution of (5.7) is rather complicated, and it is desirable to calculate the mean and the variance of the distribution $\{P_n(t)\}$ directly from the differential equations. We have for the mean

$$(5.8) \qquad M(t) = \sum_{n=1}^{\infty} nP_n(t).$$

We shall omit a formal proof that $M(t)$ is finite and that the following formal operations are justified (again both points follow readily from the solution given in problem 12). Multiplying the second equation in (5.7) by n and adding over $n = 1, 2, \ldots$, we find that the terms containing n^2 cancel, and we get

$$(5.9) \qquad M'(t) = \lambda \sum (n-1)P_{n-1}(t) - \mu \sum (n+1)P_{n+1}(t) =$$

$$= (\lambda-\mu)M(t).$$

This is a differential equation for $M(t)$. The initial population size is i, and hence $M(0) = i$. Therefore

$$(5.10) \qquad M(t) = ie^{(\lambda-\mu)t}.$$

We see that the mean tends to 0 or infinity, according as $\lambda < \mu$ or $\lambda > \mu$. The variance of $\{P_n(t)\}$ can be calculated in a similar way (cf. problem 14).

(b) *Waiting lines for a single channel.* In the simplest case of constant coefficients $\lambda_n = \lambda$, $\mu_n = \mu$ the birth-and-death process reduces to a special case of the waiting line example (7.b) when $a = 1$.

6. EXPONENTIAL HOLDING TIMES

The principal field of applications of the pure birth-and-death process is connected with trunking in telephone engineering and various types of waiting lines for telephones, counters, or machines. This type of problem can be treated with various degrees of mathematical sophistication. The method of the birth-and-death process offers the easiest approach, but this model is based on a mathematical simplification known as the *assumption of exponential holding times*. We begin with a discussion of this basic assumption.

For concreteness of language let us consider a telephone conversation, and let us assume that its length is necessarily an integral number of seconds. We treat the length of the conversation as a random variable X and assume its probability distribution $p_n = \mathbf{P}\{X = n\}$ known. The telephone line then represents a physical system with two possible states, "busy" (E_0) and "free" (E_1). When the line is busy, the probability of a change in state during the next second depends on how long the conversation has been going on. In other words, the past has an influence on the future, and our process is therefore not a Markov process (see XV,13). This circumstance is the source of difficulties, but fortunately there exists a simple exceptional case discussed at length in XIII,9.

Imagine that the decision whether or not the conversation is to be continued is made each second at random by means of a skew coin. In other words, a sequence of Bernoulli trials with probability p of success is performed at a rate of one per second and continued until the first success. The conversation ends when this first success occurs. In this case the total length of the conversation, the "holding time," has the geometric distribution $p_n = q^{n-1}p$. Whenever the line is busy, the probability that it will remain busy for more than one second is q, and the probability of the transition $E_0 \to E_1$ at the next step is p. These probabilities are now independent of how long the line was busy.

When it is undesirable to use a discrete time parameter it becomes necessary to work with continuous random variables. The role of the geometric distribution for waiting times is then taken over by the *exponential distribution*. It is the only distribution having a Markovian character, that is, endowed with complete lack of memory. In other words, the probability that a conversation which goes on at epoch x continues beyond $x + h$ is independent of the past duration of the conversation if, and only if, the probability that the conversation lasts for longer than t time units is given by an exponential $e^{-\lambda t}$. We have encountered this "exponential holding time distribution" as the zero term in the Poisson distribution (2.4), that is, as the waiting time up to the occurrence of the first change.

The method of the birth-and-death process is applicable only if the transition probabilities in question do not depend on the past; for trunking and waiting line problems this means that all holding times must be exponential. From a practical point of view this assumption may at first sight appear rather artificial, but experience shows that it reasonably describes actual phenomena. In particular, many measurements have shown that telephone conversations within a city[12] follow the exponential law to a surprising degree of accuracy. The same situation prevails for other holding times (e.g., the duration of machine repairs).

It remains to characterize the so-called incoming traffic (arriving calls, machine breakdowns, etc.). We shall assume that during any time interval of length h the probability of an incoming call is λh plus negligible terms, and that the probability of more than one call is in the limit negligible. According to the results of section 2, this means that the number of incoming calls has a Poisson distribution with mean λt. We shall describe this situation by saying that *the incoming traffic is of the Poisson type with intensity* λ.

It is easy to verify the described property of exponential holding times. Denote by $u(t)$ the probability that a conversation lasts for at least t time units. The probability $u(t+s)$ that a conversation starting at 0 lasts beyond $t + s$ equals the probability that it lasts longer than t units multiplied by the conditional probability that a conversation lasts additional s units, given that its length exceeds t. If the past duration has no influence, the last conditional probability must equal $u(s)$; that is, we must have

$$(6.1) \qquad u(t+s) = u(t)\,u(s).$$

To prove the asserted characterization of exponential holding times it would suffice to show that *monotone* solutions of this functional equation are necessarily of the form $e^{-\lambda t}$. We prove a slightly stronger result which is of interest in itself.[13]

Theorem. *Let u be a solution of* (6.1) *defined for $t > 0$ and bounded in some interval. Then either $u(t) = 0$ for all t, or else $u(t) = e^{-\lambda t}$ for some constant λ.*

Proof. Clearly

$$(6.2) \qquad u(a) = u^2(\tfrac{1}{2}a).$$

Suppose first that $u(a) = 0$ for some value a. From (6.2) we conclude by induction that $u(2^{-n}a) = 0$ for all integers n, and from (6.1) it is clear that $u(s) = 0$ implies

---

[12] Rates for long distance conversations usually increase after three minutes and the holding times are therefore frequently close to three minutes. Under such circumstances the exponential distribution does not apply.

[13] (6.1) is only a logarithmic variant of the famous Hamel equation $f(t + s) = f(t) + f(s)$. We prove that its solutions are either of the form at or else unbounded in *every* interval. (It is known that no such solution is a Baire function, that is, no such solution can be obtained by series expansions or other limiting processes starting from continuous functions.)

$u(t) = 0$ for all $t > s$. Thus $u(a) = 0$ implies that u vanishes identically. Since (6.2) obviously excludes negative values of u it remains only to consider strictly positive solutions of (6.1).

Put $e^{-\lambda} = u(1)$ and $v(t) = e^{\lambda t}u(t)$. Then

$$(6.3) \qquad\qquad v(t+s) = v(t)v(s) \qquad and \qquad v(1) = 1.$$

We have to prove that this implies $v(t) = 1$ for all t. Obviously for arbitrary positive integers m and n

$$(6.4) \qquad\qquad v\left(\frac{m}{n}\right) = v^m\left(\frac{1}{n}\right) = \sqrt[n]{v^m(1)} = 1$$

and hence $v(s) = 1$ for all rational s. Furthermore, if $v(a) = c$ then $v(na) = c^n$ for any positive or negative integer n. It follows that if u assumes some value $c \neq 1$ then it assumes also arbitrarily large values. But using (6.1) with $t + s = \tau$ it is seen that $v(\tau-s) = v(\tau)$ for all rational s. Accordingly, if a value A is assumed at some point τ, the same value is assumed in every interval, however small. The boundedness of u in any given interval therefore precludes the possibility of any values $\neq 1$.   ▶

7. WAITING LINE AND SERVICING PROBLEMS

(a) *The simplest trunking problem.*[14] Suppose that infinitely many trunks or channels are available, and that the probability of a conversation ending between t and $t+h$ is $\mu h + o(h)$ (exponential holding time). The incoming calls constitute a traffic of the Poisson type with parameter λ. The system is in state E_n if n lines are busy.

It is, of course, assumed that the durations of the conversations are mutually independent. If n lines are busy, the probability that one of them will be freed within time h is then $n\mu h + o(h)$. The probability that within this time two or more conversations terminate is obviously of the order of magnitude h^2 and therefore negligible. The probability of a new call arriving is $\lambda h + o(h)$. The probability of a combination of several calls, or of a call arriving and a conversating ending, is again $o(h)$. Thus, in the

---

[14] C. Palm, *Intensitätsschwankungen im Fernsprechverkehr*, Ericsson Technics (Stockholm), no. 44 (1943), pp. 1–189, in particular p. 57. Waiting line and trunking problems for telephone exchanges were studied long before the theory of stochastic processes was available and had a stimulating influence on the development of the theory. In particular, Palm's impressive work over many years has proved useful. The earliest worker in the field was A. K. Erlang (1878–1929). See E. Brockmeyer, H. L. Halström, and Arne Jensen, *The life and works of A. K. Erlang*, Transactions of the Danish Academy Technical Sciences, No. 2, Copenhagen, 1948. Independently valuable pioneer work has been done by T. C. Fry whose book, *Probability and its engineering uses*, New York (Van Nostrand), 1928, did much for the development of engineering applications of probability.

notation of section 5

(7.1) $\lambda_n = \lambda, \qquad \mu_n = n\mu.$

The basic differential equations (5.2)–(5.3) take the form

(7.2)
$$P_0'(t) = -\lambda P_0(t) + \mu P_1(t)$$
$$P_n'(t) = -(\lambda+n\mu)P_n(t) + \lambda P_{n-1}(t) + (n+1)\mu P_{n+1}(t)$$

where $n \geq 1$. Explicit solutions can be obtained by deriving a partial differential equation for the generating function (cf. problem 15). We shall only determine the quantities $p_n = \lim P_n(t)$ of (5.5). They satisfy the equations

(7.3)
$$\lambda p_0 = \mu p_1$$
$$(\lambda+n\mu)p_n = \lambda p_{n-1} + (n+1)\mu p_{n+1}.$$

We find by induction that $p_n = p_0(\lambda/\mu)^n/n!$, and hence

(7.4) $$p_n = e^{-\lambda/\mu}\frac{(\lambda/\mu)^n}{n!}.$$

Thus, *the limiting distribution is a Poisson distribution with parameter* λ/μ. *It is independent of the initial state.*

It is easy to find the mean $M(t) = \sum nP_n(t)$. Multiplying the nth equation of (7.2) by n and adding, we get, taking into account that the $P_n(t)$ add to unity,

(7.5) $$M'(t) = \lambda - \mu M(t).$$

When the initial state is E_i, then $M(0) = i$, and

(7.6) $$M(t) = \frac{\lambda}{\mu}(1-e^{-\mu t}) + ie^{-\mu t}.$$

The reader may verify that in the special case $i = 0$ the $P_n(t)$ are given exactly by the Poisson distribution with mean $M(t)$.

(b) *Waiting lines for a finite number of channels.*[15] We now modify the last example to obtain a more realistic model. The assumptions are the same, except that *the number a of trunklines or channels is finite. If all a channels are busy, each new call joins a waiting line and waits until a channel is freed.* This means that all trunklines have a *common* waiting line.

The word "trunk" may be replaced by *counter* at a postoffice and "conversation" by *service*. We are actually treating the general waiting

---

[15] A. Kolmogoroff, *Sur le problème d'attente*, Recueil Mathématique [Sbornik], vol. 38 (1931), pp. 101–106. For related processes see problems 6–8 and 20.

line problem for the case where a person has to wait only if all a channels are busy.

We say that *the system is in state E_n if there are exactly n persons either being served or in the waiting line.* Such a line exists only when $n > a$, and then there are $n - a$ persons in it.

As long as at least one channel is free, the situation is the same as in the preceding example. However, if the system is in a state E_n with $n > a$, only a conversations are going on, and hence $\mu_n = a\mu$, for $n \geq a$. The basic system of differential equations is therefore given by (7.2) for $n < a$, but for $n \geq a$ by

$$(7.7) \qquad P'_n(t) = -(\lambda + a\mu)P_n(t) + \lambda P_{n-1}(t) + a\mu P_{n+1}(t).$$

In the special case of a single channel $(a = 1)$ these equations reduce to those of a birth-and-death process with coefficients independent of n. The limits $p_n = \lim p_n(t)$ satisfy (7.3) for $n < a$, and

$$(7.8) \qquad (\lambda + a\mu)p_n = \lambda p_{n-1} + a\mu p_{n+1}$$

for $n \geq a$. By recursion we find that

$$(7.9) \qquad p_n = p_0 \frac{(\lambda/\mu)^n}{n!}, \qquad\qquad n \leq a$$

$$(7.10) \qquad p_n = \frac{(\lambda/\mu)^n}{a! \, a^{n-a}} p_0, \qquad\qquad n \geq a.$$

The series $\sum (p_n/p_0)$ converges only if

$$(7.11) \qquad\qquad \lambda/\mu < a.$$

Hence a limiting distribution $\{p_k\}$ cannot exist when $\lambda \geq a\mu$. *In this case $p_n = 0$ for all n, which means that gradually the waiting line grows over all bounds.* On the other hand, if (7.11) holds, then we can determine p_0 so that $\sum p_n = 1$. From the explicit expressions for $P_n(t)$ it can be shown that the p_n thus obtained really represent the *limiting distribution* of the $P_n(t)$. Table 1 gives a numerical illustration for $a = 3$, $\lambda/\mu = 2$.

(*c*) *Servicing of machines.*[16] For orientation we begin with the simplest case and generalize it in the next example. The problem is as follows.

We consider automatic machines which normally require no human care except that they may break down and call for service. The time required

---

[16] Examples (*c*) and (*d*), including the numerical illustrations, are taken from an article by C. Palm, *The distribution of repairmen in servicing automatic machines* (in Swedish), Industritidningen Norden, vol. 75 (1947), pp. 75–80, 90–94, 119–123. Palm gives tables and graphs for the most economical number of repairmen.

for servicing the machine is again taken as a random variable with an exponential distribution. In other words, the machine is characterized by two constants λ and μ with the following properties. If at epoch t the machine is in working state, the probability that it will call for service before epoch $t+h$ equals λh plus terms which are negligible in the limit $h \to 0$. Conversely, when the machine is being serviced, the probability that the servicing time terminates before $t+h$ and the machine reverts to the working state equals $\mu h + o(h)$. For an efficient machine λ should be relatively small and μ relatively large. The ratio λ/μ is called the *servicing factor*.

We suppose that *m machines with the same parameters λ and μ and working independently are serviced by a single repairman.* A machine which

TABLE 1

LIMITING PROBABILITIES IN THE CASE OF $a = 3$
CHANNELS AND $\lambda/\mu = 2$

n	0	1	2	3	4	5	6	7
Lines busy	0	1	2	3	3	3	3	3
People waiting	0	0	0	0	1	2	3	4
p_n	0.1111	0.2222	0.2222	0.1481	0.09888	0.0658	0.0439	0.0293

breaks down is serviced immediately unless the repairman is servicing another machine, in which case a waiting line is formed. We say that *the system is in state E_n if n machines are not working.* For $1 \leq n \leq m$ this means that one machine is being serviced and $n - 1$ are in the waiting line; in the state E_0 all machines work and the repairman is idle.

A transition $E_n \to E_{n+1}$ is caused by a breakdown of one among the $m - n$ working machines, whereas a transition $E_n \to E_{n-1}$ occurs if the machine being serviced reverts to the working state. Hence we have a birth-and-death process with coefficients

$$(7.12) \qquad \lambda_n = (m-n)\lambda, \qquad \mu_0 = 0, \qquad \mu_1 = \mu_2 = \cdots = \mu_m = \mu.$$

For $1 \leq n \leq m - 1$ the basic differential equations (5.2) become

$$(7.13) \quad P'_n(t) = -\{(m-n)\lambda+\mu\}P_n(t) + (m-n+1)\lambda P_{n-1}(t) + \mu P_{n+1}(t),$$

while for the limiting states $n = 0$ and $n = m$

$$(7.13a) \qquad \begin{aligned} P'_0(t) &= -m\lambda P_0(t) + \mu P_1(t), \\ P'_m(t) &= -\mu P_m(t) + \lambda P_{m-1}(t). \end{aligned}$$

This is finite system of differential equations and can be solved by standard methods. The limits $p_n = \lim P_n(t)$ are determined by

$$m\lambda p_0 = \mu p_1,$$

(7.14) $$\{(m-n)\lambda + \mu\}p_n = (m-n+1)\lambda p_{n-1} + \mu p_{n+1},$$

$$\mu p_m = \lambda p_{m-1}.$$

TABLE 2

ERLANG'S LOSS FORMULA
PROBABILITIES p_n FOR THE CASE $\lambda/\mu = 0.1$,
$m = 6$

n	Machines in Waiting Line	p_n
0	0	0.4845
1	0	0.2907
2	1	0.1454
3	2	0.0582
4	3	0.0175
5	4	0.0035
6	5	0.0003

From these equations we get the recursion formula

(7.15) $$(m-n)\lambda p_n = \mu p_{n+1}.$$

Substituting successively $n = m - 1, m - 2, \ldots, 1, 0,$ we find

$$p_{m-k} = \frac{1}{k!}\left(\frac{\mu}{\lambda}\right)^k \cdot p_m.$$

The remaining unknown constant p_m can be obtained from the condition that the p_j add to unity. The result is known as *Erlang's loss formula*:

(7.16) $$p_m = \left\{1 + \frac{1}{1!}\left(\frac{\mu}{\lambda}\right)^1 + \cdots + \frac{1}{m!}\left(\frac{\mu}{\lambda}\right)^m\right\}^{-1}.$$

Typical numerical values are exhibited in table 2.

The probability p_0 may be interpreted as the probability of the repairman's being idle (in the example of table 2 he should be idle about half the time). The *expected number of machines in the waiting line is*

(7.17) $$w = \sum_{k=1}^{m}(k-1)p_k = \sum_{k=1}^{m}kp_k - (1-p_0).$$

This quantity can be calculated by adding the relations (7.15) for $n = 0, 1, \ldots, m$. Using the fact that the p_n add to unity, we get

$$m\lambda - \lambda w - \lambda(1-p_0) = \mu(1-p_0)$$

or

(7.18) $$w = m - \frac{\lambda + \mu}{\lambda}(1-p_0).$$

In the example of table 2 we have $w = 6 \cdot (0.0549)$. Thus 0.0549 is the average contribution of a machine to the waiting line.

(*d*) *Continuation: several repairmen.* We shall not change the basic assumptions of the preceding problem, except that the m *machines are now serviced by* r *repairmen* ($r < m$). Thus for $n \leq r$ the state E_n means that $r - n$ repairmen are idle, n machines are being serviced, and no machine is in the waiting line for repairs. For $n > r$ the state E_n signifies that r machines are being serviced and $n - r$ machines are in the waiting line. We can use the setup of the preceding example except that (7.12) is obviously to be replaced by

(7.19) $$\lambda_0 = m\lambda, \qquad \mu_0 = 0,$$
$$\lambda_n = (m-n)\lambda, \qquad \mu_n = n\mu \qquad (1 \leq n \leq r),$$
$$\lambda_n = (m-n)\lambda, \qquad \mu_n = r\mu \qquad (r \leq n \leq m).$$

We shall not write down the basic system of differential equations but only the equations for the limiting probabilities p_n. For $1 \leq n < r$

(7.20a) $$\{(m-n)\lambda + n\mu\}p_n = (m-n+1)\lambda p_{n-1} + (n+1)\mu p_{n+1}$$

while for $r \leq n \leq m$

(7.20b) $$\{(m-n)\lambda + r\mu\}p_n = (m-n+1)\lambda p_{n-1} + r\mu p_{n+1}.$$

For $n = 0$ obviously $m\lambda p_0 = \mu p_1$. This relation determines the ratio p_1/p_0, and from (7.20a) we see by induction that for $n < r$

(7.21) $$(n+1)\mu p_{n+1} = (m-n)\lambda p_n;$$

finally, for $n \geq r$ we get from (7.20b)

(7.22) $$r\mu p_{n+1} = (m-n)\lambda p_n.$$

These equations permit calculating successively the ratios p_n/p_0. Finally, p_0 follows from the condition $\sum p_k = 1$. The values in table 3 are obtained in this way.

A comparison of tables 2 and 3 reveals surprising facts. They refer to the same machines $(\lambda/\mu = 0.1)$, but in the second case we have $m = 20$ machines and $r = 3$ repairmen. The number of machines per repairman

TABLE 3

PROBABILITIES p_n FOR THE CASE $\lambda/\mu = 0.1$, $m = 20$, $r = 3$

n	Machines Serviced	Machines Waiting	Repairmen Idle	p_n
0	0	0	3	0.13625
1	1	0	2	0.27250
2	2	0	1	0.25888
3	3	0	0	0.15533
4	3	1	0	0.08802
5	3	2	0	0.04694
6	3	3	0	0.02347
7	3	4	0	0.01095
8	3	5	0	0.00475
9	3	6	0	0.00190
10	3	7	0	0.00070
11	3	8	0	0.00023
12	3	9	0	0.00007

has increased from 6 to $6\frac{2}{3}$, and yet the machines are serviced more efficiently. Let us define a *coefficient of loss for machines* by

$$(7.23) \qquad \frac{w}{m} = \frac{\text{average number of machines in waiting line}}{\text{number of machines}}$$

and a coefficient of loss for repairmen by

$$(7.24) \qquad \frac{\rho}{r} = \frac{\text{average number of repairmen idle}}{\text{number of repairmen}}.$$

For practical purposes we may identify the probabilities $P_n(t)$ with their limits p_n. In table 3 we have then $w = p_4 + 2p_5 + 3p_6 + \cdots + 17p_{20}$ and $\rho = 3p_0 + 2p_1 + p_2$. Table 4 proves conclusively that for our particular machines (with $\lambda/\mu = 0.1$) *three repairmen per twenty machines are much more economical than one repairman per six machines.*

(e) *A power-supply problem.*[17] One electric circuit supplies *a* welders who use the current only intermittently. If at epoch *t* a welder uses current, the probability that he ceases using before epoch *t+h* is $\mu h + o(h)$; if at epoch *t* he requires no current, the probability that he calls for current before *t+h* is $\lambda h + o(h)$. The welders work independently of each other.

We say that the system is in state E_n if *n* welders are using current. Thus we have only finitely many states $E_0, \ldots, E_a$.

TABLE 4

COMPARISON OF EFFICIENCIES OF TWO SYSTEMS DISCUSSED
IN EXAMPLES (c) AND (d)

	(c)	(d)
Number of machines	6	20
Number of repairmen	1	3
Machines per repairman	6	$6\frac{2}{3}$
Coefficient of loss for repairmen	0.4845	0.4042
Coefficient of loss for machines	0.0549	0.01694

If the system is in state E_n, then $a - n$ welders are not using current and the probability for a new call for current within a time interval of duration *h* is $(a-n)\lambda h + o(h)$; on the other hand, the probability that one of the *n* welders ceases using current is $n\mu h + o(h)$. Hence we have a birth-and-death process with

$$(7.25) \qquad \lambda_n = (a-n)\lambda, \qquad \mu_n = n\mu, \qquad 0 \le n \le a.$$

The basic differential equations become

$$(7.26) \quad \begin{aligned} P_0'(t) &= -a\lambda P_0(t) + \mu P_1(t), \\ P_n'(t) &= -\{n\mu+(a-n)\lambda\}P_n(t) + (n+1)\mu P_{n+1}(t) + \\ &\qquad + (a-n+1)\lambda P_{n-1}(t), \\ P_a'(t) &= -a\mu P_a(t) + \lambda P_{a-1}(t). \end{aligned}$$

---

[17] This example was suggested by the problem treated (inadequately) by H. A. Adler and K. W. Miller, *A new approach to probability problems in electrical engineering*, Transactions of the American Institute of Electrical Engineers, vol. 65 (1946), pp. 630–632.

(Here $1 \leq n \leq a - 1$.) It is easily verified that *the limiting probabilities are given by the binomial distribution*

$$(7.27) \qquad p_n = \binom{a}{n} \left(\frac{\lambda}{\lambda + \mu} \right)^n \left(\frac{\mu}{\lambda + \mu} \right)^{a-n},$$

a result which could have been anticipated on intuitive grounds. (Explicit representations for the $P_n(t)$ are given in problem 17.)

8. THE BACKWARD (RETROSPECTIVE) EQUATIONS

In the preceding sections we were studying the probabilities $P_n(t)$ of finding the system at epoch t in state E_n. This notation is convenient but misleading, inasmuch as it omits mentioning the initial state E_i of the system at time zero. For the further development of the theory it is preferable to revert to the notations of section 1 and to the use of *transition probabilities*. Accordingly we denote by $P_{in}(t)$ the (conditional) probability of the state E_n at epoch $t + s$ given that at epoch s the system was in state E_i. We continue to denote by $P_n(t)$ the (absolute) probability of E_n at epoch t. When the initial state E_i is given, the absolute probability $P_n(t)$ coincides with $P_{in}(t)$, but when the initial state is chosen in accordance with a probability distribution $\{a_i\}$ we have

$$(8.1) \qquad P_n(t) = \sum_i a_i P_{in}(t).$$

For the special processes considered so far we have shown that for fixed i the transition probabilities $P_{in}(t)$ *satisfy the basic differential equations* (3.2) *and* (5.2). The subscript i appears only in the initial conditions, namely

$$(8.2) \qquad P_{in}(0) = \begin{cases} 1 & \text{for} \quad n = i \\ 0 & \text{otherwise.} \end{cases}$$

As a preparation for the theory of more general processes we now proceed to show that the same transition probabilities satisfy also a second system of differential equations. To fix ideas, let us start with the pure birth process of section 3. The differential equations (3.2) were derived by prolonging the time interval $(0, t)$ to $(0, t+h)$ and considering the possible changes during the short time $(t, t+h)$. We could as well have prolonged the interval $(0, t)$ in the direction of the past and considered the changes during $(-h, 0)$. In this way we get a new system of differential equations in which n (instead of i) remains fixed. Indeed, a transition from E_i at epoch $-h$ to E_n at epoch t can occur in three mutually exclusive ways: (1) No jump occurs between $-h$ and 0, and the system passes from the state E_i at epoch 0 to E_n. (2) Exactly one jump occurs between $-h$ and 0, and the system passes from the state E_{i+1} at epoch 0 to E_n at epoch t; (3) more than one jump occurs between $-h$ and 0. The probability of the first contingency is $1 - \lambda_i h + o(h)$, that of the second $\lambda_i h + o(h)$, while the third contingency has probability $o(h)$. As in sections 2 and 3 we conclude that

$$(8.3) \qquad P_{in}(t+h) = P_{in}(t)(1-\lambda_i h) + P_{i+1,n}(t)\lambda_i h + o(h).$$

Hence for $i \geq 0$ the new basic system now takes the form

$$(8.4) \qquad P'_{in}(t) = -\lambda_i P_{in}(t) + \lambda_i P_{i+1,n}(t).$$

These equations are called the *backward equations*, and, for distinction, equations (3.2) are called the *forward equations*. The initial conditions are (8.2). [Intuitively one should expect that

$$(8.5) \qquad P_{in}(t) = 0 \quad \text{if} \quad n < i,$$

but pathological exceptions exist; see example (9.b).]

In the case of the birth-and-death process the basic *forward equations* (for fixed i) are represented by (5.2)–(5.3). The argument that lead to (8.4) now leads to the corresponding *backward equations*

$$(8.6) \qquad P'_{in}(t) = -(\lambda_i+\mu_i)P_{i,n}(t) + \lambda_i P_{i+1,n}(t) + \mu_i P_{i-1,n}(t).$$

It should be clear that the forward and backward equations are not independent of each other; the solution of the backward equations with the initial conditions (8.2) automatically satisfies the forward equations, except in the rare situations where the solution is not unique.

Example. *The Poisson process.* In section 2 we have interpreted the Poisson expression (2.4) as the probability that exactly n calls arrive during any time interval of length t. Let us say that at epoch t the system is in state E_n if exactly n calls arrive within the time interval from 0 to t. A transition from E_i at t_1 to E_n at t_2 means that $n - i$ calls arrived between t_1 and t_2. This is possible only if $n \geq i$, and hence we have for the transition probabilities of the Poisson process

$$(8.7) \qquad \begin{aligned} P_{in}(t) &= e^{-\lambda t}\frac{(\lambda t)^{n-i}}{(n-i)!} && \text{if} \quad n \geq i, \\[2mm] P_{in}(t) &= 0 && \text{if} \quad n < i. \end{aligned}$$

They satisfy the forward equations

(8.8) $$P'_{in}(t) = -\lambda P_{in}(t) + \lambda P_{i,n-1}(t)$$

as well as the backward equations

(8.9) $$P'_{in}(t) = -\lambda P_{in}(t) + \lambda P_{i+1,n}(t). \qquad \blacktriangleright$$

9. GENERAL PROCESSES

So far the theory has been restricted to processes in which direct transitions from a state E_n are possible only to the neighboring states E_{n+1} and E_{n-1}. Moreover, the processes have been time-homogeneous, that is to say, the transition probabilities $P_{in}(t)$ have been the same for all time intervals of length t. We now consider more general processes in which both assumptions are dropped.

As in the theory of ordinary Markov chains, we shall permit direct transitions from any state E_i to any state E_n. The transition probabilities are permitted to vary in time. This necessitates specifying the two endpoints of any time interval instead of specifying just its length. Accordingly, we shall write $P_{in}(\tau, t)$ *for the conditional probability of finding the system at epoch t in state E_n, given that at a previous epoch τ the state was E_i.* The symbol $P_{in}(\tau, t)$ is meaningless unless $\tau < t$. If the process is homogeneous in time, then $P_{in}(\tau, t)$ depends only on the difference $t - \tau$, and we can write $P_{in}(t)$ instead of $P_{in}(\tau, \tau+t)$ (which is then independent of τ).

We saw in section 1 that the transition probabilities of time-homogeneous Markov processes satisfy the *Chapman-Kolmogorov equation*

(9.1a) $$P_{in}(s+t) = \sum_v P_{iv}(s)P_{vn}(t).$$

The analogous identity for non-homogeneous processes reads

(9.1b) $$P_{in}(\tau, t) = \sum_v P_{iv}(\tau, s)P_{vn}(s, t)$$

and is valid for $\tau < s < t$. This relation expresses the fact that a transition from the state E_i at epoch τ to E_n at epoch t occurs via some state E_v at the intermediate epoch s, and for Markov processes the probability $P_{vn}(s, t)$ of the transition from E_v to E_n is independent of the previous state E_i. The transition probabilities of Markov processes with countably many states are therefore solutions of the Chapman-Kolmogorov identity (9.1b) satisfying the side conditions

(9.2) $$P_{ik}(\tau, t) \geq 0, \qquad \sum_k P_{ik}(\tau, t) = 1.$$

We shall take it for granted without proof that, conversely, such solution represents the transition probabilities of a Markov process.[18] It follows that a basic problem of the theory of Markov processes consists in finding all solutions of the Chapman-Kolmogorov identity satisfying the side conditions (9.2).

The main purpose of the present section is to show that the postulates of the birth-and-death processes admit of a natural generalization permitting arbitrary direct transitions $E_i \to E_j$. From these postulates we shall derive two systems of ordinary differential equations, to be called forward and backward equations, respectively. Under ordinary circumstances each of the two systems uniquely determines the transition probabilities. The forward equations are probabilistically more natural but, curiously enough, their derivation requires stronger and less intuitive assumptions.

In the time-homogeneous birth-and-death process of section 5 the starting postulates referred to the behavior of the transition probabilities $P_{jk}(h)$ for small h; in essence it was required that the derivatives P'_{jk} exist at the origin. For inhomogeneous processes we shall impose the same condition on $P_{jk}(t, t+x)$ considered as functions of x. The derivatives will have an analogous probabilistic interpretation, but they will be functions of t.

Assumption 1. *To every state E_n there corresponds a continuous function $c_n(t) \geq 0$ such that as $h \to 0$*

$$(9.3) \qquad \frac{1 - P_{nn}(t, t+h)}{h} \to c_n(t).$$

Assumption 2. *To every pair of states E_j, E_k with $j \neq k$ there correspond transition probabilities $p_{jk}(t)$ (depending on time) such that as $h \to 0$*

$$(9.4) \qquad \frac{P_{jk}(t, t+h)}{h} \to c_j(t)p_{jk}(t) \qquad\qquad (j \neq k).$$

---

[18] The notion of a Markov process requires that, given the state E_v at epoch s, the development of the process prior to epoch s has no influence on the future development. As was pointed out in section 1, the Chapman-Kolomogorov identity expresses this requirement only partially because it involves only one epoch $\tau < s$ and one epoch $t > s$. The long-outstanding problem whether there exist non-Markovian processes whose transition probabilities satisfy (9.1) has now been solved in the affirmative; the simplest known such process is time-homogeneous and involves only three states E_j [See W. Feller, Ann. Math. Statist., vol. 30 (1959), pp. 1252–1253.] Such processes are rather pathological, however, and their existence does not contradict the assertion that *every* solution of the Chapman-Kolmogorov equation satisfying (9.2) corresponds (in a unique manner) to a Markov process.

The $p_{jk}(t)$ are continuous in t, and for every fixed t, j

$$(9.5) \qquad\qquad \sum_k p_{jk}(t) = 1, \qquad\qquad p_{jj}(t) = 0.$$

The probabilistic interpretation of (9.3) is obvious; if at epoch t the system is in state E_n, the probability that between t and $t+h$ a change occurs is $c_n(t)h + o(h)$. The coefficient $p_{jk}(t)$ can be interpreted as the conditional probability that, *if* a change from E_j occurs between t and $t+h$, this change takes the system from E_j to E_k. In the birth-and-death process $c_n(t) = \lambda_n + \mu_n$,

$$(9.6) \qquad p_{j,j+1}(t) = \frac{\lambda_j}{\lambda_j + \mu_j}, \qquad p_{j,j-1}(t) = \frac{\mu_j}{\lambda_j + \mu_j},$$

and $p_{jk}(t) = 0$ for all other combinations of j and k. For every fixed t the $p_{jk}(t)$ can be interpreted as transition probabilities of a Markov chain.

The two assumptions suffice to derive a system of backward equations for the $P_{jk}(\tau, t)$, but for the forward equations we require in addition

Assumption 3. *For fixed k the passage to the limit in (9.4) is uniform with respect to j.*

The necessity of this assumption is of considerable theoretical interest and will be discussed presently.

We proceed to derive differential equations for the $P_{ik}(\tau, t)$ as functions of t and k (forward equations). From (9.1) we have

$$(9.7) \qquad P_{ik}(\tau, t+h) = \sum_j P_{ij}(\tau, t)P_{jk}(t, t+h).$$

Expressing the term $P_{kk}(t, t+h)$ on the right in accordance with (9.3), we get

$$(9.8) \quad \frac{P_{ik}(\tau, t+h) - P_{ik}(\tau, t)}{h} =$$

$$= -c_k(t)P_{ik}(\tau, t) + h^{-1}\sum_{j \neq k} P_{ij}(\tau, t)P_{jk}(t, t+h) + \cdots$$

where the neglected terms tend to 0 with h, and the sum extends over all j except $j = k$. We now apply (9.4) to the terms of the sum. Since (by assumption 3) the passage to the limit is uniform in j, the right side has a limit. Hence also the left side has a limit, which means that $P_{ik}(\tau, t)$ has a partial derivative with respect to t, and

$$(9.9) \qquad \frac{\partial P_{ik}(\tau, t)}{\partial t} = -c_k(t)P_{ik}(\tau, t) + \sum_j P_{ij}(\tau, t)c_j(t)p_{jk}(t).$$

This is the basic system of forward differential equations. Here i and τ are fixed so that we have (despite the formal appearance of a partial derivative) a system of *ordinary differential equations*[19] for the functions $P_{ik}(\tau, t)$. The parameters i and τ appear only in the initial *condition*

$$(9.10) \qquad P_{ik}(\tau, \tau) = \begin{array}{ll} 1 & for \quad k = i \\ 0 & otherwise. \end{array}$$

We now turn to the backward equations. In them k and t are kept constant so that the transition probabilities $P_{ik}(\tau, t)$ are considered as functions of the initial data E_i and τ. In the formulation of our starting assumptions the initial variable was kept fixed, but for the derivation of the backward equations it is preferable to formulate the same conditions with reference to a time interval from $t-h$ to t. In other words, it is more natural to start from the following *alternative form for the conditions* (9.3) *and* (9.4):

$$(9.3a) \qquad \frac{1 - P_{nn}(t-h, t)}{h} \to c_n(t)$$

$$(9.4a) \qquad \frac{P_{jk}(t-h, t)}{h} \to c_j(t)p_{jk}(t) \qquad\qquad (j \neq k).$$

It is not difficult to prove the equivalence of the two sets of conditions (or to express them in a unified form), but we shall be content to start from the alternative form. The remarkable feature of the following derivation is that no analogue to assumption 3 is necessary.

By the Chapman-Kolmogorov identity (9.1b)

$$(9.11) \qquad P_{ik}(\tau-h, t) = \sum_v P_{iv}(\tau-h, \tau)P_{vk}(\tau, t),$$

and using (9.3a) with $n = i$, we get

$$(9.12) \qquad \frac{P_{ik}(\tau-h, t) - P_{ik}(\tau, t)}{h} =$$

$$= -c_i(\tau)P_{ik}(\tau, t) + h^{-1}\sum_{v \neq i} P_{iv}(\tau-h, \tau)P_{vk}(\tau, t) + \cdots.$$

---

[19] The standard form would be

$$x_k'(t) = -c_k(t)x_k(t) + \sum_j x_j(t)c_j(t)p_{jk}(t).$$

Here $h^{-1}P_{iv}(\tau-h, \tau) \to c_i(\tau)p_{iv}(\tau)$ and the passage to the limit in the sum to the right in (9.12) is always uniform. In fact, if $N > i$ we have

$$(9.13) \quad 0 \le h^{-1} \sum_{v=N+1}^{\infty} P_{iv}(\tau-h, \tau)P_{vk}(\tau, t) \le h^{-1} \sum_{v=N+1}^{\infty} P_{iv}(\tau-h, \tau) =$$

$$= h^{-1}\left\{1 - \sum_{v=0}^{N} P_{iv}(\tau-h, \tau)\right\} \to c_i(\tau)\left\{1 - \sum_{v=0}^{N} p_{iv}(\tau)\right\}.$$

In view of condition (9.5) the right side can be made arbitrarily small by choosing N sufficiently large. It follows that a termwise passage to the limit in (9.12) is permitted and we obtain

$$(9.14) \qquad \frac{\partial P_{ik}(\tau, t)}{\partial \tau} = c_i(\tau)P_{ik}(\tau, t) - c_i(\tau) \sum_v p_{iv}(\tau)P_{vk}(\tau, t).$$

These are the basic *backward differential equations*. Here k and t appear as fixed parameters and so (9.14) represents a system of *ordinary* differential equations. The parameters k and t appear only in the *initial conditions*

$$(9.15) \qquad P_{ik}(t, t) = \begin{array}{ll} 1 & for \quad i = k \\ 0 & otherwise. \end{array}$$

Example. (*a*) *Generalized Poisson process.* Consider the case where *all $c_i(t)$ equal the same constant, $c_i(t) = \lambda$, and the p_{jk} are independent of t.* In this case the p_{jk} are the transition probabilities of an ordinary Markov chain and (as in chapter XV) we denote its higher transition probabilities by $p_{jk}^{(n)}$.

From $c_i(t) = \lambda$, it follows that the probability of a transition occurring betwen t and $t + h$ is independent of the state of the system and equals $\lambda h + o(h)$. This implies that the number of transitions between τ and t has a Poisson distribution with parameter $\lambda(t-\tau)$. Given that exactly n transitions occurred, the (conditional) probability of a passage from j to k is $p_{jk}^{(n)}$. Hence

$$(9.16) \qquad P_{ik}(\tau, t) = e^{-\lambda(t-\tau)} \sum_{n=0}^{\infty} \frac{\lambda^n(t-\tau)^n}{n!} p_{ik}^{(n)}$$

(where, as usual, $p_{jj}^{(0)} = 1$ and $p_{jk}^{(0)} = 0$ for $j \ne k$). It is easily verified that (9.16) is in fact a solution of the two systems (9.9) and (9.14) of differential equations satisfying the boundary conditions.

In particular, if

$$(9.17) \qquad p_{jk} = 0 \quad for \quad k < j, \qquad p_{jk} = f_{k-j} \quad for \quad k \ge j$$

(9.16) reduces to the *compound Poisson distribution* of XII,2.   ▶

Our two systems of differential equations were first derived by A. Kolmogorov in an important paper developing the foundations of the theory of Markov processes.[20] Assuming that the sequence of coefficients $c_n(t)$ remains bounded for each t it was then shown by W. Feller that there exists a unique solution $\{P_{jk}(\tau, t)\}$ common to both systems, and that this solution satisfies the Chapman-Kolmogorov identity (9.1b) as well as the side conditions (9.2). Furthermore, in this case neither system of differential equations possesses any other solutions, and hence the two systems are essentially equivalent. However, concrete problems soon lead to equations with unbounded sequences $\{c_n\}$ and, as shown in section 4, in such cases we sometimes encounter unexpected solutions for which

$$(9.18) \qquad\qquad \sum_k P_{jk}(\tau, t) \leq 1$$

holds with the strict inequality. It has been shown[21] [without any restrictions on the coefficients $c_n(t)$] that there always exists a *minimal solution* $\{P_{jk}(\tau, t)\}$ satisfying both systems of differential equations as well as the Chapman-Kolmogorov identity (9.1b) and (9.18). This solution is called minimal because

$$(9.19) \qquad\qquad \bar{P}_{jk}(\tau, t) \geq P_{jk}(\tau, t)$$

whenever the left sides satisfy either the backward or the forward differential equations (together with the trite initial conditions (9.10)]. When the minimal solution satisfies (9.18) with the equality sign for all t, this implies that neither the backward nor the forward equations can have any probabilistically meaningful solutions besides $P_{jk}(\tau, t)$. In other words, when the minimal solution is not defective, the process is uniquely determined by either system of equations. As stated before, this is so when the coefficients $c_n(t)$ remain bounded for each fixed t.

The situation is entirely different when the minimal solution is defective, that is, when in (9.18) the inequality sign holds for some (and hence for all) t. In this case there exist infinitely many honest transition probabilities

[20] A. Kolmogoroff, *Über die analytischen Methoden in der Wahrscheinlichkeitsrechnung*, Mathematische Annalen, vol. 104 (1931), pp. 415–458.

[21] W. Feller, *On the integro-differential equations of purely discontinuous Markoff processes*, Trans. Amer. Math. Soc., vol. 48 (1940), pp. 488–515. This paper treats more general state spaces, but countable state spaces are mentioned as special case of greatest interest. This was overlooked by subsequent authors who gave more complicated and less complete derivations. The minimal solution in the time-homogeneous case is derived in XIV, 7 of volume 2 by the use of Laplace transforms. For a more complete treatment see W. Feller, *On boundaries and lateral conditions for the Kolmogorov differential equations*, Ann. Math., vol. 65 (1957), pp. 527–570.

satisfying the backward equations and the Chapman-Kolmogorov identity, and hence there exist infinitely many Markovian processes satisfying the basic assumptions 1 and 2 underlying the backward equations. Some of these may satisfy also the forward equations, but in other cases the solution of the forward equations is unique.[22]

Example. (b) *Birth processes.* The differential equations (3.2) for the time-homogeneous birth process were of the form

$$(9.20) \qquad x_0'(t) = -\lambda_0 x_0(t), \qquad x_k'(t) = -\lambda_k x_k(t) + \lambda_{k-1} x_{k-1}(t).$$

These are the forward equations. Since they form a recursive system the solution is uniquely determined by its initial values for $t = 0$. For the transition probabilities we get therefore successively $P_{ik}(t) = 0$ for all $k < i$,

$$(9.21) \qquad P_{ii}(t) = e^{-\lambda_i t}, \qquad P_{i,i+1}(t) = \frac{\lambda_i}{\lambda_i - \lambda_{i+1}} (e^{-\lambda_{i+1} t} - e^{-\lambda_i t}),$$

and finally for $k > i$

$$(9.22) \qquad P_{ik}(t) = \lambda_{k-1} \int_0^t e^{-\lambda_k s} P_{i,k-1}(t-s) \, ds.$$

To see that these transition probabilities satisfy the Chapman-Kolmogorov identity (9.1a) it suffices to notice that for fixed i and s both sides of the identity represent solutions of the differential equations (9.20) assuming the same initial values.

The backward equations were derived in (8.4) and are of the form

$$(9.23) \qquad y_i'(t) = -\lambda_i y_i(t) + \lambda_i y_{i+1}(t).$$

We have to show that this equation is satisfied by $P_{ik}(t)$ when k is kept fixed. This is trivially true when $k < i$ because in this case all three terms in (9.23) vanish. Using (9.21) it is seen that the assertion is true also when $k - i = 0$ and $k - i = 1$. We can now proceed by induction using the fact that for $k > i + 1$

$$(9.24) \qquad P_{ik}'(t) = \lambda_{k-1} \int_0^t e^{-\lambda_k s} \cdot P_{i,k-1}'(t-s) \, ds.$$

---

[22] It will be recalled that only assumptions 1 and 2 are probabilistically meaningful whereas assumption 3 is of a purely analytic character and was introduced only for convenience. It is unnatural in the sense that not even all solutions of the forward equations satisfy the imposed uniformity condition. Thus the backward equations express probabilistically meaningful conditions and lead to interesting processes, but the same cannot be said of the forward equations. This explains why the whole theory of Markov processes must be based on the backward equations (or abstractly, on semi-groups of transformations of functions rather than probability measures).

Assume that the $P_{ik}(t)$ satisfy (9.23) if $k - i \leq n$. For $k = i + 1 + n$ we can then express the integrand in (9.24) using the right side in (9.23) with the result that (9.23) holds also for $k - i = n + 1$.

We have thus proved that a system of transition probabilities $P_{ik}(t)$ is uniquely determined by the forward equations, and that these probabilities satisfy the backward equations as well as the Chapman-Kolmogorov identity.

The backward equations (9.23) may have other solutions. The asserted minimality property (9.19) of our transition probabilities may be restated as follows. For arbitrary non-negative solutions of (9.23)

$$(9.25) \qquad if \quad y_i(0) = P_{ik}(0) \qquad then \quad y_i(t) \geq P_{ik}(t)$$

for all $t > 0$. Here k is arbitrary, but fixed. This assertion is trivial for $k < i$ since in this case the right sides vanish. Given y_{i+1} the solution y_i of (9.23) can be represented explicitly by an integral analogous to (9.22), and the truth of (9.25) now follows recursively for $i = k, k - 1, \ldots$.

Suppose now that $\sum \lambda_k^{-1} < \infty$. It was shown in section 4 that in this case the quantities

$$(9.26) \qquad L_i(t) = 1 - \sum_{k=0}^{\infty} P_{ik}(t)$$

do not vanish identically. Clearly $L_i(t)$ may be interpreted as the probability that, starting from E_i, "infinity" is reached before epoch t. It is also obvious that the L_i are solutions of the differential equations (9.23) with the initial values $L_i(0) = 0$. Consider then arbitrary non-negative functions A_k and define

$$(9.27) \qquad \bar{P}_{ik}(t) = P_{ik}(t) + \int_0^t L_i(t-s)A_k(s) \, ds.$$

It is easily verified that for fixed k the $\bar{P}_{ik}(t)$ satisfy the backward differential equations and $\bar{P}_{ik}(0) = P_{ik}(0)$. The question arises whether the $A_k(t)$ can be defined in such a way that the $\bar{P}_{ik}(t)$ become transition probabilities satisfying the Chapman-Kolmogorov equation. The answer is in the affirmative. We refrain from proving this assertion but shall give a probabilistic interpretation.

The $P_{ik}(t)$ define the so-called *absorbing boundary process*: *When the system reaches infinity, the process terminates.* Doob[23] was the first to study a *return process* in which, on reaching infinity, the system instantaneously returns to E_0 (or some other prescribed state) and the process starts from scratch. In such a process the system may pass from E_0 to E_5 either in

[23] J. L. Doob, *Markoff chains—denumerable case*, Trans. Amer. Math. Soc., vol. 58 (1945), pp. 455–473.

five steps or in infinitely many, having completed one or several complete runs from E_0 to "infinity." The transition probabilities of this process are of the form (9.27). They *satisfy the backward equations* (8.4) *or* (9.23) *but not the forward equations* (9.24) *or* (8.5).   ▶

This explains why in the derivation of the forward equations we were forced to introduce the strange-looking assumption 3 which was unnecessary for the backward equations: The probabilistically and intuitively simple assumptions 1–2 are compatible with return processes, for which the forward equations (9.24) do not hold. In other words, if we start from the assumptions 1–2 then *Kolmogorov's backward equations are satisfied, but to the forward equations another term must be added.*[24]

The pure birth process is admittedly too trite to be really interesting, but the conditions as described are typical for the most general case of the Kolmogorov equations. Two essentially new phenomena occur, however. First, the birth process involves only one escape route out to "infinity" or, in abstract terminology, a single *boundary* point. By contrast, the general process may involve boundaries of a complicated topological structure. Second, in the birth process the motion is directed toward the boundary because only transitions $E_n \to E_{n+1}$ are possible. Processes of a different type can be constructed; for example, the direction may be reversed to obtain a process in which only transitions $E_{n+1} \to E_n$ are possible. Such a process can *originate* at the boundary instead of ending there. In the birth-and-death process, transitions are possible in both directions just as in one-dimensional diffusion. It turns out that in this case there exist processes analogous to the elastic and reflecting barrier processes of diffusion theory, but their description would lead beyond the scope of this book.

10. PROBLEMS FOR SOLUTION

1. In the pure birth process defined by (3.2) let $\lambda_n > 0$ for all n. Prove that for every fixed $n \geq 1$ the function $P_n(t)$ first increases, then decreases to 0. If t_n is the place of the maximum, then $t_1 < t_2 < t_3 < \dots$. *Hint:* Use induction; differentiate (3.2).

2. *Continuation.* If $\sum \lambda_n^{-1} = \infty$ show that $t_n \to \infty$. *Hint:* If $t_n \to \tau$, then for fixed $t > \tau$ the sequence $\lambda_n P_n(t)$ increases. Use (4.10).

3. *The Yule process.* Derive the mean and the variance of the distribution defined by (3.4). [Use only the differential equations, not the explicit form (3.5).]

4. *Pure death process.* Find the differential equations of a process of the Yule type with transitions only from E_n to E_{n-1}. Find the distribution $P_n(t)$, its mean, and its variance, assuming that the initial state is E_i.

---

[24] For further details see XIV,8 of volume 2.

5. *Parking lots.* In a parking lot with N spaces the incoming traffic is of the Poisson type with intensity λ, but only as long as empty spaces are available. The occupancy times have an exponential distribution (just as the holding times in section 7). Find the appropriate differential equations for the probabilities $P_n(t)$ of finding exactly n spaces occupied.

6. *Various queue disciplines.* We consider the waiting line at a single channel subject to the rules given in example (7.*b*). This time we consider the process entirely from the point of view of Mr. Smith whose call arrives at epoch 0. His waiting time depends on the queue discipline, namely the order in which waiting calls are cleared. The following disciplines are of greatest interest:

(*a*) *Last come last served,* that is, calls are cleared in the order of arrival.

(*b*) *Random order,* that is, the members of the waiting line have equal probabilities to be served next.

(*c*) *Last come first served,* that is, calls are cleared in the inverse order of arrival.[25]

It is convenient to number the states starting with -1. During Mr. Smith's actual servicetime the system is said to be in state E_0, and at the expiration of this servicetime it passes into E_{-1} where it stays forever. For $n \geq 1$ the system is in state E_n if Mr. Smith's call is still in the waiting line together with $n-1$ other calls that will, or may, be served before Mr. Smith. (The call being served is not included in the waiting line.) Denote by $P_n(t)$ the probability of E_n at epoch t. Prove that

$$P'_{-1}(t) = \mu P_0(t)$$

in all three cases. Furthermore

(*a*) Under *last come last served discipline*

$$P'_n(t) = -\mu P_n(t) + \mu P_{n-1}(t), \qquad n \geq 0.$$

(*b*) *under random order discipline* when $n \geq 2$

$$P'_n(t) = -(\lambda+\mu)P_n(t) + \frac{n\mu}{n+1} P_{n+1}(t) + \lambda P_{n-1}(t),$$

$$P'_1(t) = -(\lambda+\mu)P_1(t) + \tfrac{1}{2}\mu P_2(t)$$

$$P'_0(t) = -\mu P_0(t) + \mu P_1(t) + \tfrac{1}{2}\mu P_2(t) + \tfrac{1}{3}\mu P_3(t) + \cdots.$$

(*c*) Under *last come first served discipline* for $n \geq 2$

$$P'_n(t) = -(\lambda+\mu)P_n(t) + \mu P_{n+1}(t) + \lambda P_{n-1}(t)$$

$$P'_1(t) = -(\lambda+\mu)P_1(t) + \mu P_2(t)$$

$$P'_0(t) = -\mu P_0(t) + \mu P_1(t).$$

(See also problem 20.)

---

[25] This discipline is meaningful in information-processing machines when the latest information (or observation) carries greatest weight. The treatment was suggested by E. Vaulot, *Delais d'attente des appels téléphoniques dans l'ordre inverse de leur arrivée*, Comptes Rendues, Académie des Sciences, Paris, vol. 238 (1954), pp. 1188–1189.

7. *Continuation.* Suppose that the queue discipline is last come last served (case *a*) and that $P_r(0) = 1$. Show that

$$P_k(t) = \frac{(\mu t)^{r-k}}{(r-k)!} e^{-\mu t}, \qquad 0 \leq k \leq r.$$

8. *Continuation.* Generalize problem 6 to the case of *a* channels.

9. *The Polya process.*[26] This is a non-stationary pure birth process with λ_n depending on time:

(10.1) $$\lambda_n(t) = \frac{1 + an}{1 + at}.$$

Show that the solution with initial condition $P_0(0) = 1$ is

$$P_0(t) = (1 + at)^{-1/a}$$

(10.2)

$$P_n(t) = \frac{(1+a)(1+2a) \cdots \{1+(n-1)a\}}{n!} t^n (1+at)^{-n-1/a}.$$

Show from the differential equations that the mean and variance are t and $t(1+at)$, respectively.

10. *Continuation.* The Polya process can be obtained by a passage to the limit from the Polya urn scheme, example V, (2.c). If the state of the system is defined as the number of red balls drawn, then the transition probability $E_k \to E_{k+1}$ at the $(n+1)$st drawing is

(10.3) $$p_{k,n} = \frac{r + kc}{r + b + nc} = \frac{p + k\gamma}{1 + n\gamma}$$

where $p = r/(r+b)$, $\gamma = c/(r+b)$.

As in the passage from Bernoulli trials to the Poisson distribution, let drawings be made at the rate of one in h time units and let $h \to 0$, $n \to \infty$ so that $np \to t$, $n\gamma \to at$. Show that in the limit (10.3) leads to (10.1). Show also that the Polya distribution V, (2.3) passes into (10.2).

11. *Linear growth.* If in the process defined by (5.7) $\lambda = \mu$, and $P_1(0) = 1$, then

(10.4) $$P_0(t) = \frac{\lambda t}{1 + \lambda t}, \qquad P_n(t) = \frac{(\lambda t)^{n-1}}{(1+\lambda t)^{n+1}}.$$

The probability of ultimate extinction is 1.

12. *Continuation.* Assuming a trial solution to (5.7) of the form $P_n(t) = A(t)B^n(t)$, prove that the solution with $P_1(0) = 1$ is

(10.5) $$P_0(t) = \mu B(t), \qquad P_n(t) = \{1 - \lambda B(t)\}\{1 - \mu B(t)\}\{\lambda B(t)\}^{n-1}$$

---

[26] O. Lundberg, *On random processes and their applications to sickness and accident statistics*, Uppsala, 1940.

with

(10.6)
$$B(t) = \frac{1 - e^{(\lambda - \mu)t}}{\mu - \lambda e^{(\lambda - \mu)t}}.$$

13. *Continuation.* The generating function $P(s, t) = \sum P_n(t)s^n$ satisfies the partial differential equation

(10.7)
$$\frac{\partial P}{\partial t} = \{\mu - (\lambda + \mu)s + \lambda s^2\} \frac{\partial P}{\partial s}.$$

14. *Continuation.* Let $M_2(t) = \sum n^2 P_n(t)$ and $M(t) = \sum n P_n(t)$ (as in section 5). Show that

(10.8)
$$M_2'(t) = 2(\lambda - \mu)M_2(t) + (\lambda + \mu)M(t).$$

Deduce that when $\lambda > \mu$ the *variance* of $\{P_n(t)\}$ is given by

(10.9)
$$e^{2(\lambda - \mu)t}\{1 - e^{(\mu - \lambda)t}\}(\lambda + \mu)/(\lambda - \mu).$$

15. For the process (7.2) the generating function $P(s, t) = \sum P_n(t) s^n$ satisfies the partial differential equation

(10.10)
$$\frac{\partial P}{\partial t} = (1 - s)\left\{ -\lambda P + \mu \frac{\partial P}{\partial s} \right\}.$$

Its solution is

$$P(s, t) = e^{-\lambda(1-s)(1-e^{-\mu t})/\mu}\{1 - (1 - s)e^{-\mu t}\}^i.$$

For $i = 0$ this is a Poisson distribution with parameter $\lambda(1 - e^{-\mu t})/\mu$. *As* $t \to \infty$, *the distribution* $\{P_n(t)\}$ *tends to a Poisson distribution with parameter* λ/μ.

16. For the process defined by (7.26) the generating function for the steady state $P(s) = \sum p_n s^n$ satisfies the partial differential equation

(10.11)
$$(\mu + \lambda s) \frac{\partial P}{\partial s} = a\lambda P,$$

with the solution $P = \{(\mu + \lambda s)/(\lambda + \mu)\}^a$.

17. For the differential equations (7.26) assume a trial solution of the form

$$P_n(t) = \binom{a}{n} A^n (1 - A)^{a-n}.$$

Prove that this is a solution if, and only if,

$$A = \frac{\lambda}{\lambda + \mu} (1 - e^{-(\lambda + \mu)t})$$

18. In the "simplest trunking problem," example (7.*a*), let $Q_n(t)$ be the probability that starting from E_n the system will reach E_0 before epoch t.

Prove the validity of the differential equations

(10.12)

$$Q_n'(t) = -(\lambda+n\mu)Q_n(t) + \lambda Q_{n+1}(t) + n\mu Q_{n-1}(t), \qquad (n \geq 2)$$

$$Q_1'(t) = -(\lambda+\mu)Q_1(t) + \lambda Q_2(t) + \mu$$

with the initial conditions $Q_n(0) = 0$.

19. *Continuation.* Consider the same problem for a process defined by an arbitrary system of forward equations. Show that the $Q_n(t)$ satisfy the corresponding *backward equations* (for fixed k) with $P_{0k}(t)$ replaced by 1.

20. Show that the differential equations of problem 6 are essentially the same as the forward equations for the transition probabilities. Derive the corresponding backward equations.

21. Assume that the solution of at least one of the two systems of (forward and backward) equations is unique. Prove that the transition probabilities satisfying this system satisfy the Chapman-Kolmogorov equation (1.1).

Hint: Show that both sides satisfy the same system of differential equations with the same initial conditions.

22. Let $P_{ik}(t)$ satisfy the Chapman-Komogorov equation (1.1). Supposing that $P_{ik}(t) > 0$ and that $S_i(t) = \sum_k P_{ik}(t) \leq 1$, prove that either $S_i(t) = 1$ for all t or $S_i(t) < 1$ for all t.

23. *Ergodic properties.* Consider a stationary process with finitely many states; that is, suppose that the system of differential equations (9.9) is finite and that the coefficients c_j and p_{jk} are constants. Prove that the solutions are linear combinations of exponential terms $e^{\lambda(t-\tau)}$ where the real part of λ is negative unless $\lambda = 0$. Conclude that the asymptotic behavior of the transition probabilities is the same as in the case of *finite* Markov chains except that the periodic case is impossible.

Answers to Problems

CHAPTER I

1. (a) $\frac{3}{5}$; (b) $\frac{3}{5}$; (c) $\frac{3}{10}$.

2. The events S_1, S_2, $S_1 \cup S_2$, and $S_1 S_2$ contain, respectively, 12, 12, 18, and 6 points.

4. The space contains the two points HH and TT with probability $\frac{1}{4}$; the two points HTT and THH with probability $\frac{1}{8}$; and generally two points with probability 2^{-n} when $n \geq 2$. These probabilities add to 1, so that there is no necessity to consider the possibility of an unending sequence of tosses. The required probabilities are $\frac{15}{16}$ and $\frac{2}{3}$, respectively.

9. $\mathbf{P}\{AB\} = \frac{1}{6}$, $\mathbf{P}\{A \cup B\} = \frac{23}{36}$, $\mathbf{P}\{AB'\} = \frac{1}{3}$.

12. $x = 0$ in the events (a), (b), and (g).
$x = 1$ in the events (e) and (f).
$x = 2$ in the event (d).
$x = 4$ in the event (c).

15. (a) A; (b) AB; (c) $B \cup (AC)$.

16. Correct are (c), (d), (e), (f), (h), (i), (k), (l). The statement (a) is meaningless unless $C \subset B$. It is in general false even in this case, but is correct in the special case $C \subset B$, $AC = 0$. The statement (b) is correct if $C \supset AB$. The statement (g) should read $(A \cup B) - A = A'B$. Finally (k) is the correct version of (j).

17. (a) $AB'C'$; (b) ABC'; (c) ABC; (d) $A \cup B \cup C$;
(e) $AB \cup AC \cup BC$; (f) $AB'C' \cup A'BC' \cup A'B'C$;
(g) $ABC' \cup AB'C \cup A'BC = (AB \cup AC \cup BC) - ABC$;
(h) $A'B'C'$; (i) $(ABC)'$.

18. $A \cup B \cup C = A \cup (B-AB) \cup \{C-C(A \cup B)\} = A \cup BA' \cup CA'B'$.

CHAPTER II

1. (a) 26^3; (b) $26^2 + 26^3 = 18{,}252$; (c) $26^2 + 26^3 + 26^4$. In a city with 20,000 inhabitants either some people have the same set of initials or at least 1748 people have more than three initials.

2. $2(2^{10} - 1) = 2046$.

3. $\binom{n}{2} + n = \frac{n(n+1)}{2}$. **4.** (a) $\frac{1}{n}$; (b) $\frac{1}{n(n-1)}$.

5. $q_A = (\frac{5}{6})^6$, $\qquad q_B = (\frac{5}{6})^{12} + 12(\frac{5}{6})^{11} \cdot \frac{1}{6}$.

6. (a) $p_1 = 0.01$, $p_2 = 0.27$, $p_3 = 0.72$.

 (b) $p_1 = 0.001$, $p_2 = 0.063$, $p_3 = 0.432$, $p_4 = 0.504$.

7. $p_r = (10)_r 10^{-r}$. For example, $p_3 = 0.72$, $p_{10} = 0.00036288$. Stirling's formula gives $p_{10} = 0.0003598 \ldots$.

8. (a) $(\frac{9}{10})^k$; (b) $(\frac{9}{10})^k$; $(\frac{8}{10})^k$; (d) $2(\frac{9}{10})^k - (\frac{8}{10})^k$; (a) AB and $A \cup B$.

9. $\binom{n}{2} n! \, n^{-n}$. **10.** $9 / \binom{12}{8} = \frac{1}{55}$.

11. The probability of exactly r trials is $(n-1)_{r-1}/(n)_r = n^{-1}$.

12. (a) $[1 \cdot 3 \cdot 5 \cdots (2n-1)]^{-1} = 2^n n!/(2n)!$;

 (b) $n! \, [1 \cdot 3 \cdots (2n-1)]^{-1} = 2^n / \binom{2n}{n}$.

13. On the assumption of randomness the probability that all of twelve tickets come either on Tuesdays or Thursdays is $(\frac{2}{7})^{12} = 0.0000003 \ldots$. There are only $\binom{7}{2} = 21$ pairs of days, so that the probability remains extremely small even for any two days. Hence it is reasonable to assume that the police have a system.

14. Assuming randomness, the probability of the event is $(\frac{6}{7})^{12} = \frac{1}{6}$ appr. No safe conclusion is possible.

15. $(90)_{10}/(100)_{10} = 0.330476 \ldots$.

16. $25! \, (5!)^{-5} 5^{-25} = 0.00209 \ldots$.

17. $\dfrac{2(n-2)_r (n-r-1)!}{n!} = \dfrac{2(n-r-1)}{n(n-1)}$.

18. (a) $\frac{1}{216}$; (b) $\frac{83}{3888}$.

19. The probabilities are $1 - (\frac{5}{6})^4 = 0.517747 \ldots$ and $1 - (\frac{35}{36})^{24} = 0.491404 \ldots$.

20. (a) $(n-N)_r/(n)_r$. (b) $(1-N/n)^r$. For $r = N = 3$ the probabilities are (a) $0.911812 \ldots$; (b) $0.912673 \ldots$. For $r = N = 10$ they are (a) 0.330476; (b) $0.348678 \ldots$.

21. (a) $(1-N/n)^{r-1}$. (b) $(n)_{Nr}/((n)_N)^r$.

22. $(1-2/n)^{2r-2}$; for the median $2^{r+1} = 0.7n$, approximately.

23. On the assumption of randomness, the probabilities that three or four breakages are caused (a) by one girl, (b) by the youngest girl are, respectively, $\frac{13}{64} \approx 0.2$ and $\frac{13}{256} \approx 0.05$.

24. (a) $12!/12^{12} = 0.000054$. (b) $\binom{12}{2}(2^6-2)12^{-6} = 0.00137 \ldots$.

25. $\dfrac{30!}{2^6 6^6} \binom{12}{6} 12^{-30} \approx 0.00035 \ldots$.

26. (a) $\dbinom{n}{2r} 2^{2r} \Big/ \dbinom{2n}{2r}$; (b) $n \dbinom{n-1}{2r-2} 2^{2r-2} \Big/ \dbinom{2n}{2r}$;

(c) $\dbinom{n}{2} \dbinom{n-2}{2r-4} 2^{2r-4} \Big/ \dbinom{2n}{2r}$.

27. $\dbinom{N-3}{r-1} \Big/ \dbinom{N-1}{r-1}$.

28. $p = \dbinom{2N}{N}^2 \Big/ \dbinom{4N}{2N} \approx \sqrt{2/(N\pi)}$.

29. $p = \dfrac{\dbinom{4}{k}\dbinom{48}{13-k}\dbinom{39}{13}\dbinom{26}{13}}{\dbinom{52}{13}\dbinom{39}{13}\dbinom{26}{13}} = \dfrac{\dbinom{4}{k}\dbinom{48}{13-k}}{\dbinom{52}{13}}$.

30. Cf. problem 29. The probability is

$$\dbinom{13}{m}\dbinom{39}{13-m}\dbinom{13-m}{n}\dbinom{26+m}{13-n} \Big/ \dbinom{52}{13}\dbinom{39}{13}.$$

31. $\dbinom{4}{k}\dbinom{48}{26-k} \Big/ \dbinom{52}{26}$.

32. $\dfrac{\dbinom{13}{a}\dbinom{39}{13-a}\dbinom{13-a}{b}\dbinom{26+a}{13-b}\dbinom{13-a-b}{c}\dbinom{13+a+b}{13-c}}{\dbinom{52}{13}\dbinom{39}{13}\dbinom{26}{13}}$.

33. (a) $24p(5, 4, 3, 1)$; (b) $4p(4, 4, 4, 1)$; (c) $12p(4, 4, 3, 2)$.

34. $\dfrac{\dbinom{13}{a}\dbinom{13}{b}\dbinom{13}{c}\dbinom{13}{d}}{\dbinom{52}{13}}$. (Cf. problem 33 for the probability that the

hand contains a cards of some suit, b of another, etc.)

35. $p_0(r) = (52-r)_4/(52)_4$; $p_1(r) = 4r(52-r)_3/(52)_4$;
$p_2(r) = 6r(r-1)(52-r)_2/(52)_4$;
$p_3(r) = 4r(r-1)(r-2)(52-r)/(52)_4$; $p_4(r) = r_4/(52)_4$.

36. The probabilities that the waiting times for the first, ..., fourth ace
exceed r are

$$w_1(r) = p_0(r); \quad w_2(r) = p_0(r) + p_1(r);$$

$$w_3(r) = p_0(r) + p_1(r) + p_2(r);$$

$$w_4(r) = 1 - p_4(r).$$

Next $f_i(r) = w_i(r-1) - w_i(r)$. The medians are 9, 20, 33, 44.

37. (a) $\dbinom{4}{k}\dbinom{4-k}{k}\dbinom{48}{r-k}\dbinom{48-r+k}{r-k}\Big/\dbinom{52}{r}\dbinom{52-r}{r}$, with $k \le 2$;

(b) $\left\{\dbinom{4}{k}\dbinom{48}{r-k}\Big/\dbinom{52}{r}\right\}^2$, with $k \le 4$.

39. $\dbinom{r_1+n-1}{r_1}\dbinom{r_2+n-1}{r_2}$.　　**40.** $\dbinom{r_1+5}{5}(r_2+1)$.

41. $\dfrac{(r_1+r_2+r_3)!}{r_1!\,r_2!\,r_3!}$.　　**42.** $(49)_4/(52)_4$.

43. $\mathbf{P}\{(7)\}$　　　　　$= 10 \cdot 10^{-7}$　　　　　　　$= 0.000\,001.$

$\quad\mathbf{P}\{(6, 1)\}$　　　　$= \dfrac{10!}{8!\,1!\,1!} \cdot \dfrac{7!}{1!\,6!} \cdot 10^{-7}$　　$= 0.000\,063.$

$\quad\mathbf{P}\{(5, 2)\}$　　　　$= \dfrac{10!}{8!\,1!\,1!} \cdot \dfrac{7!}{2!\,5!} \cdot 10^{-7}$　　$= 0.000\,189.$

$\quad\mathbf{P}\{(5, 1, 1)\}$　　$= \dfrac{10!}{7!\,2!\,1!} \cdot \dfrac{7!}{1!\,1!\,5!} \cdot 10^{-7}$　$= 0.001\,512.$

$\quad\mathbf{P}\{(4, 3)\}$　　　　$= \dfrac{10!}{8!\,1!\,1!} \cdot \dfrac{7!}{3!\,4!} \cdot 10^{-7}$　　$= 0.000\,315.$

$\quad\mathbf{P}\{(4, 2, 1)\}$　　$= \dfrac{10!}{7!\,1!\,1!} \cdot \dfrac{7!}{1!\,2!\,4!} \cdot 10^{-7}$　$= 0.007\,560.$

$\quad\mathbf{P}\{(4, 1, 1, 1)\}$　$= \dfrac{10!}{6!\,3!\,1!} \cdot \dfrac{7!}{1!\,1!\,1!\,4!} \cdot 10^{-7}$　$= 0.017\,640.$

$\quad\mathbf{P}\{(3, 3, 1)\}$　　$= \dfrac{10!}{7!\,2!\,1!} \cdot \dfrac{7!}{1!\,3!\,3!} \cdot 10^{-7}$　$= 0.005\,040.$

$\quad\mathbf{P}\{(3, 2, 2)\}$　　$= \dfrac{10!}{7!\,2!\,1!} \cdot \dfrac{7!}{2!\,2!\,3!} \cdot 10^{-7}$　$= 0.007\,560.$

$\quad\mathbf{P}\{(3, 2, 1, 1)\}$　$= \dfrac{10!}{6!\,2!\,1!\,1!} \cdot \dfrac{7!}{1!\,1!\,2!\,3!} \cdot 10^{-7} = 0.105\,840.$

$\quad\mathbf{P}\{(3, 1, 1, 1, 1)\}$　$= \dfrac{10!}{5!\,4!\,1!} \cdot \dfrac{7!}{1!\,1!\,1!\,1!\,3!} \cdot 10^{-7} = 0.105\,840.$

$\quad\mathbf{P}\{(2, 2, 2, 1)\}$　$= \dfrac{10!}{6!\,3!\,1!} \cdot \dfrac{7!}{1!\,2!\,2!\,2!} \cdot 10^{-7}$　$= 0.052\,920.$

$\quad\mathbf{P}\{(2, 2, 1, 1, 1)\}$　$= \dfrac{10!}{5!\,3!\,2!} \cdot \dfrac{7!}{1!\,1!\,1!\,2!\,2!} \cdot 10^{-7} = 0.317\,520.$

$\quad\mathbf{P}\{(2, 1, 1, 1, 1, 1)\}$ $= \dfrac{10!}{4!\,5!\,1!} \cdot \dfrac{7!}{1!\,1!\,1!\,1!\,1!\,2!} \cdot 10^{-7} = 0.317\,520.$

$\quad\mathbf{P}\{(1, 1, 1, 1, 1, 1, 1,)\} = \dfrac{10!}{3!\,7!} \cdot 7! \cdot 10^{-7}$　　　$= 0.060\,480.$

44. Letting S, D, T, Q stand for simple, double, triple, and quadruple, respectively, we have

$$P\{22S\} \qquad = \frac{365!}{343!} \cdot 365^{-22} \qquad\qquad = 0.524\ 30.$$

$$P\{20S + 1D\} \quad = \frac{365!}{1!\ 344!} \cdot \frac{22!}{20!\ 2!} \cdot 365^{-22} \qquad = 0.352\ 08.$$

$$P\{18S + 2D\} \quad = \frac{365!}{2!\ 345!} \cdot \frac{22!}{18!\ 2!\ 2!} \cdot 365^{-22} \qquad = 0.096\ 95.$$

$$P\{16S + 3D\} \quad = \frac{365!}{3!\ 346!} \cdot \frac{22!}{16!\ 2!\ 2!\ 2!} \cdot 365^{-22} = 0.014\ 29.$$

$$P\{19S + 1T\} \quad = \frac{365!}{345!} \cdot \frac{22!}{19!\ 3!} \cdot 365^{-22} \qquad = 0.006\ 80.$$

$$P\{17S + 1D + 1T\} = \frac{365!}{346!} \cdot \frac{22!}{17!\ 2!\ 3!} \cdot 365^{-22} \qquad = 0.003\ 36.$$

$$P\{14S + 4D\} \quad = \frac{365!}{347!} \cdot \frac{22!}{14!\ 2!\ 2!\ 2!\ 2!} \cdot 365^{-22} = 0.001\ 24.$$

$$P\{15S + 2D + 1T\} = \frac{365!}{347!} \cdot \frac{22!}{15!\ 2!\ 2!\ 3!} \cdot 365^{-22} \qquad = 0.000\ 66.$$

$$P\{(18S + 1Q\} \quad = \frac{365!}{346!} \cdot \frac{22!}{18!\ 4!} \cdot 365^{-22} \qquad = 0.000\ 09.$$

45. Let $q = \binom{52}{5} = 2{,}598{,}960.$ The probabilities are:

(a) $4/q$; (b) $13 \cdot 12 \cdot 4 \cdot q^{-1} = \frac{1}{4165}$; (c) $13 \cdot 12 \cdot 4 \cdot 6 \cdot q^{-1} = \frac{6}{4165}$;

(d) $9 \cdot 4^5 \cdot q^{-1} = \frac{768}{216580}$; (e) $13 \cdot \binom{12}{2} 4 \cdot 4^2 \cdot q^{-1} = \frac{88}{4165}$;

(f) $\binom{13}{2} \cdot 11 \cdot 6 \cdot 6 \cdot 4 \cdot q^{-1} = \frac{198}{4165}$; (g) $13 \cdot \binom{12}{3} \cdot 6 \cdot 4^3 \cdot q^{-1} = \frac{1760}{4165}.$

CHAPTER IV

1. 99/323.   **2.** 0.21 . . . .   **3.** 1/4.   **4.** $7/2^6$.

5. 1/81 and $31/6^6$.

6. If A_k is the event that (k, k) does not appear, then from 1(.5)

$$1 - p_r = 6\left(\frac{35}{36}\right)^r - \binom{6}{2}\left(\frac{34}{36}\right)^r + \binom{6}{3}\left(\frac{33}{36}\right)^r - \binom{6}{4}\left(\frac{32}{36}\right)^r + 6\left(\frac{31}{36}\right)^r - \left(\frac{30}{36}\right)^r.$$

7. Put $p^{-1} = \binom{52}{13}$. Then $S_1 = 13\binom{48}{9}p$; $S_2 = \binom{13}{2}\binom{44}{5}p$;

$S_3 = 40\binom{13}{3}p$. Numerically, $P_{[0]} = 0.09658$; $P_{[1]} = 0.0341$; $P_{[2]} = 0.0001$,

approximately.

8. $u_r = \sum_{k=0}^{N} (-1)^k \binom{N}{k} \left(1 - \frac{k}{n}\right)^r.$

9. $u_r = \sum_{k=0}^{N} (-1)^k \binom{N}{k} \frac{(n-k)_r}{(n)_r}.$ See II, (12.18) for a proof that the two results agree.

10. The general term is $a_{1k_1} a_{2k_2} \cdots a_{Nk_N}$, where $(k_1, k_2, \ldots, k_N)$ is a permutation of $(1, 2, \ldots, N)$. For a diagonal element $k_\nu = \nu$.

12. $u_r = \sum_{k=0}^{n} (-1)^k \binom{n}{k} \frac{(ns - ks)_r}{(ns)_r}.$

14. Note that, by definition, $u_r = 0$ for $r < n$ and $u_n = n! \, s^n/(ns)_n$.

15. $u_r - u_{r-1} = \sum_{k=1}^{n} (-1)^{k-1} \binom{n-1}{k-1} \frac{(ns - ks)_{r-1}}{(ns-1)_{r-1}}.$

The limit equals $\sum_{k=0}^{n-1} (-1)^k \binom{n-1}{k} \left(1 - \frac{k+1}{n}\right)^{r-1}.$

16. $\binom{N}{2}^{-r} \binom{N}{m} \sum_{k=2}^{m} (-1)^{m-k} \binom{m}{k} \binom{k}{2}^r.$

17. Use $\binom{52}{5} S_k = \binom{4}{k} \left(\frac{52 - 13k}{5}\right).$

$P_{[0]} = 0.264,\ P_{[1]} = 0.588,\ P_{[2]} = 0.146,\ P_{[3]} = 0.002,$ approximately.

18. Use $\binom{52}{13} S_k = \binom{4}{k} \left(\frac{52 - 2k}{13 - 2k}\right).$

$$P_{[0]} = 0.780217, \qquad P_{[1]} = 0.204606, \qquad P_{[2]} = 0.014845,$$

$$P_{[3]} = 0.000330, \qquad P_{[4]} = 0.000002,\ \text{approximately.}$$

19. $m! \, N! \, u_m = \sum_{k=0}^{N-m} (-1)^k (N-m-k)!/k!.$

20. Cf. the following formula with $r = 2$.

21. $(rN)! \, x =$

$$= \binom{N}{2} r^2 (rN-2)! - \binom{N}{3} r^3 (rN-3)! + - \cdots + (-1)^N r^N (rN-N)!.$$

24. $P_{[m]} = \dfrac{\binom{n}{m}}{\binom{n+r-1}{r}} \sum_{k=0}^{n-m} (-1)^k \binom{n-m}{k} \binom{n-m+r-1-k}{r}.$

25. Use II, (12.16) and (12.4).

26. Put $U_N = A_1 \cup \cdots \cup A_N$ and note that $U_{N+1} = U_N \cup A_{N+1}$ and $U_N A_{N+1} = (A_1 A_{N+1} \cup \cdots \cup (A_N A_{N+1}).$

CHAPTER V

1. $1 - \dfrac{(5)_3}{(6)_3} = \dfrac{1}{2}$. **2.** $p = 1 - \dfrac{10 \cdot 5^9}{6^{10} - 5^{10}} = 0.61 \ldots$

3. (a) $\dbinom{35}{13} \Big/ \dbinom{39}{13} = 0.182 \ldots$ The probability of exactly one ace is

$4 \dbinom{35}{12} \Big/ \dbinom{39}{13} = 0.411 \ldots$ (b) $1 - 0.182 - 0.411 = 0.407$, approximately.

4. (a) $2 \dfrac{\dbinom{23}{10}}{\dbinom{26}{13}} = \dfrac{11}{50}$; (b) $2 \dfrac{\dbinom{23}{12}}{\dbinom{26}{13}} = \dfrac{13}{50}$.

6. $\frac{125}{345}$; $\frac{140}{345}$; $\frac{80}{345}$. **7.** $\frac{20}{21}$. **9.** $(\frac{5}{6})^2$. **10.** $1 - (\frac{5}{6})^2$.

12. $\dfrac{p}{2 - p}$. **13.** (b) $\frac{3}{5}$; (c) $2^n (1 + 2^n)^{-1}$.

14. (d) Put $a_n = x_n - \frac{4}{7}$, $b_n = y_n - \frac{1}{7}$, $c_n = z_n - \frac{2}{7}$. Then

$$|a_n| + |b_n| + |c_n| = \tfrac{1}{2}\{|a_{n+1}| + |b_{n+1}| + |c_{n+1}|\}.$$

Hence $|a_n| + |b_n| + |c_n|$ increases geometrically.

15. $p = (1 - p_1)(1 - p_2) \cdots (1 - p_n)$.

16. Use $1 - x < e^{-x}$ for $0 < x < 1$ or Taylor's series for $\log (1 - x)$; cf. II, (12.26).

18. $\dfrac{b + c}{b + c + r}$.

19. Suppose the assertion to be true for the nth drawing regardless of b, r, and c. Considering the two possibilities at the *first* drawing we find then that the probability of black at the $(n+1)$st trial equals

$$\frac{b}{b + r} \cdot \frac{b + c}{b + r + c} + \frac{r}{b + r} \cdot \frac{b}{b + r + c} = \frac{b}{b + r}.$$

20. The preceding problem states that the assertion is true for $m = 1$ and all n. For induction, consider the two possibilities at the first trial.

23. Use II, (12.9).

24. The binomial coefficient on the right is the limit of the first factor in the numerator in (8.2). Note that

$$\binom{-1/\gamma}{n} \sim \binom{-1/\gamma}{n_2} (1 + \rho)^{n_1}.$$

26. $2v = 2p(1 - p) \le \frac{1}{2}$ in consequence of (5.2).

28. (a) u^2;   (b) $u^2 + uv + v^2/4$;   (c) $u^2 + (25uv + 9v^2 + vw + 2uw)/16$.

33. $p_{11} = p_{32} = 2p_{21} = p$, $p_{12} = p_{33} = 2p_{23} = q$, $p_{13} = p_{31} = 0$, $p_{22} = \frac{1}{2}$.

CHAPTER VI

1. $\frac{5}{16}$.   **2.** The probability is $0.02804\ldots$.   **3.** $(0.9)^x \le 0.1$, $x \ge 22$.

4. $q^x \le \frac{1}{2}$ and $(1-4p)^x \le \frac{1}{2}$ with $p = \binom{48}{9} \bigg/ \binom{52}{13}$.   Hence $x \ge 263$ and $x \ge 66$, respectively.

5. $1 - (0.8)^{10} - 2(0.8)^9 = 0.6242\ldots$.

6. $\{1 - (0.8)^{10} - 2(0.8)^9\}/\{1 - (0.8)^{10}\} = 0.6993\ldots$.

7. $\binom{26}{2}\binom{26}{11} \bigg/ \binom{52}{13} = 0.003954\ldots$,   and $\binom{13}{2}\dfrac{1}{2^{13}} = 0.00952\ldots$.

8. $\binom{12}{2}\{6^{-6} - 2\cdot 12^{-6}\}$.

9. True values: $0.6651\ldots$, $0.40187\ldots$, and $0.2009\ldots$,;   Poisson approximations: $1 - e^{-1} = 0.6321\ldots$, $0.3679\ldots$, and $0.1839\ldots$.

10. $e^{-2}\sum_{4}^{\infty} 2^k/k! = 0.143\ldots$.   **11.** $e^{-1}\sum_{3}^{\infty} 1/k! = 0.080\ldots$.

12. $e^{-x/100} \le 0.05$ or $x \ge 300$.

13. $e^{-1} = 0.3679\ldots$, $1 - 2\cdot e^{-1} = 0.264\ldots$.

14. $e^{-x} \le 0.01$, $x \ge 5$.   **15.** $1/p = 649{,}740$.

16. $1 - p^n$ where $p = p(0; \lambda) + \cdots + p(k; \lambda)$.

18. q^3 for $k = 0$; pq^3 for $k = 1, 2, 3$;   and $pq^3 - pq^6$ for $k = 4$.

19. $\sum_{k=0}^{\infty} \binom{n}{k}^2 2^{-2n} = \binom{2n}{n} 2^{-2n} \approx 1/\sqrt{\pi n}$ for large n.

20. $\sum_{k=a}^{a+b-1} \binom{a+b-1}{k} p^k q^{a-b-1-k}$. This can be written in the alternative form

$p^a \sum_{k=0}^{b-1} \binom{a+k-1}{k} q^k$, where the kth term equals the probability that the ath success occurs directly after $k \le b - 1$ failures.

21. $x_r = \binom{2N-1-r}{N-1} \cdot 2^{-2N+r+1}$.

22. (a) $x = \sum_{r=1}^{N} x_r 2^{-r-1} = 2^{-2N}\sum_{r=1}^{N} \binom{2N-1-r}{N-1}$;   (b) Use II, (12.6).

23. $k_i \approx np_i$, $k_{12} \approx np_{12}$ whence $n \approx k_1 k_2/k_{12}$.

24. $\dbinom{n}{n_1} \cdot \dbinom{n-s_1}{n_2} \cdots \dbinom{n-s_{r-1}}{n_r} \cdot q^{s_r} p^{(rn-s_1-\cdots-s_r)}$

where $s_i = n_1 + \cdots + n_i$.

25. $p = p_1 q_2 (p_1 q_2 + p_2 q_1)^{-1}$.

31. By the Taylor expansion for the logarithm

$$b(0; n, p) = q^n = (1 - \lambda/n)^n < e^{-\lambda} = p(0; \lambda).$$

The terms of each distribution add to unity, and therefore it is impossible that *all* terms of one distribution should be greater than the corresponding terms of the other.

32. There are only finitely many terms of the Poisson distribution which are greater than ϵ, and the remaining ones dominate the corresponding terms of the binomial distribution.

CHAPTER VII

1. Proceed as in section 1.   **2.** Use (1.7).   **3.** $\Re(-\frac{32}{30}) = 0.143 \ldots$.

4. 0.99.   **5.** 511.   **6.** 66,400.

7. Most certainly. The inequalities of chapter VI suffice to show that an excess of more than eight deviations is exceedingly improbable.

8. $(2\pi n)^{-1} \{p_1 p_2 (1 - p_1 - p_2)\}^{-\frac{1}{2}}$.

CHAPTER VIII

1. $\beta = 21$.

2. $x = pu + qv + rw$, where u, v, w are solutions of

$$u = p^{\alpha-1} + (qv+rw)\frac{1 - p^{\alpha-1}}{1 - p}, \qquad v = (pu+rw)\frac{1 - q^{\beta-1}}{1 - q}$$

$$w = pu + qv + rw = x.$$

3. $u = p^{\alpha-1} + (qv+rw)\dfrac{1 - p^{\alpha-1}}{1 - p}$,

$$v = (pu+rw)\frac{1 - q^{\beta-1}}{1 - q}, \qquad w = (pu+qv)\frac{1 - r^{\gamma-1}}{1 - r}.$$

4. Note that $\mathbf{P}\{A_n\} < (2p)^n$, but

$$\mathbf{P}\{A_n\} > 1 - (1-p^n)^{2^n/2n} > 1 - e^{(-2p)^n/2n}.$$

If $p = \frac{1}{2}$, the last quantity is $\sim \dfrac{1}{2n}$; if $p > \frac{1}{2}$, then $\mathbf{P}\{A_n\}$ does not even tend to zero.

CHAPTER IX

1. The possible combinations are $(0, 0)$, $(0, 1)$, $(0, 2)$, $(1, 0)$, $(1, 1)$, $(2, 0)$, $(2, 1)$, $(3, 0)$. Their probabilities are 0.047539, 0.108883, 0.017850, 0.156364, 0.214197, 0.321295, 0.026775, 0.107098.

2. (*a*) The joint distribution takes on the form of a 6-by-6 matrix. The main diagonal contains the elements $q, 2q, \ldots, 6q$ where $q = \frac{1}{36}$. On one side of the main diagonal all elements are 0, on the other q. (*b*) $E(X) = \frac{7}{2}$, Var $(X) = \frac{35}{12}$, $E(Y) = \frac{161}{36}$, Var $(Y) = \frac{2555}{1296}$, Cov $(X, Y) = \frac{105}{72}$.

3. In the joint distribution of X, Y the rows are 32^{-1} times $(1, 0, 0, 0, 0, 0)$, $(0, 5, 4, 3, 2, 1,)$ $(0, 0, 6, 6, 3, 0)$, $(0, 0, 0, 1, 0, 0)$;
of X, Z: $(1, 0, 0, 0, 0, 0)$, $(0, 5, 6, 1, 0, 0)$, $(0, 0, 4, 6, 1, 0)$, $(0, 0, 0, 3, 2, 0)$, $(0, 0, 0, 0, 2, 0)$, $(0, 0, 0, 0, 0, 1)$;
Y, Z: $(1, 0, 0, 0)$, $(0, 5, 6, 1)$, $(0, 4, 7, 0)$, $(0, 3, 2, 0)$, $(0, 2, 0, 0)$, $(0, 1, 0, 0)$.
Distribution of $X + Y$: $(1, 0, 5, 4, 9, 8, 5)$ all divided by 32, and the values of $X + Y$ ranging from 0 to 6;
of XY: $(1, 5, 4, 3, 8, 1, 6, 0, 3, 1)$ all divided by 32, the values ranging from 0 to 9.
$E(X) = \frac{5}{2}$, $E(Y) = \frac{3}{2}$, $E(Z) = \frac{31}{16}$, Var $(X) = \frac{5}{4}$, Var $(Y) = \frac{3}{8}$, Var $(Z) = \frac{303}{256}$.

4. (*a*) $p/(1 + q)$; (*b*) $1/(1 + q + q^2)$; (*c*) $1/(1 + q)^2$.

8. The distribution of V_n is given by (3.5), th^2 of U_n follows by symmetry.

9. (*a*) $P\{X \leq r, Y \geq s\} = N^{-n}(r-s+1)^n$ for $r \geq s$;

$$P\{X = r, Y = s\} = N^{-n}\{(r-s+1)^n - 2(r-s)^n + (r-s-1)^n\},$$

if $r > s$, and $= N^{-n}$ if $r = s$.

(*b*) $x = \dfrac{r^{n-2} - (r-1)^{n-2}}{r^n - (r-1)^n}$ if $j < r$ and $k < r$.

$x = \dfrac{r^{n-2}}{r^n - (r-1)^n}$ if $j \leq r$ and $k = r$, or $j = r$ and $k \leq r$.

$x = 0$ if $j > r$ or $k > r$.

(*c*) $\sigma^2 \approx \dfrac{nN^2}{(n+1)^2(n+2)}$.

10. Probability for n double throws $2pq(p^2+q^2)^{n-1}$. Expectation $1/(2pq)$.

12. $P\{N = n, K = k\} = \dbinom{n}{k} p^{n-k}(qq')^k \cdot qp'$ for $k \leq n$.

$P\{N = n\} = (1-qp')^n qp'$.

$P\{K = k\} = (qq')^k qp' \sum \dbinom{-k-1}{v} (-p)^v = p'q'^k$.

13. $E\left(\dfrac{K}{N+1}\right) = \sum\limits_{k,n} k p_{k,n}/(n+1) = q^2 p'q' \sum\limits_{n=1}^{\infty} \left(1 - \dfrac{1}{n+1}\right)(p + qq')^{n-1} =$

$$= \dfrac{qq'}{1 - qp'} - \dfrac{q^2 p'q'}{(1-qp')^2} \log \dfrac{1}{qp'}.$$

$E(K) = \dfrac{q'}{p'}$; $E(N) = \dfrac{(1-qp')}{qp'}$;   Cov $(K, N) = \dfrac{q'}{qp'^2}$.

$\rho(K, N) = \sqrt{q'/(1-qp')}$.

14. (a) $p_k = p^k q + q^k p$; $\quad E(X) = pq^{-1} + qp^{-1}$;

$$\text{Var}(X) = pq^{-2} + qp^{-2} - 2.$$

(b) $q_k = p^2 q^{k-1} + q^2 p^{k-1}$; $\quad P\{X = m, Y = n\} = p^{m+1} q^n + q^{m+1} q^n$ with m, $n \geq 1$; $\quad E(Y) = 2$; $\quad \sigma^2 = 2(pq^{-1} + qp^{-1} - 1)$.

17. $\binom{n}{k} 364^{n-k} 365^{1-n}$.

18. (a) $365\{1 - 364^n \cdot 365^{-n} - n 364^{n-1} \cdot 365^{-n}\}$; (b) $n \geq 28$.

19. (a) $\mu = n$, $\sigma^2 = (n-1)n$; (b) $\mu = (n+1)/2$, $\sigma^2 = (n^2-1)/12$.

20. $E(X) = np_1$; $\quad \text{Var}(X) = np_1(1-p_1)$; $\quad \text{Cov}(X, Y) = -np_1 p_2$.

21. $-n/36$. This is a special case of problem 20.

25. $E(Y_r) = \sum_{k=1}^{r} \dfrac{N}{r - k + 1}$; $\quad \text{Var}(Y_r) = \sum_{k=1}^{r} \dfrac{N(N-r+k-1)}{(r-k+1)^2}$.

26. (a) $1 - q^k$; (b) $E(X) = N\{1 - q^k + k^{-1}\}$; (c) $\dfrac{dE(X)}{dk} = 0$.

27. $\Sigma(1 - p_j)^n$. Put $X_j = 1$ or 0 according as the jth class is not or is presented.

28. $E(X) = \dfrac{r_1(r_2+1)}{r_1 + r_2}$; $\quad \text{Var}(X) = \dfrac{r_1 r_2 (r_1 - 1)(r_2 + 1)}{(r_1 + r_2 - 1)(r_1 + r_2)^2}$.

30. $E(S_n) = \dfrac{nb}{b + r}$; $\quad \text{Var}(S_n) = \dfrac{nbr\{b + r + nc\}}{(b+r)^2(b+r+c)}$.

33. $E\left(\dfrac{X}{r}\right) = r \sum_{r=k}^{\infty} k^{-1} \binom{k-1}{r-1} p^r q^{k-r} =$

$$= \sum_{k=1}^{r-1} (-1)^{k-1} \frac{r}{r - k} \left(\frac{p}{q}\right)^k + \left(\frac{-p}{q}\right)^r r \log p.$$

To derive the last formula from the first, put $f(q) = r \sum k^{-1} \binom{k-1}{r-1} q^k$. Using II, (12.4), we find that $f'(q) = rq^{r-1}(1-q)^{-r}$. The assertion now follows by repeated integrations by part.

CHAPTER XI

1. $sP(s)$ and $P(s^2)$.

2. (a) $(1-s)^{-1} P(s)$; (b) $(1-s)^{-1} sP(s)$; (c) $\{1 - sP(s)\}/(1-s)$; (d) $p_0 s^{-1} + \{1 - s^{-1} P(s)\}/(1-s)$; (e) $\frac{1}{2}\{P(\sqrt{s}) + P(-\sqrt{s})\}$.

3. $U(s) = pqs^2/(1 - ps)(1 - qs)$. Expectation $= 1/pq$, $\text{Var} = (1 - 3pq)/p^2 q^2$.

6. The generating function satisfies the quadratic equation $A(s) = A^2(s) + s$. Hence $A(s) = \frac{1}{2} - \frac{1}{2}\sqrt{1 - 4s}$ and $a_n = n^{-1}\binom{2n - 2}{n - 1}$.

10. (a) $\Phi^r(s)F^k(s)\,|p - q|$
   (b) $\Phi^r(s)[1 + F(s) + \cdots + F^k(s)]\,|p - q|$.

11. (a) $(q/p)^r\Phi^{2r}(s)$.
   (b) $(q/p)^r\Phi^{2r}(s)U(s)$.

12. Using the generating function for the geometric distribution of $\mathbf{X}_\nu$ we have without computation

$$P_r(s) = s^r\left(\frac{N-1}{N-s}\right)\left(\frac{N-2}{N-2s}\right)\cdots\left(\frac{N-r+1}{N-(r-1)s}\right).$$

13. $P_r(s)\{N - (r-1)s\} = P_{r-1}(s)(N-r-1)s$.

14. $P_r(s) = \dfrac{s}{N - (N-1)s} \cdot \dfrac{2s}{N - (N-2)s} \cdots \dfrac{rs}{N - (N-r)s}$.

15. S_r is the sum of r independent variables with a common geometric distribution. Hence

$$P_r(s) = \left(\frac{q}{1 - ps}\right)^r, \qquad p_{r,k} = q^r p^k\binom{r+k-1}{k}.$$

16. (a) $\mathbf{P}\{R = r\} = \displaystyle\sum_{k=0}^{\nu-1}\mathbf{P}\{S_{r-1} = k\}\mathbf{P}\{X_r \geq \nu - k\} =$

$$= \sum_{k=0}^{\nu-1}q^{r-1}p^k\binom{r+k-2}{k}p^{\nu-k} = p^\nu q^{r-1}\binom{r+\nu-2}{\nu-1}.$$

$$\mathbf{E}(R) = 1 + \frac{q\nu}{p}, \qquad \mathbf{Var}(R) = \frac{\nu q}{p^2}.$$

(b) $(p_1 p_2)^N \displaystyle\sum_{\nu=1}^{\infty}\binom{N+\nu-2}{\nu-1}^2(q_1 q_2)^{\nu-1}$.

17. Note that

$$1 + s + \cdots + s^{ab-1} = (1 + s + \cdots + s^{a-1})(1 + s^a + s^{2a} + \cdots + s^{(b-1)a}).$$

21. $u_n = q^n + \displaystyle\sum_{k=3}^{n}\binom{k-1}{2}p^3 q^{k-3}u_{n-k}$ with $u_0 = 1$, $u_1 = q$, $u_2 = q^2$, $u_3 = p^3 + q^3$. Using the fact that this recurrence relation is of the convolution type,

$$U(s) = \frac{1}{1 - qs} + \frac{(ps)^3}{(1-qs)^3}\,U(s).$$

22. $u_n = pw_{n-1} + qu_{n-1}$, $v_n = pu_{n-1} + qv_{n-1}$, $w_n = pv_{n-1} + qw_{n-1}$. Hence $U(s) - 1 = psW(s) + qsU(s);$ $V(s) = psU(s) + qs \cdot V(s);$ $W(s) = psV(s) + qsW(s)$.

CHAPTER XIII

1. It suffices to show that for all roots $s \neq 1$ of $F(s) = 1$ we have $|s| \geq 1$, and that $|s| = 1$ is possible only in the periodic case.

2. $u_{2n} = \left\{\binom{2n}{n}2^{-2n}\right\}^r \sim 1/\sqrt{(\pi n)^r}$. Hence $\mathcal{E}$ is persistent only for $r = 2$.

For $r = 3$ the tangent rule for numerical integration gives

$$\sum_{n=1}^{\infty} u_{2n} \approx \frac{1}{\sqrt[3]{\pi}} \int_{\frac{1}{2}}^{\infty} \frac{1}{\sqrt[3]{x}}\, dx = 3\sqrt{\frac{2}{\pi}} \approx \frac{1}{2}.$$

3. $u_{6n} \sim \sqrt{6/(2\pi n)^5}$. Thus $u - 1 \approx \sqrt{\dfrac{6}{(2\pi)^5}} \int_{\frac{1}{2}}^{\infty} x^{-\frac{5}{2}}\, dx$. Hence $u \approx 1.047$ and $f \approx 0.045$.

4. $u_{(\lambda+1)n} = \binom{(\lambda+1)n}{n} p^{\lambda n} q^n$. The ratio of two successive terms is <1 except when $p = \lambda/(\lambda+1)$. (The assertion is also a consequence of the law of large numbers.)

6. From $\sum f_i + P\{X_1 > 0\} \leq 1$ conclude that $f < 1$ unless $P\{X_1 > 0\} = 0$. In this case all $X_i < 0$ and $\mathcal{E}$ occurs at the first trial or never.

7. Z_n = smallest integer $\geq (n - N_n)/r$. Furthermore $E(Z_n) \sim np/(q + pr)$, $\text{Var}(Z_n) \sim npq(q + pr)^{-3}$.

8. $G(s) = \dfrac{(1 - qs)q^r s^r}{1 - s + pq^r s^{r+1}}$, $F(s) = qs + psG(s)$, $\mu = q^{-r}$.

9. $G(s) = \dfrac{(1 - qs)B(qs)}{1 - s + psB(qs)}$, and $F(s)$ as in problem 8.

11. $N_n^* \approx (N_n - 714.3)/22.75$; $\mathfrak{N}(\frac{2}{3}) - \mathfrak{N}(-\frac{2}{3}) \approx \frac{1}{2}$.

12. $r_n = r_{n-1} - \frac{1}{4}r_{n-2} + \frac{1}{8}r_{n-3}$ with $r_0 = r_1 = r_2 = 1$; $R(s) = (8 + 2s^2)(8 - 8s + 2s^2 - s^3)^{-1}$; $r_n \sim 1.444248(1.139680)^{-n-1}$.

14. If a_n is the probability that an A-run of length r occurs at the nth trial, then $A(s)$ is given by (7.5) with p replaced by α and q by $1 - \alpha$. Let $B(s)$ and $C(s)$ be the corresponding generating functions for B- and C-runs. The required generating functions are $[(1 - s)U(s)]^{-1}$, where in case (a) $U(s) = A(s)$; in (b) $U(s) = A(s) + B(s) - 1$; in (c) $U(s) = A(s) + B(s) + C(s) - 2$.

15. Use a straightforward combination of the method in example (8.b) and problem 14.

16. Expected number for age k equals Npq^k.

18. $w_k(n) = v_{n-k}r_k$ when $n > k$ and $w_k(n) = \beta_{k-n}r_k/r_{k-n}$ when $n \leq k$.

19. Note that $1 - F(s) = (1-s)Q(s)$ and $\mu - Q(s) = (1-s)R(s)$, whence $Q(1) = \mu$, $2R(1) = \sigma^2 - \mu + \mu^2$. The power series for $Q^{-1}(s) = \sum (u_n - u_{n-1})s^n$ converges for $s = 1$.

CHAPTER XIV

1. $\dfrac{(q/p)^b - 1}{(q/p)^{a+b} - 1}$ if $p \neq q$, and $\dfrac{b}{a + b}$ if $p = q$.

3. When $q < p$, the number of visits is a defective variable.

4. The expected number of visits equals $p(1 - q_1)/qq_{a-1} = (p/q)^a$.

5. The probability of ruin is still given by (2.4) with $p = \alpha(1-\gamma)^{-1}$, $q = \beta(1-\gamma)^{-1}$. The expected duration of the game is $D_z(1-\gamma)^{-1}$ with D_z given by (3.4) or (3.5).

6. The boundary conditions (2.2) are replaced by $q_0 - \delta q_1 = 1 - \delta$, $q_a = 0$. To (2.4) there corresponds the solution

$$q_z = \frac{\{(q/p)^a - (q/p)^z\}(1 - \delta)}{(q/p)^a(1 - \delta) + \delta q/p - 1}.$$

The boundary conditions (3.2) become $D_0 = \delta D_1$, $D_a = 0$.

7. To (2.1) there corresponds $q_z = pq_{z+2} + qq_{z-1}$, and $q_z = \lambda^z$ is a particular solution if $\lambda = p\lambda^3 + q$, that is, if $\lambda = 1$ or $\lambda^2 + \lambda = qp^{-1}$. The probability of ruin is

$$q_z = \begin{cases} 1 & \text{if } q \geq 2p \\[2mm] \left\{ \sqrt{\frac{1}{4} + \frac{q}{p}} - \frac{1}{2} \right\}^z & \text{if } q \leq 2p. \end{cases}$$

10. $w_{z,n+1}(x) = pw_{z+1,n}(x) + qw_{z-1,n}(x)$ with the boundary conditions (1) $w_{0,n}(x) = w_{a,n}(x) = 0$; (2) $w_{z,0}(x) = 0$ for $z \neq x$ and $w_{x,0}(x) = 1$.

11. Replace (1) by $w_{0,n}(x) = w_{1,n}(x)$ and $w_{a,n}(x) = w_{a-1,n}(x)$.

12. Boundary condition: $u_{a,n} = u_{a-1,n}$. Generating function:

$$\frac{\lambda_1^z(s)\lambda_2^{a-\frac{1}{2}}(s) + \lambda_2^z(s)\lambda_1^{a-\frac{1}{2}}(s)}{\lambda_1^{a-\frac{1}{2}}(s) + \lambda_2^{a-\frac{1}{2}}(s)} = \frac{\lambda_1^{a-z-\frac{1}{2}}(s) + \lambda_2^{a-z-\frac{1}{2}}(s)}{\lambda_1^{a-\frac{1}{2}}(s) + \lambda_2^{a-\frac{1}{2}}(s)}.$$

18. $\mathbf{P}\{M_n < z\} = \sum_{x=1}^{\infty} (v_{x-z,n} - v_{x+z,n})$

$\mathbf{P}\{M_n = z\} = \mathbf{P}\{M_n < z + 1\} - \mathbf{P}\{M_n < z\}$.

19. The first passage through x must have occurred at $k \leq n$, and the particle returned from x in the following $n - k$ steps.

31. The relation (8.2) is replaced by

$$U_z(s) = s\sum_{x=1}^{a-1} U_x(s)p_{x-z} + sr_z.$$

The characteristic equation is $s \sum p_k \sigma^k = 1$.

CHAPTER XV

1. P has rows $(p, q, 0, 0)$, $(0, 0, p, q)$, $(p, q, 0, 0)$, and $(0, 0, p, q)$. For $n > 1$ the rows are (p^2, pq, pq, q^2).

2. (a) The chain is irreducible and ergodic; $p_{jk}^{(n)} \to \frac{1}{3}$ for all j, k. (Note that P is doubly stochastic.)

(b) The chain has period 3, with G_0 containing E_1 and E_2; the state E_4 forms G_1, and E_3 forms G_2. We have $u_1 = u_2 = \frac{1}{2}$, $u_3 = u_4 = 1$.

(c) The states E_1 and E_3 form a closed set S_1, and E_4, E_5 another closed set S_2, whereas E_2 is transient. The matrices corresponding to the closed sets are 2-by-2 matrices with elements $\frac{1}{2}$. Hence $p_{jk}^{(n)} \to \frac{1}{2}$ if E_j and E_k belong to the same S_r; $p_{j2}^{(n)} \to 0$; finally $p_{2k}^{(n)} \to \frac{1}{2}$ if $k = 1, 3$, and $p_{2k}^{(n)} \to 0$ if $k = 2, 4, 5$.

(d) The chain has period 3. Putting $a = (0, 0, 0, \frac{1}{3}, \frac{1}{3}, \frac{1}{3})$, $b = (1, 0, 0, 0, 0, 0)$, $c = (0, \frac{1}{2}, \frac{1}{2}, 0, 0, 0)$, we find that the rows of $P^2 = P^5 = \cdots$ are a, b, b, c, c, c, those of $P^3 = P^6 = \cdots$ are b, c, c, a, a, a, those of $P = P^4 = \cdots$ are c, a, a, b, b, b.

3. $p_{jj}^{(n)} = (j/6)^n$, $p_{jk}^{(n)} = (k/6)^n - ((k-1)/6)^n$ if $k > j$, and $p_{jk}^{(n)} = 0$ if $k < j$.

4. $x_k = (\frac{3}{4}, \frac{1}{2}, \frac{1}{4}, \frac{1}{2})$, $y_k = (\frac{1}{4}, \frac{1}{2}, \frac{3}{4}, \frac{1}{2})$.

6. For $n \geq j$

$$f_{j0}^{(n)} = \binom{n-1}{j-1} p^{n-j} q^j = \binom{j}{n-j} (-p)^j q^j.$$

Generating function $(qs)^j (1 - ps)^{-j}$. Expectation j/q.

7. $f_{00}^{(n)} = \sum_{k=1}^{n-1} v_k \binom{n-2}{k-1} p^{n-1-k} q^k$ for $n > 1$.

8. The even-numbered states form an irreducible closed set. The probability of a return to E_0 at or before the nth step equals

$$1 - v_0 + v_0(1 - v_2) + v_0 v_2(1 - v_4) + \cdots + v_0 v_2 \cdots v_{2n-2}(1 - v_{2n}) =$$
$$= 1 - v_0 v_2 v_4 \cdots v_{2n}$$

Thus the even states are persistent if, and only if, the last product tends to 0. The probability that starting from E_{2r+1} the system remains forever among the odd (transient) states equals $v_{2r+1} v_{2r+3} \cdots$.

9. $u_r = [1 - p/q](p/q)^{r-1}[1 - (p/q)^p]^{-1}$.

10. Possible states $E_0, \ldots, E_w$. For $j > 0$

$$p_{j,j-1} = j(\rho - w + j)\rho^{-2}, \qquad p_{j,j+1} = (\rho - j)(w - j)\rho^{-2},$$
$$p_{jj} = j(w - j)\rho^{-2} + (\rho - j)(\rho - w + j)\rho^{-2}$$
$$u_k = \binom{w}{k}\binom{b}{\rho - k} \Big/ \binom{2\rho}{\rho}.$$

13.
$$P = \begin{bmatrix} q & p & & & & 0 & 0 \\ 0 & 0 & 1 & & \cdots & 0 & 0 \\ 0 & 0 & 0 & 1 & \cdots & 0 & 0 \\ \cdot & \cdot & \cdot & \cdot & \cdot & \cdot & \cdot \\ 0 & 0 & 0 & 0 & \cdots & 0 & 1 \\ q & p & 0 & 0 & \cdots & 0 & 0 \end{bmatrix}.$$

14. Note that the matrix is doubly stochastic; use example $(7.h)$.

15. Put $p_{k,k+1} = 1$ for $k = 1, \ldots, N - 1$, and $p_{Nk} = p_k$.

16. $\Sigma u_j p_{jk} = u_k$, then $U(s) = u_0(1 - s)P(s)\{P(s) - s\}^{-1}$. For ergodicity it is necessary and sufficient that $\mu = P'(1) < 1$. By L'Hospital's rule $U(1) = u_0(1 - \mu)$ whence $u_0 = (1 - \mu)^{-1}$.

25. If $N \geq m - 2$, the variables $X^{(m)}$ and $X^{(n)}$ are independent, and hence the three rows of the matrix $p_{jk}^{(m,n)}$ are identical with the distribution of $\mathbf{X}^{(n)}$, namely $(\frac{1}{4}, \frac{1}{2}, \frac{1}{4})$. For $n = m + 1$ the three rows are $(\frac{1}{2}, \frac{1}{2}, 0)$, $(\frac{1}{4}, \frac{1}{2}, \frac{1}{4})$, $(0, \frac{1}{2}, \frac{1}{2})$.

CHAPTER XVII

3. $E(X) = ie^{\lambda t}$; $\quad \text{Var}(X) = ie^{\lambda t}(e^{\lambda t} - 1)$.

4. $P_n' = -\lambda n P_n + \lambda(n+1)P_{n+1}$.

$$P_n(t) = \binom{i}{n} e^{-i\lambda t}(e^{\lambda t} - 1)^{i-n} \quad (n \leq i).$$

$$E(X) = ie^{-\lambda t}; \quad \text{Var}(X) = ie^{-\lambda t}(1 - e^{-\lambda t}).$$

5. $P_n'(t) = -(\lambda + n\mu)P_n(t) + \lambda P_{n-1}(t) + (n+1)\mu P_{n+1}(t)$ for $n \leq N - 1$ and $P_N'(t) = -N\mu P_N(t) + \lambda P_{N-1}(t)$.

19. The standard method of solving linear differential equations leads to a system of linear equations.

Index